INTRODUCTION TO
SOCIOLOGY

SEAGULL

Recent Sociology Titles
from W. W. Norton

Code of the Streets by Elijah Anderson

The Cosmopolitan Canopy by Elijah Anderson

Social Problems, 2nd Edition by Joel Best

A History of Future Cities by Daniel Brook

You May Ask Yourself: An Introduction to Thinking Like a Sociologist, 3rd Edition by Dalton Conley

The Real World: An Introduction to Sociology, 4th Edition by Kerry Ferris and Jill Stein

Essentials of Sociology, 4th Edition by Anthony Giddens, Mitchell Duneier, Richard P. Appelbaum, and Deborah Carr

Mix It Up: Popular Culture, Mass Media, and Society by David Grazian

The Contexts Reader, 2nd Edition edited by Douglas Hartmann and Christopher Uggen

The Society Pages: Crime and the Punished edited by Douglas Hartmann and Christopher Uggen

The Society Pages: The Social Side of Politics edited by Douglas Hartmann and Christopher Uggen

Doing Race edited by Hazel Rose Markus and Paula M.L. Moya

Readings for Sociology, 7th Edition edited by Garth Massey

Social Construction of Sexuality, 2nd Edition by Stephen Seidman

The Sociology of News, 2nd Edition by Michael Schudson

Sex Matters: The Sexuality and Society Reader, 4th Edition edited by Mindy Stombler, Dawn M. Baunach, Wendy O. Simonds, Elroi J. Windsor, and Elisabeth O. Burgess

Naked Statistics by Charles Wheelan

Cultural Sociology: An Introductory Reader by Matt Wray

American Society: How It Really Works by Erik Olin Wright and Joel Rogers

To learn more about Norton Sociology, please visit:
wwnorton.com/soc

INTRODUCTION TO
SOCIOLOGY

SEAGULL

9E

Anthony Giddens

LONDON SCHOOL OF ECONOMICS

Mitchell Duneier

CITY UNIVERSITY OF NEW YORK—GRADUATE CENTER
PRINCETON UNIVERSITY

Richard P. Appelbaum

UNIVERSITY OF CALIFORNIA,
SANTA BARBARA

Deborah Carr

RUTGERS UNIVERSITY

W. W. NORTON & COMPANY, INC.
New York • London

W. W. NORTON & COMPANY has been independent since its founding in 1923, when William Warder Norton and Mary D. Herter Norton first published lectures delivered at the People's Institute, the adult education division of New York City's Cooper Union. The firm soon expanded its program beyond the Institute, publishing books by celebrated academics from America and abroad. By mid-century, the two major pillars of Norton's publishing program—trade books and college texts—were firmly established. In the 1950s, the Norton family transferred control of the company to its employees, and today—with a staff of four hundred and a comparable number of trade, college, and professional titles published each year—W. W. Norton & Company stands as the largest and oldest publishing house owned wholly by its employees.

Editor: Karl Bakeman
Associate editors: Kate Feighery, Nicole Sawa
Editorial assistants: Alicia González-Gross, Lindsey Thomas
Project editors: Amy Weintraub, Sandy Lifland
Production manager, College: Vanessa Nuttry
Art director: Hope Miller Goodell
Book designer: Chin-Yee Lai
Media editor: Eileen Connell
Associate media editor: Laura Musich
Media editorial assistants: Kathryn Young, Cara Folkman
Marketing managers: Natasha Zabohonski, Julia Hall
Composition: Jouve North America
Manufacturing: Courier—Westford, MA

Library of Congress Cataloging-in-Publication Data

Giddens, Anthony.
Introduction to sociology / Anthony Giddens, London School of Economics, Mitchell Duneier, City University of New York-Graduate Center, Princeton University, Richard P. Appelbaum, University of California, Santa Barbara, Deborah Carr, Rutgers University.—Ninth edition.
      pages cm
      Includes bibliographical references and index.
      ISBN 978-0-393-92223-3 (pbk)
  1. Sociology.   I. Title.
HM585.G53 2014
301—dc23   2013033082

W. W. Norton & Company, Inc., 500 Fifth Avenue, New York, NY 10110
www.ww.norton.com

W.W. Norton & Company Ltd., Castle House, 75/76 Wells Street, London W1T 3QT

1 2 3 4 5 6 7 8 9 0

Contents

Preface

We wrote this book with the belief that sociology plays a key role in modern intellectual culture and occupies a central place within the social sciences. We have aimed to write a book that combines classic theories of sociology with empirically grounded studies and examples from real life that reveal the basic issues of interest to sociologists today. The book does not bring in overly sophisticated notions; nevertheless, ideas and findings drawn from the cutting edge of the discipline are incorporated throughout. We hope it is a fair and nonpartisan treatment; we endeavored to cover the major perspectives in sociology and the major findings of contemporary American research in an evenhanded, although not indiscriminate, way.

MAJOR THEMES

The book is constructed around **eight** basic themes, each of which helps give the work a distinctive character. One of the central themes is the **micro and macro link**. At many points in the book, we show that interaction in micro-level contexts affects larger, or macro-level, social processes, and that these macro-level processes influence our day-to-day lives. We emphasize that one can better understand a social situation by analyzing it at both the micro and macro levels.

A second theme is that of the **world in change**. Sociology was born out of the transformations that wrenched the industrializing social order of the West away from the ways of life that characterized earlier societies. The world created by these changes is the primary object of sociological analysis. The pace of social change has continued to accelerate, and it is possible that we stand on the threshold of transitions as significant as those that occurred in the late eighteenth and nineteenth centuries. Sociology has prime responsibility for charting the transformations of the past and grasping the major lines of development taking place today.

Another fundamental theme is the **globalization of social life**. For far too long, sociology has been dominated by the view that societies can be studied as independent and distinctive entities. But even in the past, societies never really existed in isolation. In current times, we can see a clear acceleration in processes of global integration. This is obvious, for example, in the expansion of international trade across the world, or the use of social media, which played a key role in recent popular uprisings against repressive governments throughout the Middle East. The emphasis on globalization also connects closely with the weight given to the interdependence of the industrialized and developing worlds today.

The book also focuses on the importance of **comparative study**. Sociology cannot be taught solely by understanding the institutions of any one particular society. Although we have focused our discussion primarily on the United States, we have balanced it with a rich variety of materials drawn from other cultures. These include research carried out in other Western countries and in Russia and eastern European societies, which are currently undergoing substantial changes. The book also includes much more material on developing countries than has been usual in introductory texts. In addition, we strongly emphasize the relationship between sociology and anthropology, whose concerns often overlap. Given the close connections that now mesh societies across the world and the virtual disappearance of traditional social systems, sociology and anthropology have increasingly become indistinguishable.

A fifth theme is the necessity of taking a **historical approach** to sociology. This involves more than just filling in the historical context within which events occur. One of the most important developments in sociology over the past few years has been an increasing emphasis on historical analysis. This should be understood not solely as applying a sociological outlook to the past but as a way of contributing to our understanding of institutions in the present. Recent work in historical sociology is discussed throughout the text and provides a framework for the interpretations offered in the chapters.

Throughout the text, particular attention is given to a sixth theme—issues of **social class, gender, and race**. The study of social differentiation is ordinarily regarded as a series of specific fields within sociology as a whole—and this volume contains chapters that specifically explore thinking and research on each subject (Chapters 8, 10, and 11, respectively). However, questions about gender, race, and class relations are so fundamental to sociological analysis that they cannot simply be considered a subdivision. Thus many chapters contain sections concerned with the ways that multiple sources of social stratification shape the human experience.

A seventh theme is that a strong grasp of **sociological research methods** is crucial for understanding the world around us. A strong understanding of how social science research is conducted is crucial for interpreting and making sense of the many social "facts" that the media trumpet.

The final major theme is the relation between the **social and the personal**. Sociological thinking is a vital help to self-understanding, which in turn can be focused back on an improved understanding of the social world. Studying sociology should be a liberating experience: The field enlarges our sympathies and imagination, opens up new perspectives on the sources of our own behavior, and creates an awareness of cultural settings different from our own. Insofar as sociological ideas challenge dogma, teach appreciation of cultural variety, and allow us insight into the working of social institutions, the practice of sociology enhances the possibilities of human freedom.

ORGANIZATION

We have completely reorganized the ninth edition to include only what students need to master the sociological concepts taught in introductory courses. Every chapter now follows the same structure, making it easier for students to study. Each chapter opens with an attention-grabbing question that challenges students' misconceptions about the topic.

Each chapter is broken down into four sections:

1. Basic concepts
2. Important theories
3. Current research
4. Unanswered questions

At the end of each section, students have the opportunity to test themselves with integrated "Concept Check" quizzes. Furthermore, the ninth edition features new "Big Picture" concept maps that integrate the learning objectives, key terms, "Concept Checks," and "Thinking Sociologically" activities into a handy one-stop review tool at the end of each chapter.

The chapters follow a sequence designed to help students achieve a progressive mastery of the different fields of sociology, but we have taken care to ensure that the book can be used flexibly and will be easy to adapt to the needs of individual courses. Chapters can be deleted or studied in a different order without much loss. Each has been written as a fairly autonomous unit, with cross-referencing to other chapters at relevant points.

CHANGES IN THE NINTH EDITION

Chapter 1: We begin with an opening question about the college admissions process and lead into a new discussion of colleges looking for "best graduates" instead of "best students," or those who will be successful after graduation. Such students include athletes who may not have the highest GPAs or SAT scores. We have also added a discussion of Alan Krueger and Stacey Dale's 2002 study showing that Ivy League–accepted students who decided on state-level colleges instead were still very successful, indicating that highly motivated individuals can do well even without an Ivy League diploma.

Chapter 2: The opening question asks students their view of sociology as a science. There is a new example about researchers who studied three groups of people: those who were able to move from high-poverty to low-poverty neighborhoods, those who wanted to but could not, and those who did not want to move and then stayed. We have added to the discussion of Theda Skocpol's *States and Social Revolutions*. There is a lengthy new discussion of Andreas Wimmer's book *Waves of War*, which goes against the grain of war history by focusing on hundreds of lesser-known wars in places such as Latin America instead of only focusing on a few major European wars. The chapter touches upon the uncomfortable question of social scientists benefiting at their subjects' expense.

Chapter 3: We begin the chapter by comparing the use of the Internet by teenagers in the Silicon Valley and in Beijing. There are new examples of change and conflict as a result of globalization, including the global manufacturing of the iPhone and the meaning of headscarves in the United States, France, and Muslim countries. We have included a discussion of Marx's, Weber's, and Durkheim's analyses of the emerging industrial society. We have updated the explanation of colonialism, introducing the idea of settler colonialism and the distinction between the "global north" and the "global south." We have also added a discussion of the ways different groups use the Internet, ranging from Saudi Arabia's Internet censorship to the creation of digitally linked communities by various subcultures. There is also a new section on China's seismic cultural and economic changes in the past few decades.

Chapter 4: We have included Deborah Carr's research on women's changing roles in the past century, which illustrates the tension between older women, who were expected to embrace traditional gender roles, and their daughters, who are getting advanced degrees, delaying marriage, and having fewer children. Data on Americans who play video games have been updated. There is a new discussion of "violent video games" in the context of the confession by the perpetrator of the July 2011 massacre of 77 people in Norway.

Chapter 5: We have updated statistics on young people's use of social media for information, in particular noting that 48 percent of young people get news from Facebook.

Chapter 6: The opening story about West Point has been revised as has the discussion of Nicholas Christakis and James Fowler's 2007 obesity study. There are also updated data on the savings resulting from telecommuting.

Chapter 7: An opening question about homeless people, drug addicts, and gang members immediately challenges students about the stereotypes of these groups as deviant. We also expand on Chapter 2's discussion of Alice Goffman's "On the Run" article about the effects of police officers' use of homes, hospitals, and family members to catch suspected criminals. We have updated statistics on the death penalty in the United States, as well as discussing Americans' opinions on capital punishment.

Chapter 8: This chapter has been extensively edited to incorporate the Great Recession of 2008, starting with the opening question. Statistics have been added or updated on household assets by race, Americans' net worth, class, consumer debt, student debt, intergenerational mobility, education, job prospects, and other socioeconomic factors that were affected by the Great Recession. We have expanded the section on homelessness to include data on veterans. Annette Lareau's 2003 book, *Unequal Childhoods*, is also examined in this chapter.

Chapter 9: This chapter includes a new section on global poverty statistics, including a discussion of how China's economic boom has lifted so many Chinese out of poverty that China is now considered a middle-income country. We also discuss newly industrializing economies in East Asia that are a significant part of shaping what Fareed Zakaria calls a "post-American world." There are updated statistics throughout this chapter—on GNI, poverty, manufacturing, transnational companies, and more.

Chapter 10: We have added new statistics on women in national legislatures around the world. We have also included updated discussions of issues such as the pay gap, sex segregation in the workforce, female executives, sexual harassment, and global violence against women.

Chapter 11: Reflecting the rapidly shifting racial dynamics in the United States today, we have updated several statistics in this chapter, including immigration rates to the United States by race and ethnicity, poverty data by race, the education level of immigrants, Asian American rates of intermarriage, and the effects of immigration on the U.S. economy.

Chapter 12: We have significantly updated the chapter to reflect how the Great Recession has affected seniors' finances and well-being. We have incorporated several studies on quality of life: Rebecca Levy's 2002 study of how positive and negative attitudes affect lifespan; Luo et al.'s 2011 research into discriminatory treatment and its effects on physical and mental health; and Findsen and Formosa's 2011 study on the importance of older adults engaging in lifelong educational activities. We have included new data on Social Security and Medicare, as well as discussing Americans' opinions toward the two programs. We have also expanded the analysis of the global experience of aging and how traditional bonds of caring for the elderly are fraying under globalization and the recession.

Chapter 13: The chapter begins by asking students how many countries are "free," as determined by their citizens enjoying rights and liberties Americans may take for granted. We have incorporated several recent current events into this chapter, such as Occupy Wall Street, the Arab Spring, and *Kony 2012*. There are updated statistics for the percentage of female voters and heads of state around the world, and for global Internet usage by race, age, education, and wealth.

Chapter 14: We have updated our discussions about employment issues and the future of work, including the opening question about the Taiwanese firm Pou Chen, which is a company that makes several popular brands of athletic shoes. We have also presented recent data about housework, volunteering, financial firms, the rise of Chinese corporations on the global stage, and how unions are responding to outsourcing by focusing on occupations that cannot be exported. We have included a discussion of how Chinese companies are turning to automation in response to rising labor costs and bad publicity concerning labor conditions in that country. There are new issues throughout the chapter as a result of the Great Recession, such as questions about part-time work, longer unemployment, and more flexible (and more insecure) jobs and working conditions.

Chapter 15: We have significantly expanded the sections on two highly debated issues: the well-being of children raised by parents of the same sex, and people who live alone. We have also updated several statistics throughout the chapter, including rates for marriage, childbirth, and cohabitation by race and ethnicity, class, and sexual orientation.

Chapter 16: This chapter contains updated references—for example, on high school dropout rates and international college students. We have included recent developments in the section on No Child Left Behind, including President Obama's NCLB waivers to certain states and the administration's program Race to the Top.

There is a new section on homeschooling and how wealth, single- or two-parent households, and race influence which families choose to homeschool their children.

Chapter 17: There is new or updated information on religious believers worldwide, Americans unaffiliated with any religion, and the religion of immigrants to the United States. We have expanded the section on the rise of evangelicalism in Africa, the Middle East, Latin America, and parts of Asia. The chapter concludes with a new section, "Is Religious Violence on the Rise?," which discusses Mark Juergensmeyer's analysis of the reasons for religious violence, the religious fanaticism of Timothy McVeigh and Osama bin Laden, and the attitudes of people in Muslim countries toward foreign technology and culture, which make their lives better but also lead to the loss of traditional ways of life.

Chapter 18: We have updated statistics on Americans who are overweight and obese by race and age, the most hazardous and fatal jobs in the United States, and race-based inequalities in health and crime. We have included new references to Hui Zheng's 2012 study on whether income inequality in the United States affects poor health and mortality.

Chapter 19: There are updated statistics for global population projections, what countries will experience increases in urban dwellers, the rural-urban trends of the United States, urban poverty, and food and water shortages. We mention recent concerns over nuclear power plants, such as Japan's Fukushima plant and Germany's decision to phase out nuclear power by 2020, and update our discussion of Paul Ehrlich's Malthusian predictions.

Chapter 20: This chapter includes new discussions of globalization, including the phenomenal success of *Avatar*, and Erik Olin Wright's 2012 American Sociologist Association address focusing on egalitarian reforms. There are also updated statistics for genetically modified foods, the global film industry, free trade, and the extreme concentration of wealth and resources.

ACKNOWLEDGMENTS

During the writing of all nine editions of this book, many individuals offered comments and advice on particular chapters and, in some cases, large parts of the text. They helped us see issues in a different light, clarified some difficult points, and allowed us to take advantage of their specialized knowledge in their respective fields. We are deeply indebted to them. Special thanks go to Erik Nielsen, who worked assiduously to help us update data in all chapters and contributed significantly to the editing process.

We would also like to thank the many readers of the text who have written with comments, criticisms, and suggestions for improvements. We have adopted many of their recommendations in this new edition.

Ryan Acton, University of Massachusetts-Amherst
Ryan Alaniz, University of Minnesota
Cristina Bradatan, Texas Tech University
Rob Crosnoe, University of Texas at Austin
Nancy Downey, University of Nevada, Reno

David Embrick, Loyola University Chicago

Kelly Fulton, University of Texas at Austin

Farrah Gafford, Xavier University of Louisiana

Robert Gallagher, Broward Community College (FL)

Chad Goldberg, University of Wisconsin–Madison

Kerry Greer, Indiana University

Drew Halfmann, University of California, Davis

Ted Henken, Baruch College (CUNY)

Cedric Herring, University of Illinois at Chicago

Hanna Jokinen-Gordon, Florida State University

Xavia Karner, University of Houston

Kevin Keating, Broward Community College

Alissa King, Kirkwood Community College (IA)

Christopher Knoester, Ohio State University

Jenny Le, Texas A&M University

Alexander Lu, Indiana University

Timothy Madigan, Mansfield University (PA)

Aaron Major, University at Albany (SUNY)

Catherine Marrone, Stony Brook University (SUNY)

Mike McCarthy, New York University

Julie Netto, Western Connecticut State University

Mary Pattillo, Northwestern University

Teresa Roach, Florida State University

David Tabachnick, Muskingum University (OH)

Ahoo Tabatabai, Columbia College (MO)

Rowan Wolf, Portland Community College

Jane Zavisca, University of Arizona

We have many others to thank as well. We are especially grateful to copyeditors Jenna Dolan and Greg Lauzon, who did a marvelous job offering numerous suggestions for alterations and improvements that have contributed in important ways to the final form of the volume. We are also extremely grateful to project editor Amy Weintraub, production manager Vanessa Nuttry, associate editors Kate Feighery and Nicole Sawa, and editorial assistants Alicia González-Gross and Lindsey Thomas for managing the myriad details involved in producing this book. Media editor Eileen Connell, associate media editor Laura Musich, and media editorial assistants Kathryn Young and Cara Folkman deserve special thanks for creating all the websites, DVDs, and instructor-support materials that accompany the book. Stephanie Romeo and Julie Tesser painstakingly researched the best photos to grace these pages. Art director Hope Miller Goodell, designer Chin-Yee Lai, and Kiss Me I'm Polish showed exceptional flair and originality in designing and illustrating the book.

We are also grateful to our editors at Norton, Steve Dunn, Melea Seward, and Karl Bakeman, who have made many direct contributions to the various chapters and have ensured that we made reference to the very latest research. We would also like to register our thanks to a number of current and former graduate students—many of whom are now tenured professors at prestigious universities—whose contributions over the years have proved invaluable: Wendy Carter, Joe Conti, Francesca Degiuli, Audrey Devine-Eller, Neha Gondal, Neil Gross, Black

Hawk Hancock, Dmitry Khodyakov, Paul LePore, Alair MacLean, Ann Meier, Susan Munkres, Josh Rossol, Sharmila Rudrappa, Christopher Wildeman, David Yamane, and Kathrin Zippel.

RESOURCES FOR STUDENTS AND INSTRUCTORS

For Students

Everyday Sociology Blog
everydaysociologyblog.com

Designed for a general audience, the *Everyday Sociology* blog is an exciting and unique online forum that encourages visitors to actively explore sociology's relevance to popular culture, mass media, and everyday life. Moderated by Karen Sternheimer (University of Southern California), the blog features postings on topical subjects, video interviews with well-known sociologists, and contributions from special guests during the academic year.

Contributors include: Sally Raskoff (Los Angeles Valley College), Peter Kaufman (SUNY New Paltz), and Jon Wynn (University of Massachusetts Amherst).

Ebooks
wwnortonebooks.com

An affordable and convenient alternative, Norton eBooks retain the content and design of the print book and allow students to highlight and take notes with ease, print out chapters as needed, and search the text. Norton eBooks are available online and as downloadable PDFs. They can be purchased directly from the Norton website or with a registration folder that can be sold in bookstores.

For Instructors

Sociology in Practice DVDs

These four DVDs contain more than 12 hours of video clips drawn from documentaries by independent filmmakers. The *Sociology in Practice* DVD series has been expanded to include a new DVD of documentary clips on the family. The DVDs are ideal for initiating classroom discussion and encouraging students to apply sociological concepts to popular and real-world issues. The clips are also offered in streaming versions in Norton coursepacks. Each streamed clip is accompanied by a quiz, exercise, or activity.

Instructor Resource Disc

Available in downloadable file and CD-ROM formats, this helpful classroom presentation tool includes:

- **Enhanced Lecture PowerPoints** featuring a suggested classroom lecture script in the notes field that will be particularly helpful to first-time teachers. While the slides are easy to customize, they are also a "lecture-ready" solution for instructors who have limited preparation time.
- **"Clicker" questions** for each PowerPoint chapter enable instructors to incorporate classroom response systems into their lectures.
- **Art PowerPoints** featuring photographs and drawn figures from the text.

Testbank

Written by Sara Raley (McDaniel), Marion Hughes (Towson), Whitney Garcia (Towson), and Stephanie Arnett (Tulane), the testbank for the ninth edition is designed to help instructors prepare exams. It has been extensively revised to reflect the new edition's updates and to conform to Bloom's taxonomy of learning objectives. Each chapter includes approximately 100 questions. In addition to Bloom's taxonomy, each question is tagged with metadata placing it in the context of the chapter and a difficulty level, making it easy to construct tests that are meaningful and diagnostic. It is available online, in paperback, on CD-ROM, and in ExamView format.

Interactive Instructor's Guide

We are proud to introduce with the ninth edition the Interactive Instructor's Guide, written by Kathleen Doherty. This guide makes lecture development easy with an array of teaching resources that can be searched and browsed according to a number of criteria. Resources include chapter outlines and summaries; lecture ideas; discussion questions; recommended readings, videos, and website; DVD and You-Tube exercises with streaming video; and new Service Learning Exercises. It is available at no cost to instructors only, who can also subscribe to a mailing list to be notified of periodic updates and new content.

Coursepacks
(available for free download at wwnorton.com/instructors; BB/WebCT, Angel, Desire2Learn, Moodle, and other Learning Management Systems)

Available at no cost to professors or students, Norton coursepacks for online or hybrid courses are available in a variety of formats, including all versions of Blackboard and WebCT. With just a simple download from our Instructor Resources page, instructors can bring high-quality Norton digital media into a new or existing online course (no extra student passwords required), and it's theirs to keep forever.

The coursepacks are organized around the big concepts in each chapter. They offer an extensive array of materials, including:

- a five- to seven-question pretest that allows instructors to gauge student knowledge of key concepts and tailor lectures and assignments accordingly;
- interactive activities and assessments focused on the big concepts;
- NEW! Analyzing the Data multiple-choice quizzes on key charts and graphs (one to three per chapter);
- exercises that allow students to work with 2010 Census and Community Survey data;
- a "Writing about Sociology" section that includes practice activities and assessments;
- select readings from the previous edition with exercises and discussion questions;
- *Sociology in Practice* DVD activities that include multiple-choice assessments that connect each clip to key sociological concepts (select clips only); and
- a bank of discussion forum questions.

Part I

THE STUDY OF SOCIOLOGY

We live in a world today that is increasingly complex. What makes this possible? Why are the conditions of our lives so different from those of earlier times? How will our lives change in the future? To what extent are things that seem natural actually socially constructed? Does the individual matter? These types of questions led to the study of sociology. As you read this text, you will encounter examples from different people's lives that will help answer these important questions.

In Chapter 1, we explore the scope of sociology and learn what insights the field can bring, such as the development of a global perspective and an understanding of social change. Sociology is not a body of theories everyone agrees on. As in any complex field, the questions we raise allow for different answers. In this chapter, we compare and contrast differing theoretical traditions.

Chapter 2 explores the tools of the trade and considers how sociologists do research. A number of basic methods of investigation are available to explore the social world. We must be sure that the information underlying sociological reasoning is as reliable and accurate as possible. The chapter examines the problems encountered when gathering such information and indicates how best to deal with them.

What Is Sociology?

1

The admissions process at major American universities has:

a Always favored prettier or more handsome people.

b Always favored minorities.

c Always favored athletes.

d Undergone serious revision across time.

Turn the page for the correct answer.

he correct answer is *d*, because the criteria for admission to universities have changed across time. In the early twentieth century, college admissions began to undergo a series of major transformations, for reasons that were kept discreetly out of the public eye (Karabel, 2005; Gladwell, 2005). In 1905 the SAT was instituted, and for the first time, people started getting into college on the basis of standardized tests. Within a few years, the Harvard class became 15 percent Jewish, as Jews (not unlike Asians today) excelled at the standardized test in disproportionate numbers. Sociologists to this day disagree about whether this success can be explained by cultural characteristics or economic advantages that even relatively poor ethnic and religious minorities experience in comparison with other minority groups that don't do as well.

Nevertheless, reflecting the wider anti-Semitism of the era, the people who were running Harvard looked at this as a very undesirable turn of events. The administrators drew an analogy between the university and hotels in upstate New York—first the Jews will arrive, then the Gentiles will leave, and then the Jews will leave and nobody will be here or want to come here anymore (Zimmerman, 2010). So Harvard determined that it needed to come up with another way of conducting admissions. Rather than putting quotas on Jews, they decided to change to a system of admissions very much like the one we know today. They would start to look at "the whole person," rather than give advantages to people simply because they'd done well on a standardized test. In recent years, these institutions have generally transitioned to looking for "best graduates" rather than "best students": that is, not students who will excel academically in college, but who, instead, will become successful after college (Gladwell, 2005). Excellent high school students compete for a limited number of spots at elite American colleges, with many able candidates being rejected in favor of athletes or student leaders in lower academic standing.

Today, it seems natural that a college would want to get to know a student as a whole person. In your college application, you had to write an essay that helped define you as a total human being. You may have tried to show what an interesting person you are—the clubs you were a

LEARNING OBJECTIVES

1 BASIC CONCEPTS

Learn what sociology encompasses and how everyday topics are shaped by social and historical forces. Recognize that sociology involves not only acquiring knowledge but also developing a sociological imagination.

2 THE DEVELOPMENT OF SOCIOLOGICAL THINKING

Learn how sociology originated and understand the significance of the intellectual contributions of early sociologists.

3 MODERN THEORETICAL APPROACHES

Be able to identify some of the leading theorists and distinguish between their theoretical approaches to social life.

4 HOW CAN SOCIOLOGY HELP US?

See the practical implications of sociology.

part of and the sports you participated in. While answer *c* is not entirely correct, athletes experience a growing advantage in admissions over their peers, despite on average lower GPAs and SAT scores. Part of the reason for this may be that despite the fact athletes are not academically inclined, they are still able (and more likely) to pursue careers in high-paying professions (Bowen and Shulman, 2001a). When Ivy League schools switched to the new system, they would also send representatives to various schools around the country to interview prospective students. They didn't want too many "nerds." They wanted well-rounded, good-looking people: future leaders who would have an impact on the country, and who would make these schools look good in return. And so they would conduct interviews and keep notes on whether an applicant was tall, handsome, or pretty (by whatever standard that was determined).

There were things the admissions office simply didn't like: people with big ears, for example. Short people were also undesirable, as recommendation files from that time indicate. In the mid-1950s, Harvard, Princeton, and Yale were actually keeping records on the number of men who entered the freshman class who were over six feet tall. Today, all schools release records about their incoming freshman classes, but they are more likely to keep track of race, class, and gender variables than height or ear size. Thus, answer choice *a* is incorrect if we are considering the present day; though physical appearance was at one time a salient aspect of college admissions criteria, it is generally no longer a consideration. Indeed, when people hear statistics about incoming college freshman classes, they more frequently ask about affirmative action. Some whites might wonder, "Is it true that I can't get into some competitive schools because so many of the spaces now go to minorities?"

It's interesting how frequently this question is asked. The average person who wants to know is actually using what C. Wright Mills called the **sociological imagination**, a phrase he coined in 1959 in a now-classic book (Mills, 2000; orig. 1959). Mills tried to understand how the average person in the United States understood his everyday life. According to Mills, each of us lives in a very small orbit, and our worldview is limited by the social situations we encounter on a daily basis. These include the family and the small groups we are a part of, the school we attend, and even the dorm in which we live. All these things give rise to a certain limited perspective and point of view.

The average person, according to Mills, doesn't really understand her personal problems as part of any kind of larger framework or series of goings-on. Mills argued that we all need to overcome our limited perspective. What is necessary is a certain quality of mind that makes it possible to understand the larger meaning of our experiences. This quality of mind is the sociological imagination.

When some white college applicants wonder if they are not getting into competitive schools because so many of the spaces go to minorities, they are connecting their individual experience up with a conception of the larger **social structure**. This conception about college admissions is perpetuated as a valid idea by cable television news; by certain newspapers, magazines, and websites; and by everyday conversation.

But is it true? One thing that Mills did not discuss is that having a sociological imagination requires more than making connections between individual lives and ideas about social structure. Since Mills's time, sociologists have come to focus even more strongly than ever on the careful assessment of evidence. When you look at the data, you will realize that it is absolutely impossible for most college rejections to be due to

sociological imagination • The application of imaginative thought to the asking and answering of sociological questions. Someone using the sociological imagination "thinks himself away" from the familiar routines of daily life.

social structure • The underlying regularities or patterns in how people behave and in their relationships with one another.

affirmative action. In a current entering class at an Ivy League school, for example, out of 1,000 students there may be 100 blacks and 75 Latinos. The 1,000 students were selected from about 20,000 applicants. A significant portion of the 19,000 who were rejected may think that they didn't get in because a black or a Latino got in instead of them. But we know from the data that this is impossible: There is no way that 175 people could be keeping 19,000 people out of any school. For this reason, answer choice *b* is also incorrect.

As you can see, it's not enough to have a sociological imagination in the way that Mills intended it. We want you to learn how to sort through the evidence in a way that begins with imagination but insists on the kind of methods that can give us firmer and better answers to important sociological questions. How to do this in a rigorous way will be the subject of Chapter 2.

THE ANSWER IS D.

1 BASIC CONCEPTS

The scope of sociological study is extremely wide, but in general, sociologists ask themselves certain questions that help to focus the sociological imagination and provide them with the concepts that motivate research. These questions that orient the discipline include: How are the things that we take to be natural actually socially constructed? How is social order possible? Does the individual matter? How are the times in which we are living different from the times that came before?

Social Construction

There is a basic flaw in human reasoning that goes something like this: The things that we see before us are inevitable. They are natural and cannot be changed. What sociology teaches us is that in many ways we are freer than we think—that the things we think are natural are actually created by human beings. We might consider the question we started this chapter with as an example: The college admissions system is a **social construction** located in a specific place and time. Criteria for admission to American colleges have shifted according to historical and demographic trends and to changes in university leadership (Gladwell, 2005).

Another example comes from everyday experiences with sex and gender. A baby is born with a penis or a vagina. By way of that characteristic, the baby begins a process of being assigned to the category of "boy" or "girl." This is extremely important because it is almost always the first thing you want to know before you can interact with the baby. If you can't figure it out, you may ask the parents.

Is this true of any other characteristic? You usually don't need to know the race of a baby before you start interacting. You don't need to know the economic class of a baby. Most babies today, regardless of their economic standing, are dressed in mass-produced clothes from stores such as Baby Gap or Old Navy. Most parents in general do not try to signal the class of their baby with his or her garments. The same principle applies to race and ethnicity. There are certain parents who will dress their baby in order to affiliate with a certain race or ethnic group,

social construction • An idea or practice that a group of people agree exists. It is maintained over time by people taking its existence for granted.

but—except on holidays—such parents are less common. Not as many people feel they need to know the race of a baby in order to interact with it.

Sex is different. If you are a parent, you do not want someone coming up to your baby boy and asking, "Is it a boy or a girl?" So what do you do to avoid this scenario? You dress your baby in blue if he is a boy, or in pink if she is a girl. Some parents do not do this at the beginning—until they start getting asked that question. Then they start dressing their baby in a certain way so that people will stop asking. Of course, even if you do dress your baby in the traditional blue or pink, there may still be people who come up and ask, "Is it a boy or a girl?" But it is not something that will happen often, because most people are pretty good at reading social cues—such as a blue or pink cap.

Now, the fact that many people need to know the sex of a baby suggests that we interact differently depending on whether we think someone is a boy or a girl. If a baby is a boy, a person might walk up and say something in a traditional masculine style, such as "Hey, Bud! How you doin'?" If it's a girl, the person might say something that is more appropriate for a little girl or more in keeping with the norms of traditional femininity. Eventually, we get to the point where these interactions start to mold the kind of person the baby becomes. Children come to see themselves as being either a boy or a girl. They start to move their bodies like a little boy or a little girl. They know that this is how they are seen by others and they know that when they go out onto the street, they occupy the role of boy or girl. This happens through a process of interaction.

Even though it is not simply a natural occurrence that a person starts to behave as a boy or a girl, many of us are raised to believe that the differences between men and women are purely biological. Sociologists disagree. Does this mean that sociologists want to eliminate the role of biology? No. The goal of sociology is not to try to teach you that the biological realm is a residual category with a minor role in explaining human behavior. One purpose of sociology is to disentangle what is biological from what is socially constructed. It is in part to try to figure out how social phenomena relate to biological phenomena. Most sociologists admit that there is a place for the biological. However, there are many fascinating studies that show that the things that the average human being thinks are biological, and thus natural, are actually socially constructed.

The more you start to think about disentangling what is natural from what is socially constructed, the more rigorously you will begin to think as a sociologist.

People interact differently with babies based on the babies' gender. How do sociologists analyze these interactions?

Social Order

A professor looks out onto a lecture hall and sees a roomful of silent students taking notes and exhibiting self-control and discipline. There must be somebody in the room who wishes that she were doing yoga instead, or who would like to turn around to a friend in the back and say something to him. But the fact of the matter is that almost everyone appears to be doing the same thing: sitting quietly, listening, taking notes (or at least pretending to). How can we explain this orderly behavior? How can we explain the existence of social order in a lecture hall or in a society? We certainly need social order to get through the day, but how can we understand it?

Sociologists have offered up many different explanations to try to answer such questions. One explanation is that it is rational for individuals to act this way. Students know it is in their self-interest to sit quietly and pay, or pretend to pay, attention. Perhaps a student hopes to apply to graduate school and wants to get a letter of recommendation from the professor. This goal motivates her to respond to the classroom environment: The professor's willingness to write a letter is an incentive for good behavior. The recommendation acts as an incentive, stimulating the response of the student who wants it. The student tries to make a good impression, all the while keeping in mind that if she turns around and talks to her friend week after week instead of listening, the professor might write an unflattering letter or refuse to write one at all. This explanation based on self-interest and incentives is what economists would use to explain most things. While some sociologists adopt such theories, most find such explanations to be based on an all-too-narrow conception of human nature. They appeal to a different set of theories.

Thus, another explanation for social order is the existence of norms. It is a norm of social life that when students come into a classroom they sit and take notes and pay attention. They learn and internalize norms as young people through a process called **socialization**. Once they have internalized a norm, they tend to follow through with the expectations of the norm in most of their interactions. Norms are important to sociologists because they explain some of the ways in which we are inside society and, simultaneously, society is inside us.

Yet another explanation for social order focuses on beliefs and values. Perhaps students place a value on the classroom, on the university, or on higher education. If this is the case, then the social order upheld in classrooms is more than a norm. The lecture hall is a symbol of a greater whole, a sacred place that is part of a larger moral universe. Students sit quietly because they believe professors in this ceremonial order deserve respect, maybe even deference.

It is important to keep in mind that we do not need to choose between these theories. Multiple factors can operate together. All these explanations address the question of social order from a sociological perspective. As such, the existence of social order is not taken for granted. For the average person, the question of social order arises in response to disruptions or breaks in that order. The average person who sees an event such as the attacks on the World Trade Center and the Pentagon on September 11, 2001, or the Columbine school shooting may ask, "How could this event have happened?" The sociologist reverses that question in order to ask, "How is it that disruptions in the social order do not happen more frequently?"

socialization • The social processes through which children develop an awareness of social norms and values and achieve a distinct sense of self. Although socialization processes are particularly significant in infancy and childhood, they continue to some degree throughout life. No individuals are immune from the reactions of others around them, which influence and modify their behavior at all phases of the life course.

Agency and Structure

A long-standing debate in the social sciences revolves around questions of free will and determinism. For example, a deterministic framework would predict that where an individual ends up in life is significantly if not entirely influenced by the position into which he is born. The sociological imagination can be quite deterministic in that it pushes us to see that, in many ways, the lives of individuals are quite determined by their social roles, gender, race, and class. Yet we would not want you to take away the lesson that individuals are trapped, or controlled like puppets.

Let us return to our example of college admissions. It is true that Ivy League graduates have a significantly higher average income than graduates of state-level schools. This would suggest that the place at which one attends college is a crucial determinant of one's success in later life. However, conventional studies looked only at students who had the same SAT scores and grades; they did not factor in other, personal characteristics that may have had an effect on later success in life.

In 2002, Alan Krueger and Stacy Dale published a study comparing the average yearly incomes of students who had been admitted to and attended an Ivy League college with those who had been admitted to an Ivy League school, but who chose to attend a state-level college instead. Krueger and Dale's study found that the individual *does* matter, despite an apparent disparity in opportunities for students who attend Ivy League versus non–Ivy League universities. Contrary to the popular conception that attending elite institutions will guarantee future success, it appears that highly motivated students, rather than institutional structures, prove more a determinant of this success (2002; Gladwell, 2005).

Sociologists tend to think in probabilities. They look at the probabilities that people will end up in certain living situations on the basis of characteristics, de-emphasizing to some extent the power of the individual. However, the sociological imagination does leave room for the person to have an impact, even as we acknowledge that she is constrained.

Think about a girl from a working-class family whose parents have active sociological imaginations and a very deterministic understanding of their child's life chances. The parents did not go to college. Instead, they entered the workforce after high school, and they expect that their daughter will do the same. When the teenager tells her parents that she would like to go to college and be a lawyer, the parents might think of the probability of an individual from their class position achieving such a goal—how unlikely it is. They might tell their child to consider the odds against her and encourage her to find a different goal so that she will not be disappointed. What if she took this advice with a grain of salt and applied to college anyway? She would be no different from many of your classmates, and possibly even you. Many of you can think of people who started out just like this, with similar constraints, but who ended up in college due to their refusal to accept the odds as their fate.

Social Change

One of the questions sociologists ask is how people live in light of the social transformations of their time.

In 1831, Alexis de Tocqueville, a French aristocrat and one of the first great social theorists, visited the United States from France. He wanted to understand how the conditions of democracy and equality were possible. Ever since the publication of his resulting study, *Democracy in*

Tocqueville described nineteenth-century Americans as a nation of joiners. Is that still true?

America (1969; orig. 1835), the United States has been viewed through the lens of sociology as a nation of joiners in which, more so than in Europe, people are involved in many groups and activities. Yet sociologists constantly revisit questions about whether the way we live today is different from how we lived in earlier times, and one of the enduring questions is whether Americans are less involved than before in public-spirited activities.

Another great theorist, Max Weber (1947; orig. 1922), looked at the way the world had been changing due to the influence of massive large-scale organizations, and how the emergence of an organizational society and large bureaucratic organizations had changed and transformed social life. Karl Marx, in *Capital* (1977; orig. 1867), examined how industrialization had changed the structure of an entire society, transforming the relationships of individuals to their work and to each other from feudalism to capitalism. Émile Durkheim, in *The Division of Labor in Society* (1964; orig. 1893), discussed how the historical changes wrought by industrialization and urbanization had led to the increasing specificity of the roles individuals fulfilled, and how this specialization functioned to benefit society as a whole. These sound like abstract topics, but they were central to understanding how the world was changing at particular times.

CONCEPT CHECKS ✓

1. What is the sociological imagination, according to C. Wright Mills?
2. How does sociology help us to disentangle biological from sociological phenomena?
3. How does the concept of social structure help sociologists better understand social phenomena?

2 THE DEVELOPMENT OF SOCIOLOGICAL THINKING

When students start studying sociology, many are puzzled by the diversity of approaches they encounter. Indeed, sociologists often disagree about how to study human behavior and how best to interpret research results. Why should this be so? Why can't sociologists agree more consistently, as natural scientists seem to do? The answer is bound up with the very nature of the field. Sociology is about our lives and our behavior, and studying ourselves is the most complex endeavor we can undertake. To understand this complexity, sociologists are guided by the four questions we have discussed and that are characteristic of sociological thinking: How are the things we take to be natural actually socially constructed? How is social order possible? Does the individual matter? How are the times in which we live different from those that came before?

Theories and Theoretical Approaches

AUGUSTE COMTE

The French philosopher Auguste Comte (1798–1857) invented the word *sociology* to describe the subject he wished to establish. Comte believed that the scientific method could be applied to the study of human behavior and society, and that this new field could produce knowledge of society based on scientific evidence. Comte believed that sociology should model itself after physics, and he initially called the subject *social physics*, a term that many of his contemporaries used. In addition to the scientific study of social life, Comte felt that sociology should contribute to the welfare of humanity by using science to predict and control human behavior. His ideas about social planning were predicated on an understanding that society and the social order are not natural or preordained by a divine power but, rather, are constructed by individuals. Later in his career, Comte drew up ambitious plans for the reconstruction of French society in particular, and for human societies in general, based on scientific knowledge. The question of whether sociologists should seek to serve humanity with their work is one that sociologists still ask.

ÉMILE DURKHEIM

Although Émile Durkheim (1858–1917) drew on aspects of Comte's work, he thought that many of his predecessor's ideas were too speculative and vague and that Comte had not successfully carried out his program—to establish sociology on a scientific basis. To have a scientific basis, according to Durkheim, sociologists must develop methodological principles to guide their research. Sociology must study **social facts**—aspects of social life that shape our actions as individuals, such as the state of the economy or the influence of religion. Durkheim's famous first principle of sociology was "Study social facts as things!" By this he meant that social life can be analyzed as rigorously as objects or events in nature.

Émile Durkheim (1858–1917).

Like a biologist studying the human body, Durkheim saw society as a set of independent parts, each of which could be studied separately. Each of a body's specialized parts (such as the brain, heart, lungs, and liver) contributes to sustaining the life of the organism. These specialized parts work in harmony with one another; if they do not, the life of the organism is under threat. So it is, according to Durkheim, with society. For a society to have a continuing existence over time, its specialized institutions (such as the political system, the religion, the family, and the educational system) must function as an integrated whole. Durkheim referred to this social cohesion as **organic solidarity**. He argued that the continuation of a society depends on cooperation, which presumes a general consensus among its members over basic values and customs.

social facts • According to Émile Durkheim, the aspects of social life that shape our actions as individuals. Durkheim believed that social facts could be studied scientifically.

organic solidarity • According to Émile Durkheim, the social cohesion that results from the various parts of a society functioning as an integrated whole.

Another theme pursued by Durkheim, and by many others since, is that societies exert **social constraint** over their members' actions. Durkheim argued that society is far more than the sum of individual acts; when we analyze social structures, we study characteristics that have a "firmness" or "solidity" comparable to those of structures in the physical world. Think of a person standing in a room with several doors. The structure of the room constrains the range of the person's possible activities. The position of the walls and doors, for example, defines routes of exit and entry. Social structure, according to Durkheim, constrains our activities in a parallel way, limiting what we can do as individuals. It is "external" to us, just as the walls of the room are.

Durkheim's analysis of social change was based on the development of the **division of labor**; he saw it as gradually replacing religion as the basis of social cohesion and providing organic solidarity to modern societies. He argued that as the division of labor expands, people become more dependent on one another because each person needs goods and services that those in other occupations supply. Another of Durkheim's famous studies (1966; orig. 1897) analyzed suicide. Although suicide seems to be a personal act, the outcome of extreme personal unhappiness, Durkheim showed that social factors influence suicidal behavior—such as **anomie**, a feeling of aimlessness or despair provoked by modern social life. Suicide rates show regular patterns from year to year, he argued, and these patterns must be explained sociologically. According to Durkheim, processes of change in the modern world are so rapid and intense that they give rise to major social difficulties, which he linked to anomie. Traditional moral controls and standards, formerly supplied by religion, largely break down under modern social development, and this leaves many individuals feeling that their lives lack meaning. Durkheim later focused on the role of religion in social life. In his study of religious beliefs, practices, and rituals, *The Elementary Forms of Religious Life* (1965; orig. 1912), he explored the importance of religion in maintaining moral order in society.

social constraint • The conditioning influence on our behavior of the groups and societies of which we are members. Social constraint was regarded by Émile Durkheim as one of the distinctive properties of social facts.

division of labor • The specialization of work tasks by means of which different occupations are combined within a production system. All societies have at least some rudimentary form of division of labor, especially between the tasks allocated to men and those performed by women. With the development of industrialism, the division of labor became vastly more complex than in any prior type of production system. In the modern world, the division of labor is international in scope.

anomie • The concept first brought into wide usage in sociology by Durkheim referring to a situation in which social norms lose their hold over individual behavior.

KARL MARX

The ideas of Karl Marx (1818–1883), German economic, political, and social theorist, contrast sharply with those of Comte and Durkheim; however, Marx also sought to explain social changes arising from the Industrial Revolution. When he was a young man, his political activities brought him into conflict with the German authorities; after a brief stay in France, he settled in exile in Britain. Much of his writing concentrates on economic issues, but because he was always concerned with connecting economic problems to social institutions, his work is rich in sociological insights.

Karl Marx (1818–1883).

Marx's viewpoint was founded on what he called the **materialist conception of history**. According to this view, it is not the ideas or values human beings hold that are the main sources of social change, as Durkheim claimed. Rather, social change is prompted primarily by economic influences. The conflicts between classes—rich versus poor—provide the motivation for historical development. In Marx's words, "All human history thus far is the history of class struggles."

Though he wrote about various phases of history, Marx concentrated on change in modern times. For him, the most important changes related to the development of **capitalism**. Those who own capital—factories, machines, and large sums of money—form a ruling class. The mass of the population makes up a class of wage workers, a working class, who do not own the means of their livelihood but must find employment provided by the owners of capital. Capitalism is thus a class system in which conflict is inevitable because it is in the interests of the ruling class to exploit the working class and in the interests of the workers to seek to overcome that exploitation.

According to Marx, in the future, capitalism will be supplanted by a society with no divisions between rich and poor. He didn't mean that all inequalities would disappear. Rather, societies will no longer be split into a small class that monopolizes economic and political power and the large mass of people who benefit little from the wealth their work creates. The economic system that will develop in response to capitalist conflict will have communal ownership and will lead to a more equal society than we know at present.

Marx's work had a far-reaching effect on the twentieth-century world. Until recently, before the fall of Soviet communism, more than a third of the earth's population lived in

materialist conception of history • The view developed by Marx according to which material, or economic, factors have a prime role in determining historical change.

capitalism • An economic system based on the private ownership of wealth, which is invested and reinvested in order to produce profit.

Table 1.1
Interpreting Modern Development

DURKHEIM	1.	The main dynamic of modern development is the **division of labor** as a basis for social cohesion and **organic solidarity**.
	2.	Durkheim believed that sociology must study **social facts** as things, just as science would analyze the natural world. His study of suicide led him to stress the important influence of social factors, qualities of a society external to the individual, on a person's actions. Durkheim argued that society exerts **social constraint** over our actions.
MARX	1.	The main dynamic of modern development is the expansion of **capitalism**. Rather than being cohesive, society is divided by class differences.
	2.	Marx believed that we must study the divisions within a society that are derived from the economic inequalities of capitalism.
WEBER	1.	The main dynamic of modern development is the **rationalization** of social and economic life.
	2.	Weber focused on why Western societies developed so differently from other societies. He also emphasized the importance of cultural ideas and values on social change.

Max Weber (1864–1920).

societies whose governments derived inspiration from Marx's ideas. In addition, many sociologists have been influenced by Marx's ideas about class divisions.

MAX WEBER

Like Marx, the German-born Max Weber (pronounced "Vaber," 1864–1920) cannot be labeled simply a sociologist; his interests spanned many areas. His writings covered the fields of economics, law, philosophy, and comparative history as well as sociology, and much of his work also treated the development of modern capitalism. He was influenced by Marx but was also critical of some of Marx's major views. He rejected the materialist conception of history and saw class conflict as less significant than did Marx. In Weber's view, economic factors are important, but ideas and values have just as much effect on social change.

Some of Weber's most influential writings analyzed the distinctiveness of Western society compared with other major civilizations. He studied the religions of China, India, and the Near East, thereby making major contributions to the sociology of religion. Comparing the leading religious systems in China and India with those of the West, Weber concluded that certain aspects of Christian beliefs had strongly influenced the rise of capitalism. He argued that the capitalist outlook of Western societies had not emerged, as Marx supposed, only from economic changes. In Weber's view, cultural ideas and values shape society and affect individual actions.

One of the most persistent concerns of Weber's work was the study of **bureaucracy**. A bureaucracy is a large organization that is divided into jobs based on specific functions and staffed by officials ranked according to a hierarchy. Industrial firms, government organizations, hospitals, and schools are examples of bureaucracies. Weber saw the advance of bureaucracy as an inevitable feature of our era. Bureaucracy enables large organizations to run efficiently, but at the same time it poses problems for effective democratic participation in modern societies. Bureaucracy involves the rule of experts, who make decisions without consulting those whose lives are affected by them.

Some of Weber's writings also address the character of sociology itself. He was more cautious than either Durkheim or Marx in proclaiming sociology to be a science. According to Weber, it is misleading to imagine that we can study people by using the same procedures by which we use physics or biology to investigate the physical world. Humans are thinking, reasoning beings; we attach meaning and significance to most of what we do, and any discipline that deals with human behavior must acknowledge this.

Neglected Founders

Although Comte, Durkheim, Marx, and Weber are foundational figures in sociology, other thinkers from the same period made important contributions. Very few women or members of racial minorities had the opportunity to become professional sociologists during the "classical" period of the late nineteenth and early twentieth centuries. Even the foundational figures in sociology frequently ignored women and racial minorities, at the same time that they were

bureaucracy • A type of organization marked by a clear hierarchy of authority and the existence of written rules of procedure and staffed by full-time, salaried officials.

creating the first theories systematically to address inequality, stratification, subjective meaning, and exploitation. As a result, the few women and members of racial minorities that conducted sociological research of lasting importance often remain neglected by the field. These individuals and the theories they developed deserve the attention of sociologists today.

HARRIET MARTINEAU

Harriet Martineau (1802–1876), born and educated in England, has been called the "first woman sociologist." As with Marx and Weber, her interests extended beyond sociology. She was the author of more than 50 books as well as numerous essays, and was an active proponent of women's rights and the abolition of slavery. Martineau is now credited with introducing sociology to England through her translation of Comte's founding treatise of the field, *Positive Philosophy* (Rossi, 1973). Additionally, she conducted a systematic study of American society during her extensive travels throughout the United States in the 1830s, which is the subject of her book *Society in America* (1962; orig. 1837). Martineau is significant to sociologists today for several reasons, but in particular for her methodological insight. First, she argued that when one studies a society, one must focus on all its aspects, including key political, religious, and social institutions. Second, she insisted that an analysis of a society must include all its members, a point that drew attention to the conspicuous absence of women's lives from the sociology of that time. Third, she was the first to turn a sociological eye on previously ignored issues and institutions, including marriage, children, domestic and religious life, and race relations. Finally, like Comte, she argued that sociologists should do more than just observe; they should also act in ways to benefit society.

Harriet Martineau (1802–1876).

W.E.B. DU BOIS

W.E.B. Du Bois (1868–1963) was the first African American to earn a doctorate from Harvard University. Among his many contributions to sociology, perhaps most important is the concept of "double consciousness," a way of talking about identity through the lens of the experiences of African Americans. Du Bois made a persuasive claim that one's sense of self and one's identity are greatly influenced by historical experiences and social circumstances—in the case of African Americans, the effect of slavery and, after emancipation, segregation and prejudice. Throughout his career, Du Bois focused on race relations in the United States; as he said in an oft-repeated quote, "the problem of the twentieth century is the problem of the color line" (Du Bois, 1903). His influence on sociology today is evidenced by continued interest in the questions he raised, particularly his concern that sociology must explain "the contact of diverse races of men" (Du Bois, 1903). Du Bois was also the first social researcher to trace the problems faced by African Americans to their social and economic underpinnings, a connection that most sociologists now widely accept. Finally, he connected social

W.E.B. Du Bois (1868–1963).

analysis to social reform. He was one of the founding members of the National Association for the Advancement of Colored People (NAACP) and a longtime advocate for the collective struggle of African Americans.

Understanding the Modern World: The Sociological Debate

From Marx's time to the present, many sociological debates have centered on Marx's ideas about the influence of economics on the development of modern societies. According to Marx, the impulse behind social change in the modern era resides in the pressure toward constant economic transformation produced by the spread of capitalist production. Capitalism is a vastly more dynamic economic system than any other that preceded it. Capitalists compete to sell their goods to consumers; to survive in a competitive market, firms have to produce their wares as cheaply and efficiently as possible. This leads to constant technological innovation, because increasing the effectiveness of the technology used in a particular production process is one way in which companies can secure an edge over their rivals.

There are also strong incentives to seek new markets in which to sell goods, acquire cheap raw materials, and make use of cheap labor power. Capitalism, therefore, according to Marx, is a restlessly expanding system pushing outward across the world. This is how Marx explains the global spread of Western industry.

Subsequent Marxist authors have refined Marx's portrayal. However, numerous critics have set out to rebut Marx's view, offering alternative analyses of the influences shaping the modern world. Virtually everyone accepts that capitalism has played a major part, but other sociologists have argued that Marx exaggerated the effect of purely economic factors in producing change and that capitalism is less central to modern social development than he claimed. Most of these writers have also been skeptical of Marx's belief that a socialist system would eventually replace capitalism.

One of Marx's earliest and most acute critics was Max Weber, whose alternative position remains important today. According to Weber, noneconomic factors have played the key role in modern social development. Weber's celebrated work *The Protestant Ethic and the Spirit of Capitalism* (1977; orig. 1904) proposes that religious values—especially those associated with Puritanism—were of fundamental importance in creating a capitalistic outlook. This outlook did not emerge, as Marx supposed, only from economic changes.

Weber's understanding of the nature of modern societies, and the reasons for the spread of Western ways of life across the world, also contrasts substantially with that of Marx. According to Weber, capitalism—a distinct way of organizing economic enterprise—is one among other major factors shaping social development in the modern period. Underlying capitalist mechanisms, and in some ways more fundamental than those mechanisms, is the effect of science and bureaucracy. Science has shaped modern technology and will presumably do so in any future society, whether socialist or capitalist. Bureaucracy is the only way of organizing large numbers of people effectively, and therefore inevitably expands with economic and political growth. The developments of science, modern technology, and bureaucracy are examples of a general social process that Weber refers to collectively as **rationalization**. Rationalization means the organization of

rationalization • A concept used by Max Weber to refer to the process by which modes of precise calculation and organization, involving abstract rules and procedures, increasingly come to dominate the social world.

social, economic, and cultural life according to principles of efficiency, on the basis of technical knowledge.

Which interpretation of modern societies, that deriving from Marx or that coming from Weber, is correct? Scholars are divided on the issue. Moreover, within each camp are variations, so not every theorist agrees with all the points of one interpretation. The contrasts between these two standpoints inform many areas of sociology.

CONCEPT CHECKS

1. According to Émile Durkheim, what makes sociology a social science? Why?
2. According to Karl Marx, what are the differences between the two classes that make up a capitalist society?

3 MODERN THEORETICAL APPROACHES

Although the origins of sociology were mainly European, over the last century the subject has become firmly established worldwide, and some of the most important developments have taken place in the United States (Figure 1.1).

Symbolic Interactionism

The work of George Herbert Mead (1863–1931), a philosopher teaching at the University of Chicago, influenced the development of sociological thought, in particular through a perspective called **symbolic interactionism**. Mead placed particular importance on the study of language in

symbolic interactionism • A theoretical approach in sociology developed by George Herbert Mead that emphasizes the role of symbols and language as core elements of all human interaction.

Figure 1.1
Theoretical Approaches in Sociology

The solid lines indicate direct influence, the dotted line, an indirect connection. Mead is not indebted to Weber, but Weber's views—stressing the meaningful, purposive nature of human action—have affinities with the themes of symbolic interactionism.

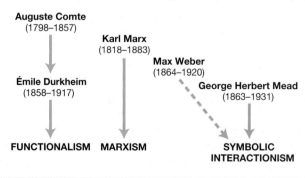

analyzing the social world. According to him, language allows us to become self-conscious beings—aware of our own individuality. The key element in this process is the **symbol**. For example, the word *tree* is a symbol by which we represent the object tree. Once we have mastered such a concept, Mead argued, we can think of a tree even if none is visible. Symbolic thought frees us from being limited in our experience to what we actually see, hear, or feel.

Unlike animals, according to Mead, human beings live in a richly symbolic universe. This applies even to our sense of self. Each of us is a self-conscious being because we learn to look at ourselves as if from the outside—as others see us. When a child begins to use "I" to refer to that object whom others call "you" (herself), she is exhibiting the beginnings of self-consciousness.

All interactions among individuals, symbolic interactionists say, involve an exchange of symbols. When we interact with others, we constantly look for clues to what type of behavior is appropriate in the context and how to interpret what others are up to. Symbolic interactionism directs our attention to the detail of interpersonal interaction and how that detail is used to make sense of what others say and do. For instance, suppose two people are on a first date. Each spends a good part of the evening sizing the other up and assessing how the relationship is likely to develop, if at all. Neither wishes to be seen doing this too openly, although each recognizes that it is going on. Both individuals are careful about their own behavior, being eager to present themselves in a favorable light; but, knowing this, both are looking for aspects of the other's behavior that would reveal his or her true opinions. A complex and subtle process of symbolic interpretation shapes their interaction.

Functionalism

Symbolic interactionism has been criticized for concentrating too much on things that are small in scope. Symbolic interactionists have found difficulty in dealing with larger-scale structures and processes—the very things that a rival tradition of thought, **functionalism**, emphasizes. Functionalist thinking in sociology was originally pioneered by Comte, who saw it as closely bound up with his overall view of the field.

To study the function of a social activity is to analyze its contribution to the continuation of the society as a whole. The best way to understand this idea is by analogy to the human body, a comparison that Comte, Durkheim, and other functionalist authors made. To study an organ such as the heart, we need to show how it relates to other parts of the body. When we learn how the heart pumps blood, we understand its vital role in the continuation of the life of the organism. Similarly, analyzing the function of some aspect of society, such as religion, means showing its part in the continued existence and health of a society. Functionalism emphasizes the importance of moral consensus in maintaining order and stability in society. Moral consensus exists when most people share the same values. Functionalists regard order and balance as the normal state of society—this social equilibrium is grounded in a moral consensus among the members of society. According to Durkheim, for instance, religion reaffirms people's adherence to core social values, thereby helping to maintain social cohesion.

Functionalism became prominent in sociology through the writings of Talcott Parsons and

symbol • One item used to stand for or represent another—as in the case of a flag, which symbolizes a nation.

functionalism • A theoretical perspective based on the notion that social events can best be explained in terms of the functions they perform—that is, the contributions they make to the continuity of a society.

Robert K. Merton, each of whom saw functionalist analysis as providing the key to the development of sociological theory and research. Merton's version of functionalism has been particularly influential.

Merton distinguished between manifest and latent functions. **Manifest functions** are those known to, and intended by, the participants in a social activity. **Latent functions** are consequences of that activity of which participants are unaware. Merton used the example of a rain dance performed by the Hopi tribe of Arizona and New Mexico. The Hopi believe that the ceremony will bring the rain they need for their crops (manifest function). This is why they organize and participate in it. But using Durkheim's theory of religion, Merton argued that the rain dance also promotes the cohesion of Hopi society (latent function). A major part of sociological explanation, according to Merton, consists in uncovering the latent functions of social activities and institutions.

Merton also distinguished between functions and dysfunctions. To look for the dysfunctional aspects of social behavior means to focus on features of social life that challenge the existing order. For example, it is mistaken to suppose that religion is always functional—that it contributes only to social cohesion. When two groups support different religions or different versions of the same religion, the result can be major social conflicts, causing widespread social disruption. Thus wars have often been fought between religious communities—as in the struggles between Protestants and Catholics in European history.

Robert K. Merton (1910–2003).

For a long while, functionalist thought was the leading theoretical tradition in sociology, particularly in the United States. In recent years, its popularity has declined. Although this was not true of Merton, many functionalist thinkers—Talcott Parsons is an example—unduly stressed factors leading to social cohesion at the expense of those producing division and conflict. In addition, many critics claim that functional analysis attributes to societies certain qualities those societies do not have. Functionalists often wrote as though societies had "needs" and "purposes," even though these concepts make sense only when applied to individual human beings.

Marxism and Class Conflict

Functionalism and symbolic interactionism are not the only modern theoretical traditions of importance in sociology. A further influential approach is **Marxism**. Marxists, of course, all trace their views back to the writings of Karl Marx, but today there are schools of Marxist thought that take very different theoretical positions.

In all its variations, Marxism differs from non-Marxist traditions of sociology in that its authors see it as a combination of sociological analysis and political reform. Marxism is supposed to generate a program of radical political change. Moreover, Marxists lay more emphasis

manifest functions • The functions of a type of social activity that are known to and intended by the individuals involved in the activity.

latent functions • Functional consequences that are not intended or recognized by the members of a social system in which they occur.

Marxism • A body of thought deriving its main elements from the ideas of Karl Marx.

on conflict, class divisions, power, and ideology than many non-Marxist sociologists do, especially those influenced by functionalism. The concept of **power** is of great importance to Marxist sociologists and to sociology in general. Power implies the capability of individuals or groups to make their own interests count, even when others resist. Power sometimes involves the direct use of force but is almost always accompanied by the development of ideas (**ideologies**), which are used to justify the actions of the powerful. Power, ideology, and conflict are always closely connected. Many conflicts are about power because of the rewards it can bring. Those who hold most power may depend on the influence of ideology to retain their dominance but are usually also able to use force if necessary.

Feminism and Feminist Theory

Feminist theory is one of the most prominent areas of contemporary sociology. This is a notable development because gender issues are scarcely central in the work of the major figures who established the discipline. The success of feminism's entry into sociology required a fundamental shift in the discipline's approach.

Many feminist theorists' experiences in the women's movement of the 1960s and '70s influenced their work as sociologists. Like Marxism, feminism links sociological theory and political reform. Many feminist sociologists have been advocates for political and social action to remedy the inequalities between women and men in both the public and the private spheres.

Feminist sociologists argue that women's experiences are central to the study of society. Sociology, like most academic disciplines, has presumed a male point of view. Concerned with women's subordination in society, feminist sociologists highlight gender relations and gender inequality as important determinants of social life in terms of both social interaction and social institutions such as the family, the workplace, and the educational system. Feminist theory emphasizes that gendered patterns and gendered inequalities are socially constructed. (We will cover this point in more detail in Chapter 10.)

Today, feminist sociology focuses on the intersection of gender, race, and class. A feminist approach to the study of inequality has influenced new fields of study, such as men's studies, sexuality studies, and gay and lesbian studies.

power • The ability of individuals or the members of a group to achieve aims or further the interests they hold. Power is a pervasive element in all human relationships. Many conflicts in society are struggles over power, because how much power an individual or group is able to achieve governs how far they are able to put their wishes into practice.

ideologies • Shared ideas or beliefs that serve to justify the interests of dominant groups. Ideologies are found in all societies in which there are systematic and ingrained inequalities between groups. The concept of ideology connects closely with that of power, since ideological systems serve to legitimize the power that groups hold.

feminist theory • A sociological perspective that emphasizes the centrality of gender in analyzing the social world and particularly the uniqueness of the experience of women. There are many strands of feminist theory, but they all share the desire to explain gender inequalities in society and to work to overcome them.

Rational Choice Theory

The sociologist Max Weber thought that all behavior could be divided into four categories: (1) behavior oriented toward higher values, such as politics; (2) behavior oriented toward habit, such as walking to school on a familiar path; (3) behavior oriented toward affect (emotions), such as falling in love; and (4) behavior oriented toward self-interest, such as making money. Behavior in the last category is often called "instrumental," or "rational," action. In recent years, many sociologists have adopted an approach that focuses on it. This has led numerous scholars to ask under what conditions human behavior can be said to constitute rational responses to opportunities and constraints.

The **rational choice approach** posits that if you could have only a single variable to explain society, self-interest would be the best one. A person who believes in this approach might even use it to explain things that seem irrational. One popular rational choice theory sees decisions to marry as maximizing self-interest in a marriage market; this might explain why marriage has declined the most in poor African American communities with low rates of employment. The explanation—that it is not in the self-interest of women to marry men who cannot support them (Wilson, 1987)—goes against competing explanations suggesting that poor African Americans don't marry because they don't share mainstream values. The rational choice argument sees the decline as having little to do with values and much to do with self-interest under existing conditions. According to this theory, if employment rates for black men were to change, so would the number of "eligible" men and the desire of women to marry them.

Rational choice theorists find few irrational mysteries in life. One of the few some note is love, which they define as the irrational act of substituting another person's self-interest for one's own (Becker, 1991). But such a definition makes it difficult to distinguish between basic altruism, friendship, and romantic love. Indeed, although a rational choice approach often can be useful, there are some aspects of life that it cannot explain. Consider an angry driver who tries to teach a tailgater a lesson by tailgating the tailgater. Self-interest does not explain this action because the "teacher" is unlikely to personally reap the benefits of a lesson well learned (Katz, 1999).

Postmodern Theory

Advocates of **postmodernism** claim that the classic social thinkers' idea that history has a shape—it "goes somewhere" and leads to progress—has collapsed. No longer do any "grand narratives," or metanarratives—overall conceptions of history or society—make any sense (Lyotard, 1985). In fact, there is no such thing as history. The postmodern world is not destined, as Marx hoped, to be a socialist one. Instead, it is dominated by the new media, which "take us out" of our past. Postmodern society is highly pluralistic and diverse. As countless films, videos, TV programs, and websites circulate images around the world, the many ideas and values we encounter have little connection with our local or personal histories. Everything seems constantly in flux: "[F]lexibility, diversity, differentiation, and mobility, communication, decentralization and internationalization are in the ascendant. In the process our own identities, our sense of self, our own subjectivities are being transformed" (Hall, Held, and McGrew, 1988).

One important theorist of postmodernity, Jean Baudrillard (1929–2007), believed that the electronic media created a chaotic, empty world. Despite being influenced by Marxism in his early years, Baudrillard argued that the spread of electronic communication and the mass media reversed the Marxist theorem that economic forces shape society. Instead, he asserted, social life is influenced above all by signs and images.

rational choice approach • More broadly, the theory that an individual's behavior is purposive. Within the field of criminology, rational choice analysis argues that deviant behavior is a rational response to a specific social situation.

postmodernism • The belief that society is no longer governed by history or progress. Postmodern society is highly pluralistic and diverse, with no "grand narrative" guiding its development.

In a media-dominated age, Baudrillard said, meaning is created by the flow of images, as in TV programs. Much of our world is now a make-believe universe in which we respond to media images rather than to real persons or places. Thus, when Diana, Princess of Wales, died in 1997, the worldwide outpouring of grief did not constitute mourning for a real person, because Diana existed for most people only through the media. Her death was more like an event in a soap opera.

Theoretical Thinking in Sociology

So far we have been discussing theoretical approaches—broad orientations to the subject matter of sociology. However, there is a distinction between theoretical approaches and theories. Theories are more narrowly focused and attempt to explain particular social conditions or types of events. They are usually formed during the research process and suggest other problems for subsequent research. An example would be Durkheim's theory of suicide.

Some theories are more encompassing than others. Opinions vary about whether it is desirable or useful for sociologists to engage in very wide-ranging theoretical endeavors. Robert K. Merton (1957), for example, argued that sociologists should concentrate on what he called theories of the middle range. Rather than attempting to create grand theoretical schemes (in the manner of Marx, for instance), we should develop more modest theories.

Middle-range theories are specific enough to be tested by empirical research, yet sufficiently general to cover a range of phenomena. Consider the theory of relative deprivation, which holds that how people evaluate their circumstances depends on whom they compare themselves to. Thus feelings of deprivation do not conform directly to the level of material poverty that individuals experience. A family living in a small home in a poor area, where everyone is in similar circumstances, is likely to feel less deprived than a family living in a similar house in a neighborhood where other homes are much larger and other people more affluent.

Indeed, the more wide-ranging and ambitious a theory is, the more difficult it is to test empirically. Yet there seems no obvious reason that theoretical thinking in sociology should be confined to the "middle range."

Assessing theories in sociology, especially theoretical approaches, is a challenging and formidable task. The fact that no theoretical approach dominates the whole of sociology might seem to be a sign of weakness in the subject. But this is not the case: The jostling of rival theoretical approaches and theories actually expresses the vitality of the sociological enterprise. In studying human beings (ourselves), theoretical variety rescues us from dogma. Because human behavior is so complicated, a single theoretical perspective could never cover all its aspects. Diversity in theoretical thinking provides a rich source of ideas for research and stimulates the imaginative capacities so essential to progress in sociological work.

microsociology • The study of human behavior in contexts of face-to-face interaction.

macrosociology • The study of large-scale groups, organizations, or social systems.

Levels of Analysis: Microsociology and Macrosociology

An important distinction among theoretical perspectives involves the level of analysis each takes. The study of everyday behavior during face-to-face interaction is **microsociology**. **Macrosociology** is the analysis of large-scale social systems, such as the political system

Microsociology focuses on face-to-face interactions (a), while macrosociology analyzes large-scale social forces (b). How might a microsociologist and a macrosociologist analyze this food court differently?

or the economic order. It also includes analysis of long-term processes of change, such as the development of industrialism. Although micro analysis and macro analysis may seem distinct from one another, in fact the two are closely connected (Giddens, 1984; Knorr-Cetina and Cicourel, 1981).

Macro analysis is essential for understanding the institutional background of daily life, because people's lives are affected by the broader institutional framework. Consider a comparison of the daily cycle of activities in a medieval culture and in an industrialized urban environment. In modern societies, we are constantly in contact with strangers. This contact may be indirect and impersonal. However, no matter how many indirect or electronic relations we enter into, even the most complex societies require the presence of other people. While we may choose to send an acquaintance just an e-mail message, we can also choose to fly thousands of miles to spend the weekend with a friend.

Micro studies illuminate broad institutional patterns. Face-to-face interaction is the basis of all forms of social organization, no matter how large scale. In studying a business corporation, we could examine face-to-face behavior to analyze, for example, the interaction of directors in the boardroom, people working in various offices, or workers on the factory floor. We would not gain a picture of the whole corporation in this way because some of its business involves printed materials, letters, the telephone, and computers. Yet we could certainly contribute significantly to understanding how the organization works.

Later chapters will give further examples of how interaction in micro contexts affects larger social processes and how macro systems affect the more confined settings of social life.

CONCEPT CHECKS

1. What are the differences between symbolic interactionism and functionalist approaches to the analysis of society?

2. How do rational choice theorists explain human behavior?

3. What role does theory play in sociological research?

4. How are macro and micro analyses of society connected?

4 HOW CAN SOCIOLOGY HELP US?

As we discussed at the beginning of the chapter, sociological thinking applies to your day-to-day life—from college admissions to falling in love. C. Wright Mills emphasized these practical applications of sociology when developing his idea of the sociological imagination.

Awareness of Cultural Differences

First, sociology allows us to see the social world from many perspectives. If we properly understand how others live, we better understand their problems. Practical policies that lack an informed awareness of the ways of life of people they affect have little chance of success. Thus a white social worker operating in an African American community won't gain the confidence of its members without having a sensitivity to the differences in social experience that separate white and black in the United States.

Assessing the Effects of Policies

Second, sociological research helps in assessments of the results of policy initiatives. For example, a program of practical reform may fail to achieve its goals or may produce unintended negative consequences. Consider the large public-housing blocks built in city centers in many countries following World War II. The goal was to provide high standards of accommodation for low-income groups from slum areas and to offer shopping amenities and other civic services close at hand. However, research later showed that many people who had moved to the large apartment blocks felt isolated and unhappy. High-rise apartment blocks and shopping malls in poorer areas often became dilapidated and provided breeding grounds for muggings and other violent crimes.

Self-Enlightenment

Third, and perhaps most important, sociology can provide us with self-enlightenment— increased self-understanding. The more we know about our own behavior and how our society works, the better chance we have to influence our futures. Sociology doesn't just help policy makers make informed decisions. Those in power may not always consider the interests of the less powerful or underprivileged when making policies. Self-enlightened groups can benefit from sociological research by using the information gleaned to respond to government policies or form policy initiatives of their own. Self-help groups such as Alcoholics Anonymous (AA) and social movements such as the environmental movement are examples of social groups that have directly sought practical reforms, with some success.

The Sociologist's Role

Finally, many sociologists address practical matters in their work as professionals—as industrial consultants, urban planners, social workers, and personnel managers, among other jobs. An understanding of society also serves those working in law, journalism, business, and medicine.

Those who study sociology frequently develop a social conscience. Should sociologists themselves agitate for programs of reform or social change? Some argue that sociology can preserve its intellectual independence only if sociologists remain neutral in moral and political controversies. Yet are scholars who remain aloof more impartial in their assessment of sociological issues than others? No sociologically sophisticated person can be unaware of the inequalities, the lack of social justice, or the deprivations suffered by millions of people worldwide. It would be strange if sociologists did not take sides on practical issues, and it would be illogical to ban them from drawing on their expertise in doing so.

We have seen that sociology is a discipline in which we often set aside our personal views to explore the influences that shape our lives and those of others. Sociology emerged as an intellectual endeavor along with the development of modern societies, and the study of such societies remains its principal concern. But sociologists are also preoccupied with the nature of social interaction and human societies in general.

Sociology has major practical implications for people's lives. Learning to become a sociologist shouldn't be a dull academic endeavor! The best way to make sure of this is to approach the subject in an imaginative way and to relate sociological ideas and findings to your own life.

CONCEPT CHECKS

1. Describe three ways that sociology can help us in our lives.
2. What skills and perspectives do sociologists bring to their work?

THE BIG PICTURE

Chapter 1
What Is Sociology?

1 **Basic Concepts**

p. 6

2 **The Development of Sociological Thinking**

p. 10

LEARNING OBJECTIVES

Learn what sociology encompasses and how everyday topics are shaped by social and historical forces. Recognize that sociology involves not only acquiring knowledge but also developing a sociological imagination.

Learn how sociology originated and understand the significance of the intellectual contributions of early sociologists.

TERMS TO KNOW

Sociological imagination • Social structure • Social construction • Socialization

Social facts • Organic solidarity • Social constraint • Division of labor • Anomie • Materialist conception of history • Capitalism • Bureaucracy • Rationalization

CONCEPT CHECKS

1. What is the sociological imagination, according to C. Wright Mills?
2. How does sociology help us to disentangle biological from sociological phenomena?
3. How does the concept of social structure help sociologists better understand social phenomena?

1. According to Émile Durkheim, what makes sociology a social *science*? Why?
2. According to Karl Marx, what are the differences between the two classes that make up a capitalist society?

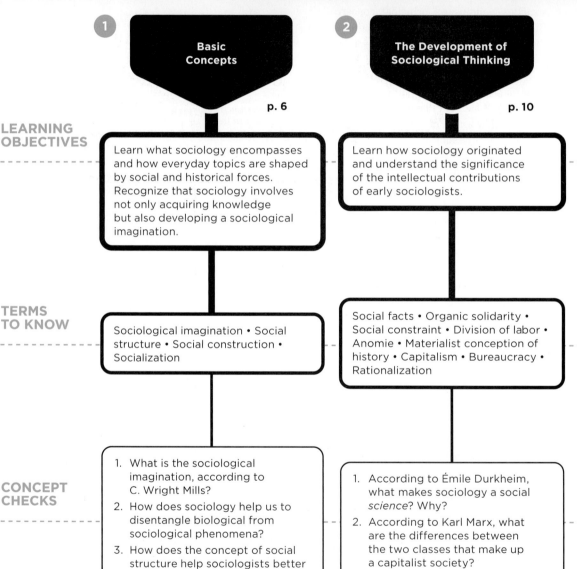

Exercises: Thinking Sociologically

1. Healthy older Americans often encounter exclusionary treatment when younger people assume they are feebleminded and thus overlook them for jobs they are fully capable of doing. How would functionalism and symbolic interactionism explain the dynamics of prejudice against the elderly?

2. Coffee drinking is a cultural fixture that says as much about us as it does about the bean itself. Coffee is more than a simple product designed to quench a person's thirst and fend off drowsiness. Discuss five sociological features of coffee consumption that show its "sociological" nature.

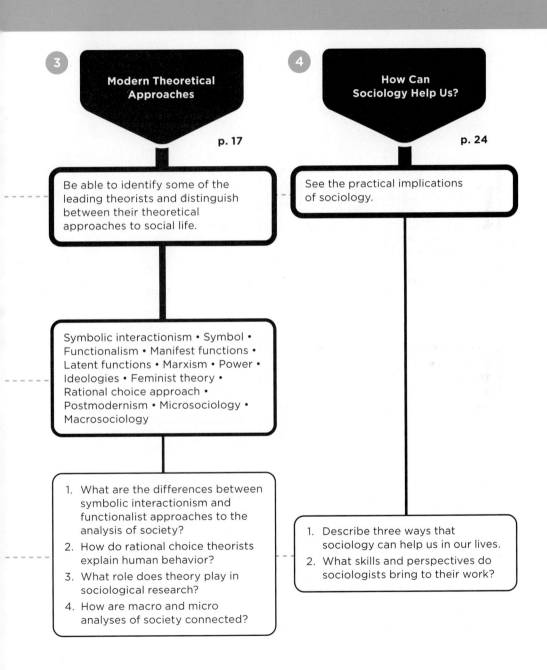

3 **Modern Theoretical Approaches**

p. 17

Be able to identify some of the leading theorists and distinguish between their theoretical approaches to social life.

Symbolic interactionism • Symbol • Functionalism • Manifest functions • Latent functions • Marxism • Power • Ideologies • Feminist theory • Rational choice approach • Postmodernism • Microsociology • Macrosociology

1. What are the differences between symbolic interactionism and functionalist approaches to the analysis of society?
2. How do rational choice theorists explain human behavior?
3. What role does theory play in sociological research?
4. How are macro and micro analyses of society connected?

4 **How Can Sociology Help Us?**

p. 24

See the practical implications of sociology.

1. Describe three ways that sociology can help us in our lives.
2. What skills and perspectives do sociologists bring to their work?

Asking and Answering Sociological Questions

2

Sociology is

a a pseudoscience

b a science like the natural sciences

c a science unlike the natural sciences

Turn the page for the correct answer.

By the end of this chapter, we hope you will understand that the answer to this question is *c*, "a science unlike the natural sciences." But if you picked *a* or *b*, you would not be unlike many educated people, and a good argument could be made for any of those positions.

If you picked *a*, "a pseudoscience," you might believe that sociology is a discipline masquerading as a science. Those who believe this have much in common with those who would call sociology a soft (not rigorous) science, thereby drawing a distinction between sociology and so-called hard (rigorous) sciences such as physics or chemistry. Yet what makes fields such as chemistry and physics rigorous is not their subject matter as much as a series of characteristics that are also true of social sciences (King, Keohane, and Verba, 1994).

When thinking about this question, it is helpful to remember the following four factors that unify all scientific endeavors.

- First, they are usually interested in studying things not for their own sake, but to develop theories that can apply to the widest class of things with similar characteristics.
- Second, all scientific conclusions are uncertain; in order for a claim to be scientific it must come with a statement that explains how much uncertainty there is as to whether it is true.
- Third, procedures must be publicized so that all studies can be repeated by others who want to see if they get the same results.
- Fourth, if correct procedures are followed, any topic can be the subject matter of science.

All these criteria might make us satisfied with answer *b*, "a science like the natural sciences," but such an answer would overstate the degree of overlap between social and natural

LEARNING OBJECTIVES

1 BASIC CONCEPTS

Learn the steps of the research process and be able to complete the process yourself. Name the different types of questions sociologists address in their research—factual, theoretical, comparative, and developmental.

2 ASKING AND ANSWERING SOCIOLOGICAL QUESTIONS: HISTORICAL CONTEXT

Contrast Park's and Ogburn's visions of sociology as a science. Understand their influence on contemporary sociological research.

3 ASKING AND ANSWERING SOCIOLOGICAL QUESTIONS TODAY: THE RESEARCH PROCESS

Familiarize yourself with the methods available to sociological researchers and know the advantages and disadvantages of each.

4 UNANSWERED QUESTIONS

See how research methods generate controversies and ethical dilemmas for sociologists.

sciences. In order to make this point, it is important to emphasize that in social science the investigator is part of the study and must be aware of the grounds of her own action. For social scientists more so than natural scientists, there is more of an acknowledgment that the investigator is a crucial part of the world she studies, and cannot necessarily divorce herself from it. Her impact on the world she studies can range from investigator effects, exploitation of human subjects, and power dynamics between her and subjects, to the way her values or personal identity impact the nature of the questions asked and the interpretation of data. While the natural sciences deal with such problems as well, these issues are more extreme in the social sciences. It is thus necessary to think of sociology as a science that is both like and unlike the natural sciences.

THE ANSWER IS C.

BASIC CONCEPTS

In order to understand the way sociology asks and answers questions, it is helpful to think of the research it does as a process. The main concepts of research design can be better understood by breaking down the process into eight stages of research—from the beginning of an investigation to the time its findings are made available in written form.

1. Defining the Research Problem

All research starts with a research problem. This may be an area of factual ignorance about, say, certain institutions, social processes, or cultures. A researcher might seek to answer questions such as: What proportion of the population holds strong religious beliefs? Are people today disaffected with "big government"? How far does the economic position of women lag behind that of men?

The best sociological research begins with problems that are also puzzles. A puzzle arises from not simply a lack of information, but also a gap in our understanding. Much of the skill in producing worthwhile sociological research consists in correctly identifying puzzles.

Rather than simply answering the question "What is going on here?" puzzle-solving research tries to illuminate why events happen as they do. Thus we might ask: Why are patterns of religious belief changing? What accounts for the recent decline in the proportion of the population voting in presidential elections? Why are women poorly represented in high-status jobs?

No piece of research stands alone. One project may lead to another because it raises issues the researcher had not previously considered. A sociologist may discover puzzles by reading the work of other researchers in books and professional journals or by being aware of social trends. For example, an increasing number of programs for treating the mentally ill encourage them to live in the community rather than being confined to hospitals. Sociologists might be prompted to ask: What has caused this shift in attitude toward the mentally ill? What are the likely consequences for the patients themselves and for the rest of the community?

2. Reviewing the Literature

Once the problem is identified, the sociologist must review related research: Have previous researchers spotted the same puzzle? How have they tried to solve it? What aspects of the problem has their research left unanalyzed? Drawing on others' ideas helps the sociologist clarify the relevant issues and the appropriate research methods.

3. Formulating a Hypothesis

A third stage involves clearly formulating the research problem. If relevant literature already exists, the researcher might gain a good notion of how to approach the problem. At this stage, hunches sometimes become **hypotheses**—educated guesses about what is going on. For the research to be effective, a hypothesis must be formulated in such a way that the factual material gathered will provide evidence either supporting or disproving it.

4. Selecting a Research Design

The researcher then decides how to collect the research materials, choosing from a range of methods based on the objectives of the study as well as the aspects of behavior under study. For some purposes, a survey (usually involving questionnaires) might be suitable. In other circumstances, interviews or an observational study might be appropriate.

5. Carrying Out the Research

Researchers then proceed to carry out the plan developed in step 4. However, during the actual research, unforeseen practical difficulties may occur. For example, it might prove impossible to contact certain questionnaire recipients or interview subjects. A business firm or government agency might not let the researcher carry out the work as planned. Such difficulties might bias the study results and lead to false interpretations. A researcher studying how business corporations have complied with affirmative-action programs for women might find that companies that have not complied do not wish to be studied.

6. Interpreting the Results

Gathering material for analysis may be just the beginning of the researcher's troubles. Working out the implications of the data and relating them to the research problem are rarely easy tasks. Although it may be possible to reach clear answers to the initial questions, many investigations are ultimately not fully conclusive.

7. Reporting the Research Findings

The research report, usually published as a journal article or book, relates the nature of the research and seeks to justify its conclusions. This is a final stage only in terms of the individual project. Most reports identify unanswered questions and suggest options for further research. All individual research investigations are part of the continuing process of research within the sociological community (Figure 2.1).

hypotheses • Ideas or guesses about a given state of affairs, put forward as bases for empirical testing.

Reality Intrudes!

The preceding sequence of steps is a simplified version of what happens in actual research projects. These stages rarely succeed each other so neatly; the difference is like that between the recipes outlined in a cookbook and the actual process of preparing a meal. Experienced cooks often don't work from recipes at all, yet they might cook better than those who do. Following fixed schemes can be unduly restricting; much outstanding sociological research would not fit rigidly into this sequence, though it would include most of the steps outlined here.

2 ASKING AND ANSWERING SOCIOLOGICAL QUESTIONS: HISTORICAL CONTEXT

When sociology began as a discipline, it was a highly theoretical field. It consisted of much armchair speculation, and many of the notions it developed about how the world worked were not well grounded in evidence. But in the 1920s there developed in American sociology, largely at the University of Chicago, a more intense commitment to the idea that such theoretical speculations were not enough—that sociology as a discipline needed to ground its concepts and theories in facts and data.

This goal for sociology was represented in two figures, both of whom were professors at the University of Chicago: Robert Park and William Ogburn. Park's beliefs about how to make social research more scientific came from his background, both as a student of philosophy in Europe and as a reporter for the *Minneapolis Star*. He was interested in

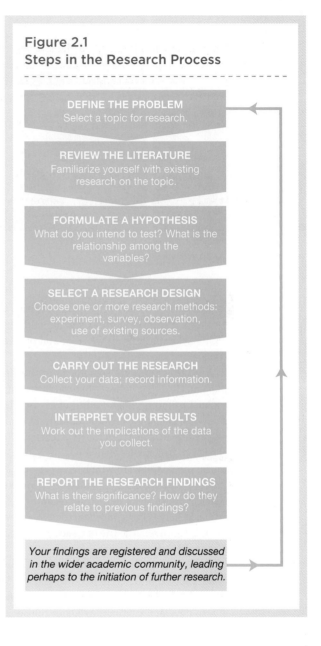

Figure 2.1
Steps in the Research Process

DEFINE THE PROBLEM
Select a topic for research.

REVIEW THE LITERATURE
Familiarize yourself with existing research on the topic.

FORMULATE A HYPOTHESIS
What do you intend to test? What is the relationship among the variables?

SELECT A RESEARCH DESIGN
Choose one or more research methods: experiment, survey, observation, use of existing sources.

CARRY OUT THE RESEARCH
Collect your data; record information.

INTERPRET YOUR RESULTS
Work out the implications of the data you collect.

REPORT THE RESEARCH FINDINGS
What is their significance? How do they relate to previous findings?

Your findings are registered and discussed in the wider academic community, leading perhaps to the initiation of further research.

CONCEPT CHECKS ✓

1. What are the seven steps in the research process?

(a) Robert Park and (b) William Ogburn.

developing theories, but wanted them to relate directly to the actual lives of people, and to be based on the careful accumulation of evidence about their lives. He told his students that they needed to get the seat of their pants dirty in real research, to wear out their shoe leather in order to discover the truth.

Park thought that the most important thing for a sociologist to do was to go around all the neighborhoods of the city and find out what was going on by meeting the people who were the subjects of the sociologists' theories. Following Park's lead, the University of Chicago's sociology department used the city as a laboratory. Its sociologists took on roles in the communities to see how the community's members lived, conducting interviews and firsthand observation. Their research reports tended to be highly systematic, well written, and oriented toward improving conditions in the city and around the United States.

Another prominent sociologist at the University of Chicago in that era was William Ogburn. He didn't believe that the future of sociology lay in shoe leather, in well-written books, in findings that could not be quantified, or in efforts to influence public policy. These, he thought, were the domain of ethics, religion, journalism, and propaganda. In his presidential address to the American Sociological Society, he argued that sociology needed to become a science (Ogburn, 1930). The goal, he argued, was not "to make the world a better place in which to live" or to set forth "impressions of life" or to "[guide] the ship of state" but only to "[discover] new knowledge." Ogburn wanted sociology to be a field that looked a lot more like the natural sciences in both its presentation and its orientation. Whereas Park had clear ideas about what the subject matter of sociology should be (immigration and the life of the city), Ogburn believed sociologists could study anything that could be measured with numbers.

These two figures, Park and Ogburn, coexisted at the University of Chicago for many years, each committed to his own vision of sociology as a science. For Park and his students, the personal, emotional, and scientific side of sociology coexisted with the aspiration to develop explanations about the social world. We can see this legacy in the work of young sociologists today. But the legacy of William Ogburn is no less significant. The value of statistics and scientific methodologies for understanding the world has never been greater, in part because of the massive amount of data and information being collected on the Internet. More than ever before, business and government need people who can analyze this material and who are disposed to think about the world in a scientific way.

CONCEPT CHECKS ✓

1. How did Park and Ogburn approach sociological research differently? In what ways did each sociologist influence researchers today?

③ ASKING AND ANSWERING SOCIOLOGICAL QUESTIONS TODAY: THE RESEARCH PROCESS

Let's look at the various **research methods** sociologists employ today (Table 2.1). Whereas many fields have one main method, modern sociology embraces a variety of methodologies. People trained in sociology end up developing a wide range of research skills, which makes them quite versatile after graduation. Here are the basic methods used today, with examples drawn from recent research.

Ethnography

Ethnography involves firsthand studies of people, using **participant observation** or interviewing. For some research projects, the investigator works or lives with a group, organization, or community, and perhaps participates in its activities. An ethnographer cannot simply be present in the group she studies, but must justify her presence to its members. She must gain and sustain the cooperation of the community to achieve worthwhile results.

For a long while, research based on participant observation excluded accounts of the hazards or problems involved, but more recently fieldworkers have been more open. Frequently, fieldworkers experience feelings of loneliness and frustration, the latter occurring especially when group members refuse to talk frankly with them. Some types of fieldwork may be physically dangerous; for instance, a researcher studying a delinquent gang might be seen as a police informer or might become unwittingly embroiled in conflicts with rival gangs.

In traditional works of ethnography, accounts provided little information about the observer because ethnographers were expected to present objective reports. More recently, ethnographers have increasingly spoken about their connection to the people under study. For example, one's race, class, or gender may affect the work, or the power differences between observer and observed may distort the dialogue between them.

A RECENT EXAMPLE

When Alice Goffman was a graduate student, she spent six years in an intensely policed poor black neighborhood. She was interested in the social situation of large numbers of black men who were on the run from the criminal justice system. She became part of the everyday life of a group of boys who were known as the 6th Street boys, writing about them in her article "On the Run" (Goffman, 2009). Goffman's research cast new light on the struggles of men who were dipping and dodging the police, worrying that any encounter would result in their imprisonment. By spending time with them every day for many years, she was able to see that for these men, activities, relations, and localities that others relied on to maintain a decent and respectable identity were transformed into a system that authorities used to locate, arrest, and confine them. The police and the courts became dangerous to interact with, as did showing up

research methods • The diverse methods of investigation used to gather empirical (factual) material. Different research methods exist in sociology, but the most commonly used are fieldwork (or participant observation) and survey methods. For many purposes, it is useful to combine two or more methods within a single research project.

ethnography • The firsthand study of people using participant observation or interviewing.

participant observation • A method of research widely used in sociology and anthropology in which the researcher takes part in the activities of the group or community being studied.

Table 2.1
Three of the Main Methods Used in Sociological Research

RESEARCH METHOD	STRENGTHS	LIMITATIONS
Ethnography	Usually generates richer and more in-depth information than other methods.	Can be used to study only relatively small groups or communities.
	Ethnography can provide a broader understanding of social processes.	Findings might apply only to groups or communities studied; not easy to generalize on the basis of a single fieldwork study.
Surveys	Make possible the efficient collection of data on large numbers of individuals.	Material gathered may be superficial; if questionnaire is highly standardized, important differences among respondents' viewpoints may be glossed over.
	Allow for precise comparisons to be made among the answers of respondents.	Responses may be what people profess to believe rather than what they actually believe.
Experiments	Influence of specific variables can be controlled by the investigator.	Many aspects of social life cannot be brought into the laboratory.
	Are usually easier for subsequent researchers to repeat.	Responses of those studied may be affected by the experimental situation.

to work or going to places such as hospitals. Instead of a safe place to sleep, eat, and find acceptance and support, their mothers' home was transformed into a "last known address," one of the first places police looked for them. Close relatives, friends, and neighbors became potential informants.

ADVANTAGES AND LIMITATIONS OF FIELDWORK

Successful ethnography provides information on the behavior of people in groups, organizations, and communities and how these people understand their own behavior. Once we look inside a given group, we can better understand not only that group but also broader social processes.

Yet fieldwork has its limitations. Only fairly small groups or communities can be studied. Much also depends on the researcher's skill in gaining the confidence of the individuals involved. Also a researcher could identify so closely with the group that he loses the perspective of an outside observer. Or a researcher might draw conclusions that are more about his own effect on the situation than he or his readers realize.

Surveys

Interpreting ethnographies usually involves problems of generalization because we cannot be sure that what we find in one context will apply in others, or even that two different researchers will draw the same conclusions when studying the same group. This is usually less problematic in **survey** research, in which questionnaires are sent or administered directly to a select group of people. This group is known as a **population**. Ethnographies are best suited for in-depth studies of small slices of social life; survey research produces information that is less detailed but can be generalized to the population as a whole.

STANDARDIZED AND OPEN-ENDED QUESTIONNAIRES

Two types of questionnaires are used in surveys. One contains a standardized, or fixed-choice, set of questions to which only a fixed range of responses is possible: Yes, No, Don't know or Very likely, Likely, Unlikely, Very unlikely. In such surveys with a small number of categories, responses are easy to count and compare. However, because they do not allow for subtleties of opinion or verbal expression, they may yield restrictive, if not misleading, information.

Other questionnaires are open-ended: Respondents have more opportunity to use their own words. Open-ended questionnaires typically provide more detailed information than do standardized ones, and the researcher can follow up answers to probe more deeply into what the respondent thinks. However, the lack of standardization means that responses may be difficult to compare statistically.

Questionnaire items are normally listed so that every member of the team of interviewers can ask the questions and record responses in the same order. All the items must be understandable to interviewers and interviewees alike. In large national surveys undertaken by government agencies and research organizations, interviews occur more or less simultaneously across the country. Those who conduct the interviews and those who analyze the results could not work effectively if they constantly had to check with one another about ambiguities in the questions or answers.

Questionnaires should also accommodate the characteristics of respondents. Will they see the point of a particular question? Might it offend them? Do they have enough information to answer usefully? Will they answer at all? A questionnaire's terminology might be unfamiliar; for instance, "What is your marital status?" might better be asked as, "Are you single, married, separated, or divorced?" Most surveys are preceded by pilot studies, which reveal problems with the survey not anticipated by the investigator. A **pilot study** is a trial run in which just a few people participate. Any difficulties can then be ironed out before the main survey takes place.

Often sociologists are interested in the characteristics of large numbers of individuals—for example, political attitudes of the American population as a whole. In such situations, researchers concentrate on a **sample**, or a small proportion of the overall group. Usually, the results from a properly chosen sample can be generalized to the total population. Studies of only two or three thousand voters, for instance, can accurately indicate the attitudes and voting intentions of the entire population. But to achieve such accuracy, the sample must be representative; the individuals studied must be typical of the population as a whole. Because **sampling** is highly complex, statisticians have developed rules for working out the correct size and nature of samples.

survey • A method of sociological research in which questionnaires are administered to the population being studied.

population • The people who are the focus of social research.

pilot study • A trial run in survey research.

sample • A small proportion of a larger population.

sampling • Studying a proportion of individuals or cases from a larger population as representative of that population as a whole.

A particularly important procedure that ensures that a sample is representative is **random sampling**, in which every member of the sample population has the same probability of being included. The most sophisticated way of obtaining a random sample is to assign each member of the population a number and then use a computer to generate a random list from which the sample is derived.

ADVANTAGES AND DISADVANTAGES OF SURVEYS

Surveys are widely used in sociological research for several reasons. Questionnaire responses can be more easily quantified and analyzed than material generated by most other research methods; large numbers of people can be studied; and, given sufficient funds, researchers can employ a specialized agency to collect the responses. The scientific method is the model for this kind of research, as surveys give researchers a statistical measure of what they are studying.

However, many sociologists are critical of the survey method. They argue that findings whose accuracy may be dubious—given the relatively shallow nature of most survey responses—can nonetheless appear to be precise. Also, levels of nonresponse are sometimes high, especially now that so many people use cell phones and no longer have phone lines at home. Furthermore, some studies that are published are based on results derived from little over half a sample, though normally there is an effort to recontact nonrespondents or to substitute them with other people. Although little is known about those who do not respond to surveys or who refuse to be interviewed, we do know that people often experience survey research as intrusive and time-consuming. One development that may hold great promise for learning about public opinion is the rise of new statistical techniques for surveying the "online conversation" that is taking place quite naturally on the Internet.

A RECENT EXAMPLE

One of the most famous surveys today is called the General Social Survey, which has been administered to Americans since 1972. It is sometimes called the "pulse of America" as it has tracked the social life of Americans for decades. Since 1985, however, it has been administered also outside the United States, to obtain comparative data. One of its most significant and controversial findings of recent years came from an analysis of the number of "friends" Americans were reporting. The results suggested that Americans had fewer confidants than in the past, and that a growing number couldn't name a single person with whom they shared "important matters." The implication was that Americans were growing lonelier (McPherson, Smith-Lovin, and Brashears, 2006).

How did the researchers evaluate whether friendships were declining over time? What accounts for this decline? The study was based on face-to-face interviews with a nationally representative sample of nearly 1,500 American adults. All had participated in the long-running General Social Survey and were asked questions about their social networks. Specifically, they were asked to identify people with whom they had discussed "matters [that are] important to [them]" in the past six months. On average, they named 2.08 people in 2004, compared to 2.94 persons in 1985. The proportion of respondents who reported that there was no one with whom they discussed important matters jumped from 10 percent in 1985 to 25 percent in 2004.

Some social scientists are not convinced that these findings support the claim that Americans are isolated or lonely. Rather, some argue

random sampling • Sampling method in which a sample is chosen so that every member of the population has the same probability of being included.

that "weak" social ties, such as those with acquaintances, may be perfectly acceptable and rewarding for some people; these people may actually prefer to have many casual acquaintances rather than a handful of deep friendships. University of Toronto sociologist Barry Wellman, for example, believes that the study offers important findings about "intimate ties," but he questions whether these findings should be taken as evidence that Americans are lonely and isolated. Rather, he notes that people's overall ties are actually increasing compared to previous decades, due in part to the Internet.

Experiments

In a typical **experiment**, people are randomly assigned to two groups. The first, called an experimental group, receives some special attention, based on the researcher's theory; the second, the control group, does not receive this attention. The subjects usually do not know to which group they have been assigned and seldom know the purpose of the experiment, though this is not always the case.

A classic example is the 1971 experiment carried out by Philip Zimbardo (1992), who set up a make-believe jail, randomly assigning some student volunteers to the role of guard and other volunteers to the role of prisoner. His aim was to see how role-playing would affect changes in attitude and behavior. The results shocked the investigators. Students who played guards quickly assumed an authoritarian manner; they displayed real hostility toward the prisoners, verbally abusing and bullying them. The prisoners, by contrast, showed a mixture of apathy and rebelliousness—a response often noted among inmates in actual prisons. These effects were so marked and the level of tension so high that the experiment had to be called off at an early stage. The results, however, were important: Zimbardo concluded that behavior in prisons is more influenced by the nature of the prison situation than by the individual characteristics of those involved.

The advantage of experimental studies is that they permit control of experimental conditions, enabling the researcher to isolate specific causes. The ability to control experimental conditions, however, is also the principal weakness of experimental studies, which in many ways are artificial. To the extent that the laboratory fails to duplicate a natural setting, it is difficult to generalize the results of laboratory experiments to the larger society. We can bring only small groups of individuals into a laboratory setting, and in such experiments, people know they are being studied and may behave unnaturally. As a result, sociologists sometimes use field experiments, in which a real-life situation is simulated as accurately as possible.

A RECENT EXAMPLE

In 1994 a group of sociologists launched an experiment to find out if it makes a difference to move people from high-poverty ghetto neighborhoods to low-poverty neighborhoods. People who responded to an advertisement offering vouchers for new apartments were randomly assigned to two groups—those who received the opportunity to move and those who did not. The first condition was called the treatment group, while the second was the control.

Why would the experimenters have compared the fate of two groups who both applied for vouchers, one of which got them and the other did not? Why not compare people who got the vouchers against those who did not apply in the first place?

experiment • A research method in which variables can be analyzed in a controlled and systematic way, either in an artificial situation constructed by the researcher or in naturally occurring settings.

STATISTICAL TERMS

Research in sociology often makes use of statistical techniques in the analysis of findings. Some are highly sophisticated and complex, but those most often used are easy to understand. The most common are **measures of central tendency** (ways of calculating averages) and **correlation coefficients** (measures of the degree to which one variable relates consistently to another).

There are three methods of calculating averages, each of which has certain advantages and shortcomings. Take as an example the amount of personal wealth (including all assets, such as houses, cars, bank accounts, and investments) owned by thirteen individuals. Suppose the thirteen own the following amounts:

1	$0	8	$80,000
2	$5,000	9	$100,000
3	$10,000	10	$150,000
4	$20,000	11	$200,000
5	$40,000	12	$400,000
6	$40,000	13	$10,000,000
7	$40,000		

The **mean** corresponds to the average, arrived at by adding together the personal wealth of all the people and dividing the result by the number of people in the sample (13). The total is $11,085,000; dividing this by 13, we calculate the mean to be $852,692.31. The mean is often a useful calculation because it is based on the whole range of data provided. However, the mean can be misleading when one or a small number of cases is very different from the majority. In this example, the mean is not in fact an appropriate measure of central tendency, because the presence of one very large figure, $10,000,000, skews the picture. One might get the impression, when using the mean to summarize these data, that most of the people own far more than they actually do.

In such instances, one of two other measures may be used. The **mode** is the figure that occurs most frequently in a given set of data. In our example, it is $40,000. The problem with the mode is that it doesn't take into account the *overall distribution* of the data—that is, the range of figures covered. The most frequently occurring case in a set of figures is not necessarily representative of the distribution as a whole and thus may not be a useful average. In this example, $40,000 is too close to the lower end of the figures.

The third measure is the **median**, which is the middle of any set of figures; here, this would be the seventh figure, again, $40,000. Our sample includes an odd number of figures, 13. If there were an even number—for instance, 12—the median would be calculated by taking the mean of the two middle cases, figures 6 and 7. As with the mode, the median gives no indication of the actual *range* of the data being measured.

Sometimes a researcher will use more than one measure of central tendency to avoid giving a deceptive picture of the average. More often, a researcher will calculate the **standard deviation** for the data in question. This is a way of calculating the **degree of dispersal**, or the range, of a set of figures—which in this case goes from $0 to $10,000,000.

Correlation coefficients offer a useful way of expressing how closely connected two (or more) variables are. When two variables correlate completely, we can speak of a perfect positive correlation, expressed as 1.0. When no relation is found between two variables—they have no consistent connection at all—the coefficient is 0.0. A perfect negative correlation, expressed as –1.0, exists when two variables are in a completely inverse relation to one another. Perfect correlations are never found in the social sciences. Correlations of the order of 0.6 or more, whether positive or negative, are usually regarded as indicating a strong degree of connection between whatever variables are being analyzed. Positive correlations on this level might be found between, say, social class background and voting behavior.

In fact, the study kept data on all three groups. The ones who applied but did not receive vouchers had more in common with the ones who got to move, because they also wanted to escape from their current circumstances. The best comparison is between two groups that wanted to move. They are alike in all characteristics except for whether they actually stayed in place or experienced a new living condition.

Following the groups since the mid-1990s, researchers made some important discoveries. For example, people who moved did not do much better in the labor market than those who stayed behind. But the movers tended to be much happier, and they experienced decreased levels of obesity when compared with those who did not get to move.

Comparative Historical Research

Comparative research is crucial in sociology because it enables researchers to document whether social behavior varies across time, place, and according to one's own social group membership. Consider the American rate of divorce—the number of divorces granted each year. Divorce rates rose rapidly in the United States after World War II, reaching a peak in the early 1980s, before declining slightly and leveling off in recent years. Current trends suggest that four in 10 couples marrying today will divorce—a statistic expressing profound changes in the area of sexual relations and family life (U.S. Bureau of the Census, 2011h). Do these changes reflect specific features of American society? We can find out by comparing divorce rates in the United States with those in other countries. The comparison reveals that although the U.S. rate is higher than that of most other Western societies, the overall trends are similar. Virtually all Western countries have experienced steadily climbing divorce rates over the past half century.

The most influential way of doing comparative research is through historical research. One classic study that investigated a much longer period and applied comparative research in a historical context was Theda Skocpol's *States and Social Revolutions* (1979), one of the best-known studies of social change. To produce a theory of the origins and nature of revolution grounded in detailed empirical study, Skocpol looked at processes of revolution in three historical contexts: the 1789 revolution in France, the 1917 revolution in Russia (which brought the Communists to power and established the Soviet Union, which was eventually dissolved in 1989), and the revolution of 1949 in China (which created Communist China).

By analyzing a variety of documentary sources, Skocpol was able to develop a powerful explanation of revolutionary change, one that emphasized underlying social structural conditions. She showed that social revolutions are largely the result of unintended consequences.

In Philip Zimbardo's make-believe jail, tension between students playing guards and students playing prisoners became dangerously real. From his experiment, Zimbardo concluded that behavior in prisons is influenced more by the nature of the prison itself than by the individual characteristics of those involved.

measures of central tendency • The ways of calculating averages.

correlation coefficients • The measure of the degree of correlation between variables.

mean • A statistical measure of central tendency, or average, based on dividing a total by the number of individual cases.

mode • The number that appears most often in a given set of data. This can sometimes be a helpful way of portraying central tendency.

median • The number that falls halfway in a range of numbers—a way of calculating central tendency that is sometimes more useful than calculating a mean.

standard deviation • A way of calculating the spread of a group of figures.

degree of dispersal • The range or distribution of a set of figures.

comparative research • Research that compares one set of findings on one society with the same type of findings on other societies.

Before the Russian Revolution, for instance, various political groups were trying to overthrow the regime, but none of these—including the Bolsheviks (Communists), who eventually came to power—anticipated the revolution that occurred. A series of clashes and confrontations gave rise to a process of social transformation that was much more radical than anyone had foreseen. At the time that Skocpol wrote, existing theories basically related the emergence of revolutions to the strength of social movements, and these to class relations. Skocpol showed, first, that state structures are as important as class relations and more important than the strength of the revolutionary movements; and second, that these state structures are heavily influenced by international events (revolutions come in the wake of a breakdown in state authority often due to lost international wars).

A RECENT EXAMPLE

Such studies as those pioneered by Theda Skocpol relied on qualitative methods of historical research, which depended on careful comparisons of a small number of cases. One of the costs of such approaches has been that sociologists have derived their understandings from some very famous revolutions or wars, while ignoring most of the world altogether. In recent years, Andreas Wimmer has taken up an alternative approach to historical sociology. He uses formal modeling and statistical techniques to analyze hundreds of cases at the same time, rather than a few famous ones. Unlike scholars who go to the library and pull existing data off the shelf, Wimmer has found it necessary to create his own datasets to answer age-old questions. In his approach, what happened in Haiti or in Latin America counts no less than what went on in Holland or in Europe more generally—though these latter places have tended to be studied much more frequently and thus count more heavily in existing theories. Wimmer's work therefore goes against the grain of most historical sociology that tends to focus mainly on Europe at the expense of Africa and the Americas. (It is not just Latin America that has figured infrequently in historical sociology; even North America is eclipsed by the usual focus on Europe.)

In a monumental new book, *Waves of War*, Wimmer has used this approach by focusing on large original datasets to study war as a sociological phenomenon. He has found that if we look at all wars that occurred throughout history, there has been a major shift. Prior to the nineteenth century most wars were driven by conquest, or the desire of states to achieve or throw off a certain balance of power in their region. More recently, wars have been driven by ethnic and nationalist concerns. According to Wimmer, whereas Karl Marx once proclaimed that the twentieth century would be the age of revolutionary class struggle, it turned into the age of ethno-nationalist conflict. Using a global dataset of his own creation, Wimmer found that the existence of nationalist organizations in a territory more than doubles the probability of war at any time. It is unlikely that a researcher using a qualitative approach with small numbers of cases would have come up with such a finding, because such an approach would have focused on positive cases (i.e., on a handful of nationalist wars), rather than systematically compared a large number of pre-nationalist contexts with nationalist ones.

CONCEPT CHECKS ✓

1. What are the main advantages and limitations of ethnography as a research method?
2. Contrast the two types of questions commonly used in surveys.
3. What is a random sample?
4. Discuss the main strengths of experiments.
5. What are the similarities and differences between comparative and historical research?

④ UNANSWERED QUESTIONS

Although the research methods of sociology have become quite advanced over the past 50 years, there are many open or unanswered questions that still cause much disagreement among sociologists.

Understanding Cause and Effect of Social Context

One of the main problems faced in research methodology is the analysis of cause and effect. One difficult causal relationship to understand is an association in which one social context produces a certain effect. Thus, if you live in a poor neighborhood, some sociologists think you are more likely to be unemployed or obese. But is the neighborhood the cause, or is it the other way around? Isn't it also possible that the kinds of people who would be unemployed or obese tend to gravitate toward living in certain kinds of neighborhoods? Although one of the main tasks of sociology is to identify causes and effects, there is a crisis of confidence among many scholars that such a goal is not as easily attained as once thought.

Human Subjects and Ethical Dilemmas

All research involving human beings can pose ethical dilemmas. A key question for sociologists is whether research poses risks to subjects that are greater than the risks those subjects face in their everyday lives. For example, ethnographers and field researchers conducting research in areas with high crime rates potentially risk getting their subjects arrested with their writings or getting themselves arrested simply for observing and participating in the lives of the people whom they are trying to understand. Although there is a great deal of sensitivity to such issues in contemporary social science, one largely unanswered question relates to exploitation. Are social scientists benefitting at their subjects' expense? Such questions are not addressed in most studies, and some social scientists are never forced to think seriously about them. The question of exploitation arises more in field studies than in statistical studies, but it must be considered whenever people's careers come to depend on the advancement of sociological knowledge.

Can We Really Study Human Social Life in a Scientific Way?

To answer this question, we must first understand what science means. **Science** is all the things just mentioned and more. It is the use of systematic methods of **empirical investigation**, the analysis of data, theoretical thinking, and the logical assessment of arguments to develop a body of knowledge about specific subject matter. According to this definition, sociology is a scientific endeavor.

However, sociology is not equivalent to a natural science. Unlike natural phenomena and animals, humans are self-aware beings who confer sense and purpose on what

> **science** • In the sense of physical science, the systematic study of the physical world. Science involves the disciplined marshaling of empirical data, combined with theoretical approaches and theories that illuminate or explain those data. Scientific activity combines the creation of bold new modes of thought with the careful testing of hypotheses and ideas. One major feature that helps distinguish science from other idea systems is the assumption that all scientific ideas are open to criticism and revision.
>
> **empirical investigation** • Factual inquiries carried out in any area of sociological study.

READING A TABLE

When reading sociological literature, you will often come across tables. They sometimes look complex but are easy to decipher if you follow the few basic steps outlined here; with practice, these will become automatic (see Table 2.2 as an example). Do not succumb to the temptation to skip over tables; they contain information in concentrated form that can be read more quickly than would be possible if the same material were expressed in words. By becoming skilled in the interpretation of tables, you will also be able to check how justified the conclusions a writer draws actually are.

1. Read the title in full. Tables frequently have long titles, which represent an attempt by the researcher to state accurately the nature of the information conveyed. The title of Table 2.2 gives, first, the *subject* of the data; second, the fact that the table provides material for comparison; and third, the fact that data are given only for a limited number of countries.

2. Look for explanatory comments, or *notes*, about the data. A footnote to Table 2.2 linked to the main column heading indicates that the data cover only licensed cars. This is important, because in some countries the proportion of vehicles properly licensed may be lower than in others. Footnotes may say how the material was collected or why it is displayed in a particular way. If the data have not

been gathered by the researcher but are based on findings originally reported elsewhere, a source will be included. The source sometimes gives you some insight into how reliable the information is likely to be and tells you where to find the original data. In Table 2.2, the source note makes clear that the data have been taken from more than one source.

3. Read the *headings* along both the top and the left-hand side of the table. (Sometimes tables are arranged with "headings" at the foot rather than the top.) These tell you what type of information is contained in each row and column. In reading the table, keep in mind each set of headings as you scan the figures. In our example, the headings on the left name the countries involved, while those at the top refer to the levels of car ownership and the years for which numbers apply.

4. Identify the units used; the figures in the body of the table may represent cases, percentages, averages, or other measures. Sometimes it may be helpful to convert the figures to a form more useful to you: If percentages are not provided, for example, it may be worth calculating them.

5. Consider the conclusions that might be reached from the information in the table. Most tables are discussed by the author, and what he has to say should of course be borne in mind. But you should also ask what further issues or questions could be suggested by the data.

they do. We can't describe social life accurately unless we grasp the concepts that people apply in their own behavior. For instance, to describe a death as a suicide means knowing what the person intended when he died. Suicide can occur only when an individual has self-destruction actively in mind. If he accidentally steps in front of a car and is killed, he cannot be said to have committed suicide.

The fact that we cannot study human beings in the same way as objects in nature is an advantage to sociological researchers, who profit from being able to pose questions directly to those they study: other human beings. In other respects, sociology encounters difficulties not present in the natural sciences. People who are aware that their activities are being scrutinized may not behave normally; they may consciously or unconsciously portray themselves in a way that differs from their usual attitudes. They may even try to "assist" the researcher by giving the responses they believe she wants.

CONCEPT CHECKS ✓

1. How are the ethical dilemmas that social scientists face different from those that other researchers encounter in the physical or the biological sciences?

2. Why should sociologists be concerned about the exploitation of the people that they study?

Table 2.2
Automobile Ownership: Comparisons of Several Selected Countries

Several interesting trends can be seen from the figures in this table. First, the level of car ownership varies considerably among different countries. The number of cars per 1,000 people is more than six times greater in the United States than in Brazil, for example. Second, there is a clear connection between car ownership ratios as a rough indicator of differences in prosperity. Third, in all the countries represented, the rate of car ownership increased between 1971 and 2009, but in some the rate of increase was higher than in others—probably indicating differences in the degree to which countries have successfully generated economic growth or are catching up.

NUMBER OF CARS PER 1,000 OF THE ADULT POPULATION[a]

COUNTRY	1971	1981	1984	1989	1993	1996	2001	2009
Brazil	12	78	84	98	96	79	95	178
Chile	19	45	56	67	94	110	133	118
China	NA	NA	NA	5[c]	6	8	12[d]	34
France	261	348	360	574	503	524	584	496
Greece	30	94	116	150	271	312	428	455
Ireland	141	202	226	228	290	307	442	434
Italy	210	322	359	424	586	674	638	596
Japan	100	209	207	286	506	552	577	454
Sweden	291	348	445	445	445	450	497	462
United Kingdom	224	317	343	366	386	399	554	460
United States	448	536	540	607	747	767	785	439
West Germany[b]	247	385	312	479	470	528	583	510

[a] Includes all licensed cars.
[b] Germany as a whole after 1989.
[c] Data for 1990.
[d] Data for 2000.
NA, not applicable.

Sources: Baltic 21 Secretariat; World Bank, 1999; International Monetary Fund, 2005; International Road Federation, 1987, p. 68; OECD, 2005; Statistical Office of the European Communities, 1991; *The Economist*, 1996; Toyota Corporation, 2001; United Nations Economic Commission for Europe, 2003; World Bank, 2005, 2011d.

1 **Basic Concepts**

p. 31

2 **Asking and Answering Sociological Questions: Historical Context**

p. 33

LEARNING OBJECTIVES

Learn the steps of the research process and be able to complete the process yourself. Name the different types of questions sociologists address in their research—factual, theoretical, comparative, and developmental.

Contrast Park's and Ogburn's visions of sociology as a science. Understand their influence on contemporary sociological research.

TERMS TO KNOW

Hypotheses

CONCEPT CHECKS

1. What are the seven steps in the research process?

1. How did Park and Ogburn approach sociological research differently? In what ways did each sociologist influence researchers today?

Exercises: Thinking Sociologically

1. Suppose the dropout rate in your local high school increased dramatically. Faced with such a serious problem, the school board offers you a $500,000 grant to study the sudden increase. Following the recommended procedures outlined in the text, explain how you would conduct your research. What hypotheses might you test? How would you prove or disprove them?

2. Explain the advantages and disadvantages of documentary research. What will it yield that will be better than experimentation, surveys, and ethnographic fieldwork? What are its limitations compared with those approaches?

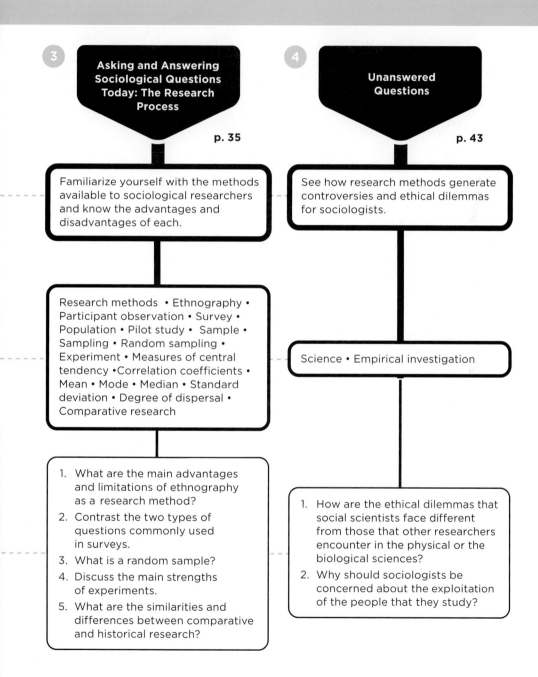

3

Asking and Answering Sociological Questions Today: The Research Process

p. 35

Familiarize yourself with the methods available to sociological researchers and know the advantages and disadvantages of each.

Research methods • Ethnography • Participant observation • Survey • Population • Pilot study • Sample • Sampling • Random sampling • Experiment • Measures of central tendency •Correlation coefficients • Mean • Mode • Median • Standard deviation • Degree of dispersal • Comparative research

1. What are the main advantages and limitations of ethnography as a research method?
2. Contrast the two types of questions commonly used in surveys.
3. What is a random sample?
4. Discuss the main strengths of experiments.
5. What are the similarities and differences between comparative and historical research?

4

Unanswered Questions

p. 43

See how research methods generate controversies and ethical dilemmas for sociologists.

Science • Empirical investigation

1. How are the ethical dilemmas that social scientists face different from those that other researchers encounter in the physical or the biological sciences?
2. Why should sociologists be concerned about the exploitation of the people that they study?

Part II

THE INDIVIDUAL AND SOCIETY

We start our exploration of sociology by looking at the connections between individual development and culture and by analyzing types of society from the past and present. Although our personalities and outlooks are influenced by our culture and society, we actively re-create and reshape the cultural and social contexts in which our activities occur.

Chapter 3 examines the unity and diversity of human culture. We consider how human beings differ from and resemble nonhuman animals, and we analyze variations among human cultures.

Chapter 4 discusses socialization, concentrating on how the human infant develops into a social being. Because socialization continues throughout the life span, we also analyze the relationships among young, middle-aged, and older people.

Chapter 5 explores how people interact in everyday life and identifies the mechanisms people use to interpret what others say and do. The study of social interaction reveals a great deal about the larger social environment.

Chapter 6 focuses on social groups, networks, and organizations, and how individuals interact in various settings.

Chapter 7 looks at deviance and crime. We can learn about the way a population behaves by studying people whose behavior deviates from accepted patterns.

49

Culture and Society

3

Who is more likely to use the latest Internet social networking technologies to develop networks of online friends, mostly persons they have never met: teenage students in Silicon Valley, Beijing, London, or New York?

a Silicon Valley

b Beijing

c London

d New York

Turn the page for the correct answer.

W hile teenagers around the world are likely to be immersed in a digital world, Beijing and Silicon Valley stand out, according to a recent Stanford Business School survey. High school students in both places reported heavy Internet use, including texting and social networking. The study, conducted for the Stanford Program on Regions of Innovation and Entrepreneurship,

> . . . suggested the emergence of a "digital tribe" of teens transcending cultures and geographic borders, especially in tech hotspots such as Silicon Valley and Beijing. "In certain urban locations, today's teens are native 'netizens,'" said Marguerite Gong Hancock, associate director of SPRIE. "Most teens in our survey in both Palo Alto and Beijing have had mobile phones since the age of 12. They lead a large part of their daily lives online" (Shao, 2011).

Differences, however, did exist. The Silicon Valley students spent substantially more time online, while the Beijing students were more often technologically adept. While both groups engaged in social networking, the Beijing students were more likely to have only online friends. Interestingly, while both groups of students reported that their main online activity during the week involved doing schoolwork, on weekends they diverged: The Beijing students continued to prioritize schoolwork, while the Silicon Valley students favored social networking.

China—not so long ago a country in which the only products one could buy were made in state-owned factories and sold in state-owned stores—is now the place where much of the world's consumer goods are made, and where a growing proportion is consumed as well. China is Apple's second-largest market, after the United States; young people flock to Apple stores every time there is a new release of an iPhone or iPad. China has by far the world's largest number of mobile phone users, Internet users, and smartphone users. It has its own version of Google (Baidu), Facebook (Renren), and Twitter (SinaWeibo)—

LEARNING OBJECTIVES

1 BASIC CONCEPTS

Know what culture consists of and recognize how it differs from society.

2 THE SOCIOLOGICAL STUDY OF CULTURE

Learn about the "cultural turn" and sociological perspectives on culture. Understand the processes that changed societies over time.

3 RESEARCH TODAY: UNDERSTANDING THE MODERN WORLD

Recognize the legacies of colonialism and the effects of globalization on your own life and the lives of people around the world.

4 UNANSWERED QUESTIONS

Understand the debate over the influence of biological and cultural factors on behavior. Learn how the Internet and global culture influence local cultures.

all started by Chinese who had either studied in the United States or previously worked for a U.S. corporation.

Is there indeed a common digital culture emerging among young people around the globe, one that involves doing schoolwork online, developing friendships online, and spending hours on social networking sites or downloading movies and music? Or is the Internet producing a bewildering variety of new youthful "tribes," globally interconnected by shared beliefs and values? What happens when those beliefs and values differ significantly from those of their parents, religious teachers, or government leaders?

One thing is clear: The lives of everyone on the planet are becoming increasingly interdependent. As businesses and people move about the globe in increasing numbers in search of new markets and economic opportunities, the cultural map of the world changes: Networks of peoples span national borders and continents, providing cultural connections between their birthplaces and their adoptive countries (Appadurai, 1986). A handful of languages becomes dominant, and in some cases replaces, the thousands of languages that were once spoken on the planet. Thanks to the Internet, information now spans the world in nanoseconds. Money, or music, crosses borders effortlessly, reshaping people's experiences and understandings with the click of a mouse.

It is increasingly impossible for cultures to exist as islands. Few places on earth can escape radio, television, air travel (and its throngs of tourists), or the computer. A generation ago, some tribes' ways of life were untouched by the rest of the world. Today these peoples use tools made in the United States or Japan, wear clothing manufactured in the Dominican Republic or Guatemala, and take medicine manufactured in Germany or Switzerland to combat diseases contracted through contact with outsiders. Within a generation or two, all the world's once-isolated cultures will be touched by global culture, despite their efforts to preserve their age-old ways of life.

The forces that contribute to a global culture are discussed throughout this book. These include:

- Television, which brings U.S. culture into homes throughout the world daily, and which adapts other cultural products for the U.S. audience;
- The emergence of a unified global economy, with businesses whose factories, management structures, and markets span continents and countries;
- "Global citizens," such as managers of large corporations, who may spend so much time crisscrossing the globe that they identify with a global, cosmopolitan culture rather than with their own nation's culture;
- A host of international organizations—including UN agencies, regional trade and mutual defense associations, multinational banks and other global financial institutions, and international labor and health organizations—that are creating a global political, legal, and military framework;
- Electronic communications (telephone, fax, e-mail, the Internet, and the World Wide Web), which make instantaneous communication with almost any part of the planet an integral part of daily life in the business world; and
- The exploding use of smartphones and other devices, and the associated rise of social media such as Facebook and Twitter.

Yet the emergence of a global culture is far from self-evident. In fact, there is considerable evidence to the contrary. The Internet, while exposing billions of people around the world to ideas that often challenge some of their most cherished cultural beliefs and values, also has resulted in a strengthening of those beliefs and values in many places. Although the force of globalization can often seem to be irresistible, sweeping away everything in its path, globalization has also resulted in outright resistance to the homogenization of local cultures along European and North American lines.

In this chapter we explore the nature of culture and society in their many forms, and how they are being reshaped by the many changes occurring in the world today.

THE ANSWER IS A'.

BASIC CONCEPTS

The sociological study of culture and society began with Émile Durkheim in the nineteenth century. The work of early sociologists strongly reflected the values of highly educated Europeans who often assumed that "primitive" cultures were inferior, the reason their societies were viewed as lagging behind modern European "civilization." However, two destructive world wars, fought largely between European countries that claimed to be the most "civilized" cultures on earth, helped discredit that belief. Sociologists now recognize that there are many different cultures and societies, each with distinctive characteristics. The task of social science is to understand this diversity, which is best done by avoiding value judgments.

Culture and Society

Culture consists of the values the members of a group hold, the norms they follow, the material goods they create, and the languages and symbols they use to construct their understanding of the world, including both speech and writing. Some elements of culture, especially people's beliefs and expectations about one another and about the world they inhabit, are components of all social relations. Culture therefore refers to the ways of life of individual members or groups within a society: how they dress, their marriage customs and family life, their patterns of work, their religious ceremonies, and their leisure pursuits. The concept also covers the goods they create—bows and arrows, plows, factories and machines, computers, books, dwellings. We should think of culture as a "design for living" or a "tool kit" of practices, knowledge, and symbols acquired through learning, rather than by instinct, that enable people to live in society (Kluckhohn, 1949; Swidler, 1986). Without culture, we would have no language in which to express ourselves and no sense of self-consciousness; our ability to think or reason would be severely limited.

When common features of human behavior are found in virtually all societies, they are called **cultural universals**. For example, there is no known culture without a grammatically complex language. Also, all cultures possess some recognizable form of family system, in which there are values and norms associated with the care of children. The institution of

culture • The values, norms, and material culture characteristic of a given group. Like the concept of society, the notion of culture is widely used in sociology and the other social sciences (particularly anthropology). Culture is one of the most distinctive properties of human social association.

cultural universals • Values or modes of behavior shared by all human cultures.

marriage is a cultural universal, as are religious rituals and property rights—although what constitutes marriage, how many spouses one is entitled to, and what is considered acceptable behavior both within and outside the marriage can vary considerably from culture to culture. All cultures also practice some form of incest prohibition—the banning of sexual relations between close relatives. Other cultural universals include art, dancing, bodily adornment, games, gift giving, joking, and rules of hygiene.

There are clearly variations within each category. Consider the prohibition against incest. Most often, incest is regarded as sexual relations between members of the immediate family; but among some peoples it includes cousins, and in some instances all people bearing the same family name. There have also been societies in which a small proportion of the population engages in incestuous practices. This was the case within the ruling class of ancient Egypt, when brothers and sisters were permitted to have sex with each other.

Among the cultural characteristics shared by all societies, two stand out in particular. All cultures incorporate ways of expressing communication, and all depend on material means of production. In all cultures, *language* is the primary vehicle of meaning and communication. It is not the only such vehicle, however. *Material culture* itself carries meanings, as we shall show.

A **society** is a *system of interrelationships* that connects individuals. The word *society*—like the word *social*—derives from a Latin term for the ties that bind people together, ties that make sustained human interaction possible. Such bonds can be informal, such as friendship or family; or formal, such as religious organizations, businesses, or entire nations. One characteristic of societies, at least as sociologists see them, is that they are relatively enduring over time. For this to occur, societies require some degree of common culture—a set of shared values and norms to guide behavior. No society could exist without culture, and conversely, no culture could exist without a society.

Values and Norms

Values are abstract ideals. For example, being faithful to a single marriage partner is a prominent value in most Western societies, but in some other cultures a person may have several wives or husbands. Some cultures value individualism, whereas others emphasize shared needs. In the United States, for example, striving to get ahead is a widely accepted value. According to this value, all it takes is hard work and anybody can go from rags to riches; celebrating one's achievements might even get you on *America's Got Talent*. In China there is a much stronger belief in the importance of collective effort. Modesty is a strongly held virtue, as reflected in the adage (attributed to Confucius) "When walking in the company of three, there must be one I can learn from." Although an American who boasts about her self-made success might seem vulgar to a Chinese, some Chinese seem to

marriage • A socially approved sexual relationship between two individuals. Marriage almost always involves two persons of opposite sexes, but in some cultures, types of homosexual marriage are tolerated. Marriage normally forms the basis of a family of procreation—that is, it is expected that the married couple will produce and bring up children. Some societies permit polygamy, in which an individual may have several spouses at the same time.

society • A group of people who live in a particular territory, are subject to a common system of political authority, and are aware of having a distinct identity from other groups. Some societies, such as hunting and gathering societies, are small, numbering no more than a few dozen people. Others are large, numbering millions—modern Chinese society, for instance, has a population of more than a billion people.

values • Ideas held by individuals or groups about what is desirable, proper, good, and bad. What individuals value is strongly influenced by the specific culture in which they happen to live.

be changing their values in this regard: *China's Got Talent* premiered in 2010 on a Shanghai TV station!

Even within American society, values may conflict. Some groups or individuals might value traditional religious beliefs, whereas others might favor progress and science. Some people might prefer lavish material comfort, whereas others might favor simplicity. In the modern age characterized by the global movement of people, ideas, goods, and information, cultural values will inevitably conflict. Sociological research suggests that such conflicts foster a sense of frustration and isolation (Bellah et al., 1985).

Norms are principles or rules of social life that everyone is expected to observe. Norms of behavior in marriage include the way husbands and wives are supposed to behave toward their in-laws: In some societies, they are expected to develop a close relationship; in others, they keep a clear distance. Like the values they reflect, norms vary across cultures. Among most Americans, for example, while a woman might wear a hat if it is in fashion, most would not cover their hair and neck with a headscarf except for occasional protection against the cold. In some more traditional Muslim cultures, there is often a norm calling for women to wear headscarves as a religiously required sign of modesty. While a few highly conservative Muslim cultures might enforce this rule on some women who prefer to dress otherwise, cultural norms regarding dress are also often widely accepted; as a result, women in traditional Muslim cultures often prefer to wear headscarves and other forms of more traditional clothing.

Cultural conflict occurs when norms perceived as culturally incompatible collide. The use of headscarves by Muslim women in predominantly Christian countries, for example, has led to cultural conflict in France (which in 2004 considered banning headscarves in public schools) and some other European countries with large immigrant populations from the Middle East or North Africa. In the United States, Europe, and even predominantly Muslim Turkey, religious Muslim women who insist on wearing headscarves often clash with prevailing beliefs that emphasize the separation of church and state, or the belief that a headscarf symbolizes women's subservience to male-generated beliefs and thus threatens women's rights (Elver, 2012).

Norms, like the values they reflect, also change over time. For example, beginning in 1964, with a U.S. Surgeon General's report that linked smoking with serious health problems, the U.S. government waged a highly effective campaign to discourage people from smoking. A strong social norm favoring smoking—once associated with independence, sex appeal, and glamour—has now given way to an equally strong social norm depicting smoking as unhealthful, unattractive, and selfish. Today, only 19 percent of American adults smoke (Centers for Disease Control and Prevention [CDC], 2013), which is half the rate of 1964, when the Surgeon General's report was issued.

norms • Rules of conduct that specify appropriate behavior in a given range of social situations. A norm either prescribes a given type of behavior or forbids it. All human groups follow definite norms, which are always backed by sanctions of one kind or another, varying from informal disapproval to physical punishment.

material culture • The physical objects that a society creates that influence the ways in which people live.

Material Culture

Material culture consists of the physical objects that a society creates and that influence the ways people live. These include consumer goods, from clothes to cars to houses; the tools and technologies used to make those goods, from sewing machines to computerized factories; and the towns and cities that serve as places for people to live and work. A central aspect of a society's material culture is technology.

Muslim women in Jakarta, Indonesia, protest the French government's plan to ban headscarves in public schools.

Today, material culture is rapidly becoming globalized, largely through modern information technology such as the computer and the Internet. Although the United States has been in the forefront of this technological revolution, most other industrial countries are catching up. In fact, it no longer makes sense to speak of an exclusively "U.S. technology" any more than it makes sense to speak of a U.S. car. The iPod, with more than 450 parts manufactured across the planet, embodies technology developed in Japan, the United States, and Europe (Linden, Kraemer, and Dedrick, 2007). Another example of the globalization of material culture is the way classrooms and department stores the world over increasingly resemble one another, and the fact that McDonald's restaurants are now found on nearly every continent.

Language

Language demonstrates both the unity and the diversity of human culture, because there are no cultures without language, and there are thousands of languages spoken in the world. Although languages with similar origins have words in common with one another—for example, German and English—most major language groups have no words in common at all.

Language is involved in virtually all our activities. In the form of ordinary speech, it is the means by which we organize most of what we do. (We will discuss the importance of talk and conversation in social life in Chapter 5.) However,

language • The primary vehicle of meaning and communication in a society, language is a system of symbols that represent objects and abstract thoughts.

language is involved not just in mundane activities but also in ceremony, religion, poetry, and many other spheres. One of its most distinctive features is that it allows us to extend the scope of our thought and experience. Using language, we can convey information about events remote in time or space and can discuss things we have never seen. We can develop abstract concepts, tell stories, and make jokes.

Languages—indeed, all symbols—are representations of reality. Symbols may signify things we imagine, such as mathematical formulas or fictitious creatures, or they may represent (that is, "re-present," or make present again in our minds) things initially experienced through our senses. Human behavior is oriented toward the symbols we use to represent "reality," rather than toward the reality itself—and these symbols are determined within a particular culture. When you see a four-footed furry animal, for example, you must determine which cultural symbol to attach to it. Do you decide to call it a dog, a wolf, or something else? If you determine it is a dog, what cultural meaning does that convey? In American culture, dogs are typically regarded as household pets and lavished with affection. In Guatemalan Indian culture, however, dogs are more often seen as guards or scavengers, and are treated with an indifference that might seem cruel to Americans. Among the Akha of northern Thailand, dogs are seen as food, and are treated accordingly. The diversity of cultural meanings attached to the word *dog* thus requires an act of interpretation. In this way, human beings are freed, in a sense, from being directly tied to the physical world.

In the 1930s the anthropological linguist Edward Sapir and his student Benjamin Lee Whorf advanced the **linguistic relativity hypothesis**, which argues that language influences our perceptions of the world. That is because we are more likely to be aware of things if we have words for them (Lucy, 1997; Wolff and Holmes, 2011). For example, expert skiers and snowboarders use terms such as *black ice, corn, powder,* and *packed powder* to describe different snow and ice conditions to more readily perceive potentially life-threatening situations that would escape the notice of a novice. In a sense, then, experienced winter athletes have a different perception of the world—or, at least, a different perception of the alpine slopes—than do novices.

Language also helps give permanence to a culture and identity to a people. Language outlives any particular speaker or writer, affording a sense of history and cultural continuity. It may seem that the English language is becoming increasingly global, as a primary language of both business and the Internet. Yet local attachments to language persist, often out of cultural pride. For example, the French-speaking residents of the Canadian province of Quebec are so passionate about their linguistic heritage that they often refuse to speak English, the dominant language of Canada, and periodically seek political independence from the rest of Canada. Minority languages are sometimes even outlawed by the majority government: Turkey restricts the use of the Kurdish language, and the "English-only" movement in the United States seeks to restrict the language of education and government to English, even though numerous other languages are spoken throughout the country.

linguistic relativity hypothesis • A hypothesis, based on the theories of Sapir and Whorf, that perceptions are relative to language.

symbols • Items used to stand for or represent another—as in the case of a flag, which symbolizes a nation.

signifier • Any vehicle of meaning and communication.

Symbols

The **symbols** expressed in speech and writing are the chief ways in which cultural meanings are formed and expressed. But they are not the only ways. Both material objects and aspects of behavior can generate meanings. A **signifier** is any vehicle of meaning—any set of elements used to communicate. The sounds made in speech are signifiers, as are the marks made on paper or other materials in writing. Other signifiers include dress, pictures or visual signs, modes of eating, forms of building or architecture, and many other material features of culture (Hawkes, 1977). Styles of dress, for example, normally signify differences between the sexes. Until relatively recently, women in our culture wore skirts and men pants. In some other cultures, this is reversed: Women wear pants and men skirts (Leach, 1976).

Semiotics—the analysis of nonverbal cultural meanings—opens up a fascinating field for sociology because it allows us to contrast the ways in which different cultures are structured. For example, the buildings in cities are not simply places where people live and work; they often have a symbolic character. In traditional cities, the main temple or church usually sat on high ground in or near the city center to symbolize the all-powerful influence of religion. In modern societies, by contrast, the skyscrapers of big business often occupy that symbolic position. Of course, material culture is not simply symbolic but also includes actual, practical objects vital for catering to physical needs—for example, the tools or technology used to acquire food, make weaponry, construct dwellings, and so forth. We have to study both the practical and the symbolic aspects of material culture to understand it completely.

Speech and Writing

All societies use speech as a vehicle of language. However, there are other ways of expressing language—most notably, writing. The invention of writing marked a major transition in human history. Writing first began as the drawing up of lists: Marks made on wood, clay, or stone served to keep records about significant events, objects, or people. For example, a mark, or sometimes a picture, might represent each tract of land possessed by a particular family or set of families (Gelb, 1952). Writing began as a means of storing information and as such was closely linked to the administrative needs of the early civilizations. A society that possesses writing can locate itself in time and space. Documents can be accumulated that record the past, and information can be gathered about present-day events and activities.

Written documents, or *texts*, have qualities distinct from the spoken word. The effect of speech is limited to the contexts in which words are uttered. Ideas and experiences can be passed down through generations in cultures without writing, but only by word of mouth. Texts, on the other hand, can endure for thousands of years, and through them those from past ages can address us directly. This is why documentary research is so important to historians.

> ### CONCEPT CHECKS
>
> 1. Describe the main elements of culture.
> 2. What roles does culture play in society?
> 3. Why is language considered to be a cultural universal?
> 4. What is the linguistic relativity hypothesis?

② THE SOCIOLOGICAL STUDY OF CULTURE

It is easy to assume that we are so thoroughly shaped by culture that we never escape its influence. In fact, that is how most sociologists

semiotics • The study of the ways in which nonlinguistic phenomena can generate meaning—as in the example of a traffic light.

thought about culture until the 1990s (Inglis, 2005). Most sociologists took for granted the importance of culture without seriously considering how it worked in daily life.

Culture and Change: A "Cultural Turn" in Sociology?

The phrase **cultural turn** describes sociology's recent emphasis on understanding the role of culture in daily life. One result has been to challenge the assumption that culture rigidly determines our values and behaviors. Instead, the sociologist Ann Swidler (1986) has characterized culture as a "tool kit" from which people select different understandings and behaviors. Thus some people can choose to dye their hair, wear nose rings, and tattoo their bodies but still accept their parents' traditional ideas about sexual restraint. Because people participate in many different (and often conflicting) cultures, the tool kit can be quite large and its contents varied (Bourdieu, 1990; Sewell, 1992; Tilly, 1992).

Our cultural tool kits include a variety of "scripts" that we can draw on—and even improvise on—to shape our beliefs, values, and actions. The more appropriate the script is to a particular set of circumstances, the more likely we will be to follow it—and recall events that conform to it long after they have occurred (D'Andrade, 1995; DiMaggio, 1997). For example, imagine that you are a woman walking alone in an unfamiliar city late at night and suddenly encounter a male stranger who begins to cross the street toward you, stating as he approaches, "Excuse me, may I ask you a question?" Your choice of cultural script will shape your response. A popular cultural script—honed by film and television entertainment, reality TV, and politicians—is to fear such encounters, especially if you are female (Glassner, 1999). As a result, instead of hearing him out, you quickly turn and head for the safety of a nearby all-night restaurant. Later, when retelling the story, you might recall the stranger as taller and more dangerous than he was, perhaps even that he was brandishing a weapon—traits consistent with American cultural scripts about such encounters.

Now imagine that you are the male in this encounter, perhaps an out-of-town businessman trying to find your hotel in an unfamiliar neighborhood. You see a woman walking on the other side of the street, and as you cross to ask directions, she turns and disappears into a restaurant. Your experience would be very different from that of the woman: You are concerned about the late hour, worried about being lost, and stunned by her sudden actions. Perhaps when you return home you will describe this event as evidence that people in this city are cold and indifferent to strangers.

In studying this case in light of the cultural turn, sociologists would attempt to understand the different cultural scripts involved and why each person might have chosen those scripts. How did physical appearance influence their different experiences? What words were spoken, and what meanings did those words convey? What did the two people's "body language" communicate? Sociologists would also consider alternative scripts that might have altered the experience of each participant. For example, the woman might have chosen the script of "good Samaritan," viewing the approaching stranger as potentially in need of assistance and thereby offering to help. Or the man might have recognized that a lone woman would feel threatened and instead chosen a less confrontational script—perhaps remaining on

cultural turn • Sociology's recent emphasis on the importance of understanding the role of culture in daily life.

his side of the street and beginning with a soft-spoken, "Excuse me, can you please tell me the way to my hotel? I seem to be lost."

The cultural turn in sociology reveals that there is no single "reality" to social encounters and that multiple cultural scripts can play out in any situation. The challenge of sociology is to understand people's differing realities, the scripts that they follow, and the reasons they choose one set of scripts over another (Bonnell and Hunt, 1999; Chaney, 1994; Glassner, 1999; Hays, 2000; Long, 1997; Seidman, 1997; Sewell, 1999; Smith and West, 2000; Swidler, 2001).

Early Human Culture: Greater Adaptation to Physical Environment

Human culture and human biology are intertwined. Understanding how culture is related to the physical evolution of the human species can help us understand the central role of culture in shaping our lives. To understand the forms of society that existed before modern industrialism, we call on the historical dimension of the sociological imagination.

Given the archaeological evidence, and the similarities in blood chemistry and genetics between chimpanzees and humans, scientists believe that humans evolved from apelike creatures on the African continent some 4 million years ago. The first evidence of human-like culture dates back 2 million years. Early humans fashioned stone tools, hunted animals and gathered nuts and berries, harnessed the use of fire, and established a highly cooperative way of life. Because early humans planned their hunts, they must have had some ability for abstract thought.

Culture enabled early humans to compensate for their physical limitations, such as lack of claws, sharp teeth, and running speed relative to that of other animals (Deacon, 1998). It freed humans from dependence on the instinctual responses to the environment that are characteristic of other species. The larger, more complex human brain permitted greater adaptive learning in dealing with major environmental changes such as the Ice Age. For example, humans figured out how to build fires and sew clothing for warmth. Through greater flexibility, humans could survive unpredictable challenges in their surroundings and shape the world with their ideas and their tools. In an instant of geological time, we became the dominant species on the planet.

Yet early humans were closely tied to their physical environment because they lacked the technological ability to modify their surroundings significantly (Bennett, 1976; Harris, 1975, 1978, 1980). Their ability to secure food and make clothing and shelter depended on physical resources close at hand. Cultures varied widely according to geographic and climatic conditions, from deserts to rain forests, the frozen Arctic to temperate areas. Human inventiveness spawned a rich tapestry of cultures around the world. As you will see later in this chapter, however, modern technology and other forces of globalization pose both challenges and opportunities for future global cultural diversity.

The Earliest Societies: Hunters and Gatherers

For all but a tiny part of our existence on this planet, human beings have lived in small **hunting and gathering societies**, often numbering no more than 30 or 40 people (see Table 3.1). Hunters and gatherers gain their livelihood from

hunting and gathering societies • Societies whose mode of subsistence is gained from hunting animals, fishing, and gathering edible plants.

hunting, fishing, and gathering wild edible plants. Such cultures still exist in some parts of the world, such as in a few arid parts of Africa and the jungles of Brazil and New Guinea. Most such cultures, however, have been destroyed or absorbed by the spread of Western culture. Currently, fewer than a quarter of a million people in the world support themselves through hunting and gathering—only 0.001 percent of the world's population.

Compared with larger societies—particularly modern societies, such as the United States—there was little inequality in most hunting and gathering groups; everyone lived in what would today be regarded as extreme poverty. Because necessary material goods were limited to weapons for hunting, tools for digging and building, traps, and cooking utensils, there was little difference among members of the society in the number or kinds of material possessions—there were no divisions between rich and poor. Differences in position or rank were based on age and gender; men were almost always the hunters, while women gathered wild crops, cooked, and brought up the children.

The oldest and most experienced men usually had an important say in major decisions affecting the group, but differences in power were much less distinct than in larger types of society. Hunting and gathering societies were usually participatory rather than competitive: All adult male members assembled in the face of important decisions or crises.

Table 3.1
Types of Human Society

TYPE	PERIOD OF EXISTENCE	CHARACTERISTICS
Hunting and gathering societies	50,000 B.C.E. to the present. Now on the verge of complete disappearance.	Consist of small numbers of people gaining their livelihood from hunting, fishing, and the gathering of edible plants. Few inequalities. Differences of rank limited by age and gender.
Agrarian societies	12,000 B.C.E. to the present. Most are now part of larger political entities and losing their distinct identity.	Based on small rural communities, without towns or cities. Livelihood gained through agriculture, often supplemented by hunting and gathering. Stronger inequalities than among hunters and gatherers. Ruled by chiefs.
Pastoral societies	12,000 B.C.E. to the present. Today mostly part of larger states; their traditional ways of life are being undermined.	Range from a few hundred people to many thousands. Depend on the tending of domesticated animals for their subsistence. Marked by distinct inequalities. Ruled by chiefs or warrior kings.
Traditional societies or civilizations	6000 B.C.E. to the nineteenth century. All traditional states have disappeared.	Very large in size, some numbering millions of people (though small compared with larger industrialized societies). Some cities exist, in which trade and manufacture are concentrated. Based largely on agriculture. Major inequalities exist among different classes. Distinct apparatus of government headed by a king or emperor.

Hunters and gatherers moved about a good deal within fixed territories, around which they migrated from year to year. Because they lacked animal or mechanical means of transport, they could take very few goods or possessions with them. Many hunting and gathering communities did not have a stable membership; people often moved between camps, or groups split up and joined others within the same territory.

Hunters and gatherers had little interest in developing material wealth; their main concerns were with religious values and ritual activities. Members participated regularly in elaborate ceremonies and often spent time preparing the dress, masks, paintings, or other sacred objects used in such rituals.

Hunters and gatherers are not merely primitive peoples whose ways of life no longer hold interest for us. Studying their cultures demonstrates that some of our institutions are far from natural features of human life. We shouldn't idealize the circumstances in which hunters and gatherers lived, but the lack of inequalities in wealth and power and the emphasis on cooperation are reminders that the world of modern industrial civilization cannot necessarily be equated with progress.

Pastoral and Agrarian Societies

About 15,000 years ago, some hunting and gathering groups started raising domesticated animals and cultivating fixed plots of land as their means of livelihood. **Pastoral societies** relied mainly on domesticated livestock, whereas **agrarian societies** grew crops (practiced agriculture). Some societies had mixed pastoral and agrarian economies.

Depending on the environment, pastoralists reared cattle, sheep, goats, camels, or horses. Some pastoral societies exist in the modern world, especially in areas of Africa, the Middle East, and Central Asia. They are usually found in regions of dense grasslands or in deserts or mountains. Such regions are not amenable to agriculture, but may support livestock.

At some point, hunting and gathering groups began to sow their own crops rather than simply collecting those growing in the wild. This practice developed as *horticulture*, in which small gardens were cultivated by the use of simple hoes or digging instruments. Like pastoralism, horticulture provided a more reliable food supply than hunting and gathering and therefore could support larger communities. Because they were not on the move, people who practiced horticulture could develop larger stocks of material possessions than people in either hunting and gathering or pastoral communities.

From about 6000 B.C.E. onward, we find evidence of societies larger than and different from any that existed before. These societies, which were based on settled agriculture and the development of cities, led to pronounced inequalities in wealth and power, and were ruled by kings or emperors. Because writing was present and science and art flourished, these societies are often called *civilizations*.

The earliest civilizations developed in the Middle East, mostly in fertile river areas. The Chinese Empire originated in about 1800 B.C.E., at which time powerful states also existed in what are now India and Pakistan. By the fifteenth century A.D., large civilizations also existed in Mexico and Latin America, including the Aztecs of the Mexican peninsula and the Incas of Peru.

Most traditional (premodern) civilizations were also empires: They conquered and incorporated other peoples (Kautsky, 1982). This was true, for instance, of traditional Rome and China. At its height in the first century A.D., the Roman

pastoral societies • Societies whose subsistence derives from the rearing of domesticated animals.

agrarian societies • Societies whose means of subsistence are based on agricultural production (crop growing).

Empire stretched from Britain in northwest Europe to beyond the Middle East. The Chinese Empire covered most of the massive region of East Asia now occupied by modern China.

Industrial Societies

What happened to destroy the forms of society that dominated the whole of history up to two centuries ago? The answer, in a word, is **industrialization**—the emergence of machine production based on the use of inanimate power resources (such as steam or electricity). The industrialized, or modern, societies differ from any previous type of social order in several key respects, and their development has had consequences stretching far beyond their European origins.

Industrialization originated in eighteenth-century Britain as a result of the Industrial Revolution, a complex set of technological changes between 1750 and 1850 that affected people's means of gaining a livelihood. These changes included the invention of new machines (such as the spinning jenny for creating yarn, patented in 1770), the harnessing of power resources (especially water and steam) for production, and the use of science to improve production methods. Because discoveries and inventions in one field led to more in others, the pace of technological innovation in **industrialized societies** is extremely rapid compared with that of traditional social systems.

In even the most advanced of traditional civilizations, most people worked on the land. By contrast, in industrialized societies today, the majority of the employed population works in factories, offices, or shops. And over 90 percent of people live and work in towns and cities. The largest cities are vastly larger than the urban settlements of traditional civilizations. In the cities, social life becomes impersonal and anonymous, and many encounters are with strangers. Large-scale organizations, such as business corporations or government agencies, influence the lives of virtually everyone.

The political systems of modern societies are more developed than forms of government in traditional states; in the latter, monarchs and emperors had little influence on the customs of most of their subjects, who lived in self-contained villages. With industrialization, transportation and communication became much more rapid, promoting a more integrated "national" community.

The industrialized societies were the first **nation-states**—political communities with clearly delimited borders and shared culture, rather than vague frontier areas that separated traditional states. Nation-state governments have extensive powers over many aspects of citizens' lives, framing laws that apply to all those living within their borders. The United States is a nation-state, as are virtually all other societies in the world today.

The application of industrial technology not only has served peaceful processes of economic development but also has altered ways of waging war, creating weaponry and modes of military

industrialization • The process of the machine production of goods. See also industrialized societies.

industrialized societies • Strongly developed nation-states in which the majority of the population works in factories or offices rather than in agriculture, and most people live in urban areas.

nation-states • Particular types of states, characteristic of the modern world, in which governments have sovereign power within defined territorial areas, and populations are citizens who know themselves to be part of single nations. Nation-states are closely associated with the rise of nationalism, although nationalist loyalties do not always conform to the boundaries of specific states. Nation-states developed as part of an emerging nation-state system, originating in Europe; in current times, they span the whole globe.

organization much more advanced than those of nonindustrial cultures. Together, superior economic strength, political cohesion, and military superiority account for the worldwide spread of Western culture over the past two centuries.

Sociology first emerged as a discipline as industrial societies developed in Europe and North America, and was strongly influenced by the changes taking place. As we saw in Chapter 1, the major nineteenth-century sociological theorists (Marx, Weber, and Durkheim) all sought to explain the sweeping changes taking place. While they differed in their understanding and their predictions about the future, all shared one thing: a belief that industrial society was here to stay, and that as a result, the future would in many ways resemble the past.

For Durkheim, this meant the increasing importance of what he termed "organic solidarity"—a growing division of labor, with all members of society engaged in highly specialized roles (or *functions*, in Durkheim's terminology), with functional interdependence resulting in ties that bind the members of society together. Marx, on the other hand, argued that industrial society's division into social classes hampered its technological potential, since the capitalist class reaped all the benefits of advanced technologies at the expense of the working class. In his view, a working-class revolution was required to create a classless society, a new form of industrial society in which everyone prospered. Weber focused on the rise of what he termed *rational-legal society*, best seen in modern bureaucracies. This he viewed as a highly efficient form of social organization that was, unfortunately, at the same time destructive of human freedom and potential—in his memorable phrase, an "iron cage." While Weber anticipated that, from time to time, charismatic leaders might emerge to challenge this trend, ultimately their power would become routinized, and the long march of the bureaucrat would continue.

While Marx, Weber, and Durkheim's theoretical understanding of the emerging industrial society still has relevance, contemporary theorists have shed new light on the ways in which culture and society are changing in the modern world. In Chapter 14, we will take up the question of whether there is such a thing as a "postindustrial" society. In the next section of this chapter, however, we will consider recent research on some of the issues that confront societies in the world today.

CONCEPT CHECKS

1. Compare the three main types of premodern societies.

2. What transformations led to the development of civilizations?

3. What does the concept industrialization mean?

4. How has industrialization weakened traditional social systems?

---

③ RESEARCH TODAY: UNDERSTANDING THE MODERN WORLD

From the seventeenth to the early twentieth century, Western countries established colonies in numerous areas previously occupied by traditional societies. Although all these colonies have by now attained independence, the process of **colonialism** helped shape the social map

colonialism • The process whereby Western nations established their rule in parts of the world away from their home territories.

of the globe as we know it today. In some regions, such as North America, Australia, and New Zealand, which were only thinly populated by hunting and gathering or pastoral communities, Europeans became the majority population. In North America, the native population was greatly reduced by the spread of European diseases for which they lacked immunity, as well as through conquest (Diamond, 1999). This form of colonialism is sometimes referred to as settler colonialism, because it took the form of large-scale European settlement (Veracini, 2010). In other areas, including much of Asia, Africa, and South America, the local populations remained in the majority, and were administered by the colonial powers, largely for the benefit of the home country.

Societies created through settler colonialism, including the United States, have become industrialized. Those with large native populations ruled by colonial administrators experienced a much lower level of industrial development, largely because much of the wealth produced in these societies was realized by the colonial powers. These included South Asia, as well as much of Africa and Latin America. Colonialism had come to an end by the mid-twentieth century, and today many of these societies are rapidly growing economically. Some, such as India and Brazil, are currently major drivers of global economic growth (Nederveen Pieterse, 2011).

There is no agreed-upon way of classifying countries in terms of their degree of industrialization. While it was once common to distinguish between "developed" and "developing" countries, it is not surprising that members of the latter category objected to being characterized as "developing," on the grounds that it privileged the "developed" countries of the world as somehow more advanced. They saw this both as an invidious cultural judgment and as ignoring the role of colonialism in shaping their adverse economic situations. Among sociologists, a commonly used distinction is between the "global north" and the "global south," since most (but not all) of what was once referred to as the industrialized world is found in the Northern Hemisphere, while most (but not all) of what was called the developing world lies in the Southern Hemisphere.

These different ways of characterizing the world today show the importance of language, and reflect an increased sensitivity, at least among scholars of globalization, to the ways in which words can shape our perceptions, unconsciously elevating some societies (for example, those in the "global north") to a more "advanced" status, while unconsciously denigrating others. We shall use the terms *global north* and *global south*, imperfect as they are, because they are least likely to imply a judgment as to which is culturally preferable.

The Global South

As previously mentioned, the majority of countries in the global south are in areas that underwent colonial rule in South Asia, Africa, and South America. A few colonized areas gained independence early, such as Haiti, which became the first autonomous black republic in 1804. The Spanish colonies in South America acquired their freedom in 1810, while Brazil broke away from Portuguese rule in 1822.

Some countries that were never ruled from Europe were nonetheless strongly influenced by colonial relationships. China, for example, was compelled from the seventeenth century on to enter into trading agreements with European powers, which assumed government control over certain areas, including major seaports. Hong Kong was the last of these. Most nations in the global south have become independent states only since World War II, often following bloody anticolonial struggles. Examples include India, which shortly after achieving self-rule split into India and Pakistan; a range of other Asian countries (such as Malaysia, Myanmar, and Singapore); and countries in Africa (such as Algeria, the Democratic Republic of Congo, Kenya, Nigeria, and Tanzania).

Although they may include peoples living in traditional fashion, these countries differ from earlier forms of traditional society. Their political systems, following Western models, make them nation-states. Although most of the population still lives in rural areas, a rapid process of city development is occurring. Although agriculture remains the main economic activity, many crops are produced for sale in world markets. These countries are not merely societies that have somehow "lagged behind" the more industrialized areas; they have been created by contact with Western industrialism, which has undermined the more traditional systems.

As of 2012, there were 1.4 billion people living on $1.25 or less per day, almost all of them in the global south (United Nations Food and Agriculture Organization [UN FAO], 2012a). About a third of the world's poor, and two-thirds of the world's hungry people, live in South Asia, in countries such as Cambodia, India, and Myanmar. China, however, has made great strides, reducing by half the number of people living in poverty since 1990. New research methods have been used to estimate that there are more poor people in India than in sub-Saharan Africa (Burke, 2010). However, a substantial proportion lives on the doorstep of the United States—in Central and South America. Despite progress toward achieving the Millennium Development Goals, which call for halving the percentage of the world's population that suffers from hunger and extreme poverty by 2015, major challenges remain. The global economic crisis has had an acutely destructive impact on people living in poverty, particularly women (United Nations Economic and Social Commission for Asia and the Pacific [UNESCAP], 2010). In fact, most of the gains in reducing global poverty and hunger have resulted from economic growth in China and East Asia.

Global poverty shouldn't be seen as remote from the concerns of Americans. Whereas in previous generations the bulk of immigrants to the United States came from European countries, recent years have seen waves of Hispanic immigrants, nearly all from Latin America. Some U.S. cities, such as Los Angeles and Miami, have become international gateways to Latin America and are bursting with new immigrants and also maintain trading connections with their home countries.

In most societies, poverty is worst in rural areas. Malnutrition, lack of education, low life expectancy, and substandard housing are most severe in the countryside, especially where arable land is scarce, agricultural productivity low, and drought or floods common. Women are usually more disadvantaged than men. For instance, they often work longer hours and, when paid at all, earn lower wages. (See Chapter 10 for a lengthier discussion of gender inequality.)

The poor in the global south live in conditions almost unimaginable to North Americans. Many have no permanent dwellings apart from shelters

Women waiting in line for food in Calcutta, India. Why does poverty disproportionately affect women around the world?

made of cartons or loose pieces of wood. Most have no running water, sewage systems, or electricity. Nonetheless, millions of poor people also live in the United States, and there are connections between poverty in America and global poverty. Almost half of the impoverished people in the United States emigrated from poor countries. This is true of the descendants of the black slaves brought over by force centuries ago, and it is true of more recent, and willing, immigrants who have arrived from Latin America, Asia, and elsewhere.

Some formerly impoverished countries have successfully embarked on a process of industrialization. Referred to as the **emerging economies**, they include Argentina, Brazil, Chile, China, India, Mexico, Singapore, South Korea, and Taiwan. The rates of economic growth of the most successful countries, such as those in East Asia, are several times those of the Western industrial economies.

The East Asian emerging economies are investing abroad as well as promoting growth at home. China is investing in mines and factories in Africa, elsewhere in East Asia, and in Latin America. South Korea's production of steel has doubled in the last decade, and its shipbuilding and electronics industries are among the world's leaders. Singapore is becoming the major financial and commercial center of Southeast Asia. Taiwan is an important presence in the manufacturing and electronics industries. All these changes have directly affected the United States. In fact, the "rise of the rest" (Zakaria, 2009) is arguably the most important aspect of global economic change in the world today.

It is worth noting that a country's economic growth does not necessarily mean that its citizens are happier or feel more secure. There is a growing body of research that suggests the opposite: as countries industrialize, their general sense of well-being does not increase, and may even decline. Even in China, despite unprecedented rates of economic growth that have elevated hundreds of millions of Chinese into middle-class status, the most recent research suggests that people's happiness—at least as measured on a "life satisfaction" index—is actually lower than it was two decades ago, before China's "growth miracle" took off (Easterlin, 2001, 2003, 2010; Easterlin and Sawangfa, 2010; Easterlin et al., 2010, 2012; Inglehart, 1997).

Contemporary Industrial Societies: Cultural Conformity or Diversity?

The study of cultural differences highlights the influence of cultural learning on behavior, which can vary widely from culture to culture. For example, in the United States, we eat oysters but not kittens or puppies, both of which are regarded as delicacies in some other parts of the world. Westerners regard kissing as a normal part of sexual behavior, but in other cultures the practice is either unknown or regarded as disgusting.

CULTURAL CONFORMITY

American culture involves a range of values shared by many, if not all, Americans—such as a belief in the merits of individual achievement or in equality of opportunity. These values are connected to norms: For example, people are expected to work hard to achieve occupational success (Bellah et al., 1985; Parsons, 1964; orig. 1951). These norms also involve the use of material goods created mostly through modern industrial technology, such as cars, mass-produced food, and clothing.

emerging economies • Formerly impoverished countries that over the past two or three decades have begun to develop a strong industrial base, such as India or Singapore.

All cultures serve as an important source of conformity. For example, when you say that you subscribe to a particular value, you are probably voicing the beliefs of your family members, friends, teachers, or others who are significant in your life. When you choose a word to describe some personal experience, that word acquires its meaning in a language you learned from others.

American high school and college students often see themselves as especially nonconformist. Like the body piercers and tattooists of today, the hippies of the 1960s and the punks of the 1980s all sported distinctive clothing styles, haircuts, and other forms of bodily adornment. Yet how individualistic were they? Were their styles actually "uniforms," just as navy blue suits or basic black are "uniforms" among conservative businesspeople?

There is, in fact, an aspect of conformity to their behavior—conformity to their own group. When you buy a seemingly unique article of clothing to express your individuality, that garment was likely created by the design department of a global manufacturer that studied the current tastes of consumers and then ordered the mass production of your "unique" garment. When you listen to music, it is most likely the same kind that your friends listen to.

One of the challenges for all cultures is to instill in people a willingness to conform. This is accomplished in two ways (Parsons, 1964). First, members learn the norms of their culture starting from childhood, with parents playing a key role. When learning is successful, the ingrained norms become unquestioned ways of thinking and acting; they appear "normal." (Note the similarity between the words *norm* and *normal*.) Second, *social control* comes into play when a person fails to conform adequately to a culture's norms. Social control often involves informal punishment, such as rebuking friends for minor breaches of etiquette, gossiping behind their backs, or ostracizing them from the group. Formal forms of discipline might range from issuing parking tickets to imprisonment (Foucault, 1979). Émile Durkheim argued that punishment not only helps guarantee conformity among those who would violate a culture's norms and values but also vividly reminds others what the norms and values are.

Cultures differ, however, in how much they value conformity. Research shows that Chinese culture lies at one extreme in terms of valuing conformity (Hofstede, 1997; Minkov and Hofstede, 2012), while at the other extreme lies American culture, ranking among the world's highest in cherishing individualism. Americans pride themselves on their independence of spirit, represented by the lone bald eagle, the U.S. national symbol. Globalization—from Starbucks and McDonald's to the widespread use of the Internet or smartphones—is exposing many young Chinese to more individualistic Western values.

CULTURAL DIVERSITY

Small societies tend to be culturally uniform, but industrialized societies involving numerous **subcultures** are themselves culturally diverse, or multicultural. As processes such as slavery, colonialism, war, migration, and contemporary globalization have led to populations settling in new areas, societies have emerged that are cultural composites: Their population comprises groups from diverse cultural and linguistic backgrounds. In modern cities, for example, many subcultural communities live side by side.

Subcultures not only imply different cultural backgrounds or different languages within a larger society, but also include segments of the population that have different cultural patterns.

subcultures • Values and norms distinct from those of the majority, held by a group within a wider society.

Subcultures might include Goths, computer hackers, hippies, Rastafarians, and fans of hip-hop. Some people identify with a particular subculture, whereas others move among several.

Culture helps perpetuate the values and norms of a society, yet it also offers opportunities for creativity and change. Subcultures and countercultures—groups that reject prevailing values and norms—can promote views that represent alternatives to the dominant culture. Social movements or groups with common lifestyles are powerful forces of change within societies, allowing people to express and act on their opinions, hopes, and beliefs.

U.S. schoolchildren are frequently taught that the United States is a vast melting pot that assimilates subcultures. **Assimilation** is the process by which different cultures are absorbed into a mainstream culture. Although virtually all peoples living in the United States take on some common cultural characteristics, many groups strive to retain a unique identity. In fact, identification based on race or country of origin persists in the United States, particularly among African Americans and immigrants from Asia and Latin America (Parekh, 2010). Research has found that migrants to the United States have gradually adopted the label of "American." Scholars still point to a segmented assimilation where certain groups have better opportunities by which to enter U.S. society (Sezgin, 2012).

A more appropriate metaphor for American society than the assimilationist melting pot might be the culturally diverse salad bowl, in which all the ingredients, though mixed together, retain their original flavor and integrity, thereby contributing to the richness of the salad as a whole. This viewpoint, termed **multiculturalism**, calls for respecting cultural diversity and promoting equality of different cultures (Anzaldua, 1990).

As we have seen, in many modern industrial nations young people have their own subcultures. Youth subcultures typically revolve around musical preferences and distinctive styles of dress, language (especially slang), and behavior. Like all subcultures, however, they still accept most of the norms and values of the dominant culture.

Consider the patchwork that is hip-hop. Although it emerged as a subculture in the Bronx, New York, in the mid-1970s, hip-hop owes much of its identity to Jamaica. The first important hip-hop DJ, Kool Herc, was a Jamaican immigrant, and rapping derives from the Jamaican DJ tradition of "toasting," chanting stories into microphones over records. The story of hip-hop is a lesson in the fluidity of contemporary cultural identity. The music is built around beats from other records, but in "sampling" from recordings, hip-hop artists often do something more significant: They sample identities, taking on the characteristics of subcultures that can be considerably foreign to them.

Hip-hop's reach has widened over time. Rappers and rap groups from Queens and Long Island—such as Run-DMC, LL Cool J, and Public Enemy—recorded some of the first great hip-hop albums. By the end of the 1980s, the music had a national presence in the United States, as Los Angeles artists such as N.W.A and Ice T developed gangsta rap, which soon had outposts in Oakland, New Orleans, Houston, and elsewhere. White rappers such as Kid Rock and Eminem, following in the footsteps of the Beastie Boys, pioneered a rap-rock synthesis, and a Filipino American crew known as the Invisibl Skratch Piklz revolutionized turntable techniques. Hip-hop soon became a global form, with British hip-hop artists such as Dizzee Rascal and Lady Sovereign and French rappers such

assimilation • The acceptance of a minority group by a majority population in which the new group takes on the values and norms of the dominant culture.

multiculturalism • A condition in which ethnic groups exist separately and share *equally* in economic and political life.

as MC Solaar. Mathangi "Maya" Arulpragasam, better known by her stage name "M.I.A.," has become a global sensation in hip-hop. M.I.A. is of Sri Lankan Tamil descent and used the cultural milieu of West London to help shape her specific style.

The sampled beats of hip-hop can contain nearly anything. The secret is transformation: A portion of an earlier song, recast to fit a new context, can take on an entirely different meaning while still retaining enough of its former essence to create a complicated and richly meaningful finished product. In many ways, hip-hop is a music of echoes: rappers revisiting the funk music and "blaxploitation" films of the 1970s (black action movies often criticized for glorifying violence and presenting blacks in negative stereotypes); suburban fans romanticizing inner-city street styles. Hip-hop is the soundtrack to an emerging global culture that treats the looks, sounds, and byways of particular subcultures, or particular moments in time, as raw material for the creation of new styles.

What does hip-hop tell us about cultural diversity? On the one hand, its history of incorporating an ever-wider circle of influences and participants demonstrates that what is "normal" in one community can quickly be adopted in another community far away, through dissemination via vinyl records, digital samples, and other media. On the other hand, the controversies that hip-hop has generated suggest that such cultural crossings also bring uncertainty, misperception, and fear. Finally, hip-hop's evolution suggests that even in a global culture, subcultural distinctions retain an important aura of authenticity. Even today, hip-hop describes aspects of social realities that most Americans would prefer not to contemplate.

Subcultures also develop around types of work associated with unique cultural features. Long-distance truckers, coal miners, Wall Street stockbrokers, computer programmers, professional athletes, corporate lawyers, and artists, for example, form subcultures that value (respectively) physical strength, bravery, shrewdness, knowledge, speed, material wealth, and creativity. However, they seldom stray far from the dominant culture. Even professional thieves share most of the values of U.S. society: They marry and raise children; like most Americans, they want to accumulate wealth, power, and prestige; they eat with knives and forks, drive on the right side of the road, and try to avoid trouble as much as possible (Chambliss, 1988).

Cultural Identity and Ethnocentrism

Every culture displays unique patterns of behavior. If you have traveled abroad, you know that aspects of daily life taken for granted in your own culture may not be part of everyday life elsewhere. Even in countries that share the same language, you might find customs to be quite different. The expression *culture shock* is an apt one. Often people feel disoriented when immersed in a new culture because they have lost familiar cultural reference points and have not yet learned how to navigate in the new culture.

Almost any familiar activity will seem strange if described out of context. Western cleanliness rituals are no more or less bizarre than the customs of some Pacific groups who knock out their front teeth to beautify themselves or of certain South American tribal groups who place discs inside their lips to make them protrude, believing that this enhances their attractiveness.

We cannot understand these practices and beliefs separately from the wider cultures of which they are a part. A culture must be studied in terms of its own meanings and values—a

(a) The origins of hip-hop culture can be traced back to DJ Kool Herc, who brought the Jamaican disc jockey tradition of "toasting" to New York in the mid-1970s. (b) M.I.A. represents one aspect of the widening appeal of hip-hop across cultural lines, arguably for better and for worse.

key presupposition of sociology. Sociologists seek to avoid **ethnocentrism**, which is the judging of other cultures in terms of the standards of one's own. We must remove our own cultural blinders to see the ways of life of different peoples in an unbiased light. The practice of judging a society by its own standards is called **cultural relativism**.

Applying cultural relativism can be fraught with uncertainty and challenge. Not only is it hard to see things from a completely different point of view, but sometimes troubling questions arise. Does cultural relativism mean that all customs and behaviors are equally legitimate? Are there any universal standards to which all humans should adhere? Consider the ritual acts of what opponents have called "genital mutilation" in some societies. Numerous young girls in certain African, Asian, and Middle Eastern cultures undergo clitoridectomies, a painful cultural ritual in which the clitoris and sometimes all or part of the vaginal labia are removed with a knife or a sharpened stone and the two sides of the vulva are partly sewn together as a means of controlling sexual activity and increasing the sexual pleasure of the man.

ethnocentrism • The tendency to look at other cultures through the eyes of one's own culture, and thereby misrepresent them.

cultural relativism • The practice of judging a society by its own standards.

In cultures where clitoridectomies have been practiced for generations, they are regarded as normal. A study of 2,000 men and women in two Nigerian communities found that 9 out of 10 women interviewed had undergone clitoridectomies in childhood and that the large majority favored the procedure for their own daughters, primarily for cultural reasons. Yet a significant minority believed that the practice should be stopped (Ebomoyi, 1987). Clitoridectomies are regarded with abhorrence by most people from other cultures and by a growing number of women in the cultures where they are practiced (el Dareer, 1982; Johnson-Odim, 1991; Lightfoot-Klein, 1989). These differences in views can result in a clash of cultural values, especially when people from cultures where clitoridectomies are common migrate to countries where the practice is illegal.

France is an example. France has a large North African immigrant population, in which many African mothers arrange for traditional clitoridectomies to be performed on their daughters. Some have been tried and convicted under French law for mutilating their daughters. These African mothers have argued that they were engaging in the same cultural practice that their own mothers had performed on them, that their grandmothers had performed on their mothers, and so on. They have complained that the French are ethnocentric, judging traditional African rituals by French customs. Feminists from Africa and the Middle East, while themselves strongly opposed to clitoridectomies, have criticized Europeans and Americans who sensationalize the practice by calling it "backward" or "primitive" without seeking any understanding of the underlying cultural and economic circumstances (Wade, 2011; Knop, Michaels, Riles, 2012). In this instance, globalization has led to a clash of cultural norms and values that has forced members of both cultures to confront some of their most deeply held beliefs. The role of the sociologist is to avoid knee-jerk responses and to examine complex questions carefully and from as many angles as possible.

CONCEPT CHECKS

1. Give examples of subcultures that are typical of American society.
2. What is the difference between cultural ethnocentrism and cultural relativism?

4 UNANSWERED QUESTIONS

There are many unanswered questions in the sociological study of culture and society. One of the oldest debates has to do with whether we are more likely to be shaped by biological factors or social ones. More recently, many debates have focused on the role of the Internet, and on globalization more generally, in shaping the modern world. We now turn to some of these unanswered questions.

Nature or Nurture?

Because humans evolved as part of the world of nature, one would assume that human thinking and behavior are the result of biology and evolution. In fact, one of the oldest (and still unresolved) controversies in the social sciences is the "nature/nurture" debate: Are we shaped by our biology, or are we products of learning through life's experiences—that is, of nurture? Whereas biologists and some psychologists emphasize biological factors, sociologists stress the role of learning and culture. They also argue that because human beings can make conscious choices, neither biology nor culture wholly determines human behavior.

The nature/nurture debate has raged for more than a century. For example, in the 1930s and 1940s, many social scientists focused on biological factors, with some seeking (unsuccessfully) to prove that a person's physique determined his personality. In the 1960s and 1970s, scholars in different fields emphasized culture. Some social psychologists argued that even severe mental illness was the result of society labeling some behavior as unusual, rather than resulting from biochemical processes (Scheff, 1966). Today, partly because of new understandings in genetics and brain neurophysiology, the pendulum is again swinging toward the side of biology.

The resurgence of biological explanations for human behavior began in 1975, when the evolutionary biologist Edward O. Wilson published *Sociobiology: The New Synthesis.* The term **sociobiology** refers to the application of biological principles to explain the social activities of animals, including human beings. Wilson argued that genes influence not only physical traits but also behavior. For instance, some species of animals perform elaborate courtship rituals leading to sexual union and reproduction. Human courtship and sexual behavior, according to sociobiologists, involve similar rituals. Also, in most species, males are larger and more aggressive than females. Some suggest that genetic factors explain why, in all known human societies, men tend to hold positions of greater authority than women.

One way in which sociobiologists illuminate the relations between the sexes is through the idea of "reproductive strategy." A reproductive strategy is a pattern of behavior developed through evolutionary selection that favors the chances of survival of offspring. The female body has a larger investment in its reproductive cells than the male—a fertilized human egg takes nine months to develop. Thus women will not squander that investment and are not driven to have sexual relations with many partners; their overriding aim is the care and protection of children. Men, on the other hand, desire to have sex with many partners, which is a sound strategy in terms of preserving the species. This view, it has been suggested, explains differences in sexual behavior and attitudes between men and women.

Sociobiologists do not argue that genes determine 100 percent of our behavior. For example, depending on the circumstances, men can choose to act in nonaggressive ways. Yet even though this argument seems to add culture as another explanatory factor in describing human behavior, social scientists have condemned sociobiology for claiming that a propensity for particular behaviors, such as violence, is somehow "genetically programmed" (Seville Statement on Violence, 1990).

Different biological factors interact with and respond to environmental inputs. It has been difficult to find compelling, substantive data on the interaction between biology and experience. But more evidence is coming out of studies of brain development. Beginning in the womb, genes interact with hormones to shape the development of the child (Stiles, 2011).

Most sociologists today acknowledge a role for nature in determining attitudes and behavior, but with strong qualifications. For example, no one questions that newborn babies have basic human reflexes, such as "rooting" for the mother's nipple and responding to the human face (Cosmides and Tooby, 1997; Johnson and Morton, 1991). But it is a leap to conclude that because babies have human reflexes, adult behavior is governed by **instincts**—biologically fixed patterns of action found in all cultures.

Sociologists now ask how nature and nurture interact to produce human behavior. They

sociobiology • An approach that attempts to explain the behavior of both animals and human beings in terms of biological principles.

instincts • Fixed patterns of behavior that have genetic origins and that appear in all normal animals within a given species.

acknowledge that all known human cultures have some common characteristics—for example, language, forms of emotional expression, rules for raising children or engaging in sexual behavior, and standards of beauty (Brown, 1991). But they also recognize that there is enormous variety in *how* these common characteristics play out: It is not some biological disposition that makes American males feel attracted to a *particular* type of woman. Rather, it's their exposure to magazine ads, TV commercials, and film stars that transmit culturally specific standards of female beauty.

Because humans think and act in many different ways, sociologists do not believe that "biology is destiny." If biology were all-important, we would expect all cultures to be similar, if not identical. Yet this is hardly the case. For example, pork is forbidden to religious Jews and Muslims, but it is a dietary staple in China. All cultures have standards of beauty and ornamentation, but what constitutes beauty in one culture may constitute the opposite in another (Elias, 1987; Elias and Dunning, 1987; Foucault, 1988). For example, the half-starved body of a typical *Vogue* model or the bulked-up body of a weight lifter would be grossly unattractive to the Borneo forest dweller, although the tattoos now sported by many Bornean young people would be easily accepted (tattooing being a common feature of Bornean culture).

Sociologists' main concern, therefore, is with how behavior is learned through interactions with family, friends, schools, television, and every other facet of the social environment. Early child rearing is especially relevant to this kind of learning. Human babies have a large brain, requiring birth relatively early in their fetal development, while their heads can still pass through the birth canal. As a result, human babies must spend a number of years in the care of adults, during which time the child learns his society's culture. All cultures therefore provide for childhood socialization, but the processes vary greatly from culture to culture. An American child learns the multiplication table from a classroom teacher, whereas a child in the forests of Borneo learns to hunt with older members of the tribe.

Perhaps recent scientific advances in brain neurophysiology and genetics will tip the balance more toward emphasizing the role of nature in shaping human behavior. But for the present, most sociologists would conclude that both nature and nurture interact in complex and as yet imperfectly understood ways to shape who we are and how we behave.

Does the Internet Promote a Global Culture?

Many believe that the rapid worldwide growth of the Internet is hastening the spread of a global culture resembling the cultures of Europe and North America. Belief in such values as equality between men and women, the right to speak freely, democratic participation in government, and the pursuit of pleasure through consumption are diffused throughout the world over the Internet. Moreover, Internet technology itself seems to foster such values: Global communication, seemingly unlimited (and uncensored) information, and instant gratification all characterize the new technology.

Yet it may be premature to conclude that the Internet will sweep aside traditional cultures. Evidence shows that the Internet is in many ways compatible with traditional cultural values, perhaps even a means of strengthening them. This is especially likely to be true in countries that seek to control the Internet, censoring or blocking unwanted content and punishing those whose postings violate traditional values. One example is Saudi Arabia, a monarchy that officially enforces a highly conservative form of traditional Islam. Cyber cafes are routinely monitored, and cyber dissidents—for example, those who defend women's rights or criticize traditional religious beliefs—are likely to receive steep fines and severe punishment. Yet at the same time, even under such repressive conditions, the Internet provides a space for self-expression and discussion, albeit within limits. Women, for example, who comprise more than half of all Internet users in Saudi Arabia, are able to engage in Internet discussions that would be forbidden in public, such as on women's health issues. Reporters Without Borders (2010) includes Saudi Arabia among a group of 10 countries that it identifies as "Internet Enemies" because their governments not only routinely filter or block Internet content, but also use it to disseminate official propaganda.

The Internet has sometimes been described as an echo chamber, in which people seek out like-minded others whose postings reinforce their own beliefs (Manjoo, 2008; Sunstein, 2012). For example, one study of a Jewish ultraorthodox religious group found that the Internet helped to strengthen the community, providing a forum for communication and the sharing of ideas (Barzilai-Nahon and Barzilai, 2005). In this sense, the Internet may be splitting society into what can be thought of as digitally linked tribes with their own unique cultural beliefs and values—sometimes even in conflict with the dominant culture. Examples from youth subcultures in recent years would include hippies, punks, skinheads, Rastas, Goths, vampires, rappers, and dancehall enthusiasts. Such subcultures sometimes emerge when ethnic minority youth seek to create a unique cultural identity within the dominant culture, often through music, dress, hairstyle, and bodily adornment such as tattoos and piercing. They are often hybrids of existing cultures: For example, dancehall, like reggae, which originated as part of a youth culture in Jamaica's poor neighborhoods, today has spread to the United States, Europe, and anywhere there has been a large Caribbean migration (Niahh, 2010).

Finally, of course, the Internet can be used to build a community around ideas that directly threaten the dominant culture. Al-Qaeda and other radical Islamist jihadists rely on the Internet to spread their ideas, attract new recruits, and organize acts of violence (National Coordinator for Counterterrorism [NCTb], 2007). Suicide bombers routinely make videos celebrating their imminent deaths, videos that are posted on jihadist websites (and occasionally even YouTube) in order to reach a wider audience of current and potential believers. Extremist groups from all faiths (Christian, Jewish, Muslim) have found the Internet to be a useful tool (Juergensmeyer, 2008).

Does Globalization Weaken or Strengthen Local Cultures?

The world has become a single *social system* as a result of growing ties of interdependence, both social and economic, that affect everyone. But it would be a mistake to think of increasing globalization simply as the growth of world unity. Rather, it is primarily the reordering of *time and distance* in social life as our lives are increasingly influenced by events far removed from our everyday activities.

Globalizing processes have brought many benefits to Americans, such as a much greater variety of goods and foodstuffs. At the same time, those processes have helped create some of the most serious problems American society faces, such as global climate change, the threat of terrorism, and the loss of jobs to low-wage countries.

The growing global culture has provoked numerous reactions at the local level. Many local cultures remain strong or are experiencing rejuvenation, partly out of the concern that a global culture, dominated by North American and European cultural values, will corrupt the local culture. For example, extremist Islamist movements in Afghanistan, in the tribal areas of Pakistan, in Yemen, and elsewhere in the Middle East seek to impose traditional, tribal values, often abolishing the use of alcohol, requiring men to grow full beards, and forbidding women from working outside their home or being seen in public with men who are not their spouses or relatives. In some cases, violations of these rules are punished, sometimes by death. These movements can be understood partly as a rejection of the spread of Western culture—what Osama bin Laden referred to as "Westoxification" (Juergensmeyer, 2001).

The resurgence of local cultures is evident in the rise of **nationalism**, a sense of identification with one's people expressed through a common set of strongly held beliefs. Nationalism can be highly political, involving attempts to assert the power of a nation based on a shared ethnic or racial identity over people of a different ethnicity or race. The strife in the former Yugoslavia, and in parts of Africa and the former Soviet Union, bear tragic witness to the power of nationalism. The world of the twenty-first century may well witness responses to globalization that celebrate ethnocentric nationalist beliefs, promoting intolerance and hatred rather than acceptance of diversity.

New nationalisms, cultural identities, and religious practices are constantly being forged throughout the world. When you socialize with students from the same cultural background or celebrate traditional holidays with friends and family, you are sustaining your culture. The very technology that helps foster globalization also supports local cultures: The Internet enables you to communicate with others who share your cultural identity, even when they are dispersed around the world. A casual search of the Web reveals thousands of pages devoted to different cultures and subcultures.

Although sociologists do not fully understand these processes, they often conclude that despite the powerful forces of globalization, local cultures remain strong. But it is too soon to tell whether and how globalization will result in the homogenization of the world's cultures, the flourishing of many individual cultures, or both.

How Easily Do Cultures Change?

China has undergone a transformation in recent years that is in many ways historically unprecedented. Thirty years ago, China was completely closed to foreign businesses. Government bureaucrats, who controlled every economic institution, ran its economy. From large factories to small businesses to collective farms—all were owned and run by the state. The Chinese government also sought to control most aspects of Chinese culture: Media were state-run, education was tightly managed to promote values the ruling Communist Party deemed appropriate, and any signs of disagreement were closely monitored and often punished. Wall posters would denounce behavior that deviated from acceptable norms, while many universities and public places had loudspeaker systems that would frequently broadcast inspirational messages or criticize bad behavior.

Today, China appears to be a vastly different place, especially in the more developed coastal and large metropolitan areas. While some key industries remain state-owned, most of the economy is now in private hands. European, American, Japanese, and other foreign firms are flocking to China in large numbers, bringing with them the cultural values of their home countries. China's rapidly growing economy has lifted hundreds of millions of people into middle-class status, turning them into consumers not only of products, but also of information. China now claims

nationalism • A set of beliefs and symbols expressing identification with a national community.

Thousands of customers await the release of the iPhone 4S at a Beijing Apple store.

more than a billion mobile phone users (Savitz, 2012), opening up many Chinese to foreign sources of information and culture. Although the Chinese government still censors search engines, websites, blogs, and Twitter feeds it deems critical of central government policies, a great deal of dissent is now tolerated. Importantly, many Chinese are now exposed to cultural norms and values that 30 years ago were considered unthinkable.

Have these changes significantly altered Chinese culture so that it is becoming more Western? While superficially this may seem to be the case, in some ways traditional Chinese culture has remained remarkably durable. Take one example: instilling in China's leading scientists and engineers a strong cultural value for the kinds of innovative thinking that can lead to technological breakthroughs. In the United States, such thinking is highly culturally valued. In business, one result has been the creation of such innovative brands as Apple, Facebook, and Twitter. Such brands often achieve worldwide cachet—so much so that when the iPhone 4S was introduced in January 2012, a thousand Chinese showed up to buy one at an Apple store in Beijing—and rioted when the store failed to open its doors as expected (LaFraniere, 2012).

To date, China's economic growth has been based largely on manufacturing and assembling products for foreign firms, rather than innovating new brands that capture global markets. Chinese scientists and engineers are known for their strong work ethic—for putting in long hours at diligent labor in their effort to innovate. Yet thus far the results have been mainly improving on foreign designs, rather than developing truly unique Chinese breakthroughs. During the past decade, the Chinese government has sought to change this. It has invested vast sums of money in higher education and science parks, in the hope of spurring technological breakthroughs that will result in Chinese brand-name products consumers the world over will want to buy. Yet so far these efforts have not succeeded. Why haven't they?

There are many reasons, but one has to do with a long-standing cultural tradition emphasizing the importance of memorization and rote learning, which produces stunning results on standardized tests but discourages the kind of "outside-the-box," more analytical thinking that can contribute to truly innovative breakthroughs (Wilsdon and Keeley, 2007). The Chinese cultural value that emphasizes test taking as the key measure of one's ability dates back to the sixth and seventh centuries, when entrance into prestigious government jobs was first based on passing a difficult examination (Miyazaki, 1981). Every year, millions of Chinese students now take the dreaded two- to three-day exam known as the *gaokao*, which determines not only whether they will go to college, but what college they will go to, and ultimately their life prospects. Hopeful parents often hire expensive private tutors, and students spend months (if not years) in preparation (Sudworth, 2012).

As a result, Chinese students do extraordinarily well when tested. In 2009, on a standardized test administered to nearly a half million 15-year-olds in 65 countries, Chinese students scored higher than students from any other country on science, reading, and math. U.S. students, by way of comparison, ranked 23rd in science, 17th in reading, and 32nd in math (OECD, 2009). Yet despite their superior performance, Chinese students do not often come up with creative, breakthrough ideas after they graduate, whether in the laboratory or in business (Parker and Appelbaum, 2012). In an effort to change this, the Chinese government recently instituted an educational reform plan calling for more flexible college admissions policies modeled, in part, on the U.S. approach; letters of recommendation and extracurricular activities are now supposed to be taken into account (Wang, 2010; *Chronicle of Higher Education*, 2010). There is little evidence, however, that such official edicts have had any effect on students' relentless preparation for the *gaokao*, or on college admissions committees' decisions.

Cultural beliefs and practices that have been in existence for nearly 1,500 years do not change easily.

CONCEPT CHECKS ✓

1. Explain the nature/nurture debate.
2. How does global culture influence local cultures?
3. How is the Internet transforming local cultures?

1 Basic Concepts p. 54

2 The Sociological Study of Culture p. 59

LEARNING OBJECTIVES

Know what culture consists of and recognize how it differs from society.

Learn about the "cultural turn" and sociological perspectives on culture. Understand the processes that changed societies over time.

TERMS TO KNOW

Culture • Cultural universals • Marriage • Society • Values • Norms • Material culture • Language • Linguistic relativity hypothesis • Symbols • Signifier • Semiotics

Cultural turn • Hunting and gathering societies • Pastoral societies • Agrarian societies • Industrialization • Industrialized societies • Nation-states

CONCEPT CHECKS

1. Describe the main elements of culture.
2. What roles does culture play in society?
3. Why is language considered to be a cultural universal?
4. What is the linguistic relativity hypothesis?

1. Compare the three main types of premodern societies.
2. What transformations led to the development of civilizations?
3. What does the concept *industrialization* mean?
4. How has industrialization weakened traditional social systems?

1. Mention at least two cultural traits that you would claim are universals; mention two others you would claim are culturally specific traits. Use case study materials from different societies to show the differences between universal and specific cultural traits. Are the cultural universals you have discussed derivatives of human instincts? Explain your answer.

2. What does it mean to be ethnocentric? How is ethnocentrism dangerous in conducting social research? How is ethnocentrism problematic among nonresearchers in their everyday lives?

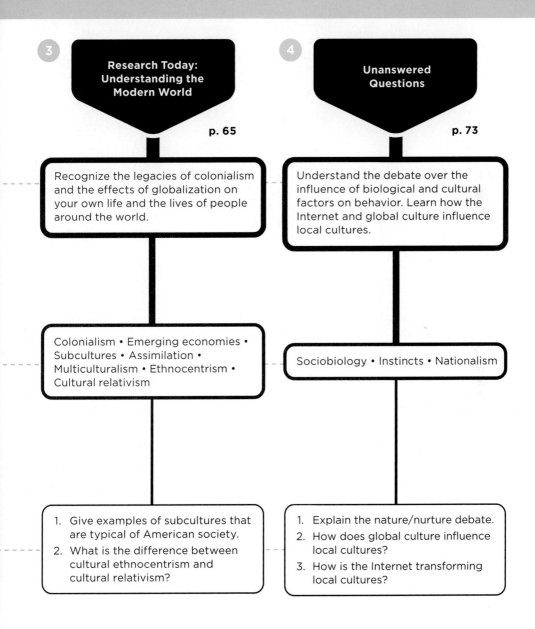

3

Research Today: Understanding the Modern World

p. 65

Recognize the legacies of colonialism and the effects of globalization on your own life and the lives of people around the world.

Colonialism • Emerging economies • Subcultures • Assimilation • Multiculturalism • Ethnocentrism • Cultural relativism

1. Give examples of subcultures that are typical of American society.
2. What is the difference between cultural ethnocentrism and cultural relativism?

4

Unanswered Questions

p. 73

Understand the debate over the influence of biological and cultural factors on behavior. Learn how the Internet and global culture influence local cultures.

Sociobiology • Instincts • Nationalism

1. Explain the nature/nurture debate.
2. How does global culture influence local cultures?
3. How is the Internet transforming local cultures?

Socialization and the Life Cycle

If a child does well on a crossword puzzle, the best response is:

a You're so smart!

b You worked so hard!

c How did you do that?

Turn the page for the correct answer.

I f you, like many parents and teachers, believe that positive reinforcement is the best way to teach and empower a child to succeed, then it might make sense to choose any of the three answers just suggested. In fact, 85 percent of American parents think it's important to tell their kids that they're smart. However, recent studies have shown that it is too simplistic to assume that all praise produces the same result.

Stanford University psychologist Carol Dweck attempted to address this question through a series of experiments in which a group of fifth-grade students were asked to complete an easy puzzle. All completed the puzzle successfully. A randomly selected half of the students were told "you must be smart at this," while the other half were told "you must have worked really hard." The children then had the opportunity to choose another puzzle—either one that was easy, or another one from which they were told they would "learn a lot." Fully 90 percent of those who were told they were smart chose the easy puzzle, while the majority of those who were praised for their effort opted for the more challenging puzzle. Dweck concluded that when children are told they're smart, they're afraid to make mistakes, for fear of no longer looking smart. Emphasizing effort, by contrast, allows the children "to see themselves as in control of their success" (Bronson and Merryman, 2009, p. 15). Moreover, the ability to plow through difficult challenges by exerting more effort—instead of giving up out of fear of looking "dumb"—is an important predictor of persistence and the ability to rebound in the face of failure.

The example just cited illustrates a crucial element of raising children within a society. **Socialization** is the process whereby the helpless infant gradually becomes a self-aware, knowledgeable person, skilled in the ways of her culture. Socialization among the young contributes to **social reproduction**—the process whereby societies have structural continuity over time. During socialization, especially in the early years, children learn the ways of their elders, thereby perpetuating their values, norms, and social practices. All societies have characteristics that endure over time, even though their members change as individuals

LEARNING OBJECTIVES

① BASIC CONCEPTS

Learn about how the four main agents of socialization contribute to social reproduction. Learn the stages of the life course and see the similarities and differences among cultures.

② THEORIES OF SOCIALIZATION

Learn the theories of child development according to Mead, Piaget, Freud, and Chodorow.

③ RESEARCH ON SOCIALIZATION TODAY

Learn how recent research on midlife and child-care challenges assumptions about midlife, gender roles, and child care.

④ UNANSWERED QUESTIONS ABOUT SOCIALIZATION

Learn more about the debate over the influence of media on gender role socialization.

are born and die. American society, for example, has many distinctive social and cultural characteristics that have persisted for generations—such as the fact that English is the main language spoken.

Socialization connects different generations to one another (Turnbull, 1983). The birth of a child alters the lives of those who are responsible for his upbringing—who themselves therefore undergo new learning experiences. Older people, while of course remaining parents, forge a new set of relationships with another generation when they become grandparents. Although cultural learning is much more intense in infancy and early childhood than later, learning and adjustment go on through the whole life cycle.

In the sections to follow, we continue the theme of nature interacting with nurture introduced in the previous chapter. We first analyze human development from infancy to early childhood, identifying the main stages of change. Different writers have offered a number of theoretical interpretations of how and why children develop as they do, and we describe and compare these, including theories that explain how people develop gender identities. Finally, we discuss the main groups and social contexts that influence socialization during the various phases of life.

THE ANSWER IS B.

BASIC CONCEPTS

Agents of Socialization

Sociologists often speak of socialization as occurring in two broad phases, involving numerous **agents of socialization**—that is, groups or social contexts in which significant processes of socialization occur. Primary socialization, which occurs in infancy and childhood, is the most intense period of cultural learning. It is the time when children learn language and basic behavioral patterns that form the foundation for later learning. The family is the main agent of socialization during this phase. Secondary socialization occurs later in childhood and in maturity. In this phase, other agents of socialization, such as schools, peer groups, organizations, the media, and the workplace, become socializing forces. Social interactions in these contexts help people learn the values, norms, and beliefs of their culture.

THE FAMILY

Because family systems vary widely, the infant's range of family contacts is not standard across cultures. The mother everywhere is normally the most important individual in the child's early life, but the nature of relationships between mothers and their children is influenced by the form and regularity of their contact. This, in turn, is conditioned by the character of family institutions and their relation to other groups in society.

In modern societies, most early socialization occurs within a small-scale family context. Most American children grow up within a domestic

socialization • The social processes through which children develop an awareness of social norms and values and achieve a distinct sense of self. Although socialization processes are particularly significant in infancy and childhood, they continue to some degree throughout life. No individuals are immune to the reactions of others around them, which influence and modify their behavior at all phases of the life course.

social reproduction • The process of perpetuating values, norms, and social practices through socialization, which leads to structural continuity over time.

agents of socialization • Groups or social contexts within which processes of socialization take place.

unit containing mother, father, and perhaps one or two other children. In many other cultures, by contrast, aunts, uncles, and grandparents are part of a single household and serve as caretakers even for very young infants. Yet even within American society there are variations in family contexts. Some children grow up in single-parent households; some have two mothering and/or two fathering agents (divorced parents, stepparents, or same-sex parents). Many women with families are employed outside the home and return to their paid work soon after the birth of their children. In spite of these variations, the family normally remains the major agent of socialization from infancy to adolescence and beyond, in a sequence of development connecting the generations.

Families have varying "locations" within the overall institutions of a society. In most premodern societies, the family into which a person was born determined the individual's lifelong social position. In modern societies, social position is not inherited at birth, yet the region and social class of the family have a distinct effect on patterns of socialization. Children pick up ways of behavior characteristic of their parents or others in their neighborhood or community.

Varying patterns of child rearing and discipline, together with contrasting values and expectations, are found in different sectors of large societies. It is easy to understand the differing influence of family background if we imagine the life of, say, a child growing up in a poor black family in a run-down city neighborhood compared with one born into an affluent white family living in an all-white suburb (Kohn, 1977).

Of course, few children unquestioningly adopt their parents' outlook. This is especially true in the modern world, in which change is pervasive. Moreover, the very existence of a range of socializing agents in modern societies leads to divergences among the outlooks of children, adolescents, and parents.

SCHOOLS

Another important socializing agent is school. Schooling is a formal process: students pursue a definite curriculum of subjects. Yet schools are agents of socialization in more subtle respects. Children must be quiet in class, be punctual at lessons, and observe rules of discipline. They must accept the authority of the teaching staff. Reactions of teachers affect the expectations children have of themselves, which in turn become linked to their job experience when they leave school. Peer groups are often formed at school, and the system of age-based classes reinforces their influence.

PEER RELATIONSHIPS

The **peer group** consists of individuals of a similar age. In some cultures, particularly small traditional societies, peer groups are formalized as **age-grades** (normally confined to males), with ceremonies or rites that mark the transition from one age-grade to another. Those within a particular age-grade generally maintain close connections throughout their lives. A typical set of age-grades consists of childhood, junior warriorhood, senior warriorhood, junior elderhood, and senior elderhood. Men move through these grades not as individuals but as whole groups.

Although the family's importance in socialization is obvious, it is less apparent, especially in Western societies, how significant peer groups are. Yet even without formal age-grades, children over the age of four or five usually spend a great

peer group • A friendship group composed of individuals of similar age and social status.

age-grade • The system found in small traditional cultures by which people belonging to a similar age-group are categorized together and hold similar rights and obligations.

deal of time in the company of friends the same age. Given the high proportion of women now in the workforce whose children play together in day-care centers, peer relations are even more important today than before (Corsaro, 1997; Harris, 1998).

In her book *Gender Play* (1993), sociologist Barrie Thorne explores how children learn what it means to be male and female. (You will learn three classic theories of gender socialization later in this chapter.) Rather than seeing children as passively learning the meaning of gender from their parents and teachers, Thorne examines how children actively create and re-create the meaning of gender in their interactions with one another. The social activities that schoolchildren do together can be as important as other agents for their socialization.

Thorne spent two years observing fourth- and fifth-graders at two schools in Michigan and California, sitting in the classroom with them and observing their activities outside the classroom. She watched games—such as "chase and kiss," "cooties," and "goin' with," as well as children teasing one another—to learn how children construct and experience gender meanings in the classroom and on the playground.

Thorne found that peer groups greatly influence gender socialization, particularly as children talk about their changing bodies. The social context determined whether a child's bodily change was experienced with embarrassment or pride. As Thorne (1993) observed, "if the most popular girls started menstruating or wearing bras (even if they didn't 'need to'), then other girls wanted those changes too. But if the popular girls didn't wear bras and hadn't . . . gotten their periods, then these developments were seen as less desirable."

Peer relations have a significant effect beyond childhood and adolescence. Informal groups of people of similar ages, at work and in other situations, are usually of enduring importance in shaping individuals' attitudes and behavior.

Thorne's research is a powerful reminder that children are social actors who help create their social world and influence their own socialization. Still, the effect of societal and cultural influences is also tremendous: children's activities and values are also determined by influences such as the media.

THE MASS MEDIA

Newspapers, periodicals, and journals flourished in the West from the early 1800s onward but had a limited readership. It was not until the early 1900s that such printed material became part of the daily experience of millions of people, influencing their attitudes and opinions. The spread of **mass media** soon included electronic communication—radio, television, audio recordings, and videos. American children now spend the equivalent of almost a hundred school days per year watching television.

Much research has assessed the effects of television programs on audiences, particularly children. Perhaps the most commonly researched topic is the effect of television on propensities to crime and violence.

The most extensive studies to date are those by George Gerbner and his collaborators, who analyzed samples of prime-time and weekend daytime TV for all the major American networks each year since 1967. They charted the number and frequency of violent acts and episodes for a range of programs, defining violence as physical force directed against the self or others, in which physical harm or death occurs. Television drama emerged as highly violent. On average, 80 percent of programs contained violence, with a rate of 7.5 violent episodes per hour. Children's programs showed even higher levels of

> **mass media** • Forms of communication, such as newspapers, magazines, radio, and television, designed to reach mass audiences.

violence, although killing was less common. Cartoons depict the highest number of violent acts and episodes of any type of television program (Gerbner et al., 1986).

Research on the effects of television has tended to treat children as passive and undiscriminating. However, Robert Hodge and David Tripp (1986) emphasize that children's responses to TV involve interpreting, or reading, what they see, not just registering content. Hodge and Tripp suggest that most research has not considered the complexity of children's mental processes. TV watching, even of trivial programs, is not an inherently low-level intellectual activity; children read programs by relating them to other systems of meaning in their lives. According to Hodge and Tripp, it is not the violence alone that affects behavior but rather the general framework of attitudes within which it is both presented and read.

As home video games became widespread, social codes developed based on the games and their characters. The games are often linked to the characters or stories in films and TV programs. Television programming, in turn, has been based on Nintendo games. In 2008, more than 201 million video game units amounting to almost $11.7 billion were sold in the United States alone (Siwek, 2010). Over 70 percent of American households play computer or video games. The average age of gamers is 37 (Entertainment Software Association, 2011). In his book *Video Kids* (1991), Eugene Provenzo analyzes the effect of Nintendo. Video games, Provenzo concludes, have become a key part of the culture and experience of childhood today. Roughly 57 percent of parents believe that playing video games helps families spend more time together (Entertainment Software Association, 2011).

But is this effect a negative one? It is doubtful that a child's involvement with Nintendo harms her achievement at school. However, when strong pressures from other influences deflect students' interest in schoolwork, absorption with TV or video pursuits will reinforce these attitudes. Video games and TV then can become a refuge from a disliked school environment.

At the same time, video games may hone skills that might be relevant both to formal education and to wider participation in a society that depends on electronic communication. According to media scholar Marsha Kinder (1993), her son's adeptness at Nintendo transferred fruitfully to other spheres. For example, the better he became at video games, the more interested and skillful he was at drawing cartoons. Patricia Greenfield (1993) has argued that "video games are the first example of a computer technology that is having a socializing effect on the next generation on a mass scale, and even on a world-wide basis."

Mass media are an important influence on socialization in all forms of society. Few societies in current times, even among more traditional cultures, remain untouched by the media. Electronic communication is accessible even to those who cannot read or write; and in the most impoverished parts of the world, it is common to find people owning radios and television sets.

WORK

Work is, in all cultures, an important agent of socialization, although only in industrial societies do large numbers of people go to places of work separate from the home. In communities where people farmed nearby land or had workshops in their dwellings, work was not as distinct from other activities. In industrialized countries the work environment often poses unfamiliar demands, perhaps calling for major adjustments in the person's outlook or behavior.

SOCIAL ROLES

Through socialization, individuals learn about **social roles**—socially defined expectations for a person in a given social position. The social role of doctor, for example, encompasses a set of behaviors that all doctors should assume, regardless of their personal opinions or outlooks. Because all doctors share this role, we can speak in general terms about the professional role behavior of doctors.

Some sociologists, particularly those associated with the functionalist school, regard social roles as unchanging parts of a society's culture. They are social facts. According to this view, individuals learn the expectations for social positions in their culture and perform these roles largely as they have been defined. Social roles do not involve negotiation or creativity. Rather, they direct an individual's behavior. Through socialization, individuals internalize social roles and learn how to carry them out.

This view, however, is mistaken. It suggests that individuals simply take on roles rather than creating or negotiating them. In fact, socialization is a process in which humans can exercise agency; they are not passive subjects waiting to be instructed or programmed. Individuals come to understand and assume social roles through an ongoing process of social interaction.

Identity

The cultural settings in which we grow up influence our behavior, but that does not mean that humans lack individuality or free will. The fact that from birth to death we are involved in interaction with others certainly conditions our personalities, values, and behavior. Yet socialization is also at the origin of our individuality and freedom. In the course of socialization, each of us develops a sense of identity and the capacity for independent thought and action.

The concept of identity in sociology is multifaceted. Broadly speaking, **identity** relates to people's understandings about who they are and what is meaningful to them. These understandings are formed in relation to certain attributes that take priority over other sources of meaning. Some of the main sources of identity are gender, sexual orientation, nationality, ethnicity, and social class. Sociologists often speak of two types of identity: social identity and self-identity (or personal identity). These types are analytically distinct but closely related to one another. **Social identity** refers to the characteristics that other people attribute to an individual—markers that indicate who, in a basic sense, that individual is. At the same time, these characteristics place that individual in relation to others who share the same attributes. Examples of social identities are student, mother, lawyer, Catholic, homeless, Asian, dyslexic, and married.

All individuals have more than one social identity, thereby reflecting the many dimensions of their lives. A person could simultaneously be a mother, an engineer, a Muslim, and a city council member. This plurality of social identities can be a source of conflict. Most individuals organize meaning and experience in their lives around a primary identity that is continuous across time and place.

Social identities involve a collective dimension. They mark ways that individuals are the

social roles • Socially defined expectations of an individual in a given status or social position.

identity • The distinctive characteristics of a person's or group's character that relate to who he is and what is meaningful to him. Some of the main sources of identity include gender, sexual orientation, nationality or ethnicity, and social class.

social identity • The characteristics that are attributed to an individual by others.

same as others. Shared identities—predicated on common goals, values, or experiences—aside from forming an important base for social movements, serve as a powerful source of personal meaning or self-worth.

If social identities mark ways in which individuals are the same as others, **self-identity** (or personal identity) sets us apart as distinct individuals. Self-identity refers to the process of self-development through which we formulate a unique sense of ourselves and our relationship to the world. The notion of self-identity draws heavily on the work of symbolic interactionists. It is our constant negotiation with the outside world that shapes our sense of self, linking our own personal and public worlds. Though the cultural and social environment is a factor in shaping self-identity, individual agency and choice are key.

Tracing the changes in self-identity from traditional to modern societies, we can see a shift away from the fixed, inherited factors that previously guided identity formation, such as membership in social groups bound by class or nationality. People's identities are now more multifaceted and less stable owing to urban growth, industrialization, and the breakdown of earlier social formations. Individuals have become more socially and geographically mobile. Freed from the homogeneous communities of the past, people now find that other sources of personal meaning, such as gender and sexual orientation, play a greater role in their sense of identity.

Today we have unprecedented opportunities to create our own identities. We are our own best resources in defining who we are, where we have come from, and where we are going. Now that the traditional signposts of identity have become less essential, the social world confronts us with a dizzying array of choices about who to be, how to live, and what to do, without offering much guidance about which selections to make. The decisions we make in our everyday lives—about what to wear, how to behave, and how to spend our time—help make us who we are. Through our capacity as self-conscious, self-aware human beings, we constantly create and re-create our identities.

Socialization through the Life Course

The transitions through which individuals pass during their lives seem to be biologically fixed—from childhood to adulthood and eventually to death. But the stages of the human life course are social as well as biological. They are influenced by cultural differences and material circumstances in various types of societies. For example, in the modern West, death is usually thought of in relation to old age, because most people enjoy a life span of seventy years or more. In traditional societies of the past, however, more people died in younger age groups than survived to old age.

CHILDHOOD

In modern societies, childhood is considered a distinct stage of life between infancy and the teen years. Yet the concept of childhood has developed only over the past two or three centuries. In earlier societies, the young moved directly from a lengthy infancy into working roles within the community. The French historian Philippe Ariès (1965) has argued that childhood did not exist in medieval times. In the paintings of medieval Europe, children are portrayed as little adults, with mature faces and the same style of dress as their elders. Children took part in the same work and play activities

self-identity • The ongoing process of self-development and definition of our personal identity through which we formulate a unique sense of ourselves and our relationship to the world around us.

as adults, rather than in the childhood games we now take for granted.

Right up to the twentieth century, in the United States and most other Western countries, children were put to work at what now seems a very early age. There are countries in the world today, in fact, where young children do full-time work, sometimes in physically demanding circumstances (for example, in coal mines). The ideas that children have rights and that child labor is morally repugnant are recent developments.

Because of the long period of childhood that we recognize today, societies now are in some respects more child-centered than traditional ones. But a child-centered society, it must be emphasized, is not one in which all children experience love and care from parents or other adults. The physical and sexual abuse of children is a commonplace feature of family life in present-day society, although the extent of such abuse has only recently come to light. Child abuse has clear connections to what seems to us today the frequent mistreatment of children in premodern Europe.

It is possible that as a result of changes in modern societies the separate character of childhood is again diminishing. Some observers have suggested that children now grow up so fast that this is in fact the case. They point out that even small children may watch the same television programs as adults, thereby becoming much more familiar early on with the adult world than did preceding generations.

Duccio da Buoninsegna's *Madonna and Child*, painted in the thirteenth century, depicts the infant Jesus with a mature face. Until recently, children in Western society were viewed as little adults.

THE TEENAGER

The idea of the teenager also didn't exist until recently. The biological changes involved in puberty (the point at which a person becomes capable of adult sexual activity and reproduction) are universal. Yet in many cultures, these do not produce the turmoil and uncertainty often found among young people in modern societies. In cultures that foster age-grades, for example, which hold ceremonies that signal a person's transition to adulthood, the process of psychosexual development seems easier to negotiate. Adolescents in such societies have less to "unlearn" because the pace of change is slower. There is a time in Western societies when children are required to put away their toys and break with childish pursuits. In traditional cultures, in which children already work alongside adults, this process of unlearning is much less jarring.

In Western societies, teenagers are betwixt and between: They often try to follow adult ways, but they are treated by law as children. They may wish to go to work, but they are constrained to stay in school. Teenagers in the West live in between childhood and adulthood, growing up in a society subject to continuous change.

YOUNG ADULTHOOD

Young adulthood seems increasingly to be a stage in personal and sexual development in modern societies (Goldscheider and Waite, 1991). Particularly among affluent groups, people in their early twenties take the time to travel and explore sexual, political, and religious affiliations. The importance of this postponement of the responsibilities of full adulthood is likely to grow, given the extended period of education many people now undergo.

MATURE ADULTHOOD

Most young adults in the West today can expect to live well into old age. In premodern times, few could anticipate such a future. Death through sickness or injury was much more frequent among all age groups than it is today, and women faced a high rate of mortality in childbirth.

However, some of the strains we experience now were less pronounced in previous times. People usually maintained a closer connection with their parents and other kin than in today's mobile populations, and their work routines were the same as those of their forebears. In current times, major uncertainties must be resolved in marriage, family life, and other social contexts. We have to make our own lives more than people did in the past. The creation of sexual and marital ties, for instance, now depends on individual initiative and selection rather than being fixed by one's parents. This represents greater freedom for the individual, but the responsibility can also impose difficulties.

Keeping a forward-looking perspective in middle age has become particularly important in modern societies. Most people do not expect to do the same thing all their lives, as in traditional cultures. Individuals who have spent their lives in one career may find the level they have reached in middle age unsatisfying and further opportunities blocked. Women who have spent their early adulthood raising a family and whose children have left home may feel they lack social value. The midlife crisis is very real for many middle-aged people. A person may feel that she has thrown away the opportunities that life had to offer or that she will never attain goals cherished since childhood. Yet growing older need not lead to resignation or despair; a release from childhood dreams can be liberating.

OLD AGE

In traditional societies, older people were accorded great respect. Among cultures that included age-grades, the elders usually had a major—often the final—say in matters of importance to the community. Within families, the authority of both men and women increased with age. In industrialized societies, by contrast, older people tend to lack authority within both the family and the social community. Having retired from the labor force, they may be poorer than ever before in their lives. At the same time, there has been a great increase in the proportion of the population over age 65. In 1900 only one in 30 people in the United States was over age 65, whereas in 2011, 13 percent of the population was over the age of 65 (U.S. Bureau of the Census, 2011o). The same trend is found in all industrially advanced countries.

Transition to the age-grade of elder in a traditional culture often marked the pinnacle of an individual's status. In modern societies, retirement brings the opposite. No longer living with their children and often having retired from paid work, older people may find it difficult to make the final period of their life rewarding. People used to think that those who successfully coped with old age relied on their inner resources, becoming less interested in the material rewards of social life. Although this may be true, it seems likely that in a society in which many are physically healthy in old age, an outward-looking view will become more prevalent. Those in retirement might find renewal in the "third age," in which a new phase of education begins. (See also Chapter 12 on lifelong learning.)

CONCEPT CHECKS

1. What is social reproduction? What are some specific ways the four main agents of socialization contribute to social reproduction?

2. Compare and contrast social roles and social identities.

3. What are the five stages of the life course, and what are some of the defining features of each stage?

4. Describe how the life course stage of childhood has changed since medieval times.

② THEORIES OF SOCIALIZATION

One of the most distinctive features of human beings, compared with other animals, is that they are self-aware. How should we understand the emergence of a sense of self—the awareness that the individual has a distinct identity separate from others? During the first months of life, the infant possesses little or no understanding of differences between human beings and material objects and has no awareness of self. Children do not grasp concepts such as I, me, and you until the age of two or later. Only gradually do they understand that others have distinct identities, consciousness, and needs separate from their own.

The problem of the emergence of self is much debated among contrasting theoretical perspectives. To some extent, this is because the most prominent theories about child development emphasize different aspects of socialization. The American philosopher and sociologist George Herbert Mead mainly considered how children learn to use the concepts of I and me. Jean Piaget, the Swiss student of child behavior, studied many aspects of child development, but his best-known writings concern **cognition**—the ways in which children learn to think about themselves and their environment.

G. H. Mead and the Development of Self

Because Mead's ideas underlie a general tradition of theoretical thinking, symbolic interactionism, they have had a broad impact in sociology. Symbolic interactionism emphasizes that interaction between human beings occurs through symbols and the interpretation of meanings (see Chapter 1). But Mead's work also describes the main phases of child development, concentrating on the emergence of a sense of self.

According to Mead, infants and young children develop as social beings by imitating the actions of those around them. Play is one way in which this occurs. A small child will make mud pies, having seen an adult cooking, or will dig with a spoon, having observed someone gardening. Children's play evolves from simple imitation to more complicated games in which a child of four or five years old will act out an adult role. Mead called this "taking the role of the other." It is only at this stage that children acquire a developed sense of self. Children

cognition • Human thought processes involving perception, reasoning, and remembering.

Using their toy wheelbarrows to help their father with the gardening, these boys are, according to Mead, "taking on the role of the other" and achieving an understanding of themselves as separate social agents.

achieve an understanding of themselves as separate agents—as a "me"—by seeing themselves through the eyes of others.

We achieve self-awareness, according to Mead, when we learn to distinguish the me from the I. The I is the unsocialized infant, a bundle of spontaneous wants and desires. The me is the **social self**. Individuals develop **self-consciousness**, Mead argued, by coming to see themselves as others see them. A further stage of child development occurs when the child is eight or nine years old, the age at which children take part in organized games rather than unsystematic play. At this period children begin to understand the values and morality that govern social life. To learn organized games, children must understand the rules of play and notions of fairness and equal participation. Children at this stage learn to grasp what Mead termed the **generalized other**—the general values and moral rules of the culture in which they are developing.

Jean Piaget and the Stages of Cognitive Development

Piaget emphasized the child's active capability to make sense of the world. Children do not passively soak up information, but instead select and interpret what they see, hear, and feel. Piaget described distinct stages of cognitive development during which children learn to think about themselves and their environment. Each stage involves the acquisition of new skills and depends on the successful completion of the preceding ones.

Piaget called the first stage, from birth up to about age two, the **sensorimotor stage**, because infants learn mainly by touching objects, manipulating them, and physically exploring their environment. Until age four months or so, infants cannot differentiate themselves from their environment. For example, a child will not realize that her own movements cause the sides of her crib to rattle. Objects are not differentiated from persons, and the infant is unaware that anything exists outside her range of vision. The infant gradually learns to distinguish people from objects, realizing that both have an existence independent of her immediate perception of them. The main accomplishment of this stage is children's understanding that their environment has distinct and stable properties.

social self • The basis of self-consciousness in human individuals, according to the theory of G. H. Mead. The social self is the identity conferred upon an individual by the reactions of others. A person achieves self-consciousness by becoming aware of this social identity.

self-consciousness • Awareness of one's distinct social identity as a person separate from others. Human beings are not born with self-consciousness but acquire an awareness of self as a result of early socialization. The learning of language is of vital importance to the processes by which the child learns to become a self-conscious being.

generalized other • A concept in the theory of G. H. Mead, according to which the individual takes over the general values of a given group or society during the socialization process.

sensorimotor stage • According to Piaget, a stage of human cognitive development in which the child's awareness of its environment is dominated by perception and touch.

The next phase, the **preoperational stage**, is the one to which Piaget devoted the bulk of his research. During this stage, which lasts from age two to seven, children master language and use words to represent objects and images in a symbolic fashion. A four-year-old might use a sweeping hand, for example, to represent the concept airplane. Piaget termed the stage "preoperational" because children are not yet able to use their developing mental capabilities systematically. Children in this stage are egocentric in the sense that they interpret the world exclusively in terms of their own position. The child does not understand, for instance, that others see objects from a different perspective. Holding a book upright, the child may ask about a picture in it, not realizing that the person sitting opposite can see only the back of the book.

Children at the preoperational stage are not able to hold connected conversations with another person. With **egocentric** speech, what each child says is more or less unrelated to what the other speaker has said. Children talk together, but not to one another in the same sense as adults. During this stage, children have no general understanding of categories of thought that adults take for granted: concepts such as causality, speed, weight, or number. Even if the child sees water poured from a tall, thin container into a shorter, wider one, she will not understand that the volume of water remains the same—and she will conclude that there is less water because the water level is lower.

A third period, the **concrete operational stage**, lasts from age seven to 11. During this phase, children master abstract, logical notions such as causality. A child at this stage of development will recognize the false reasoning involved in the idea that the wide container holds less water than the narrow one, even though the water levels are different. The child becomes capable of carrying out the mathematical operations of multiplying, dividing, and subtracting. Children by this stage are much less egocentric. In the preoperational stage, if a girl is asked, "How many sisters do you have?" she may correctly answer, "One." But if asked, "How many sisters does your sister have?" she will probably answer, "None," because she cannot see herself from the point of view of her sister. The concrete operational child can easily answer such a question.

The years from 11 to 15 cover the **formal operational stage**. During adolescence, the developing child becomes able to grasp highly abstract and hypothetical ideas. When faced with a problem, children at this stage are able to review all the possible ways of solving it and go through them theoretically to reach a solution. The young person at the formal operational stage can understand why some questions are trick ones. To the question "What creatures are both poodles and dogs?" the individual might not be able to give the correct reply but will understand why the answer "poodles" is right and will appreciate the humor in it.

According to Piaget, the first three stages of development are universal; but not all adults reach the formal operational stage. The development of formal operational thought depends in part on processes of schooling. Adults of limited educational attainment tend to continue to think in more concrete terms and retain large traces of egocentrism.

preoperational stage • A stage of cognitive development, in Piaget's theory, in which the child has advanced sufficiently to master basic modes of logical thought.

egocentric • According to Piaget, the characteristic quality of a child during the early years of her life. Egocentric thinking involves understanding objects and events in the environment solely in terms of one's own position.

concrete operational stage • A stage of cognitive development, as formulated by Piaget, in which the child's thinking is based primarily on physical perception of the world. In this phase, the child is not yet capable of dealing with abstract concepts or hypothetical situations.

formal operational stage • According to Piaget's theory, a stage of cognitive development at which the growing child becomes capable of handling abstract concepts and hypothetical situations.

Freud's Theory

Perhaps the most influential, and controversial, theory of the emergence of gender identity is that of Sigmund Freud. According to Freud, the learning of gender differences in infants and young children centers on the possession or absence of the penis. "I have a penis" is equivalent to "I am a boy," while "I am a girl" is equivalent to "I lack a penis." Freud is careful to say that it is not just the anatomical distinctions that matter; the possession and absence of the penis are symbolic of masculinity and femininity.

At around age four or five, the theory goes, a boy feels threatened by the discipline and autonomy his father demands of him, fantasizing that the father wishes to remove his penis. Partly consciously, but mostly unconsciously, the boy recognizes the father as a rival for the affections of his mother. In repressing erotic feelings toward the mother and accepting the father as a superior being, the boy identifies with the father and becomes aware of his male identity. The boy gives up his love for his mother out of an unconscious fear of castration by his father. Girls, on the other hand, supposedly suffer from "penis envy" because they do not possess the visible organ that distinguishes boys. The mother becomes devalued in the little girl's eyes, because she also lacks a penis and is unable to provide one. When the girl identifies with the mother, she takes over the submissive attitude involved in the recognition of being "second best."

Once this phase is over, the child has learned to repress his erotic feelings. The period from about five years of age to puberty, according to Freud, is one of latency—sexual activities are suspended until the biological changes of puberty reactivate erotic desires. The latency period, covering the early and middle years of school, is the time at which same-sex peer groups are most important in the child's life.

Major objections have been raised against Freud's views, particularly by feminists but also by many other authors (Coward, 1984; Mitchell, 1975). First, Freud seems to identify gender identity too closely with genital awareness; other, more subtle factors are surely involved. Second, the theory seems to depend on the notion that the penis is superior to the vagina, which is thought of as just a lack of the male organ. Yet why shouldn't the female genitals be considered superior to those of the male? Third, Freud treats the father as the primary disciplining agent, whereas in many cultures the mother is more significant in imposing discipline. Fourth, Freud believed that gender learning is concentrated at age four or five. Later authors have emphasized the importance of earlier learning, beginning in infancy.

Chodorow's Theory

Although many writers have used Freud's approach in studying gender development, they have modified it in major respects. An important example is the sociologist Nancy Chodorow (1978, 1988), who argues that learning to feel male or female derives from the infant's attachment to the parents from an early age. She emphasizes much more than Freud the importance of the mother rather than the father. Children become emotionally involved with the mother because she is the most dominant influence in their early lives. At some point this attachment has to be broken for the child to achieve a separate sense of self—to become less closely dependent.

Chodorow argues that the breaking process occurs in a different way for boys and girls. Girls remain closer to the mother—able, for example, to go on hugging and kissing her and imitating what she does. Because there is no sharp break from the mother, the girl, and later the adult woman, develops a sense of self that is more continuous with other people. Her identity is more likely to be merged with or depend on another's: first her mother's, later a man's. In Chodorow's view, this fosters sensitivity and emotional compassion in women.

Boys gain a sense of self via a more radical rejection of their original closeness to the mother, forging their understanding of masculinity from what is not feminine. They learn not to be "sissies" or "mama's boys." As a result, boys are relatively unskilled in relating closely to others; they develop more analytical ways of looking at the world. They take a more active view of their lives, emphasizing achievement, but they have repressed their ability to understand their own feelings and those of others.

To some extent, Chodorow reverses Freud's emphasis. Masculinity, rather than femininity, is defined by a loss, the forfeiting of continued close attachment to the mother. Male identity is formed through separation; thus men later in life unconsciously feel that their identity is endangered if they become involved in close emotional relationships with others. Women, on the other hand, feel that the absence of a close relation to another person threatens their self-esteem. These patterns are passed on from generation to generation, because of women's primary role in the early socialization of children. Women express and define themselves mainly in terms of relationships. Men have repressed these needs and adopt a more manipulative stance toward the world.

Chodorow's work has met with various criticisms. Janet Sayers (1986), for example, has suggested that Chodorow does not explain the struggle of women, particularly in current times, to become autonomous, independent beings. Women (and men), Sayers points out, are more contradictory in their psychological makeup than Chodorow's theory suggests. Femininity may conceal feelings of aggressiveness or assertiveness, which are revealed only obliquely or in certain contexts (Brennan, 1988). Chodorow has also been criticized for her narrow conception of the family based on a white, middle-class model. What happens, for example, in one-parent households or, as in many Chicano communities, in families where children are cared for by more than one adult (Segura and Pierce, 1993)?

These criticisms don't undermine Chodorow's ideas, which remain important, as they teach us a good deal about the nature of femininity and help us understand the origins of "male inexpressiveness"—the difficulty men have in revealing their feelings to others (Balswick, 1983).

Gilligan's Theory

Carol Gilligan (1982) further developed Chodorow's analysis, concentrating on the images adult women and men have of themselves and their attainments. Women, she agrees with Chodorow, define themselves in terms of personal relationships and judge their achievements in terms of their ability to care for others. Women's place in the lives of men is traditionally that of caretaker and helpmate. But the qualities developed in these tasks are devalued by men, who see their own emphasis on individual achievement as the only form of success. Women's concern with relationships appears to men as a weakness rather than as the strength that in fact it is.

Gilligan carried out intensive interviews with about 200 American women and men of varying ages and social backgrounds. She asked a range of questions concerning their moral outlook and conceptions of self. Consistent differences emerged between the men's and women's views. When asked, "What does it mean to say something is

CONCEPT CHECKS ✓

1. According to Mead, how does a child develop a social self?

2. What are the four stages of cognitive development, according to Piaget?

3. How do Chodorow's and Gilligan's theories help us understand socialization influence on gender?

morally right or wrong?" the men mentioned abstract ideals of duty, justice, and individual freedom, whereas the women raised the theme of helping others.

The women were more tentative in their moral judgments than the men, seeing possible contradictions between following a strict moral code and avoiding harming others. Gilligan suggests that this outlook reflects the traditional situation of women, anchored in caring relationships, rather than the outward-looking attitudes of men. Women's views of themselves are based on successfully fulfilling the needs of others, rather than on pride in individual achievement (Gilligan, 1982).

RESEARCH ON SOCIALIZATION TODAY

Women in the Workforce

Sociologist Deborah Carr researches how the world has changed for women in the past century. Throughout much of the twentieth century, most middle-class women were expected to settle down with a husband after high school, bear children, and embrace a life of motherhood. A career was a man's pursuit. For him, changing jobs was often a sign that he couldn't hold down a stable position. Families would live for decades in one community, and gender expectations in American culture were relatively clear.

Carr has spent years studying the changes that have taken place in that scenario and how they influence the choices people make about their lives. Take the issue of women's work. In 1947 less than one-third of women worked outside the home, a proportion that doubled to almost 60 percent by 2010. What was a comparatively rare phenomenon in the mid-twentieth century had become the norm just 50 years later (Blau and Kahn, 2005; U.S. Department of Labor, 2010b). Not only are women working more but they are also delaying marriage, living longer, graduating college in unprecedented numbers, and having fewer children on average than they did in 1950. In other words, women are living very different lives from the ones their mothers did just a generation ago.

As gender roles continue to blur, Carr's research has focused on the choices women make during a period she calls the "new midlife." For many women, this is not an end but a time for new beginnings. More and more, women are feeling empowered to exit stale marriages, start their own businesses, learn from their daughters, and pick up new hobbies.

Part of Carr's challenge as a public sociologist is to translate private troubles into public issues—to point out to individual women that they are not alone. This process of reinvention can be painful and emotionally complicated. Without the benefit of a road map or a script, "women are always questioning if what they're feeling is OK." Whereas psychologists may focus on the individual or couple when finding solutions to marital woes, the task for sociologists is simultaneously to balance two levels, the micro and the macro. For example, there are currently 43 million American women aged 40 to 60 passing through middle age, and many of them are probably confronting similar feelings of excitement, confusion, and regret.

In a study titled, "My Daughter Has a Career: I Just Raised Babies," Carr (2004) describes the tension that can arise between mothers and daughters growing up in different eras. For women who came of age in the 1950s and 1960s, maintaining a sense of self-worth in the midst of changing cultural norms can be very difficult. Having grown up amid considerable pressure to have children and ignore professional pursuits, many women in Carr's study watched with mixed feelings as their daughters took on new challenges: On the one hand, the pursuit of education and professional esteem was a sign of progress and liberation; but on the other hand, daughters experienced considerable difficulty balancing work and family life. Carr comments:

> Social changes since the late 1960s have created a new normative context in which women and men are expected to be both successful workers and involved parents. Given this shift, midlife women who complied with the mid-twentieth century expectation that they should stay home with their children (rather than work for pay outside the home) may suffer regret or self-criticism, especially if they use the contemporary cultural ideal as the standard for evaluating their past decisions and experiences. (Carr, 2004, p. 132)

By connecting these individual-level anxieties to massive social shifts, Carr's research often sparks conversations beyond the classroom. Carr states, "As sociologists, we must never forget that the data points in our surveys are actually real people." The effects of women entering the workforce and the changing dynamics of gender relations will remain a major issue moving forward into the twenty-first century.

Many women who complied with the pressure to stay at home and raise children in the 1950s and 1960s have struggled with their sense of self-worth as they watched their daughters enter the workforce.

Early Child Care and Youth Development

Throughout the past decade, many parents wrestled with the tough question "Should I pull my child out of daycare and stay with him at home?" The study was based on data from the National Institute of Child Health and Human Development (NICHD) Study of Early Child Care and Youth Development, the nation's longest-running study of child care in the United States (Belsky et al., 2007). The researchers, led by Dr. Jay Belsky of Birkbeck University of London, tracked more than 1,300 children from birth through sixth grade. They collected detailed data on how the children were cared for and what proportion of their lives they spent in a variety of different care settings. The study's authors were particularly interested in comparing children who were cared for by relatives, by nonrelatives, and by paid child-care providers. They also measured the "quality" of the care received, based on periodic observations of the child-care centers. They examined whether the site, duration, and quality of care were associated with outcomes such as performance on vocabulary tests, social skills, work habits, emotional adjustment, behavior problems, and relationships with their schoolteachers.

Belsky and his colleagues did indeed find that children who spent more time in child-care centers had more behavior problems in elementary school, even after the researchers "held constant" or statistically controlled for other possible risk factors for problematic behaviors, such as parents' socioeconomic resources and mental health. However, the researchers did not jump to the conclusion that child care "caused" behavior problems. Rather, they honestly noted that the effect sizes were very modest—that is, that the differences in behavior problems between those children in child care and those in family care were quite small.

Moreover, the scientists believed that several of their other findings were much more important. First, they found that children who were in high-quality child-care settings went on to have higher vocabulary scores than other children. Second, they found that the quality of parenting mattered much more than where a child was cared for. The authors wrote that "parenting quality significantly predicted all the developmental outcomes and much more strongly than did any of the child care predictors." One reason parents matter more than child-care arrangements is that they are an enduring presence in the children's lives, while day care is often just a short-term experience. As Belsky and his coauthors noted, "most children . . . experienced multiple different classrooms and after-school arrangements subsequent to school entry. In comparison, family experiences and parenting were relatively stable."

As more and more women enter the workforce, the debate over benefits and losses related to daycare continue. Belsky's research offers important insight into this phenomenon that is bound to continue in the coming years.

CONCEPT CHECKS ✓

1. According to Carr, what is the "new midlife?" What is the significance of this new stage in the life course for women, in particular?

2. What does Belsky's research tell us about the influence of day-care on childhood development?

---

4 UNANSWERED QUESTIONS ABOUT SOCIALIZATION

Although studies of socialization have become quite advanced over the past century, there are many open or unanswered questions that are still the subject of much disagreement among sociologists. Perhaps the most significant has to do with **gender socialization**—the learning of **gender roles** through social factors such as the family and the media.

Gender Socialization: Reactions of Parents and Adults

Many studies have examined the degree to which gender differences are the result of social influences. Studies of mother-infant interaction show differences in the treatment of boys and girls even when parents believe their reactions to both are the same. Adults asked to assess the personality of a baby give different answers according to whether they believe the child is a girl or a boy. In one experiment, five young mothers were observed interacting with a six-month-old called Beth. They smiled at her often and offered her dolls to play with. She was seen as "sweet," and as having a "soft cry." The reaction of a second group of mothers to a child the same age, named Adam, was noticeably different. They offered him a train or other "male" toys

gender socialization • The learning of gender roles through social factors such as schooling, the media, and family.

gender roles • Social roles assigned to each sex and labeled as masculine or feminine to play with. Beth and Adam were actually the same child, dressed in different clothes (Will, Self, and Datan, 1976).

Gender Learning

Gender learning by infants is almost certainly unconscious. Before a child can label itself as either a boy or a girl, it receives preverbal cues. For instance, male and female adults usually handle infants differently. Women's cosmetics contain scents different from those the baby might associate with males. Systematic differences in dress, hairstyle, and so on provide visual cues for the infant in the learning process. By age two, children have a partial understanding of what gender is. They know whether they are boys or girls, and they can usually categorize others accurately. Not until age five or six, however, does a child know that a person's sex does not change, that everyone has gender, and that sex differences between girls and boys are anatomically based.

Children's toys, picture books, and television programs all tend to emphasize male and female attributes. Toy stores and mail-order catalogs usually categorize their products by gender. Even some toys that seem gender neutral are not so in practice. For example, toy kittens and rabbits are recommended for girls, whereas lions and tigers are seen as more appropriate for boys.

Vanda Lucia Zammuner (1986) studied the toy preferences of children between 7 and 10 years of age in Italy and Holland; stereotypically masculine and feminine toys and toys presumed not to be gender-typed were included. The children and their parents were asked which toys were suitable for boys and which for girls. There was close agreement between the adults and the children. On average, the Italian children chose gender-differentiated toys more often than the Dutch children—a finding that conformed to expectations, because Italian culture holds a more traditional view of gender divisions than does Dutch society. As in other studies, girls from both societies chose gender-neutral or boys' toys far more often than boys chose girls' toys.

Storybooks and Television

In the 1970s, Lenore Weitzman and her colleagues analyzed gender roles in some of the most widely used preschool children's books and found several clear differences in gender roles (Weitzman et al., 1972). Males played a much larger part in the stories and pictures than did females, outnumbering females by a ratio of 11 to 1. When animals with gender identities were included, the ratio was 95 to 1. The activities of males and females also differed. The males engaged in adventurous pursuits and outdoor activities demanding independence and strength. When girls did appear, they were portrayed as passive and were confined mostly to indoor activities. Girls cooked and cleaned for the males or awaited their return. Much the same was true of the adult characters. Women who were not wives and mothers were imaginary creatures such as witches and fairy godmothers. There was not a single woman in all the books analyzed who held an occupation outside the home. By contrast, the men were depicted as fighters, policemen, judges, kings, and so forth.

More recent research suggests a slight change, but notes that the bulk of children's literature remains the same (Davies, 1991). Fairy tales, for example, embody traditional attitudes toward gender and expectations for boys' and girls' ambitions. In versions of fairy tales from several centuries ago, the idea that "someday my prince will come" usually implied that a girl from a poor family might dream of wealth and fortune. Today that notion is tied to the ideals of romantic love. Some feminists have tried to rewrite some of the most celebrated fairy tales, reversing their usual emphases: "He's not nearly as attractive as he seemed the other night. So I think I'll just pretend that this glass slipper feels too tight" (Viorst, 1986). However, these rewrites, like this version of "Cinderella," are directed mainly to adult audiences and have hardly affected the tales told in innumerable children's books.

Although there are exceptions, analyses of children's television programs match the findings about children's books. In the most popular cartoons, most leading figures are male, and males dominate the active pursuits. Similar images appear in the commercials that air throughout the programs.

The Difficulty of Nonsexist Child Rearing

June Statham (1986) studied a group of parents committed to nonsexist child rearing. Thirty adults in 18 families were involved in the research, which included children ages six months to 12 years. The parents were middle class, mostly teachers or professors. Most of the parents did not simply try to modify traditional gender roles by seeking to make girls more like boys, but wanted to foster new combinations of the feminine and masculine. They wished boys to be more sensitive to others' feelings and capable of expressing warmth, while they encouraged girls to seek opportunities for learning and self-advancement. All the parents found existing patterns of gender learning difficult to combat. They were reasonably successful at persuading the children to play with gender-neutral toys, but even this proved more difficult than they had expected. One mother commented:

> If you walk into a toy shop, it's full of war toys for boys and domestic toys for girls, and it sums up society the way it is. This is the way children are being socialized: it's all right for boys to be taught to kill and hurt. . . . I try not to go into toy shops, I feel so angry. (Statham, 1986)

Practically all the children possessed, and played with, gender-typed toys, given to them by relatives.

There are now some storybooks available with strong independent girls as the main characters, but few depict boys in nontraditional roles. The mother of a five-year-old boy told of her son's reaction when she reversed the sexes of the characters in a story she read to him:

> In fact he was a bit upset when I went through a book which has a boy and a girl in very traditional roles, and changed all the he's to she's and she's to he's. When I first started doing that, he was inclined to say "you don't like boys, you only like girls." I had to explain that that wasn't true at all, it's just that there's not enough written about girls. (Statham, 1986)

Clearly, gender socialization is very powerful, and challenges to it can be upsetting. Once a gender is "assigned," society expects individuals to act like females and males. It is in the practices of everyday life that these expectations are fulfilled and reproduced (Bourdieu, 1990; Lorber, 1994).

The Question of Video Games

In recent years, video games have come under critical scrutiny from researchers and public policy officials. As early as April of 2012, a flurry of media attention resulted from a confession by Anders Breivik, the Norwegian right-wing extremist who killed 77 people in the Utoya Massacre of July 2011, that he trained for the mass murders by playing *Grand Theft Auto IV*. The confession spawned an outpouring of public debate, waged on the op-ed pages of national news sources and online blogs. Journalists, pundits, bloggers, and the public at large became obsessed with answering the question of whether video games caused violence.

Research conducted in 2005 by Douglas Gentile, who runs the Media Research Lab at Iowa State University, shows a strong correlation between violent video games and aggression in children.

Combined with lax parenting, negligence, and drug use, playing violent video games adds, according to Gentile, another ingredient to a potentially explosive mix. But even children who have no predisposition for hostility are more likely to get into physical fights if they play violent video games, he said.

His study of 607 eighth- and ninth-graders found 38 percent of the children with "low hostility" who played violent video games got into fights, compared with only 4 percent of those who did not play at all. And the more they played, the more violent they wanted the game to be.

According to Gentile, violent video games and media violence contribute to a culture that teachers around the country have become quite familiar with: pushing and shoving in the corridors, verbal aggression, disrespect, and impolite behavior.

Leaders of the American Medical Association, the American Academy of Pediatrics, the American Psychological Association, and the American Academy of Child and Adolescent Psychiatry also believe in the link, citing 3,500 studies during a Congressional Public Health Summit a few years ago.

But the Entertainment Software Association, along with some scientists, beg to differ. "There are no studies that show a causal effect," said Carolyn Rauch, a former senior vice president of ESA. "Even the weakest links have serious methodological defects. It's totally subjective. Video games are today's rock n' roll in the '60s. Older people want to believe it's bad, but they don't understand it."

On the association's website, several studies are quoted, from the Australian government to the Surgeon General to the Department of Social and Health Services of Washington State, calling evidence of a correlation "ambiguous" or "lacking consensus" at best.

Karen Sternheimer, sociologist at the University of Southern California and author of *It's Not the Media: The Truth About Pop Culture's Influence on Children* (2003), said many studies use contrived definitions of aggression to prove their point. For example, she said some measured the trait by how much a player of violent video games would fine his opponent in Monopoly, how loudly he would blow a horn, or how fast he could read a list of aggressive words.

In any case, the debate regarding whether video game violence translates into real-world violence is far from settled. A recent study conducted by Christopher Ferguson and published in the *Journal of Psychiatric Research* demonstrated that children who played violent video games were *not* "more violent than other kids, nor harmed in any other identifiable fashion" (Ferguson, 2011). His longitudinal study produced results that run counter to those initially produced by Gentile.

CONCEPT CHECKS

1. How do the media contribute to gender role socialization?

2. How do parents and other adults reinforce gender roles?

THE BIG PICTURE

Chapter 4
Socialization and the Life Cycle

1 **Basic Concepts**

p. 85

2 **Theories of Socialization**

p. 93

p. 85
p. 93

LEARNING OBJECTIVES

Learn about how the four main agents of socialization contribute to social reproduction. Learn the stages of the life course and see the similarities and differences among cultures.

Learn the theories of child development according to Mead, Piaget, Freud, and Chodorow.

TERMS TO KNOW

Socialization • Social reproduction • Agents of socialization • Peer group • Age-grades • Mass media • Social roles • Identity • Social identity • Self-identity

Cognition • Social self • Self-consciousness • Generalized other • Sensorimotor stage • Preoperational stage • Egocentric • Concrete operational stage • Formal operational stage

CONCEPT CHECKS

1. What is social reproduction? What are some specific ways the four main agents of socialization contribute to social reproduction?
2. Compare and contrast social roles and social identities.
3. What are the five stages of the life course, and what are some of the defining features of each stage?
4. Describe how the life course stage of childhood has changed since medieval times.

1. According to Mead, how does a child develop a social self?
2. What are the four stages of cognitive development, according to Piaget?
3. How do Chodorow's and Gilligan's theories help us understand socialization influence on gender?

Exercises: Thinking Sociologically

1. Concisely review how an individual becomes a social person according to the three leading theorists discussed in this chapter: G. H. Mead, Jean Piaget, and Sigmund Freud. Which theory seems most appropriate and correct to you? Explain why.

2. Consuming alcoholic beverages is one of many things we do as a result of socialization. Suggest how the family, peers, schools, and mass media help establish the desire to consume alcoholic drinks. Of these influences, which force is the most persuasive? Explain.

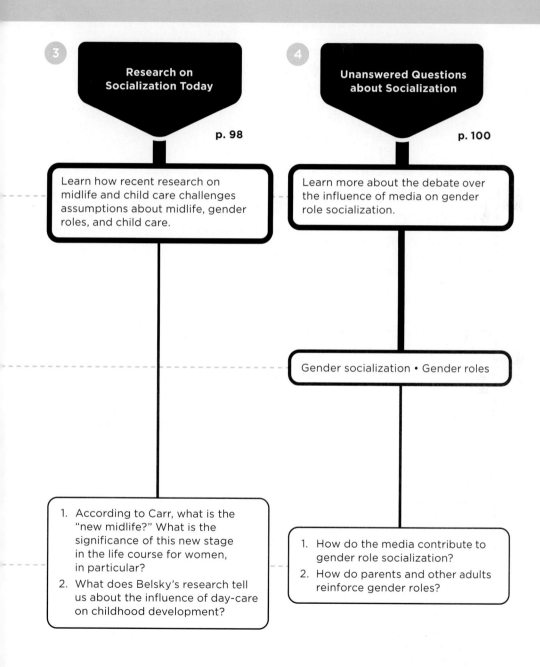

3

Research on Socialization Today

p. 98

Learn how recent research on midlife and child care challenges assumptions about midlife, gender roles, and child care.

1. According to Carr, what is the "new midlife?" What is the significance of this new stage in the life course for women, in particular?
2. What does Belsky's research tell us about the influence of day-care on childhood development?

4

Unanswered Questions about Socialization

p. 100

Learn more about the debate over the influence of media on gender role socialization.

Gender socialization • Gender roles

1. How do the media contribute to gender role socialization?
2. How do parents and other adults reinforce gender roles?

Social Interaction and Everyday Life in the Age of the Internet

5

Imagine you are in need of assistance in a crowded subway car. A person nearby who is listening to her iPod will probably:

- a Willingly provide you help
- b Begrudgingly provide you help
- c React angrily to your request for help
- d Ignore your request for help altogether

Turn the page for the correct answer.

D oes the use of an iPod affect public social conduct? This is the question asked by Christine Miranda, a junior at Princeton University who wanted to know whether the use of iPods had an impact on users' receptivity to strangers. Comparing the behavior of iPod users and nonusers, she embarked on a study in New York's subway system and began to document interactions with iPod users (and nonusers) on the 6 train on the East Side of Manhattan.

You might expect that iPod users on the subway would be unwilling or unhappy to speak with you (answers *b, c,* or *d*). Given that people listening to music via headphones appear to be less interested in conversation, you are probably wary about approaching someone pre-occupied with another task. People not wearing the trademark white earbuds likely appear more open to conversation, (literally) more able to hear what you have to say.

Miranda's study put this commonsense hypothesis to the test. Boarding a subway car, she took note of whether people possessed iPods; their positioning in relation to her; and their race, sex, and approximate age. In addition to observing users' and nonusers' responses to interactions, she took note of cues such as body language and facial gestures, and recorded exchanges between users and nonusers, as well as interactions involving auditory interruptions, invasions of physical space, and sexual offenses.

Sometimes Miranda simply observed naturally occurring interactions: for example, the responses of users and nonusers to a panhandler petitioning for donations. At other times, she acted as the "confederate," or intruder, interrupting an iPod user to ask about the train's last stop. She asked similar questions of nonusers as well, seeking to determine whether iPod users were less eager or less willing to respond.

What Miranda found was that iPod users seemed just as open to providing useful infor-mation as nonusers. Thus, answer *a* is actually correct. Among the iPod users, no one she asked seemed to mind removing headphones long enough to provide an answer; indeed, the users she asked seemed more courteous than the nonusers. Having offered the information requested, however, iPod users promptly went back to listening to their music. (Similarly,

LEARNING OBJECTIVES

① BASIC CONCEPTS

Understand the core concepts of the "impression management" perspective. See how we use impression management techniques in everyday life.

② THEORIES OF SOCIAL INTERACTION

Learn about sociological theories of interaction, ethnomethodology, and conversation analysis.

③ CONTEMPORARY RESEARCH ON SOCIAL INTERACTION

Understand how social interaction and broader features of society are closely related.

④ UNANSWERED QUESTIONS

See how face-to-face interactions remain important in the age of the Internet.

nonusers who were reading when she asked them went back to their newspapers or books, and those engaged in conversation went back to talking.)

Corroborating the popular hypothesis just detailed, most subway riders, Miranda discovered, perceived iPod users as less approachable. So while most users seemed happy to offer information that was requested of them, they were less likely than nonusers to be asked in the first place. "The personal stereo presents an opportunity to block off the outside environment and to reduce the likelihood of being approached, but when social conduct does occur, the user's behavior is not much different from the non-user's."

Miranda concluded that while the personal stereo presents the illusion of separation, making a user appear less approachable, "this wall can be easily broken when we simply disrupt a person's personal space with words or actions." It may initially take a bit more effort to get the attention of an iPod user, whose senses may be somewhat dulled compared with those of a more alert nonuser.

When a true attempt is made to get an iPod user to interact (for example, by asking a pointed question), the iPod user seems as open to interruption as the nonuser. After the interaction, however, it is generally understood that iPod users will go about their own business without acknowledging those around them.

THE ANSWER IS A.

BASIC CONCEPTS

When we published the first edition of this book, the study of face-to-face communication was a well-settled territory. There is reason to think, however, that social interaction over the past decade or so has undergone a major transformation because of the Internet. In this chapter, we will review the traditional findings of the field, but we will also ask how those findings must be modified in light of the rise of e-mail, Internet chatting, and social networking sites such as Facebook. We will first learn about the nonverbal cues (facial expressions and bodily gestures) all of us use when interacting with one another. We then move on to analyze everyday speech—how we use language to communicate to others the meanings we wish to convey. Finally, we focus on the ways in which our lives are structured by daily routines, paying particular attention to how we coordinate our actions across space and time.

The World as a Stage

Sociologist Erving Goffman and other writers on social interaction often use notions from theater in their analyses. The concept of the social role, for example, originated in a theatrical setting. Broadly speaking, **roles** are socially defined expectations that a person in a given **status** (or **social position**) follows. To be a teacher is to hold a specific

roles • The expected behaviors of people occupying particular social positions. The idea of social role originally comes from the theater, referring to the parts that actors play in a stage production. In every society, individuals play a number of social roles.

status • The social honor or prestige that a particular group is accorded by other members of a society. Status groups normally display distinct styles of life—patterns of behavior that the members of a group follow. Status privilege may be positive or negative. Pariah status groups are regarded with disdain or treated as outcasts by the majority of the population.

social position • The social identity an individual has in a given group or society. Social positions may be general in nature (those associated with gender roles) or more specific (occupational positions).

How are technologies such as webcams, e-mail, and mobile phones transforming the ways we interact with each other?

position; the teacher's role consists of acting in specified ways toward pupils. Goffman (1973) sees social life as played out by actors on a stage (or on many stages) because how we act depends on the roles we play at a given time. People are sensitive to how they are seen by others and use many forms of impression management to compel others to react to them in the ways they wish. Although we may sometimes do this in a calculated way, usually it is among the things we do without conscious attention. When someone attends a business meeting, he wears a suit and is on his best behavior; that evening, when going to a club, he may wear "sexy" garments. This is **impression management**, or more colloquially, "striking a pose."

A central insight of social interaction based on Goffman's work is that every human being possesses a self that is fragile and vulnerable to embarrassment or even humiliation at every turn. People are intensely attuned to what others think of them and how they are being viewed. Seeking approval and respect, they want to "save face" at every turn. In social interactions, human beings tend to collaborate with others to make sure that the interaction ends without embarrassment for anyone. As a stage, social life has many players, and they must collaborate to make each scene work.

Think of examples from your own life when people did not collaborate with you. If you go to a club and someone whom you don't want to meet approaches you, you will likely try to end the interaction in a way that is least embarrassing to the other person. If you were simply to tell the person, "Get lost!" rather than help her save face, that would be highly unusual. This is because there is a norm of collaboration by which human beings try to move through life without embarrassing or humiliating others. When this collaboration does not occur, the interaction stands out.

The pose that we adopt depends a great deal on our social role, but no particular role implies any specific presentation of self. A person's demeanor can be different depending on the social context. For instance, as a student, you have a certain status and are expected to act a certain way when you are around your professors. Some pupils will enact the self-presentation of the dutiful student, while others will assume an uncaring or apathetic pose. In many poor schools whose student body comprises largely minorities, students afraid of being accused of "acting white" will adopt an oppositional stance. Yet this appearance may not give an accurate sense of what is going on inside them. A student who takes on the demeanor of the "street" may be studying just as hard as one who appears to act in accordance with old-fashioned propriety.

Adopting Roles

For an example of collaboration in impression management that also borrows from the theater, let's look at one particular study in some

impression management • Preparing for the presentation of one's social role.

detail. James Henslin and Mae Biggs (1971, 1997) studied a specific, highly delicate type of encounter: a woman's visit to a gynecologist. At the time of the study, most pelvic examinations were carried out by male doctors, hence the experience was (and sometimes still is) fraught with potential ambiguities and embarrassment for both parties. Men and women in the West are socialized to think of the genitals as the most private part of the body, and seeing, and particularly touching, the genitals of another person is ordinarily associated with intimate sexual encounters. Some women feel so worried by the prospect of a pelvic examination that they refuse to visit the doctor, male or female, even when they suspect there is a strong medical reason to do so.

Henslin and Biggs analyzed material collected by Biggs, a trained nurse, from a large number of gynecological examinations. They interpreted what they found as occurring in several typical stages. Adopting a dramaturgical metaphor, they suggested that each phase could be treated as a distinct scene, in which the parts the actors play alter as the episode unfolds. In the prologue, the woman enters the waiting room preparing to assume the role of patient and temporarily discarding her outside identity. Called into the consulting room, she adopts the "patient" role, and the first scene opens. The doctor assumes a businesslike, professional manner and treats the patient as a proper and competent person, maintaining eye contact and listening politely to what she has to say. If he decides an examination is called for, he tells her so and leaves the room; scene one is over.

As he leaves, the nurse comes in. She is an important stagehand in the main scene shortly to begin. She soothes any worries the patient might have, acting as both a confidante—knowing some of the "things women have to put up with"—and a collaborator in what is to follow. Crucial to the next scene, the nurse helps alter the patient from a person to a "nonperson" for the vital scene—which features a body, part of which is to be scrutinized, rather than a complete human being. In Henslin and Biggs's study, the nurse not only supervises the patient's undressing but also takes over aspects that normally the patient would control. Thus she takes the patient's clothes and folds them. Most women wish their underwear to be out of sight when the doctor returns, and the nurse makes sure that this is so. She guides the patient to the examining table and covers most of the patient's body with a sheet before the physician returns.

The central scene now opens, with the nurse as well as the doctor taking part. The presence of the nurse helps ensure that the interaction between the doctor and the patient is free of sexual overtones and provides a legal witness should the physician be charged with unprofessional conduct. The examination proceeds as though the personality of the patient were absent; the sheet across her separates the genital area from the rest of her body, and her position does not allow her to watch the examination itself. Save for any specific medical queries, the doctor ignores her, sitting on a low stool, out of her line of vision. The patient collaborates in becoming a temporary nonperson, not initiating conversation and keeping any movements to a minimum.

In the interval between this and the final scene, the nurse again plays the role of stagehand, helping the patient become a full person once more. After the doctor has left the room, the two may again engage in conversation, the patient expressing relief that the examination is over. Having dressed and groomed herself, the patient is ready to face the concluding scene. The doctor reenters and, in discussing the results of the examination, again treats the patient as a complete person. Resuming his polite, professional manner, he conveys that his reactions to her are in no way altered by the intimate contact with her body. The epilogue is played out when the patient leaves the physician's office, resuming her identity in the outside world. The patient and the doctor have thus collaborated in such a way as to manage the interaction and the impression each participant forms of the other.

Audience Segregation

Although people cooperate to help one another "save face," they also endeavor individually to preserve their own dignity, autonomy, and respect. One of the ways in which people do this is by arranging for "audience segregation" in their lives. In each of their roles they act somewhat differently, and they try to keep what they do in each role distinct from what they do in their other roles. This means that they can have multiple selves. Frequently these selves are consistent with each other, but sometimes they are not. People find it very stressful when boundaries break down or when they cannot reconcile their role in one area of their life with their role in another. For example, some people have two friends who do not like each other. Rather than choose between them, they spend time with both friends but never mention to either friend that they are close with the other. Or some people live very different lives at home and at work. For example, due to discrimination against gays and lesbians, some people will appear "straight" at work and gay at home. Like all people who engage in "audience segregation," they show a different face to different people, "striking a (different) pose" in each context (Brekhus, 2003).

Goffman saw social life as a precarious balancing act, but he also studied those instances in which audience segregation could not be maintained. He conducted an ethnographic study of St. Elizabeth's, a mental hospital in Washington, D.C., described in his book *Asylums*. St. Elizabeth's was a place where the barriers between different spheres of life (sleep, play, and work) did not exist. In such an environment, which Goffman called a "total institution," human beings need to adapt to the fact that their private spheres are limited. Other examples of "total institutions," in which all aspects of life are conducted in the same place, include prisons, monasteries, and army boot camps.

Civil Inattention

When passersby, either strangers or intimates, quickly glance at each other and then look away again, they demonstrate what Goffman (1967, 1971) calls the **civil inattention** we require of each other in many situations. Civil inattention is not the same as merely ignoring another person. Each individual indicates recognition of the other person's presence but avoids any gesture that might be taken as too intrusive. Can you think of examples of civil inattention in your own life? Perhaps when you are walking down the hall of a dormitory, trying to decide where to sit in the cafeteria, or simply walking across campus? Civil inattention to others is something we engage in more or less unconsciously, but it is of fundamental importance to the existence of social life, which must proceed efficiently and sometimes among total strangers, without fear. When civil inattention occurs among passing strangers, an individual implies to another person that she has no reason to suspect his intentions, be hostile to him, or in any other way specifically avoid him.

The best way to see the importance of this is by thinking of examples when it doesn't apply. When a person stares fixedly at another, allowing her face to openly express a particular emotion, it is frequently with a lover, family member, or close friend. Strangers or chance acquaintances, whether encountered on the street, at work, or at a party, virtually never hold the gaze of another in this way. To do so may be taken as an indication of hostile intent. It is only where two groups are strongly antagonistic to one another that strangers might indulge in

civil inattention • The process whereby individuals in the same physical setting demonstrate to one another that they are aware of each other's presence.

such a practice—for example, when whites in the United States have been known to give a "hate stare" to blacks walking past. Even friends in close conversation need to be careful about how they look at one another. Each individual demonstrates attention and involvement in the conversation by regularly looking at the eyes of the other but not staring into them. To look too intently might be taken as a sign of mistrust about, or at least failure to understand, what the other is saying. Yet if each party does not engage the eyes of the other at all, each is likely to be thought evasive, shifty, or otherwise odd.

Social interaction requires numerous forms of **nonverbal communication**—the exchange of information and meaning through facial expressions, gestures, and body movements. Nonverbal communication is sometimes referred to as "body language," but this is misleading, because we characteristically use such nonverbal cues to eliminate or expand on what we say with words.

Face, Gestures, and Emotion

One major aspect of communication is the facial expression of emotion. Paul Ekman and his colleagues have developed what they call the Facial Action Coding System (FACS) for describing movements of the facial muscles that give rise to particular expressions (Ekman and Friesen, 1978). By this means, they have tried to inject some precision into an area notoriously open to inconsistent or contradictory interpretations—for there is little agreement about how emotions are to be identified and classified. Charles Darwin, one of the originators of evolutionary theory, claimed that basic modes of emotional expression are the same in all human beings. Although some have disputed the claim, Ekman's research among people from widely different cultural backgrounds seems to confirm Darwin's view. Ekman and W. V. Friesen carried out a study of an isolated community in New Guinea whose members had previously had virtually no contact with outsiders. When they were shown pictures of facial expressions conveying six emotions (happiness, sadness, anger, disgust, fear, and surprise), the New Guineans were able to identify these emotions.

According to Ekman, the results of his own and similar studies of different peoples support the view that the facial expression of emotion and its interpretation are innate in human beings. He acknowledges that his evidence does not conclusively demonstrate this, and it may be that widely shared cultural learning experiences are involved; however, his conclusions are supported by other types of research. I. Eibl-Eibesfeldt (1972) studied six children born deaf and blind to see how far their facial expressions were the same as those of sighted and hearing individuals in particular emotional situations. He found that the children smiled when engaged in obviously pleasurable activities, raised their eyebrows in surprise when sniffing at an object with an unaccustomed smell, and frowned when repeatedly offered a disliked object. Because the children could not have seen other people behaving in these ways, it seems that these responses must be innately determined.

Using the FACS, Ekman and Friesen identified a number of the discrete facial muscle actions in newborn infants that are also found in adult expressions of emotion. Infants seem, for example, to produce facial expressions similar to the adult expression of disgust (pursing the lips and frowning) in response to sour tastes. But although the facial expression of emotion seems to be partly innate, individual and cultural factors influence what exact form facial movements take and the contexts in which

nonverbal communication • Communication between individuals based on facial expression or bodily gesture rather than on language.

Paul Ekman's photographs of facial expressions from a tribesman in an isolated community in New Guinea helped test the idea that basic modes of emotional expression are the same among all people. Here the instructions were to show how your face would look if (a) your friend had come and you were happy, (b) your child had died, (c) you were angry and about to fight, and (d) you saw a dead pig that had been lying there a long time.

they are deemed appropriate. How people smile—for example, the precise movement of the lips and other facial muscles—and how fleeting the smile is both vary among cultures.

There are no gestures or bodily postures that have been shown to characterize all, or even most, cultures. In some societies, for instance, people nod when they mean no, the opposite of Anglo-American practice. Gestures that Americans tend to use a great deal, such as pointing, seem not to exist among certain peoples (Bull, 1983). Similarly, a straightened forefinger placed in the center of the cheek and rotated is used in parts of Italy as a gesture of praise but appears to be unknown elsewhere.

Like facial expressions, gestures and bodily posture are continually used to fill out utterances and to convey meanings when nothing is actually said. All three can be used to joke, show irony, or express skepticism. The nonverbal impressions that we convey often inadvertently indicate that what we say is not quite what we actually mean. Blushing is perhaps the most obvious example, but innumerable other subtle indicators can be picked up by other people. Genuine facial expressions tend to evaporate after four or five seconds. A smile that lasts longer could indicate deceit. An expression of surprise that lasts too long may indicate deliberate sarcasm—to show that the individual is not in fact surprised after all.

On the Internet, it is very difficult to capture dimensions of emotion that are present only with facial expression. At first, the need that Internet users felt to approximate facial gestures resulted in at least two common faces:

:) or :-)

As time passed, a need for greater subtlety resulted in other widely understood variations, such as this winking smiley face:

;-)

which means that a comment is meant to be taken with a grain of salt.

E-mail may once have been devoid of facial expression, but today the average e-mail user expects to insert different emotions into a message. The strong need that human beings feel to communicate with their faces has also led to other innovations, such as the Web camera (webcam), which has become a relatively inexpensive and widely used technology. But in general, people who communicate over the Internet or even the telephone lack the benefit of seeing the faces of their conversational partners as they speak.

How might this matter? On the telephone, I might talk longer for a stretch of time than I would in face-to-face conversation with you. Unable to see your face, I can't as readily adjust what I say in response to a sense that you already "get it" or think I'm going down an unproductive (or silly) path. Yet the telephone maintains at least some immediacy of feedback that e-mail lacks. This is why, in e-mail disputes, people who are unable to make mutual adjustments in response to verbal or facial cues will end up saying much more—communicated in the form of long messages—than they would say in conversation.

Which is better? Would you prefer to make your point in e-mail or in person? Using sociological insights such as these might make you prefer electronic communication at some times and face-to-face communication at others. For example, if you are dealing with a powerful person and want to get your thoughts across, you may want to avoid a situation where the person can signal with facial gestures that your idea is silly and thus intimidate you, inhibiting you from making all your points. The power to signal with facial gestures is one of the things people do to control the flow of a conversation. On the other hand, face-to-face communication gives you an opportunity to try out an idea on someone more powerful than you without going too far down the road if the person is actually unreceptive.

Focused and Unfocused Interaction

In many social situations, we engage in what Goffman calls **unfocused interaction** with others. Unfocused interaction takes place whenever individuals exhibit awareness of one another's presence. This is usually the case anywhere large numbers of people are assembled, as on a busy street, in a theater crowd, or at a party. When people are in the presence of others, even if they do not directly talk to them, they continually communicate nonverbally through their posture and facial and physical gestures.

Focused interaction occurs when individuals directly attend to what others say or do. Goffman calls an instance of focused interaction an **encounter**. Much of our day-to-day life consists of encounters with other people (family, friends, colleagues), frequently occurring against the background of unfocused interaction with others. Small talk, seminar discussions, games, and routine face-to-face contact (with ticket clerks, waiters, shop assistants, and so forth) are all examples of encounters.

Encounters always need "openings," which indicate that civil inattention is being discarded. When strangers meet and begin to talk at a party, the moment of ceasing civil inattention is always risky because misunderstandings can easily occur about the nature of the encounter being established (Goffman, 1971). Hence making eye contact may first be ambiguous and tentative. A person can then act as though she made no direct move if the overture is not accepted. In focused interaction, each person communicates as much by facial expression and gesture as by the words actually exchanged.

Goffman distinguishes between the expressions an individual "gives" and those he "gives

unfocused interaction • Interaction occurring among people present in a particular setting but not engaged in direct face-to-face communication.

focused interaction • Interaction between individuals engaged in a common activity or in direct conversation with one another.

encounter • A meeting between two or more people in a situation of face-to-face interaction. Our daily lives can be seen as a series of different encounters strung out across the course of the day. In modern societies, many of those encounters are with strangers rather than people we know.

off." The first are the words and facial expressions he uses to produce certain impressions on others. The second are the cues that others may spot to check his sincerity or truthfulness. For instance, a restaurant owner listens with a polite smile to the statements of customers about how much they are enjoying their meal. At the same time, he is noting how pleased they seemed to be while eating the food, whether a lot is left over, and the tone of voice they use to express their satisfaction.

Think about how Goffman's concepts of focused and unfocused interaction, developed mainly to explain face-to-face social encounters, apply to the current age. Can you think of a way in which unfocused interaction occurs in Gmail chatting, Facebook, or websites that have a chat forum? In some of these online communities, anyone can have an awareness of who else is online without being in direct contact with them. On some sites, people are constantly broadcasting elements of what they are doing or their current situation through status messages. These status messages make it possible for people in unfocused interaction to have even more control over how they are perceived than people who are merely in one another's presence. Instead of unconsciously revealing their facial expression or posture as they would in face-to-face encounters, people in such situations can consciously choose what message they wish to broadcast.

Response Cries

Certain kinds of utterances are not talk but consist of muttered exclamations, or what Goffman (1981) has called **response cries**. Consider Lucy, who exclaims, "Oops!" after knocking over a glass of water. "Oops!" seems to be merely an uninteresting reflex response to a mishap, rather like blinking your eye when a person moves a hand sharply toward your face. It is not a reflex, however, as shown by the fact that people do not usually make the exclamation when alone. "Oops!" is normally directed toward others present. The exclamation demonstrates to witnesses that the lapse is only minor and momentary, not something that should cast doubt on Lucy's command of her actions.

"Oops!" is used only in situations of minor failure, rather than in major accidents or calamities—which also demonstrates that the exclamation is part of our controlled management of the details of social life. Moreover, the word may be used by someone observing Lucy rather than by Lucy herself, or it may be used to sound a warning to another. *Oops* is normally a short sound, but the *oo* may be prolonged in some situations. Thus someone might extend the sound to cover a critical moment in performing a task. For instance, a parent may utter an extended "Oops!" or "Oopsadaisy!" when playfully tossing a child in the air. The sound covers the brief phase when the child may feel a loss of control, reassuring him and probably at the same time developing his understanding of response cries.

This may all sound very contrived and exaggerated. Why bother to analyze such an inconsequential utterance in such detail? Surely we don't pay as much attention to what we say as this example suggests? Of course we don't—on a conscious level. The crucial point, however, is that we take for granted the immensely complicated, continuous control of our appearance and actions. In situations of interaction, we are never expected simply to be present. Others expect, as we expect of them, that we will display what Goffman calls controlled alertness. A fundamental part of being human is continually demonstrating to others our competence in the routines of daily life.

response cries • Seemingly involuntary exclamations individuals make when, for example, they are taken by surprise, drop something inadvertently, or want to express pleasure.

Interaction in Time and Space

Understanding how activities are distributed in time and space is fundamental to analyzing encounters and understanding social life in general. All interaction is situated—it occurs in a particular place and has a specific duration in time. Our actions over the course of a day tend to be "zoned" in time as well as in space. Thus, for example, most people spend a zone—say, from 9:00 A.M. to 5:00 P.M.—of their daily time working. Their weekly time is also zoned: they are likely to work on weekdays and spend weekends at home, altering the pattern of their activities on the weekend days. As they move through the temporal zones of the day, they often are also moving across space; to get to work, they may take a bus from one area of a city to another or perhaps commute in from the suburbs. When we analyze the contexts of social interaction, therefore, it is often useful to look at people's movements across **time-space**.

The concept of **regionalization** will help us understand how social life is zoned in time-space. Take the example of a private home. A modern house is regionalized into rooms, hallways, and floors (if there is more than one story). These spaces are not just physically separate areas but are zoned in time as well. The living room and kitchen are most used in the daylight hours; the bedrooms, at night. The interaction that occurs in these regions is bound by both spatial and temporal divisions. Some areas of the house form back regions, with "performances" taking place in the others. At times, the whole house can become a back region. Once again, this idea is beautifully captured by Goffman (1973):

> On a Sunday morning, a whole household can use the wall around its domestic establishment to conceal a relaxing slovenliness in dress and civil endeavor, extending to all rooms the informality that is usually restricted to kitchen and bedrooms. So, too, in American middle-class neighborhoods, on afternoons the line between children's playground and home may be defined as backstage by mothers, who pass along it wearing jeans, loafers, and a minimum of make-up. . . .

Clock Time

In modern societies, the zoning of our activities is strongly influenced by **clock time**. Without clocks and the precise timing of activities, and thereby their coordination across space, industrialized societies could not exist (Mumford, 1973). Today measuring of time by clocks is standardized across the globe, making possible the complex international transport systems and communications we now depend on. World standard time was first introduced in 1884 at a conference of nations held in Washington, D.C. The globe was then partitioned into 24 time zones, one hour apart, and an exact beginning of the universal day was fixed.

Fourteenth-century monasteries were the first organizations to try to schedule the activities of their inmates precisely across the day and week. Today, there is virtually no group or organization that does not do so—the greater the number of people and resources involved, the more precise the scheduling must be. Eviatar Zerubavel (1979, 1982) demonstrated this in his study of the temporal structure of a large modern hospital. A hospital must operate on a 24-hour

time-space • When and where events occur.

regionalization • The division of social life into different regional settings or zones.

clock time • Time as measured by the clock, in terms of hours, minutes, and seconds. Before the invention of clocks, time reckoning was based on events in the natural world, such as the rising and setting of the sun.

basis, and coordinating the staff and resources is a highly complex matter. For instance, the nurses work for one time period in ward A, another time period in ward B, and so on, and are called on to alternate between day- and night-shift work. Nurses, doctors, and other staff, plus the resources they need, must be integrated both in time and in space.

Social Life and the Ordering of Space and Time

The Internet is another example of how closely forms of social life are bound up with our control of space and time. The Internet makes it possible for us to interact with people we never see or meet, in any corner of the world. Such technological change rearranges space—we can interact with anyone without moving from our chair. It also alters our experience of time, because communication on the electronic highway is almost immediate. Until about 50 years ago, most communication across space required a duration of time. If you sent a letter to someone abroad, there was a time gap while the letter was carried by ship, train, truck, or plane, to the person to whom it was written.

People still write letters by hand today, of course, but instantaneous communication has become basic to our social world. Our lives would be almost unimaginable without it. We are so used to being able to switch on the TV and watch the news or make a phone call or send an e-mail message to a friend in another state that it is hard for us to imagine what life would be like otherwise.

CONCEPT CHECKS ✓

1. What is impression management?
2. Why do we segregate our audiences in daily life?
3. What is nonverbal communication?
4. Describe several ways that individuals communicate their emotions to one another.
5. Compare and contrast focused and unfocused interaction.
6. How does time structure human life?

② THEORIES OF SOCIAL INTERACTION

Erving Goffman

Many of the concepts we have already reviewed were developed by Erving Goffman, the sociologist who did the most to create a new field of study called *microsociology* or **social interaction**. Goffman believed that sociologists needed to concern themselves with seemingly trivial aspects of social behavior. Passing someone on the street or exchanging a few words with a friend seem minor and uninteresting activities, things we do countless times a day without giving them any thought. Goffman argued that the study of such apparently insignificant forms of social interaction is of major importance in sociology and, far from being uninteresting, is one of the most absorbing of all areas of sociological investigation. There are three reasons for this.

First, our day-to-day routines, with their almost constant interactions with others, give structure and form to what we do; we can learn a great deal about ourselves as social beings, and about social life itself, from studying them. Our lives are organized around the repetition of similar patterns of behavior from day to day, week to week, month to month, and year to

social interaction • The process by which we act and react to those around us.

year. Think of what you did yesterday, for example, and the day before that. If they were both weekdays, in all probability you got up at about the same time each day (an important routine in itself). You may have gone off to class fairly early in the morning, making a journey from home to school or college that you make virtually every weekday. You perhaps met some friends for lunch, returning to classes or private study in the afternoon. Later, you retraced your steps back home, possibly going out later in the evening with other friends.

Of course, the routines we follow from day to day are not identical, and our patterns of activity on weekends usually contrast with those on weekdays. If we make a major change in our life, such as leaving college to take a job, alterations in our daily routines are usually necessary, but then we establish a new and fairly regular set of habits again.

Second, the study of everyday life reveals to us how humans can act creatively to shape reality. Although social behavior is guided to some extent by forces such as roles, norms, and shared expectations, individuals perceive reality differently according to their backgrounds, interests, and motivations. Because individuals are capable of creative action, they continuously shape reality through the decisions and actions they take. In other words, reality is not fixed or static—it is created through human interactions.

Third, studying social interaction in everyday life sheds light on larger social systems and institutions. All large-scale social systems, in fact, depend on the patterns of social interaction we engage in daily. This is easy to demonstrate. Consider the case of two strangers passing on the street. Such an event may seem to have little direct relevance to large-scale, more permanent forms of social organization. But when we take into account many such interactions, they are no longer irrelevant. In modern societies, most people live in towns and cities and constantly interact with others whom they do not know personally. Civil inattention, a concept discussed earlier, is one of the mechanisms that give public life, with its bustling crowds and fleeting, impersonal contacts, the character it has.

personal space • The physical space individuals maintain between themselves and others.

Edward T. Hall—Personal Space

There are cultural differences in the definition of **personal space**. In Western culture, people usually maintain a distance of at least three feet when engaged in focused interaction with others; when standing side by side, they may stand closer together. In the Middle East, people often stand closer to each other than is thought acceptable in the West. Westerners visiting that part of the world are likely to find themselves disconcerted by this unexpected physical proximity.

Edward T. Hall (1969, 1973), who worked extensively on nonverbal communication, distinguishes four zones of

Cultural norms frequently determine the acceptable boundaries of personal space. In the Middle East, for example, people frequently stand closer to each other than is common in the West.

personal space. Intimate distance, of up to one and a half feet, is reserved for very few social contacts. Only those involved in relationships in which regular bodily touching is permitted, such as lovers or parents and children, operate within this zone of private space. Personal distance, from one and a half to four feet, is the normal spacing for encounters with friends and close acquaintances. Some intimacy of contact is permitted, but this tends to be strictly limited. Social distance, from four to twelve feet, is the zone usually maintained in formal settings such as interviews. The fourth zone is that of public distance, beyond twelve feet, preserved by those who are performing to an audience.

In ordinary interaction, the most fraught zones are those of intimate and personal distance. If these zones are invaded, people try to recapture their space. We may stare at the intruder as if to say, "Move away!" or elbow her aside. When people are forced into proximity closer than they deem desirable, they might create a kind of physical boundary: A reader at a crowded library desk might physically demarcate a private space by stacking books around its edges (Hall, 1969, 1973).

Harold Garfinkel: Ethnomethodology

Ethnomethodology is the study of the "ethnomethods"—folk or lay methods—that people use to make sense of what others do and particularly of what they say. We all apply these methods, normally without giving any conscious attention to them. This field was created by Harold Garfinkel, who, after Goffman, was the most important figure in the study of micro interaction.

Garfinkel argued that in order to understand the way people use context to make sense of the world, sociologists need to study the "background expectancies" with which we organize ordinary conversations. He highlighted these in some experiments he undertook with student volunteers (1963). The students were asked to engage a friend or relative in conversation and to insist that casual remarks or general comments be actively pursued to make their meaning precise. If someone said, "Have a nice day," the student was to respond, "Nice in what sense, exactly?" "Which part of the day do you mean?" and so forth. One of the exchanges that resulted ran as follows (S is the friend; E, the student volunteer) (Garfinkel, 1963):

> S: *How are you?*
> E: *How am I in regard to what? My health, my finances, my school work, my peace of mind, my . . . ?*
> S: *(red in the face and suddenly out of control): Look! I was just trying to be polite. Frankly, I don't give a damn how you are.*

Why do people get so upset when apparently minor conventions of talk are not followed? The answer is that the stability and meaningfulness of our daily social lives depend on the sharing of unstated cultural assumptions about what is said and why. If we weren't able to take these for granted, meaningful communication would be impossible. Any question or contribution to a conversation would have to be followed by a massive "search procedure" of the sort Garfinkel's subjects were told to initiate, and interaction would simply break down. What seem at first sight to be unimportant conventions of talk, therefore, turn out to be fundamental to the very fabric of social life, which is why their breach is so serious.

ethnomethodology • The study of how people make sense of what others say and do in the course of day-to-day social interaction. Ethnomethodology is concerned with the "ethnomethods" by which people sustain meaningful interchanges with one another.

Note that in everyday life, people on occasion deliberately feign ignorance of unstated knowledge. This may be done to rebuff others, poke fun at them, cause embarrassment, or call attention to a double meaning in what was said. Consider, for example, this classic exchange between parent and teenager:

P: *Where are you going?*
T: *Out.*
P: *What are you going to do?*
T: *Nothing.*

The responses of the teenager are effectively the opposite of those of the volunteers in Garfinkel's experiments. Rather than pursuing inquiries where this is not normally done, the teenager declines to provide appropriate answers at all—essentially saying, "Mind your own business!"

The first question might elicit a different response from another person in another context:

A: *Where are you going?*
B: *I'm going quietly round the bend.*

B deliberately misreads A's question to convey worry or frustration ironically. Comedy and joking thrive on such deliberate misunderstandings of the unstated assumptions involved in talk. There is nothing threatening about this, so long as the parties concerned recognize that the intent is to provoke laughter.

Conversation Analysis: Social Rules and Talk

SOCIAL CONTEXT AND SHARED UNDERSTANDINGS CONVERSATION

We can make sense of what is said in conversation only if we know the social context, which does not appear in the words themselves. Take the following conversation (Heritage, 1985):

A: *I have a fourteen-year-old son.*
B: *Well, that's all right.*
A: *I also have a dog.*
B: *Oh, I'm sorry.*

What do you think is happening here? What is the relationship between the speakers? What if you were told that this is a conversation between a prospective tenant and a landlord? The conversation then becomes sensible: Some landlords accept children but don't permit their tenants to keep pets. Yet if we don't know the social context, the responses of individual B seem to bear no relation to the statements of A. Part of the sense is in the words, and part is in the way in which the meaning emerges from the social context.

SHARED UNDERSTANDINGS

The most inconsequential forms of daily talk presume complicated, shared knowledge brought into play by those speaking. In fact, our small talk is so complex that it has so far proved impossible to program even the most sophisticated computers to converse with human beings. The words used in ordinary talk do not always have precise meanings, and we "fix" what we want to say through the unstated assumptions that back it up. If Maria asks Tom, "What did you do yesterday?" the words in the question themselves suggest no obvious answer. A day is a long time, and it would be logical for Tom to answer, "Well, at seven sixteen,

I woke up. At seven eighteen, I got out of bed, went to the bathroom, and started to brush my teeth. At seven nineteen, I turned on the shower . . ." We understand the type of response the question calls for by knowing Maria, what sort of activities she and Tom consider relevant, and what Tom usually does on a particular day of the week, among other things.

Although we routinely use nonverbal cues in our own behavior and in making sense of the behavior of others, much of our interaction is done through talk—casual verbal exchange—carried on in informal conversations with others. Sociologists have always accepted that language is fundamental to social life. However, an approach has been developed that is specifically concerned with how people use language in the ordinary contexts of everyday life.

Conversations are one of the main ways in which our daily lives are maintained in a stable and coherent manner. We feel most comfortable when the tacit conventions of small talk are adhered to; when they are breached, we can feel threatened, confused, and insecure. In most everyday talk, conversants are carefully attuned to the cues they get from others—such as changes in intonation, slight pauses, or gestures—to facilitate smooth conversation. By being mutually aware, conversants "cooperate" in opening and closing interactions and in taking turns to speak. Interactions in which one party is conversationally "uncooperative," however, can give rise to tensions.

③ CONTEMPORARY RESEARCH ON SOCIAL INTERACTION

Interactional Vandalism

Garfinkel's students created tense situations by intentionally undermining conversational rules as part of a sociological experiment. But what about situations in the real world in which people make trouble through their conversational practices? One study investigated verbal interchanges between pedestrians and street people in New York City to understand why such interactions are often seen as problematic by passersby. The researchers used a technique called conversation analysis to compare a selection of street interchanges with samples of everyday talk. **Conversation analysis** is a methodology that examines all facets of a conversation for meaning—from the smallest filler words (such as *um* and *ah*) to the precise timing of interchanges (including pauses, interruptions, and overlap).

conversation analysis • The empirical study of conversations, employing techniques drawn from ethnomethodology. Conversation analysis examines details of naturally occurring conversations to reveal the organizational principles of talk and its role in the production and reproduction of social order.

The study looked at interactions between black men—many of whom were homeless, alcoholic, or drug addicted—and women who passed by them on the street. The men often tried to initiate conversations with passing women by calling out to them, paying them compliments, or asking them questions. But something "went wrong" in these conversations, because the women rarely responded as they would have in a normal interaction. Even though the men's comments were rarely hostile in tone, the women tended to quicken their step and stare fixedly ahead. The following shows attempts by Mudrick, a black man in his late fifties, to engage women in conversation (Duneier and Molotch, 1999):

Mudrick begins this interaction when a white woman who looks about 25 approaches at a steady pace:

1. *Mudrick:*   *I love you, baby.*

She crosses her arms and quickens her walk, ignoring the comment.

2. *Mudrick:*   *Marry me.*

Next, it is two white women, also probably in their mid-twenties:

3. *Mudrick:*   *Hi, girls, you all look very nice today. You have some money? Buy some books.*

They ignore him. Next it is a young black woman.

4. *Mudrick:*   *Hey, pretty. Hey, pretty.*

She keeps walking without acknowledging him.

5. *Mudrick:*   *'Scuse me. 'Scuse me. I know you hear me.*

Then he addresses a white woman in her thirties.

6. *Mudrick:*   *I'm watching you. You look nice, you know.*

She ignores him.

Negotiating smooth "openings" and "closings" to conversations is a fundamental requirement for urban civility. These crucial aspects of conversation were highly problematic between the men and women in this study. Where the women resisted the men's attempts at opening conversations, the men ignored the women's resistance and persisted. Similarly, if the men succeeded in opening a conversation, they often refused to respond to cues from the women to close the conversation once it had gotten under way (Duneier and Molotch, 1999):

1. *Mudrick:*   *Hey, pretty.*
2. *Woman:*   *Hi, how you doin'.*
3. *Mudrick:*   *You alright?*
4. *Mudrick:*   *You look very nice, you know. I like how you have your hair pinned.*

Mudrick, pictured below, approaches a woman on the sidewalk in New York City.

5.	*Mudrick:*	*You married?*
6.	*Woman:*	*Yeah.*
7.	*Mudrick:*	*Huh?*
8.	*Woman:*	*Yeah.*
9.	*Mudrick:*	*Where the rings at?*
10.	*Woman:*	*I have it home.*
11.	*Mudrick:*	*Y'have it home?*
12.	*Woman:*	*Yeah.*
13.	*Mudrick:*	*Can I get your name?*
14.	*Mudrick:*	*My name is Mudrick, what's yours?*

She does not answer and walks on.

In this instance, Mudrick made 9 out of the 14 utterances in the interaction to initiate the conversation and to elicit further responses from the woman. From the transcript alone, it is quite evident that the woman is not interested in talking, but when conversation analysis is applied to the tape recording, her reluctance becomes even clearer. Even when she does respond, the woman delays all her responses, while Mudrick replies immediately, his comments sometimes overlapping hers. Timing in conversations is a very precise indicator; delaying a response by even a fraction of a second is adequate in most everyday interactions to signal the desire to change the course of a conversation. By betraying these tacit rules of sociability, Mudrick was practicing conversation in a way that was "technically" rude. The woman, in return, was also technically rude in ignoring Mudrick's repeated attempts to engage her in talk. It is the technically rude nature of these street interchanges that make them problematic for passersby to handle. When standard cues for opening and closing conversations are not adhered to, individuals feel a sense of profound and inexplicable insecurity.

The term **interactional vandalism** describes cases like these in which a subordinate person breaks the tacit rules of everyday interaction that are of value to the more powerful person. The men on the street often do conform to everyday forms of speech in their interactions with one another, local shopkeepers, the police, relatives, and acquaintances. But when they choose to, they subvert the tacit conventions for everyday talk in a way that leaves passersby disoriented. Even more than physical assaults or vulgar verbal abuse, interactional vandalism leaves victims unable to articulate what has happened.

This study of interactional vandalism provides another example of the two-way links between micro-level interactions and forces that operate on the macro level. To the men on the street, the women who ignore their attempts at conversation appear distant, cold, and bereft of sympathy—legitimate "targets" for such interactions. The women, meanwhile, may often take the men's behavior as proof that they are indeed dangerous and best avoided. Interactional vandalism is closely tied up with overarching class, gender, and racial structures. The fear and anxiety generated in such mundane interactions help constitute the outside statuses and forces that, in turn, influence the interactions themselves. Interactional vandalism is part of a self-reinforcing system of mutual suspicion and incivility.

How would issues of this kind play themselves out on the Internet? Timing is a far less precise indicator in electronic communications. In the exchange just given, the woman's long pauses signaled that she wanted to end the exchange with Mudrick. In online chat rooms, pauses are very hard to interpret. They may be commonplace as one partner is temporarily called away from the computer or even merely to another computer window. On the other hand,

interactional vandalism • The deliberate subversion of the tacit rules of conversation.

the very possibility that someone has been called away can make intentional pauses seem like a gentler way to prevent conversation than can nonresponsiveness in physical space.

Can we think of ways in which less powerful people who engage in electronic communications undermine the taken-for-granted rules of interaction that are of value to the more powerful? The very existence of the Internet creates spaces in which less powerful people can make their superiors accountable in ways they never were before. Think of all the blogs in which workers talk anonymously about their bosses, or the common situations in which workers forward rude messages from their boss to other employees.

Women and Men in Public

Take, for example, a situation that may seem micro on its face: A woman walking down the street is verbally harassed by a group of men. In a study published as *Passing By: Gender and Public Harassment,* Carol Brooks Gardner (1995) found that in various settings, most famously the edges of construction sites, these types of unwanted interaction occur and are something women frequently experience as abusive.

Although the harassment of a single woman could be analyzed in microsociological terms by looking at a single interaction, it is not fruitful to view it that simply. Such harassment is typical of street talk involving men and women who are strangers (Gardner, 1995). These kinds of interactions cannot be understood without also looking at the larger background of gender hierarchy in the United States. In this way we can see how microanalysis and macroanalysis are connected. For example, Gardner linked the harassment of women by men to the larger system of gender inequality, represented by male privilege in public spaces, women's physical vulnerability, and the omnipresent threat of rape.

Without making this link between microsociology and macrosociology, we can have only a limited understanding of these interactions. It might seem as though they were isolated instances or that they could be eliminated by teaching people good manners. Understanding the link between micro and macro helps us see that to attack the problem at its root cause, one would need to focus on eliminating the forms of gender inequality that give rise to such interactions.

Blacks and Whites in Public

Have you ever crossed to the other side of the street when you felt threatened by someone behind you or someone coming toward you? One sociologist who has tried to understand simple interactions of this kind is Elijah Anderson. In his book *Streetwise: Race, Class, and Change in an Urban Community* (1990), Anderson describes social interaction on the streets of two adjacent urban neighborhoods, noting that studying everyday life sheds light on how social order is created by the individual building blocks of infinite micro-level interactions. He is particularly interested in understanding interactions when at least one party was viewed as threatening. Anderson shows that the ways many blacks and whites interact on the streets of a northern city in the United States have a great deal to do with the structure of racial stereotypes, which itself is linked to the economic structure of society. In this way, he reveals the link between micro interactions and the larger macro structures of society.

Anderson begins by recalling Erving Goffman's description of how social roles and statuses come into existence in particular contexts or locations: "When an individual enters the presence of others, they commonly seek to acquire information about him or bring into play information already possessed. . . . Information about the individual helps to define the situation, enabling others to know in advance what he will expect of them and they may expect of him" (Anderson, 1990).

Following Goffman's lead, Anderson (1990) asked what types of behavioral cues and signs make up the vocabulary of public interaction. He concluded that skin color, gender, age, companions, clothing, jewelry, and the objects people carry help identify them, allowing assumptions to be formed and communication to occur. Movements (quick or slow, false or sincere, comprehensible or incomprehensible) further refine this public communication. Factors such as time of day or an activity that "explains" a person's presence can also affect how and how quickly the image of "stranger" is neutralized. If a stranger cannot pass inspection and be assessed as "safe," the image of predator may arise, and fellow pedestrians may try to maintain a distance consistent with that image.

According to Anderson, the people most likely to pass inspection are those who do not fall into commonly accepted stereotypes of dangerous persons: "children readily pass inspection, while women and white men do so more slowly, black women, black men, and black male teenagers most slowly of all." In showing that interactional tensions derive from outside statuses such as race, class, and gender, Anderson makes clear that we cannot develop a full understanding of the situation by looking at the micro interactions themselves. This is how he makes the link between micro interactions and macro processes.

Anderson argues that people are streetwise when they develop skills such as "the art of avoidance" to deal with their felt vulnerability toward violence and crime. According to Anderson, whites who are not streetwise do not recognize the difference between different kinds of black men (e.g., middle-class youths versus gang members). They may also not know how to alter the number of paces to walk behind a suspicious person or how to bypass bad blocks at various times of day.

CONCEPT CHECKS ✓

1. Describe the purpose of interactional vandalism.
2. What does Anderson mean by the term "streetwise?"
3. How would you explain the street harassment that women often experience?

---

④ UNANSWERED QUESTIONS

Impression Management in the Internet Age

The concept of "audience segregation" helps us understand some of the dilemmas of electronic communication. Many people are very sensitive about having things sent to their business e-mail address if they don't want their coworkers or supervisors to know about these. Thus, they maintain different addresses for home ("**back region**") and office ("**front region**"), a practice that is increasingly important because many companies have policies against sending personal e-mails from a company's computer. In 2007, New Jersey employees of PNC Bank learned the hard way how important it is to maintain such boundaries; Heidi Arace was

back region • Areas apart from front-region performance, as specified by Erving Goffman, in which individuals are able to relax and behave informally.

front region • Settings of social activity in which people seek to put on a definite "performance" for others.

fired in 2007 after forwarding a picture of a bare-breasted woman attached to Hillary Clinton's face.

Or consider the social situation of a copied message. You write a message to a friend asking her whether she prefers to go to the early show or the late show. You also tell your friend that you have a new boyfriend whom you hope she'll like. She replies and copies the other people who are thinking of going to the movie, many of whom you never intended to tell about the new romance. Suddenly the audience segregation you had imagined has broken down.

In recent years, undergraduate students have posted pictures of themselves drinking at parties or even naked only to discover that future employers have found these and other postings on the Web before making a hiring decision. Some of these items remain on the Internet long after anyone remembers the situation that gave rise to them. Disasters such as this, and ones far worse, occur frequently in the age of e-mail. One of the most troublesome of breakdowns occurs due to "autofill," the tool on e-mail that fills in the rest of an address. Here is one common story:

> My worst e-mail disaster was not too long ago, when I composed an e-mail using my work e-mail (MS Outlook) asking my friend Krista for a link to a porn site. My e-mail was something like "Yo, Krista! where's the link to that porn site? I need to forward it to Jenny!"
>
> Anyone who uses MS Outlook knows that it has this autofill feature for the "To:" field, and instead of selecting "Krista," I selected "Kirsten," who's a coworker!
>
> I had no idea I sent it to the wrong person until Kirsten e-mailed me back, asking if the e-mail I just sent her was meant for her or "someone else"!
>
> I still can't look Kirsten in the eye. And I never send personal e-mail using my work e-mail account. EVER.

The Compulsion of Proximity

In modern societies, we are constantly interacting with others whom we may never see or meet. Almost all our everyday transactions, such as buying groceries or making a bank deposit, bring us into contact—but indirect contact—with people who may live thousands of miles away. The banking system, for example, is international. Any money you deposit is a small part of the financial investments the bank makes worldwide.

Some people are concerned that the rapid advances in communication technology such as e-mail, the Internet, and social media will only increase this tendency toward indirect interactions. Our society is becoming "devoiced," some claim, as the capabilities of technology grow ever greater. According to this view, as the pace of life accelerates, people are increasingly isolating themselves; we now interact more with our televisions and computers than with our neighbors or members of the community.

Now that e-mail, instant messages, electronic discussion groups, and chat rooms have become facts of life for many people in industrialized countries, what is the nature of these interactions and what new complexities are emerging from them? One study conducted at Stanford University found that about 20 percent of Internet users employ the medium to communicate with people whom they do not know (Nie et al., 2004). At the same time, the study found that Internet use reduces face-to-face socializing, TV watching, and sleep. In another study, of office workers, conducted in 1997 by Raymond Friedman and Steven Currall, almost half of the respondents said that the Internet had replaced their need for face-to-face communication. A third of them admitted to using e-mail deliberately to avoid direct communication. Others reported that the sending of abusive or offensive e-mails within the workplace had resulted in a complete breakdown in certain office relations. The substitution of e-mail for face-to-face communication in the office had led to a weakening of social ties and a disruption of techniques used in personal dialogue for avoiding conflict. As a result, online communication seemed to have allowed more room for misinterpretation, confusion, and abuse than more traditional forms of communication did (Friedman and Currall, 2003). An MSN survey in 2001 reported that for the age group under 25, e-mail was fast replacing face-to-face contact. For instance, 44 percent of the respondents felt that e-mail was an acceptable medium for sending thank-you notes; some 27 percent had sent an electronic card for a seasonal or birthday greeting; and about 10 percent of the women surveyed said that they had used e-mail to end a relationship. By 2011 the social networking site Facebook had roughly 800 million users, or more than 1 in 13 people on the planet. Over 48 percent of young people said that they got their news from Facebook (Online Schools, 2011).

> The problem lies in the nature of human communication. We think of it as a product of the mind, but it's done by bodies: faces move, voices intone, bodies sway, hands gesture . . . On the Internet, the mind is present but the body is gone. Recipients get few clues about the personality and mood of the person, can only guess why messages are sent, what they mean, what responses to make. Trust is virtually out the window. It's a risky business (Locke and Pascoe, 2000).

Many Internet enthusiasts, however, disagree. They argue that far from being impersonal, online communication has many inherent advantages that cannot be claimed by more traditional forms of interaction such as the telephone and face-to-face meetings. The human voice, for example, may be far superior in terms of expressing emotion and subtleties of meaning, but it can also convey information about the speaker's age, gender, ethnicity, or social position—information that could be used to the speaker's disadvantage. Electronic communication, it is noted, masks all these identifying markers and ensures that attention focuses strictly on the content of the message. This can be a great advantage for women or other traditionally disadvantaged groups whose opinions are sometimes devalued in other settings (Locke and Pascoe, 2000). Electronic interaction is often presented as liberating and empowering because people can create their own online identities and can speak more freely than they would elsewhere.

Who is right in this debate? How far can electronic communication substitute for face-to-face interaction? There is little question that new media forms are revolutionizing the way people communicate, but even when it is more expedient to interact indirectly, humans still value direct contact—possibly even more highly than before. People in business, for instance, continue to attend meetings, sometimes flying halfway around the world to do so when it would seem much simpler and more effective to transact business through a conference call or video link. Family members could arrange virtual reunions or holiday gatherings using electronic real-time communications, but we all recognize that these would lack the warmth and intimacy of face-to-face celebrations.

Deirdre Boden and Harvey Molotch (1994) have studied what they call the Carol Brooks Gardner **compulsion of proximity**—the need of individuals to meet with one another in situations of copresence, or face-to-face interaction. People put themselves out to attend meetings, Boden and Molotch suggest, because situations of copresence (for reasons

compulsion of proximity • People's need to interact with others in their presence.

These Israeli-Palestinian peace talks are an example of what Molotch and Boden call the compulsion of proximity. Individuals prefer face-to-face interactions, because these situations provide richer information about how other people think or feel.

documented by Goffman in his studies of interaction) supply much richer information about how other people think and feel, as well as their sincerity, than any form of electronic communication.

Only by actually being in the presence of people who make decisions affecting us in important ways do we feel able to learn what is going on and feel confident that we can impress them with our own views and our sincerity. "Co-presence," Boden and Molotch (1994) say, "affects access to the body part that 'never lies': the eyes, the 'windows on the soul.' Eye contact itself signals a degree of intimacy and trust; co-present interactants continuously monitor the subtle movements of this most subtle body part."

One reminder of the need for proximity is when people who meet through e-mail or a listserv feel the need to be together physically. One listserv for fans of the television show *My So-Called Life*, which ran for one season in 1994/1995, resulted in eleven couples. In some cases, one or both partners moved to a different country in order to live together.

The seven children these couples have already produced are perhaps the best possible evidence for the compulsion of proximity!

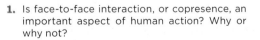

CONCEPT CHECKS ✓

1. Is face-to-face interaction, or copresence, an important aspect of human action? Why or why not?

Chapter 5

Social Interaction and Everyday Life in the Age of the Internet

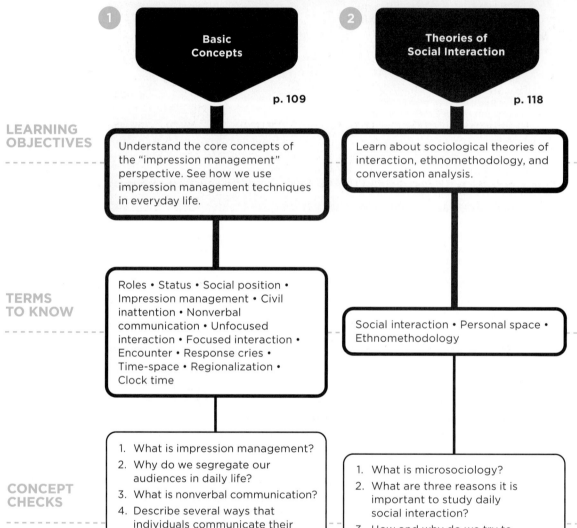

1 **Basic Concepts**

p. 109

2 **Theories of Social Interaction**

p. 118

LEARNING OBJECTIVES

Understand the core concepts of the "impression management" perspective. See how we use impression management techniques in everyday life.

Learn about sociological theories of interaction, ethnomethodology, and conversation analysis.

TERMS TO KNOW

Roles • Status • Social position • Impression management • Civil inattention • Nonverbal communication • Unfocused interaction • Focused interaction • Encounter • Response cries • Time-space • Regionalization • Clock time

Social interaction • Personal space • Ethnomethodology

CONCEPT CHECKS

1. What is impression management?
2. Why do we segregate our audiences in daily life?
3. What is nonverbal communication?
4. Describe several ways that individuals communicate their emotions to one another.
5. Compare and contrast focused and unfocused interaction.
6. How does time structure human life?

1. What is microsociology?
2. What are three reasons it is important to study daily social interaction?
3. How and why do we try to protect our "personal space"?
4. Why do we make small talk?
5. What do ethnomethodologists do?

Exercises: Thinking Sociologically

1. Identify the important elements to the dramaturgical perspective. This chapter shows how such a perspective might be applied in viewing the ministrations of a nurse to his or her patient. Apply the theory to account for a plumber's visit to a client's home. Are there any similarities? Explain.

2. Smoking cigarettes is a pervasive habit found in many parts of the world and a habit that could be explained by both microsociological and macrosociological forces. Give an example of each that would be relevant to explain the proliferation of smoking. How might your suggested micro- and macro-level analyses be linked?

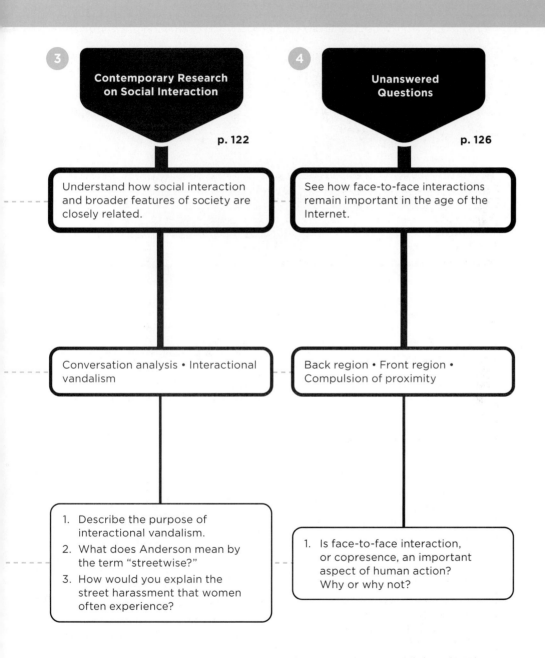

3 **Contemporary Research on Social Interaction**

p. 122

Understand how social interaction and broader features of society are closely related.

Conversation analysis • Interactional vandalism

1. Describe the purpose of interactional vandalism.
2. What does Anderson mean by the term "streetwise?"
3. How would you explain the street harassment that women often experience?

4 **Unanswered Questions**

p. 126

See how face-to-face interactions remain important in the age of the Internet.

Back region • Front region • Compulsion of proximity

1. Is face-to-face interaction, or copresence, an important aspect of human action? Why or why not?

Groups, Networks, and Organizations

6

Military discipline at West Point Academy is most heavily dependent on:

- a Fear of punishment by superiors
- b Positive reinforcement from superiors
- c Group loyalty and conformity to social norms
- d Personal motivation and self-discipline

Turn the page for the correct answer.

The U.S. Military Academy (West Point) is very hard to get into. More than 50,000 high school students open files at the academy, of whom perhaps 12,000 are qualified to apply. Another 4,000 are nominated by a congressional representative, a senator, or the White House. Yet out of all these, barely 2,000 pass the physical fitness test, and only 1,200 are admitted.

From "Reception Day" (R-Day) on, the academy emphasizes conformity to group norms:

At R-Day you surrender your old self in stages. You've already left behind family and control over your environment. In the fluorescent Thayer hallways, you hand over your belongings, then file to the treasurer's office to give up your cash; any sum greater than forty dollars gets banked. . . . "No talking," cadre announces. "Do not move, do not smile. Hands will remain cupped at all times. You need to look at anything, look at my wall." Unless you had an unlucky home life, this is the first time anybody has spoken to you this way. The candidates are just blank eyes now, mouths so tight the lips appear to be hiding. . . . Now the army demands your clothing. In their dressing room, male candidates tuck on black gym shorts and white T-shirts with a speed that suggests graded events. "You *must* put on a jockstrap," a TAC-NCO commands. "Let's go—move with a purpose." . . . Then the academy takes custody of your actual skin. "If you have," the sergeant booms, "any tattoo, brand or body piercing, regardless of whether it is visible while wearing a uniform, you must declare it at this time to the registration desk at my rear." . . . Then the army takes your hair. . . . Every few minutes the guy working the push broom sweeps away what looks like a whole discarded wig.

LEARNING OBJECTIVES

1 BASIC CONCEPTS

Learn the variety and characteristics of groups as well as the effect groups have on individual behavior. Know how to define an organization and understand how organizations developed over the last two centuries.

2 THEORIES OF GROUPS, ORGANIZATIONS, AND NETWORKS

Learn Max Weber's theory of organizations and view of bureaucracy. Understand the importance of the physical setting of organizations and Michel Foucault's theory of surveillance. Understand the importance of social networks and the advantages they give some people.

3 CONTEMPORARY RESEARCH ON GROUPS AND NETWORKS

Learn what the term "McDonaldization" means. Understand how social networks can influence you in unexpected ways. See how the Internet has transformed relationships between groups and social networks.

4 UNANSWERED QUESTIONS

Become familiar with alternatives to bureaucracy that have developed in other places and in recent times. Think about the influence of technology on organizations.

(The barbers place bets on R-Day yield.) . . . Now you're shorn of everything. You look, act, dress like everyone beside you, for maybe the first time in your life. In five hours, West Point has reduced you to just the meat your parents made, topped by its frenetic, calculating brain. . . . The cadre introduces [you] to the basics of the Army body language: how to stand, how to listen, how to respond with the grammar of obedience. (Lipsky, 2003)

If it were the case that individuals at West Point *were* extraordinary—extremely disciplined individuals who intuitively surrender themselves to directives from superiors—such measures would likely be unnecessary. After all, what business would the army have to reduce you to "just the meat your parents made," if you were already well versed in the language of subordination to your superiors?

Having said that, you might expect that this subordination to authority would result from fear of punishment (answer *a*). Given the brutal nature of military punishment represented in the mass media (being forced to scrub the floor or do additional push-ups), you might suspect that new entrants would live in mortal fear of being on the receiving end of such a shameful treatment.

David Lipsky, a writer for *Rolling Stone* who tried to understand how and why cadets at West Point would "subject themselves to the intense discipline," conducted a four-year study that culminated in the publication of his book *Absolutely America: Four Years at West Point* (Lipsky, 2003). What he discovered was a place where people tried their best and where most at least looked out for one another. Though they liked to complain, the cadets at West Point were the happiest young people he had met. Part of the reason, he concluded, was the military value system, which emphasizes self-sacrifice, discipline, honor, respect, and loyalty and leads to the *unit cohesion* that bonds cadets. As Lipsky points out, "In battle, what often drives soldiers isn't simply courage but a complicated version of crisis loyalty, the desire not to let down their friends" (Lipsky, 2003). Thus, the answer is *c*.

It is, of course, possible that each of the other elements listed in the question just posed also contributes in some small way to the disciplined social life of West Point; certainly, we are not disregarding the existence of self-motivation among the cadets, nor the possibility that fear of one's superiors might factor into social order. However, what Lipsky's study shows is that it is a strong sense of group loyalty and a willingness to conform to norms that structures the ordered social world at West Point.

In this chapter, we will examine the ways in which all of us, not just West Point cadets, are creatures of human groups and organizations. We will look at the rise of the network as a key social form in modern society.

THE ANSWER IS C.

BASIC CONCEPTS

Groups

Much of importance in life occurs through some type of social group. You and your roommate make up a social group, as do the members of your sociology class. A **social group** is a collection

> **social group** • A collection of people who regularly interact with one another on the basis of shared expectations concerning behavior and who share a sense of common identity.

of people who have a common identity and who regularly interact with one another on the basis of shared expectations concerning behavior. People who belong to the same social group identify with each other, expect each other to conform to certain ways of thinking and acting, and recognize the boundaries that separate them from other groups or people. In our need to congregate and belong, we have created a rich and varied group life that gives us our norms, practices, and values—our whole way of life.

We sometimes feel alone, yet we are seldom far from one kind of group or another. Every day nearly all of us move through various social situations. We hang out with friends, study with classmates, play team sports, and go online to find new friends or people who share our interests.

But just because people find themselves in one another's company does not make them a social group. People milling around in crowds, waiting for a bus, or strolling on a beach make up what is called a **social aggregate**—a collection of people who happen to be together in a particular place but do not significantly interact or identify with one another. People waiting together at a bus station, for example, may be aware of each other, but they are unlikely to think of themselves as a "we"—the group waiting for the next bus to Poughkeepsie or Des Moines. By the same token, people may make up a **social category**—people sharing a common characteristic such as gender or occupation—without necessarily interacting or identifying with one another.

Group life differs greatly in how intensely members experience it. Beginning with the family—the first group to which most of us belong—many of the groups that shape our personalities and lives are those in which we experience strong emotional ties. This is common not only for families but also for groups of friends, including gangs and other peer groups, all of which are known as primary groups. **Primary groups** are usually small groups characterized by face-to-face interaction, intimacy, and a strong sense of commitment. Members of primary groups often experience unity, a merging of the self with the group into one personal "we." The sociologist Charles Horton Cooley (1864–1929) termed such groups "primary" because he believed that they were the basic form of association, exerting a long-lasting influence on the development of our social selves (Cooley, 1964; orig. 1902).

In contrast, **secondary groups** are large and impersonal and seldom involve intense emotional ties, enduring relationships, powerful commitments to the group itself, or experiences of unity. Examples of secondary groups include businesses, schools, work groups, athletic clubs, and governmental bodies. We rarely feel we can be ourselves in a secondary group; rather, we are often playing a role, such as employee or student. Cooley argued that people belong to primary groups mainly because it is fulfilling, but people join secondary groups to achieve a specific goal: to earn a living, get a college degree, or compete on a sports team. Secondary groups may, of course, become primary groups. For example, when students taking a course together socialize after class, they create bonds of friendship that constitute a primary group.

For most of human history, nearly all interactions took place within primary groups. This began to change with the emergence of larger,

social aggregate • A simple collection of people who happen to be together in a particular place but do not significantly interact or identify with one another.

social category • People who share a common characteristic (such as gender or occupation) but do not necessarily interact or identify with one another.

primary groups • Groups that are characterized by intense emotional ties, face-to-face interaction, intimacy, and a strong, enduring sense of commitment.

secondary groups • Groups characterized by large size and by impersonal, fleeting relationships.

agrarian societies, which included such secondary groups as those based on governmental roles or occupations. Today most of our waking hours are spent within secondary groups, although primary groups remain a basic part of our lives.

Some early sociologists, such as Cooley, worried about a loss of intimacy as more and more interactions revolved around large, impersonal organizations. However, what Cooley saw as the growing impersonality and anonymity of modern life may also offer increasing tolerance of individual differences. Primary groups often enforce strict conformity to group standards (Durkheim, 1964; orig. 1893; Simmel, 1955). Secondary groups are more likely to be concerned with accomplishing a task than with enforcing conformity.

Conformity

Not so long ago, the only part of the body that American teenage girls were likely to pierce was the ears—one hole per ear, enough to hold a single pair of earrings. For the vast majority of boys, piercing was not an option. Today, earrings are common for males. From teenage boys to male professional athletes to college students, a growing number of males now sport multiple earrings, navel rings, and even studs in their tongues. Pressure to conform to the latest styles is especially strong among teenagers and young adults, among whom the need for group acceptance is often acute.

While wearing navel rings or the latest style of jeans—or rigidly conforming to the military code of West Point—may seem relatively harmless, conformity to group pressure can lead to destructive behavior, such as drug abuse or even murder. For this reason, sociologists and social psychologists have long sought to understand why most people tend to go along with others and under what circumstances they do not.

GOING ALONG WITH THE GROUP: ASCH'S RESEARCH

Some of the earliest studies of conformity to group pressures were conducted by psychologist Solomon Asch (1952). In a classic experiment, Asch asked subjects to decide which of three lines of different length most closely matched the length of a fourth line (Figure 6.1). The differences were obvious; subjects had no difficulty making the correct match. Asch then arranged a version of the experiment in which the subjects were asked to make the matches in a group setting, with each person calling out the answer in turn. In this version, all but one of the subjects were actually Asch's confederates. Each confederate picked as matches two lines that were clearly unequal in length. The unwitting subject, one of the last to answer, felt enormous group pressure to make the same match. Amazingly, one-third of the subjects gave the same answer as the others in the group at least half the time, even though that answer was clearly wrong. They sometimes stammered and fidgeted when doing so, but they nonetheless yielded to the unspoken pressure to conform to the group's decision. Asch's experiments clearly showed that many people are willing to discount their own perceptions rather than buck group consensus.

OBEDIENCE TO AUTHORITY: MILGRAM'S RESEARCH

Another classic study of conformity was Stanley Milgram's (1963) research. Milgram's work was intended to shed some light on what had happened in Nazi Germany during World War II. How could ordinary German citizens have gone along with, and even participated in, the mass extermination of millions of Jews, Romanies (Gypsies), homosexuals, intellectuals, and others who were judged inferior or undesirable by the Nazis?

Obedience is a kind of conformity. Milgram sought to find its limits. He wanted to see how far a person would go when ordered by a scientist to give another person increasingly powerful electric shocks. He set up an experiment that he told the subjects was about memorizing pairs of words. In reality, it was about obedience to authority. Milgram's study would not be permitted today because its deception of subjects and its potential for doing psychological harm would violate current university ethics standards.

The subjects who volunteered for the study were supposedly randomly divided into "teachers" and "learners." In fact, the learners were Milgram's assistants. The teacher was told to read pairs of words from a list that the learner was to memorize. Whenever the learner made a mistake, the teacher was to give him an electric shock by flipping a switch on a fake but real-looking machine. The control board indicated shock levels ranging from "15 volts—slight shock" to "450 volts—danger, severe shock." For each mistake, the voltage was to be increased, until it reached the highest level. In reality, the learner, who was usually concealed from the teacher by a screen, received no shocks.

As the experiment progressed, the learner began to scream out in pain, begging the teacher to stop delivering the shocks. (The screams, increasingly louder as the voltage rose, had actually been prerecorded.) However, the Milgram assistant who was administering the experiment exercised his authority as a scientist and, if the teacher tried to quit, ordered the teacher to continue administering shocks. The assistant would say such things as "the experiment requires that you continue," even when the learner was tearfully protesting—even when he shrieked about his "bad heart."

The teacher was confronted with a major moral decision: Should he obey the scientist and go along with the experiment, even if it meant injuring another human being? Much to Milgram's surprise, over half the subjects administered the shocks until the maximum voltage was reached and the learner's screams had subsided into an eerie silence as he presumably died of a heart attack. How could ordinary people so easily obey orders that would turn them into possible accomplices to murder?

The answer, Milgram found, was deceptively simple. Although it is obvious that soldiers in training, such as first-year plebes at West Point, will obey orders given by someone in a position of power or authority, ordinary citizens will often do the same—even if those orders have horrible consequences. From this we can learn something about Nazi atrocities during World War II, which were Milgram's original concern. Many of the ordinary Germans who participated in the mass executions in concentration camps did so on the grounds that they were just following orders. Milgram's research has sobering implications for anyone who

(a) The Milgram experiment required participants to "shock" the confederate learner (seated). The research participant (left) helped apply the electrodes that would be used to shock the learner. (b) An obedient participant shocks the learner in the "touch" condition. More than half obeyed the experimenter in this condition. (c) After the experiment, all the participants were introduced to the confederate learner so they could see he was not actually harmed.

- -

thinks that only "others" will always knuckle under to authority but "not me" (Zimbardo, Ebbesen, and Maslach, 1977).

Organizations

People frequently band together to pursue activities that they cannot do by themselves. A principal means of accomplishing such cooperative actions is the **organization**—a group with an identifiable membership that engages in concerted collective actions to achieve a common purpose (Aldrich and Marsden, 1988). An organization can be a small primary group, but it is more likely a larger, secondary one. Universities, religious bodies, and business corporations are all examples of organizations. Such organizations are a central feature of all societies, and their study is a core concern of sociology today.

Organizations tend to be highly formal in modern industrial and postindustrial societies. A **formal organization** is designed to achieve its objectives, often by means of explicit rules, regulations, and procedures. The modern bureaucratic organization, discussed later in this chapter, is a prime example of a formal organization. As Max Weber (1979; orig. 1921) recognized almost a century ago, there has been a long-term trend in Europe and North America toward formal organizations, in part because formality is often a requirement for legal standing. For a college or university to be accredited, for example, it must satisfy explicit written standards governing everything from grading policy to faculty performance to fire codes. Today formal organizations are the dominant form of organization throughout the world.

Social systems in the traditional world developed as a result of custom and habit. Modern organizations are designed with definite aims and housed in buildings or physical settings constructed to help realize those aims. Organizations play a more important part in our everyday lives

organization • A large group of individuals with a definite set of authority relations. Many types of organizations exist in industrialized societies, influencing most aspects of our lives. While not all organizations are bureaucratic, there are close links between the development of organizations and bureaucratic tendencies.

formal organization • A group that is rationally designed to achieve its objectives, often by means of explicit rules, regulations, and procedures.

than ever before. Besides delivering us into this world (hospital), they also mark our progress through it (school) and see us out of it when we die (hospital, funeral home). Even before we are born, our mothers, and often our fathers, are involved in birthing classes, pregnancy checkups, and so forth, all carried out within hospitals and other medical organizations. Today every child born is registered by government organizations, which collect information on all of us from birth to death. Most people today die in a hospital—not at home, as was once the case—and each death must be formally registered with the government.

It is easy to see why organizations are so important today. In the premodern world, families, relatives, and neighbors provided for most needs—food, the instruction of children, work, and leisure-time activities. In modern times, many of our requirements are met by people we never meet and who might live and work thousands of miles away. Substantial coordination of activities and resources (which organizations provide) is needed in such circumstances.

But the tremendous influence organizations have on our lives cannot be seen as wholly beneficial. Organizations often take things out of our own hands and put them under the control of officials or experts over whom we have little influence. For instance, we are required to do certain things the government tells us to do—pay taxes, obey laws, fight wars—or face punishment. As sources of social power, organizations can subject people to dictates they may be powerless to resist.

Networks

"Who you know is often as important as what you know." This adage expresses the value of having "good connections." Sociologists refer to such connections as **networks**—all the direct and indirect connections that link a person or a group with other people or groups. Your personal networks thus include people you know directly (such as your friends) as well as people you know indirectly (such as your friends' friends). Personal networks often include people of similar race, class, ethnicity, and other types of social background, but some networks have a different basis. For example, if you subscribe to an online mailing list, you are part of a network that consists of all the people on the list, who may be of different racial or ethnic backgrounds. Because groups and organizations, such as sororities or religious groups, can also be networked—for example, all the chapters of Gamma Phi Beta or Hillel belong to their respective national organizations—belonging to such groups can greatly extend your reach and influence.

Social groups are an important source for acquiring networks, but not all networks are social groups. Many networks lack the shared expectations and sense of common identity that are the hallmarks of social groups. For example, you are not likely to share a sense of identity with the subscribers to an online mailing list, nor will you probably even know the neighbors of most of your coworkers at the office, even though they do form part of your social network.

Networks serve us in many surprising ways that we will take up shortly.

CONCEPT CHECKS ✓

1. What is the difference between social aggregates and social groups? Give examples that illustrate this difference.
2. Describe the main characteristics of primary and secondary groups.
3. What role do organizations play in contemporary society?

---

networks • Sets of informal and formal social ties that link people to each other.

---

② THEORIES OF GROUPS, ORGANIZATIONS, AND NETWORKS

In-Groups and Out-Groups

The "sense of belonging" that characterizes social groups is sometimes strengthened by scorning other groups (Sartre, 1965; orig. 1948). This is especially true of racist groups, which promote their identity as superior by hating "inferior" groups. In the United States, Jews, Catholics, African Americans and other people of color, immigrants, and gay people are often the targets of such hatred. This sense of group identity created through scorn is dramatically illustrated by the website rantings of a racist skinhead group called Combat 18 (1998): "We are the last of our warrior race, and it is our duty to fight for our people. The Jew will do everything to discredit us, but we hold that burning flame in our hearts that drove our ancestors to conquer whole continents."

Such proud, disdainful language illustrates the sociological distinction between in-groups and out-groups. **In-groups** are groups toward which one feels loyalty and respect—the groups that "we" belong to. **Out-groups** are groups toward which one feels antagonism and contempt—"those people." At one time or another, many of us have used in-group/out-group imagery to trumpet what we believe to be our group's strengths vis-à-vis another group's presumed weaknesses. For example, fraternity or sorority members may bolster their feelings of superiority—in academics, sports, or campus image—by ridiculing the members of a different house. Similarly, an ethnic group may prefer its sons and daughters to marry only within the group, a religion often holds up its truths as the only ones, and immigrants are sometimes accused of ruining the country for "real" Americans.

Reference Groups

We often judge ourselves by how we think we appear to others, which Cooley termed the "looking-glass self." Groups as well as individuals provide the standards by which we make self-evaluations. Robert K. Merton (1968; orig. 1938) elaborated on Cooley's work by introducing the concept of the **reference group**—a group that provides a standard for judging one's attitudes or behaviors (see also Hyman and Singer, 1968). The family is typically one of the crucial reference groups in our lives, as are peer groups and coworkers. However, you don't have to belong to a group for it to be a reference group. Regardless of his station in life, a person may identify with the wealth and power of Fortune 500 corporate executives, admire the contribution of Nobel Prize–winning scientists, or be captivated by the glitter of Hollywood stars. Although few of us interact socially with such reference groups, we may take pride in identifying with them, glorify their accomplishments, and even imitate the behavior of their members. This is why it is critical for children—minority children in particular, whose groups are often represented with negative stereotypes in the media—to be exposed to reference groups that will provide positive standards of behavior.

Reference groups may be primary (such as the family) or secondary (such as a group of soldiers). They may even be fictional. One of the chief functions of advertising is to create a set of imaginary reference groups that will influence consumers' buying habits. For example, when cosmetic ads

in-groups • Groups toward which one feels particular loyalty and respect—the groups to which "we" belong.

out-groups • Groups toward which one feels antagonism and contempt—"those people."

reference group • A group that provides a standard for judging one's attitudes or behaviors.

feature thin models with flawless complexions, the message is simple: "If you want to look as though you are part of an in-group of highly attractive, eternally youthful women, buy this product." In reality, the models seldom have the unblemished features depicted; instead, the ideal features are constructed through artful lighting, photographic techniques, and computer enhancement. Similarly, the happy-go-lucky, physically perfect young men and women seen sailing or playing volleyball or hang-gliding in beer commercials have little to do with the reality of most of our lives—or, indeed, with the lives of the actors in those commercials. The message, however, is otherwise: "Drink this beer, and you will be a member of the carefree in-group in this ad."

The Effects of Size

Size is also an important characteristic of groups. Sociological interest in group size can be traced to Georg Simmel (1858–1918), a German sociologist who studied the effect of small groups on people's behavior. Since Simmel's time, small-group researchers have examined the effects of size on both the quality of interaction in the group and the effectiveness of the group in accomplishing certain tasks (Bales, 1953, 1970; Homans, 1950; Mills, 1967).

DYADS

The simplest group, which Simmel (1955) called a **dyad**, consists of two people (Figure 6.2). Simmel reasoned that dyads, which involve both intimacy and conflict, are likely to be simultaneously intense and unstable. To survive, they require the full attention and cooperation of both parties. If one person withdraws from the dyad, it vanishes. Dyads are typically the source of our most elementary social bonds, often constituting the group in which we are likely to share our deepest secrets. But dyads can be fragile. That is why, Simmel believed, numerous cultural and legal supports for marriage are found in societies in which marriage is an important source of social stability.

TRIADS

Adding a third person changes the group relationship. Simmel used the term **triad** to describe a group of three people. Triads tend to be more stable than dyads because the presence of a third person relieves some of the pressure on the other two members to always get along and energize the relationship. In a triad, one person can temporarily withdraw attention from the relationship without necessarily threatening it. In addition, if two of the members have a disagreement, the third can play the role of mediator, as when you try to patch up a falling-out between two of your friends.

On the other hand, alliances (sometimes termed coalitions) may form between two members of a triad, enabling them to gang up on the third and thereby destabilize the group. Alliances are most likely to form when no one member is clearly dominant and when all three members are competing for the same thing—for example, when three friends are given a pair of tickets to a concert and have to decide which two will go. The TV series *Survivor* provides many examples of alliance formation, as the program's characters forge special relationships with one another to avoid being eliminated in the weekly group vote. In forming an alliance, a member of a triad is most likely to choose the weaker of the two other members as a partner, if there is one. In what have been termed revolutionary coalitions, the two weaker members form an alliance to overthrow the stronger one (Caplow, 1956, 1959, 1969).

dyad • A group consisting of two persons.
triad • A group consisting of three persons.

LARGER GROUPS

Going from a dyad to a triad illustrates an important sociological principle first identified by Simmel: In most cases, as groups grow in size, their intensity decreases and their stability increases. Increasing a group's size tends to decrease its intensity of interaction, simply because there is the potential for more smaller group relationships to exist as outlets for individuals who are not getting along with other members of the group. In a dyad, only one relationship is possible; in a triad, three two-person relationships can occur. Adding a fourth person leads to six possible two-person relationships without counting the potential subgroups of three. In a ten-person group, the number of possible two-person relationships explodes to forty-five! When one relationship doesn't work out, you can easily move to another, as you probably often do at large parties.

At the same time, larger groups tend to be more stable than smaller ones because they can survive the withdrawal of some members. A marriage or love relationship falls apart if one person leaves, whereas an athletic team or drama club routinely survives, though it may temporarily suffer from the loss of its graduating seniors.

Larger groups also tend to be more exclusive because it is easier for members to limit social relationships to the group itself and to avoid relationships with non-members. This sense of being part of an in-group or clique is sometimes found in fraternities, sororities, and other campus organizations. Cliquishness is especially likely to occur when a group's members are similar in such social characteristics as age, gender, class, race, or ethnicity. People from rich families, for example, may be reluctant to fraternize with working-class groups, men may prefer to go to the basketball court with other men, and students who belong to a particular ethnic group (for example, African Americans, Latinos,

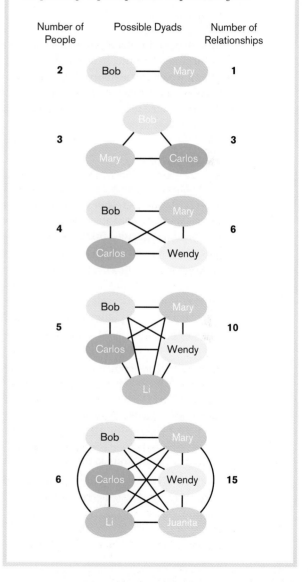

Figure 6.2
Dyads

The larger the number of people, the greater the possible number of relationships. Note that this figure illustrates only dyads; if triads and more complex coalitions were to be included, the numbers would be still greater (four people yield ten possibilities). Even a 10-person group can produce 45 possible dyads!

Number of People	Possible Dyads	Number of Relationships
2	Bob — Mary	1
3	Bob, Mary, Carlos	3
4	Bob, Mary, Carlos, Wendy	6
5	Bob, Mary, Carlos, Wendy, Li	10
6	Bob, Mary, Carlos, Wendy, Li, Juanita	15

or Asian Americans) may seek out one another in the dorm or cafeteria. Even so, groups do not always restrict relationships with outsiders. A group with a socially diverse membership is likely to foster a high degree of interaction with people outside the group (Blau, 1977). For example, if your social group or club has members from different social classes or ethnic groups, it is more likely that you will come to appreciate such social differences from firsthand experience and seek them out in other aspects of your life. Beyond a certain size (perhaps a dozen people), groups tend to develop a formal structure. Formal leadership roles may arise, such as president or secretary, and official rules may be developed to govern what the group does. We will discuss formal organizations later in this chapter.

ORGANIZATIONS

Max Weber developed the first systematic interpretation of modern organizations. Organizations, he argued, are ways of coordinating the activities of human beings or the goods they produce in a stable way across space and time. Weber emphasized that the development of organizations depends on the control of information, and he stressed the central importance of writing in this process. An organization needs written rules to function and files in which its "memory" is stored. Weber saw organizations as strongly hierarchical, with power tending to concentrate at the top. Was Weber right? It matters a great deal, for Weber detected a clash as well as a connection between modern organizations and democracy, which he believed had far-reaching consequences for social life.

Bureaucracy

All large-scale organizations, according to Weber, tend to be bureaucratic. The word *bureaucracy* was coined by Jean-Claude Marie Vincent de Gournay in 1745, who added the word *bureau*, meaning both an office and a writing table, to *cracy*, a term derived from the Greek verb meaning "to rule." **Bureaucracy** is thus the rule of officials. The term was first applied only to government officials, but it gradually came to refer to large organizations in general.

From the beginning, the concept was used disparagingly. De Gournay spoke of the developing power of officials as "an illness called bureaumania." The nineteenth-century French novelist Honoré de Balzac saw bureaucracy as "the giant power wielded by pygmies." This view persists today. Bureaucracy is frequently associated with red tape, inefficiency, and wastefulness. Others, however, have seen bureaucracy as a model of carefulness, precision, and effective administration. Bureaucracy, they argue, is the most efficient form of human organization, because in it all tasks are regulated by strict procedures.

Weber's account of bureaucracy steers between these two extremes. A limited number of bureaucratic organizations, he pointed out, existed in traditional civilizations. For example, a bureaucratic officialdom in imperial China was responsible for the overall affairs of government. But it is only in modern times that bureaucracies have developed fully.

According to Weber, the expansion of bureaucracy is inevitable in modern societies; bureaucratic authority is the only way of coping with the administrative requirements of large-scale social systems. However, as we will see, Weber also believed bureaucracy exhibits a number of major failings that have important implications for modern social life.

To study the origins and nature of bureaucratic organizations, Weber constructed an **ideal type** of bureaucracy. (*Ideal* here refers not to what is most desirable but to a pure form of bureaucratic organization, one that accentuates

bureaucracy • A type of organization marked by a clear hierarchy of authority and the existence of written rules of procedure and staffed by full-time, salaried officials.

ideal type • A "pure type," constructed by emphasizing certain traits of a social item that do not necessarily exist in reality. An example is Max Weber's ideal type of bureaucratic organization.

certain features of real cases so as to pinpoint essential characteristics.) Weber (1979; orig. 1921) listed several characteristics of the ideal type of bureaucracy:

1. There is a clear-cut hierarchy of authority. Tasks in the organization are distributed as "official duties." A bureaucracy looks like a pyramid, with the positions of highest authority at the top. There is a chain of command stretching from top to bottom, thus making possible the coordination of decisions. Each higher office controls and supervises the one below it in the hierarchy.
2. Written rules govern the conduct of officials at all levels of the organization. This does not mean that bureaucratic duties are just a matter of routine. The higher the office, the more the rules tend to encompass a wide variety of cases and to demand flexibility in their interpretation.
3. Officials work full time and are salaried. Each job in the hierarchy has a definite and fixed salary attached to it. Individuals are expected to make a career within the organization. Promotion is possible on the basis of capability, seniority, or a combination of the two.
4. There is a separation between the tasks of an official within the organization and his life outside. The home life of the official is distinct from his activities in the workplace and is also physically separated from it.
5. No members of the organization own the material resources with which they operate. The development of bureaucracy, according to Weber, separates workers from the control of their means of production. In traditional communities, farmers and craft workers usually had control over their processes of production and owned the tools they used. In bureaucracies, officials do not own the offices they work in, the desks they sit at, or the office machinery they use.

Weber believed that the more an organization approaches the ideal type of bureaucracy, the more effective it will be in reaching its goals. He likened bureaucracies to sophisticated machines operating according to rational principles (see Chapter 1). Yet he also recognized that bureaucracy could be inefficient and that many bureaucratic jobs are dull, offering little opportunity for creativity. Although Weber feared that the rationalization of society could have negative consequences, he concluded that bureaucratic routine and the authority of officialdom were the prices we pay for the technical effectiveness of bureaucratic organizations. Since Weber's time, the rationalization of society has become more widespread. Critics of this development who share Weber's initial concerns have questioned whether the efficiency of rational organizations comes at a cost greater than Weber imagined. The most prominent of these costs is known as "the McDonaldization of society" and will be discussed later in this chapter.

FORMAL AND INFORMAL RELATIONS WITHIN BUREAUCRACIES

Weber's analysis of bureaucracy gave prime place to **formal relations** within organizations, relations as stated in the rules of the organization. Weber had little to say about the informal connections and small-group relations that exist in all organizations. But in bureaucracies, informal ways of doing things often allow for a flexibility that couldn't otherwise be achieved.

In a classic study, Peter Blau (1963) looked at **informal relations** in a government agency that investigated possible income-tax violations. Agents who came across difficult cases

formal relations • Relations that exist in groups and organizations, laid down by the norms, or rules, of the official system of authority.

informal relations • Relations that exist in groups and organizations developed on the basis of personal connections; ways of doing things that depart from formally recognized modes of procedure.

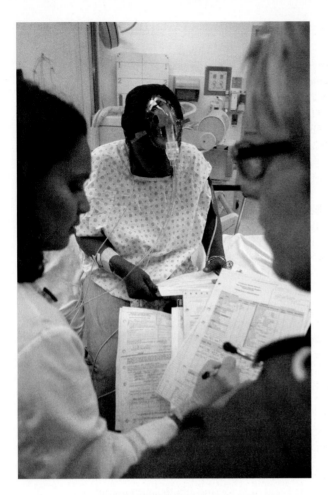

A woman suffering from severe asthma fills out paperwork in an emergency room at San Francisco General Hospital. Modern hospitals are complex organizations with impersonal structures and procedures—but they are designed for a personal outcome.

were supposed to discuss them with their immediate supervisor; the rules of procedure stated that they should not consult colleagues at the same level as they. Most agents were wary about approaching their supervisors, however, because they felt it might suggest a lack of competence on their part and reduce their chances for promotion. Hence they usually consulted one another, violating the official rules. This breaking of the rules not only helped provide concrete advice but also reduced the anxieties involved in working alone. A cohesive set of loyalties of a primary group kind developed among those working at the same level. The problems these workers faced, Blau concludes, were probably addressed more effectively as a result. The group was able to develop informal procedures that allowed for more initiative and responsibility than were provided for by the formal rules of the organization.

Informal networks tend to develop at all levels of organizations. At the top, personal ties and connections may be more important than the formal situations in which decisions are supposed to be made. For example, meetings of boards of directors and shareholders supposedly determine the policies of business corporations. In practice, a few members of the board often run the corporation, making their decisions informally and expecting the rest of the board to approve them. Informal networks of this sort can also stretch across different corporations. Business leaders from different firms frequently consult one another in an informal way and may belong to the same clubs and leisure time associations.

John Meyer and Brian Rowan (1977) argue that formal rules and procedures are usually quite distant from the practices actually adopted by an organization's members. Formal rules, in their view, are often "myths" that people profess to follow but that have little substance in reality. The rules serve to legitimate (to justify) ways in which tasks are carried out, even while these ways may diverge greatly from how things are "supposed to be done." Formal procedures, Meyer and Rowan point out, often have a ceremonial or ritual character. People make a show of conforming to them but get on with their real work using other, more informal procedures. For example, rules governing ward procedure in a hospital help justify how nurses act toward patients. Thus a nurse will faithfully fill in the chart at the end of a patient's bed but will actually check progress by means of other, informal criteria— how the patient looks and whether the patient seems alert and lively. Rigorously keeping up the charts impresses the patients and keeps the doctors happy but is not always essential to the nurse's assessments.

Deciding how much informal procedures help or hinder the effectiveness of organizations is not simple. Systems that resemble Weber's ideal type tend to give rise to a multitude of unofficial ways of doing things. This is partly because the flexibility that is lacking ends up being achieved by unofficial tinkering with formal rules. For those in dull jobs, informal procedures often create a more satisfying work environment. Informal connections among officials in higher positions may be effective in ways that aid the organization as a whole.

The Control of Time and Space

Michel Foucault (1971, 1975) showed that the architecture of an organization is directly involved with its social makeup and system of authority. By studying the physical characteristics of organizations, we can shed new light on the problems Weber analyzed. The offices Weber discussed abstractly are also architectural settings—rooms, separated by corridors. The buildings of large firms are sometimes actually constructed as a hierarchy, in which the more elevated one's position, the nearer to the top of the building one's office is; not for nothing does "the top floor" refer to those who hold ultimate power in an organization.

In many other ways, the geography of an organization affects its functioning, especially when systems rely heavily on informal relationships. Physical proximity makes forming primary groups easier, whereas physical distance can polarize groups, resulting in a "them" and "us" attitude between departments.

The arrangement of rooms, hallways, and open spaces in an organization's buildings provides basic clues to how the organization's system of authority operates. In some organizations, people work collectively in open settings. Because of the dull, repetitive nature of certain kinds of industrial work, such as assembly line production, regular supervision is needed to ensure that workers sustain the pace of labor. The same is often true of routine work carried out by telephone operators who respond to calls for information and who sit together where their activities are visible to their supervisors. Foucault laid great emphasis on how visibility, or lack of it, in the architectural settings of modern organizations influences and expresses patterns of authority. The level of visibility determines how easily subordinates can be subject to **surveillance**—the supervision of activities in organizations. In modern organizations, everyone, even those in relatively high positions of authority, is subject to surveillance; but the lowlier a person is, the more her behavior tends to be scrutinized.

Surveillance takes two forms. One is the direct supervision of the work of subordinates by superiors. Consider the example of a school classroom. Pupils sit at tables or desks, usually arranged in rows, all in view of the teacher. They are supposed to look alert or be absorbed in their work. Of course, how far this actually happens depends on the abilities of the teacher and the inclinations of the children to do what is expected of them.

The second type of surveillance is subtler but equally important. It consists of keeping files, records, and case histories about people's work lives. Weber realized the importance of written records (nowadays usually computerized) in modern organizations but did not fully explore how they could be used to regulate behavior. Employee records usually provide complete work histories, including personal details and often character evaluations. Such records are used to monitor employees' behavior

surveillance • The supervising of the activities of some individuals or groups by others in order to ensure compliant behavior.

and assess recommendations for promotion. In many businesses, individuals at each level in the organization prepare annual reports on the performances of those in the level just below them. In schools, transcripts are used to monitor students' performance as they move through the organization. Records are kept on file for academic staff, too.

Organizations cannot operate effectively if employees' work is haphazard. In business firms, as Weber pointed out, people are expected to work regular hours. Activities must be consistently coordinated in time and space, something promoted both by the physical settings of organizations and by the precise scheduling of detailed timetables. **Timetables** regularize activities across time and space—in Foucault's words, they "efficiently distribute bodies" around the organization. Timetables are a condition of organizational discipline, because they organize, or schedule, the activities of large numbers of people. If a university did not observe a lecture timetable, for example, it would soon collapse into complete chaos.

The Strength of Weak Ties

Networks serve us in many ways. Sociologist Mark Granovetter (1973) demonstrated that there can be enormous strength in *weak ties*, particularly among higher socioeconomic groups. Granovetter showed that upper-level professional and managerial employees are likely to hear about new jobs through connections such as distant relatives or remote acquaintances. Such weak ties can be beneficial because relatives or acquaintances tend to have very different sets of connections than one's close friends, whose social contacts are likely to be similar to one's own. Among lower socioeconomic groups, Granovetter argued, weak ties are not necessarily bridges to other networks and so do not really increase opportunities (see also Knoke, 1990; Marsden and Lin, 1982; Wellman, Carrington, and Hall, 1988). After graduation, you may rely on good grades and a strong résumé to find a job. But it also may help that your second cousin went to school with a top person in the organization in which you are seeking work.

Most people depend on personal networks to gain advantages, but not everyone has equal access to powerful networks. Some sociologists argue that women's business and political networks are weaker than men's, so that women's power in these spheres is reduced (Brass, 1985). The Bohemian Grove is a case in point. This is an annual political gathering that has been held on the Russian River, north of San Francisco, each summer since 1879. Its all-male membership includes Republican leaders, the heads of major corporations, businessmen, and entertainers. The highly exclusive weekend includes horseback riding, meetings, entertainment, "lakeside talks," informal discussion groups—and some serious deal making. In 1999 the Bohemians included former president George H. W. Bush, then-Texas governor (and later president) George W. Bush, former secretary of state Henry Kissinger, retired general Colin Powell (later secretary of state), and former Speaker of the House Newt Gingrich (Bohan, 1999; Domhoff, 1974).

In general, sociologists have found that women's job market networks comprise fewer ties than do men's, meaning that women know fewer people in fewer occupations (Marsden, 1987; Moore, 1990). Meager networks tend to channel women into typically "female" jobs, which usually offer lower pay and fewer opportunities for advancement (Drentea, 1998; Roos and Reskin, 1992). Still, as more and more women move into higher-level positions, the resulting networks can foster further advancement. One study found that women are more likely to be hired or promoted into job levels that already have a high proportion of women (Cohen, Broschak, and Haveman, 1998).

timetables • The means by which organizations regularize activities across time and space.

Networks confer more than economic advantage. You are likely to rely on your networks for a broad range of contacts, from obtaining access to your congressperson to finding a date for Saturday night. Similarly, when you visit another country to study a foreign language or to vacation, your friends, school, or religious organization may steer you to its overseas connections, who can then help you find your way around the unfamiliar environment. When you graduate, your alumni group can further extend your network of social support.

CONCEPT CHECKS ✓

1. When groups become large, why does their intensity decrease but their stability increase?
2. What does the term *bureaucracy* mean?
3. Describe five characteristics of an ideal type of bureaucracy.
4. According to Granovetter, what are the benefits of weak ties? Why?

③ CONTEMPORARY RESEARCH ON GROUPS AND NETWORKS

The "McDonaldization" of Society?

George Ritzer (1993) used a vivid metaphor to express his view of the transformations in industrialized societies. He argues that we are witnessing the "McDonaldization" of society—the process by which the principles of the fast-food restaurants are coming to dominate more and more sectors of American society as well as the rest of the world. Ritzer uses the four guiding principles of McDonald's restaurants—efficiency, calculability, uniformity, and control through automation—to show that our society is becoming ever more rationalized.

If you have visited a McDonald's in two different countries, you will have noticed that there are few differences between them. The interior decoration may vary slightly, and the language used will most likely differ, but the layout, the menu, the procedure for ordering, the uniforms, the tables, the packaging, and the "service with a smile" are virtually identical. The McDonald's experience is designed to be the same whether you are in Bogota or Beijing. No matter where they are, McDonald's customers can expect quick service with a minimum of fuss and a standardized product that is reassuringly consistent. The McDonald's system is constructed to maximize efficiency and minimize human responsibility and involvement in the process. Except for certain key tasks such as taking orders and pushing the Start and Stop buttons on cooking equipment, the restaurants' functions are highly automated and largely run themselves.

Ritzer argues that society as a whole is moving toward this highly standardized and regulated model. Many aspects of our daily lives, for example, now involve automated systems and computers instead of human beings. E-mail and voice mail are replacing letters and phone calls; e-commerce is threatening to overtake trips to the store; bank machines outnumber bank tellers; and prepackaged meals provide a quicker option than cooking. And if you have recently tried to call a large organization such as an airline, you know that it is almost impossible to speak to a human being. Automated touch-tone information services are designed to answer your requests; only in certain cases will you be connected to a live employee. Ritzer, like Weber before him, is fearful of the harmful effects of rationalization on the human spirit and creativity. He argues that McDonaldization is making social life more homogeneous, more rigid, and less personal.

Personal Taste

Are our music choices a matter of personal taste or an example of conforming behavior? We tend to think of the music we listen to as an intensely personal choice made independently of the people around us and one that reflects our individual personalities and preferences. How much, however, do our group memberships and social networks shape our most personal of decisions such as our aesthetic tastes?

Social scientists Matthew Salganik, Peter Dodds, and Duncan Watts (2006) conducted research to test the effects of the influence of social networks on musical choices. To do so, they created an artificial cultural market on a website named Music Lab. More than 14,000 participants registered with the site and were asked to listen to music by bands with which they were unfamiliar and then rate how much they liked the songs. If they liked the music, they could download songs. The researchers first divided their sample into two groups. Those in the control group were unable to use the website to see what other participants were listening to. Members of the experimental, or "treatment," group, the "social influence" group, were able to see what other participants on the site were listening to as well as downloading. The social influence group was further placed into eight "worlds," and participants could see only the rankings and number of downloads of people in their world.

The researchers found that in the social influence groups, the most popular songs were more popular than those in the control group—that is, when participants knew what songs were favored by others, they were more likely to favor those songs themselves. The most popular song in each world was also different, providing further evidence of the importance of group influence. This suggests that the determinants of popularity in music were based on the listener's social "world." That is, the "intrinsic" quality of the music mattered less than the number of people in each world who were listening to the song, giving it high ratings, and downloading it. The authors of the study described the effect of social networks as a "cumulative advantage" where "if one object happens to be slightly more popular than another at just the right point, it will tend to become more popular still. As a result, even tiny, random fluctuations can blow up, generating potentially enormous long-run differences among even indistinguishable competitors—a phenomenon that is similar in some ways to the famous 'butterfly effect' in chaos theory" (Watts, 2007). The butterfly effect proposes that small variations may produce large variations in the long-term behavior of a system or organism. Salganik, Dodd, and Watts's study revealed the impact of our social networks, which are now increasingly virtual networks, on our music decisions.

Studying how consumers make decisions is a part of a much deeper sociological tradition that is concerned with conformity, propaganda, and the question of how leaders have persuaded whole populations to take part in horrific deeds. The Holocaust, which claimed the lives of more than six million Jews and millions of others, left many social scientists searching to understand how, why, and under what conditions ordinary people will conform to authority. Many students who have seen or read about Stanley Milgram's laboratory experiments or the "make-believe jail" experiment (discussed in Chapter 2) tend to think that they would not conform to the demands of an authority figure as the study participants did. Yet the music lab study reveals how social environments affect our behavior and how we all, at times, conform to the movements of larger social groups, even in something as personal as the music we like.

Obesity

One major public health problem that sociologists have studied in recent years is obesity. In the United States today, the number of obese people has been growing steadily. More than one-third (35.7 percent)of adults are obese, and 18.4 percent of children and teenagers age 12–19 are overweight (CDC, 2012d). Although obesity may have a significant biological component, there are also significant social factors that should not be ignored. Most obviously, sociologists have discovered that particular communities, sometimes known as "food deserts," are short of healthy food options. More controversial has been the finding by sociologist Nicholas Christakis of Harvard Medical School and James Fowler of the University of California–Davis that having fat friends can make you fat.

Their study, entitled "The Spread of Obesity in a Large Social Network over 32 Years," published in *The New England Journal of Medicine* (2007), showed that obesity was "contagious." Christakis and Fowler found that if one person became obese, then persons closely connected to him had a greater chance of becoming obese. If a person once considered a "friend" became obese, then one's own chances of becoming obese increased by 57 percent. However, a mere neighbor's weight change had no effect on one's body weight.

The media were eager to report the findings of the Christakis and Fowler study. It was the first-ever study to examine the ways that one's social networks affected one's body weight. The researchers had access to a unique data source that allowed them to ask questions such as: How do one's friends affect one's weight? Does it matter if one's friends live nearby or far away? Christakis and Fowler analyzed data from a sample of 12,067 adults who were followed over a period of 32 years, from 1971 to 2003. These adults were participants in the renowned Framingham Heart Study. The data source revealed whom the study participants were friends with and who was a spouse or sibling or neighbor. It also obtained information on each person's address and body weight at each interview point.

Because of their unique data and rigorous methodology, the researchers could rule out competing explanations for their findings. For example, because they had data from many time points throughout the 32-year study, they could ascertain the order in which events unfolded. It was not the case that obese people would simply seek out similar-weight people as friends. Rather, Christakis noted, there was a "direct, causal relationship." Christakis and Fowler also found that it didn't matter whether one's friend lived near or far—they found that a friend who lived 500 miles away had just as powerful an impact on one's own weight as a friend who lived across the street.

The study also found that the "contagion" of body weight was not due to the fact that friends might share lifestyles, hobbies, and dietary choices—such as eating large meals together or discouraging one another from exercising. If it's not the "birds of a feather flock together" explanation or "gluttony loves company" explanation, what accounts for the spread of body weight? The authors believe that their study is a testimony to the power of social norms. People develop their ideas about what is an acceptable body type by looking at the people around them. Christakis notes, "People come to think that it is okay to be bigger since those around them are bigger, and this sensibility spreads."

However, the researchers were adamant that Americans should not come away thinking that it is wise or healthy to abandon their obese friends. Rather, Christakis noted, it is good for one's health to have friends, period: "It is unlikely that severing ties with people on the basis of any of their particular traits—as some have supposed that our results might suggest—would necessarily be beneficial." Instead, they suggest that overweight or obese people could befriend a healthy-weighted person and then allow themselves to be influenced by the positive model set by the healthy-weight friend. Other researchers have criticized their methods. Lyons (2011) argued in a scathing critique that the researchers did not properly use their statistics and that most of the association was due to error.

The Internet as Social Network

The advantages and potential reach of networks are evident in an increasingly productive means of networking all but unknown 10 years ago: the Internet. Internet use has exploded in recent years. Until the early 1990s, when the World Wide Web was developed, there were few Internet users outside university and scientific communities. According to one national survey, 74 percent of American adults (over 18 years of age) use the Internet, and on any given day in the United States, 55 percent of American adults are connected to it wirelessly (Pew Research Center, 2012d). With such rapid communication and global reach, it is now possible to radically extend one's personal networks. The Internet is especially useful for networking with like-minded people in areas such as politics, business, hobbies, and romance (Southwick, 1996; Wellman et al., 1996). It also enables people who might lack face-to-face contact with others to become part of global networks. For example, shut-ins can join chat rooms, and people in rural communities can take distance-learning courses on the Web.

The Internet fosters the creation of relationships, often without the emotional and social baggage or constraints that are part of face-to-face encounters. Although this might lead to fleeting, impersonal relationships, it also creates opportunities for the expression of intimate feelings or discussion of topics that might be suppressed in face-to-face encounters. For example, chat rooms offer support for lesbians and gay men who can't find acceptance in their local communities. Some websites for teenagers provide answers to important questions on health and sexuality that teens may be shy about asking their parents. Internet communication also helps us to strengthen bonds between friends and acquaintances who would otherwise seldom see each other (Wellman et al., 1996).

Without the usual physical and social cues, such as skin color and home address, people can meet electronically on the basis of shared interests. Such factors as social position, wealth, race, ethnicity, gender, and physical disability are less likely to cloud social interaction (Coate, 1994; Jones, 1995; Kollock and Smith, 1996). The Internet thus enables people to communicate first and then decide if the relationship is worth continuing in person. As a consequence, Internet-based social networks may be socially broader than other networks (Wellman, 1994). Whether this strengthens social diversity (or downgrades its importance) is a matter of ongoing debate.

The Internet can also help people join organizations they otherwise might not have access to. In particular, it has become instrumental in politics (Townsend, 2002), as demonstrated by MoveOn.org's fund-raising for the 2004 presidential election and by the mobilization of protests against the war in Iraq that drew 8 million demonstrators into the streets of cities around the world on February 15, 2003 (Ali, 2003). Of course, there is a downside to these opportunities, as in the case of hate groups that use the Internet to recruit members. Some evidence indicates that hate groups concentrate on the Internet, where potential members and lone wolves who are attracted to racist notions but not fully committed to the movement can participate without exposing their identities (Southern Poverty Law Center, 2001).

Another issue is that not everyone has equal access to the Internet. Though gender, racial, and class differences affect who is using the Internet and what they use it for, the most pronounced differences affecting Internet use are age and education (Nie and Ebring, 2000). Still, within the span of a few years, Internet use has become much more widespread among all groups (Nielsen Company, 2001; Pew Research Center, 2005). In the words of one study that tracked Internet use among different socioeconomic groups, "The Internet was, at first, an elitist country club reserved only for individuals with select financial abilities and technical skills. . . . Now nearly every socioeconomic group is aggressively adopting the Web"

(Nielsen Company, 2012). The Pew project tracking Internet usage in American life reports similar findings. Pew found that of adults in the United States, 75 percent of Hispanics, 77 percent of (non-Hispanic) blacks, and 84 percent of (non-Hispanic) whites use the Internet (Pew Research Center, 2012d). Roughly 45 percent of adults in the United States use "smart-phones"—phones with Internet and other capabilities. The percentage of blacks (47) and Hispanics (49) who use smartphones is higher than the percentage of whites who use smart-phones (42) (Pew Research Center, 2012f).

The United States has one of the highest rates of Internet use in the world. Alongside North America, Internet use is highest in the wealthy countries of Europe and emerging economies of East Asia. Some sociologists think that the Internet's inevitable strength-ening of global ties may come at the expense of local ones. Being able to connect with anyone in the world who has similar inter-ests may mean that one's own community becomes less important. If this happens, will the ties that have bound people to locality throughout human history slowly disappear?

CONCEPT CHECKS

1. What does Ritzer mean by the term "McDon-aldization of society?"
2. How do Christakis and Fowler explain the spread of obesity through social networks? Why are some researchers critical of their findings?
3. What evidence do Watts et al. have for their claims about social influence on personal taste?

④ UNANSWERED QUESTIONS

Is Democracy Meaningless in the Face of Increasingly Powerful Bureaucratic Organizations?

Even in democracies such as the United States, government organizations hold enormous amounts of information about us, from records of our birth dates, schools attended, and jobs held to data on income used for tax collecting and information for issuing driver's licenses and allocating Social Security numbers. Because we don't have access to the files of most government agencies, such surveillance activities can infringe on the principle of democracy.

The diminishing of democracy with the advance of modern forms of organization worried Weber a great deal (see also Chapter 13). What especially disturbed him was the prospect of rule by faceless bureaucrats. After all, Weber reasoned, bureaucracies are necessarily specialized and hierarchical. Those near the bottom of the organization inevi-tably carry out mundane tasks and have no power over what they do; power resides with those at the top. Weber's student Robert Michels (1967; orig. 1911) invented a phrase: "Who says organization says oligarchy." It has come to refer to this loss of power, in large-scale organizations and, more generally in a society dominated by organizations. He called this the **iron law of oligarchy**. **Oligarchy** means rule by the few. According to Michels, the flow of power toward the top is an inevitable part of an increasingly bureaucratized world—hence the "iron law."

iron law of oligarchy • A term coined by Weber's student Robert Michels meaning that large organizations tend toward centralization of power, making democracy difficult.

oligarchy • Rule by a small minority within an organization or society.

Was Michels right? It surely is true that large-scale organizations involve the centralizing of power. Yet there is reason to believe that the iron law of oligarchy is not quite as hard and fast as Michels claimed. The connections between oligarchy and bureaucratic centralization are more ambiguous than he supposed.

First, unequal power is not just a function of size. Marked differences of power exist even in modest-size groups. In a small business, for instance, in which the activities of employees are directly visible to the directors, much tighter control might be exerted than in larger organizations. As organizations expand in size, power relationships often become looser. Those at the middle and lower levels may have little influence over policies forged at the top. However, because of the specialization and expertise involved in bureaucracy, people at the top may lose control over many of the administrative decisions made by those lower down.

In many modern organizations, power is often delegated downward from superiors to subordinates. The heads of huge corporations are so busy coordinating different departments, coping with crises, and analyzing budget and forecast figures that they have little time for original thinking. Consequently, they delegate consideration of policy issues to others, whose task is to develop proposals. Many corporate leaders admit that, for the most part, they simply accept the conclusions given to them.

How Are Late-Modern Organizations Reinventing Themselves?

For quite a long while in Western societies, Weber's model, closely mirrored by Foucault's, held fast. In government, hospital administration, universities, and business organizations, bureaucracy was dominant. Even though, as Peter Blau showed, informal social groups always develop in bureaucratic settings, and are in fact effective, it seemed as though the future might be what Weber had anticipated: constantly increasing bureaucratization.

Bureaucracies still exist in the West, but Weber's idea that a clear hierarchy of authority, with power and knowledge concentrated at the top, is the only way to run a large organization is starting to look archaic. Numerous organizations are overhauling themselves to become less, rather than more, hierarchical.

In the 1960s, Burns and Stalker concluded that traditional bureaucratic structures could stifle innovation and creativity in cutting-edge industries. In today's electronic economy, few would dispute these findings. Departing from rigid vertical command structures, many organizations are turning to "horizontal," collaborative models to become more responsive to fluctuating markets. In this section we examine some of the forces behind these shifts, including globalization and information technology, and consider some of the ways in which late-modern organizations are reinventing themselves.

The development of **information and communication technology**—computers and electronic communication media such as the Internet—is another factor currently influencing organizational structures (Attaran, 2004; Bresnahan, Brynjolfsson, and Hitt, 2002; Castells, 2000, 2001; Kanter, 1991; Kobrin, 1997; Zuboff, 1988). Anyone who draws money from a bank or buys an airline ticket depends on a computer-based communication system. Because data can be processed instantaneously in any part of the world linked to such a system, there is no need for physical proximity among those involved. As a result, new technology has allowed

information and communication technology • Forms of technology based on information processing and requiring microelectronic circuitry.

many companies to "reengineer" their organizational structures. Such changes, while good for efficiency, can have negative as well as positive consequences for the individuals within the organization.

For example, one company found the sales of some of its products falling and needed to reduce costs. The traditional route would have been to lay off staff. Instead, the firm set up as independent consultants those who would have been laid off and established a computerized support network called Xanadu to provide basic office services to each of them working out of their homes. The company then bought back a substantial proportion of the former employees' working time for a number of years but also left them free to work for other clients. The idea was that the new arrangement would provide the corporation with access to the skills of its former employees but at a cheaper rate because it no longer provided office space or company benefits (pension, health insurance, and so on). The former employees, in turn, had the opportunity to build up their own businesses. Initially, at least, the arrangement has worked well for both parties. In such a scheme, though, the burden is on the former employees, because they have to compensate for the loss of benefits with new business.

This is just one example of how large organizations have become more decentralized and flexible (Burris, 1998). Another example is the rise of telecommuting. A good deal of office work can now be carried out by telecommuters using the Internet and other mobile technologies, such as cell phones, to work at home or somewhere other than their employer's primary office. The number of Americans working out of their home (or remote location other than the office) at least one day per month, not including self-employed or unpaid volunteers, was about 16 million in 2010. The number of workers who list their home as the primary place of work is 3.1 million people, or 2.5 percent of the workforce. It is estimated that 50 percent of American jobs are compatible with at least part-time work from home (Telework Research Network, 2012). Worldwide, about 17 percent of employees telecommute frequently, and 7 percent of those employees work from home every day (Ipsos/Reuters, 2012). Telecommuters in the United States are typically males from the Northeast and West who have college degrees and work in professional or managerial positions (Davis and Polonko, 2001; WorldatWork, 2009). To reduce costs and increase productivity, large firms may have set up information networks connecting employees who work from home with the main office. In 2009 the computer company Cisco released a study of its own employees, which found that telecommuting significantly increased productivity, work-life flexibility, and job satisfaction. The company reportedly accrued annual savings of $277 million in productivity by allowing employees to telecommute and telework. In addition to productivity gains, Cisco estimates that its telework and telecommuting policies have resulted in a reduction of the company's carbon footprint, saving approximately 47,320 metric tons of greenhouse gas emissions due to avoided travel (Cisco, 2009). It is estimated that if all the workers whose jobs are compatible with working at home could do so, the savings would total $900 billion and reduce the need for Persian Gulf oil imports by 46 percent (Telework Research Network, 2011).

One reason that telecommuting increases productivity is that it eliminates commuting time, thereby permitting greater concentration of energy on work. Hartig, Johansson, and Kylin (2003) found that telecommuters actually spend more time on paid work when working at home than their counterparts do when working in the office. Employers view these longer hours as a primary benefit of telecommuting (ITAC, 2004). However, these new work arrangements are not perfect. First, the employees lose the human side of work; computer terminals are no substitute for face-to-face interaction with colleagues and friends at work. Second, telecommuters experience isolation, distraction, and conflicting demands of work and home responsibilities (Ammons and Markham, 2004). In addition, female telecommuters face more stress from increased housework and child-care responsibilities (Ammons and Markham, 2004; Olson, 1989; Olson and Primps, 1984). On the plus side for telecommuters, management cannot easily monitor employees working off-site (Dimitrova, 2003; Kling, 1996). While this may create problems for employers, it allows employees greater flexibility in managing their nonwork roles, thus contributing to increased worker satisfaction (Davis and Polonko, 2001). According to surveys by *Computer World* (2002) magazine, in the information technology field, the possibility of telecommuting is significant in determining the desirability of a job. Telecommuting also creates new possibilities for older and disabled workers to remain independent, productive, and socially connected (Bricourt, 2004). Finally, telecommuting is contributing to new trends in housing and residential development as space for home offices becomes more of a priority. With people able to work at a distance from city centers, residential development no longer need be tied to commuting practices.

Although computerization has resulted in increased flexibility and a reduction in hierarchy, it has created a two-tier occupational structure composed of technical "experts" and less-skilled production or clerical workers. In these restructured organizations, jobs have been redefined more in terms of technical skill than rank or position. For "expert" professionals, traditional bureaucratic constraints are relaxed to allow for creativity and flexibility (Burris, 1993). Although professionals benefit from this expanded autonomy, computerization makes production and service workers more visible and vulnerable to supervision (Wellman et al., 1996; Zuboff, 1988). For instance, organizations can now monitor work patterns to the point where they can count the number of seconds per phone call or keystrokes per minute, which in turn can lead to higher levels of stress for employees.

Granted, workplace computerization does have some positive effects. It has made some of the mundane tasks of clerical jobs more interesting. It can also promote social networking (Wellman et al., 1996). Office computers can be used for recreation; private exchanges with coworkers, friends, or family; and work-related interaction. But in most workplaces, computerization benefits the professionals who possess the knowledge and expertise on how to gain from it. It has not brought commensurate improvements in the career opportunities or salaries of the average worker (Kling, 1996).

Can the Traditional Organization Survive?

Traditionally, identifying the boundaries of organizations has been fairly straightforward. Until recently, organizations were generally located in defined physical spaces, such as an office building, a suite of rooms, or, in the case of a hospital or university, a campus. In addition, the mission or tasks of an organization were usually clear cut. A central feature of bureaucracies, for example, was adherence to a defined set of responsibilities and procedures for carrying them out. Weber's bureaucracy was a self-contained unit that intersected with outside entities at limited and designated points.

We have already seen how the physical boundaries of organizations are being broken down by the capacity of information technology to transcend countries and time zones. The same process is affecting the work that organizations do and the way in which it is coordinated. Many organizations no longer operate as independent units. A growing number are finding that they run more effectively when they are part of a web of complex relationships with other organizations and companies. No longer is there a clear dividing line between the organization and outside groups. Globalization, information technology, and trends in occupational patterns mean that organizational boundaries are more open and fluid than they once were.

In *The Rise of the Network Society* (1996), Manuel Castells argues that the "network enterprise" is the organizational form best suited to a global, informational economy. By this he means that it is increasingly impossible for organizations (large corporations or small businesses) to survive if they are not part of a network. What enables networking to occur is the growth of information technology, whereby organizations around the world are able to enter into contact and coordinate joint activities through an electronic medium. Castells cites several examples of organizational networking that originated in diverse cultural and institutional contexts but nevertheless all represent "different dimensions of a fundamental process"—the disintegration of the traditional, rational bureaucracy.

An example of organizations as networks is the powerful alliances formed between top companies. Increasingly, the large corporation is less and less a big business and more an "enterprise web"—a central organization that links together smaller firms. IBM, for example, used to be a highly self-sufficient corporation, wary of partnerships with others. Yet in the 1980s and early 1990s, IBM joined with dozens of U.S.-based companies and more than 80 foreign-based firms to share strategic planning and cope with production problems.

Decentralization is another process that contributes to organizations functioning as networks. When change becomes more profound and more rapid, highly centralized Weberian-style bureaucracies are too cumbersome and too entrenched in their ways to cope. Stanley Davis (1988) argues that as business firms and other organizations come to be networks, they go through a process of decentralization by which power and responsibility are devolved downward throughout the organization, rather than remaining concentrated at the top.

Networked organizations offer at least two advantages over more bureaucratic ones: They can foster the flow of information, and they can enhance creativity. As we've seen, bureaucratic hierarchy can impede the flow of information: One must go through the proper channels, fill out the right forms, and avoid displeasing people in higher positions. These processes not only hinder the sharing of information but also stifle creative problem solving. In networked organizations, when a problem arises, instead of writing a memo to your boss and waiting for a reply, you can simply pick up the phone or dash off an e-mail to the person responsible for working out a solution. As a result, members of networked organizations learn more easily from one another than do bureaucrats. It is therefore easier to solve routine dilemmas and to develop innovative solutions to all types of problems (Hamel, 1991; Powell and Brantley, 1992; Powell, Koput, and Smith-Doerr, 1996).

CONCEPT CHECKS

1. How is technology and globalization transforming traditional organizations?
2. What is the difference between networked and bureaucratic organizations?

1 **Basic Concepts**

p. 135

2 **Theories of Groups, Organizations, and Networks**

p. 141

LEARNING OBJECTIVES

Learn the variety and characteristics of groups as well as the effect groups have on individual behavior. Know how to define an organization and understand how organizations developed over the last two centuries.

Learn Max Weber's theory of organizations and view of bureaucracy. Understand the importance of the physical setting of organizations and Michel Foucault's theory of surveillance. Understand the importance of social networks and the advantages they give some people.

TERMS TO KNOW

Social group • Social aggregate • Social category • Primary groups • Secondary groups • Organization • Formal organization • Networks

In-groups • Out-groups • Reference group • Dyad • Triad • Bureaucracy • Ideal type • Formal relations • Informal relations • Surveillance • Timetables

CONCEPT CHECKS

1. What is the difference between social aggregates and social groups? Give examples that illustrate this difference.
2. Describe the main characteristics of primary and secondary groups.
3. What role do organizations play in contemporary society?

1. When groups become large, why does their intensity decrease but their stability increase?
2. What does the term *bureaucracy* mean?
3. Describe five characteristics of an ideal type of bureaucracy.
4. According to Granovetter, what are the benefits of weak ties? Why?

1. According to George Simmel, what are the primary differences between dyads and triads? Explain, according to his theory, how the addition of a child would alter the relationship between a husband and wife. Does the theory fit this situation?

2. The advent of computers and the computerization of the workplace may change our organizations and relationships with coworkers. Explain how you see modern organizations changing with the adoption of newer information technologies.

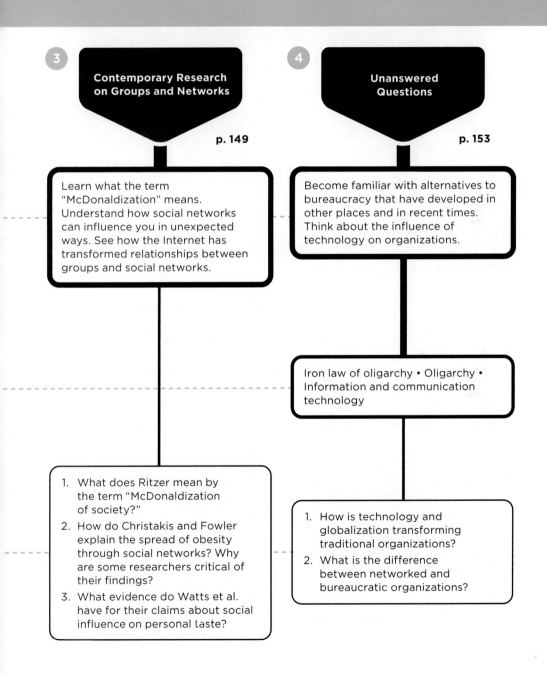

3

Contemporary Research on Groups and Networks

p. 149

Learn what the term "McDonaldization" means. Understand how social networks can influence you in unexpected ways. See how the Internet has transformed relationships between groups and social networks.

1. What does Ritzer mean by the term "McDonaldization of society?"
2. How do Christakis and Fowler explain the spread of obesity through social networks? Why are some researchers critical of their findings?
3. What evidence do Watts et al. have for their claims about social influence on personal taste?

4

Unanswered Questions

p. 153

Become familiar with alternatives to bureaucracy that have developed in other places and in recent times. Think about the influence of technology on organizations.

Iron law of oligarchy • Oligarchy • Information and communication technology

1. How is technology and globalization transforming traditional organizations?
2. What is the difference between networked and bureaucratic organizations?

Conformity, Deviance, and Crime

7

Homeless people, drug addicts, and gang members are individuals who:

a   follow no codes of social behavior.

b   are crazy.

c   follow strict codes of social behavior.

d   have no role in larger society.

Turn the page for the correct answer.

he three groups cited in the question just posed are generally regarded as social deviants—those who refuse to live by the rules the majority follows. Sometimes social deviants are violent criminals, vagrants, or down-and-outs who don't fit normal standards of acceptability. These are the cases that seem easy to identify, and indeed, if you chose answer *a* or *d*, you might think these individuals are asocial, totally divorced from society at large, or perhaps even biologically incapable of engaging with society (answer *b*).

We have learned in previous chapters that social life is governed by **norms** that define some kinds of behavior as appropriate in particular contexts and others as inappropriate. Norms are principles or rules people are expected to observe; they represent the dos and don'ts of society. Orderly behavior on the highway, for example, would be impossible if U.S. drivers didn't observe the rule of driving on the right. No deviants here, you might think, except for drunken or reckless drivers. If you did think this, you would be incorrect. When we drive, most of us are not merely deviants but criminals, for most of us regularly exceed the legal speed limit—assuming there isn't a police car in sight. In such cases, breaking the law is normal behavior!

We are all rule breakers as well as conformists. We are all also rule creators. Most American drivers may break the law on the freeways, but in fact they've evolved informal rules superimposed on the legal rules. When the legal speed limit is 65 mph, most drivers don't go above 75 mph or so, and they drive more slowly through urban areas.

As a result, when we study deviant behavior, we must consider which rules people are observing and which ones they are breaking. Nobody breaks all rules, just as no one conforms to all rules. Even someone who doesn't seem to be part

norms • Rules of conduct that specify appropriate behavior in a given range of social situations. A norm either prescribes a given type of behavior or forbids it. All human groups follow definite norms, which are always backed by sanctions of one kind or another, varying from informal disapproval to physical punishment.

LEARNING OBJECTIVES

① BASIC CONCEPTS

Learn how we define deviance and how it is related to social power and social class. See the ways in which conformity is encouraged.

② SOCIETY AND CRIME: SOCIOLOGICAL THEORIES

Know the leading sociological theories of crime and how each is useful in understanding deviance.

③ RESEARCH ON CRIME AND DEVIANCE TODAY

Recognize the helpfulness and limitations of crime statistics. Understand that some individuals or groups are more likely than others to commit or be the victims of crime. Familiarize yourself with some of the varieties of crime.

④ UNANSWERED QUESTIONS

Think about the best solutions to reduce crime. Consider the ways in which individuals and governments can address crime.

of respectable society, such as a drug dealer or gang member, is likely to follow many rules of the groups he belongs to. Indeed, some "deviant" groups such as the homeless have informal but strict codes of social behavior. As a result, answer *c* to the question just posed is correct: social deviants are *not* asocial beings; rather, they adhere to a set of norms that may or may not differ from the ones that you, or society at large, adhere to. These groups have different definitions of who is "deviant" and who is "conformist." As with society at large, those who deviate from these codes may be expelled from the group.

The study of deviant behavior reveals that none of us is as normal as we think. It also shows that people whose behavior appears incomprehensible or alien can be seen as rational beings when we understand why they act as they do.

The study of deviance directs our attention to social power and the influence of social class—the divisions between rich and poor. When we look at deviance from or conformity to social rules or norms, we always have to ask, Whose rules? As we shall see, social norms are strongly influenced by divisions of power and class.

THE ANSWER IS C.

BASIC CONCEPTS

What Is Deviance?

Deviance may be defined as nonconformity to a set of norms that are accepted by a significant number of people in a community or society. No society can be simply divided between those who deviate from norms and those who conform to them, because most people sometimes transgress generally accepted rules of behavior.

Norms and Sanctions

We follow social norms because, as a result of socialization, we are used to doing so. Individuals become committed to social norms through interactions with people who obey the law. Through these interactions, we learn self-control. The more numerous these interactions, the fewer opportunities there are to deviate from conventional norms. Over time, the longer we interact in conventional ways, the more we have at stake in continuing to act in those ways (Gottfredson and Hirschi, 1990).

All social norms carry sanctions that promote conformity and protect against nonconformity. A **sanction** is any reaction from others that is meant to ensure that a person or group complies with a given norm. Sanctions may be positive (the offering of rewards for conformity) or negative (punishment for behavior that does not conform). They can also be formal or informal. Formal sanctions are applied by a specific group or agency to ensure that a particular set of norms is followed. Informal sanctions are less organized and more spontaneous reactions to nonconformity, such as

deviance • Modes of action that do not conform to the norms or values held by most members of a group or society. What is regarded as deviant is as variable as the norms and values that distinguish different cultures and subcultures from one another. Forms of behavior that are highly esteemed by one group are regarded negatively by others.

sanction • A mode of reward or punishment that reinforces socially expected forms of behavior.

when a student's friends teasingly accuse him of working too hard or being a "nerd" if he spends an evening studying rather than going to a party.

Courts and prisons represent the main types of formal sanctions in modern societies. The police are charged with bringing offenders to trial and possibly to imprisonment. **Laws** are norms defined by governments as principles their citizens must follow; sanctions are used against people who do not conform to those principles. Where there are laws, there are also crimes, because crime constitutes any type of behavior that breaks a law.

It is important to recognize, however, that the law is only a guide to a society's norms.

CONCEPT CHECKS ✓

1. How do sociologists define deviance?

② SOCIETY AND CRIME: SOCIOLOGICAL THEORIES

Any satisfactory account of the nature of **crime** must be sociological, for what crime is depends on the social institutions of a society. Sociological thinking about crime especially emphasizes the interconnections between conformity and deviance in different social contexts (see Figure 7.1). Modern societies contain many subcultures, and behavior that conforms to the norms of one subculture may be regarded as deviant outside it; for instance, there may be strong pressure on a member of a boys' gang to prove himself by stealing a car. Moreover, wide divergences of wealth and power in society greatly influence criminal opportunities for different groups. Theft and burglary are carried out mainly by people from the poorer segments of the population; embezzling and tax evasion tend to be committed by persons in positions of affluence.

Functionalist Theories

Functionalist theories see crime and deviance resulting from structural tensions and a lack of moral regulation within society. If the aspirations of individuals and groups do not coincide with available rewards, the disparity between desires and fulfillment will be felt in the deviant motivations of some of the society's members.

Crime and Anomie: Durkheim and Merton

The notion of **anomie** was introduced by Émile Durkheim, who suggested that in modern societies traditional norms and standards become undermined without being replaced by new ones. Anomie exists when there are no clear standards to guide behavior in a given area of social life. Under such circumstances, Durkheim believed, people feel disoriented and anxious; anomie therefore heightens dispositions to suicide.

laws • Rules of behavior established by a political authority and backed by state power.

crime • Any actions that contravene the laws established by a political authority. Although we may think of criminals as a distinct subsection of the population, there are few people who have not broken the law in one way or another during their lives. While laws are formulated by state authorities, it is not unknown for those authorities to engage in criminal behavior in certain situations.

anomie • A concept first brought into wide usage in sociology by Durkheim, referring to a situation in which social norms lose their hold over individual behavior.

Durkheim saw crime and deviance as inevitable and necessary elements in modern societies. According to Durkheim, people in the modern age are less constrained than they were in traditional societies. Because there is more room for individual choice in the modern world, inevitably there will be some nonconformity. Durkheim recognized that no society would ever be in complete consensus about the norms and values that governed it.

Deviance is also necessary for society, according to Durkheim. First, deviance has an adaptive function: By introducing new ideas and social challenges, deviance brings about change. Second, deviance promotes boundary maintenance between "good" and "bad" behavior. A criminal event can provoke a collective response that heightens group solidarity and clarifies social norms. For example, residents of a neighborhood facing a problem with drug dealers might join together in the aftermath of a drug-related shooting and commit themselves to maintaining the area as a drug-free zone.

Durkheim's ideas on crime and deviance helped shift attention from individual explanations to social forces. His notion of anomie was applied by the American sociologist Robert K. Merton (1957), who located the source of crime within the very structure of American society.

Merton modified the concept of anomie to refer to the strain put on individuals' behavior when accepted norms conflict with social reality. In American society—and to some degree in other industrial societies—values emphasize material success through self-discipline and hard work. Accordingly, it is believed that people who work hard can succeed regardless of their starting point in life. This idea is not in fact valid, because most disadvantaged people have limited or no conventional opportunities for advancement. Yet those who do not "succeed" are condemned for their apparent inability to make material progress. Thus there is pressure to get ahead by any means, legitimate or illegitimate. According to Merton, then, deviance is a by-product of economic inequalities.

Merton split people into five possible types based on how they responded to the tensions between socially endorsed values and the limited means of achieving them: *Conformists* accept generally held values and the conventional means of realizing them, whether or not they meet with success (Figure 7.2). Most of the population falls into this category. *Innovators* accept socially approved values but use illegitimate or illegal means to follow them. Criminals who acquire wealth through illegal activities exemplify this type. *Ritualists* conform to socially accepted standards, though they have lost sight of their underlying values. They compulsively follow rules for their own sake. A ritualist might dedicate herself to a boring job, even though it has no career prospects and provides few rewards. *Retreatists* have abandoned the competitive outlook, rejecting both the dominant values and the approved means of achieving them. An example would be members of a self-supporting commune. Finally, *rebels* reject both the existing values and the means

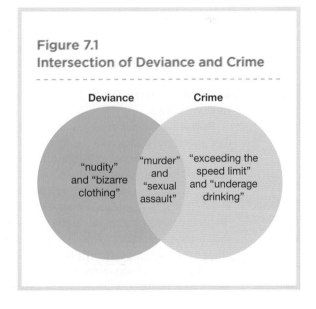

Figure 7.1
Intersection of Deviance and Crime

Deviance   Crime

"nudity" and "bizarre clothing"   "murder" and "sexual assault"   "exceeding the speed limit" and "underage drinking"

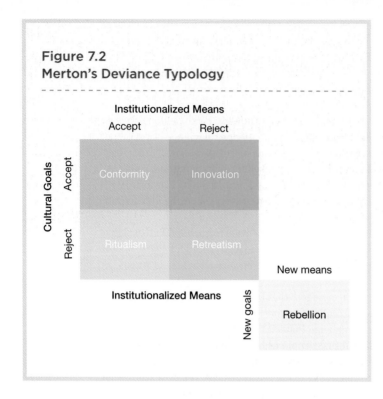

Figure 7.2
Merton's Deviance Typology

Institutionalized Means

	Accept	Reject
Cultural Goals Accept	Conformity	Innovation
Reject	Ritualism	Retreatism

Institutionalized Means

New means

New goals — Rebellion

of achieving them but work to substitute new ones and reconstruct the social system. The members of radical political groups fall into this category.

Merton's writings addressed one of the main puzzles in the study of criminology: At a time when society was becoming more affluent, why did crime rates continue to rise? By emphasizing the contrast between rising aspirations and persistent inequalities, Merton identified a sense of relative deprivation as an important element in deviant behavior.

SUBCULTURAL EXPLANATIONS

Later researchers examined subcultural groups that adopt norms that encourage or reward criminal behavior. Like Merton, Albert Cohen saw the contradictions within American society as the main cause of crime. But while Merton emphasized individual deviant responses, Cohen saw the responses occurring collectively through subcultures. In *Delinquent Boys* (1955), Cohen argues that frustrated boys in the lower working class often join delinquent subcultures, such as gangs. These subcultures replace middle-class values with norms that celebrate nonconformity and defiance, such as delinquency.

Richard A. Cloward and Lloyd E. Ohlin (1960) agree with Cohen that most delinquent youths emerge from the lower working class. But they argued that such gangs arise in subcultural communities where the chances of achieving success legitimately are slim, as among deprived ethnic minorities. Cloward and Ohlin's work emphasizes connections between conformity and deviance. Lack of opportunity for success as defined by the wider society is the differentiating factor between those who engage in criminal behavior and those who do not.

Research by sociologists has examined the validity of claims that immediate material deprivation can lead people to commit crimes. A survey of homeless youth in Canada, for instance, shows a strong correlation between hunger, lack of shelter, and unemployment on the one hand, and theft, prostitution, and violent crime on the other (Hagan and McCarthy, 1992).

Functionalist theories rightly emphasize connections between conformity and deviance in different social contexts. We should be cautious, however, about accepting the idea that people in poorer communities aspire to the same things as more affluent people. Most adjust their aspirations to the reality of their situation. Merton, Cohen, and Cloward and Ohlin can all be criticized for presuming that middle-class values are accepted throughout society. It would also be wrong to suppose that only the less privileged experience a mismatch of aspirations and opportunities. There are pressures toward criminal activity among other groups, too, as indicated by the white-collar crimes of embezzlement, fraud, and tax evasion, which we will study later.

Interactionist Theories

Sociologists studying crime and deviance in the interactionist tradition focus on deviance as a socially constructed phenomenon. Rejecting the idea that some types of conduct are inherently "deviant," they ask how behaviors get defined as deviant and why only certain groups get labeled as deviant.

According to interactionists, it's not the act of smoking marijuana that makes one a deviant, but the way others react to marijuana smoking.

LEARNED DEVIANCE: DIFFERENTIAL ASSOCIATION

In 1949, Edwin H. Sutherland advanced a notion that influenced much interactionist work: He linked crime to what he called **differential association**. In a society with a variety of subcultures, some social environments encourage illegal activities, whereas others do not. Individuals become delinquent through associating with people who follow criminal norms. According to Sutherland, criminal behavior is learned within primary groups, particularly peer groups. This theory contrasts with the view that psychological differences separate criminals from other people; it sees criminal activities as learned in the same way that law-abiding ones are, and as serving the same needs and values. Thieves, just like other people, try to make money; they simply do so illegally.

LABELING THEORY

One of the most important interactionist approaches to understanding criminality is **labeling theory**. It was originally associated with Howard S. Becker's (1963) studies of marijuana smokers. In the early 1960s, marijuana use was a marginal activity of subcultures rather than the mainstream lifestyle choice it is today (Hathaway, 1997). Becker found that becoming a marijuana smoker depended on one's acceptance by and close association with experienced users and on one's attitudes toward nonusers. Because labeling theorists such as Becker interpret deviance as a process of interaction between deviants and nondeviants, it is not the act of marijuana smoking that makes one a deviant but the way others react to it. Thus, in order to understand the nature of deviance itself, labeling theorists seek to discover why some people become labeled "deviant."

People who represent law and order or who impose definitions of morality on others do most of the labeling. Thus the rules by which deviance is defined express the power structure of society; such rules are framed by the wealthy for the poor,

differential association • An interpretation of the development of criminal behavior proposed by Edwin H. Sutherland, according to whom criminal behavior is learned through association with others who regularly engage in crime.

labeling theory • An approach to the study of deviance that suggests that people become "deviant" because certain labels are attached to their behavior by political authorities and others.

by men for women, by older people for younger people, and by ethnic majorities for minority groups. For example, many children wander into other people's gardens, steal fruit, or skip school. In an affluent neighborhood, parents, teachers, and police might regard such activities as relatively innocent. When they are committed by children in poor areas, they might be considered acts of juvenile delinquency.

Once a child is labeled a delinquent, teachers and prospective employers may consider him to be untrustworthy. The child then relapses into further criminal behavior, widening the gulf between himself and orthodox social conventions. Edwin Lemert (1972) called the initial act of transgression **primary deviation. Secondary deviation** occurs when the individual accepts the label and sees himself as deviant. One study examining self-appraisals of a random national sample of young men showed that such appraisals are strongly tied to higher levels of criminality (Matsueda, 1992).

Consider Luke, who smashes a shop window while out on the town with friends. The act may be called the accidental result of overly boisterous behavior, an excusable characteristic of young men. Luke might escape with a reprimand and a small fine—a likely result if he is from a respectable background and is seen as being of good character. The window smashing stays at the level of primary deviance. If, however, the police and courts hand out a suspended sentence and make Luke report to a social worker, the incident could become the first step on the road to secondary deviance. The process of "learning to be deviant" tends to be reinforced by the very organizations set up to correct deviant behavior: prisons and social agencies.

Labeling theory assumes that no act is intrinsically criminal but may become so through the formulation of laws and their interpretation by police, courts, and correctional institutions. Although some critics of labeling theory argue that certain acts—such as murder, rape, and robbery—are prohibited across all cultures, this view is surely incorrect; even within our own culture, killing is not always regarded as murder. In times of war, killing the enemy is approved, and until recently, the laws in most U.S. states did not recognize sexual intercourse forced on a woman by her husband as rape.

We can criticize labeling theory on more convincing grounds, though. First, labeling theorists neglect the processes that lead to acts being defined as deviant. Indeed, labeling certain activities as deviant is not arbitrary; differences in socialization, attitudes, and opportunities influence how far people engage in behavior likely to be labeled deviant. For instance, children from deprived backgrounds are more likely to steal from shops than are richer children. It is not the labeling that leads them to steal so much as their background.

Second, it is not clear whether labeling actually has the effect of increasing deviant conduct. Delinquent behavior tends to increase after a conviction, but is this the result of the labeling itself? Other factors, such as increased interaction with other delinquents or learning about new criminal opportunities, may be involved.

primary deviation • According to Edwin Lemert, the actions that cause others to label one as a deviant.

secondary deviation • According to Edwin Lemert, following the act of primary deviation, secondary deviation occurs when an individual accepts the label of deviant and acts accordingly.

conflict theory • Argument that deviance is deliberately chosen and often political in nature.

Conflict Theory

Conflict theory draws on elements of Marxist thought to argue that deviance is deliberate and often political. Conflict theorists deny that deviance is "determined" by factors such as biology, personality, anomie, social disorganization, and labels. Rather, they argue, individuals choose to engage in deviant behavior in response to the inequalities of the capitalist system. Thus members of countercultural groups regarded as deviant—such as supporters of the black power movement or gay liberation movement—are engaging in political acts that challenge the social order. Conflict theorists analyze crime and deviance in terms of the social structure and the preservation of power among the ruling class.

For example, they argue that laws serve the powerful to maintain their privileged positions. These theorists reject the idea that laws are applied evenly across the population. Instead, as inequalities increase between the ruling class and the working class, law becomes the key instrument for the powerful to maintain order. This dynamic is evident in the criminal justice system, which has become increasingly oppressive toward working-class offenders, or in tax legislation that disproportionately favors the wealthy. This power imbalance is not restricted to the creation of laws, however. The powerful also break laws, scholars argue, but are rarely caught. These crimes are much more significant than the everyday crime and delinquency that attract the most attention. But, fearful of the implications of pursuing white-collar criminals, law enforcement instead targets less powerful members of society, such as prostitutes, drug users, and petty thieves (Chambliss, 1988; Pearce, 1976).

These studies and others broadened the debate about crime and deviance to include questions about social justice, power, and politics. They emphasized that crime occurs in the context of inequalities and competing interests among social groups.

Control Theory

Control theory posits that crime results from an imbalance between impulses toward criminal activity and the social or physical controls that deter it. Control theory assumes that people act rationally and that, given the opportunity, everyone would engage in deviant acts. One of the best-known control theorists, Travis Hirschi, argues that humans are fundamentally selfish beings who make calculated decisions about whether to engage in criminal activity by weighing the benefits and risks. In *Causes of Delinquency* (1969), Hirschi identifies four types of bonds that link people to society and law-abiding behavior, thus maintaining social control and conformity: attachment, commitment, involvement, and belief. If these bonds are weak, delinquency and deviance may result. Hirschi's approach suggests that delinquents have low levels of self-control that result from inadequate socialization at home or at school (Gottfredson and Hirschi, 1990).

Some control theorists see the growth of crime as an outcome of the increasing number of opportunities and targets for crime in modern society. As the population grows more affluent and consumerism becomes more central, more people own goods such as televisions, video equipment, computers, cars, and designer clothing—favorite targets for thieves. Residential homes are increasingly empty during the daytime as more women work outside the home. Motivated offenders can select from a broad range of suitable targets.

Many official approaches to crime prevention in recent years have focused on limiting the opportunities for crime via target hardening—making it more difficult for crimes to occur by intervening in potential crime situations. Control theorists argue that rather than changing the criminal, the best policy is to take practical measures to control the criminal's ability to commit crime.

control theory • A theory that views crime as the outcome of an imbalance between impulses toward criminal activity and controls that deter it. Control theorists hold that criminals are rational beings who will act to maximize their own reward unless they are rendered unable to do so through either social or physical controls.

Target-hardening techniques and zero-tolerance policing have been successful at curtailing crime in some contexts, but these measures do not address the underlying causes of crime. The growing popularity of private security services, car alarms, house alarms, guard dogs, and gated communities suggests that segments of the population feel compelled to defend themselves against others. This tendency is occurring not only in the United States but also in countries such as South Africa, Brazil, and those of the former Soviet Union, where a fortress mentality has emerged among the privileged.

There is another unintended consequence of such policies: as popular crime targets are hardened, patterns of crime may simply shift from one domain to another. Target-hardening and zero-tolerance approaches may simply displace criminal offenses from better-protected areas to more vulnerable ones.

The Theory of Broken Windows

Target hardening and zero-tolerance policing are based on a theory known as broken windows (Wilson and Kelling, 1982), which arose from a study by the social psychologist Philip Zimbardo (1969). Zimbardo abandoned cars without license plates and with their hoods up in two social settings: the wealthy community of Palo Alto, California, and a poor neighborhood in the Bronx, New York. In both places, the cars were vandalized once passersby, regardless of class or race, sensed that the vehicles had been abandoned. Extrapolating from this study, Wilson and Kelling argued that any sign of social disorder in a community, even the appearance of a broken window, encourages more serious crime. One unrepaired broken window is a sign that no one cares, so breaking more windows—that is, committing more serious crimes—is a rational response by criminals to this situation of social disorder. Thus minor acts of deviance lead to a spiral of crime and social decay.

In the late 1980s and '90s, the broken windows theory underpinned policing strategies that aggressively focused on minor crimes such as traffic violations and drinking or using drugs in public. Studies have shown that proactive policing directed at maintaining public order can reduce the occurrence of more serious crimes such as robbery (Sampson and Cohen, 1988). However, one flaw in the broken windows theory is that it lacks a systematic definition of disorder, and thus the police can see almost anything as a sign of disorder and anyone as a threat. In fact, as crime rates fell throughout the 1990s, the number of complaints of police abuse and harassment went up, particularly by young, urban black men who fit the "profile" of a potential criminal.

Theoretical Conclusions

The contributions of the sociological theories of crime and deviance are twofold. First, these theories emphasize the continuities between criminal and respectable behavior and demonstrate that the contexts in which particular activities are seen as deviant and/or punishable by law vary widely. Second, all agree that context is important; whether someone engages in

CONCEPT CHECKS ✓

1. How do Merton's and Durkheim's definitions of anomie differ?
2. What is the core idea behind differential association theory?
3. What are two criticisms of labeling theory?
4. What are the root causes of crime, according to conflict theorists?
5. How does the theory of broken windows exemplify the core ideas of control theory?

a criminal act or comes to be regarded as a criminal is influenced by social learning and social surroundings.

In spite of its deficiencies, labeling theory is perhaps the most widely used approach to understanding crime and deviant behavior. It explains how some activities become defined in law as punishable, the power relations that form such definitions, and the circumstances in which particular individuals fall afoul of the law.

The way in which crime is understood affects the policies developed to combat it. For example, if crime is seen as the product of deprivation or social disorganization, policies might be aimed at reducing poverty and strengthening social services. If criminality is seen as freely chosen, attempts to counter it will take a different form.

③ RESEARCH ON CRIME AND DEVIANCE TODAY

"Defining Deviancy Down"

Many people assume that a well-structured society is designed to prevent deviant behavior. But Émile Durkheim argued otherwise. He believed that deviance is important in a well-ordered society, because by defining what is deviant we become aware of the standards we share as members of a society. Thus we should aim not to completely eliminate deviance but to keep it within acceptable limits.

Seventy years after Durkheim's work appeared, the sociologist Kai Erikson published *Wayward Puritans*, a study of deviance in seventeenth-century New England. Erikson (1966) sought "to test [Durkheim's] notion that the number of deviant offenders a community can afford to recognize is likely to remain stable over time." His research led him to conclude that a community's capacity for dealing with deviance could be approximated by counting its prison cells, hospital beds, policemen, psychiatrists, courts, and clinics. Agencies assigned the task of controlling society often saw their job as keeping deviance in check as opposed to eliminating it altogether. In addition, Erikson hypothesized that societies needed their quotas of deviance and functioned in such a way as to keep those quotas intact.

What does a society do when the level of deviant behavior gets out of hand? In a controversial 1993 article, "Defining Deviancy Down," former New York senator Daniel Patrick Moynihan argued that levels of deviance in American society had increased so much that the concept needed to be redefined in order to exempt previously stigmatized conduct and raise some behavior previously considered abnormal to a "normal" level. Moynihan cites the deinstitutionalization movement in the mental health profession that began in the 1950s. Instead of being forced into institutions, the mentally ill began to be treated with tranquilizers and released. As a result, the number of psychiatric patients in New York dropped from 93,000 in 1955 to 1,000 by 1992.

What happened to all those psychiatric patients? Many of them are the homeless who today sleep in doorways. According to Moynihan, people sleeping on the street are defined not as insane but as lacking affordable housing. At the same time, the normal acceptable level of crime has risen. Moynihan pointed out that whereas in 1929 the nation was outraged at the murder of seven gangsters in one day, by 1993 violent gang murders were so common that there was hardly any public reaction. Moynihan also saw the underreporting of crime as another form of normalizing it. As he concluded, "We are getting used to a lot of behavior that is not good for us."

Reporting on Crime and Crime Statistics

Does American society *really* have more crime than other societies? Most TV and newspaper reporting is based on official crime statistics collected by the police and published by the government. But many crimes—possibly half of all serious crimes, such as robbery with violence—are never reported to the police. The proportion of less serious crimes that go unreported, especially small thefts, is even higher. Since 1973 the U.S. Bureau of the Census has been interviewing households across the country in its National Crime Victimization Survey, which confirms that the *overall* rate of crime is higher than the index of *reported* crime. For instance, in 2004 only 50 percent of violent crime was reported, including just 36 percent of rapes, 61 percent of robberies, 45 percent of simple assaults, and 53 percent of burglaries. Auto theft is the crime most frequently reported to the police (85 percent) (Catalano, 2005).

Public concern in the United States focuses on crimes of violence—murder, assault, and rape—even though only 13.4 percent of all crimes are violent (Figure 7.3). In the United States, the most common victims of murder and other violent crimes (with the exception of rape) are young, poor African American men in the larger cities. The rate of murder among black male teenagers is more than five times the rate for their white counterparts, although this disparity has declined in recent years. In general, whether indexed by police statistics

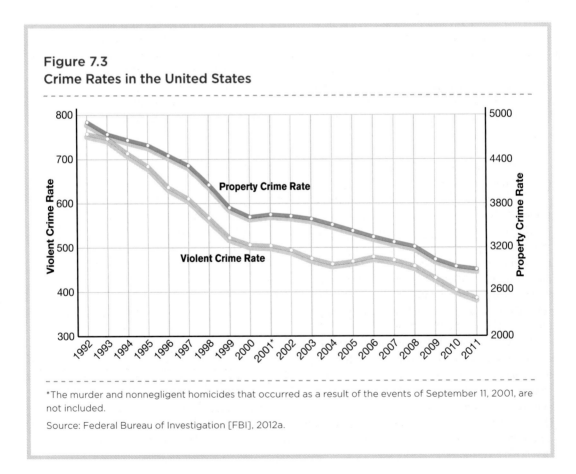

Figure 7.3
Crime Rates in the United States

*The murder and nonnegligent homicides that occurred as a result of the events of September 11, 2001, are not included.

Source: Federal Bureau of Investigation [FBI], 2012a.

or by the National Crime Victimization Survey, violent crimes, such as burglary and car theft, are more common in cities than in suburbs, and more common in suburbs than in smaller towns. The most likely explanation for the overall high level of violent crime in the United States is a combination of the availability of firearms, the general influence of the frontier tradition, and the subcultures of violence in the large cities.

In the 1990s the overall U.S. crime rate dropped to its lowest levels since 1973, when the victimization survey was first used. Rates of violent crime dropped substantially: murders by 31 percent and robberies by 32 percent. There is no prevailing explanation among sociologists for this decline. Aggressive efforts by local police to stop the use of guns contributed to the decrease in homicides, but other social factors were also at work, including the declining market for crack cocaine and the stigmatization of crack among young urban dwellers. Another factor was the booming economy of the 1990s, which provided job opportunities for those who may otherwise have worked in the drug trade (Butterfield, 1998).

A notable feature of most crimes of violence is their mundane character. Most assaults and homicides bear little resemblance to the murderous, random acts of gunmen or the carefully planned homicides highlighted in the media. Murders generally happen in the context of family and other interpersonal relationships; the victim usually knows the murderer.

Victims and Perpetrators of Crime

Are some individuals or groups more likely to commit crimes or to become the victims of crime? Criminologists say yes—research and crime statistics show that crime and victimization are not randomly distributed among the population. Men are more likely than women, for example, to commit crimes; the young are more often involved than older people.

The likelihood of someone becoming a victim of crime is linked to the area where she lives. Inner-city residents run a much greater risk of becoming victims than do residents of affluent suburban areas. The fact that ethnic minorities are concentrated in inner-city regions appears to be a significant factor in their higher rates of victimization.

GENDER AND CRIME

Like other areas of sociology, criminological studies have traditionally ignored half the population: Women are largely invisible in both theoretical considerations and empirical studies. Since the 1970s, important feminist works have noted the way in which criminal transgressions by women occur in different contexts from those by men and how women's experiences with the criminal justice

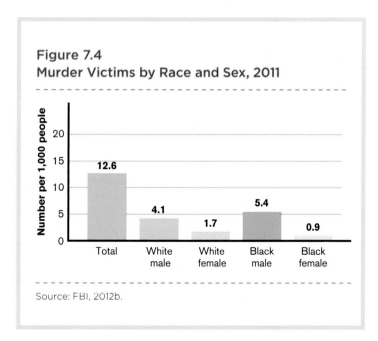

Figure 7.4
Murder Victims by Race and Sex, 2011

Number per 1,000 people

Total	12.6
White male	4.1
White female	1.7
Black male	5.4
Black female	0.9

Source: FBI, 2012b.

system are influenced by assumptions about appropriate male and female roles. Feminists have also highlighted the prevalence of violence against women, both at home and in public.

Male and Female Crime Rates The statistics on gender and crime are startling. For example, of all crimes reported in 2011, an overwhelming 74.1 percent of arrestees were men (FBI, 2012c). There is also an enormous imbalance in the ratio of men to women in prison, not only in the United States but in all the industrialized countries. Women made up just under 7 percent of the U.S. prison population in 2010 (U.S. Bureau of Justice Statistics [BJS], 2012). There are also contrasts between the types of crimes men and women commit. Women's offenses rarely involve violence and are almost all small scale. Petty thefts such as shoplifting and public order offenses such as prostitution and public drunkenness are typical female crimes.

Perhaps the real gender difference in crime rates is smaller than the official statistics show. In the 1950s, Otto Pollak suggested that certain crimes perpetrated by women go unreported because women's domestic role enables them to commit crimes at home and in the private sphere. Pollak regarded women as naturally deceitful and highly skilled at covering up their crimes. He claimed this was grounded in biology, as women had learned to hide the pain and discomfort of menstruation from men and were able to fake interest in sexual intercourse in a way that men could not! Pollak (1950) also argued that female offenders are treated more leniently because male police officers adopt a "chivalrous" attitude toward them.

Pollak's portrayal of women as conniving and deceptive is based in groundless stereotypes, yet the suggestion that the criminal justice system treats them more leniently has prompted much debate. The *chivalry thesis* has been applied in two ways. First, police and other officials may indeed regard female offenders as less dangerous than men and excuse activities for which males would be arrested. Second, in sentencing for criminal offenses, women get sent to prison much less often than men. A number of empirical studies have tested the chivalry thesis, but the results remain inconclusive. One difficulty is assessing the relative influence of gender compared with other factors such as age, class, and race. For example, older women offenders tend to be treated less aggressively than their male counterparts. Other studies have shown that black women receive worse treatment than white women at the hands of the police.

Another perspective, which feminists have adopted, examines how social understandings about femininity affect women's experiences in the criminal justice system. One argument is that women receive harsher treatment when they have allegedly deviated from the norms of female sexuality. For example, young girls who are perceived to be sexually promiscuous are more often taken into custody than boys. Such young women are seen as doubly deviant—not only breaking the law but also flouting appropriate female behavior. In such cases, they are judged less on the nature of the offense and more on their deviant lifestyle. Thus the criminal justice system operates under a double standard, considering male aggression and violence as natural but female offenses as reflecting psychological imbalances (Heidensohn, 1985).

To make female crime more visible, feminists have conducted detailed investigations on female criminals—from girl gangs to female terrorists to women in prison. Such studies have shown that violence is not exclusively a characteristic of male criminality. Women are much less likely than men to participate in violent crime but are not always inhibited from doing so. Why, then, are female rates of criminality so much lower than those of men?

Some evidence shows that female lawbreakers often avoid coming before the courts because they persuade the police or other authorities to see their actions in a particular light. They invoke the *gender contract*—the implicit contract between men and women whereby to be a woman is to be erratic and impulsive on the one hand and in need of protection on the other (Worrall, 1990).

Yet differential treatment cannot account for the vast difference between male and female rates of crime. The reasons are probably the same as those that explain gender differences in other spheres: Male crimes remain "male" because of differences in socialization and because men's activities are still more nondomestic than those of most women.

Ever since the late nineteenth century, criminologists have predicted that gender equality would reduce or eliminate the differences in criminality between men and women, but as yet, crime remains a gendered phenomenon.

Crimes against Women In certain categories of crime—domestic violence, sexual harassment, sexual assault, and rape—men are overwhelmingly the aggressors and women the victims. Although each of these has been practiced by women against men, they remain almost exclusively crimes against women. It is estimated that one-quarter of women are victims of violence at some point, but all women face the threat of such crimes either directly or indirectly.

The Gulabi Gang, also known as the Pink Vigilantes, fights against police corruption, domestic violence, and sexual abuse by physically attacking police men who refuse to register rape cases and husbands who hit their wives. The group is comprised of some of India's poorest women from the lowest castes.

For many years these offenses were ignored by the criminal justice system; victims had to persevere tirelessly to gain legal recourse. Even today, the prosecution of crimes against women is hardly straightforward. Yet feminist criminology has raised awareness of crimes against women and integrated such offenses into mainstream debates on crime. In this section we examine the crime of rape, leaving discussions of domestic violence and sexual harassment to other chapters (see Chapters 10 and 15).

The extent of rape is very difficult to assess accurately. Only a small proportion of rapes comes to the attention of the police and is recorded in the statistics. In 2005, 127,430 cases of rape or attempted rape and 61,530 cases of sexual assault were reported. However, from surveys of victims, we know that only about 38 percent of rapes are reported to the police (BJS, 2005b). At the same time, data from a nationally representative survey indicates that 1 in 6 women and 1 in 33 men in the United States have been victims of a completed or attempted rape (Tjaden and Thoennes, 2010). There are many reasons that a woman might not report sexual violence. The majority of rape victims either wish to put the incident out of their minds or are unwilling to participate in the humiliating process of medical examination, police interrogation, and courtroom cross-examination. The legal process takes a long time and can be intimidating. Courtroom procedure is public, and the victim must face the accused. Proof of penetration, the identity of the rapist, and the fact that the act occurred without the woman's consent all have to be forthcoming. A woman may feel that *she* is the one on trial, particularly if her own sexual history is examined publicly, as is often the case.

Recently, women's groups have sought change in both legal and public thinking about rape, stressing that rape should not be seen as a sexual offense but as a violent crime. It is not just a physical attack but an assault on an individual's integrity and dignity. Rape is clearly related to the association of masculinity with power, dominance, and toughness. It is not primarily the result of overwhelming sexual desire but of the ties between sexuality and feelings of power and superiority. The sexual act itself is less significant than the debasement of the woman (Estrich, 1987). This campaign has managed to change legislation, and rape is today generally recognized in law as a type of criminal violence.

In a sense, all women are victims of rape. Women who have never been raped may be afraid to go out alone at night, even on crowded streets, and may be almost equally fearful of being alone in a house or apartment. Susan Brownmiller (1975) has argued that rape is part of a system of male intimidation that keeps all women in fear. Those who are not raped are affected by the anxieties thus provoked and by the need to be more cautious in everyday aspects of life than men have to be.

CRIMES AGAINST GAYS AND LESBIANS

Feminists claim that understandings of violence are highly gendered and are influenced by perceptions about risk and responsibility. Because women are considered less able to defend themselves, common sense holds that they should modify *their* behavior to reduce the risk of victimhood. For example, not only should women avoid walking in unsafe neighborhoods alone and at night but they also should not dress provocatively or behave in a manner that could be misinterpreted. Women who fail to do so can be accused of "asking for trouble." In a court setting, their behavior can be a mitigating factor in considering the perpetrator's act of violence (Dobash and Dobash, 1992; Richardson and May, 1999). It has been suggested that a similar logic applies in violent acts against gay men and lesbians.

Victimization studies reveal that homosexuals experience a high incidence of violent crime and harassment. Data collected for the 2011 Hate Crime Statistics (FBI, 2011) suggests that in that year, there were 1,293 anti-GLBT incidents affecting 1,572 victims. A national survey of more than 4,000 gay men and women found that in the previous five years, one-third of gay men and one-quarter of lesbians had been the victim of at least one violent attack. One-third had experienced some form of harassment, including threats or vandalism. Fully 75 percent had been verbally abused in public (Mason and Palmer, 1996).

Because sexual minorities remain stigmatized and marginalized in many societies, they are more often treated as deserving of crime rather than as innocent victims. Homosexual relationships are still seen as belonging to the private realm, whereas heterosexuality is the norm in public spaces. Lesbians and gay men who display their homosexual identities in public are often blamed for making themselves vulnerable to crime, in a sense even provoking it. This notion ultimately denies both the essential personhood and rights of the victim. Such crimes have led many social groups to call for hate crime legislation to protect the human rights of groups who remain stigmatized.

CRIMES OF THE POWERFUL

Although there are connections between crime and poverty, it would be a mistake to suppose that crime is concentrated among the poor. Crimes by people in positions of power and wealth can have farther-reaching consequences than the often petty crimes of the poor.

The term **white-collar crime**, introduced by Edwin Sutherland (1949), refers to crime by affluent people. This category of criminal activity includes tax fraud, antitrust violations, illegal sales practices, securities and land fraud, embezzlement, the manufacture or sale of dangerous products, and illegal environmental pollution, as well as straightforward theft. The distribution of white-collar crimes is even harder to measure than that of other types of crime; most do not appear in the official statistics at all.

Efforts to detect white-collar crime are limited, and rarely do those who are caught go to jail. Although the authorities regard white-collar crime more tolerantly than crimes of the less privileged, the amount of money involved in white-collar crime in the United States is 40 times greater than the amount involved in crimes against property, such as robberies, burglaries, larceny, forgeries, and car thefts (President's Commission on Organized Crime, 1986). Some forms of white-collar crime, moreover, affect more people than lower-class criminality does. An embezzler might rob thousands—or today, via computer fraud, millions—of people.

Corporate Crime **Corporate crime** describes the offenses committed by large corporations. Pollution, product mislabeling, and violations of health and safety regulations affect much larger numbers of people than does petty criminality. The increasing power and influence of large corporations and their global reach mean that they touch our lives in many ways—from producing the cars we drive and the food we eat to affecting the natural environment and the financial markets.

Quantitative and qualitative studies of corporate crime have concluded that many corpora-

white-collar crime • Criminal activities carried out by those in white-collar, or professional, jobs.

corporate crime • Offenses committed by large corporations in society. Examples of corporate crime include pollution, false advertising, and violations of health and safety regulations.

One of the most high-profile white-collar criminals in recent memory is Bernie Madoff, a financier who choreographed a $50 million Ponzi scheme to defraud thousands of people and organizations.

tions do not adhere to legal regulations (Slapper and Tombs, 1999). Corporate crime is pervasive and widespread. Studies have revealed six types of violations: *administrative* (paperwork or noncompliance), *environmental* (pollution, permit violations), *financial* (tax violations, illegal payments), *labor* (working conditions, hiring practices), *manufacturing* (product safety, labeling), and *unfair trade practices* (anticompetition, false advertising).

Sometimes there are obvious victims, as in environmental disasters such as the 2010 Upper Big Branch coal mine explosion in West Virginia and the health dangers posed to women by silicone breast implants. The most famous recent case of white-collar crime with obvious victims was the Bernard Madoff scandal, in which Madoff turned his wealth management business into the largest Ponzi scheme in history, defrauding his victims of billions of dollars. The victims included pension holders, employees, and investors. Recently those injured in car crashes or relatives of those who were killed have called for the executives of car manufacturers to be brought to trial when the companies have shown negligence. But very often victims of corporate crime do not see themselves as such. Distances in time and space mean that victims may not realize they have been victimized or may not know how to seek redress.

The effects of corporate crime are often experienced unevenly within society. Those who are disadvantaged by other socioeconomic inequalities suffer disproportionately. For example, safety and health risks in the workplace tend to occur in low-paying occupations. Many of the risks from healthcare products and pharmaceuticals have affected women more than men, as in the case of contraceptives and fertility treatments with harmful side effects (Slapper and Tombs, 1999).

Violent aspects of corporate crime are less visible, but they are just as real—and may have much more serious consequences. For example, the flouting of regulations regarding the preparation of new drugs, safety in the workplace, or pollution may cause physical harm or death to large numbers of people. Deaths from hazards at work far outnumber murders, although precise statistics about job accidents are difficult to obtain. Of course, we cannot assume that all, or even the majority, of these deaths and injuries are the result of employer negligence in relation to safety factors for which the employers are legally liable. Nevertheless, there is some basis for supposing that many involve the neglect of legally binding safety regulations by employers or managers.

CYBERCRIME

It seems certain that the information and telecommunications revolution will change the face of crime. In 2007 a survey of computer security practitioners conducted by the FBI found that nearly 46 percent of companies experienced a security incident related to their computer systems and that **cybercrime** cost almost $67 million to American businesses (Computer Security Institute, 2007). Yet only 29 percent of security violations were reported to the police out of fears that negative publicity would damage the company's stock price or that competitors would steal valuable information. A similar survey in the United Kingdom reported that 89 percent of respondents had experienced unauthorized access to their firm's computer networks and that computer crime cost those businesses over £2.4 billion in 2004 (National High-Tech Crime Unit, 2005). Internet-based fraud is one of the fastest-growing categories of crime in the United States. The FBI now ranks cybercrime as the third-greatest threat to U.S. national security, after nuclear war and other weapons of mass destruction (PBS *NewsHour*, 2009).

cybercrime • Criminal activities by means of electronic networks or involving the use of information technologies. Electronic money laundering, personal identity theft, electronic vandalism, and monitoring electronic correspondence are all emergent forms of cybercrime.

The global reach of telecommunications crime poses challenges for law enforcement in terms of detecting and prosecuting crimes. Police from the countries involved must determine the jurisdiction in which the act occurred and agree on extraditing the offenders and providing evidence for prosecution. Although police cooperation across national borders may improve with the growth of cybercrime, at present, cybercriminals have a great deal of room to maneuver.

At a time when financial, commercial, and production systems in countries worldwide are being integrated electronically, rising levels of Internet fraud and unauthorized electronic intrusions are potent warnings of the vulnerability of computer security systems. From the FBI to the Japanese government's antihacker police force, governments are scrambling to contend with new and elusive forms of cross-national computer activity.

SOCIAL DEVIANTS "ON THE RUN"

Today, the prison population in the United States is larger than at any time in the nation's history. The number of people with convictions for felonies is therefore at an all-time high. One of the things that this statistic does not reveal is the massive number of people who live their lives trying to avoid being picked up for various offenses.

In her article "On the Run" (see Chapter 2), Alice Goffman sheds new light on the struggles of men who were "dipping and dodging" the police, worrying that any encounter would result in their imprisonment. She shows that, for these men, activities, relations, and localities that others rely on to maintain a decent and respectable identity are transformed into a system the authorities make use of to locate, arrest, and confine them. The police and the courts become dangerous to interact with, as does showing up to work or going to places such as hospitals. Instead of a safe place to sleep, eat, and find acceptance and support, their mother's home is transformed into a "last known address," one of the first places the police will look for them. Close relatives, friends, and neighbors become potential informants.

Goffman argues that issuing warrants on a large scale for low-level violations leads men to live anguished existences caused by their need to resort to extreme secrecy and dangerous activities. Her study argues that assigning fugitive status to large numbers of poor black men rolls back the gains in citizenship that African Americans made through the civil rights movement, and deprives them of basic rights to family, employment, and safety from harm.

In looking at the ways in which the police use a hospital as a key site to make arrests, Goffman shows how society works in ways that differ from traditional expectations. While many of us think of going to the doctor as a routine occurrence, poor black men in Philadelphia neighborhoods find that it is fraught with risk; if they seek medical care, they are likely to be stopped and searched, and have their names run in a police database. What some take to be natural and normal (a routine doctor's visit) is actually socially constructed (see Chapter 1), differing in its meaning depending on who is walking through the doors.

Goffman found that those with close contact to wanted men are under considerable pressure from the police to act as informants, and that this, too, leads wanted men to be secretive and unpredictable, so that their friends and relatives are not able to notify the authorities of their whereabouts.

Goffman found that men often gave their wanted status as an explanation for their inability to find jobs, use banks, seek medical care, call the police, or attend family functions. Goffman wanted to know how much of the young men's behavior was attributable to the warrants and how much would have occurred even without them. To answer this question, Goffman compared what young men said to what they did. She found that while nearly all the men justified their behavior on the basis of their legal entanglements, only a few in fact attempted to get a job, secure a bank account, seek medical care, or see their children regularly when they were not wanted by the police. Goffman thus learned that a warrant was both a constraining condition and an excuse for a variety of failures that may have occurred for other reasons.

GANGS AND LEADERS OF GANGS

Sudhir Venkatesh's *Gang Leader for a Day* is a memoir of a sociologist's experiences studying the inner city through firsthand observation. Venkatesh is a man of Indian descent who grew up in the lily-white San Diego suburbs before attending graduate school at the University of Chicago. It was there that he had his initial encounters with urban poverty. Under the direction of the eminent sociologist William Julius Wilson, he was sent to housing projects to ask residents, "How does it feel to be black and poor?"

When he approached one group of young men, they thought his question was naïve and offensive. Venkatesh did not know what he had gotten himself into. He ended up getting kidnapped by the men, who turned out to be members of the Black Kings, a drug-dealing gang. Having never encountered a South Asian, some of them thought he was a Mexican gang member, and they held him hostage for what might have been the longest 24 hours of his life.

The gang's leader, J.T., finally ordered his subordinates to release Venkatesh. "Go back to where you came from," he told him, "and be more careful when you walk around the city." Then, as the sociologist began packing his belongings, J.T. told him, "You shouldn't go around asking them silly-ass questions. With people like us, you should hang out, get to know what they do, how they do it. . . . You need to understand how young people live on the streets."

Without knowing it, what J.T. was suggesting to Venkatesh was a method that actually had a very long history at the University of Chicago, where the field of sociology was founded on the basis of studying people firsthand by, for example, "hanging out" with them. (This method, known as ethnography, was discussed in Chapter 2.) Over the previous century, dozens of books had been written about communities all over the city based on participating in and observing everyday life.

Venkatesh was about to become part of that tradition, known as the Chicago School of sociology. He took J.T. up on his offer. In exchange, J.T. offered Venkatesh the protection he would need for this endeavor, and so invited him to come back again and become an observer of the gang's affairs. Thus began Venkatesh's immersion in the everyday life of a criminal gang in the Robert Taylor housing projects, one of the most impoverished and notorious communities in the United States.

deviant subcultures • Subcultures whose members hold values that differ substantially from those of the majority.

Venkatesh's research revealed the corporate structure of the gang. Over time, he so won the trust of J.T. that he was given access to all the gang's receipts and finances. The books showed that the gang operated just like many other "legitimate" businesses. They also revealed how little money the average drug dealer made—so little, in fact, that frequently drug dealers still lived with their mothers. Venkatesh came to see the drug dealers as people with aspirations similar to many middle-class people who go into business, but without the requisite opportunities to succeed in the formal economy. In fact, many of the people Venkatesh introduced in the book were quite intelligent but had been held back from succeeding in school by some combination of social circumstances and personal failures.

There is a long-standing tradition of research in sociology on criminals and the underworld. When scholars immerse themselves in **deviant subcultures**, they are often exposed to the ugly realities of this lawless world. There are times they wish they were not present. Venkatesh ended up witnessing a great deal of illegal activity, and sometimes the boundary between witnessing and participating could not be easily drawn. For example, on one occasion J.T. beat up a crackhead who had abused a woman in the projects. Venkatesh got so swept up in the emotion of the moment that he found himself kicking the person as well.

Venkatesh's fieldwork was conducted right before universities began tightly regulating research conducted by their professors. Today, committees for the protection of human subjects mandate that participants in studies such as Venkatesh's sign off on forms that explain the possible risks of participating in them.

It is harder to conduct this kind of study today because it would be very difficult to go up to subjects and ask them to sign a form in advance of getting to know them. Why would any gang member sign a legal contract giving permission to a researcher to study him, especially when the researcher could be an undercover cop? But although studies of deviants and criminals are likely to be more difficult in the future as a result of such regulations, they will not disappear. Sociologists such as Venkatesh, who are committed to immersing themselves in the underworld, will nevertheless find ways to gain access and bring back news about how that world works.

CONCEPT CHECKS

1. What are the main sources of crime data in the United States?
2. Describe crime trends in the 1970s through today.
3. How would sociologists explain the high rate of violent crime in the United States?
4. Contrast the following two explanations for the gender gap in crime: behavioral differences and biases in reporting.
5. What are some consequences of white-collar crime?

④ UNANSWERED QUESTIONS

Are Prisons the Answer?

Although, as measured by police statistics (problematic, as we have seen), rates of violent crime have declined since 1990, many people in the United States view crime as their most serious social concern. Americans favor tougher prison sentences for all but relatively minor crimes. The price of imprisonment, however, is enormous; it costs an average of $29,000 to keep a prisoner in the federal prison system for one year (Palazzolo, 2013). Moreover, even if the prison system were expanded, it wouldn't significantly reduce the level of serious crime. Only about one-fifth of all serious crime known to the police results in arrest, and no more than half of those arrests result in conviction. Even so, America's prisons are so overcrowded (Figure 7.5) that the average convict serves only a third of his sentence.

The United States already locks up more people (nearly all men) per capita than any other country, and has by far the most punitive justice system in the world. More than 2.2 million people are presently incarcerated in American prisons, with another 4.6 million falling under the jurisdiction of the penal system (U.S. Department of Justice, 2011; McDonough, 2005; Slevin, 2005). Although the United States makes up only 4.5 percent of the world's overall population, it accounts for 23 percent of the world's prisoners (International Centre for Prison Studies, 2007).

The American prison system employs more than 750,000 people (Slevin, 2005) and costs nearly $200 billion annually to maintain (BJS, 2005c). It has also become partially

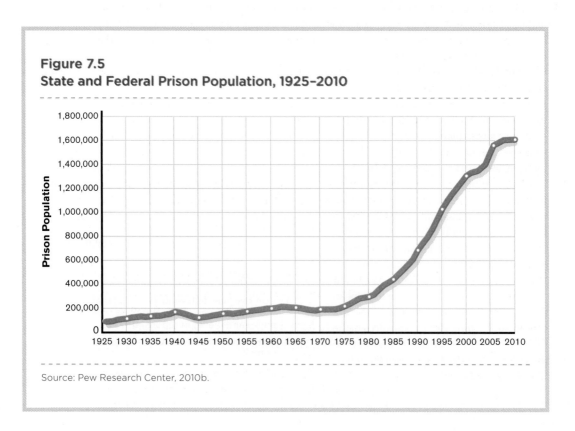

Figure 7.5
State and Federal Prison Population, 1925–2010

Source: Pew Research Center, 2010b.

privatized, with private companies building and administering prisons to accommodate the growing inmate population. Critics claim that a "prison-industrial complex" has emerged. Large numbers of people—including bureaucrats, politicians, and prison employees—have vested interests in the existence and further expansion of the prison system.

Support for capital punishment (the death penalty) is high in the United States. In 2011, approximately 62 percent of adults surveyed said they believed in capital punishment; 31 percent opposed it (Pew Research Center for the People and the Press, 2012a). This represents a significant shift from 1965, when 38 percent of those surveyed supported the death penalty and 47 percent were opposed. However, given the choice between the death penalty and life imprisonment, the share of those supporting the death penalty falls to 50 percent (ABC News/Washington Post Poll, 2006). The number of individuals awaiting execution has climbed steadily since 1977, when the Supreme Court upheld state capital punishment laws. Since that time there have been 1,307 executions in the United States (Death Penalty Information Center, 2012). Nearly two-thirds of these executions have taken place in five states: Texas (486), Virginia (109), Oklahoma (100), Missouri (68), and Florida (73). At the end of 2012, a total of 3,170 prisoners were held on death row. The group was 98 percent men, 43 percent white, 42 percent black, and 12 percent Latino. In 1995 there were 312 death sentences. Death sentences have been declining yearly to today. In 2011 there were 78 death sentences (Death Penalty Information Center, 2012).

More than one-quarter of African American men are either in prison or under the control of the penal system. In some major urban areas, counting those currently in prison, more than half of working-age African American men have criminal records (Alexander, 2011).

There is little evidence to support the view that imprisoning large numbers of people or stiffening sentences deters individuals from committing crimes. In fact, sociological studies have demonstrated that prisons often make offenders more hardened criminals. The harsher and more oppressive prison conditions are, the more likely it is that inmates will be brutalized by the experience. Yet if prisons were attractive and pleasant places to live, would they have a deterrent effect?

Although prisons do keep some dangerous men (and a tiny minority of dangerous women) off the streets, evidence suggests a need for other means to deter crime. Robert Gangi, director of the Correctional Association of New York, says that "building more prisons to address crime is like building more graveyards to address a fatal disease" (quoted in Smolowe, 1994). A sociological interpretation of crime makes clear that there are no quick fixes. The causes of crime, especially crimes of violence, are bound up with structural conditions of American society, including widespread poverty, the condition of the inner cities, and the deteriorating life circumstances of many young men.

Situational Crime Prevention

"Situational" crime prevention—such as target hardening and surveillance systems—has become a popular approach. Policy makers often favor such techniques because they are relatively simple to introduce alongside existing policing techniques, and they reassure citizens by giving the impression of decisive action against crime. Yet because such techniques do not address underlying causes of crime, they mainly just protect certain segments of the population and displace delinquency to other realms.

This dynamic is evident in the physical exclusion of certain categories of people from common spaces—such as libraries, parks, and street corners—in an attempt to reduce crime and its perceived risk. Practices such as police monitoring, private security teams, and surveillance systems are aimed at protecting the public from potential risks. In shopping malls, for example, security measures are part of a contractual bargain between businesses and consumers; to attract and maintain a customer base, businesses must ensure the safety and comfort of their clients. Young people are disproportionately excluded from such spaces, being perceived as a greater security threat because malls typically create "locations of trust" for consumers.

Police forces have also expanded in response to growing crime and public clamor for more protection. Governments eager to appear decisive on crime favor increasing the number and resources of the police. But it is not clear that a greater police presence translates into lower crime rates. In the United States, official statistics on violent crime rates and number of police cast doubt on such a link (Figure 7.6). This raises puzzling questions: If increased policing does not prevent violent crime, why does the public demand a visible police presence? What role does policing play in our society, and what role should it play?

Policing

Some sociologists and criminologists have suggested that visible policing techniques, such as patrolling the streets, are reassuring for the public. Such activities support the perception that the police actively control crime, investigate offenses, and support the criminal justice system. But sociologists also see a need to reassess the role of policing in the late modern age. Policing, they argue, is now less about controlling crime and more about detecting and managing risks. Mostly it involves communicating knowledge about risk to other institutions in society that demand such information (Ericson and Haggerty, 1997).

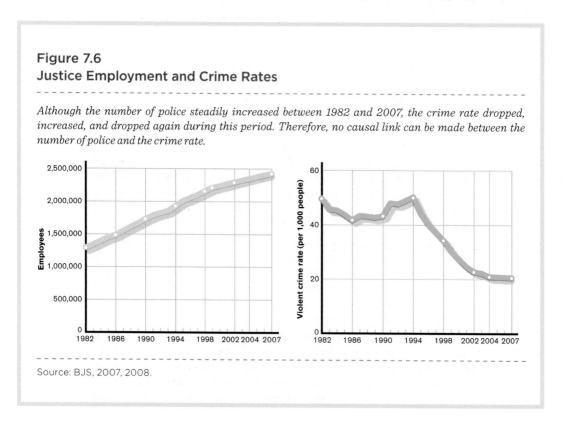

Figure 7.6
Justice Employment and Crime Rates

Although the number of police steadily increased between 1982 and 2007, the crime rate dropped, increased, and dropped again during this period. Therefore, no causal link can be made between the number of police and the crime rate.

Source: BJS, 2007, 2008.

According to this view, police are primarily "knowledge workers," spending time processing information, drafting reports, or communicating data. Consider the "simple" case of an automobile accident in Ontario, Canada. A police officer is called to the scene of an automobile accident involving two vehicles, with minor injuries and one drunk driver. The investigation takes one hour; the drunk driver is criminally charged with the impaired operation of a motor vehicle, causing bodily harm, and operating a motor vehicle under the influence of excess alcohol. The driver's license is automatically suspended for twelve hours.

Following this routine investigation, the officer spends three hours writing up 16 reports. Here the role of police as brokers of information becomes clear:

- The provincial motor registry requires information about the location of the accident and the vehicles and people involved. This is used for risk profiling in accident prevention initiatives, traffic management, and resource allocation.
- The automobile industry needs to know about the vehicles involved to improve safety standards, to report to regulatory agencies, and to provide safety information to consumer groups.
- The insurance companies involved need information to determine responsibility and to make awards in the case. They also require police information to develop statistical profiles of risk to set premiums and compensation levels for clients.
- The public health system requires details on the injuries. This knowledge is used for statistical profiles and to plan emergency service provision.
- The criminal courts require police information as material for the prosecution and as proof that the scene was properly investigated and evidence collected.
- The police administration itself requires reports on the incident for both internal records and national computer databases.

This example reveals how police work is increasingly about "mapping" and predicting risk within the population.

The informational demands of other institutions, such as the insurance industry, now require that police gather and report information in a way that is compatible with the needs of outside agencies. Computerized systems and forms define the way in which police report information. Rather than writing narrative accounts, police input the facts of a case into standardized forms by checking off boxes and choosing among available options. The information is used to categorize people and events as part of creating risk profiles. But such close-ended reporting formats influence what police observe and investigate, how they understand and interpret an incident, and the approach they take in resolving a problem. This emphasis on information collection and processing can alienate and frustrate many police officers, who see a distinction between real police work (e.g., investigating crimes) and the bureaucratic "donkey work" of reports and paper trails (Figure 7.7).

Crime and Community

Preventing crime and reducing fear of crime are both closely related to rebuilding strong communities. As we saw in our earlier discussion of the broken windows theory, one of the most significant discoveries in criminology in recent years is that the decay of day-to-day civility relates directly to criminality. For a long time, attention was focused almost exclusively on serious crime: robbery, assault, and other violent crime. More minor crimes and

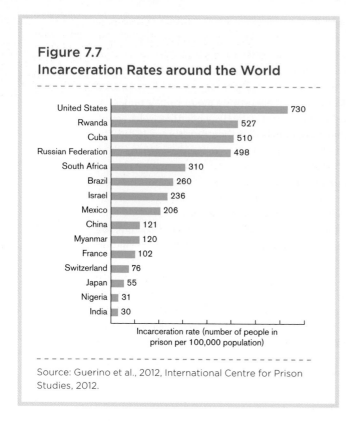

Figure 7.7
Incarceration Rates around the World

Incarceration rate (number of people in prison per 100,000 population)

- United States: 730
- Rwanda: 527
- Cuba: 510
- Russian Federation: 498
- South Africa: 310
- Brazil: 260
- Israel: 236
- Mexico: 206
- China: 121
- Myanmar: 120
- France: 102
- Switzerland: 76
- Japan: 55
- Nigeria: 31
- India: 30

Source: Guerino et al., 2012, International Centre for Prison Studies, 2012.

forms of public disorder, however, tend to have a cumulative effect. When asked to describe their problems, residents of troubled neighborhoods mention abandoned cars, graffiti, prostitution, youth gangs, and similar phenomena.

People act on their anxieties about these issues; they leave the areas in question if they can, buy heavy locks for their doors and bars for their windows, and abandon public places. Fearful citizens stay off the streets, avoid certain neighborhoods, and curtail their normal activities and associations. As they withdraw physically, they also withdraw from roles of mutual support for fellow citizens, thereby relinquishing the social controls that formerly helped maintain civility within the community.

COMMUNITY POLICING

One popular idea to combat this development is to have police work closely with citizens to improve local community standards and civil behavior, using education, persuasion, and counseling instead of incarceration.

Community policing implies not only involving citizens but also changing the outlook of police forces. A renewed emphasis on crime prevention rather than law enforcement can support a reintegration of policing with the community and reduce the siege mentality that develops when police have little regular contact with ordinary citizens.

To be successful, partnerships among government agencies, the criminal justice system, local associations, and community organizations have to include all economic and ethnic groups (Kelling and Coles, 1997). Government and business can act together to repair urban decay. One model is the creation of business improvement districts, which provide tax breaks for corporations that participate in strategic planning and that invest in designated areas. Such schemes demand a long-term commitment to social objectives.

Emphasizing these strategies does not mean denying the links between unemployment, poverty, and crime. Rather, when coordinated with community-based approaches to crime prevention, these approaches can contribute directly and indirectly to furthering social justice. Where social order has decayed along with public services, other opportunities, such as new jobs, decline also. Improving the quality of life in a neighborhood by providing job

community policing • A renewed emphasis on crime prevention rather than law enforcement to reintegrate policing within the community.

opportunities and public services can lead to a revival of such areas.

SHAMING AS PUNISHMENT

The current emphasis on imprisonment as a means of deterring crime can cripple the social ties within certain communities. In recent years, **shaming**—a form of punishment that maintains the ties of the offender to the community—has grown in popularity as an alternative to incarceration. Some criminologists see the fear of being shamed within one's community as an important deterrent to crime. As a result, the public's formal disapproval could deter crime as effectively as incarceration, without the high costs of building and maintaining prisons.

> **shaming** • A way of punishing criminal and deviant behavior based on rituals of public disapproval rather than incarceration. The goal of shaming is to maintain the ties of the offender to the community.

Criminologist John Braithwaite (1996) has suggested that shaming practices can take two forms: *reintegrative shaming* and *stigmatizing shaming*. Stigmatizing shaming is related to labeling theory, discussed earlier, by which a criminal is labeled as a threat to society and is treated as an outcast. The labeling process and society's efforts to marginalize the individual reinforce that person's criminal conduct, perhaps leading to future criminal behavior and higher crime rates. The much different practice of reintegrative shaming works as follows. People central to the criminal's immediate community—such as family members, employers and coworkers, and friends—are brought into court to state their condemnation of the offender's behavior. At the same time, these people must accept responsibility for reintegrating the offender back into the community. The goal is to rebuild the social bonds of the individual to the community as a means of deterring future criminal conduct.

Japan, with one of the lowest crime rates in the world, has successfully implemented this approach. The process is based on a voluntary network of more than 500,000 local crime prevention associations dedicated to facilitating reintegration into the community, and on a criminal justice system that attempts to be lenient for this purpose. As a result, in Japan only 5 percent of convicted individuals serve time in prison, compared with 30 percent in the United States. Reintegrative shaming is already a familiar practice in American social institutions such as the family. When a child misbehaves, the parent may express disapproval and try to make the child feel ashamed of her conduct but at the same time reassure her that she is a loved member of the family.

Could reintegrative shaming succeed in the U.S. criminal justice system? In spite of the beliefs that these tactics are "soft" on crime, that Americans are too individualistic to participate in community-based policing, and that high-crime areas are less community oriented, community networks have successfully worked with the police in preventing crime. These social bonds could also be fostered to increase the power of shame and to reintegrate offenders into local networks of community involvement.

CONCEPT CHECKS

1. How does imprisonment affect the life chances of ex-cons?
2. Why has the U.S. prison population increased steeply over the past three decades?
3. What are police officersí primary tasks each day?
4. What are two specific ways community members can combat local crime?

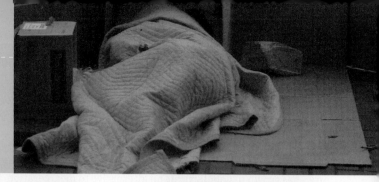

1 Basic Concepts

p. 163

2 Society and Crime: Sociological Theories

p. 164

LEARNING OBJECTIVES

Learn how we define deviance and how it is related to social power and social class. See the ways in which conformity is encouraged.

Know the leading sociological theories of crime and how each is useful in understanding deviance.

TERMS TO KNOW

Norms • Deviance • Sanction • Laws

Crime • Anomie • Differential association • Labeling theory • Primary deviation • Secondary deviation • Conflict theory • Control theory

CONCEPT CHECKS

1. How do sociologists define deviance?

1. How do Merton's and Durkheim's definitions of anomie differ?
2. What is the core idea behind differential association theory?
3. What are two criticisms of labeling theory?
4. What are the root causes of crime, according to conflict theorists?
5. How does the theory of broken windows exemplify the core ideas of control theory?

Exercises: Thinking Sociologically

1. Summarize several leading theories explaining crime and deviance presented in this chapter: differential association, anomie, labeling, conflict, and control theories. Which theory appeals to you the most? Explain why.

2. Explain how differences in power and social influence can play a significant role in defining and sanctioning deviant behavior.

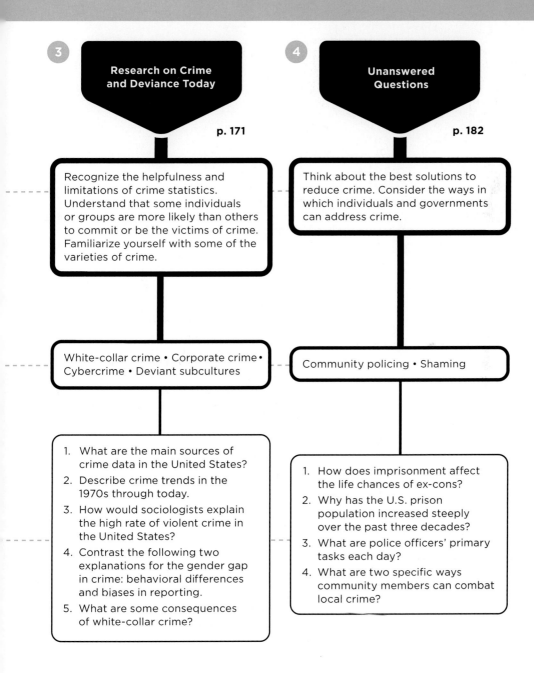

3

Research on Crime and Deviance Today

p. 171

Recognize the helpfulness and limitations of crime statistics. Understand that some individuals or groups are more likely than others to commit or be the victims of crime. Familiarize yourself with some of the varieties of crime.

White-collar crime • Corporate crime • Cybercrime • Deviant subcultures

1. What are the main sources of crime data in the United States?
2. Describe crime trends in the 1970s through today.
3. How would sociologists explain the high rate of violent crime in the United States?
4. Contrast the following two explanations for the gender gap in crime: behavioral differences and biases in reporting.
5. What are some consequences of white-collar crime?

4

Unanswered Questions

p. 182

Think about the best solutions to reduce crime. Consider the ways in which individuals and governments can address crime.

Community policing • Shaming

1. How does imprisonment affect the life chances of ex-cons?
2. Why has the U.S. prison population increased steeply over the past three decades?
3. What are police officers' primary tasks each day?
4. What are two specific ways community members can combat local crime?

Part III

STRUCTURES OF POWER

Power is an ever-present phenomenon in social life. In all human groups, some individuals have more authority or influence than others, and groups themselves have varying degrees of power. Power and inequality are closely linked. The powerful are able to accumulate valued resources, such as property and wealth; possession of such resources in turn generates more power.

In this part, we explore some of the main systems of power and inequality. Chapter 8 discusses stratification and class structure—the ways in which inequalities are distributed within societies. Chapter 9, on global inequality, examines the ways in which inequalities are distributed across societies. Chapter 10 analyzes the differences and inequalities between men and women and how these inequalities relate to others based on class and race. Chapter 11, on ethnicity and race, examines the tensions between people who are physically or culturally different from one another. Chapter 12 discusses the experience of growing old and analyzes related social problems. Chapter 13 examines the state, political power, and social movements. Governments are specialists in power; they are the source of the directives that influence many of our daily activities. However, they are also the focus of resistance and rebellion, political action that can lead to political and social change.

Stratification, Class, and Inequality

8

Which income group lost the greatest percentage of its wealth during the Great Recession of 2008?

a The upper class
b The middle class
c The lower class

Turn the page for the correct answer.

D id you ever consider how the effects of the Great Recession of 2008 might be felt differently by different parts of the U.S. population? One of the ways in which we might consider these differences is by looking at social class as a determinant of one's experiences. Take, for example, the question just posed.

If you thought the upper class (answer *a*) experienced the greatest percentage loss of wealth during the Great Recession, you are incorrect. While the upper class lost the most in absolute dollars (ultra-rich and high-net-worth individuals lost $2.6 trillion), members of this group fared much better than their less wealthy counterparts as a percentage of total wealth (Wolff, Owens, and Burak, 2011). Thus, while the upper class had many more assets to lose, the Great Recession had less an impact on their wealth relative to the middle and lower classes.

If you thought the lower class (answer *c*) was the correct answer, you are also incorrect. Unlike for the upper class, home ownership is the principal source of wealth for the lower and middle classes. The lower class had the smallest amount of wealth to begin with, but, surprisingly, it also experienced a lower percentage drop in home value than did either the middle class or the wealthiest Americans. The lower class not only purchased less expensive homes, but also took on smaller mortgages relative to the value of those homes. As a result, when the real estate market collapsed and housing prices plummeted, the lower class lost a smaller percentage of its wealth, on average, than either the middle class or the upper class (Wolff, Owens, and Burak, 2011). And because far fewer members of the lower class than middle or upper classes own homes, a smaller proportion faced the risk of a declining home value.

The correct answer to the opening question, therefore, is *b*, the middle class. Since the middle class has higher incomes, it would seem as if it would be less likely to default on mortgages than lower-class families. But, in comparison to the upper and lower classes, a larger

LEARNING OBJECTIVES

1 BASIC CONCEPTS

Learn about social stratification and the importance of social background in an individual's chances for material success.

2 THEORIES OF STRATIFICATION IN MODERN SOCIETIES

Know the most influential theories of stratification—including those of Karl Marx, Max Weber, and Erik Olin Wright.

3 RESEARCH ON SOCIAL STRATIFICATION TODAY

Know the class differences in U.S. society, what influences them, and how they are defined and determined. Recognize the ways in which the gap between rich and poor has grown larger. Learn the processes by which people become marginalized in a society and the forms this marginalization takes.

4 UNANSWERED QUESTIONS

Learn about competing explanations for why poverty exists, and means for combating it. Understand your own social mobility chances. Learn how changes in the American economy since the 1970s have led to growing inequalities.

proportion of the middle class tended to purchase houses it had difficulty paying for, and did so by taking out higher mortgage debt, through refinancing and secondary mortgages, relative to its actual home values (Wolff, Owens, and Burak, 2011). So when the housing market collapsed, the middle class was the hardest hit.

The differences explained here are directly related to the existence of inequalities within American society that result from class disparities. In this chapter, we will introduce a key concept of sociology, **social stratification**. By this we mean inequalities among individuals and groups that are determined not so much by individual personality or small-scale social situations but, more broadly, by attributes such as gender, age, religious affiliation, and military rank. In this chapter, we focus on stratification with regard to societal inequalities based on social class: aspects of wealth, income, education, and lifestyle. In later chapters, we will consider how gender (Chapter 10), race and ethnicity (Chapter 11), and age (Chapter 12) contribute to stratification.

Individuals and groups enjoy unequal access to rewards depending on their position within the larger stratification scheme. Stratification can thus be defined as **structured inequalities** between different groups of people such as classes, races, and genders. Sociologists see these inequalities as built into the economic and political system, rather than resulting from individual differences or chance occurrences, such as being the most handsome or beautiful person in a class. We can think of stratification like the geological layering of rock in the earth's surface. Societies consist of strata in a hierarchy, with the more favored at the top and the less privileged nearer the bottom.

BASIC CONCEPTS

Systems of Stratification

Historically, a few basic systems of stratification have existed in human societies: slavery, caste, and class. **Slavery** is an extreme form of inequality in which some individuals are literally owned by others as property. As a formal institution, slavery is illegal in every country and has almost completely disappeared. **Caste** is associated with the cultures of the Indian subcontinent and the Hindu belief in rebirth. It is believed that individuals who fail to abide by the rituals and duties of their caste will be reborn in an inferior position in their next life. Caste systems structure the type of contact that can occur between members of different ranks. **Class systems** differ in many respects from slavery and castes. We can define a **class** as a large-scale grouping of people who share common economic resources that strongly influence the type of lifestyle they are able to lead. Class systems differ from slavery and castes in four

social stratification • The structuring of inequalities between groups in society, in terms of their access to material or symbolic rewards. While all societies involve some forms of stratification, only with the development of state-based systems did wide differences in wealth and power arise. The most distinctive form of stratification in modern societies is class divisions.

structured inequalities • Social inequalities that result from patterns in the social structure.

slavery • A form of social stratification in which some people are literally owned by others as their property.

caste • A social system in which one's social status is held for life.

class systems • A system of social hierarchy that allows individuals movement between classes. The four chief bases of class are ownership of wealth, occupation, income, and education.

class • Although it is one of the most frequently used concepts in sociology, there is no clear agreement about how the notion should be defined. Most sociologists use the term to refer to socioeconomic variations between groups of individuals that create variations in their material prosperity and power.

main ways: Class systems are fluid and movement is possible; positions are partly achieved; classes are economically based; and class systems are large-scale and impersonal. The four chief bases of class are: ownership of wealth, occupation, income, and education.

Let's begin our exploration of classes in modern societies by looking at basic divisions of income, wealth, educational attainment, and occupational status within the population as a whole.

Income

As reflected in the answer to the question we posed earlier, income serves as an important determinant of one's social position, and therefore has a powerful effect on one's experience of the 2008 recession. **Income** refers to wages and salaries earned from paid occupations, plus money received from investments. One of the most significant changes over the past century has been the rising real income of the majority of the working population. (*Real income* is income excluding rises due to inflation, to provide a fixed standard of comparison from year to year.) Blue-collar workers, who typically perform physical labor such as manufacturing or construction work, now earn three to four times as much in real income in Western societies as their counterparts in the early 1900s, although they have seen their real income drop in the first two decades of the twenty-first century. Gains for managerial and professional workers, often known as "white-collar workers," have been higher still. In terms of earnings per person (per capita) and the range of goods and services that can be purchased, the majority of the population today is vastly more affluent than any peoples have previously been in human history. One of the most important reasons for this is *increasing productivity*—output per worker—through technological development in industry.

Nevertheless, income distribution both before and after the Great Recession remains unequal; some see this unequal distribution as a contributing factor in the resultant economic instability that precipitated this economic downturn. In 2011 the top 5 percent of households in the United States received 22.3 percent of total income, the highest 20 percent obtained 51.1 percent, and the bottom 20 percent received only 3.2 percent (Figure 8.1) (U.S. Bureau of the Census, 2012o). Between 1974 and 2006, income inequality increased dramatically and has continued to grow during the recession that started in 2007. The mean household earnings (calculated at 2010 dollars) of the bottom 20 percent of people in the United States was about the same in both 1974 and 2010 (U.S. Bureau of the Census, 2012j, 2012o). During the same period, by contrast, the richest fifth saw their incomes grow by almost 50 percent, while for the richest 5 percent of the population, income rose by more than 65 percent.

Wealth

Wealth refers to all assets individuals own: cash, savings and checking accounts; investments in stocks, bonds, real estate properties; and so on. Debt, by contrast, refers to all one's assets minus what one owes on those assets, such as outstanding home or health-care payments. Although most people make money from work, the wealthy often derive the bulk of their money from interest on their investments, some of them inherited. Some scholars argue that wealth, not income, is the real indicator of social class because it is less sensitive to fluctuations due to shifting work hours, health, and other factors that might affect one's income in a given year.

income • Money received from paid wages and salaries or earned from investments.

wealth • Money and material possessions held by an individual or group.

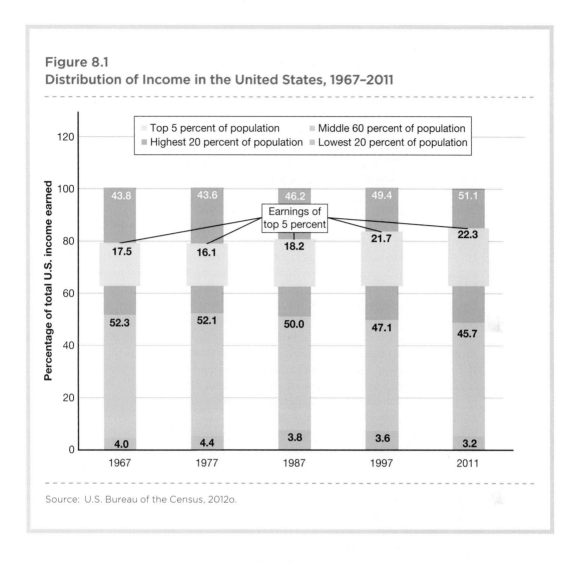

Figure 8.1
Distribution of Income in the United States, 1967–2011

Legend:
- Top 5 percent of population
- Highest 20 percent of population
- Middle 60 percent of population
- Lowest 20 percent of population

Y-axis: Percentage of total U.S. income earned

Earnings of top 5 percent

Year	1967	1977	1987	1997	2011
Highest 20 percent	43.8	43.6	46.2	49.4	51.1
Top 5 percent	17.5	16.1	18.2	21.7	22.3
Middle 60 percent	52.3	52.1	50.0	47.1	45.7
Lowest 20 percent	4.0	4.4	3.8	3.6	3.2

Source: U.S. Bureau of the Census, 2012o.

The best source of information about wealth comes from the national Survey of Consumer Finances, conducted every three years by the Governors of the Federal Reserve Bank (Bricker et al., 2012). These data show that, in the United States, wealth is highly concentrated, with enormous differences according to income, age, and education. Families with incomes in the top 10 percent in 2010, for example, had a median net worth of $1,194,300—more than 192 times as much as the lowest quintile of families, whose median net worth was only $6,200. Also, the median net worth of college graduates is more than 12 times greater than that of high school dropouts. Owning a home makes a great difference, because homes are the principal asset for most families: Homeowners' median net worth was $174,500 in 2010, compared with only $5,100 for renters. Age matters also: Net worth, like income, increases with age, although it typically peaks by age 65, after which savings are generally used as income and often are depleted among very old adults, who spend their assets on long-term care. However, the recession created an exception to this general rule. By 2010 the median net worth of younger age groups fell much more steeply due to the recession than that of the older group. As a result, the median wealth of those over 75 was still higher than that of younger groups.

When comparisons use a slightly different measure of assets, one that excludes the ownership of cars and homes—which are not sources of wealth that can be used to pay the bills or to get richer—the difference in wealth between high-income families and everyone else is even more pronounced. Net financial assets are far lower for minority groups than for whites (Oliver and Shapiro, 2006). Between 1983 and 2007 the median net financial assets of white Americans nearly tripled, from $19,900 to $67,000. Most African Americans began to accumulate net financial assets only in the 1990s; by 2000 the median net worth for their group was $6,166. For Hispanic households, median financial net worth grew from effectively $0 in 1998 to $6,766 in 2000, surpassing that of African American households. In the recent recession, the median assets of all households fell, but white non-Hispanic Americans, on average, experienced less loss of assets than their Hispanic or African American counterparts (Bricker et al., 2012).

What are some of the reasons for the racial disparity in wealth? Is it simply that blacks have less money to purchase assets? To some degree, the answer is yes. The old adage "It takes money to make money" is a fact of life for those who start with little or no wealth. Because whites historically have enjoyed higher incomes and levels of wealth than blacks, whites can accrue even more wealth, which they pass on to their children (Conley, 1999). But family advantages are not the only factors. Melvin Oliver and Thomas Shapiro (2006) argue that it is easier for whites to obtain assets, even when they have fewer resources than blacks, because discrimination affects the racial gap in home ownership. Blacks are rejected for mortgages 60 percent more often than whites, even when they have the same qualifications and credit worthiness. When blacks do receive mortgages, they are more likely to take "subprime" mortgage loans that charge much higher interest rates. In 2006, 30.3 percent of blacks took out subprime home loans, compared with 24.0 percent of Hispanics and 17.7 percent of whites. Research shows that subprime loans are offered by only a few lenders, but those lenders focus on minority communities, whereas the prime lenders are unable or unwilling to lend in those communities (Avery, Canner, and Cook, 2005). These issues are particularly important because home ownership constitutes American families' primary means for accumulating wealth. According to a *New York Times* analysis of mortgage lending in New York City, black households making more than $68,000 a year were nearly five times as likely to hold high-interest subprime mortgages as whites of similar or lower income levels (Powell, 2009).

In 2007 the bottom 60 percent of Americans held less than 2 percent of the country's total net worth (Wolff, 2010). For this group, accumulating stocks or bonds in the hope of cashing them in to pay for their children's college education is not even a fantasy. In fact, it is more likely that people in this group owe far more than they own. In recent years, as credit has become more available, many Americans have gone increasingly into debt, using credit cards and refinancing their home mortgages to pay for their lifestyles rather than relying on their earnings. In 2009 there were 980.1 million bank-issued Visa and MasterCard credit and debit card accounts in the United States. Total U.S. consumer debt (which includes installment debt but not mortgage debt) totaled $2.43 trillion in May 2011 (Woolsey and Schulz, 2012). The mean amount owed on credit cards, among those with at least one card, was $3,000. Increased debt means less net worth, which for Americans as a whole has declined in the first years of the twenty-first century for the first time since the government began recording such figures in 1945 (Leonhardt, 2001).

College students often live on credit, and rack up purchases that far surpass their income sources; in 2012, 35 percent of college students owned credit cards. Although this is down from earlier numbers, about a quarter of students carry a balance of more than $500, and about 1 in 10 owes more than $2,000 (Sallie Mae, 2012). Older adults also have fallen increasingly into debt; between 2006 and 2009 those aged 65 years and older experienced on average a 26 percent increase in credit card debt, with $10,235 in debt (*USA Today*, 2009).

Wealth is even more unequal globally. The world's richest 500 individuals have a combined income greater than that of the poorest 416 million. The poorest 40 percent of the developing world's population (those living on less than two dollars per day) account for only 5 percent of global income, but the richest 10 percent, who all live in high-income countries, account for 54 percent of global income (United Nations, 2005; World Bank, 2010a). But even the poorest 10 percent of Americans are better off than two-thirds of the world population (*The Guardian*, 2002). We'll come back to this in Chapter 20.

Differences in wealth often take the form of differences in privilege, which affect life chances as much as income differences do. Members of Congress, high-level military officers at the Pentagon, and White House staff members do not have gargantuan salaries like the chief executive officers of corporations. What they do have, however, are privileges that translate into wealth. They enjoy access to limousines and military aircraft, not to mention expense accounts that pay for many of their meals and hotel bills when they travel. Likewise, wealthy elites often have social connections that give them and their children access to elite schools, highly sought-after professional positions, membership in elite social organizations, and access to romantic partners and potential spouses who hail from very wealthy backgrounds. In these ways, wealth and its rewards are perpetuated across the generations (Khan, 2012).

Education

Education is an important dimension of social stratification. The value of a college education has increased significantly in recent years as a result of the increased demand for and wages paid to educated workers in the computer- and information-based economy (Danziger and Gottschalk, 1995). In fact, education is one of the strongest predictors of occupation, income, and wealth later in life. As we will see later in this chapter, how much education one receives is often influenced by the social class of one's parents. However, as we shall also see later in this chapter, for current cohorts of college graduates who face a recession and difficult job market after graduation, a college degree may not be the same ticket to success as it was for their older siblings and parents.

Racial differences in levels of education persist, which partly explains why racial differences in income and wealth also persist. In 2009, 94 percent of whites between the ages of 18 and 24 who were not enrolled in high school had completed high school, whereas only 77 percent of Hispanics and 87 percent of unenrolled African Americans had a high school degree or GED (Chapman et al., 2011).

Occupation

In the United States and other industrialized societies, occupation is an important indicator of social standing. In studies in which people rate jobs in terms of how "prestigious" they are, those requiring the most education are ranked most highly (Treiman, 1977). Research shows that physicians, college professors, lawyers, and dentists are at the top of the scale, whereas garbage collectors and gas station attendants are at the bottom. At the middle are jobs such as registered nurse, computer programmer, and insurance sales representative. Similar rankings occur regardless of who does the ranking and in what country (Table 8.1).

Table 8.1
Relative Social Prestige of Selected U.S. Occupations

OCCUPATION	PRESTIGE SCORE	WHITE-COLLAR OCCUPATION	BLUE-COLLAR OCCUPATION
Physician	86	X	
Lawyer	75	X	
Architect	73	X	
Dentist	72	X	
Member of the clergy	69	X	
Registered nurse	66	X	
Secondary-school teacher	64	X	
Veterinarian	62	X	
Sociologist	61	X	
Police officer	60		X
Actor	58	X	
Aircraft mechanic	53		X
Firefighter	53		X
Realtor	49	X	
Machinist	47		X
Musician/composer	47	X	

Class and Lifestyle

In analyzing class location, sociologists have traditionally relied on measures that are primarily economic, such as income or wealth. Some recent authors, however, seek to include cultural factors such as lifestyle and consumption patterns. According to this perspective, symbols and markers related to *consumption* are playing an ever-greater role in daily life. Individual identities are structured more around *lifestyle choices*—such as how to dress, what to eat, how to care for one's body, and where to relax—and less around traditional class indicators such as employment.

The French sociologist Pierre Bourdieu saw social class groups as identifiable according to their levels of *cultural and economic capital* (Bourdieu, 1984). Increasingly, individuals distinguish themselves not according to economic or occupational factors but on the basis of cultural tastes and leisure pursuits. Consider the proliferation of "need merchants"—people who present and represent goods and services, either symbolic or actual, for consumption. Advertisers, marketers, fashion designers, style consultants, interior designers, personal trainers, therapists, and Web page designers, to name but a few, are all involved in influencing cultural tastes and promoting lifestyle choices.

It would be difficult to dispute that stratification within classes as well as between classes now depends not only on occupational differences but also on differences in consumption and lifestyle. The rapid expansion of the service economy and the entertainment

OCCUPATION	PRESTIGE SCORE	WHITE-COLLAR OCCUPATION	BLUE-COLLAR OCCUPATION
Bank teller	43	X	
Welder	42		X
Farmer	40		X
Carpenter	39		X
Child-care worker	36		X
File clerk	36	X	
Bulldozer operator	34		X
Auto body repairperson	31		X
Retail apparel salesperson	30	X	
Truck driver	30		X
Cashier	29	X	
Taxi driver	28		X
Waiter/waitress	28		X
Bartender	25		X
Door-to-door salesperson	22		X
Janitor	22		X

Source: National Opinion Research Center, 2001.

and leisure industry, for example, reflects an increasing emphasis on consumption within industrialized countries. Modern societies have become consumer societies, and in some respects a consumer society is a "mass society" where class differences are overridden; thus people from different class backgrounds may all watch similar television programs or shop for clothing in the same stores. Yet class differences can also become *intensified* through variations in lifestyle and "taste" (Bourdieu, 1984).

Despite the importance of cultural capital in signifying class, however, we must not ignore the critical role of economic factors in the reproduction of social inequalities. For the most part, individuals experiencing extreme social and material deprivations are not doing so as part of a lifestyle choice. Rather, their circumstances are constrained by factors relating to the economic and occupational structure (Crompton, 1988). Some Americans may not necessarily "choose" to buy clothes at Walmart and eat at McDonald's; they may simply not be able to afford to shop at Neiman-Marcus and dine at exclusive gourmet restaurants.

CONCEPT CHECKS

1. What are the three shared characteristics of socially stratified systems?
2. What are two examples of caste systems in the world today?
3. How is the concept of class different from that of caste?
4. What are two examples of noneconomic indicators of one's social class?

② THEORIES OF STRATIFICATION IN MODERN SOCIETIES

In this section, we look at some broad theories regarding stratification. The most influential approaches were developed by Karl Marx and Max Weber. Most contemporary theories of stratification are heavily indebted to their ideas.

Marx: Means of Production and the Analysis of Class

For Marx, the term *class* refers to people who have a common relationship to the **means of production**—the means by which they gain a livelihood. In modern societies, the two main classes are those who own the means of production (industrialists, or **capitalists**) and those who earn their living by selling their labor to them (the working class). The relationship between classes, according to Marx, is exploitative. During the working day, workers produce more than employers actually need to repay the cost of hiring them. This **surplus value** is the source of profit, which capitalists put to their own use.

Marx (1977; orig. 1867) believed that the maturing of industrial capitalism would cause an increasing gap between the wealth of the minority and the poverty of the mass of the population. In his view, the wages of the working class could never rise far above subsistence level, while wealth would pile up in the hands of those owning capital. In addition, laborers would daily face work that is physically wearing and mentally tedious, as in many factories. At the lowest levels of society, particularly among those frequently or permanently unemployed, there would develop an "accumulation of misery, agony of labor, slavery, ignorance, brutality, moral degradation."

Marx was right about the persistence of poverty in industrialized countries and in anticipating continued inequalities of wealth and income. He was wrong in supposing that the income of most of the population would remain extremely low. Most people in Western countries today are much better off materially than were comparable groups in Marx's day.

Weber: Class and Status

There are two main differences between Weber's theory and that of Marx. First, according to Weber, class divisions derive not only from control or lack of control of the means of production but also from economic differences that have nothing to do with property. Such resources include people's skills and credentials. Those in managerial or professional occupations earn more and enjoy more favorable conditions at work, for example, than people in blue-collar jobs. Their qualifications, such as degrees, diplomas, and skills they have acquired, make them more "marketable" than others without such qualifications. At a lower level, among blue-collar workers, skilled craft workers secure higher wages than the semi-skilled or unskilled.

means of production • The means whereby the production of material goods is carried on in a society, including not just technology but the social relations between producers

capitalists • People who own companies, land, or stocks (shares) and use these to generate economic returns.

surplus value • The value of a worker's labor power, in Marxist theory, left over when an employer has repaid the cost of hiring the worker.

Second, Weber distinguished another aspect of stratification, which he called "status." **Status** refers to differences between groups in the social honor, or prestige, that others accord them. Status distinctions can vary independently of class divisions. Social honor may be either positive or negative. For instance, doctors and lawyers have high prestige in American society. **Pariah groups**, on the other hand, are negatively privileged status groups subject to discrimination that prevents them from taking advantage of opportunities open to others. The Jews were a pariah group in medieval Europe, banned from participating in certain occupations and from holding official positions.

status • The social honor or prestige a particular group is accorded by other members of a society. Status groups normally display distinct styles of life—patterns of behavior that the members of a group follow. Status privilege may be positive or negative. Pariah status groups are regarded with disdain or treated as outcasts by the majority of the population.

pariah groups • Groups who suffer from negative status discrimination—they are looked down on by most other members of society. The Jews, for example, have been a pariah group throughout much of European history.

Possession of wealth normally confers high status, but there are exceptions. In Britain, for instance, individuals from aristocratic families enjoy social esteem even after their fortunes have been lost, but individuals with "new money" are often scorned by the well-established wealthy.

Whereas class is an objective measure, status depends on people's subjective evaluations of social differences. Classes derive from the economic factors associated with property and earnings; status is governed by the varying lifestyles that groups follow.

Weber's writings on stratification show that other dimensions besides class strongly influence people's lives. Most sociologists hold that Weber's scheme offers a more flexible and sophisticated basis for analyzing stratification than Marx's.

Davis and Moore: The Functions of Stratification

Kingsley Davis and Wilbert E. Moore (1945) provided a functionalist explanation of stratification, arguing that it has beneficial consequences for society. They claimed that certain positions in society are functionally more important than others, such as brain surgeon, and these positions require special skills. However, only a few individuals have the talents or experience appropriate to these positions. To attract the most qualified people, rewards need to be offered, such as money, power, and prestige. Davis and Moore determined that because the benefits of different positions in any society must be unequal, all societies must be stratified. They concluded that social stratification and social inequality are functional because they ensure that the most qualified people, attracted by the rewards bestowed by society, fill the roles that are most important to a smoothly functioning society.

Davis and Moore's theory suggests that a person's social position is based solely on innate talents and efforts. It is not surprising that their theory has been criticized by other sociologists. For example, Melvin Tumin (1953) argued that the functional importance of a particular role is difficult to measure and that the social rewards bestowed on those in "important" roles do not reflect these people's actual importance. For instance, who is more important, a lawyer or a schoolteacher? If, on average, a lawyer earns four or five times the amount a schoolteacher earns, does that accurately reflect his relative importance to society? Tumin also argued that Davis and Moore overlooked the ways in which stratification limits the discovery of talent in a society. As we have seen, the United States is not entirely a meritocratic society. Those at the top have special access to economic and cultural resources, such as the highest-quality education, that help transmit their privileged status from one generation to the next. For those without access to these resources, even those with superior talents, social inequality is a barrier to reaching their full potential.

Erik Olin Wright: Contradictory Class Locations

The American sociologist Erik Olin Wright (1978, 1985, 1997) developed a theoretical position that owes much to Marx but also incorporates ideas from Weber. According to Wright, there are three dimensions of control over economic resources in modern capitalist production, and these allow us to identify the major classes:

1. Control over investments or money capital
2. Control over the physical means of production (land or factories and offices)
3. Control over labor power

Members of the capitalist class have control over each of these dimensions of the production system. Members of the working class have control over none of them. Between these two main classes, however, are the groups whose position is more ambiguous: managers and white-collar workers. These people are in what Wright calls **contradictory class locations**, because they can influence some aspects of production but lack control over others. White-collar and professional employees, for example, have to contract their labor power to employers to make a living, in the same way manual workers do. Yet they have a greater degree of control over the work setting than do most people in blue-collar jobs. Wright terms the class position of such workers "contradictory," because they are neither capitalists nor manual workers, yet they share certain common features with each.

A large segment of the population—85 to 90 percent, according to Wright (1997)—falls into the category of those who must sell their labor because they do not control the means of production. Yet within this population is a great deal of diversity, ranging from the traditional manual working class to white-collar workers. To differentiate class locations within this large population, Wright considers two factors: the relationship to authority and the possession of skills or expertise. First, many middle-class workers, such as managers and supervisors, enjoy *relationships to authority* that are more privileged than those of the working class. Such individuals assist capitalists in controlling the working class—for example, by monitoring the work of other employees or by conducting personnel reviews and evaluations—and are rewarded by earning higher wages and receiving regular promotions. Yet these individuals remain under the control of the capitalist owners. In other words, they are both exploiters and exploited.

The second factor that differentiates class locations within the middle classes is the *possession of skills and expertise*. According to Wright, middle-class employees possessing skills that are in demand in the labor market have a specific form of power in the capitalist system: They can earn a higher wage. The lucrative positions available to information technology specialists in the knowledge economy illustrate this point. Moreover, Wright argues, because employees with knowledge and skills are more difficult to monitor and control, employers secure their loyalty and cooperation by rewarding them accordingly.

contradictory class locations • Positions in the class structure, particularly routine white-collar and lower managerial jobs, that share characteristics with the class positions both above and below them.

Annette Laureau on Parenting Styles: "Concerted Cultivation" versus the "Development of Natural Growth"

A final, more recent American theory of inequality comes from the work of the sociologist Annette Lareau (2011) Lareau's work has its conceptual roots in Bourdieu's writings on cultural capital. Her book *Unequal Childhoods* focuses on the way social class influences parenting in poor and middle-class families. She found that different styles of parenting are associated with different class positions. Middle-class parents engage in a style of "concerted cultivation," in which children are scheduled in multiple activities and learn teamwork, time management, and assertiveness with adults. Working-class parents raise their children with what Lareau calls "the development of natural growth." They are not scheduled in many activities and end up playing freely in the neighborhood with other kids. They tend not to learn to challenge authority, but instead become deferential to it. They thrive in unstructured time and never learn to be assertive with adults. The result is that they end up with fewer skills that are valued by the most powerful institutions, and feel a sense of constraint when operating in them. Lareau argues that the different kinds of parenting emerge from the different classes and tend to reproduce those classes.

> ### CONCEPT CHECKS
>
> 1. According to Karl Marx, what are the two main classes and how do they relate to one another?
> 2. What are the two main differences between Max Weber's and Karl Marx's theories of social stratification?
> 3. According to Kingsley Davis and Wilbert E. Moore, how does social stratification contribute to the functioning of society? What is wrong with this argument, according to Melvin Tumin?
> 4. According to Annette Lareau, how do middle-class and working-class parents differ in their child-rearing styles?

③ RESEARCH ON SOCIAL STRATIFICATION TODAY

A Contemporary Portrait of the U.S. Class Structure

As we have already learned, a person's social class position can make an enormous difference in terms of lifestyle. Most sociologists identify social classes in terms of wealth, income, and occupation, noting how social class makes a difference in terms of consumption, education, health, and access to political power. The purpose of the following discussion is to describe broad class differences in the United States. Bear in mind that there are no sharply defined boundaries between the classes.

THE UPPER CLASS

The **upper class** consists of the very wealthiest Americans—those households earning more than $180,800, or approximately 5 percent of all

upper class • A social class broadly composed of the more affluent members of society, especially those who have inherited wealth, own businesses, or hold large numbers of stocks (shares).

American households (U.S. Bureau of the Census, 2012h). Most Americans in the upper class are wealthy but not super-rich. They are likely to own a large suburban home as well as a town house or a vacation home, to drive expensive automobiles, to fly first class to vacations abroad, to educate their children in private schools and colleges, and to have their desires attended to by a staff of servants. Their wealth stems in large part from their substantial investments, from stocks and bonds to real estate, and from the interest income derived from those investments. They are politically influential at the national, state, and local levels. The upper class includes people who acquired their wealth in a variety of ways: celebrities; professional athletes; the heads of major corporations; people who have made large amounts of money through investments or real estate; and those fortunate enough to have inherited great wealth from their parents.

At the very top of this group are people who have accumulated vast fortunes that permit them to enjoy a lifestyle unimaginable to most Americans. The superrich are conscious of their unique and privileged social class position; some give generously to such worthy causes as the fine arts, hospitals, and charities. Their homes are often lavish and sometimes filled with collections of fine art. Their common class identity is strengthened by such things as being listed in the social register or having attended the same exclusive private secondary schools (to which they also send their children). They sit on the same corporate boards of directors and belong to the same private clubs. They contribute large sums of money to their favorite politicians and are likely to be on a first-name basis with members of Congress and perhaps even with the president (Domhoff, 1998).

The turn of the twenty-first century saw extraordinary opportunities for the accumulation of such wealth. Globalization is one reason. Entrepreneurs who are able to invest globally often prosper, both by selling products to foreign consumers and by making profits cheaply by using low-wage labor in developing countries. The information revolution is another reason for the accumulation of wealth. Young entrepreneurs with startup high-tech companies, such as Facebook founder Mark Zuckerberg and Yahoo! cofounder Jerry Yang, made legendary fortunes. In May 2012, Zuckerberg was estimated to be worth $16 billion (Dolan, 2012).

As a consequence of globalization and the information revolution, the number of superrich Americans has exploded in recent years. At the end of World War II, there were only 13,000 people worth $1 million or more in the United States. Today, there are 5.22 million, making up 4.5 percent of U.S. households (*Forbes*, 2011). The 400 richest Americans are worth more than $1.37 trillion—equal to approximately one-tenth the gross domestic product of the United States and more than the gross domestic product of Mexico (*Forbes*, 2011). Unlike "old money" families such as the Rockefellers or the Vanderbilts, who accumulated their wealth in earlier generations and thus are viewed as a sort of American aristocracy, this "new wealth" is held primarily by entrepreneurs.

While Americans have long glamorized and aspired to be part of this extraordinarily wealthy elite, perceptions of the superrich have changed in recent years. The current recession, rampant scandals on Wall Street, and the Bernie Madoff fraud case have triggered movements such as Occupy Wall Street, in which protesters sought to bring attention to what they saw as greed, corruption, and undeserved political power among the very wealthy. Further, a recent Pew Research Center poll showed that two-thirds of Americans in 2011 felt there were "strong" or "very strong" conflicts between the rich and the poor today (up from just 47 percent in 2009). The same poll showed that nearly half (46 percent) of Americans believe that most rich people "are wealthy mainly because they know the right people or were born into wealthy families." However, a sizeable minority (43 percent) of Americans believe the wealthy have rightfully earned their status through "their own hard work, ambition or education" (Morin, 2012).

THE MIDDLE CLASS

When Americans are asked to identify their social class, the majority claims to be middle class (Boushey and Hersh, 2012). The reason is partly the pervasive cultural belief that the United States is relatively free of class distinctions. Few people want to be identified as being too rich or too poor. Most Americans seem to think that others are not very different from their immediate family, friends, or coworkers (Kelley and Evans, 1995). Since people seldom interact with those outside their social class, they tend to see themselves as like "most other people," whom they then regard as being "middle class" (Kelley and Evans, 1995).

Middle class is a catchall term for a diverse group of occupations, lifestyles, and people who earn stable and sometimes substantial incomes at primarily white-collar and highly skilled blue-collar jobs. The middle class grew throughout much of the first three-quarters of the twentieth century, then shrank during most of the last quarter century. During the late 1990s, however, economic growth halted this decline. Whether this trend will continue depends on whether the economy expands or contracts during the next several years. Currently, the middle class includes slightly more than half of all American households. While the middle class was once largely white, today it is increasingly diverse, both racially and culturally, including African Americans, Asian Americans, and Latinos.

Another, less desirable change is that the level of financial security enjoyed by the middle class has eroded in recent years, with many worrying about their ability to make home payments, pay for health care, and provide their children with the same opportunities they had while growing up (Boushey and Hersh, 2012). These concerns are more acute among persons who are lower middle class versus upper middle class (U.S. Department of Commerce, 2010). A brief sketch of both follows.

The Upper Middle Class The *upper middle class* consists of highly educated professionals (for example, doctors, lawyers, engineers, and professors), mid-level corporate managers, people who own or manage small businesses and retail shops, and some large farm owners. Household incomes range quite widely, from about $100,000 to perhaps $180,000. The lower end of the income category would include college professors, for example, while the higher end would include corporate managers and small business owners. The upper middle class includes approximately 15 percent of all American households (U.S. Bureau of the Census, 2012h). Its members are likely to be college educated (as are their children), with advanced degrees. They own comfortable homes, drive expensive late-model cars, have some savings and investments, and are often active in local politics and civic organizations. However, they tend not to enjoy the same high-end luxuries, social connections, or extravagancies as members of the upper class. Historically, their jobs have been secure and provide retirement, pension, and health benefits, yet in the recent economic downturn, many upper-middle-class persons—especially those working in finance

middle class • A social class composed broadly of those working in white-collar and lower managerial occupations.

and media—have been susceptible to layoffs and have seen their pension and home value wealth shrink (U.S. Department of Commerce, 2010).

The Lower Middle Class The *lower middle class* consists of trained office workers (for example, secretaries and bookkeepers), elementary and high school teachers, nurses, salespeople, police officers, firefighters, and others who provide skilled services. This group, which includes about 40 percent of American households, is the most varied of the social class strata, and may include college-educated persons with relatively modest earnings, such as public elementary school teachers, and quite highly paid persons with high school diplomas only, such as skilled craftsmen (e.g., plumbers) and civil servants with many years of seniority. Household incomes in this group range from about $38,000 to $100,000 (U.S. Bureau of the Census, 2012h). Members of the lower middle class may own a modest house, although many live in rental units. Their automobiles may be late models, but not the more expensive ones. Almost all have a high school education, and some have college degrees. They want their children to attend college, although this usually requires work-study programs and student loans. They are rarely politically active beyond exercising their right to vote.

Like upper-middle-class persons, lower-middle-class workers have seen their job security and financial security decline during the recession, and these threats have disproportionately struck African Americans and persons who work in the public sector (Pitts, 2011). While firefighters, police officers, and schoolteachers have historically enjoyed job security, this is no longer the case. Between 2009 and 2011, state and local governments throughout the United States have laid off 429,000 workers (Pitts, 2011). For example, in June 2012 the New Orleans school system announced the layoffs of 200 teachers (Vanacore, 2012), while the impoverished city of Camden, New Jersey, witnessed the layoffs of nearly 250 firefighters, police officers, and city employees in 2011, and public workers in dozens of other American cities have seen their pensions threatened (Kaplan and Eligon, 2012).

THE WORKING CLASS

The **working class**, about 20 percent of all American households, includes primarily blue-collar workers such as mechanics and pink-collar laborers such as clerical aids. Household incomes range from about $20,000 to $38,000 (U.S. Bureau of the Census, 2012h), and at least two household members work to make ends meet. Family income is just enough to pay the rent or the mortgage, to put food on the table, and perhaps to save for a summer vacation. The working class includes factory workers, mechanics, office workers, sales clerks, restaurant and hotel workers, and others who earn a modest weekly paycheck at a job that involves little control over the size of their income or working conditions. As you will see later in this chapter, many manufacturing jobs in the United States are threatened by economic globalization, and so members of the working class today are likely to feel insecure about their own and their family's future.

The working class is racially and ethnically diverse. While older members of the working class may own a home that was bought a number of years ago, younger members are likely to rent. The home or apartment is likely to be in a lower-income suburb or a city neighborhood. The household car, a lower-priced model, is unlikely to be new. Most members of the working class are not likely to be politically active even in their own community, although they may vote in some elections.

working class • A social class broadly composed of people working in blue-collar, or manual, occupations.

Children of working-class families often bypass college and instead seek full-time work immediately after graduating high school. However, in the current recessionary years, high school graduates' employment prospects are increasingly bleak. Rutgers University researchers studied high school graduates from the classes of 2009 to 2011 who did not go on to college; as of 2011, only 16 percent were working full time while 37 percent were unemployed and looking for work, 17 percent were unemployed and had given up on finding work, and 13 percent were hoping to up their current work hours from part time to full time (Van Horn et al., 2012). Of those who had found jobs, the median hourly wage was $7.50, just $0.25 above federal minimum wage. These bleak employment prospects bode poorly for their futures; two-thirds of the high school graduates viewed important life transitions such as starting a family or owning a home as many years off in the future.

The **lower class**, roughly 20 percent of American households, includes some full-time low-wage workers and those who work part time or not at all; annual household income is typically lower than $20,000 (U.S. Bureau of the Census, 2012h). Most lower-class individuals are found in cities, although some live in rural areas and earn a little money as farmers or part-time workers. Some manage to find employment in semiskilled or unskilled manufacturing or service jobs, ranging from making clothing in sweatshops to cleaning houses. Their jobs, when they can find them, are dead-end jobs, since years of work are unlikely to lead to promotion or substantially higher income. Their work is probably part time and highly unstable, without benefits such as medical insurance, disability, or Social Security. Even if they are fortunate enough to find a full-time job, there are no guarantees that it will be around next month or even next week. Many people in the lower class live in poverty. Very few own their own homes. Most of the lower class rent, and some are homeless. If they own a car at all, it is likely to be a used car. A higher percentage of the lower class is nonwhite than is true of other social classes (Lin and Harris, 2010). Its members do not participate in politics, and they seldom vote.

THE "UNDERCLASS"

In the lower class, some sociologists have recently identified a group they call the **underclass** because they are "beneath" the class system in that they lack access to the world of work and mainstream patterns of behavior. Located in the highest-poverty neighborhoods of the inner city, the underclass is sometimes called the "new urban poor."

The underclass includes many African Americans who have been trapped for more than one generation in a cycle of poverty from which there is little possibility of escape (Wacquant, 1993, 1996; Wacquant and Wilson, 1993; Wilson, 1996). These are the poorest of the poor. As we will explore later in this chapter, their numbers have grown rapidly over the past quarter century and today include unskilled and unemployed men, young single mothers and their children on welfare, teenagers from welfare-dependent families, and many of the homeless. They live in poor neighborhoods troubled by drugs, gangs, and high levels of violence. They are the truly disadvantaged, people with extremely difficult lives who have little realistic hope of ever making it out of poverty.

In recent years some sociologists have argued that members of the underclass perpetuate their own inequality because the difficult conditions they face have made them "ill-suited to the requirements of the formally rational sector of

lower class • A social class comprised of those who work part time or not at all and whose household income is typically lower than $17,000 a year.

underclass • A class of individuals situated at the bottom of the class system, normally composed of people from ethnic minority backgrounds.

the economy" (Wacquant, 2002). Although these scholars see the sources of such behavior in the social structure, they believe the culture of the underclass has taken on a life of its own, serving as both cause and effect. Such claims have generated considerable controversy, inspiring a number of studies that have taken issue with this viewpoint. Those who stand on the other side argue that although the urban poor comprise an immobile stratum, they are not simply a "defeated" and disconnected class, as theorists of the underclass believe. Thus, studies of fast-food workers and homeless street vendors have argued that the separations between the urban poor and the rest of society are not as great as scholars of the underclass believe (Newman, 2000; Duneier, 1999).

Social Mobility: Moving Up and Down the Ladder

The United States has long been hailed as the land of opportunity. "Rags-to-riches" stories abound, offering inspiring accounts of people such as Liz Murray, the homeless daughter of drug-addicted parents who ultimately graduated Harvard University (Murray, 2010). Movies and novels recount the triumphs of the secretary or mailroom worker who became a corporate vice president. Is it possible for a young person from a poor or working-class background to transcend class roots and become an upper-class professional? If yes, what factors contribute to one's ascent up the social ladder?

Answers to these questions can be found in the study of **social mobility**, which refers to the movement of individuals and groups between different class positions as a result of changes in occupation, wealth, or income. Mobility can occur in one of two forms. **Intergenerational mobility** refers to social movement across generations; we can analyze where children are on the scale compared with their parents or grandparents. **Intragenerational mobility**, by contrast, refers to how far an individual moves up or down the socioeconomic scale during his working life. Another important distinction is between structural mobility and exchange mobility. In a hypothetical society with complete equality of opportunity—in which each person has the same chance of success as everyone else—there would be a great deal of downward as well as upward mobility. This is **exchange mobility**—an exchange of positions, such that more talented people in each generation move up the economic hierarchy, while the less talented move down.

In practice, no society approaches full equality of opportunity. Most mobility, whether intragenerational or intergenerational, is **structural mobility**—upward mobility made possible by an expansion of better-paid occupations at the expense of poorly paid ones. Most mobility in the United States since World War II has depended on continually increasing prosperity. Levels of downward mobility, therefore, have been historically low, although levels have seen an uptick during the recent recession (Acs, 2011).

One of the groups disproportionately impacted by the period of unemployment in the early 1980s was new entrants to the workforce. Younger workers who entered the labor market during this period suffered long-term consequences that had negative effects on their ability to improve their

social mobility • Movement of individuals or groups between different social positions.

intergenerational mobility • Movement up or down a social stratification hierarchy from one generation to another.

intragenerational mobility • Movement up or down a social stratification hierarchy within the course of a personal career.

exchange mobility • The exchange of positions on the socioeconomic scale such that talented people move up the economic hierarchy while the less talented move down.

structural mobility • Mobility resulting from changes in the number and kinds of jobs available in a society.

social class. In fact, even displaced workers—those who were simply finding new jobs in the market—were more vulnerable to downward mobility, with nearly half earning less than what they made in their previous jobs, and a quarter making over 20 percent less than what they used to make (Newman and Pedulla, 2010).

Opportunities for Mobility: Who Gets Ahead?

Is social mobility a fairy tale or a reality? If a reality, what factors contribute to one's ascent up the social ladder? Sociologists have sought to answer this question by trying to understand which social factors are most influential in determining an individual's status or position in society.

In a classic study of intergenerational mobility in the United States, the sociologists Peter Blau and Otis Dudley Duncan (1967) found that long-range intergenerational mobility—that is, from working class to upper middle class—was rare. Why? Blau and Duncan concluded that the key factor behind occupational status was educational attainment. But a child's education is influenced by family social status; this, in turn, affects the child's social position later in life. Sociologists William Sewell and Robert Hauser (1980) later confirmed Blau and Duncan's conclusions. They added to the argument by claiming that the connection between family background and educational attainment occurs because parents, teachers, and friends influence the educational and career aspirations of the child, and that these aspirations then become an important influence on the schooling and careers obtained throughout the child's life.

As we learned earlier in this chapter, French sociologist Pierre Bourdieu (1984, 1988) also has examined the importance of family background to social status, but his emphasis is on the cultural advantages that parents can provide to their children. Bourdieu argued that among the factors responsible for social status, the most important is the transmission of cultural capital, or the cultural advantages that coming from a "good home" confers. Wealthier families are able to afford to send their children to better schools, an economic advantage that benefits the children's social status as adults. Parents from the upper and middle classes are mostly highly educated themselves and tend to be more involved in their children's education—reading to them, helping with homework, purchasing books and learning materials, and encouraging their progress. Bourdieu noted that working-class parents are concerned about their children's education, but they lack the economic or cultural capital to make a difference.

Although Bourdieu focused on social status in France, the socioeconomic order in the United States is similar. Those who already hold positions of wealth and power can ensure that their children have the best available education, and this will often lead them into the best jobs. Studies consistently show that the large majority of people who have "made money" did so on the basis of inheriting or being given at least a modest amount initially—which they then used to make more. In U.S. society, it's better to start at the top than at the bottom (Jaher, 1973; Rubinstein, 1986; Duncan et al., 1998).

One of the most important avenues to upward intergenerational mobility is higher education. A college degree opens the door to well-paying managerial and professional occupations. Fully 60 percent of Americans in the top fifth of income earners graduated college, whereas in the bottom fifth of earners, just 6 percent hold a college degree. However, the returns on education, or the economic payoff received in the workplace for each additional year of schooling or academic degree, is not equal for all Americans. As we will learn in subsequent chapters, each additional academic degree brings much richer financial and occupational rewards for men versus women, and whites versus blacks and Latinos.

That said, the Great Recession of 2008 has deemphasized the centrality of educational attainment as a predictor of upward mobility. College graduates entering a weak labor market following the Great Recession are likely to experience long-term consequences, including underemployment and lower wages. Lisa Kahn of the Yale School of Management conducted a study of white male college graduates who entered the job market during the 1980s, the last period in which unemployment stood at over 10 percent. Fifteen years after the recession, these workers continued to face significantly lower wages (Newman and Pedulla, 2010). Graduates who entered the job market during this downturn could suffer similar consequences.

Further, the very process of applying for, being accepted to, and graduating from college, especially prestigious colleges, is shaped by one's social background. In order to obtain a "behind-the-scenes" look at who is accepted to prestigious colleges, sociologist Mitchell Stevens (2009) conducted ethnography in which he spent a year and a half working in the admissions office of an elite New England college. The college was proud of its high academic standards, social conscience, and commitment to diversity. In practice, however, the admissions process often reproduced preexisting inequalities, Stevens found. Although admissions officers did strive for diversity in each entering class, they typically targeted black and Latino students from economically advantaged backgrounds, rather than those from disadvantaged communities in the inner city or rural areas. Working-class whites and ethnic minorities, even those with quite stellar records, often were left out in the cold.

Downward Mobility

Downward mobility is less common than upward mobility, yet the current recession has seen an uptick in the proportion of Americans who have moved down the social ladder—either down from their parents' status or down from their own earlier economic status. For example, the recent Pew study "Downward Mobility from the Middle Class: Waking up from the American Dream" finds that a middle-class upbringing does not guarantee the same status over the course of a lifetime (Acs, 2011). One-third of Americans raised in the middle class—defined as those who grew up in households between the 30th and 70th percentiles of the income distribution—fall out of the middle class as adults.

Downward intergenerational mobility also has increased in recent years. During the late 1980s and early '90s, corporate America was flooded with instances in which middle-aged men lost their jobs because of company mergers, takeovers, or bankruptcies. These executives either had difficulty finding new jobs or could find only jobs that paid less than their previous ones (Newman, 1999). Among the industries most strongly affected by the current economic downturn are finance, construction, and real estate, which primarily employ men. The most common type of downward intergenerational mobility is short-range downward mobility. Here, a worker moves from one job to another that is similar in pay and prestige (for example, from a routine office job to semiskilled blue-collar work). Although such moves may seem fairly minor, they often are accompanied by quite serious psychological costs, and may create family strains. Men and women who stake their identity on having a well-paying and rewarding job may find themselves despondent working in a job that provides neither rich earnings nor the prestige and satisfaction that accompanied their prior job (Warner, 2010).

For women, both inter- and intragenerational downward mobility may have an additional source: divorce. The 2011 Pew study found that women who divorced were between 31 and 36 percentage points more likely than their married counterparts to fall down the economic ladder (Acs, 2011). Similarly, qualitative studies show that the fortunes of adult women change dramatically upon divorce. Newman (1999) tracked the experiences of upper-middle-class suburban mothers who found themselves struggling to maintain their former lifestyles upon divorce. At the other end of the class ladder, Schwarz and Volgy (1992) traced the experience of a poor young mother who divorced her abusive husband and lived a hand-to-mouth existence after she left him. Sandra Bolton, the subject of the study, worked evenings as a supermarket checkout clerk. As a result of divorce, both the upper-middle-class and low-income women sank from a life of some comfort and stability to one of financial uncertainty. As we will learn about further in Chapter 15, women's standard of living drops by as much as 33 percent upon divorce.

Ironically, the Great Recession has actually contributed to higher rates of female labor force participation. As in the Great Depression, women are generally paid less, and maintain jobs that do not feel the effects of the economic downturn in the same way that predominantly male professions (e.g., construction or manufacturing) do. As a result, some scholars refer to the recent economic downturn as a "man-cession," in which men suffer greater job losses than women (Newman and Pedulla, 2010).

Poverty in the United States

At the bottom of the class system in the United States are the millions of people who live in poverty. Many do not maintain a proper diet and often live in neighborhoods marked by high crime rates, exposure to dangerous environmental conditions, and run-down, dilapidated homes. Poor persons are more likely than their richer counterparts to suffer from every possible health condition, ranging from heart disease to diabetes, and consequently their average life expectancy is lower than that of the majority of the population. In addition, the number of poor individuals and families who have become homeless has increased greatly over the past 20 years.

In defining poverty, a distinction is usually made between absolute and relative poverty. **Absolute poverty** means that a person or family simply can't get enough to eat. People living in absolute poverty are undernourished and, in situations of famine, may even starve to death. Absolute poverty is common in the poorer developing countries.

In industrial countries, by contrast, **relative poverty** is essentially a measure of inequality. It means being poor as compared with the standards of living of the majority. It is reasonable to call a person poor in the United States if he lacks the basic resources needed to maintain a decent standard of housing and healthy living conditions.

MEASURING POVERTY

When President Lyndon B. Johnson began his War on Poverty in 1964, around 36 million Americans lived in poverty. In 2010, this number sat at 46 million people, or roughly 15.1 percent of the population—the highest level recorded since 1993 (DeNavas-Walt, Proctor, and Smith, 2011). The rate of child poverty is even worse; more than one in five children lives in a household with income levels beneath the poverty line (Figure 8.2). A recent UNICEF study reported that among the 35 wealthiest nations in the world, the United States has the second-highest child poverty rate, falling just behind Romania (UNICEF, 2012). The largest concentrations of poverty in the United States are found in the South and the Southwest, in inner cities, and in rural areas. Among the poor, 20.5 million Americans (or 6.7 percent of the

absolute poverty • The minimal requirements necessary to sustain a healthy existence.

relative poverty • Poverty defined according to the living standards of the majority in any given society.

country) live in extreme poverty: Their incomes are only half of the official poverty level, meaning that they live at near-starvation levels (DeNavas-Walt, Proctor, and Smith, 2011).

What does it mean to be poor in the world's richest nation? The U.S. government calculates the **poverty line** as an income equal to three times the cost of a nutritionally adequate diet—a strict, no-frills budget assumes that a nutritionally adequate diet could be purchased in 1999 for only $3.86 per day for each member, with about $7.72 spent on all other items (including rent and utilities, clothing, medical expenses, and transportation). For a family of four in 2011, this works out to an annual cash income of $22,350 (Federal Register, 2011).

How realistic is this formula? Some critics believe it overestimates the amount of poverty. They point out that the current standard fails to take into account noncash forms of income available to the poor, such as food stamps, Medicare, Medicaid, and public housing subsidies, as well as "under-the-table" pay obtained from work at odd jobs that is concealed from the government. Other critics counter that the government's formula greatly underestimates the amount of poverty, because it overemphasizes the proportion of a family budget spent on food and severely underestimates the share spent on housing. According to some estimates, poor families today may spend as much as three-quarters of their income on housing alone (Dolbeare, 1995; Joint Center for Housing Studies of Harvard University, 2005). Still others observe that this formula dramatically underestimates the proportion of older adults (age 65+) who live in poverty, because they spend a relatively small proportion of their income on food yet are faced with high health care costs (Carr, 2010).

poverty line • An official government measure to define those living in poverty in the United States.

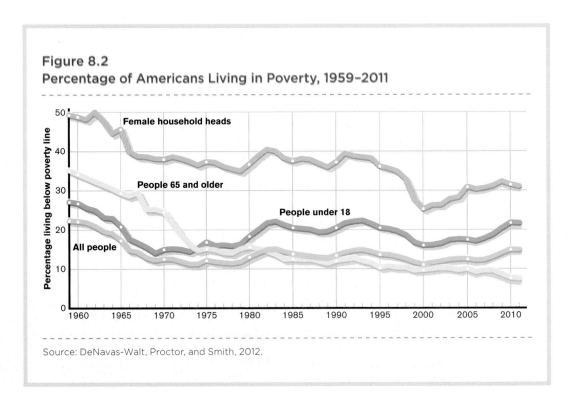

Figure 8.2
Percentage of Americans Living in Poverty, 1959–2011

Source: DeNavas-Walt, Proctor, and Smith, 2012.

Who Are the Poor?

Most Americans think of the poor as people who are unemployed or on welfare. Surveys repeatedly show that the majority of Americans regard the poor as responsible for their plight and are antagonistic to those who live on "government handouts." For example, a Gallup poll (1998) found that 55 percent of the public believed that lack of effort by the poor was the principal reason for poverty. Nearly two-thirds believed that government-assistance programs reduced incentives to work. Another poll, in 2001, reported similar findings: 48 percent of those interviewed believe that the poor are responsible for their own condition (National Public Radio [NPR], 2001). Yet these views are out of line with the realities of poverty. The poor are as diverse as other groups. A recent report by the research organization Demos, working with Brandeis University, estimated that a substantial segment of the middle class—one-fifth of white families, one-third of black families, and two-fifths of Latino families—will be in danger of downward social mobility and, ultimately, poverty should the nation's recession continue (Wheary, Shapiro, and Draut, 2010).

THE WORKING POOR

Many Americans are the **working poor**—that is, people who work but whose earnings are not high enough to lift them above poverty. The federal minimum wage, the legal floor for wages in the United States, was first set in 1938, at $0.25 an hour. As of July 24, 2011, the minimum wage was $7.25 per hour, although individual states can set higher minimum wages than the federal standard. Eighteen have chosen to do so; the highest is in the state of Washington, at $8.80 per hour (U.S. Department of Labor, 2010a, 2011). Although the federal minimum wage has increased over the years, since 1965 it has failed to keep up with inflation.

About one-third of those age 16 and older who are officially living in poverty have worked in the past year. In 2010 the number of working poor Americans climbed to its highest level in the last two decades, according to the U.S. Bureau of Labor Statistics. About 10.6 million Americans, or 7.2 percent of the labor force in 2010, weren't earning enough to stay out of poverty (BLS, 2012h). Of those working poor, roughly 5.5 million usually worked full time, and another 5.1 million usually worked part time. Most poor people, contrary to popular belief, do not receive welfare payments, because they earn too much to qualify for welfare. Only 5 percent of all low-income families with a full-time, full-year worker receive welfare benefits, and over half rely on public health insurance rather than employer-sponsored insurance. The working poor are disproportionately nonwhite and immigrant (Urban Institute, 2005; BLS, 2012h). Qualitative research on low-wage fast-food workers further reveals that many working poor lack adequate education, do not have health insurance to cover medical costs, and are trying to support families on poverty-level wages (Newman, 2000).

Poverty, Race, and Ethnicity

Poverty rates in the United States are much higher among most minority groups than among whites, even though more than two-thirds of the poor are white (Figure 8.3). Blacks and Latinos continue to earn around two-thirds of what whites earn in the United States, while experiencing three times the poverty rate that whites experience. This is because they often work at the lowest-paying jobs and because of racial discrimination. Asian Americans have the highest income

> **working poor** • People who work but whose earnings are not enough to lift them above the poverty line.

of any group, but their poverty rate is also slightly more than that of whites, reflecting the recent influx of relatively poor Asian immigrant groups.

Hispanics have somewhat higher incomes than blacks, although their poverty rate is comparable. Nonetheless, the number of blacks living in poverty has declined considerably in recent years. In 1959, 55.1 percent of blacks were living in poverty; by 2010, that figure had dropped to 27.6 percent. A similar pattern holds for Hispanics: Poverty grew steadily between 1972 and 1994, peaking at 30.7 percent of the Hispanic population. By 2010, however, the poverty rate for Hispanics had fallen to 27.6 percent (DeNavas-Walt, Proctor, and Smith, 2011). This is mainly because the economic expansion of the 1990s created new job opportunities (DeNavas-Walt, Proctor, and Lee, 2005).

The Feminization of Poverty

Much of the growth in poverty is associated with the **feminization of poverty**, an increase in the proportion of the poor who are female. Growing rates of divorce, separation, and single-parent families have placed women at a particular disadvantage, since it is extremely difficult for unskilled or semiskilled, low-income, poorly educated women to raise children by themselves while also holding down a job that could raise them out of poverty. As a result, in 2010, 31.6 percent of all single-parent families headed by women were poor, compared with only 6.2 percent of married couples with children (DeNavas-Walt, Proctor, and Smith, 2011).

The feminization of poverty is particularly acute among families headed by Hispanic women. Although the rate declined by about 25 percent since its peak in the mid-1980s (64 percent in 1985), 44.5 percent of all female-headed Hispanic families lived in poverty in 2010. A similar proportion (40.9 percent) of female-headed African American families also live in poverty; both considerably higher than either white (31.2 percent) or Asian (21.5 percent) female-headed households (U.S. Bureau of the Census, 2011m, 2011n).

A single woman attempting to raise children alone is caught in a vicious circle (Edin and Kefalas, 2005). If she has a job, she must find someone to take care of her children, since she cannot afford to hire a babysitter or pay for day care. From her standpoint, she will take in more money if she accepts welfare payments from the government and tries to find illegal part-time jobs that pay cash not reported to the government rather than a regular full-time job paying minimum wage. Even though welfare will not get her out of poverty, if she finds a regular job, she will lose her welfare altogether, and she and her family may even be worse off economically.

feminization of poverty • An increase in the proportion of the poor who are female.

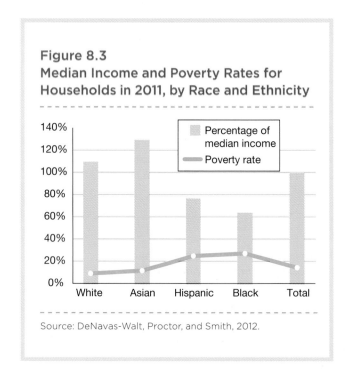

Figure 8.3
Median Income and Poverty Rates for Households in 2011, by Race and Ethnicity

Source: DeNavas-Walt, Proctor, and Smith, 2012.

Children in Poverty

Given the high rates of poverty among families headed by single women, it follows that children are the principal victims of poverty in the United States. As we noted earlier, the United States ranks second among the world's wealthiest nations with respect to its child poverty rate. Nonetheless, that rate has varied considerably over the last 40 years, declining when the economy expands or the government increases spending on antipoverty programs and rising when the economy slows and government antipoverty spending falls. The child poverty rate declined from 27.3 percent of all children in 1959 to 14.4 percent in 1973, a period associated with both economic growth and the War on Poverty declared by the Johnson administration (1963–1969). During the late 1970s and 1980s, as economic growth slowed and cutbacks were made in government antipoverty programs, child poverty grew, exceeding 20 percent during much of the period. The economic expansion of the 1990s saw a drop in child poverty rates, and by 2002 the rate had fallen to 16.3 percent, a 20-year low (U.S. Bureau of the Census, 2003b).

However, these patterns have reversed in recent years, due in part to the current recession. A recent study by the Annie E. Casey Foundation found that child poverty surged in 38 states during the past decade, and erased many of the gains in child well-being made in the last 20 years. In 2009, 15 million children lived in poor families, and another 31 million children lived in families where the loss of just two paychecks would produce economic catastrophe, according to the report. Taken together, this means that about 43 percent of the nation's children live in economically insecure households. The study also found that 4 percent of children had been directly affected by a foreclosure and 11 percent had at least one parent who had lost a job since the recession began (Annie E. Casey Foundation, 2011).

The economic well-being for racial minority children and children of single mothers is even more dire. In 2010, 11.7 percent of white, non-Hispanic children were poor; as were 38.1 percent of black children, 13.3 percent of Asian children, 34.6 percent of Hispanics, and 46.9 percent of children who lived in a single-mother household (U.S. Bureau of the Census, 2011j; Figure 8.4).

The Elderly in Poverty

Although relatively few persons age 65 and older live in poverty (9.0 percent), this aggregate statistic conceals vast gender, race, and marital status differences in the economic well-being of older adults. In 2010, elderly poverty rates ranged from just 3.1 percent

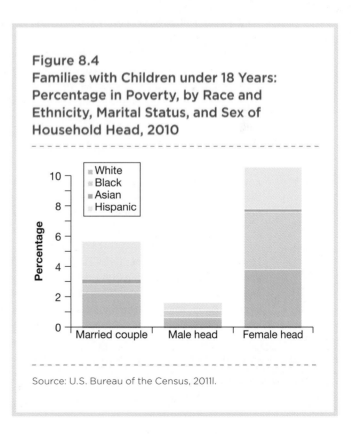

Figure 8.4
Families with Children under 18 Years: Percentage in Poverty, by Race and Ethnicity, Marital Status, and Sex of Household Head, 2010

Source: U.S. Bureau of the Census, 2011l.

among white married men to an astounding 31.4 percent for black women who live alone and 40.8 percent for Hispanic women living alone (U.S. Bureau of the Census, 2011a). As we noted earlier, these estimates may underestimate how widespread elderly poverty is, because poverty rates fail to consider the high (and rising) costs of medical care, which disproportionately strike older adults (Carr, 2010).

Because older people have for the most part retired from paid work, their income is based primarily on Social Security and private retirement programs. Social Security and Medicare have been especially important in lifting many elderly people out of poverty. Yet people who depend solely on these two programs for income and healthcare coverage are likely to live modestly at best. Social Security accounts for only about 40 percent of the income of the typical retiree; most of the remainder comes from investments and private pension funds, and sometimes earnings. In 2010, Social Security was the main source of income for a majority of households headed by individuals or couples 65 or older. Low-income households in particular are likely to rely heavily on Social Security: The lowest income group of adults 65 and older—the 20 percent with income under $12,554 annually—obtained an average of 84 percent of its income from Social Security benefits (Social Security Administration, 2012b). Yet even the combination of Social Security and private pensions results in modest retirement incomes for most people—in 2010 the median income for retirees without job-related earnings was only about $33,000 even for retirees with multiple additional sources of income (Social Security Administration, 2012b).

A Special Case of Poverty: Homelessness

No discussion of poverty is complete without reference to the people who are traditionally seen as at the very bottom of the social hierarchy, the **homeless**. The growing problem of homelessness is one of the most distressing signs of changes in the American stratification system. The homeless are a common sight in nearly every U.S. city and town and are increasingly found in rural areas as well. Two generations ago the homeless were mainly elderly, alcoholic men who were found on the skid rows of the largest metropolitan areas. Today they are primarily young single men, often of working age.

Because it is extremely difficult to count people who do not have a stable residence (Appelbaum, 1990), estimates of the number of homeless vary widely. The most recent estimate is that 636,017 persons live in emergency shelters, transitional housing, and on the streets on any given night, while 107,148 are chronically homeless in the United States. This last number has declined in recent years due to an increase in the number of permanent supportive housing for formerly homeless individuals (National Alliance to End Homelessness, 2012).

The fastest-growing group of homeless, however, consists of families with children, who make up as much as a third of those currently homeless (National Law Center on Homelessness and Poverty [NLCHP], 2009). Approximately 42 percent of those children are under the age of five. In 2004 the National Law Center on Homelessness and Poverty estimated that 41 percent of homeless persons are single men and 14 percent are single women. Equal shares of the homeless population are black and white (40 percent), while 11 percent are Hispanic and 8 percent are Native American. Very few homeless are Latino or Asian American immigrants, possibly because these groups enjoy close-knit family and community ties that provide a measure of security against homelessness (Waxman and Hinderliter, 1996).

homeless • People who have no place to sleep and either stay in free shelters or sleep in public places not meant for habitation.

Sadly, veterans, or the men and women who have served their country in the armed forces, have particularly high rates of homelessness, due in part to work-limiting physical and mental health problems triggered in combat. An estimated 68,000 veterans are currently homeless in the United States. Within that number, at least 14,000 have been homeless for a year or more and suffer from at least one chronic—and costly-to-treat—health condition (Haggerty, 2012). The National Coalition for Homeless Veterans documents that veteran homelessness, like other forms of poverty, varies by race. Approximately 56 percent of all homeless veterans are African American or Hispanic, despite accounting for only 12.8 percent and 15.4 percent of the U.S. population respectively (NCHV, 2011).

There are many reasons why people become homeless. About two-thirds reported having a problem with alcohol at some point during their lives, another two-thirds reported having a problem with drugs at some point, and nearly 60 percent have experienced a mental health problem (NLCHP, 2004). One reason for the widespread incidence of such problems among the homeless is that many public mental hospitals have closed their doors. The number of beds in state mental hospitals has declined by as many as half a million since the early 1960s, leaving many mentally ill people with no institutional alternative to a life on the streets or in homeless shelters. Such problems are compounded by the fact that many homeless people lack family, relatives, or other social networks to provide support.

The rising cost of housing is another factor, particularly in light of the increased poverty noted elsewhere in this chapter. Declining incomes at the bottom, along with rising rents, create an affordability gap between the cost of housing and what poor people can pay in rent (Dreier and Appelbaum, 1992). The share of renters paying more than 30 percent of income for rent more than doubled since the 1960s, from 23 percent to 50 percent (Joint Center for Housing Studies of Harvard University, 2011). The burden of paying rent is extremely difficult for low-income families whose household heads work for minimum wage or slightly higher. Paying so much in rent leaves them barely a paycheck away from a missed rental payment and eventual eviction (National Low Income Housing Coalition, 2000).

CONCEPT CHECKS

1. What are two pieces of statistical evidence used to support the claim that the gap between the rich and the poor is growing in the United States?

2. How would you explain the wealth gap between blacks and whites in the United States today?

3. According to classic studies of mobility in the United States, how does family background affect one's social class in adulthood?

4. What is the poverty line, and how does the U.S. government calculate this statistic?

5. What are the main reasons that people become homeless?

4 UNANSWERED QUESTIONS

Sociologists of social stratification have documented and explained important trends in recent years, but new, fascinating, and policy-relevant questions are continually emerging. Here, we highlight four critical questions and, in the following section, provide preliminary answers. First, is inequality declining or increasing in the United States? Second, why are poverty rates rising in the United States? Third, what can be done to combat poverty? Fourth, how will these economic patterns affect your life?

Is Inequality Declining or Increasing in the United States?

In 1955 the Nobel Prize–winning economist Simon Kuznets proposed a hypothesis that came to be widely accepted: the **Kuznets curve**, a formula showing that inequality increases during the early stages of capitalist development, then declines, and eventually stabilizes at a relatively low level (Figure 8.5). Studies of European countries, the United States, and Canada all suggested that inequality peaked in these places before World War II, declined through the 1950s, and remained roughly the same through the 1970s (Berger, 1986; Nielson, 1994). In the post–World War II era, inequality was due in part to economic expansion in industrial societies, which created opportunities for people at the bottom to move up, and in part to government health insurance, welfare, and other programs aimed at reducing inequality.

Was Kuznets's prediction correct? Have we seen stabilization in levels of inequality? There is evidence that some capitalist economies have entered a fourth phase, one in which inequality is again increasing. In the United States, for example, during the past 30 years the rich have gotten much richer, middle-class incomes have stagnated, and the poor have grown in number and are poorer than they have been since the 1960s. The gap between rich and poor is the largest since 1947, when the Census Bureau started measuring it (U.S. Bureau of the Census, 2012o), and the largest in the industrial world. One statistical analysis found that the United States had the most unequal distribution of household income among all 21 industrial countries studied (Sweden had the most equal; OECD, 2010).

Most people are aware that the gap between rich Americans and all others has increased significantly since the Great Recession. But did you know that the gap had been widening long before the recession? The reasons for this are many and debated, but globalization (whose role we consider in the next chapter) and the declining role of governments (discussed in Chapter 13) are likely two factors that have led to rising inequality not only in the United States and Europe but also in much of the world.

How much did inequality in the United States grow before the Great Recession? Table 8.2 compares the average after-tax income of five income groups in 2010 with the income each group would have had if

Figure 8.5
The Kuznets Curve

The Kuznets curve, named for the Nobel Prize–winning economist who first advanced the idea in 1955, argues that inequality increases during early industrialization, then decreases during later industrialization, eventually stabilizing at low levels. There is some evidence that inequality may increase once again during the transition to postindustrial society.

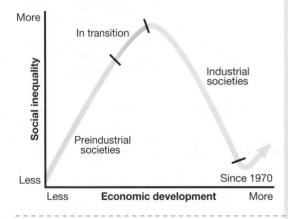

Source: Nielsen, 1994.

Table 8.2

How Has an Increase in Income Inequality Affected American Households during the Last Thirty-Five Years?

INCOME CATEGORY	ACTUAL 2009 MEAN INCOME ($)[a]	2009 INCOME IF INEQUALITY HAD NOT CHANGED FROM 1974 ($)[b]	DIFFERENCE: HOW MUCH POORER OR RICHER ($)
Lowest fifth	11,552	12,698	-1,664
Second fifth	29,257	31,560	-2,924
Middle fifth	49,534	50,860	-1,551
Fourth fifth	78,694	73,454	+5,586
Highest fifth	170,844	130,141	+39,492
Top 5 percent	295,388	197,814	+89,872

Source: (a) U.S. Bureau of the Census, 2012j; (b) calculations based on historical inflation rate change of 353.1 percent between January 1974 and January 2011, inflationdata.com/inflation/inflation_Rate /InflationCalculator.asp (accessed fall 2012).

its share of total income had remained the same as in 1974—that is, if inequality had not increased during the thirty-six-year period. Three of the groups were worse off in 2010 than they would have been had inequality not increased. The top 20 percent, on the other hand, were on average $39,492 richer; the top 5 percent, $89,872 richer. Another indication of growing inequality (again, long before the Great Recession) was the growing earnings gap between top corporate officials and average working Americans. According to data provided by *Forbes* magazine (2007), the average annual pay of the 25 best-paid chief executive officers (CEOs) in the United States in 2007 was $125 million, at a time when the average blue-collar worker in the United States was earning $35,000 (BLS, 2007). Between 1990 and 2004, CEO pay increased by 300 percent, while production worker pay increased by only 4.5 percent (Domhoff, 2005).

Since the Great Recession, the growing gap between the rich and everybody else has accelerated (Smeeding, Thompson, Levanon, and Burak, 2011). Most gains in income, for example, have gone to the wealthiest 5 percent of the population, while income declined for the bottom 60 percent. Rising unemployment badly hurt lesser-skilled workers: between May 2007 and October 2009, for example, 7.5 million jobs were lost, while the nation's unemployment rate more than doubled, from 4.4 percent to 10.1 percent. Worse, much of this unemployment has been persistent: by 2010, two-fifths of the unemployed said they had been looking for work for at least six months (Grusky, Western, and Wimer, 2011).

Although the income gap between the rich and the majority of Americans grew sharply during the Great Recession, was the same true of wealth? After all, as we have seen, the rich enjoy not only more income than other economic groups, but also greater wealth: they own stocks and bonds, real estate, multiple homes, expensive cars, fine art, and other forms of investment. One measure of those investments, the stock market, lost more than half its value between October 2007 and March 2009 (Grusky, Western, and Wimer, 2011). As we noted at the beginning of this chapter, the rich and superrich saw their wealth decline by $2.6 trillion (Wolff, Owens, and Burak, 2011). The average value of all homes—the principal form of wealth for all but the wealthiest Americans—dropped sharply, with average home prices falling 26 percent. Millions of families lost their homes, unable to pay their mortgages. Yet also, as we saw at the beginning of this chapter, as a percentage of total wealth, the middle class suffered a greater decline than either the wealthiest or the poorest homeowners (Wolff, Owens, and Burak, 2011).

President Barack Obama's response to the Great Recession involved $600 billion in government spending between 2009 and 2010, intended to stimulate the national economy. Federal dollars provided direct-income assistance to households, tax relief to state and local governments, and government spending on technology and infrastructure. Although this spending did not halt the economic decline for most households, it did slow that decline somewhat. It was successful, in other words, in somewhat reducing the level of inequality that otherwise would have resulted from the recession (Burtless and Gordon, 2011).

The limited success of the Obama stimulus program did not make it popular, however; a majority of Americans polled at the time believed the stimulus to be wasteful (Burtless and Gordon, 2011). The current political climate, where voters are nervous about government spending, makes it unlikely that even the Great Recession will result in government policies that slow or end the current growth in inequality (Grusky, Western, and Wimer, 2011).

The ideas behind the Kuznets curve may have held true for much of the nineteenth and twentieth centuries, but whether it will hold true for the twenty-first century remains an open question.

Why Are Poverty Rates Rising in the United States? The Sociological Debate

The poor are most deeply affected by economic downturns, and the current recession was no exception. One study estimates that the percentage of Americans living in poverty grew from 12.5 percent in 2007 to 15.0 percent in 2010, a trend that most economists agree will continue for some years (Smeeding, Thompson, Levanon, and Burak, 2011).

Some theories see poor individuals as responsible for their own poverty, and other theories view poverty as produced and reproduced by structural forces in society. These approaches are sometimes described as "blame the victim" and "blame the system" theories, respectively. We shall briefly examine each.

There is a long history of attitudes holding the poor responsible for their own disadvantaged positions. For example, the poorhouses of the nineteenth century were grounded in a belief that the poor were unable—due to lack of skills, moral or physical weakness, absence of motivation, or below-average ability—to succeed in society. Social standing was seen to reflect a person's talent and effort; those who deserved to succeed did so, while others less capable were doomed to fail.

Such outlooks reemerged in the 1970s and '80s as the political emphasis on entrepreneurship and ambition rewarded those who "succeeded" and held those who did not succeed responsible for their unfortunate circumstances. Often, explanations for poverty targeted the lifestyles and attitudes of poor people. Oscar Lewis (1968) proposed one of the most influential theories, which argues that poverty results from a larger social and cultural atmosphere into which poor children are socialized. The **culture of poverty** is transmitted across generations because young people see little point in aspiring to something more. Instead, they resign themselves to a life of impoverishment.

The culture of poverty thesis was taken further by Charles Murray (1984), who placed individuals who are poor through "no fault of their own"—such as widows or widowers, orphans, or the disabled—into a different category from those who are part of the **dependency culture**. This term refers to poor people who rely on welfare rather than entering the labor market. Murray argued that the growth of the welfare state undermines personal ambition and the capacity for self-help: Welfare erodes people's incentive to work.

Such theories seem to resonate among the U.S. population. Surveys have shown that the majority of Americans regard the poor as responsible for their own poverty, and are suspicious of those who live "for free" on "government handouts." Many believe that people on welfare could find work if they were determined to do so. Yet, as we have seen, these views are out of line with the realities of poverty. One recent study (OECD, 2008) found that nearly half of Americans surveyed believed that poverty is due to laziness—a far higher percentage than in other industrial countries (in Germany, for example, only about 10 percent shared this opinion).

A second approach to explaining poverty emphasizes larger social processes that are difficult for individuals to overcome. In this view, structural forces within society— differences in opportunity that are associated with race, class, gender, ethnicity, occupational position, educational attainment, and so forth—shape the way in which resources are distributed (Wilson, 1996, 2011). Advocates of this approach argue that the perceived lack of achievement among the poor is a consequence of their constrained situations, not a cause of it. Reducing poverty thus requires policy measures aimed at distributing income and resources more equally throughout society, such as child-care subsidies, a minimum hourly wage, and guaranteed income levels for families.

Both theories play a role in public debates about poverty. Critics of the "culture of poverty" thesis accuse its advocates of blaming the poor for circumstances beyond their control. They see the poor as victims, not as freeloaders. Yet we cannot accept uncritically the view that poverty originates exclusively in the structure of society. Such an approach implies that the poor passively accept their difficult situations.

culture of poverty • The thesis, popularized by Oscar Lewis, that poverty is not a result of individual inadequacies but is instead the outcome of a larger social and cultural atmosphere into which successive generations of children are socialized. The culture of poverty refers to the values, beliefs, lifestyles, habits, and traditions that are common among people living under conditions of material deprivation.

dependency culture • A term popularized by Charles Murray to describe individuals who rely on state welfare provision rather than entering the labor market. The dependency culture is seen as the outcome of the "paternalistic" welfare state that undermines individual ambition and people's capacity for self-help.

What Can Be Done to Combat Poverty?

In past economic downturns—beginning with the New Deal policies enacted by the Franklin Roosevelt administration during the Great Depression of the 1930s—government transfers helped to blunt the effects. Unemployment insurance, welfare benefits, antipoverty programs, and government stimulus spending helped to create jobs, benefiting those at the bottom, and thereby reducing inequality. These reforms helped to reduce inequality in the long run as well, by transferring wealth (in the form of higher taxes) from richer Americans to poorer Americans. Can contemporary government policies effectively reduce poverty?

Critics of government spending on poverty alleviation argue that it promotes "welfare dependency," meaning that poor people become materially and psychologically dependent on the very programs that are supposed to enable them to become independent. Others deny that such dependency is widespread. "Being on welfare" is a source of shame, they say, and most people on welfare usually try to escape from it.

President Bill Clinton enacted sweeping welfare reform, designed to get people off the welfare rolls. In a sense, this law provided a test case of the "welfare dependency" thesis. The Temporary Assistance for Needy Families (TANF) program, which took effect in 1997, replaced earlier welfare programs by requiring that welfare recipients begin work after receiving benefits for only two years; families would be cut off entirely after a cumulative five years of assistance. Before this reform, there were no time limits or work requirements imposed by the federal government for welfare recipients, many of whom are single mothers.

On the one hand, the welfare-to-work approach was a resounding success: it reduced welfare claims from 5.1 million families to 2.7 million families in their first three years (Figure 8.6). Employment rates did increase somewhat among welfare recipients, and the 61 percent of those who left welfare were able to find work.

On the other hand, nearly one out of every five welfare recipients was unable to find work (or, indeed, any source of independent income), while another fifth was forced to rely on romantic partners, family members, or private charities for support. About half of those who did get a job wound up earning less than they received on welfare; less than a quarter had health insurance through their employer (Loprest, 1999). For low-income mothers, the costs of leaving welfare for work can outweigh the advantages, since they face expenses for food, rent, child care, and other necessities that often exceed their income. In addition, their jobs tend to be less stable and to pay less than welfare (Edin and Lein, 1997).

Thus critics argue that the apparent success of welfare-to-work initiatives conceals troublesome patterns in the experiences of those who lose their welfare benefits. Moreover, even the most hopeful studies were conducted during a period of economic expansion.

Figure 8.6
Percentage of the U.S. Population on Welfare since 1960

Source: U.S. Department of Health and Human Services, 2004.

When growth slows, or declines, it becomes difficult, if not impossible, for welfare recipients to find any jobs at all.

How Will These Economic Patterns Affect Your Life?

Sometime in the next four years, you will graduate from college and face the prospect of starting a new career. Do you have any idea what you will do? Perhaps you will start your own business or will work your way up the hierarchy of an organization in a formal career. Some of you may go to graduate school, or take an unpaid internship, or volunteer for an organization such as the Peace Corps. After reading this chapter, have your hopes and plans changed in any way? Research findings on social stratification and mobility may have important implications for your economic future. Managerial and professional jobs may continue to expand relative to lower-level positions. Those who have earned a college degree are most likely to fill these openings and make a high income. Indeed, 61 percent of Americans in the top fifth of income earners graduated from college, whereas in the bottom fifth, just 12 percent hold a college degree (Brooks and Weidrich, 2012). Educational attainment seems to be the key variable for upward mobility in the United States (Urahn et al., 2012).

Research indicates, however, that the effect of education on mobility chances has decreased somewhat (Hout, 1988; Hout and Lucas, 1996). Because you are a college student, chances are that one of or both your parents are college educated, and that you grew up enjoying a middle-class lifestyle. If this was the case, what are the chances that you will wind up better off than your parents?

Based on their projections into the future, Smeeding, Thompson, Levanon, and Burak (2011) concluded that "the twenty-first century is already on its way to becoming the century of wealth and that such a development will further exacerbate income inequality . . . over the longer term, traditional upward routes to the middle class, in manufacturing and construction jobs, will continue to disappear."

In addition, as a result of global economic competition, not nearly enough well-paid positions are open for all who wish to enter them. Even if a higher proportion of jobs is created at managerial and professional levels, the overall number of jobs available in the future may not keep pace with the number of people with college degrees seeking work. Reasons for this include the growing number of women entering the workforce and the increasing use of information technology in production processes. Because computerized machinery can now handle tasks—even highly complicated ones—that only humans could do before, many jobs may be eliminated.

Moreover, China, India, Brazil, and other countries are now part of a global workforce in which U.S. workers must compete for jobs. While this has been the case for some time with regard to manufacturing jobs—from automobiles to apparel to electronics—it is increasingly true for higher-skilled, high-wage jobs as well. As we shall see in Chapter 14, many so-called "emerging economies" are now educating a growing number of scientists, engineers, and professionals, who will be competing for jobs with U.S. college graduates. Although we are increasingly moving toward an interdependent, global economy, how these shifts will affect your jobs and careers—and stratification in the United States—is difficult to foresee.

CONCEPT CHECKS

1. How has globalization affected the life chances of young adults in the United States today?

2. Contrast the "culture of poverty" argument and structural explanations for poverty.

1 Basic Concepts

p. 195

2 Theories of Stratification in Modern Societies

p. 202

LEARNING OBJECTIVES

Learn about social stratification and the importance of social background in an individual's chances for material success.

Know the most influential theories of stratification—including those of Karl Marx, Max Weber, and Erik Olin Wright.

TERMS TO KNOW

Social stratification • Structured inequalities • Slavery • Caste • Class systems • Class • Income • Wealth

Means of production • Capitalists • Surplus value • Status • Pariah groups • Contradictory class locations

CONCEPT CHECKS

1. What are the three shared characteristics of socially stratified systems?
2. What are two examples of caste systems in the world today?
3. How is the concept of class different from that of caste?
4. What are two examples of noneconomic indicators of one's social class?

1. According to Karl Marx, what are the two main classes and how do they relate to one another?
2. What are the two main differences between Max Weber's and Karl Marx's theories of social stratification?
3. According to Kingsley Davis and Wilbert E. Moore, how does social stratification contribute to the functioning of society? What is wrong with this argument, according to Melvin Tumin?
4. According to Annette Lareau, how do middle-class and working-class parents differ in their child-rearing styles?

Exercises: Thinking Sociologically

1. If you were doing your own study of status differences in your community, how would you measure people's social class? Explain why you would take the particular measurement approach you've chosen. What would be its value(s) and shortcoming(s) compared with those of alternative measurement procedures?

2. Using occupation and occupational change as your mobility criteria, view the social mobility within your own family and explain why you think people in your family have moved up, moved down, or remained at the same status level. Apply these terms: *vertical* and *horizontal mobility*, *upward* and *downward mobility*, *intragenerational* and *intergenerational mobility*.

3. Research on Social Stratification Today

p. 205

Know the class differences in U.S. society, what influences them, and how they are defined and determined. Recognize the ways in which the gap between rich and poor has grown larger. Learn the processes by which people become marginalized in a society and the forms this marginalization takes.

Upper class • Middle class • Working class • Lower class • Underclass • Social mobility • Intergenerational mobility • Intragenerational mobility • Exchange mobility • Structural mobility • Absolute poverty • Relative poverty • Poverty line • Working poor •Feminization of poverty • Homeless

1. What are two pieces of statistical evidence used to support the claim that the gap between the rich and the poor is growing in the U.S.?
2. How would you explain the wealth gap between blacks and whites in the United States today?
3. According to classic studies of mobility in the United States, how does family background affect one's social class in adulthood?
4. What is the poverty line, and how does the U.S. government calculate this statistic?
5. What are the main reasons that people become homeless?

4. Unanswered Questions

p. 219

Learn about competing explanations for why poverty exists, and means for combating it. Understand your own social mobility chances. Learn how changes in the American economy since the 1970s have led to growing inequalities.

Kuznets curve • Culture of poverty • Dependency culture

1. How has globalization affected the life chances of young adults in the United States today?
2. Contrast the "culture of poverty" argument and structural explanations for poverty.

Global Inequality

Who was the world's richest person in 2012?

- **a** Bill Gates, founder of Microsoft
- **b** Warren Buffett, investor, CEO of Berkshire Hathaway
- **c** Carlos Slim Helú, head of Grupo Carso, a global conglomerate based in Mexico

Turn the page for the correct answer.

If you went out on a limb and guessed Carlos Slim Helú, you were right!

Even though most Americans have never heard of Mr. Slim, in 2012 he was the wealthiest person in the world, with a net worth (the value of everything he owned minus everything he owed) of $69 billion. Mr. Slim—a Mexican citizen of Lebanese descent—actually achieved this lofty position in 2010, surpassing both Bill Gates and Warren Buffett. It was the first time in more than a decade and a half that someone other than an American had topped the list, and the first time—ever—that someone from an emerging economy had done so. Mr. Slim's fortune derives from a vast array of Mexican companies and investments he has acquired, including telecommunications (the lion's share of Mexico's landlines and mobile phone systems), hotels, retailers, tobacco, and financial services. As his wealth grew, he diversified into global businesses as well, including investments in Saks Fifth Avenue and the *New York Times*.

Behind Mr. Slim is Microsoft founder Bill Gates, whose fortune (worth $61 billion) is based largely on ownership of his company's stock, and who seems to be the personification of American entrepreneurialism: a computer nerd turned capitalist. During the late 1990s, Mr. Gates was the first person in history to have a net worth in excess of $100 billion.

Mr. Gates is followed by the financier Warren Buffett, at $44 billion. Mr. Buffett is an investor and CEO of Berkshire Hathaway, Inc., which owns companies such as GEICO auto insurance, MidAmerican Energy Holdings, Fruit of the Loom, Dairy Queen, and See's Candies. The fourth and fifth wealthiest are Bernard Arnault of France, worth $41 billion, and Armancio Ortega of Spain, worth $37.5 billion. Rounding out the top ten: Lawrence Ellison of the United States has a net worth of $36 billion; followed by Eike Batista of Brazil, worth $30 billion; Stefan Persson of Sweden, worth $26 billion; Li Ka-Shing of Hong Kong, worth $25.5 billion; and Karl Albrecht of Germany, worth $25.4 billion (*Forbes*, 2012).

The past quarter century has seen the appearance of more global billionaires than ever before. In 2011 there were 1,210 billionaires worldwide—up from 1,011 two years before. The

LEARNING OBJECTIVES

1   BASIC CONCEPTS

Understand the systematic differences in wealth and power among countries.

2   THEORIES OF GLOBAL INEQUALITY

Recognize the impact of different economic standards of living on people throughout the world.

3   RESEARCH ON GLOBAL INEQUALITY TODAY

Analyze the success of newly industrializing economies.

4   UNANSWERED QUESTIONS

Consider various theories explaining why some societies are wealthier than others, as well as how global inequality can be overcome. Learn how globalization might shape global inequality in the future.

combined net worth of the world's billionaires in 2011 was $4.5 trillion—greater than the total gross national income of all but the top ten economies of the world (calculated from World Bank, 2012e). This was the first time that countries other than the United States produced more than 100 billionaires. China had 155; Russia 101 (*Forbes*, 2012). For the first time, China (including Hong Kong) had the most billionaires outside the United States (*Forbes*, 2012).

Globalization—the increased economic, political, and social interconnectedness of the world—has produced opportunities for unthinkable wealth but also widespread poverty and suffering. Consider Bina Khatun, who worked at a Chinese-owned garment factory in Bangladesh where thousands of workers labored long hours, often thirteen hours a day, six days a week, for which the higher-paid workers might earn $11 per week. Bina and her coworkers made sweaters for major European retailers—sweaters that sell for upward of $50 each. When Bina complained to the factory management about being sexually stalked by her supervisor, she was beaten for speaking out (Kernaghan, 2012). Billions of workers such as Bina are being drawn into the global labor force, many working in oppressive conditions that would be unacceptable, if not unimaginable, under U.S. labor laws. And these are the fortunate ones: Those outside the global economy are frequently even worse off.

In the previous chapter, we noted vast differences in individuals' income, wealth, work, and quality of life. Just as we can speak of rich or poor individuals within a country, so we can talk about rich or poor countries in the world system. A country's position in the global economy affects how its people live, work, and die. In this chapter, we examine the differences in wealth and power among countries in the late twentieth and early twenty-first centuries. We discuss differences in economic standards of living and then turn to a discussion of different theories on the causes of global inequality and what can be done about it. We conclude by considering some unanswered questions concerning economic inequality in an age of globalization.

THE ANSWER IS C.

① BASIC CONCEPTS

Global inequality refers to the systematic differences in wealth and power between countries. These differences exist alongside differences within countries: Even the wealthiest countries have growing numbers of poor people, while less wealthy nations are producing many of the world's superrich. Sociology's challenge is not merely to identify such differences but to explain why they occur—and how they might be overcome.

One way to classify countries in terms of global inequality is to compare the wealth produced by each country for its average citizen. The *gross national income (GNI)* is a measure of a country's yearly output of goods and services per person. The World Bank, an international lending organization that provides loans for development

globalization • The development of social and economic relationships stretching worldwide. In current times, we are all influenced by organizations and social networks located thousands of miles away. A key part of the study of globalization is the emergence of a world-system—for some purposes, we need to regard the world as forming a single social order.

global inequality • The systematic differences in wealth and power between countries projects in poorer countries, uses this measurement to classify countries as high-income (an annual 2012 GNI of $12,476 or more, in 2012 dollars), upper-middle-income ($4,036–$12,475), lower-middle-income ($1,026–$4,035), or low-income (under $1,025) (World Bank, 2012a). This system of classification will help show the vast differences in living standards among countries. According to these classifications, the World Bank identifies 70 countries as high-income, 54 as upper-middle-income, 54 as lower-middle-income, and 36 as low-income (World Bank, 2012g).

Figure 9.1 shows how the World Bank divides 214 countries' economies into the four economic classes. Although nearly 40 percent of the world's population lives in low-income countries, less than 16 percent live in high-income countries. Because this classification is based on *average* income for each country, it masks income inequality *within* each country. Such differences can be significant, although we do not focus on them in this chapter. For example, the World Bank classifies India as a low-income country, yet despite widespread poverty, India also boasts a large and growing middle class. China, in contrast, was reclassified in 1999 from low- to middle-income on the basis of its GNI, yet it has hundreds of millions of people living in poverty.

Comparing countries on the basis of economic output alone may be misleading, because GNI includes only goods and services produced for cash sale. Many people in low-income countries produce only for their own families or for barter, which involves noncash transactions. The value of their crops and animals is not reflected in the statistics. Furthermore, economic output is not a country's whole story: Poor countries are no less rich in history and culture than their wealthier neighbors, even though the lives of their people are much harsher.

High-Income Countries

High-income countries are generally those that industrialized first, a process that began in England some 250 years ago and then spread to the rest of Europe, the United States, and Canada. Beginning about a half century ago, Japan joined their ranks, while Singapore, Hong Kong, and Taiwan did so only within the last decade or so.

High-income countries have 14.2 percent of the world's population, yet they command 66 percent of the world's total income (World Bank, 2012e). Although high-income countries often have large numbers of poor people, they offer decent housing, adequate food, drinkable water, and other comforts—a standard of living unimaginable by the majority of the world's people.

Middle-Income Countries

Middle-income countries (including lower- and upper-middle) are primarily found in East and Southeast Asia and also include the oil-rich countries of the Middle East and North Africa, a few countries in the Americas (Mexico, some Central American countries, Cuba, and other countries in the Caribbean, and most countries in South America), and the once-Communist republics that formerly made up the Soviet Union and its East European allies (Global Map 9.1). Having begun to industrialize relatively late in the twentieth century, most are not yet as developed (nor as wealthy) as the high-income countries. The countries of the former Soviet Union, however, are highly industrialized, although their living standards have eroded as a result of the collapse of communism and the move to capitalist economies. In Russia, for example, the wages of ordinary people dropped by nearly a third between 1998 and 1999, while retirement pensions dropped by

Figure 9.1

GLOBAL INEQUALITY

Comparing Quality of Life Among Countries

	LOW-INCOME COUNTRIES	LOWER MIDDLE INCOME COUNTRIES	UPPER MIDDLE INCOME COUNTRIES	HIGH INCOME COUNTRIES
GROSS NATIONAL INCOME PER CAPITA* *Current U.S. $	$567	$1,760	$6,530	 $41,144
TOTAL POPULATION	816.8 million	2.533 billion	2.489 billion	1.039 billion
ANNUAL POPULATION GROWTH	2.1%	1.6%	0.7%	0.5%
LIFE EXPECTANCY AT BIRTH	59 59 years	66 66 years	73 73 years	80 80 years
FERTILITY RATE	4.1 Births per woman	2.9 Births per woman	1.8 Births per woman	1.7 Births per woman
INFANT MORTALITY RATE* *Per 1,000 live births	 63 per 1,000	46 per 1,000	16 per 1,000	5 per 1,000

Source: World Bank, 2013b, "World DataBank: 2011."

Global Map 9.1
Rich and Poor Countries: The World by Income, 2011

Like individuals in a country, the countries of the world as a whole can be seen as economically stratified. In general, those countries that experienced industrialization the earliest are the richest, while those that remain agricultural are the poorest. An enormous, and growing, gulf separates the two groups.

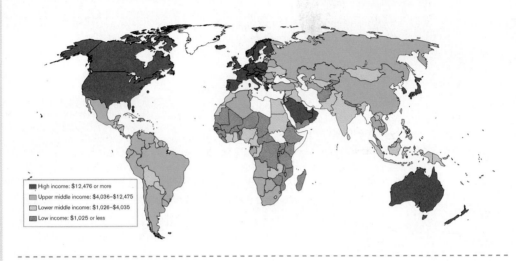

High income: $12,476 or more
Upper middle income: $4,036–$12,475
Lower middle income: $1,026–$4,035
Low income: $1,025 or less

Source: World Bank, 2011b.

nearly half (CIA, 2000). Since then, the Russian economy has recovered somewhat, with foreign investment gradually increasing and the energy market booming.

In 2010, middle-income countries were home to 71.7 percent of the world's population (4.91 billion people) but accounted for only 31 percent of the output produced that year. Although many residents are substantially better off than their neighbors in low-income countries, most do not enjoy anything resembling the standard of living common in high-income countries.

Low-Income Countries

The *low-income countries* include much of eastern, western, and sub-Saharan Africa; Cambodia, and North Korea in East Asia; Nepal, and Bangladesh in South Asia; and Haiti in the Caribbean. They have mostly agricultural economies and are just beginning to industrialize. Scholars debate the reasons for their late industrialization and widespread poverty, as we will see later.

In 2011 the low-income countries included nearly 12 percent of the world's population (816 million people) but just 7 percent of the world's GNI (World Bank, 2012e). Moreover, this inequality is increasing—partly as a result of higher fertility, for large families provide additional farm labor or otherwise contribute to family income. In fact, the populations of low-income countries (with the principal exception of India) grew 2.6 times as fast as those of high-income countries between 1990 and 2005.

In many low-income countries, people struggle with poverty, malnutrition, and starvation. Most people live in rural areas, although recently hundreds of millions of people have been moving to densely populated cities, where they live either in dilapidated housing or on the streets (see Chapter 19).

CONCEPT CHECKS ✓

1. Explain how the World Bank measures global inequality, and discuss some of the problems associated with measuring global inequality.

2. Compare and contrast high-income, middle-income, and low-income countries.

② THEORIES OF GLOBAL INEQUALITY

Four kinds of theories have been advanced to explain global inequality: market-oriented theories, dependency theories, world-systems theory, and global commodity chains theory. Each theory has strengths and weaknesses. One shortcoming of all four is that they underemphasize the role of women in economic development. By putting the theories together, however, we should be able to answer a question facing the 86 percent of the world's population living outside high-income countries: How can they move up in the world economy?

Market-Oriented Theories

Market-oriented theories assume that the best economic consequences will result if individuals are free—from governmental constraint—to make their own economic decisions. Unrestricted capitalism is seen as the avenue to economic growth. Government bureaucracy should not dictate which goods to produce, what prices to charge, or how much to pay workers. According to market-oriented theorists, governmental direction of the economies of low-income countries blocks economic development; thus, local governments should get out of the way of development (Berger, 1986; Ranis, 1996; Ranis and Mahmood, 1992; Rostow, 1961; Warren, 1980).

Market-oriented theories reflect the belief that "any country can make it if it does it 'our way'"—that is, like the United States and other similar high-income countries. These theories inspired U.S. government foreign-aid programs that provided money, expert advisers, and technology to low-income countries, paving the way for U.S. corporations to make investments there.

One influential proponent of such theories was W. W. Rostow, an economic adviser to former U.S. president John F. Kennedy, whose ideas helped shape U.S. foreign policy toward Latin America during the 1960s. Rostow's explanation, termed **modernization theory**, argues that low-income societies can develop economically only if they

market-oriented theories • Theories about economic development that assume that the best possible economic consequences will result if individuals are free to make their own economic decisions, uninhibited by governmental constraint.

modernization theory • A version of market-oriented development theory that argues that low-income societies develop economically only if they give up their traditional ways and adopt modern economic institutions, technologies, and cultural values that emphasize savings and productive investment.

adopt modern economic institutions, technologies, and cultural values that emphasize savings and productive investment.

According to Rostow (1961), the traditional cultural values and social institutions of low-income countries impede the countries' economic effectiveness. For example, many people in low-income countries, in Rostow's view, lack a strong work ethic: They would sooner consume today than invest for the future. Large families also contribute to "economic backwardness," since a breadwinner with many mouths to feed can hardly save money for investment purposes.

To some modernization theorists, the problems in low-income countries run even deeper, because their cultures support a value system that views hardship and suffering as unavoidable. Acceptance of one's lot in life discourages people from being thrifty and working hard to overcome their fate. In this view, a country's poverty is due largely to the cultural failings of the people themselves, which are reinforced by government policies that set wages and control prices and generally interfere in the operation of the economy. How can low-income countries break out of their poverty? Rostow viewed economic growth as going through several stages, which he likened to the journey of an airplane:

1. Traditional stage. This stage is characterized by low rates of savings, the supposed lack of a work ethic, and a fatalistic value system. The airplane is not yet off the ground.
2. Takeoff to economic growth. Economic takeoff occurs when poor countries begin to jettison their traditional values and institutions and start to save and invest money for the future. Wealthy countries, such as the United States, can facilitate this growth by financing birth-control programs or providing low-cost loans for electrification, road and airport construction, and new industries.
3. Drive to technological maturity. With the help of money and advice from high-income countries, the airplane of economic growth would taxi down the runway, pick up speed, and become airborne. The country would then approach technological maturity and climb to cruising altitude, improving its technology, reinvesting its recently acquired wealth in new industries, and adopting the institutions and values of the high-income countries.
4. High mass consumption. Now people can enjoy the fruits of their labor by achieving a high standard of living. The airplane (country) cruises on automatic pilot, having entered the ranks of high-income countries.

Rostow's ideas remain influential. Indeed, the prevailing view among economists today, **neoliberalism**, argues that free-market forces, achieved by minimizing governmental restrictions on business, provide the only route to economic growth. Neoliberalism holds that global free trade will enable all countries to prosper; eliminating governmental regulation is necessary. Neoliberal economists therefore seek an end to restrictions on trade and often challenge minimum-wage and other labor laws, and environmental restrictions on business.

neoliberalism • The economic belief that free-market forces, achieved by minimizing government restrictions on business, provide the only route to economic growth.

Sociologists, however, focus on the cultural aspects of Rostow's theory: whether and how certain beliefs and institutions hinder development (So, 1990). These include religious values, moral beliefs, belief in magic, folk traditions and practices, and the belief that moral decay and social unrest accompany business and trade.

Dependency Theories

During the 1960s, a number of sociologists and economists from the low-income countries of Latin America and Africa rejected the idea that their countries' economic underdevelopment was due to their own cultural or institutional faults. Instead, they built on the theories of Karl Marx, who argued that world capitalism would create a class of countries manipulated by more powerful countries, just as capitalism within countries leads to the exploitation of workers. Adherents to **dependency theories** argue that the poverty of low-income countries stems from their exploitation by wealthy countries and the multinational corporations based in those wealthy countries. In their view, global capitalism has locked their countries into a downward spiral of exploitation and poverty.

According to dependency theories, the exploitation began with **colonialism**. Powerful nations colonized other countries to procure raw materials (such as petroleum, copper, and iron) for their factories and to control markets for the manufactured products. Although colonialism typically involved European countries establishing colonies in North and South America, Africa, and Asia, some Asian countries (such as Japan) had colonies as well.

Even though colonialism largely ended after World War II, the exploitation did not: Transnational corporations continued to reap enormous profits from their branches in low-income countries. According to dependency theories, these global companies, often with the support of the powerful banks and governments of rich countries, established factories in poor countries, using cheap labor and raw materials to maximize production costs without governmental interference. In turn, the low prices for labor and raw materials prevented poor countries from accumulating the profit necessary to industrialize themselves. Local businesses that might have competed with foreign corporations were prevented from doing so. In this view, poor countries were forced to borrow from rich countries, thereby increasing their economic dependency.

Low-income countries are seen not as underdeveloped but as misdeveloped (Amin, 1974; Emmanuel, 1972; Frank, 1966, 1969a, 1969b, 1979; Prebisch, 1967, 1971). Except for a few local politicians and businesspeople serving the interests of the foreign corporations, people fall into poverty. Peasants must choose between starvation and working at near-starvation wages on foreign-controlled plantations and in foreign-controlled mines and factories. Most dependency theorists reject such exploitation and call for revolutionary changes that would push foreign corporations out of their countries altogether (Frank, 1966, 1969a, 1969b).

> **dependency theories** • Marxist theories of economic development arguing that the poverty of low-income countries stems directly from their exploitation by wealthy countries and by the multinational corporations that are based in wealthy countries.
>
> **colonialism** • The process whereby Western nations established their rule in parts of the world away from their home territories.

Two British generals are served tea in Bangalore, India. India was part of the British Empire until 1947.

Whereas market-oriented theorists usually ignore political and military power, dependency theorists regard the exercise of power as central to enforcing unequal economic relationships: Whenever local leaders question such unequal arrangements, their voices are suppressed. Unionization is usually outlawed, and labor organizers are jailed or killed. When people elect a government opposing these policies, it is likely to be overthrown by the country's military, often backed by armed forces of the industrialized countries. Dependency theorists cite many examples, such as the role of the CIA in overthrowing the Marxist governments of Guatemala in 1954 and Chile in 1973 and in undermining support for the leftist government in Nicaragua in the 1980s. In the view of dependency theories, global economic inequality is backed up by force: Economic elites in poor countries, backed by their counterparts in wealthy ones, use police and military power to keep the local population under control.

The Brazilian sociologist Fernando Henrique Cardoso argued that some degree of **dependent development** was nonetheless possible—that under certain circumstances, poor countries can still develop economically, although only in ways shaped by their reliance on wealthier countries (Cardoso and Faletto, 1979). In particular, the governments of these countries could help steer a course between dependency and development (Evans, 1979). Once Cardoso was elected as Brazil's president (1995–2002), however, he changed his thinking, calling for greater integration of Brazil into the global economy—although on terms more favorable to Brazil.

World-Systems Theory

While dependency theories hold that individual countries are economically tied to one another, **world-systems theory** argues that the world capitalist economic system of countries engaging in diplomatic and economic relations with one another must be understood as a single unit. This approach is identified with the work of Immanuel Wallerstein and his colleagues. Wallerstein (1974a, 1974b, 1979, 1990, 1996) showed that capitalism has functioned as a global economic system ever since the extension of markets and trade in Europe in the fifteenth and sixteenth centuries (Hopkins and Wallerstein, 1996). According to this theory, the world system comprises four overlapping elements (Chase-Dunn, 1989):

1. A world market for goods and labor;
2. The division of the population into different economic classes, particularly capitalists and workers;
3. An international system of formal and informal political relations among the most powerful countries, whose competition helps shape the world economy; and
4. The division of the world into three unequal economic zones, with the wealthier zones exploiting the poorer ones.

dependent development • The theory that poor countries can still develop economically, but only in ways shaped by their reliance on the wealthier countries.

world-systems theory • Pioneered by Immanuel Wallerstein, this theory emphasizes the interconnections among countries based on the expansion of a capitalist world economy. This economy is made up of core, semiperiphery, and periphery countries.

World-systems theorists term the zones mentioned in the fourth element as *core*, *periphery*, and *semiperiphery*; understanding the relationships among these three zones is central to understanding global inequality.

- The **core** includes the most advanced industrial countries, taking the greatest profits from countries in the other two zones. Core countries include Japan, the United States, and the countries of western Europe.
- The **periphery** comprises low-income, largely agricultural countries that are often manipulated by core countries for their own economic advantage. Examples are found throughout Africa and to a lesser extent in Latin America and Asia. Natural resources, such as agricultural products, minerals, and other raw materials, flow from periphery to core—as do the profits. The core, in turn, sells finished goods to the periphery, also at a profit—essentially making itself wealthy while limiting the economic development of peripheral countries.
- Finally, the **semiperiphery** comprises semi-industrialized, middle-income countries that extract profits from the more peripheral countries and in turn yield profits to the core countries. Examples include Mexico in North America; Argentina, Brazil, and Chile in South America; and the newly industrializing economies (NIEs) of East Asia. The semiperiphery, though to some degree controlled by the core, can exploit the periphery. Moreover, the greater economic success of the semiperiphery holds out to the periphery the promise of similar development.

Although the world system changes very slowly, once-powerful countries in the core eventually lose their economic power to others. For example, some five centuries ago the Italian city-states of Venice and Genoa dominated the world capitalist economy, but eventually they were superseded by the Dutch, then the British, and currently the United States. Today, American dominance may be giving way to a more "multipolar" world where economic power will be shared among the United States, Europe, and Asia (Arrighi, 1994).

According to world-systems theory, the ability of countries to move from one zone to another is severely limited, but it does sometimes happen. Many East Asian countries, for example, have moved from the periphery to the semiperiphery—and some regions of those countries, such as those containing their leading cities, increasingly resemble the core. The reasons for their success are debated, but world-system theory would attribute the success of some of these countries at least in part to their strong states. Unlike market-oriented theories, world-systems theory argues that appropriate government policies do not interfere with economic development but, rather, can be key in promoting it. Considerable research now suggests that in some regions, such as East Asia, successful economic development has been state led. Strong governments contributed in various ways to economic growth in the East Asian NIEs during the 1980s and '90s (Amsden, Kochanowicz, and Taylor, 1994; Appelbaum and Henderson, 1992; Cumings, 1997; Evans, 1995; World Bank, 1997):

- East Asian governments have sometimes aggressively acted to ensure political stability while keeping labor costs low. They have accomplished this by outlawing trade unions, banning strikes, jailing labor leaders, and, in

core • According to world-systems theory, describes the most advanced industrial countries, which take the lion's share of profits in the world economic system.

periphery • Describes countries that have a marginal role in the world economy and are thus dependent on the core producing societies for their trading relationships.

semiperiphery • Countries that supply sources of labor and raw materials to the core industrial countries and the world economy but are not themselves fully industrialized societies.

general, silencing the voices of workers. The governments of Taiwan, South Korea, and Singapore in particular have engaged in such practices.

- East Asian governments have frequently sought to steer economic development in desired directions. For example, state agencies have provided cheap loans and tax breaks to businesses that invest in industries favored by the government. Sometimes this strategy has backfired, resulting in bad loans held by the government (one of the causes of the region's economic problems during the late 1990s). Some governments have prevented businesses from investing their profits in other countries, forcing them to invest in economic growth at home. Sometimes governments have owned and controlled key industries.

- East Asian governments have often been heavily involved in social programs such as low-cost housing and universal education. The world's largest public housing systems (outside socialist or formerly socialist countries) have been in Hong Kong and Singapore, where government subsidies keep rents extremely low. Because workers don't require high wages to pay for housing, they can compete better with American and European workers in the global labor market. In Singapore, which has an extremely strong central government, well-funded public education and training provide workers with the skills they need to compete in the global labor market. The Singaporean government also requires businesses and individual citizens alike to save a large percentage of their income for investment in future growth.

Other factors, also debated among scholars, include benefiting from a long period of economic growth, the cold war between the Soviet Union and the United States (which led the United States and its allies to invest heavily in the region to discourage the spread of communism), a cultural emphasis on hard work and respect for authority, and a colonial legacy that weakened the power of large landowners. (For a more detailed discussion, see Appelbaum and Henderson, 1992.)

Global Commodity Chains Theory

An important offshoot of the world-systems approach is a concept that emphasizes the global nature of economic activities. **Global commodity chains** are worldwide networks of labor and production processes yielding a finished product. These networks consist of all pivotal production activities that form a tightly interlocked "chain" extending from the raw materials to the final consumer (Appelbaum and Christerson, 1997; Gereffi, 1995, 1996; Hopkins and Wallerstein, 1996).

The commodity-chain approach sees manufacturing as becoming increasingly globalized. Manufacturers accounted for approximately three-quarters of the world's total economic growth during the period 1990–1998. The sharpest growth was among middle-income countries: Manufacturers accounted for only 54 percent of these countries' exports in 1990, compared with 71 percent in 1998. In 2010 the export volume of manufactured goods increased by 18 percent—the highest growth in a decade (WTO, 2011a). Between 2006 and 2010 there was a 19 percent increase in the number of companies exporting from the United States to other countries (*The Economist*, 2012a). China, which moved from the ranks of low- to middle-income countries largely because of its exports of manufactured goods, partly accounts for this trend. Yet the most profitable activities in the commodity chain—engineering, design, and advertising—usually

global commodity chains • Worldwide networks of labor and production processes yielding a finished product.

occur in core countries, whereas the least profitable activities, such as factory production, occur in peripheral countries.

Consider the manufacture of Barbie, one of the most profitable toys in history. Although she sells mainly in the United States, Europe, and Japan, she can also be found in 140 other countries. She is a truly global citizen (Tempest, 1996), not only in sales but also in terms of her birthplace. The first doll was made in Japan in 1959, when that country was recovering from World War II and wages were low. As wages rose in Japan, Barbie moved to other low-wage countries in Asia. Her multiple origins today tell us a great deal about the operation of global commodity chains.

Barbie is designed in the United States, where her marketing and advertising strategies are devised and where most of the profits are made. But the only physical aspect of Barbie that is "Made in the U.S.A." is her cardboard packaging, along with some of the paints and oils used to decorate her. Barbie's body and wardrobe span the globe in their origins:

- Barbie begins her life in Saudi Arabia, where oil is extracted and refined into the ethylene that is used to create her plastic body.
- Taiwan's state-owned oil importer, the China National Petroleum Corporation, buys the ethylene and sells it to Taiwan's Formosa Plastics Corporation, the world's largest producer of polyvinyl chloride (PVC) plastics, which are used in toys. Formosa Plastics converts the ethylene into the PVC pellets that will be shaped to make Barbie's body.
- The pellets are shipped to one of the four Asian factories that make Barbie—two in southern China, one in Indonesia, and one in Malaysia. The plastic-mold injection machines that shape her body, which are the most expensive part of Barbie's manufacture, are made in the United States and shipped to the factories.
- Once Barbie's body is molded, she gets her nylon hair from Japan. Her cotton dresses are made in China, with Chinese cotton—the only raw material in Barbie that actually comes from the country where most Barbies are made.
- Hong Kong plays a key role in the manufacturing process of the Chinese Barbies. Nearly all the material used in her manufacture is shipped into Hong Kong and then trucked to the factories in China. The finished Barbies leave by the same route. Some 23,000 trucks make the daily trip between Hong Kong and southern China's toy factories.

So where is Barbie actually from? The cardboard and cellophane box containing the "My First Tea Party" Barbie is labeled "Made in China," but almost none of the materials that go into making her originate there. For a $20 Barbie, China gets only about $0.70, mainly in wages paid to the 11,000 peasant women who assemble her in the two factories. Back in the United States, however, Mattel makes about $2 in profits.

What about the rest of the money that is made when Barbie is sold for $20? Only $0.65 is needed to cover the plastics, cloth, nylon, and other materials used in her manufacture. Most of the money covers machinery and equipment, transoceanic shipping and domestic trucking, advertising and merchandising, retail floor space—and, of course, the profits of Toys R Us and other retailers.

Although manufacturing in the global commodity chain typically takes place in peripheral countries, an exception has developed. Low-wage, low-profit factories known as sweatshops are reappearing in core countries, sometimes for the first time in half a century or more. A sweatshop is a small factory that violates numerous wage, health, and safety laws. In New York City and Los Angeles, for example, more than 100,000 workers labor in tiny garment factories that make many of the brands of clothing sold in major department

(a) Female workers make Barbie dolls at a toy factory in the Guangdong province of China. (b) Barbie, the quintessentially American doll, has never actually been produced in the United States. Since she was first made in Japan in 1959, rising wages in Asia have moved Barbie production from one low-wage country to another. The four factories that currently make Barbie are located in southern China, Indonesia, and Malaysia.

stores. Many laborers work for less than minimum wage, in buildings described by government officials as firetraps.

The private experiences of these workers are shaped by larger social forces. First, garment workers in New York City and Los Angeles are in direct competition with workers in the Caribbean and Mexico, where wages are a tenth of those in the United States. If workers in New York City and Los Angeles want to keep their jobs, they must settle for sweatshop wages and conditions. Otherwise, the work will be moved to another country. Second, most garment workers are illegal immigrants. If they complain about their working conditions, they risk losing their jobs and being deported.

The global economy not only has brought sweatshops back to the United States, but has also provided the immigrants to work in them.

Evaluating Theories of Global Inequality

Each of the four sets of theories of global inequality has strengths and weaknesses. Together, they enable us to better understand the causes and cures for global inequality.

1. **Market-oriented theories recommend the adoption of modern capitalist institutions to promote economic development.** They further argue that countries can develop economically only if they open their borders to trade, and they cite evidence to support this argument. But market-oriented theories overlook economic ties between poor countries and wealthy ones—ties that can impede economic growth under some conditions and enhance it under others. They blame low-income countries for their poverty rather than acknowledging outside factors, such as the business operations of more powerful nations. Market-oriented theories also ignore the ways government can work with the private sector to spur economic development. Finally, they fail to explain why some countries take off economically while others remain grounded in poverty and underdevelopment.

2. **Dependency theories emphasize how wealthy nations have exploited poor ones.** However, although these theories account for much of the economic

backwardness in Latin America and Africa, they cannot explain the occasional success stories such as Brazil, Argentina, and Mexico, or the rapidly expanding economies of China and East Asia. In fact, some formerly low-income countries have risen economically despite the presence of multinational corporations. Even some former colonies, such as Hong Kong and Singapore, are among the success stories.

3. **World-systems theory analyzes the world economy as a whole, looking at the complex global web of political and economic relationships that influence development and inequality in poor and rich nations alike.** It is thus well suited to understanding the global economy at a time when businesses are increasingly free to set up operations anywhere, acquiring an economic importance rivaling that of many countries. One challenge faced by world-systems theory lies in the difficulty of modeling a complex and interdependent world economy. It has also has been criticized for emphasizing economic and political forces at the expense of cultural ones, such as the combination of nationalism and religious belief that is currently reshaping the Middle East. Finally, world-systems theory has been said to place too much emphasis on the role of nation-states in a world economy increasingly shaped by transnational corporations that operate independently of national borders (Robinson, 2004; Sklair, 2000).

4. **The theory of global commodity chains focuses on global businesses and their activities rather than relationships between countries.** While this approach provides important insights into how different countries and regions are affected (positively or negatively) by the ways in which they connect with global commodity claims, it also tends to emphasize the importance of business decisions over other factors, such as the roles of workers and governments in shaping a country's economy (Amsden, 1989; Cumings, 1997; Deyo, 1989; Evans, 1995; see also the collection of essays in Bair, 2009).

CONCEPT CHECKS

1. Describe the main assumptions of market-oriented theories of global inequality.
2. Why are dependency theories of global inequality often criticized?
3. Compare and contrast core, peripheral, and semiperipheral nations.
4. How have strong governments of some East Asian nations contributed to the economic development of that region?

③ RESEARCH ON GLOBAL INEQUALITY TODAY

Wealth and poverty make life different in a host of ways. For instance, about one-third of the world's poor are undernourished, and almost all are illiterate and lack access to even primary school education. Between 2011 and 2050 the world population is expected to grow from 7 billion to well over 9 billion (U.N., 2012). Over half the world's population now lives in urban areas. The global urban population is projected to gain 2.7 billion, growing from 3.6 billion in 2011 to 6.3 billion in 2050 (U.N., 2012). Many of the poor come from tribes or racial and ethnic groups that differ from the dominant groups, and their poverty is partly the result of discrimination (Narayan, 1999).

Health

People in high-income countries are far healthier than their counterparts in low-income countries. Low-income countries generally suffer from inadequate health facilities, and the few hospitals or clinics seldom serve the poorest people. Residents of low-income countries also lack proper sanitation, drink polluted water, and risk contracting infectious diseases. They are more likely to suffer malnourishment, starvation, and famine. All these factors contribute to physical weakness and poor health. There is growing evidence that the high rates of HIV infection in many African countries reflect the weakened health of impoverished people (Stillwagon, 2001). One interesting caveat here is that in the United States and other advanced industrial countries, illnesses that have been all but eradicated are starting to resurface, due in large part to the fact that many parents are electing not to immunize their children over fears of a link between immunization and autism. An example of this is the notable increase in deaths stemming from pertussis (whooping cough), a disease that is easily preventable through childhood vaccination. According to a report aired on National Public Radio, there were 140 deaths resulting from pertussis in the United States between 2000 and 2005 (NPR, 2009). An outbreak in the first few months of 2012 numbered 17,000 cases and 9 deaths (CDC, 2012c).

Because of poor health conditions, people in low-income countries are more likely to die in infancy and less likely to live to old age than people in high-income countries. Infants are 13 times more likely to die at birth and—if they survive birth—are likely to live 20 fewer years. Children often die of illnesses that are readily treated in wealthier countries, such as measles or diarrhea. In some parts of the world, such as sub-Saharan Africa, a child is more likely to die before the age of five than to enter secondary school (World Bank, 2005). Still, conditions are improving somewhat. Between 1980 and 2010, for example, the infant mortality rate dropped from 97 (per 1,000 live births) to 70 in low-income countries and from 60 to 38 in middle-income countries (World Bank, 2012b). HIV/AIDS and growing poverty have increased infant mortality in the poorest countries in recent years.

Since the early 1980s, some improvements have occurred in most of the middle-income countries and in some of the low-income ones: Infant mortality has been cut in half, and average life expectancy has increased by 10 years or more because of the wider availability of modern medical technology, improved sanitation, and rising incomes.

Hunger, Malnutrition, and Famine

Hunger, malnutrition, and famine have always been global sources of poor health. What seems to be new is their extent—the fact that so many people today are on the brink of starvation (Global Map 9.2). The United Nations Food and Agriculture Organization (UN FAO, 2010) estimates that 925 million people go hungry every day, virtually all of them in the global south. (For a discussion of the use of this term, instead of the commonly used term *developing countries*, please see Chapter 14.) FAO defines "hunger" as a diet of 1,800 calories or less a day—an amount insufficient to provide adults with the nutrients required for active, healthy lives. According to FAO, 147 million of the world's hungry are children under the age of five; they are underweight because they lack adequate food (UN FAO, 2010). Every five seconds, a child dies because of hunger (UN FAO, 2007). Every year, 10.9 million children under the age of five die; 60 percent of those deaths are a result of hunger. Every year, another 17 million children are born with low birth weight stemming from inadequate maternal nutrition (United Nations World Food Programme [UNWFP],

Global Map 9.2
Hunger Is a Global Problem

Hunger is a global problem, although it is disproportionately found in the poorest regions of the world. The world's great concentrations of hunger are in central and sub-Saharan Africa, followed by the Indian subcontinent. It is estimated that at any given time, 870 million people worldwide are undernourished, 852 million of which are in developing countries. The map shows percentages of undernourishment throughout the world, from countries with very low undernourishment to countries with very high undernourishment.

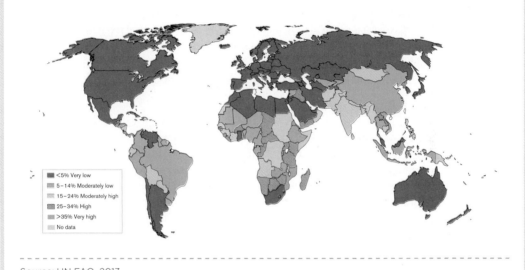

<5% Very low
5–14% Moderately low
15–24% Moderately high
25–34% High
>35% Very high
No data

Source: UN FAO, 2013.

2004). Yet a large majority of all malnourished children under the age of five lives in countries that produce a food surplus (Lappe, Collins, and Rosset, 1998).

Most famine and hunger today are the result of a combination of natural and social forces. Drought alone affects an estimated 100 million people. In countries such as Afghanistan, Eritrea, Ethiopia, Guinea, Indonesia, Sierra Leone, Sudan, and Tajikistan, the combination of drought and internal warfare has wrecked food production, resulting in starvation and death for millions. The role of conflict and warfare in creating hunger is increasing: Conflict and economic problems were cited as the main cause of 35 percent of food shortages between 1992 and 2003, compared with 15 percent between 1986 and 1991 (UN FAO, 2005). In Latin America and the Caribbean, 53 million people (11 percent of the population) are malnourished—a number that rises to 239 million (30 percent) in sub-Saharan Africa and 578 million (17 percent) in Asia (UN FAO, 2010). Two-thirds of the hungry live in just seven countries: Bangladesh, China, Democratic Republic of Congo, Ethiopia, India, Indonesia, and Pakistan (UN FAO, 2010).

The HIV/AIDS epidemic has also contributed to food shortages and hunger, killing many working-age adults. One study by the UN FAO (2001) predicted that HIV/AIDS-caused deaths in the 10 African countries most afflicted by the epidemic will reduce the labor force by 26 percent by the year 2020. UNAIDS (2010a) estimates that 33.3 million people were living with HIV/AIDS at the end of 2009, compared with 26.2 million in 1999—a 27 percent increase. Fully a third of them live in sub-Saharan Africa. On the more hopeful side, between 2001 and 2009 the incidence of HIV/AIDS fell by more than 25 percent due to more access to treatment and the natural course of the illness; sub-Saharan Africa accounted for 22 of the 33 countries that experienced a drop in HIV/AIDS. Still, in sub-Saharan Africa, where the majority of new HIV infections continue to occur, an estimated 1.8 million people became infected in 2009—down from 2.2 million in 2001, but still an enormous number of unfortunate people. The epidemic can be devastating to nutrition, food security, and agricultural production, affecting the entire society's survival.

The countries affected by famine and starvation are too poor to pay for new technologies that would increase food production. Nor can they afford sufficient food imports. At the same time, paradoxically, as world hunger grows, food production continues to increase, often in the very countries experiencing hunger emergencies (UN FAO, 2010). This growth, however, is not evenly distributed around the world. In much of Africa, for example, food production per person has declined. Surplus food produced in high-income countries such as the United States is seldom affordable to the countries that need it most.

Education and Literacy

Education and literacy are important routes to economic development. Lower-income countries are therefore disadvantaged because they lack high-quality public education systems. Thus children in high-income countries get more schooling, and adults in those countries are more likely to be literate. While virtually all high school–age males and females attend secondary school in high-income countries, in 2005 only 78 percent in middle-income countries did so and only 43 percent in low-income countries. In 2010, 30 percent of male adults and 56 percent of female adults in low-income countries were unable to read and write. The adult literacy rate in low-income countries was only 63 percent. One reason for these differences is that high-income countries spend a much larger percentage of their national income on education than do low-income countries (World Bank, 2005, 2012h).

Education is important for several reasons. First, it contributes to economic growth, because people with advanced schooling provide the skilled workforce necessary for high-wage industries. Second, education offers the only hope for escaping the cycle of harsh working conditions and poverty; poorly educated people are condemned to low-wage, unskilled jobs. Finally, educated people have fewer children, thus slowing the global population explosion that contributes to global poverty (see Chapter 19).

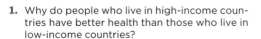

CONCEPT CHECKS ✓

1. Why do people who live in high-income countries have better health than those who live in low-income countries?

4 UNANSWERED QUESTIONS

Since the mid-1970s the overall standard of living in the world has generally risen. Illiteracy is down, infant deaths and malnutrition are less common, people are living longer, and average income is higher. Does this mean that global poverty is being eliminated, or that inequality within nations—or, for that matter, between nations—is declining? What is the future of inequality in our rapidly globalizing world?

There are no clear-cut answers to any of these questions, perhaps because during a time of rapid changes, it is difficult accurately to assess the social forces at play, even with the tools of social science. The debates, however, are informative, and have produced some useful understandings, even if agreement is lacking.

Is Global Poverty Increasing or Decreasing?

The number of people living in extreme poverty, defined by the World Bank as less than $1.25 a day, is declining. In a recent study (2012j), the World Bank reported that "in every region of the developing world, the percentage of people living on less than $1.25 a day and the number of poor declined between 2005–2008 . . . This across-the-board reduction over a three-year monitoring cycle marks a first since the Bank began monitoring extreme poverty." According to the report, preliminary estimates for 2010 indicate that the percentage of people living on less than $1.25 a day was only half the rate in 1990.

But these positive trends mask some disturbing differences between regions and countries. The steep drop in the *percentage* of people living in extreme poverty is not matched, unfortunately, by an equally steep drop in the *number* of people. This is because the world population has grown during the past 30 years. The total number of people living in extreme poverty has declined somewhat—by less than a third, from 1.9 billion to 1.3 billion people. While this is clearly progress, the World Bank forecasts that as many as a billion people will still be in this unfortunate category by 2015, a situation the Bank characterizes as "intolerable" (World Bank, 2012j).

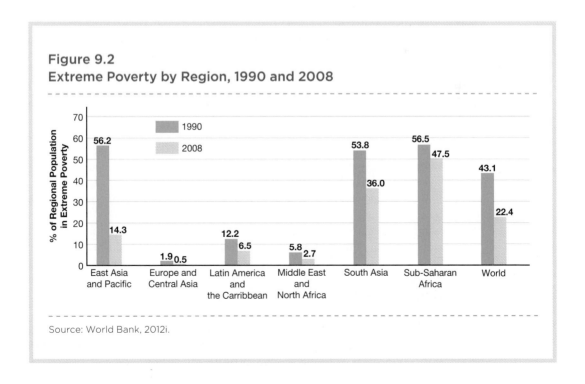

Figure 9.2
Extreme Poverty by Region, 1990 and 2008

Source: World Bank, 2012i.

Moreover, all countries or regions have not shared equally in the gains that have been made. Sub-Saharan Africa, the poorest region in the world, did experience a slight decline in the *percentage* living in extreme poverty, from 56.5 percent in 1990 to 47.5 percent in 2008. Because of overall population growth, however, the *number* of extremely poor people grew sharply, from 290 million to 386 million during the same period (see Figure 9.2).

In fact, a good part of the global reduction in extreme poverty can be attributed to a single country: China. Between 1990 and 2008 the number of Chinese subsisting on less than $1.25 a day declined from 683 million to 173 million. China's economic boom has lifted more than a half billion Chinese out of extreme poverty in the past 30 or so years—roughly the same number as for the world as a whole, where declines in extreme poverty in East Asia, Europe, and Latin America have been more than offset by increases in the Middle East, Africa, and South Asia (see Figure 9.2).

What about Inequality between Countries?

Between 1983 and 2011, average GNI increased nearly fourfold in high-income countries, but barely doubled in low-income countries, widening the global gap between rich and poor (Figure 9.3). Inequality between rich and poor countries has clearly grown during the past 30 years. In 2012 the average person in a typical high-income country earned nearly $36,000, which is almost 150 times greater than the $250 earned by his or her counterpart in Burundi that same year (World Bank, 2012e).

Yet there is at least one hopeful sign: Most of the growth in GNI in low-income countries has occurred in the past 10 years, while such growth in high-income countries has stagnated. If this trend continues, perhaps the gap between the two will decline in coming years. Another hopeful sign is what Fareed Zakaria (2009) has called "the rise of the rest"—the rapid growth of once-poor economies throughout the world that is helping to shape what he calls a "post-American world."

As noted previously, a number of low-income countries in East Asia have undergone rapid economic growth in recent years. This process began with Japan in the 1950s but quickly extended to what were called the **newly industrializing economies (NIEs)** in East Asia. (Today the more widely used term is *emerging economies*.) The East Asian NIEs included Hong Kong in the 1960s and Singapore, South Korea, and Taiwan in the 1970s and '80s. Other Asian countries followed in the 1980s and the early 1990s, including China, Indonesia, Malaysia, and Thailand. Many of these countries averaged 7–8 percent annual growth from 1980 to 1999, a rate that is extraordinary by world standards (World Bank, 2000–2001). By 1999 the GNI in Singapore was the same as that in the United States. Today, most of these countries are middle-income, and some—such as Hong Kong, Singapore, South Korea, and Taiwan—have reached the high-income category.

China, the world's most populous country, has one of the most rapidly growing economies on the planet. According to projections by the International Monetary Fund, China ranks first in terms of gross domestic product (GDP) growth among all economies listed in the World Economic Outlook Projections (*Xinhua*, 2010). At an average annual growth rate of 10 percent between 1980 and 2010, the Chinese economy has more than doubled, and is today the world's second-largest economy, having surpassed Japan in 2010.

newly industrializing economies (NIEs) • Developing countries that over the past two or three decades have begun to develop a strong industrial base, such as Singapore and Hong Kong.

Figure 9.3
GNI in Low-, Middle-, and High-Income Countries, 1983–2011

Despite overall growth in the global economy, the gap between rich and poor countries has not declined in recent years. Between 1984 and 2011, the GNI in low-income countries increased an average of 3.01 percent a year, far less than in high-income countries (5.44 percent). As a consequence, the average person in a high income country earned roughly 70 times as much as the average person in a low-income country. Average GNI in middle-income countries split the difference and increased by an average 6.29 percent.

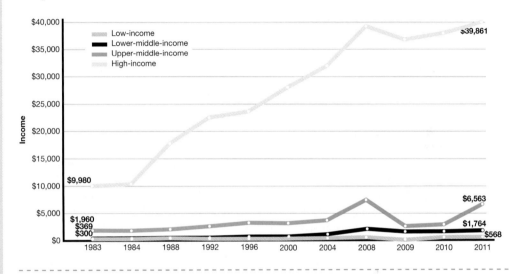

Source: World Bank, 2013a.

What Does Rapid Globalization Mean for the Future of Global Inequality?

Today, the social and economic forces leading to a single global capitalist economy seem irresistible. The principal challenge to this outcome, socialism, came to an end with the collapse of the Soviet Union in 1991.

Many future scenarios are possible. In one, our world might be dominated by large, global corporations, with falling wages for many people in high-income countries and rising wages for a few in low-income countries (see again Robinson, 2004; Sklair, 2000). Average income worldwide might level out, although at a level much lower than that currently enjoyed in the United States and other industrialized nations. In this scenario, the polarization between the haves and the have-nots within countries would grow, as the whole world would be divided into those who benefit from the global economy and those who do not. Such polarization could fuel conflict between ethnic groups and even nations, as those suffering from economic globalization would blame others for their plight (Hirst and Thompson, 1992; Wagar, 1992).

In another, more hopeful scenario, a global economy could mean greater opportunity for everyone, as the benefits of modern technology stimulated worldwide economic growth. The republics of the former Soviet Union and the formerly socialist countries of Eastern Europe will eventually become high-income countries. Economic growth will spread to Latin America, Africa, and the rest of the world. Because capitalism requires that workers be mobile, the remaining caste societies will be replaced by class-based societies, which will experience enhanced opportunities for upward mobility. Indeed, the most successful countries in Asia and South America might be a sign of things to come. China and India, the world's two most populous countries, together have middle-class populations totaling as many as several hundred million people, while Brazil, the world's fifth-most-populous country, is also growing rapidly.

One challenge to this more hopeful scenario, however, is the widening technology gap between rich and poor countries. The gap is a result of the disparity in wealth among nations, but it also serves to reinforce those disparities. Poor countries cannot easily afford modern technology—yet, in the absence of modern technology, they face major barriers to overcoming poverty. They are caught in a vicious downward spiral. Jeffrey Sachs (2000), director of the Earth Institute and professor of sustainable development and health policy and management at Columbia University—and an adviser to the United Nations—claims that the world is divided into three classes: technology innovators, technology adopters, and the technologically disconnected:

- *Technology innovators* are regions that provide most of the world's technological inventions; they represent around 15 percent of the world's population.
- *Technology adopters* are regions that adopt technologies invented elsewhere, applying them to production and consumption; they account for 50 percent of the world's population.
- Finally, the *technologically disconnected* are regions that neither innovate nor adopt technologies developed elsewhere; they account for 35 percent of the world's population.

Innovation requires a critical mass of ideas and technology to become self-sustaining. That is why technological innovation in the United States is concentrated in regions rich in universities and high-tech firms: for example, California's Silicon Valley. Poor countries are ill equipped to develop such high-tech regions; most lack even a science adviser to their government. Sachs urges the governments of wealthy countries, along with international lending institutions, to provide loans and grants for scientific and technological development. Universities in wealthy nations could establish overseas research and training institutes that would foster collaborative research projects. As long as major regions of the world remain technologically disconnected, it seems unlikely that global poverty will be eradicated.

There is, however, a hopeful sign here as well: the rapid growth of international collaboration in scientific research, which is helping to spread the most advanced technologies throughout the world. Carolyn Wagner (2008) has termed this "the new invisible college"; it involves the globalization of knowledge. Scientists, engineers, social scientists, and humanities scholars increasingly operate across borders. It is possible that future years will see an increasing willingness to bring human knowledge and understanding to bear on finding solutions to our most pressing global problems.

CONCEPT CHECKS ✓

1. What is the role of technology in deepening existing global inequalities?

What is the future of global inequality? It is difficult to be entirely optimistic. Global economic growth has slowed, and the economic crisis of 2008 continues to send shock-waves around the world. The Russian economy, in its move from socialism to capitalism, has encountered many pitfalls, leaving many Russians poorer than ever. The European Union, once thought to be a pillar of the global economy, is facing many challenges. While many countries have experienced economic growth, many have not; the gap between rich and poor remains large.

The future of global inequality remains an open question—one whose answer will depend, in large part, on whether global economic expansion can be sustained in the face of ecological constraints and a global economy that has proven to be surprisingly fragile.

Chapter 9
Global Inequality

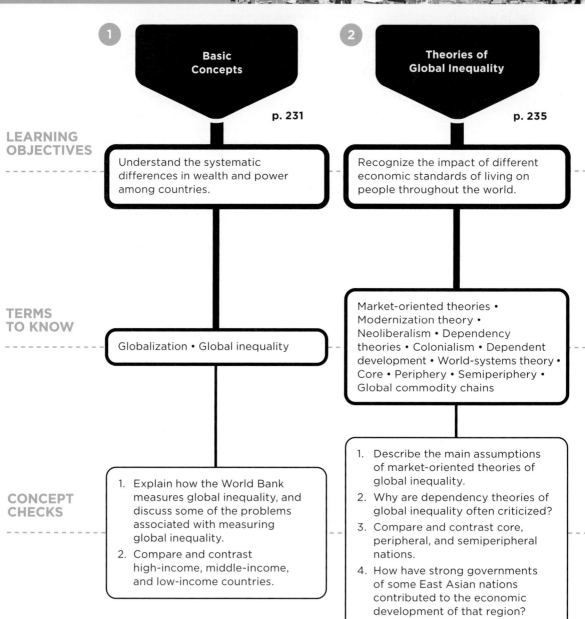

1 **Basic Concepts**

p. 231

2 **Theories of Global Inequality**

p. 235

LEARNING OBJECTIVES

Understand the systematic differences in wealth and power among countries.

Recognize the impact of different economic standards of living on people throughout the world.

TERMS TO KNOW

Globalization • Global inequality

Market-oriented theories • Modernization theory • Neoliberalism • Dependency theories • Colonialism • Dependent development • World-systems theory • Core • Periphery • Semiperiphery • Global commodity chains

CONCEPT CHECKS

1. Explain how the World Bank measures global inequality, and discuss some of the problems associated with measuring global inequality.
2. Compare and contrast high-income, middle-income, and low-income countries.

1. Describe the main assumptions of market-oriented theories of global inequality.
2. Why are dependency theories of global inequality often criticized?
3. Compare and contrast core, peripheral, and semiperipheral nations.
4. How have strong governments of some East Asian nations contributed to the economic development of that region?

1. Summarize the four types of theories that explain why there are gaps between nations' economic development and resulting global inequality: market-oriented theories, dependency theories, world-systems theory, and state-centered theories. Briefly discuss the distinctive characteristics of each type of theory and how it differs from the others. Which theory do you feel best explains economic developmental gaps?

2. This chapter states that global economic inequality has personal relevance and importance to people in advanced, affluent economies. Briefly review this argument. Explain whether you were persuaded by it or not.

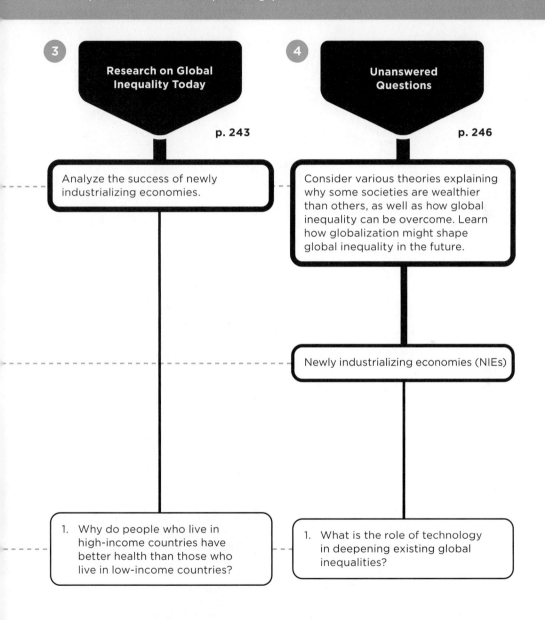

3

Research on Global Inequality Today

p. 243

Analyze the success of newly industrializing economies.

1. Why do people who live in high-income countries have better health than those who live in low-income countries?

4

Unanswered Questions

p. 246

Consider various theories explaining why some societies are wealthier than others, as well as how global inequality can be overcome. Learn how globalization might shape global inequality in the future.

Newly industrializing economies (NIEs)

1. What is the role of technology in deepening existing global inequalities?

Gender Inequality

10

In the year 2012, what proportion of all CEOs of *Fortune* 1000 companies were women?

- **a** 4 percent
- **b** 24 percent
- **c** 54 percent
- **d** 74 percent

Turn the page for the correct answer.

Most of us know that far fewer women than men hold leadership positions in business and politics today, yet we also know that women have made tremendous strides in education, politics, and the workplace over the past century. Business magazines regularly tout the accomplishments of women such as Marissa Mayer, who became CEO of Yahoo! in 2012, and Ginni Rometty, the president and CEO of IBM. Given these highly visible accomplishments of women in business and technology, we might think that one-quarter (answer *b*) or roughly one-half (answer *c*) is the correct answer. Yet according to *Fortune* magazine, which tracks the CEOs of the nation's 1,000 top revenue-generating companies, women held just 3.8 percent of *Fortune* 500 CEO positions and 4.0 percent of *Fortune* 1000 CEO positions in 2012 (Catalyst, 2012).

Why do so few women hold leadership positions in business? This is an important question because women make up half the total workforce in the United States but are CEOs at just 4 percent of major corporations and 3 percent of financial companies (Torregrossa, 2012). Few would point to outright discrimination as the culprit, yet most experts say that discrimination often takes place in subtle and hard-to-prove ways. Climbing to the top-tier positions at competitive Wall Street firms requires round-the-clock work along with "really macho kinds of behavior," including aggressiveness and even ruthlessness, according to Ilene Lang, president of Catalyst, a research organization focused on gender and work. These traits are at odds with traditional gender role socialization; "it is behavior that's admired in men but despised in women," Lang observes. Others point to lack of female mentors in corporate upper echelons, and the tendency of some male decision makers to hold stereotypical and incorrect beliefs about what women are capable of. Others say that women are kicked off the corporate "fast track" when they start having children, and their colleagues view them as unfit for competitive and time-consuming work.

LEARNING OBJECTIVES

❶ BASIC CONCEPTS

Understand the ways that differences between women and men reflect biological factors, sociocultural influences, and the complex interplay between the two.

❷ SOCIOLOGICAL THEORIES OF GENDER INEQUALITIES

Recognize and contrast competing explanations for gender inequality. Learn some feminist theories about gender equality.

❸ RESEARCH ON GENDER TODAY: DOCUMENTING AND UNDERSTANDING GENDERED INEQUALITIES

Learn the forms that both between and within-gender inequalities take. Understand the ways in which women worldwide experience economic and political inequality.

❹ UNANSWERED QUESTIONS: WHY DO GENDERED INEQUALITIES PERSIST?

Learn about gender-based inequalities in the workplace and violence against women.

Women are striking back against both overt and subtle forms of gender discrimination at major Wall Street firms. In the past decade, banks including Goldman Sachs, Wells Fargo, Deutsche Bank, Citigroup, and others have been targets of sex discrimination lawsuits. Charlotte Hanna, a former vice president at Goldman Sachs, filed a sex discrimination lawsuit against her employer in 2010. Hanna alleged that after she returned from her first maternity leave in 2005, Goldman Sachs made her feel like an outsider in what had become a "boys only" club. She worked only part time after her first child was born, taking advantage of her firm's flexible work program. However, she subsequently hit a "glass ceiling" with respect to pay and advancement. She was demoted, and said that she was regularly excluded from company decisions and social functions. Hanna had a second child, in 2009, and was fired while on maternity leave. Prior to that time, she had enjoyed a long and successful career at Goldman; she joined the firm in 1998 as an associate and was promoted to vice president two years later, having received strong praise for her work. Her lawsuit said that 75 percent of "those selected for termination" in her work group had recently taken a maternity leave.

A very similar case was filed against Deutsche Bank by Kelley Voelker, who was a vice president with the bank's securities lending desk for 14 years. In a lawsuit filed in September 2011, Voelker claimed that despite consistently high performance reviews, Deutsche Bank denied her a promotion and eventually demoted her, one of its few female vice presidents, solely because of her gender and recent childbirth. Voelker said that shortly before she took her maternity leave for her first child, in 2003, her supervisor aired his doubts that she would return to work. In her lawsuit, Voelker claimed that her supervisors "never took her seriously because she was a woman starting a family, and this was seen as a huge negative within the company." She also pointed to excessively "macho" behavior from some of her male colleagues—including vulgar language in the office and taking clients to strip clubs—as further evidence that her work climate was not friendly to women.

It's not only female corporate executives who experience obstacles to their career advancement. One of the largest and most famous gender discrimination lawsuits was filed against Walmart by Betty Dukes, a cashier. When Dukes started her job at Walmart in 1994, she had more than 20 years' experience in retail, and was eager to advance her career. When she approached her store manager about her desire to work her way up the ladder, she was brusquely dismissed. Betty was undeterred. She performed well as a cashier, earning regular raises in her hourly wage. She repeatedly asked her manager for a promotion, and she requested opportunities to learn more about the store and take on more challenging assignments. She continued to be denied promotions and was not informed of postings for available positions or management training programs at the retailer. All the while, she

From right: Betty Dukes, Patricia Surgenson, Stephanie Odle, and Christine Kwapnoski charged that Walmart, including its Sam's Club division, systematically discriminated against its hourly and salaried female employees by denying them promotions and equal pay.

watched her male associates become promoted, and she later learned that they were paid more than she was for the same job—although she had more years of work experience in retail and greater seniority at the company (U.S. Supreme Court, 2011).

The final straw came when Dukes was demoted from cashier to greeter. She contacted a lawyer and subsequently sued Walmart on the grounds that the retailer was violating the 1964 Civil Rights Act, which makes it illegal for employers to discriminate on the basis of gender, race, or religion. Dukes alleged that Walmart systematically paid women less than men who did the same jobs, and promoted men to higher ranks at faster rates than women. When Dukes filed her case, her lawyer told her she wasn't alone, and that many other women had also complained that they weren't getting ahead with the multinational firm. The class-action lawsuit that was eventually filed on behalf of roughly 1 million "similarly situated" plaintiffs eventually made its way to the Supreme Court. Dukes and her fellow female Walmart employees were disappointed and angry when the Supreme Court threw out their case in June 2011. Observers say the verdict does not mean that discrimination did not happen in Dukes's case. Rather, all nine Supreme Court justices thought there was not "significant proof" that Walmart "operated under a general policy of discrimination" against each and every one of the million or so women who filed the suit. Nor did they find proof that all the women were systematically victimized by a discriminatory "corporate culture" at Walmart (Toobin, 2011).

We have not heard the final chapter on the Goldman Sachs and Deutsche Bank lawsuits; both cases are pending. Regardless of the legal verdicts, however, these three cases raise awareness about the overt and subtle ways that gender shapes all aspects of our lives. Many people who encounter someone such as Betty Dukes might make certain assumptions about her life. They might assume, for example, that a disproportionate number of women become cashiers because it is "natural" for women to have certain kinds of occupations, including retail or secretarial jobs. People who hear the story of Charlotte Hanna or Kelley Voelker might assume that women prefer to work part time, or do so because part-time work is compatible with childrearing, while full-time work on Wall Street might be "bad for the children." It is the job of sociologists to analyze these assumptions and to adopt a much wider view of our society. Sociology allows us to understand why women make up only a minuscule proportion of all top CEOs in the United States, why women are more likely than men to work in low-paying clerical and retail jobs, why women are likely to spend more time on child care, and why women on the whole have less economic and political power in society than men.

In this chapter, we will take a sociological approach to the exploration of gender differences and gender inequality. Gender is a way for society to divide people into two categories: "men" and "women." According to this socially created division, men and women have different identities and social roles. Men and women are expected to think and act in different ways, across most life domains. Gender also serves as a social status, since in almost all societies men's roles are valued more than women's roles. Sociologists are interested in explaining how society differentiates between women and men, and how these differences serve as the basis for social inequalities (Chafetz, 1990). Yet sociologists recognize that gender alone does not shape our life experiences. Rather, there are pronounced differences in women's (and men's) lives on the basis of race, social class, age, birth cohort, religion, nation of origin, and even one's marital or parental status (Choo and Ferree, 2010).

We will first identify core concepts related to sex and gender. We next provide an overview of influential sociological and feminist theories that guide our understanding of gender. We then review cutting-edge research on the ways that gender shapes our lives in the United States and throughout the world. We conclude by addressing several unanswered and controversial questions about the importance of gender in contemporary society.

THE ANSWER IS A.

1 BASIC CONCEPTS

Before we explore the origins of differences between men and women, boys and girls, it is important that we define and differentiate those attributes and processes that make us male or female. One critical distinction is between sex and gender. **Sex** refers to physical differences of the body, whereas **gender** concerns the psychological, social, and cultural differences between males and females, such as personality, goals, and social roles. The distinction between sex and gender is fundamental because many of the most important differences between males and females are not biological. While sex is something we are born with, gender is something that we both *learn* and *do*.

Gender role socialization is the process through which we *learn* about male- and female-typed roles and practices through social agents such as the family and the media (see also Chapter 4). For example, boys may learn how to engage in rambunctious and aggressive play by watching their favorite male superheroes on TV, while young girls may learn how to nurture their younger siblings by following the model set by their mothers or grandmothers. Through contact with primary and secondary agents of socialization, children internalize the social norms and expectations that correspond with their sex. Gender differences are not biologically determined; they are culturally produced.

We also learn how to "do" gender. Some scholars argue that gender is more than learning to act like a girl or boy; we all "do gender" in our daily interactions with others (West and Zimmerman, 1987). Our fashion choices, how we wear our hair, even the pitch and intonation of our voice are all indications of how we "do gender" each day. This process of "doing gender" underscores the notion that gender is "socially constructed." Theorists who believe in the **social construction of gender** reject all biological bases for gender differences. Gender identities emerge, they argue, in relation to perceived sex differences in society, and in turn help shape those differences. For example, a society in which ideas of masculinity are characterized by physical strength and tough attitudes will encourage men to cultivate a specific body image and set of mannerisms (Butler, 1989; Connell, 1987; Scott and Morgan, 1993). We will elaborate these four concepts—sex, gender, gender role socialization, and social construction of gender—in the following sections; as you will soon see, our identities as "male" or "female" are not as simple as they seem.

sex • The biological and anatomical differences distinguishing females from males.

gender • Social expectations about behavior regarded as appropriate for the members of each sex. Gender refers not to the physical attributes distinguishing men and women but to socially formed traits of masculinity and femininity. The study of gender relations has become one of the most important areas of sociology in recent years.

gender role socialization • The learning of gender roles through social factors such as schooling, the media, and family.

social construction of gender • The learning of gender roles through socialization and interaction with others.

Understanding Sex Differences: The Role of Biology

How much are differences in the behavior of women and men the result of sex—that is, biological differences—rather than gender? Some researchers assert that innate behavioral differences between the sexes appear in some form in all cultures; the findings of sociobiology strongly support this (Goldberg, 1999). For example, the fact that in almost all cultures men rather than women take part in hunting and warfare indicates that men possess biologically based tendencies toward aggression that women lack. Scholars who endorse this perspective might also look at current occupational patterns and attribute them to biology. In 2010, 98 percent of dental hygienists, 97 percent of all secretaries, and 91 percent of registered nurses in the United States were women, whereas 99 percent of auto mechanics and 94 percent of welders were male (Institute for Women's Policy Research [IWPR], 2010; Marsh, 2012). Supporters of the "nature" perspective might point out that women are "wired" to choose jobs that are supportive and nurturing, whereas men hold jobs that require more physical strength or mechanical ability.

Most sociologists are unconvinced by these "nature" arguments. Men's physical strength and aggressiveness, they say, varies widely between cultures, and women are expected to be more passive or gentle in some cultures than in others. Further, some argue that women are just as aggressive as men; however, women use strategies that are consistent with gender role socialization. For instance, women will use "interpersonal aggression" such as malicious gossip or "bad-mouthing" rather than physical fights (Bjorkqvist, 1994; Bjorkqvist, Lagerspetz, and Osterman, 2006). Theories of "natural difference" are often grounded in data on animal behavior, critics say, rather than in anthropological or historical evidence about human behavior, which reveals variation over time and place. In the majority of cultures, most women spend a significant part of their lives caring for children and therefore cannot readily participate in hunting or war.

Despite critiques of the "nature" perspective, the hypothesis that biological factors determine behavior patterns cannot be wholly dismissed. Studies document persuasively that biological factors, including genetics, hormones, and brain physiology, differ by gender, and that these biological differences are associated with some social behaviors, including language skills, interpersonal interactions, and physical strength. However, nearly all social scientists agree that theories based *solely* on an innate predisposition neglect the vital role of social interaction in shaping human behavior.

What does the evidence show? One group of studies investigates gender differences in hormonal makeup. Some have claimed that the male sex hormone, testosterone, is associated with a propensity for violence (Rutter and Giller, 1984). Research has indicated, for instance, that male monkeys castrated at birth become less aggressive than noncastrated monkeys; conversely, female monkeys given testosterone become more aggressive than normal females. However, it has also been found that providing monkeys with opportunities to dominate others actually increases testosterone levels. It is not the case that the hormone causes increased aggression; instead, aggressive behavior may affect production of the hormone.

Another source of evidence is direct observation of animal behavior. Researchers who connect male aggression with biological influences often emphasize male aggressiveness among the higher animals. Among chimpanzees, they say, males are consistently more aggressive than females. Yet critics note that there are large differences between types of animals. Gibbons, for instance, show few sex differences in aggression. Moreover, many female apes or monkeys are highly aggressive in some situations, such as when their young are threatened.

Other evidence comes from studies of identical twins, who derive from a single egg and have exactly the same genetic makeup. In one anomalous but particularly highly talked-about case, one identical male twin was seriously injured while being circumcised, and the decision was made by his physician and parents to reconstruct his genitals as female. He was thereafter raised as a girl. The twins at age six demonstrated typical male and female traits as found in Western culture. The little girl enjoyed playing with other girls, helped with the housework, and wanted to get married when she grew up. The boy preferred the company of other boys, his favorite toys were cars and trucks, and he wanted to become a firefighter or police officer.

For some time, this case was treated as conclusive evidence of the overriding influence of social learning on gender differences. However, when the girl was a teenager she was interviewed during a television program and revealed some unease about her gender identity, even wondering if perhaps she was "really" a boy after all. She had by then learned of her unusual background, and this knowledge may have led to an altered perception of herself (Ryan, 1985).

Technological advances in the last two decades have provided a new source of evidence: brain imaging research, which has identified several key differences between men's and women's brains (Brizendine, 2007, 2010). For example, Burman and colleagues (2007) found that the brains of school-age girls were more highly "activated," or worked harder, than the brains of school-age boys when presented with spelling and writing tasks. This greater level of activation has been associated with greater accuracy in performing such tasks. The authors do not conclude that girls' language skills are superior to boys, yet they do argue that their data show that girls and boys learn language in different ways. A mounting body of research concludes that gender differences in brain functioning may contribute, in part, to a wide range of social outcomes including communication style, empathy, depression, anxiety, and fear. However, most scholars conducting this research are careful to point out that biological differences are almost always exacerbated or fostered by social contexts and norms (Hines, 2003).

Gender Socialization: How Gender Differences Are Learned

As we noted earlier, gender socialization describes the processes through which we learn what it means to be "male" or "female" in our society (see also Chapter 4). This approach distinguishes between biological sex and social gender—an infant is born with sex and develops a gender. Children are guided in this process by positive and negative sanctions, that is, socially applied forces that reward or restrain behavior. For example, a young boy could be positively sanctioned for complying with masculine expectations ("What a brave boy you are!") or negatively sanctioned for violating these expectations ("Boys don't play with dolls. What are you, a sissy?"). If an individual develops gender practices that do not correspond with his or her biological sex—that is, if he or she is deviant—the explanation given is inadequate socialization. According to functionalist perspectives, socializing agents help maintain the smooth continuation of the existing social order by overseeing the smooth gender socialization of new generations. (See Chapter 1 for a review of the core themes of functionalism.)

This rigid interpretation of sex roles and socialization has been criticized on a number of fronts. Many writers argue that gender socialization is not an inherently smooth process; different agents such as the family, schools, and peer groups may be at odds with one another. Moreover, socialization theories ignore individuals' ability to reject or modify the social expectations surrounding sex roles.

Humans are not passive objects or unquestioning recipients of gender programming, as some sociologists have suggested. People actively create and modify roles for themselves. Although any wholesale adoption of the sex roles approach may be inadvisable, many studies have shown that, to some degree, gender identities *are* a result of social influences.

Consider the following two scenes. Two newborns a few hours old lie in the nursery of a hospital maternity ward. One, a male, is wrapped in a blue blanket; the other, a female, is in a pink blanket. Their grandparents are seeing them for the first time. The conversation between one pair of grandparents runs along these lines:

Grandma A: There he is—our first grandchild, and a boy.

Grandpa A: Hey, isn't he a hefty little fellow? Look at that fist he's making. He's going to be a regular little fighter, that guy is. (Grandpa A smiles and throws out a boxing jab to his grandson.) Atta boy! [. . .]

Grandma A: Let's go and congratulate the parents. I know they're thrilled about little Fred. They wanted a boy first.

Grandpa A: Yeah, and they were sure it would be a boy, too, what with all that kicking and thumping going on even before he got here.

When they depart to congratulate the parents, the grandparents of the other child arrive. The dialogue between them goes like this:

Grandma B: There she is . . . the only one with a pink bow taped to her head. Isn't she darling.

Grandpa B: Yeah—isn't she little. Look at how tiny her fingers are. Oh, look—she's trying to make a fist.

Grandma B: Isn't she sweet. . . . You know, I think she looks a little like me.

Grandpa B: Yeah, she sorta does. She has your chin.

Grandma B: Oh, look, she's starting to cry. . . . Poor little girl. (To the baby) There, there, we'll try to help you.

Grandpa B: Let's find the nurse. I don't like to see her cry . . .

Grandma B: Hmm. I wonder when they will have their next one. I know Fred would like a son, but little Fredericka is well and healthy. After all, that's what really matters.

Grandpa B: They're young yet. They have time for more kids. I'm thankful too that she's healthy.

(Walum, 1977)

The contrast between the two conversations sounds so exaggerated that it's tempting to think they were made up. In fact, they are composed of transcripts of actual dialogue recorded in a maternity ward. The first question usually asked of a new parent—in Western culture, at least—is "Is it a boy or a girl?" In fact, expectant parents today can buy over-the-counter tests to determine the sex of their fetus, and a new trend is "gender reveal" parties, where expectant parents share pink or blue cakes with their friends, as a celebratory way to announce the sex (O'Connor, 2012). The implication is that sex matters, because parents will raise boys and girls in different ways (Nugent, 2012).

Once the infant is born and is marked as male or female, everyone who interacts with the child will treat it in accordance with its gender. They do so on the basis of the society's assumptions, which lead people to treat women and men differently, even as opposites (Renzetti and Curran, 1995).

Clearly, gender socialization is very powerful, and challenges to it can be upsetting. Once a gender is "assigned," society expects individuals to act like "females" and "males." These expectations are fulfilled and reproduced in the practices of everyday life (Bourdieu, 1990; Lorber, 1994).

The Social Construction of Gender: How We Learn to "Do" Gender

Recently, socialization and gender role socialization theories have been criticized by a growing number of sociologists. Rather than seeing sex as biologically determined and gender as culturally learned, they argue that both sex and gender are socially constructed products. Not only is gender a purely social creation that lacks a fixed essence, but the human body itself is subject to social forces that shape and alter it in various ways.

Scholars who focus on gender roles and role learning accept that there is a biological basis for some gender differences. Adherents to socialization perspectives believe that the biological distinction between the sexes is the starting point for differences that become culturally elaborated and amplified in society. In contrast, theorists who believe in the social construction of gender reject all biological bases for gender differences.

Proponents of this view argue that gender is more than learning to act like a girl or boy; rather, it is something that we continually "do" in our daily interactions with others (West and Zimmerman, 1987). Our physical appearances, how we walk, and even the pitch of our voices are all indications of how we "do gender" each day. These taken-for-granted practices are vividly brought to life by journalist Norah Vincent, in her book *Self-Made Man: One Woman's Year Disguised as a Man* (2006). Vincent spent 18 months disguised as a man, to understand not only how men behave when women aren't around, but also to reveal the ways that men (and, in Vincent's case, a woman!) "do masculinity" in everyday life.

At 5 feet, 10 inches, and 155 pounds, Vincent passed as a medium-build man she called Ned. Her transformation began with a buzz cut, baggy men's clothes, and a too-small sports bra to flatten her breasts. Vincent underwent months of training with a professional voice teacher to learn how to sound like a man. She then went undercover in a range of typically male settings, including a bowling league, a strip club, a monastery, and a men's support group. She also observed the importance of gender in even the most ordinary everyday encounters—including shopping for a new car at a dealership. When she went into the showroom as Norah, the salesman's pitch quickly turned flirtatious, but when she returned to the same salesman as her disguised alter ego, Ned, the tone was all business and the talk was all about the car's performance. As *Self-Made Man* reveals, gender is powerfully shaped by social context and transcends one's biology.

SOCIAL CONSTRUCTION OF GENDER IN OTHER CULTURES

The subtle ways in which we do gender are so much a part of our lives that we don't notice them until they are missing or radically altered. Cross-cultural research conducted by anthropologists, in particular, helps us recognize how deeply entrenched gendered categories are in the United States and shows us strong evidence that gender is fluid and socially constructed.

The !Kung The !Kung of the Kalahari Desert have specific gender roles, but it is very common for both men and women to engage in child care. Due to the nonconfrontational

Mehran Rafaat, left, with her twin sisters. Mehran was formerly called Manoush and is regarded as a boy by her family.

parenting practices of the !Kung, who oppose violent conflict and physical punishment, children learn that aggressive behavior will not be tolerated by either men or women. Although the !Kung abide by the seeming traditional arrangement where "men hunt and women gather," the vast majority of the tribe's food actually comes from the gathering activities of women (Draper, 1975). Women return from their gathering expeditions armed not only with food for the community but also with valuable information for hunters.

The *Bacha Posh* in Afghanistan In contemporary Afghanistan, boys are so highly prized that families with only daughters often experience shame and pity; as a result, some transform one young daughter into a son. The parents cut the girl's hair short, dress her in boy's clothes, change her name to a boy's name, and encourage her to participate in "boys' activities" such as bicycling and playing cricket. These children are called *"bacha posh,"* which translates into "dressed up as a boy."

Parents of *bacha posh* believe that boys are afforded so many advantages in Afghan culture that it is helpful, rather than cruel, to transform their girls into boys. A *bacha posh* can more easily receive an education, work outside the home, even escort her sisters in public, allowing freedoms that are unheard of for girls in a society that strictly segregates men and women. In most cases, a return to womanhood takes place when the child enters puberty, a decision almost always made by her parents (Nordberg, 2010).

Multiple Genders The understanding that only two genders (i.e., male and female) exist is not universal. The Spaniards who came to both North and South America in the seventeenth century noticed men in the native tribes who had taken on the mannerisms of women, and women who occupied male roles.

Several Native American cultures hold a special honor for persons of "integrated genders." For example, the Navaho term *nádleehí* literally means "one who constantly transforms," and refers to a male-bodied person with a feminine nature, a special gift according to Navajo culture. The Navajo believe that to maintain harmony, there must be a balanced interrelationship between the feminine and the masculine within a single individual. Native activists working to renew their cultural heritage adopted the English term *two-spirit* as useful shorthand to describe the entire spectrum of gender and sexual expression that is better and more completely described in their own languages (Nibley, 2011).

Taken together, anthropologists' studies of gender reveal that culture, not biology, underlies gender differences. Sociologists have noted that while society teaches "masculine" and "feminine" gender roles, such an approach does not explain where these roles come from or how they can be changed. For this, we need to delve into classic and contemporary theoretical perspectives that shed light on how gender roles and gendered inequalities are built into social institutions (Lorber, 1994).

CONCEPT CHECKS ✓

1. What is the difference between sex and gender?
2. How do both biology and gender socialization contribute to differences between men and women?
3. What is the "social construction" of gender?
4. Name two or three ways that we "do gender" in our daily lives.

② SOCIOLOGICAL THEORIES OF GENDER INEQUALITIES

Sociologists try to explain why gender inequalities exist and persist. Explanations vary widely, from functionalist approaches, which view such differences as an essential key to societal stability, to radical feminist approaches, which view gender inequalities as a product of male oppression. These perspectives have been advanced to explain men's enduring dominance over women—in the realm of economics, politics, the family, and elsewhere. In this section, we review the main theoretical approaches to explaining gender inequality in society.

Functionalist Approaches

Functionalist approaches see society as a system of interlinked parts that, when in balance, operate smoothly to produce social solidarity. Thus functionalist and functionalist-inspired perspectives on gender argue that gender differences, and specifically men and women's specialization in different tasks, contribute to social stability and integration. Though popular in the 1950s and '60s, these perspectives have been heavily criticized for neglecting social tensions at the expense of consensus and for perpetuating a conservative view of the social world.

Scholars who support the concept of natural differences argue that women and men perform those tasks for which they are biologically best suited. The anthropologist George Murdock (1949) saw it as practical and convenient that women should concentrate on domestic and family responsibilities while men worked outside the home. On the basis of a cross-cultural study of more than 200 societies, Murdock concluded that the sexual division of labor is present in all cultures and that, although not the result of biological programming, it is the most logical and efficient basis for the organization of society.

Sociologist Talcott Parsons studied the role of the family in industrial societies (Parsons and Bales, 1955). He was particularly interested in the socialization of children and believed that stable, supportive families were the key to successful socialization. He saw the family as operating most efficiently with a clear-cut sexual division of labor in which women carry out *expressive* roles, providing care and security to children and offering them emotional support, and men perform an *instrumental* role—namely, being the breadwinner. Because of the stressful nature of men's role, women's expressive and nurturing tendencies should also be used to comfort and care for men. This complementary division of labor, springing from a biological distinction between the sexes, would ensure the solidarity and stability of the family, according to Parsons.

Another perspective on gender differences that is consistent with core themes of functionalist theories is attachment theory—advanced by psychologist John Bowlby (1953). Bowlby argued that the mother is crucial to the primary socialization of children. If the mother is absent or if a child is separated from the mother at a young age, the child may be inadequately socialized. This can lead to serious social and psychological difficulties later in life, including antisocial and psychopathic tendencies. Bowlby argued that a child's well-being and mental health require a close, personal, and continuous relationship with the mother or a female mother substitute. Bowlby's *maternal deprivation* thesis has been used by some to argue that working mothers are neglectful of their children.

Feminists have sharply criticized claims of a biological basis for the sexual division of labor. They argue that women are not prevented from pursuing occupations on the basis of biological features; rather, humans are socialized into roles that are culturally expected. Further, a steady stream of evidence suggests that the maternal deprivation thesis is questionable—studies have shown that children's educational performance and personal development are in fact enhanced when both parents work outside the home at least part of the time (e.g., Brooks-Gunn, Han, and Waldfogel, 2010).

Parsons's view on the "expressive" female also has been attacked for implicitly condoning the subordination of women in the home. There is no basis for the belief that the "expressive" female is necessary for the smooth operation of the family—rather, the role is promoted largely for the convenience of men.

In addition, cross-cultural studies show that societies vary greatly in terms of the degree to which they differentiate and assign tasks as exclusively men's or women's (Baxter, 1997; Gornick and Meyers, 2003). The extent to which certain tasks can be shared, and even how open groups and societies are to women performing men's activities and roles, differs across cultures, across time, and in different political and economic contexts. Finally, cultures differ in the degree to which men are seen as "naturally" dominant over women. Thus gender inequalities do not seem to be fixed or static.

Biological determinists see gender inequalities and differences based on gender as inevitable and unchangeable because they are consequences of biological necessities, not of social processes. Feminist scholars do not deny that men and women have distinctive biological characteristics, yet they argue that physical differences alone cannot explain the stark gender differences in men's and women's social and economic roles (e.g., Grosz, 1994). Sociological approaches, in general, hold that society more than biology guides gendered roles, interactions, and status differences today. Sociologists also emphasize that gender inequality is tied to issues of race and class. Women—rich and poor, black and white, immigrant and native-born—may share similar biological characteristics, yet their social experiences are vastly different (Rothenberg, 2007).

Feminist Theories

Feminist theories address gender inequalities and sets forth an agenda for overcoming them. Feminist writers are all concerned with women's unequal position in society, but their explanations for it vary substantially. There is no one "feminism." Rather, different schools cite a variety of deeply embedded social processes, such as sexism, patriarchy, capitalism, and racism. The following sections look at the arguments behind four main feminist perspectives—liberal, radical, black, and postmodern feminism.

LIBERAL FEMINISM

Liberal feminism sees gender inequalities as rooted largely in social and cultural attitudes. Unlike radical feminists, liberal feminists do not see women's subordination as part of a larger system or structure. Instead, they identify many separate factors that contribute to inequalities—for example, sexism and discrimination in the workplace, in educational institutions, and in the media. They focus on establishing and protecting equal opportunities for women through legislation and other democratic means. Liberal feminists actively supported legal advances such as the Equal Pay Act and the Sex Discrimination Act, arguing that mandating equality in law is essential to eliminating discrimination against women. Because liberal feminists seek to work through and within the existing political and economic systems to bring about reforms in a gradual way, they are more moderate in their aims and methods than radical feminists, who call for an overthrow of the existing system (Tong, 2009).

Critics charge that liberal feminists are unsuccessful in dealing with the root cause of gender inequality and do not acknowledge the systemic nature of women's oppression in society (Bryson, 1999). Liberal feminists say that by focusing on independent deprivations—sexism, discrimination, the glass ceiling, unequal pay—they draw attention to larger, more persistent features of society. Radical feminists accuse liberal feminists of encouraging women to accept an unequal society and its competitive character.

RADICAL FEMINISM

At the heart of **radical feminism** is the belief that men are responsible for and benefit from the exploitation of women. The analysis of patriarchy—the systematic domination of females by males—is of central concern, being viewed as a universal phenomenon that has existed across time and cultures. Radical feminists identify the family as one of the primary

feminist theories • Sociological perspectives that emphasize the centrality of gender in analyzing the social world and particularly the uniqueness of the experience of women. There are many strands of feminist theory, but they all share the desire to explain gender inequalities in society and to work to overcome them.

liberal feminism • The form of feminist theory that posits that gender inequality is produced by unequal access to civil rights and certain social resources, such as education and employment, based on sex. Liberal feminists tend to seek solutions through changes in legislation that ensure that the rights of individuals are protected.

radical feminism • The form of feminist theory that posits that gender inequality is the result of male domination in all aspects of social and economic life.

sources of women's oppression. They argue that men both exploit women by relying on their unpaid domestic labor in the home and, as a group, deny women access to positions of power and influence in society (Tong, 2009).

Radical feminists differ in their interpretations of the basis of patriarchy, but most agree that it involves some form of appropriation of women's bodies and sexuality. Shulamith Firestone (1970) argues that because men control women's roles in reproduction and child rearing, women become dependent materially on men for protection and livelihood. This "biological inequality" is socially organized in the nuclear family. Firestone argues that women can be emancipated only through the abolition of the family and the power relations that characterize it.

Other radical feminists point to male violence against women as central to male supremacy. In this view, intimate partner violence, rape, and sexual harassment are all part of the systematic oppression of women, rather than isolated cases of pathological or criminal perpetrators. Even interactions in daily life—such as nonverbal communication, patterns of listening and interrupting, and women's sense of comfort in public—contribute to gender inequality. Moreover, popular conceptions of beauty and sexuality are imposed on women by men to produce a certain type of femininity. For example, social and cultural norms emphasizing a slim body, youthful face, and caring, nurturing attitude toward men perpetuate women's subordination. The objectification of women through the media, fashion, and advertising turns women into sexual objects whose main role is to please and entertain men (Kilbourne, 2010).

Radical feminists do not believe that women can be liberated from sexual oppression through legislative reforms or gradual attitudinal change. Because patriarchy is a systemic phenomenon, they argue, gender equality can be attained only by overthrowing the patriarchal order.

In asserting that "the personal is political," radical feminists have drawn attention to the many linked dimensions of women's oppression. Their emphasis on male violence and the objectification of women has brought these issues into the heart of mainstream debates about women's subordination.

Many objections can be raised to radical feminist views. A key objection is that the concept of patriarchy is inadequate as a general explanation for women's oppression (Tong, 2009). Critics argue that the conception of patriarchy as a universal phenomenon does not leave room for historical or cultural variations. It also ignores the influence of race, class, and ethnicity on the nature of women's subordination; in short, it fails to recognize that not all men have equal power to act as oppressors, and not all women are equally subjugated. In fact, seeing patriarchy as a universal phenomenon risks *biological reductionism*—attributing all the complexities of gender inequality to a simple distinction between men and women.

bell hooks.

BLACK FEMINISM

Do the versions of feminism just described apply equally to the experiences of both white women and women of color? Many black feminists and feminists from developing countries claim they do not. They argue that the main feminist schools of thought address the dilemmas of white, predominantly middle-class women living in industrialized societies and in traditional two-parent families, and that it is not valid to generalize theories about women's subordination from the experience of a specific group. Moreover, the very idea of a unified form of gender oppression experienced equally by all women is problematic (Collins, 2008).

Dissatisfaction with existing forms of feminism has led to the emergence of **black feminism**, which concentrates on the problems facing black women. Black feminist writings emphasize aspects of the past that inform current gender inequalities in the black community: the legacy of slavery, segregation, and the civil rights movement. They point out that early black suffragettes supported the campaign for women's rights but realized that the question of race could not be ignored, because black women were discriminated against on the basis of race *and* gender. In recent years, black women have not been central to the women's liberation movement in part because their race informed their identities and political allegiances more than their gender did (Collins, 2008).

Author, feminist, and social activist bell hooks argues that explanatory frameworks favored by white feminists—for example, the view of the family as a mainstay of patriarchy—may not apply in black communities, where the family often is headed by a woman and provides a safe, supportive haven against racism. In other words, the oppression of black women may be found in different locations than that of white women.

Black feminists contend that any theory of gender equality that does not take racism into account cannot adequately explain black women's oppression. Likewise, social class cannot be neglected. Some black feminists hold that the strength of black feminist theory is its focus on the interplay between race, class, and gender concerns. When these three factors interact, they reinforce and intensify one another (Brewer, 1993).

POSTMODERN FEMINISM

Like black feminism, **postmodern feminism** challenges the idea that all women share a single basis of identity and experience. (Postmodern approaches in sociology were introduced in Chapter 1, and it may be helpful to review that section.) This strand of feminism draws on the cultural phenomenon of postmodernism in the arts, architecture, philosophy, and economics. Postmodern feminists reject the claim that there is a grand theory that can explain the position of women in society or that there is any universal category of "woman." Consequently, these feminists reject the accounts given by others to explain gender inequality—such as patriarchy, race, or class—as "essentialist" (Beasley, 1999).

Instead, postmodern feminism encourages the acceptance of many different standpoints, representing very different experiences (heterosexuals, lesbians, black women, working-class women, and so on). The "otherness" of different groups and individuals is celebrated in all its diverse forms. Emphasis on the positive side of

black feminism • A strand of feminist theory that highlights the multiple disadvantages of gender, class, and race that shape the experiences of nonwhite women. Black feminists reject the idea of a single, unified gender oppression that is experienced evenly by all women, and argue that early feminist analysis reflected the specific concerns of white, middle-class women.

postmodern feminism • The feminist perspective that challenges the idea of a unitary basis of identity and experience shared by all women. Postmodern feminists reject the claim that there is a grand theory that can explain the position of women in society, or that there is any single, universal essence or category of "woman." Instead, postmodern feminism encourages the acceptance of many different standpoints as equally valid.

CONCEPT CHECKS ✓

1. Contrast functionalist and feminist approaches to understanding gender inequality.

2. What are the key ideas of liberal feminism? What are criticisms of this perspective?

3. What are the key ideas of radical feminism? What are criticisms of this perspective?

4. Do you think that postmodern feminism is incompatible with liberal, radical, and black feminist perspectives? Why or why not?

otherness is a major theme in postmodern feminism and symbolizes plurality, diversity, difference, and openness: There are many truths, roles, and constructions of reality (Tong, 2009).

Postmodern feminism is said to have the most difficult relationship with the strands of feminism just discussed (Tong, 2009). This is largely because of its belief that many feminists are mistaken in assuming that it is possible to provide overarching explanations for women's oppression and to find steps toward its resolution.

③ RESEARCH ON GENDER TODAY: DOCUMENTING AND UNDERSTANDING GENDERED INEQUALITIES

As we have learned so far, gender is one of the main dimensions along which we differentiate humans in society. Yet men and women are not merely viewed as different in most societies; in many domains, men and women experience unequal treatment, with men consistently holding more political, economic, and social power. Male dominance in a society is **patriarchy**. Although men are favored in almost all societies, the degree of patriarchy varies. In the United States, women have made tremendous progress in education, work, politics, and economics, but several forms of gender inequality persist.

patriarchy • The dominance of men over women. All known societies are patriarchal, although there are variations in the degree and nature of the power that men exercise as compared with women. One of the prime objectives of women's movements in modern societies is to combat existing patriarchal institutions.

gender inequality • The inequality between men and women in terms of wealth, income, and status.

Sociologists define **gender inequality** as the difference in the status, power, and prestige that women and men have in groups, collectives, and societies. In the following sections, we will review contemporary research that documents both the magnitude of and the explanations for gendered inequalities across multiple domains, including education, the workplace, the family, and politics. We will focus primarily on the U.S. context, but will also demonstrate that the disparities in the United States pale in comparison to those in other nations, where the cultural devaluation of women is widespread.

Gendered Inequalities in Education: Unequal Treatment in the Classroom

Schools foster gender differences in outlook and behavior. In the past, school regulations compelling girls to wear dresses or skirts served as an obvious means of gender typing. The consequences went beyond mere appearance. As a result of their clothes, girls lacked the freedom to sit casually, to join in rough-and-tumble games, or to run as fast as they were able. Although strict enforcement of school dress has become rare, differences in informal styles of dress persist, still influencing gender behavior in school. School reading texts also perpetuate gender images. Although this, too, is changing, storybooks in elementary school often portray boys showing initiative and independence, and girls as more passive and watching their brothers. Stories written especially for girls often have an element of adventure, but usually in a domestic or school setting. Boys' adventure stories are more wide ranging, with heroes who travel to distant places or who, in other ways, are sturdily independent (Statham, 1986).

In general, people interact differently with men and women, and boys and girls (Lorber, 1994)—even in elementary schools. Studies document that teachers interact differently, and often inequitably, with male and female students in terms of the frequency and content of teacher-student interactions. Such patterns are based on, and perpetuate, traditional assumptions about male and female behavior and traits.

One study shows that regardless of the sex of the teacher, male students interact more with their teachers than female students do. Boys receive more teacher attention and instructional time than girls do. This is partly because boys are more demanding than girls (American Association of University Women [AAUW], 1992). Another study reported that boys are eight times more likely to call out answers in class, thus grabbing their teachers' attention, and that even when boys do not voluntarily participate in class, teachers are more likely to solicit information from them than from girls. However, when girls try to bring attention to themselves by calling out in class without raising their hands, they are reprimanded by comments such as "In this class, we don't shout out answers, we raise our hands" (Sadker and Sadker, 1994).

In addition, the content of teacher-student interactions differs depending on the sex of the students. After observing elementary school teachers and students over many years, researchers found that teachers helped boys in working out the correct answers, whereas they simply gave girls the correct answers and did not engage them in the problem-solving process. In addition, teachers posed more academic challenges to boys, encouraging them to think through their answers to find the best possible response (Sadker and Sadker, 1994).

Boys were disadvantaged in several ways, however. Because of their rowdy behavior, they were more often scolded and punished than girls. Moreover, boys outnumber girls in special education programs by startling percentages. Sociologists have argued that school personnel may be mislabeling boys' behavioral problems as learning disabilities.

The differential treatment of boys and girls perpetuates stereotypic gender role behavior. Girls are trained to be quiet and well behaved and to turn to others for answers, while boys are encouraged to be outspoken, active problem solvers. Female children from ethnic minorities may be doubly disadvantaged. A study of what it was like to be a black female pupil in a white school reported that while the black girls were, like the boys, initially enthusiastic about school, they altered their attitudes because of the difficulties they encountered. Even when the girls were young, age seven or eight, teachers would disperse them if they were chatting in a group on the playground, while tolerating similar behavior among white children. Once treated as "troublemakers," the black girls rapidly became so (Bryan, Dadzie, and Scafe, 1987).

Gendered Inequalities in the Workplace

Gender plays a powerful role in shaping workplace experiences. Everything from the jobs we hold, to how much we earn, even to our treatment at the hands of coworkers, is powerfully shaped by gender. Although women have seen tremendous progress both in rates of labor force participation and in entry to a wide variety of occupations over the past century, as we shall see, stark inequities persist.

Women currently account for roughly half the total workforce, and almost 60 percent of women are now employed outside the home (U.S. Bureau of Labor Statistics [BLS], 2013c). Although women's entry into the paid labor force is a fairly contemporary phenomenon, dating back only to the early 1970s, some women have always worked for pay. Poor, immigrant, and ethnic minority women have always had relatively high rates of employment. For example, in the United States in 1910, the female labor force consisted mainly of young, single women and children. More than a third of gainfully employed women were maids or house servants. When women or girls worked in factories or offices, employers often sent their wages to their parents. When young women married, they typically withdrew from the labor force.

Since then, women's participation in the paid labor force has risen more or less continuously, especially since the 1950s (Figure 10.1). The U.S. Bureau of Labor Statistics reports that 58.6 percent of all women were in the labor market in 2011 (compared with 40 percent in 1975 and 38 percent in 1960) and that women outnumbered men in the workforce for the first time in 2010 (BLS, 2011e). According to BLS data, 64.2 million payroll employees were women and only 63.4 million were men in January 2010. Some economists say that women now outnumber men in the labor force because the ongoing recession has disproportionately struck male-dominated industries, including finance, insurance, real estate,

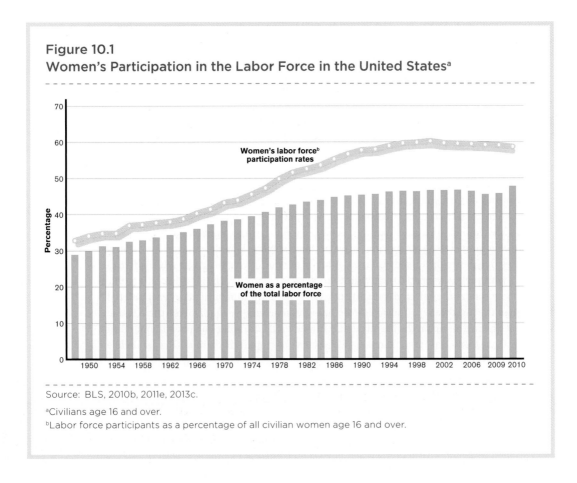

Figure 10.1
Women's Participation in the Labor Force in the United States[a]

Source: BLS, 2010b, 2011e, 2013c.

[a]Civilians age 16 and over.
[b]Labor force participants as a percentage of all civilian women age 16 and over.

and construction. Some pundits have dubbed the current economic climate a "he-cession" or "man-cession" to reflect the fact that 80 percent of the jobs lost in the current recession were jobs held by men. Some would argue further that women's employment is essential for families' financial well-being during this difficult economic period.

Perhaps an even greater change in labor force participation has occurred among married mothers of young children. In 1978, only 14 percent of married women with pre-school-age children worked full time year round, yet this figure had increased to 64.8 percent by 2012 (BLS, 2013a).

One impetus behind women's increased entry into the labor force was the increasing demand for clerical and service workers in the mid-twentieth century, as the U.S. economy expanded and changed (Oppenheimer, 1970). From 1940 until the late 1960s, labor force activity increased among women who were past their prime child-rearing years, such as "empty nest" women whose children had left the family home. During the 1970s and '80s, as the marriage age rose, fertility declined, and women's educational attainment increased, the growth in labor force participation spread to younger women. Many women now postpone marriage and childrearing to complete their education and establish themselves in the labor force. Despite family obligations, today a majority of women of all educational levels work outside the home during their child-rearing years (Padavic and Reskin, 2002).

OCCUPATIONAL SEGREGATION

Until recently, women were overwhelmingly concentrated in routine, poorly paid occupations. The clerk (office worker) provides a good illustration. In 1850 in the United States, clerks held responsible positions requiring accountancy skills and carrying managerial responsibilities; fewer than 1 percent were women. The twentieth century saw a general mechanization of office work (starting with the introduction of the typewriter in the late nineteenth century), accompanied by a downgrading of the clerk's status—together with a related occupation, secretary—into a routine, low-paid occupation. Women filled these occupations as the jobs' pay and prestige declined. Today, most secretaries and clerks are women (Reskin and Roos, 1990).

Studies of certain occupations reveal how **gender typing** occurs in the workplace. Expanding areas of lower-level work, such as secretarial positions or retail sales, attract a substantial proportion of women. These jobs are poorly paid and hold few career prospects. Men with good educational qualifications aspire to something higher, whereas others choose blue-collar work. Once an occupation has become gender typed, inertia sets in. Job hierarchies are built around the assumption that men will occupy superior positions, while a stream of women will flow through subordinate jobs. Employers are guided in future hiring decisions by gender labels. And the very conditions of most female jobs lead to adaptive responses on the part of women—low job commitment, few career ambitions, high turnover, the seeking of alternative rewards in social relations—which fortify the image of women as suitable for only lower-level jobs (Lowe, 1987).

These social conditions reinforce outlooks produced by early gender socialization, as women may grow up believing that they should put their husbands' careers before their own. (Men also are frequently brought up to believe the same thing.)

Women have recently made inroads into occupations once defined as "men's jobs" (Figure 10.2).

gender typing • Women holding occupations of lower status and pay, such as secretarial and retail positions, and men holding jobs of higher status and pay, such as managerial and professional positions.

Figure 10.2
Women at Work

Of all jobs in a given occupation, the following shows the proportion held by women for each year (percentage).

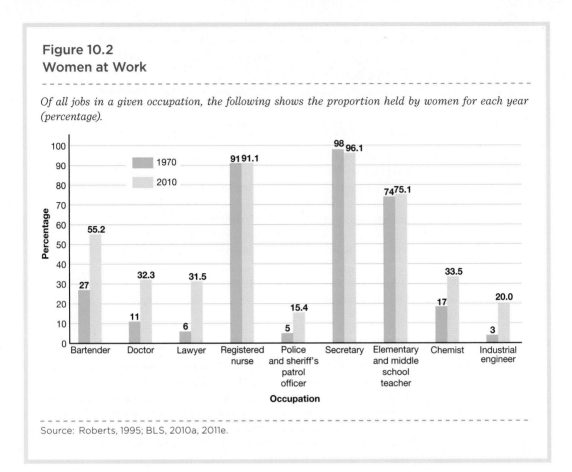

Source: Roberts, 1995; BLS, 2010a, 2011e.

By the 1990s, women dominated previously male-dominated professions such as accounting, journalism, psychology, and public service. In fields such as law, medicine, and engineering, women's proportion has risen substantially since 1970. Women now account for about one-third of all lawyers and physicians, and outnumber men in both law school and medical school (National Center for Education Statistics [NCES], 2009). Further, for the first time ever, in the 2008/2009 academic year, American women earned more doctoral degrees than men, according to the Council of Graduate Schools (Bell, 2010): approximately 51 percent of awarded doctorates. However, the CGS report also noted that men continue to earn a majority of doctorates in traditionally male-dominated fields such as engineering (78.4 percent) and mathematics and computer sciences (73.2 percent).

THE "GLASS CEILING"

Although women are increasingly entering traditionally male jobs, they may not be seeing increases in pay—or increases in occupational mobility—because of the **glass ceiling**, a promotion barrier that prevents women's upward mobility. The glass ceiling is particularly problematic in male-dominated occupations and professions, such as investment banking,

glass ceiling • A promotion barrier that prevents a woman's upward mobility within an organization.

as we learned earlier in this chapter. Women's progress is blocked not by virtue of innate inability or lack of basic qualifications but by lack of the sponsorship of powerful senior colleagues to articulate the women's value to the organization or profession (Alvarez et al., 1996). As a result, women progress into middle-management positions but do not, in proportionate numbers, move beyond. The examples of Kelley Voelker and Charlotte Hanna show that, even today, women are subtly blocked access to high-level positions such as managing director (Lattman, 2010).

One explanation for women's blocked mobility is that dated gender stereotypes persist. Research shows that college-educated white males in professional jobs identify potential leaders as people who are like them. Women are thus assessed negatively because they deviate from this norm (Cleveland, 1996).

Ironically, men who work in female-dominated professions do not face similar obstacles to promotion. To the contrary, they enjoy a boost up the corporate ladder. The sociologist Christine Williams coined the term "glass escalator" (1992) to reflect men's rapid ascent up the hierarchy when they work in female-dominated professions. She found that employers singled out male workers in traditionally female jobs, such as nurse, librarian, elementary school teacher, and social worker, and promoted them to top administrative jobs in disproportionately high numbers. These men often "face invisible pressures to move up in their professions. Like being on a moving escalator, they have to work to stay in place," writes Williams (1992). These pressures may take positive forms, such as close mentoring and encouragement from supervisors, or they may be the result of prejudicial attitudes of those outside the profession, such as clients who prefer to work with male rather than female executives.

The glass ceiling phenomenon is one of several reasons women continue to earn less than men, although the gender pay gap has narrowed considerably in recent years. Between 1970 and 2011, the ratio of women's to men's earnings among full-time, year-round workers increased from 62 to 81 percent. Moreover, this ratio increased among all races and ethnic groups. Despite the decreasing gender gap in pay, men still earn substantially more than women (Figure 10.3). Scholars disagree as to why the gender gap persists; we will delve more deeply into these competing perspectives later in the chapter. However, pay disparities

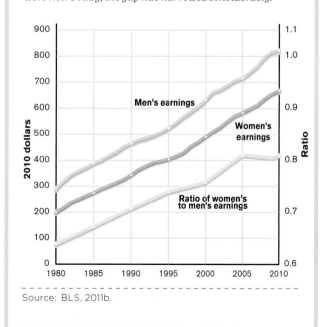

Figure 10.3
The Gender Pay Gap

This figure, in which weekly earnings are shown in constant 2010 dollars, illustrates what has been happening to the gender pay gap over time. After narrowing gradually for years, it widened a little after 1993, when men's inflation-adjusted earnings were increasing slightly and women's were not. Today, the gap has narrowed considerably.

Source: BLS, 2011b.

are not the only disadvantage women face in the labor market; they are also more likely than men to experience discriminatory treatment, including sexual harassment.

SEXUAL HARASSMENT IN THE WORKPLACE

Although most sociological research on gendered inequalities in the workplace focuses on occupational status and earnings, in recent years scholars have identified another important source of inequitable treatment: sexual harassment. **Sexual harassment** is unwanted or repeated sexual advances, remarks, and behavior that are offensive to the recipient and cause discomfort or interference with job performance. Power imbalances facilitate harassment; even though women can and do sexually harass subordinates, it is more common for men to harass women because men usually hold positions of authority (Padavic and Reskin, 2002).

The U.S. courts have identified two types of sexual harassment. One is the quid pro quo, in which a supervisor demands sexual acts from a worker as a job condition or promises work-related benefits in exchange for sexual acts. The other is the "hostile work environment," in which a pattern of sexual language, sexual advances, or even sexually explicit or demeaning posters makes a worker so uncomfortable that it is difficult for her to do her job (Padavic and Reskin, 2002).

Recognition of sexual harassment and women's willingness to report it have increased substantially since the testimony of Anita Hill to the Senate Judiciary Committee during the confirmation hearings for Clarence Thomas's 1991 nomination to the U.S. Supreme Court. Hill's recounting of Thomas's harassment raised public awareness of the problem and encouraged more women to report incidents (Figure 10.4). In the first six months of 1992 alone, the number of workplace harassment complaints increased by more than 50 percent (Gross, 1992).

sexual harassment • The making of unwanted sexual advances by one individual toward another, in which the first person persists even though it is clear that the other party is resistant.

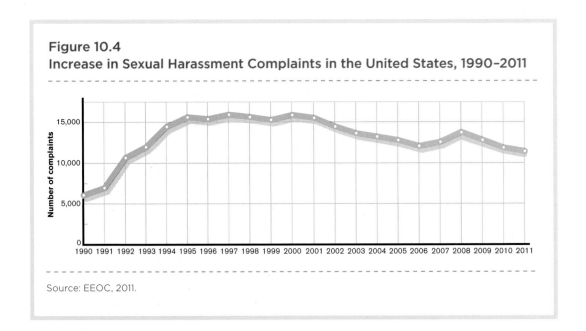

Figure 10.4
Increase in Sexual Harassment Complaints in the United States, 1990–2011

Source: EEOC, 2011.

Through most of the first decade of the twenty-first century, an average of 12,000 sexual harassment complaints are filed each year (U.S. Equal Employment Opportunity Commission [EEOC], 2012).

Despite increased awareness, sociologists have observed that "the great majority of women who are abused by behavior that fits legal definitions of sexual harassment—and who are traumatized by the experience—do not label what has happened to them as sexual harassment" (Paludi and Barickman, 1991). Women's reluctance to report may be due to the following factors: (1) many still do not recognize that sexual harassment is an actionable offense; (2) victims may be reluctant to make complaints, fearing that they will not be believed, that their charges will not be taken seriously, or that they will be subject to reprisals; and (3) it may be difficult to differentiate between harassment and joking on the job (Giuffre and Williams, 1994).

In 1998 the U.S. Supreme Court ruled that the Civil Rights Act outlaws harassment between members of the same sex. The case involved a man who had to quit his job on an offshore oil rig because he had been repeatedly grabbed, ridiculed, and threatened by two male supervisors. The Court ruled that neither "roughhousing" among men, nor "flirtations" between men and women, nor even some types of "verbal or physical harassment" are illegal, but that when sexual harassment is so "severely hostile or abusive" that it prevents workers from doing their jobs, it violates the Civil Rights Act—regardless of whether the offender and the harassed person are of the same or the opposite sex (Savage, 1998).

Global Gendered Inequalities in Economic Well-Being

The United States is not alone in having a history of gender inequality in the workplace. Across the globe, men outpace women in most workplace and economic indicators. Yet, as in the United States, most nations have witnessed tremendous strides in women's economic progress in recent decades.

Women now make up more than 52 percent of the world's paid workforce in all regions except northern Africa, South Asia, and parts of the Middle East (ILO, 2008). Women around the world work in the lowest-wage jobs and are likely to make less than men doing similar work—although there is some evidence that the wage gap is slowly decreasing, at least in industrialized countries (ILO, 2007). Because women throughout the world also perform housework and childcare at the end of the paid work, often dubbed the "second shift," women also work longer hours than men in most countries. A recent UN report found that women in the United States worked on average 25 minutes each day more than men—a difference that was considerably smaller than that in Austria (45 minutes) or Italy (103 minutes). Because of persistent discrimination, higher unemployment, and lower wages, women represent 60 percent of the world's 550 million working poor (ILO, 2004a). This gap is considerably worse in developing nations. On average, women worked 165 minutes more than men in Benin, 105 minutes more in Mexico, 66 minutes more in India, 59 in South Africa, 58 in the Republic of Korea, 51 in Madagascar, 44 in Mongolia, and 24 in Mauritius (UNICEF, 2006).

Women remain in the poorest-paying industrial and service-sector jobs in all countries, and in the less industrialized nations, they are concentrated in the declining agricultural sector. The feminization of the global workforce has brought with it the increased exploitation of young, uneducated, largely rural women around the world. These women labor under conditions that are often unsafe and unhealthy, at low pay and with nonexistent job security.

Yet, at the same time, even poor-paying factory jobs may enable some women to achieve a measure of economic independence and power. The ILO (2004a) found that while the gap between the number of men and women in the labor force has been decreasing in all regions of the world since 1993, this decrease has varied widely. Although women in developed economies and East Asia—where the number of women working per 100 men is 82 and 79, respectively—have nearly closed the gap, in other regions of the world such as the Middle East, North Africa, and South Asia, fewer than 45 women to 100 men work (ILO, 2008). Some scholars and activists argue further that women's economic empowerment has contributed in large part to China's meteoric rise as an economic power. An estimated 80 percent of the factory workers in China's Guangdong province are female, and 6 of the 10 richest self-made women in the world are Chinese (Kristof and WuDunn, 2009).

At the other end of the occupational spectrum, a recent study by the ILO concludes that women throughout the world still encounter a "glass ceiling" that restricts their movement into the top positions. Even though women have made progress in moving into managerial and professional positions, globally they still hold only 2 to 3 percent of the top corporate jobs, and those who do make it to the top typically earn less than men. In Japan, for example, women are especially likely to face barriers to upper-level positions: When college-educated Japanese women interview for managerial jobs, they are typically assigned to noncareer secretarial work. As many as 40 percent of Japanese companies hire no women college graduates for management-level positions (French, 2001). On the other hand, in the United States, women own about 30 percent of all business (American Express OPEN, 2013). Female participation in senior management has reached nearly 22 percent in the Netherlands, 21 percent in Canada, and over 36 percent in Hungary, although it remains low (13.6 percent) in the United States (ILO, 2004b). In the European Union as a whole, women make up only 32 percent of "heads of businesses" and only 10 percent of board members (ILO, 2008). In some developing countries, progress has been even greater: In Thailand, for example, 45 percent of senior managers are women; in Malaysia, 31 percent are women (Grant Thornton Business Report, 2011).

Women's share of professional jobs is highest in Eastern Europe and the former Soviet Union: Lithuania (70.2 percent in 2002), Latvia (67.0 percent), Estonia (66.0 percent), Georgia (64.8 percent), Ukraine (63.7 percent), Slovakia (63.1 percent), Poland (60.9 percent), and Moldova (60.3 percent). The reason for these countries' high proportion of women in professional jobs is their long-standing policies supporting working mothers (ILO, 2004b).

Gendered Inequalities in the Family: Division of Household Labor

Early in this chapter, we saw how the careers of two highly accomplished women, Kelley Voelker and Charlotte Hanna, were derailed after they returned from maternity leave. One key reason that women face compromised labor force prospects relative to men is that household duties, ranging from child care to elder care to daily housework, are disproportionately borne by women. Over the past three decades, sociologists have documented that work and family are competing social roles, and women's family lives often impede their career and professional prospects.

Although there have been revolutionary changes in women's status in the United States in recent decades, including the entry of women into male-dominated professions, one area of work has lagged far behind: housework. Because of the increase of married women in the workforce and the resulting change in status, it was presumed that men would contribute more to housework. On the whole, this has not been the case. Although men now do more housework than they did three decades ago, a large gender gap persists. In 1976, women performed 26.0 hours of housework per week, although this number dropped to 16.5 hours by 2005. By contrast, men's housework increased from 6 to 12 hours per week between 1976 and 2005. However, this means that women still put in significantly more time than their spouses (Achen and Stafford, 2005).

Further investigation shows that it is the intersection of gender, marital status, and parental status that most powerfully shapes housework. A recent study shows that whereas women save their husbands an hour of housework a week, husbands create an additional 7 hours of housework for wives every week. Childless women do an average of 10 hours of housework a week before marriage and 17 hours after marriage. Childless men, by contrast, do 8 hours before marriage and 7 hours afterward. Married women with more than three kids are the most overworked, reporting an average of about 28 hours, while married men with more than three kids logged only 10 hours of housework a week (University of Michigan Institute for Social Research, 2008).

One reason that wives—even full-time employed, high-earning women—perform more hours of housework than their husbands is that women and men specialize in different chores. The chores that women typically perform are more time-consuming and happen on a daily rather than a sporadic basis. Wives do most of the daily chores, such as cooking and routine cleaning, while husbands take on more occasional tasks, such as mowing the lawn and doing home repairs. The major difference is the amount of control the individual has over when the work gets done. Women's household jobs bind them to a fixed schedule, whereas men's are more discretionary. Women also spend more time on child-rearing responsibilities, which reflects pervasive assumptions that women are "naturally" the primary caregiver (Shelton, 1992). Sociologists argue that underlying this inequitable distribution of tasks is the implicit understanding that men and women are responsible for different spheres. Men are expected to be providers, women to be caretakers—even if they are breadwinners as well as mothers. By reproducing in everyday life these roles learned during childhood socialization, men and women "do gender" and reinforce it as a means for society to differentiate between the sexes.

Some sociologists have further suggested that women's greater burden at home is best explained as a result of economic forces: Household work is exchanged for economic support. Because women earn less than men, they are more likely to remain economically dependent on their husbands and thus perform the bulk of the housework. Until the earnings gap is narrowed, women will likely remain in their dependent position.

Yet, ironically, the gender gap in housework and child care contributes to women's inferior economic position. Part of the reason that family responsibilities create obstacles for women is that their employers and colleagues may hold stereotypical ideas about women workers—especially the belief that mothers are less committed to their careers and thus less appropriate candidates for promotion than non-mothers. Research by Stanford University sociologist Shelley Correll and colleagues (Correll, Benard, and Paik, 2007) find that mothers are 44 percent less likely to be hired than non-mothers who have the same work experience and qualifications; and mothers are offered significantly lower starting pay than equally qualified non-mothers (an average of $11,000 lower in this study) for the same job.

Similar findings emerged in a qualitative study conducted in Great Britain. Homans (1987) investigated the views of managers interviewing female applicants for positions as technical staff in the health services. They found that the interviewers always asked the women about whether they had, or intended to have, children. (This is now illegal in the United States.) They virtually never followed this practice with male applicants. When asked why, two themes ran through their answers: Women with children may require extra time off for school holidays or if a child falls sick, and responsibility for child care is a mother's problem rather than a parental one. Some managers thought their questions indicated an attitude of "caring" toward female employees. Women were seen as likely to interrupt their careers to care for young children, no matter how senior a position they might have reached.

Women's struggles with the work-family balance clearly illustrate the powerful ways that gender shapes our daily lives. As long as most of the population takes it for granted that parenting cannot be shared on an equal basis by both women and men, the problems facing women employees such as Voelker and Hanna will persist. It will remain a fact of life, as one of the managers put it, that women are disadvantaged, compared with men, in their career opportunities.

Gender Inequality in Politics

Women are playing an increasingly important role in U.S. politics, although they are still far from achieving full equality. Before 1993 there were only two women in the U.S. Senate (out of 100 Senate members), and 29 in the U.S. House of Representatives (out of 435). Just 20 years later, however, the 113th Congress has a record-high number of women. The 2012 elections swept in an all-time-high total of 20 women (16 Democratic and 4 Republican) senators, while there will be a record 78 women (58 Democratic and 20 Republican) in the House in 2013.

Women are continuing to make strides in other elected offices, although at a slow pace. In 2013, just 5 of the nation's 50 governors were women (Center for American Women and Politics, 2013a). The U.S. Supreme Court had its first woman justice appointed in 1981, and its second 12 years later. Three women currently occupy seats on the Supreme Court—Ruth Bader Ginsburg, Elena Kagan, and Sonya Sotomayor—marking an all-time high. It was not until 1984 that a woman was nominated as the vice-presidential candidate of either major party, neither of which has ever nominated a woman for the presidency—despite strides made by Hillary Clinton in the 2008 Democratic primaries.

Women politicians are overwhelmingly affiliated with the Democratic Party. In the U.S. Congress nearly three-quarters of women are Democrats, and

Women members of the Democratic Caucus gather on Capitol Hill to celebrate the record-high number of women in the 113th Congress.

in state legislatures, over 60 percent of women legislators are Democrats (National Conference of State Legislatures [NCSL], 2011). However, the Republican Party and especially the "Tea Party" movement prominently feature women leaders, including former Alaska governor Sarah Palin, Minnesota congresswoman Michele Bachmann, and South Carolina governor Nikki Haley.

Typically, the more local the political office, the more likely it is to be occupied by a woman. One reason is that local politics is often part-time work, especially in smaller cities and towns. Local politics can thus be good "women's work," offering low pay, part-time employment, flexible hours, and the absence of a clear career path (Carr, 2008). The farther from home the political office, the more likely it is to be regarded as "man's work," providing a living wage, full-time employment, and a lifetime career.

American women are not alone in their recent strides in elected politics. Women are playing an increasingly major role in politics throughout the world. Yet of the 192 countries that belong to the United Nations, only 20 are presently headed by women. Since World War II, 38 countries have been headed by women; the United States is not among them.

As of 2011, women made up only 19.3 percent of the combined membership of the national legislatures throughout the world. Only in Rwanda (56.3 percent), Andorra (53.6 percent), Sweden (45.0 percent), South Africa (44.5 percent), Cuba (43.2 percent), Iceland (42.9 percent), and Finland (42.5 percent) do women make up a significant part of parliament; in the Arab states, the figure is only 10.7 percent (Women in National Parliaments [WNP], 2011). It is interesting that Rwanda, which rates very low on the UN's Human Development Index, is close to Sweden for the highest share of women in the lower house of the parliament. The U.S. Congress is 19 percent female, placing the United States roughly 70th out of 187 countries for which data exist (WNP, 2011). Women are most likely to hold seats in national legislatures in countries in which women's rights are a strong cultural value— where women have long had the right to vote and are well represented in the professions (Kenworthy and Malami, 1999).

CONCEPT CHECKS ✓

1. Do you believe that girls or boys are more disadvantaged in the classroom? Why?

2. Describe at least three examples of how gender inequalities emerge in the workplace. How would a sociologist explain these inequities?

3. How do inequalities in the home, especially with regard to housework and child care, reflect larger gender inequities in society?

4. What are some important differences between men's and women's political participation?

4 UNANSWERED QUESTIONS: WHY DO GENDERED INEQUALITIES PERSIST?

We have demonstrated the many forms that gender inequalities take in society, in the workplace, in the family, in politics, and throughout the globe. Yet many readers of this textbook may wonder why gendered inequalities still persist, especially during an era when young women outnumber young men in the college classroom and a record-high number of women were elected to the U.S. Congress in 2012. How and why can we see so much progress in some domains, but so little in others?

There are no easy answers to questions of why gendered inequalities persist in the United States and throughout the world. In this section, we will delve into two particularly vexing questions about inequality, and will provide competing insights into why the gender pay gap persists and why are women disproportionately the target of sexual violence, whether on the college campuses of the United States or the war-torn deserts in parts of Africa.

The Gender Pay Gap: Why Do Women Earn Less Than Men?

The "gender gap" in pay is widely recognized. As we learned earlier in this chapter, women currently earn about 80 cents per every dollar earned by a man (BLS, 2013b). While the gender gap is now at its narrowest in history, experts believe that much of the recent convergence reflects the fact that men's wages are particularly hurt by the current recession. In other words, men are losing ground relative to women, and women are not necessarily seeing an objective improvement in their economic standing. What factors account for women's persistent disadvantage?

Many sociologists view sex segregation as a cause of the gender gap in earnings. **Sex segregation** refers to the concentration of men and women in different occupations. For instance, in 2010, occupations with the highest proportion of women included secretary, child-care worker, hairdresser, cashier, bookkeeper, receptionist, elementary school teacher, librarian, and nurse. Fully 97 percent of secretaries, more than 90 percent of registered and licensed practical nurses, and more than 80 percent of elementary school teachers were women. Occupations with the highest proportion of male workers included construction worker, truck driver, taxi driver, plumber, electrician, carpenter, firefighter, auto mechanic, and machinist (IWPR, 2010).

Sex segregation is problematic because the gender composition of a job is associated with the pay received for that job. This finding has emerged in numerous studies. An analysis of 1980 census data (England, 1992) showed that both women and men are disadvantaged by employment in an occupation that is predominantly female. Even "after adjusting for cognitive, social, and physical skill demands, amenities, disamenities, demands for effort, and industrial and organization characteristics, jobs pay less if they contain a higher proportion of females" (England, 1992).

The Equal Pay Act, established in 1963, requires employers to provide equal pay to workers in the *same job*. But it has done little to eradicate pay differences attributable to gender, because men and women rarely work at the same jobs. Two pay solutions have been proposed, in recognition of the limits of the Equal Pay Act. First, the Paycheck Fairness Act is being considered by Congress; the act is an update of the Equal Pay Act, and aims to close long-standing loopholes and strengthen incentives to prevent pay discrimination (National Organization for Women, 2010). Second, pay-equity policies such as "comparable worth" policies may help to minimize the gender pay gap. Such policies remunerate workers on the basis of the worth of their work and not the sex, race, or other personal characteristics of the majority of workers in a job (Stryker, 1996).

Economists and sociologists differ in explaining *how* occupational segregation leads to a gender gap in pay. Economists focus on women's occupational choices, while sociologists focus on the constraints women face. Many economists—as well

sex segregation • The concentration of men and women in different occupations.

human capital theory • The argument that individuals make investments in their own "human capital" in order to increase their productivity and earnings.

as employers and public-policy makers— endorse a **human capital theory** explanation. Developed by Gary Becker (1964), the theory argues that individuals make investments in their own "human capital" (such as formal schooling, on-the-job training, and work experience) to increase their productivity and earnings. Those who invest more in their own skills and knowledge are considered more productive and consequently are paid higher wages.

Human capital theorists reason that women select occupations that are easy to move in and out of, and that offer flexible or part-time hours while still providing moderately good incomes. Central to this argument is the assumption that women's primary allegiance is to home and family;

The Equal Pay Act of 1963 mandated equal pay for equal work. Studies indicate, however, that even when men and women work in the same job, men take home larger paychecks.

they seek undemanding or flexible jobs that require little personal investment in training or skills acquisition so that they can better tend to household responsibilities. When women leave the labor force to rear children, their job skills deteriorate, and they suffer a wage penalty when they reenter. Moreover, employers may "invest" less in women workers because they believe women will work less continuously than men.

Feminist sociologists criticize human capital theory on several grounds. For example, they dispute the claim that women "choose" certain occupations. In fact, the forces blocking women from freely choosing a career may be indirect or direct. For instance, childhood socialization promoting traditional gender roles may lead young women to choose occupations that are viewed as compatible with feminine traits such as warmth and nurturance— for example, teaching or nursing. More direct obstacles include discouragement from guidance counselors and college advisers, and discrimination on the part of bosses, coworkers, and customers. Also, workplace "gatekeepers" prohibit women from entering certain occupations. For example, in 1992 State Farm Insurance was forced to provide back pay to 814 women who were denied jobs as insurance agents because of their sex. More recently, class-action lawsuits were brought up against Walmart and Costco. The suit against Walmart alleged that the company discriminated against 1.6 million former and current female employees in making promotions, job assignments, and pay decisions, and that it retaliated against women who complain about such practices (Greenhouse, 2010). A similar class-action case was brought against Costco, by more than 700 women workers, on the grounds that store management practices prevented women from securing jobs as assistant managers or general managers (Greenhouse and Barbaro, 2007).

Sociologists further argue that human capital theory neglects power differentials between men and women in the workplace and society. Numerous studies reveal that even when men and women are in the same job, men are paid more (IWPR, 2010).

Because women's work is devalued by society and by employers, women are rewarded less for their work. Moreover, women's relative powerlessness prevents them from redefining the work they do as "skilled." As long as jobs predominantly filled by women, such as caring for children and the elderly, are viewed as "unskilled" or even "intuitive," and thus requiring little training, wages in women's jobs will remain low.

These competing explanations have very different implications for the future. According to human capital theory, the gender gap in pay could disappear if women and men received equal amounts of education and workplace training and if they took equal responsibility for family commitments such as child care. If feminist sociologists are correct in arguing that women's work is devalued, a drastic change in gender ideology must occur if men and women are to become equally rewarded for their participation in the workplace.

COMPARABLE WORTH: A POTENTIAL POLICY SOLUTION?

Some scholars propose that **comparable-worth policies** are potential mechanisms for attacking the gender pay gap. Comparable-worth policies compare pay levels of jobs held disproportionately by women with pay levels of jobs held disproportionately by men and try to adjust pay so that the women and men working in female-dominated jobs are not penalized. The policy presumes that jobs can be ranked objectively according to skill, effort, responsibility, and working conditions. After such a ranking, pay is adjusted so that equivalently ranked male- and female-dominated jobs receive equivalent pay (Hartmann et al., 1985).

Only a handful of U.S. states have instituted comparable-worth policies for public-sector employees (Blum, 1991), partly because such policies raise technical, political, and economic issues. Perhaps most important is the issue of job evaluation, or the identification of common denominators of skill, effort, responsibility, and working conditions so jobs can be compared and ranked independent of the race and gender of job incumbents (Stryker, 1996). Effective implementation requires that job evaluations be free from gender bias. However, substantial research shows that it is very difficult to make gender-neutral assessments of jobs and required job skills. Once men and women know which jobs are predominantly male and which are predominantly female, they attribute to those jobs the content that best fits with gender stereotypes (Steinberg, 1990).

Opposition to comparable-worth policies comes from both economists and feminists. Economists worry that comparable worth is inflationary and will cause wage losses and unemployment for some (disproportionately women) because of benefits enacted for others. Feminists counter that comparable worth reinforces gender stereotyping rather than breaking down gender barriers at work (Blum, 1991). Comparable worth also has faced obstacles in the courts. It suffered its biggest setback in 1985 when the Ninth Circuit Federal Court of Appeals rejected a comparable-worth job evaluation as evidence of discrimination. In a case involving the government employees' union (AFSCME) versus the state of Washington, the court upheld the state's right to base pay on market wages rather than on a job evaluation, writing, "Such hotly contested debates show that the jobs [that] society values are determined not by their market or societal worth but by power relations" (Blum, 1991).

Why Are Women So Often the Targets of Violence?

One of the most disturbing trends documented by gender scholars is the high rate of violence, including sexual violence, against women. From date rape on college campuses, to the systematic use of rape during wartime, sexual violence remains a pressing concern for scholars and policy makers alike. Why does such violence persist?

VIOLENCE AGAINST WOMEN: CONCEPTS AND PATTERNS

Before discussing the reasons why gendered-based violence persists, it is important that we first review data describing the magnitude and pervasiveness of such violence. Violence directed against women is found in many societies, including the United States. Violence takes multiple forms, including physical and sexual abuse, mutilation, and murder. Studies indicate that between one-quarter and one-half of all women around the world have been abused in some way by intimate partners (Stop Violence Against Women, 2006). One in five worldwide will be a victim of rape or attempted rape in her lifetime (UNFPA, 2005). In India, an estimated 8,172 women were killed in dowry-related deaths in 2008, a 14.4 percent rise from the 1998 level (National Crime Records Bureau [NCRB], 2008); these are deaths of young women who are murdered or driven to suicide by continuous harassment and torture by husbands and in-laws in an effort to extort more resources and property from a bride when she marries. It has been estimated that more than 130 million girls and women worldwide have been subjected to "genital mutilation" (UNICEF, 2005), and about 101 million are "missing," partly as the result of female infanticide in cultures in which boys are more highly valued than girls (Klasen and Wink, 2003).

Rape is an all-too-common subtype of violence against women, and refers to the forcing of nonconsensual vaginal, oral, or anal intercourse. The vast majority of rapes are committed by men against women, although men rape other men in prisons and other all-male institutional environments. However, recent studies have documented cases where women take sexual advantage of young men who may be insecure, intoxicated, or of a lower status (Anderson and Struckman-Johnson, 1998).

Rape is an act of violence, often carefully planned rather than performed on the spur of the moment to satisfy some uncontrollable sexual desire. Many rapes involve beatings, knifings, and even murder. In some instances, sexual assault is facilitated by alcohol, or women having their drinks spiked with the sedative Rohypnol (i.e., a "roofie") or drugs referred to as "date-rape drugs" (Michigan Department of Community Health, 2010). Even when rape leaves no physical wounds, it is a highly traumatic violation of the victim's person that leaves long-lasting psychological scars.

It is difficult to know how many rapes actually occur because most rapes go unreported. In one comprehensive study of American sexual behavior, 22 percent of the women surveyed reported having been forced into a sexual encounter. Yet the same study found that only 3 percent of the men admitted to having forced a woman into sex, a discrepancy the study's authors attribute to different perceptions between men and women regarding what constitutes forced sex (Laumann et al., 1994). The U.S. Department of Justice estimated that in 2009 there were 222,000 sexual assaults on women.

Although media reports sensationalize "stranger rapes," most rapes are committed by relatives (fathers or stepfathers, brothers, uncles), partners, or acquaintances. Among college students, most rapes are committed by boyfriends, former boyfriends, or classmates. The National Institute of Justice Sexual Victimization of College Women study (NCWSV) presents a chilling picture of violence against women on campuses across the country (Fisher et al., 2000). The study, conducted during spring semester 1997, asked college women about their experience with rape, attempted rape, coerced sex, unwanted sexual contact, and stalking during the 1996/1997 academic year. Overall, within the first seven months of a new school year, 1.7 percent had been the victim of a completed rape, and 1.1 percent of an attempted rape.

rape • The forcing of nonconsensual vaginal, oral, or anal intercourse.

Moreover, fully a tenth of the female students surveyed had been raped before the period of the study, and a tenth had been the victims of attempted rape. For both completed and attempted rapes, 9 out of 10 offenders were known to the victim. About 55 percent of rape victims used physical force in an effort to thwart the rape, as did 69 percent of attempted rape victims.

The incidence of other forms of victimization reported in the study was substantially higher than that of rape. Nearly one out of six female students reported being the target of attempted or completed sexual coercion or unwanted sexual contact during the academic year of the study, half involving the use or threat of physical force. More than a third reported a threatened, attempted, or completed unwanted sexual assault at some time during their lives. And about one out of every eight reported having been stalked during that academic year, almost always by someone they knew—typically a former boyfriend or classmate. Stalking, it was reported, was emotionally traumatizing, and in 15 percent of the incidents, it involved actual or threatened physical harm.

WHY DOES VIOLENCE PERSIST? COMPETING PERSPECTIVES

Some radical feminist scholars claim that men are socialized to regard women as sex objects and that this partly explains the high levels of victimization of women (Dworkin, 1987; Griffin, 1979). Susan Brownmiller (1975), for example, claims that the constant threat of rape contributes to a "rape culture" in which male domination fosters a state of continual fear in women. One aspect of a rape culture is male socialization to a sense of sexual entitlement, which may encourage sexual conquest and promote insensitivity to the difference between consensual and nonconsensual sex (Scully, 1990). From seemingly innocent high school locker room jokes, to television commercials and magazine ads depicting women as sexually inviting, to television and movie images equating masculinity with the conquest of women, many males learn to believe that women exist for their pleasure. Under such circumstances, rape is all too "normal" (Wolf, 1992).

The fact that "acquaintance rapes" occur suggests that some men feel entitled to sexual access if they already know the woman. In a survey of nearly 270,000 first-year college students, 55 percent of male students agreed with the following statement: "If two people really like each other, it's all right for them to have sex even if they've known each other only for a very short time." Only 31 percent of female students agreed (American Council on Education [ACE], 2001). Another national survey reported that 43 percent of all men believed that a woman is partly to blame if she is raped after changing her mind about having sex (Yankelovich, 1991). When a man goes out on a date with sexual conquest on his mind, he may force his attentions on an unwilling partner, overcoming her resistance through the use of alcohol, persistence, or both. While such an act may not be legally defined as rape, it would be experienced as such by many women.

Because some men are socialized to feel sexual entitlement, rapes are most common when men believe that norms condemning rape do not apply—for example, in times of war. Indeed, war-related rapes are as old as human history. Followers of Rome's legendary founder, Romulus, were reputed to have captured and raped Sabine women to populate Rome. Japanese soldiers raped as many as 20,000 women when they conquered the city of Nanking in China in 1937 (Chang and Kirby, 1997). American soldiers committed rapes during the U.S. Civil War and the Vietnam War.

Rape is an especially potent instrument of war, since it dehumanizes the victims and—where sexual mores are highly restrictive—can break apart families and weaken the resolve of victims to resist their aggressors. David Rosen, professor of sociology and anthropology who has long studied war crimes in Africa, argues that the systematic rape by armed militias of women in Darfur is intended to destroy their communities and ultimately serve as a means of ethnic cleansing (Rosen, 2008). A study of rape in ethno-national conflicts supports this conclusion; it reports that rape is far more likely when the future existence of the state is threatened (Hayden, 2000).

During World War II, for example, Japanese soldiers forced as many as 200,000 young women and girls to serve as "comfort women" for Japanese troops. These women—mainly Korean but also taken from other Asian countries conquered by the Japanese—were forced to work as sex slaves in military brothels throughout the Pacific. Many died in captivity; others committed suicide (Stetz and Oh, 2001). Rape was widely used as a Serbian strategy in the wars in Kosovo and Bosnia in the 1990s. By systematically raping and impregnating Muslim women, the Serbian forces hoped to humiliate the Muslim population into fleeing their homelands (Allen, 1996). Similarly, rape is used as a weapon of war in the Congo, where groups of armed rebels rape women and children to humiliate them and their families—a context that journalist Nicholas Kristof (2010) has referred to as "the world capital of rape, torture and mutilation."

Sexual assault is devastating to its victims, yet the consequences are particularly dire for those living in cultures that devalue women and women's sexuality. For example, in their book *Half the Sky*, journalists Nicholas Kristof and Sheryl WuDunn (2009) recount the harrowing experience of Hawa, a young student living in a refugee camp in Sudan's Darfur region. Hawa was attacked and gang-raped by members of the government-sponsored Janjaweed militia. When her friends attempted to get her medical treatment for her injuries in a small clinic staffed by foreign doctors, local police arrested her. Premarital sexual intercourse is a crime in Sudan. For the police, the act of seeking medical attention constituted proof of Hawa's sexual engagement, and without the required four male witnesses to testify to the rape, she was presumed to be guilty. Contrast Hawa's experience with the emotional support that sexual assault victims may receive on some college campuses, whether through counseling centers or "Take Back the Night" events.

Feminist scholars are pessimistic that gendered inequalities, whether pay inequalities or sexual violence, will be eradicated anytime soon. However, Kristof and WuDunn (2009) provide insights into ways that these problems might be attacked, slowly and gradually. They describe the eradication of gendered inequalities as "the paramount moral challenge" of this century, and believe that the education and financial empowerment of women is a first essential step. A similar recommendation is offered by the United Nations. On July 2, 2010, in a historic moment, the UN General Assembly voted unanimously to establish the UN Entity for Gender Equality and Empowerment, to be known as UN Women. With the establishment of UN Women, UN secretary-general Ban Ki-moon said, "UN Women is recognition of a simple truth: Equality for women and girls is not only a basic human right, it is a social and economic imperative. Where women are educated and empowered, economies are more productive and strong. Where women are fully represented, societies are more peaceful and stable" (Fifth World Conference on Women, 2010).

> ## CONCEPT CHECKS
>
> 1. Name three possible explanations for the gender pay gap.
> 2. Discuss at least two reasons why women are so often the targets of sexual violence.

1 **Basic Concepts**

p. 259

2 **Sociological Theories of Gender Inequalities**

p. 265

LEARNING OBJECTIVES

Understand the ways that differences between women and men reflect biological factors, sociocultural influences, and the complex interplay between the two.

Recognize and contrast competing explanations for gender inequality. Learn some feminist theories about gender equality.

TERMS TO KNOW

Sex • Gender • Gender role socialization • Social construction of gender

Feminist theories • Liberal feminism • Radical feminism • Black feminism • Postmodern feminism

CONCEPT CHECKS

1. What is the difference between sex and gender?
2. How do both biology and gender socialization contribute to differences between men and women?
3. What is the "social construction" of gender?
4. Name two or three ways that we "do gender" in our daily lives.

1. Contrast functionalist and feminist approaches to understanding gender inequality.
2. What are the key ideas of liberal feminism? What are criticisms of this perspective?
3. What are the key ideas of radical feminism? What are criticisms of this perspective?
4. Do you think that postmodern feminism is incompatible with liberal, radical, and black feminist perspectives? Why or why not?

Exercises: Thinking Sociologically

1. What does cross-cultural evidence from tribal societies in New Guinea, Afghanistan, Africa, and North America suggest about the differences in gender roles? Explain.

2. Why are minority women likely to think very differently about gender inequality than white women? Explain.

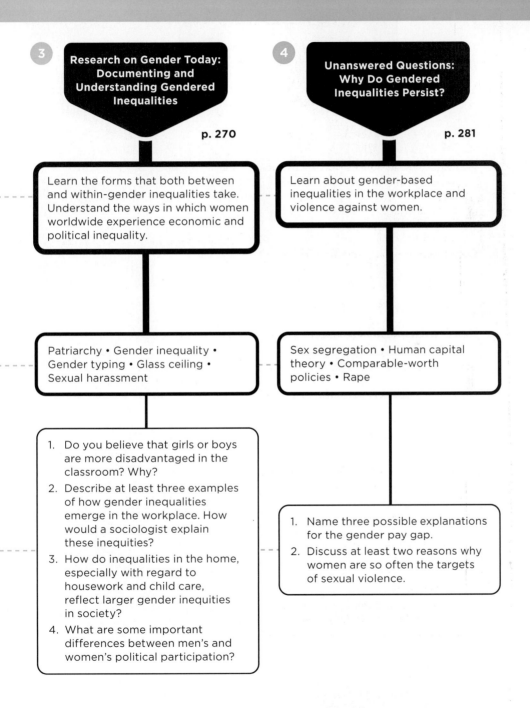

3 Research on Gender Today: Documenting and Understanding Gendered Inequalities

p. 270

Learn the forms that both between and within-gender inequalities take. Understand the ways in which women worldwide experience economic and political inequality.

Patriarchy • Gender inequality • Gender typing • Glass ceiling • Sexual harassment

1. Do you believe that girls or boys are more disadvantaged in the classroom? Why?
2. Describe at least three examples of how gender inequalities emerge in the workplace. How would a sociologist explain these inequities?
3. How do inequalities in the home, especially with regard to housework and child care, reflect larger gender inequities in society?
4. What are some important differences between men's and women's political participation?

4 Unanswered Questions: Why Do Gendered Inequalities Persist?

p. 281

Learn about gender-based inequalities in the workplace and violence against women.

Sex segregation • Human capital theory • Comparable-worth policies • Rape

1. Name three possible explanations for the gender pay gap.
2. Discuss at least two reasons why women are so often the targets of sexual violence.

Ethnicity and Race

11

Which of the following is true about race in many parts of the world today?

- **a** It is learned.
- **b** It is simply a figment of the imagination.
- **c** It is strictly a matter of descent.

Turn the page for the correct answer.

You have no doubt used the term *race* many times, but do you know what it means? For many Americans, race is viewed as a matter of physical appearance and descent. Others view it as a social construction, a figment of the imagination. The truth is somewhere in between. If race were *completely* a social construction, then the descent of people would not matter at all. In fact, there is a strong connection between physical characteristics and racial characteristics, though they are hardly definitive for any individual. For this reason, it is an overstatement to say that race is simply a figment of humans' imagination. Instead, sociologists have observed that while grounded in the lived reality of descent, race is something more than that. It is learned.

Consider the example of Maureen, a 45-year-old black woman who was born in the Caribbean and came to England at age 12 with her family. She is the social services manager for Home Care in Leicester, a city located 90 miles north of London. She has three brothers and 10 nieces and nephews. All her brothers have established families with white English women. She describes six of her nieces and nephews as "dual heritage." Yet she also believes that these racially mixed children will be classified as "black" by those outside the family. Here she sums up her view of one of her white sisters-in-law, whom she respects: "She very much wants the child to have a black identity. So, every Sunday she would bring [my niece] up to my mum's house so that she knows her black family. If you say, 'Do this for her hair,' she'd be religiously doing it. And she's asked for advice about her hair. And you'd see her plaiting it. And her hair is always so pretty." Maureen and her other black Caribbean family members consider her niece to be "racially" black although she has a white birth mother. They recognize that in spite of having a white mother, this girl will be classified as black because

LEARNING OBJECTIVES

① BASIC CONCEPTS

Learn the cultural bases of race and ethnicity and how racial and ethnic differences create sharp divisions. Learn the leading psychological theories and sociological interpretations of prejudice and discrimination.

② HISTORICAL PERSPECTIVES ON RACE AND ETHNICITY

Familiarize yourself with the history and social dimensions of ethnic relations in America. Recognize the importance of the historical roots of ethnic conflict, particularly in the expansion of Western colonialism. Understand the different models for a multiethnic society.

③ RESEARCH ON RACE AND ETHNICITY TODAY

Learn the forms of inequality experienced by racial and ethnic groups in the United States. See that the history of prejudice and discrimination against ethnic minorities has created hardship for many but that some have succeeded despite societal barriers.

④ UNANSWERED QUESTIONS

Understand global migration patterns and their effects.

of her physical appearance, and that she should thus learn to identify herself as a black. The labor required of Maureen's white sister-in-law demonstrates how "race," like ethnicity, is learned. Race and ethnicity are "socially constructed."

In 2001, according to the U.K. census, almost 50 percent of U.K.-born men described their ethnic group as "black" and almost 30 percent of "black Caribbean" men were married to women outside their black ethnic group, in most cases white women (U.K. Statistics Authority, 2001). Sociologist France Winddance Twine found in her research among multiracial families in the United States and the United Kingdom that some parents train their children to develop what she terms **racial literacy** skills to help them cope with racial hierarchies and to integrate multiple ethnic identities. Twine (2003) defines one dimension of racial literacy as antiracist training that helps children recognize the forms of racism they might encounter. Twine identifies gaps between how parents view their children racially, their children's own racial self-identification, and how they have been socially classified outside the home. For example, in her studies there were shifts and intense struggles among parents, extended family members, and teachers over a child's racial and ethnic classification (Twine, 1991, 1997, 2004). Such research illustrates the difficulty of defining the conditions of racial and ethnic group membership for some multiracial individuals. In recent decades, a number of sociologists have addressed this problem of multiracial identity and racial classification schemes, arguing that a "static measure of race" is not useful for multiracial individuals who assert different identities in different social contexts (Goldstein and Morning, 2000; Harris, 2003; Harris and Sim, 2000).

THE ANSWER IS C.

BASIC CONCEPTS

Ethnicity

Ethnicity refers to the cultural practices and outlooks of a given community that have emerged historically and that set people apart. Members of ethnic groups see themselves as culturally distinct from other groups and are seen as distinct by those other groups. Different characteristics may distinguish ethnic groups from one another, but the most common are some combination of language, history, religious faith, ancestry (real or imagined), and style of dress or adornment. Examples of ethnic groups in the United States are Irish Americans, Jewish Americans, Italian Americans, Cuban Americans, and Japanese Americans. Ethnic differences are learned.

Race is a kind of ethnicity but has certain characteristics that make it different from ethnicity. First, at certain historical moments some ethnic differences become the basis of stigmas that cannot be removed by conversion or

racial literacy • The skills taught to children of multiracial families to help them cope with racial hierarchies and to integrate multiple ethnic identities.

ethnicity • Cultural values and norms that distinguish the members of a given group from others. An ethnic group is one whose members share a distinct awareness of a common cultural identity, separating them from other groups. In virtually all societies, ethnic differences are associated with variations in power and material wealth. Where ethnic differences are also racial, such divisions are sometimes especially pronounced.

assimilation. Second, these stigmas become the basis of extreme hierarchy.

Race

Race can be understood as a classification system that assigns individuals and groups to categories that are ranked or hierarchical. But there are no clear-cut "races," only a range of physical variations among human beings. Differences in physical type arise from population inbreeding, which varies according to the degree of contact between different social or cultural groups. Human population groups are a continuum, and the genetic diversity *within* a population that shares visible physical traits is as great as the diversity *between* it and other populations. Racial distinctions do more than describe human differences—they also affect patterns of power and inequality within society.

The process by which people use understandings of race to classify individuals or groups is **racialization**. Historically, certain groups of people were seen to constitute distinct biological groups on the basis of innate physical features. From the fifteenth century onward, as Europeans increased their contact with different regions of the world, they attempted to systematize their expanding knowledge by categorizing and explaining both natural and social phenomena. Non-European populations were "racialized" in opposition to

Four schoolboys represent the "racial scale" in South Africa: black, Indian, half-caste, and white.

the European "white race." In some instances this racialization took codified institutional forms, as in the case of slavery in the former British, French, and Spanish colonies in the Americas; slavery in the United States; and the establishment of apartheid in South Africa after World War II. More commonly, everyday political, educational, legal, and other institutions become racialized through legislation. With the civil rights movement in the United States, de facto racial segregation and racial hierarchies persisted even after state-sanctioned segregation was dismantled. Within a racialized system, an individual's social life and overall life chances—including education, employment, incarceration, housing, health care, and legal representation—are all shaped by the racial assignments and racial hierarchies within that system.

race • Differences in human physical characteristics used to categorize large numbers of individuals.

racialization • The process by which understandings of race are used to classify individuals or groups of people. Racial distinctions are more than ways of describing human differences; they are also important factors in the reproduction of patterns of power and inequality.

Minority Groups

The term *minority group* can be confusing because it refers to political power and is not simply a numerical distinction. There are many minorities in a numerical or statistical sense, such as people having red hair or weighing more than 250 pounds, but these are not minorities according to the sociological concept. In sociology, members of a **minority group** are disadvantaged as compared to the dominant group (a group possessing more wealth, power, and prestige) and thus have some sense of group solidarity. Subjection to prejudice and discrimination usually heightens feelings of common loyalty and interests.

Members of minority groups, such as Spanish speakers in the United States, often see themselves as distinct from the majority. Minority groups are sometimes, but not always, physically and socially isolated from the larger community. Although they tend to live in certain neighborhoods, cities, or regions of a country, their children often intermarry with members of the dominant group. People who belong to minority groups sometimes promote *endogamy* (marriage within the group) to keep alive their cultural distinctiveness.

The idea of a minority group is more confusing today than ever before. Some groups that were once clearly identified as minorities, such as Asians and Jews, now have more resources, intermarry at greater rates, and experience less discrimination. This highlights the fact that the concept of a minority group is really about disadvantage in terms of power, rather than a numerical distinction.

Racism and Antiracism

Both *racism* and *antiracism* are fairly new terms. *Racism* did not come into use until the 1930s; *antiracism* did not appear in regular usage until the 1960s. Both terms can be defined in many ways because there are different definitions of what constitutes racism in different national contexts.

RACISM

Some people see **racism** as a system of domination operating in social processes and social institutions; others see it as operating in the individual consciousness. *Racism* can also refer to explicit beliefs in racial supremacy such as the systems established in Nazi Germany, before the civil rights movement in the United States, and under apartheid in South Africa.

Yet many have argued that racism is more than the ideas held by bigoted individuals, and that it is, in fact, embedded in the structure and operation of society in institutions—such as the police, the health care industry, and the educational system—that promote policies favoring certain groups while discriminating against others.

The idea of **institutional racism** was developed in the United States in the late 1960s by black power activists Stokeley Carmichael and Charles Hamilton, and was taken up by civil rights campaigners who believed that white supremacy structured all social relations. In

minority group • A group of people in a given society who, because of their distinct physical or cultural characteristics, find themselves in situations of inequality compared with the dominant group within that society.

racism • The attribution of characteristics of superiority or inferiority to a population sharing certain physically inherited characteristics. Racism is one specific form of prejudice, focusing on physical variations between people. Racist attitudes became entrenched during the period of Western colonial expansion, but seem also to rest on mechanisms of prejudice and discrimination found in human societies today.

institutional racism • Patterns of discrimination based on ethnicity that have become structured into existing social institutions.

subsequent years, the existence of institutional racism became widely accepted and openly acknowledged. A 1990s investigation into the practices of the Los Angeles Police Department following the beating of a black man named Rodney King found that institutional racism is pervasive within the Los Angeles police force and the criminal justice system. Similar cases occurred in 1999 in New York City, when police officers shot and killed an unarmed African man from Guinea, Amadou Diallo, and in 2006, when plainclothes New York City police detectives shot and killed another unarmed man, 23-year-old Sean Bell, on the day Bell was to be married. In culture and the arts, institutional racism has been found in Hollywood films and television broadcasting (via negative or limited portrayals of racial and ethnic minorities in programming).

PREJUDICE AND DISCRIMINATION

Prejudice refers to opinions or attitudes held by members of one group toward another. These preconceived views are often based on hearsay and are resistant to change even in the face of direct evidence or new information. People may harbor favorable prejudices toward groups with which they identify and negative prejudices against others.

Discrimination refers to *actual behavior* toward another group. Evident in activities that distribute rewards and benefits unequally based on membership in the dominant ethnic groups, discrimination involves excluding or restricting members of some racial or ethnic groups from opportunities that are available to other groups. For example, blacks have been excluded from and remain underrepresented in entire job categories despite the emergence of an educated black middle class. Discrimination does not necessarily derive directly from prejudice. For example, white homebuyers might avoid properties in predominantly black neighborhoods not because of hostility toward African Americans but because of worries about declining property values. Prejudiced attitudes in this case bring about discrimination, but indirectly.

prejudice • The holding of preconceived ideas about an individual or group, ideas that are resistant to change even in the face of new information. Prejudice may be either positive or negative.

discrimination • Behavior that denies to the members of a particular group resources or rewards that can be obtained by others. Discrimination must be distinguished from prejudice: Individuals who are prejudiced against others may not engage in discriminatory practices against them; conversely, people may act in a discriminatory fashion toward a group even though they are not prejudiced against that group.

stereotyping • Thinking in terms of fixed and inflexible categories.

displacement • The transferring of ideas or emotions from their true source to another object.

scapegoats • Individuals or groups blamed for wrongs that were not of their doing.

STEREOTYPES AND SCAPEGOATS

Prejudice operates mainly through **stereotyping**, which means thinking in terms of inflexible categories. Stereotyping is linked to the psychological mechanism of **displacement**, in which feelings of hostility or anger are directed against objects that are not at the root of those feelings. Stereotyping leads people to blame **scapegoats** for problems that are not their fault. Scapegoating is common when two deprived ethnic groups compete with one another for economic rewards. People who direct racial attacks against African Americans, for example, are often in a similar economic position to them. They blame blacks for grievances whose real causes lie elsewhere.

Scapegoating is normally directed against groups that are relatively powerless, because they make for easy targets. Protestants, Catholics, Jews, Italians, racial minorities, and others have played the unwilling role of scapegoat at various times throughout Western history.

Scapegoating frequently involves *projection*, the unconscious attribution to others of one's own desires or characteristics. For example, research has consistently demonstrated that when members of a dominant group practice violence against a minority and exploit it sexually, they are likely to believe that the minority group itself displays traits of sexual violence. In the United States before the civil rights movement, for instance, some white men's ideas about the lustful nature of African American men probably originated in their own frustrations, since sexual access to white women was limited by the formal nature of courtship. Similarly, in apartheid South Africa, black males were thought to be sexually dangerous to white women—but in fact, virtually all criminal sexual contact was initiated by white men against black women (Simpson and Yinger, 1986).

FROM "OLD RACISM" TO "NEW RACISM"

Just as the concept of biological race has been discredited, so the concept of "biological" racism based on differences in physical traits is rarely expressed today. The end of state-sanctioned segregation in the United States in 1954 and the collapse of apartheid in South Africa in 1994 were important turning points in the rejection of biological racism. But racist attitudes have not disappeared from modern societies. Rather, as some scholars argue, they have been replaced by a more sophisticated "new racism" (or cultural racism), which excludes certain groups on the basis of cultural differences (Barker, 1981).

According to this view, hierarchies of superiority and inferiority are constructed according to the values of the majority culture. Groups that stand apart from the majority can be marginalized or vilified for their refusal to assimilate.

ANTIRACISM

Antiracism is a concept that began to appear in regular usage in the 1960s. Alistair Bonnett (2000) defines it as:

> forms of thought and/or practice that seek to confront, eradicate and/or ameliorate racism. Anti-racism implies the ability to identify a phenomenon— racism—and to do something about it. Different forms of anti-racism exist because there are different definitions of what constitutes racism in different national contexts.

Some governments embrace opposition to racism as a way to protect their political interests. Affirmative-action programs, which are a form of antiracism, vary tremendously across national contexts. In India and Malaysia, antiracism has served as a component of national identity and a symbol of national allegiance (Bonnett, 2000). For example, in the aftermath of the 1969 race riots between Malays and Chinese in Kuala Lumpur, the Malaysian government implemented affirmative-action programs. These programs established a quota in which 40 percent of jobs in most industries were reserved for Malays and a target of 30 percent was established for Malay ownership of commercial and industrial enterprises. Another measure empowered the government to require universities to lower their qualification entrance requirements for Malay students (Nesiah, 1997). Antiracism measures in India provide constitutional safeguards for what are known as the scheduled castes and tribes. Articles 330 and 332 of the Indian Constitution

antiracism • Forms of thought and/or practice that seek to confront, eradicate and/or ameliorate racism.

reserve a percentage of the legislative seats in the Lower Parliament for members of these groups. These quotas constitute a stronger form of affirmative action than do programs in the United States.

Sociologists have only recently begun to study antiracism, particularly white antiracism. Becky Thompson (2001) interviewed white antiracists all over the United States to understand their political trajectories and how they formed an antiracist constituency and community after World War II.

② HISTORICAL PERSPECTIVES ON RACE AND ETHNICITY

To fully analyze ethnic relations, we must start with a historical and comparative perspective. It is impossible to understand ethnic divisions today without considering the effect of Western colonialism on the rest of the world (Global Map 11.1), as global migratory movements resulting from colonialism helped create ethnic divisions by placing different peoples in close proximity.

Global Map 11.1
Colonization and Ethnicity

This map shows the massive movement of peoples from Europe who colonized the Americas, South Africa, Australia, and New Zealand, resulting in the ethnic composition of populations there today. People from Africa were brought to the Americas to be slaves.

45 Million

20 Million

15 Million

17 Million

To Australia and New Zealand

Ethnic Antagonism: A Historical Perspective

From the fifteenth century onward, Europeans ventured into seas previously uncharted and unexplored by them, pursuing exploration and trade but also conquering native peoples and settling in new areas. Europeans also occasioned a large-scale movement of people from Africa to the Americas via the slave trade. The following extraordinary shifts in population have occurred in the past 350 years or so:

1. **Europe to North America.** Since the seventeenth century, some 45 million people have emigrated from Europe to what are now the United States and Canada. About 200 million people in North America today trace their ancestry to this migration.

2. **Europe to Central and South America.** About 20 million people, mostly from Spain, Portugal, and Italy, have migrated to Central and South America. Some 50 million people in these areas today are of European ancestry.

3. **Europe to Africa and Australasia.** Approximately 17 million people in Africa and Australasia are of European ancestry. In Africa, the majority of emigrants went to the state of South Africa, which was colonized mainly by the British and the Dutch.

4. **Africa to the Americas.** Starting in the sixteenth century, about 10 million blacks were unwillingly transported to the North and South American continents. Fewer than 1 million arrived in the sixteenth century; some 1.3 million in the seventeenth century; 6 million in the eighteenth century; and 2 million in the nineteenth century.

These population flows underlie the current ethnic composition of the United States, Canada, the countries of Central and South America, South Africa, Australia, and New Zealand. In all these societies, the indigenous populations were decimated by disease, war, and genocide and subjected to European rule. They are now impoverished ethnic minorities. Because the Europeans themselves had diverse national and ethnic origins, they transplanted ethnic hierarchies and divisions to their new homelands. At the height of the colonial era, Europeans also ruled over native populations in South Asia, East Asia, the South Pacific, and the Middle East.

Throughout European expansion, ethnocentric attitudes caused many colonists to believe that, as Christians, they were on a civilizing mission to the rest of the world. Europeans of all political persuasions believed themselves superior to the peoples they colonized and conquered. The fact that many of those peoples possessed technologies, agricultural skills, and knowledge that the Europeans embraced and incorporated (for example, the civil service system in India) seemed irrelevant, because the Europeans possessed the power to institutionalize their interpretation of the relationship between Europeans and the rest of the world. The early period of colonization coincided with the rise of scientific racism, and ever since then, the legacy of colonization has generated ethnic divisions that have affected regional and global conflicts. In particular, racist views distinguishing the descendants of Europeans from those of Africans became central to European racist attitudes.

The Rise of Racism

Why has racism flourished? There are several reasons. The first reason lies in the exploitative relations that Europeans established with the peoples they conquered. The slave trade could not have been carried on had Europeans not constructed a belief system that allowed them to justify their actions by claiming that Africans belonged to an inferior race. Racism helped justify colonial rule over nonwhites and denied them the rights of political participation being won by whites in the colonists' European homelands. The relations between whites and nonwhites varied according to different patterns of colonial settlement and were influenced by cultural differences among Europeans themselves.

Second, an opposition between the colors white and black as cultural symbols was deeply rooted in European culture. White had long been associated with purity, and black with evil. (There is nothing natural about this symbolism; in some other cultures, it is reversed.) The symbol of blackness held negative meanings *before* the West came into extensive contact with black peoples. These symbolic meanings infused the Europeans' reactions to blacks when they first encountered them on African shores. The sense that there was a radical difference between black and white peoples, combined with the "heathenism" of the Africans, led many Europeans to regard blacks with disdain and fear.

A third factor was the invention and diffusion of the concept of race itself. Racist attitudes have existed for thousands of years. In China of 300 B.C.E., for example, we find descriptions of barbarian peoples "who greatly resemble monkeys from whom they are descended." But the notion of race as a cluster of inherited characteristics comes from European thought. Count Joseph Arthur de Gobineau (1816–1882), sometimes called the father of modern racism, proposed that three races exist: white, black, and yellow. The white race possessed superior intelligence, morality, and willpower, and these inherited qualities underlay the spread of Western influence across the world. Blacks were the least capable, marked by an animal nature, a lack of morality, and emotional instability.

The ideas of Gobineau and other similar views were presented as supposedly scientific theories. Although completely without factual value, the notion of the superiority of the white race remains a key element of white racism—in the ideology of the Ku Klux Klan, for example—and was the basis of **apartheid** in South Africa.

African Americans in the United States

By 1780 there were nearly four million slaves in the American South. Slaves had no rights in law whatsoever. But they did not passively accept the conditions their masters imposed on them. The struggles of slaves sometimes took the form of direct opposition or disobedience to orders, and occasionally rebellion, though collective slave revolts were more common in the Caribbean than in the United States. On a more subtle level, their response involved a cultural creativity—a mixing of aspects of African cultures, Christian ideals, and cultural threads from their new environments. Some of the art forms they developed—for example, jazz—were genuinely new.

Hostility toward blacks on the part of whites was in some respects stronger in states where slavery had never existed than in the South itself. As the French political observer Alexis de Tocqueville noted in 1835, "The prejudice of race appears to be stronger in the states that have abolished slavery than in those where it still exists; and nowhere is it so intolerant as in those states where servitude has never been known." Moral rejection of slavery was confined to a few more educated groups. The main factors underlying the Civil War were political and economic; most northern leaders were more interested in sustaining the Union than in abolishing slavery, although the abolition of slavery was an eventual outcome of the conflict. The formal abolition of slavery barely changed the real conditions of life for African Americans in the South. The "black codes"—laws limiting the rights of blacks—restricted the behavior of the former slaves and punished their transgressions in much the same way they had under slavery. Acts legalizing segregation of blacks from whites in public places were passed. One kind of slavery was thus replaced by another: that of social, political, and economic discrimination.

INTERNAL MIGRATION FROM SOUTH TO NORTH

Industrial development in the North combined with the mechanization of agriculture in the South produced a progressive movement of African Americans northward. In 1900, more than 90 percent of African Americans lived in the South, mostly in rural areas. Today, three-quarters of the black population live in northern urban areas. African Americans used to be farm laborers and domestic servants, but in the course of little more

apartheid • The system of racial segregation established in South Africa.

than two generations they have become mainly urban, industrial, and service-economy workers. But African Americans have not assimilated into the wider society in the way white immigrants did. They still face conditions of neighborhood segregation and poverty that other immigrants faced only upon arrival. Together with those of Anglo-Saxon origin, African Americans have lived in the United States far longer than most other immigrant groups. What was a transitional experience for most of the later, white immigrants has become a seemingly permanent experience for blacks.

THE CIVIL RIGHTS MOVEMENT

In contrast to other racial and ethnic minorities, blacks and Native Americans have largely been denied opportunities for self-advancement. The National Association for the Advancement of Colored People (NAACP) and the National Urban League were founded in 1909 and 1910, respectively, to promote black civil rights. However, they did not have a significant effect until after World War II, when the NAACP instituted a campaign against segregated public education. This struggle came to a head when the organization sued five school boards, challenging the concept of separate but equal schooling. In 1954, in

Martin Luther King Jr. addresses a large crowd at a civil rights march on Washington in 1963. Born in 1929, King was a Baptist minister, civil rights leader, and winner of the 1964 Nobel Peace Prize. He was assassinated by James Earl Ray in 1968.

Brown v. Board of Education of Topeka, Kansas, the U.S. Supreme Court unanimously ruled that "separate educational facilities are inherently unequal."

This decision underpinned struggles for civil rights from the 1950s to the 1970s. The strength of the resistance from many whites persuaded black leaders that mass militancy was necessary. In 1955 a black woman, Rosa Parks, was arrested in Montgomery, Alabama, for declining to give up her seat on a bus to a white man. As a result, nearly the entire African American population of the city, led by a Baptist minister, Martin Luther King Jr., boycotted the transportation system for 381 days. Eventually the city was forced to abolish segregation on public transportation.

Further boycotts and sit-ins followed, with the objective of desegregating other public facilities. The marches and demonstrations began to achieve a mass following from blacks and white sympathizers. In 1963 a quarter of a million civil rights supporters staged a march on Washington and cheered as King announced, "We will not be satisfied until justice rolls down like the waters and righteousness like a mighty stream." In 1964 the Civil Rights Act was passed by Congress and signed into law by President Lyndon B. Johnson, banning discrimination in public facilities, education, employment, and any agency receiving government funds. Subsequent bills outlawed discrimination in housing and ensured that African Americans became fully registered voters.

Although civil rights marchers were beaten up and some lost their lives, and in spite of some barriers to full realization of the Civil Rights Act's provisions, the law was fundamentally important. Its principles applied not just to African Americans but also to anyone subject to discrimination, including other ethnic groups and women. It spurred a range of movements asserting the rights of oppressed groups.

How successful has the civil rights movement been? On one hand, a substantial black middle class has emerged. Many African Americans—such as the writer Toni Morrison, the literary scholar Henry Louis Gates Jr., former secretary of state Condoleezza Rice, media mogul Oprah Winfrey, basketball player Michael Jordan, and President Barack Obama—have achieved positions of power and influence. On the other hand, a significant African American underclass remains trapped in the ghettos. Scholars have debated whether this underclass has resulted primarily from economic disadvantage or from dependency on the welfare system. Later in this chapter we will examine the forms of inequality still experienced by African Americans and other minority groups.

Latinos in the United States

The wars of conquest that created the boundaries of the contemporary United States were directed not only against the Native American population but also against Mexico. The territory that later became California, Nevada, Arizona, New Mexico, and Utah—along with its quarter of a million Mexicans—was taken by the United States in 1848 as a result of the American war with Mexico. The terms *Mexican American* and *Chicano* refer to the descendants of these people, together with subsequent immigrants from Mexico. The term *Latino* refers to anyone from Spanish-speaking regions living in the United States.

The three main groups of Latinos in the United States come from Mexico (around 32.9 million), Puerto Rico (4.6 million), and Cuba (1.8 million). A further 9.6 million Spanish-speaking residents are from countries in Central and South America and other Hispanic or Latino regions (Pew Research Hispanic Center, 2010b). The Latino population increased by 43 percent between 2000 and 2010 (Pew Hispanic Research Center,

Table 11.1
Racial and Ethnic Populations in the United States, 2010

RACE OR ETHNICITY	POPULATION	SHARE OF TOTAL POPULATION*
Total US Population	308,745,538	100.00
White (non-Hispanic)	196,817,552	63.7
Hispanic or Latino	50,477,594	16.3
Black or African American	38,929,319	12.6
Asian	14,674,252	4.8
American Indian and Alaska Native	2,932,248	0.9
Native Hawaiian and Other Pacific Islander	540,013	0.2
Some other race	19,107,368	6.2
Two or more races	9,009,073	2.9

*Percentages do not total 100 percent because Hispanics or Latinos can be of any race.

Source: U.S. Bureau of the Census, 2011i.

2011a). The majority of unauthorized immigrants in the United States come from Mexico (58 percent). However, since 2008 there has been a sharp downward trend in net migration. In 2007 the number of unauthorized immigrants from Mexico peaked at 7 million. By 2011 that number had fallen to 6.1 million. During that same period, the number of authorized immigrants from Mexico rose from 5.6 million in 2007 to 5.8 million by 2011 (Pew Hispanic Research Center, 2012a). Latino residents now slightly outnumber African Americans.

MEXICAN AMERICANS

Mexican Americans reside mainly in California, Texas, and other southwestern states, although there are substantial groups in the Midwest and in northern cities as well. The majority work at low-paying jobs. In the post–World War II period up to the early 1960s, Mexican workers were admitted without much restriction. This was succeeded by a phase of quotas on legal immigrants and deportations of illegal immigrants. Today, illegal immigrants continue to cross the border. Large numbers are intercepted and sent back each year, but most simply try again, and four times as many escape officials as are stopped.

Since Mexico is a relatively poor neighbor of the wealthy United States, this flow of people northward is unlikely to diminish. Illegal immigrants can be employed more cheaply than indigenous workers, and they perform jobs that most of the rest of the population would not accept. Legislation passed by Congress in 1986 has enabled illegal immigrants living in the United States for at least five years to claim legal residence. Unfortunately, however, partly due to the broader economy, the number of Hispanics in poverty in the United States increased from 23 percent in 2000 to 25 percent by 2010 (Pew Research Hispanic Center, 2012b).

Over 60 percent of Mexicans in the United States are proficient in English. However, only 9 percent hold bachelor's degrees (Pew Research Hispanic Center, 2012b). Many Mexican Americans resist assimilation into the dominant English-speaking culture and increasingly display pride in their own cultural identity within the United States.

PUERTO RICANS AND CUBANS

Puerto Rico was acquired by the United States through war, and Puerto Ricans have been American citizens since 1917. The island is poor, and many of its inhabitants have migrated to the mainland United States to seek a better life. Puerto Ricans who emigrated originally settled primarily in New York City, but since the 1960s they have also settled elsewhere. In a trend of reverse migration, more Puerto Ricans have left the mainland than have arrived since the 1970s. One of the most important issues facing Puerto Rican activists is the political destiny of their homeland. Puerto Rico is a commonwealth, not a full state. For years, Puerto Ricans have been divided about whether the island should retain its present status, opt for independence, or attempt to become the 51st state of the Union.

A third Latino group, the Cubans, differs from the others in key respects. Half a million Cubans fled communism after the rise of Fidel Castro in 1959, and the majority of these settled in Florida. Unlike other Latino immigrants, most were educated people from white-collar and professional backgrounds. They have thrived within the United States, many finding positions comparable to those they abandoned in Cuba. As a group, Cubans have the highest family income of all Latinos.

A further wave of Cuban immigrants of less affluent origin arrived in 1980 and live in circumstances closer to the rest of the Latino communities in the United States. Both sets of Cuban immigrants are mainly political refugees rather than economic migrants. The later immigrants have become the "working class" for the earlier immigrants. They are paid low wages, but Cuban employers hire them in preference to other ethnic groups. In Miami, nearly one-third of all businesses are owned by Cubans, and 75 percent of the labor force in construction is Cuban.

In this 1942 photo, young Japanese Americans wait for baggage inspection upon arrival at a World War II Assembly Center in Turlock, California. From here they were transported to one of several internment camps for Japanese Americans.

Asian Americans

About 5.8 percent of the population of the United States is of Asian origin—18.2 million people (Pew Research Center for the People and the Press, 2012b). Chinese, Japanese, and Filipinos form the largest groups, but now there are also significant

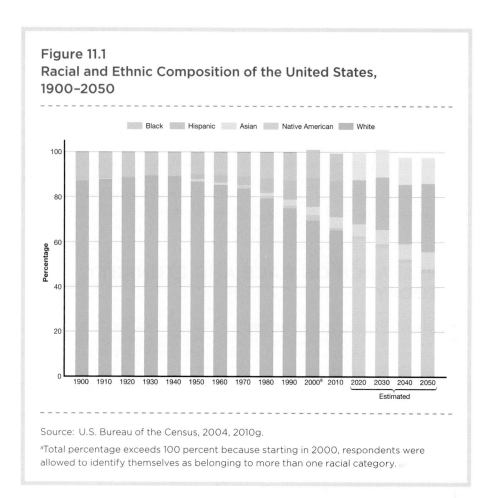

Figure 11.1
Racial and Ethnic Composition of the United States, 1900–2050

Legend: Black, Hispanic, Asian, Native American, White

Source: U.S. Bureau of the Census, 2004, 2010g.

[a]Total percentage exceeds 100 percent because starting in 2000, respondents were allowed to identify themselves as belonging to more than one racial category.

numbers of Asian Indians, Pakistanis, Koreans, and Vietnamese. As a result of the war in Vietnam, some 350,000 refugees from that country alone entered the United States in the 1970s.

Most of the early Chinese immigrants settled in California and worked in heavy industries, such as mining and railroad construction. The retreat of the Chinese into distinct Chinatowns was a response to the hostility they faced. Since Chinese immigration was legally banned in 1882, the Chinese remained isolated from the wider society, at least until recently.

The early Japanese immigrants also settled in California and the other Pacific states. During World War II, after the attack on Pearl Harbor by Japan, all Japanese Americans in the United States were taken to remote "relocation centers" surrounded by barbed wire and gun turrets. Even though most were American citizens, they were compelled to live in the hastily established camps for the duration of the war. Paradoxically, this situation promoted their greater integration within the wider society because, after the war, Japanese Americans did not return to their previously separate neighborhoods. Since then, they have attained high levels of education and income, marginally outstripping whites. The rate of intermarriage of Japanese Americans with non-Asians is now over 50 percent.

CONCEPT CHECKS ✓

1. What are three reasons racism has flourished in the United States?
2. According to Table 11.1, which ethnic minority group is the largest in American society?
3. How did the civil rights movement help minority groups achieve equal rights and opportunities?

Roughly 37 percent of Asian American brides have married non-Asian American grooms (Pew Research Center for the People and the Press, 2012b).

After passage of a new immigration act in 1965, large-scale immigration of Asians again took place. Foreign-born Chinese Americans today outnumber those brought up in the United States. The newly arrived Chinese have avoided the Chinatowns in which the long-established Chinese remain.

3 RESEARCH ON RACE AND ETHNICITY TODAY

Models of Ethnic Integration

In today's age of globalization and rapid social change, the rich benefits and complex challenges of ethnic diversity are confronting a growing number of states. As international migration accelerates along with the global economy, the mixing of populations will intensify. Meanwhile, ethnic tensions and conflicts continue, threatening the existence of some multiethnic states and hinting at protracted violence in others. How can ethnic diversity be accommodated and ethnic conflict be averted? Within multiethnic societies, what should be the relationship between ethnic minority groups and the majority population? Four primary models of ethnic integration address these challenges: assimilation, the "melting pot," pluralism, and multiculturalism. These will be discussed shortly.

For many years, the two most common positive models of political ethnic harmony in the United States were those of assimilation and the melting pot. **Assimilation** meant that new immigrant groups would assume the attitudes and language of the dominant white community. The idea of the **melting pot** involved merging different cultures and outlooks by stirring them all together. A newer model of ethnic relations is **pluralism**, in which ethnic cultures exist separately yet participate in the larger society's economic and political life. A recent outgrowth of pluralism is **multiculturalism**, in which ethnic groups exist separately and *equally*. It seems possible to create a society in which ethnic groups are separate and equal, as in Switzerland, where French, German, and Italian groups coexist in the same society. But this situation is unusual, and it is unlikely that the United States will mirror this achievement in the near future.

assimilation • The acceptance of a minority group by a majority population, in which the new group takes on the values and norms of the dominant culture.

melting pot • The idea that ethnic differences can be combined to create new patterns of behavior drawing on diverse cultural sources.

pluralism • A model for ethnic relations in which all ethnic groups retain their independent and separate identities yet share equally in the rights and powers of citizenship.

multiculturalism • The condition in which ethnic groups exist separately and share equally in economic and political life.

Global Migration

Floods of refugees and emigrants move restlessly across different regions of the globe, either escaping conflicts or fleeing poverty in search of a better life. Often they reach a new country only to face resentment from people whose forebears were immigrants themselves. Sometimes there are reversals, as in some areas of the United States along the Mexican border. Much of what is now California was once part of Mexico. Today, some Mexican Americans might say the new waves of Mexican immigrants are reclaiming what used to be their heritage—except that most of the existing groups in California don't quite see things this way.

MIGRATORY MOVEMENTS

Migration is accelerating as part of the process of global integration. Worldwide migration patterns reflect the rapidly changing economic, political, and cultural ties among countries. It has been estimated that the world's migrant population in 1990 was more than 80 million people, 20 million of whom were refugees. In 2009 the number of migrants was estimated at 214 million (U.N. Population Division, 2008a). The number will likely continue to increase in the twenty-first century, prompting some scholars to label this the "age of migration" (Castles and Miller, 1993).

Immigration, the movement of people into a country to settle, and **emigration**, the process by which people leave a country to settle in another, combine to produce global migration patterns linking countries of origin and countries of destination. Migratory movements add to ethnic and cultural diversity and affect demographic, economic, and social dynamics. Rising immigration rates in many Western societies have challenged commonly held notions of national identity and have forced a reexamination of concepts of citizenship.

Scholars offer four models of migration to describe the main global population movements since 1945. The *classic model* applies to countries such as Canada, the United States, and Australia, which developed as nations of immigrants. These countries have encouraged immigration and promised citizenship to newcomers, although restrictions and quotas limit the annual intake. The *colonial model* of immigration, pursued by countries such as France and the United Kingdom, grants preferences to immigrants from former colonies.

Countries such as Germany, Switzerland, and Belgium have followed the *guest workers model*: Immigrants are admitted on a temporary basis, often to fulfill demands within the labor market, but do not receive citizenship rights, even after long periods of settlement. Finally, *illegal models* of immigration are increasingly common because of tightening immigration laws in many industrialized countries. Immigrants who gain entry into a country either secretly or under a nonimmigration pretense often live illegally, outside the realm of official society. Examples include Mexican undocumented immigrants in many southern U.S. states and the refugees smuggled across national borders (part of a growing international business).

What are the forces behind global migration, and how are they changing as a result of globalization? Many early theories focused on push and pull factors. *Push factors* are dynamics within a country of origin that force people to emigrate, such as war, famine, political oppression, and population pressures. *Pull factors* are features of destination

immigration • The movement of people into one country from another for the purpose of settlement.

emigration • The movement of people out of one country in order to settle in another.

countries that attract immigrants, such as prosperous labor markets, better living conditions, and lower population density.

Recently, push and pull theories have been criticized for offering overly simplistic explanations of a multifaceted process. Instead, scholars of migration are regarding global migration patterns as systems produced through interactions between macro-level and micro-level processes. *Macro-level* factors refer to overarching issues such as the political situation in an area, laws and regulations controlling immigration and emigration, and changes in the international economy. *Micro-level* factors are concerned with the resources, knowledge, and understandings that the migrant populations possess.

The intersection of macro and micro processes is evident in Germany's large Turkish immigrant community. On the macro level are factors such as Germany's economic need for labor, its policy of accepting foreign "guest workers," and the state of the Turkish economy, which prevents many Turks from earning at a satisfactory level. On the micro level are the informal networks and channels of mutual support within the Turkish community in Germany and the strong links to family and friends in Turkey. Among potential Turkish migrants, knowledge about Germany and its "social capital"—its human or community resources—make Germany one of the most popular destination countries. Supporters of the migration systems approach emphasize that no single factor can explain the process of migration. Rather, each migratory movement, like that between Turkey and Germany, is the product of an interaction among macro- and micro-level processes.

Stephen Castles and Mark Miller (1993) identified four tendencies that they claim will characterize migration patterns in the coming years:

1. Acceleration. Migration across borders is occurring in greater numbers than ever before.
2. Diversification. Most countries now receive immigrants of many different types—in contrast with earlier times, when particular forms of immigration, such as labor immigration or refugees, were predominant.
3. Globalization. Migration has become more global, involving a greater number of countries as both senders and recipients (Global Map 11.2).
4. Feminization. A growing number of migrants are women, making contemporary migration much less male-dominated than previously. The increase reflects changes in the global labor market, including the growing demand for domestic workers, the expansion of sex tourism, "trafficking" in women, and the "mail-order brides" phenomenon.

GLOBAL DIASPORAS

The term **diaspora** refers to the dispersal of an ethnic population from a homeland into foreign areas, often in a forced manner or under traumatic circumstances. Although members of a diaspora are scattered geographically, they are held together by factors such as a shared history, a collective memory of the homeland, or a common ethnic identity that is nurtured and preserved.

Robin Cohen has argued that diasporas occur in various forms, although the most commonly cited examples are those that result from persecution

diaspora • The dispersal of an ethnic population from an original homeland into foreign areas, often in a forced manner or under traumatic circumstances.

Global Map 11.2
Global Migratory Movements since 1973

Arrow dimensions do not indicate the size of movements

Source: Castles and Miller, 1993, p. 6.

and violence. In *Global Diasporas* (1997), Cohen adopts a historical approach and identifies five categories of diasporas: *victim* (e.g., African, Jewish, and Armenian), *imperial* (British), *labor* (Indian), *trade* (Chinese), and *cultural* (Caribbean). In certain cases, such as that of the Chinese, large-scale population movements have occurred on a voluntary basis.

Despite the diversity of forms, all diasporas share certain key features (Cohen, 1997):

- A forced or voluntary movement from a homeland to a new region or regions;
- A shared memory about the homeland, a commitment to its preservation, and a belief in the possibility of eventual return;
- A strong ethnic identity sustained over time and distance;
- A sense of solidarity with members of the same ethnic group also living in areas of the diaspora;
- A degree of tension in relation to the host societies; and
- The potential for valuable and creative contributions to pluralistic host societies.

Some scholars have accused Cohen of simplifying complex and distinctive migration experiences into a narrow typology by associating categories of diasporas with particular ethnic groups. Others argue that his conceptualization of diaspora is not sufficiently precise. Yet Cohen's study is valuable for demonstrating that diasporas are nonstatic, ongoing processes of maintaining collective identity and preserving ethnic culture in a rapidly globalizing world.

UNANSWERED QUESTIONS

Do New Immigrants Help or Hinder the Nation's Economy?

The cultural and social landscape of the United States is viewed as an amalgam of diverse cultures, largely because of our nation's history as a refuge for immigrants. Today, however, policy makers and social scientists disagree over the social and economic costs of immigration.

Before discussing this debate, it is important to understand the current state of immigration to the United States. There are more than 39 million foreign-born individuals in the United States, roughly 13 percent of the total population; a number not seen since the 1920s (American Community Survey, 2012). In the decade of the 1990s, more than 977,000 legal immigrants arrived each year, and an additional 300,000 entered and stayed in the country illegally (U.S. Bureau of the Census, 2006). From 2002 to 2006, an average of 1,021,884 legal immigrants was admitted each year, and another 500,000 illegal immigrants entered the country (Migration Policy Institute, 2007). In contrast to the major wave of immigration of the 1880s and 1890s, fewer than 10 percent of immigrants admitted into the United States in the 1980s and 1990s were of European origin. In fact, between 1989 and 1993, more than half came from Mexico, the Philippines, Vietnam, and El Salvador. This change is attributed to two government acts: the 1965 Immigration and Nationality Act Amendments, which abolished preference for northern and western European immigrants and gave preference to "family reunification"—rather than occupational skills—as a reason for accepting immigrants; and the 1986 Immigration Reform and Control Act, which provided amnesty for many illegal immigrants. Recently, Asian Americans surpassed Hispanic Americans as the largest population of new immigrants (Pew Research Center for the People and the Press, 2012b).

Consequently, much of the debate focuses on new immigrants' ability to secure employment and achieve economic self-sufficiency. In his 1994 essay "The Economics of Immigration," economist George Borjas argues that since the 1980s, the United States has attracted "lower-quality" immigrants with less education and few marketable job skills. Moreover, they are less skilled than both natives (i.e., people born in the United States) and earlier migrants; thus they are more reliant on government assistance. It is estimated that 36 percent of immigrants use some form of social assistance, compared with 22 percent of the native-born (Center for Immigration Studies, 2012). Borjas estimates that recent immigrants will likely earn 20 percent less than native-born Americans for most of their working lives.

In terms of the effect of immigrants on natives' economic prospects, Borjas argues that large-scale migration of less-skilled workers harms the economic opportunities of less-skilled natives—particularly African Americans. This occurs because immigrants increase the number of workers in the economy; as they create additional competition in the labor market, wages of the least-skilled workers fall.

Other economists and policy analysts claim that recent immigration has had either a positive effect or no influence on the U.S. economy. Economist Julian Simon (1981, 1989) has argued that immigrants benefit the U.S. economy by joining the labor force and paying into the federal revenue system for their whole lives. By the time they retire and collect government benefits such as Social Security and Medicare, their children will be covering these costs by working and paying into the tax system. Simon's arguments, however, assume that immigrants earn the same wages and are as employable as natives—an assumption refuted by Borjas's research.

Simon also holds that immigrants are a cultural asset to the United States. In fact, he claims that "the notion of wanting to keep out immigrants to keep our institutions and our values pure is prejudice" (quoted in Brimelow, 1995). He argues, moreover, that because human beings have the intelligence to adapt to their surroundings, the more immigrants that come to the United States, the larger the pool of potential innovators and problem solvers our nation will have.

Studies conducted by Simon and the Urban Institute, a nonprofit research organization, acknowledge that although some recent immigrants may benefit from federally funded programs such as welfare, these costs to the government are often quite short term. Immigrant children who benefit from the U.S. educational system go on to become productive, taxpaying workers.

The National Immigration Forum has estimated that immigrant workers contribute significantly to the national economy. Even though most immigrants work in low-wage and hard-labor jobs, without them the gross domestic product of the United States would be $1 trillion less (Rodriguez, 2004). Assessing the fiscal costs of immigration proves difficult, however. Although much of the public debate focuses on the costs of providing services to illegal immigrants, actual statistics documenting the number of illegal immigrants are difficult to obtain and verify. Moreover, few policy analysts can predict whether U.S. immigration policy—or the characteristics of immigrants themselves—will change drastically in the future.

Has Real Progress Been Made Since the Civil Rights Movement of the 1960s?

On the one hand, an increasing number of blacks joined the middle class by acquiring college degrees, professional jobs, and new homes. On the other hand, blacks are far more likely than whites to live in poverty and be socially isolated from good schools and economic opportunity. Also, many immigrants came to the United States throughout the 1980s and '90s to find new economic opportunity. Yet some of these groups, particularly Mexicans, have among the lowest levels of educational achievement and live in dire poverty. Most sociologists agree on the facts about racial and ethnic inequality but disagree on how to interpret them. Are the improving economic conditions for minority groups part of a long-term process, or were they temporary reflections of the booming 1990s economy? Is racial and ethnic inequality primarily the result of a person's racial or ethnic background, or does it reflect a person's class position? In this section, we examine how racial and ethnic inequality is reflected in educational and occupational attainment, income, health, residential

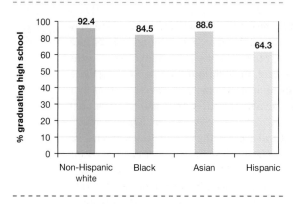

Figure 11.2A
High School Graduation Rates by Race and Ethnicity, 2011

Source: U.S. Bureau of the Census, 2011c.

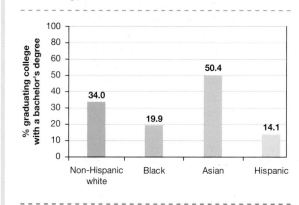

Figure 11.2B
College Graduation Rates by Race and Ethnicity, 2011

Source: U.S. Bureau of the Census, 2011c.

segregation, and political power. We then consider divergent social statuses within the largest racial and ethnic groups. We conclude by examining how sociologists try to explain racial inequality.

EDUCATIONAL ATTAINMENT

Differences between blacks and whites in levels of educational attainment have decreased, but these seem more the result of long-established trends than the direct outcome of the struggles of the 1960s. Young African Americans are for the first time close to whites in terms of finishing high school. The number of blacks over the age of 25 with high school degrees increased from about 20 percent in 1960 to 84.5 percent in 2011. By contrast, about 92.4 percent of whites have completed high school (Figure 11.2A). However, while more blacks are attending college now than in the 1960s, a much higher proportion of whites than blacks graduates from college (Figure 11.2B). In today's global economy and job market, which value college degrees, the result is a wide disparity in incomes between whites and blacks (see the next section, "Employment and Income"). Still, the number of associate degrees awarded to blacks rose 89 percent from 1990 to 2009 (U.S. Department of Education, 2012).

Another trend is the large gap in educational attainment between Hispanics and both whites and blacks. Hispanics have by far the highest high school dropout rate of any group in the United States, and only 1 in 10 Hispanic high school dropouts has a General Educational Development (GED) credential (Pew Research Hispanic Center, 2010a). While rates of college attendance and graduation have improved for other groups, the rate for Hispanics has held relatively steady since the mid-1980s. Only about 14.1 percent hold a college degree (U.S. Bureau of the Census, 2011c). It is possible that these poor results reflect the large number of poorly educated immigrants from Latin America since the 1980s, many of whom have limited English-language skills and whose children encounter difficulties in school. One study found, however, that even among Mexican Americans whose families have lived in the United States for three generations or more, there has been a decline in educational attainment (Bean et al., 1994). For Hispanics with low levels of education and poor language skills, living in the United States has been "the American nightmare, not the American dream" (Holmes, 1997).

EMPLOYMENT AND INCOME

As a result of increased educational attainment, blacks now hold slightly more managerial and professional jobs than they did in 1960, though still not in proportion to their overall numbers. In 2012, out of about 54 million managerial or professional positions in the United States, blacks held 8.7 percent; Hispanics, 8.4 percent, and Asians, 6.9 percent (BLS, 2012b).

The unemployment rate of black and Hispanic men outstrips that of whites by the same degree today as in the early 1960s. While the total unemployment rates for all groups jumped after the economic crisis of 2007, the total unemployment rate for blacks and Hispanics is higher than that for whites. The percentage of unemployed whites increased from 3.5 in 2005 to 7.5 in 2010, while the percentage of unemployed blacks increased from 7.5 in 2005 to 13.4 in 2010 and the percentage of unemployed Hispanics increased from 4.8 in 2005 to 10.8 in 2010 (U.S. Bureau of the Census, 2012p). There has also been debate about whether employment opportunities for minorities have improved or worsened. Statistics on unemployment don't adequately measure economic opportunity because they reflect only those known to be looking for work. A higher proportion of disillusioned blacks and Hispanics have simply opted out of the occupational system, neither working nor looking for work. Unemployment figures also do not reflect the increasing numbers of young minority men in prison (see also Chapter 7).

Nevertheless, the disparities between the earnings of blacks and whites are gradually diminishing. As measured in terms of median weekly income, black men now earn 75.6 percent of the level of pay of white men (BLS, 2012f), compared to 49 percent in 1959. In terms of household family income (adjusted for inflation), blacks are the only social group to have seen an improvement in the 1990s. By 2000, poverty rates for African Americans had fallen to their lowest rates since 1955, when the government started tracking the figure. These signs of improvement for African Americans have been occurring across the country. Some scholars have warned, however, that the gains could be reversed in the wake of the financial crisis of 2007. They also point out that large gaps between African Americans and whites still exist in terms of college degrees, infant mortality, poverty rates, and household income (Figure 11.3).

Prospects for Hispanics stagnated or worsened since 2000, as well. Between 2000 and 2005, Hispanic household incomes (adjusted for inflation) decreased significantly. Yet the rate of Hispanic household poverty has remained very similar to that of blacks (in 2003–2005 the weighted average poverty rate for Hispanics was 20.3 percent versus 22.4 percent for blacks). By 2011 the poverty rate for Hispanics was 26.7 and 27.5 percent for blacks (Pew Research Hispanic Center, 2011a). The large influx of poor immigrants explains some of the decline in average income, but even among Hispanics born in the United States, income levels have declined. As one Latino group leader commented, "Most Hispanic residents are caught in jobs like gardener, nanny, and restaurant worker that will never pay well and from which they will never advance" (quoted in Goldberg, 1997).

HEALTH

Jake Najman (1993) surveyed the evidence linking health to racial and economic inequalities. He also considered strategies for improving the health of the poorer groups in society. After studying data for a number of countries, including the United States, he concluded

Figure 11.3
Real Median Household Income by Race, 1980–2011

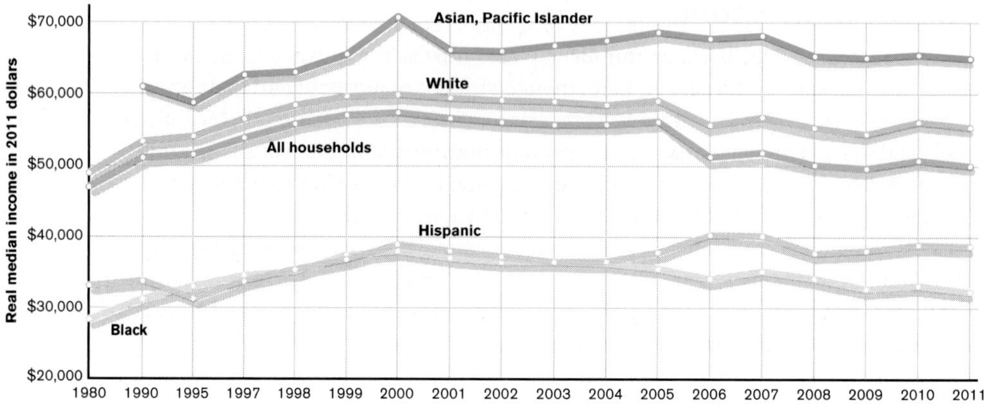

Source: DeNavas-Walt, Proctor, and Smith, 2012.

that for people in the poorest 20 percent, as measured in terms of income, the death rates were 1.5–2.5 times those of the highest 20 percent of income earners. In the United States, the rate of infant mortality for the poorest 20 percent was four times higher than for the wealthiest 20 percent. When differences were measured between whites and African Americans in the United States, rather than only in terms of income, the contrast in infant mortality rates was even higher—five times higher for blacks than for whites. The contrast between races is also apparent in life expectancy. In 2007, whites on average could expect to live 5.3 years longer than African Americans (Arias, 2007).

How might the influence of poverty and race on health be countered? Extensive programs of health education and disease prevention are one possibility. But such programs work better among prosperous, well-educated groups and usually produce only small changes in behavior. Increased accessibility to health services would help, but probably to a limited degree. The only truly effective policy option, it is argued, would be to attack poverty itself, so as to reduce the income gap between rich and poor (Najman, 1993).

RESIDENTIAL SEGREGATION

Neighborhood segregation seems to have declined little over the past quarter century. Studies show that discriminatory practices between black and white clients in the housing market continue (Lake, 1981). This is why black and white children still tend to attend the same schools in most rural areas of the South and in many smaller and medium-size cities throughout the country. Most black college students now also attend the same colleges and universities as whites, instead of all-black institutions (Bullock, 1984). Yet in the larger cities, a high level of educational segregation persists as a result of the continuing movement of whites to suburbs or rural areas.

In *American Apartheid* (1993), Douglas S. Massey and Nancy A. Denton argue that the history of racial segregation and its urban form, the black ghetto, are responsible for the perpetuation of black poverty and the continued polarization of black and white. Even many middle-class blacks still find themselves segregated from white society. For them, as for poor blacks, this becomes a self-perpetuating cycle. Affluent blacks who could afford to live in predominantly white neighborhoods may choose not to because of the struggle for acceptance they might face. The black ghetto, the authors conclude, was constructed through a series of well-defined institutional practices of racial discrimination—private behavior and public policies by which whites sought to contain growing urban black populations. Until policy makers, social scientists, and private citizens recognize the crucial role of such institutional discrimination in perpetuating urban poverty and racial injustice, the United States will remain a deeply divided and troubled society.

POLITICAL POWER

Blacks have made gains in holding local elective offices; the number of black public officials increased from 40 in 1960 to 9,101 as of January 2001, the most recent year for which data are available (Bositis, 2001). Blacks have been voted into every major political office. Most notably, in 2008, Barack Obama became the first African American to be elected president. He won by a large margin, and he was reelected in 2012. In spite of high-profile victories such as Obama's, most elected black officials hold relatively minor local positions, although they do include quite a few mayors and judges. The share of representation that Latinos and African Americans have in Congress is not proportionate to their percentage of the population. In 2013 there were 43 black members of the U.S. House of Representatives, out of a total of 435 (9.8 percent of the total). As of 2013, there were two black senators: William "Mo" Cowan from Massachusetts and Tim Scott from South Carolina. Three Latinos—Bob Menendez from New Jersey, Marco Rubio from Florida, and Ted Cruz from Texas—do serve in the U.S. Senate.

How Can Ethnic Conflict Be Reduced?

The most extreme and devastating form of group relations involves **genocide**—the systematic destruction of a racial, political, or cultural group. The most horrific recent instance of brutal destruction of such a group was the massacre of six million Jews in the German concentration camps during World War II. Other examples of mass genocide in the twentieth century span the globe. Between 1915 and 1923, more than a million Armenians were killed by the Ottoman Turkish government. In the late 1970s, two million Cambodians died under the Khmer Rouge. During the 1990s, in the African country of Rwanda, hundreds of thousands of the minority Tutsis were massacred by the dominant Hutu group. In the former Yugoslavia, Bosnian and Kosovar Muslims were executed by the Serb majority. And in the Darfur region of Sudan, the conflict between the Arabic-speaking, nomadic Janjaweed and the non-Arab Sudanese who speak African languages escalated to genocide, with hundreds of thousands of people killed and approximately two million forced to flee their homes.

The conflicts in the former Yugoslavia involved **ethnic cleansing**—the creation of ethnically homogeneous areas through the mass expulsion of other ethnic populations via targeted violence, harassment, threats, and campaigns of terror.

genocide • The systematic, planned destruction of a racial, political, or cultural group.

ethnic cleansing • The creation of ethnically homogeneous territories through the mass expulsion of ethnic populations.

Croatia, for example, became a "monoethnic" state after a costly war in which thousands of Serbs were expelled from the country. The war—which broke out in Bosnia in 1992 between Orthodox Serbs, Catholic Croats, and Bosnian Muslims—involved the ethnic cleansing of the Bosnian Muslim population at the hands of the Serbs. Thousands of Muslim men were forced into internment camps, and Muslim women were systematically raped. The war in Kosovo in 1999 was prompted by charges that Serbian forces were ethnically cleansing the Kosovar Albanian (Muslim) population from the province.

In Bosnia and Kosovo, ethnic conflict became internationalized. Hundreds of thousands of refugees fled to neighboring areas, further destabilizing the region. Western states intervened diplomatically and militarily to protect the human rights of targeted ethnic groups. In the short term, such interventions succeeded, yet they had unintended consequences as well. The fragile peace in Bosnia has persisted only through the presence of peacekeeping troops and the partitioning of the country into separate ethnic enclaves. In Kosovo, reverse ethnic cleansing ensued after the North Atlantic Treaty Organization (NATO) bombing campaign. Ethnic Albanian Kosovars began to drive the local Serb population out of Kosovo; the presence of NATO-led Kosovo Force troops was inadequate to prevent ethnic tensions from reigniting.

Violent conflicts worldwide are increasingly civil wars with ethnic dimensions. In a world of growing interdependence and competition, international factors become even more important in shaping ethnic relations, while the effects of internal ethnic conflicts are felt well outside national borders—sometimes provoking military intervention, sometimes requiring international war crimes tribunals. Responding to and preventing ethnic conflicts have become key challenges facing individual states and international political structures.

In some areas of the world, the concept of group closure has been institutionalized in the form of **segregation**—a practice whereby racial and ethnic groups are kept physically separate by law, thereby maintaining the superior position of the dominant group. For instance, in apartheid-era South Africa, laws forced blacks to live separately from whites and forbade sexual relations between races. In the United States, African Americans experienced numerous legal forms of segregation, including, until 1967, the prohibition of interracial marriage, which had been criminalized for more than 270 years in every state except Alaska and Hawaii. Even today, segregated residential areas still exist in many cities, leading some to claim that an American system of apartheid has developed (Massey and Denton, 1993).

CONFLICT AND ECONOMIC POWER

Many commentators have argued that the best way to reduce ethnic conflicts is to establish democracy and a free market; this would promote peace by giving everyone a say in running the country and by giving all people access to the prosperity that comes from trade. In *World on Fire: How Exporting Free Market Democracy Breeds Ethnic Hatred and Global Instability* (2003), Amy Chua, a professor at Yale University, contests this view.

Chua's starting point is that in many developing countries a small ethnic minority enjoys disproportionate economic power. One example is the white minority that exploited nonwhite ethnic groups in apartheid South Africa. Chua argues that the massacre of Tutsis by Hutus in Rwanda in 1994 and the hatred felt by Serbs toward Croats in the former Yugoslavia were partly related to the economic advantage enjoyed by the Tutsis and the Croats in their respective countries.

segregation • The practices of keeping racial and ethnic groups physically separate, thereby maintaining the superior position of the dominant group.

Chua often mentions the Chinese ethnic minority in Indonesia, where the free-market policies of the former dictator General Suharto enriched the country's tiny Chinese minority. In turn, Chinese Indonesians supported the Suharto dictatorship. By 1998, the year that mass pro-democracy demonstrations forced Suharto to resign, Chinese Indonesians controlled 70 percent of Indonesia's private economy but made up just 3 percent of its population. The end of Suharto's regime was accompanied by violent attacks against the Chinese minority. Chua (2003) writes, "The prevailing view among the pribumi [ethnic] majority was that it was 'worthwhile to lose 10 years of growth to get rid of the Chinese problem once and for all.'"

As Suharto's dictatorship collapsed, the United States and other Western countries called for the introduction of democratic elections. Yet Chua argues that introducing democracy to countries with what she calls "market dominant minorities," such as the Chinese in Indonesia, is not likely to bring peace but, instead, a backlash from the country's ethnic majority. Political leaders will emerge who scapegoat the resented minority and encourage the ethnic majority to reclaim the country's wealth for the "true" owners of the nation, as the pribumi majority in Indonesia did against the Chinese minority.

Chua's account illustrates that although democracy and the market economy are in principle beneficent forces, they must be grounded in an effective system of law and civil society. Where they are not, new and acute ethnic conflicts can emerge.

CONCEPT CHECKS

1. What are some of the main reasons there is a large gap in educational attainment between Hispanics and blacks in the United States?

2. How do Massey and Denton explain the persistence of residential segregation?

3. Some sociologists argue that racial inequalities should be explained in terms of class rather than race. What are some of the problems associated with social class–based explanations of racial inequalities?

4. Compare and contrast three forms of ethnic conflict.

1 **Basic Concepts**

p. 293

2 **Historical Perspectives on Race and Ethnicity**

p. 298

LEARNING OBJECTIVES

Learn the cultural bases of race and ethnicity and how racial and ethnic differences create sharp divisions. Learn the leading psychological theories and sociological interpretations of prejudice and discrimination.

Familiarize yourself with the history and social dimensions of ethnic relations in America. Recognize the importance of the historical roots of ethnic conflict, particularly in the expansion of Western colonialism. Understand the different models for a multiethnic society.

TERMS TO KNOW

Racial literacy • Ethnicity • Race • Racialization • Minority group • Racism • Institutional racism • Prejudice • Discrimination • Stereotyping • Displacement • Scapegoats • Antiracism

Apartheid

CONCEPT CHECKS

1. Explain the difference between ethnicity and race.
2. What does the term *racialization* refer to?
3. How does prejudice operate in society?
4. Why are Hispanics and African Americans considered to be minority groups in American society?

1. What are three reasons racism has flourished in the United States?
2. According to Table 11.1, which ethnic minority group is the largest in American society?
3. How did the civil rights movement help minority groups achieve equal rights and opportunities?

Exercises: Thinking Sociologically

1. Review the discussion of the assimilation of different American minorities. Then write a short essay comparing the assimilation experiences of Asians and Latinos. In your essay, identify the criteria for assimilation and discuss which group has assimilated most readily. Then explain the sociological reasons for the difference in assimilation between the two groups.

2. Does affirmative action still have a future in the United States? On the one hand, increasing numbers of African Americans have joined the middle class by acquiring college degrees, professional jobs, and new homes. On the other hand, blacks are still far more likely than whites to live in poverty, to attend poor schools, and to lack economic opportunity. Given these differences and other contrasts mentioned in the text, do we still need affirmative action?

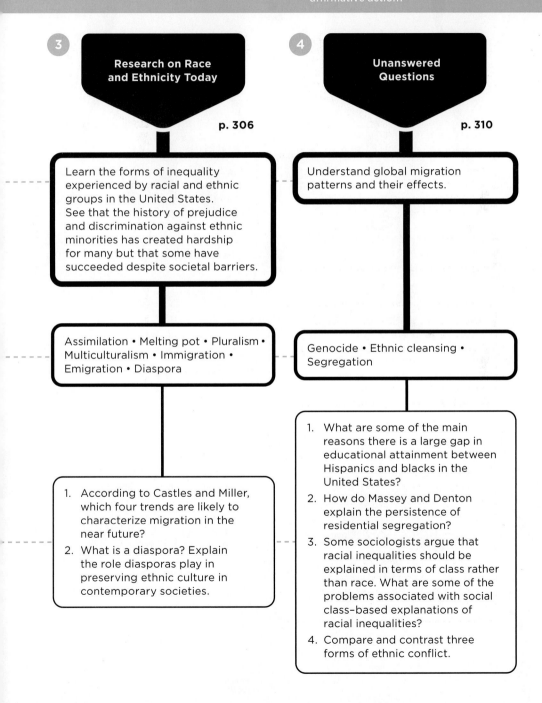

3 — **Research on Race and Ethnicity Today**

p. 306

Learn the forms of inequality experienced by racial and ethnic groups in the United States.
See that the history of prejudice and discrimination against ethnic minorities has created hardship for many but that some have succeeded despite societal barriers.

Assimilation • Melting pot • Pluralism • Multiculturalism • Immigration • Emigration • Diaspora

1. According to Castles and Miller, which four trends are likely to characterize migration in the near future?
2. What is a diaspora? Explain the role diasporas play in preserving ethnic culture in contemporary societies.

4 — **Unanswered Questions**

p. 310

Understand global migration patterns and their effects.

Genocide • Ethnic cleansing • Segregation

1. What are some of the main reasons there is a large gap in educational attainment between Hispanics and blacks in the United States?
2. How do Massey and Denton explain the persistence of residential segregation?
3. Some sociologists argue that racial inequalities should be explained in terms of class rather than race. What are some of the problems associated with social class–based explanations of racial inequalities?
4. Compare and contrast three forms of ethnic conflict.

Aging

12

Which of the following is true about older adults (persons age 65+) in the United States today?

a Physical illness and senility are inevitable aspects of aging.

b Older adults are economically well off, because benefits such as Social Security and Medicare provide a stable income and free health insurance.

c The most common residence for older adults is nursing homes.

d Older adults are a highly heterogeneous group, with their health and well-being varying widely by age, race, gender, and social class.

Turn the page for the correct answer.

What does the term *senior citizen, elderly,* or *old age* conjure up in your mind? For many Americans, old age is viewed as a time of senility, poverty, loneliness, and celibacy. Others view old age as a "golden" time, when cash-flush retirees sell their homes, move to Florida, and live the good life, surrounded by their golf buddies and devoted grandchildren (Wilken, 2008). The truth is somewhere in between. Older adults, persons ages 65 and older, are a highly diverse group, with some enjoying good health, wealth, and happiness, and others suffering from poverty, physical disability, and loneliness. Often the trajectories that set one on the path toward a rewarding or distressing later life begin decades earlier, sometimes as early as childhood.

Witness the cases of Judy Hofstadter and Alice Garvin. Judy Hofstadter, 81, lives in New York City and works full time as a financial planner at a large firm. She keeps up a vigorous exercise regimen, shops weekly at the local farmers' market for healthy food, devotes time to organizations promoting peace in the Middle East, and donates her time and money to political candidates she believes in. In 2006, while going door to door before midterm elections, she tripped and broke her wrist. "I sacrificed my hand in service to my country," Judy says, laughing. Although she now suffers from breast cancer, significant hearing loss, a serious case of glaucoma, and excruciating neck and back pain, "she has learned to make lemonade from everything," according to her son David Tuller (2009).

Judy learned at a young age how to overcome challenges with her sense of humor intact. Born into a middle-class Jewish family that promoted academic achievement, Judy entered Harvard Law School in 1951, joining only the second class to admit women. She married a physician who was physically abusive, so she gathered up the courage to take her two children and leave him. To preserve her spirit during those difficult years, "she funneled her

LEARNING OBJECTIVES

1 BASIC CONCEPTS

Learn some basic facts about the increase in the proportion of the U.S. population that is age 65 and older. Recognize that aging is a combination of biological, psychological, and social processes. Understand how technological advances affect each of the three aging processes.

2 GROWING OLD: THEORIES OF AGING

Understand key theories of aging, particularly those that focus on how society shapes the social roles of older adults and that emphasize aspects of age stratification.

3 RESEARCH ON AGING IN THE UNITED STATES TODAY

Evaluate the experience of growing old in the United States and how this experience is shaped by race, social class, gender, and birth cohort.

4 UNANSWERED QUESTIONS: THE POLITICAL AND ECONOMIC IMPACT OF POPULATION AGING

Understand and analyze the politics of generational equity. Assess the social issues of graying on a global level.

energy and passion into political and social causes. She fought for integrated housing and civil liberties, and infused [her children] with her progressive spirit" (Tuller, 2009).

Her fighting spirit hasn't waned in later life. When she was first diagnosed with breast cancer, "she investigated the issue like a lawyer . . . she scoured the literature, interrogated researchers at medical conferences, and joined the boards of breast cancer advocacy groups." Her son proudly describes her as "my model . . . for how to age with grace, compassion and vitality." According to Judy, "I think having passions takes you outside of yourself and animates your life . . . It makes you want to take care of yourself so you can keep on going. I still look forward to the next adventure."

Judy is fortunate to have had a prestigious education, a comfortable Manhattan apartment, an intellectually challenging and well-paying career, two emotionally supportive and financially secure children—one a professor, the other a therapist—and a well-honed sense of problem solving. Not all older adults are so lucky. Just a few miles away, in Brooklyn, 77-year-old Alice Garvin has been dealt a much worse hand.

Alice Garvin is now fighting foreclosure, while also struggling to support her children, grandchildren, great-grandson, and grand-nephew. Alice, a retired home health aide, first faced foreclosure four years ago, when she found an eviction notice on the front door of her apartment building (Mascia, 2009). The second time, the loss of her apartment was a blessing in disguise; she was evicted from a rundown apartment in a dangerous neighborhood "she couldn't wait to leave" because of gunshots outside and "bugs falling from the ceiling" (Mascia, 2009). In both cases, "foreclosure was beyond her control: she is not a homeowner, but a tenant." Alice was saved by a local charity that provided her with money so that she could move into a new apartment big enough for her and her large extended family.

Now in her new apartment, Alice continues to struggle financially. Her family "survives on a patchwork of welfare," including Social Security for Alice, disability payments for her children and grandchildren, and an occasional visit to a food pantry. Foreclosure and economic struggles are difficult for anyone, but for Alice "it is just the latest blow in a lifetime filled with difficulty." Born in South Carolina, Alice was "an orphan by the time she was 14; she was 36 when her husband died from an alcohol-related illness. Four of her six children have died"—one from the effects of Agent Orange exposure in the Vietnam War, two from pneumonia, and one from AIDS.

Alice is caregiver and financial provider to her two surviving sons; one cannot work because of a congenital heart problem, and the other was nearly beaten to death in a mugging 20 years ago and cannot work due to frequent seizures. Her two teenage grandsons and grand nephew were born addicted to cocaine, and have lingering behavioral problems. And this past spring, Alice became a great-grandmother. Despite her seemingly insurmountable responsibilities, she keeps a positive attitude: "I try to look forward, not back. I have a lot to keep me going now."

Growing old can be a fulfilling and rewarding experience, as Judy Hofstadter knows. Or it can be filled with adversity and stress, as Alice Garvin has discovered. For most older Americans, the experience of aging lies somewhere in between. How we experience old age is shaped by our gender, race, social class, and historical context. Yet aging also is a cumulative process, and is molded by our experiences, resources, and struggles in earlier life. How older adults navigate their later years reflects not only their personal resources, such as optimism, problem-solving skills, and energy, but also structural factors such as economic opportunities and public policies.

Although old age is often accompanied by physical and cognitive declines and economic and psychological distress—as the lives of Judy Hofstadter and Alice Garvin reveal—more Americans are leading longer, healthier, and more productive lives than ever before. In

2010, more than 40 million Americans were age 65 or older, including some 5.5 million over 85 years old (Federal Interagency Forum on Aging-Related Statistics [FIFARS], 2012). In this chapter, we examine the nature of aging in U.S. society, exploring what it means to grow old in a world that is rapidly changing. We first review the core concepts of aging, including the graying of the U.S. population and biological, psychological, and social aspects of aging. We next look at sociological theories that describe how people adapt to growing old. This will lead us to a discussion of contemporary research on aging in the United States, focusing on some of the special challenges facing older adults, including social isolation, health declines, and elder abuse. We next delve into important although unresolved questions regarding political and economic issues surrounding the aging of the American population, including Social Security and Medicare. The future of these programs affects the lives of all Americans, and will gain increasing importance given the growing numbers of elderly people. We conclude with a discussion of the graying of the world population, and what this means for individuals, governments, and societies.

THE ANSWER IS D.

1 BASIC CONCEPTS

The Graying of Society

The United States and other industrial societies are said to be **graying**—that is, experiencing an increase in the proportion of the population that is **elderly**. Older adults, or the elderly, are generally considered to be persons ages 65 and older, although, as we will see later in this chapter, aging is a multifaceted process. Graying is the result of two long-term trends in industrial societies: the tendency of families to have fewer children (discussed in Chapter 15) and the fact that people are living longer.

For most of human history the average life expectancy at birth was less than 20 years; the main reason was that many people died in infancy or during early childhood. As such, the "average" age at which a person died was very low. About 2,000 years ago, the average newborn baby in Rome could expect to live to just 22. In 1900 in the United States, the average baby could expect to live to about age 47. Today, by contrast, the average baby born in the United States can expect to live until age 78 (National Center for Health Statistics, 2010). However, there is enormous variation in life expectancy depending on where a baby is born—from 83 years in Japan to 48 years in sub-Saharan African nations such as Lesotho and Democratic Republic of the Congo (World Bank, 2011c). Even within the United States today, life expectancy varies widely; a black baby boy born today can expect to live until 71, whereas a white baby girl will live an average of 10 years longer, until age 81 (National Center for Health Statistics, 2010).

What explains the aging of U.S. and other societies? Modern agriculture, sanitation systems, epidemic control, improved nutrition, and medicine have all contributed to a decline in mortality and an increase in life expectancy throughout the world. In most societies today, fewer children die

graying • A term used to indicate that an increasing proportion of a society's population is elderly.

elderly • Adults ages 65 and older.

in infancy and more adults survive until their seventies, eighties, and even older. The U.S. population, like that of other industrial societies, is aging even faster than less industrialized nations. Given the growing numbers of older adults and declining numbers of younger persons, the median age of the population is rising. In 1850, half the U.S. population was older than 19. Today, half is over 35; by 2050, half will be over 40 (Figure 12.1).

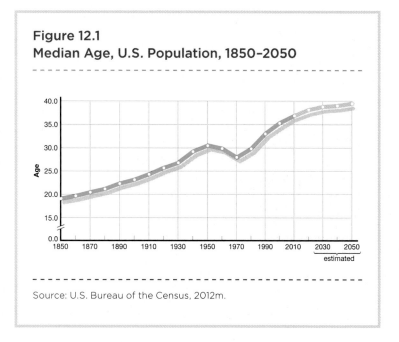

Figure 12.1
Median Age, U.S. Population, 1850–2050

Source: U.S. Bureau of the Census, 2012m.

Because of the graying of the American population, the number of older adults in the United States is expected to increase from 40 million in 2010 to 72 million by the year 2030 (FIFARS, 2012). According to U.S. Bureau of the Census estimates, 25 percent of all people reaching age 65 today will live to be 90. By the middle of the twenty-first century, that figure is expected to rise to 42 percent. According to some projections, by that time there may be as many as two million living Americans who have celebrated their 100th birthday (Healthful Life Project, 2003). These trends have enormous importance for the future of American society. In a culture that often worships eternal youth, what will happen when a quarter of the population is over 65?

How Do People Age?

In examining the nature of aging, we will draw on studies of **social gerontology**, a discipline concerned with the study of the social aspects of aging. Studying aging requires a "sociological imagination." How people experience old age is shaped by social and historical context (Riley, Foner, and Waring, 1988). For Americans born in the first quarter of the twentieth century, a high school education was regarded as more than sufficient for most available jobs, and most people did not expect to live much past their sixties—and then only at the cost of suffering a variety of disabilities. Today those very same people find themselves in their seventies and eighties; many are relatively healthy, unwilling to disengage from work or social life, and in need of more schooling than they ever dreamed would be necessary to compete in today's information-based economy.

What does it mean to age? **Aging** can be defined as the combination of biological, psychological, and social processes that affect people as they grow older (Abeles and Riley, 1987; Atchley, 2000; Riley, Foner, and Waring, 1988). These processes can be thought of as three different, although interrelated, developmental clocks: (1) biological, which refers to the

social gerontology • The study of aging and the elderly.

aging • The combination of biological, psychological, and social processes that affect people as they grow older.

Figure 12.2
Average Life Expectancy at Birth for Males and Females, 1900–2010, in the United States

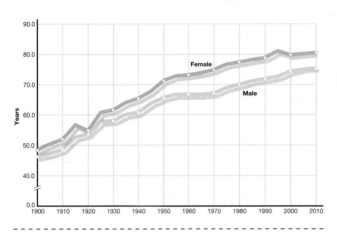

Source: U.S. Bureau of the Census, 2010b.

physical body; (2) psychological, which refers to the mind, including one's mental, emotional, and cognitive capabilities; and (3) social, which refers to cultural norms, values, and role expectations having to do with age. There is an enormous range of variation in all three of these processes. The very meaning of old age is changing rapidly, both because research is dispelling many outdated notions about aging and because advances in nutrition, health, and medical technology now enable many people to live longer, healthier lives than ever before.

BIOLOGICAL AGING

The biological effects of aging are well established, although the exact chronological age at which they occur varies greatly, depending on one's genes, lifestyle, and luck. In general, for men and women alike, biological aging typically means:

- Declining vision, as the eye lens loses its elasticity;
- Hearing loss, first of higher-pitched tones, then of lower-pitched ones;
- Wrinkles, as the skin's underlying structure becomes more and more brittle;
- A decline in muscle mass and an accompanying accumulation of fat, especially around the abdomen;
- A drop in cardiovascular efficiency, as less oxygen can be inhaled and used during exercise.

The normal processes of aging are inevitable, but they can be partly delayed by good health, low to modest levels of stress, proper diet and nutrition, and regular participation in vigorous exercise (Butler, 2010). Lifestyle can make a significant health difference for people of all ages. Some scientists have even argued that with a proper lifestyle and advances in medical technology, more and more people will be able to live relatively illness-free lives until they reach their biological maximum, experiencing only a brief period of sickness just before death (Fries, 1980; Vaupel et al., 1998). Eventually, of course, the biological clock runs out for everyone. About 90 to 100 years seems to be the upper end of the genetically determined age distribution for most human beings, although some have argued that it may be as high as 120 (Fries, 1980; Olshansky, Carnes, and Grahn, 2003).

Gerontologists agree that *senescence*, or physical decline that accompanies aging, is inevitable. However, today's older adults now have unprecedented access to many *assistive technologies* that enable them to live full and active lives. These are products that increase, maintain, or improve the functional capabilities of individuals with disabilities. Such products range from hearing aids and eyeglasses to canes, walkers, and "grabbers" (which help frail older adults reach a box of cereal on a high shelf in their kitchen), to computer screen magnifiers and oversize kitchen utensils. Gerontologists also consider household modifications, such as chair lifts, wheelchair ramps, and grab bars in the shower, as assistive devices.

About 14 to 18 percent of all older adults use assistive devices (Cornman, Freedman, and Agree, 2005) and two-thirds of older people reporting difficulty with personal care activities use a device to meet daily needs (Agree and Freedman, 2000). One of the most important benefits of such devices is that they enable older adults to maintain their independence, keep up daily routines, and stay in their own homes (rather than moving to an assisted-living facility) for as long as possible. These devices are particularly helpful for preventing falls; one-third of persons over age 65 report a fall each year, making falls the leading cause of accidents and a common trigger of hospitalizations among older adults (Center for Technology and Aging, 2010). In this way, technological advances have altered the impact of biological aging on older adults' lives.

PSYCHOLOGICAL AGING

The psychological effects of aging are less well established than the physical effects. Even though memory, intelligence, reasoning skills, and both the capacity and motivation to learn are widely assumed to decline with age, research into the psychology of aging suggests a much more complicated process (Schaie and Willis, 2010). For most people, memory and learning ability, for example, do not decline significantly until very late in life, although the speed with which one recalls or analyzes information may slow somewhat, giving the false impression of mental impairment. For most elderly people whose lives are stimulating and rich, such mental abilities as motivation to learn, clarity of thought, creativity, and problem-solving capacity do not decline significantly until the late eighties (Atchley, 2000; Cohen, 2005).

Even **Alzheimer's disease**—the progressive deterioration of brain cells that is the primary cause of dementia in old age—is relatively rare in noninstitutionalized persons under 75, although it may afflict as many as half of all people over 85 (Alzheimer's Association, 2012). Given the projected steep growth in the number of persons 85 and older in the coming decades, caring for and treating Alzheimer's patients will be an important challenge. More than 5 million older adults currently suffer from Alzheimer's disease, and this number will increase in coming decades. Scientists have recently developed new technologies that enable an earlier and more accurate detection of dementia and Alzheimer's. This advance holds great promise for treating patients before the disease progresses too far (Alzheimer's Association, 2012). Former president Ronald Reagan is perhaps the most famous example of someone who suffered from Alzheimer's; his wife Nancy Reagan has spoken out publicly about the profound physical and emotional challenges of providing care to an Alzheimer's patient and has called for the use of stem-cell research to find a cure (Collins, 2004). Gerontologists are cautiously optimistic about the promise of science to help fight the ravages of Alzheimer's disease.

SOCIAL AGING

Social aging refers to the norms, values, and roles that are culturally associated with a particular chronological age. Historically, social roles in the United States have been closely tied to one's age. The role of "student" was held by young people, while the roles of "worker"

Alzheimer's disease • A degenerative disease of the brain resulting in progressive loss of mental capacity.

social aging • The norms, values, and roles that are culturally associated with a particular chronological age.

(typically, for men) and "parent" (typically, for women) were held by young adults and middle-aged persons, and the role of "retiree" was reserved for older adults. Social roles also were highly age-segregated; the only "old" person in a college classroom was typically the professor.

Throughout the twentieth century, however, links between age and social roles have grown more tenuous, and social roles have become less age-segregated. For example, as young people stay in school longer and graduate school later, they delay the traditional markers of "adulthood"—full-time employment, marriage, childbearing, and home ownership—to their thirties, forties, and even later. Young people in their twenties and thirties are living with their parents, unable to afford their own apartments against the backdrop of the Great Recession (Parker, 2012). People who become new parents for the first time in their forties are parents to young adults at age 65, while in prior generations, most people aged 65 were happily settled into the role of grandparent or even great-grandparent.

Similarly, changes in the labor force mean that adults are working into late life, and many need to retrain or retool their skills. "Nontraditional age" students now represent nearly 50 percent of college enrollment. Many older adults have seen their pension wealth, home values, and savings evaporate in the recession that began in 2007, forcing them to delay their retirement past age 65. Some remain in their lifelong jobs, while others cut back to part-time hours or take "bridge" (transitional) jobs between their full-time lifelong job and retirement (Sackmann and Wingens, 2003). Yet retirement is no longer the exclusive domain of older adults. Some middle-aged adults, especially those in high-paying jobs, may be forced to retire early if their companies can no longer afford to employ them—instead hiring less skilled, less costly younger workers.

Social aging, like biological and psychological aging, has been transformed by technology. In earlier decades, older adults (especially women) were considered physically undesirable because they defied the cultural standard of youthful beauty. Today, cosmetic surgery helps older women (and men, to a lesser extent) maintain a taut, dewy complexion via processes such as Botox injections and face lifts, and a svelte physique via procedures such as tummy tucks and liposuction (Elliott, 2008). The cultural belief that older adults are uninterested in sex or incapable of maintaining a healthy sex life has been shattered by the development of impotence drugs such as Viagra (Loe, 2004). In the United States today, virility drugs top $5 billion in annual sales. Social scientists agree that more than ever before, age is "just a number."

CONCEPT CHECKS ✓

1. What is the "graying" of the U.S. population?
2. By how much will the U.S. elderly population increase over the next five decades?
3. Compare and contrast biological, psychological, and social aging processes.
4. How has technology affected the processes of biological, psychological, and social aging?

② GROWING OLD: THEORIES OF AGING

Social gerontologists have developed several influential theories of aging in Western society. Some of the earliest theories emphasized individual adaptation to changing social roles as a person grows older. Later theories focused on how society shapes the social roles of the elderly, often in inequitable ways, and emphasized various aspects of age stratification.

The most recent theories emphasize micro-macro links and focus on how elderly persons actively create their lives within specific institutional and historical contexts (Bengston, Putney, and Johnson, 2005).

The First Generation of Theories: Functionalism

The earliest theories of aging reflected the functionalist approach that was dominant in sociology during the 1950s and '60s. These early theories often assumed that aging brings with it physical and psychological decline and that changing social roles should take into account this decline (Hendricks, 1992). Functionalist theories, in particular, emphasized how individuals adjusted to changing social roles as they aged and how the roles fulfilled by older adults were useful to society.

Talcott Parsons (1960), one of the most influential functionalist theorists of the 1950s, argued that U.S. society needs to find roles for older persons that are compatible with their advanced age. He expressed concern that the United States, with its emphasis on youth and its denial of death, had failed to provide roles that adequately drew on the potential wisdom and maturity of its older citizens. This failure could lead to older people becoming discouraged and alienated from society. To achieve a "healthy maturity," Parsons (1960) argued, the elderly need to adjust psychologically to their changed circumstances, while society needs to redefine the social roles of the elderly.

Disengagement Theory

Parsons's ideas set the stage for the development of **disengagement theory**, which asserts that it is functional for society to relieve people of their traditional roles when they become old, thereby freeing up those roles for other, younger persons (Cumming and Henry, 1961; Estes, Binney, and Culbertson, 1992). According to this perspective, given the increasing frailty, illness, and dependency of elderly persons, it becomes increasingly dysfunctional for them to occupy roles they are no longer capable of adequately fulfilling. Older adults should therefore retire from their jobs, pull back from civic life, and eventually withdraw from their other activities and relationships. Disengagement is assumed to be functional for society because it opens up roles formerly filled by the elderly for younger people, who presumably will carry them out with fresh energy and new skills. Disengagement also is assumed to be functional for the elderly because it enables them to abandon potentially taxing social roles and instead invest their energies in more private introspective activities as they prepare for their eventual demise.

Although there is some empirical support and ample anecdotal evidence for the validity of disengagement theory, the idea that elderly people should completely disengage from the larger society presumes that old age necessarily involves frailty and dependence. Recent studies suggest that selective disengagement from some roles—rather than complete disengagement from all roles—can be healthy if the older adult chooses which roles to drop and which to maintain. For example, most retirees report quite high levels of life satisfaction; however, the happiest retirees are those in good health, with strong social ties, adequate financial resources, and engagement in other productive activities such as volunteering or part-time work (Atchley, 2000; Barnes and Parry, 2004).

disengagement theory • A functionalist theory of aging that holds that it is functional for society to remove people from their traditional roles when they become elderly, thereby freeing up those roles for others.

Scholars also have found that older adults may cut back on the number of social relationships they maintain, often dropping those relationships that are not a source of great joy or support. **Socioemotional selectivity theory** states that older adults selectively choose to maintain fewer, but higher-quality, relationships as they age and experience declines in health. Casual, less rewarding ties may lapse while only the most meaningful relationships are maintained (Carstensen, Isaacowitz, and Charles, 1999).

Activity Theories

Given this strong evidence that disengagement from all social roles is rare, and such disengagement does not ease the aging process, the very assumptions of disengagement theory have been challenged, often by some of the theory's original proponents (Cumming, 1963, 1975; Hendricks, 1992; Henry, 1965; Hochschild, 1975; Maddox, 1965, 1970). These challenges gave rise to another functionalist theory of aging, which drew conclusions quite opposite to those of disengagement theory: activity theory.

According to **activity theory**, people who are busy and engaged, leading fulfilling and productive lives, can be functional for society. The guiding assumption is that an active individual is much more likely to remain healthy, alert, and socially useful. In this view, people should remain engaged in their work and other social roles as long as they are capable of doing so. If a time comes when a particular role becomes too difficult or taxing, then other roles can be sought—for example, volunteer work in the community.

Activity theory is supported by research showing that continued activity well into old age—whether volunteering, paid employment, hobbies, or visits with friends and family—is associated with enhanced mental and physical health (Birren and Bengston, 1988; Rowe and Kahn, 1987; Schaie, 1983). Yet critics observe that not all activities are equally valuable, giving rise to the development of **continuity theory**. This theory specifies that older adults' well-being is enhanced when they participate in activities that are consistent with their personality, preferences, and activities earlier in life (Atchley, 1989). For instance, a retired elementary school teacher may find volunteering at a local elementary school to be much more satisfying than taking bus trips to Atlantic City or playing bingo at a local community center.

Critics of functionalist theories of aging argue that these theories emphasize the need for the elderly to adapt to existing conditions, either by disengaging from socially useful roles or by actively pursuing them, but that they do not question whether the circumstances faced by the elderly are just. In response to this criticism, another group of theorists arose—those growing out of the social conflict tradition (Hendricks, 1992).

socioemotional selectivity theory • The theory that adults maintain fewer relationships as they age, but that those relationships are of higher quality.

activity theory • A functionalist theory of aging that holds that busy, engaged people are more likely to lead fulfilling and productive lives.

continuity theory • The theory that older adults' well-being is enhanced when their activities are similar to those done earlier in life.

The Second Generation of Theories: Social Conflict

Unlike their predecessors, who emphasized the ways older adults could be integrated into society, the second generation of theorists focused on sources of social conflict between the elderly and the larger society (Hendricks, 1992). Like other theorists who were studying social conflict in U.S. society during the 1970s and early 1980s, these theorists stressed the ways in which the larger social structure helped shape the opportunities available to older adults; unequal opportunities were seen as creating the potential for conflict.

According to this view, many of the problems of aging—such as poverty, poor health, or inadequate health care—are systematically produced by the routine operation of social institutions. A capitalist society, the reasoning goes, favors those who are most economically powerful. While there are certainly some older people who have "made it" and are set for life, many have not—and these people must fight to get even a meager share of society's scarce resources.

conflict theories of aging • Arguments that emphasize the ways in which the larger social structure helps to shape the opportunities available to the elderly. Unequal opportunities are seen as creating the potential for conflict.

life course • The various transitions and stages people experience during their lives.

Conflict theories of aging flourished during the 1980s, when a shrinking job base and cutbacks in federal spending threatened to pit different social groups against each other in the competition for scarce resources. Older persons were seen as competing with the young for increasingly scarce jobs and dwindling federal dollars. Conflict theorists further pointed out that even among the elderly, those who fared worst were women, low-income people, and ethnic minorities (Atchley, 2000; Estes, 2011; Hendricks, 1992; Hendricks and Hendricks, 1986). As we will see later in this chapter, the concerns articulated by conflict theorists persist today. For example, while poverty rates among older adults have plummeted over the past 60 years, with less than 10 percent of older adults now living in poverty, this figure is as high as 40 percent among unmarried black and Hispanic older women (Carr, 2010).

The Third Generation of Theories: Life Course Perspectives

Life course theorists reject what they regard as the one-sided emphases of both functionalism and conflict theories, where older adults are viewed either as merely adapting to the larger society (functionalism) or as victims of the stratification system (social conflict). Rather, life course theorists view older persons as playing an active role in determining their own physical and mental well-being, yet recognize the constraints imposed by social structural factors.

According to the life course perspective, the aging process is shaped by historical time and place; factors such as wars, economic shifts, or the development of new technologies shape how people age. Yet this perspective also emphasizes *agency*, where individuals make choices that reflect both the opportunities and the constraints facing them. The most important theme of the life course perspective is that *aging is a lifelong process*; relationships, events, and experiences of early life have consequences for later life.

Mounting research shows that our physical and mental health in later life is closely linked to the advantages and disadvantages we faced early in life, dating back as far as childhood and infancy. People who begin life in a position of social advantage generally are better positioned to acquire additional resources than those who begin life at the bottom of the stratification system. Those born into well-off families enjoy richer economic resources, better health, and more educational opportunities in early life—all of which set the stage for rewarding jobs, good health, and emotional well-being in later life. Those with adversities earlier in life, like Alice Garvin, often are blocked access to the opportunities that ensure a happy and healthy old age. Researchers have found that childhood and adolescent experiences—including parental death (Slavich, Monroe, and Gotlib, 2011), parental divorce (Amato, 2000), child abuse victimization (Slopen et al., 2010), poverty (Duncan, Ziol-Guest, and Kalil, 2010), and living in an unsafe neighborhood (Vartanian and Houser, 2010)—have harmful implications for health among older adults. Often, these early adversities put young people at risk of poor health behaviors, economic strains, marital troubles, and other difficulties in young adulthood that may contribute to lifelong health problems. In other words, adversities in early life give rise to difficulties in adulthood, which accumulate to make the aging process very difficult for the disadvantaged.

③ RESEARCH ON AGING IN THE UNITED STATES TODAY

Who Are America's Older Adults?

Older adults reflect the diversity of U.S. society that we've noted elsewhere in this textbook: They are rich, poor, and middle class; they belong to all racial and ethnic groups; they live alone and in families of various sorts; they vary in their political views; and they are gay and lesbian as well as heterosexual. Furthermore, like other Americans, they are diverse with respect to health: Although some suffer from mental and physical disabilities, most lead active, independent lives.

A portrait of older Americans reveals that whites are overrepresented among persons age 65 and older (Figure 12.3). Fully 80 percent of Americans age 65 and older in 2010 were white, just 8 percent were black, 7 percent Hispanic (of any race), 3 percent Asian/Pacific Islander, and less than 1 percent Native American (U.S Bureau of the Census, 2010d). This reflects both whites' longer life expectancy relative to blacks and the fact that many older Latino immigrants return to their home countries in later life, so that they can spend their final years with their families.

Currently, 3.9 million of the elderly population in the United States are foreign born (U.S. Bureau of the Census, 2008a). In California, New York, Hawaii, and other states that receive large numbers of immigrants, as many as one-fifth of the elderly population were born outside the United States (Shin and Kominski, 2010). Most elderly immigrants either do not speak English well or do not speak it at all. Integrating elderly immigrants into U.S. society poses special challenges: Some are highly educated, but most are not. Many require special education and training programs. Most lack a retirement income, so that they depend on their families or public assistance for support.

Finally, as people live to increasingly older ages, the elderly are becoming diverse in terms of age itself. It is useful to distinguish between different age categories of the elderly, such as the **young old** (ages 65 to 74), the **old old** (ages 75 to 84), and the **oldest old** (ages 85 and older) (Figure 12.4). The young old are most likely to be

young old • Sociological term for persons age 65 to 74.

old old • Sociological term for persons age 75 to 84.

oldest old • Sociological term for persons age 85 and older.

Figure 12.3
Projected Population Aged 65 and Over by Race for the United States: 2010 to 2050

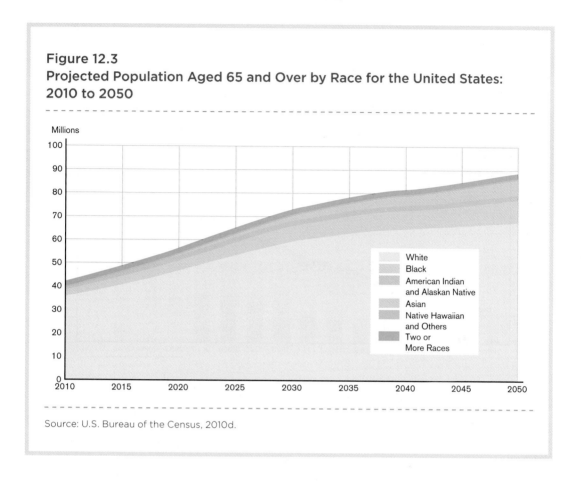

Source: U.S. Bureau of the Census, 2010d.

economically independent, healthy, active, and engaged; the oldest old, the fastest-growing segment of the elderly population, are most likely to encounter difficulties such as poor health, financial insecurity, isolation, and loneliness.

These differences are not necessarily due only to the effects of aging; they may also reflect one's birth cohort. The young old came of age during the post–World War II period of strong economic growth, and benefited as a result: They are more likely to be educated; to have acquired wealth in the form of a home, savings, or investments; and to have had many years of stable employment. These advantages are much less likely to be enjoyed by the oldest old, partly because their education and careers began at an earlier time, when economic conditions were not so favorable and medical technologies were less well developed (Alwin, 2008; Idler, 1993; Manton et al., 2008).

What is the experience of growing old in the United States today? Although older adults do face some special challenges, many lead relatively healthy, satisfying lives. In this section, we describe contemporary sociological studies that document differences among the elderly in the United States, and investigate some of the common problems that they confront. In the next section, we delve into several debates about the impact of aging on society, and the ways that older persons, governments, and societies can adjust and adapt to the challenges of population aging.

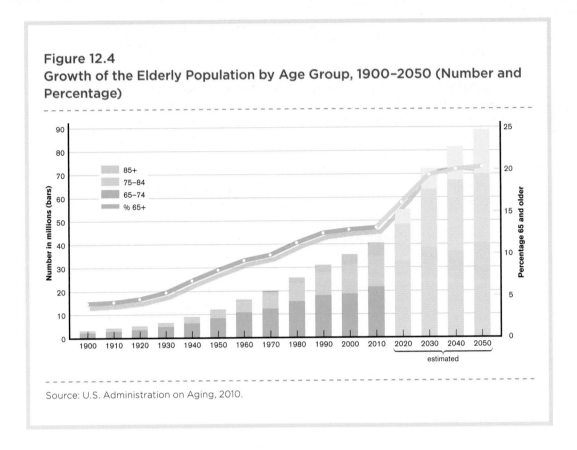

Figure 12.4
Growth of the Elderly Population by Age Group, 1900–2050 (Number and Percentage)

Source: U.S. Administration on Aging, 2010.

Poverty

Fewer than 10 percent of persons age 65 and older currently live in poverty, although some of the very poorest Americans are elderly, particularly among minorities and women (U.S. Administration on Aging, 2011). Because most older people have retired from full-time work, their income is based primarily on **Social Security** and private retirement programs. Social Security and **Medicare** have been especially important in lifting many elderly people out of poverty. An estimated 55 million older adults received monthly Social Security checks in 2010. Yet people who depend solely on these two programs for income and health care coverage are likely to live modestly at best.

In 2008, Social Security provided 37 percent of the average older adult's income, earnings provided 30 percent, pensions provided 19 percent, and asset income accounted for 13 percent. Low-income households in particular are likely to rely heavily on Social Security. Among older adults in the lowest fifth of the income distribution, Social Security accounts for 83 percent of aggregate income, and cash public assistance for another 8 percent. By contrast, for those whose income is in the highest income category, Social Security, pensions, and asset income each account for almost a fifth of income, and earnings accounts for the remaining two-fifths

Social Security • A government program that provides economic assistance to persons faced with unemployment, disability, or agedness.

Medicare • A program under the U.S. Social Security Administration that reimburses hospitals and physicians for medical care provided to qualifying people over 65 years old.

(FIFARS, 2012). Yet even the combination of Social Security and private pensions results in modest retirement incomes for most people (Krueger, 1995); the median income of older households in 2007 was just under $30,000.

The economic conditions of the elderly have improved steadily since the 1970s. As Figure 12.5 shows, in 1959, 35 percent of all people 65 or older lived in poverty. That figure began to drop during President Lyndon B. Johnson's War on Poverty in the mid-1960s, when Medicare was enacted and Social Security benefits increased. By the early 1970s, poverty rates among the elderly had dropped to below 15 percent, and today they hover around 9 percent. Contrast this with the rate of poverty among children under 18 years, 22 percent of whom were poor in 2010 (FIFARS, 2012). However, the low overall poverty rate among older adults conceals two serious problems: the economic strains facing the near-elderly, or those ages 55 to 64, and tremendous race and gender gaps in late-life poverty rates.

POVERTY AMONG THE NEAR-ELDERLY

The current recession, which began in 2007, has taken a very severe toll on persons on the brink of retirement, those ages 55 to 64. These "nearly old" persons are among the older members of the large baby boom cohort, the 75 million babies born between roughly 1945 and 1964. The unemployment rates for workers between 55 and 64 more than doubled during the recession, from 3.1 percent in 2007 to 7.1 percent in 2010. According to a recent U.S. government study, unemployed older workers have more difficulty finding new jobs

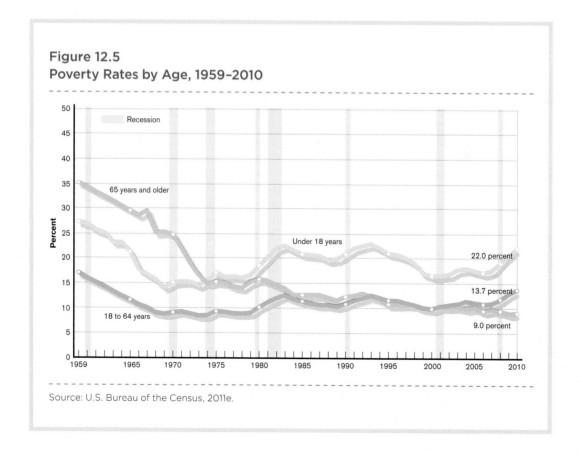

Figure 12.5
Poverty Rates by Age, 1959–2010

Source: U.S. Bureau of the Census, 2011e.

and remain unemployed for a longer period than their younger counterparts (U.S. Government Accountability Office [GAO], 2011). Some face discrimination by potential employers, who believe that older workers may be less able to acquire new skills. Others may have early-onset health problems that limit the kind of work they can do. Due to the cohort's large size, unemployed persons in their late fifties and early sixties may face stiff competition from their peers who are also seeking work. To make matters worse, many older Americans have seen their retirement savings and home values plummet due to volatility in the stock and housing markets. The average income for adults 55 to 64 fell by 6 percent during the recessionary period of 2007 to 2010, and the median household net worth dropped nearly 14 percent between 2007 and 2009. Due in part to their long spells of unemployment and evaporating assets, many near-old adults were pushed into poverty during the Great Recession. Poverty rates for adults age 55 to 64 rose from 8.6 percent in 2007 to 10.1 percent in 2010. As older Americans lose their employer-provided health insurance or exhaust their savings, many are forced to delay their medical care, or receive Social Security early, at the age of 62, with a resulting 25 percent reduction in benefits.

It's not surprising, then, that these aging baby boomers are very pessimistic about their financial situation. According to a 2012 poll conducted by the American Association of Retired Persons (AARP), only 54 percent of adults ages 50–64 are satisfied with their financial situation. As such, fully two-thirds say that they will delay their retirement, while one-half say they may never retire (Kiger, 2012). Each of these strains and anxieties may set the stage for a difficult transition to old age; only future research will tell whether the well-being of older adults declines for future cohorts (GAO, 2011).

SUBGROUP DIFFERENCES IN ELDERLY POVERTY RATES

The low overall poverty rate also conceals stark race, gender, and marital status differences in poverty among the elderly (Figure 12.6). Poverty rates range from just 3.1 percent among older white married men to an astounding 37.5 percent for Hispanic women who live alone and 40.5 percent for black women living alone. In other words, older women of color who live alone are more than 10 times as likely as their white married male counterparts to be poor.

Despite tremendous improvements in overall economic well-being among older adults during the past half century, the future looks uncertain—at least for some elders. Some policy experts argue that the current government indicator of poverty (see Chapter 8) does not adequately capture the economic realities of late life. The federal government has proposed a new calculation that takes into account rising health care costs. Under this new formula, the proportion of older adults living in poverty would double from just over 9 percent to 18.6 percent (Carr, 2010).

To make matters worse, for the first time since 1975, Social Security recipients did not get an automatic cost-of-living increase in their benefits in 2010 or 2011. Annual increases are tied to inflation, and inflation was negative in 2009 and 2010. To offset the flat payments, President Barack Obama sent all seniors a one-time $250 payment each year. However, this payment was little consolation to those older adults with declining assets and investment income due to the collapse of the housing bubble, failed investments, and falling stock prices. Fortunately, in 2012, Social Security benefits were increased by an average of 3.6 percent, bringing the average monthly payment up from $1,186 to $1,229 (Luhby, 2011). Although some older adults may find their retirement years to be "golden," others may need to continue working far past age 65 just to maintain a minimum standard of living (Carr, 2010).

Social Isolation

Old age historically has been considered a time of social isolation. Disengagement theory, which we learned about earlier in this chapter, proposed that it was beneficial for both the older adult and society if the elder gradually withdrew from his social roles and relationships (Cumming and Henry, 1961). Similarly, classic role theories held that the loss of the work role for men (via retirement) and loss of the wife role for women (via widowhood) would leave older adults socially isolated and despondent (Biddle, 1986). More recent research counters, however, that while loneliness and social isolation are problematic, they are neither inevitable nor universal features of aging.

Most older adults have family members and friends they can turn to. Four out of five older people have living children, and the vast majority of them can rely on their children for support if necessary. More than 9 out of 10 adult children say that maintaining parental contact is important to them, including the provision of financial support if it is needed (Suitor et al., 2011). The reverse is also true: Many studies have found that elderly parents continue to provide support for their adult children, particularly during times of difficulty, such as divorce. Most elderly parents and adult children report feeling that the amount of support they receive from the other is fair, and that their relationship is close and loving (Birditt, Jackey, and Antonucci, 2009). Most older adults have regular contact with their children and live near them; about 85 percent of older persons live within an hour of one of their children. However, relatively few live with their children. This arrangement is exactly what they want; studies repeatedly show that older adults—even those with serious physical health limitations—prefer to remain independent and reside in their own homes. They want "intimacy at a distance" (Gans and Silverstein, 2006).

Over the past three decades, researchers have discovered that loneliness is not triggered by a quantitative lack of relationships, but by a lack of satisfaction with the number or quality of one's relationships. Contemporary researchers have identified distinct types of loneliness: **Emotional loneliness** refers to the absence of an intimate confidant, while **social loneliness** refers to the absence of a broader social network. The two types often overlap; widowed persons, those living alone, or those living far away from their friends and families consistently report higher levels of both types of loneliness than persons who are more socially integrated, such as married persons or those who live with their adult children (de Jong Gierveld and Havens, 2004).

Figure 12.6
Percentage Poor: White, Black, and Hispanic Elderly, 2010

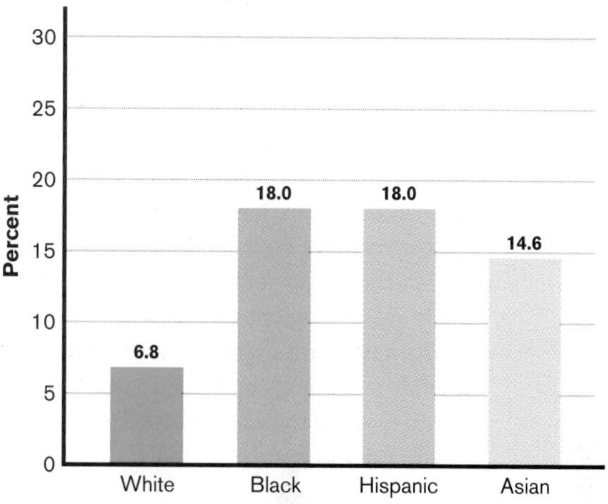

Source: U.S. Administration on Aging [AOA], 2011.

emotional loneliness • The absence of an intimate confidant.

social loneliness • The absence of a broader social network.

The mere presence of personal relationships does not ward off loneliness, however. An estimated 25 percent of older married persons report emotional and social loneliness; this pattern is particularly common among persons whose spouses are ill, who have a dissatisfying (or nonexistent) sexual relationship, and who have infrequent or conflicted conversations (de Jong Gierveld et al., 2009). As de Jong Gierveld and Havens (2004) noted, loneliness depends on one's "standards as to what constitutes an optimal network of relationships."

Despite its subjective nature, loneliness is a serious problem for many older adults; it is linked to sleep problems, poor cardiovascular health, and elevated blood pressure, each of which carries long-term consequences for mortality risk (Cacioppo et al., 2002). Loneliness also may be a particularly serious social problem for older adults in future generations. Smaller families and increased rates of divorce and childlessness among future cohorts of older adults may create a context where older persons maintain objectively fewer relationships, thus triggering social loneliness (Manning and Brown, 2011). More important, however, some have argued that current cohorts of midlife adults have unrealistically high expectations for what their social relationships should provide (e.g., one's partner should be their "soul mate"); if these lofty expectations go unfulfilled, then older adults may report higher levels of emotional loneliness as well (Carr and Moorman, 2011).

WHO SUFFERS MORE: WOMEN OR MEN?

Researchers continue to debate whether men or women are more socially isolated in later life. Women are less likely than men to be married, yet they tend to have richer social and emotional ties to children and friends. This reflects patterns of lifelong gender socialization, where women are raised to emphasize social relationships, and men are raised to be independent and autonomous (Carr and Moorman, 2011).

Statistics confirm that older women are far less likely than men to be married. Because men die younger than women, women are more likely than men to become widowed. Women also are more likely than men to remain widowed; a dearth of eligible male partners prevents most older women from remarrying. Among people 65 and older there are 1.5 women per man, and this gap increases to 3.0 women for every man by age 85. As a result, only 13 percent of men ages 65 and older were widowers in 2010; by contrast, 40 percent of older women were widowed (AOA, 2011). Given the stark gender gap in widowhood, women are much more likely than men to live alone (37 versus 19 percent). By age 75, nearly half of women live alone (AOA, 2011).

However, as we have just learned, being single and living alone does not necessarily mean loneliness. Many older women report that they have little interest in dating and remarrying. Carr (2004) estimated that 18 months after becoming widowed, only 10 percent of older women (yet 20 percent of men) were dating, and just 15 percent of women (yet nearly 40 percent of men) said that they would like to date. Some older women report that they do not want to remarry because they do not want to take on the homemaking and caregiving responsibilities that often accompany marriage to an elderly man (van den Hoonard, 2002).

Women's more emotionally intimate social relations over the life course are an important resource as they adjust to spousal loss and social isolation. Older widows receive more practical and emotional support from their children than do widowers, given mothers' closer relationships with their children throughout the life course. Women also are more likely to have larger and more varied friendship networks than men, and these friendships provide an important source of support to women as they cope with the strains of late life (Ha, 2008).

Men, by contrast, are more likely than women to experience physical health declines, increased disability, and heightened risk of mortality after their spouses die. While popular lore claims that widowers may "die of a broken heart," research shows that it is the loss of a helpmate and caretaker that is actually the culprit. Wives typically monitor their husbands' diets, remind them to take their daily medications, and urge them to give up vices such as smoking and drinking (Umberson, Wortman, and Kessler, 1992). For many older men, wives often are their primary (or only) source of social support and integration; when a man loses his wife, he also loses an important connection to his social networks.

Prejudice

Discrimination on the basis of age is prohibited by federal law. The Age Discrimination in Employment Act of 1967 (ADEA) protects job applicants and employees 40 years of age and older from discrimination on the basis of age in hiring, firing, promotion, and pay. Nonetheless, prejudices based on false stereotypes are common. **Ageism** is prejudice and/or discrimination based on age; like all prejudices, it is fueled in part by stereotypes. The elderly are frequently seen as lonely, sad, frail, forgetful, dependent, senile, old-fashioned, inflexible, and embittered.

There are a number of reasons for such prejudice. Americans' obsession with youthful beauty and vigor, reflected in popular entertainment and advertising, leads many younger people to disparage their elders, frequently dismissing them as irrelevant. Associated with the emphasis on youthfulness is a fear-filled avoidance of reminders of death and dying. Such fear carries over into negative attitudes toward the elderly, who serve as a constant reminder of one's mortality (Fry, 1980). The new information technology culture undoubtedly reinforces these prejudices, because youthfulness and computer abilities seem to go hand in hand. In the fast-paced world of Twitter and dot-com businesses that seem to flourish and perish overnight, young people may come to view the elderly as anachronistic.

These stereotypes are harmful in several ways. First, merely believing negative stereotypes about aging can take a toll on the health and longevity of older adults. Rebecca Levy (2002) and her colleagues asked a sample of older adults how much they agreed or disagreed with statements such as "As you get older, you are less useful." When researchers followed up with the study participants 10 years later, they found that 87 percent of those with positive attitudes, yet just 66 percent of those with negative attitudes, were still alive. The pattern was even more pronounced at the 22-year follow-up, when 50 percent of those with positive attitudes, yet just 27 percent of those with negative attitudes, were still alive. Even after statistically controlling for possible explanatory pathways such as health, socioeconomic status, and health behaviors, these patterns persisted, suggesting that harmful beliefs can exact a physical toll, although researchers are not certain as to why.

Second, older adults can be harmed if other people's ageist beliefs are translated into discriminatory treatment. For example, one recent study found that nearly two-thirds of older adults reported that they had been the victim of ageism, with their experiences ranging from minor slights such as being treated as if they were not smart or receiving poor service at a restaurant, to more serious experiences such as job or health care

ageism • Discrimination or prejudice against a person on the grounds of age.

discrimination. Moreover, those persons who had experienced such mistreatment later experienced poorer physical and mental health than their peers who had not been victimized (Luo et al., 2011).

If ageist stereotypes are so harmful, why do they persist? Age-based stereotypes, like all stereotypes, have a kernel of truth (LeVine and Campbell, 1972). Prior cohorts of older adults often were less vigorous, healthy, financially well-off, integrated into society, and technologically savvy than both their younger counterparts and current cohorts of older adults. These patterns are less a reflection of older persons themselves than of society's failure to afford equal opportunities to older adults. Current cohorts of older adults, by contrast, are healthier, more integrated into society, and technologically savvier than ever before.

These patterns, in turn, may start to chip away at outdated and inaccurate notions of what old age is. Consider that Bruce Springsteen graced the cover of *AARP* magazine in 2009, the year he turned 60 (Swartley, 2009). That same year, Springsteen and the E Street Band had the second-highest-grossing concert tour—topped only by 51-year-old Bono and his bandmates in U2. Just as older adults are a vital part of popular culture, they are becoming an increasingly large presence online. About 38 percent of Americans 65 and older go online, according to a 2009 Pew Internet and American Life Project survey. And older adults—especially women age 55 and older—make up the fastest-growing group of Facebook users, increasing by 35 percent in the first six months of 2010 alone (Rocheleau, 2010). Experts agree that baby boomers may play a critical role in further helping to dissolve stereotypes of the frail, out-of-it older adult.

Bruce Springsteen on the cover of AARP magazine.

Elder Abuse

The National Research Council (NRC) report *Elder Mistreatment: Abuse, Neglect, and Exploitation* (Bonnie and Wallace, 2003) defines elder abuse as "(a) intentional actions that cause harm or create a serious risk of harm, whether or not intended, to a vulnerable elder by a caregiver or other person who stands in a trust relationship to the elder, or (b) failure by a caregiver to satisfy the elder's basic needs or to protect the elder from harm." Mistreatment may take many forms; it may include physical, sexual, emotional, or financial abuse, neglect, or abandonment.

Elder mistreatment is very difficult to measure and document. Older adults who are embarrassed, ashamed, or fearful of retaliation by their abusers may be reluctant to report such experiences. As a result, official prevalence rates are low. Worldwide, it is estimated that between 4 and 6 percent of the elderly experience some form of abuse at home (Hood, 2002). Nationwide it is estimated that between one and two million Americans over age 65 have been injured, exploited, or otherwise mistreated. But financial abuse, for example, may be grossly underreported: It is estimated that only 1 in 25 cases is reported, suggesting that there may be 5 million financial abuse victims every year (National Center on Elder Abuse, 2005).

The National Social Life, Health, and Aging Project (NSHAP) is the first nationally representative population-based survey to ask older adults about their recent experiences of mistreatment. Edward Laumann and colleagues (Laumann, Leitsch, and Waite, 2008) found that 9.0 percent of older adults reported verbal mistreatment, 3.5 percent financial mistreatment, and less than 1.0 percent reported physical mistreatment by a family member. Women and persons with physical disabilities were particularly likely to report abuse.

It is widely believed that abuse results from the anger and resentment that adult children feel when confronted with the need to care for their infirm parents (King, 1984; Steinmetz, 1983). Most studies have found this to be a false assumption, however. In the NSHAP study, most mistreatment was perpetrated by someone other than a member of the elder's immediate family. Of those who reported verbal mistreatment, 26 percent named their spouse or romantic partner as the perpetrator, 15 percent named their child, and 57 percent named someone other than a spouse, parent, or child. Similarly, 56 percent of elders who reported financial mistreatment said that someone other than a family member was responsible; of family members, though, children were mentioned most often, while spouses were rarely named (Laumann, Leitsch, and Waite, 2008).

Health Problems

The prevalence of chronic disabilities among the elderly has declined in recent years, and most elderly people rate their health as reasonably good and free of major disabilities (FIFARS, 2012). From 2000 through 2009, roughly 40 percent of noninstitutionalized people over age 65 considered their health to be "excellent" or "very good," although this proportion declined steadily with age (AOA, 2011). Still, older people obviously suffer from more health problems than most younger people, and the number and intrusiveness of health difficulties often increase with advancing age. Whereas only about 1 in 10 people between the ages of 65 and 75 reports needing daily assistance due to poor health, the figure rises to 1 in 5 for people between 75 and 79, and to 1 in 3 for people between 80 and 84. Half of all people over age 85 require assistance (U.S. Bureau of the Census, 1996).

One reason many older adults need assistance is that they have health conditions that limit their ability to participate in many activities of daily life, such as maintaining a home or going grocery shopping. In 2009, more than half of all noninstitutionalized persons over 65 reported having at least some problems with hypertension (FIFARS, 2012) and about a third reported suffering from such ailments as arthritis, heart disease, and hearing loss (AOA, 2011).

Further, recent evidence suggests that the most disadvantaged members of the baby boom cohort may fare particularly poorly as they reach later life; a recent analysis of National Health and Nutrition Examination Survey data shows that persons between 60 and 69 are more disabled than prior generations of young old adults (Seeman et al., 2009); the authors attribute this to rising rates of obesity among young and middle-aged Americans, especially blacks and Latinos.

Almost all elderly (93 percent) receive health insurance, via the Medicare program. Although 48.6 million Americans (about 15.7 percent of the population) lacked health insurance in 2011 (DeNavas-Walt, Proctor, and Smith, 2012), less than 1 percent of the elderly lacked coverage in 2010 (AOA, 2011). However, Medicare covers about half the total health care expenses of the elderly, so more than 85 percent of older adults supplement this coverage with either their own private insurance, military insurance, or some other type of supplementary coverage. The rising costs of private insurance, unfortunately, have made this option impossible for a growing number of the elderly.

Health insurance is essential for older adults, given the high and rising costs of medical care. Since 1977 the percentage of elderly with out-of-pocket health care expenses increased from 83 percent to over 95 percent. In 2010, older consumers averaged out-of-pocket health care expenditures of $4,843, an increase of 49 percent since 2000. Older Americans spent 13.2 percent of their total expenditures on health, more than twice the proportion spent by all consumers (6.6 percent). Average health costs for older adults in 2010 consisted of $3,085 (65 percent) for insurance, $795 (18 percent) for medical services, $805 (17 percent) for drugs, and $158 (3.0 percent) for medical supplies (AOA, 2011).

Annual costs rise even higher for the oldest old adults, or those requiring institutional care. When the elderly become physically unable to care for themselves, they may end up in nursing homes or assisted-living facilities. A relatively small percentage (4.1 percent) of the 65+ population in 2009 lived in institutional settings such as nursing homes (1.3 million). However, the percentage increases dramatically with age, ranging (in 2009) from

Table 12.1
What Is Your Biggest Fear about Growing Old?

- -

When it comes to growing old, most Americans fear losing their health and independence far more than being alone or living in a nursing home.

Losing your health	73%
Losing ability to care for yourself	70%
Losing mental abilities	69%
Running out of money	60%
Not being able to drive/travel on own	59%
Being a burden on your family	54%
Winding up in a nursing home	52%
Not being able to work or volunteer	49%
Being alone	39%
Losing your looks	22%

- -

Source: Cohen and Lange, 2005.

1.1 percent for persons 65–74 years to 3.5 percent for persons 75–84 years and 13.2 percent for persons 85+ (AOA, 2011).

The average cost of a semiprivate room in a nursing home is now over $75,000 a year, while the annual cost of a room at an assisted-living facility averages $40,000 (Genworth Financial, 2012). As a result of these high costs, many nonpoor elderly who require such institutionalization may see their lifetime savings quickly depleted (a process dubbed "spending down"). Some also receive Medicaid coverage; Medicaid is the government program that provides health insurance for the poor; it covers long-term supervision and nursing costs, although only when most of one's assets (except for one's home) have been used up.

Although older adults have often been reluctant to reside in nursing homes, the quality of care in most homes has improved in recent years because federal programs such as Medicaid help cover the cost of care and because of federal quality regulations. Further, long-term care offers diverse options to older adults, ranging from apartments with partial nursing care and meals to units that provide round-the-clock medical assistance. Many also offer a wide array of cultural, social, and recreational programs for their residents (Genworth Financial, 2012).

Lifelong Learning

As more and more people live well beyond the age of retirement, they enter a new stage of life for which there are few socially prescribed roles (Moen, 1995). Many people can look forward to 10 or 20 years of relatively healthy living, free from the obligations of paid work and raising a family. Furthermore, the elderly population will be increasingly well educated, because young people today are much more likely than their parents or grandparents to have gone to college (FIFARS, 2012).

These trends suggest that the elderly are much more likely to remain a part of mainstream society rather than to become isolated (Jarvis, 2007). It is important for older adults to maintain a readiness to learn, stimulated by participation in a wide variety of learning activities; this engagement can contribute to mental alertness, a positive psychological attitude, and even improved physical health (Findsen and Formosa, 2011).

Many two-year and four-year colleges today recognize the importance of lifelong learning; an estimated 60 percent of accredited degree-granting educational institutions offer tuition waivers for older adults, according to the American Council on Education (2008). For example, Rutgers University in New Jersey permits retired state residents, age 62 or older, to audit university courses for free, where classroom space is available. Community colleges play a particularly important role in lifelong learning. According to the American Council on Education (2008), about half of college-going adults age 50 and older attend community colleges, primarily for fun, to connect with other people, and to retool for a new career.

CONCEPT CHECKS

1. Contrast the young old, old old, and oldest old.

2. Describe four common problems older Americans often confront.

3. What characteristics differentiate those older adults who are emotionally and physically well from those who face great distress in later life?

4 UNANSWERED QUESTIONS: THE POLITICAL AND ECONOMIC IMPACT OF POPULATION AGING

Older adults are a potent voice in Washington, due both to their large and rapidly growing numbers and to their high levels of political engagement. **AARP** (formerly the American Association of Retired People) is a highly effective advocate for the elderly. It is a nonprofit organization that boasts a membership of over 39 million Americans age 50 and older—reportedly the largest member-based organization in the world next to the Roman Catholic Church, and over 10 times larger than the National Rifle Association (Birnbaum, 2005). Those 65 and older have high voter turnout rates—71.9 percent in the 2012 presidential election—compared to just 41.2 percent of those 18 to 24 years old (U.S. Bureau of the Census, 2013). This is not to suggest that all older adults hold the same political views; on the contrary, they are as politically heterogeneous as the other age groups. But on issues they perceive as affecting their interests, such as retirement pensions and health care reform, they are likely to have strong opinions. Moreover, because cuts in programs for the elderly would shift the burden of supporting them to their families, opposition to significant reductions in these programs is likely to be widespread.

Because there is "strength in numbers," some observers have argued that older adults have undue political influence, and that they may benefit from government programs more than younger persons. Others counter, however, that older adults are entitled to programs such as Social Security and Medicare on the grounds of both equity and social justice (Kotlikoff and Burns, 2012). Yet as the large baby boom cohort, 75 million strong, enters later life, social scientists and policy makers are in heated debates over whether the federal government can afford to provide these benefits to older adults in coming years (Urban Institute, 2010). Such debates extend beyond the borders of the United States; throughout the globe, social scientists and policy makers wrestle with whether and how the planet can fairly provide services to an unprecedented number of older adults, sometimes dubbed the "gray tsunami" (O'Neill, 2009).

AARP • U.S. advocacy group for people age 50 and over, formerly the American Association of Retired Persons.

Protestors at a rally in Olympia, Washington. The demonstrators were asking lawmakers not to cut the budgets for long-term health care facilities such as nursing homes and assisted-living facilities.

Do Elderly Americans Get an Unfair Amount of Government Support?

The costs of providing for the elderly come largely out of taxes paid by working people. In the United States, the growing ratio of the elderly to the working-age population has alarmed policy makers. They point out that for every 100 people of working age (18 to 64 years old) in 2011 there are roughly 21 persons 65 and older; this figure will increase to 34 by the year 2029. A rapidly aging population will pose serious challenges to public policy throughout this century (AOA, 2011).

Do government programs adequately promote **generational equity**—the striking of a balance between the needs and interests of members of different generations? The issue of generational equity was first raised by an organization called Americans for Generational Equity (AGE), created in 1984 by David Durenberger, a U.S. senator from Minnesota, to challenge the notion that elderly people are entitled to Social Security benefits (Quadagno, 1989).

AGE argued that as the U.S. population ages, those who are working will bear an increasing burden for those who are not. AGE also argued that Social Security unfairly favors retirees over other needy groups in society. For example, AGE pointed out that retirees are sometimes wealthier than the working people whose taxes fund Social Security. For example, in 2011, 21.9 percent of persons under age 18 (16.1 million) and 13.7 percent of adults age 18 to 64 (26.4 million) lived at or below the poverty line, while just 8.7 percent of persons age 65 and older (3.6 million) did so (DeNavas-Walt, Proctor, and Smith, 2012). The difficulty arises from the fact that there are fewer and fewer working-age people to shoulder the tax burden necessary to support more and more retirees.

In practice, however, there is limited evidence that the average American is concerned about generational equity and the potential threat of older adults disproportionately benefiting from public programs. For example, opinion poll data show that younger Americans report greater support for increased spending on Social Security than do older persons, while older adults are most likely to favor increased spending on education (Street and Cossman, 2006). Further, most Americans support Medicare and Social Security; a 2011 survey found that nearly 90 percent feel that both programs are "good for the country." However, the same survey shows concern about exactly how these programs operate; one-third of Americans say the entitlement programs "need major changes," and another 20 percent believe they "need to be completely rebuilt" (Pew Research Center, 2011d).

Americans may recognize that the old and young generations are not in competition; rather, benefits provided to one generation may help the other. At the same time, Americans' anxieties about how to fund such benefits are well founded, as we will see in the next section.

Can Medicare and Social Security Survive the "Graying" of America?

The two principal governmental programs that provide financial support for the elderly are Medicare, which was instituted in 1965, and Social Security, whose benefits were increased at about the same time. (The program itself was begun in 1935.) The full benefits of Medicare and Social Security are available at age 65 for current cohorts of older adults, although partial benefits are available to some people a few years earlier. For birth cohorts born in 1960 and later, however, Social Security benefits will start for most people at age 67.

Social Security and Medicare are financed by workers' payroll deductions, employer contributions, and taxes on those who are self-employed. Working Americans pay into these programs today so they can be eligible for benefits when they are no longer able to earn a living. By providing a degree of economic support for the elderly, such programs also make it economically possible to retire; in the absence of the economic security such programs provide, elderly people would be under greater economic

generational equity • The striking of a balance between the needs and interests of members of different generations.

pressure to continue working as long as they are physically capable. In 2009, more than 51 million Americans received $672 billion in Social Security benefits. About 69 percent of benefits went to retired workers and their dependents; the remainder went to disabled workers and their dependents and to survivors of deceased workers. Although the program was not initially designed to be the sole financial resource for retirees, an estimated one-quarter of older adults rely on Social Security for 90 percent or more of their income (Urban Institute, 2010).

The monthly benefit one receives under Social Security depends in part on earnings before retirement. The average monthly benefit in January 2012 was $1,229 for retired workers, $1,111 for disabled workers, and $1,184 for nondisabled widows and widowers (Social Security Administration, 2012a). Because retired women are less likely than men to have had continuous paid employment throughout their lives, their average retirement income is typically lower than men's.

As these figures suggest, Social Security provides a minimal level of support for older adults—by itself, barely enough to keep recipients out of poverty (Sullivan, 2012). Still, without such benefits an estimated three-quarters of all older adults would live in poverty (Carr, 2010).

Medicare is the nation's largest health insurer. In 2010 it provided health insurance to 48 million Americans—40 million people age 65 and older and 8 million younger people with disabilities (Henry J. Kaiser Family Foundation, 2011). The estimated budget for the 2012 fiscal year was $536 billion, or about 16 percent of the federal budget (Henry J. Kaiser Family Foundation, 2012). Because it reaches so many people, Medicare has made an enormous difference in the elderly population's access to adequate health care—although at a high cost.

Programs such as Social Security and Medicare will become increasingly costly as more and more Americans retire and live long lives after they retire; further, the share of the population funding Social Security is shrinking. As a result, the worker-to-beneficiary ratio has fallen, from 16.5:1 in 1950 to 2.8:1 today. By 2033, it will be 2.1:1 (Social Security Administraion, 2013a). At that point, the trust fund reserves will be depleted (Social Security Administration, 2013b; Urban Institute, 2010). There is particular concern over whether the Social Security system will remain financially sound as retiring baby boomers collect their pensions. It is currently expected to have sufficient assets to pay full benefits until at least 2029, although if it is to avoid running out of money in the long run, changes will have to be made in the way the system works.

A variety of solutions have been proposed, including: charging co-payments for home health care services, requiring beneficiaries to pay higher premiums, and requiring drug companies to provide discounts (Pear, 2011). One controversial proposal would involve "means testing," or allocating benefits based on an older person's financial means and needs. In the past decade, there also have been calls to privatize at least part of Social Security—that is, to enable workers to invest part of their Social Security withholdings in the stock market, rather than simply paying it all into a government fund. The effectiveness of this approach depends, of course, on how well the stock market performs in the future. Although it looked promising in the 1990s, when stocks were soaring, today it does not look nearly so hopeful. In his February 2005 State of the Union address, President George W. Bush argued for the privatization of Social Security. As of 2011, President Barack Obama stated that he "strongly opposes" privatization or raising the retirement age, but supports raising the cap on the payroll tax to help fund the program, as well as increasing the

Medicare eligibility age from 65 to 67 (Pear, 2011). The future of Social Security and Medicare will likely remain at the center of one of the major political debates of this century.

How Will Nations of the World Cope with Global Aging?

An "elder explosion" is sweeping the world today. According to the United Nations, in 1950 there were 205 million persons age 60 and older on the planet; 50 years later, in 2000, this number had jumped to 606 million. The United Nations projects that by 2050, an astounding 2 billion older adults will inhabit the planet. The world's average life expectancy grew from age 46 in 1950 to age 50 in 1985 and will reach age 71 by 2025. Globally, the population of older persons is growing by 2 percent each year, considerably faster than the population as a whole (United Nations, 2005).

Global aging, such as the graying of the U.S. population, is largely a women's issue. Women outnumber men by roughly 4 to 3 at age 65 or older, and by roughly 2 to 1 at age 80 or above. These patterns are due primarily to women's life expectancy advantage in most nations of the world. The Central Intelligence Agency (2013) has identified just 12 nations where older men outnumber older women: these generally are places that have higher maternal mortality rates, lower levels of schooling among women, and higher levels of gender oppression.

The extent to which nations are "graying" varies widely. Older adults made up 21 percent of the population in more developed countries in 2009; this proportion is projected to reach 33 percent by 2050 (Bremner et al., 2010). The percentage of people age 65 and older in less developed nations is considerably lower due to three important factors that suppress life expectancy: poverty, disease, and malnutrition. In 1950, 4 percent of the population in less developed countries was age 65+. As of 2010 that proportion had risen to nearly 6 percent and is projected to reach nearly 15 percent by mid-century (Haub, 2011).

Just as population composition varies starkly worldwide, the experiences of older adults in less developed nations differ tremendously from those of their peers in wealthier nations. Retirement is "an unaffordable luxury" for most older adults in Africa, and many in Latin America and parts of Asia (Bremner et al., 2010). Four out of five older adults worldwide receive no retirement income from pensions or government entitlement programs. Many must continue to work or rely on their families for financial support. Some work in the informal economy, such as selling products in street markets or working on farms with no benefits or health protection.

Although children and grandchildren historically have cared for their aging parents and grandparents, this support is eroding in some parts of the world. For example, in many parts of Africa, young people are moving to urban areas to work, while others are dying prematurely due to HIV/AIDS, and others still are grappling with their own poverty and cannot support their parents. As a result, many older adults are left to take care of themselves. These challenges are compounded by the fact that many frail elders unexpectedly find themselves as caretakers to their grandchildren, when their own children (that is, the grandchildren's parents) have died due to ravages such as the AIDS epidemic (Bremner et al., 2010).

Worldwide, the "gray tsunami" (O'Neill, 2009) has enormous implications for social policy. As we learned earlier, when a large share of the population enters into older ages, there are fewer working-age people to support them. The number of working-age adults per older adult worldwide will drop steeply between 2010 and 2050, from 9 to 4. By 2050, demographers predict that there will be just 2 working-age adults per older adult in more devolved nations, 4 in less developed nations, and 9 in the least-developed nations.

With fewer people working and paying into the system and more taking out, policy makers are concerned about the solvency of social programs. Countries vary widely in what they are doing to cope with their growing numbers of older people. More than 150 nations currently provide public assistance for people who are elderly or disabled or for their survivors when they die. As we have seen already, the United States relies primarily on Social Security and Medicare to serve the financial and health needs of the elderly. Other industrial nations provide a much broader array of services.

In Japan, one of the oldest nations in the world, 23 percent of men and women are now 65 and older. Many older adults remain active well into old age because the Japanese culture encourages this activity and because business policies often support post-retirement work with the same company one worked for before retirement. A number of national laws in Japan support the employment and training of older workers, and private businesses also support retraining (Statistics Bureau Japan, 2012).

Societies that have large extended families and practice ancestor worship historically have been more likely to treasure their elders, honoring them at public events and seeking their counsel in political matters. East Asian nations, in particular, have a tradition of following the Confucian teaching of filial piety. Children care for their parents in old age out of gratitude for the care they received when young (Sung, 2000). As a result, parents historically have lived with and are cared for by their children when they are no longer able to care for themselves (Cowgill, 1968; Falk, Falk, and Tomashevich, 1981).

This pattern of parent-child co-residence in Asia is starting to fade, however, due to economic development and globalization. Economic development in wealthier Asian nations now enables older adults to live on their own, if they choose to do so. For example, improvements in the health and financial status of older persons now enable Japanese older adults to maintain their own homes and the desirable status of "intimacy at a distance" (Kumagai, 2010).

Globalization also has altered the treatment and status of the elderly throughout the world (Cowgill, 1986; Foner, 1984; Fry, 1980; Holmes, 1983). As previously agrarian societies become part of the emerging global economy, traditional ways of thinking and behaving are likely to change. For example, adult children in China are now abandoning their rural villages to seek jobs in urban regions. Yet these moves often mean leaving behind their aging parents, who are responsible for supporting themselves, often by working in arduous agricultural jobs. Although economic conditions require that children move, cultural beliefs still condemn such moves. In one high-visibility case from 2006, a 60-year-old Chinese widow successfully sued her son and daughter for abandonment. The courts ruled that she was allowed to live with her daughter, and obliged her son to pay her monthly support (French, 2006).

CONCEPT CHECKS ✓

1. Describe the debate surrounding the future of Social Security and Medicare programs in the United States.
2. What is generational equity?
3. What is the graying of the world's population?
4. What two long-term processes have contributed to this graying?
5. What is the feminization of global aging?
6. What are the implications of the graying world population for social policy?

The combination of graying and globalization will shape the lives of elderly people throughout the world well into this century. Traditional patterns of family care will be challenged, as family-based economies continue to give way to labor on the farms and in the offices and factories of global businesses. Like the industrial nations earlier in the twentieth century, all societies will be challenged to find roles for their aging citizens. This challenge will include identifying new means of economic support, often financed by government programs. It will also entail identifying ways to incorporate rather than isolate the elderly, by drawing on their considerable reserves of experience and talent.

1
Basic Concepts

p. 324

2
Growing Old: Theories of Aging

p. 328

LEARNING OBJECTIVES

Learn some basic facts about the increase in the proportion of the U.S. population that is age 65 and older. Recognize that aging is a combination of biological, psychological, and social processes. Understand how technological advances affect each of the three aging processes.

Understand key theories of aging, particularly those that focus on how society shapes the social roles of older adults and that emphasize aspects of age stratification.

TERMS TO KNOW

Graying • Elderly • Social gerontology • Aging • Alzheimer's disease • Social aging

Disengagement theory • Socioemotional selectivity theory • Activity theory • Continuity theory • Conflict theories of aging • Life course

CONCEPT CHECKS

1. What is the "graying" of the U.S. population?
2. By how much will the U.S. elderly population increase over the next five decades?
3. Compare and contrast biological, psychological, and social aging processes.
4. How has technology affected the processes of biological, psychological, and social aging?

1. Summarize the three theoretical frameworks used to describe the nature of aging in U.S. society.
2. What are the main criticisms of functionalism and conflict theory?
3. What are three themes of the life course perspective?
4. Describe the processes of cumulative adversity and advantage over the life course.

Exercises: Thinking Sociologically

1. Briefly discuss the competing theories about growing old that are presented in this chapter. How do these theories compare with each other? Which theory do you feel is most appropriate to explain aging, and why do you feel this way about that theory?

2. What do you think the United States could do socially and politically to alleviate the problems of aging for its elder citizens? How likely is it that your suggestions for alleviating the problems of age could be adopted into the American political process, and why?

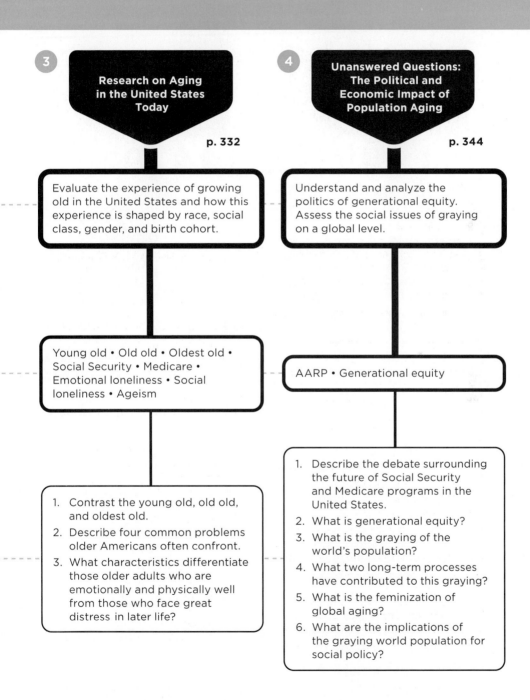

3 **Research on Aging in the United States Today**

p. 332

Evaluate the experience of growing old in the United States and how this experience is shaped by race, social class, gender, and birth cohort.

Young old • Old old • Oldest old • Social Security • Medicare • Emotional loneliness • Social loneliness • Ageism

1. Contrast the young old, old old, and oldest old.
2. Describe four common problems older Americans often confront.
3. What characteristics differentiate those older adults who are emotionally and physically well from those who face great distress in later life?

4 **Unanswered Questions: The Political and Economic Impact of Population Aging**

p. 344

Understand and analyze the politics of generational equity. Assess the social issues of graying on a global level.

AARP • Generational equity

1. Describe the debate surrounding the future of Social Security and Medicare programs in the United States.
2. What is generational equity?
3. What is the graying of the world's population?
4. What two long-term processes have contributed to this graying?
5. What is the feminization of global aging?
6. What are the implications of the graying world population for social policy?

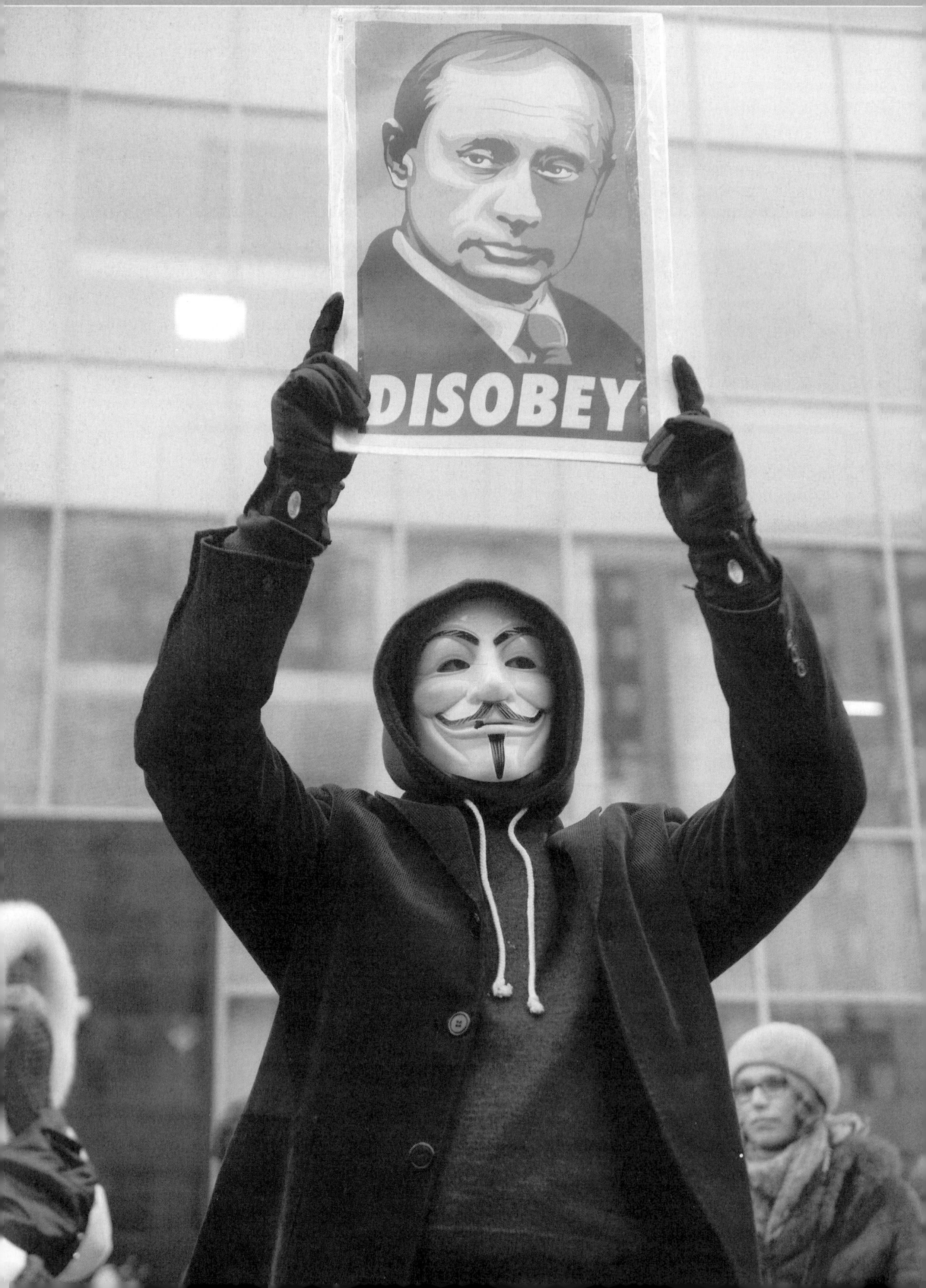
DISOBEY

Government, Political Power, and Social Movements

13

Approximately what percentage of the world's population lives in countries that enjoy the following rights: freedom to participate freely in politics, including voting in fair and open elections for accountable representatives; freedom of expression and belief, including the right to freely assemble; a just and equitable legal system; and access to economic opportunity, including the right to own property?

- a 35 percent
- b 45 percent
- c 55 percent
- d 65 percent
- e 75 percent

Turn the page for the correct answer.

Every year, an organization called Freedom House (2012) classifies countries as either "free," "partly free," or "not free" based on a country-by-country survey of political rights (including open and fair elections, a multiparty system, and the absence of governmental corruption) and civil liberties (including freedom of expression and association, the rule of law, and individual rights). By these measures, in 2012 less than half the world's population (45 percent) lived in countries that were classified as "free;" 31 percent were classified as "partly free," while the rest—numbering some 2.3 billion people living in 48 countries—were classified as "not free." Freedom House also reports that on some measures, the percentage of people who would be classified as "free" has increased in recent years. For example, in 1989 only 41 percent of the 167 countries surveyed were classified as places in which people could vote for their elected officials in open and honest elections; by 2011 the figure had increased to 60 percent (of 195 countries surveyed). But the major gains over the past two decades resulted when India was reclassified from "partly free" to "free," which added nearly a billion people to the "free" category.

This points out one of the principal limitations of such broad-stroke classifications: Although India now formally enjoys a wide range of political rights and civil liberties and a growing economy and middle class, as many as a half billion people in India still live in grinding poverty. Whatever freedom they may have on paper is severely limited by economic hardship and corrupt or indifferent local officials, a situation that has led to widespread discontent, protests, and a thriving Communist movement. Or, to take an example closer to home, candidates for the 2012 U.S. elections and their supporters are estimated to have spent as much as $6 billion on campaigns, suggesting that extremely wealthy individuals, large corporations, organized labor, and lobbying groups have an enormous ability to shape electoral outcomes to reflect their interests. Moreover, any trend toward greater freedom is not irreversible: Since 2004, freedom has significantly declined in Russia and the former Soviet states in Central Europe (Freedom House, 2012; Shkolnikov, 2010).

LEARNING OBJECTIVES

1 BASIC CONCEPTS

Understand basic ideas underlying modern nation-states and social movements.

2 WHO RULES? THEORIES OF DEMOCRACY

Learn some theories about power in a democracy.

3 RECENT RESEARCH ON U.S. POLITICS AND SOCIAL MOVEMENTS

Learn about some of the trends associated with modern-day democracy. Assess the effect of globalization and technology on social movements today. Learn about nationalism and the importance of nationalist movements.

4 UNANSWERED QUESTIONS

Evaluate whether or not democracy is in trouble. Understand why voter turnout is low. Examine whether the Internet is encouraging democracy.

What difference does it make whether a country is free or not? The answer is that it clearly matters how the decisions are made that affect its citizens' lives. Furthermore, most people (and their governments) at least profess to believe that people should enjoy basic political and social freedoms. The second paragraph of the Declaration of Independence famously says, "We hold these truths to be self-evident, that all men are created equal, that they are endowed by their Creator with certain unalienable Rights, that among these are Life, Liberty and the pursuit of Happiness . . . That to secure these rights, Governments are instituted among Men, deriving their just powers from the consent of the governed."

Is greater freedom spreading around the world? Is the idea of freedom contagious, as some have suggested? Before turning to theories and research that address this issue, it is first necessary to define some basic concepts.

BASIC CONCEPTS

Democracy

The terms *freedom* and *democracy* are sometimes used interchangeably, since the latter is intended to guarantee the former. The word *democracy* has its roots in the Greek term *demokratia*, from *demos* (people) and *kratos* (rule). Its basic meaning is a political system in which the people rule. But what does it mean to be "ruled by the people"? Many questions can be raised about this seemingly obvious phrase (see, for example, Held, 2006).

Regarding the "people," who exactly are they? Everyone? Only people who are affected by the decisions? What should be the proper voting age? What about people who are currently in jail or once were? What about people who are not citizens but who have lived in the country for years and have a strong stake in any decisions that might affect them? What if there are strong differences of opinion among "the people"—how are the rights of the minority protected? What about people who choose not to participate or who find it difficult to participate, because of work or family obligations, or lack of understanding of complex issues?

Regarding "rule," how, exactly, is rule exercised? By periodic voting? Actual participation in all decisions that might affect one's life? Does "rule" refer only to government decisions or to other spheres of life as well, such as the economy? Does it encompass the daily administrative decisions of governments, or should it refer only to major policy decisions? Are all rules equally binding? Should rule breaking be punished, and if so, how severely? How much (and what forms of) dissent should be tolerated? If some people believe that the rules are unjust, do they have the right to disobey them?

PARTICIPATORY DEMOCRACY

Answers to these questions have varied over time and in different societies. For example, during U.S. history "the people" have been variously understood as owners of property, white men, educated men, men, and adult men and women. In some societies, democracy is limited to the political sphere; in others, it extends to other areas of social life. Moreover, in modern societies it is not really feasible to have everybody "rule." This has led to at least two different forms of democracy: participatory democracy and liberal democracy.

Participatory democracy (or **direct democracy**) exists when decisions are made communally by those affected by them. This was the original type of democracy practiced in ancient Athens, where the citizens, constituting a small minority of Athenian society (women and slaves were excluded), regularly assembled to consider policies and make major decisions. Participatory democracy has limited importance in modern societies, where the mass of the population has political rights and it would be impossible for everyone to participate in making all the decisions that affected them. (Some New England towns still hold annual town meetings that are a form of participatory democracy.)

Liberal democracies exist in countries where voters can choose between two or more political parties and in which the mass of the adult population has the right to vote. Liberal democracies are also characterized by the rule of law, including the guaranteed freedoms that make voting more than a purely symbolic act. The United States, the western European countries, Japan, Australia, and New Zealand all fall into this category. Some developing countries, such as India, also have liberal democratic systems.

MONARCHIES AND LIBERAL DEMOCRACIES

Not all countries today claim to be democratic. In a handful of countries (e.g., Saudi Arabia, Jordan, and some small Middle Eastern emirates), **monarchies** (rule by unelected kings or queens) still exist. While this was a common form of government well into the nineteenth century, true monarchies are rare today. **Constitutional monarchs** are still found (the queen of England, the king of Sweden, the emperor of Japan), but they are monarchs in name only. Their actual power is severely restricted by their countries' constitutions, which vest authority in the elected representatives of the people.

The Concept of the State

When we say "the people rule," we are typically referring such a right to an entity called a **nation-state**—an entity comprised of a **nation** (people with a common identity that ideally includes shared culture, language, and feelings of belonging) and a **state** (a political apparatus or government that rules over a territory). A modern state includes institutions such as a congress or parliament, a president or prime minister, judges, and other public officials; its authority is often backed by a legal system and the ability to use military force to implement its policies.

CHARACTERISTICS OF THE STATE

All modern states claim specific territories, have formalized codes of law, and are backed by the control of military force. The notion of national **sovereignty**—that a government possesses

participatory democracy • A system of democracy in which all members of a group or community participate collectively in making major decisions.

direct democracy • A form of participatory democracy that allows citizens to vote directly on laws and policies.

liberal democracies • Systems of democracy based on parliamentary institutions, coupled to the free-market system in the area of economic production.

monarchies • Systems of government in which unelected kings or queens rule.

constitutional monarchs • Kings or queens who are largely figureheads. Real power rests in the hands of other political leaders.

nation-states • Particular types of states, characteristic of the modern world, in which governments have sovereign power within defined territorial areas, and populations are citizens who know themselves to be part of single nations.

nation • People with a common identity that ideally includes shared culture, language, and feelings of belonging.

state • A political apparatus (government institutions plus civil service officials) ruling over a given territorial order, whose authority is backed by law and the ability to use force.

sovereignty • The undisputed political rule of a state over a given territorial area.

authority over an area with clear-cut borders, within which it is the supreme power—is a relatively modern one. All modern nation-states are sovereign states. **Failed states** exist when the central government has lost authority over large parts of its national territory, and resorts to the use of deadly force, often against civilian populations, in an effort to retain some degree of power. Examples today include Chad, the Democratic Republic of Congo, Somalia, Sudan, and Zimbabwe (*Foreign Policy,* 2012).

Nationalism   Nation-states are associated with the rise of **nationalism**, which can be defined as a set of symbols and beliefs providing the sense of membership in a single political community—such as being American, Canadian, or Russian. Although people may have always identified with their family, village, or religious community, nationalism appeared only with the development of the modern state. It is the main expression of identity with a distinct political community.

Nationalistic loyalties do not always fit the physical borders marking nations' territories. Because all nation-states comprise communities of diverse backgrounds, **local nationalism** frequently arises in opposition to that fostered by the state—such as nationalist feelings among the French-speaking population in Quebec, Canada. Yet, while the relation between the nation-state and nationalism is complicated, the two are part of the same process. (We will return to nationalism when we explore its effect on international politics.)

Power and Authority   For states to operate effectively they must have **power**—the ability of individuals or groups to make their own interests or concerns count, even when others resist. Power therefore sometimes involves the use of force. It is present in almost all social relationships: between parent and child, professor and student, employer and employee. The exercise of power is, in turn, almost always accompanied by belief systems that justify its use. **Authority** is a form of power that is seen as rightfully exercised, or (to use a term preferred by sociologists and political scientists) "legitimate." Those who are subject to a government's authority voluntarily consent to it. Contrary to what many believe, democracy is not the only type of legitimate government. Dictatorships can have legitimacy as well, as can states governed by religious leaders.

Citizenship   Before the emergence of modern societies, most people lacked awareness or even interest in those who governed them; moreover, they had no political rights or influence. Normally only the dominant classes or richest groups felt a sense of belonging to a political community. In modern societies, by contrast, most people living within the borders of the political system are **citizens**, individuals having common rights and duties, who know they are members of a common national community (Brubaker, 1992). Although some people are political refugees or

failed state • States in which the central government has lost authority and resorts to deadly force to retain power.

nationalism • A set of beliefs and symbols expressing identification with a national community.

local nationalism • The belief that communities that share a cultural identity should have political autonomy, even within smaller units of a nation-state.

power • The ability of individuals or the members of a group to achieve aims or further the interests they hold. Power is a pervasive element in all human relationships. Many conflicts in society are struggles over power, because how much power an individual or group is able to achieve governs how far they are able to put their wishes into practice.

authority • A government's legitimate use of power.

citizens • Members of a political community, having both rights and duties associated with that membership.

Civil rights demonstrators march in 1964 in St. Augustine, Florida.

are "stateless," almost everyone in the world today identifies as a member of some national political order.

Citizenship Rights Three types of rights are associated with citizenship (Marshall, 1973). First, **civil rights** are rights of the individual as established by law; these include privileges that took a long while to achieve and are not fully recognized in all countries. Examples are the freedom of individuals to live where they choose, freedom of speech and religion, the right to own property, and the right to equal justice before the law. These rights were not fully established in most European countries until the early nineteenth century, and not all groups were allowed the same privileges. Although the U.S. Constitution granted such rights to Americans well before most European states had them, African Americans were excluded until the midnineteenth century. Even after the Civil War, when blacks legally obtained these rights, they were unable to exercise them. Blacks were assured full legal equality only with the passage of the Civil Rights Act of 1964—and that only because of more than a decade of marches, demonstrations, and nonviolent civil disobedience led by Dr. Martin Luther King Jr. and countless others in the civil rights movement (Branch, 1989).

The second type of citizenship rights consists of **political rights**, especially the right to participate in elections and to run for public office. Again, these were not won easily or quickly. Except in the United States, the achievement of full voting rights even for all men is relatively recent, and occurred only after the African American struggle for civil rights. In most European countries, the vote was at first limited to male citizens owning a certain amount of property—in other words, an affluent minority. In most Western countries, the vote for women was achieved partly through the efforts of women's movements and partly as a consequence of women entering the formal economy early in the twentieth century, during World War I.

The third type of citizenship rights consists of **social rights**—the right of every individual to enjoy a minimum standard of economic welfare and security. Social rights include sickness benefits, unemployment benefits, and a guaranteed minimum wage—in other words, welfare provisions. In most societies, social rights developed last because the establishment of civil and political rights underpinned the fight for social rights. Social rights have been won largely through poorer groups' political strength, expressed after obtaining the vote.

Social rights are typically achieved through a **welfare state**, which exists when government

civil rights • Legal rights held by all citizens in a given national community.

political rights • Rights of political participation, such as the right to vote in local and national elections, held by citizens of a national community.

social rights • Rights of social and welfare provision held by all citizens in a national community, including, for example, the right to claim unemployment benefits and sickness payments provided by the state.

welfare state • A political system that provides a wide range of welfare benefits for its citizens.

organizations provide material benefits for citizens. Some of these benefits are intended to help those who cannot support themselves adequately through paid employment—the unemployed, the sick, the disabled, and the elderly. Many benefits go as well to the middle class: free or low-cost public education, from kindergarten through state colleges and universities (although the cost of the latter is rapidly rising in many states), freeways, and Social Security, to name a few examples. In many poorer countries, welfare benefits, especially for the poor, are simply nonexistent. In Western countries, however, an extensive welfare state has been considered the ideal expression of citizenship rights for more than half a century.

Finally, social change sometimes occurs outside the established political system. **Revolutions** occur when an existing political order is overthrown by means of a mass movement that emerges when desired changes cannot be achieved within the system, often using violence (Foran, 1997, 2005). Yet for all their high drama, revolutions occur relatively infrequently. More commonly, political change is achieved through **social movements**—collective attempts to further a common interest or secure a common goal through action outside the sphere of established institutions. Social movements are as evident in the contemporary world as are the formal, bureaucratic organizations they often oppose. Many contemporary social movements are international and utilize information technology in linking local campaigners to global issues.

CONCEPT CHECKS ✓

1. Why is it problematic for contemporary states to have participatory democracy?
2. Describe three characteristics of the state.
3. What is the welfare state?

② WHO RULES? THEORIES OF DEMOCRACY

Classical sociology offers three different ideas of how modern democracies actually function: through rule by elites who possess the necessary expertise, but are accountable to the electorate; through interest groups that compete for influence, providing a form of checks and balances against one another; and through an elite of the wealthy and powerful that operates in the background, thereby shaping policy in their interest.

Democratic Elitism

One of the most influential views of the nature and limits of modern democracy was set out by Max Weber and, in modified form, by economist Joseph Schumpeter (1983; orig. 1942). Their ideas are called the theory of **democratic elitism**.

Weber held that direct democracy is impossible as a means of regular government in

revolutions • A process of political change involving the mobilizing of a mass social movement, which by the use of violence successfully overthrows an existing regime and forms a new government.

social movements • Large groups of people who seek to accomplish, or to block, a process of social change. Social movements normally exist in conflict with organizations whose objectives and outlook they oppose. However, movements that successfully challenge power, once they become institutionalized, can develop into organizations.

democratic elitism • A theory of the limits of democracy that holds that in large-scale societies democratic participation is necessarily limited to the regular election of political leaders.

large-scale societies—not only for the logistical reason that millions of people cannot meet to make political decisions, but also because running a complex society demands *expertise*. Participatory democracy, Weber believed, can succeed only in small organizations where the work is straightforward. When complicated decisions or policies are involved, even in modest-size groups, such as a small business firm, specialized knowledge and skills are necessary. Because experts carry out their jobs on a continuous basis, positions requiring expertise cannot be subject to regular election by people with vague knowledge of the necessary skills and information. Although higher officials, responsible for overall policy decisions, are elected, there must be a large substratum of full-time bureaucratic officials who play a large part in running a country (Weber, 1979; orig. 1921).

In Weber's view, the development of mass citizenship, which is closely connected with the idea of general democratic participation, greatly expands the need for bureaucratic officialdom. For example, provision for welfare, health, and education requires permanent, large-scale administrative systems.

Representative multiparty democracy, according to Weber, helps defend against both arbitrary decision making on the part of political leaders (because they are subject to popular elections) and power being completely usurped by bureaucrats (because elected officials set overall policy). But under these circumstances, the contribution of democratic institutions falls short of achieving pure democracy. "Rule by the people" is possible in only a very limited sense. To achieve power, political parties must become organized in a systematic way—they must become bureaucratized. "Party machines" then develop that threaten the autonomy of parliaments or congresses in discussing and formulating policies. If a party with a majority representation can dictate policy, and if that party is run by officials who are permanently in control, then the level of democracy is low.

For democratic systems to be effective, Weber argued, two conditions must be met. First, there must be parties that represent different interests and have different outlooks. If the policies of competing parties are basically the same, voters lack any effective choice. Weber held that one-party systems cannot be democratic in any meaningful way. Second, there must be political leaders with imagination and the courage to escape the inertia of bureaucracy. Weber emphasized the importance of *leadership* in democracy, which is why his view is known as democratic elitism: Rule by elites is inevitable; ideally they will represent our interests in an innovative and insightful fashion. Parliaments and congresses give rise to political leaders who can counter the influence of bureaucracy and command mass support. Weber valued multiparty democracy more for the quality of leadership it generates than for the mass participation in politics it makes possible.

Joseph Schumpeter (1983) agreed with Weber about the limits of mass political participation and about democracy being important as a method of generating effective and responsible government. Democracy, Schumpeter stated, is the rule of *the politician,* not *the people.* To achieve voting support, however, politicians must be minimally responsive to the demands and interests of the electorate. Only if there is competition to secure votes can arbitrary rule be avoided.

Pluralist Theories

Pluralists accept that individual citizens can have little or no *direct* influence on political decision making. But they argue that the presence of interest groups can limit the centralization of power in the hands of government officials. Competing interest groups or factions are vital to democracy because they divide up power, reducing the exclusive influence of any one group or class (Truman, 1981).

In the pluralist view, bargaining among interest groups—business organizations, trade unions, ethnic groups, environmental organizations, religious groups, and so forth—influences government policies in a democracy. A democratic political order involves a balance among competing interests, all having some effect on policy but none dominating the mechanisms of government. Elections are also influenced by this situation, for to achieve a majority of votes, the parties must be responsive to diverse interest groups. In the view of pluralist theorists, the United States is one of the most pluralistic of industrialized societies and, therefore, the most democratic. Competition among interest groups occurs not only at the national level but also within the states and in local communities.

The Power Elite

C. Wright Mills's celebrated work *The Power Elite* (1956) takes a view different from that of pluralist theories. According to Mills, early in its history American society did show flexibility and diversity at all levels; however, this has since changed.

Mills argued that during the twentieth century a process of institutional centralization occurred in the political order, the economy, and the military. On the political side, individual state governments used to be very powerful and were loosely coordinated by the federal government. But political power by the mid-twentieth century, Mills argued, had become tightly coordinated at the federal level. Similarly, the economy once comprised many small units, businesses, banks, and farms, but now was dominated by a cluster of very large corporations. Finally, since World War II, the military, once restricted in size, had grown to a giant establishment at the heart of the country's institutions.

Not only had each sphere become more centralized, according to Mills, but all had increasingly merged into a unified system of power. Those holding the highest positions in all three institutional areas had similar social backgrounds, enjoyed parallel interests, and often knew one another personally. They had become a **power elite** that ran the country and, given the international position of the United States, influenced much of the rest of the world.

According to Mills, the power elite is composed mainly of white Anglo-Saxon Protestants (WASPs) who are from wealthy families, attended the same prestigious universities, belong to the same clubs, and sit on government committees with one another. They have closely connected concerns. Business and political leaders work together, and both have close relationships with the military through weapons contracting and the supply of goods for the armed forces. There is considerable movement among top positions in the three spheres. Politicians have business interests; business leaders often run for public office; higher military personnel sit on the boards of the large companies. In opposition to pluralist interpretations, Mills saw three distinct levels of power in the United States. The power elite occupies the highest level, formally and informally making key decisions affecting both domestic and foreign policy. Interest groups operate at the middle levels of power, together with local government agencies. Their influence over major policy decisions is limited. At the bottom is the mass of the population, who have virtually no influence on policy decisions because these are made within closed settings by the power elite. Because the power elite spans the top of both

power elite • Small networks of individuals who, according to C. Wright Mills, hold concentrated power in modern societies.

President Dwight Eisenhower at his farewell radio-television address, where he warned against the "military-industrial complex."

party organizations, the choices open to voters in presidential and congressional elections are so small as to be of little consequence.

Since Mills published his study, other researchers have analyzed the social background and interconnections of leading figures in American society (Dye, 1986). All studies find that the social backgrounds of those in leading positions are highly unrepresentative of the population as a whole (Domhoff, 1971, 1979, 1983, 1998).

The main argument among sociologists about the distribution of power in the United States now focuses on the relative power of government officials and of the business leaders who run large corporations. Some scholars argue that true power lies with politicians in government and that business leaders are much less powerful (Amenta, 1998; Orloff, 1993; Skocpol, 1992). Other scholars hold that corporate business executives and families of great wealth form a capitalist class that greatly influences government officials and experts through lobbying, campaign contributions, the sponsorship of think tanks, and the appointment of top corporate leaders to important government positions (Domhoff, 1998). Both sides agree, however, that it is not inevitable for business leaders or government officials always to be dominant. Although an elite class—whether elected, expert, or corporate—rules America, the power of groups can change over time, leaving open the possibility that those who are now powerless could be dominant in the future.

THE ROLE OF THE MILITARY

Mills's argument that the military plays a central role in the power elite was buttressed by a well-known warning from a former military hero and U.S. president, Dwight David Eisenhower. In his farewell address in 1961, Eisenhower warned, "In the councils of government, we must guard against the acquisition of unwarranted influence, whether sought or unsought, by the military-industrial complex. The potential for the disastrous rise of misplaced power exists and will persist" (Eisenhower, 1961). Eisenhower's experience lent considerable credence to his assertion: He served for eight years as president (1953–1961), held the top rank of five-star army general, and had been Supreme Commander of the Allied forces in Europe during World War II. In 1989, at the end of the cold war, U.S. defense spending—which had reached $300 billion in that year—began to decline slightly. With the collapse of the Soviet Union in 1991, the United States became the world's unrivaled military superpower; there was even talk of a "peace dividend" to spend on improving schools, repairing highways, or other domestic needs. But the decline proved to be short lived. By 2001, military spending once

CONCEPT CHECKS ✓

1. Compare and contrast pluralist theories of modern democracy and the power elite model.
2. According to Weber, what are the necessary conditions for democratic systems to be effective?

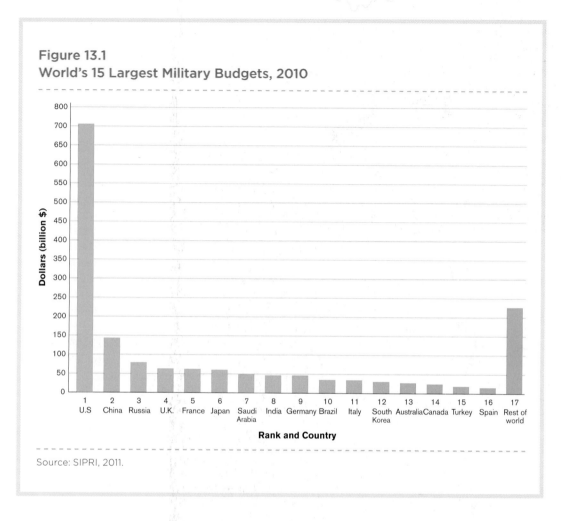

Figure 13.1
World's 15 Largest Military Budgets, 2010

Source: SIPRI, 2011.

again topped $300 billion annually. It reached $400 billion in 2004, and over $700 billion in 2010 (Shah, 2011; Figure 13.1). Wars in Iraq and Afghanistan added to the total. The global war on terrorism has triggered another cycle of military spending. The U.S. defense budget for 2013 was projected to be $613.9 billion (U.S. Department of Defense, 2012). Total military spending in the United States is greater than that for nearly all other countries in the world combined. Eisenhower's dire warning seems no less true today than when he uttered it half a century ago.

③ RECENT RESEARCH ON U.S. POLITICS AND SOCIAL MOVEMENTS

In this section we look first at research on the U.S. political system. We then turn to a discussion of the role of social movements in fostering political and social change, before concluding with an examination of terrorism as a means of achieving political objectives on a global scale.

Democracy in the United States

The United States is a representative democracy in which political participation is achieved through elected representatives. Political parties have come to play a key role in elections, while interest groups have significant (and, some would argue, growing) influence behind the scenes and on electoral politics. Two important (and relatively recent) changes in the U.S. political system are the increased political participation of women and the impact of the Internet.

POLITICAL PARTIES

A *political party* is an organization of individuals with broadly similar political aims, oriented toward achieving legitimate control of government through an electoral process. Two parties dominate political systems where elections are based on the principle of winner take all, as in the United States. The candidate who gains the most votes wins the election, no matter what proportion of the overall vote he or she gains (Duverger, 1954). Exceptions to this general rule in the United States involve presidential elections, which are decided by the Electoral College. Under this system, each state has a number of electors equal to its total congressional representation: the number of seats it holds in the House of Representatives (which is proportional to its population), plus its two senators. Whichever candidate gets the largest number of votes in a state gets that state's entire electoral vote.

As a result, a tiny margin of victory in a populous state such as California, New York, or Florida can swing an election. At three times in American history, one candidate won the majority of votes from citizens (the popular vote) but still lost the Electoral College vote. This occurred most recently in 2000, when Al Gore outpolled George W. Bush by about 500,000 votes but still lost the electoral vote by 271 to 267, since although Bush won Florida by only 537 votes, he received all 25 of that state's electoral votes, which were sufficient to tip the election in his favor. Where elections are based on different principles, such as proportional representation (in which seats in a representative assembly are allocated according to the proportions of the vote attained), five or six or more parties may be represented in the assembly. When no single party has a majority, some of the parties have to form a *coalition*, an alliance with one another, to form a government.

As a consequence of the winner-take-all electoral system, the United States effectively has only two significant political parties, Republicans and Democrats, since it is virtually impossible for minor parties to garner sufficient electoral votes to win presidential elections. Two-party systems often lead to a concentration on the middle ground, where most votes are found, although in recent years the two parties in the United States have become increasingly polarized. While the Democratic Party remains divided between its dominant, more liberal base and its more conservative members (the so-called "Blue Dog Democrats"), the Republican Party has become much more consistently conservative.

Multiparty systems, on the other hand, allow more direct expression of divergent interests and provide scope for the representation of radical alternatives. Green Party representatives and representatives of far right or far left parties, found in some European parliaments, are cases in point. However, often no single party can achieve an overall majority, and the resulting government by coalition may lead either to a stalemate (if compromises can't be made) or to a rapid succession of elections and new governments, none remaining in power for long.

Some writers have studied the connection between voting patterns and class differences. Liberal and leftist parties gain most votes from lower-class voters, whereas conservative and rightist parties often win the vote of the affluent (see, for example, Bartels, 2008; Lipset, 1981; Pew Research Center for the People and the Press, 2005; Stonecash, 2000). Although the Democratic Party has tended to appeal more to lower-class groups, and the Republicans have drawn support from the more affluent sectors, the connections are not absolute. In recent years, while the poorest voters (annual household income under $19,000 in 2005) overwhelmingly identify as Democrats, lower-middle-income households ($19,000–$35,000) increasingly identify as Republican—although Democrats still enjoy a slight edge in this group (Pew Research Center for the People and the Press, 2005). The reasons that support for Democrats has eroded somewhat among lower-middle-income voters have been much debated (Bartels, 2006, 2008; Frank, 2004, 2005). Two factors, however, seem especially important: race and union membership. In all income groups except the poorest, white voters tend to identify as Republican—with the exception of those who belong to unions, who remain more likely to call themselves Democrats. As union membership has declined, so has support for Democrats (Francia and Bigelow, 2010; Pew Research Center for the People and the Press, 2005).

POLITICS AND VOTING

The founders of the American governmental system did not foresee a role for parties in the political order. George Washington recognized that interest groups would develop, but he warned against "the harmful effects of the spirit of party." Thomas Jefferson echoed these sentiments but in fact became the leader of one of the earliest party organizations. The early parties endorsed candidates for Congress, and the subsequent national division of parties spread to the state legislatures. Soon the parties developed into state organizations representing specific interests and points of view. A two-party system was well established by the 1830s, and its fundamental nature has not altered greatly to this day. Building mass support for a party in the United States is difficult, because the country is so large and includes so many regional, cultural, and ethnic groups. The parties have all cultivated electoral strength by forging broad regional bases of support and by campaigning for very general political ideals.

As measured by levels of membership, party identification, and voting support, both of the major American parties are in decline. In 1964, 51 percent of adults identified as Democrat, 25 percent as Republican, and 23 percent as independent. After 45 years of gradual but fairly steady decline, by 2009 the number of self-identified Democrats had dropped to 30 percent in 2012. Twenty-eight percent identified as Republicans, while the largest percentage of people (41 percent) now described themselves as independent (Gallup, 2012).

The decline in party identification reflects a steadily growing distrust of politics among American voters. According to one survey conducted in March 2010, only 22 percent of adults reported they could trust the government "almost always or most of the time"—one of the lowest ratings in 50 years. The reasons for this are many: An economic recession that left 1 out of every 10 American workers jobless; partisan fighting in Congress; and a growing polarization between the Democratic and Republican parties (Pew Research Center for the People and the Press, 2010b). Mistrust toward government is especially high among "Tea Partiers," a conservative movement strongly identified with the Republican Party, which first appeared on the scene in 2009. The Tea Party is not actually a political party; its name comes from the Boston Tea Party protests of 1773, in which the colonists dumped tea into Boston Harbor, protesting British taxes on tea exported to the colonies. The Tea Party is a well-organized social movement opposed to what its adherents view as the Obama administration's excessive interference in the economy, as seen in its efforts to end the recession through federal spending, its partial takeover of failing corporations, and its push for universal health care coverage. Tea Party protests and rallies in Washington garnered widespread media attention, as well as strong support among Republicans, 45 percent of whom reported agreeing with the movement as of March 2010. Among all adults, however, the same poll found that only a quarter agreed: Nearly two-thirds either had never heard of the Tea Party movement, or had no opinion (Pew Research Center for the People and the Press, 2010b).

There is also a distrust of the economic system and Wall Street in particular. Following the Arab Spring and protests in Spain, the Occupy Wall Street movement began in the United States and occupied Zuccotti Park, in the Financial District of Manhattan. Though not stating any specific demands nor having specific leaders, the movement spread to all parts of the country, where similar sentiments were expressed. By the end of 2011 and the beginning of 2012, it had spread to massive demonstrations on college campuses against tuition cuts and the "financialization" of society. Roughly 48 percent of the public agrees with the concerns of the Occupy movement, though nearly the same percentage disagrees with its tactics. Seventy-seven percent of the American public believes that the economic system is unfair and that power is concentrated in too few hands (Pew Research Center for the People and the Press, 2011c).

The 2008 elections resulted in a decisive victory for the Democrats, when Barack Obama became the first black American to be elected president, winning by a decisive margin (52 to 46 percent) over Republican John McCain. Democrats also won large majorities in both houses of Congress, although Republicans regained a majority in the House of Representatives in the 2010 elections.

Obama's victory also revealed deep divisions by race, class, and age within the American electorate. While he received 95 percent of the black vote and 66 percent of the Latino vote, he lost decisively among white voters, 55 percent of whom voted for McCain. Although the two candidates polled evenly among middle- and upper-income voters, Obama won decisively among voters earning less than $50,000 (60 to 38 percent); he also carried younger voters (18–29 years of age) by a substantial margin (60 to 38 percent) (Keeter, 2008; Kohut, 2008).

The 2012 election between Obama and Republican challenger Mitt Romney revealed an even more polarized electorate. Black, Hispanic, and Asian voters chose Obama by 93 percent, 71 percent, and 73 percent, respectively, but white voters chose Romney by 59 percent. Voters earning more than $50,000 voted for Romney by slightly more than 50 percent, while 60 percent of those earning less than $50,000 chose Obama. Young voters once again turned out in significant numbers for Obama: 18-29-year-olds voted for him 60 to 37 percent, while those 65 and older voted for him 44 to 56 percent (*Washington Post*, 2012).

Whether these divisions portend a longer-term shift in American political identifications remains to be seen, although at least one trend would seem to favor the Democrats: The United States is predicted to become majority-minority by 2050, with whites declining to less than half (47 percent) of the population, from 67 percent in 2005. This change will result almost entirely from a substantial increase in the historically Democrat-identified

Latino population, whose share will double between 2005 and 2050 (from 14 to 29 percent; Passel and Cohn, 2008).

INTEREST GROUPS

An **interest group** is any organization that attempts to persuade elected officials to consider its aims when deciding on legislation. The American Medical Association, the National Organization for Women, and the National Rifle Association are three examples. Some interest groups are national; others are statewide. Some are permanently organized; others are short lived. *Lobbying* is the act of persuading influential officials to vote in favor of a cause or otherwise lend support to the aims of an interest group.

The U.S. Lobbying Disclosure Act of 1995 requires all organizations employing lobbyists to register with Congress and to disclose whom they represent, whom they lobby, what they are lobbying for, and how much they are paid. In 2009 nearly 14,000 different lobbyists were registered (Center for Public Integrity, 2010). To run as a political candidate is enormously expensive, and interest groups provide much of the funding at all levels of political office. The Republican candidate for the November 2008 presidential election, John McCain, raised over $360 million, and the Democratic candidate, Barack Obama, raised over $639 million (CRP, 2008). In the 2012 presidential election, the Democratic incumbent and subsequent winner, Barack Obama, raised $715 million, and the Republican candidate, Mitt Romney, raised $446 million (CRP, 2012a, 2012c). Even to run for the House or Senate costs a small fortune.

Incumbents clearly have an enormous advantage in soliciting money. In the 2012 congressional election, 90 percent of incumbents running for reelection to the House of Representatives beat their challengers (CRP, 2012d). Incumbents raised nearly three and a half times more money than their challengers—$635 million compared with $295 million (CRP, 2011). Incumbents are preferred as fund-raisers partly because they can curry favor with special interests and other contributors, since they are in a position to ensure favorable votes and obtain spending on their contributors' pet issues. Incumbency also provides familiarity—a formidable obstacle for most challengers to overcome. The cost of beating an incumbent has increased significantly in the last few decades, which is perhaps why roughly two out of every five congressional representatives and senators are millionaires.

Corporations, which have a strong stake in getting favorable legislation and government contracts, are the largest contributors to campaigns, accounting for almost three-quarters of the total in the 2012 election cycle (Figure 13.2). About three-fifths of all corporate contributions go to Republican candidates. Labor unions overwhelmingly favor Democrats. About a third of the funding in congressional elections comes from *political action committees* (PACs), which are set up by interest groups to raise and distribute campaign funds. The top 20 PACs contributed over $52 million to candidates in the 2011-2012 election cycle. The National Association of Realtors made the largest contribution, totaling $3.9 million, and close behind was the National Beer Wholesalers Association at $3.3 million (CRP, 2013b). Labor unions also weigh in heavily, accounting for nearly half of the largest contributors. Since 1989 the American Federation of State, County, and Municipal Employees (AFSCME) has been the largest overall donor, giving over $61 million between 1989 and 2012 to various candidates for office (CRP, 2013a).

interest group • A group organized to pursue specific interests in the political arena, operating primarily by lobbying the members of legislative bodies.

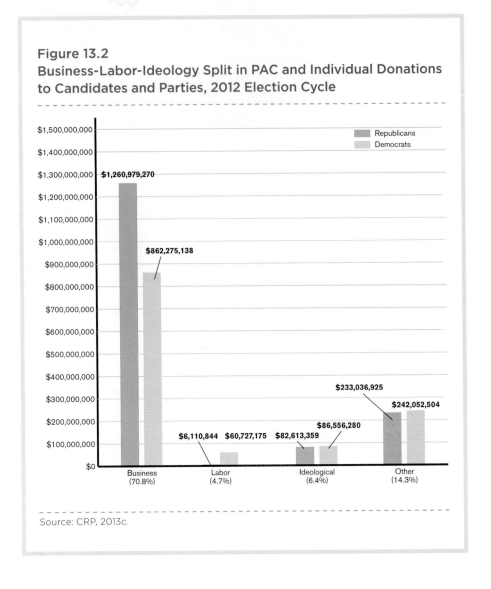

Figure 13.2
Business-Labor-Ideology Split in PAC and Individual Donations to Candidates and Parties, 2012 Election Cycle

Republicans
Democrats

$1,500,000,000

$1,400,000,000

$1,300,000,000   **$1,260,979,270**

$1,200,000,000

$1,100,000,000

$1,000,000,000

$900,000,000   **$862,275,138**

$800,000,000

$700,000,000

$600,000,000

$500,000,000

$400,000,000

$300,000,000   **$233,036,925**

                                                            $242,052,504

$200,000,000   **$86,556,280**

            $6,110,844 **$60,727,175** **$82,613,359**

$100,000,000

$0
        Business   Labor   Ideological   Other
        (70.8%)   (4.7%)   (6.4%)   (14.3%)

Source: CRP, 2013c.

Paid lobbyists play a significant role in influencing the outcome of votes in Congress and decisions by the president. The Center for Responsive Politics (CRP, 2010) reported that businesses, unions, and other advocacy groups spent some $3.5 billion in 2009—a third of which went to influence health care reform. The Affordable Care Act, signed into law by President Obama in 2010, overhauled the U.S. health care system. Among other provisions, it extended insurance coverage to an additional 30 million Americans, and prohibited insurance companies from denying care for preexisting conditions. When the debate over health care reform began, the White House was seriously considering a "public option," an approach Obama had promoted during his campaign for president. Under this approach, the government would have offered its own competing health care insurance program, in the hope of forcing private insurance companies to lower their premiums. Once in the White House, however, Obama found it impossible to get a public option endorsed by Congress—even though the Democrats held solid majorities in both the House and Senate, and despite the fact that public opinion polls showed that a majority of Americans favored this approach (Pew Research Center for the People and the Press, 2009). Lobbyists for pharmaceutical companies, hospitals, and insurance companies spent millions of dollars in an effort to shape the final outcome (Eggen, 2009). A study by the Center for Public Integrity found that nearly 1,800 firms and other organizations hired more than 4,500 lobbyists to influence the outcome of the health care debate—effectively eight lobbyists for each member of Congress (Eaton and Pell, 2010).

In 2002, Congress passed the McCain-Feingold Campaign Finance Reform Act, which severely restricted unlimited campaign contributions. Under federal laws, corporations and labor unions are prohibited from contributing to federal campaigns. Legal loopholes, however, had permitted unlimited "soft-money" contributions to the political parties' "nonfederal accounts," supposedly destined for party-building activities unrelated to federal campaigns. In fact, almost all the money found its way back into presidential and congressional elections (Common Cause, 2002). The McCain-Feingold law closed those loopholes. Candidates for federal elections were once again restricted to raising money from individuals—$2,000 per candidate, $25,000 to political parties. However, campaigns have already found a new loophole: so-called "527" organizations (named after the provision in the tax code that provides them with tax-exempt status). These groups are political organizations that campaign and lobby for candidates and are funded by unlimited soft-money donations. They cannot coordinate their actions with any of the candidates, but they typically support one party or the other. In the 2012 presidential campaign, 527s such as the Service Employees International Union, National Association of Realtors, and the Plumbers/Pipefitters Union spent more than $415 million (CRP, 2012b).

In 2010 the U.S. Supreme Court, in a narrow 5–4 decision (*Citizens United v. Federal Election Commission*), overturned a 63-year-old law that limited corporate and union spending in elections. The conservative majority on the Court reasoned that corporations and unions were protected under First Amendment free speech rights, and so were free to spend as much as they chose in order to express their independent opinions on candidates—so long as these were not coordinated with candidates' campaigns (Liptak, 2010). This decision has raised concern among liberals that businesses will now be able to saturate the airwaves with political ads during elections, thereby exerting undue influence on voters. This, they reason, will further tip the balance of political influence toward those corporations that have deep pockets. Instead of "one person, one vote," it will more likely be "one dollar, one vote," with those having the most dollars able to garner the largest number of votes (Johnson, 2010).

The Political Participation of Women

The early women's movements saw the vote as the symbol of political freedom and as the means of achieving greater economic and social equality. In the United States, women did not get the right to vote until 1920; in France, not until 1944. Women's leaders underwent considerable hardships to reach this end. Even today, in many countries women do not have the same voting rights as men.

Women's obtaining the vote has not greatly altered the nature of politics, although women's votes did contribute significantly to Obama's victory in 2008 and again in 2012. Women's voting patterns, like those of men, are shaped by party preferences, policy options, and the choice of candidates. In the 2012 election, 55 percent of women voted for Obama over Romney (*New York Times*, 2012a). Whether women's preference for the Democratic Party candidate in the last two elections is evidence of a longer-term trend remains to be seen.

Women such as Hillary Clinton, Nancy Pelosi, and Nikki Haley now play central roles in American politics. Still, women remain underrepresented in government. In 2013 there were only 20 women in the Senate (out of 100 members), and only 78 in the House of Representatives (18 percent of total House membership). While these percentages might seem low, from a historical perspective they represent a sea change in women's roles in politics. Just 40 years ago, in 1970, there was only a single woman in the Senate, and just 10 in the House.

Since 1990, female candidates have been successful when they have run for office. The critical factor seems to be that political parties (which are run largely by men) have not recruited as many women to run for office. The factors that impede women's advancement in the economy also operate in the realm of politics. Rising within a political organization requires considerable effort and time, which women shouldering major domestic burdens can rarely generate. That is perhaps why women are more likely to run for local elected positions such as city council or mayor, rather than for statewide or national offices, which would require them to relocate far from their families. But there may be an additional influence in political life, where a high level of power is concentrated: Perhaps men are especially reluctant to abandon their dominance in such a sphere.

The influence of women on U.S. politics cannot be assessed solely through voting patterns and elected officials, however. Feminist groups have impacted political life independently of the franchise, particularly in recent decades. Since the early 1960s, the National Organization for Women (NOW) and other women's groups in the United States have been instrumental in the passing of equal opportunity acts and in getting a range of issues directly affecting women on the political agenda. Such issues include equal rights at work, the availability of abortion, changes in family and divorce laws, and lesbian rights. In 1973, women achieved a legal victory when the Supreme Court ruled in *Roe v. Wade* that women had a legal right to abortion. The 1989 Court ruling in *Webster v. Reproductive Health Services*, which placed restrictions on that right, caused a resurgence of involvement in the women's movement.

Although women in the United States may have achieved increased political power in recent decades, in terms of global comparisons the country still has a long way to go. The Inter-Parliamentary Union (IPU, 2012) compiles a ranking of 186 countries, based on the percentage of women in each country's lower legislative house (comparable with the U.S. House of Representatives). As of 2012 the United States ranked only 78th. Rwanda—an African country where intertribal genocide claimed more than 800,000 lives in 1994—ranked first, with more than half of all seats (56 percent) held by women. Countries in which more than 40 percent of seats were held by women included Sweden (44 percent), Cuba (48 percent), Seychelles (43 percent), Finland (42 percent), South Africa (42 percent), and Nicaragua (40 percent). Since 1960, 69 different women have served as heads of state (as presidents or prime ministers) in 46 countries around the world, including such predominantly Muslim nations as Bangladesh, Pakistan, and Turkey. As of January 2013, countries with female heads of state included Argentina, Australia, Bangladesh, Brazil, Costa Rica, Denmark, Germany, Iceland, Jamaica, Kosovo, Liberia, Lithuania, Malawi, Slovakia, South Korea, Thailand, and Trinidad and Tobago (Headhoncha, 2012; Center for American Women and Politics, 2013b; McCullough, 2013). The United States, which has never had a female president, is a striking exception.

The Internet and Political Participation

The Internet transcends national and cultural borders, facilitating the global spread of ideas. More and more people worldwide access the Internet regularly and consider it important to their lifestyles. According to one service that tracks global Internet usage, as of 2011 nearly 2.3 billion people were using the Internet in some form—32.7 percent of the world's population. Internet use, of course, reflects global inequalities as well. Internet usage ranged from highs of 78.0 percent in North America and 61.0 percent in Europe, to only 13.5 percent in Africa and 26.0 percent in Asia. Still, this picture is rapidly changing: Internet usage in Africa has grown 24-fold during the past 10 years, by far the highest rate of increase in the world (Internet World Stats, 2012).

While a December 2012 survey by the Pew Internet and American Life Project found that 82 percent of Americans report using the Internet, those most likely to do so are young (97 percent of those 18–29, compared with only 53 percent of those 65 and older), relatively wealthy (97 percent of those earning over $75,000, compared with 71 percent of those earning less than $30,000), and educated (95 percent of those with a college education, compared with only 58 percent of high school dropouts). Racial differences were not nearly as pronounced; for example, African Americans are more likely to use cell phones and other forms of mobile computing than whites (Pew Research Center, 2012a, 2012d). Americans increasingly use the Internet on an array of devices and gadgets. Younger people, age 18–29, are much more likely to use cellphones (95 percent) and laptops (75 percent), compared with the 68 percent cellphone usage and 32 percent ownership by those aged 65 and older. People aged 30–45 are most likely to use tablets and e-readers (Pew Research Center, 2012a). The inequalities in technology use are reflected in politics: While the Pew survey found that more than a third of adults earning at least $100,000 engaged in two or more online political activities, the figure dropped to only 8 percent for those earning less than $20,000 (Pew Research Center, 2009c). Generational differences were significant: Young adults (ages 18–32) seem most interested in listening to music and watching videos, playing games, instant-messaging, and social-networking; their parents (ages 55–63) prefer shopping, banking, seeking out health information, and visiting governmental websites (Pew Research Center, 2009d).

With the click of a mouse (thanks to Google and other search engines), it is now possible to obtain, instantly and effortlessly, information on any topic (including, of course, term papers). During the ongoing conflicts in Iraq and Afghanistan, people who tired of news reports by NBC or CNN—or Fox or MSNBC—could choose among dozens of other news sources from around the world, from official U.S. military sites to the Arab news service Al Jazeera. Concerned citizens can e-mail their opinions to their elected representatives, while blogging and tweeting their thoughts to anyone who cares to read them (and everyone who does not). Even YouTube has become a major outlet for would-be opinion makers, from military experts to middle school students with iPhones. The YouTube video posting *Kony 2012*, which sought to bring public attention to the atrocities committed by indicted Ugandan war criminal Joseph Kony, went viral with some 100 million viewings overnight, and contributed to efforts (unsuccessful as of 2012) to bring him to justice. On the other hand, the most widely viewed YouTube video of all time, garnering 1.6 billion viewers, was hardly a posting intended to mobilize public protest against atrocities committed by an African warlord: It was Psy's "Gangnam Style." YouTube has clearly become a powerful (and popular) medium for people to express their views in a user-friendly manner. But whether Americans use this technology to become better informed and more involved is clearly another matter.

One prominent example of the political role of the Internet is MoveOn.org, a liberal organization originally created in 1998 to electronically mobilize opposition to the impeachment of then-president Bill Clinton. MoveOn.org played a central role in the antiwar protest on February 15, 2003, when millions of people peacefully demonstrated in cities worldwide to express opposition to U.S. plans for military intervention in Iraq. The Web-based organization, at the time with a paid staff of only four people, found out about the protest only a month before it was scheduled to occur. It used its website to spread the word, enlist volunteers, and coordinate organization in numerous cities. Today MoveOn.org claims more than eight million members. In 2008, political organizations and presidential candidates applied the lessons learned from MoveOn.org's 2003 campaign. Barack Obama mobilized grassroots support via the Internet and raised contributions totaling a record-breaking $639 million. His campaign also used his website to organize volunteers for phone banks and get-out-the-vote efforts. Conservatives have also learned the lesson: The conservative Tea Party movement has mobilized house parties and marches on Washington through its creative use of the Web and social networking (not to mention more conventional media such as Fox News), and has become a significant force in electoral politics and in issues such as health care reform.

The Internet is playing a growing role throughout the world. In Iran, texting was widely used by the pro-democracy Green Movement during the 2009 presidential elections to mobilize millions of people in peaceful protests against the Ahmadinejad government. The Internet played a key role in contributing to the mass mobilizations that produced what came to be called the Arab Spring in 2011, which toppled dictatorships in Egypt, Libya, and Yemen; sparked a civil war in Syria; and threatened monarchies elsewhere in the Middle East. In China, citizens and journalists have used the Internet to bring public attention to a host of problems, from toxic rivers to dismal working conditions in factories. When a Shanghai-based financial reporter blew the whistle on a corrupt but well-connected business, government officials initially put him on the country's "Most Wanted" list. The reporter went into hiding, but his continued blogging turned him into a media celebrity, and the Chinese government eventually reversed itself, going after the corrupt businessmen instead (*Global Times*, 2010). And between 2006 and 2008, China vetted a proposed labor law that would give workers greatly expanded rights. While this law has been strongly opposed by foreign businesses in China, workers felt differently, and were encouraged to weigh in on a public website. The debate, which lasted for two years, elicited more than 200,000 comments in the first month alone; the law was revised three times before the final version was adopted (Wang et al., 2009).

Political and Social Change through Social Movements

Political life is by no means carried out only within the framework of political parties, voting, and representation in legislative and governmental bodies. When groups' objectives or ideals cannot be achieved within, or are blocked by, this framework (as under authoritarian regimes), political and social change may require other forms of political action. Social movements, which operate outside the established political system, have been an important source of social change throughout U.S. history. Terrorism can be seen as an extreme form of social movements—one that is willing to use violence, often directed against civilian populations, to achieve its goals.

WHY DO SOCIAL MOVEMENTS OCCUR?

Because mass social movements have been so important around the world over the past two centuries, many theories try to account for them. Some theories were formulated early in the history of the social sciences; the most important were those of Karl Marx. He intended his views not just to analyze the conditions of revolutionary change but actually to promote such change. Indeed, Marx's ideas had an immense practical effect on twentieth-century social change.

We examine four frameworks for the study of social movements, many of which were developed in the context of revolution: economic deprivation, resource mobilization, structural strain, and fields of action.

Economic Deprivation   Marx's view of social movements arises from his interpretation of human history (see Chapter 1). According to Marx (1983; 2008, orig. 1867; see also Marx and Engels, 2008, orig. 1848), the development of societies involves periodic class conflicts that lead to revolutionary change. Class struggles derive from the *contradictions*—irresolvable tensions—in societies. In any stable society, there is a balance among the economic structure, social relationships, and the political system. As the forces of production change, contradictions intensify, leading to open clashes between classes—and ultimately to revolution.

Marx applied this model to the past development of feudalism and to the future evolution of industrial capitalism. The feudal societies of Europe were based on peasant (serf) production under a class of wealthy lords. Economic changes gave rise to towns and cities, where trade and manufacturing developed. This new economic system, created *within* feudal society, threatened that society's very basis. Rather than being founded on the traditional lord-serf relationship, the emerging economic order encouraged industrialists to produce goods for sale in open markets. The contradictions between the old feudal economy and the emerging capitalist one eventually took the form of violent conflicts between the rising capitalist class and the feudal landowners. Revolution was the outcome, the most important example being the French Revolution of 1789. Through such revolutions and revolutionary changes occurring in other European societies, Marx argued, the capitalist class achieved dominance.

But industrial capitalism, according to Marx, sets up new contradictions, which in his view would lead to revolutions prompted by ideals of socialism or communism (Appelbaum, 1988). Industrial capitalism, an economic order based on the private pursuit of profit and on competition between firms to sell their products, requires individual capitalists to continually cut costs in order to remain competitive. This is accomplished in two principal ways: firms reduce wages at home, often by replacing workers with the latest "labor-saving" technologies, and they move their production to low-wage countries overseas. Both these strategies, while enabling businesses to survive, create a gulf between a rich minority that controls the industrial resources and an increasingly impoverished majority of waged workers. The resulting wealth disparity not only is seen as unjust by workers, fueling their revolutionary fervor, but also creates a fatal economic contradiction: Even though businesses produce an ever-increasing supply of goods, the growing masses of workers become too poor to buy them. This results, in the long run, in declining profits and economic stagnation. Capitalism, in other words, is the first economic system in history to suffer from producing too many goods rather than too few. The resulting economic crises, Marx predicted, would eventually lead the workers to overthrow the capitalist system and set up an alternative one in which they could better enjoy the fruits of their own labor. When a dominant class is particularly entrenched, Marx believed, violence is necessary to achieve the required transition. In other circumstances, this process might happen peacefully through parliamentary action; a revolution (in the sense just defined) would not be necessary.

Contrary to Marx's expectations, revolutions failed to occur in the advanced industrialized societies of the West. Why? One reason is that capitalism proved to be more resilient than Marx had predicted, finding ways to resolve the economic contradictions Marx believed would eventually lead to its collapse. The welfare state, enacted throughout Europe and North America in response to the Great Depression of the 1930s, was one solution: Raise taxes, especially upon wealthier individuals, to provide a "social safety net" for those who are less well off. Examples include government-funded retirement programs such as Social Security, unemployment compensation, welfare payments to the poor, and universal health care. Globalization provides another solution: While the loss of jobs to low-wage countries hurts many workers, it also results in ever-cheaper commodities, enabling people to buy products they otherwise might not be able to afford. A third solution is the credit economy: Even when their incomes are stagnant or declining, people are able to consume goods (at least for a while). Whether these approaches will suffice in the longer run remains a matter of debate.

Sociologist James Davies (1962), a critic of Marx, offered another explanation for the absence of revolutions in industrialized societies. Davies identified periods in history when people lived in dire poverty but did not rise up in protest. Constant poverty or deprivation does not make people into revolutionaries; rather, they usually endure such conditions with resignation or mute despair. Social protest, and ultimately revolution, is more likely when people's living conditions *improve*. Then their expectations also go up. If improvement in actual conditions subsequently slows down, propensities to revolt develop because rising expectations are frustrated.

Thus it is not absolute deprivation that leads to protest but **relative deprivation**— the discrepancy between people's actual lives and what they think could realistically be achieved. Davies's theory illuminates the connections between revolution and modern social and economic development. The ideals of progress, together with expectations of economic growth, induce rising hopes, which, if frustrated, spark protest. Such protest gains strength from the ideas of equality and democratic political participation, which were key not only in the American Revolution of 1776 and the Russian Revolution of 1917 but also in the revolutions of 1989 in Europe.

As Charles Tilly (1978) has pointed out, however, Davies's theory does not explain how and why different groups mobilize to seek revolutionary change. Protest might often occur against a backdrop of rising expectations; to understand how it becomes a mass social movement, we need to identify how groups collectively organize to make effective political challenges.

Resource Mobilization In *From Mobilization to Revolution*, Tilly (1978) analyzed processes of revolutionary change in the context of broader forms of protest and violence. He distinguished four main components of **collective action** taken to contest or overthrow an existing social order:

relative deprivation • Deprivation a person feels by comparing himself with a group.

collective action • Action undertaken in a relatively spontaneous way by a large number of people assembled together.

1. The *organization* of the group or groups involved. Protest movements are organized in many ways, varying from the spontaneous formation of crowds to tightly disciplined revolutionary groups. The Russian Revolution, for example, began as a small group of activists.

2. *Mobilization*, the ways in which a group acquires resources to make collective action possible. Such resources may include material goods, political support, and weaponry. Lenin acquired material and moral support from a sympathetic peasantry, together with many townspeople.

3. The *common interests* of those engaging in collective action, what they see as the gains and losses resulting from their policies. Common goals always underlie mobilization to collective action. Lenin built a broad coalition of support because many people had a common interest in removing the existing government.

4. *Opportunity*. Chance events may provide opportunities to pursue revolutionary aims. Numerous forms of collective action, including revolution, are influenced by such incidental events. Lenin's success depended on contingent factors, including success in battle. If Lenin had been killed, would there have been a revolution?

Collective action can be defined as people acting together in pursuit of shared interests—for example, gathering to demonstrate in support of their cause. Some of the people may be intensely involved; others may lend more passive or irregular support. Effective collective action, such as action that culminates in revolution, usually moves through all four stages.

Social movements, in Tilly's view, develop as a way of mobilizing group resources either when people have no institutionalized means of voicing their concerns or when the state authorities repress their needs. Although collective action at some point involves open confrontation with the political authorities, it is not likely to affect established patterns of power unless groups who are systematically organized support it.

Modes of collective action and protest vary with historical and cultural circumstances. In the United States today, for example, most people are familiar with mass marches, large assemblies, and street riots. Other types of collective protest (such as fights between villages, machine breaking, or lynching) have become less common or have disappeared. Protesters can also build on examples taken from other places; for instance, guerrilla movements proliferated in various parts of the world once disaffected groups learned how successful guerrilla actions could be against regular armies. And, as discussed earlier, new forms of social protest are now being accomplished through the Internet, as exemplified in the voter mobilization for the 2008 elections among liberals, and the Tea Party movement that began the following year among conservatives.

When and why does collective action become violent? After studying many incidents in western Europe since 1800, Tilly concluded that most collective violence develops from action that is not initially violent. Whether violence occurs depends not so much on the nature of the activity as on other factors—in particular, how the authorities respond. Consider the street demonstration: The vast majority of such demonstrations occur without damage to people or property. A few lead to violence and are then labeled as riots. Sometimes the authorities step in when violence has already occurred; more often, the historical record shows, the authorities are the originators of violence and, in fact, are responsible for most deaths and injuries. This is not surprising given their special access to arms and military discipline. The groups they attempt to control, conversely, do greater damage to objects and property.

Revolutionary movements, according to Tilly, are a type of collective action that occurs in situations of **multiple sovereignty**—when a government lacks full control over the areas it is supposed

multiple sovereignty • A situation in which there is no single sovereign power in a society.

to administer. Multiple sovereignty can arise as a result of external war, internal political clashes, or both. Whether a revolutionary takeover of power succeeds depends on how far the ruling authorities maintain control over the armed forces, the extent of conflicts within ruling groups, and the level of organization of the protest movements trying to seize power.

Tilly's concepts have wide application, and his use of them is sensitive to the variability of historical time and place. How social movements are organized, the resources they mobilize, the common interests of groups contending for power, and chance opportunities are all important facets of social transformation.

Tilly says little, however, about the circumstances underlying multiple sovereignty—a serious omission. According to Theda Skocpol (1979), Tilly assumes that social movements are guided by the deliberate pursuit of interests and that successful revolutionary change occurs when people realize these interests. Skocpol, in contrast, sees social movements as more ambiguous and indecisive in their objectives. Revolutions, she emphasizes, emerge largely as unintended consequences of more partial aims:

> In fact, in historical revolutions, differently situated and motivated groups have become participants in complex unfoldings of multiple conflicts. These conflicts have been powerfully shaped and limited by existing social, economic and international conditions. And they have proceeded in different ways depending upon how each revolutionary situation emerged in the first place. (Skocpol, 1979)

Skocpol's argument seems correct when we analyze the revolutionary changes that occurred in Eastern European societies in 1989, compared with earlier revolutionary episodes.

Structural Strain Neil Smelser (1963) distinguished six conditions underlying the origins of collective action in general and social movements in particular: structural conduciveness, structural strain in society, generalized beliefs, precipitating factors, effective leadership, and the nature of social control directed against the social movement.

1. *Structural conduciveness* refers to the social conditions promoting or inhibiting the formation of social movements. In Smelser's view, the sociopolitical system of the United States leaves open certain avenues of mobilization for protest because there is little or no state regulation in those areas. For example, there is no state-sponsored religion. People are free to exercise their religious beliefs. This creates a conducive environment in which religious movements might compete for individuals, so long as they do not transgress criminal or civil law.

2. Conducive conditions are not enough to bring a social movement into being. There must be **structural strain**—tensions (in Marx's terminology, contradictions) that produce conflicting interests. Uncertainties, anxieties, ambiguities, and direct clashes of goals are expressions of such strains. Sources of strain may be general or specific. Thus sustained inequalities between ethnic groups create overall tensions; these may become focused in specific conflicts when, say, blacks begin to move into a previously all-white area.

3. Social movements do not develop simply as responses to vaguely felt anxieties or hostilities. They are shaped by the influence of *generalized beliefs*—definite ideologies—that crystallize grievances and suggest courses of action to remedy those grievances. Revolutionary

structural strain • Tensions that produce conflicting interests within societies.

movements, for instance, are based on ideas about why injustice occurs and how it can be alleviated by political struggle.

4. *Precipitating factors* are events that trigger direct action by those involved in the movement. In 1955, when a black woman named Rosa Parks refused to give up her seat to a white man on a bus in Montgomery, Alabama, her action helped spark the civil rights movement (see Chapter 11).

5. The first four conditions combined might occasionally lead to street disturbances or outbreaks of violence, but such incidents do not promote the development of social movements unless a coordinated group mobilizes for action. *Leadership* and some means of *regular communication* among participants, together with funding and material resources, are necessary for a social movement to exist.

6. Finally, the manner in which a social movement develops is influenced by the *operation of social control*. The governing authorities may respond initially by intervening in the conditions of conduciveness that gave rise to the

Rosa Parks's refusal to give up her seat to a white man on a bus sparked the civil rights movement and is an example of a precipitating factor.

movement. For instance, steps might be taken to reduce the ethnic inequality that generates resentment and conflict. Other important aspects of social control concern the responses of the police or armed forces. A harsh response might spark further protest and help solidify the movement. Also, doubt and divisions within the police and military can be crucial in deciding the outcome of confrontations with revolutionary movements.

Smelser's model is useful for analyzing the sequences in the development of social movements and collective action in general. Each stage "adds value" to the overall outcome; also, each stage is a necessary condition for the next one. But Smelser's theory bears some criticism as well. For example, some social movements become strong without precipitating incidents. Conversely, a series of incidents might highlight the need to establish a movement to change the circumstances that gave rise to the incidents. Also, a movement itself might create strains, rather than develop in response to them. For example, the women's movement has sought to identify and combat gender inequalities where previously those had gone unquestioned. Smelser's theory treats social movements as responses to situations, rather than acknowledging that members might spontaneously organize to achieve desired social changes. In this respect, his ideas contrast with the approach developed by Alain Touraine.

Fields of Action Alain Touraine (1977, 1981) developed his analysis of social movements on the basis of four main ideas. The first, which he called **historicity**, explains why there are many more social movements in the modern world than in earlier times. In modern societies, individuals and groups know that social activism can achieve social goals and reshape society.

Second, Touraine focused on the *rational objectives* of social movements. Such movements are not irrational responses to social divisions or injustices; rather, they develop from specific views and rational strategies for overcoming injustices.

Third, Touraine saw a process of *interaction* in the shaping of social movements. Movements develop in deliberate antagonism with established organizations and sometimes with rival social movements. According to Touraine, other theories of social movements have not adequately considered how the objectives of a social movement are shaped by encounters with others holding divergent positions and by the ways in which they themselves influence their opponents' outlooks and action. For instance, the objectives and outlook of the women's movement were shaped in opposition to the male-dominated institutions the women's movement seeks to alter. The movement's goals and outlook have shifted in relation to its successes and failures and have influenced men's perspectives. These changed perspectives in turn have stimulated a reorientation in the women's movement.

Fourth, social movements and change occur in the context of "fields of action." A **field of action** comprises the connections between a social movement and the forces or influences against it. Mutual negotiation among antagonists in a field of action may produce the social changes sought by the movement as well as changes in the movement itself and in its antagonists. In either circumstance, the movement may evaporate or become institutionalized as a permanent organization. For example, labor union movements became formal organizations when they achieved the right to strike and to engage in types of bargaining acceptable to both workers and employers. These changes were forged out of earlier processes involving widespread violent confrontation on both sides. Where there are continuing sources of conflict (as in the relation between unions and employers), new movements still tend to emerge.

Touraine's analysis can also be applied to movements concerned with individual change. For instance, Alcoholics Anonymous is a movement based on medical findings about the harmful effects of alcohol on people's health and social activities. The movement has been shaped by its own opposition to advertising that encourages alcoholic drinking and by its attempt to confront the pressures faced by alcoholics in a society that readily tolerates drinking.

TECHNOLOGY AND SOCIAL MOVEMENTS

Recently, two of the most influential forces in late modern societies—information technology and social movements—have come together with astonishing results. Social movements worldwide can now join in huge regional and international networks, including nongovernmental organizations, religious and humanitarian groups, human rights associations, consumer protection advocates, environmental

historicity • The use of an understanding of history as a basis for trying to change history—that is, producing informed processes of social change.

field of action • The arena within which social movements interact with established organizations, the ideas and outlook of the members of both often becoming modified as a result.

activists, and others campaigning in the public interest. These electronic networks can respond immediately to events as they occur; gain access to and share sources of information; and put pressure on corporations, governments, and international bodies as part of their campaigning strategies. The enormous protests against the World Trade Organization (WTO) that took place in Seattle in 1999, Prague in 2000, Genoa in 2001, and Geneva in 2009, for example, were organized in large part through Internet-based networks. As we have seen, web-based organizations such as MoveOn.org have been influential in the anti–Iraq War movement, the election of Barack Obama in 2008, and the Arab Spring of 2011. The Internet has been at the forefront of these changes, although mobile phones, fax machines, and satellite broadcasting also hastened their evolution.

The ability to electronically coordinate international political campaigns is worrisome for governments and inspiring to participants in social movements. Indeed, the number of international social movements has grown steadily with the spread of the Internet. From global protests in favor of canceling developing world debt to the international campaign to ban land mines (which culminated in a Nobel Peace Prize), the Internet has united campaigners across national and cultural borders. Some observers argue that the information age is witnessing a migration of power away from nation-states and toward new nongovernmental alliances and coalitions.

Manuel Castells (1997) examines social movements that, although dissimilar, have all attracted international attention to their cause through the effective use of information technology. The Mexican Zapatista rebels, the American militia movement, the Japanese Aum Shinrikyo cult, and al Qaeda have all used media skills to spread their message of opposition to the effects of globalization and to express their anger at losing control over their own destinies.

According to Castells, each of these movements relies on information technologies as its organizational infrastructure. Without the Internet, for example, the Zapatista rebels would have remained an isolated guerrilla movement in southern Mexico. Instead, within hours of their armed uprising in January 1994, local, national, and international support groups had emerged online to promote the rebels' cause and to condemn the Mexican government's brutal repression of the rebellion. The Zapatistas used telecommunications, videos, and media interviews to voice their objections to trade policies, such as the North American Free Trade Agreement (NAFTA), that further exclude impoverished Indians of the Oaxaca and Chiapas areas from the benefits of globalization. With their cause highlighted in the online networks of social campaigners, the Zapatistas managed to force negotiations with the Mexican government and draw international attention to the harmful effects of free trade on indigenous populations.

GLOBALIZATION AND SOCIAL MOVEMENTS

Social movements vary widely. Some have only a few dozen members; others include thousands or millions of people. Although some social movements operate within the law, others are illegal or underground groups. Protest movements operate near the margins of what is legally permissible.

Social movements often seek change on a public issue, such as expanding civil rights for a segment of the population. In response, counter movements sometimes arise in defense of the status quo. The campaign for women's right to abortion, for example, has been challenged by anti-abortion ("pro-life") activists, who believe that abortion should be illegal.

Often, laws or policies are altered as a result of the action of social movements. These changes can have far-ranging effects. For example, it used to be illegal for workers' groups to call their members out on strike, and striking was punished with varying degrees of severity in different countries. Eventually, however, the laws were amended, making the strike a permissible tactic of industrial conflict.

The last few decades have seen an explosion of social movements around the globe. These movements—ranging from the civil rights and feminist movements of the 1960s and '70s, respectively, to the antinuclear and ecological movements of the 1980s, to the gay rights campaign of the 1990s—are called **new social movements**. They are often concerned with the quality of private life as much as with political and economic issues, calling for changes in the way people think and act.

What makes new social movements "new" is that, unlike conventional social movements, they are not based on single-issue objectives related to the distribution of economic resources or power. Rather, they seek collective identities based on entire lifestyles, often calling for sweeping cultural changes. New social movements have emerged around issues such as ecology, peace, gender and sexual identity, gay and lesbian rights, women's rights, alternative medicine, and opposition to globalization.

Because new social movements involve new collective identities, they can provide a strong incentive for action. Participation is viewed as a moral obligation (and even a pleasure) rather than a calculated effort to achieve some specific goal. Moreover, the forms of protest chosen by new social movements constitute an "expressive logic" whereby participants make a statement about who they are: Protest is an end in itself, a way of affirming one's identity as well as a means of achieving concrete objectives (Polletta and Jasper, 2001).

The rise of new social movements is a reflection of the changing risks facing human societies. Traditional political institutions are increasingly unable to cope with the challenges before them, such as threats to the natural environment, the potential dangers of nuclear energy and genetically modified organisms, and the powerful effects of information technology. Because existing democratic political institutions cannot fix these problems, they go ignored or avoided until a full-blown crisis occurs.

As a cumulative effect of these new challenges and risks, people feel less secure and more isolated—a combination that leads to a sense of powerlessness. By contrast, corporations, governments, and the media appear to be dominating more aspects of people's lives, heightening the sensation of a runaway world. There is a growing sense that globalization presents ever-greater risks to citizens' lives.

Although faith in traditional politics seems to be waning, the growth of new social movements is evidence that citizens in late modern societies are not apathetic or uninterested in politics. Rather, there is a belief that direct action and participation are more useful than reliance on politicians and political systems. More than ever before, people are supporting social movements as a way of putting complex moral issues at the center of social life. In this respect, new social movements are helping revitalize civic culture and **civil society**—the sphere between the state and the marketplace occupied by family, community associations, and other noneconomic institutions.

new social movements • A set of social movements that have arisen in Western societies since the 1960s in response to the changing risks facing human societies. New social movements such as feminism, environmentalism, the antinuclear movement, opposition to genetically modified food, and the antiglobalization movement differ from earlier social movements in that they are single-issue campaigns oriented to nonmaterial ends and draw support from across class lines.

civil society • The realm of activity that lies between the state and the market, including the family, schools, community associations, and noneconomic institutions. Civil society, or civic culture, is essential to vibrant democratic societies.

NATIONALIST MOVEMENTS

Some of the most important social movements today are nationalist movements. Although the countries of the world have become more interdependent, especially since the 1970s, this interdependence has not spelled the end of nationalism. It may even have helped intensify it. Recent thinkers have contrasting ideas about why this is so. There are also disagreements about the stage of history at which nationalism, the nation, and the nation-state came into being.

Nationalism and Modern Society According to one of the best-known current scholars of nationalism, Anthony Smith (1988), nations have direct lines of continuity with earlier ethnic communities, groups that share ideas of common ancestry, a common cultural identity, and a link with a specific homeland. Many nations, Smith points out, have premodern continuities, and in earlier times there were ethnic communities resembling nations. Jews, for example, formed a distinct ethnic community that has lasted more than 2,000 years. At certain periods, Jews clustered in communities that had some of the characteristics of nations. But only after World War II were all these elements brought together in the nation-state of Israel. Like most other nation-states, Israel was not formed from a single ethnic community. The Palestinian minority in Israel traces its origins to a different ethnic background and claims that the creation of the Israeli state has displaced the Palestinians from their ancient homelands—hence their persistent tensions with Jews in Israel, the tensions between Israel and most surrounding Arab states, and the violence between Palestinians and Israelis that has escalated in the twenty-first century.

Different nations have followed divergent patterns of development in relation to ethnic communities. In some, including most of the nations of western Europe, a single ethnic community expanded and pushed out earlier rivals. Thus, in France in the seventeenth century, several other languages were spoken and different ethnic histories were linked to them. As French became the dominant language, most of these rivals disappeared. Yet remnants persist in a few areas. One is in the Basque country overlapping the French and Spanish frontiers. The Basque language is different from either French or Spanish, and the Basques claim a separate cultural history. Some Basques want their own nation-state. Although there has been nothing like the level of violence seen in other areas—such as East Timor, or Chechnya in southern Russia—separatist groups in the Basque country have sporadically used bombing campaigns to further their goal of independence.

Nations without States The persistence of well-defined ethnic communities within established nations leads to the phenomenon of **nations without states**. These situations reflect many essential characteristics of a nation, but those who make up the nation lack an independent political community. Separatist movements are driven by the desire to establish an autonomous, self-governing state.

Several types of nations without states can be recognized, depending on the relationship between the ethnic community and the nation-state in which it exists (Guibernau, 1999):

- In some situations, a nation-state may accept the cultural differences among its minorities and allow them a certain amount of active development. Thus in Great Britain, Scotland and Wales are recognized as having histories and cultural features partly divergent from the rest

> **nations without states** • Instances in which the members of a nation lack political sovereignty over the area they claim as their own.

of the United Kingdom, and to some extent they have their own institutions. The majority of Scots, for instance, are Presbyterians, and Scotland has long had a separate educational system from that of England and Wales. Scotland and Wales achieved further autonomy within the United Kingdom with the creation of a Scottish Parliament and a Welsh Assembly in 1999.

Some nations without states have a higher degree of autonomy. In Quebec (the French-speaking province of Canada) and Flanders (the Dutch-speaking area in western Belgium), regional political bodies have the power to make major decisions without being fully independent. They also contain nationalist movements agitating for complete independence.

- Some nations completely lack recognition from the state that contains them. In such cases, the larger nation-state uses force to deny recognition to the minority. The Palestinians are an example. Others include the Tibetans in China, and the Kurds, whose homeland overlaps parts of Iran, Iraq, Syria, and Turkey.

Nations and Nationalism in Developing Countries In most of the developing world, the course followed by nationalism, the nation, and the nation-state has been different from that of industrial societies. Most less-developed countries were once colonized by Europeans and achieved independence in the second half of the twentieth century. In many of these countries, boundaries between colonial administrations that were set arbitrarily in Europe ignored economic, cultural, or ethnic divisions among the population being colonized. As a consequence, most colonized areas contained a mosaic of ethnic communities and other groups.

Given this background, when former colonies achieved independence it was hard to create a sense of nationhood. Although nationalism played a great part in securing the independence of colonized areas, it was confined to small groups of activists and did not reflect the majority of the population. Even today, many postcolonial states are continually threatened by internal rivalries and competing claims to political authority.

The continent that was most completely colonized was Africa. Nationalist movements promoting independence in Africa following World War II sought to free the colonized areas from European domination. Once this had been achieved, the new leaders faced enormous problems trying to create national unity. Many of the leaders in the 1950s and 1960s had been educated in Europe or the United States, and there was a vast gulf between them and their citizens, most of whom were illiterate, poor, and unfamiliar with the rights and obligations of democracy. Under colonialism, some ethnic groups had prospered more than others; these groups had different interests and goals, and legitimately saw each other as enemies.

Civil wars broke out in several postcolonial states in Africa, such as Nigeria, Sudan, and Zaire, while ethnic rivalries and antagonisms characterized many others in both Africa and Asia. In Sudan, about 40 percent of the population spoke Arabic and claimed Arabic ethnic origins. Elsewhere in the country, particularly in the south, Arabic was barely spoken at all. Once the nationalists took power, they set up a program for national integration, with Arabic as the national language. The attempt was only partly successful, and the stresses it produced are still visible. In January 2011 a referendum was held in South Sudan, with nearly 100 percent of those voting supporting independence. South Sudan became an independent country as a result, although conflicts and open fighting between the two countries remain.

The ongoing civil wars in Sudan have displaced more than 4 million people. Some have fled to southern cities, such as Juba; others have trekked as far north as Khartoum and even into Egypt, Ethiopia, Kenya, Uganda, and other neighboring countries. These refugees are unable to grow food or earn money to feed themselves, and malnutrition and starvation are widespread. Lack of investment has also created what international humanitarian organizations call a "lost generation," whose members lack educational opportunities and access to basic health care services and who have few prospects for employment in the small and weak economies of the south and the north.

In summary, most states in the developing world underwent different processes of nation formation from those in the industrialized world. States were imposed externally on areas that often had no prior cultural or ethnic unity, leading to problems that are very difficult to overcome. Modern nations have arisen most effectively either in areas that were never fully colonized or where there was already much cultural unity—such as Japan, Korea, and Thailand.

The Nation-State, National Identity, and Globalization

In some parts of Africa, nations and nation-states are not yet fully formed. Yet in other areas of the world, some writers are speaking of the "end of the nation-state" in the face of globalization. According to Japanese writer Kenichi Ohmae (1995), we live in a borderless world in which national identity is weakening.

How valid is this point of view? All states are certainly affected by globalizing processes. The very rise of "nations without states" is probably bound up with globalization. As globalization progresses, people often revive local identities to achieve security in the rapidly changing world. Nations have less economic power of their own than they used to have, as a result of the spreading global marketplace.

Yet it wouldn't be accurate to say that we are witnessing the end of the nation-state. In some ways the opposite is the case. Today the nation-state has become a universal political form. Until quite recently it still had rivals; after all, for most of the twentieth century, colonized areas and empires existed alongside nation-states. It is arguable that the last empire disappeared only in 1990, with the collapse of Soviet communism. The satellite states constituting the Soviet Union's former empire in Eastern Europe now have become independent nation-states, as have many areas inside the former Soviet Union itself. There are far more sovereign nations today than there were 25 years ago.

A more accurate way of framing the current situation would be to think of two powerful forces at play today—the international world of nation-states and the transnational forces of globalization that are challenging the nation-state. Nation-states remain important in the world today; they alone have governments and legal structures, along with the means to enforce laws—both internally (through police powers) and externally (through military means). Nation-states are the recognized actors in international organizations such as the United Nations and the World Trade Organization; they form economic and military alliances with one another, and all too often wage wars to achieve their objectives. Yet the economic, political, environmental, and cultural power of nation-states is everywhere being challenged by globalizing forces that show little regard for national borders. Trillions of dollars cross borders with the click of a mouse, while products that are designed in one country give jobs to workers half a world away. As we discuss in the next section, military force seems to be of limited value against stateless enemies such as al Qaeda, which operates in many countries yet pledges allegiance to none. Global warming and environmental degradation threaten everyone on the planet, regardless of which country is the immediate source of the problem. YouTube, the Internet, and popular culture generally flow freely around the world, despite the efforts of authoritarian regimes to control them.

Whether the outcome of this titanic conflict between nation-states and globalization will ultimately favor one or the other is uncertain—one reason globalization has become such a fascinating topic for sociologists and other social scientists to study.

④ UNANSWERED QUESTIONS

Among the many unanswered questions having to do with politics and social movements, in this final section we focus on four. Three have to do with some challenges faced by democracies in the United States and elsewhere: low voter turnout, the impact of the Internet, and the future of democracy. We also look at questions surrounding terrorism, and the appropriate response of governments.

Why Is Voter Turnout So Low in the United States?

Since the early 1960s, voter turnout in the United States has generally decreased, although recent elections suggest a possible reversal of that trend. In the 1960 presidential election, 64 percent of the eligible voting age population turned out to vote; by the year 2000, that figure had dropped to 56 percent. In 2004 and 2008, however, turnout grew once again, to roughly 61 percent. The reasons for this increase are not clear, although higher-than-usual youth turnouts, mobilized by Rock the Vote and other organizations, undoubtedly account for part. The turnout for midterm congressional elections is usually only around 40 percent (Kuhn, 2008; McDonald and Popkin, 2001; U.S. Bureau of the Census, 2010e). Furthermore, there are significant differences in turnout by race and ethnicity, age, educational attainment, and income. Turnout is highest among whites and lowest among Hispanics, with blacks and Asian Americans in between. Generally, turnout increases with age: Only a little more than a third of all voters age 18–24 voted for president in 2000, compared with nearly three-quarters of voters in their sixties. However, in the

Residents of Miami line up for early voting before the 2012 presidential election. Why have some states, like Florida, adopted early voting policies?

2012 presidential election, the number of young voters swelled to about 23 million (49 percent of all eligible voters under 30) because of an effective voter mobilization campaign (Center for Information and Research on Civic Learning and Engagement [CIRCLE], 2012). Education also influences voting behavior: 38 percent of persons who lacked a high school diploma voted in 2012, compared with 75 percent of those with bachelor's degrees. Turnout was only about less than half among voters whose family income was less than $20,000, rising to over 70 percent among voters whose family income was over $75,000 (U.S. Bureau of the Census, 2012q).

Voter turnout in the United States is among the world's lowest. Many studies have found that countries with high rates of literacy, high average incomes, and well-established political freedoms and civil liberties have high voter turnouts (International Institute for Democracy and Electoral Assistance [IIDEA], 2004). Even though the United States ranks high on all these measures, it fails to motivate people to vote. Sweden's International Institute for Democracy and Electoral Assistance tracked voter turnout in all countries holding national elections during the period 1945–2002. Voter turnout in the United States averaged only 48 percent overall, earning it 138th place (out of 169 countries). In comparison, voter turnout in Europe averaged 74 percent; Asia, 70 percent; South America, 62 percent; Mexico, Central America, and the Caribbean, 60 percent; and Africa, 55 percent (Pintor and Gratschew, 2002).

Why is voter turnout so low in the United States? People give many reasons for not voting. In one study of the 2000 presidential election, when turnout was relatively low, two out of five nonvoters felt that voting was not worth the effort: 21 percent reported they were "too busy," while another 20 percent stated they either didn't like the candidates or simply weren't interested. Many of the remaining nonvoters cited an illness or other emergency, lack of transportation or some other inconvenience, bad weather, being out of town, or forgetfulness. Only 7 percent cited problems in registering to vote, although this is likely a greater difficulty for lower-income voters (National Election Studies, 2003). Clearly, voting is not a high priority among many Americans. Whereas throughout Europe compulsory registration is common and registration is easy, in the United States voters must register well in advance of elections; many fail to do so and are thus disqualified from voting. Thirty-three countries now practice compulsory voting. Even where enforcement is weak or nonexistent, voter turnout is higher when voting is required by law (Pintor and Gratschew, 2002).

Another reason may be that because winner-take-all elections discourage the formation of third parties, voters may feel a lack of viable choices. A staunch environmentalist may see no point in voting if the Green Party candidate has no chance of winning a seat in Congress; an antigovernment voter may draw the same conclusion in regard to the Libertarian Party's chances. In many countries (including most European countries), some system of proportional representation is practiced, under which parties receive seats in proportion to the vote they get in electoral districts. Thus, for example, if a district has 10 seats in Parliament, and the Conservative Party gets 30 percent of the vote, that district would send three Conservative representatives to Parliament. Under this system, even small parties can often muster sufficient support to elect one or two representatives. When voters have a wider range of choices, they are more likely to vote.

Finally, the range of elections for offices at all levels—including sheriffs, judges, city treasurers, and many other posts—is much more extensive in the United States than in other Western societies. Americans are entitled to do about three or four times as much electing as citizens elsewhere. Low voter turnout thus must be balanced against the wider extent of voter choice.

Does the Internet Promote Democracy?

The Internet is a potentially democratizing force, although it can also have the opposite effect—for example, when governments control what is acceptable on the Internet, or when extremists use their websites to mobilize support for acts of violence. The Internet fosters social networking: It allows like-minded people to find one another in cyberspace. While this may contribute to increased dialogue and debate on political issues, it often has the opposite effect: It can create an "echo chamber" in which people seek out only information that confirms and therefore reinforces their existing beliefs or prejudices (Jameson and Cappella, 2009; Wallsten, 2005).

Governments may perceive the spread of the Internet as a threat because of the potential of online activity to subvert state authority. Although the Internet has existed more or less freely in most countries, some governments are curbing its use. In Iran, the government responded to the Green Movement mass mobilizations during the 2009 elections by shutting down texting and Gmail, as well as violently suppressing the protests. Malaysian authorities have demanded that cyber cafés keep lists of all individuals who use their computers. In Russia, local Internet service providers (ISPs) must join an electronic monitoring scheme overseen by the federal security service. In the United States, when 90,000 intelligence documents about the war in Afghanistan were posted on the WikiLeaks website in July 2010, the U.S. government obtained court orders to seize the documents, arguing that their publication compromised the war efforts and endangered soldiers and their Afghan collaborators. As of August 2010, according to Reporters Without Borders (2010), 116 "cyberdissidents" were being held around the world for their Internet activities, two-thirds of them in China.

China has seen the number of Internet users increase 18-fold in ten years, reaching 538 million in 2012, nearly a third of the country's population (Russell, 2012). The Chinese Communist leadership views the Internet as threatening state security, claiming that sensitive information on the country's military and technological capacities has been published on Chinese websites. The government is also concerned that the Internet can be used to enable political opposition groups to coordinate their activities. In response to such concerns, the government has banned the publication of "state secrets" on the Internet, has blocked direct and indirect links between domestic Chinese and foreign websites, and has initiated a system of Web censors to monitor the context of news and information exchanged on the Internet. The government also requires ISPs to report detailed information on users and Internet activities, censoring all "subversive" content—which includes information on HIV/AIDS and stories about democracy and Tibet.

Foreign firms are not immune from government control in China. The U.S. companies that provide the software in China facilitate much of the filtering just discussed. Google, in order to operate in China, had to agree to governmental censorship, which it permitted from 2006 to 2010. When its computers were hacked by Chinese government authorities in 2010, however, Google had had enough, and announced it would avoid censorship by redirecting search queries to Google Hong Kong, which enjoys greater freedom. China responded by briefly banning all Google searches. While the ban was eventually lifted, Google users are now referred to the company's Hong Kong website. At the same time, China's homegrown competitor to Google, Baidu, has thrived, in part because it is far less concerned about government censorship. Or, to take another example, prior to the 2008 Olympics in Beijing, the Chinese government announced it would not allow journalists access to banned websites such as Amnesty International, Human Rights Watch, or sites focusing on Tibet. But after an outcry from foreign correspondents (thousands of whom were in Beijing to cover the games), the government backed down and allowed unrestricted Internet access. As the example of China illustrates, the degree to which the Internet promotes democratization remains an open question: While it makes possible a great degree of governmental control, it also creates spaces for resistance and protest, which even tight government control often cannot afford to ignore.

The U.S. government expanded its Internet surveillance activities after the attacks of September 11, 2001. The FBI immediately requested all major ISPs to install Carnivore software, which would allow the ISPs to record, filter, and store e-mails on the basis of specific words. Internet surveillance was further strengthened by the USA Patriot Act, enacted in October 2001, which expanded the types of Internet activity records that could be obtained without the consent of a judge. The Pentagon's Information Awareness Office is developing software to track Internet use, including credit card and airline ticket purchases, while the FBI is reportedly working on "magic lantern" software, which can secretly record the keystrokes of an Internet user, enabling the agency to overcome surveillance barriers posed by encryption software (Hentoff, 2002). The disclosure that the U.S. government has conducted secret monitoring of telephone conversations, e-mail, and Internet communication between U.S. citizens and suspected foreign terrorists has raised the question of whether such spying (without a warrant) violates U.S. laws and even the Constitution (Risen and Lichtblau, 2005).

Is Democracy in Trouble?

Democracy almost everywhere is in some peril. This is not only because it is hard to set up a stable democratic order in places such as Russia and other formerly Communist societies. Democracy is in trouble even in its countries of origin—such as the United States. For example, as just noted, voter turnout in presidential and other elections has generally declined. In surveys, many people say they don't trust politicians.

In 1964, confidence in government was fairly high: Nearly four out of five people answered "most of the time" or "just about always" when asked, "How much of the time do you trust the government in Washington to do the right thing?" This level of confidence dropped steadily for the following 20 years, rose somewhat in the 1980s, then dropped to a low of one in five in 1994. Following the terrorist attacks of September 11, 2001, a solid majority (55 percent) of Americans reported that they trusted the government "most of the time" or "just about always." Recently, however, trust in the government has declined as a result of disillusionment over the wars in Iraq and Afghanistan, the economic collapse of 2008, the tepid recovery that followed, and government paralysis in Washington. In 2010, just 22 percent of Americans said they could trust the government in Washington almost always or most of the time (Pew Research Center for the People and the Press, 2010b); by 2011 that number had fallen even further, to 14 percent (Pew Research Center for the People and the Press, 2011a). Of those expressing trust in government, most vote in presidential elections; of those who lack trust, most do not vote. Today, with economic growth stagnant, historically high levels of unemployment in the United States, and concerns over congressional deadlock, anger and frustration are often directed at government (Pew Research Center for the People and the Press, 2011b).

Among the major industrial democracies, the United States spends the lowest proportion of its total economy on government at the federal, state, and local levels: roughly one-third of its gross domestic product (GDP). In comparison, Sweden devotes more than half its GDP to government spending; the European Union, 44 percent; and all industrial countries combined, 38 percent. Americans have lower taxes than other industrial democracies, but they also receive lower levels of support for health care, housing, education, unemployment compensation, and social services in general. This may be another reason for low levels of confidence in government and poor voter turnout: Americans expect less, and get less, from their government. Finally, for the past quarter century there has been a steady stream of well-financed (and highly effective) criticism from conservative think tanks, news media, and politicians who share the belief that government is part of the problem, rather than part of the solution. This has been highly effective in changing the national discourse on the role of government (Fried and Harris, 2001; Hibbing and Theiss-Morse, 2001).

Why are so many people dissatisfied with the very political system that seems to be sweeping across the world? The answers may be bound up with the very factors that help spread democracy—the effect of capitalism and the globalizing of social life. For instance, while capitalist economies generate more wealth than any other type of economic system, the wealth is unevenly distributed (see Chapter 8). And economic inequalities influence who votes, joins parties, and gets elected. Wealthy individuals and corporations back interest groups that lobby elected officials to support their aims when deciding on legislation. Not being subject to election, interest groups are not accountable to the majority of the electorate (Lessig, 2011).

Economic inequalities also create an underclass of people living in poverty—about 20 percent of the population of liberal democracies. Most Western liberal democracies establish policies to reduce poverty levels, but they vary in spending to achieve that aim. Societies that implement a complex welfare system require a higher level of taxation and a larger nonelected government bureaucracy. The question arises as to how much of an economic and political price a society is willing to pay to reduce poverty, who pays for it, and what the effect is of this cost.

Two theories have been put forward to account for this changing political situation. One is the theory of **state overload** (Britain, 1975; Nordhaus, 1975). In this view, governments in the twentieth century acquired more responsibilities than they could fund and manage, from establishing public ownership of industries, utilities, and transportation to creating extensive welfare programs. One reason is that political parties tried to woo voters by promising too many benefits and services. Governments were unable to deliver because state expenditures rose beyond the resources provided by tax revenues: State responsibilities were overloaded (Etzioni-Halévy, 1985). Consequently, voters have become skeptical about claims made by governments and political parties. For example, the Democratic Party in the United States and leftist parties elsewhere have lost some of their traditional support from lower-class groups, who need the promised (but undelivered) services. The rise of new right politics reflects an attempt to cope with this situation by trimming back the state and encouraging private enterprise.

state overload • A theory that modern states face major difficulties as a result of being overburdened with complex administrative decisions.

legitimation crisis • The failure of a political order to generate a sufficient level of commitment and involvement on the part of its citizens to be able to govern properly.

A rival theory, developed by Jürgen Habermas (1975), is that of **legitimation crisis** (Offe, 1984, 1985). In this theory, modern governments lack the legitimacy to carry out tasks they are required to undertake, such as providing highways, public housing, and health care. People who feel that they pay most for these services through higher taxes, the more affluent, may believe that they gain the least from them. On the one hand, governments must take more responsibility for providing health care for those who cannot afford it; on the other, taxpayers either resist increases in taxation or want taxes reduced. Governments cannot cope with the contradictory demands of lower taxes and more responsibilities, leading to decreased public support and general disillusionment about government's capabilities. According to Habermas, legitimation crises could probably be overcome if the electorate were persuaded to accept high taxation in return for a wide range of government services.

As sociologist Daniel Bell (1976) observed, national government is too small to address the big questions, such as the influence of global economic competition or the destruction of the world's environment, but it has become too big to address the small questions, such as issues affecting cities or regions. Governments have little power, for instance, over giant business corporations, the main actors within the global economy. A U.S. corporation may shut down its production plants in America and set up a new factory in Mexico instead, to lower costs and compete with other corporations. The result is that thousands of American workers lose their jobs and expect the government to do something, but national governments cannot control processes bound up with the world economy. All a government can do is soften the blow—for example, by providing unemployment benefits or job retraining.

At the same time that governments have shrunk in relation to global issues, they have become more remote from the lives of most citizens. Many Americans resent that "power brokers" in Washington—party officials, interest groups, lobbyists, and bureaucratic officials—make decisions affecting their lives. They also believe that government is unable to address important local issues, such as crime and homelessness. Thus Americans' faith in government has dropped substantially, which affects Americans' willingness to participate in the political process.

CONCEPT CHECKS

1. What are the reasons that voter turnout is so low? How could it be improved?
2. How might the Internet be used to stifle movements for democracy?

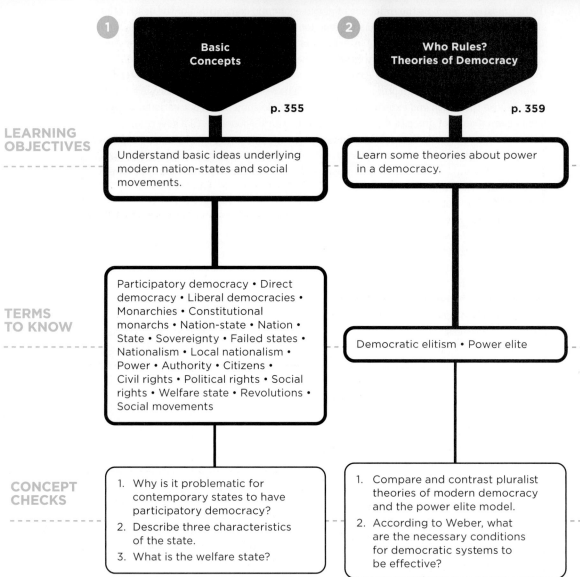

1 **Basic Concepts**

p. 355

2 **Who Rules? Theories of Democracy**

p. 359

LEARNING OBJECTIVES

Understand basic ideas underlying modern nation-states and social movements.

Learn some theories about power in a democracy.

TERMS TO KNOW

Participatory democracy • Direct democracy • Liberal democracies • Monarchies • Constitutional monarchs • Nation-state • Nation • State • Sovereignty • Failed states • Nationalism • Local nationalism • Power • Authority • Citizens • Civil rights • Political rights • Social rights • Welfare state • Revolutions • Social movements

Democratic elitism • Power elite

CONCEPT CHECKS

1. Why is it problematic for contemporary states to have participatory democracy?
2. Describe three characteristics of the state.
3. What is the welfare state?

1. Compare and contrast pluralist theories of modern democracy and the power elite model.
2. According to Weber, what are the necessary conditions for democratic systems to be effective?

Exercises: Thinking Sociologically

1. Discuss the differences between the pluralistic and the power elite theories of democratic political processes. Which theory do you find most appropriate to describe U.S. politics in recent years?

2. Your textbook offers a variety of explanations on the formation of social movements. Briefly review the predisposing conditions for social movements, and then discuss their relevance to the rise of nationalist movements in the developing world.

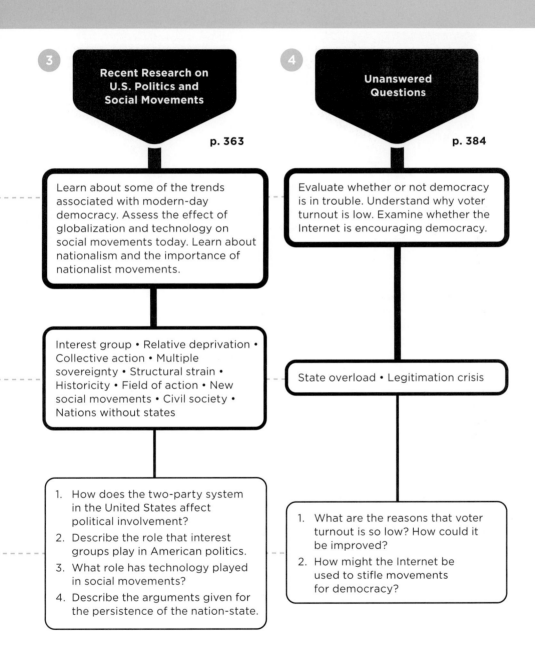

3

Recent Research on U.S. Politics and Social Movements

p. 363

Learn about some of the trends associated with modern-day democracy. Assess the effect of globalization and technology on social movements today. Learn about nationalism and the importance of nationalist movements.

Interest group • Relative deprivation • Collective action • Multiple sovereignty • Structural strain • Historicity • Field of action • New social movements • Civil society • Nations without states

1. How does the two-party system in the United States affect political involvement?
2. Describe the role that interest groups play in American politics.
3. What role has technology played in social movements?
4. Describe the arguments given for the persistence of the nation-state.

4

Unanswered Questions

p. 384

Evaluate whether or not democracy is in trouble. Understand why voter turnout is low. Examine whether the Internet is encouraging democracy.

State overload • Legitimation crisis

1. What are the reasons that voter turnout is so low? How could it be improved?
2. How might the Internet be used to stifle movements for democracy?

Part IV

SOCIAL INSTITUTIONS

Social institutions are the cement of social life. They are the basic living arrangements that human beings work out with one another, by means of which continuity is achieved across the generations.

We begin in Chapter 14 with work and economic life. Although the nature of work varies widely both within and across societies, work is one of the most pervasively important of all human pursuits.

In Chapter 15, we look at the institutions of kinship, marriage, and the family. Although the social obligations associated with kinship vary depending on the type of society, the family is everywhere the context within which the young are provided with care and protection. Marriage is more or less universally connected to the family because it is a means of establishing new kin connections and forming a household in which children are brought up. In traditional cultures, much of the direct learning a child receives occurs within the family context. In modern societies, children spend many years of their lives in special places of instruction outside the family—schools and colleges. They also are constantly fed images and information from the mass media. Chapter 16 looks at the ways in which formal education is organized, concentrating particularly on how the educational system relates to the mass media.

The subject of Chapter 17 is religion. Although religious beliefs and practices are found in all cultures, the changes affecting religion in modern societies have been particularly acute. We analyze the nature of these changes, considering in what ways traditional types of religion still maintain their influence.

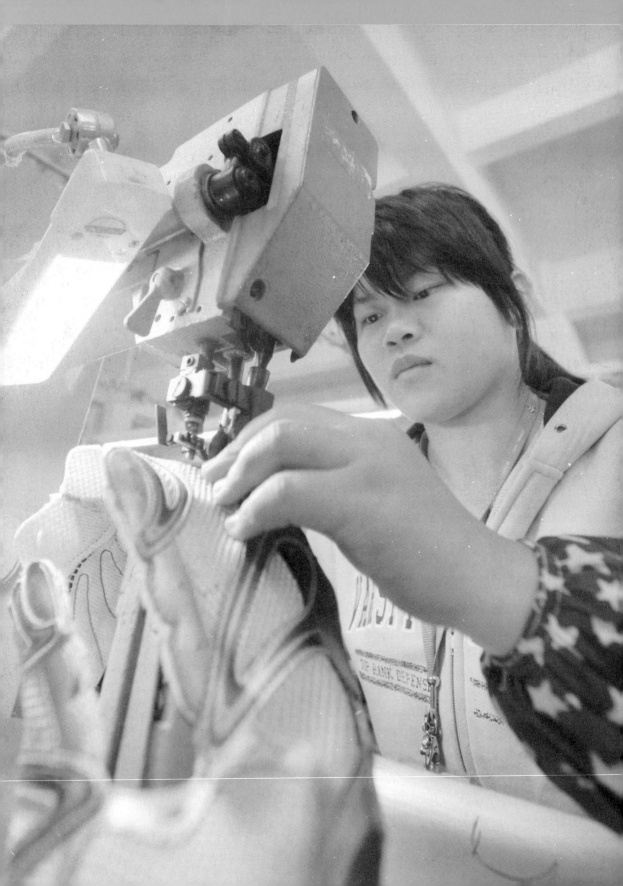

Work and Economic Life

14

Which company makes your favorite athletic shoe?

- **a** Nike
- **b** Reebok
- **c** Asics
- **d** Adidas
- **e** Puma
- **f** New Balance
- **g** Converse
- **h** Skechers
- **i** Timberland
- **j** Rockport
- **k** FILA
- **l** Pou Chen

Turn the page for the correct answer.

Y ou may suspect that this is a trick question—but it isn't! Nor is it an infomercial for leading athletic shoe brands. Whatever your preferred brand, one thing is certain: Your favorite brand did not actually make the shoe you are wearing. Whether you buy a branded athletic shoe for running, walking, cycling, or whether you prefer basketball, tennis, or soccer, your favorite brand's job was to design the shoe, launch an effective marketing campaign, and eventually convince you—and millions of others—that this particular shoe, in this particular style, and most likely at this (often seemingly outrageous) price, is the key to your athletic success, whether you are a weekend walker or a national track star.

The company that actually made your favorite athletic shoe has a one-in-six chance of bearing a name that you most likely have never heard of: Yue Yuen, the Hong Kong subsidiary of a Taiwanese firm, Pou Chen, which specializes in footwear manufacture. Pou Chen is a transnational corporation and the largest manufacturer of branded athletic footwear in the world. Its nearly 300,000 workers in China, Vietnam, and Indonesia turn out 250 million pairs of shoes every year, accounting for one out of every six branded athletic shoes sold in the world today. Its sprawling factory in Dongguan, in southern China, employs 110,000 workers to produce nearly a million pairs of athletic shoes a month for Nike, Adidas, Reebok, and practically every other major brand. Working with its many brands, it engages in research to develop the best materials that can be used in its products; has developed its own advanced manufacturing technology; and is engaged in high-tech logistics, coordinating its global supply chain to ensure that all the components required in shoe manufacture are acquired in a timely fashion (Appelbaum and Lichtenstein, 2006; Yue Yuen, 2007).

Pou Chen is an example of an important development in the global economy, one that is reshaping the nature of work throughout the world. Nations once referred to as "developing countries" are playing an increasingly important role as suppliers and assemblers of the products consumed throughout the world. Design and marketing may remain

LEARNING OBJECTIVES

1 BASIC CONCEPTS

Assess the social significance of work and the sociological ramifications of paid and unpaid work.

2 THEORIES OF WORK AND ECONOMIC LIFE

Understand that modern economies are based on the division of labor and economic interdependence. Learn Marx's theory of alienation.

3 CURRENT RESEARCH ON WORK AND ECONOMIC LIFE

See the importance of the rise of large corporations; consider particularly the global effect of transnational corporations.

4 UNANSWERED QUESTIONS

Learn about the effect of global economic competition on employment. Consider how work will change over the coming years.

centered in the United States, Europe, Japan, and a few other advanced economies, but the actual goods are produced by independently owned factories throughout the world. Giant transnational corporations, owned by individuals from China, Hong Kong, South Korea, and Taiwan, operate apparel, electronic assembly, and other consumer goods factories around the world. When you buy a pair of jeans, whatever its brand might be, it may well have been made in Mexico, Nicaragua, or the African country of Lesotho, in a factory owned by the Nien Hsing, a Taiwanese textile firm that makes clothing for such well-known brands and retailers as Target, C&Y Sportswear, Kohl's, GAP, and Levi's (Nien Hsing, 2012). The sweatshirt or hoodie sold in your campus bookstore—the one that bears your college's logo or name—was certainly not made by your college; nor was it made by Nike, Russell Athletic, or Knights Apparel, three of the leading brands that design products specifically for the college market. It, too, was made in a factory overseas, anywhere from the Caribbean to China.

How does this affect work and economic life? Many manufacturing jobs are moving to low-wage countries. What kinds of jobs are replacing them back home? What does it mean for the nature of work when brands such as Nike or retailers such as Walmart rely on foreign firms halfway around the world to actually manufacture the products that bear their names or are sold on their shelves?

Work and economic life are central to our daily lives. In this chapter we will examine their changing nature, before turning to some important unresolved questions about our economic future.

THE ANSWER IS L.

① BASIC CONCEPTS

Work can be defined as the carrying out of tasks that require the expenditure of mental and physical effort, which has as its objective the production of goods and services that cater to human needs. An **occupation**, or job, is work that is done in exchange for a regular wage, or salary. In all cultures, work is the basis of the economic system, or **economy**. The economy consists of institutions that provide for the production and distribution of goods and services.

Modern societies are capitalistic. **Capitalism** is a way of organizing economic life that is distinguished by the following important features: private ownership of the means of production; profit as incentive; free competition for markets to sell goods, acquire cheap materials, and use cheap labor; and restless expansion and investment to accumulate capital. Capitalism, which began to spread

work • The activity by which people produce from the natural world and so ensure their survival. Work should not be thought of exclusively as paid employment. In traditional cultures, there was only a rudimentary monetary system, and few people worked for money. In modern societies, there remain types of work that do not involve direct payment (e.g., housework).

occupation • Any form of paid employment in which an individual regularly works.

economy • The system of production and exchange that provides for the material needs of individuals living in a given society. Economic institutions are of key importance in all social orders. What goes on in the economy usually influences other areas of social life. Modern economies differ substantially from traditional ones because the majority of the population is no longer engaged in agricultural production.

capitalism • An economic system based on the private ownership of wealth, which is invested and reinvested in order to produce profit.

technology • The application of knowledge of the material world to production; the creation of material instruments (such as machines) used in human interaction with nature.

with the growth of the Industrial Revolution in the early nineteenth century, is a vastly more dynamic economic system than any other that preceded it in history. Although the system has had many critics, such as Marx, it is now the most widespread form of economic organization in the world.

Most adults spend the better part of their waking hours at work in capitalist economies. The jobs they do determine their economic prospects, shape their lifestyle, and provide them with friends and acquaintances. Yet the nature of work is often determined by forces far beyond our control, and sometimes even beyond our understanding. In this chapter, we analyze the nature of work in modern societies and look at the major changes affecting economic life today. We investigate the changing nature of industrial production, the ownership structure of large business corporations, and the changing nature of work itself. Modern industry, as has been stressed in other parts of this book, differs in a fundamental way from premodern systems of production, which were based above all on agriculture. In modern societies, in contrast, most people no longer work on farms or in fields. Nor do large numbers work in factories, as was the case for much of the twentieth century. Rather, today's jobs involve providing services to others—services that range from those provided by high-paid professionals, such as managers of giant corporations, to those provided by low-paid workers requiring limited skills and training, such as sales clerks at Walmart.

The study of economic institutions is of major importance in sociology, because the economy influences all segments of society and, therefore, social life in general. And economic institutions are themselves always changing. One reason for such change is **technology**, which harnesses science to machinery in order to produce an ever-increasing variety of goods more cheaply. Another reason is globalization, which creates global competition among not only firms but also workers: Whether you are an auto worker in a Detroit factory, an engineer in Silicon Valley, or a graphic designer in New York City, there is likely to be someone half a world away with the skill, talent, and drive to challenge you for your job.

To tackle these issues, we need to relate work to the broad contours of our society and to industrial organization as a whole. We often associate the notion of work with drudgery—with a set of tasks that we want to minimize and, if possible, escape altogether. (You may have this very thought in mind as you set out to read this chapter!) Is this most people's attitude toward their work, and if so, why? We will try to find out in the following pages.

Work has more going for it than drudgery, or people would not feel so lost and disoriented when they became unemployed. How would you feel if you thought you would never get a job? In modern societies, having a paid job is important for maintaining self-esteem as well as paying the bills. Even where work conditions are relatively unpleasant, and the tasks involved dull, work tends to be a structuring element in people's psychological makeup and the cycle of their daily activities. Several characteristics of work are relevant here.

- *Money*. A wage or salary is the main resource many people depend on to meet their needs. Without such an income, anxieties about coping with day-to-day life tend to multiply.
- *Activity level*. Work often provides a basis for the acquisition and exercise of skills and capacities. Even where work is routine, it offers a structured environment in which a person's energies may be absorbed. Without it, the opportunity to exercise such skills and capacities may be reduced.

- *Variety*. Work provides access to contexts that contrast with domestic surroundings. In the working environment, even when the tasks are relatively dull, individuals may enjoy doing something different from home chores.
- *Structuring one's time*. For people in regular employment, the day is usually organized around the rhythm of work. Although work may sometimes be oppressive, it provides a sense of direction in daily activities. Those who are out of work frequently find boredom a major problem and develop a sense of apathy about time. As one unemployed man remarked, "Time doesn't matter now as much as it used to . . . There's so much of it" (Fryer and McKenna, 1987).

housework • Unpaid work carried out in the home, usually by women; domestic chores such as cooking, cleaning, and shopping. Also called *domestic labor*.

division of labor • The specialization of work tasks by means of which different occupations are combined within a production system. All societies have at least some rudimentary form of division of labor, especially between the tasks allocated to men and those performed by women. With the development of industrialism, the division of labor became vastly more complex than in any prior type of production system. In the modern world, the division of labor is international in scope.

- *Social contacts*. The work environment often provides friendships and opportunities to participate in shared activities with others. Separated from the work setting, a person's circle of possible friends and acquaintances is likely to dwindle.
- *Personal identity*. Work is usually valued for the sense of stable social identity it offers. For men in particular, self-esteem is often bound up with the economic contribution they make to the maintenance of the household. In addition, job conditions—such as the opportunity to work in jobs that are challenging, not routinized, and not subject to close supervision—are known to affect a person's sense of self-worth (Kohn, 1977).

Against the backdrop of this formidable list, it is not difficult to see why being without paid employment may undermine individuals' confidence in their social value. Yet even though we often think of work as equivalent to having a paid job, in fact this is an oversimplified view. **Housework**, which has traditionally been carried out mostly by women, is usually unpaid. But it is work nonetheless, sometimes satisfying, often difficult and exhausting. Unpaid housework includes such things as having primary responsibility for raising children, cleaning, shopping, and attending to countless (and unending) household chores. It typically involves one of the most important tasks of any society: the socialization of children, a crucial step in preparing them for adulthood. One recent study found that in 1965, women put in an average of 40 hours per week on household work; today, as an increasing number of women have joined the paid workforce, it is estimated that, on average, women now spend only 26 hours a week on household labor. Men have not exactly taken up the slack: their weekly contribution in 1965 was 14 hours; today it is 17. The study estimates that if housework were monetized—that is, paid according to its true value—it would have increased the U.S. GDP by 26 percent in 2010 (Bridgeman et al., 2012). Another form of unpaid labor that has an important social role involves volunteer work for charities or other organizations. According to one estimate, in 2010 nearly 64 million people—a quarter of all American adults—contributed 8.1 billion hours of volunteer service, estimated as worth $173 billion (Independent Sector, 2012).

One of the most distinctive characteristics of the economic system of modern societies is the existence of a highly complex **division of labor**: Work has become divided into an enormous number of different occupations in which people specialize. In traditional societies, nonagricultural work entailed the mastery of a craft. Craft skills were learned through a lengthy period of apprenticeship, and the worker normally carried out all aspects of the production process from beginning to end. For example, a metal-worker making a plow would forge the iron, shape it, and assemble the implement itself. With the rise of modern industrial production, most traditional crafts have disappeared altogether, replaced by skills that form part of more large-scale production processes. An electrician working in an industrial setting today, for instance, may inspect and repair only a few parts of one type of machine; different people will deal with the other parts and other machines.

The contrast in the division of labor between traditional and modern societies is truly extraordinary. Even in the largest traditional societies, there usually existed no more than 20 or 30 major craft trades, together with such specialized pursuits as merchant, soldier, and priest. In a modern industrial system, there are literally thousands of occupations. The U.S. Bureau of the Census lists some 20,000 distinct jobs in the American economy. In traditional communities, most of the population worked on farms and were economically self-sufficient. They produced their own food, clothes, and other necessities of life.

One of the main features of modern societies, by contrast, is an enormous expansion of **economic interdependence**. We all depend on an immense number of other workers—today stretching right across the world—for the products and services that sustain our lives. With few exceptions, the vast majority of people in modern societies do not produce the food they eat, the houses in which they live, or the material goods they consume.

CONCEPT CHECKS

1. Describe six characteristics that shape one's everyday experiences at work.
2. Contrast the division of labor in traditional and modern societies.

② THEORIES OF WORK AND ECONOMIC LIFE

To better understand the social organization of work, we first consider the different forms that capitalism has taken, before turning to a discussion of two broad types of economic organization in modern society that play a central role in shaping the kinds of jobs people are likely to find: Fordism and post-Fordism.

Types of Capitalism

There have been four general stages in the development of business corporations, although each overlaps the others and all continue to coexist today. The first stage, characteristic of the nineteenth and early twentieth centuries, was dominated by **family capitalism**. Large firms were run either by individual entrepreneurs or by members of the same family, and then passed on to their descendants. The famous corporate dynasties, such as the Rockefellers and Fords, belong in this category. These individuals and families did not just own a single large corporation but held a diversity of economic interests and stood at the apex of economic empires.

economic interdependence • The fact that in the division of labor, individuals depend on others to produce many or most of the goods they need to sustain their lives.

family capitalism • Capitalistic enterprise owned and administered by entrepreneurial families.

Most of the big firms founded by entrepreneurial families have since become *public companies*—that is, shares of their stock are traded on the open market—and have passed into managerial control. But important elements of family capitalism remain, even within some of the largest corporations, such as News Corporation, the world's third-largest media conglomerate, owner of Fox Films, Fox Broadcasting, HarperCollins, Dow Jones, *The Wall Street Journal*, and a host of newspapers, cable networks, and satellite broadcasters around the world. News Corporation's Australian-born CEO, Rupert Murdoch, who turned 81 in 2012, took over his father's struggling media business in 1953, building it into a global media empire. Among small firms, such as local shops run by their owners, small plumbing and house-painting businesses, and so forth, family capitalism continues to dominate. Some of these firms, such as shops that remain in the hands of the same family for two or more generations, are also dynasties, albeit on a minor scale. However, the small-business sector is highly unstable, and economic failure is common; the proportion of firms owned by members of the same family for extended periods of time is minuscule.

In the large corporate sector, family capitalism was increasingly succeeded by **managerial capitalism**. As managers came to have more and more influence through the growth of very large firms, the entrepreneurial families were displaced. The result has been described as the replacement of the family in the company by the company itself. The corporation emerged as a more defined economic entity. In studying the 200 largest manufacturing corporations in the United States, Michael Allen (1981) found that in cases in which profit showed a decline, family-controlled enterprises were unlikely to replace their chief executive, but manager-controlled firms did so rapidly.

There is no question that managerial capitalism has left an indelible imprint on modern society. The large corporation drives not only patterns of consumption but also the experience of employment in contemporary society—it is difficult to imagine how different the work lives of many Americans would be in the absence of large factories or corporate bureaucracies. Sociologists have identified another area in which the large corporation has left a mark on modern institutions. **Welfare capitalism** refers to a practice that sought to make the corporation—rather than the state or trade unions—the primary shelter from the uncertainties of the market in modern industrial life. Beginning at the end of the nineteenth century, large firms began to provide certain services to their employees, including child care, recreational facilities, profit-sharing plans, paid vacations, and group life and unemployment insurance. These programs often had a paternalistic bent, such as sponsoring "home visits" for the "moral education" of employees. Viewed in less benevolent terms, welfare capitalism had as one of its major objectives coercion, as employers deployed all manner of tactics, including violence, to avoid unionization. As such, conventional histories typically suggest that welfare capitalism met its demise in the Great Depression years, as labor unions achieved unprecedented levels of influence and as the New Deal administration began to guarantee many of the benefits provided by firms. In contrast to this standard interpretation, others argue that welfare capitalism did not die but instead went underground during the height of the labor movement (Jacoby, 1998). In firms that avoided unionization during the period between the 1930s and, '60s—such as Kodak, Sears, and Thompson Products—welfare capitalism was modernized, shedding blatantly paternalistic aspects and routinizing benefit programs. When

managerial capitalism • Capitalistic enterprise administered by managerial executives rather than by owners.

welfare capitalism • The practice by which large corporations protect their employees from the vicissitudes of the market.

the union movement began to weaken after 1970, these companies offered a model to many other firms, which were then able to press their advantage against flanking unions, reasserting the role of the firm as "industrial manor" and workers as "industrial serfs."

Despite the overwhelming importance of managerial capitalism in shaping the modern economy, many scholars now see the contours of a fourth, different phase emerging in the evolution of the corporation. They argue that managerial capitalism has today partly ceded place to **institutional capitalism**. This term refers to the emergence of a consolidated network of business leadership, concerned not only with decision making within single firms but also with the development of corporate power beyond them. Institutional capitalism is based on the practice of corporations holding shares in other firms. In effect, interlocking boards of directors exercise control over much of the corporate landscape. This reverses the process of increasing managerial control because the large blocks of shares owned by other corporations dwarf the managers' shareholdings. One of the main reasons for the spread of institutional capitalism is the shift in patterns of investment that has occurred since the 1970s. Rather than investing directly by buying shares in a business, individuals now invest in money market, trust, insurance, and pension funds that are controlled by large financial organizations, which in turn invest these grouped savings in industrial corporations.

Fordism and Scientific Management (Taylorism)

Alongside these changes in the nature of capitalist economic systems, there has also been a change in the predominant type of industrial organization in capitalist economies. This change involves a shift from mass production in large bureaucratic organizations for a mass consumer market to more flexible forms of production through global networks of suppliers, tailored to more individualized consumer tastes. Because the former emerged with the modern automobile industry, it is often referred to as "Fordism." **Fordism**, therefore, is the name given to designate the system of mass production tied to the cultivation of mass markets.

Affixing the prefix *post* to *Fordism* suggests that Fordism is being replaced by something entirely new, signaling the end of the Fordist era. This is misleading, since both forms of industrial organization are found throughout the world today, although these new forms are becoming increasingly important, as we shall see.

Writing some two centuries ago, Adam Smith, one of the founders of modern economics, identified advantages that the division of labor provides in terms of increasing productivity. His most famous work, *The Wealth of Nations* (1776), opens with a description of the division of labor in a pin factory. A person working alone could perhaps make 20 pins per day. By breaking down that worker's task into a number of simple operations, however, 10 workers carrying out specialized jobs in collaboration with one another could collectively produce 48,000, pins per day. The rate of production per worker, in other words, is increased from 20 to 48,000, with each specialist operator producing 240 times more than he could working alone.

institutional capitalism • Capitalistic enterprise organized on the basis of institutional shareholding.

Fordism • The system of production pioneered by Henry Ford, in which the assembly line was introduced.

More than a century later, these ideas reached their most developed expression in the writings of Frederick Winslow Taylor, an American management consultant. Taylor's approach to what he called "scientific management" involved the detailed study of industrial processes to break them down into simple operations that could be precisely timed and organized. **Taylorism**, as scientific management came to be called, was not merely an academic study. It was a system of production designed to maximize industrial output, and it had a widespread effect not only on the organization of industrial production and technology but on workplace politics as well. In particular, Taylor's time and motion studies wrested control over knowledge of the production process from the worker and placed such knowledge firmly in the hands

One of Henry Ford's most significant innovations was the introduction of the assembly line, which allowed for mass production of the Model T.

of management, eroding the basis on which craft workers maintained autonomy from their employers (Braverman, 1974). As such, Taylorism has been widely associated with the de-skilling and degradation of labor.

The principles of Taylorism were adopted by the industrialist Henry Ford. In 1908, Ford designed his first auto plant in Highland Park, Michigan, to manufacture only one product, the Model T, thereby allowing the introduction of specialized tools and machinery designed for speed, precision, and simplicity of operation. One of Ford's most significant innovations was the introduction of the assembly line, said to have been inspired by Chicago slaughterhouses, in which animals were disassembled section by section on a moving conveyor belt. Each worker on Ford's assembly line was assigned a specialized task, such as fitting the left-side door handles as the car bodies moved along the line. By 1929, when production of the Model T ceased, more than 15 million cars had been assembled.

Ford was among the first to realize that mass production requires mass markets. He reasoned that if standardized commodities such as the automobile were to be produced on an ever-greater scale, the presence of consumers who were able to buy those commodities must also be ensured. In 1914, Ford took the unprecedented step of unilaterally raising wages at his Dearborn, Michigan, plant to five dollars for an eight-hour day—a very generous wage at the time and one that ensured a working-class lifestyle that included owning such an automobile. As David Harvey (1989) remarks, "The purpose of the five-dollar, eight-hour day was only in part to secure worker compliance with the discipline required to work the highly productive assembly-line system. It was coincidentally meant to provide workers with sufficient income and leisure time to consume the mass-produced products the corporations were about to turn out in ever vaster quantities." Ford also enlisted the services of a small army of social workers, who were sent into the homes of workers to educate them in the proper habits of consumption.

"Fordism" is also sometimes used to refer to a historical period in the development of post–World War II capitalism in which mass production was associated with stability in labor relations and a high degree of unionization. Under Fordism, firms made long-term

Taylorism • A set of ideas, also referred to as "scientific management," developed by Frederick Winslow Taylor, involving simple, coordinated operations in industry.

low-trust systems • Organizational or work settings in which people are allowed little responsibility for, or control over, the work task.

high-trust systems • Organizations or work settings in which individuals are permitted a great deal of autonomy and control over the work task.

alienation • The sense that our own abilities as human beings are taken over by other entities. The term was originally used by Karl Marx to refer to the projection of human powers onto gods. Subsequently he used the term to refer to the loss of workers' control over the nature and products of their labor.

commitments to workers, and wages were tightly linked to productivity growth. As such, collective bargaining agreements—formal agreements negotiated between firms and unions that specified working conditions such as wages, seniority rights, and benefits—created a virtuous circle that ensured worker consent to automated systems of production, as well as sufficient demand for mass-produced commodities. The system is generally understood to have broken down in the 1970s, giving rise to greater flexibility and insecurity in working conditions.

The reasons for the declining importance of Fordism are complex and intensely debated. As firms in a variety of industries adopted Fordist production methods, the system encountered certain limitations. Fordism was not suitable for all industries; it could be applied successfully only to industries that produced standardized commodities for large markets. At one time, it looked as though Fordism represented the likely future of industrial production as a whole. This has not proven to be the case. Setting up mechanized production lines is enormously expensive, and once a Fordist system is established, it is quite rigid; to alter a product, for example, substantial reinvestment is needed. Fordist production is easy to copy if sufficient funding is available to set up the plant. But firms in countries in which labor power is expensive find it difficult to compete with those where wages are cheaper. This was one of the factors originally leading to the rise of the car industry in Japan (although Japanese wage levels today are no longer low), followed by South Korea, and most recently China.

Fordism and Taylorism involve what some industrial sociologists call **low-trust systems**. Jobs are set by management and are geared to machines. Those who carry out the work tasks are closely supervised and are allowed little autonomy of action. Where there are many low-trust positions, the level of worker dissatisfaction and absenteeism is high, and industrial conflict is common. **High-trust systems** are those in which workers are permitted to control the pace and even the content of their work, within overall guidelines. Such systems are usually concentrated at the higher levels of industrial organizations.

Karl Marx was one of the first writers to grasp that the development of modern industry would reduce many people's work to dull, uninteresting tasks, resulting—to use today's language—in low-trust systems. According to Marx, the division of labor alienates human beings from their work. For Marx, **alienation** refers to feelings of estrangement and even hostility—initially to one's job and eventually to the overall framework of capitalist industrial production. In Marx's view, workers in capitalist society lack ownership of the products they make, which they often cannot even afford to buy; they are dehumanized by tedious and demeaning labor processes over which they have no control; and they find themselves in competition with their fellow workers for scarce jobs. Marx saw this as counter to human nature, which he believed involved creativity, control over one's activities, and cooperation with others (Marx, 2000; orig. 1844). In traditional societies, he pointed out, work was often exhausting—peasant farmers sometimes had to toil from dawn to dusk. Yet peasants held a real measure of control over their work, which required much knowledge and skill. Many industrial workers, by contrast, have little control over their jobs, contribute only a fraction to the creation of the overall product, and have no influence over how or to whom it is eventually sold. Work thus appears as something alien, a task that the worker must carry out to earn an income but that is in itself unsatisfying.

post-Fordism • The period characterized by the transition from mass industrial production, using Fordist methods, to more flexible forms of production favoring innovation and aimed at meeting market demands for customized products.

Post-Fordism

Since the 1970s, flexible practices have been introduced in a number of spheres, including product development, production techniques, management style, the working environment, employee involvement, and marketing. Group production, problem-solving teams, multitasking, and niche marketing are just some of the strategies adopted by companies attempting to restructure themselves under shifting conditions. Some commentators have suggested that, taken collectively, these changes represent a radical departure from the principles of Fordism; they contend that we are now operating in a period that can best be understood as **post-Fordism** (Table 14.1). *Post-Fordism*, a term initially popularized by Michael Piore and Charles Sabel in *The Second Industrial Divide* (1984), describes a new era of capitalist economic production in which flexibility and innovation are maximized to meet market demands for diverse, customized products—albeit often with adverse impacts on the workforce.

The idea of post-Fordism is somewhat problematic, however. The term is used to refer to a set of overlapping changes that occur not only in the realm of work and economic life but throughout society as a whole. Some writers argue that the tendency toward post-Fordism can be seen in spheres as diverse as party politics, welfare programs, and consumer and lifestyle choices. While observers of late modern societies often point to many of the same changes, there is no consensus about the precise meaning of post-Fordism or, indeed, if this is even the best way of understanding the phenomenon we are witnessing.

Regardless of the confusion surrounding the term *post-Fordism*, several distinctive trends within the world of work have emerged in recent decades that seem to represent a clear departure from earlier Fordist practices. These include the replacement of highly bureaucratic, vertically organized business structures with more flexible, horizontally organized networked approaches; the transition from mass production to mass customization; a shift from in-house production to global outsourcing; and the resulting severe erosion in job security for employees. We now consider each of these in turn.

Table 14.1
Fordist versus Post-Fordist Production Systems

FORDISM	POST-FORDISM
Bureaucratic/vertical	Flexible/horizontal
Mass production	Mass customization
Most work in-house (local)	Most work outsourced (global)
Job security (high wage, long term, full time, high career advancement)	Job insecurity (low wage, short term, part time, low career advancement)

FLEXIBLE BUSINESS STRUCTURES

One of the most important changes in worldwide production processes over the past few years has been an increase in the organizational flexibility of many large firms. For much of the twentieth century, the most important business organizations were large manufacturing firms that controlled both the making of goods and their final sales. Giant automobile companies such as Ford and General Motors typified this approach. Such companies employed tens of thousands of factory workers to make everything from components to the final cars, which were then sold in the manufacturers' showrooms. Such manufacture-dominated production processes were organized as large bureaucracies, often controlled by a single firm.

If General Motors represented the prototypical corporation of the twentieth century, Walmart may well prove to be symbolic of the twenty-first. Sociologist Gary Hamilton has described a world in which "big buyers"—global retailers—are becoming increasingly dominant in the global economy, not only reshaping business structures but also driving economic development in those regions (such as East Asia) that supply their products (Petrovic and Hamilton, 2006). While both General Motors and Walmart are giant transnational corporations, GM was organized vertically: Most of its production was done under its own roof, controlled by its own management structure in a highly bureaucratized fashion. GM designed, marketed, and produced the cars that it sold. Control, in other words, was highly centralized. Walmart, by way of contrast, designs very little of what it sells and produces next to nothing. Walmart sells products designed by others—the thousands of brands and labels that are available in its stores. Those brands and labels, in turn, seldom actually make the products they design: That task falls to factories around the world. Like GM, Walmart exerts control over its suppliers—but in this case, the suppliers are outside the firm rather than part of it.

The resulting network of retailers, brands, and factories enables each to respond quickly to changes in market conditions, in a way that the more vertically organized GM never could hope to do. If an economic slowdown or changing buyer tastes caused a drop in sales for GM, the corporation still had to cover the cost of expensive plants and equipment, as well as meet the payroll of hundreds of thousands of employees, from management to the factory floor. While Walmart has plenty of stores to maintain (some 4,000 in the United States and an additional 5,600 worldwide), its situation is markedly different from GM's: If Sony flat-panel TVs are not moving, Walmart can simply tell Sony it is reducing its orders and shift to Panasonic. Sony, in turn, can respond by canceling orders in some of the contract factories that are its suppliers. Those factories then either switch to other labels (perhaps Panasonic) or else lay off workers.

Walmart controls its suppliers through the information technology (IT) that has revolutionized the field of supply chain management. In today's world of flexible production, there are complex networks of buyers and suppliers: A clothing company such as the Gap may have thousands of independently owned factories supplying its stores, while each of those factories may in turn be making clothing for many competing brands. Coordinating these activities requires sophisticated computer technology—electronic data interchange (EDI) software systems that enable firms to share relevant data, beginning with the information on the bar code attached to each product that is scanned at the time of purchase. The most advanced systems, such as those pioneered by Walmart, enable firms to order just the right number of products to meet demand, to shift their orders among different suppliers, and to respond "nimbly"—a favored term of business—to changing market conditions. Today, even large automobile manufacturers such as GM have moved down the post-Fordist path, outsourcing as much work as possible and using advanced information systems to manage their supply chains.

MASS CUSTOMIZATION

Controlling such far-flung networks of suppliers is only part of the challenge faced by modern businesses. They must also cater to the changing demands of their customers—demands that are shaped, in turn, by a constant flow of advertising in magazines, newspapers, television, radio, and films such as *Spider-Man* (in its various incarnations), which are always accompanied by a deluge of toys based on the movie. Although Taylorism and Fordism successfully produced mass products (that were all the same) for mass markets, they were completely unable to produce small orders of goods, let alone goods specifically made for an individual customer. GM or Ford changed the overall design of its cars every couple of years, and the changes were often largely cosmetic: Large tail fins adorned cars in the 1950s, marketed as providing "greater stability on the nation's highways."

Mass customization has changed all this (Pine, 1999). It combines the large-volume production associated with Fordism with the flexibility required to tailor products to consumers' needs. Computer-aided designs, coupled with other types of computer-based technology such as EDI, now permit factories to alter their assembly lines for small-batch production, serving (and creating) particular market niches. Information can be solicited about individual consumers and analyzed to determine the key types of consumer preferences for particular products, which are then manufactured to those specifications. In a modern car factory, several different models can even be built on the same assembly line.

Dell was one of the first computer companies to carry mass customization to a high level: It is now commonplace for consumers to custom-design their computer online, charge the purchase to their credit card, and within a week receive the custom-made computer at their door. Dell is often thought of as a computer manufacturing company, but in fact the company does not make any significant computer components. Instead, it assembles components produced by others, controlling its supply chains through EDI. In effect, Dell has turned traditional ways of doing business upside down. Firms used to build a product first, then worry about selling it. Now mass customizers such as Dell sell first and build second. Such a shift has important consequences for industry. The need to hold stocks of parts on hand, a major cost for manufacturers, has been dramatically reduced. In addition, an increasing share of production is outsourced. Thus, the rapid transfer of information between manufacturers and suppliers is essential to the successful implementation of mass customization.

GLOBAL OUTSOURCING

Changes in industrial production include not only how products are manufactured but also where they are manufactured. In **flexible production** systems, there is truly a global assembly line: The companies that design and sell products seldom make them in their own factories, instead **outsourcing** production to factories around the world. For example, the 30-gigabyte Apple iPod is made by dozens of

flexible production • Process in which computers design customized products for a mass market.

outsourcing • A business practice that sends production of materials to factories around the world. The components of one final product often originate from many different countries and then are sent elsewhere to be put together and sold. Factories from different countries must compete with one another to obtain business.

companies in half a dozen countries. Of the approximately $300 retail price, less than half goes to pay for the 451 component parts whose manufacture is outsourced; the bulk is for retailing, marketing, distribution, and Apple's revenues (Linden, Kraemer, and Dedrick, 2007).

Few if any industries are as globalized as the industry that makes the clothing and footwear that fill your closet. Almost no major U.S. companies today make their own apparel or footwear; rather, they outsource to independently owned factories that do the work for them. These factories are found in more than 100 different countries and range from tiny sweatshops to giant plants owned by transnational corporations. Sociologists Edna Bonacich and Richard Appelbaum (2000), for example, show that most so-called garment manufacturers actually employ no garment workers at all. Instead, they rely on thousands of factories around the world to make their apparel, which they then sell in department stores and other retail outlets. Clothing manufacturers do not own any of these factories and are therefore free to use them or not, depending on their needs. While this provides the manufacturers with the flexibility previously discussed, it creates great uncertainty both for the factories, which must compete with one another for orders, and for the workers in those factories, who may lose their jobs if their factory loses business.

JOB INSECURITY

Flexible production has produced some benefits for consumers and the economy as a whole, but the effect on workers has not been wholly positive. Though some workers undoubtedly do learn new skills and have less monotonous jobs, the majority find their work lives less secure than before. For many workers inside the United States, the long-term employment, rising wages, career advancement, and health and retirement benefits once associated with a job at a General Motors or Ford plant have become a thing of the past. To keep their jobs, as previously noted, U.S. workers have had to accept pay cuts and reduced benefits packages. And, of course, many have lost their jobs to overseas competition.

For workers in low-wage countries, the downside of flexible production can be onerous. Given the far-flung nature of global supply chains, it is virtually impossible to know where all the components that go into a product are made. Bonacich and Appelbaum (2000) argue that such flexible production, driven by global competition, has resulted in a global "race to the bottom," in which retailers and manufacturers will go anyplace on earth where they can find the lowest wages, the fewest environmental restrictions, and the most lax governmental regulations. This is a system that invites abuses—as evidenced by the well-publicized cases of toxic toys made in Chinese factories under contract to leading U.S. brands such as Mattel.

THE INFORMAL ECONOMY

Many types of work do not conform to orthodox categories of paid employment—they cannot be classified as either Fordist or post-Fordist. Much of the work done in all societies, for example, is performed outside formal business firms, and indeed outside the formal economy itself. The term **informal economy** refers to transactions outside the sphere of regular employment, sometimes involving the exchange of cash for goods and services provided, for which no official records are kept, and which therefore escape government notice. Your television

informal economy • Economic transactions carried on outside the sphere of orthodox paid employment.

In what ways do college students participate in the informal economy?

repairman might be paid in cash, "off the books," without any receipt being given or details of the job recorded; the same may be true of the person who cleans your house or does your gardening, if you have such services. In poor countries, a significant part of the national economy consists of such informal work; one study estimates that informal work accounts for nearly four-fifths of all nonagricultural employment in Africa, contributing as much as 40 percent of GDP in the sub-Saharan part of the African continent (Becker, 2004). In the United States the informal economy was estimated to add only 9 percent to the GDP in the year 2000—which, given the large size of the American economy, amounts to nearly $1 trillion in goods and services exchanged that never appears in any official government accounts (Schneider and Enste, 2002; Barnes, 2009). The informal economy includes not only "hidden" cash transactions but also many forms of *self-provisioning*, which people carry on inside and outside the home.

> ## CONCEPT CHECKS
>
> 1. What are the main stages of capitalism?
> 2. What are two key differences between Taylorism and Fordism?
> 3. What are some of the changes that occurred in the occupational structure in the twentieth century? How can they be explained?
> 4. Define and provide an example of an informal economy.

Do-it-yourself activities and household appliances and tools, for instance, provide goods and services that would otherwise have to be purchased.

Finally, illegal drugs constitute a major part of the informal economy in some countries, estimated to range globally from only several hundred billion dollars to as much as $2.1 trillion, or nearly 4 percent of global GDP (United Nations Development Programme [UNDP], 1999; United Nations Office on Drugs and Crime [UNODC], 2011). There is widespread disagreement over the exact numbers—not surprising, perhaps, given the illicit and secretive nature of the global drug trade. Moreover, drug enforcement agencies have an interest in showing that there is a significant need for their services, which may result in inflated estimates of the problem (Blickman, 2003; Thoumi, 2003; Reuter and Greenfield, 2001).

3 CURRENT RESEARCH ON WORK AND ECONOMIC LIFE

The changes we have just described affect many aspects of work and economic life. These changes have generally favored the growing power of corporations relative to their workers. We first look at the growth of transnational corporations and how this is reshaping the nature of economic organization in the twenty-first century, before turning to a discussion of workers, unions, and the challenges they face. We conclude the discussion of current research by looking at some forms of industrial conflict that occur when labor and management fail to agree.

Corporations and Corporate Power

So far in this chapter, we have been looking at industry mostly from the perspective of occupations and employees. We have studied the changes in patterns of work and the factors influencing the development of labor unions. But we also have to concern ourselves with the nature of the business firms in which the workforce is employed. (Many people today are employees of government organizations, although we will not consider these here.) What is happening to business corporations today, and how are they run?

Since the turn of the twentieth century, modern capitalist economies have been more and more influenced by the rise of large business **corporations**. The share of total manufacturing assets held by the 200 largest *manufacturing* firms in the United States has increased by 0.5 percent each year from 1900 to the present day; these 200 corporations now control more than half of all manufacturing assets. The 200 largest *financial* organizations—banks, building societies, and insurance companies—account for more than half of all financial activity. There are numerous connections among large firms. For example, financial institutions hold well over 30 percent of the shares of the largest 200 manufacturing firms.

Of course, there still exist thousands of smaller firms and enterprises within the American economy. In these companies, the image of the **entrepreneur**—the boss who owns and runs the firm—is by no means obsolete. The large corporations are a different matter. Ever since Adolf Berle and Gardiner Means published their celebrated study *The Modern Corporation and Private Property* (1982; orig. 1932), it has been accepted that most of the largest firms are not run by those who own them. In theory, large

corporations • Business firms or companies.

entrepreneur • The owner/founder of a business firm.

corporations are the property of their shareholders, who have the right to make all important decisions. But Berle and Means argue that because share ownership is so dispersed, actual control has passed into the hands of the managers who run the firms on a day-to-day basis. *Ownership* of corporations is thus separated from their *control*.

Whether they are run by owners or managers, the power of the major corporations is very extensive. When one or a handful of firms dominate in a given industry, they often cooperate in setting prices rather than freely competing with one another. Thus the giant oil companies normally follow one another's lead in the price charged for gasoline. When one firm occupies a commanding position in a given industry, it is said to be in a **monopoly** position. More common is a situation of **oligopoly**, in which a small group of giant corporations predominates. In situations of oligopoly, firms are able more or less to dictate the terms on which they buy goods and services from the smaller firms that are their suppliers.

The emergence of the global economy has contributed to a wave of mergers and acquisitions on an unprecedented scale, which have created oligopolies in industries such as communications and media. In 1998 the German automaker Daimler-Benz purchased Chrysler for $38 billion, and Exxon purchased the oil giant Mobil for $86 billion. In 1999, AT&T acquired the media corporation MediaOne for $5 billion, to create what was at the time the world's largest cable company. Also in 1999, CBS purchased Viacom for $35 billion. In 2000, Britain's Vodafone Airtouch took over Germany's Mannesmann for $130 billion in the world's largest hostile takeover. In that same year, Time Warner and the Internet service provider America Online announced the largest merger in history—worth $165 billion (PBS *NewsHour,* 2003). In 2010 some 3,000 mergers and acquisitions, worth a total of $131 billion, involved Chinese enterprises—one index of China's growing presence in the global economy (Chapman and Li, 2011).

A number of factors have contributed to this trend, including: technological advances, which have lowered global transportation and communications costs; a relaxation of regulation of corporate business activities; and new and efficient ways of financing and pooling the large sums of capital needed to conduct a merger or acquisition. Yet over 70 percent of the mergers and acquisitions have been between businesses competing in the same industry (United Nations Conference on Trade and Development [UNCTAD], 2005). This suggests that the primary aim of the recent wave of business consolidations has been to eliminate direct competition and productive overcapacity. Overcapacity is a problem that occurs when businesses produce more goods than the market will consume. Following the logic of supply and demand, this leads to decline in the value of the goods produced and to a decline in profits. Consolidation of firms is an attempt to avoid this problem. Yet it doesn't always work. In response to the declining success of AOL, Time Warner dropped AOL from its name and posted a $99 billion loss for 2002 (PBS *NewsHour,* 2000).

Transnational Corporations

With the intensifying of globalization, most large corporations now operate in an international economic context. When they establish branches in two or more countries, they are referred to as **transnational** or **multinational corporations**. *Transnational* is the preferred term, indicating that these companies operate across many different national boundaries.

monopoly • The domination of a single firm in a given industry.

oligopoly • The domination of a small number of firms in a given industry.

transnational (or multinational) corporations • Business corporations located in two or more countries.

Swiss researchers identified more than 43,000 transnational corporations networked together across the globe in 2007. They found that only 147 of these corporations controlled almost 40 percent of the total monetary value of the entire network; 737 firms accounted for 80 percent. The top 50 firms are primarily financial institutions such as Barclays, JPMorgan Chase, and Merrill Lynch, which strongly suggests that the financial services industry has a great deal of power and influence in the global economy (Vitali, Glattfelder, and Battiston, 2011).

The largest transnationals are gigantic; their wealth outstrips that of many countries (Table 14.2). The scope of these companies' operations is staggering. The combined revenues of the world's 500 largest transnational corporations totaled $9.75 trillion in 2009

Table 14.2
Corporate Globalization: The World's 50 Largest Economies Are Not All Countries (in billions of dollars)

1	European Union	17,549.2	26	**Royal Dutch Shell**	**484.4**
2	United States of America	15,094.0	27	**Exxon Mobil**	**453.0**
3	China	7,298.1	28	**Wal-Mart Stores**	**447.0**
4	Japan	5,867.2	29	Argentina	446.0
5	Germany	3,570.6	30	Austria	418.5
6	France	2,773.1	31	South Africa	408.2
7	Brazil	2,476.7	32	**BP**	**386.5**
8	United Kingdom	2,431.6	33	**Sinopec Group**	**375.2**
9	Italy	2,194.8	34	United Arab Emirates	360.3
10	Russia	1,857.8	35	**China National Petroleum**	**352.3**
11	India	1,848.0	36	Thailand	345.6
12	Canada	1,736.1	37	Denmark	332.7
13	Spain	1,491.0	38	Colombia	332.0
14	Australia	1,372.0	39	Iran	331.0
15	Mexico	1,155.3	40	Venezuela	316.5
16	South Korea	1,116.2	41	Greece	299.0
17	Indonesia	847.0	42	Malaysia	279.0
18	Netherlands	836.3	43	Finland	266.1
19	Turkey	773.1	44	**State Grid**	**259.1**
20	Switzerland	636.6	45	Chile	249.0
21	Saudi Arabia	577.0	46	**Chevron**	**246.0**
22	Sweden	538.1	47	Hong Kong	244.0
23	Poland	514.5	48	Israel	243.0
24	Belgium	511.5	49	Singapore	240.0
25	Norway	486.0	50	Portugal	238.0

Sources: CNN, 2012b; World Bank, 2012c.

(CNN, 2012a). To give an idea of the magnitude of that number, in 2009, $58 trillion in goods and services were produced by the *entire world* (International Monetary Fund, 2010). Royal Dutch Shell, one of the world's largest corporations, had 2011 revenues of $5 trillion, generating 17 percent of the total Global 500 revenue. In fact, 8 of the top 10 largest corporations were in the energy business. Of the top 500 transnational corporations in the world, 139 are based in the United States, contributing about 30 percent of the total revenues of all 500. The share of American companies has, however, fallen in recent years, as the number of transnational corporations based in other countries—especially Asian countries such as South Korea and China—has increased. As seen in Table 14.3, between 2005 and 2012, among the world's largest 500 transnational corporations, the U.S. share declined from 176 to 132, while Japan's share declined from 81 to 73. In 2002 there were 11 Chinese firms on the Global 500. By 2012, 68 Chinese companies made the list. While U.S.- and European-based transnational corporations continue to dominate the global economy by a wide margin, China has begun to have a significant presence and may well emerge as the equal of Japan within the next decade or so.

Contrary to common belief, three-quarters of all foreign direct investments are made among industrialized countries. Of the 500 largest transnational corporations, four are based in Russia and one each is based in Mexico, Saudi Arabia, Poland, and Turkey. The rest are all based in North America, Europe, and Asia; none is from Latin America or Africa. Nevertheless, the involvements of transnationals in developing countries are extensive, with Brazil, India, and Mexico showing the highest levels of foreign investment. The most rapid rate of increase in corporate investment by far has been in the newly industrializing economies (NIEs) of Asia: China, Hong Kong, Malaysia, Singapore, South Korea, and Taiwan.

Transnational corporations have assumed an increasingly important place in the world economy over the course of this century. They are of key importance in the **international division of labor**—the specialization in producing goods for the world market that divides regions into zones of industrial or agricultural production or high- or low-skilled labor (Fröbel, Heinrichs, and Kreye, 1979; McMichael, 1996). Just as national economies have become increasingly concentrated—dominated by a limited number of very large companies—so has the world economy. In the case of the United States and several of the other leading industrialized countries, the firms that dominate nationally also have a wide-ranging international presence. Many sectors of world production (such as agribusiness) are oligopolies. Over the past two or three decades, international oligopolies have developed in the automobile, microprocessor, and electronics industries and in the production of some other goods marketed worldwide.

international division of labor • The specialization in producing goods for the world market that divides regions into zones of industrial or agricultural production or high- or low-skilled labor.

Table 14.3
The World's 500 Largest Transnational Corporations—Number by Leading Economies

	2005	2012
European Union	161	148
United States	176	132
Japan	81	73
China	16	68
Korea	11	13

Source: CNN, 2012a.

The reach of the transnationals since the mid-1970s would not have been possible without advances in transportation and communications. Air travel now allows people to move around the world at a speed that would have seemed inconceivable even 60 years ago. Technological innovations allowing *containerization* have permitted the rapid movement and distribution of bulk goods around the world. The best example of containerization is the development of extremely large oceangoing vessels (superfreighters) that carry tractor trailers full of goods. These trailers can be easily loaded and sealed at the point of manufacture, loaded onto ships, and moved across an ocean, then transferred onto a train or truck and delivered to a store, where the trailers are finally opened and unloaded.

Telecommunications technologies now permit more or less instantaneous communication from one part of the world to another. Satellites have been used for commercial telecommunications since 1965. The first satellite could carry 240 telephone conversations at once; current satellites can carry 12,000 simultaneous conversations! The larger transnationals now have their own satellite-based communications systems. The Mitsubishi Corporation, for instance, has a massive network across which 5 million words are transmitted to and from its headquarters in Tokyo each day.

TRANSNATIONAL CORPORATIONS PLAN GLOBALLY

The global corporations have become the first organizations able to plan on a truly world scale. Coca-Cola ads reach billions. A few companies with developed global networks are able to shape the commercial activities of diverse nations. There are four webs of interconnecting commercial activity in the new world economy. These are what Richard Barnet and John Cavanagh (1994) call the global cultural bazaar, the global shopping mall, the global workplace, and the global financial network.

The global cultural bazaar is the newest of the four but already the most extensive. Global images and global dreams are diffused through movies, TV programs, music, videos, games, toys, and T-shirts, sold on a worldwide basis. All over the earth, even in the poorest developing countries, people use the same electronic devices to see or listen to the same commercially produced songs and shows.

The global shopping mall is a "planetary supermarket with a dazzling spread of things to eat, drink, wear and enjoy," according to Barnet and Cavanagh. It is more exclusive than the global cultural bazaar because the poor do not have the resources to participate—they have the status only of window shoppers. Of the 6.7 billion people who make up the world's population, nearly three out of five lack the cash or credit to purchase any consumer goods.

The third global web, the global workplace, is the increasingly complex global division of labor that affects all of us. It consists of the massive array of offices, factories, restaurants, and millions of other places where goods are produced and consumed or information is exchanged. This web is closely bound up with the global financial network, which it fuels and is financed by. The global financial network consists of billions of bits of information stored in computers and portrayed on computer screens. It entails almost endless currency exchanges, credit card transactions, insurance plans, and buying and selling of stocks and shares.

The Twenty-First-Century Corporation: Different from Its Twentieth-Century Counterpart

There are big differences between the large corporation of the early twenty-first century and its mid-twentieth-century counterpart. Many of the names are the same—General Motors, Ford, IBM, AT&T—but these have been joined by other giant firms, largely unknown in the 1950s, such as Walmart, Microsoft, and Intel. They all wield great power, and their top executives still inhabit the large buildings that dominate so many city centers.

But below the surface similarities between today and half a century ago, some profound transformations have taken place. The origin of these transformations lies in a process we have encountered often in this book: globalization. Since the 1950s, the giant corporations have become more and more caught up in global competition; as a result, both their internal composition and, in a way, their very nature have altered.

More than 20 years ago, former U.S. labor secretary Robert Reich (1991) wrote:

> Underneath, all is changing. America's core corporation no longer plans and implements the production of a large volume of goods and services; it no longer invests in a vast array of factories, machinery, laboratories, inventories, and other tangible assets; it no longer employs armies of production workers and middle-level managers. . . . In fact, the core corporation is no longer even American. It is, increasingly, a façade, behind which teems an array of decentralized groups and subgroups continuously contracting with similarly diffuse working units all over the world.

The large corporation is less a big business than an "enterprise web"—a central organization that links together smaller firms. IBM, for example, which used to be one of the most jealously self-sufficient of all large corporations, in the 1980s and early 1990s, joined with dozens of U.S.-based companies and more than 80 foreign-based firms to share strategic planning and cope with production problems. Nelson Lichtenstein (2006), a labor historian who spent many years studying Walmart, has characterized this as a shift from General Motors to Walmart, which he describes as "a template for twenty-first-century capitalism":

> GM workers were often life-time employees so factory turnover was exceedingly low: these were the best jobs around, and they were jobs that rewarded longevity. . . . At Wal-Mart, in contrast, employee turnover approaches 50 percent a year, which means it must be even higher for those hired at an entry level wage. . . . The hours of labor, the very definition of a full work day, constitutes the other great contrast dividing America's old industrial economy from that of its retail future . . . at Wal-Mart a 32 hour work week is considered "full time" employment. This gives managers great flexibility and power, enabling them to parcel out the extra hours to fill in the schedule, reward favored employees, and gear up for the holiday rush. But the social consequences of this policy are profound: Unlike General Motors, Wal-Mart is not afraid to hire thousands of new workers each year, but employee attachment to their new job is low, and millions of Americans find it necessary, and possible, to moonlight with two part time jobs.

Walmart, Lichtenstein points out, provides us with a steady stream of low-cost products, making it possible for millions of Americans of limited means to feed and clothe their families. Walmart thus permits many Americans to enjoy a lifestyle of consumption that would otherwise not be possible. The giant retailer also provides jobs, although most are not nearly as well paying as the millions of manufacturing jobs that have been lost in recent years. The one place where jobs have been gained, and in large numbers, is the developing world. Manufacturing has boomed in China, where as many as 100 million new workers now labor under harsh conditions, in millions of factories that turn out everything from running shoes to flat-panel TVs to iPads. China's factories provide the goods that are sold in Walmart's thousands of U.S. stores, linking the economies of both countries tightly together. Walmart's global supply chains, along with those of all corporations that design, make, and sell products today, link the world in a web of production networks that now reach every place on the planet. For better or for worse, the lives and work of all of us—indeed, of all people everywhere—are increasingly intertwined.

Some corporations remain strongly bureaucratic and centered in the United States. However, most are no longer so clearly located anywhere. The old transnational corporation used to work mainly from its American headquarters, from where its overseas production plants and subsidiaries were controlled. Now, with the transformation of space and time noted earlier (Chapter 5), groups situated in any region of the world are able, via telecommunications and computer, to work with others. Nations still try to influence flow of information, resources, and money across their borders. But modern communication technologies make this more and more difficult, if not impossible. Knowledge and finances can be transferred across the world, as electronic blips moving at nearly the speed of light.

Even the production of the technology that makes the global activities of transnational corporations possible is spread out over the globe. The California-based computer chip manufacturer Intel had, as of 2006, 94,100 employees; 13 production sites; 11 assembly sites spread over 7 countries; and 20,000 research and development employees in 30 countries, including China, India, and the Russian Federation. One-third of its workforce is located outside the United States. Intel is especially interested in China, where it has been operating laboratories, manufacturing facilities, and testing facilities for more than 20 years. Its new $2.5 billion chip fabrication plant in Dalian, China, is the first such plant the company has located in a developing country. The reason China was selected? Not low labor costs (chip fabrication depends on expensive equipment rather than cheap labor), but rather, China's growing supply of talented engineers, along with generous financial incentives provided by the Chinese government (UNCTAD, 2005; Kanellos, 2007).

The products of the transnational companies similarly have an international character. When is something "Made in America," and when not? There is no longer any clear answer. What could be more American than a Ford? Today, the answer may be a Toyota or Honda. Automobiles contain more than 20,000 different parts, and the production of vehicles has become a truly globalized system. Including direct employment, dealerships, and suppliers, Toyota employs roughly 365,000 people in the United States, invests $18 billion, and spends $25 billion on parts and components (Toyota, 2012). The Toyota Avalon, for example, built at a production facility in Kentucky, is made up of 80 percent U.S. or Canadian parts; Toyota also plans to begin building its popular hybrid, the Prius, in the United States in 2015. Nissan makes its all-electric vehicle, the Leaf, in Tennessee, while Honda manufactures a wide range of its cars in the United States. Foreign companies have moved some of their production facilities to the United States to take advantage of closer access to a principal market and a productive workforce (which, interestingly, can be less costly than workers in Europe and even Japan).

Workers and Their Challenges

The idea of work is actually a complex one. All of us work in many ways besides in paid employment. Cleaning the house, planting a garden, and going shopping are plainly all work. But for two centuries or more, Western society has been built around the central importance of paid work. The experience of unemployment—being unable to find a job when one wants it—is still a largely negative one. And unemployment does bring with it unfortunate effects, including, sometimes, falling into poverty.

GROWING UNEMPLOYMENT

Rates of unemployment fluctuated considerably over the course of the twentieth century. In Western countries, unemployment reached a peak during the Great Depression in the early 1930s, when some 20 percent of the workforce was out of work in the United States. Economist John Maynard Keynes, who strongly influenced public policy in Europe and the United States during the post–World War II period, believed that unemployment results from consumers' lacking sufficient resources to buy goods. Governments can intervene to increase the level of demand in an economy, leading to the creation of new jobs, and the newly employed then have the income with which to buy more goods, thus creating yet more jobs for people who produce them. State management of economic life, most people came to believe, meant that high rates of unemployment belonged to the past. Commitment to full employment became part of government policy in virtually all Western societies. Until the 1970s, these policies seemed successful, and economic growth was more or less continuous.

During the 1970s and 1980s, however, Keynesianism was largely abandoned. In the face of economic globalization, governments lost the capability to control economic life as they once did. At the same time, there was a growing belief, particularly among economists, that the "free market" by itself, rather than the government, was best equipped to ensure economic prosperity. These ideas were especially appealing to conservative politicians, initially in the United States and Britain in the 1980s and, to a lesser extent, in other Western industrialized economies. During the same period, unemployment rates shot up in many countries.

Several factors probably explain the increase in unemployment levels in Western countries at that time. One was the rise of international competition in industries on which Western prosperity used to be founded. For example, in 1947, 60 percent of steel production in the world was carried out in the United States. Today, the figure is only about 8 percent, whereas steel production has tripled in Hong Kong, Japan, Singapore, and Taiwan (Worldsteel.org, 2008). A second factor was the worldwide economic recession of the late 1980s and the more severe global recession that began in 2008. A third reason was the increasing use of microelectronics in industry, the net effect of which has been to reduce the need for labor power. Finally, beginning in the 1970s more women sought paid employment, meaning that more people were chasing a limited number of available jobs.

During this time, rates of unemployment tended to be lower in the United States, for example, than in some European nations. This is perhaps because the sheer economic strength of the country gives it more power in world markets than smaller, more fragile economies. Alternatively, it may be that the exceptionally large service sector in the United States provides a greater source of new jobs than in countries where more of the population has traditionally been employed in manufacturing. As we have noted, many of these jobs provide low pay and limited job security. A final explanation, based on research by Chris Kollmeyer (2003), is that most European countries provide much longer-term unemployment compensation than the United States, along with universal health insurance and other forms of social protection. As a result, European workers are under less economic pressure to find work when they are laid off and so are able to wait until a relatively good job comes along.

In the United States, Kollmeyer finds, workers are more likely to take any job that comes along in order to maintain some income. The trade-off, he concludes, is that European countries are willing to accept higher levels of longer-term unemployment for the benefit of having access to higher-quality jobs. In the United States, on the other hand, the choice is for lower levels of shorter-term unemployment but at the cost of moving into lower-quality jobs. At the present time, this may be changing, as many European governments are cutting back on various forms of social welfare spending, in order to reduce their national debts.

Within countries, unemployment is not equally distributed. It varies by race or ethnic background, by age, and by industry and geographic region. Ethnic minorities living in central cities in the United States have much higher rates of long-term unemployment than the rest of the population. A substantial proportion of young people are among the long-term unemployed, again especially among minority groups.

DECLINING LABOR UNION STRENGTH

Although their levels of membership and the extent of their power vary widely, union organizations exist in all Western countries, which also all legally recognize the right of workers to strike in pursuit of economic objectives. Why have unions become a basic feature of Western societies? Why does union-management conflict seem to be a more or less ever-present possibility in industrial settings?

In the early development of modern industry, workers in most countries had no political rights and little influence over the conditions of work in which they found themselves. Unions developed as a means of redressing the imbalance of power between workers and employers. Whereas workers had virtually no power as individuals, through collective organization their influence was considerably increased. An employer can do without the labor of any particular worker but not without that of all or most of the workers in a factory or plant. Unions originally were mainly "defensive" organizations, providing the means whereby workers could counter the overwhelming power that employers wielded over their lives.

Workers today have voting rights in the political sphere, and there are established forms of negotiation with employers, by means of which economic benefits can be pressed for and grievances expressed. However, union influence, both at the level of the local plant and nationally, still remains primarily veto power. In other words, using the resources at their disposal, including the right to strike, unions can only block employers' policies or initiatives, not help formulate them in the first place. There are exceptions to this—for instance, when unions and employers negotiate periodic contracts covering conditions of work.

Earnings tend to be higher in those industries that are more heavily unionized. For example, unionized construction workers had median weekly earnings of $938 in 2012; manufacturing workers, $729. Unionization rates are highest in the government sector, and those workers saw a steady increase in earnings between 2000 and 2009 (Figure 14.1), with median weekly earnings reaching $947 by 2009, before falling to $878 in 2011 (BLS, 2010d, 2011d).

The post–World War II period witnessed a dramatic reversal in the positions of unions in advanced industrial societies. In most developed countries, the period from 1950 to 1980 was a time of steady growth in **union density**—a statistic that represents the number of union members as a percentage of the number of people who could potentially be union members. Union density across the Western economies was highly variable, however. In the United States, for example, union density peaked in the late 1950s, much earlier than in Europe. Countries that reached the highest levels of union density—Belgium, Denmark, Finland, and Sweden, with more than 80 percent of all workers belonging to labor unions in 1985—had three features in common (Western, 1997). First, strong working-class political parties created favorable conditions for labor organizing. Second, bargaining between firms and labor unions was coordinated at the national level rather than occurring separately in different industries, or at the local level. Third, unions rather than the state directly administered unemployment insurance, ensuring that workers who lost their jobs did not leave the labor movement. Countries lacking one or more of these factors had lower rates of union density, ranging between two-fifths and two-thirds of the working population.

After 1980, unions suffered declines across the advanced industrial countries. In the United States, the decline began even earlier; unionization peaked at more than a third of the workforce during the 1950s, and has been declining steadily since that time, to only 11.9 percent in 2011 (Dickens and Leonard, 1985; BLS, 2011d). There is, however, considerable variation in union membership by occupation and industry (BLS, 2010d). For example, while only about 6.9 percent of all private-sector wage and salary workers were unionized in 2011, the rate was three times higher in transportation and utilities (21.9 percent) and twice as high in construction (14 percent); it was much lower in agriculture and related industries (1.4 percent) and in financial services (1.6 percent). The highest rates of unionization were among public-sector workers, nearly five times higher on average than the private sector: more than a third (37.4 percent) of all government employees belonged to unions in 2009, reaching 43.3 percent for local government.

There are several possible explanations for the difficulties confronted by unions since 1980. Perhaps the most common is the decline of the older manufacturing industries and the rise of the service sector. The United States, for example, has lost many manufacturing jobs during recent years, and manufacturing has traditionally been a stronghold for organized labor, whereas jobs in such services as wholesale and retail trade, education, health services, and leisure and hospitality have historically been more resistant to unionization. Yet it is precisely these sorts of service-sector jobs that have grown most rapidly (U.S. Bureau of the Census, 2008a).

Some of the largest employers of the growing number of service workers have been highly effective at stifling all efforts of their workforce to unionize. Walmart, the world's largest corporation, is one example: Its nearly 2

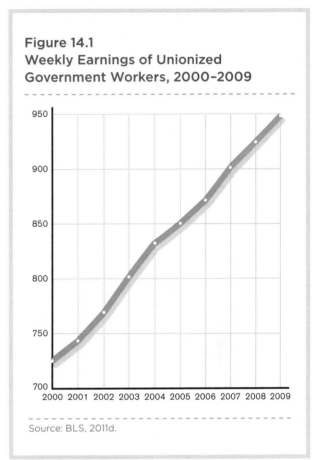

Figure 14.1
Weekly Earnings of Unionized Government Workers, 2000–2009

Source: BLS, 2011d.

union density • A statistic that represents the number of union members as a percentage of the number of people who could potentially be union members.

million employees worldwide, with few exceptions, have not been allowed to form unions. (Under pressure from the Chinese government, Walmart recently allowed its growing number of stores in China to be unionized, although by the official governmental union rather than more independent ones.)

Attributing the decline of unionization to the rise of service-sector employment, however, has a number of weaknesses. Sociologist Bruce Western (1997) argues that this factor alone cannot account for the experience of the 1970s in many advanced industrial economies, which was generally a good period for unions—the United States was an exception—and yet was also characterized by a shift from manufacturing to services. Moreover, at least some of the growth in service-sector employment in the United States has been in areas that have been successfully unionized in recent years. The fastest-growing U.S. labor union is the Service Employees International Union (SEIU), which has 2.1 million members in such diverse areas as health care, janitorial work, security, state and local government, public school employees, bus drivers, and child care (SEIU, 2012).

The rapid fall in union membership in the United States is due to a combination of factors, chief among which is the loss of once-unionized manufacturing jobs to low-wage countries around the world, particularly in East Asia, and most notably China—a country where independent labor unions are illegal. Such job loss, real or threatened, has greatly weakened the bargaining power of unions in the manufacturing sector, and as a result has lowered their appeal to workers. Why join a union and pay union dues if the union cannot deliver wage increases or job security? Unionization efforts in the United States have also been hampered in recent years by decisions of the National Labor Relations Board (NLRB), the government agency responsible for protecting the right of workers to form unions and engage in collective bargaining. The NLRB has proven ineffective at protecting efforts to unionize workplaces, failing to take aggressive action when businesses harass or fire union organizers (Estlund, 2006; Clawson and Clawson, 1999).

It is significant that the service jobs that have been successfully unionized by such unions as SEIU are precisely those that cannot be exported to other countries: janitors, nurses, and state and local government employees. These are all jobs that are tied to a specific location, where well-organized workers can still achieve some measure of job security and wage gains without fear that their place of employment will close shop and move to a low-wage country. Labor unions traditionally tied to manufacturing have recognized this and now are actively seeking new members in those service sectors where the jobs cannot be exported. The United Auto Workers (UAW), for example, has branched out to organize technical, office, and professional workers, including graduate students at the University of California and some 20 other colleges and universities. United Steelworkers members now include workers in offices, nursing homes, hospitals, hotels, restaurants, and colleges and universities—in fact, as their website boasts, "in just about every job imaginable" (United Steelworkers, 2008).

In the United States, unions clearly face a crisis of even greater dimensions than their counterparts in most European countries. Union-protected working conditions and wages have eroded in major industries over the past 30 years. Workers in the trucking, steel, and car industries have all accepted lower wages than those previously negotiated. The unions came out second best in several major strikes, beginning with the crushing of the air traffic controllers' union in the early 1980s. In recent years the UAW has been forced to reach agreements with Ford, Chrysler, and General Motors that conceded wage cuts, in exchange for a freeze on outsourcing jobs, along with promises of employer support for retired workers' health care.

One consequence of the erosion of workers' power has been a revolt within the labor movement itself. A number of unions have challenged the dominance of the once-powerful American Federation of Labor and Congress of Industrial Organizations (AFL-CIO), a confederation of 57 unions representing 12.2 million workers (AFL-CIO, 2011). Frustrated with the AFL-CIO's inability to organize more workers or achieve significant gains, in 2005 seven leading unions broke off to form Change to Win, a more militant federation that is composed in large part of 6 million women and minority service-sector workers. The unions that made up this new organization at the time represented more than a third of the original membership of the AFL-CIO. The revolt was led by SEIU and its charismatic leader, Andy Stern, and originally included the SEIU, Teamsters, and five other unions. Change to Win concentrated its organizing in areas where the jobs could not be sent overseas: for example, Walmart employees, hotel workers, and truckers who move goods from U.S. container ports. Among their demands was the passage of the Employee Free Choice Act, which would require employers to recognize a union if the majority of its workers signed cards saying they were in favor. This "card check" approach to union membership would bypass elections, as currently required by law. Proponents claim that elections are seldom democratic, because companies often harass or fire union organizers, threaten workers who support the union, and coerce workers into voting against union formation. Since its formation, however, Change to Win has lowered its expectations, now describing itself as a "strategic organizing center" rather than a new federation of labor unions. More generally, as the U.S. organized labor movement has shrunk, it has also splintered, which has greatly hampered its effectiveness (Early, 2011).

INDUSTRIAL CONFLICT

There have long been conflicts between workers and those in economic and political authority over them. Riots against conscription and high taxes and food riots at periods of harvest failure were common in urban areas of Europe in the eighteenth century. These "premodern" forms of labor conflict continued up to not much more than a century ago in some countries. For example, there were food riots in several large Italian towns in 1868 (Geary, 1981). Such traditional forms of confrontation were not just sporadic, irrational outbursts of violence: The threat or use of violence had the effect of lowering the price of grain and other essential foodstuffs (Booth, 1977; Rudé, 1964; Thompson, 1971).

Industrial conflict between workers and employers at first tended to follow these older patterns. In situations of confrontation, workers would quite often leave their places of employment and form crowds in the streets; they would make their grievances known through their unruly behavior or by engaging in acts of violence against the authorities. Workers in some parts of France in the late nineteenth century would threaten disliked employers with hanging (Holton, 1978). Use of the strike as a weapon, today commonly associated with organized bargaining between workers and management, developed only slowly and sporadically.

Strikes We can define a **strike** as a temporary stoppage of work by a group of employees to express a grievance or enforce a demand (Hyman, 1984). All the components of this definition are important in separating strikes from other forms of opposition and conflict. A strike is *temporary* because workers intend to return to the same job with the same employer; when workers quit altogether, the term *strike* is not appropriate. As a *stoppage of work*, a strike

> **strike** • A temporary stoppage of work by a group of employees in order to express a grievance or enforce a demand.

is distinguishable from an overtime ban or "slowdown." A *group* of workers has to be involved, because a strike is a collective action, not the response of one individual worker. That those involved are *employees* serves to separate strikes from protests such as may be conducted by tenants or students. Finally, a strike involves seeking to make known a grievance or to press a demand; workers who miss work to go to a ball game could not be said to be on strike.

Workers choose to go on strike for many specific reasons. For much of the twentieth century, U.S. workers typically went on strike to secure higher wages, better hours, safer working conditions, and security of employment, and occasionally to protest against technological changes that would make their work duller or lead to layoffs. In all these circumstances the strike is essentially a mechanism of power: a weapon of people who are relatively powerless in the workplace and whose working lives are affected by managerial decisions over which they have little or no control. It is usually a weapon of last resort, to be used when other negotiations have failed, because workers on strike either receive no income or depend on union funds, which might be limited.

Throughout much of the latter half of the twentieth century, at least in the automobile, steel, and other industries where labor unions were strong, strikes were usually successful. An expanding economy, coupled with well-organized labor militancy, ensured that workers would share in economic growth. During the past quarter century, however, globalization has eroded many of these gains. Competition with low-wage labor elsewhere in the world has resulted in factory closures and layoffs, undermining the effectiveness of strikes and other militant forms of labor action. As Figure 14.2 shows, the number of strikes plummeted after the mid-1970s, and today strikes are increasingly rare. Workers in many industries have instead accepted pay cuts in the hope of keeping their jobs, and as we will discuss in the next section, labor union membership has declined significantly.

Lockouts and "Work to Rule" Strikes represent only one aspect or type of conflict in which workers and management may become involved. Other closely related expressions of organized conflict are *lockouts*—in which the employers rather than the workers bring about a stoppage of work—output restrictions, and clashes in contract negotiations. "Work to rule" is a form of organized labor action in which workers do the minimum work that is legally required of them, carefully following health, safety, and other regulations. Work to rule usually results in costly slowdowns for the firm because workers routinely exceed the requirements of their contracts and often may even violate health, safety, and wage and hour regulations in order to get the job done. Work to rule is typically done in situations where strikes may be illegal, such as among schoolteachers, whose contracts often forbid strikes. Less-organized expressions of conflict may include high labor turnover, absenteeism, and interference with production machinery.

WHAT DO WORKERS WANT?

An individual's quality of life depends on his or her position in the labor market. Arguably this is truer in the United States than in any other comparably developed economy. Americans spend more time at work than do citizens of other advanced industrial countries. U.S. living standards also reflect income and employment-related benefits more directly than do living standards in other comparably developed countries where governments universally guarantee paid vacation, job training, and health insurance. There is also more variability in terms of pay and work conditions in the U.S. labor market than elsewhere. Yet, in spite of the overwhelming importance of the labor market for the life conditions of working

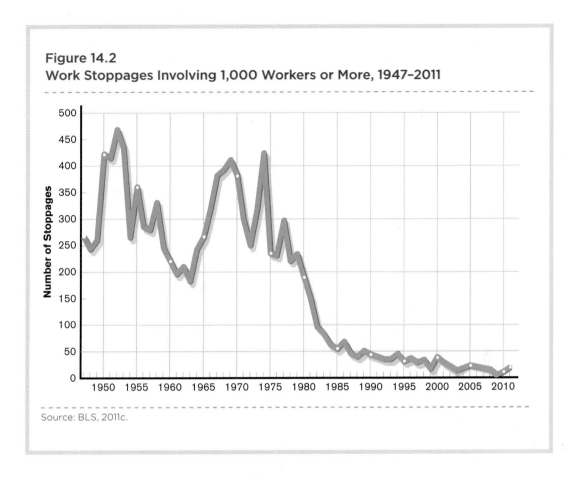

Figure 14.2
Work Stoppages Involving 1,000 Workers or More, 1947–2011

Source: BLS, 2011c.

Americans, there has been relatively little investigation of how workers view the framework through which the U.S. labor market is governed.

For this reason, Richard Freeman of Harvard University and Joel Rogers of the University of Wisconsin set out to find out what workers want in regard to the conditions under which they labor. Freeman and Rogers (1999) designed the Worker Representation and Participation Survey (WRPS) to canvass workers systematically in a wide variety of professions for their opinions on their employment and how their workplaces could be improved. Freeman and Rogers's findings are based on a national telephone survey of 2,400 workers in private-sector establishments that employ 25 or more people. They excluded top managers, the self-employed, owners of firms or their relatives, public-sector workers, and employees in small firms. Overall, the population from which survey respondents were selected covers approximately 75 percent of all private-sector workers. The findings range across a wide variety of aspects of people's work lives, including causes of worker dissatisfaction, attitudes toward unionization, views of management, and worker knowledge of protective labor legislation. In-depth follow-up interviews were conducted with 801 workers, who were asked about their views of alternative institutional designs for American workplaces.

The overwhelming finding of Freeman and Rogers's study is that what workers want is more influence at work. American workers believe that if they had more say over how production were carried out, not only would they enjoy work more but also their firms would be more competitive and problems would be solved more effectively. Furthermore, influence is associated with a wide range of attitudes about work: Workers satisfied with their degree of influence report that they enjoy going to work, grade employee-management relations as excellent, and trust their employer. In contrast, workers who are dissatisfied with their degree of influence tend to dislike going to work, report poor relations with management, and distrust their employers.

One of the most surprising findings of the WRPS concerns the kind of institutional arrangement workers consider ideal for achieving greater say. Contrary to what Freeman and Rogers expected, workers prefer an organization run jointly by workers and management to one run by employees alone. Workers were also asked to choose between two hypothetical organizations, "one that management cooperated with in discussing issues, but had no power to make decisions," and "one that had more power but management opposed." Sixty-three percent of all employees chose the former organization, whereas only 22 percent stated that they would prefer the latter. These results—in which workers effectively indicated that they would prefer weaker to stronger organizations, in spite of the fact that they also reported wanting more say at work—make sense in light of another question on Freeman and Rogers's survey. When asked if they thought an organization could be effective without managerial support, three-quarters of all respondents indicated that they believed an employee organization could function only with management cooperation.

CONCEPT CHECKS

1. What are three defining characteristics of transnational corporations?
2. What is a labor union? Why have unions in the United States suffered from a decline in membership since the 1980s?
3. According to Freeman and Rogers's research, how can workplaces be changed to better meet the desires of modern workers?
4. In your opinion, how will globalization change the nature of work?

4 UNANSWERED QUESTIONS

The nature of work and economic life in the United States—indeed, throughout the world—is rapidly changing. Advances in technology, global supply chains, the information revolution, a revolution in shipping—all these are transforming the world at a pace unprecedented since the Industrial Revolution of the eighteenth and nineteenth centuries. As a result, the occupational structure in all industrialized countries has changed substantially since the beginning of the twentieth century, and the United States is no exception (Figure 14.3). In 1900, about three-quarters of the employed American population were in manual work, either farming or blue-collar work such as manufacturing. White-collar professional and service jobs were much fewer in number. By 1960, however, more people worked in white-collar professional and service jobs than in manual labor. By 1993 the occupational system had basically reversed its structure from 1900. Today, almost three-quarters of the employed population work in white-collar professional and service jobs, while the rest work in blue-collar and farming jobs. The reasons for this, and how they will play out in terms of job opportunities for young people today, remain poorly understood. Perhaps because we are in the midst of such a significant transformation, there are disagreements over its causes and consequences.

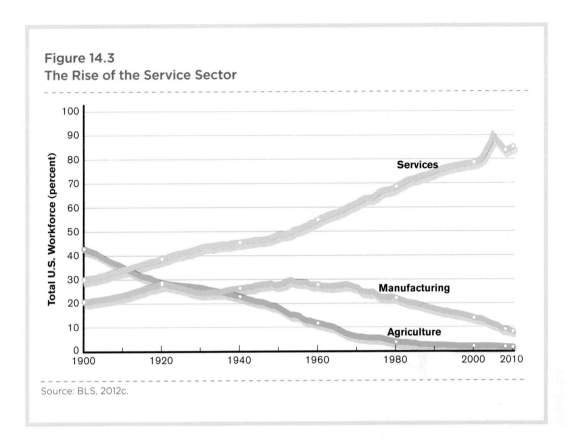

Figure 14.3
The Rise of the Service Sector

Total U.S. Workforce (percent)

Services

Manufacturing

Agriculture

1900   1920   1940   1960   1980   2000   2010

Source: BLS, 2012c.

Will Automation Make Things Better or Worse for Workers?

The relationship between technology and work has long been of interest to sociologists. How is our experience of work affected by the type of technology involved? As industrialization has progressed, technology has assumed an ever-greater role at the workplace— from factory automation to the computerization of office work. The current information technology revolution has attracted renewed interest in this question. Technology can lead to greater efficiency and productivity, but how does it affect the way work is experienced by those who carry it out? For sociologists, one of the main questions is how the move to more complex systems influences the nature of work and the institutions in which it is performed.

The concept of **automation**, or programmable machinery, was introduced in the mid-1800s, when Christopher Spencer, an American, invented the first fully automatic turret lathe, a programmable lathe that made screws, nuts, and gears. Automation has thus far affected relatively few industries, but with advances in the design of industrial robots, its effect is certain to become greater. A robot is an automatic device that can perform functions ordinarily

automation • Production processes monitored and controlled by machines with only minimal supervision from people.

done by human workers. The term *robot* comes from the Czech word *robota*, or serf, popularized about 50 years ago by the playwright Karel Čapek.

The majority of the robots used in industry worldwide is to be found in automobile manufacture. Although one of the first industrial robots was used in a General Motors plant, the Japanese automobile industry pioneered their extensive use. Most recently, and perhaps significantly, China has begun to mass-produce its Chery automobile for the global market, persuading one of the world's leading automation firms, ABB Robotics, to relocate its corporate headquarters from Detroit to Shanghai. While it may seem likely that automated production will spread rapidly in coming years, as robots decline in cost while becoming increasingly sophisticated, their usage may well have peaked, at least for the time being: Robots have proven costly to maintain, leading many automobile manufacturers to emphasize more efficient management practices over the latest high-tech automation (Bradsher, 2000).

The use of robots, or at least robotic arms, is spreading from automobiles to a wide range of other industries. As one report describes it (Markoff, 2012),

> At the Philips Electronics factory on the coast of China, hundreds of workers use their hands and specialized tools to assemble electric shavers. That is the old way. At a sister factory here in the Dutch countryside, 128 robot arms do the same work with yoga-like flexibility. Video cameras guide them through feats well beyond the capability of the most dexterous human. One robot arm endlessly forms three perfect bends in two connector wires and slips them into holes almost too small for the eye to see. The arms work so fast that they must be enclosed in glass cages to prevent the people supervising them from being injured. And they do it all without a coffee break—three shifts a day, 365 days a year.

The world's largest electronics assembly company, Foxconn, currently relies on more than a million workers worldwide to assemble Apple, Dell, HP, and other major brands' computers, smartphones, and other electronic equipment. Foxconn, however, says it plans to install a million robots in its Chinese factories in the near future. As Terry Gou, Foxconn CEO, explained it during an interview given in a Chinese zoo, "as human beings are also animals, to manage one million animals gives me a headache" (Markoff, 2012). As wages have gone up in China, there is growing incentive to replace more costly workers with low-cost robots that work tirelessly around the clock, never complain, never go on strike, and never embarrass clients (e.g., Apple) by committing suicide, as has happened with a number of Foxconn workers in recent years.

The spread of automation provoked a heated debate among sociologists and experts in industrial relations over the effect of the new technology on workers, their skills, and their level of commitment to their work. In his now-classic *Alienation and Freedom*, Robert Blauner (1964) examined the experience of workers in four different industries with varying levels of technology. Using the ideas of Durkheim and Marx, Blauner measured the extent to which workers in each industry experienced alienation in the form of powerlessness, meaninglessness, isolation, and self-estrangement. He concluded that workers on assembly lines were the most alienated of all, but that levels of alienation were somewhat lower at workplaces using automation. In other words, Blauner argued that the introduction of automation to factories was responsible for reversing the otherwise steady trend toward increased worker alienation. Automation helped integrate the workforce and gave workers a sense of control over their work that had been lacking with other forms of technology.

A very different thesis was set forth by Harry Braverman in his highly influential *Labor and Monopoly Capital* (1974). In Braverman's eyes, automation was part of the overall "de-skilling" of the industrial labor force. By imposing Taylorist organizational techniques and breaking up the labor process into specialized tasks, managers were able to exert control over the workforce. In both industrial settings and modern offices, the introduction of technology contributed to this overall degradation of work by limiting the need for creative human input. Instead, all that was required was an unthinking, unreflective body capable of endlessly carrying out the same unskilled task.

A somewhat more recent study sheds more light on this debate. Sociologist Richard Sennett (1998) studied the people who worked in a bakery that had been bought by a large food conglomerate and automated with the introduction of high-tech machinery. Computerized baking radically altered the way bread was made. Instead of using their hands to mix the ingredients and knead the dough, and their noses and eyes to judge when the bread was done baking, the bakery's workers had no physical contact with the materials or the loaves of bread. In fact, the entire process was controlled and monitored via computer screen. Computers decided oven temperature and baking time. Although at times the machines produced excellent-quality bread, at other times the results were burned, blackened loaves. The workers at this bakery (it would be erroneous to call them bakers) were hired because they were skilled with computers, not because they knew how to bake bread. Ironically, these workers used very few of their computer skills. The production process involved little more than pushing buttons on a computer. In fact, one time, when the computerized machinery broke down, the entire production process was halted because none of the bakery's "skilled" workers was trained or empowered to repair the problem. The workers that Sennett (1998) observed wanted to be helpful, to make things work again, but they could not, because automation had diminished their freedom to make decisions. The introduction of computerized technology in the workplace has led both to a general increase in all workers' skills, but also to a split workforce composed of a small group of highly skilled professionals with high degrees of flexibility and freedom in their jobs and a larger group of clerical, service, and production workers who lack such autonomy.

Whether or not automation replaces workers with impersonal robots, or upgrades their skills while robots engage in the tedious labor, remains an unresolved issue. Part of the problem is that the widespread use of robots is relatively recent, so the jury is still out on its long-term impact. Another problem is more conceptual, however. As feminist researchers have argued, what constitutes "skill" is itself socially constructed (Steinberg, 1990). As such, conventional understandings of "skilled" work tend to reflect the social status of the typical incumbent of the job rather than the difficulty of the task in an objective sense. The history of occupations is rife with examples of jobs in which the very same task was assigned a different skill level (and even renamed!) once women entered the field (Reskin and Roos, 1990). To take but one example, "private secretary" was once a prestigious male occupation. Once a growing number of women moved into secretarial positions in the twentieth century, however, the job became reclassified as merely a clerical position, its tasks were downgraded, and it ceased to be a step on the ladder to management positions (Davies, 1983). The same, of course, holds for other low-status workers, such as racial minorities. Even where gender and racial biases are not in operation, skill has multiple dimensions; the same job may be downgraded on one dimension while simultaneously upgraded on another (Block, 1990).

Thus opinions as to whether automation has de-skilled work depend on which dimension of skill is examined. In his comprehensive review of the skill debate, Spenner

(1983) notes that studies examining skill in terms of the actual complexity of tasks have tended to support the "up-skilling" position, whereas those that have examined skill in terms of the autonomy and/or control exercised by the worker have tended to find that work has in fact been "de-skilled" through automation (Vallas and Beck, 1996; Zuboff, 1988).

What Will the Economy of the Future Look Like?

During the period 2000–2010, the United States lost 5.7 million manufacturing jobs. During the same period, the largest growth occurred in the service sector. The share of the workforce engaged in the service sector grew from 73 percent in 2000 to 78 percent in 2010 (BLS, 2012c). Employment in professional and business services, which pay relatively high wages, grew by 1.2 million. But most service-sector growth occurred in areas, such as wholesale and retail trade, education, leisure and hospitality, and health care, which typically pay lower wages than the manufacturing jobs that were lost.

By 2014, blue-collar work will have declined even further, with most of the increase in new jobs occurring in lower-wage service industries. Of the 15 occupations predicted to grow the most between 2004 and 2014, just one will require a two-year college degree (registered nurses), while only four will require a college degree or higher (elementary school teachers, accountants, auditors, managers, and college teachers). Together, these five relatively high-paying occupations are predicted to add slightly more than 2 million new jobs. The rest—adding twice as many jobs and paying low wages—will require, for the most part, only on-the-job training. The largest increase, 736,000 jobs, is predicted for retail salespeople, such as workers for Walmart (U.S. Bureau of the Census, 2008d).

Some observers suggest that what is occurring today is a transition to a new type of society no longer based primarily on manufacturing or low-paying service work. We are entering, they claim, a phase of development beyond the industrial era altogether. A variety of terms have been coined to describe this new social order, such as the *postindustrial society*, the *information age*, and the *"new" economy*. The term that has come into most common usage, however, is **knowledge economy**.

A precise definition of *knowledge economy* is difficult to formulate, but in general it refers to an economy in which ideas, information, and forms of knowledge underpin innovation and economic growth. In a knowledge economy, much of the workforce is involved in research and development; advanced technologies; and the design, marketing, sales, and service of innovative products, rather than in their physical production. Employees in this economy can be termed "knowledge workers." The knowledge economy is dominated by the constant flow of information and opinions and by the powerful potential of science and technology.

knowledge economy • A society no longer based primarily on the production of material goods but instead on the production of knowledge. Its emergence has been linked to the development of a broad base of consumers who are technologically literate and have made new advances in the computing, entertainment, and telecommunications part of their lives.

How widespread is the knowledge economy at the start of the twenty-first century? The World Bank Institute (2012) created a Knowledge Economy Index (KEI) to gauge the extent of the knowledge economy among developed nations by measuring the percentage of each country's overall business output attributable to knowledge-based industries. Knowledge-based industries are understood broadly to include high technology, education and training, research and development, and the financial and investment sector. Knowledge economy jobs are typically said to include: scientists and engineers engaged in innovative research and development, and research scholars more generally; highly skilled occupations that involve the use of advanced technology; financial management and services; and, in general, any occupation or profession that requires the ability to think symbolically and analytically (and that typically involves higher education and specialized skills) (Castells, 2000).

The KEI uses several measures to gauge a country's knowledge economy performance: its degree of educational attainment at the secondary and college levels; access to communications, including telephones, computers, and the Internet; scientific accomplishments, as measured by publications in scientific journals, patents, and royalty payments; adherence to the rule of law; an effective regulatory environment; and openness to free trade with other countries. By these measures, the list is topped by Scandinavian countries, followed by other European countries, and by the United States. Taiwan is the highest-ranked non-European country on the KEI. However, since 2000, several countries in Asia and Latin America have continually risen in the rankings. In 2012 the United States ranked 12th, just ahead of Taiwan (World Bank Institute, 2012).

Investments in the knowledge economy—in the form of public education, software development, and research and development—now make up a significant part of many countries' budgets. Sweden, for example, invested nearly 11 percent of its overall gross domestic product in the knowledge economy in 1995. France was a close second because of its extensive spending on public education. China is rapidly moving up the scale, investing large sums of public money in higher education, science parks, and high-tech research.

In light of the effect of the knowledge economy and the demand for a flexible labor force, some sociologists and economists have argued that more and more people in the future will become **portfolio workers**—that is, they will have a skill portfolio (a number of different job skills and credentials) that they will use to move between several jobs during the course of their working lives. Only a relatively small proportion of workers will have continuous careers in the current sense. Some see this move to the portfolio worker in a positive light: Workers will not be stuck in the same job for years on end and will be able to plan their work lives in a creative way (Handy, 1994). Others hold that flexibility in practice means that organizations can hire and fire more or less at will, undermining any sense of security their workers might have. Employers will have only a short-term commitment to their workforces and will be able to minimize the paying of extra benefits or pension rights.

What does this portend for the United States? No one can say for sure, but it seems unlikely that the American workforce—which in July 2012 included 142.2 million employed people, along with another 13 million looking for work (BLS, 2012d)—will all somehow become knowledge economy workers. Will current economic changes produce another period of sustained economic growth, in which workers at all levels become a scarcity, with wages and salaries steadily rising, as they did in the post–World War II period? Or will the American workforce increasingly be split into two categories: those with the educational background, skills, and good fortune to thrive as knowledge workers, and everyone else,

portfolio workers • Workers who possess a diversity of skills or qualifications and are therefore able to move easily from job to job.

who may find themselves chasing after a dwindling number of manufacturing jobs and lower-paying service work?

How Permanent Is Your Job Likely to Be?

This leads to another question: Does the future of work mean the end of the full-time, life-long career with one or at best a few employers?

Since the mid-1980s, in all the industrialized countries except the United States, the average length of the working week has become shorter. Workers still undertake long stretches of overtime, but some governments are beginning to introduce new limits on permissible working hours. In France, for example, annual overtime is restricted to a maximum of 130 hours a year. In most countries, there is a general tendency toward shortening the average working career. More people would probably quit the labor force at age 60 or earlier if they could afford to do so.

If the amount of time given over to paid employment continues to shrink, and the need to have a job becomes less central, the nature of working careers might become substantially reorganized. Job sharing or flexible working hours, which arose primarily as a result of the increasing numbers of working parents trying to balance the commitments of workplace and family, for example, might become more common. Some work analysts have suggested that sabbaticals of the university type should be extended to workers in other spheres: People would be entitled to take a year off to study or pursue some form of self-improvement. Perhaps more individuals will engage in life planning, in which they arrange to work in different ways (paid, unpaid, full or part time, etc.) at different stages in their lives. Thus some people might choose to enter the labor force in their late thirties, having followed a period of formal education in their early twenties with time devoted to pursuits such as travel. People might opt to work part time throughout their lives rather than being forced to because of a lack of full-time employment opportunities.

The Future of Work program, funded by the Russell Sage and Rockefeller foundations, studied nearly 500 businesses in 25 industries, surveying some 10,000 workers and conducting interviews with more than 1,700 managers and workers. The research offers a complex picture of the changing workplace, particularly for lower-wage workers. In some cases, workers are being displaced by advanced technologies—think about the last time you made a phone call and spoke to an electronic voice rather than an actual person, or ordered something online rather than speaking with a salesperson. In other cases, businesses have partnered with their employees to develop creative ways to combine new technologies with upgraded (and higher-paying) work. The study found that even the temporary work industry does not always lead to dead-end jobs: About half of all temp jobs lead eventually to permanent ones (Appelbaum, Murnane, and Bernhardt, 2003).

Sociologist Joyce Rothschild (2000), who has studied workplace trends for many years, offers a hopeful picture of the possibility for greater worker participation in the workplace. She argues that the move toward more networked forms of business organization could result in a democratization of the workplace. She identifies a number of trends in support of this possibility. These include a drive toward flatter, more team-based forms of organization, sometimes called "quality circles" or "total quality management"; workplaces in which the workers help shape the use of technology; the inclusion of women and minorities on teams; and even worker-based management of firms.

Another important employment trend of the past decade has been the replacement of full-time workers by part-time workers, who are hired and fired on a contingency basis.

Most temporary workers are hired for the least-skilled, lowest-paying jobs. But many of the portfolio workers whom we've just discussed take jobs on a part-time basis as well. As a general rule, part-time jobs do not include the benefits associated with full-time work, such as medical insurance, paid vacation time, or retirement benefits. Because employers can save on the costs of wages and benefits, the use of part-time workers has become increasingly common. By 2005, researchers estimated that contingency workers already made up approximately 4 percent of the American workforce, or about 5.7 million people (BLS, 2005).

The temporary employment agency Manpower, Inc., founded in Milwaukee, Wisconsin, in 1948, has become a global leader in the provision of temporary workers. This company employed 5 million temps (which Manpower refers to as "associates") in 80 countries in 2007 and was the 120th-largest corporation in the United States and 408th on the *Fortune* list of the Global 500 (Manpower, Inc., 2008). Manpower provides labor on a flexible basis to virtually all Fortune 500 companies. Clearly, temporary labor has become a critical component of the worldwide organization of work and occupations. Moreover, since the economic downturn of 2008, over 54 percent of the jobs created in all sectors have been temporary. By the end of 2011, approximately 1 in every 50 workers held a temporary position (Baden, 2011).

There has been some debate over the psychological effects of part-time work on the workforce. Many temporary workers fulfill their assignments promptly and satisfactorily, but others rebel against their tenuous positions by shirking their responsibilities or sabotaging their results. Some temporary workers have been observed trying to "look busy" or to work longer than necessary on rather simple tasks. Finally, contingency workers have tried to avoid emotionally intensive work that would require them to become psychologically committed to their employer.

However, some recent surveys of work indicate that part-time workers register higher levels of job satisfaction than those in full-time employment. Some individuals seem to find reward precisely in the fact that they are able to balance paid work with other activities and enjoy a more varied life. Others might choose to "peak" their lives, giving full commitment to paid work from their youth to their middle years, then perhaps changing to a second career, which would open up new interests.

How will work change in the future? It appears very likely that people will take a more active look at their lives than in the past, moving in and out of paid work at different points. These are positive options, however, only when they are deliberately chosen. The reality for most is that regular paid work remains the key to day-to-day survival and that unemployment is experienced as a hardship rather than an opportunity.

CONCEPT CHECKS

1. Why does automation lead to worker alienation?

2. What are the fastest growing job sectors? Based on these trends, what are the implications for careers in the future?

Chapter 14
Work and Economic Life

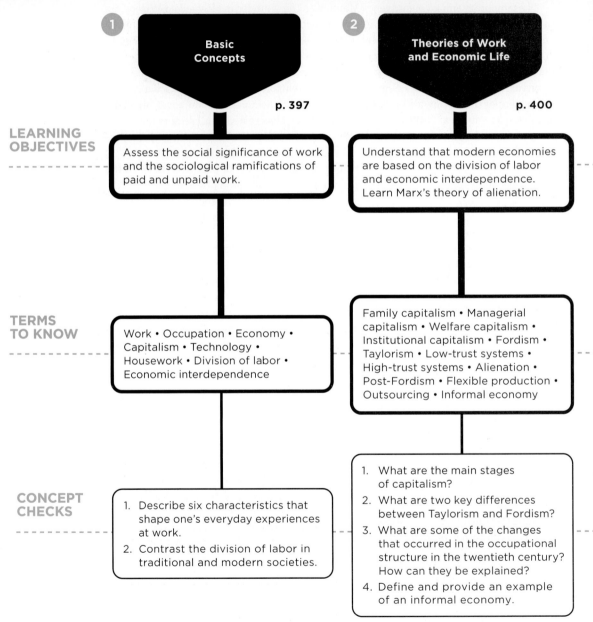

1 Basic Concepts

p. 397

2 Theories of Work and Economic Life

p. 400

LEARNING OBJECTIVES

Assess the social significance of work and the sociological ramifications of paid and unpaid work.

Understand that modern economies are based on the division of labor and economic interdependence. Learn Marx's theory of alienation.

TERMS TO KNOW

Work • Occupation • Economy • Capitalism • Technology • Housework • Division of labor • Economic interdependence

Family capitalism • Managerial capitalism • Welfare capitalism • Institutional capitalism • Fordism • Taylorism • Low-trust systems • High-trust systems • Alienation • Post-Fordism • Flexible production • Outsourcing • Informal economy

CONCEPT CHECKS

1. Describe six characteristics that shape one's everyday experiences at work.
2. Contrast the division of labor in traditional and modern societies.

1. What are the main stages of capitalism?
2. What are two key differences between Taylorism and Fordism?
3. What are some of the changes that occurred in the occupational structure in the twentieth century? How can they be explained?
4. Define and provide an example of an informal economy.

Exercises: Thinking Sociologically

1. Explain the meaning of globalization of the modern economy. Explain how this textbook sees globalization affecting workers in third world countries and in advanced industrial societies.

2. Discuss some of the important ways that the nature of work will change for the contemporary worker as companies apply more automation and larger-scale production processes and as oligopolies become more pervasive. Explain each of these trends and how they affect workers, both now and in the future.

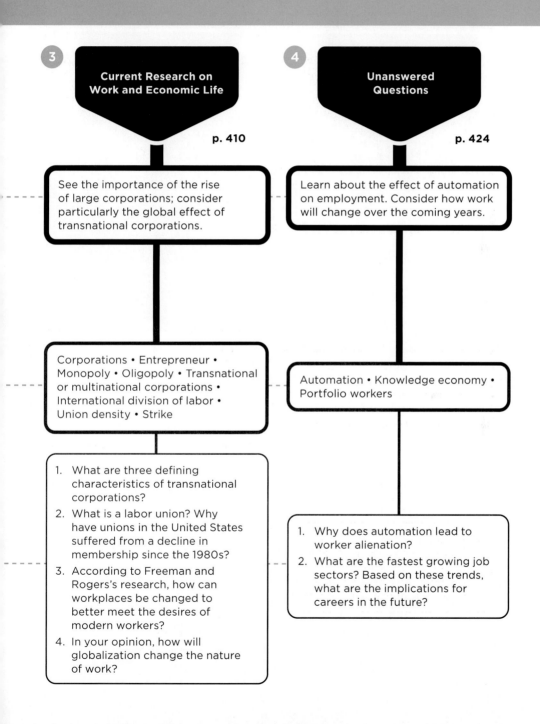

3

Current Research on Work and Economic Life

p. 410

See the importance of the rise of large corporations; consider particularly the global effect of transnational corporations.

Corporations • Entrepreneur • Monopoly • Oligopoly • Transnational or multinational corporations • International division of labor • Union density • Strike

1. What are three defining characteristics of transnational corporations?
2. What is a labor union? Why have unions in the United States suffered from a decline in membership since the 1980s?
3. According to Freeman and Rogers's research, how can workplaces be changed to better meet the desires of modern workers?
4. In your opinion, how will globalization change the nature of work?

4

Unanswered Questions

p. 424

Learn about the effect of automation on employment. Consider how work will change over the coming years.

Automation • Knowledge economy • Portfolio workers

1. Why does automation lead to worker alienation?
2. What are the fastest growing job sectors? Based on these trends, what are the implications for careers in the future?

Families and Intimate Relationships

15

The "typical" American family is made up of a mother, father, and children who live with their parents.

True or false?

Turn the page for the correct answer.

I f you answered "true," you would be incorrect. But ours is a bit of a "trick" question—most scholars agree that there is no such thing as a "typical" American family in the early twenty-first century. As popular television shows such as *Modern Family* and *The New Normal* reveal, there is no one family form or structure that accounts for the majority of American households today. Data from the U.S. Census show that just 21 percent of all households in 2010 were made up of a married couple with children under age 18. And the notion that the "typical" household includes a breadwinner dad, a stay-at-home mom, and two perfect children is even more dated. Just 23 percent of two-parent households had a stay-at-home mother in 2010 (U.S. Bureau of the Census, 2011b). Families today include people who live alone, single parents with children, stepfamilies, grandparents who share a home with their grandchildren, gay and lesbian couples both with and without children, cohabiters both with and without children, and even divorced spouses who share a home because they can't afford their own places during these difficult recessionary times.

Census data can tell us what the "statistical" norm is, or those behaviors that are objectively more or less common in the United States today. Sociologists, by contrast, help us to shed light on what the "cultural" norm is—and why. Are there family forms that are considered "best" for the health and well-being of U.S. society? Or are all family forms equally healthy and desirable? And if so, why do so many Americans still hold on to the beliefs that some family forms are superior to others? Sociologists David Popenoe and Judith Stacey offer vastly differing perspectives. Popenoe (1993, 1996) argues that the family has changed for the worse since 1960. Over the past five or six decades, divorce, nonmarital births, and cohabitation rates have increased, while marriage and marital fertility rates have decreased. He claims these trends underlie social ills such as child poverty, adolescent pregnancy, substance abuse, and juvenile crime. Increasing rates of divorce and nonmarital births have created millions of female-headed households and have removed men from the child-rearing process. Popenoe argues that this is harmful for children.

Stacey (1998, 2011) counters that the "traditional" American family of the 1950s—praised by Popenoe and conservative politicians as the panacea for all social problems—is a dated and oppressive institution. According to Stacey, the "modern family" with

---

LEARNING OBJECTIVES

① **BASIC CONCEPTS**

Learn how sociologists define and describe families.

② **THEORETICAL AND HISTORICAL PERSPECTIVES ON THE FAMILY**

Review the development of sociological thinking about families. Learn how the family has changed over the last five hundred years.

③ **RESEARCH ON FAMILIES TODAY**

Learn about patterns of marriage, childbearing, and divorce. Analyze how these patterns today differ from those of other periods.

④ **UNANSWERED QUESTIONS**

Recognize alternatives to traditional marriage and family patterns.

"breadwinner-father and child-rearing-mother" perpetuated the "segregation of the sexes by extracting men from, and consigning white married women to, an increasingly privatized domestic domain." The modern family has been replaced by the "postmodern family"—single mothers, blended families, cohabiting couples, lesbian and gay partners, communes, and two-worker families. The postmodern family is well suited to meet the challenges of the current economy and is an appropriate setting for raising children, who need capable, loving caretakers—regardless of their gender, marital status, or sexual orientation, argues Stacey.

Popenoe agrees that children need capable, loving caretakers, yet he maintains that "two parents—a father and a mother—are better for a child than one parent." He claims that biological fathers make "distinctive, irreplaceable contributions" to their children's welfare. Fathers offer a strong male role model to sons, act as disciplinarian for trouble-prone children, provide daughters with a male perspective on heterosexual relationships, and, through their unique play styles, teach their children about teamwork, competition, independence, self-fulfillment, self-control, and regulation of emotions. Mothers, on the other hand, teach their children about communion, the feeling of being connected to others. Both needs can be met only through the gender-differentiated parenting of a mother and father, Popenoe argues.

Stacey retorts that the postmodern family is better suited to the postmodern economy, in which employment has shifted from unionized heavy industries to nonunionized clerical, service, and new industrial sectors. The loss of union-protected jobs means that many men no longer earn enough to support a wife and children. And during the recessionary years of the early twenty-first century, men who suffer long-term unemployment often rely on their wives to fully support their families. At the same time, demand for clerical and service labor, escalating consumption standards, increases in women's educational attainment, and continuing high divorce rates have led women to seek employment outside the home.

Stacey also disagrees with media rhetoric and claims by conservatives, such as Popenoe, who elevate the married, two-parent family as the ideal family form. Their condemnation of other family forms is particularly harmful to the millions of children who live with gay or lesbian parents. Rather than condemning nontraditional family forms, Stacey reasons, family sociologists and policy makers should develop strategies to mitigate the harmful effects of divorce and single parenthood on children. She suggests restructuring work schedules and benefit policies to accommodate familial responsibilities; redistributing work opportunities to reduce unemployment rates; enacting comparable-worth standards of pay equity to enable women as well as men to earn a family wage; providing universal health care, prenatal and child care, and sex education; and rectifying the economic inequities of divorce.

Claiming that "marriage must be re-established as a strong social institution," Popenoe argues that employers should stop relocating married couples with children and should provide more generous parental leave. He also supports a two-tiered system of divorce law. Marriages without minor children would be relatively easy to dissolve, but marriages with young children would be dissolvable only by mutual agreement or on grounds involving a wrong by one party against the other. The proposal has encountered skepticism among feminist scholars, who address the costs for children and adults alike of reinstating grounds of fault for divorce.

Where does the "truth" lie—with Stacey, with Popenoe, or somewhere in between? In this chapter we will learn about what families actually look like today, how families have changed through history, the wide range of forms that families take, and some of the challenges family members face in the early twenty-first century.

THE ANSWER IS FALSE.

1 BASIC CONCEPTS

A **family** is a group of people directly linked by kin connections, the adult members of which take care of the children. **Kinship** ties are connections among individuals, established either through marriage, through the lines of descent that connect blood relatives (mothers, fathers, offspring, grandparents, etc.), or through adoption. **Marriage** can be defined as a socially acknowledged and approved sexual union between two adult individuals. When two people marry, they become kin to one another; however, the marriage bond also connects a wider range of kinspeople. Parents, brothers, sisters, and other blood relatives become relatives of the partner through marriage.

All societies contain what sociologists and anthropologists call the **nuclear family**, two adults living together in a household with their own or adopted children. In most traditional societies, the nuclear family was part of a larger kinship network. When close relatives in addition to a married couple and children live either in the same household or in a close and continuous relationship with one another, we speak of an **extended family**. An extended family may include grandparents, brothers and their wives, sisters and their husbands, aunts, nephews, and so on.

Whether nuclear or extended, families can be divided into **families of orientation** and **families of procreation**. The first is the family into which a person is born or adopted; the second is the family into which one enters as an adult and within which a new generation of children is brought up. A further distinction concerns place of residence. In the United States, when two people marry, they do not necessarily set up their own household in the same area where the bride's or groom's parents live, although they often do so. In some other societies, however, married couples live close to or within the same dwelling as the parents of the bride or groom. When the couple lives near or with the bride's parents, the arrangement is **matrilocal**. In a **patrilocal** pattern, the couple lives near or with the groom's parents.

In Western societies, marriage is associated with **monogamy**. It is illegal for a man or woman to be married to more than one individual at any time. But monogamy is not the only type of

family • A group of individuals related to one another by blood ties, marriage, or adoption, who form an economic unit, the adult members of which are responsible for the upbringing of children. All known societies involve some form of family system, although the nature of family relationships varies widely. While in modern societies the main family form is the nuclear family, extended family relationships are also found.

kinship • A relation that links individuals through blood ties, marriage, or adoption. Kinship relations are by definition part of marriage and the family, but extend much more broadly. While in most modern societies few social obligations are involved in kinship relations extending beyond the immediate family, in other cultures kinship is of vital importance to social life.

marriage • A socially approved sexual relationship between two individuals. Marriage almost always involves two persons of opposite sexes, but in some cultures, types of homosexual marriage are tolerated. Marriage normally forms the basis of a family of procreation—that is, it is expected that the married couple will produce and bring up children. Some societies permit polygamy, in which an individual may have several spouses at the same time.

nuclear family • A family group consisting of a wife, a husband (or one of these), and dependent children.

extended family • A family group consisting of more than two generations of relatives living either within the same household or very close to one another.

families of orientation • The families into which individuals are born.

families of procreation • The families individuals initiate through marriage or by having children.

matrilocal • A family system in which the husband is expected to live near the wife's parents.

patrilocal • A family system in which the wife is expected to live near the husband's parents.

monogamy • A form of marriage in which each married partner is allowed only one spouse at any given time.

marriage worldwide. In a comparison of several hundred early twentieth-century societies, George Murdock (1949) found that **polygamy**, a marriage that allows a husband or wife to have more than one spouse, was permitted in over 80 percent. There are two types of polygamy: **polygyny**, in which a man may have two or more wives at the same time, and **polyandry**, much less common, in which a woman may have two or more husbands simultaneously.

CONCEPT CHECKS

1. Contrast a family of orientation and a family of procreation.
2. Provide an example of a nuclear versus an extended family.
3. What are several alternatives to monogamy?

② THEORETICAL AND HISTORICAL PERSPECTIVES ON THE FAMILY

The study of the family and family life encompasses contrasting approaches. Many perspectives adopted even a few decades ago now seem less convincing in light of recent research and changes in the social world. Nevertheless, it is valuable to trace the evolution of sociological thinking before discussing contemporary approaches to the study of the family. We discuss two of the main theories used to understand the contemporary family, functionalism and feminist approaches, and then provide a historical context for understanding contemporary families.

Sociological Theories of the Family

FUNCTIONALISM

According to the functionalist perspective, families perform important tasks that contribute to society's basic needs and help perpetuate social order. Sociologists in the functionalist tradition regard the nuclear family as fulfilling specialized roles in modern societies. With the advent of industrialization, the family became less important as a unit of economic production and more focused on bearing, rearing, and socializing children.

According to American sociologist Talcott Parsons, the two main functions of families are *primary socialization* and *personality stabilization* (Parsons and Bales, 1955). **Primary socialization** is the process by which children learn their society's cultural norms. Because this happens during early childhood, the family is the most important site for the development of the human personality. **Personality stabilization** refers to the role of the family in assisting adult family members emotionally. Marriage between two adults is the arrangement through which personalities are supported and kept healthy. In industrial societies, the role of the family in

polygamy • A form of marriage in which a person may have two or more spouses simultaneously.

polygyny • A form of marriage in which a man may simultaneously have two or more wives.

polyandry • A form of marriage in which a woman may simultaneously have two or more husbands.

primary socialization • The process by which children learn the cultural norms of the society into which they are born. Primary socialization occurs largely in the family.

personality stabilization • According to the theory of functionalism, the family plays a crucial role in assisting its adult members emotionally. Marriage between adult men and women is the arrangement through which adult personalities are supported and kept healthy.

stabilizing adult personalities becomes critical because the nuclear family is often geographically distant from its extended kin and cannot draw on larger kinship ties.

Parsons regarded the nuclear family as best equipped to handle the demands of industrial society. In the "conventional" family, one adult can work outside the home while the second adult cares for the home and children. In practical terms, this specialization of roles historically has meant the husband adopting the "instrumental" role as breadwinner and the wife assuming the "affective," or emotional support, role in domestic settings.

Today, Parsons's view of the family seems inadequate and outdated. Yet viewed in historical context, his theories are more understandable. The immediate post–World War II years (when Parsons proposed his theories) saw women returning to their traditional roles of wives, mothers, and homemakers and men reassuming positions as sole breadwinners. We can criticize functionalist views of families on other grounds, however. In emphasizing the importance of the family, such theories neglect the role of other social institutions—such as government, media, peers, and schools—in socializing children. The theories also neglect family forms that do not reflect the nuclear family. Families that did not conform to the white, suburban, middle-class ideal were considered deviant, including childless families or families in which husbands were not primary breadwinners.

FEMINIST APPROACHES

For many people, the family provides solace and comfort, love and companionship. Yet it can also be a locus for exploitation, loneliness, and profound inequality. In this regard, feminism has challenged the vision of the family as harmonious and protective. In 1965 the American feminist Betty Friedan wrote of "the problem with no name"—the isolation and boredom of many suburban American housewives trapped in an endless cycle of child care and housework. Others followed, exploring the phenomenon of the "captive wife" (Gavron, 1966) and the damaging effects of "suffocating" family settings on interpersonal relationships (Laing, 1971).

During the 1970s and '80s, feminist perspectives dominated debates and research on the family. Where previously the sociology of the family had focused on family structures, the historical development of the nuclear and extended family, and the importance of kinship ties, feminism directed attention inside families to examine women's experiences in the domestic sphere. Many feminist writers questioned the vision of the family as a cooperative unit based on common interests and mutual support, arguing instead that unequal power relationships within the family meant that certain family members benefited more than others.

Among a broad spectrum of topics, three main feminist themes are particularly important. One is the *domestic division of labor*—the way in which tasks are allocated among household members, where women often specialize in homemaking and childrearing and men specialize in breadwinning. Feminists disagree about the historical emergence of this division. While some see it as an outcome of industrial capitalism, others link it to patriarchy and thus see it as predating industrialization. Although a domestic division of labor probably did exist before industrialization, capitalist production caused a sharper distinction between the domestic and work realms. This process resulted in the crystallization of "male spheres" and "female spheres" and the power relationships that persist today. Until recently, the male breadwinner model has been widespread in most industrialized societies.

Feminist sociologists have studied the way men and women share domestic tasks, such as child care and housework. They have investigated the validity of claims such as that of the "symmetrical family" (Young and Willmott, 1973)—the belief that, over historical time, family roles and responsibilities are becoming more egalitarian. Findings have shown that women still bear the main responsibility for domestic tasks and enjoy less leisure time than men, even though more women are working in paid employment outside the home than before (Gershuny, Godwin, and Jones, 1994; Hochschild and Machung, 1989; Sullivan, 1997). Data from a national study of time use in the United States show that as recently as 2011, men were much less likely than women to do housework, and when they did, they spent 20 percent less time doing it (BLS, 2011e).

Some sociologists have examined the contrasting realms of paid and unpaid work, focusing on the contribution of women's unpaid domestic labor to the overall economy (Oakley, 1974). Others have investigated the distribution of resources among family members and the patterns of access to and control over household finances (Pahl, 1989).

A second theme is the *unequal power relationships* within many families, especially the phenomenon of domestic violence. Wife battering, marital rape, incest, and the sexual abuse of children have all received more public attention as a result of feminists' claims that the violent and abusive sides of family life have long been ignored in both academic contexts and legal and policy circles. Feminist sociologists consider how the family serves as an arena for gender oppression and physical abuse.

Caring activities constitute a third theme that feminists address. This broad realm encompasses a variety of processes, from attending to a family member who is ill to looking after an elderly relative over a long period. Sometimes caring means simply being attuned to someone else's psychological well-being. Not only do women shoulder concrete tasks such as cleaning and child care, but they also invest significant emotional labor in maintaining personal relationships (Pinquart and Sorensen, 2006). While caring activities are grounded in love and deep emotion, they also require an ability to listen, perceive, negotiate, and act creatively. Caring activities often involve long spells of unpaid labor, and these responsibilities often limit women's ability to work for pay outside the home. In these ways, caregiving indirectly contributes to women's relative economic disadvantage in society.

CONTEMPORARY PERSPECTIVES IN THE SOCIOLOGY OF THE FAMILY

Recent theoretical and empirical studies conducted from a feminist perspective have generated increased interest in the family among both academics and the general population. Terms such as the *second shift*—referring to women's dual roles at work and at home—have entered our vocabulary. But because feminist studies often focused on issues within the domestic realm, they did not always address trends and influences outside the home.

Since the 1990s an important body of sociological literature on the family has emerged that draws on feminist perspectives but is not strictly informed by them. Of primary concern are the larger transformations in family forms—the formation and dissolution of families and households and the evolving expectations within personal relationships. The rise in divorce and single parenting, the emergence of "reconstituted families" (i.e., remarriages) and gay families, and the popularity of cohabitation are all topics of inquiry. In the recent recessionary years, scholars also have focused on shifting gender roles within families, where men's and women's "traditional" roles have converged or even crossed over. As the recession has disproportionately struck "male" industries such as finance and manufacturing, an increasing number of households now have breadwinner wives and dads who either stay at home with children or juggle part-time work with childrearing (Rampell, 2009). The popular media in recent years are replete with images of "stay-at-home dads" (A. Williams, 2012) and women who "wear the pants in the family" (Rosin, 2012). These transformations within our families are inextricably tied to the larger changes occurring at the societal, and even global, level.

Historical Perspectives on Families

Sociologists and laypersons alike tend to romanticize the ways families were in the past, when extended families prevailed and family members were mutually dependent on and supportive of one another. However, the notion that the extended family was the predominant form of family in premodern Western Europe has been disproved. Historical research shows that the nuclear family has long been preeminent. Premodern household size was indeed larger than it is today, but not by much. In the United States, for example, throughout the seventeenth, eighteenth, and nineteenth centuries the average household size was 4.75 persons. The current average is 2.59 (U.S. Bureau of the Census, 2011j). This seemingly large gap in size is a bit misleading, because the earlier figure includes domestic servants, whereas the latter reflects the growth of single-dweller households, often older widows.

In the premodern United States and Europe, children as young as age seven or eight often worked, helping their parents on the farm. Most who did not remain in the family enterprise left the parental household at an early age to do domestic work for others or to follow apprenticeships. Children who went away to work rarely saw their parents again.

Other factors made family groups then even more impermanent than they are now. Rates of mortality (numbers of deaths per 1,000 of the population in any one year) for people of all ages were much higher. A quarter or more of all infants in early modern Europe did not survive beyond the first year of life, and women frequently died in childbirth. The notion of staying married until "old age" often was not realized, due to mortality. The death of children or of one or both spouses often shattered family relations.

THE DEVELOPMENT OF FAMILY LIFE

Historical sociologist Lawrence Stone (1980) distinguished three phases in the development of the family from the 1500s to the 1800s. Early in this period, from the 1500s to the early seventeenth century, the main form was a type of nuclear family that lived in fairly small households but maintained deeply embedded relationships within the community, including with other kin. According to Stone (although some historians have challenged this), the family was not a major focus of emotional attachment or dependence for its members, in the way we associate with family life today. Individual freedom of choice in marriage and other matters of family life were subordinated to the interests of parents, other kin, or the community. Sex within marriage was not regarded as a source of pleasure but as a necessity to produce children. Outside aristocratic circles, where it was sometimes actively encouraged, erotic or romantic love was regarded by moralists and theologians as a sickness. As Stone (1980) put it, the family during this period "was an open-ended, low-keyed, unemotional, authoritarian institution. . . . It was also very short-lived, being frequently dissolved by the death of the husband or wife or the death or very early departure from the home of the children."

Next came a transitional form of family that lasted from the early seventeenth century to the beginning of the eighteenth. Although largely a feature of the upper reaches of society, this form was very important because from it spread attitudes that have since become almost universal. The nuclear family became a more separate entity, distinct from other kin and the local community. There was a growing stress on marital and parental love, although the authoritarian power of fathers also increased.

The third phase, which emerged in the mid-eighteenth century and persisted through the mid-twentieth century, gave rise to the type of family system widespread in the West today. This family is a group tied by close emotional bonds, domestic privacy, and child rearing. It is marked by **affective individualism**, marriage ties based on personal selection, and sexual attraction or romantic love. Sexual aspects of love became glorified within marriage instead of in extramarital relationships. The family became

affective individualism • The belief in romantic attachment as a basis for contracting marriage ties.

geared to consumption rather than production, as a result of workplaces being separate from the home. Women became associated with domesticity and men with being the breadwinners. Originating among affluent groups, this family type became fairly universal in Western countries with the spread of industrialization.

In premodern Europe, marriage usually began as a property arrangement, was in its middle mostly about raising children, and only in the end was about love. Few couples married for love, but many grew to love each other as they jointly managed their household, reared their offspring, and shared life's experiences. By contrast, in most of the modern West, marriage *begins* with love; in its middle, it is still mostly about raising children (if there are children); and in the end, it is, often, about property, by which point love is absent or a distant memory (Boswell, 1995).

MYTHS OF THE TRADITIONAL FAMILY

As we discussed in this chapter's introduction, many people today feel that family life is being undermined. They contrast the apparent decline of the family with more traditional forms of family life. Was the family of the past as harmonious as many people recall it, or is this an idealized fiction? As Stephanie Coontz (1992, 2005) points out, the rosy light shed on the "traditional family" dissolves when we study previous times.

Many admire the Colonial family as disciplined and stable, but it suffered from the same disintegrative forces as its counterparts in Europe. Especially high death rates meant that

the average marriage lasted less than twelve years, and more than half of all children saw the death of at least one parent by the time they were 21. The much-admired discipline of the Colonial family was rooted in the strict authority of parents over their children, which would seem exceedingly harsh by today's standards.

The Victorian family of the 1850s was also less than ideal. In this period, wives were more or less forcibly confined to the home. Women were supposed to be strictly virtuous, while men were sexually licentious. In fact, wives and husbands often had little to do with one another, communicating only through their children. Moreover, domesticity wasn't even an option for poorer groups. African American slaves

Television shows like *Father Knows Best* painted an idyllic portrait of family life in the 1950s. In reality, though, women often felt trapped in the domestic sphere while their emotionally distant husbands pursued extramarital affairs.

in the South lived and worked in appalling conditions. In the factories and workshops of the North, white families worked long hours with little time for home life. Child labor was widespread.

Many people regard the 1950s as the time of the "ideal" American family captured in old television shows such as *Father Knows Best* and *Leave It to Beaver*, where women worked only in the home and men earned the family wage. Yet many women felt miserable and trapped in their domestic role. They had held paid jobs during World War II as part of the war effort but lost those jobs when men returned from the war. Moreover, men were still emotionally removed from their wives and often observed a sexual double standard, seeking sexual adventures for themselves but setting strict codes for their spouses.

Betty Friedan's best-selling book *The Feminine Mystique* appeared in 1963, but its research referred to the 1950s. Friedan struck a chord in the hearts of thousands of women when she spoke of the oppressive domestic life bound up with child care, domestic drudgery, and a husband who was rarely home and who allowed little emotional communication. Even more severe were the alcoholism and violence suffered within some families during a time when society was unprepared to confront these issues.

Let's now examine the changes affecting personal life, marriage, and the family today. No doubt some of these changes are profound and far-reaching. But interpreting their likely implications, particularly in the United States, means acknowledging just how unrealistic it is to contrast present conditions with a mythical view of the traditional family.

CONCEPT CHECKS

1. According to the functionalist perspective, what are the two main functions of the family?

2. According to feminist perspectives, what three aspects of family life are sources of concern? Why are these three aspects troubling to feminists?

3. Briefly describe changes in family size over the past three centuries.

4. Stephanie Coontz has dispelled the myth of the peaceful and harmonious family believed to exist in past decades. Give two examples of problems facing the family in past centuries.

③ RESEARCH ON FAMILIES TODAY

Contemporary research on families both in the United States and worldwide is unified by four key themes. First, family structure continues to change and evolve. Second, there is tremendous variation in what families look like; our family experiences are powerfully shaped by our social group memberships, including race, social class, religion, sexual orientation, and age. Third, families are an important influence on the health and well-being of both adults and children. And finally, while the family has been historically thought of as a safe haven, it also has a dark side where family members may inflict abuse and pain on one another. We review recent research on the ways families are today and suggest ways they may change in future decades.

Changes in Family Patterns Worldwide

Many family forms exist today. In some areas, such as remote regions in Asia, Africa, and the Pacific Rim, traditional family systems are essentially unchanged. In most developing countries, however, changes are occurring rapidly. Among the complex origins of these changes, one is the spread of Western ideals of romantic love. Another is the development of centralized government in areas previously comprising autonomous smaller societies. People's lives become influenced by their involvement in a national political system; moreover, governments attempt to alter traditional ways of behavior. Because of rapid population growth, states frequently introduce programs advocating smaller families, the use of contraception, and so forth.

Another influence is large-scale migration from rural to urban areas. Often men go to work in towns or cities, leaving family members in the home village. Alternatively, a nuclear family group moves to the city. In both cases, traditional family forms and kinship systems may weaken. Finally, and perhaps most important, employment opportunities away from the land and in organizations such as government bureaucracies, mines, plantations, and industrial firms disrupt family systems previously centered on landed production in the local community.

These changes are creating a worldwide movement toward the predominance of the nuclear family, breaking down extended-family systems and other types of kinship groups. This was first documented by William J. Goode in his book *World Revolution in Family Patterns* (1963) and has been borne out by subsequent research.

The most important changes occurring worldwide over the past half century are:

1. Clans and other kin groups are declining in influence.
2. There is a general trend toward the free choice of a spouse.
3. The rights of women are more widely recognized, with respect both to initiating marriage and to making decisions within the family.
4. Kin marriages are less common.
5. Higher levels of sexual freedom are developing in societies that were formerly very restrictive.
6. There is a general trend toward extending children's rights.

There are differences in the speed at which change is occurring, and reversals and counter trends. A study in the Philippines, for example, found a higher proportion of extended families in urban areas than in rural regions. Leaving the rural areas, cousins, nephews, and nieces go to live with their relatives in the cities to take advantage of employment opportunities there. Parallel examples have also been noted elsewhere (Stinner, 1979), including in some industrialized nations. Certain regions of Poland, for instance, show a rejuvenation of the extended family. Many industrial workers in Poland have farms that they tend part time. In the cities, grandparents move in with their children's family, run the household, and bring up the grandchildren, while the younger generation takes outside employment (Turowski, 1977).

Given the ethnically diverse character of the United States, there are considerable variations in family and marriage within our country. Some of the most striking include differences between white and African American family patterns. After considering these differences, we will examine divorce, remarriage, and stepparenting in relation to contemporary patterns of family life.

Marriage and the Family in the United States

The United States has long had high marriage rates; over 90 percent of adults in their mid-fifties today are or have previously been married (U.S. Bureau of the Census, 2011b). The age at which first marriages occur has risen, however, over the past 30 years. There are several explanations for this trend. Some researchers contend that increases in cohabitation among younger people account for the decreases (or delays) in marriage among this group.

Others argue that increases in postsecondary school enrollment, especially among women, are partially responsible. Similarly, women's increased participation in the labor force means many women establish careers before marrying and starting a family (Copen et al., 2012). Labor force participation also increases economic independence among women and leads to a relative deterioration of men's economic position that makes them less attractive as mates and less ready to marry. Some researchers cite this "marriageable men hypothesis" to explain the especially low marriage rates among blacks, because black men have suffered the worst economic conditions in recent decades (Wilson, 1987). Finally, some researchers believe that modernization and a secular change in attitudes promote individualism and downplay the importance of marriage. Although the true reason for the decline in marriage rates is likely a combination of all these factors, we must be careful in making comparisons. Whereas some have argued that the trend since 1970 toward later marriage is a break from tradition, age of first marriage now is close to what it was in the period 1890–1940. To say that people today are postponing marriage is true only if we compare ourselves with the 1950s generation. It might be more accurate to say that the 1950s generation married at an unusually young age.

In 1960 the average age of first marriages was 22.8 for men and 20.3 for women. Comparable ages in 2010 were 28.2 for men and 26.1 for women in 2010 (U.S. Bureau of the Census, 2010j). If we examine the proportions of people who remain unmarried before a certain age (Figure 15.1), we find that in 1960 just 28 percent of women under 24 years of age had never married. In 2009 that proportion was more than 75 percent. The U.S. Census now incorporates a category of "unmarried couples sharing the same household." As the practice of cohabitation is relatively new, it is not easy to make direct comparisons with earlier years. Nonetheless, we can estimate that the number of younger-age couples who have ever lived

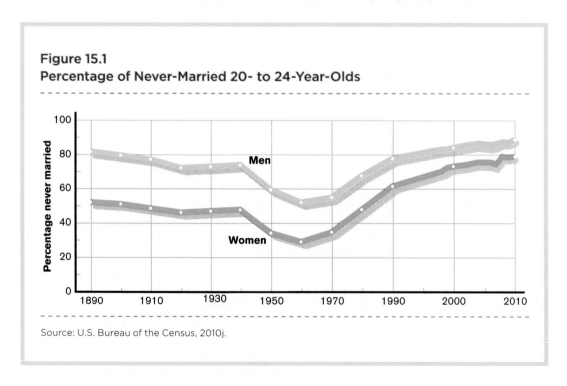

Figure 15.1
Percentage of Never-Married 20- to 24-Year-Olds

Source: U.S. Bureau of the Census, 2010j.

together without being married has risen steeply from half a million couples around 1970 to almost 3.0 million in 1990. By 2010, more than 7.5 million couples were cohabiting in the United States (Kreider, 2010). By age 30, more than 50 percent of women will have cohabited outside marriage (Bramlett and Mosher, 2002).

No one knows how the trend toward cohabitation will develop in the future, but we can get useful information from other industrial countries. In France, cohabiting relationships are more widespread, and last longer, than in the United States. A survey in that country published in the late 1980s found that over half of cohabiting couples "did not think about marriage." For most people in the United States, cohabitation is seen as a precursor to marriage, yet a sizeable minority also says they're not sure if they will ever marry their cohabiting partner (Rhoades, Stanley, and Markman, 2009; Sassler, 2004). We return to the topic of cohabitation as an alternative to marriage later in this chapter.

An extraordinary increase in the proportion of people living alone in the United States has also occurred recently—a phenomenon that partly reflects the high levels of marital separation and divorce. More than one in every four households (27 percent) now consists of one person, a rise of 44 percent since 1960 (U.S. Bureau of the Census, 2010j). There has been a particularly sharp rise for individuals living alone in the 24–44 age bracket.

As we noted in this chapter's introduction, some people still think the "average" American family consists of a husband who works in paid employment and a wife who looks after the home, living together with their two children. However, only about one-fifth of children live in households that fit this picture (U.S. Bureau of the Census, 2010a). One reason is the rising divorce rate: A substantial proportion of the population lives either in single-parent households or in stepfamilies, or both. Another is the high proportion of women who work. Dual-career marriages and single-parent families are now the norm (Figure 15.2). The majority of married women working outside the home also cares for one or more children. Although many working women have poor or nonexistent promotion prospects, the standard of living of many American couples depends on the wife's income as well as her unpaid work in the home (see also Chapter 14).

There are also significant differences in patterns of childbearing between parents in the 1950s and later generations. The birth rate rose sharply just after World War II and again during the 1950s. Women in the 1950s had their first child earlier than later generations did, and subsequent children were born closer together. Since the late 1960s the average age at which women have their first child has risen. And women are leaving larger gaps between children. In 1976 only 20 percent of births were to women over age 30. By 2005 this proportion had grown to 37.3 percent, even though the proportion of women in the population aged 30 to 34 years declined between 2000 and 2005. The number of births to women 35 to 39 years old has increased even more dramatically—by over 52 percent between 1990 and 2010 (CDC, 2010a).

RACE, ETHNICITY, AND THE AMERICAN FAMILY

Asian American Families The Asian American family historically has been characterized by interdependence among members of the extended family. In many Asian cultures, family concerns take priority over individual concerns. Family interdependence also helps Asian Americans prosper financially. In fact, family and friend networks often pool money to help their members start a business or buy a house; this help is reciprocated through contributions to the others. The result is a median family income for Asian Americans that is higher than that for non-Hispanic whites. As each generation of Asian Americans grows

Figure 15.2
The Changing Structure of American Families with Children

Percentage of American children 17 and younger living in each of four types of families, 1790–1990.

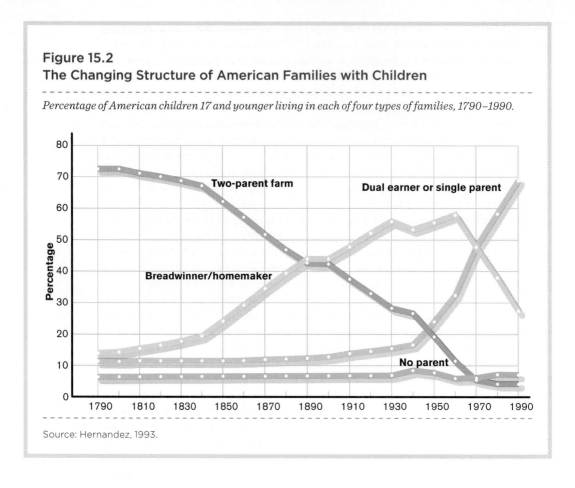

Source: Hernandez, 1993.

increasingly acculturated to life in the United States, however, scholars predict that they will come to resemble white families more and more (Pew Research Center for the People and the Press, 2012b).

Although there is less research on differences between various Asian American subgroups than among Hispanic subgroups, some fertility differences have been established. Chinese American and Japanese American women have much lower fertility rates than do any other racial or ethnic group, due partly to their high levels of educational attainment. Chinese, Japanese, and Filipino families have lower levels of nonmarital fertility than all other racial or ethnic groups, including non-Hispanic whites. Low levels of nonmarital fertility combined with low levels of divorce for most Asian American groups demonstrate the emphasis on marriage as the appropriate forum for family formation and maintenance.

Native American Families Kinship ties are very important in Native American families. As Cherlin (1999) notes, "kinship networks constitute tribal organization; kinship ties confer identity" for Native Americans. However, for those who live in cities or away from reservations, kinship ties may be less prominent. Furthermore, Native Americans have higher rates of intermarriage than any other racial or ethnic group. In fact, in 1990, fewer than half of all married Native Americans were married to other Native Americans (Sandefur and Liebler, 1997).

Native American women have a high percentage of nonmarital fertility but a low overall birth rate: At 11 babies per 1,000 women aged 15–44, it is the lowest of any ethnic group in the United States, a drastic change from 20 years ago, when the 1990 birth rate of Native American women was 19 per 1,000 women—one of the highest rates in the United States (Martin et al., 2012). However, compared to all U.S. women, a high proportion of Native American births were to women under age 20 (16 percent compared to 9 percent for women of all ethnicities) and the youngest mean age of mother at first birth (22.3). Furthermore, over 65 percent of all Native American women giving birth in 2010 were not married (Martin et al., 2012). Sandefur and Liebler (1997) also report a high divorce rate for Native Americans. Native Americans also are at particularly high risk of domestic violence; yet as we will see later in this chapter, family violence can afflict persons of any ethnicity (T. Williams, 2012).

Latino Families Hispanics are heterogeneous when it comes to family patterns. Mexicans, Puerto Ricans, and Cubans are the three largest Hispanic subgroups. In the U.S. Decennial Census of 2010, Mexicans constituted 63.0 percent of the Hispanic population, Puerto Ricans constituted 9.0 percent (down from 12.0 percent in 1990), and Cubans were just 3.5 percent; the rest of the Hispanic population was made up of much smaller groups from many Latin American nations (Ennis, Ríos-Vargas, and Albert, 2011).

Mexican American families live primarily in multigenerational households and have a high birth rate. Economically, Mexican American families are more successful than Puerto Rican families but less so than Cuban families. Defying cultural stereotypes of a Mexican American home with a male breadwinner and female homemaker, more than half of all Mexican American women are in the labor force (BLS, 2012e). However, this is because of necessity rather than desire. Many Mexican American families would prefer the breadwinner-homemaker model but are constrained by finances (Hurtado, 1995).

Although Puerto Rico is a U.S. commonwealth, Puerto Ricans are still considered part of the umbrella category of Hispanics. However, because of their status as U.S. citizens, Puerto Ricans move freely between Puerto Rico and the mainland without the difficulties encountered by immigrants. When barriers to immigration are high, only the most able (physically, financially, and so on) members of a society can move to another country; but because Puerto Ricans face fewer barriers, even the least able can manage the migration process. Thus they are the most economically disadvantaged of all the major Hispanic groups. Puerto Rican families have a higher percentage of children born to unmarried mothers than any other Hispanic group—65.2 percent in 2010 (Martin et al., 2012). Only African Americans (72.1 percent) and Native Americans (65.6 percent) had higher rates of births to unmarried women (Martin et al., 2012). However, consensual unions—cohabiting relationships in which couples consider themselves married but are not legally married—are often the context for births to unmarried mothers. Nancy Landale and Kelly Fennelly (1992) studied the marital experiences of Puerto Rican women and found that many lived in consensual unions. They suggest that Puerto Ricans respond to tough economic times by forming consensual unions as the next best option to a more expensive legal marriage.

Cuban American families are the most prosperous of all the Hispanic groups but less prosperous than whites. Most Cuban Americans have settled in the Miami area, forming enclaves in which they rely on other Cubans for their business and social needs (such as banking, schools, and shopping). The relative wealth of Cuban Americans is driven largely by family business ownership. In terms of childbearing, Cuban Americans have lower levels of fertility than non-Hispanic whites and equally low levels of nonmarital fertility.

African American Families There are important differences in white and black family patterns. Blacks have higher rates of childbearing outside marriage, are less likely ever to marry, and are less likely to marry after having a nonmarital birth. These differences are of particular interest to sociologists because single parenthood in the United States is associated with high rates of poverty (Harknett and McLanahan, 2004).

More than 40 years ago, Senator Daniel Patrick Moynihan (1965) described black families as "disorganized" and caught up in a "tangle of pathology." Moynihan, among others, sought reasons for this in the history of the black family. For one thing, the circumstances of slavery prevented blacks from maintaining the cultural customs of their societies of origin; for example, members of similar tribal groups were dispersed to different plantations. Also, although some owners treated their slaves considerately and fostered their family life, others regarded them as little better than livestock and inherently promiscuous and, therefore, unworthy of marriage.

After emancipation, new cultural experiences and structural factors wreaked havoc on black families. Among these were new forms of discrimination against African Americans, changes in the economy such as the development of sharecropping in the South after the Civil War, and the migration of black families to northern cities early in the twentieth century (Jones, 1986).

The divergence between black and white family patterns has become greater since the 1960s, when Moynihan's study was published, and we look mainly to present-day influences to explain them. In 2010, 52 percent of white families included a married couple, compared to 29 percent of black families (U.S. Bureau of the Census, 2012b). In 1960, women headed 21 percent of African American families; among white families in 2010, the proportion was 8 percent. By 2010, the proportion (including married but spouse absent, divorced, separated, never married, and widowed categories) for black families had risen to 53.3 percent, while that for white families was 21.8 percent (U.S. Bureau of the Census, 2011b) (Figure 15.3). Female-headed families are more prominently represented among poorer blacks. One social condition that has exacerbated this situation is a shortage of what sociologist William Julius Wilson calls "marriageable" black men (1990). Marriage opportunities for women are constrained if there are not enough men employed in the formal labor market. Recent research confirms that one of the best predictors of whether parents marry after a nonmarital birth is the availability of eligible partners in a geographic area (Harknett and McLanahan, 2004), demonstrating the continued importance of marriage markets even after the birth of a child.

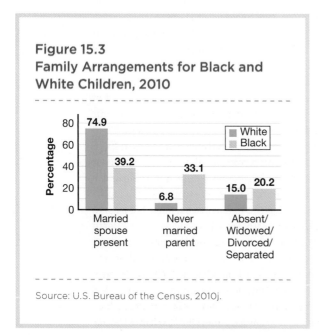

Figure 15.3
Family Arrangements for Black and White Children, 2010

Source: U.S. Bureau of the Census, 2010j.

African Americans are often embedded in larger and more complex family networks than whites, but these ties are a source of both support and strain. White anthropologist Carol Stack (1997) lived in a black ghetto community in Illinois to study the support systems that poor black families formed. Getting to know the kinship system from the inside, she demonstrated that families adapted to poverty by forming large, complex support networks. Thus a mother heading a one-parent family is likely to have a close and supportive network of relatives to depend on. Yet these family ties often place demands—especially on older African American women, who are more likely than any other group to live with and raise their grandchildren. They step into this role when their own children, or the grandchildren's parents, can no longer adequately fulfill their parenting role. For many older black women, family ties are a source of strain and demand as well as social support (Hughes et al., 2007).

CLASS AND THE AMERICAN FAMILY

While Stack's arguments addressed racial differences in the organization of the extended family, contemporary researchers have concluded that "the differences between black and white extended family relationships are mainly due to contemporary differences in social and economic class positions of group members. Cultural differences are less significant" (Sarkisian and Gerstel, 2004).

This leads to an interesting question: Are racial differences in family formation due primarily to economic or to cultural factors? Consider an example of four individuals, all women, who are the heads of their households: (1) a black doctor, (2) a white doctor, (3) a black nurse's aide, and (4) a white nurse's aide. The cultural argument suggests that blacks and whites are different, which means that the black doctor and black nurse's aide should have family lives that are more similar to each other than they are to the family lives of the white doctor or white nurse's aide. The class argument argues the opposite: that the two nurse's aides and the two doctors will be more similar to each other than they will be to people of the same race but from a different class position.

Recent studies show that race and class each have distinctive and often complicated influences on family behavior. For instance, while whites from working-class and poor backgrounds—often residing in the southern United States—report very strong support for marriage and bearing children within marriage, their behaviors often depart from these conservative ideals. White young adults of lower- and working-class backgrounds are much more likely than their wealthier peers to get pregnant prior to marriage, to marry young, and subsequently to divorce (Cahn and Carbone, 2010). Because they often do not attend college, they marry young and bear children young—often before they are financially or emotionally prepared. As a result, they often struggle unsuccessfully with the challenges of marriage and babies, and ultimately divorce. Middle-class young adults, by contrast, often cohabit while in school or working in their first jobs, so they marry later and bear children later. Delaying marriage until they are emotionally and financially ready, however, is one of the key reasons college-educated young whites have lower rates of divorce than their more economically disadvantaged counterparts (Cahn and Carbone, 2010).

Research comparing middle-class blacks with their less advantaged counterparts was very scarce until the past decade, when scholars began to explore in depth middle-class black families (Lacy, 2007; Landry and Marsh, 2011; Pattillo-McCoy, 1999). Although middle-class black families are much more likely than their less economically advantaged peers to live in married couple households, recent studies detect a new form of middle-class black family: the single-person household, especially among young adults. Due in part to the shortage of marriageable men described earlier, college-educated black women often must live on their own without a romantic partner (Marsh et al., 2007). Studies of intersectionality, or the complex interplay between race and class, provide important insights into the ways both culture and structure shape family lives.

Nonmarital Childbearing Nonmarital childbearing continues to be one of the most hotly debated and well-researched areas of family sociology. This intense interest is driven, in part, by the fact that the number of children born out of wedlock today is more than six times higher than it was in the 1950s. In 2010, 73 percent of all births to black non-Hispanic women, 66 percent of births of American Indian or Alaskan native women, and 53 percent of births to Hispanic women occurred outside marriage, compared with 29 percent for white non-Hispanic women and 17 percent for Asian or Pacific Islander women (Child Trends, 2012). Yet these numbers can be misleading because they suggest that babies are being born to women without a male partner, thus denying the children a "father figure." Recent studies show, however, that nearly one-half of all nonmarital births take place in cohabiting unions (Child Trends, 2012), meaning that many of these children are raised by two parents who just happen not to be legally married to one another. A key question addressed by sociologists is: Why do women have children out of wedlock? This is an important concern to policy makers because children born to unmarried mothers are more likely to grow up in a single-parent household, experience instability in living arrangements, and live in poverty. As these children reach adolescence, they are more likely to have low educational attainment, engage in sex at younger ages, and have a premarital birth. As young adults, children born outside marriage are more likely to be idle (neither in school nor employed), have lower occupational status and income, and have more troubled marriages and more divorces than those born to married parents. Of course, most studies conclude that it is not single mothers who are the problem, but rather, the economically disadvantaged conditions that both give rise to and follow from nonmarital childbearing (Child Trends, 2012). This is a topic we revisit in our consideration of single-parent families.

Kathryn Edin and Maria Kefalas (2005) ask why low-income women continue to have children out of wedlock when they can hardly afford to do so. Following in the tradition of scholars such as Carol Stack and Elijah Anderson, Edin and Kefalas lived with their subjects—among poor blacks, whites, and Puerto Ricans in Philadelphia and in Camden, New Jersey. Their interviews with 165 low-income single mothers in black and white neighborhoods led them to argue that single mothers were not eschewing marriage. To the contrary, women of all ethnicities whom they interviewed highly valued marriage but believed that getting married at that time would make things worse, either committing them to terrible relationships or leading to divorce. As one woman told Edin and Kefalas, "I'd rather say I had a child out of wedlock than that I married this idiot." Or, as others said, a failed marriage would be worse than having children on their own. In an environment in which more men than ever were going to prison or were unemployed, these women needed to be able to fend for themselves.

Two-thirds of the pregnancies in the study were neither planned nor actively avoided. In these poor communities, women stop using contraception when the relationship becomes serious, even if the woman and man have not planned to have children together. But why do women have children out of wedlock in the first place? For one thing, the researchers find that young people in poor communities feel very confident about their ability to raise children, more so than most middle-class people do. This is because most of the pregnant mothers came from social environments in which young people helped raise the other children in a family or in a building.

Second, the poor place an extraordinarily high value on children, perhaps an even higher value than do middle-class families. They also have fewer things to make their lives meaningful. For them, one of the worst things is to be childless. Finally, many women in the study reported that having a child actually saved their lives, bringing order to an otherwise chaotic life (Edin and Kefalas, 2005).

A third reason to "retreat from marriage" has to do with the changing meaning of marriage in low-income communities. Although low-income women do value marriage, what qualifies a man as a potential marital partner has changed over the last 50 years. Edin and Kefalas comment that "in the 1950s all but the most marginally employed men found women who were willing to marry them. Now, however, even men who are stably employed at relatively good jobs at the time of the child's birth . . . aren't automatically deemed marriageable." This suggests that women have become more selective. When women who value motherhood highly also set the bar higher for marriage, higher rates of nonmarital fertility follow. Through Edin and Kefalas's (2005) work, we can understand the worldviews of black, white, and Puerto Rican young people who are having children out of wedlock.

Class-Based Cultural Practices

The relationship between social class and family life in the contemporary United States is central to another recent work of field-based sociology. Annette Lareau (2011) closely observed 12 families—6 white, 5 black, and 1 interracial—and found that middle-class and working-class people have different cultural practices for raising children.

Middle-class parents engage in "concerted cultivation," working hard to cultivate their children's talents through many non-school-based activities as well as continuous linguistic interaction. Working-class and poor parents adopt a different style of child rearing, the "accomplishment of natural growth": Talk is brief and instrumental, children learn to be more compliant with adult directives, and they have few organized activities outside school. They learn to occupy themselves, often playing with neighborhood friends.

As a result of these child-rearing strategies, Lareau claims, middle-class children develop a sense of entitlement and value an individualized sense of self. They become comfortable questioning authority and making demands on adults and institutions. In contrast, the working-class child-rearing strategy promotes a sense of constraint in children, who become more cautious in dealing with adults, bureaucratic institutions, and authority. Like Stack, Lareau also finds that working-class and low-income parents stress close ties to kin; thus these children develop closer relationships with their siblings, cousins, and other relatives.

Lareau argues that there are important signs of hidden advantages and disadvantages "being sown at early ages"; but because her research subjects were young, it was not possible to make claims about the way these child-rearing strategies affect adult outcomes. Further research would benefit from testing some of Lareau's hypotheses in large samples of children.

Like Edin and Kefalas, Lareau recognizes that social class is crucial to understanding family life in the contemporary United States. Her work sets a new standard in showing both how these differences emerge and operate and their potential implications. She emphasizes that the differences between working-class and middle-class culture do not reflect radically different values and priorities but, instead, vastly different levels of income and wealth. Her evidence suggests that if poor and working-class people had more money, their child-rearing strategies would change.

DIVORCE AND SEPARATION

Recent decades have seen major increases in divorce rates and more relaxed attitudes toward divorce. Whereas for centuries in the West marriage was regarded as indissoluble, today most countries are making divorce more easily available.

Divorce rates (based on the number of divorces per 1,000 married men or women per year) have fluctuated in the United States in different periods (Figure 15.4). They rose, for example, after World War II, then dropped off before increasing steeply from the 1960s to 1980 (thereafter declining somewhat). It used to be common for divorced women to move back to their parents' homes; today most set up their own households.

Divorce has an enormous impact on children. Since 1970, more than 1 million American children per year have been affected by divorce. In one calculation, about half of children born in 1980 became members of a one-parent family. Since two-thirds of women and three-fourths of men who are divorced eventually remarry, most of these children nonetheless grew up in a family environment. Only 4 percent of children under 18 in the United States today are not living with either parent (U.S. Bureau of the Census, 2012b). The remarriage figures are substantially lower for African Americans. Only 32 percent of black women and 55 percent of black men who divorce remarry within 10 years. Black children are half as likely as white children to live with both parents or one parent and a stepparent (Cherlin, 1992).

Lenore Weitzman (1985) has argued that no-fault divorce laws have helped recast the psychological context of divorce positively (reducing some of the hostility it once generated) but have negatively affected the economic position of women. Laws designed to be gender neutral have had the unintended consequence of depriving divorced women of the financial protections provided under the old laws. Women are expected to be as capable as men of supporting themselves after divorce. Yet because most women's careers are still secondary to their work as homemakers, they may lack the qualifications and earning power of men. The living standards of divorced women and their children fell by 27 percent in the first year following the divorce settlement. The average standard of living of divorced men, by contrast, rose by 10 percent. Most court judgments left the former husband with a high proportion of his income intact; therefore, he had more to spend on his own needs than while he was married (Peterson, 1996).

Reasons for Divorce Divorce rates are not a direct index of marital unhappiness. For example, they do not include separated people who are not legally divorced. Moreover, unhappily married people may stay together because they believe in the sanctity of marriage, worry about the consequences of breaking up, or decide to remain together for the sake of the children.

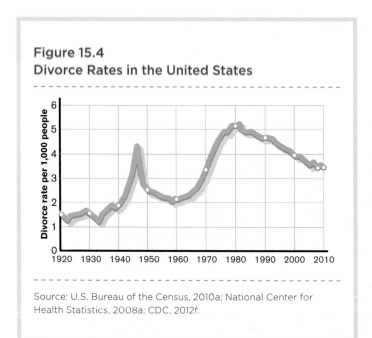

Figure 15.4
Divorce Rates in the United States

Source: U.S. Bureau of the Census, 2010a; National Center for Health Statistics, 2008a; CDC, 2012f.

Why has divorce become more common? There are several reasons, which involve the wider changes in modern societies and social institutions. First, changes in the law have made divorce easier. Second, except for a few wealthy people, marriage no longer reflects the desire to perpetuate property and status across generations. As women become more economically independent, it is easier for them to establish a separate household (Lee, 1982). The fact that little stigma now attaches to divorce is partly the result of these developments but also adds momentum to them. Third, there is a growing tendency to evaluate marriage in terms of personal satisfaction. Rising divorce rates do not indicate dissatisfaction with marriage as such, but an increased determination to make it a rewarding and satisfying relationship (Cherlin, 1990).

Other factors showing a positive correlation to the likelihood of divorce include:

- Parental divorce (people whose parents divorce are more likely to divorce);
- Premarital cohabitation (people who cohabit before marriage have a higher divorce rate);
- Premarital childbearing (people who marry after having children are more likely to divorce);
- Marriage at an early age (people who marry as teenagers have a higher divorce rate);
- A childless marriage (couples without children are more likely to divorce);
- Low incomes (divorce is more likely among couples with low incomes) (White, 1990).

The Experience of Divorce It is extremely difficult to draw up a balance sheet of the social advantages and costs of high levels of divorce. More tolerant attitudes toward divorce mean less social ostracism. However, marriage breakup is almost always emotionally stressful and may create financial hardship, especially for women.

Diane Vaughan (1986) interviewed 103 recently separated or divorced people (mainly from middle-class backgrounds) to chart the transition from living together to living apart. Her notion of "uncoupling" refers to the social separation that occurs before the actual physical parting—at least one of the partners develops a new life pattern, following new pursuits and making new friends in contexts apart from the other. This usually means keeping secrets—especially when a relationship with a lover is involved.

According to Vaughan's research, uncoupling often begins unintentionally. One individual—the "initiator"—becomes more dissatisfied with the relationship than the other and creates an independent "territory" of activities. Before this, the initiator may have tried unsuccessfully to change the partner, foster shared interests, and so forth. Ultimately feeling that this attempt has failed and that the relationship is fundamentally flawed, the initiator becomes preoccupied with the ways in which the relationship or the partner is defective. Vaughan suggests that this is the opposite of the process of falling in love.

Divorce and Children The effects of divorce on children are difficult to gauge. How contentious the relationship is between the parents before separation; the ages of the children; whether there are siblings, grandparents, and other relatives; the children's relationship with their individual parents; and how frequently the children continue to see both parents—all affect the adjustment process. Because children whose parents are unhappy but stay together may also be affected, assessing the consequences of divorce for children is doubly problematic.

Research indicates that children often suffer marked emotional anxiety right after their parents' separation, yet these effects are relatively short-lived. Judith Wallerstein and Joan Kelly (1980) studied 131 children of 60 families in Marin County, California, after the separation of the parents. They contacted the children at the time of the divorce, a year and a half after, and five years after. Almost all the children experienced intense emotional disturbance at the time of the divorce. Preschool-age children were confused and frightened, blaming themselves for the separation. Older children better understood their parents' motives for the split but worried about its effects on their future and expressed anger over it. At the end of the five-year period, however, two-thirds were coping reasonably well with their home lives and their commitments outside. A third remained dissatisfied, were subject to depression, and expressed feelings of loneliness, even when the parent they were living with had remarried.

Wallerstein continued studying 116 of the original 131 subjects at the end of 10-year and 15-year periods (1980, 1989, 2000). She found that these children brought memories and feelings of their parents' divorce into their own romantic relationships. Almost all felt they had suffered from their parents' mistakes. Most of them shared a hope for something their parents had failed to achieve—a good, committed marriage based on love and faithfulness. Nearly half entered adulthood as "worried, underachieving, self-deprecating, and sometimes angry young men and women." Although many of them got married, the legacy of their parents' divorce lived with them. Those who appeared to manage the best had supportive relationships with one or both parents.

Can we reasonably conclude, then, that divorce is bad for children? Despite the many strengths of the Wallerstein study, including an unusually long follow-up period, it also had many limitations that undermine its generalizability. The parents and children studied all came from an affluent white area and might or might not have been representative of the wider population. Moreover, the families were self-selected: They had approached counselors. Those who actively seek counseling might be less (or more) able to cope with separation than those who do not. In general, studies based on "clinical" or help-seeking samples tend to overstate problems; by definition, the study participants were troubled enough that they had sought professional help.

A more recent study based on a population-based sample found that the majority of people with divorced parents did not have serious mental health problems. The researchers did find small differences in mental health between those whose parents divorced and those whose parents stayed together (favoring those whose parents stayed together), but much of the difference had been identified in the children at age seven, before the families experienced divorce (Cherlin, Chase-Lansdale, and McRae, 1998). The most prominent sociologist of the family in the United States, Andrew Cherlin (1999), has argued that these are the general effects of divorce on children:

- Almost all children experience an initial period of intense emotional upset after their parents separate;
- Most resume normal development without serious problems within two years after the separation; and
- A minority of children experiences some long-term problems as a result of the breakup that may persist into adulthood.

REMARRIAGE AND STEPPARENTING

Before 1900, almost all marriages in the United States were first marriages. Most remarriages involved at least one widowed person. With the progressive rise in the divorce rate, the level of remarriage also began to climb, and in an increasing proportion of remarriages at least one person was divorced.

Today, around one-third of marriages involve at least one previously married person. Up to age 35, the majority of remarriages is between divorced people. After that age, the proportion of remarriages with widows or widowers rises. By age 55, the proportion of such remarriages is larger than those following divorce (Sweeney, 2010).

People who have been married and divorced are more likely to marry again than single people in similar age groups are to marry for the first time. At all age levels, divorced men are more likely to remarry than divorced women. Many divorced individuals choose to cohabit instead of remarry.

In statistical terms at least, remarriages are less successful than first marriages: Divorce rates are higher. This does not mean that second marriages are doomed to fail. Divorced people may have higher expectations of marriage than those who remain with their first spouses; hence they may be more ready to dissolve new marriages. The second marriages that endure are usually more satisfying than the first.

A **stepfamily** may be defined as a family in which at least one of the adults is a stepparent. Many who remarry become stepparents of children who regularly visit rather than live in the same household. By this definition, the number of stepfamilies is much greater than official statistics indicate, because the statistics usually refer only to families with whom stepchildren live. Stepfamilies give rise to kin ties resembling those of some traditional societies in non-Western countries. Children may now have two "mothers" and two "fathers"—their natural parents and their stepparents. Some stepfamilies regard all the children and close relatives (including grandparents) from previous marriages as part of the family.

Certain difficulties arise in stepfamilies. First, there is usually a biological parent living elsewhere whose influence over the child or children remains powerful. Cooperative relations between divorced individuals often become strained when one or both remarry. Consider a woman with two children who marries a man with two children, all six living together. If the "outside" parents demand the same times of visitation as previously, the pressures on the newly established family will likely be intense. It may prove impossible to have the new family all together on weekends.

Second, since most stepchildren belong to two households, the possibilities of clashes of habits and outlooks are considerable. There are few established norms defining the relationship between stepparent and stepchild. Should a child call a new stepparent by name, or is "Dad" or "Mom" more appropriate? Should the stepparent play the same part in disciplining the children as the natural parent? How should a stepparent treat the new spouse of his or her previous partner when picking up the children?

Research on family-structure effects on children shows that girls experience more detrimental outcomes from stepfamily living, whereas boys demonstrate more negative outcomes from single-parent family living. The more negative effects for boys may be because single-parent family living generally means living with a mother only, without a male role model. Girls are more likely to bond with their mothers in this type of family. A remarriage that introduces a stepfather may cause girls to feel that their close relationship with their mother is threatened. This may be why girls living in stepfamilies experience more negative outcomes (Sweeney, 2010).

SINGLE-PARENT HOUSEHOLDS

As a result of increasing divorce rates and births before marriage, about one-half of all children spend some time in a single-parent family (Furstenberg and Cherlin, 1991). In 2011, more than

stepfamily • A family in which at least one partner has children from a previous marriage, living either in the home or nearby.

20.0 million children under the age of 18 lived with one parent, 17.6 million with their mother and 2.6 million with their father (U.S. Bureau of the Census, 2012i). The vast majority of such families are headed by women, because the mother usually obtains custody of the children after a divorce (in a few single-parent households, the individual, again almost always a woman, has never been married). There were 11.76 million single-parent households with children under age 18 in the United States in 2011, 10 million single-mother and 1.7 million single-father families (Figure 15.5), constituting 33.8 percent of all families with dependent children (U.S. Bureau of the Census, 2012f, 2012k). They are among the poorest groups in contemporary society. Many single parents, whether previously married or not, still face social disapproval as well as economic insecurity.

The category of single-parent household is internally diverse. For instance, more than half of widowed mothers are homeowners, but the majority of never-married single mothers live in rented accommodations. Single parenthood tends to be a changing state. For a person who is widowed, the break is clear-cut—although he or she might have been living alone for some while if the partner was hospitalized before death. About 60 percent of single-parent households today, however, are the result of separation or divorce. In such cases, individuals may live together sporadically over a quite lengthy period.

Most people do not wish to be single parents, but a growing minority chooses to have a child or children without the support of a spouse or partner. "Single mothers by choice" aptly describes some parents who possess sufficient resources to manage as a single-parent household. For the majority of unmarried or never-married mothers, however, the reality is different: There is a high correlation between the rate of births outside marriage and indicators of poverty and social deprivation. These are key influences underlying the high proportion of single-parent households among families of African American background in the United States.

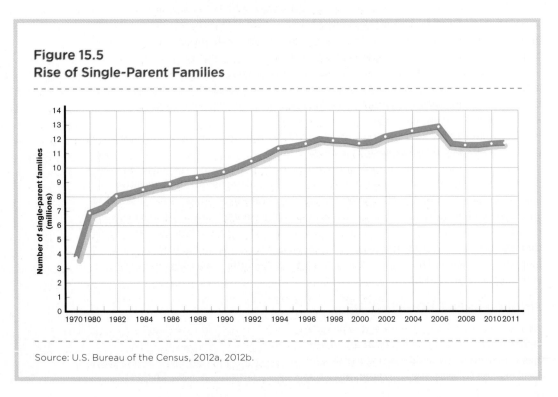

Figure 15.5
Rise of Single-Parent Families

Source: U.S. Bureau of the Census, 2012a, 2012b.

Sociologists debate the effect on children of growing up with a single parent. Empirical research by Sara McLanahan and Gary Sandefur (1994) rejects the claim that children raised by only one parent do just as well as children raised by both parents. A large part of the reason is economic: the sudden drop in income associated with divorce. Other reasons include inadequate parental attention and lack of social ties. Separation or divorce weakens the connection between child and father, and the link between the child and the father's network of friends and acquaintances. The authors conclude it is a myth that strong support networks or extended family ties are usually available to single mothers. Others have also pointed out that although most children growing up in single-parent homes are disadvantaged, it is better for children's mental health if parents in extremely high-conflict marriages divorce rather than stay together (Amato, Loomis, and Booth, 1995). Divorce may benefit children growing up in high-conflict households while harming children whose parents have relatively low levels of marital conflict before divorcing.

SAME-SEX COUPLES

Many gay men and lesbian women now live in stable relationships as couples today. According to data from the American Community Survey collected by the U.S. government, there were approximately 594,000 same-sex-couple households in the United States in 2010, a very slight increase over the 581,000 households reported in 2009. About 1 percent of households in the United States today are of same-sex couples (Lofquist, 2011). Approximately one-fifth of same-sex-couple households have children; most of these children (73 percent) are the biological child of one of the two partners, while roughly one-fifth of the children are either stepchildren or adopted. To date, the majority of same-sex households includes unmarried partners, because gays and lesbians still are denied the right to legally marry in most states. However, there is a swiftly developing movement afoot to legally recognize these unions as marriages. Recent decisions in the United States, Canada, Mexico, and several European nations demonstrate the current pulse of this movement.

Passed by Congress and signed by President Bill Clinton in 1996, the Defense of Marriage Act (DOMA) allowed states the right to refuse to recognize same-sex marriages from other states (section 2) and defined marriage as one man and one woman at the federal level (section 3; Defense of Marriage Act, 1996). Although no state at the time permitted same-sex marriage, courts and legislatures were already addressing the issue.

In 1998, voters in Hawaii approved a state constitutional amendment limiting legal marriages to one man and one woman. Before the issue was put to the electorate, the Hawaii Supreme Court was close to legalizing gay marriage. In fact, in 1993 the state's Supreme Court ruled that restricting marriage to heterosexual couples was sex discrimination, and the court asked the state of Hawaii to show a compelling reason for the restriction. Many legal observers believe the court would have ruled for gay marriage if not for the vote on the constitutional amendment.

In 1999 the Supreme Court of Canada ruled that same-sex couples are entitled to equal legal treatment (i.e., the same benefits) as married couples. The case was initiated when a lesbian filed for spousal support from her former partner. Initially, Ontario's Family Law Act had permitted only partners of the opposite sex to make a claim for spousal support after a breakup. The court therefore decided first to resolve the constitutional issue of whether same-sex couples have a right to seek spousal support. The Supreme Court's decision was that the Family Law Act's restriction to opposite-sex partners was unconstitutional.

Another decision on the issue of same-sex couples came in July 2000, when the Vermont legislature voted to allow same-sex partners to register their "civil unions" with town clerks, thereby gaining access to all the state-granted rights, privileges, and responsibilities of marriage. Though this was a big victory for gay and lesbian marriage advocates, the measure fell short of calling the partnerships "marriage" and instead opted for "civil unions." In 2003 the Massachusetts Supreme Judicial Court ruled that the state constitution does not forbid gay men and lesbians to marry, and gave the Massachusetts state legislature six months to rewrite the state's marriage laws to permit gay marriages. On May 17, 2004, the nation's first legal same-sex marriage was performed in Massachusetts. Just three months earlier, the mayor of San Francisco, Gavin Newsom, started issuing marriage licenses to gay and lesbian couples. Mayor Newsom argued that the state referendum passed in 2000, which defined marriage as between a man and a woman, violated the state constitution, which prevents discrimination against any social group. This prompted a response from California's governor to order the state attorney general to halt the action and for President George W. Bush to publicly endorse a constitutional amendment "defining and protecting marriage as a union of a man and woman as husband and wife" (CNN, 2004). (The president did not call for a ban on civil unions between homosexuals, which would be left up to the states to determine.)

Since 2005, more states and countries have shown support for same-sex marriage. As of 2013, California, Connecticut, Delaware, Iowa, Maine, Maryland, Massachusetts, Minnesota, New Hampshire, New York, Rhode Island, Vermont, Washington, and Washington, D.C. allowed or will implement same-sex marriage. Civil unions are options in Colorado, Hawaii, Illinois, and New Jersey, in addition to the states that allow same-sex marriage (NCSL, 2013).

Jessica Vandermark-Martinez (left) holds hands with Jodie Vandermark-Martinez at their wedding ceremony outside the Polk County administrative office in Des Moines, Iowa.

In June 2013, the U.S. Supreme Court decided that section 3 of DOMA was unconstitutional, but left section 2 intact. As a result, the federal government defined same-sex spouses as married, and thus eligible for benefits already granted to opposite-sex spouses, including joint taxes, health insurance, and immigration sponsorship (Peralta, 2013). However, marriage is still defined by each state, and 35 states ban same-sex marriage (NCSL, 2013).

Fifteen countries have legalized same-sex marriage, including Argentina, Canada, Norway, Spain, and most recently Denmark, Uruguay, New Zealand, and France. Similar to the United States, only some jurisdictions in Mexico recognize same-sex marriage: Mexico City and the state of Quintana Roo (Pew Research Center, 2013).

Although the ultimate outcome—whether state law will respect these marriages—is yet to be determined, these events demonstrate the growing social movement toward legalizing same-sex marriage.

The Dark Side of the Family

Family life encompasses the whole range of emotional experience. Family relationships—between wife and husband, parents and children, brothers and sisters, or more distant relatives—can be warm and fulfilling. But they can equally be extremely tense, driving people to despair or imbuing them with anxiety and guilt. The dark side of family life belies the rosy images of family harmony frequently depicted in TV commercials and programs. It can take many forms. Among the most devastating are the incestuous abuse of children and domestic violence.

FAMILY VIOLENCE

Violence within families is primarily a male domain. The two broad categories of family violence are child abuse and spousal abuse. Because of the sensitive and private nature of violence within families, it is difficult to obtain national data on levels of domestic violence. Data on child abuse are particularly sparse because of the cognitive development and ethical issues involved in studying child subjects.

Child Abuse The most common definition of child abuse is serious physical harm (trauma, sexual abuse with injury, or willful malnutrition) with intent to injure. One national study of married or cohabiting adults indicates that about 3 percent of respondents abused their children in 1993, though cohabiting adults are no more or less likely to abuse their children than married couples (Brown, 2004; Sedlak and Broadhurst, 1996). More recent statistics are based on national surveys of child welfare professionals. However, these surveys miss children who are not seen by professionals or reported to state agencies. Researchers estimate that as many as 50 to 60 percent of child deaths from abuse or neglect are not recorded (U.S. Department of Health and Human Services [DHHS], 2008). In the 1993 National Incidence Study (NIS) of Child Abuse and Neglect, almost half of all substantiated cases of child abuse and neglect fell into the neglect category (47 percent). Physical abuse was the next most common violation (25 percent), followed by sexual abuse (15 percent) (Sedlak and Broadhurst, 1996). The most recent statistics based on the National Child Abuse and Neglect Data System (NCANDS) indicate that in 2010 more than 695,000 children were determined to be victims of abuse or neglect. Of these, 78.3 percent suffered neglect, 17.6 percent suffered physical abuse, 8.1 percent suffered from emotional maltreatment, and 9.2 percent were sexually abused (Child Welfare Information Gateway, 2012). Also, 81.2 percent of child abuse or neglect is perpetrated by the child's parents, and

6.1 percent by other relatives of the victim. Almost half (44.8 percent) of all victims of child abuse or neglect are white and 21.9 percent are black (Child Welfare Information Gateway, 2012). In 1990 there were 860,000 reported victims of child abuse or neglect; the number of victims rose to just over 1 million in 1994, before declining to 695,000 in 2010.

Spousal Abuse A 1985 study by Murray Straus and his colleagues found that spousal violence had occurred at least once in the past year in 16 percent of all marriages and at some point in the marriage in 28 percent of all marriages. This does not, however, distinguish between severe acts, such as beating up and threatening with or using a gun or knife, and less severe acts, such as slapping, pushing, grabbing, or shoving. When the authors disaggregated this number, they found that approximately 3 percent of all husbands admitted perpetrating at least one act of severe violence on their spouse in the previous year, and this is likely an underestimate.

The national survey by Straus and his colleagues also uncovered a somewhat surprising finding: Women reported perpetrating about the same amount of violent acts as men. This contrasts with much of the literature based on crime statistics, hospital records, and shelter administrative records, which all indicate that spousal violence is almost exclusively man-on-woman violence.

Michael Johnson (1995) untangled these inconsistencies, recognizing that the data generating such conflicting findings came from two very different samples. In the shelter samples, respondents are generally women who were severely beaten by their husbands or partners. The severity of their situation had drawn them to a shelter. In contrast, those responding to a national survey are generally living at home and have the time, energy, and wherewithal to complete a survey. It is unlikely that individuals experiencing extreme violence in the home would respond to a national survey. Furthermore, it is unlikely that those experiencing less severe violence (e.g., slapping) would end up in a shelter. Therefore, the two groups of people are very different.

Johnson argued that the spousal abuse in the two samples was also different in character. The extreme abuse experienced by many in the shelter samples was "patriarchal terrorism," perpetuated by feelings of power and control. The violence reported in national surveys is "common couple violence," which generally relates to a specific incident and is not rooted in power or control.

CONCEPT CHECKS ✓

1. Explain the nature/nurture debate.
2. Why do sociologists disagree with the claim that biology is destiny?
3. Give examples of subcultures that are typical of American society.
4. What is the difference between cultural ethnocentrism and cultural relativism?
5. Why is language considered to be a cultural universal?
6. What is the linguistic relativity hypothesis?

---

④ UNANSWERED QUESTIONS

As you have learned so far, the family is an ever-evolving institution. As the family changes and new questions arise about these new forms, sociologists face the challenge of developing rigorous research to address these questions. Some of the most pressing questions facing family sociologists today focus on family forms that were once considered "nontraditional" or even "deviant," such as cohabiting families, same-sex couples with children, and persons who choose to forgo marriage and live life on their own. Each of these fascinating groups has grown rapidly in number over the past half decade, prompting sociologists to explore new and unanswered questions.

Is Cohabitation a Substitute for Marriage?

Cohabitation—in which a couple lives together in a sexual relationship without being married—has become increasingly widespread in most Western societies. Until a few decades ago, cohabitation was regarded as somewhat scandalous, but during the 1980s, the number of unmarried men and women sharing a household went up sharply. Cohabitation has become widespread among college and university students, although they did not initiate this trend. Larry Bumpass and coworkers (Bumpass, Sweet, and Cherlin, 1991) found that the cohabitation phenomenon started with lower-educated groups in the 1950s—probably as a substitute for marriage, which may involve economic constraints.

While, for some, cohabitation today may be a substitute for marriage, for many it is a stage in the process of relationship building that precedes marriage. Young people usually come to live together by drifting into it, rather than through calculated planning. A couple having a sexual relationship spend increasing time together, eventually giving up one of their individual homes. While in the 1980s and '90s cohabiting couples said their main reason for cohabiting was to "be sure they are compatible before marriage" (Bumpass, Sweet, and Cherlin, 1991), very different reasons are given by cohabiters in the early twenty-first century. One study of cohabiters found that the main reasons a couple moved in together were because the partners "loved spending time together" and to share love, intimacy, and space (see Figure 15.6) (Rhoades, Stanley, and Markman, 2009).

For most couples, cohabitation is a temporary state—leading either to marriage or to a breakup. The chances of a cohabiting union transitioning to a first marriage is related to several socioeconomic factors. For instance, the probability that a cohabiting couple will marry within five years is 75 percent for white women but only 61 percent for Hispanic women and 48 percent for black women. Similarly, the likelihood of a first marriage resulting from cohabitation is positively associated with higher education, the absence of children during cohabitation, and higher family income. It is also more likely in communities with low male unemployment rates (Bramlett and Mosher, 2002). For many people, however, cohabitation does not end in marriage. Only about 35 percent of cohabiters married their partners within three years of starting to live together. Increasingly, evidence shows that rather than being a "stage in the process" between dating and marriage, cohabitation may be an end in itself.

For some couples, though, cohabitation is "marriage-like" in that it is a context for bearing and rearing children. In the early 1980s, 29 percent of all nonmarital births were to those in cohabiting unions. In the 2006–2010 period, about half of all nonmarital births are to cohabiting couples. Among first births to Hispanic women, more than one in four (29.9 percent) occurred within cohabiting unions, compared with one in five of first births to white women (20 percent) and to black women (19 percent) (Martinez, Daniels, and Chandra, 2012).

Part of the reason more babies are born into cohabiting unions is that pregnant women today don't feel the same social pressure to marry their partner as they would have in past years. In the past, couples who got pregnant before they were

cohabitation • Two people living together in a sexual relationship of some permanence without being married to one another.

Figure 15.6
Reasons for Cohabiting

Researchers interviewed 123 heterosexual cohabiting couples and asked them how strongly they agreed or disagreed with each of 29 reasons for cohabiting with their partners. A score of 1 meant "strongly disagree," and a score of 7 meant "strongly agree." Here are the top five and bottom five reasons listed, with the average "agreement" score.

Top Five Reasons

Because I love spending time with him/her.

Because I wanted to spend more time with him/her.

So that we could have more daily intimacy and sharing.

Because I want us to have a future together.

Because we were spending most nights together anyway.

Bottom Five Reasons

Because I had doubts about how well I could handle being in a serious relationship.

Because I was concerned that he/she might not make a good husband/wife and thought living together would be a good way to find out.

Because it was inconvenient to have some of my stuff at my place and some at my partner's.

Because I wanted to find out how much work he/she would do around the house before deciding about marriage.

Because I was concerned about how my partner handles money and wanted time to test out my concerns before marriage.

Source: Rhoades et al., 2009.

married might have had a "shotgun" marriage before the birth of the baby. Currently, however, only 11 percent of single women who have a pregnancy that results in a live birth are married by the time the child is born. Fewer unmarried couples—whether cohabiting or not—are marrying before the birth of their child. There has, however, been an increase in the rate at which unmarried women begin cohabiting with their partner once they find out they are pregnant: Currently, 11 percent of single women who have a pregnancy that results in a live birth begin cohabiting by the time the baby is born—the same number as marry to "legitimate" a pregnancy.

Although cohabitation is increasingly like marriage in that it is entered into for love, companionship, support, and childrearing, it does differ from marriage in one important way: Cohabitation is less stable than marriage. Whereas the likelihood of a first marriage ending in separation or divorce within 5 years is 20 percent, there is a 49 percent chance that a premarital cohabitation will break up within 5 years. Similarly, after 10 years, the probability of a first marriage ending is 33 percent, compared with 62 percent for cohabitations (Bramlett and Mosher, 2002). Overall, scholars tend to believe that cohabitation is a highly varied experience, with some enjoying long-term satisfying unions that are "marriage-like" and others living together as a trial, and view cohabitation as a more serious form of "dating."

Does Living Together Help Reduce the Chances for Divorce?

A second important puzzle faces researchers of cohabitation: Does living together for marriage help reduce the chances for divorce, perhaps by serving as a "trial" marriage where couples can resolve their issues and adjust to each other's quirks? The belief that living together allows people to make better decisions about marriage dates back to the countercultural revolution of the 1960s and to scholars such as anthropologist Margaret Mead (1966). There is some truth that cohabitation helps to weed out ill-suited couples and serves as a training ground for well-matched couples: The act of living together is a kind of trial marriage that can help poorly matched couples avoid a failed marriage (Elwert, 2005).

Yet many people would be surprised to learn that couples who live together before marrying are more likely to divorce than those who do not. How could this be so? Researchers propose two competing arguments: the social explanation and social causation explanation.

THE SOCIAL SELECTION EXPLANATION

One compelling explanation suggests that there is nothing about living together that promotes cohabitation. This explanation cites the fact that people who live together are more likely to divorce whether or not they lived together first. This might sound odd until we recognize that the condition of living together may not be the cause of more divorce. Instead, perhaps the very people who choose to cohabit differ from those who do not. For example, people who cohabit are less religious, and people who refuse to cohabit are more religious (Dush, Cohan, and Amato, 2003). People who are less religious would be less likely to stay married in any event, whereas people who are more religious would be more likely to stay married. So people who elect to cohabit are the ones who are less religious and more likely to get divorced anyway.

THE SOCIAL CAUSATION (OR EXPERIENCE OF LIVING TOGETHER) EXPLANATION

This explanation suggests that living together is the kind of experience that erodes beliefs in the experience of marriage. Particularly as people go through their twenties living with various partners, they see that relationships can be started and ended more easily and that they have many options for intimate relations outside marriage (Teachman, 2003).

Which explanation is right? The best evidence seems to indicate that while cohabitation may slightly increase the probability of divorce, the majority of divorces among those who cohabit is due to the fact that people who choose to live together before marrying have characteristics (such as low levels of religiosity) that would make divorce more likely for them anyway.

One other interesting fact bears on this discussion. People who cohabit only with the person they marry have as low a divorce rate as people who never cohabit. Perhaps this is because such people don't live together with enough partners to get a sense that relationships can be started and ended at will. Or perhaps it is because the very kinds of people who would live with only one partner have characteristics, such as higher religiosity, that keep divorce down. Overall, though, sociologists agree that there is little evidence that living together "causes" divorce.

Do Children Raised by Gay Parents Fare Differently from Children Raised by Straight Parents?

As we noted earlier, more than 115,000 same-sex-couple households today are raising children (Lofquist, 2011). The legal, cultural, and technological landscapes facing gay parents and their children have changed dramatically in recent years. Increasingly tolerant attitudes toward homosexuality have been accompanied by a growing tendency for courts to allocate custody of children to mothers living in lesbian relationships. All but two U.S. states (Utah and Mississippi) now allow same-sex couples to adopt children (Tavernise, 2011). Techniques of artificial insemination mean that lesbians may have children and become same-sex families without any heterosexual contact. Popular media images in recent years, such as the film *The Kids Are All Right,* depict same-sex parents as providing the same love and guidance as heterosexual parents.

But what do sociological studies show? Does parental sexual orientation shape how children turn out? This question continues to generate heated political debates today, although most sociological data reveal that the children of same-sex parents fare no better or worse than the children of heterosexual parents, provided the parents have a stable relationship. Although one recent and controversial study argued that children of parents who had ever had a same-sex relationship would go on to face greater adversity, this study has since been discredited for its serious methodological limitations. The most persuasive and comprehensive studies to date, including the American Psychological Association's (2005) review of 59 studies, have concluded that "not a single study has found children of lesbian or gay parents to be disadvantaged in any significant respect relative to children of heterosexual parents." For example, Rosenfeld (2010) finds that children of gay parents are just as likely as the children of straight parents to progress successfully throughout their school grades without being left back. Part of the reason children fare equally well regardless of parental sexual orientation is that sexual orientation has no bearing on one's capacity to be a loving parent. Moreover, children of same-sex couples usually share a common peer and school environment with children of heterosexual couples. As such, their experiences at school and with peers are very similar regardless of their parents' romantic preferences (Rosenfeld, 2010).

Although children of neither gay nor straight parents are significantly advantaged or disadvantaged, some studies point out a small number of differences. For example, in one of the most comprehensive studies to date, sociologists Judith Stacey and Timothy Biblarz (2001) reviewed 21 studies dating back to the 1980s and found that children in gay households are more likely to buck stereotypical male-female behavior. For example, boys raised by lesbians appear to be less aggressive and more nurturing than boys raised in heterosexual families. Daughters of lesbians are more likely to aspire to become doctors, lawyers, engineers, and astronauts. Heterosexual mothers tend to encourage sons to participate in historically "masculine" games and activities, such as Little League, and daughters in more "feminine" pursuits, such as ballet. In contrast, lesbian mothers had no such interest; their preferences for their children's play were gender neutral. The balance of evidence shows that children of gay parents are just as happy, healthy, and academically successful as their peers raised by heterosexual parents, and they may have more flexible views of gender and gender-typed behaviors.

Are Single People Less Happy Than Married People?

The number of people living alone in U.S. society has increased dramatically in recent decades. Several factors have combined to create this trend. First, people are marrying later than ever. The average age at first marriage today is 28.2 for men and 26.1 for women (U.S. Bureau of the Census, 2010j). That means that more and more people in their twenties, thirties, and even forties are living alone, waiting for the "right one" to come along. Second, the rise and stabilization of divorce rates over the past half century mean that many more people are living on their own when their marriage ends. Third, the "graying of the U.S. population" (see Chapter 12) is accompanied by growing numbers of older adults whose partners have died and who now live alone as widows and widowers. Fourth, the "stigma" of being single has diminished, due in part to television shows such as *Sex and the City*, which glamorized the lifestyles of "single and fabulous" women. As such, many more Americans are happily choosing to live their lives on their own (Byrne and Carr, 2005; Klinenberg, 2012a).

Yet are people really happy on their own, or are they better off being married? A large literature dating back to Émile Durkheim's classic *Suicide* (1966; orig. 1897) argues that social ties, especially marriage and parenthood, are essential to one's physical, social, and emotional well-being. Recent contemporary studies also show that divorced and widowed people report more sickness, depression, and anxiety compared with their married counterparts, although much of this disadvantage reflects the strains that precede a marital transition (such as a husband's illness or marital strife) as well as the strains that follow from the dissolution, such as financial worries or legal battles (Carr and Springer, 2010).

But what about people who are long-term singles or who choose to live alone without a spouse or partner? Are their lives marked by loneliness and desolate evenings at home eating frozen dinners alone? New research by sociologist Eric Klinenberg (2012a) and others finds that living alone can "promote freedom, personal control, and self-realization—all prized aspects of contemporary life" (Klinenberg, 2012b). After interviewing more than 300 people who live alone, he found that they had more rather than less social interaction than their married counterparts, and much of their social interactions were those they sought out by choice: encounters with friends, volunteering, arts events, classes, and other meetings that rounded out their lives. These patterns hold among older adults and younger adults alike. As Klinenberg observes, for many people, living alone and being able to choose how and with whom they spend their time is a sought-after luxury. Taken together, research showing that people who live alone (by choice) are no better or worse off than their partnered peers underscores one of the core themes of sociology of family: there is no one "best" or "typical" way in which Americans arrange their social lives. It is the freedom to choose one's relationships that is essential to one's happiness.

> ## CONCEPT CHECKS
>
> 1. Does cohabitation "cause" divorce? Why or why not?
> 2. What differences have researchers detected when comparing the children of gay versus straight parents?
> 3. Contrast the social lives and well-being of persons who live alone versus those who live with a spouse or partner.

1 **Basic Concepts**

p. 438

2 **Theoretical and Historical Perspectives on the Family**

p. 439

LEARNING OBJECTIVES

Learn how sociologists define and describe families.

Review the development of sociological thinking about families. Learn how the family has changed over the last five hundred years.

TERMS TO KNOW

Family • Kinship • Marriage • Nuclear family • Extended family • Families of orientation • Families of procreation • Matrilocal • Patrilocal • Monogamy • Polygamy • Polygyny • Polyandry

Primary socialization • Personality stabilization • Affective individualism

CONCEPT CHECKS

1. Contrast a family of orientation and a family of procreation.
2. Provide an example of a nuclear versus an extended family.
3. What are several alternatives to monogamy?

1. According to the functionalist perspective, what are the two main functions of the family?
2. According to feminist perspectives, what three aspects of family life are sources of concern? Why are these three aspects troubling to feminists?
3. Briefly describe changes in family size over the past three centuries.
4. Stephanie Coontz has dispelled the myth of the peaceful and harmonious family believed to exist in past decades. Give two examples of problems facing the family in past centuries.

Exercises: Thinking Sociologically

1. Compare the structures and lifestyles among contemporary white non-Hispanic, Asian American, Hispanic, and African American families using the text's presentation.

2. Increases in cohabitation and single-parent households suggest that marriage may be losing ground in contemporary society. However, this chapter claims that marriage and the family remain firmly established social institutions. Explain the rising patterns of cohabitation and single-parent households, and show how these seemingly paradoxical trends can be reconciled with the claims offered by this textbook.

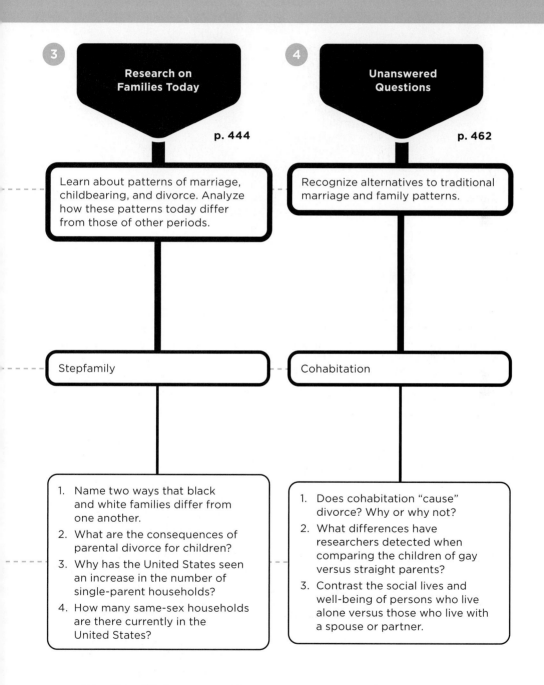

3

Research on Families Today

p. 444

Learn about patterns of marriage, childbearing, and divorce. Analyze how these patterns today differ from those of other periods.

Stepfamily

1. Name two ways that black and white families differ from one another.
2. What are the consequences of parental divorce for children?
3. Why has the United States seen an increase in the number of single-parent households?
4. How many same-sex households are there currently in the United States?

4

Unanswered Questions

p. 462

Recognize alternatives to traditional marriage and family patterns.

Cohabitation

1. Does cohabitation "cause" divorce? Why or why not?
2. What differences have researchers detected when comparing the children of gay versus straight parents?
3. Contrast the social lives and well-being of persons who live alone versus those who live with a spouse or partner.

Education

16

What was the United States' high school graduation rate in 2009?

- **a** 90 percent
- **b** 75 percent
- **c** 50 percent
- **d** 35 percent

Turn the page for the correct answer.

I f you answered *a*, you would be very optimistic, but you would be incorrect. In 2009, just 75.5 percent of public high school students earned a high school diploma within four years of entering the ninth grade, so *b* is the correct response. Rates are even lower among blacks and Hispanics, who have graduation rates of just 66.5 and 63.5 percent respectively, compared to 82.0 percent among whites and 91.8 percent among Asians (Balfanz et al., 2012). Our nation's overall high school graduation rate trails behind most other wealthy Western nations. In 2008, Finland, Ireland, Japan, New Zealand, Norway, Portugal, Slovenia, Switzerland and the United Kingdom all boasted rates at or above 90 percent (OECD, 2011). However, a 90 percent graduation rate is exactly what President Obama and U.S. secretary of education Arne Duncan have stated as their goal for the United States by the year 2020.

One of the key motivations behind the goal of a 90 percent high school graduation rate is to improve the life chances of young Americans. High school dropouts have much higher unemployment rates than other Americans and are particularly vulnerable during economic downturns. For example, during the recessionary year of 2011, high school dropouts suffered a 14.3 percent unemployment rate, compared to rates of just 9.6 percent for high school graduates and 4.3 percent for college graduates (Alliance for Excellent Education, 2011). In 2009 the average annual income of high school graduates ($19,540) was less than half that of college graduates ($46,930) (Alliance for Excellent Education, 2011). These disparities accumulate dramatically during one's working life: over the course of his or her lifetime, a high school dropout earns an average of $260,000 less than a high school graduate. The costs of high school dropout transcend the individual and affect our nation as a whole. As such, a secondary goal of President Obama's 90 percent plan is to increase the economic well-being of the United States. Some researchers have estimated that if all dropouts from the high school graduating class of 2006 had graduated, the United States would have saved more than $17 billion in Medicaid and expenditures for

LEARNING OBJECTIVES

1 BASIC CONCEPTS

Learn sociologists' explanations for achievement gaps between different groups of students.

2 SOCIOLOGICAL THEORIES OF EDUCATION

Understand the social functions of schooling. Learn three major sociological perspectives on the role of schooling in society.

3 RESEARCH ON EDUCATION TODAY

Become familiar with the most important research on whether education reduces or perpetuates inequality. Learn the social and cultural influences on educational achievement.

4 UNANSWERED QUESTIONS

Identify some of the current educational issues that concern sociologists.

uninsured health care over the course of these young people's lives (Alliance for Excellent Education, 2010).

Why do so many young Americans drop out of high school when the costs of doing so are so potentially devastating? One way to answer this question is by looking at national statistics: Students attending poor and underperforming schools, students with poor attendance and failing grades, students who come from economically disadvantaged backgrounds, and students who have very little interest or engagement in school are most likely to drop out (Alliance for Excellent Education, 2010). However, another way to understand the reasons young people drop out of school is to think about the personal experiences of one dropout.

Christine is an eighteen-year-old Puerto Rican American who lives in the Bronx, New York. She is a bright young woman who for many years has dreamed of becoming a doctor. When she graduated from eighth grade, she was assigned to a notoriously dangerous, low-performing public high school called UPHS, about two miles away from her home. UPHS, like many urban schools around the country, was in the process of being dismantled and made into several small, theme-based schools. Small schools had become the latest trend in urban school restructuring. Often, a group of public school educators will team up with a community-based organization or a private company to create a school for students interested in a particular profession. Many of these small schools have good reputations, and there is a perception among students and parents that the small schools have better resources, such as state-of-the-art computers, than the traditional large public high schools. When Christine arrived at UPHS, she was pleased to learn that a new small school that partnered with a local hospital had opened up. The school was designed for students with an interest in the medical professions. Christine applied and was informed by her counselor that all slots for the new school had already been filled. The counselor explained to Christine that he would put her on the list for another small school about to open up for students interested in careers in law enforcement.

Christine's father died when she was nine and her mother suffered chronic and serious medical problems, so Christine had no one to advocate for her. For two years, she attended classes and waited for the new small school to be established. Christine enjoyed some of her classes but felt ambivalent about others. Some classes were overcrowded, and there was immense pressure on teachers to prepare students for state-mandated standardized tests. To make matters worse, several of Christine's classmates were underprepared for high school–level work, and they often misbehaved and disrupted class. Not all teachers had the patience or the ability to deal with the difficult situation effectively. Christine also had to contend with the general disorder and violence in the school and the heavy police presence that had been added to the school in an effort to restore order. From time to time, Christine would hear of a disturbing incident in which a classmate or friend was seriously injured in a fight. But it was becoming an even more common occurrence to hear that a friend had gotten into a confrontation with the police in the school hallways and ended up getting arrested. Like many of the students at UPHS, Christine came to view the heavy policing of students as another reason school was becoming less and less welcoming and enjoyable.

Several times during that period, Christine's mother was hospitalized, and Christine was placed in foster care. Christine moved in with a foster mother who lived several miles from the school. She began having trouble making it to school on time or at all. She would meet with her counselor at school regularly to express her interest in a transfer. She believed she would do better in a school closer to where she was living and one that offered a more flexible or accelerated program, as she was beginning to fall behind with her course credits and wanted very much to graduate on time.

At the beginning of her junior year, Christine finally transferred to a new school and was back living with her mother. Things were going well for a while, but she felt pressured to earn money, as her mother was living on a fixed income and had no spare money for her daughter. Christine worked at a supermarket for a while, and then at a restaurant. But the competing demands of school and paid work proved overwhelming. Unable to keep the difficult pace, Christine ultimately dropped out of high school, although she vowed that she would eventually enter a GED (General Educational Development) program and earn her high school equivalency degree.

There are many aspects of Christine's life that hurt her chance of high school graduation—including her family background, her neighborhood, the economy, and the structure and organization of her school. Children from poor homes often must take part-time jobs to support their families financially, making it hard to find time to study and excel in schools. Parents who struggle with economic or health problems of their own often cannot help their children with their studies, or advocate for their children when they face academic challenges. Changes in family structure, such as a parent's divorce or even a major illness, often mean that a child must move to a new home and new school, which can be highly disruptive to one's academic progress. Dangerous school systems are uninviting if not intimidating, leading many students to decide that being a high school dropout can't be worse than risking physical violence at school.

What happens to young people after they drop out? Some flounder, engage in criminal activity, and spend time in prison. Others, such as Christine, try to find their way—despite the daunting odds. Today, Christine works full-time in a supermarket, and she also was recruited to attend a *proprietary* (or for-profit) school that offers training and a credential in medical billing. Christine has given up on her dream of being a doctor and now has a new and shorter-term goal: a career in medical billing. The tuition at her proprietary school is high enough that it will use up whatever financial aid and savings she would have used for college.

Christine is working hard to succeed; she is getting good grades but occasionally misses class because of her grueling schedule. She still needs to pass her GED exam. Christine, like so many other young working-class people today, is struggling without much help and without good options to gain financial security.

Christine's story touches on many of the issues of interest to sociologists of education today. Education is a social institution that teaches individuals how to be members of society. Through education, we become aware of the common characteristics we share with other members of the same society and have at least some sort of knowledge about our society's geographical and political position in the world and its past history. The educational system both directly and indirectly exposes young people to the lessons they will need to learn to become players in other major social institutions, such as the economy and the family.

In this chapter, we will provide a historical and theoretical overview of the sociology of education. We will also review cutting-edge research and investigate several puzzles that researchers continue to grapple with. In doing so, we will reveal the many complex and fascinating ways our lives are shaped by the social institution of education.

THE ANSWER IS B.

① BASIC CONCEPTS

Before we delve into complex theories of the ways that education shapes our everyday lives, we first define several key concepts that are essential to our understanding of this major social institution.

One of the core concepts in the sociology of education is the notion of educational inequalities, or an **achievement gap** between different groups of students. What this means is that certain groups, such as African Americans and other minorities, have achieved lower scores on standardized tests and other measures of academic success (such as high school graduation rates and entrance into college) relative to their white counterparts. Sociologists have sought to explain achievement gaps in a variety of ways and highlight influences such as social background—or the educational and economic resources of one's parents—as well as intelligence.

Intelligence may seem like a simple concept, but it is both complex and potentially controversial. For years, psychologists, geneticists, statisticians, and others have debated whether there exists a single human capability that can be called **intelligence**, and if so, whether it rests on innately determined differences. Intelligence is difficult to define because, as the term is usually employed, it covers qualities that may be unrelated to one another. We might suppose, for example, that the "purest" form of intelligence is the ability to solve abstract mathematical puzzles. However, people who are very good at such puzzles sometimes show low capabilities in other areas, such as history or art. Scholars today increasingly believe there are multiple forms of intelligence, including aptitudes in art, music, language, interpersonal relations, and spatial skills, to name a few. Some scholars have also argued that **emotional intelligence** is just as important to professional and personal success as is the more intellect-based types of intelligence (Gardner and Hatch, 1989). Emotional intelligence is generally defined as the ability to identify, assess, and control the emotions of oneself or others (Goleman, 1996).

Because the concept of intelligence has proven so resistant to accepted definition, some psychologists have proposed (and many educators have by default accepted) that intelligence should simply be regarded as "what **IQ (intelligence quotient)** tests measure." Most IQ tests consist of a mixture of conceptual and computational problems. The tests are constructed so that the average score is 100 points: Anyone scoring below is thus labeled "below-average intelligence," and anyone scoring above is "above-average intelligence." In spite of the fundamental difficulty in measuring intelligence, IQ tests are widely used in

achievement gap • Disparity on a number of educational measures between the performance of groups of students, especially groups defined by gender, race, ethnicity, ability, and socioeconomic status.

intelligence • Level of intellectual ability, particularly as measured by IQ (intelligence quotient) tests.

emotional intelligence • The ability to identify, assess, and control the emotions of oneself or others.

IQ (intelligence quotient) • A score attained on tests of symbolic or reasoning abilities.

CONCEPT CHECKS ✓

1. Name at least three factors that contribute to high school dropout.
2. What is the "achievement gap"?
3. Define and contrast different types of intelligence.

research studies and in schools and businesses. However, sociologists remain critical and wary of the concept. Researchers have found that IQ is powerfully affected by the socio-economic resources of one's parents, thus calling into question the belief that intelligence is "innate" or "inborn" (Fischer et al., 1996). Later in this chapter we will delve further into the debates surrounding the meaning and influences on intelligence.

② SOCIOLOGICAL THEORIES OF EDUCATION

When we think of education, we tend to see it from an individual perspective. We may think of our own reasons for attending college: to cultivate our intelligence, to enjoy a fun and social "college experience," or to prepare for a career. We also tend to think of education as a means of upward mobility. But sociologists look beyond the individual student and his or her goals to connect these to the larger social functions of schools. We discuss three major sociological theories of the role schooling plays in the larger society: schooling as a process of assimilation or acculturation, schooling as a credentialing mechanism, and schooling as a process of social, or cultural, reproduction.

Assimilation

The first perspective, schooling as a process of assimilation, focuses on what might be called the "official" curriculum and looks at questions such as how learning a common language and the facts of a common history and geography creates a sense of "affinity" among members of society, which is something less than full consensus (Shils, 1972). The official curriculum promotes feelings of nationalism and is instrumental in the development of national societies, constituted of citizens from different regions who would then know the same history and speak a common language (Ramirez and Boli, 1987; Shils, 1972). In this approach, the content of education is particularly important in creating a common culture. For example, public schools historically have taught the children of immigrants about "American" foods, holidays, legends, and heroes to help them (and their immigrant parents) become fully steeped in our nation's culture. But even children whose parents are part of the country's dominant culture depend upon the official curriculum to develop an image of themselves as Americans with a common history.

Credentialism

A second influential perspective is credentialism. Adherents to this way of thinking place less emphasis on the content of an official curriculum. They argue that the specific skills and information that students learn in the classroom are much less relevant to their later achievements than the actual diploma. The primary social function of mass education derives from the need for degrees to determine one's credentials for a job, even if the work involved has nothing to do with the education one has received (Collins, 1979). Over time, the practice of credentialism results in demands for higher credentials, which require higher levels of educational attainment. Jobs that thirty years ago would have required a high school diploma, such as that of a sales representative, now require a college degree. Since educational attainment is closely related to class position, credentialism reinforces the class structure within a society.

Hidden Curriculum

A third perspective, described as "critical" or Marxist, places the emphasis on social reproduction. In the context of education, *social reproduction* refers to the ways in which schools help perpetuate social and economic inequalities across the generations. A number of sociologists have argued that the *hidden curriculum* is the mechanism through which social reproduction occurs. The **hidden curriculum** refers to the idea that students from different social class backgrounds are provided different types of education, in terms both of curricular materials and the kinds of interactions in which they are engaged by their teachers. More specifically, the notion of the hidden curriculum suggests that the expansion of education was brought about by employers' needs for certain personality characteristics in their workers—self-discipline, dependability, punctuality, obedience, and the like—which are all taught in schools.

In their classic study of social reproduction, Samuel Bowles and Herbert Gintis (1976) provide an example of how the hidden curriculum works. They argue that modern education is a response to the economic needs of industrial capitalism. Schools help provide the technical and social skills required by industrial enterprise, and they instill discipline and respect for authority in the labor force. Schools also socialize children to get along with one another. Being able to "play well with others" is, after all, an important characteristic of a good worker.

Authority relations in school, which are hierarchical and place strong emphasis on obedience, directly parallel those dominating the workplace. The rewards and punishments held out in school also replicate those found in the world of work. Schools help motivate some individuals toward "achievement" and "success" while discouraging others, who find their way into low-paying jobs. You might even have noticed this in your own high school, where students from wealthier backgrounds took college prep courses, while their classmates from more disadvantaged backgrounds were tracked into vocational or secretarial programs.

A cruder way of putting this is that schools facilitate the ruling class's need to exploit a docile or cooperative workforce. Here the emphasis is on the fact that much of what is learned in school has nothing directly to do with the formal content of lessons. Schools, by the nature of the discipline and regimentation they entail, tend to teach students an uncritical acceptance of the existing social order. These lessons are not consciously taught; they are implicit in school procedures and organization. Thus, the hidden curriculum teaches children from underprivileged backgrounds that their role in life is "to know their place and to sit still with it" (Illich, 1983). Children spend long hours in school, and they learn a great deal more in the school context than is contained in the lessons they are actually taught. Children get an early taste of what the world of work will be like, learning that they are expected to be punctual and to apply themselves diligently to the tasks that those in authority set for them. From this perspective, even if a student in a poor inner-city school learned very little in her classes, the basic training she received in arriving on time for class would end up serving her well as a worker at a fast-food restaurant. Such an analysis can be quite depressing, but it may be a realistic way of understanding the place of education in the lives of such people.

Adherents to this perspective don't completely dismiss the content of the official curriculum.

hidden curriculum • Traits of behavior or attitudes that are learned at school but not included in the formal curriculum—for example, gender differences.

They accept that the development of mass education has had many beneficial consequences. Illiteracy rates are low compared with premodern times, and schooling provides access to learning experiences that are intrinsically self-fulfilling. Yet because education has expanded mainly as a response to economic needs, the school system falls far short of what enlightened reformers had hoped for from it. That is, according to this perspective, schooling has not become the "great equalizer"; rather, within the current economic and political system, schooling reproduces social class stratification.

Pierre Bourdieu and Cultural Capital

Another seminal figure who wrote about education and reproduction is the French sociologist Pierre Bourdieu, who argued that schools reproduce social class inequality by rewarding certain cultural norms over others (1984, 1988). Bourdieu's focus on the role of culture in the process of reproduction distinguished his theory from a strict Marxist analysis that focused on how schools mirrored and reproduced economic class structures. For this reason he used the term *cultural reproduction*. In relation to his theory of cultural reproduction, Bourdieu argued that there were many kinds of capital that people could possess other than financial capital. Specifically, he was concerned with the existence of what he called **cultural capital**. That is, his theory of cultural reproduction proposes that middle- and upper-class children come to schools with a certain kind of cultural capital—speech patterns, demeanors, tastes, and so on—that is valued, and thus rewarded, by the school. Bourdieu argues that children from low-income or working-class homes, however, do not possess these same cultural characteristics valued by the school and thus are placed at a disadvantage in schools.

Another important concept Bourdieu offers is the notion of habitus. *Habitus* refers to a class-based set of dispositions, such as taste, language use, and demeanor. For Bourdieu, these dispositions are internalized unconsciously through social practices within one's social group. Put simply, poor and working-class children are socialized into a particular habitus—one that is not valued within the school system. In arguing that working-class individuals are unconsciously socialized into a working-class culture (and therefore are not likely to obtain the dispositions required for school success), Bourdieu, like Bowles and Gintis, ultimately proposes a theory of reproduction in which the cycle of domination seems unbreakable.

These kinds of theories have been challenged by the notion of schools as *contested spaces* (Aronowitz and Giroux, 1985; Willis, 1977). It has been proposed that social reproduction does not happen without struggle or opposition from oppressed groups. Written over 30 years ago, but still important today, Paul Willis's influential ethnographic study of working-class British youth known as "the lads" shows how working-class students exhibit an implicit understanding that schooling is not structured to benefit their group (industrial factory workers) as a whole. The lads express their understanding that schooling is not designed to better their own conditions as members of the working class by embracing a working-class culture that valorizes manual labor and a counter-school culture. In doing so, they participate in the reproduction of their own class subordination.

cultural capital • The advantages that well-to-do parents usually provide their children.

Willis suggests that these insights demonstrate that working-class youth are not passive dupes in the process of reproduction. Willis also suggests that the emphasis on the lads' being in control of their destiny points to possibilities for organized resistance. A number of subsequent studies of resistance in schooling in the U.S. context (Foley, 1994; McLaren, 1994; McLeod, 1995; Solomon, 1992; Valenzuela, 1999) have expanded our understanding of schools as contested spaces.

Let's return for a moment to Christine's story. What sociological theories might be relevant to her experience of schooling? Christine was very likely assimilated into a common American culture to some extent through her schooling experiences. She also attempted to gain credentials through the proprietary school in order to enter a particular profession. But perhaps a theory of reproduction is most relevant to Christine's experience. What do you think Christine's future will hold? How have school curricula, interactions with school personnel, and her own choices impacted that future? One thing is for sure: One's educational path is often quite complicated and shaped by myriad influences. It is also important to recognize that, whatever we are left thinking after examining these theories, Christine's future is not written in stone. She is resourceful and intelligent. And recent sociological research offers us some reason to believe that Christine will one day find herself in a satisfying job in the medical profession.

CONCEPT CHECKS

1. Contrast credentialism and social reproduction perspectives on education.
2. What is cultural capital?
3. According to Wills, how do working-class boys view the formal educational system?

3 RESEARCH ON EDUCATION TODAY

In the previous sections, we learned that the purpose and function of schooling have been viewed from a variety of perspectives. On the one hand, education has consistently been seen as a means of equalization. Access to universal education, it has been argued, could help reduce disparities in wealth and power. On the other hand, some theorists have argued that schools serve to perpetuate, or reproduce, inequalities. Are educational opportunities equal for everyone? Has education in fact proven to be a great equalizer? There is a vast amount of research that examines these questions. Next, we outline some of the important research related to educational equality and differential outcomes (when one group consistently does better than another group in terms of educational achievement). The concepts offered here help to frame recent debates in education in the United States. We also report on recent studies that help us understand the development and proliferation of the Internet, and "digital gaps," or disparities, in its access and use.

Macrosocial Influences on Student Outcomes: Do Schools and Neighborhoods Matter?

Many of us believe that if we are intelligent and hardworking, and receive encouragement from our teachers, parents, and peers, we can succeed in school. This is true—to a point—but the types of school we attend, the types of classes we take, and the experiences we have within those schools also may affect our lives. The notion that schools may matter dates back to the classic studies of sociologist James Coleman in the 1960s. The ways that schools shape our daily lives both today and in our futures have been documented dramatically by author Jonathan Kozol. Yet a large and controversial body of research on school tracking emphasizes that even within a single school, one's outcomes are powerfully shaped by the types of classes to which one is assigned.

COLEMAN'S STUDY OF BETWEEN-SCHOOL EFFECTS IN AMERICAN EDUCATION

The study of "between-school effects," or the ways students' experiences at School A differ from those at School B, has been the focus of sociological research for more than five decades. One of the classic investigations of educational inequality was undertaken in the United States in the 1960s. The Civil Rights Act of 1964 required the commissioner of education to prepare a report on educational inequalities resulting from differences in ethnic background, religion, and national origin. James Coleman, a sociologist, was appointed director of the research program. The outcome was a study based on one of the most extensive research projects ever carried out in sociology (Coleman et al., 1966).

Information was collected on more than half a million pupils who were given a range of achievement tests assessing verbal and nonverbal abilities, reading levels, and mathematical skills. Sixty thousand teachers also completed forms providing data for about 4,000 schools. The report found that a large majority of children went to schools that effectively segregated black from white. Almost 80 percent of schools attended by white students contained only 10 percent or fewer African American students. White and Asian American students scored higher on achievement tests than did blacks and other ethnic minority students. Coleman had supposed his results would also show mainly African American schools to have worse facilities, larger classes, and more inferior buildings than schools that were predominantly white. But, surprisingly, the results showed far fewer differences of this type than had been anticipated.

Coleman, therefore, concluded that the material resources provided in schools made little difference to educational performance; the decisive influence was the children's backgrounds. The report stated, "Inequalities imposed on children by their home, neighborhood, and peer environment are carried along to become the inequalities with which they confront adult life at the end of school" (Coleman et al., 1966). There was, however, some evidence that students from deprived backgrounds who formed close friendships with those from more favorable circumstances were likely to be more successful educationally.

Not long after Coleman's study, Christopher Jencks and coworkers (1972) produced an equally celebrated work that reviewed empirical evidence accumulated on education and inequality up to the end of the 1960s. Jencks reaffirmed two of the earlier study's conclusions: First, educational and occupational attainment are governed mainly by family background and nonschool factors, and second, on their own, educational reforms can produce only minor effects on existing inequalities. Jencks's work has been criticized on methodological grounds, but the study's overall conclusions remain persuasive. Subsequent research has tended to confirm them.

CHILDREN LEFT BEHIND

Between 1988 and 1990, the journalist Jonathan Kozol studied schools in about 30 neighborhoods around the United States. There was no special logic to the way he chose the schools, except that he went where he happened to know teachers, principals, or ministers. What startled him most was the segregation within these schools and the inequalities among them. Kozol brought these terrible conditions to the attention of the American people in his books, including *Savage Inequalities* (1991) and *Amazing Grace* (1995).

In his passionate opening chapter of *Savage Inequalities*, he first took readers to East St. Louis, Illinois, a city that is 98 percent black, had no regular trash collection, and had few jobs. Three-quarters of its residents were living on welfare at the time. City residents were forced to use their backyards as garbage dumps, which attracted a plague of flies and rats during the hot summer months. One resident told Kozol about "rats as big as puppies" that lived in his mother's yard. City residents also contended with fumes from two major chemical plants in the city. Another public health problem resulted from raw sewage, which regularly backed up into people's homes. East St. Louis had some of the sickest children in the United States, with extremely high rates of infant death, asthma, and poor nutrition and extremely low rates of immunization. Only 55 percent of the children had been fully immunized for polio, diphtheria, measles, and whooping cough. Among the city's other social problems were crime, dilapidated housing, poor health care, and lack of education.

Kozol showed how the problems of the city often spilled over into the schools—in this case, literally. Over the course of two weeks, raw sewage backed up into the school on three occasions, each time requiring the evacuation of students and the cancellation of classes. Kozol documented other problems, which he argued stemmed from inadequate and disparate funding. Teachers often had to hold classes without chalk or paper. One teacher commented, "Our problems are severe. I don't even know where to begin. I have no materials with the exception of a single textbook given to each child. If I bring in anything else—books or tapes or magazines—I bring it in myself. The high school has no VCRs. They are such a crucial tool. So many good things run on public television. I can't make use of anything I see unless I unhook my VCR and bring it into school. The AV equipment in the school is so old that we are pressured not to use it." Comments from students reflected the same concerns. "I don't go to physics class, because my lab has no equipment," one student said. Another added, "The typewriters in my typing class don't work." A third said, "I wanted to study Latin but we don't have Latin in this school." Only 55 percent of the students in this high school ultimately graduate, about one-third of whom go on to college.

Kozol also wrote about the other end of the inequality spectrum, taking readers into a wealthy suburban school in Westchester County, outside New York City. This school had 96 computers for the 546 students. Most studied a foreign language (including Latin) for four or five years. Two-thirds of the senior class were enrolled in an advanced placement (AP) class. Kozol visited an AP class to ask students about their perceptions of inequalities within the educational system. Students at this school were well aware of the economic advantages that they enjoyed at both home and school. In regard to their views about students less well off than they, the general consensus was that equal spending among schools was a worthy goal, but it would probably make little difference because poor students lacked motivation and would fail because of other problems. These students also realized that equalizing spending could have adverse effects on their school. As one student said, "If you equalize the money, someone's got to be short-changed. I don't doubt that [poor] children are getting a bad deal. But do we want *everyone* to get a mediocre education?"

More than two decades later, Kozol went back and revisited the neighborhoods and children he studied, to find out what had happened to them. His portraits are often depressing, with many of the children growing up to be troubled adults—their lives often were derailed by alcohol abuse, unwanted pregnancies, murders, prison time, and even death by suicide. Yet Kozol did find that a handful of the students succeeded despite the odds. Most of these resilient children had been fortunate to have especially devoted parents, the support from their religious community, or a serendipitous scholarship opportunity. As Kozol notes, "these children had unusual advantages: someone intervened in every case." For example, one young girl named Pineapple, who met Kozol when she was a kindergartner, went on to graduate college and become a social worker. Pineapple had attended a school that Kozol described as "almost always in a state of chaos because so many teachers did not stay for long." A local minister helped her get scholarships to private schools. The daughter of Spanish-speaking immigrants, Pineapple had to work hard to overcome deficits in reading, writing, and basic study skills, but she and her older sister both were the first in their family to finish high school and go to college (Kozol, 2012).

It is impossible to read Kozol's work without believing that the extremes of wealth and poverty in the public schools and their surrounding neighborhoods are being exposed. Indeed, Kozol's poignant journalistic account of educational inequality has become part of our nation's conventional wisdom on the subject of educational inequality. But many sociologists have argued that although Kozol's book (1991) is a moving portrait, it provides an inaccurate and incomplete view of educational inequality. Why would Kozol's research not be compelling? There are several reasons, including the unsystematic way he chose the schools he studied. Other sociologists have proposed a variety of theories and have identified myriad factors contributing to inequality and differential outcomes.

TRACKING AND WITHIN-SCHOOL EFFECTS

Kozol's work vividly revealed the vast disparities between schools found in wealthy versus impoverished school districts. Yet sociologists are also interested in inequalities even within a single school. The practice of **tracking**, also referred to as ability grouping—dividing students into groups that receive different instruction on the basis of assumed similarities in ability or attainment—is common in American schools. In some schools, students are tracked only for certain subjects; in others, for all subjects. Sociologists have long believed that tracking is entirely negative in its effects and that its use partly explains why schooling seems to have little effect on existing social inequalities, since being placed in a particular track labels a student as either able or otherwise. As we have seen in the case of labeling and deviance, once attached, such labels are hard to break away from. Children from more privileged backgrounds, in which academic work is encouraged, are likely to find themselves in the higher tracks early on—and by and large stay there.

A now-classic study by Jeannie Oakes (1985) examined tracking in 25 junior and senior high schools, both large and small and in both urban and rural areas. She concentrated on differences *within* schools rather than between them. She found that although several schools claimed they did not track students, virtually all of them had mechanisms for sorting students into groups that seemed to be alike in ability and achievement, to make teaching easier. In other words, they employed tracking but did not choose to use the term *tracking*. Even where tracking existed only in this informal fashion, Oakes found strong labels developing—"high ability," "low-achieving," "slow," "average," and so on. Individual students in these groups came to be defined by teachers, other students, and themselves in terms of such labels. A student in a "high-achieving" group was considered a high-achieving *person*—smart and quick. Pupils in a "low-achieving" group came to be seen as slow, below average—or, in more colloquial terms, as "dummies," "sweathogs," or "yahoos." What is the effect of tracking on students in the low group? A subsequent study by Oakes (1990) found that these students received a poorer education in

tracking • Dividing students into groups that receive different instruction on the basis of assumed similarities in ability or attainment.

terms of the quality of the courses, teachers, and textbooks made available to them. More-over, the negative effect of tracking affected mostly African American, Latino, and poor students.

The usual reason given for tracking is that bright children learn more quickly and effec-tively in a group of others who are equally able and that clever students are held back if placed in mixed groups. Surveying the evidence, Oakes attempted to show that these assumptions are wrong. The results of later research investigations are not wholly consistent, but a path-breaking study by sociologist Adam Gamoran and his colleagues (1995) concluded that Oakes was partially correct in her arguments. They agreed with Oakes's conclusions that tracking reinforces previously existing inequalities for average or poor students but coun-tered her argument by asserting that tracking does have positive benefits for "advanced" students. The debate about the effects of tracking is sure to continue as scholars analyze more data. Yet nearly two decades after Gamoran's study was published, tracking was still considered "one of the most divisive issues" facing educators and school administrators today (*Education Week*, 2004).

SCHOOL DISCIPLINE

In the past two decades, scholars and educators have been increasingly interested in another aspect of school culture that may affect student outcomes: school discipline. Some sociologists have noted that there has been a shift in school discipline toward more puni-tive policies that mirror current trends in our nation's criminal justice system. Moreover, this shift has been most acute among schools located in poor areas and which are attended largely by members of ethnic minority groups. One of the major changes in school discipline came in 1995, when the Gun-Free School Zones Act was amended by Congress. This act and subsequent federal mandates established a "zero-tolerance" policy for weapons and drugs in schools. Zero tolerance was initially meant to address school violence by mandating sus-pension or expulsion for possession of drugs or weapons in school. However, as it was imple-mented nationwide, it was expanded to include a broad range of misbehavior. Critics of the policy argue that it has led to unnecessary police intervention in schools and has increased racial bias. Activists and educators opposed to zero tolerance have coined the term *school-to-prison pipeline* as a way of emphasizing the negative impact of the policies.

Disciplinary practices in schools, it has been argued, also appear to be influenced by media representations and negative images of black and Latino youth. Ann Arnett Fergu-son's ethnographic study of middle-school children (2000), for example, shows how insti-tutional discourses (such as the use of prison metaphors), the subjective views of teachers, and the treatment black boys receive in school influence the ways in which black boys see themselves—that is, as criminally oriented.

Other researchers have noted that punitive school discipline policies appear to be, in part, a response to low performance in inner-city schools populated by low-income, minor-ity students. Based on ethnographic research in an urban school, Kathleen Nolan and Jean Anyon (2004) theorize that, within our current economy, criminalizing school discipline policies are a means to manage an economically and educationally marginalized group. They also contend that when students embrace an oppositional culture, they may no lon-ger be participating in the reproduction of their status as manual laborers, as Paul Willis argued (1977). Instead, as misbehavior comes to be managed by the police in schools, stu-dents may be participating in the reproduction of themselves as "criminalized subjects," or as individuals who will spend a lifetime entangled in one way or another (incarceration, parole, probation) in the criminal justice system.

Cultural and Social-Psychological Influences on Student Outcomes

Sociologists are not interested only in the ways schools and socioeconomic factors affect children's educational backgrounds; some are interested also in the ways cultural and psychological factors affect children's educational opportunities and outcomes. These explanations are typically invoked to explain race and gender differences in student's academic outcomes. In general, these theories propose that ethnic minorities and women are more likely than whites and men to be socialized in a way that may disadvantage them in education (and in the workplace). Although race and gender disparities in many important educational outcomes have narrowed over the past half century, a number of gaps persist; sociologists are intent on figuring out why.

RACE AND THE "ACTING WHITE" THESIS

As we saw in this chapter's opening, black and Latino students lag behind white and Asian students in their rates of graduating high school. Yet even at younger ages, an "achievement gap" has been documented. For example, analyses by the National Center for Education Statistics (NCES) in 2009 and 2011 showed that black and Hispanic students trailed their white peers by an average of more than 20 test score points on the standardized math and reading assessments at fourth and eighth grades, a difference of about two grade levels. These gaps persisted even though the score differentials between black and white students narrowed between 1992 and 2007 in fourth-grade math and reading and eighth-grade math (NCES, 2009, 2011).

In attempting to explain these declining yet persistent racial achievement gaps in education, anthropologists John Ogbu and Signithia Fordham (1986) proposed the **"acting white" thesis**. Based on ethnographic research of the educational experiences of black students, Ogbu and Fordham concluded that the achievement gap can be partially explained through black students' reluctance to embrace school norms, which the black students associate with white culture. In subsequent years, however, the "acting white thesis" has been challenged by a number of researchers. For example, Roslyn Mickelson's research (1990) on the achievement attitudes of African American students revealed that students held both **abstract and concrete attitudes** toward schooling. Their abstract attitudes were consistent with mainstream attitudes that placed a high value on education and the attainment of academic credentials for future success. However, these students also held concrete antiachievement attitudes that were based on their experiences in school and their perception that there were few options for them in terms of entrance into higher education or lucrative careers even if they were to obtain a high school diploma.

More recently, sociologist Prudence Carter's study (2005) of the experiences of high school students in New York City revealed that black and Latino students overwhelmingly believe in the importance of school and the need for educational credentials. Carter notes that black and Latino students' academic and social experiences are heterogeneous, and the most successful students are not necessarily the ones who assimilate to white, mainstream speech patterns, styles, and tastes. Instead, students whom she calls

"acting white" thesis • The thesis that black students do not aspire to or strive to get good grades because it is perceived as "acting white."

abstract and concrete attitudes • Abstract attitudes are ideas that are consistent with mainstream societal views, while concrete attitudes are ideas that are based on actual experience.

cultural navigators—those who draw from resources from both their home culture and the mainstream culture—tend to be highly successful in school. Ultimately, Carter argues, schools must promote intercultural communication and understanding with communities, parents, and students to mitigate unequal academic outcomes.

GENDER AND ACHIEVEMENT

For many years, girls did better on average than boys in terms of standardized tests until they reached the middle years of secondary education. They then fell behind: Boys did better than girls, particularly in math and science. However, in recent years we have seen a convergence and, in some cases, a reversal in the gender gap (College Board, 2012). In 2012, boys and girls scored roughly the same on the critical reading section of the SAT (Scholastic Aptitude Test), while boys outpaced girls by 33 points on math (532 versus 499), and girls slightly outpaced boys on the writing component of the test (494 versus 481). Moreover, girls are more likely than boys to attend a four-year college immediately following high school graduation, and this gap is particularly pronounced among African Americans. Since the mid-1990s, a higher proportion of women than men graduated four-year colleges each year (Pollard, 2011).

Given this evidence, most scholars concur that today's **gender gap** places girls ahead of boys. Sociologists have attempted to explain the reversal in the gender gap in a variety of ways. Some have argued that girls are doing better in schools today because of changes in the economy that have created more opportunities for women in the new service economy, while factory jobs, traditionally a male terrain, have decreased in number because of new technologies and the relocation of manufacturing industries to developing countries. Other studies focus on the achievements made within the women's movement and its effect on women's self-esteem and expectations. Another important impact of the women's movement is that teachers have become more aware of gender discrimination in the classroom and have taken steps to avoid gender stereotyping. Many teachers now incorporate learning materials that are free of gender bias, and they encourage girls to explore traditionally "male" subjects.

Some sociologists today are wary of all the attention directed at underachieving boys. They contend that, although girls have forged ahead, they are still less likely than boys to choose subjects in school leading to careers in technology, science, and engineering. Boys pull away from girls by about age eleven in science and continue to outperform girls through college. And women continue to be disadvantaged in the job market despite the fact that they are entering college at higher rates than young men. The question of "Who fares worse, boys or girls?" will continue to challenge social scientists and educators in future generations, as they strive to develop programs and policies to enhance gender equity.

STEREOTYPE THREAT

Differential outcomes between white students and minority students and between girls and boys have also been explained in social psychological terms. Claude Steele and Joshua Aronson's influential work (Steele and Aronson, 1995, 2004) on **stereotype threat** suggests that when African

cultural navigators • People who draw from both their home culture and mainstream culture to create an attitude that allows them to succeed.

gender gap • The differences between women and men, especially as reflected in social, political, intellectual, cultural, or economic attainments or attitudes.

stereotype threat • The idea that when African American students believe they are being judged not as individuals but as members of a negatively stereotyped social group they will do worse on tests.

American students (or female students) believe they are being judged not as individuals but as members of a negatively stereotyped social group, they will do worse on tests.

Public-Policy Influences on Student Outcomes

We have described the ways that macrosocial factors such as social class and school organization, as well as microsocial processes such as stereotype threat, may account for educational inequalities. However, a third set of factors also has a powerful influence on student outcomes: public policies.

EDUCATIONAL REFORM IN THE UNITED STATES

Research done by sociologists has played a major role in reforming the educational system. These reforms, in turn, have had a powerful impact on the lives of children who are affected by such policies. The object of James Coleman's research, commissioned as part of the 1964 Civil Rights Act, was not solely academic; it was undertaken to influence policy. And influence policy it certainly did. On the basis of the act, it was decided in the courts that segregated schools violated the rights of minority pupils. But rather than attacking the origins of educational inequalities directly, as Christopher Jencks's later work suggested was necessary, the courts decided that the schools in each district should achieve a similar racial balance. Thus began the practice of busing students to other schools.

In 1970 a U.S. judge in North Carolina ordered that black students be bused to white schools and that white students be bused to black schools. It was hoped that this crosstown school busing would end the de facto segregation of public schools caused by white students living in predominantly white neighborhoods and black students living in predominantly black neighborhoods.

Busing provoked a great deal of opposition, particularly from parents and children in white areas, and led to episodes of violence at the gates of schools where the children were bused in from other neighborhoods. White children paraded with placards reading, "We don't want them!" Still, busing met with a good deal of success, reducing levels of school segregation quite steeply, particularly in the South. But busing has also produced a number of unintended consequences. Some white parents reacted to busing either by putting their children into private schools or by moving to mainly white suburbs where busing wasn't practiced. As a result, in the cities, some schools are virtually as segregated as the old schools were in the past. Busing, however, was only one factor prompting the "white flight" to the suburbs. Whites also left as a reaction to urban decay: to escape city crowding, housing problems, and rising rates of crime.

While busing is less prominent today as an issue, another problem regarding the American educational system has become an important focus of research: functional illiteracy. Most of the U.S. population can read and write at a very basic level, but the Department of Education estimates that about 13 percent of all 17-year-olds (i.e., high school seniors) are functionally illiterate—when they leave school, they can't read or write at the fourth-grade level (NCES, 2005). Among minority youth, an estimated 44 percent of 17-year-olds are functionally illiterate. Of course, the United States is a country of immigrants, who, when they arrive, may not be able to read and write, and who may also have trouble with English. But this doesn't explain why the United States lags behind most other industrial countries in terms of its level of functional illiteracy, because many functionally illiterate people are not recent immigrants at all.

What is to be done? Some educators have argued that the most important change that needs to be made is to improve the quality of teaching, either by increasing teachers' pay or by introducing performance-related pay scales, with higher salaries going to the teachers who are most effective in the classroom. Others have proposed giving schools more control over their budgets (a reform that has been carried out in Britain). The idea is that more responsibility for and control over budgeting decisions will create a greater drive to improve the school. Further proposals include the refunding of federal programs such as Head Start to ensure healthy early child development and thus save millions of dollars in later costs. Another proposal that has gained numerous supporters in recent years is that public education should be privatized.

EDUCATION POLICY TODAY

Education has long been a political battleground. In the 1960s, some politicians, educators, and community activists pushed for greater equality and universal access to education through such initiatives as busing programs to mitigate racial segregation, bilingual education programs, multicultural education, open admissions to college, the establishment of ethnic studies programs on campuses, and more equitable funding schemes. Such initiatives were seen as supporting civil rights and equality. Educational policies in the twenty-first century have similarly intended to provide quality education for all children and to close the achievement gap. However, scholars disagree about how successful recent policies have been in meeting this goal.

The most significant piece of federal legislation influencing education in the past two decades is the No Child Left Behind (NCLB) Act enacted by Congress in 2001 and signed into law by President George W. Bush in 2002. NCLB reauthorized the 1965 Elementary and Secondary Education Act but also expands it by implementing a host of policies meant to improve academic outcomes for all children and to close the achievement gap. Indeed, NCLB is the most expansive and comprehensive piece of legislation passed since 1965, addressing virtually every aspect of education—including, for example, testing, school choice, teacher quality, the education of English-language learners, military recruitment in schools, and school discipline. At the top of its agenda is instituting standardized testing as a means of measuring students' academic performance. The act also provides a strong push for school choice—that is, in the spirit of competition, parents are to be given choices as to where to send their children to school. Low-performing schools, at risk of losing students, thus jeopardize their funding and become subject to being closed. Another significant implication of NCLB is that, for the first time since 1968, states are not required to offer non-English-speaking students bilingual education. Instead, the act emphasizes learning English over using students' native language to support learning objectives and favors

English-only program models. NCLB also provides support for a zero-tolerance approach to school discipline that was first mandated in the 1990 Gun-Free School Zone Act.

The NCLB has been widely criticized, as teachers must "teach to the test." Critics have argued that the emphasis on **standardized testing**—that is, where all students in a state take the same test under the same conditions—as the means of assessment encourages teachers to teach a narrow set of skills that will increase students' test performance, rather than helping them to acquire an in-depth understanding of important concepts and skills (Hursh, 2007). Others have condemned the program as a punitive model of school reform (i.e., teachers and principals at underperforming schools risk job loss) and note that achievement gaps have not changed and that the policy neglects the important fact that the broader socioeconomic context affects school functioning.

Recognizing that the NCLB may not be effective for all school systems, however, in 2012, President Barack Obama granted waivers from NCLB requirements to 27 states, allowing them to develop their own standards and exempting them from the 2014 targets set by the law. In exchange for that flexibility, those states "have agreed to raise standards, improve accountability, and undertake essential reforms to improve teacher effectiveness," the White House said in a statement. The Obama administration also implemented its own program, entitled Race to the Top, a contest created to spur innovation and reforms in state and local district K–12 education. States were awarded points for satisfying certain educational policies, such as performance-based standards (often referred to as "annual professional performance reviews") for teachers and principals, meeting nationwide standards, promoting charter schools and privatization of education, and computerization.

Like NCLB, RTT has been criticized by teachers and policy makers. Teachers' unions and educators have complained that the tests are an inaccurate way to measure teachers, and that such measures haven't worked in the past. Political conservatives say it imposes federal control on state schools. Critics say that high-stakes testing is unreliable, that charter schools weaken public education, or that the federal government should not influence local schools (Dillon, 2010).

The crisis in American schools won't be solved in the short term, and it won't be solved by educational reforms alone, no matter how thoroughgoing. In fact, a 2006 study by the U.S. Department of Education found that schools identified for improvement were disproportionately urban, high-poverty schools, and that "school poverty and district size better predicted existing improvement status than the improvement strategies undertaken by the schools." A further unintended consequence of the current emphasis on testing is that schools have narrowed their course offerings to focus much more heavily on tested subject areas while cutting time in science, social studies, music, art, and physical education (McMurrer, 2007).

The lesson of sociological research is that inequalities and barriers in educational opportunity reflect wider social divisions and tensions. While the United States remains racked by racial tensions, and the polarization between decaying cities and affluent suburbs persists, the crisis in the school system is likely to prove difficult to turn around. Jean Anyon's (2006) analysis of how political and economic forces influence schooling helps clarify these challenges. Anyon argues that not until educational reform is linked to more sweeping economic reforms, such as job creation and training programs and corporate tax reform, will schools improve.

standardized testing • A situation in which all students take the same test under the same conditions.

Global Perspectives: Education and Literacy in the Developing World

You have already learned about vast educational inequalities in the United States. However, from a global perspective, another disparity is of tremendous concern: cross-national disparities in literacy. Literacy is the "baseline" of education. Without it, schooling cannot proceed. We take it for granted in the West that the majority of people are *literate*, but as has been mentioned, this is only a recent development in Western history, and in previous times no more than a tiny proportion of the population had any literacy skills.

Today, roughly 15 percent of the world population, or 775 million persons, are illiterate. Women are more likely than men to be illiterate, with rates of 20 percent versus 11 percent. When we focus on developing nations only, we see that over 23 percent of the population of these countries is still illiterate (Global Map 16.1). However, younger generations are faring better than their parents; youth literacy rates in nearly every region of the world are higher than adult literacy rates—although these generational gaps vary widely by region. Youth literacy rates refer to persons ages 15 to 24, while adult literacy rates apply to the population age 15 and older.

Worldwide, the lowest literacy rates are observed in sub-Saharan Africa (63 percent of adults and 72 percent of youth) and in South and West Asia (63 percent of adults and 81 percent of youth). However, even within regions there is great heterogeneity; for example, adult literacy rates range from just 29 percent in Niger to 94 percent in Equatorial Guinea. By contrast, Central Asia, and Central and Eastern Europe, enjoy literacy rates of nearly 100 percent. Although countries have instituted literacy programs, these have made only a small contribution to a problem of large-scale dimensions. Television, radio, the Internet, and other electronic media can be used, where they are available, to skip the stage of

Global Map 16.1
Adult Literacy Rates Worldwide (15 years and older)

Adult literacy rate
- Less than 50%
- 50% to 59%
- 60% to 69
- 70% to 79%
- 80% to 89%
- 90% to 100%
- No data

Source: UNESCO, 2012a.

learning literacy skills and to convey educational programs directly to adults. But educational programs are usually less popular than commercialized entertainment.

What accounts for these marked gaps in global literacy rates? Sociologists believe that these patterns are best understood in a historical perspective and reflect enduring consequences of colonialism. During the period of colonialism, governments regarded education with some trepidation. Until the twentieth century, most colonial governments believed indigenous populations were too primitive to be worth educating. Later, education was seen as a way of making local elites responsive to European interests and ways of life. But to some extent, the result was to spark discontent and rebellion. The majority of those who led anticolonial and nationalist movements were educated elites who had attended schools or colleges in Europe; they were able to compare firsthand the democratic institutions of the European countries with the absence of democracy in their lands of origin.

The education that the colonizers introduced usually pertained to Europe, not the colonial areas themselves. Educated Africans in the British colonies knew about the kings and queens of England and read Shakespeare and Milton, but they knew next to nothing about their own countries' histories or past cultural achievements. Policies of educational reform since the end of colonialism have not completely altered the situation even today.

Partly as a result of the legacy of colonial education, which was not directed toward the majority of the population, the educational system in many developing countries is top-heavy: Higher education is disproportionately developed, relative to primary and secondary education. The result is a correspondingly overqualified group who, having attended colleges and universities, cannot find white-collar or professional jobs. Given the low level of industrial development, most of the better-paid positions are in government, and there are not enough of those to go around.

In recent years, some developing countries, recognizing the shortcomings of the curricula inherited from colonialism, have tried to redirect their educational programs toward the rural poor, in an effort to raise literacy rates. They have had limited success because usually there is insufficient funding to pay for the scale of the necessary innovations. As a result, countries such as India have begun programs of self-help education. Communities draw on existing resources without creating demands for high levels of finance. Those who can read and write and who perhaps possess job skills are encouraged to take others on as apprentices, whom they coach in their spare time.

The Impact of the Media and Educational Technology on Everyday Life

While we spend hours a day using technology for "fun" and for socializing, technology also has shaped where, how, and with whom we learn. The spread of information technology looks set to influence education in a number of different ways, some of which may perhaps be quite fundamental. The new technologies are affecting the nature of work, replacing some types of human work by machines. The sheer pace of technological change is creating a much more rapid turnover of jobs than once was the case. Education can no longer be regarded as a stage of preparation before an individual enters work. As technology changes, necessary skills change, and even if education is seen from a purely vocational point of view—as providing skills relevant to work—most observers agree that lifelong exposure to education will be needed in the future.

TECHNOLOGIES OF EDUCATION

The rise of education in its modern sense was connected with a number of other major changes happening in the nineteenth century. One was the development of the school. One might naïvely think that there was a demand for education and that schools and universities were set up to meet that demand. But that was not how things happened. Schools arose, as Michel Foucault (1975) has shown, as part of the administrative apparatus of the modern state. The hidden curriculum was about discipline and about the control of children.

A second influence was the development of printing and the arrival of "book culture." The mass distribution of books, newspapers, and other printed media was as distinctive a feature of the development of industrial society as were machines and

The mass distribution of textbooks, like Noah Webster's *The American Spelling Book*, contributed to the rise of education in the nineteenth century.

factories. Education developed to provide skills of literacy and computation, giving access to the world of printed media. Nothing is more characteristic of the school than the schoolbook or textbook.

In the eyes of many, all this is set to change with the growing use of computers and multimedia technologies in education. It has been said that "around 70–80 percent of telecommunications trials conducted in the emerging multimedia technologies around the world involve education or at least have an education component" (quoted in Kenway et al., 1995).

As in many other areas of contemporary social life, markets and information technology are major influences on educational change. The commercializing and marketizing of education also reflect such pressures. Schools are being reengineered to resemble business corporations.

Many of those likely to enter the education field will be organizations whose relation to schooling was previously marginal or nonexistent. These include cable companies, software houses, telecommunication groups, filmmakers, and equipment suppliers. Their influence will not be limited to schools or universities. They are already forming part of what has been called "edutainment"—a sort of parallel education industry linked to the software industry in general and to museums, science parks, and heritage areas.

EDUCATION AND THE TECHNOLOGY GAP

Whether the new technologies will have the radical implications for education that some claim is still an open question. Critics have pointed out that, even if they do have major effects, these may act to reinforce educational inequalities. **Information poverty** might be added to the material deprivations that currently have such an effect

information poverty • The state of people who have little or no access to information technology, such as computers.

on schooling. The sheer pace of technological change and the demand of employers for computer-literate workers may mean that those who are technologically competent "leapfrog" over people who have little experience with computers.

Some already fear the emergence of a "computer underclass" within Western societies. Although developed countries have the highest levels of computer and Internet usage in the world, there are stark inequalities in computer use within those societies. Many schools and colleges are suffering from underfunding and long-standing neglect; even if these institutions become beneficiaries of schemes that distribute secondhand computer hardware to schools, they must gain the technical expertise and ability to teach information technology skills to pupils. Because the market for computer specialists is so strong, many schools are struggling to attract and keep information technology teachers, who can earn far greater incomes in the private sector.

Yet the technology gap within Western societies appears minor when compared with the digital divide separating Western classrooms from their counterparts in the developing world. As the global economy becomes increasingly knowledge based, there is a real danger that poorer countries will become even more marginalized because of the gap between the information rich and the information poor.

Internet access has become a new line of demarcation between the rich and the poor. Information technology enthusiasts argue that computers need not result in greater national and global inequalities—that their very strength lies in their ability to draw people together and to open up new opportunities. Schools in Asia and Africa that lack textbooks and qualified teachers can benefit from the Internet, it is claimed. Distance-learning programs and collaboration with colleagues overseas could be the key to overcoming poverty and disadvantage. When technology is put in the hands of smart, creative people, they argue, the potential is limitless.

Technology can be breathtaking and can open important doors, but there is no such thing as an easy "techno-fix." Underdeveloped regions that struggle with mass illiteracy and lack telephone lines and electricity need an improved educational infrastructure before they can truly benefit from distance-learning programs. The Internet cannot be substituted for direct contact between teachers and pupils under these conditions.

LIFELONG LEARNING

New technologies and the rise of the knowledge economy are transforming traditional ideas about work and education. The sheer pace of technological change is creating a much more rapid turnover of jobs than once was the case. Training and the attainment of qualifications now occur throughout people's lives, rather than just early in life. Mid-career professionals are choosing to update their skills through continuing education programs and Internet-based learning (or "online" courses). Many employers now allow workers to participate in on-the-job training as a way of enhancing loyalty and improving the company skills base.

As our society continues to transform, the traditional beliefs and institutions that underpin it are also undergoing change. The idea of education—implying the structured transmission of knowledge within a formal institution—is giving way to a broader notion of learning that takes place in diverse settings. The shift from education to learning is not an inconsequential one. Learners are active, curious social actors who can derive insights from a multiplicity of sources, not just within an institutional setting. Emphasis on learning acknowledges that skills and knowledge can be gained through all types of encounters—with friends and neighbors, at seminars and museums, in conversations at the local café, through the Internet and other media, and so forth.

The shift in emphasis toward *lifelong learning* can already be seen within schools themselves, where there is a growing number of opportunities for pupils to learn *outside* the confines of the classroom. The boundaries between schools and the outside world are breaking down, not only via **cyberspace**, but in the physical world as well. "Service learning," for example, has become a mainstay of many American secondary schools. As part of their graduation requirements, pupils devote a certain amount of time to volunteer work in the community. Partnerships with local businesses have also become commonplace in the United States, fostering interaction and mentor relationships between adult professionals and pupils.

Lifelong learning should and must play a role in the move toward a knowledge society. Not only is it essential to a well-trained, motivated workforce, but learning should also be seen in relation to wider human values. Learning is both a means and an end to the development of a well-rounded and autonomous self-education in the service of self-development and self-understanding. There is nothing utopian in this idea; indeed, it reflects the humanistic ideals of education developed by educational philosophers. An example already in existence is lifelong learning programs for the elderly, which provide retired people with the opportunity to educate themselves as they choose, developing whatever interests they care to follow.

> # CONCEPT CHECKS
>
> 1. How do Coleman's findings differ from the results of Kozol's research? Whose theory, in your opinion, can better explain race and class gaps in educational achievement?
> 2. What effect does tracking have on academic achievement?
> 3. What are the goals of No Child Left Behind and Race to the Top? What are criticisms of these policies?
> 4. What are some of the reasons there are high rates of illiteracy in developing nations?
> 5. Researchers have documented a "digital gap." Which populations have low rates of Internet use? Why?

4 UNANSWERED QUESTIONS

As you have learned in this chapter, the sociological study of education and the media is a rapidly evolving field. With each new technological development or the implementation of a new public policy, new issues and challenges arise. Sociologists continue to grapple with important questions about the media and education, and answers to these questions are often challenging and contested. We focus here on three "unanswered" questions: Is intelligence shaped by genes or environment? Is homeschooling a substitute for formal education? And who benefits from international education?

Is Intelligence Shaped by Genes or Environment?

What social or biological factors shape how "intelligent" we are? This question has been at the center of hotly contested debates for nearly five decades. Understanding the sources of IQ is an important goal for educational researchers, because scores on IQ tests correlate highly with academic performance (which is not surprising, because IQ tests were originally developed to predict success in school). They therefore

cyberspace • Electronic networks of interaction between individuals at different computer terminals.

also correlate closely with social, economic, and ethnic differences, because these are associated with variations in levels of educational attainment. Another reason scholars are interested in factors that shape IQ is because answers to this question may help remedy the achievement gap we learned about earlier in this chapter. White students score better, on average, than African Americans or members of other disadvantaged minorities. An article published by Arthur Jensen in 1969 caused a furor by attributing IQ differences between blacks and whites in part to genetic variations (see also Jensen, 1979). Most sociologists argue that such attributions are incomplete and misleading.

Later, the psychologist Richard J. Herrnstein and the sociologist Charles Murray reopened the debate about IQ in a controversial way. They argued in their book *The Bell Curve* (1994) that the accumulated evidence linking IQ to genetic inheritance was now overwhelming. The significant differences in intelligence between various racial and ethnic groups, they said, must in part be explained in terms of heredity. According to Herrnstein and Murray, the available evidence strongly indicated that some ethnic groups on average had higher IQs than other groups. Asian Americans, particularly Japanese Americans and Chinese Americans, on average possessed higher IQs than whites, although the difference was not large. The average IQs of Asians and whites, however, were substantially higher than those of blacks. Summarizing the findings of 156 studies, Herrnstein and Murray found an average difference of 16 IQ points between these two racial groups. The authors argued that such differences in inherited intelligence contributed in an important way to social divisions in American society. The smarter an individual is, the greater the chance he or she will rise in the social scale. Those at the top are there partly because they are smarter than the rest of the population—from which it follows that those at the bottom remain there because, on average, they are not as smart.

Herrnstein and Murray's claim created a great deal of controversy and raised the ire and indignation of countless liberals, social scientists, and members of the African American community. Although Herrnstein and Murray's claims may be seen as racist and reprehensible, is this sufficient reason to attack their work? Or are their conclusions based on faulty social research? The answer to both questions is a resounding yes. A team of sociologists at the University of California at Berkeley later reanalyzed much of the data that Herrnstein and Murray based their conclusions on and came up with quite different findings.

In the original analysis, Herrnstein and Murray analyzed data from the National Longitudinal Study of Youth (NLSY), a survey of more than 10,000 young Americans who were interviewed multiple times over more than a decade. As part of this study, subjects were given the Armed Forces Qualifying Test (AFQT), a short test that assesses IQ. Herrnstein and Murray then conducted statistical analyses, which used the AFQT score to predict a variety of outcomes. They concluded that having a high IQ was the best predictor of later economic success and that low IQ was the best predictor of poverty later in life.

The Berkeley sociologists, in their 1996 book *Inequality by Design* (Fischer et al., 1996), countered that the AFQT does not necessarily measure intelligence, but only how much a person has learned in school. Moreover, they found that intelligence is only one factor among several that predict how well people do in life. Social factors, including education, gender, community conditions, marital status, current economic conditions, and (perhaps most important) parents' socioeconomic status, better predict one's occupational and economic success. In the original analysis, Herrnstein and Murray measured parents' socioeconomic status by taking an average of mother's education, father's education, father's occupation, and family income.

The Berkeley sociologists recognized that each of these four factors matters differently in predicting a child's occupational outcomes and thus weighted the four components differently. Their analysis showed that the effects of socioeconomic background on a young adult's risk of later poverty were substantially greater than Herrnstein and Murray originally found. The Berkeley sociologists also recognized that IQ is closely associated with one's level of education. They reanalyzed the NLSY data, taking into consideration the individuals' level of education, and found that Herrnstein and Murray drastically overestimated the effects of IQ on a person's later achievements.

The relationship between race and intelligence is also best explained by social rather than biological causes, according to the Berkeley sociologists. All societies have oppressed ethnic groups. Low status, often coupled with discrimination and mistreatment, leads to socioeconomic deprivation, group segregation, and a stigma of inferiority. The combination of these forces often prevents racial minorities from obtaining education, and consequently their scores on standardized intelligence tests are lower.

The average lower IQ score of African Americans in the United States is remarkably similar to that of deprived ethnic minorities in other countries—such as the "untouchables" in India (who are at the very bottom of the caste system), the Maori in New Zealand, and the *burakumin* of Japan. Children in these groups score an average of 10 to 15 IQ points below children belonging to the ethnic majority. The *burakumin*—descendants of people who in the eighteenth century, as a result of local wars, were dispossessed from their land and became outcasts and vagrants—are a particularly interesting example. They are not in any way physically distinct from other Japanese, although they have suffered from prejudice and discrimination for centuries. In this case, the difference in average IQ results cannot derive from genetic variations because there are no genetic differences between them and the majority population; yet the IQ difference is as thoroughly fixed as that between blacks and whites. *Burakumin* children in America, where they are treated like other Japanese, do as well on IQ tests as other Japanese.

Such observations strongly suggest that the IQ variations between African Americans and whites in the United States result from social and cultural differences. This conclusion receives further support from a comparative study of 14 nations (including the United States) showing that average IQ scores have risen substantially over the past half century for the population as a whole (Coleman, 1987). IQ tests are regularly updated. When old and new versions of the tests are given to the same group of people, they score significantly higher on the old tests. Present-day children taking IQ tests from the 1930s outscored 1930s groups by an average of 15 points—just the kind of average difference that currently separates blacks and whites. Children today are not innately superior in intelligence to their parents or grandparents; the shift presumably derives from increasing prosperity and social advantages. The average social and economic gap between whites and African Americans is at least as great as that between the different generations and is sufficient to explain the variation in IQ scores. Although there may be genetic variations between individuals that influence scores on IQ tests, these have no overall connection to racial differences.

Is Homeschooling a Substitute for Traditional Schooling?

Homeschooling has increased dramatically in popularity in recent decades. Between 2000 and 2010, the number of students who were homeschooled increased steadily; an estimated 1.5 to 2.0 million (or 2.9 percent of all) children are currently homeschooled (Murphy, 2012; U.S. Department of Education, 2008). Homeschooling means that a child is taught by his or her parents, guardians, or a team of adults who oversee the child's educational development. The curricula studied by homeschooled children vary widely from state to state, with some states mandating quite strict curricula, whereas others are much more lax and provide the parent with great leeway. A survey conducted by the U.S. Department of Education (2008) queried parents about their motivation for homeschooling their children. The most frequently cited reasons were: a concern about the school environment (85 percent), a desire to provide religious or moral instruction (72 percent), and dissatisfaction with the academic instruction at other schools (68 percent).

However, it remains to be seen how well homeschooling prepares young adults for the future challenges of college or employment in the United States. Some studies suggest that homeschooled children are just as well prepared for college as their traditionally educated counterparts, while others say that homeschooling deprives children of important life lessons. However, before we can ascertain whether homeschooling is beneficial, we need to consider that homeschooling is a "selective" process, and the traits that "select" people into homeschooling may also affect their later prospects.

White students (3.9 percent) had a higher homeschooling rate than blacks (0.8 percent) and Hispanics (1.5 percent), but were not measurably different from students from other racial/ethnic groups (3.4 percent). Students in two-parent households made up 89 percent of the homeschooled population, and those in two-parent households with one parent in the labor force made up 54 percent of the homeschooled population. The latter group of students had a higher homeschooling rate than their peers: 7 percent, compared with 1 to 2 percent of students in other family circumstances. In 2007, students in households earning between $25,001 and $75,000 per year had higher rates of homeschooling than their peers in households earning $25,000 or less a year. Thus, many children who are homeschooled have several social advantages, including wealthier or more stable families.

It is much harder to ascertain whether homeschooled children fare better on outcomes such as standardized test scores or success in college, because little data are available on these topics. Most studies concluding that homeschoolers outperform traditional students are criticized on the grounds that they are focused on biased samples (e.g., Oplinger and Willard, 2004; Rudner, 1999). Experts also argue that it is hard to describe definitively the experience of homeschoolers because they are such a diverse group, representing every possible religious, political, and spiritual orientation (Murphy, 2012).

Who Benefits from "International Education"?

How many international students are enrolled in your sociology course? How many international students are there at your university? In 1943 approximately 8,000 foreign students were enrolled in American colleges and universities. By 2011–12 this number had skyrocketed to an all-time high of 764,495 (Institute of International Education [IIE], 2012). Most foreign students today come from Asia—China, Japan, Taiwan, India, and South Korea all send sizeable contingents of students abroad. The United States takes in more foreign students than any other country. What do foreign students in the United States study? At the undergraduate level, more than 21 percent focus on business and management, 19 percent study engineering, and 9 percent each concentrate on physical and life sciences; math and computer sciences; and social sciences (IIE, 2011).

Some scholars regard the exchange of international students as a vital component of globalization. Foreign students, in addition to serving as global "carriers" of specialized technical and scientific knowledge, play an important cultural role in the globalizing process. Cross-national understandings are enhanced, and xenophobic and isolationist attitudes are minimized, as native students in host countries develop social ties to their foreign classmates and as foreign students return to their countries of origin with an appreciation for the cultural mores of the nation in which they have studied.

Yet there is considerable debate in the United States about what is sometimes called the "internationalization of education." On most college and university campuses, it is not hard to find disgruntled students who complain that the influx of foreign students deprives deserving Americans of educational opportunities—especially given the increasingly competitive nature of the U.S. higher education system. Moreover, although more than two-thirds of foreign students receive nothing in the way of scholarships, some top-notch foreign students *are* given financial inducements to attend American schools. The outcry against this practice has been loudest at public universities, which receive support from tax revenues. Critics charge that U.S. taxpayers should not shoulder the financial burden of educating foreign students whose families have not paid U.S. taxes and who are likely to return home after earning their degrees.

Supporters of international education find such arguments unconvincing. Some Americans may lose out to foreign students in the competition for slots at prestigious universities, but this is a small price to pay for the economic, political, and cultural benefits the United States receives from having educated millions of foreign business executives, policy makers, scientists, and professionals over the years—many of whom became sympathetically disposed to the United States as a result of their experiences here. And although some foreign students receive scholarships from American universities, most are supported by their parents. In fact, it is estimated that foreign students pump hundreds of millions of dollars each year into the U.S. economy—over $21 billion in 2011, including tuition, housing, and related purchases (IIE, 2011). Rather than curtail the number of foreign students admitted to American universities, supporters of international education suggest that even more should be done to encourage the exchange of students.

On the one hand, greater effort should be made to recruit foreign students, to help them select the university and program that will best meet their needs, and to provide them with a positive social and educational experience while they are in the United States. On the other hand, more Americans should be encouraged to study abroad. American students are notorious for having poor or no foreign-language skills and for knowing little about global geography, much less about the cultures of other nations. This cultural and linguistic ignorance puts the United States at a disadvantage relative to other countries as the world becomes increasingly globalized; encouraging Americans to study overseas may be the best way to inculcate a global worldview.

Should there be a greater focus on international education in American colleges and universities? Should the international exchange of students be expanded? These are among the issues that educational institutions are forced to confront in the context of globalization. Still, more and more U.S. students are studying abroad—273,996 U.S. students studied abroad for credit during the academic year 2010/2011, compared with 270,604 the previous year and a 1.3 percent increase over the year before (IIE, 2012). Most scholars agree that, in our increasingly global society, international education, combined with expanded use of the Internet as a means of sharing news and information, is essential to having a well-informed, open-minded, and forward-looking population.

CONCEPT CHECKS

1. Explain the relationship between race and intelligence. Do you find the evidence compelling?
2. What are three reasons parents decide to homeschool their children?
3. Describe several characteristics of the "typical" international student enrolled at a U.S. college or university.

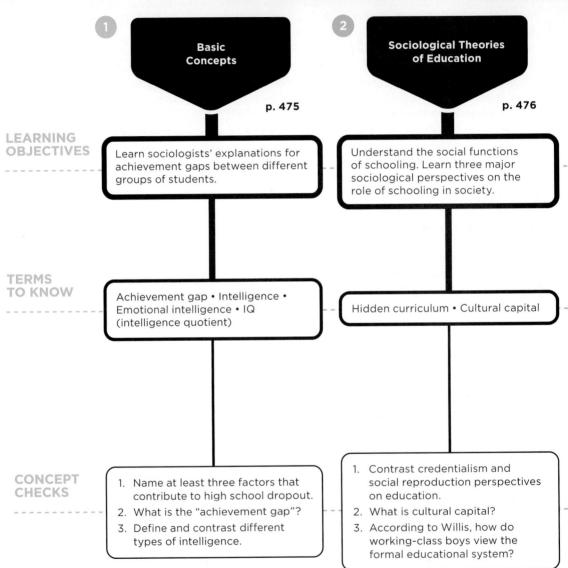

1 Basic Concepts

p. 475

2 Sociological Theories of Education

p. 476

LEARNING OBJECTIVES

Learn sociologists' explanations for achievement gaps between different groups of students.

Understand the social functions of schooling. Learn three major sociological perspectives on the role of schooling in society.

TERMS TO KNOW

Achievement gap • Intelligence • Emotional intelligence • IQ (intelligence quotient)

Hidden curriculum • Cultural capital

CONCEPT CHECKS

1. Name at least three factors that contribute to high school dropout.
2. What is the "achievement gap"?
3. Define and contrast different types of intelligence.

1. Contrast credentialism and social reproduction perspectives on education.
2. What is cultural capital?
3. According to Willis, how do working-class boys view the formal educational system?

Exercises: Thinking Sociologically

1. From your reading of this chapter and your own educational experiences, describe what might be the principal advantages and disadvantages of having children go to private versus public schools in the United States at this time. Assess whether privatization of our public schools would help improve them.

2. Back in 1964, Marshall McLuhan argued that radio and television helped to produce a global village—that is, a world linked by instantaneous media coverage of worldwide events and news. Explain how the advent of the Internet and cell phones is extending the concept of the global village even further and faster.

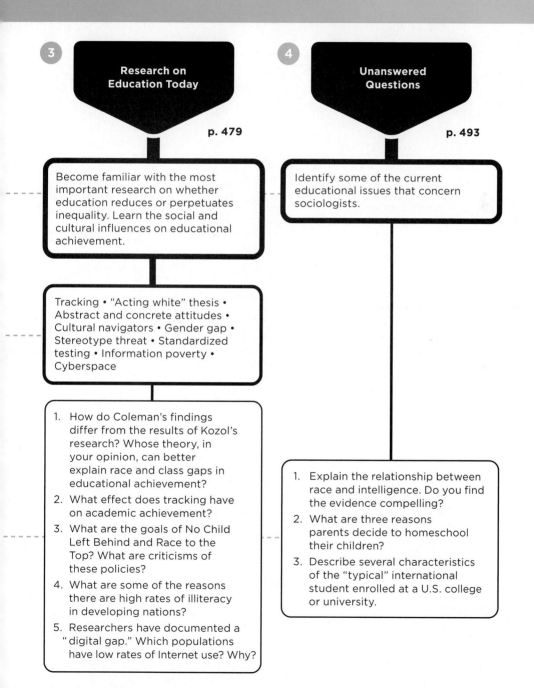

3

Research on Education Today

p. 479

Become familiar with the most important research on whether education reduces or perpetuates inequality. Learn the social and cultural influences on educational achievement.

Tracking • "Acting white" thesis • Abstract and concrete attitudes • Cultural navigators • Gender gap • Stereotype threat • Standardized testing • Information poverty • Cyberspace

1. How do Coleman's findings differ from the results of Kozol's research? Whose theory, in your opinion, can better explain race and class gaps in educational achievement?
2. What effect does tracking have on academic achievement?
3. What are the goals of No Child Left Behind and Race to the Top? What are criticisms of these policies?
4. What are some of the reasons there are high rates of illiteracy in developing nations?
5. Researchers have documented a "digital gap." Which populations have low rates of Internet use? Why?

4

Unanswered Questions

p. 493

Identify some of the current educational issues that concern sociologists.

1. Explain the relationship between race and intelligence. Do you find the evidence compelling?
2. What are three reasons parents decide to homeschool their children?
3. Describe several characteristics of the "typical" international student enrolled at a U.S. college or university.

Religion in Modern Society

17

Can you rank the following list of some of the world's major religions from fastest growing to slowest growing?

- **a** Christianity
- **b** Islam
- **c** Judaism
- **d** Hinduism
- **e** Sikhism
- **f** Bahai

T his is a difficult question—if you failed to answer it correctly, you are in good company. Very few Americans would get this question right. The correct order is Islam, Bahai, Sikhism, Hinduism, Christianity, and Judaism. Islam is the world's second-largest religion, with an estimated 1.6 million adherents; it is growing at a rate of 1.8 percent each year. Christianity, the world's largest religion with some 2.3 billion adherents, is the second-slowest-growing on the list, increasing by 1.4 percent per year. Judaism, with less than 15.0 million adherents, is small in numbers and is growing at less than 1 percent a year (some estimates have it at close to zero growth worldwide) (Pew Research Center, 2011c; *Foreign Policy*, 2007).

Christianity, Islam, and Judaism are all most likely familiar to you—they are the so-called "Abrahamic faiths," because they all trace their origins to Abraham and all accept the Old Testament of the Bible as an authoritative religious source (although Christianity, unlike Judaism, is founded on the New Testament of the Bible as well, and Islam looks to the Koran as authoritative). Hinduism is less likely to be familiar, although yoga and meditation—practices associated with Hinduism and popularized in the United States—may provide at least superficial familiarity with a 4,000-year-old religion that includes nearly 900 million people. Sikhism, an offshoot of Hinduism, is unlikely to be familiar to most Americans, even though an estimated quarter million Sikhs live in the United States. Nor is Bahai likely to be well known, even though it is a global religion with an estimated 8 million adherents (*Foreign Policy*, 2007).

Toward the end of the nineteenth century, the German philosopher Friedrich Nietzsche announced, "God is dead." Religions, he argued, used to be a point of reference for our sense of purpose and meaning. Henceforth, we would have to live without this security. Living in a world without God would mean creating our own values and getting used to

LEARNING OBJECTIVES

1 BASIC CONCEPTS

Learn the elements that make up a religion.

2 SOCIOLOGICAL THEORIES OF RELIGION

Understand the sociological approaches to religion developed by Marx, Durkheim, and Weber; the contemporary debate over secularization; and the religious economy approach.

3 THE SOCIOLOGY OF RELIGION: CURRENT RESEARCH

Know the forms religion take in traditional and modern societies. Learn about sociological dimensions of religion in the United States. Recognize the changing interrelationships between gender and religion.

4 UNANSWERED QUESTIONS

Learn about the sociological debates surrounding trends such as fundamentalism, secularization, and religious violence.

what Nietzsche called "the loneliness of being"—understanding that our lives are without purpose and that no superior entities watch over our fate. Nietzsche believed that with the rise of science and technology, **secularization**—the movement of a society away from religious beliefs and institutions—would triumph.

Nietzsche was clearly wrong in his prediction. Religion is one of the most truly global of all social institutions, affecting many aspects of life. Throughout the world today there is a religious revival. While religious revival is not limited to any particular socioeconomic group, it has especially taken root among those who are the most dispossessed. While globalization has brought benefits to many, it has brought hardship to many as well. Grinding poverty, in combination with the erosion of long-standing cultural values and traditions, is fertile ground for religious revival—especially among young people, who comprise a large part of the population in countries in the global south. One major study of secularization and religious revival in nearly 200 societies around the world concluded that religious revival is likely to win out over secularization among people who lack what the authors term "existential security"—"the feeling that survival is secure enough that it can be taken for granted" (Norris and Inglehart, 2004).

Why is it important to have better knowledge of the world's religions? One reason is that it provides a better understanding of the global social changes of recent decades, in which religion has played a central role. In Vietnam in the 1960s, Buddhist priests burned themselves alive to protest the policies of the South Vietnamese government, contributing to the emergence of an antiwar movement in the United States, where the self-immolations were viewed on television. Today, Buddhist monks living in exile in India have set themselves on fire to protest Chinese rule over Tibet, while Buddhist monks in Thailand are protesting deforestation and inadequate care for victims of AIDS. During the latter part of the twentieth century, an activist form of Catholicism, **liberation theology**, combined Catholic beliefs with a passion for social justice for the poor, particularly in Central and South America and in Africa. Catholic priests and nuns organized farming cooperatives, built health clinics and schools, and challenged government policies that impoverished the peasantry; many paid with their lives for their activism, which government and military leaders often regard as subversive. Islamic socialists in Pakistan and Buddhist socialists in Sri Lanka have played a similar role (Berryman, 1987; Juergensmeyer, 1993; Sigmund, 1990). In some central and eastern European countries once dominated by the former Soviet Union, long-suppressed religious organizations had a key role in overturning socialist regimes during the early 1990s. In Poland, for example, the Catholic Church was allied with the Solidarity movement, which toppled the socialist government in 1989. Churches and religious leaders played a key role in the abolition of slavery in the United States in the nineteenth century and the civil rights movement in the twentieth century.

Religion has also been central in reviving ancient ethnic and tribal hatreds. In Bosnia and elsewhere in the former Yugoslavia, for example, religious differences helped justify "ethnic cleansing," with Christian Serbs and Croats engaging in the mass murder, rape, and deportation of Muslims from communities and farmlands where they had lived for centuries. When

secularization • A process of decline in the influence of religion. Although modern societies have become increasingly secularized, tracing the extent of secularization is a complex matter. Secularization can refer to levels of involvement with religious organizations (such as rates of church attendance), the social and material influence wielded by religious organizations, and the degree to which people hold religious beliefs.

liberation theology • An activist Catholic religious movement that combines Catholic beliefs with a passion for social justice for the poor.

religious beliefs align with strong national feelings, violence can be the result. And as we shall see, religious violence is not limited to any particular religion. While all major religions profess love and compassion, all have also given rise to offshoots that justify the use of violence to achieve their religious beliefs (Juergensmeyer, 2001, 2008). Another reason it is important to better understand world's religions is that ignorance can fuel suspicion, prejudice, and hate.

On August 5, 2012, Wade Michael Page, a 40-year-old guitarist associated with hate rock bands, walked into a Sikh temple in Oak Creek, Wisconsin, and opened fire on the worshippers. Before police respondents arrived and shot him, he killed six people and wounded others. Page's reasons for shooting innocent worshippers may never be fully known; he died at the scene. But it is known that he was a white supremacist who hated Muslims and had reportedly called for massive bombing of the Middle East after September 11, 2001 (Goffard and Hennessy-Fiske, 2012). It seems likely that Page went on his shooting rampage intending to kill Muslims, not realizing that Sikhism is unrelated to Islam. To Page's bigoted eye, the turbaned Sikh men, with their long black beards, were likely indistinguishable from Muslims.

If Page indeed was venting his anger against people he believed to be Muslims, he was not alone in harboring negative stereotypes. A nationwide survey conducted in 2011 found that only 57 percent of Americans have a favorable opinion of Muslims, compared with 89 percent for Christians and 82 percent for Jews. Among those polled, roughly half believe that some religions are more prone to violence than others; fully 70 percent of those with such beliefs also claim that Islam is the most violent religion, compared with 9 percent for Christianity and 2 percent for Judaism. In fact, nearly half (45 percent) of all Americans polled stereotype Islam as violent, with 7 out of 10 reporting being concerned about Muslim extremism in the United States (Pew Research Center, 2011b).

Religion plays a key role in the world today. Religious groups have been a major force in the so-called 2011 "Arab Spring" that began with the self-immolation of Mohamed Bouazizi, a poor Tunisian street vendor who set himself on fire to protest harassment by corrupt local officials who had made it impossible for him to eke out a living selling produce from a cart. Bouazizi's sacrifice, seen around the world on YouTube and other social media, sparked revolutions in the Middle East and North Africa that overturned dictatorships in Egypt, Libya, and Yemen and sparked a civil war in Syria. The Muslim Brotherhood, a large and important influential religious organization throughout the Arab world, had been forced underground in Egypt and elsewhere. Today it is one of the leading political parties in Egypt.

THE ANSWER IS B, F, E, D, A, C.

 # BASIC CONCEPTS

Religion is one of the oldest human institutions. According to anthropologists, there have probably been about 100,000 religions throughout human history (Hadden, 1997a). When sociologists study religion, they hope to better understand its historical and contemporary role in shaping society and, conversely, the historical and contemporary social forces that shape religion itself (Hamilton, 2001).

Sociologists define **religion** as a cultural system of commonly shared beliefs and rituals that provides a sense of ultimate meaning and purpose by creating an idea of reality that is sacred, all-encompassing, and supernatural (Berger, 1967; Durkheim, 1965, orig. 1912; Wuthnow, 1988). There are three key elements in this definition:

1. Religion is a form of *culture*, which consists of the shared beliefs, values, norms, and material conditions that create a common identity among a group of people. Religion has all these characteristics.
2. Religion involves beliefs that take the form of ritualized practices—special activities in which believers take part and that identify them as members of the religious community.
3. Religion provides a feeling that life is ultimately meaningful. It does so by explaining coherently and compellingly what transcends or overshadows everyday life, in ways that other aspects of culture (such as an educational system or a belief in democracy) cannot (Geertz, 1973; Wuthnow, 1988).

What is absent from the sociological definition of religion is just as important as what is included: Nowhere is there mention of a god. We often think of **theism**—a belief in one or more supernatural deities—as basic to religion, but this is not necessarily the case. As we shall see, some religions, such as Buddhism, believe in spiritual forces rather than a singular god.

How Sociologists Think about Religion

When sociologists study religion, they do so as unbiased scientists and not as believers (or disbelievers) in any particular faith. This stance has a number of implications:

- Sociologists are not concerned with whether religious beliefs are true or false. The sociological perspective regards religions as socially constructed by human beings. Thus sociologists put aside their personal beliefs and address the human rather than the divine aspects of religion. Sociologists ask: How is the religion organized? What are its principal beliefs and values? How is it related to the larger society? What explains its success or failure in recruiting and retaining believers? The question of whether a particular belief is "good" or "true" is not something that sociologists can address. (As individuals, they may have strong opinions on the matter, but as sociologists, they must keep these opinions from biasing their research.)
- Sociologists are especially concerned with the social organization of religion. Not only are religions a primary source of the deepest-seated norms and values, but they are practiced through an enormous variety of social forms. Within Christianity and Judaism, for example, religious practice often occurs in formal organizations, such as churches or synagogues. Yet within Hinduism and Buddhism, religious practices occur in the home as well as in temples or other natural settings. The sociology of religion considers how different religious institutions and organizations actually function. The earliest European religions were often indistinguishable from the larger

religion • A set of beliefs adhered to by the members of a community, incorporating symbols regarded with a sense of awe or wonder together with ritual practices. Religions do not universally involve a belief in supernatural entities.

theism • A belief in one or more supernatural deities.

society, as beliefs and practices were incorporated into daily life. In modern industrial society, however, some religions have become established in separate, often bureaucratic, organizations (Hammond, 1992). This institutionalization has led some sociologists to view religions in the United States and Europe as similar to business organizations, competing with one another for members (Warner, 1993).

- Sociologists have often viewed religions as a major source of social solidarity in that they offer believers a common set of norms and values. Religious beliefs, rituals, and bonds create a "moral community" in which all members know how to behave (Wuthnow, 1988). If a single religion dominates a society, the religion may be an important source of social solidarity—although it may also be oppressive if it requires absolute conformity to a particular set of beliefs and punishes those who deviate, as is the case in Afghanistan under Taliban rule.

- If a society's members adhere to competing religions, religious differences may lead to destabilizing social conflicts. Recent examples of religious conflict within a society include struggles among Sikhs, Hindus, and Muslims in India; clashes between Muslims and Christians in Bosnia and other parts of the former Yugoslavia; conflicts between Shiite and Sunni Muslims in Iraq; and "hate crimes" against Jews, Muslims, and other religious minorities in the United States.

- Sociologists explain the appeal of religion in terms of social forces rather than personal, spiritual, or psychological factors. Sociologists do not question the depth of believers' transcendent feelings and experiences, yet they also do not limit themselves to a purely spiritual explanation of religious commitment. In fact, some researchers argue that people often turn to, or "get," religion when their fundamental sense of social order is threatened by economic hardship, loneliness, loss or grief, physical suffering, or poor health (Berger, 1967; Glock, 1976; Schwartz, 1970; Stark and Bainbridge, 1980). In explaining the appeal of religious movements, sociologists are more likely to focus on problems in the social order than on the individual's psychological response.

What Do Sociologists of Religion Study?

Several types of social forces are of special interest to sociologists of religion. First, sociologists study the ways in which a crisis in prevailing beliefs promotes religious fervor. Such a crisis occurred in the United States during the 1960s as a result of the civil rights movement, opposition to the Vietnam War, social movements among racial and ethnic minorities, and the youth-oriented counterculture. Large numbers of people were attracted to religious teachers, ranging from Indian gurus to fundamentalist preachers, who offered everything from meditation and yoga to astrology and New Age religions (Wuthnow, 1988, 1998). There is currently a resurgence of religious fervor throughout the world among Christians, Muslims, and Jews; while the reasons for this are not fully understood, part of the explanation has to do with the global changes sweeping the world today (Juergensmeyer, 2008). These include the failure of nonreligious institutions, particularly governments, to promote political and economic security in many parts of the world; the global spread of cultural norms and values and their perceived threat to traditional beliefs and values; and the explosion of new forms of media, especially the Internet, which has made it easier for religiously like-minded people to share their beliefs and build their religious institutions.

Second, sociologists study how competition among religious organizations leads some to thrive and others to perish. This study has sparked an increased interest in the organizational dynamics of religious groups (Finke and Stark, 1988, 2005; Hammond, 1992; Roof and McKinney, 1990; Stark and Bainbridge, 1987).

Third, sociologists address the relationship between religion, ethnic identity, and politics. This is seen in the resurgence of ethnically based religion in pluralist societies such as the United States and in the rise of religious nationalism worldwide (Juergensmeyer, 1993, 2008; Lawrence, 1989; Merkyl and Smart, 1983; Sahliyeh, 1990; see the following discussion of religious nationalism).

Although the sociology of religion has long included non-European religions, there has been a tendency to view all religions through concepts based in the European experience. For example, notions such as *denomination*, *sect*, and *cult* (defined later) presuppose formally organized religious institutions; they are of questionable utility in studying religions that emphasize spiritual practice as a part of daily life or that pursue the complete integration of religion with civic and political life. Recently, there has been an effort to create a comparative sociology of religion that examines religious traditions from within their own frames of reference (Juergensmeyer, 1993; Smart, 1989; van der Veer, 1994; Wilson, 1982).

Types of Religious Organizations

Early theorists such as Max Weber (1963; orig. 1922), Ernst Troeltsch (1931), and Richard Niebuhr (1929) described religious organizations according to the degree to which they were well established and conventional: In their view, churches are conventional and well established, cults are neither, and sects fall somewhere in the middle. These distinctions were based on a study of European and U.S. religions. There is much debate over how well they apply to the non-Christian world.

CHURCHES AND SECTS

Churches are large, established religious bodies; one example is the Roman Catholic Church. They normally have a formal, bureaucratic structure with a hierarchy of officials. Churches often represent the conservative face of religion, because they are integrated within the existing institutional order. Most of their adherents are born into and grow up with the church.

Sects are smaller, less organized groups of committed believers, usually set up in protest against an established church. Sects aim at following the "true way" and either try to change the surrounding society or withdraw into communities of their own, a process known as *revival*. The members of sects often regard established churches as corrupt. Many sects have few or no officials, and all members are equal participants. For the most part, people are not born into sects but join them to further personal beliefs.

DENOMINATIONS

A **denomination** is a sect that has become an institutionalized body rather than an activist protest group. Sects that survive over time become denominations. Calvinism, Methodism, and Mormonism were sects during their early period, when they generated great fervor among their members, but over the years they have

churches • Large bodies of people belonging to an established religious organization. The term is also used to refer to the place in which religious ceremonies are carried out.

sects • Religious movements that break away from orthodoxy.

denomination • A religious sect that has lost its revivalist dynamism and become an institutionalized body, commanding the adherence of significant numbers of people.

become established denominations. (Calvinists today are called Presbyterians.) Denominations are recognized as legitimate by churches, often cooperating harmoniously with them. Other examples of Christian denominations would include Baptists, Lutherans, and many of the evangelical Christian groups that have gained adherents and become more mainstream during recent decades.

CULTS

Cults resemble sects, but their emphases are different. The most loosely knit and transient of all religious organizations, cults comprise individuals who reject the values of the outside society. They are a form of religious innovation rather than revival. Their focus is on individual experience, bringing like-minded people together. Like sects, cults often form around the influence of an inspirational leader.

Cults are often in a high degree of tension with the larger society. In 1997, 39 members of Heaven's Gate, a cult whose members believed they were destined for a "higher level," took their lives to ascend to a spaceship they believed lurked behind the Hale-Bopp comet. The Japanese cult Aum Shinrikyo ("Om Supreme Truth") once claimed as many as 20,000 members. It combined elements of Buddhism and Christianity, including Christian predictions about a pending global apocalypse derived from the Book of Revelations and the writings of the sixteenth-century Christian Nostradamus. (Such doomsday predictions are not uncommon in Christian cults as well.) Aum Shinrikyo's members regarded the group's founder and leader, Shoko Asahara, as Christ. In 1995, cult members released the deadly nerve gas sarin on five Tokyo subway trains; 12 people died and thousands were injured, some seriously. Investigations revealed that the cult had previously spread germs at numerous locations in Japan, although fortunately with no toxic effects. A large number of the cult members were subsequently tried and convicted in Japan for the subway gassing and other crimes; some, including Asahara, were sentenced to death. In 2000, Aum Shinrikyo changed its name to Aleph, reportedly moderated its teachings, and now claims 1,000 or so members (Juergensmeyer, 2008).

Like sects, cults flourish when there is a breakdown in well-established societal belief systems. This is happening worldwide today, in places as diverse as Japan, India, and the United States. When such a breakdown occurs, cults may either originate within the society itself or be "imported" from outside. In the United States, examples of homegrown, or indigenous, cults include New Age religions based on spiritualism, astrology, and religious practices adapted from Asian or Native American cultures. Examples of imported cults include the Reverend Sun Myung Moon's Unification Church (whose members are popularly, if derogatively, known as "Moonies"), which originated in South Korea, and the Transcendental Meditation movement, which was promoted by the Maharishi Mahesh Yogi in India. A cult arising out of the Siddha Yoga tradition was brought to the United States in the 1970s by Swami Muktananda; since his death in 1982, the global spiritual movement—it has centers in nearly three dozen countries—has been led by his female disciple, Gurumayi Chidvilasananda, making it one of the few major cults led by a woman.

A cult in one country may be an established religious practice in another. When Indian gurus practice in the United States, what might be considered an established religion in India is regarded as a cult in the United States. Christianity began as an indigenous cult in ancient Jerusalem, and in many Asian countries today evangelical Protestantism is regarded as a cult imported from the United States. A leading

cults • Fragmentary religious groupings to which individuals are loosely affiliated but that lack any permanent structure.

sociologist of religion, Jeffrey K. Hadden (1997a), points out that all the approximately 100,000 religions that humans have devised were once new; most were initially despised cults from the standpoint of respectable religious belief of the times. For example, Jesus was crucified because his ideas threatened the established order of the Roman-dominated religious establishment of ancient Judaea.

> ### CONCEPT CHECKS
>
> 1. What are the three main components of religion as a social institution?
> 2. How do sociologists differ from other scholars in their approach to studying religion?
> 3. Describe four types of religious organizations.

SOCIOLOGICAL THEORIES OF RELIGION

Sociological approaches to religion are strongly influenced by the ideas of Marx, Durkheim, and Weber. None of the three theorists was religious himself, and each argued that religion was fundamentally an illusion: The very diversity of religions and their obvious connection to different societies and regions made their advocates' claims inherently implausible, according to these early theorists.

The Classical View

Marx, Weber, and Durkheim all wrote about religion but drew radically different conclusions. For Marx, religion was a form of false consciousness, blinding people to the underlying causes of inequality. Durkheim viewed religion as an important source of social solidarity, while Weber analyzed the relationship between religion and the emergence of capitalism.

MARX: RELIGION AND INEQUALITY

Karl Marx never studied religion in any detail. His thinking on religion was derived mostly from the writings of Ludwig Feuerbach, who believed that through a process he called **alienation**, human beings attribute their own culturally created values and norms to alien, or separate, beings (i.e., divine forces or gods) because they do not understand their own history. Thus the story of the Ten Commandments given to Moses by God is a mythical version of the origins of moral precepts that govern the lives of Jewish and Christian believers.

Marx accepted Feuerbach's view that religion represents human self-alienation. In a famous phrase, he declared that religion was the "opium of the people":

> Religion is the sigh of the oppressed creature, the heart of a heartless world, just as it is the spirit of a spiritless situation. It is the opium of the people. The abolition of religion as the illusory happiness of the people is required for their real happiness. (Marx, 1994; orig. 1843–44)

Religion defers happiness and rewards to the afterlife, Marx argued, teaching a resigned acceptance of conditions in the earthly life—including inequalities and injustices. Religion contains a strong ideological element: Religious

alienation • The sense that our own abilities as human beings are taken over by other entities. The term was originally used by Marx to refer to the projection of human powers onto gods. Subsequently he used the term to refer to the loss of workers' control over the nature and products of their labor.

belief can provide justifications for those in power. For example, "The meek shall inherit the earth" suggests humility and nonresistance to oppression. In Marx's view, people had to shed their religious beliefs in order to better understand the social forces that were oppressing them. Only then, he argued, would people rise up, overthrow the oppressive order, and create a society that truly served their interests.

DURKHEIM: RELIGION AND FUNCTIONALISM

In contrast to Marx, Émile Durkheim extensively studied religion; unlike Marx, he connected religion not with social inequalities or power but with the overall nature of a society's institutions. In *The Elementary Forms of the Religious Life* (1965; orig. 1912), Durkheim concentrated on *totemism*, the worship of objects such as animals or plants believed to embody mystical spirits. Durkheim studied totemism as practiced by Australian aboriginal societies, arguing that such totemism represents religion in its most "elementary" form.

Durkheim defined religion in terms of a distinction between the sacred and the profane. Sacred objects and symbols, he held, are treated as apart from routine aspects of day-to-day existence—the realm of the **profane**. A totem

profane • Describing that which belongs to the mundane, everyday world.

Max Weber categorized Eastern religions as "otherworldly" and Christianity as a "salvation religion." Weber believed that Hinduism stressed escaping material existence to locate a higher plane of being, which cultivated an attitude of passivity. In contrast, he argued that Christianity and its emphasis on salvation and constant struggle could stimulate revolt against the existing order.

(an animal or plant believed to have symbolic significance), Durkheim argued, is a **sacred** object, regarded with veneration and surrounded by ritual activities that bind the members of groups together.

Durkheim's theory of religion is a good example of the functionalist tradition. To analyze the function of a social behavior or social institution such as religion is to study its contribution to the continuation of a group, community, or society. According to Durkheim, religion promotes a coherent society by ensuring that people meet regularly to affirm common beliefs and values.

WEBER: WORLD RELIGIONS AND SOCIAL CHANGE

Whereas Durkheim based his arguments on a restricted range of examples, Max Weber conducted a massive study of religions worldwide. No scholar before or since has undertaken a task of the scope Weber attempted. Weber's writings on religion differ from those of Durkheim because they concentrate on the connection between religion and social change, and they contrast with those of Marx because Weber argued that religion was not necessarily a conservative force; on the contrary, religiously inspired movements have often produced dramatic social transformations. Thus Protestantism, particularly Puritanism, according to Weber, was the source of the capitalist outlook found in the modern West. The early entrepreneurs were mostly Calvinists. Their drive to succeed, which helped initiate Western economic development, was originally prompted by a desire to serve God. Material success was considered a sign of divine favor. But because Calvinists also believed that one should not ostentatiously flaunt one's wealth, Calvinist entrepreneurs were likely to reinvest their wealth in their enterprises, rather than spend it on personal consumption. Such "worldly asceticism," as Weber called it, resulted in capital accumulation—the hallmark of a successful capitalist system.

Weber's discussion of the effect of Protestantism on the development of the West was connected to a comprehensive attempt to understand the influence of religion on social and economic life in various cultures. After analyzing the Eastern religions, Weber concluded that they prevented the widespread development of industrial capitalism because they were oriented toward different values, such as escape from the toils of the material world.

In traditional India and China, Weber held, periodic development of commerce, manufacturing, and urbanism did not generate the radical patterns of social change that led to industrial capitalism in the West. In his view, Indian and Chinese belief systems significantly inhibited such change. Hinduism in India, he argued, sees material reality as a veil hiding the true spiritual concerns to which humankind should be oriented; one should focus on spiritual development, rather than the material world. In China, according to Weber, Confucianism also directs activity away from economic "progress" because it emphasizes harmony with the world rather than promoting an active mastery of it. Although China was long the most powerful and most culturally developed civilization in the world, its dominant religious values acted as a brake on a stronger commitment to economic development. It is interesting to note that a century later, sociologists have attributed the current economic growth of China and other East Asian countries, at least in part, to the same set of beliefs that Weber saw as a deterrent, drawing parallels between certain aspects of Confucianism and the Protestant ethic (Tu, 1989; Berger, 1988).

Weber regarded Christianity as a *salvation religion*—one in which human beings can be

sacred • That which inspires attitudes of awe or reverence among believers in a given set of religious ideas.

"saved" if they accept the beliefs of the religion and follow its moral tenets. The notions of sin and of being rescued from sinfulness by God's grace generate an emotional dynamism absent from the Eastern religions. Whereas Eastern religions cultivate an attitude of passivity or acceptance, Christianity demands a constant struggle against sin and thereby can stimulate revolt against the existing order. Religious leaders—such as Luther or Calvin—have arisen who reinterpret doctrines in such a way as to challenge the existing power structure.

CRITICAL ASSESSMENT OF THE CLASSICAL VIEW

Marx was right to claim that religion often has ideological implications, serving to justify the interests of ruling groups at the expense of others. There are innumerable examples in history. Consider the European missionaries who sought to convert "heathen" peoples to Christian beliefs; their motivations may have been sincere, yet their teachings reinforced the destruction of traditional cultures and the imposition of white domination. Also, almost all Christian denominations tolerated or endorsed slavery in the United States and other parts of the world into the nineteenth century. Doctrines were developed proclaiming slavery to be based on divine law, with disobedient slaves being considered guilty of an offense against God as well as their masters (Stampp, 1956).

But Weber was also correct in emphasizing the unsettling and often revolutionary effect of religious ideals on the established social order. In spite of the churches' early support for slavery in the United States, church leaders later played a key role in fighting to abolish the institution. Religious beliefs have at times prompted social movements against unjust systems of authority. Religious sentiments were prominent in the civil rights movements of the 1960s, where black churches played the key role. Dr. Martin Luther King Jr., a Baptist minister, was a cofounder of the Southern Christian Leadership Conference, an organization of southern black churches dedicated to ending racial segregation through nonviolent protests (Branch, 1989, 1999, 2007).

The divisive influences of religion find little mention in Durkheim's work, which emphasized the role of religion in promoting social cohesion. Yet it is not difficult to redirect his ideas toward explaining religious division, conflict, and change as well as solidarity. After all, much of the strength of feeling generated against other religious groups derives from the commitment to religious values that binds each community of believers.

Durkheim's emphasis on ritual and ceremony is important. All religions hold regular assemblies of believers, at which ritual prescriptions are observed. As Durkheim rightly points out, ritual activities also mark the major transitions of life—birth, entry to adulthood, marriage, and death (van Gennep, 1977; orig. 1908).

Marx, Durkheim, and Weber based their theories of religion on their studies of societies in which a single religion predominated. Thus it seemed reasonable to examine the relationship between a predominant religion and the society as a whole. However, since the 1950s, some U.S. sociologists have challenged this classical view. Living in a society that is highly tolerant of religious diversity, contemporary theorists have focused on religious pluralism rather than on religious domination. In contrast, Marx, Durkheim, and Weber believed religion reflects and reinforces society's values, or at least the values of those who are most powerful; provides solidarity and social stability; and is an engine of social change. According to this view, religion is threatened by **secular thinking**, particularly as seen in the rise of science, technology, and rational thought.

secular thinking • Worldly thinking, particularly as seen in the rise of science, technology, and rational thought in general.

Secularization, as we have noted previously, involves a decrease in religious belief and involvement and therefore results in a weakening of the social and political power of religious organizations. Peter Berger (1967) has described religion in premodern societies as a "sacred canopy" that covers all aspects of life and is seldom questioned. In modern society, however, the sacred canopy is more like a quilt, a patchwork of different religious and secular belief systems. When beliefs are compared, it becomes increasingly difficult to sustain the idea that there is any single true faith.

Contemporary Approaches: Religious Economy

One influential recent approach to the sociology of religion is tailored to societies such as the United States that encompass many different faiths. Taking their cue from economic theory, sociologists who favor the **religious economy** approach argue that religions can be understood as organizations in competition with one another for followers (Finke and Stark, 1988, 2005; Hammond, 1992; Moore, 1994; Roof and McKinney, 1990; Stark and Bainbridge, 1980, 1985, 1987; Warner, 1993). These sociologists argue that competition is preferable to monopoly when it comes to ensuring religious vitality. Whereas the classical theorists Marx, Durkheim, and Weber assumed that religion weakens when challenged by different religious or secular viewpoints, the advocates of the religious economy perspective argue that competition increases the overall level of religious involvement in society. First, the competition makes each religious group try that much harder to win followers. Second, the presence of numerous religions means there is likely something for everyone. In a culturally diverse society, a single religion will probably appeal to a limited range of followers, whereas the presence of, say, Hindu gurus and fundamentalist preachers, in addition to mainline churches, will likely encourage a high level of religious participation.

This analysis is adapted from the business world, in which competition presumably encourages the emergence of specialized products appealing to specific markets. In fact, religious economists borrow the language of business in describing the conditions that lead to the success or failure of a particular religious organization. According to Finke and Stark (2005), a successful religious group must be well organized for competition, have eloquent preachers who are effective "sales reps" in spreading the word, offer beliefs and rituals that are packaged as an appealing product, and develop effective marketing techniques. Television evangelists have been especially good businesspeople in selling religious products. As Finke and Stark (2005) put it, "The churching of America was accomplished by aggressive churches committed to vivid otherworldliness." Religious economy scholars thus do not see competition as undermining religious beliefs and contributing to secularization. Rather, they argue that modern religion constantly renews itself through active marketing and recruitment.

Although a large body of research supports the notion that competition is good for religion, not all studies come to this same conclusion (Land, Deane, and Blau, 1991). Some have argued that the religious economy approach overestimates the extent to which people rationally choose a religion. According to this view, among deeply committed believers, even in societies where people can choose among religions, most practice their childhood religion without considering alternatives.

religious economy • A theoretical framework within the sociology of religion that argues that religions can be fruitfully understood as organizations in competition with one another for followers.

Wade Clark Roof's 1993 study of 1,400 baby boomers found that a third remained loyal to their childhood faith, while another third continued to profess their childhood beliefs although they no longer belonged to a religious organization. Thus only a third were actively seeking a new religion, making the sorts of choices presumed by the religious economy approach. Yet a recent study by the Pew Forum on Religion and Public Life found Americans to be more religiously fickle than was previously believed to be the case. The study, based on thousands of interviews, concluded, "Americans change religious affiliation early and often" (Pew Research Center, 2009a). The survey found that 44 percent of all Americans change their affiliation at least once, typically before they turn 24; many change more than once. Even among the 56 percent who professed loyalty to their original faith, one out of six reported having changed faiths at one time during their life. Fifteen percent of those raised as Protestants have changed to a different Protestant denomination. Americans—especially young people—more than ever seem to be a nation of seekers.

Secularization: The Sociological Debate

The debate over secularization is one of the most complex areas in the sociology of religion. Basically, the disagreement is between supporters of the secularization thesis (who see religion as diminishing in power and importance in the modern world) and opponents (who argue that religion remains a significant force, albeit often in new and unfamiliar forms).

There is little consensus about how secularization should be measured or even how religion should be defined. Some argue that religion is best understood in terms of the world's traditional faiths; others seek a much broader view to include dimensions such as personal spirituality and deep commitment to certain values.

We can evaluate secularization according to a number of dimensions. Some are objective, such as the *level of membership* of religious organizations—how many people belong to a church or other religious body and attend services or other ceremonies. With the exception of the United States, the industrialized countries have all experienced considerable secularization according to this index. The pattern of religious decline seen in Britain is found in most of Western Europe, including predominantly Catholic countries such as France and Italy. More Italians than French attend church regularly and participate in the major rituals (such as Easter Communion), but the overall pattern of declining religious observance is similar in both cases. In France and Germany, fewer than 10 percent attend weekly religious services; in Belgium, the Netherlands, the United Kingdom, and Germany, 10–15 percent are regular churchgoers. Regular attendance is only marginally higher in Spain (21 percent), Portugal (29 percent), and Italy (31 percent) (Manchin, 2004). The United States is by far the most religious country among the advanced industrialized nations; approximately 43 percent of Americans report attending church on a weekly basis (Saad, 2009; Swanbrow, 2003; Newport, 2010). Indeed, when sociologists Pippa Norris and Ronald Inglehart (2004) examined data from four World Values Surveys conducted over a 20-year period in 80 societies, they concluded that the United States is one of the most religious nations in the world.

In the global south, the story is quite different. In the poorest countries, where people are most vulnerable, religiosity is thriving. This is especially true in parts of the Islamic world, but it can also be seen in the growing strength of Christianity, especially in Africa.

People who live in the poorest nations are not only more religious than people who live in industrialized ones; they also have much higher fertility rates, so their population is growing more rapidly as well. As Norris and Inglehart (2004) succinctly put it, "The world as a whole now has more people with traditional religious views than ever before—and they constitute a growing proportion of the world's population."

A second dimension of secularization concerns how far churches and other religious organizations maintain their *social influence, wealth,* and *prestige.* In earlier times, religious organizations wielded considerable influence over governments and social agencies and commanded high respect in the community. How much is this still the case? By the twenty-first century, religious organizations had lost much of their former social and political influence, particularly in the advanced industrial nations. Church leaders could no longer expect to be as influential with the powerful. Although some established churches remain very wealthy and some new religious movements have rapidly built up fortunes, the material circumstances of many long-standing religious organizations have become insecure. In the United States, however, since the 1970s there has been a resurgence in the power of churches, particularly what has come to be known as the Christian Right. We shall discuss this further later on in this chapter.

A third dimension of secularization concerns beliefs and values—the dimension of *religiosity.* As in the other dimensions, we need an accurate understanding of the past to see how far religiosity has declined today. Supporters of the secularization thesis argue that in the past, religion was far more important to daily life than it is now. The church was at the heart of local affairs and strongly influenced family and personal life. Yet critics of this thesis argue that just because people attended church more regularly does not prove that they were more religious. As two leading sociologists of religion have noted, most Americans during Colonial times were far from puritanical, even though American schoolchildren are raised on images of pious Pilgrims bowed in prayer over Thanksgiving turkey. According to Roger Finke and Rodney Stark (2005), "Boston's taverns were probably fuller on Saturday night than were its churches on Sunday morning." Finke and Stark go on to argue that Americans are in fact more religious today on the whole than they were in Colonial times—largely because there are more religions to choose from, as we shall see in the following section of this chapter.

On balance, it does seem that the hold of religious ideas today is weaker than in the traditional world—particularly if we include the range of the supernatural. Most of us no longer experience our environment as permeated by divine or spiritual entities that need to be worshiped and placated, lest they do us harm. It is certainly true that some of the major tensions in the world today—such as those afflicting the Middle East or the violence perpetrated by the al Qaeda terrorist network—derive from religious differences. But the majority of conflicts and wars remains secular, concerned with divergent political goals or material interests, although these may coincide with ethnic and religious differences.

CONCEPT CHECKS

1. Why did Karl Marx call religion "the opium of the people"?

2. What are the differences between classical and contemporary approaches to understanding religion?

3. Does the Pew study provide support for the religious economy approach? Why or why not?

③ THE SOCIOLOGY OF RELIGION: CURRENT RESEARCH

If for classical theorists it seemed that religious beliefs were giving way to scientific thought and secularization, today it is clear that a religious revival has been occurring, both globally and in the United States. In our review of current research, we first present a current picture of trends in world religions and religion in the United States, before turning to two topics that are of particular interest to many sociologists of religion: gender and religion, and the global rise of religious nationalism.

World Religions

Although there are thousands of religions worldwide, three of them—Christianity, Islam, and Hinduism—are embraced by nearly three-quarters of the people on earth (Figure 17.1 and Global Map 17.1).

CHRISTIANITY

With its estimated 2.3 billion followers—roughly a third of the world's population—Christianity encompasses enormously divergent denominations, sects, and cults. Common to all is the belief that Jesus of Nazareth was the Christ (Messiah, or "anointed one") foretold in the Hebrew Bible. Christianity is a form of **monotheism**—belief in a single all-knowing, all-powerful God—although in most Christian faiths God is also regarded as a trinity embracing a heavenly Father, His Son the Savior, and His sustaining Holy Spirit.

When Christianity emerged in ancient Palestine some 2,000 years ago, it was a persecuted sect outside mainstream Jewish and Roman religious practices. Yet within four centuries, Christianity had become the official religion of the Roman Empire. In the eleventh century, Christianity divided into the Eastern Orthodox Church (based in Constantinople, now Istanbul) and the Catholic Church (based in Rome). A second great split occurred within the Catholic branch in the sixteenth century, when the Protestant Reformation gave rise to numerous Protestant denominations, sects, and cults. Protestants emphasize a direct relationship between the individual and God, with each person being responsible for his or her own salvation. Catholics, in contrast, emphasize the importance of the Church hierarchy as the means to salvation, with the pope in Rome being the highest earthly authority.

monotheism • Belief in a single god.

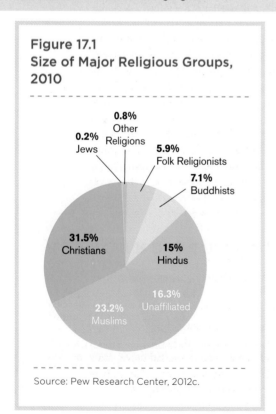

Figure 17.1
Size of Major Religious Groups, 2010

- 0.2% Jews
- 0.8% Other Religions
- 5.9% Folk Religionists
- 7.1% Buddhists
- 15% Hindus
- 16.3% Unaffiliated
- 23.2% Muslims
- 31.5% Christians

Source: Pew Research Center, 2012c.

Christianity was spread through conquest and missionary work. The European colonization of much of Africa, Asia, and North and South America that began in the fifteenth century brought Christian teachings, churches, and large-scale conversion of native peoples. In some places, converts were people from the impoverished classes, for whom Christianity was a means of social mobility. Only in Asia are Christians a small minority, largely because countries such as Japan and China successfully resisted most colonization and its accompanying Christianization.

Recently, Protestant evangelical groups have increased their efforts to convert people throughout the world, making significant inroads in traditionally Catholic countries. Protestant missionaries from the United States not only "spread the Word"; they also build homes and orphanages, help local people start small businesses, and engage in a variety of relief and development projects in the global south (Wuthnow, 2010). Local Protestant missionaries also play a key role. In Mexico, for example, the number of evangelical Protestants grew from 900,000 to 6.1 million between 1970 and 2000, owing to the efforts of local (Mexican) missionaries. Most of this increase has been in rural areas, including those areas where indigenous people predominate. The growth of evangelical Christianity may prove difficult to sustain. It makes considerable demands on its followers, so it remains to be seen whether the children of new converts will stay true to their parents' faith once they become adults (Bowen, 1996; Dow, 2005).

ISLAM

As mentioned earlier, Islam is the second-largest, and the fastest-growing, religion in the world today. There were about 1.6 billion Muslims in the world in 2011; that number is predicted to increase 35 percent, to 2.2 billion, by 2035 (Pew Research Center, 2011c). (*Muslim* is the word for those who practice *al-islam*, an Arabic term meaning submission without reservation to God's will.) This represents about a quarter of the world population. Islam began as a faith of the Arabs and other peoples of the Middle East and has spread into Africa, Central Asia, China, Europe, India, Indonesia, Pakistan, and Russia. Today, some 50 countries have Muslim-majority populations, while more than 60 different ethnic groups of a million or more people practice Islam. In fact, far more non-Arabs than Arabs identify themselves as Muslims. Indonesia, for example, is by far the largest Muslim country in the world. With nearly 203 million adherents, it is home to nearly one out of every six Muslims in the world (Pew Research Center, 2009b). A number of non-Muslim countries have large Muslim minorities, among them Hindu-majority India, with 161 million Muslims (13 percent of the population), Ethiopia (28 million, or 34 percent), and Russia (16 million, or 12 percent). Although fewer than 2 percent of China's population is Muslim, the numbers are nonetheless large (22 million). Thirty-eight million Muslims live in Europe, about 5 percent of the total European population (Pew Research Center, 2009b), mostly immigrants seeking better economic opportunities. By 2035 it is projected that roughly 26.4 percent of the world's population will practice Islam (Pew Research Center, 2011c), with a majority living in Asia.

Muslims believe in absolute, unquestioning, positive devotion to Allah (God) (Aslan, 2006). Although modern Islam dates to the Arab prophet Muhammad (c. 570–632), Muslims trace their religion to the ancient Hebrew prophet Abraham, also regarded as the founder of Judaism. The precepts of Islam are believed to have been revealed to Muhammad and are contained in a sacred book dictated to his followers called the Koran (the common English form of the book's name, which means "recitation"; another is *Qur'ān*, which is closer to the Arabic pronunciation). Muhammad's ideas were not accepted in his birthplace of Mecca, so in 622 he and his followers moved to Medina (both in what is today Saudi Arabia). This migration, called the *hegira*, marks the beginning of Islam, which soon spread throughout Arabia. Muslims do not worship Muhammad but regard him as a great teacher and prophet, the last in a line that includes Abraham, Noah, Moses, and Jesus.

Islam is an all-encompassing religion. The sacred *sharia* ("way") includes prescriptions for worship, daily life, ethics, and government. Although U.S. standards might find Muslim beliefs to be extremely restrictive, Muslims frequently view American life as spiritually undisciplined, corrupt, and immoral (Abdul-Rauf, 1975; Arjomand, 1988; Esposito, 1984; Kedouri, 1992; MacEnoin and al-Shahi, 1983; Martin, 1982).

Islam, like Christianity, comprises different religious groups. The principal division is between Sunnis (about 87–90 percent of all Muslims) and Shiites (about 10–13 percent). Sunni Muslims follow a series of traditions deriving from the Koran that tolerate a diversity of opinion, in contrast to the more rigid views of Shiites. Shiism split from the main body of orthodox Islam early in its history and has remained influential ever since. Iran (once known as Persia) is the only major Islamic country that is overwhelmingly Shiite, although there are Shiite majorities in several other countries, including Iraq. There are large numbers of Shiites in other Middle Eastern countries and in Turkey, Afghanistan, India, and Pakistan. A sect known as Sufism encompasses more mysticism and rituals than the practice by Sunnis and Shia (Pew Research Center, 2012g).

Shiism has been the official religion of Iran since the sixteenth century and was fundamental to the religiously conservative Iranian Revolution of 1978–1979. The Shiites trace their beginnings to Imam Ali, a seventh-century religious and political leader who showed outstanding virtue and personal devotion to God. Ali's descendants were considered the rightful leaders of Islam because they were held to belong to the prophet Muhammad's family, unlike the dynasties actually in power. The Shiites believed that the rule of Muhammad's rightful heir would eventually be instituted, doing away with the tyrannies and injustices associated with existing regimes. Muhammad's heir would be a leader directly guided by God, governing in accordance with the Koran.

There is no separation of church and state in a few highly religious Islamic societies, such as Iran. In most Muslim countries, however, religious leaders live in uneasy alliance with secular governments. Algeria, Egypt, Indonesia, and Turkey, for example, are all predominantly Muslim societies in which mosque and state are separate. As we noted in Chapter 13, even in countries such as Jordan, Morocco, and Turkey, where more religiously traditional Islamist parties have won recent elections, there has not been a loss of basic democratic values or the fundamental separation of mosque and state.

JUDAISM

With just under 15 million followers worldwide, Judaism is by far the smallest of the world's major religions. Jews were among the first people to practice monotheism, the worship of a single, all-powerful, all-knowing God, rather than multiple deities. According to Jewish beliefs, some 3,500 years ago God entered into a covenant with Abraham, a descendant of Noah: Abraham was to spread the word of God, and he in turn would father a "great nation" (Genesis 12:2) in the land that now includes Israel. As a symbol of this covenant, all the male descendants of Abraham were to be circumcised in a ritual ceremony eight days after birth.

The story of Abraham and his descendants is told in the first five books of the Bible, referred to as the Torah ("teachings" or "law"), which provides a foundation for Jewish religious beliefs (as well as those of the other "Abrahamic" traditions, Christianity and Islam). These teachings include the Ten Commandments, which according to the Torah were among the laws revealed by God to Moses during the 40 years the Jews were wandering in the Sinai Desert after escaping from Egyptian slavery. According to Jewish tradition, the entire Torah is read in an annual cycle during religious services. The Jewish Bible is made up of 24 books: the Torah, the writings of the prophets, philosophical works (for example, the Book of Job), and poetry (such as the Psalms). In the Christian tradition these are collectively referred to as the Old Testament, to distinguish them from the New Testament, which focuses on the story and teachings of Jesus. Later texts that are central to Jewish beliefs include the Talmud, a compendium of the debates and teachings of Jewish rabbis (religious teachers) over many centuries.

After their desert wanderings, the Jews eventually conquered the land promised by God to Abraham, encompassing what is today Israel, Lebanon, and the west bank of the Jordan River, along with coastal parts of Jordan, Egypt, and Syria. Jerusalem became the religious center and political capital of the Jewish nation some 3,000 years ago, although it was conquered a number of times by various empires during the next thousand years. During times of conquest some Jews began to flee to other countries, in what later became known as the Diaspora (exile or "scattering"). During the first century after Jesus, the Diaspora became complete: Following an unsuccessful revolt against their Roman conquerors, the remaining Jews were forced to settle throughout Europe and parts of North Africa and the Middle East. Throughout this period religious Jews lamented the loss of Jerusalem; every year, after recounting the escape of the Jews from Egyptian slavery during the ritual Passover meal called the *seder* ("order"), the vow was made: "next year in Jerusalem."

Judaism has exerted an influence greater than its limited numbers would suggest. First, as noted, it is the source of the world's two largest religions, Christianity and Islam. Second, in European and U.S. culture, Jews have played a role disproportionate to their numbers in such diverse fields as music, literature, science, education, and business. Third, the existence of Israel as a Jewish state since 1948 has given the Jewish faith international prominence. Israel has existed in nearly constant tension with many of its neighboring Arab countries since its founding and has seldom been out of the news.

Jews have often suffered persecution. From the twelfth century on, European and Russian Jews were often forced to live in special districts termed "ghettos," where they lacked full rights as citizens and were sometimes the target of harassment, attacks, and murders. Partly in reaction to these conditions, and partly because the Torah identifies the city of Jerusalem as the center of the Jewish homeland, some Jews embraced *Zionism*, a movement calling for the return of Jews to ancient Palestine and the creation of a Jewish state. (Zion is a biblical name for the ancient city of Jerusalem.) Although secular Zionists viewed Israel as a country where persecuted Jews could seek refuge, religious Zionists saw it as the one Jewish homeland and returning to it as fulfilling biblical prophecies. Zionists established settlements in Palestine early in the twentieth century, living relatively peacefully with their Arab and Palestinian neighbors. However, after World War II and the Nazi extermination of 6 million Jews during the Holocaust, the League of Nations and subsequently the United Nations approved the creation of the state of Israel as a homeland for the survivors. This action ended the once relatively peaceful relationship between Zionists and their neighbors.

HINDUISM

Hinduism, which dates to about 2000 B.C.E. and is one of the world's oldest religions, is the source of Buddhism and Sikhism. It is not based on the teachings of any individual, and its followers do not trace their national origins to a single god. Hinduism is an ethical religion that calls for an ideal way of life. Today there are nearly 900 million Hindus worldwide, primarily in India. The census of India estimated that 80 percent of its population—amounting to more than 827 million people—was Hindu (Census of India, 2011).

As we saw in Chapter 8, India's social structure is characterized by a caste system in which people are believed to be born into a certain status that they occupy for life. Although the caste system was officially abolished in 1949, it remains powerful. The caste system has its origins in Hindu beliefs that hold that an ideal life is partly achieved by performing the duties appropriate to one's caste.

Perhaps because Hinduism does not have a central organization or leader, its philosophy and practice are extremely diverse. Religious teachings direct all aspects of life, but in a variety of ways—ranging from promoting the enjoyment of sensual pleasures to advising the renunciation of earthly pursuits. Mohandas Gandhi was a modern example of a man who devoted his life to the Hindu virtues of "honesty, courage, service, faith, self-control, purity, and nonviolence" (Potter, 1992).

Despite the teaching that life is *maya*, or "illusion," Hindu religious beliefs have an earthly quality. For example, although temples and pilgrimage centers are located on sacred sites, any location may be a place of devotion. Hindus believe in the godlike unity of all things, yet their religion also has aspects of **polytheism**—the belief that different gods represent various categories

polytheism • Belief in two or more gods.

Global Map 17.1
Major Religions of the World

Missionaries and military force are two reasons that the majority of people in the world profess only a handful of religions today. Although Christianity (Catholicism and Protestantism) is the most widespread religion, its followers are becoming outnumbered by followers of Islam. Many of the predominantly Catholic countries of Central and South America have strong and, in some cases, growing Protestant minorities.

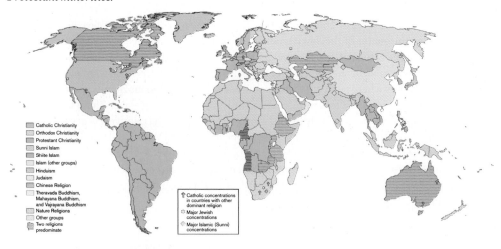

Catholic Christianity
Orthodox Christianity
Protestant Christianity
Sunni Islam
Shiite Islam
Islam (other groups)
Hinduism
Judaism
Chinese Religion
Theravada Buddhism,
Mahayana Buddhism,
and Vajrayana Buddhism
Nature Religions
Other groups
Two religions
predominate

Catholic concentrations
in countries with other
dominant religion
Major Jewish
concentrations
Major Islamic (Sunni)
concentrations

Source: Chaliand and Rageau, 1992.

of natural forces. For example, Hindus worship gods representing aspects of the whole, such as the divine dimension of a spiritual teacher (Basham, 1989; Kinsley, 1982; Potter, 1992; Schmidt, 1980).

Religion in the United States

As we have noted earlier, in comparison with the citizens of other industrial nations, Americans are highly religious. Even though secularization may have weakened the power of religious institutions in the United States, it has not diminished the strength of religious beliefs.

More than half (56 percent) of all Americans surveyed in 2007 claimed religion was "very important" in their lives (Pew Forum on Religion and Public Life, 2008). According to public opinion polls, most Americans believe in God (71 percent) and claim they pray one or more times a day (58 percent) (Pew Research Center, 2008). The 2004 General Social Survey, a random sample survey of American adults, reports that over 90 percent of people who believe now have always believed in God. More than 8 out of 10 Americans report that they believe in an afterlife, and a substantial majority claim to believe in the devil as well (Roof, 1999).

Yet one long-term measure of religiosity, based on indicators such as belief in God, religious membership, and attendance at religious services, found that the index reached its highest levels in the 1950s and has declined ever since—in part because post–World War II baby boomers were less religious, at least in the traditional sense, than their predecessors (Roof, 1999). In one national survey, overwhelming majorities of Catholics, liberal Protestants, and conservative Protestants reported attending church on a weekly basis while they were children, although their attendance had dropped sharply by the time they reached their early twenties. Among the three groups, attendance had declined the most among liberal Protestants and the least among conservative Protestants (Roof, 1999).

Another survey of nearly 114,000 adults in 1990 and more than 50,000 adults in 2001 found that religious identification had declined sharply during the 11-year period. In 1990, 90 percent of all respondents identified with some religious group; in 2001, only 81 percent. The principal decline was among self-identified Christians. This decline was not because more respondents identified with other religions; rather, it was because the number of respondents identifying with no religion whatsoever had grown from 8 percent to 14 percent of the survey population. Membership in religious institutions showed a parallel decline (Kosmin, Mayer, and Keysar, 2001). A more recent survey (Pew Research Center, 2009a) found that the fastest-growing religious category is "unaffiliated": Although only 7 percent of adult Americans report that when they were growing up their families lacked a formal religious affiliation, today more than twice as many (16 percent) report being unaffiliated. Five percent of U.S. citizens say they do not believe in a God or any sort of universal spirit. Of this 5 percent, only 24 percent consider themselves atheists; most consider themselves agnostics, or don't identify with any label (Pew Research Center, 2008). One in four "Millennials" is unaffiliated and considers himself "atheist," "agnostic," or "unaffiliated" (Figure 17.2) (Pew Research Center, 2010c).

CIVIL RELIGION

Although there is a constitutional separation of church and state in the United States, its presidents have all attended church, and some have been deeply and publicly religious.

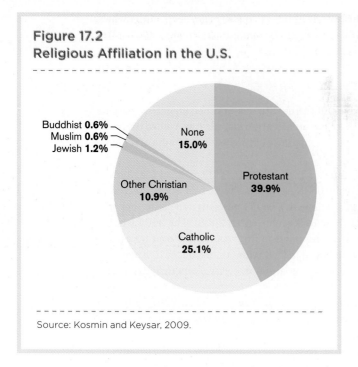

Figure 17.2
Religious Affiliation in the U.S.

- Buddhist **0.6%**
- Muslim **0.6%**
- Jewish **1.2%**
- None **15.0%**
- Protestant **39.9%**
- Other Christian **10.9%**
- Catholic **25.1%**

Source: Kosmin and Keysar, 2009.

In fact, sociologists have argued that the United States has a **civil religion**—a set of religious beliefs through which a society interprets its own history in light of some conception of ultimate reality (Bellah, 1968, 1975). Civil religion usually consists of "god-language used in reference to the nation," including "historical myths about the society's divine origins, beliefs about its sacred historical purpose, and occasionally religious restrictions on societal membership" (Wuthnow, 1988). The notion that westward expansion in the nineteenth century was America's "Manifest Destiny" is one example. The importance of civil religion in the United States is seen in the Pledge of Allegiance. By referring to "one nation, under God," the pledge infuses civic life with a religious belief derived from the Judeo-Christian heritage. Congress added the phrase "under God" in 1954, during the height of cold war fears about "godless communism." Even though the Bill of Rights of the U.S. Constitution calls for a separation of church and state, the pledge posits a theistic religious belief as central to U.S. citizenship. Every president of the United States, whether religious or not, professes to be so and regularly attends church.

Constitutional separation of church and state notwithstanding, many Americans believe that the United States is fundamentally a Christian nation. Growing religious diversity is challenging this assumption. While Americans often pride themselves on the right of everyone to pursue their own faiths freely, they seldom actually interact with people who do not share the same beliefs and so have little understanding of religious differences. Sociologist Robert Wuthnow (2007), whose research focuses on the effects of religious diversity, calls for a strategy of "reflective pluralism" as a means to promote greater religious understanding.

The need for such understanding is seen in the questioning of whether President Barack Obama is "truly a Christian." Even though Obama had worshiped at the 8,500-member Trinity United Church of Christ for the 20 years he lived in Chicago, the question was raised because his father, although not a practicing Muslim, was a Kenyan from a Muslim family. Even though Obama had seen his father only once after age three, the belief that Obama is a Muslim has grown, fueled by conservative talk show hosts and some right-wing Christian religious leaders. According to one group of surveys, in October 2008, just prior to the presidential election, more than half (51 percent) of Americans believed Obama was Christian, while only 12 percent thought he was a Muslim. Less than two years later, in August

civil religion • A set of religious beliefs through which a society interprets its own history in light of some conception of ultimate reality.

2010, barely a third of Americans still believed he was a Christian (34 percent), while 18 percent now thought him to be a Muslim—a figure that was much higher (34 percent) among conservative Republicans. Those who "didn't know" grew in number during the same period, from 32 percent to 43 percent (Pew Research Center for the People and the Press, 2010a). Calling Obama's Christianity into question has been seen by his opponents as one way to weaken his popular support: Not only does it tap into widespread post-9/11 fear of Islamic terrorism, but being a churchgoing (Christian) American is part of the country's civil religion, at least to many Americans.

TRENDS IN RELIGIOUS AFFILIATION

It is difficult to estimate the number of people belonging to religious organizations, because the U.S. government cannot require people to provide such data. Nonetheless, based on occasional surveys, public opinion polls, and church records, sociologists of religion have concluded that church membership has grown steadily since the United States was founded. About one in six Americans belonged to a religious organization at the time of the Revolutionary War, one in three at the time of the Civil War, one in two at the turn of the nineteenth century, and two in three in the 1990s (Finke and Stark, 2005).

One reason so many Americans are religiously affiliated is that religious organizations are an important source of social ties and friendship networks. Churches, synagogues, and mosques are communities of people with shared beliefs and values who support one another during times of need. Religious communities thus often play a family-like role.

Another reason so many people belong to religious organizations is that the United States has more than 1,500 religions one can belong to (Melton, 1989). Yet the vast majority of people belong to a relatively small number of religions (Figure 17.2). About 40 percent of Americans identify themselves as Protestant, 25 percent as Catholic, 1.2 percent as Jewish, and 2 percent as "other," a category that includes Hindu, Buddhist, and Muslim. The remainder (15 percent) have no religious affiliation at all (U.S. Bureau of the Census, 2012n).

Roof's (1993) study of baby boomers, *A Generation of Seekers*, found that even though two out of three had dropped out of a church or synagogue in their teens, most still remain. Increasingly, however, religious experience is sought outside established religions, often in a highly personalized fashion.

PROTESTANTISM: THE GROWING STRENGTH OF CONSERVATIVE DENOMINATIONS

A clearer picture of trends in American religion emerges if we break down the Protestant category into major subgroups. According to the U.S. Religious Landscape Survey of nearly 36,000 adults in 2007, Baptist households account for 34 percent of all Protestants—well over twice the percentage of the second-largest group, Methodists (12 percent). There were far fewer Lutherans (9 percent), Presbyterians (5 percent), and Episcopalians (3 percent). Forty-four percent of all Christians (and approximately half of all Protestants) describe themselves as "born again" or "evangelicals" (Pew Research Center, 2008).

These figures indicate the growing strength of conservative Protestants, who emphasize a literal interpretation of the Bible, morality in daily life, and conversion through evangelizing. In contrast are the more historically established liberal Protestants, who adopt a more flexible, humanistic approach to religious practice. Somewhere in between are moderate Protestants.

Since the 1960s, both liberal and moderate Protestant churches have experienced declining membership, whereas the number of conservative Protestants has exploded.

The conservative denominations inspire deep loyalty and commitment, and they are highly effective at recruiting new members, particularly young people. Today 26 percent of Americans belong to evangelical Protestant churches, compared with only 18 percent belonging to mainline ones (Pew Research Center, 2008). Liberal Protestantism in particular has suffered. The aging members of the liberal Protestant denominations have not been replaced, commitment is low, and some current members are switching to other faiths. From 1965 to 1989—a time when mainline Protestant denominations began to decline in favor of evangelical churches—losses were substantial for Lutherans, United Methodists, the United Church of Christ, Episcopalians, Presbyterians, and Disciples of Christ. Together these six denominations lost nearly 23 million members—almost the same number that was gained by such conservative Protestant denominations as the Southern Baptists, the Church of the Nazarene, the Seventh-Day Adventists, the Assemblies of God, the Church of God, and the Church of Jesus Christ of Latter-Day Saints. Between 1990 and 2008, the four largest mainline denominations—Methodists, Lutherans, Presbyterians, and Episcopalians—lost an additional 4 million members, a decline of 13 percent from 1990 (U.S. Bureau of the Census, 2012n). At the same time, black Protestant churches have thrived in the United States, as their members move into the middle class and achieve economic and political prominence (Finke and Stark, 2005; Roof and McKinney, 1990).

CATHOLICISM

Catholics have made up about a quarter of the U.S. population for several decades. As the U.S. population has increased, the number of Catholics has grown accordingly, increasing by 11 million (24 percent) between 1990 and 2008 (U.S. Bureau of the Census, 2012n). Despite this growth in numbers, Catholics have lost more adherents during the past generation than any other religious group: While nearly a third of all American adults report being raised as Catholic, only a quarter still identify with the Catholic Church. Half of those who have left the Church are now Protestants; half are unaffiliated (Pew Research Center, 2008).

If so many Catholics have turned away from the Church in recent years, how can the number of Catholics be growing? While some Protestants have converted to Catholicism, the main source of growth in the Catholic Church has been through emigration from Mexico and Central America. Among immigrants, almost half are Catholic; 45 percent of Catholics under 30 are Hispanic (Pew Research Center, 2008). Since immigrants also tend to have larger families than native-born Americans, even should immigration slow, the number of Catholics can be expected to continue increasing in the near future.

Yet even as the number of Catholics has grown, church attendance among Catholics has declined. In 1975, according to Gallup surveys (Saad, 2009), 75 percent of Catholics reported going to church at least once a week. By 2005 that figure had dropped to 45 percent, where it has remained since. The figure for Protestants, by way of comparison, has remained at roughly 40–45 percent over the same period. While church attendance has declined for Catholics of all ages, the drop has been sharpest for young Catholics (21 to 29); currently, only about 30 percent of young Catholics attend church every week. While the reasons for such declines are unclear, one reason likely has to do with the 1968 papal encyclical *Of Human Life* (*Humane Vitae*) that reaffirmed the ban on all forms of artificial contraception by Catholics. People whose conscience allowed for the use of contraceptives were faced with disobeying the Church, and many did just that. The General Social Survey (Smith, 1998) found that three out of five Catholics say that contraceptives should be available to teens even without parental approval.

OTHER RELIGIOUS GROUPS

Judaism in the United States has historically been divided into three major movements: Orthodox, which believes in the divine origins of the Jewish Bible (as previously noted, called by Christians the Old Testament) and follows highly traditional religious practices; Conservative, which is a blend of traditional and more contemporary beliefs and practices; and Reform, which rejects most traditional practices and is progressive in its ritual practices (services, for example, are more likely to be conducted in English than in Hebrew). Both Conservative and Reform Judaism reflect efforts by Jewish immigrants (or their descendants) to develop beliefs and rituals that turned away from "Old World" ones, developing forms more consistent with their new homeland.

Despite (or perhaps partly because of) these efforts to modernize Judaism, the number of Jews in the United States has declined as a result of low birthrates, intermarriage, and assimilation—from 3.1 million in 1990 to 2.6 million in 2010 (U.S. Bureau of the Census, 2012n). Yet even assimilated Jews often identify themselves as Jewish, and there has been a resurgence of interest among some younger American Jews in rediscovering Orthodox practices. Recent forms of Judaism, such as the Jewish Renewal movement and Reconstructionist Judaism, have sought to reinvigorate Jewish worship with a combination of more traditional practices (such as greater use of Hebrew in services), the use of music, an emphasis on spirituality and social justice, and equal roles for women in worship.

Among Muslims, growing emigration from Asia and Africa may change the U.S. religious profile. For example, reliable estimates of the number of Muslims in the United States run as high as 2.5 million in 2009 (Pew Research Center, 2009b), although official government statistics report only roughly half that number (U.S. Bureau of the Census, 2011k). The low estimates may be because in the post-9/11 political climate, many Muslims are reluctant to disclose their religious affiliation—only 30 percent of Americans held a favorable view of Islam in 2010 (Pew Research Center for the People and the Press, 2010b). Two-thirds of U.S. Muslims are foreign-born (Pew Research Center, 2008); many come from Pakistan or are African refugees from countries such as Somalia and Ethiopia. A majority of Muslim Americans are first-generation immigrants to the United States (63 percent), with almost half that number having moved to the United States since 1990. Thirty-seven percent of Muslim Americans were born in the United States, and of those, 15 percent have at least one immigrant parent. Despite the high number of Muslim Americans who were born abroad, eighty-one percent of Muslim Americans are citizens of the United States (Pew Research Center, 2011a).

New Religious Movements

Today, sociologists are aware that the terms *sect* and *cult* have negative connotations, so instead, they sometimes use the phrase *new religious movements* to characterize novel religious organizations lacking the respectability that comes with being well established for a long period (Hadden, 1997b; Hexham and Poewe, 1997). **New religious movements** encompass an enormously diverse range of religious and spiritual groups, cults, and sects that have emerged in Western countries, including the United States, alongside mainstream religions.

> **new religious movements** • The broad range of religious and spiritual groups, cults, and sects that have emerged alongside mainstream religions. New religious movements range from spiritual and self-help groups within the New Age movement to exclusive sects such as the Hare Krishnas.

One example is the Unification Church, founded by the Korean Sun Myung Moon. The cult boasts a membership of 50,000 in the United States and 3 million worldwide (Melton, 1996). Other new religious movements include Scientology, Wicca, Eckankar, Druid, Santería, and Rastafarianism. Their beliefs might seem unusual mixtures of traditional and modern religious ideas, but in fact all long-established religions mix elements from diverse cultural sources.

This change in characterization has proven to be controversial, however. A loosely knit "anti-cult movement" composed of academics, church groups, families of cult members, and some former cult members themselves argues that regarding cults simply as "new religious movements" masks their identity as fringe organizations that can be dangerous and even deadly. (See the collection of writings by scholars representing both perspectives in Zablocki and Robbins, 2001.)

Janja Lalich, a sociologist who at one time belonged to a political organization she now views as a cult, argues that cults can be distinguished from new religious movements on the basis of the virtually total control they exert over the daily lives and thinking of their members. Cult members, she argues, exist in a situation of "bounded choice": However seemingly irrational, harmful, or even fatal their acts (as in the examples of Heaven's Gate and Aum Shinrikyo), they are done "in a context that makes perfect sense at the time to those who [perform the acts] and are, in fact, consistent with an ideology or belief system that [the members] trust represents their highest aspirations" (Lalich, 2004). Cult members are socialized into a way of thinking that is all encompassing; they are not permitted to question the authority of the cult leader and so come to view the cult's beliefs, however bizarre or dangerous, as normal.

From the new religious movement perspective, cults—like all **religious movements**—can be best understood sociologically as a subtype of social movements. A religious movement is an association of people who spread a new religion or promote a new interpretation of an existing religion. From this perspective, all sects and cults can be classified as religious movements. Examples of religious movements include the groups that originally founded and spread Christianity in the first century, the Lutheran movement that split Christianity in Europe about 1,500 years afterward, and the groups involved in the more recent Islamic Revolution (discussed later in the chapter).

Religious movements pass through phases of development. In the first phase, the movement derives life and cohesion from a powerful leader. Max Weber classified such leaders as **charismatic**—that is, having inspirational qualities capable of capturing the imagination and devotion of a mass of followers. (Charismatic leaders in Weber's formulation could include political as well as religious figures—revolutionary China's Mao Zedong, for example, as well as Jesus and Muhammad.) The leaders of religious movements usually criticize the religious establishment and proclaim a new message. In their early years, religious movements are fluid; they do not have an established authority system. Their members are normally in direct contact with the charismatic leader, and together they spread the new teachings.

The second phase occurs following the death of the charismatic leader, when the movement must face what Weber termed the "routinization of charisma." To survive, the movement has to

religious movements • Associations of people who join together to seek to spread a new religion or to promote a new interpretation of an existing religion.

charismatic • Describing the inspirational quality capable of capturing the imagination and devotion of a mass of followers.

create formalized rules and procedures, because it can no longer depend on the central role of the original leader in organizing the followers. Many movements fade away when their leaders die or lose influence. A movement that takes on a permanent character becomes a church—a formal organization of believers with an established authority system and established symbols and rituals. The church itself might later become the origin of other movements that question its teachings and either set themselves up in opposition or break away.

Many new religious movements are derived from mainstream religious traditions, such as Hinduism, Christianity, and Buddhism, whereas others have emerged from traditions that were almost unknown in the West until recently. Some new religious movements are creations of the charismatic leaders who head their activities. This is the case with the previously mentioned Unification Church, led by the Reverend Sun Myung Moon, whose members are expected to fraternize only with one another, to donate their property to the church, and to obey Moon's commands. This new religious movement was introduced into the United States at the beginning of the 1960s, and it appealed to many who were rejecting traditional religion and looking for insight in Eastern religious teachings. Membership in new religious movements mostly consists of converts rather than individuals brought up in a particular faith. Members are usually well educated and from middle-class backgrounds.

Various theories explain the popularity of new religious movements. Some observers argue that they reflect liberalization and secularization within society and within traditional churches. People who feel that traditional religions have become ritualistic and devoid of spiritual meaning may find comfort and a greater sense of community in smaller, less impersonal new religious movements.

Others see new religious movements as an outcome of rapid social change (Wilson, 1982). As traditional social norms are disrupted, people search for explanations and reassurance. The rise of groups and sects emphasizing personal spirituality, for example, suggests that many individuals need to reconnect with their own values or beliefs in the face of instability and uncertainty.

Furthermore, new religious movements may appeal to people who feel alienated from mainstream society. The collective, communal approaches of sects and cults, some authors argue, can offer support and a sense of belonging. For example, today's middle-class youth are not marginalized from society in a material sense, but they may feel isolated emotionally and spiritually. Membership in a cult can overcome this alienation (Wallis, 1984).

New religious movements fall into three broad categories: *world-affirming, world-rejecting,* and *world-accommodating* movements. Each category is based on the relationship of the group to the larger social world. The enduring popularity of new religious movements presents another challenge to the secularization thesis. Opponents point to the diversity and dynamism of new religious movements and argue that religion and spirituality remain central facets of modern life. As traditional religions lose their hold, they claim, religion is not disappearing but is heading in new directions. Not all scholars agree, however. Proponents of secularization hold that these movements remain peripheral to society, even if they profoundly impact the lives of their followers. New religious movements are fragmented and relatively unorganized; they also suffer from high turnover rates. Compared to a serious religious commitment, proponents argue, participation in a new religious movement appears to be little more than a hobby or lifestyle choice.

WORLD-AFFIRMING MOVEMENTS

World-affirming movements are more like self-help or therapy groups than conventional religious groups. These movements often lack rituals, churches, or formal theologies, focusing instead on members' spiritual well-being. World-affirming movements do not reject the outside world or its values. Rather, they seek to enhance their followers' abilities to perform and succeed in that world by unlocking human potential.

The Church of Scientology is one such group. Founded by L. Ron Hubbard, it has grown from its original base in California to include a large membership worldwide. Scientologists believe people are all spiritual beings but have neglected their spiritual nature. Through training that makes them aware of their real spiritual capacities, people can recover forgotten supernatural powers, clear their minds, and reveal their full potential.

Many strands of the so-called **New Age movements** are world-affirming movements. The New Age movement emerged from the counterculture of the 1960s and '70s and encompasses a broad spectrum of beliefs, practices, and ways of life. Pagan teachings (Celtic, Druidic, Native American, and others), shamanism, forms of Asian mysticism, Wiccan rituals, and Zen meditation are among activities thought of as New Age.

The mysticism of the New Age movement appears to contrast with the modern societies in which it is favored. Followers of New Age movements develop alternative ways of life to cope with the challenges of modernity. Yet New Age activities should not be interpreted as simply a radical break with the present. They are also part of a larger cultural trajectory exemplifying mainstream culture. In modern societies, individuals possess unparalleled degrees of autonomy and freedom to chart their own lives. In this respect, the aims of the New Age movement

"World-affirming groups," such as the Church of Scientology, focus on members' spiritual well-being and do not reject the outside world's values. Science fiction writer L. Ron Hubbard established Scientology in 1954.

world-affirming movements • Religious movements that seek to enhance followers' ability to succeed in the outside world by helping them unlock their human potential.

New Age movements • A general term to describe the diverse spectrum of beliefs and practices oriented on inner spirituality. Paganism, Eastern mysticism, shamanism, alternative forms of healing, and astrology are all examples of New Age activities.

coincide closely with the modern age: People are encouraged to move beyond traditional values and expectations and to live actively and reflectively.

WORLD-REJECTING MOVEMENTS

World-rejecting movements are highly critical of the outside world and often demand significant lifestyle changes from their followers—such as living ascetically, changing their dress or hairstyle, or following a certain diet. World-rejecting movements are frequently exclusive, in contrast to world-affirming movements, which are inclusive. Some world-rejecting movements display characteristics of **total institutions**; members subsume their individual identities into that of the group, follow strict ethical codes or rules, and withdraw from activity in the outside world.

Most world-rejecting movements demand more of their members, in terms of time and commitment, than older established religions. Some groups use the technique of "love bombing" to gain the individual's total adherence. A potential convert is overwhelmed by attention and constant displays of affection until he or she is drawn emotionally into the group. The Unification Church reportedly employs this technique. Some new movements, in fact, have been accused of brainwashing their adherents—robbing them of the capacity for independent decision making (Lalich, 2004).

Many world-rejecting cults and sects have come under the intense scrutiny of state authorities, the media, and the public. Certain extreme cases have attracted much concern, such as the Japanese group Aum Shinrikyo, which staged a fatal attack on the Tokyo subway system. The Branch Davidian cult, based in Waco, Texas, became embroiled in a deadly confrontation with federal authorities in 1993 after accusations of child abuse and weapons stockpiling. Eighty members of the cult (including 19 children) burned to death in their compound during an assault by federal officials that ended a lengthy armed standoff. Federal officials maintain that the cult members were virtual prisoners of their charismatic leader, David Koresh, who was allegedly stockpiling illegal weapons, had numerous wives, and was having sex with some of the children. Controversy remains over whether the fire was ordered by Koresh, who reportedly preferred mass suicide to surrender, or whether the actions of the federal authorities caused the tragedy (Tabor and Gallagher, 1995).

WORLD-ACCOMMODATING MOVEMENTS

World-accommodating movements emphasize the importance of inner religious life over more worldly concerns. Members of such groups seek to reclaim the spiritual purity that they believe has been lost in traditional religious settings. Whereas followers of world-rejecting and world-affirming groups may alter their lifestyles in accordance with their religious activity, many adherents of world-accommodating movements carry on their lives and careers with little visible change. One example is Pentecostalism, a Christian renewal movement that emphasizes the direct, ecstatic experience of God that its adherents believe existed at the time of Christ. Pentecostalists believe that the Holy Spirit can be heard through individuals who are granted the gift of "speaking in tongues."

world-rejecting movements • Religious movements that are exclusive in nature, highly critical of the outside world, and demanding of their members.

total institutions • Groups who exercise control over their members by making them subsume their individual identities in that of the group, compelling them to adhere to strict ethical codes or rules, and sometimes forcing them to withdraw from activity in the outside world.

world-accommodating movements • Religious movements that emphasize the importance of inner religious life and spiritual purity over worldly concerns.

Religious Affiliation and Socioeconomic Status

Substantial socioeconomic and regional differences exist among the principal religious groupings in the United States. *Liberal Protestants* are well educated, somewhat upper income, and middle or upper class. They are concentrated in the Northeast and, to a small extent, in the West. Ethnically, they comprise white Anglo-Saxon Protestants (WASPs) of British or German origins. *Moderate Protestants* have a lower level of education, income, and social class. In fact, they are typical of the national average on these measures. They live in the Midwest and, to some extent, in the West. Moderate Protestants are from a variety of European ethnic backgrounds, including British, German, Scandinavian, Irish, and Dutch. *Black Protestants* are the least educated and poorest of any of the religious groups listed. *Conservative Protestants* have a similar profile, although they are at a slightly higher level on all these measures. They comprise a diverse profile of European ethnicities, although some are African American as well.

Catholics strongly resemble moderate Protestants in terms of their socioeconomic profile. They are largely concentrated in the Northeast, although many live in the West and the Southwest. The largest ethnic group is European in origin (primarily German, Italian, Slavic, and Irish, and to a lesser extent English and French), followed by Latinos from Mexico and Central and South America.

Jews have the highest socioeconomic profile. Most are college graduates in middle- or upper-income categories. One study found that Jewish educational and occupational attainment was significantly higher than that of other whites. Jews are largely European in origin, particularly Eastern European and German, although some are from northern Africa. Whereas the large majority of Jews once lived in the Northeast, today only half do. One recent study suggests that their high degree of geographical mobility is associated with lowered involvement in Jewish institutions. Jews who move throughout the country are less likely to belong to synagogues or temples, have Jewish friends, or be married to Jewish spouses (Goldstein and Goldstein, 1996; Hartman and Hartman, 1996; Pew Research Center, 2008; Roof and McKinney, 1990).

In sum, Jews and liberal Protestants are the most heavily middle and upper class; moderate Protestants and Catholics are somewhat in the middle (although the growing number of poor Catholic Latino immigrants may be changing this position); conservative and black Protestants are overwhelmingly lower class. These groupings correspond roughly with social and political liberalism and conservatism as well. In terms of civil liberties, racial justice, and women's rights, Jews are by far the most tolerant. Liberal Protestants and Catholics are somewhat more tolerant than the average American, while moderate Protestants and black Protestants are somewhat less tolerant. Conservative Protestants are the least tolerant of all religious groupings (Roof and McKinney, 1990).

There are political differences across religious groups as well. Jews are the most heavily Democratic; fundamentalist and evangelical Christians, the most Republican. The more moderate Protestant denominations are somewhere in between (Kosmin, Mayer, and Keysar, 2001).

Gender and Religion

Like other social institutions, churches and denominations have on the whole excluded women from power. The following sections examine some of the interrelations of religion and gender. This is an area in which significant changes are occurring.

RELIGIOUS IMAGES

In Christianity, although Mary, the mother of Jesus, is sometimes treated as having divine qualities, God is "the Father," a male figure, and Jesus took the human shape of a man. Genesis, the first book of the Bible, teaches that woman was created from a man's rib. These facts have not gone unnoticed by women's movements. Over a hundred years ago, Elizabeth Cady Stanton published a series of commentaries on the Scriptures, titled *The Woman's Bible.* In her view, the deity had created women and men as beings of equal value, and the Bible should fully reflect this fact. The "masculinist" character of the Bible reflected the fact that it was written by men. In 1870 the Church of England established a Revision Committee to revise and update the biblical texts, but the committee contained no women. Stanton asserted that there was no reason to suppose that God is a man, because it was clear in the Scriptures that all human beings were fashioned in the image of God. She subsequently organized the Women's Revision Committee in America, composed of 23 women, to advise her in preparing *The Woman's Bible,* which was published in 1895.

In some Buddhist orders, especially Mahayana Buddhism, women are represented in a favorable light. But on the whole, Buddhism is "an overwhelmingly male-created institution dominated by a patriarchal power structure," in which the feminine is mostly "associated with the secular, powerless, profane, and imperfect" (Paul, 1985). The contrasting pictures of women that appear in the Buddhist texts no doubt mirror the ambiguous attitudes of men toward women in the secular world: Women are portrayed as wise, maternal, and gentle, yet also as mysterious, polluting, and destructive, threatening evil.

THE ROLE OF WOMEN IN RELIGIOUS ORGANIZATIONS

In both Buddhism and (later) Christianity, women were allowed to express strong religious convictions by becoming nuns. Although the first orders for women were probably established in the twelfth century, their membership remained small until the 1800s. At that time, many women took religious vows to become teachers and nurses because these occupations were largely controlled by the religious orders. Nonetheless, female religious orders remained subject to a male hierarchy, and elaborate rituals reinforced this subjugation. For example, all nuns were regarded as "brides of Christ." Until some orders made changes in the 1950s and '60s, "marriage" ceremonies were carried out during which the novice would cut her hair, receive her religious name, and sometimes be given a wedding ring. After several years, a novice would take a vow of perpetual profession, after which she was required to receive dispensation if she chose to leave.

Women's orders today show considerable diversity. In some convents, nuns still dress in traditional habit and live in communities removed from the secular world. In other convents, nuns wear ordinary dress and live in apartments or houses. Traditional restrictions such as not talking to others at certain periods of the day or walking with hands folded and hidden under the habit are rarely evident.

Despite such liberalization, women have filled only lower-status positions in religious organizations. This situation is changing, in line with changes affecting women in society generally. In recent years, women's groups have pressed for equal status in religious orders. Increasingly, the Catholic and Episcopalian churches are under strong pressure to allow women an equal voice in their hierarchies. Yet in 1977 the Sacred Congregation for the Doctrine of the Faith in Rome declared that women could not be admitted to the

Catholic priesthood; the reason was that Jesus had not called a woman to be one of his disciples. Ten years later, 1987 was officially designated the "Year of the Madonna," in which women were advised to recall their traditional role as wives and mothers. The barriers to Catholic women in the hierarchy of the church thus remain formidable. In a letter published in May 1994, Pope John Paul II reaffirmed the Roman Catholic Church's ban on the ordination of women. And in July 2010, in response to widely publicized scandals involving priests who had sexually abused children, the Vatican strengthened its rules on such abuses, characterizing them as "grave crimes"—but the same decree also extended the list of "grave crimes" to include any priest who ordained a woman. Catholic organizations that favored the ordination of women priests complained that the decree implied that female ordination and pedophilia were equally grave offenses (Bates, 2010; CWO, 2010).

The Episcopal Church has allowed women into its priesthood since 1976. Altogether, women have been ordained as ministers in about half the Protestant denominations in the United States, including the Presbyterian Church (U.S.A.), the Evangelical Lutheran Church in America, the African Methodist Episcopal Church, and the United Methodist Church. And except within Orthodox Judaism, women in the United States can become rabbis as well.

WOMEN AND ISLAM

Despite the resurgence of traditional Islamist views in some parts of the Muslim world in recent years, Muslim women in most countries continue to experience a high degree of freedom and equality. As noted in Chapter 13, women have served as heads of state in such predominantly Muslim nations as Bangladesh, Pakistan, and Turkey. In Afghanistan, before the militant Islamic nationalists known as the Taliban took over in 1996, women played prominent roles: Shafiqa Habibi was the country's most popular television news anchor, her face (uncovered) known throughout the country. During the Taliban's rule, she spent her time at home hidden from public view. When she ventured out, her body had to be covered by a *burka*, a traditional tentlike garment with a screen sewn into the fabric over her face to hide her eyes but allow some ability to see (Filkins, 1998).

Habibi's experience was shared by all Afghan women. The Taliban's extreme Islamic beliefs forbade women from working outside the home, attending school, or appearing in public without covering their bodies from head to toe. Women seen in public with any man who was not their husband or relative were brutally beaten or killed. Since the overthrow of the Taliban in 2001, women have begun to regain their rights in Afghanistan, at least in the capital city of Kabul. But throughout much of the rest of the country, local religious leaders, including the Taliban, have begun to make a comeback, and women are afraid to exercise their legal rights for fear of retribution.

There is a debate among Muslim scholars as to whether Islam in fact requires severe restrictions on the role of women. At one extreme, the highly conservative interpretation sometimes referred to as Wahhabism (after the name of its nineteenth-century founder) has led to the severe treatment of women practiced by the Taliban. This strict version of Islam is strongly practiced in oil-rich Saudi Arabia, which has funded *madrassas* ("schools") throughout the Muslim world, where Wahhabism is taught. A more moderate view of women's roles—which still calls for restrictions such as veiling—was advanced by the prominent Iranian philosopher Ali Shariati. In his view, women should be veiled both because this reflects the chastity and piety of Muhammad's daughter Fatima, and because it represents defiance of the Western view of women (Aslan, 2006; Shariati, 1971). A feminist view is offered by Amina Wadud in her book *Qur'an and Woman: Rereading the Sacred Text from a Woman's Perspective* (1999). Wadud argues that women's inferior status in some Muslim countries results partly from Islam's seventh-century Arabian origins, when women were relegated to an inferior status, and partly from the hostility toward women that has characterized centuries of male-centered interpretations of the Koran. Reza Aslan (2006), an Iranian-born American sociologist who has written extensively on Islam, states the feminist position succinctly:

> As Shirin Ebadi proudly declared while accepting the 2003 Nobel Peace Prize for her tireless work in defending the rights of women in Iran, "God created us all as equals.... By fighting for equal status, we are doing what God *wants* us to do." ... The so-called Muslim women's movement is predicated on the idea that Muslim men, not Islam, have been responsible for the suppression of women's rights. For this reason, Muslim feminists throughout the world are advocating a return to the society Muhammad originally envisioned for his followers.

The Bible, like the Koran, provides a range of moral teachings, many in conflict with one another, that were rooted in the moral beliefs of the time. Some of these teachings would be regarded by most Christians and Jews today as completely unacceptable. Examples include:

> "If . . . no proof of the girl's virginity can be found, she shall be brought to the door of her father's house and there the men of her town shall stone her to death." (Deuteronomy 22:20–21)
> "Women should remain silent in the churches. They are not allowed to speak, but must be in submission, as the Law says." (1 Corinthians 14:34)
> "I do not permit a woman to teach or to have authority over a man, but to be in silence." (Timothy 2:12)

From a sociological perspective, it is important to ask not only how such beliefs arose a thousand or more years ago, but also how they are being interpreted today—and how these interpretations find their way into new religious movements and social practices.

The Global Rise of Religious Nationalism

Religious nationalism involves the linking of deep religious convictions with beliefs about a people's social and political destiny. In numerous countries, religious nationalist movements call for a revival of traditional religious beliefs that are embodied in the nation and its leadership (Beyer, 1994). These movements represent a strong reaction against the impact of technological and economic modernization on local religious beliefs. In particular, religious nationalists oppose what they regard as the destructive aspects of Western influence on local culture and religion, ranging from U.S. television to the missionary efforts of foreign evangelicals.

Religious nationalist movements accept many aspects of modern life, including modern

religious nationalism • The linking of strongly held religious convictions with beliefs about a people's social and political destiny.

technology, politics, and economics. For example, Islamic fundamentalists fighting the Russian army in Chechnya have developed websites to spread their views. Even Osama bin Laden used video and television to reach millions of Muslims worldwide. However, Islamic fundamentalists also emphasize a strict interpretation of religious values and reject the notion of secularization. Nationalist movements do not simply revive ancient religious beliefs. Rather, they partly "invent" the past, drawing on different traditions and reinterpreting events to serve their current beliefs and interests. Violent conflicts between religious groups sometimes result from their differing interpretations of the same historical event (Anderson, 1991; Juergensmeyer, 1993, 2001, 2009; van der Veer, 1994).

Religious nationalism is rising because in times of rapid social change, unshakable ideas have strong appeal. The collapse of the Soviet Union, the end of the cold war, and today's sweeping global economic and political changes have led many nations to reject the secular solutions offered by the United States and its former socialist enemies and to look instead to their own past and cultures (Juergensmeyer, 1995). In the Middle East, many Palestinian Muslims as well as Israeli Orthodox Jews renounce the notion of a secular democratic state, arguing for a religious nation purged of nonbelievers. In India, Hindus, Muslims, and Sikhs face off against one another.

Islamic nationalism has triumphed in Iran, Sudan, and until 2001, Afghanistan; today it is making a resurgence in that country. It has also made significant inroads in Algeria, Egypt, Malaysia, Pakistan, Palestine, Turkey, and elsewhere. Since the 1970s, Islamic nationalism has shaped the contours of both national and international politics. To understand this phenomenon, we must look both to aspects of Islam as a traditional religion and to secular changes affecting countries where its influence is pervasive.

ISLAMIC NATIONALISM

Islam, like Christianity, has continually stimulated activism. The Koran is full of instructions to believers to "struggle in the way of God" against both unbelievers and those within the Muslim community who introduce corruption. Over the centuries there have been successive generations of Muslim reformers, and Islam has become as internally divided as Christianity.

ISLAM AND THE WEST

During the Middle Ages, there was continuous struggle between Christian Europe and the Muslim states. During the height of Islamic power, the *caliphs* (Islamic rulers) ruled over an area extending from what later became Spain, Greece, the former Yugoslavia, Bulgaria, and Romania to India, Pakistan, and Bangladesh. Europeans eventually reclaimed most of these lands, and many Muslim areas in North Africa were colonized in the eighteenth and nineteenth centuries. These reversals were catastrophic for Muslim religion and civilization, which Islamic believers held to be the highest and most advanced possible. In the late nineteenth century, the inability of the Muslim world to resist the spread of Western culture led to reform movements seeking to restore Islam to its original purity and strength. A key idea was that Islam should respond to the Western challenge by affirming the identity of its beliefs and practices.

This idea developed in various ways in the twentieth century and underlay Iran's Islamic Revolution of 1978–1979, which was fueled initially by internal opposition to the shah ("the king"), Mohammad Reza Pahlavi (1941–1979). When the shah's premier, Mohammad Mossadeq, nationalized the oil industry in 1951, a conflict ensued between the pro-West shah and the supporters of the nationalistic Mossadeq. The shah eventually fled the country but returned in 1953, when a U.S.- and British-led coup overthrew Mossadeq. The shah tried to promote forms of modernization modeled on the West—for example, land reform, extending the vote to women, and developing secular education. He also used the army and secret police to brutally repress those who opposed his regime. The fact that he had been installed by Western powers helped fuel nationalist sentiments that eventually led to the revolution that overthrew him. A dominant figure in the revolution was Ayatollah Ruhollah Khomeini, a religious leader exiled in France during the shah's reign, who provided a radical reinterpretation of Shiite ideas.

Khomeini established a government in strict accordance with traditional Islamic law, fusing religion and the state. The government made Islam the basis of all social, political, and economic life in Iran. Men and women were kept rigorously segregated, women had to cover their heads in public, homosexuals could be shot by a firing squad, and women accused of adultery were stoned to death. The strict code reflected a pronounced nationalistic outlook, strongly rejecting Western influences.

The aim of the Islamic republic in Iran was to organize government and society so that Islamic teachings would dominate all spheres. The Guardian Council of religious leaders determines whether laws, policies, and candidates for Parliament conform to Islamic beliefs, even though Iran has a U.S.-style constitution providing for elected officials and the separation of powers.

Recent years have seen a growing movement to liberalize the country. The reform-minded president Mohammad Khatami and his allies recaptured control of Parliament in the 2000 elections. But that victory proved to be short-lived: The Guardian Council disqualified 2,400 liberal candidates (nearly a third of all candidates) during the 2004 elections, and Mahmoud Ahmadinejad, a conservative candidate close to Iran's religious leaders, won the presidency. The pro-democracy Green Movement mobilized millions of people in peaceful protests against the Ahmadinejad government during the 2009 presidential elections but was brutally repressed as a consequence (see Chapter 13 for further discussion).

THE SPREAD OF ISLAMIC REVIVALISM

Although the ideas underlying the Iranian Revolution were supposed to unite the whole Islamic world against the West, governments of countries where the Shiites are in a minority have not aligned themselves with the Islamic Revolution in Iran. Yet Islamic fundamentalism (often referred to as "Islamism," the complete adherence to Islamic law along with rejection of most non-Islamic influences) has become popular in most of these states, and various forms of Islamic revivalism elsewhere have been stimulated by it.

Although Islamic fundamentalist movements have grown in many countries in North Africa, the Middle East, and South Asia, they have won power in only two states: Sudan and Afghanistan. Sudan has been ruled since a 1989 military coup by Omar al-Bashir, who heads the National Congress Party. The fundamentalist Taliban regime consolidated its hold on the fragmented state of Afghanistan in 1996 but was ousted at the end of 2001 by Afghan opposition forces and the U.S. military, which as of 2010 was committing additional troops in an effort to quell rising Taliban power. In many other states (such as Algeria, Egypt, and Turkey), however, Islamic fundamentalist uprisings have been suppressed by the state or the military.

Islamist opposition is building in states such as Malaysia and Indonesia. Several provinces in Nigeria have implemented sharia (strict Islamic law), and the war in Chechnya has attracted Islamic militants who support the establishment of an Islamic state in that region.

Al Qaeda is an example of a loosely knit transnational network of militant religious fundamentalists with a global vision. Founded by Osama bin Laden, al Qaeda seeks to overthrow what it regards as corrupt Muslim governments, drive Western influence from the Middle East, and eventually establish a religiously based government that would encompass a billion Muslims throughout Europe, Africa, and Asia. Islamic rule would be subject to strict religious discipline, as it was during the rule of the Taliban in Afghanistan.

Such Islamic revivalism cannot be understood wholly in religious terms. It largely represents a reaction against what Iranian writer Jalal Al Ahmad (1997; orig. 1962) called "Weststruckedness" or "Westoxification"—the seductive (and, in his view, corrupting) power of Western cultural beliefs and practices. In countries where as much as half the population is under age 15, where poverty is widespread, and where many well-educated young men and women face a life of marginal employment and uncertainty, such beliefs find fertile ground.

The strong Western presence in the Middle East has provided additional fuel for anti-Western sentiments. In his *fatwas* (opinions that he claimed to be grounded in Islamic law), bin Laden repeatedly condemned U.S. troop presence in Saudi Arabia (which, as the land of Muhammad, is regarded by Islam as its most sacred place), U.S. support for Israel in its conflict with the Palestinians, the first Gulf War against Iraq, and what bin Laden claimed were a million deaths resulting from the postwar economic sanctions against Iraq. In a videotaped statement that was televised worldwide after the September 11 attacks, bin Laden also stated that "what the United States tastes today is a very small thing compared to what we have tasted for tens of years. Our nation has been tasting this humiliation and contempt for more than 80 years" (BBC News, 2001). He was referring to the collapse of the Ottoman Empire after World War I, when more than a thousand years of Islamic rule came to an end.

CONCEPT CHECKS ✓

1. What three religious groups are the largest in the world?

2. What are the reasons so many Americans belong to religious organizations?

3. To what extent does the treatment of women reflect social conditions, and to what extent is it derived from holy writings such as the Bible and the Koran?

4. What is religious nationalism? Why can't it be viewed as a reaction to economic modernization of local religious beliefs and Westernization?

④ UNANSWERED QUESTIONS

The resurgence of religion throughout the world has posed some challenges to the sociological study of religion. For much of the early twentieth century, it was widely argued that the rise of science, technology, and the critical thinking associated with modernity would prove a decisive challenge to religious thought, which is based in large part on faith rather than scientifically acceptable standards of evidence. Yet religious beliefs, in all religions, have proven to be remarkably durable. This raises a number of important questions that have yet to be conclusively answered by the sociology of religion.

Is America Experiencing Secularization or Religious Revival?

According to Philip Hammond (1992), there have been three historical periods in the United States when religion has undergone **disestablishment**—that is, the political influence of established religions has been successfully challenged. The first such disestablishment occurred with the 1791 ratification of the Bill of Rights, which calls for the separation of church and state. Some sociologists see this separation as characteristic of the industrial societies of Europe and North America, in which different institutions specialize in different functions—from economics to medicine and from education to politics. Religion is no exception (Chaves, 1993, 1994; Parsons, 1951, 1960). The second disestablishment occurred between the 1890s and the 1920s, fed by an influx of about 17 million immigrants (mainly European), many of whom were Catholic. The long-standing notion of a predominantly Protestant United States was challenged, and the mainstream Protestant churches never fully regained their influence in politics or in defining national values. The third disestablishment occurred during the 1960s and 1970s, when the anti–Vietnam War movement, the fight for racial equality, and experimentation with alternative lifestyles eroded core religious beliefs and values. Fundamental challenges arose in areas such as sexuality, family authority, sexual and lifestyle preferences, women's rights, and birth control (Glock, 1976; Hammond, 1992; Hunter, 1987; Roof and McKinney, 1990; Wuthnow, 1976, 1978, 1990).

This disestablishment of religion brought challenges to the political influence of religion. Did it also mean that religion was less important to individuals, or that secular influences were on the rise? Even during the 1960s and 1970s, when the third disestablishment was at its peak, the religious beliefs of many Americans appeared to be stronger than ever (Roof, Carroll, and Roozen, 1995). For many people, religious beliefs became increasingly private as more people sought spiritual experiences outside established religious organizations (Roof, 1993; Wuthnow, 1998). In fact, the third religious disestablishment arguably contributed to the growing strength of conservative religious denominations, whose adherents reacted strongly to what they perceived as the bankruptcy of liberal theology. Conservative evangelicals effectively helped to shape public debate, bringing moral issues such as abortion, sexuality, and lifestyle into political discourse. While liberal theology dominated the mainline churches, conservative theology became increasingly influential in politics (Wuthnow, 1990). Beginning with the Reverend Jerry Falwell's Moral Majority in the 1970s, evangelical groups, especially those with fundamentalist values, have become increasingly involved in the Christian Right in national politics, particularly in the conservative wing of the Republican Party (Kiecolt and Nelson, 1991; Simpson, 1985; Woodrum, 1988). The Christian Right has emerged as a significant force in politics, waging what it views as the "culture wars" between liberalism and traditional religious values.

disestablishment • A period during which the political influence of established religions is successfully challenged.

How Resurgent Is Evangelicalism?

Evangelicalism, a belief in spiritual rebirth (being "born again"), is a response to growing secularism, religious diversity, and the decline of once-core Protestant values in public life (Wuthnow, 1988, 1990). Recent years have seen enormous growth in evangelical denominations in the United States, paralleled by a decline in mainstream Protestant religious affiliations—although Finke and Stark (2005) argue that "the trend of growing upstart sects and declining mainline denominations has been in place since at least 1776." Many Protestants are seeking the more direct, personal, and emotional religious experience promised by evangelical denominations. Although some evangelicals combine a modern lifestyle with traditional religious beliefs, others strongly reject many aspects of contemporary life. **Fundamentalists** are evangelicals who are antimodern, calling for strict codes of morality and conduct. These frequently include taboos against drinking, smoking, and other "worldly evils," a belief in biblical infallibility, and a strong emphasis on Christ's impending return to earth (Balmer, 1989).

Evangelical organizations have been especially effective at mobilizing resources to achieve their religious and political objectives. They have become extremely competitive "spiritual entrepreneurs" in the "religious marketplace" (Hatch, 1989). Some evangelicals use radio and television as marketing technologies to reach a wider audience, although the heyday of "televangelists"—preachers with huge television audiences who preached a "gospel of prosperity"—appears to have peaked. Still, the current large number of religious television networks includes the Christian Broadcasting Network, the Eternal Word Television Network, the Trinity Broadcasting Network, Sky Angel Faith and Family Television, and FamilyNet. Some scholars argue that these ministries are stronger today than ever before (Hadden, 2004). The 2010 U.S. Census reported that the number of people who self-identify as belonging to denominations that would be classified as evangelical grew from roughly 42 million in 1990 to 45 million in 2001, to 49 million in 2008, when they accounted for one out of every six adult Americans. Yet the vast majority claimed to be Baptist, a diverse denomination whose different churches are not always evangelical in nature. If Baptists are excluded, the number of self-identified evangelicals grew from 8 million to 13 million between 1990 and 2008—a 57 percent increase, but still comprising less than 6 percent of adult Americans (calculated from U.S. Bureau of the Census, 2012n).

The growth of evangelicalism may have peaked in the United States, but it is growing rapidly throughout the world, spurred by evangelical missionary zeal (Figure 17.3). In a 2011 survey of nearly 2,200 evangelical leaders throughout the world, only 44 percent of those who lived in the United States, Europe, and other advanced industrial countries expected that the state of evangelical Christianity in their countries would be better in five years than it is today; 33 percent expected it to be worse. U.S. evangelical leaders are the most pessimistic, with nearly half (48 percent) expecting things to be worse in five years, compared with only 31 percent who expected things to be better. By way of contrast, those who lived in Africa, the Middle East, Latin America, and parts of Asia were overwhelmingly optimistic about the future: 71 percent expected the state of evangelical Christianity to be better, while only 12 percent expected it to be worse. When

evangelicalism • A form of Protestantism characterized by a belief in spiritual rebirth (being "born again").

fundamentalists • A group within evangelicalism that is highly antimodern in many of its beliefs, adhering to strict codes of morality and conduct.

asked about the principal threats to evangelical Christianity, 71 percent of the global evangelical leaders cited the influence of secularism—including 92 percent of U.S. leaders (Pew Research Center, 2011d).

In 2010, 8 out of 10 white evangelical Protestants believed that religion's influence on U.S. politics and government leaders was declining. Almost all saw this as a bad thing—and while fewer than one in five viewed the Democratic Party as friendly to religion, slightly more than half viewed the Republican Party favorably (Pew Research Center, 2011d). The Tea Party movement, discussed in Chapter 13, represents an effort by political conservatives, many with strong religious roots, to exert influence through a Republican Party that more closely reflects their views. White evangelical Protestants have become a core constituency of the Republican Party, whose program reflects fundamentalist religious beliefs on such topics as opposition to gay marriage and abortion and a reduced role for government in the economy.

Is Religious Violence on the Rise?

It is important to remember that before the September 11, 2001, attack on the World Trade Center and the Pentagon by Islamist fanatics associated with Osama bin Laden and al Qaeda, the worst terrorist attack on U.S. soil occurred at the hands of a Christian fanatic. On April 19, 1995, Timothy McVeigh, a former U.S Army soldier who believed the United States was dominated by an anti-Christian conspiracy, ignited a truck laden with explosives in front of the Alfred P. Murrah Federal Building in downtown Oklahoma City. One hundred and sixty-eight people died in the enormous blast, including 19 children under six years old in the building's day-care center. Nearly 700 additional people were injured in the blast, which also damaged hundreds of other nearby buildings. McVeigh, who was later executed for the attack, believed he was waging a "cosmic war" against his version of the unfaithful (Juergensmeyer, 2008).

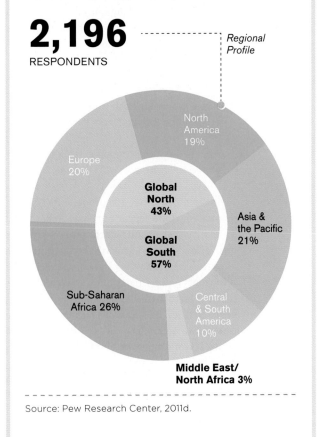

Figure 17.3
Profile of Evangelical Leaders Surveyed

Evangelicalism is fastest growing in the global south, where the number of evangelicals is now estimated to be greater than in the global north. North America—the United States and Canada—now accounts for fewer than one out of every five evangelicals in the world.

2,196
RESPONDENTS

Regional Profile

North America 19%

Europe 20%

Asia & the Pacific 21%

Global North 43%

Global South 57%

Sub-Saharan Africa 26%

Central & South America 10%

Middle East/ North Africa 3%

Source: Pew Research Center, 2011d.

Understandably, since September 11, many Americans have been concerned about the global spread of Islamic violence, a concern that contributes to false stereotypes about a relationship between Islam and violence, previously mentioned. How could Islamic religious views—or any religious views—give rise to such a culture of violence? Sociologist Mark Juergensmeyer (2001, 2008; see also Aslan, 2009) has come to a startling conclusion: Even though all major religious traditions call for compassion and understanding, violence and religion nonetheless go hand in hand. Juergensmeyer, who has studied religious violence among Muslims, Sikhs, Jews, Hindus, Christians, and Buddhists, argues that under the right conditions ordinary conflicts can become recast as religious "cosmic wars" between good and evil that must be won at all costs. He argues that a violent conflict is most likely to seek religious justification as a cosmic war when (1) the conflict is regarded as decisive for defending one's basic identity and dignity—for example, when one's culture is seen as threatened—and (2) when losing the conflict is unthinkable, although (3) winning the conflict is unlikely.

If any of these conditions is present, Juergensmeyer says, it is more likely that:

> a real-world struggle may be perceived in cosmic terms as a sacred war. The occurrence of all three simultaneously strongly suggests it. A struggle that begins on worldly terms may gradually take on the characteristics of a cosmic war as solutions become unlikely and awareness grows of how devastating it would be to lose.

In such instances, the proponents of cosmic warfare justify the loss of innocent lives as serving God's larger purpose. According to Juergensmeyer, bin Laden and al Qaeda exemplify such cosmic warfare in seeking to defend Islam against an all-engulfing Westernization. He also argues that responding to al Qaeda's violence with still greater violence runs the risk of showing the Islamic world that the conflict is indeed cosmic, particularly if the most powerful nations on earth become embroiled. Based on interviews with proponents of terrorism, Juergensmeyer concludes that this is just what al Qaeda wants—to be elevated from the status of a minor criminal terrorist organization to a worthy opponent in a global war against the West. This will increase the appeal of al Qaeda to a wider group of young Islamic men who blame the West for declining Islamic influence and growing hardships faced by many Muslims worldwide.

To what extent are bin Laden's views about "Westoxification" shared in the Muslim world? The Pew Research Center for the People and the Press (2003) polled 50,000 people worldwide in 2002 and 2003, not long after the September 11 attacks. Large majorities, including Muslims, reported that such things as television, the Internet, and cellular phones were making their lives better. (Pakistan, one of the world's largest Islamic countries, was a notable exception.) Most people (including most Muslims) felt that foreign TV, movies, and music were a "good thing" (again, except in Pakistan). At the same time, large majorities of Muslims and others also believed that their traditional ways of life were being lost and needed protection against foreign influence.

Although expressing concern that "there are serious threats to Islam today," the vast majority rejected suicide bombings and other forms of violence against civilians as a legitimate means of "defending Islam against its enemies." A recent Pew Forum on Religion and Public Life survey found very little support for al Qaeda in Muslim countries; favorable ratings for al Qaeda ranged from a high of 19 percent in Egypt, to a low of 2 percent in Lebanon. Fewer than 2 out of every 10 Muslims had a favorable view of the Taliban, the extreme group that imposed its strict views of Islam when it ruled Afghanistan before the U.S. invasion in 2003 and which is now fighting to regain control in Afghanistan as well as neighboring border areas in Pakistan (Pew Research Center, 2012e).

Bin Laden's belief that "Westoxification" is a serious problem calling for a violent solution is clearly not widely shared among ordinary Muslims.

CONCEPT CHECKS

1. How do sociologists explain the resurgence of evangelicalism in the United States in the late twentieth century?

2. Based on demographic trends, is the United States becoming more or less secular? Why?

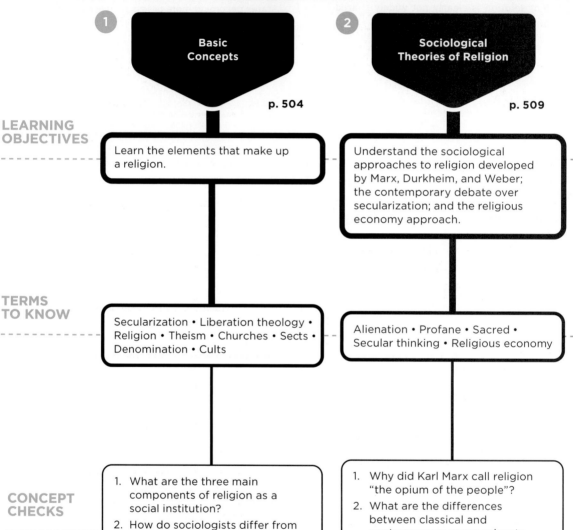

1 Basic Concepts

p. 504

2 Sociological Theories of Religion

p. 509

LEARNING OBJECTIVES

Learn the elements that make up a religion.

Understand the sociological approaches to religion developed by Marx, Durkheim, and Weber; the contemporary debate over secularization; and the religious economy approach.

TERMS TO KNOW

Secularization • Liberation theology • Religion • Theism • Churches • Sects • Denomination • Cults

Alienation • Profane • Sacred • Secular thinking • Religious economy

CONCEPT CHECKS

1. What are the three main components of religion as a social institution?
2. How do sociologists differ from other scholars in their approach to studying religion?
3. Describe four types of religious organizations.

1. Why did Karl Marx call religion "the opium of the people"?
2. What are the differences between classical and contemporary approaches to understanding religion?
3. Does the Pew study provide support for the religious economy approach? Why or why not?

1. Karl Marx, Émile Durkheim, and Max Weber had different viewpoints on the nature of religion and its social significance. Briefly explain the viewpoints of each. Which theorist's views have the most to offer in explaining the rise of national and international fundamentalism today? Why?

2. Drawing on this textbook's discussion, summarize the role of religion for most Americans today and assess whether religion is increasing or decreasing in importance for most people. Explain what it means for people to become more secular or fundamentalist in their religious practices. Are Americans becoming more secular or fundamentalist in their religious observances?

3

The Sociology of Religion: Current Research

p. 516

Know the forms religion takes in traditional and modern societies. Learn about sociological dimensions of religion in the United States. Recognize the changing interrelationships between gender and religion.

Monotheism • Polytheism • Civil Religion • New religious movements • Religious movements • Charismatic • World-affirming movements • New Age movements • World-rejecting movements • Total institutions • World-accommodating movements • Religious nationalism

1. What three religious groups are the largest in the world?
2. What are the reasons so many Americans belong to religious organizations?
3. To what extent does the treatment of women reflect social conditions, and to what extent is it derived from holy writings such as the Bible and the Koran?
4. What is religious nationalism? Why can't it be viewed as a reaction to economic modernization of local religious beliefs and Westernization?

4

Unanswered Questions

p. 536

Learn about the sociological debates surrounding trends such as fundamentalism, secularization, and religious violence.

Disestablishment • Evangelicalism • Fundamentalists

1. How do sociologists explain the resurgence of evangelicalism in the United States in the late twentieth century?
2. Based on demographic trends, is the United States becoming more or less secular? Why?

Part V

SOCIAL CHANGE IN THE MODERN WORLD

Throughout human history, the pace of social change was slow; most people followed ways of life similar to those of their forebears. By contrast, today's world is subject to dramatic and continuous transformation. In the remaining chapters, we consider some of the major areas of change.

The growing field known as sociology of the body addresses one of the most far-reaching influences of globalization. Chapter 18 examines how global processes affect our bodies, including diet, health, and sexual behavior.

The globalizing of social life both influences and is influenced by changing patterns of urbanization, the subject of Chapter 19. This chapter also analyzes the tremendous growth in world population and the increasing threat of environmental problems.

The concluding chapter explores some of the major processes of social change from the eighteenth century to the present, offers general interpretations of the nature of social change, and considers where global change is likely to lead us in the twenty-first century.

The Sociology of the Body: Health, Illness, and Sexuality

18

Physical aspects of our body, such as our body weight, how long we live, and the diseases we suffer from:

- **a** are due to our genetic makeup.
- **b** are a consequence of our personal choices.
- **c** are due to whether one can afford resources such as a healthy diet, medicine, and health insurance.
- **d** all of the above.

Turn the page for the correct answer.

If you answered *d*, you would be correct. Some of us might have answered *a*, thinking that our bodies are handed down to us through our genes; you might have a friend who says that she gets her slender physique from "her mom's side of the family," while another friend may say that he was "just born big-boned." Others might think the answer is *b*—that our bodies reflect our personal choices about what to eat and drink, or our willpower in getting up and going to the gym every morning. Students who have taken many sociology courses might think that *c* is correct—that social class, including where we live, the foods we can afford, and whether we have access to a doctor, affects our health and well-being. Each of these answers is partly correct in that each and every one of these things contributes to our health, leading us to the correct response of *d*. Aspects of our physical body, including how much we weigh, the diseases we suffer from, how long we live, and even aspects of our sexuality and sexual behavior reflect a range of social, biological, and economic factors, including our genetic makeup, the activities that fill our day, and even our beliefs about what constitutes a "beautiful" body.

To illustrate this point, let's think about a social phenomenon that many observers refer to as the "obesity epidemic" in the United States. Obesity is considered the top public health problem facing Americans today. **Obesity**, or excessive body weight, increases an individual's risk for a wide range of health problems, including heart disease and diabetes (Haslam and James, 2005). Yet excessive body weight may also take a social and psychological toll. Overweight and obese Americans are more likely than their thinner peers to experience

obesity • Excessive body weight, indicated by a body mass index (BMI) over 30.

LEARNING OBJECTIVES

① BASIC CONCEPTS

Understand how social, cultural, and historical contexts shape attitudes toward health, illness, and sexual behavior.

② THEORIES AND HISTORICAL APPROACHES TO UNDERSTANDING HEALTH, ILLNESS, AND SEXUALITY

Learn about theoretical perspectives on health and illness in contemporary society, as well as the approaches to studying sexuality throughout history.

③ RESEARCH ON HEALTH, ILLNESS, AND SEXUALITY TODAY

Learn about the social and cultural differences in the distribution of disease. Understand the causes underlying high rates of infectious diseases in developing nations. Learn more about HIV/AIDS as a sociological phenomenon. Explore the cultural differences in sexual behavior and patterns of sexual behavior today.

④ UNANSWERED QUESTIONS ON HEALTH, ILLNESS, AND SEXUALITY

Understand the debates over the relationships between health inequality and income, the relationships between traditional medicine and complementary and alternative medicine (CAM), as well as the debate about the importance of biological versus social and cultural influences on human sexual behavior.

employment discrimination, discrimination by healthcare providers, and daily experiences of teasing, insults, and shame (Carr and Friedman, 2005). Negative attitudes toward overweight and obese persons develop as early as elementary school. In one classic sociological study (Richardson et al., 1961), a sample of 10- and 11-year-old boys and girls were given six images of children and were asked to report how much they liked each child. The six drawings included an obese child and children with various physical disabilities and disfigurements. The obese child was ranked dead last—a finding that has been replicated many times in more recent studies (e.g., Latner and Stunkard, 2003).

Part of the reason why overweight and obese Americans are the targets of teasing and discrimination is that a thin ideal prevails today. Simply pick up a fashion magazine or turn on a television and it will be clear that, today, beauty is equated with slenderness. But this has not always been the case. In most premodern societies, the ideal female shape was a fleshy one. Thinness was not desirable, partly because it was associated with poverty, starvation, and illness. Even in Europe in the 1600s and 1700s, the ideal female shape was curvaceous—as evident in paintings by Rubens, for example. The notion of slimness as the desirable feminine shape originated among some middle-class groups in the late nineteenth century, but it became generalized as an ideal for most women only recently. As a result, even young girls who are genetically disposed to a fuller figure may work very hard to fight their biology as they strive to achieve a thin ideal (Haberstick et al., 2010).

Sociologists are fascinated with the puzzle facing our nation today. Negative attitudes toward overweight and obese persons persist, yet at the same time, these individuals currently make up the statistical majority of all Americans. According to the Centers for Disease Control, roughly 60 percent of adults are now overweight (see Table 18.1 for technical definitions of weight categories). More than a third of American adults (36 percent of both men and women) are currently obese (Flegal et al., 2012). This proportion varies widely by race; for example, 59 percent of black and 51 percent of Mexican American women are now obese, compared with just 36 percent of non-Hispanic white women (Flegal et al., 2012). An even more troubling trend is the increase in the proportion of American children and adolescents who are overweight. Between 1976 and 1980, just 6.5 percent of children (ages 6 to 11) and 5 percent of teens (ages 12 to 19) were overweight (National Center for Health Statistics, 2009). By contrast, in 2009–2010, 17 percent of children and adolescents were overweight (Ogden et al., 2012).

Table 18.1
What Is Your Body Mass Index?

People are classified into one of six weight categories based on their body mass index (BMI), which reflects one's current height and weight. BMI can be calculated using the following formula:

$$BMI = 703 \times \frac{weight \text{ (lb)}}{height^2 \text{ (in}^2)}$$

WEIGHT CATEGORY	BODY MASS INDEX (BMI)
Starvation	less than 16.5
Underweight	from 16.5 to 18.5
Normal	from 18.5 to 25
Overweight	from 25 to 30
Obese	from 30 to 35
Clinically Obese	from 35 to 40
Morbidly Obese	greater than 40

Source: National Heart, Lung, and Blood Institute, 2008.

Global Map 18.1
Percentage of U.S. Adults Classified as Obese (BMI > 30)

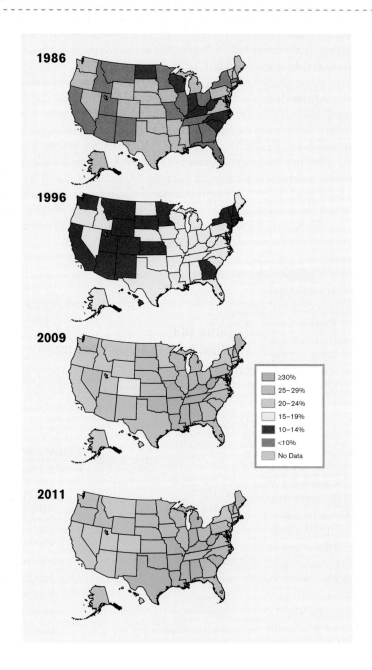

Source: CDC, 2010c, "U.S. Obesity Trends 1986 to 2009"; CDC, 2012e, "Prevalence of Self-Reported Obesity among U.S. Adults."

If body weight reflected biology alone, then we would expect that rates of overweight and obesity would be fairly constant across history—because human physiology has changed little throughout the millennia.

The reasons behind the obesity crisis are widely debated. Some argue that the apparent increase in the overweight and obese population is a statistical artifact. The proportion of the U.S. population who are middle-aged has increased rapidly since the mid-1980s, as the large baby boom cohort reached middle age. Middle-aged persons, due to slowing metabolism, are at greater risk of excessive body weight. Others attribute the pattern—especially the childhood obesity increase—to compositional factors. The proportion of children in the United States who are black or Hispanic is higher today than in earlier decades, and both these ethnic groups are at a much greater risk of becoming overweight than their white peers. Still others argue that the measures used to count and classify obese persons have shifted, thus leading to an excessively high count. Finally, some observers believe that public concern over obesity is blown out of proportion and reflects more of a "moral panic" than a "public health crisis" (Campos et al., 2006; Saguy, 2012).

Most public health experts believe, however, that obesity is a very real problem caused by what Kelly Brownell calls the "obesogenic environment"—or a social environment that unwittingly contributes to weight gain. Among adults today, desk jobs have replaced physical work such as farming. Children are more likely to spend their after-school hours sitting in front of a computer or television than playing tag or riding bikes around the neighborhood. Parents are pressed for time given their hectic work and family schedules and turn to unhealthy fast food rather than home-cooked meals. Restaurants, eager to lure bargain-seeking patrons, provide enormous serving sizes at low prices. A Big Mac is less expensive than a healthy salad in most parts of the country (Brownell and Horgen, 2004). The social forces that promote high fat and sugar consumption and that restrict the opportunity to exercise are particularly acute for poor persons and ethnic minorities. Small grocery stores in poor neighborhoods rarely sell fresh or low-cost produce. Large grocery stores are scarce in poor neighborhoods and in predominantly African American neighborhoods (Morland et al., 2002). High crime rates and high levels of traffic in inner-city neighborhoods make exercise in public parks or jogging on city streets potentially dangerous (Brownell and Horgen, 2004).

Policy makers and public health professionals have proposed a broad range of solutions to the obesity crisis. Some have proposed (unsuccessfully) practices that place the burden directly on the individual. For example, some schools have considered having a "weight report card," where children and parents would be told the child's **body mass index (BMI)**, in an effort to trigger healthy behaviors at home (Dogloff, 2010). Yet most experts endorse solutions that attack the problem at a more macro level, such as making healthy low-cost produce more widely available; providing safe public places for fitness, free exercise classes, and instruction in health and nutrition to poor children and their families; and requiring restaurants and food manufacturers to note clearly the fat and calorie content of their products.

First Lady Michelle Obama's Let's Move! is held up as an outstanding initiative because it includes programs to help children and their families maintain healthy lifestyles (White House, 2010). Let's Move! provides parents with the tools and information they need to make healthier food choices for their children; for instance, an updated food pyramid and new food package labels will help point consumers

body mass index (BMI) • A measure of body fat based on height and weight.

sociology of the body • A field that focuses on how our bodies are affected by social influences. Health and illness, for instance, are determined by social and cultural influences.

sociology of sexuality • A field that explores and debates the importance of biological versus social and cultural influences on human sexual behavior.

health • "A state of complete physical, mental, and social well-being and not merely the absence of disease or infirmity."

to healthy food choices. Increased funding for school lunch and breakfast programs, encouraging school food suppliers to deliver healthy low-fat and low-salt meals to schools, funding inner-city farmers' markets, and implementing programs to increase children's fitness levels are all steps that may help eradicate the childhood obesity epidemic. Only in attacking the "public issue" of the obesogenic environment will the private trouble of excessive weight be resolved (Brownell and Horgen, 2004).

Taken together, the "obesity epidemic" debate and its proposed solutions illustrate many core themes of sociology. First, they illustrate the ways in which a "personal trouble" such as suffering from obesity-related health problems also reflects "public issues" such as a social context that prevents poor individuals from buying costly low-fat foods or accessing public parks and other spaces that allow for regular exercise. Second, they reveal that social inequalities based on race, class, and geographic region can shape our bodies. Third, they reveal that there is no "single-bullet" explanation that can account for major social and public health issues; rather, the source of the problem often encompasses a range of biological, social, economic, and technological factors.

The study of body weight is just one topic investigated by sociologists specializing in the subfield known as **sociology of the body**. These scholars investigate how and why our bodies are affected by our social experiences and the norms and values of the groups to which we belong. Another central theme in the sociology of the body is the increasing separation of the body from "nature." Our bodies are affected by science and technology in diverse ways ranging from life-sustaining machines, to the chemicals in our food, to reproductive technologies. A closely related subfield, **sociology of sexuality**, explores and debates the importance of biological versus social and cultural influences on human sexual behavior, an important facet of sociology of the body. Only recently have sociologists recognized the profound interconnections between social life and the body. Therefore, this field is quite new and exciting. Using these two interrelated frameworks, in this chapter we analyze the social dimensions of health and illness in the United States and worldwide and examine social and cultural influences on our sexual behavior, identities, and practices.

THE ANSWER IS D.

 BASIC CONCEPTS

Before we can delve into theories describing the social and biological influences on health, illness, and sexuality, it is important that we first identify key terms and concepts.

Changing Conceptions of Health, Illness, and Medicine

What does it mean to be "healthy"? The simplest and most widely accepted definition is the one provided by the World Health Organization (1948): "**Health** is a state of complete

552 CHAPTER 18 The Sociology of the Body

physical, mental and social well-being and not merely the absence of disease or infirmity." In practice, however, cultures differ in what they consider healthy and in what they see as appropriate "treatment" for ill health. All cultures have known concepts of physical health and illness, but most of what we now recognize as medicine is a consequence of developments in Western society over the past three centuries.

In premodern cultures, the family was the main institution for coping with sickness or affliction. There have always been individuals who specialized as healers, using a mixture of physical and magical remedies, and many such traditional systems survive today in non-Western cultures. For instance, ayurvedic medicine (traditional healing) has been practiced in India for nearly 2,000 years. It is founded on a theory of the equilibrium of psychological and physical facets of the personality, imbalances of which are treated by nutritional and herbal remedies. Chinese folk medicine similarly aims to restore harmony among aspects of the personality and bodily systems, involving the use of herbs and acupuncture for treatment.

Modern medicine sees the origins and treatment of disease as physical and explicable in scientific terms. Indeed, the application of science to medical diagnosis and cure underlay the development of modern health care systems. Other features were the acceptance of the hospital as the setting within which to treat serious illnesses and the development of the medical profession as a body with codes of ethics and significant social power. The scientific view of disease was linked to the requirement that medical training be systematic and long term; self-taught healers were excluded. Although professional medical practice is not limited to hospitals, the hospital has provided an environment in which doctors can treat and study large numbers of patients, in circumstances permitting the concentration of medical technology.

On rare occasions, however, tensions may arise when physicians adhere to modern medical models and their patients adhere to folk or spiritual models of health. These cultural tensions are portrayed poignantly in the book *The Spirit Catches You and You Fall Down: A Hmong Child, Her American Doctors, and the Collision of Two Cultures* (Fadiman, 1997). The book recounts the experience of the Lee family, ethnic Hmong immigrants from Laos whose infant daughter had epilepsy. The Lees believed their daughter's illness stemmed from spiritual causes, while doctors believed the condition was biological and could be alleviated with anti-convulsive drugs. After trying to comply with a difficult medication regimen, the Lees stopped administering the drugs, and their daughter was placed in foster care, with tragic results.

Just as cultural beliefs about health and illness change across time and place, the very illnesses from which individuals suffer, and the illnesses' causes and cures, vary widely by sociohistorical context. In medieval times, the major illnesses were infectious diseases such as tuberculosis, cholera, malaria, and bubonic plague. Whereas the fourteenth-century epidemic of the plague, or Black Death, killed a quarter of the population of England and devastated large areas of Europe, infectious diseases have by now become a minor cause of death in industrialized countries, replaced by noninfectious diseases such as cancer and heart disease. Although in premodern societies the highest rates of death were among infants and young children, today death rates (the proportion of the population who die each year) rise with increasing age. The leading causes of death today, heart disease and cancer, disproportionately strike persons age 65 and older.

In spite of the prestige that modern medicine has acquired, improvements in medical care accounted for only a minor part of the decline in death rates before the twentieth century. Effective sanitation, better nutrition, water purification, milk pasteurization, control of sewage, and improved hygiene were more consequential (Dowling, 1977). Drugs, advances in surgery, and antibiotics did not significantly decrease death rates until well into the twentieth century. Antibiotics used to treat bacterial infections first became available in the 1930s and '40s; most immunizations (against diseases such as polio) were developed later.

Diverse Conceptions of Human Sexuality

Human sexuality, like health, illness, and medicine, is a complex concept, tightly tied to cultural beliefs and contexts. Judith Lorber (1994) distinguishes as many as 10 different sexual identities: straight (heterosexual) woman, straight man, lesbian woman, gay man, bisexual woman, bisexual man, transvestite woman (a woman who regularly dresses as a man), transvestite man (a man who regularly dresses as a woman), transsexual woman (a man who becomes a woman), and transsexual man (a woman who becomes a man). Sexual practices themselves are even more diverse. Sigmund Freud argued that human beings are born with a wide range of sexual tastes that are ordinarily curbed through socialization— although some adults may follow these tastes even when, in a given society, they are regarded as immoral or illegal. Freud began his research during the Victorian period, when many people were sexually prudish; yet his patients still revealed an amazing diversity of sexual pursuits. Freud's work notions underscore the complex ways that biology and social contexts shape human sexuality.

Among possible sexual practices are the following: A man or woman can have sexual relations with women, men, or both. This can happen with one partner at a time or with two or more partners participating. One can have sex with oneself (masturbation) or with no one (celibacy). One can have sexual relations with transsexuals or with people who erotically cross-dress; use pornography or sexual devices; practice sadomasochism (the erotic use of bondage and the inflicting of pain); and so on (Lorber, 1994). In most societies, sexual norms encourage some practices and discourage or condemn others. Such norms, however, vary across cultures. Homosexuality is an example. As we will discuss later, some cultures have tolerated or actively encouraged homosexuality in certain contexts. Among the ancient Greeks, for instance, the love of men for boys was idealized as the highest form of sexual love.

Accepted types of sexual behavior also vary between cultures, which indicates that most sexual responses are learned. The most extensive cross-cultural study was carried out by Clellan Ford and Frank Beach (1951), using anthropological evidence from more than 200 societies. Striking variations were found in what was regarded as "natural" sexual behavior and in norms of sexual attractiveness. For example, in some cultures, extended foreplay is desirable and even necessary before intercourse; in others, foreplay is nonexistent. In some societies, it is believed that overly frequent intercourse leads to physical debilitation or illness.

In most cultures, norms of sexual attractiveness (held by both females and males) focus more on physical looks for women than for men, a situation that may be changing in the West as women become active in spheres outside the home. The traits seen as most important in female beauty, however, differ greatly. In the modern West, a slim, small physique is admired, while in other cultures a more generous shape is attractive. Sometimes the breasts are not considered a source of sexual stimulus, whereas some societies attach erotic significance to them. Some societies value the shape of the face, whereas others emphasize the shape and color of the eyes or the size and form of the nose and lips. Although anthropologists and sociologists focus on cross-cultural differences in mate selection processes, evolutionary theorists emphasize universals, as these purportedly universal practices contribute to the continuation of the human species. For instance, research by David Buss reveals widespread male preference for a relatively low waist-to-hip ratio in women, as it can be seen as an indicator of a woman's reproductive fitness, or her ability to bear healthy offspring. Women, by contrast, are drawn to men with ambition and economic stability, which are considered indications of an ability to adequately provide for offspring (Buss, 2003).

SEXUAL ORIENTATION

Sexual orientation is an important component of human sexuality, because it involves the direction of one's sexual or romantic attraction. The term *sexual preference*, which is sometimes incorrectly used instead of *sexual orientation*, is misleading and is to be avoided because it implies that one's sexual or romantic attraction is entirely a matter of personal choice. As you will see, sexual orientation results from a complex interplay of biological and social factors not yet fully understood.

The most commonly found sexual orientation in all cultures, including the United States, is *heterosexuality*, a sexual or romantic attraction for persons of the opposite sex. In the United States, heterosexuals are also sometimes referred to as "straight." It is important to note that although heterosexuality may be the prevailing norm in most cultures, it is not "normal" in the sense of being dictated by some universal moral or religious standard. Like all behavior, heterosexual behavior is socially learned within a particular culture.

Homosexuality involves a sexual or romantic attraction for persons of one's own sex. Today, the term *gay* is used to refer to male homosexuals, *lesbian* for female homosexuals, and *bi* as shorthand for *bisexual*, which is used to describe people who experience sexual or romantic attraction for persons of either sex. Although it is difficult to know for sure because of the stigma attached to homosexuality, which may result in the underreporting of sexuality in demographic surveys, researchers estimate that approximately 4 to 8 percent of the population in the United States identifies as homosexual or bisexual (Gates, 2012; Laumann et al., 1994).

The term *homosexual* was first used by the medical community in 1869 to characterize what was then regarded as a personality disorder. The American Psychiatric Association did not remove homosexuality from its list of mental illnesses until 1973, or from its influential *Diagnostic and Statistical Manual of Mental Disorders* (DSM) until 1980. These long-overdue steps were taken only after prolonged lobbying and pressure by homosexual rights organizations. The medical community was belatedly forced to acknowledge that no scientific research had ever found homosexuals as a group to be psychologically unhealthier than heterosexuals (Burr, 1993). However, the DSM-IV continues to classify other aspects of sexuality as "disorders," including disorders of desire (e.g., low interest in sex), disorders of sexual arousal (e.g., lubrication and erectile problems), and orgasmic disorders (American Psychiatric Association, 2000).

In a small number of cultures, same-sex relationships are the norm in certain contexts and do not necessarily signify what today is termed *homosexuality*. For example, the anthropologist Gilbert Herdt (1981, 1984, 1986) reported that among more than 20 tribes in Melanesia and New Guinea, ritually prescribed same-sex encounters among young men

relation between populations and their environments, producing harmful effects on health patterns. The Europeans introduced new farming methods, upsetting the ecology of whole regions. For example, wide tracts of East Africa today are completely devoid of cattle owing to the uncontrolled spread of the tsetse fly, which multiplied as a result of the changes the intruders introduced. (The tsetse fly carries illnesses that are fatal to both humans and livestock.) Before the Europeans' arrival, Africans successfully maintained large herds in these same areas (Kjekshus, 1977).

The most significant consequence of the colonial system was its effect on nutrition and, therefore, on levels of resistance to illness as a result of the changed economic conditions involved in producing for world markets. In many parts of Africa, the nutritional quality of native diets became substantially depressed as cash crop production supplanted the production of native foods.

This was not a one-way process, however. Indeed, early colonialism also radically changed Western diets, having a paradoxical impact in terms of health. On the one hand, Western diets benefited from the addition of new foods, such as bananas, pineapples, and grapefruit. On the other hand, the importation of tobacco, together with raw sugar (which found uses in all manner of foods), has had harmful consequences. Smoking tobacco, especially, has been linked to cancer and heart disease. Thus, the diseases from which we suffer are shaped by not only human biology, but also complex macrosocial influences such as globalization, colonialism, and the development of technologies that foster the growth of particular crops.

Sociological Theories of Health and Illness

One of contemporary sociologists' main concerns is the experience of disease or illness—how individuals experience being sick, chronically ill, or disabled and how these experiences are shaped by one's social interactions with others. If you have ever been ill, even for a short period, you know that patterns of daily life are temporarily modified and your interactions with others change. This is because the normal functioning of the body is a vital, but often taken for granted part of our daily lives. Our sense of self is predicated on the expectation that our bodies will facilitate, not impede, our social interactions and daily activities.

Illness has both personal and public dimensions. When we become ill, not only do we experience pain, discomfort, confusion, and other challenges, but others are affected as well. Our friends, families, and coworkers may extend sympathy, care, support, and assistance with practical tasks. They may struggle to understand our illness or to adjust the patterns of their own lives to accommodate it. Many try to make sense of the illness or to figure out the cause of the health problem. Those we encounter react to our illness; their reactions, in turn, shape our own interpretations and can pose challenges to our sense of self. For instance, a long-time smoker who develops lung disease may be made to feel guilt or shame by family members, who provide constant reminders of the link between smoking and lung disease.

Two ways of understanding the experience of illness have been particularly influential in sociological thought. The first perspective, associated with the functionalist school, proposes that "being sick" is a social role, just as "worker" or "mother" is a social role. As such, unhealthy persons are expected to comply with a widely agreed-upon set of behavioral expectations. The second perspective, favored by symbolic interactionists, explores how the meanings of illness are socially constructed and how these meanings influence people's behavior.

FUNCTIONALIST PERSPECTIVES: SICK ROLE THEORY

The functionalist theorist Talcott Parsons (1951) developed the notion of the **sick role** to describe patterns of behavior that the sick person adopts to minimize the disruptive impact of illness. Functionalist thought holds that society usually operates in a smooth and consensual manner. Illness is, therefore, seen as a dysfunction that can disrupt the flow of this normal state. A sick individual, for example, might be unable to perform standard responsibilities or be less reliable and efficient than usual. Because sick people cannot carry out their normal roles, the lives of people around them are disrupted: Assignments at work go unfinished and cause stress for coworkers, responsibilities at home are not fulfilled, and so forth.

According to Parsons, people learn the sick role through socialization and enact it, with the cooperation of others, when they fall ill. As with other social roles, such as gender roles, sick persons face societal expectations for how to behave; at the same time, other members of society abide by a generally agreed-upon set of expectations for how they will treat the sick individual. The sick role is distinguished by three sets of normative expectations:

1. The sick person is not held personally responsible for his or her poor health. Illness is seen as the result of physical causes beyond the individual's control.
2. The sick person is entitled to certain rights and privileges, including a release from normal responsibilities. Since the sick person bears no responsibility for the illness, he or she is exempted from certain duties, roles, and behaviors. For example, a sick adult might be released from normal household duties; a sick child, excused from attending school. Behavior that is not as polite or thoughtful as usual or an unkempt appearance might be excused. The sick person gains the right to stay in bed, for example, or to take time off from work.
3. The sick person is expected to take sensible steps to regain his or her health, such as consulting a medical expert and agreeing to become a patient. In order to occupy the sick role, the sick person's claim of illness should be corroborated by a medical professional who legitimates the claim. Such confirmation allows those surrounding the sick person to accept the validity of his or her claims. Without such confirmation, the sick person may be viewed as a malingerer, or one who feigns health problems to avoid his or her obligations. A sick person who refuses to consult a doctor or who does not heed the advice of a medical authority puts his or her sick role status in jeopardy.

Over the past six decades, sociologists have refined Parsons's sick role theory. They argue that the experience of the sick role varies with the type of illness, since people's reactions to a sick person vary according to the severity of the illness and their perception of its nature and cause. Thus not all people will uniformly experience the rights and privileges that accompany the sick role. Eliot Freidson (1970) identified three versions of the sick role that correspond with different types of illness. The *conditional* sick role applies to individuals suffering from a temporary condition that ultimately will be cured. The sick person is expected to get well and receives some rights and privileges according to the severity of the illness. For example, someone with bronchitis would reap more benefits than someone with a common cold. The *unconditionally legitimate* sick role refers to individuals who are suffering from incurable terminal illnesses.

Because the sick person cannot do anything to get well, he or she is automatically entitled to occupy the sick role. The expectation that one will

sick role • A term associated with the functionalist Talcott Parsons to describe the patterns of behavior that a sick person adopts in order to minimize the disruptive impact of his illness on others.

seek timely medical care may be relaxed, because care seeking may be futile for some health conditions. The unconditionally legitimate role might apply to individuals with alopecia (total hair loss) or severe acne (in both cases there are no special privileges but rather an acknowledgment that the individual is not responsible for the illness), or with cancer or Parkinson's disease, which result in important privileges and the right to abandon many duties.

The third sick role is the *illegitimate* role, which applies when an individual suffers from a disease or condition that is stigmatized by others. In such cases, there is a sense that the individual might be partially responsible for his or her illness; additional rights and privileges are not necessarily granted. HIV/AIDS is perhaps the most vivid example of a stigmatized illness that affects a sufferer's perceived right to assume the sick role. Some AIDS patients may be held "responsible" for their condition and may be judged negatively for having engaged in high-risk behaviors such as unprotected sex or the use of unclean needles. Pediatric AIDS patients, those who contracted AIDS through a tainted blood transfusion, or other persons perceived to be "innocent" victims, by contrast, may be spared stigmatization.

Critiques of Sick Role Theory Although the sick role model reveals how the ill person is an integral part of a larger social context, a number of criticisms can be leveled against it. Some argue that the sick role formula does not adequately capture the *lived experience* of illness. Others point out that it cannot be applied across all contexts, cultures, and historical periods. For example, it does not account for instances when doctors and patients disagree about a diagnosis or have opposing interests. It also fails to explain illnesses that do not necessarily lead to a suspension of normal activity, such as alcoholism, certain disabilities, and some chronic diseases. Furthermore, assuming the sick role is not always a straightforward process. Some individuals who suffer for years from chronic pain or from misdiagnosed symptoms are denied the sick role until they get a clear diagnosis. Other sick people, such as young women with autoimmune diseases, often appear physically healthy despite constant physical pain and exhaustion; because of their "healthy" outward appearance, however, they may not be readily granted sick role status. In other cases, social factors such as race, class, and gender can affect whether and how readily the sick role is granted. The sick role cannot be divorced from the social, cultural, and economic influences that surround it.

The realities of life and illness are more complex than the sick role suggests. The leading causes of death today are heart disease and cancer, two diseases that are associated with unhealthy behaviors such as smoking, a high-fat diet, and a sedentary lifestyle. Given the emphasis on taking control over one's health and lifestyle in our modern age, individuals bear ever-greater responsibility for their own well-being. This contradicts the first premise of the sick role—that the individual is not to blame for his or her illness. Moreover, in modern societies the shift away from acute infectious disease and toward chronic illness has made the sick role less applicable. Whereas it might be useful for understanding acute illness, it is less useful for understanding chronic illness because there is no single formula for chronically ill or disabled people to follow. Moreover, chronically ill persons often find that their symptoms fluctuate, so that they feel and appear healthy on some days, yet experience disabling symptoms on other days. Living with illness is experienced and interpreted in multiple ways.

SYMBOLIC INTERACTIONIST APPROACHES: ILLNESS AS "LIVED EXPERIENCE"

Adherents to symbolic interactionist theories examine the ways people interpret the social world and the meanings they ascribe to it. Many sociologists have applied this approach to health and illness and view this perspective as a partial corrective to the limitations of functionalist approaches to health. Symbolic interactionists are not concerned with identifying risk factors for specific illnesses. Rather, they address questions such as: How do people react and adjust to news about a serious illness? How does illness shape individuals' daily lives? How does living with a chronic illness affect an individual's self-identity?

One theme that sociologists address is how chronically ill individuals cope with the practical and emotional implications of their illness. Certain illnesses require regular treatments or maintenance that can affect daily routines. Undergoing dialysis or insulin injections or taking large numbers of pills requires individuals to adjust their schedules. Some illnesses have unpredictable effects, such as violent nausea or sudden loss of bowel or bladder control. People suffering from such conditions often develop strategies for managing their illness in daily life. These include practical considerations—such as noting the location of the restrooms when in an unfamiliar place—as well as skills for managing interpersonal relations, both intimate and commonplace. Although symptoms can be embarrassing and disruptive, people develop coping strategies to live as normally as possible (Kelly, 1992).

At the same time, the experience of illness can pose challenges to and changes in people's sense of self. These develop not only through the reactions of other people but also through the ill person's perception of those reactions. For the chronically ill or disabled, routine social interactions become tinged with risk or uncertainty, and interpretations of common situations may differ substantially. An ill person may need assistance but not want to appear dependent, for example. A healthy individual may feel sympathy for someone diagnosed with an illness but might be unsure whether to address the subject directly. The changed context of social interactions can precipitate transformations in self-identity.

Some sociologists have investigated how chronically ill individuals manage their illnesses within the overall context of their lives (Jobling, 1988; Williams, 1993). Illness can place enormous demands on people's time, energy, strength, and emotional reserves. Serious illness can also tax the emotional resources of loved ones. Corbin and Strauss (1985) identified three types of "work" incorporated in the everyday strategies of the chronically ill. *Illness work* refers to activities involved in managing the condition, such as treating pain, doing diagnostic tests, or undergoing physical therapy. *Everyday work* pertains to the management of daily life, such as maintaining relationships with others, running household affairs, and pursuing professional or personal interests. *Biographical* work involves the process of incorporating the illness into one's life, making sense of it, and developing ways of explaining it to others. Such a process can help chronically ill people restore meaning and order to their lives.

Each of these processes of adaptation may be particularly difficult for those who suffer from a stigmatized health condition, such as obesity, alcoholism, HIV/AIDS, or lung cancer. Sociologist Erving Goffman (1963) developed the concept of stigma, which refers to any personal characteristic that is devalued in a particular social context. Stigmas typically come in one of three forms: "abominations of the body" (such as disfigurement, disability, or obesity), "tribal stigma of race, nation, or religion" (such as belonging to a historically denigrated racial or ethnic group), and "blemishes of individual character" (such as laziness, lack of personal control, or immorality). Stigmatized individuals and groups often are treated with suspicion, hostility, or discrimination. Some ill persons, particularly those marked by "abominations of the body," may arouse feelings of sympathy or compassion, especially if they are not held responsible for their illness. They may even receive special privileges. However, when a health condition is viewed as indicative of a "character blemish," such as sexual promiscuity or gluttony, then the healthy population may reject the sufferers.

For example, one study showed that adolescents offered much less critical appraisals of overweight persons when they believed that the weight was caused by a thyroid problem, and thus was due to a biological factor rather than to a character flaw such as laziness or lack of self-control (Dejong, 1993). Similarly, throughout history many infectious diseases, especially those contracted by the poor, often were stigmatized and viewed as indicators of shame and dishonor. This occurred in the Middle Ages with leprosy, when people were isolated in leper colonies. HIV/AIDS often provokes such stigmatization today—in spite of the fact that, as with leprosy, the risk of contracting the disease in ordinary situations is almost nonexistent. For instance, the Joint United Nations Programme on HIV/AIDS reports incidences in Kerala, India, when children infected with HIV have been barred from schools and denied any interaction with other children (U.N. Joint Programme on HIV/AIDS [UNAIDS], 2003). Stigmas are, however, rarely based on valid understandings or scientific data. They spring from stereotypes or perceptions that may be false or only partially correct. Further, the nature of a stigma varies widely across sociocultural contexts: The extent to which a trait is devalued depends on the values and beliefs of those who do the stigmatizing.

History of Sexuality in Western Culture

Just as particular diseases have been subject to stigmatization throughout history, sexual behavior has also been judged as "normal" or not across differential sociohistorical contexts. Western attitudes toward sexual behavior were for nearly 2,000 years molded primarily by Christianity, whose dominant view was that all sexual behavior is suspect except that needed for reproduction. During some periods this view produced an extreme prudishness, but at other times many people ignored the Church's teachings and engaged in practices such as adultery. The idea that sexual fulfillment can and should be sought through marriage was rare.

In the nineteenth century, religious presumptions about sexuality were partly replaced by medical ones. Most early writings by doctors about sexual behavior, however, were as stern as the views of the Church. Some argued that any type of sexual activity unconnected with reproduction would cause serious physical harm. Masturbation was said to cause blindness, insanity, heart disease, and other ailments, while oral sex was claimed to cause cancer. In Victorian times, sexual hypocrisy abounded. Virtuous women were believed to be indifferent to sexuality, accepting their husbands' advances only as a duty. Yet in the expanding towns and cities, prostitution was rife and often tolerated (Kuefler, 2007).

Many Victorian men—who appeared to be sober, well-behaved citizens, devoted to their wives—regularly visited prostitutes or kept mistresses. Such behavior was accepted, whereas "respectable" women who took lovers were regarded as scandalous and shunned in polite society. The differing attitudes toward the sexual activities of men and women formed a double standard, which persists today.

Currently, traditional attitudes exist alongside much more permissive attitudes, which developed especially rapidly in the 1960s. Some people, particularly those influenced by Christian teachings, believe that premarital sex is wrong; they frown on all forms of sexual behavior except heterosexual activity within marriage—although it is now more commonly accepted that sexual pleasure is an important feature of marriage. Others approve of premarital sex and tolerate different sexual practices. Sexual attitudes have undoubtedly become more permissive over recent decades in most Western countries. Movies and plays include scenes that previously would have been unacceptable, and pornographic material is available to most adults who want it (Kuefler, 2007).

EARLY RESEARCH ON SEXUAL BEHAVIOR: KINSEY'S STUDY

Much of what we know about human sexuality in the twentieth century is due to the path-breaking research of pioneering scientist Alfred Kinsey. When Kinsey began his research in the United States in the 1940s and '50s, it was the first major investigation of sexual behavior. Kinsey and his co-researchers (1948, 1953) faced condemnation from religious organizations, and his work was denounced in the newspapers and in Congress as immoral. But he persisted, thus making his study the largest rigorous study of sexuality at that time, although his sample was not representative of the overall American population.

Kinsey's results were surprising because they revealed a tremendous discrepancy between prevailing public expectations of sexual behavior and actual sexual conduct. He found that almost 70 percent of men in his study had ever visited a prostitute and 84 percent had had premarital sexual experience. Yet, following the double standard, 40 percent of men expected their wives to be virgins at the time of marriage. More than 90 percent of males had engaged in masturbation and nearly 60 percent in oral sexual activity. Among women, about 50 percent had had premarital sexual experiences, although mostly with the man whom they eventually married. Some 60 percent had masturbated, and the same percentage had engaged in oral-genital contact.

The gap between publicly accepted attitudes and actual behavior was probably especially pronounced just after World War II, the time of Kinsey's study. A phase of sexual liberalization had begun in the 1920s, when many younger people felt freed from the strict moral codes that had governed earlier generations. Sexual behavior probably changed, but issues concerning sexuality were not openly discussed. People participating in sexual activities that were still strongly disapproved of on a public level concealed them, not realizing that others were engaging in similar practices. The more permissive 1960s brought openly declared attitudes more into line with the realities of behavior. As we will see in subsequent sections, as research methods have improved, social scientists have been able to get a more accurate handle on adult sexual behavior. Yet as we will also see, the more things change, the more they stay the same. Even in the twenty-first century, some sexual behaviors continue to be judged harshly as "not normal," and some individuals continue to face stigmatization and discrimination due to their sexual behavior and preferences.

CONCEPT CHECKS ✓

1. Describe how the primary causes of death have changed between colonial times and the present day.

2. How do functionalist theorists and symbolic interactions differ in their perspectives on health and illness?

3. Describe several changes in sexual practices over the past two centuries.

4. What are the most important contributions of Alfred Kinsey's research on sexuality?

---

③ RESEARCH ON HEALTH, ILLNESS, AND SEXUALITY TODAY

The twentieth century witnessed a significant increase in life expectancy for people living in industrialized countries. Diseases such as polio, scarlet fever, and diphtheria have been all but eradicated. Infant mortality rates have dropped precipitously, leading to an increase in the average age of death in the developed world. Compared with other parts of the world, standards of health and well-being are high. Many advances in public health have been attributed to the power of modern medicine. It is commonly assumed that medical research has been, and will continue to be, successful in uncovering the biological causes of disease and in developing effective treatments.

Although this view has been influential, it is somewhat unsatisfactory for sociologists because it ignores the important role of social and environmental influences on patterns of health and illness. The improvements in overall public health over the past century cannot conceal the fact that health and illness occur unevenly throughout the population, both within the United States and across the globe. Research has shown that certain groups of people enjoy much better health than others. These *health inequalities* appear to reflect larger socioeconomic patterns.

Sociologists and scientists in social **epidemiology**—the science that studies the distribution and incidence of disease and illness within the population—have attempted to explain the link between health and variables such as social class, gender, race, age, and geography. While most scholars acknowledge the strong positive correlation between socioeconomic resources and good health, they do not agree about the nature of the connection or about how to address health inequalities. One of the main areas of debate involves the relative importance of individual variables (e.g., lifestyle, behavior, diet, and cultural patterns) versus environmental or structural factors (e.g., income distribution, poverty, and access to health care). In this section, we examine cutting-edge research on health patterns in the United States according to social class, gender, and race, and we review some competing explanations for those patterns' persistence. We also discuss current research on social and cultural influences on sexual practices and attitudes, with a particular focus on changing acceptance of homosexuality. We conclude by highlighting the ways our bodies—something we think of as "natural"—are increasingly shaped and affected by a further aspect of the macrosocial context: science and technology.

Social Patterning of Health and Illness in the United States

One of the most enduring patterns documented by social epidemiologists is the persistence of health inequalities, where members of those social groups with more status, prestige, power, and economic resources typically enjoy better health. Although we see some exceptions to this rule—for example, women currently live longer than men in the United States despite persistent earnings differences between the two groups—the social class and black-white gaps have remained persistent, and have even widened, over the last several decades. We now provide evidence of these patterns and offer explanations for why they persist.

SOCIAL CLASS-BASED INEQUALITIES IN HEALTH

In Chapter 8 we defined *social class* as a concept that encompasses education, income, occupation, and assets. In American society, people with more education, higher incomes, and more prestigious occupations have better health. What is fascinating is that each of these dimensions of social class may be related to health and mortality for different reasons.

Income is the most obvious dimension. In countries such as the United States, where medical care is expensive and many people lack

epidemiology • The study of the distribution and incidence of disease and illness within a population.

insurance, those with the richest financial resources have better access to physicians and medicine. But inequalities in health also persist in countries that have national health insurance, such as Great Britain. For example, the landmark *Black Report* revealed that social inequalities in health and mortality in the United Kingdom had not diminished since the implementation of the National Health Service (NHS) but had instead increased (Townsend and Davidson, 1982). Yet, part of this growing gap was due to improvements in mortality among the wealthier classes and not to declines among the lower socioeconomic groups. This suggested that the upper classes were making greater (or somehow "better") use of the improved access to medical resources. Thus we must think beyond income and consider the other dimensions of social class: occupational status and education.

Differences in occupational status may lead to inequalities in health and illness even when medical care is fairly evenly distributed. One study of health inequalities in Great Britain (Townsend and Davidson, 1982) found that manual workers had substantially higher mortality rates than professional workers, even though Britain's health service had made great strides in equalizing the distribution of health care. Indeed, different occupations are associated with different levels of health risks. Those who work in offices or in domestic settings have less risk of injury or exposure to hazardous materials. According to the U.S. Bureau of Labor Statistics, the ten most "fatal" jobs in 2011 were manual labor jobs, including fisherman, logger, trash collector, roofer, steel worker, farmer, truck driver, power line installer, and taxi driver. Each of these jobs is particularly susceptible to sudden or accidental death on the job (BLS, 2012g). Other jobs are hazardous because they expose their workers to dangerous conditions over time, ultimately leading to disease and death. However, industrial-based disease is difficult to calculate, because it is hard to determine whether an illness is acquired from working conditions or from other sources. However, some work-related diseases are well documented: Lung disease is widespread in mining, as a result of dust inhalation; work with asbestos has been shown to produce certain types of cancer (BLS, 2012g).

Education is also a powerful predictor of health, where those with higher levels of education have longer life spans than persons with fewer years of schooling. In recent years, the least educated Americans have actually experienced a reversal in life expectancy, while all other groups have experienced gains. High school dropouts not only die younger than persons with higher levels of education, but also have experienced an absolute decline in life expectancy, or the number of years they live, since the 1990s (Olshansky, Antonucci, and Berkman et al., 2012). What accounts for the steep educational gradient in life span today? Better-educated people are significantly more likely to engage in aerobic exercise and to know their blood pressure (Shea et al., 1991) and are less likely to smoke (Kenkel, Lillard, and Mathios, 2006) or be overweight (Himes, 1999). By contrast, poorly educated people engage in more cigarette smoking; they also have more problems with cholesterol and body weight (Winkleby et al., 1992). People with low levels of education also are less likely to have health insurance and more likely to misuse and even overdose on prescription medications (Tavernise, 2012). More highly educated people also respond differently to health threats. One study of smokers found that after suffering a heart attack, highly educated persons were much more likely than poorly educated persons to quit smoking (Wray et al., 1998).

Most social epidemiologists view education as the most important of the three dimensions of socioeconomic status in predicting health, because education is associated with a broad range of traits that promote positive health behaviors, including high levels of perceived control over one's environment (Mirowsky and Ross, 2005) and **health literacy**, which refers to one's capacity to obtain, process, and understand the basic health information and services needed to make appropriate health decisions (Zarcadoolas et al., 2006). Understanding one's health risks and having the means to do something about them are core components of the health belief model (Becker, 1974; Rosenstock, 1974), which provides a framework for understanding why some individuals participate in positive health behaviors and others do not. The model proposes that individuals' decisions to engage in positive health behaviors (or to change their health behaviors) are based on their evaluation of the possible threat posed by a health condition and the perceived benefits of and barriers to taking action to prevent getting the health condition. Both evaluating one's level of threat and developing a strategy to minimize risk are clearly shaped by social structural factors.

RACE-BASED INEQUALITIES IN HEALTH

Life expectancy at birth in 2008 was about 81 years for white and Hispanic females but just over 77 for black females. Likewise, life expectancy at birth in 2008 was almost 76 years for white and Hispanic males yet less than 71 years for black males (U.S. Bureau of the Census, 2012e). An even more startling gap emerges when early-life mortality is considered: Black infants have more than twice the mortality rate of white infants. Roughly 14 black infants per every 1,000 born in 2008 died in their first year of life, compared to fewer than 6 deaths per 1,000 for white and Hispanic infants (Mathews and MacDorman, 2012).

Racial differences in health reveal the complex interplay between race, social class, and culture. A powerful example of the multiple ways that race affects health is the Hispanic health paradox: Although Hispanics in the United States have poorer socioeconomic resources than whites, on average, their health—and especially the health of their infants—is just as good as if not better than that of whites. Blacks, by contrast, face economic disadvantages that are similar to those of Hispanics, yet blacks do not enjoy the health benefits enjoyed by Hispanics. Experts attribute Hispanics' health advantage relative to blacks' to cultural factors such as social cohesion but also to methodological factors. Studies of Hispanic health in the United States focus on those Latinos who successfully migrated to the United States; as such, they are believed to be in better health, or more robust, than those who remained in their native countries (Franzini, Ribble, and Keddie, 2001).

A closer inspection of blacks' health and mortality disadvantage further reveals the multiple ways that race matters for health. One of the main reasons for blacks' health disadvantage is that blacks as a group have less money than whites. In 2009 the median wealth of white households was 20 times that of black households and 18 times that of Hispanic households (Taylor et al., 2011). And the median income of a black man is only 67 percent of that of a white man (U.S. Bureau of the Census, 2009). Yet the differences in black and white health go beyond economic causes and reflect other important aspects of the social and cultural landscape. Consider racial gaps in mortality. Homicide victimization rates for all races have declined considerably over the past 15 years, yet the stark racial gap persists. The murder rate for young black males is currently more than 7.5 times higher than for their white peers (U.S. Bureau of the Census, 2011d). This rise in violent crime in the late 1980s accompanied the rise of widespread crack cocaine addiction, mainly affecting

health literacy • One's capacity to obtain, process, and understand basic health information and services needed to make appropriate health decisions.

poor African American neighborhoods plagued by high levels of unemployment (Wilson, 1996).

Other race-based inequalities in health status, health behaviors, and health care are also stark. There is a higher prevalence of hypertension among blacks, especially black men—a difference that may be partly biological. There are racial differences in cigarette smoking, with blacks smoking significantly more than whites. This may be due partly to cultural differences and to the cigarette industry's targeting of African Americans as a market.

Despite the persistence of such inequalities, some progress has been made in eradicating them. According to the Centers for Disease Control (CDC, 2010b), racial differences in cigarette smoking have decreased. In 1965, half of white men and 60 percent of black men age 18 and over smoked cigarettes. By 2008, 28.8 percent of white men and 33.7 percent of black men smoked. In 1965, roughly equal proportions of black and white women age 18 and older smoked (33 to 34 percent). This equivalence was preserved in 2008, with 26.9 percent of black and white women smoking.

Hypertension among blacks also has been greatly reduced, yet rates remain high. In the early 1970s, half of black adults between ages 20 and 74 suffered from hypertension. By 2008, roughly 42 percent of black adults over the age of 18 suffered from hypertension (CDC, 2011b). Despite the overall decline, this rate is still high and may reflect the currently high and rising rates of obesity among black women. Two-thirds of black women are classified as obese, contrasted with one-half of white women (Ogden et al., 2006), a pattern partly attributed to cultural differences in definitions of an attractive female physique (Hebl and Hetherton, 1998). By contrast, black and white men are equally likely to be overweight or obese. Black women also are far less likely than white women to exercise regularly, a pattern that most social scientists attribute to their hectic schedules of juggling work and family and the high costs of fitness programs and gym memberships (August and Sorkin, 2010). However, in 2011, U.S. surgeon general Regina M. Benjamin drew attention and some ridicule by suggesting that black women avoid exercise because it may ruin their hair; black women often spend much time and money on treatments such as hair relaxer (O'Connor, 2011).

Patterns of physician visitation, hospitalization, and preventive medicine also have improved, yet racial equity remains elusive. For example, black women historically have been less likely than white women to receive mammograms. This gap has narrowed in recent years, however. In 2010, roughly equal proportions of white (72.8 percent) and black (73.2 percent) women age 40 and older had received mammograms within the past two years (CDC, 2012a). However, some studies suggest that black women delay receiving mammograms, and thus those with breast cancer have their condition detected at a later—and more dangerous—stage of the disease's progression. Tumors in more advanced stages increase one's mortality risk and impede the effectiveness of potential treatments (Smith-Bindman et al., 2006). Thus, while some progress has been made in minimizing black-white differences in health, important disparities persist—reflecting the complex ways that biological, social, and economic factors shape health.

GENDER-BASED INEQUALITIES IN HEALTH

Women in the United States generally live longer than men—a relatively recent phenomenon. In the United States, there was only a two-year difference in female and male life expectancies in 1900. By 1940 this gap had increased to 4.4 years; by 1970, to 7.7 years. The gender gap declined to 5.0 years by 2008; women's life expectancy at birth is now 80.5 years, while men can expect to live 75.5 years. By 2015, demographers project that women and men can expect to live 76 and 81 years, respectively (Cleary, 1987; U.S. Bureau of the Census, 2012e).

The main reason for the gender gap is that the leading causes of death have changed since the turn of the century—and the main causes of death today disproportionately strike men. In 1900 the leading cause of death was infectious disease, which struck men, women, and children equally. Since mid-century, however, heart disease and cancer have been the leading causes of death for American adults. Both are influenced by lifestyle, diet, and behavior—all of which are shaped by the distinctive experiences of women and men in contemporary society.

Social explanations for women's mortality advantage focus on behavioral differences between men and women, including smoking, drinking, and preventive health behaviors. Men are more likely to smoke cigarettes than are women, and smoking is associated with heart disease and various types of cancer. Likewise, higher proportions of men drink alcoholic beverages, binge-drink, and smoke marijuana (National Center for Health Statistics, 2009). However, in recent years, female high school dropouts have experienced a decrease in life expectancy, due to poor health behaviors such as smoking, drinking, and prescription drug misuse (Olshansky, Antonucci, and Berkman et al., 2012). As a result, the gender gap in life expectancy has narrowed for those with the least education, yet this is due to declines in women's health rather than improvement in men's.

Sociologists also point to the ways that psychological factors contribute to the gender gap in health. Men historically have been socialized to equate risk with masculinity (Mahalik et al., 2007). Men also are less likely than women to seek regular preventive care, reflecting both women's need for regular checkups during their reproductive years (Bertakis et al., 2000) and men's belief that they should be strong, self-sufficient, and able to care for themselves, thus eschewing regular annual checkups (Springer and Mouzon, 2011).

Sociologists generally focus on societal factors in explaining the gender gap in life expectancy, but biological factors may also pertain. Disentangling the effects of biology from social context is very difficult, however, given that gender shapes one's social experiences from the moment of birth (see Chapter 10). One study from the 1950s used an innovative design in its attempts to identify the distinctive effects of biology versus social environment on mortality risk. The researchers focused on a subpopulation of men and women who were believed to have identical lifestyles, diets, and levels of stress: nuns and monks (Madigan, 1957). The nuns lived longer than the monks, and both had life expectancies essentially the same as that for the rest of the population. Because the living environments were equalized for the two groups, lifestyle elements such as diet, drinking, and stress could be ruled out as explanatory factors (Madigan, 1957). However, critics note that the monks smoked more than the nuns did, so that lifestyle differences were not entirely accounted for. Further, the study could not account for the gender-related lifestyle factors that existed prior to the time persons entered the religious order.

A number of studies spanning the fields of biology and epidemiology provide suggestive evidence that women have a biological advantage. Recent studies suggest that estrogen helps protect women against heart disease by reducing circulatory levels of harmful cholesterol, whereas testosterone increases low-density lipoprotein. Women also have stronger immune systems, in part because testosterone causes immunosuppression (Ness and Kuller, 1999).

Biologists have also cited genetic factors. Humans have 23 pairs of chromosomes, one of which determines sex. Males have XY sex chromosomes, while females have two X chromosomes. The X chromosome carries more genetic information than the Y, including some defects that can lead to physical abnormalities. Instead of making females more vulnerable to X-linked disorders, this seems to give females a genetic advantage. A female typically needs two defective X chromosomes for most genetically linked disorders to manifest themselves; otherwise, one healthy X chromosome can override the abnormal one. A male who has a defective X chromosome will have a genetically linked disease because there is no other X chromosome to cancel it out. This may account for the higher number of miscarriages of male foetuses, of male infant deaths, and of deaths at all ages due to congenital abnormalities and weaker cardiopulmonary systems (Hayflick, 1994; Hill and Upchurch, 1995). However, biology alone cannot explain gender difference in mortality, especially because this relationship differs substantially over time and across nations.

Despite the female advantage in mortality, most large surveys show that women more often report poor health. Women have higher rates of illness from acute conditions and nonfatal chronic conditions, including arthritis, osteoporosis, and depressive and anxiety disorders. They are slightly more likely to report their health as fair to poor, they spend about 40 percent more days in bed each year, and their activities are restricted due to health problems about 25 percent more than are men's. In addition, they make more physician visits each year and undergo twice the number of surgical procedures as do men (National Center for Health Statistics, 2008b).

There are two main explanations for this: First, women live longer than men; greater life expectancy and age bring poorer health. Second, women make greater use of medical services, including preventive care (National Center for Health Statistics, 2008b). Men may experience as many health symptoms as women or more, but may ignore their symptoms, underestimate the extent of their illness, or utilize preventive services less often (Waldron, 1986). As medical sociologists and epidemiologists look to the future, however, they question whether women's life expectancy advantage relative to men may start to erode as women increasingly take on stressful work roles and male-typed health risks (Olshansky et al., 2012).

Global Health Inequalities

We've just documented stark disparities in health and mortality in the United States. Yet when we step back and look at health through a global lens, we see even bleaker disparities. Some economically disadvantaged societies struggle to maintain basic living standards that are necessary for good health, such as adequate food, basic medical supplies, and clean water. Although the past two decades have witnessed major strides in reducing, and in some cases eliminating, infectious diseases—such as malaria—in the developing world, they remain far more common there than in wealthier nations in the West. The most important example of a disease that has almost completely disappeared is smallpox, which as recently as the 1960s was a scourge of Europe and many other regions. Campaigns against malaria have been much less successful. When the insecticide DDT was first produced, it was hoped that the mosquito, the prime carrier of malaria, could be eradicated. At first there was considerable progress, but this has slowed because some strains of mosquito have become resistant to DDT. An estimated 860,000 deaths occur from malaria each year; rates are highest in sub-Saharan Africa, and children are at a particularly high risk (Global Health Facts, 2009).

An obstacle to fighting disease in the developing world effectively is that basic medical resources are still lacking in many nations. The relatively few hospitals and trained doctors are concentrated in urban areas, where the affluent minority monopolizes their services. Most developing countries have introduced some form of national health service, organized by the central government, but the medical services are limited. The wealthy use private health care, sometimes traveling to the West for sophisticated medical treatment.

Conditions in many developing world cities, particularly in the shantytowns, make the control of infectious diseases very difficult: Many shantytowns lack basic services such as water, sewage systems, and garbage disposal.

Water and sanitation are critical factors for public health, yet many nations fall short on both dimensions. The World Health Organization and UNICEF (2012) report that in 2010, 780 million people lacked access to improved water sources, which represented 11 percent of the global population. Further, in 2010, 2.5 billion people lacked access to adequate sanitation, which represented 37 percent of the world's population. The vast majority of those without improved sanitation live in Asia and sub-Saharan Africa. These conditions are breeding grounds for diseases such as diarrhea, malaria, and trachoma, although the means of transmission varies based on the disease. For example, trachoma—an infectious eye disease that can cause blindness—is strongly related to lack of face washing, given the lack of water supply. This example vividly and sadly illustrates the powerful and varied ways that poverty affects health.

HUMAN IMMUNODEFICIENCY VIRUS (HIV) AND ACQUIRED IMMUNODEFICIENCY SYNDROME (AIDS)

A devastating exception to the trend of eliminating infectious diseases in the developing world is HIV/AIDS, which has become a global epidemic. More than 34 million people worldwide were living with HIV at the end of 2010 (UNAIDS, 2011). In 2009 alone, 1.8 million people died from AIDS-related illnesses (Avert.org, 2010). Using middle-range estimates, about 820,000 people are living with HIV/AIDS in Western and Central Europe, 1.5 million in North America, 1.6 million in Latin America and the Caribbean, and 22.5 million in sub-Saharan Africa (Global Map 18.2) (UNAIDS, 2010a). The main effect of the epidemic is still to come because of the time it takes for HIV infection to develop into full-blown AIDS.

The majority of people affected in the world today are heterosexuals. As of 2009, about half were women. In sub-Saharan Africa, young women are more than one and a half times as likely as men to be infected. Worldwide, at least four HIV infections are contracted heterosexually for every homosexually contracted case.

In high-income countries, the rate of new infections has declined, yet the demographics are striking. Just as we reported on racial gaps in infant mortality and life expectancy earlier in this chapter, we now highlight stark black-white differences in rates of HIV infection and treatment effectiveness. In the United States, approximately 50,000 people become infected with HIV each year, and roughly 1.2 million people are living with HIV infection (UNAIDS, 2010a). Although African Americans represent just 14 percent of the U.S. population, they account for 44 percent of new HIV infections. In 2009 the rate of new HIV infections among black men was 6.5 times as high as that among white men and 2.5 times as high as that among Hispanic men, while the rate of new HIV infections among black women was 15 times that of white and more than 3 times that of Hispanic women (CDC, 2011a). Heterosexuals accounted for 27 percent of new infections in 2009, while men who have sex with men accounted for another 61 percent. The remainder of cases are attributed to intravenous drug use (CDC, 2011a).

Although there was a steep drop in AIDS-related deaths after the introduction of antiretroviral therapy, African Americans are less likely than whites to benefit from such life-prolonging treatments. The Joint United Nations Program on HIV/AIDS reports that African Americans are half as likely as white Americans to be receiving antiretroviral treatment (UNAIDS, 2005).

Stigmatization of people with HIV/AIDS remains a major barrier to successful treatment. The stigma that associates HIV-positive status with sexual promiscuity, homosexuality, and IV drug use results in avoidance of HIV/AIDS prevention and treatment programs.

In the United States, 20 percent of people living with HIV/AIDS do not know that they are infected (CDC, 2012b). Part of the reason is the high level of fear and denial associated with being diagnosed as HIV positive. The stigma of having HIV/AIDS and the discrimination against people living with these infections are major barriers to the treatment of the epidemic worldwide. A 2002 survey found that 1 in 10 doctors and nurses in Nigeria have refused treatment to a person because of his or her HIV/AIDS status. In India, 70 percent of people living with HIV/AIDS have reported discrimination by health care workers (UNAIDS, 2003).

Although the spread of AIDS in Western societies has slowed, the opposite has been true in the developing world, where health education is limited and the medical establishment is poor. In low- and middle-income countries, the percentage of pregnant women who receive health care services aimed at preventing mother-to-child HIV transmission rose from 9 percent in 2004 to 59 percent in 2010 (WHO; UNICEF; UNAIDS, 2011). In 2009, 370,000

Global Map 18.2
The Number of HIV-Positive People around the World

The effect of HIV/AIDS will be greatest in sub-Saharan Africa. In 2009 alone, there were 1.8 million new HIV infections in sub-Saharan Africa; over three-quarters of all AIDS-related deaths occurred there. In Botswana, Namibia, and Swaziland, nearly 40 percent of the population is infected with HIV/AIDS.

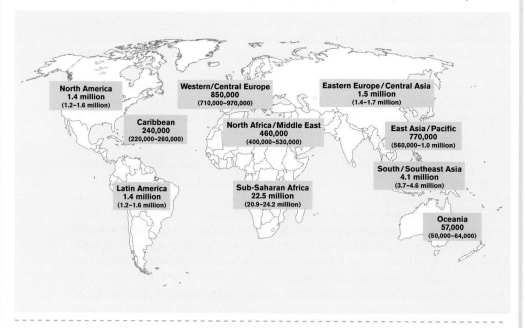

Source: UNAIDS, 2010a, "Report on the Global AIDS Epidemic."

children, a drop of 24 percent from five years earlier, were infected with HIV through mother-to-child transmission. Besides the devastation to individuals who suffer from it, the AIDS epidemic is creating severe social consequences, including sharply rising numbers of orphaned children. Frail older adults are increasingly called on to provide physical care to their adult children who suffer from AIDS (Knodel, 2006). Worldwide, the parents of an estimated 16.6 million children have died as a result of HIV/AIDS; 14.8 million are in sub-Saharan Africa (UNAIDS, 2010a). In Uganda alone, 77 percent of the population is under the age of 18; 30 percent of those are orphans (AIDS Orphans Educational Trust, 2003). In 2009 there were 1.2 million AIDS orphans in Uganda. The decimated population of working adults combined with the surging population of orphans sets the stage for massive social instability; economies break down, and governments cannot provide for the social needs of orphans, who become targets for recruitment into gangs and armies.

Contemporary Research on Sexual Behavior

Scholars who document patterns of health, illness, and sexuality in the current day owe a debt of gratitude to Alfred Kinsey; in the 1950s his research was pioneering in that it was among the first truly scientific studies of adult sexuality. Despite its methodological flaws, the work was pathbreaking in that it revealed the vast diversity in American adults' sexual preferences. Since that time, public interest in and research on sexuality have flourished. Part of this research and interest was driven by the cultural zeitgeist at the time. In the 1960s, social movements that challenged the existing order, such as those associated with countercultural lifestyles, broke with existing sexual norms. These movements preached sexual freedom, and the introduction of the contraceptive pill allowed sexual pleasure to be separated from reproduction. Women's groups also started pressing for greater independence from male sexual values, rejection of the double standard, and the need for women to achieve greater sexual satisfaction in their relationships. Until recently, it was unclear to what extent sexual behavior had changed since the time of Kinsey's research.

In the late 1980s, Lillian Rubin (1990) interviewed 1,000 Americans between the ages of 13 and 48 to identify changes in sexual behavior and attitudes over the previous 30 years or so. Her findings indicate significant changes. Sexual activity begins at a younger age; moreover, teenagers' sexual practices are as varied and comprehensive as those of adults. There is still a double standard, but it is not as powerful as before. One of the most important changes is that women now expect, and actively pursue, sexual pleasure in relationships—a phenomenon that Rubin argues has major consequences for both sexes.

Women are more sexually available than before, which most men applaud, but women also have a new assertiveness that men find difficult to accept. The men Rubin talked to often said they "felt inadequate," were afraid they could "never do anything right," and found it "impossible to satisfy women these days."

Men feel inadequate? Doesn't this contradict much of what this textbook has said so far? After all, in modern society, men still dominate in most spheres, and they are generally much more violent toward women than women are toward men. Such violence substantially seeks to control and subordinate women. Yet several authors argue that masculinity is a burden as much as a source of reward. Much male sexuality, they add, is compulsive rather than satisfying (Kimmel, 2003).

In 1994, a team of researchers led by Edward Laumann published *The Social Organization of Sexuality: Sexual Practices in the United* States, the most comprehensive study of sexual behavior since Kinsey. Their findings reflect an essential sexual conservatism

Looking AIDS in the face: Anonymous (covering face) is a student at Maputo University in Mozambique. Due to the extreme stigma he might face, he chose not to include any of his clothes in the photograph for fear of being identified. "I can't be identified because it may have a bad impact on my position as a university student. . . . Here in Mozambique there is discrimination promoted by the government. In one of his speeches the prime minister said Mozambique should not invest in educating people with AIDS as there is no hope for them. . . . If my faculty discovered my status . . . they would try all sorts of devious means to get rid of me."

among Americans. For instance, 83 percent of their subjects had had only one partner (or no partner at all) in the preceding year, and among married people the figure rose to 96 percent. Fidelity to one's spouse was also quite common: Only 10 percent of women and less than 25 percent of men reported having an extramarital affair during their lifetime. According to the study, Americans average only three partners during their entire lifetime. Despite the apparent ordinariness of sexual behavior, some distinct historical changes were revealed in this study, the most significant being a progressive increase in the level of premarital sexual experience, particularly among women. In fact, over 95 percent of Americans getting married today are sexually experienced.

In addition, sexual permissiveness among young people is much greater today than it was in the 1970s. According to the National Center for Health Statistics (2005), in 2003 nearly half (47 percent) of all high school students reported having had sexual intercourse, and 14 percent reported having had four or more partners. Both figures represent declines from 1991, when more than 54 percent of high school students had had sex and nearly 19 percent had had four or more sex partners. U.S. rates are far higher than those in Japan and China (Tang and Zuo, 2000; Toufexis, 1993). Youthful sexual activity varies widely, depending on teenagers' other characteristics, however. One study of the sexual behavior of American middle and high school students concluded that early sexual activity was higher among students from single-parent families, those of a lower socioeconomic status, those who demonstrated lower school performance, those with lower measures of intelligence, those who had lower religiosity, and, interestingly, among students with high levels of "body pride" (Halpern et al., 2000; Lammers et al., 2000).

Although documenting and monitoring the sexual behavior of young people remains a widespread concern even in the twenty-first century, researchers are increasingly documenting sexual activity among older persons. Older persons, once considered either uninterested in or physically incapable of having satisfying sexual relations, reveal high levels of both sexual activity and satisfaction. The National Social Life, Health, and Aging Project (NSHAP), a new study of sexuality among American women and men ages 57 to 85, reports that most married older persons have had sex in the last year. Although sexual problems do arise, they were reported by a minority of respondents. Women tended to report more sexual problems than men; commonly reported problems included lack of sexual interest, inability to climax, pain, and lack of pleasure during intercourse. Among men, by contrast, sexual problems included climaxing too early and performance anxiety (Lindau et al., 2007).

METHODOLOGICAL ADVANCES IN STUDYING SEXUAL BEHAVIOR IN THE UNITED STATES

Sociologists frequently use survey questionnaires to gain information on human behavior. However, obtaining detailed information on sexual behavior and attitudes is difficult. The two most comprehensive studies of sexuality in the United States—the Kinsey studies (1948, 1953) and the Laumann study (1994)—offer very different portraits of sexual preferences and behaviors. Do these conflicting results reflect historical changes in sexual mores, or are the differences an outcome of methodological approaches?

In stark contrast to Kinsey's results, which found that a high proportion of men had premarital or extramarital sex, in the Laumann study, 83 percent of survey respondents said they had had only one or no sexual partners in the year prior to the study. Moreover, only 10 percent of women and fewer than 25 percent of men reported ever having had an extramarital affair. It's possible that Americans have become more sexually conservative—perhaps from fear of AIDS and other sexually transmitted diseases.

An alternative explanation for the discrepant findings is the researchers' different methodological approaches. Kinsey, an evolutionary biologist, first gave a questionnaire about sexual practices to students in his zoology classes. Finding this method unsatisfactory, he next conducted face-to-face interviews and then focused on specific social groups. He and his colleagues eventually interviewed nearly 18,000 people.

Kinsey recognized that the ideal survey would be random, and thus results would represent the general population. However, he did not believe it was possible to persuade a randomly selected group of Americans to answer deeply personal questions about their sexual behavior. Consequently, his survey respondents were primarily college students living in sorority and fraternity houses, prisoners, psychiatric patients, and friends. To make his data more credible, Kinsey made every effort to interview 100 percent of the members of each group, such as all students living in a given fraternity house. Because Kinsey's data are based on a convenience sample, they are not representative of the American public. Moreover, many of his survey respondents volunteered to participate in the study. Thus they may have been different from nonvolunteers in having wider sexual experiences or a greater interest in sexuality. Further, many of his study questions asked about "lifetime" behavior or whether one had ever engaged in a particular practice; such a question will necessarily yield a greater number of positive responses than a question that focuses on a limited time frame, such as the past 12 months.

The Laumann study, in contrast, is based on data from the National Health and Social Life Survey (NHSLS). The NHSLS data were obtained from a nationally representative random sample of more than 3,000 American men and women age 18 to 59 who spoke English. In addition, Laumann's team purposely oversampled among blacks and Hispanics so that they would have enough members of these minority groups to analyze their survey responses separately with confidence that findings were statistically reliable and valid.

Recognizing that people are often hesitant to discuss sexuality, Laumann's team paid particular attention to choosing nonjudgmental language in their questionnaire. The team also built several "checks" into their questionnaire to ensure the veracity of responses. Several questions were redundant but were asked in different ways throughout the interview to gauge whether respondents were answering truthfully. The team also included eleven questions that had been asked previously on another national random sample survey of Americans. Comparisons of responses to the two sets of questions provided Laumann's researchers with assurance that their results were consistent with others' findings.

Although the Kinsey and Laumann studies are influential works on human sexuality, they also demonstrate that the process through which sociological knowledge is obtained can be as important as the actual research findings.

THE PERSISTENCE OF HOMOPHOBIA

The research we have reviewed so far reveals that Americans' attitudes toward human sexuality have grown increasingly expansive and open-minded throughout much of the twentieth and twenty-first centuries. Yet does this open-mindedness extend to all groups? Some contend that homophobia persists, and that gay, lesbian, and transgender Americans still do not enjoy the same rights and privileges as their heterosexual peers. **Homophobia**, a term coined in the late 1960s, refers to attitudes and behaviors marked by an aversion to or hatred of homosexuals, their lifestyles, and their practices. It is a form of prejudice reflected not only in overt acts of hostility and violence toward lesbians and gays but also in forms of verbal abuse that are widespread in American culture, for example, using words such as *fag* or *homo* to insult heterosexual males or using female-related offensive terms such as *sissy* or *pansy* to insult gay men.

One recent survey of more than 7,500 high school students found that nearly 44 percent of gay male and 40 percent of lesbian teens said they had been bullied in the previous year, compared with just 26 and 15 percent of heterosexual boys and girls, respectively (Berlan et al., 2010). Another study of homophobia in U.S. schools concluded that the estimated 2 million lesbian, gay, and bisexual middle and high school students are frequently the targets of humiliating harassment and, sometimes, physical abuse. Interviews with lesbian, gay, and bisexual students, and with youth service providers, teachers, administrators, counselors, and parents in seven states, found harassment to be a common and painful experience among lesbian, gay, and bisexual students (Bochenek and Brown, 2001).

Although some may discount teasing as harmless, this is a faulty assumption because verbal abuse often escalated into physical abuse. In one well-publicized incident, an openly gay Wisconsin student was verbally humiliated, spat

homophobia • An irrational fear of or disdain for homosexuals.

and urinated on, hit, subjected to a mock rape conducted by classmates in a science lab, and brutally beaten, suffering serious injuries. When he complained to the school principal after the mock rape, she reportedly told him that "boys will be boys" and that his open gayness was causing the problem (Bochenek and Brown, 2001). This unhappy student twice attempted suicide—a tragically common occurrence because lesbian, gay, and bisexual youths are at a four times greater risk for suicide than their straight peers (Gibson, 1989). Yet the vast majority of victims of homophobic violence never report the incident, for fear of being "outed" (New York City Anti-Violence Project, 1996).

The Stonewall Inn nightclub raid in 1969 is regarded as the first shot fired in the battle for gay rights in the United States. The twenty-fifth anniversary of the event was commemorated in New York City with a variety of celebrations as well as discussions on the evolution and future of gay rights.

Homophobia is widespread in U.S. culture, although it is slowly starting to erode. Public figures who use homophobic language are publicly upbraided. In 2007, when actor Isaiah Washington of the popular television show *Grey's Anatomy* referred to a gay costar as a "faggot," Washington was demonized by the national media and was released from his contract with the television show. That same year, the Gallup Poll found that 57 percent of Americans viewed homosexuality as an acceptable lifestyle (Saad, 2007), and in 2011, for the first time in its history, the Gallup Poll found that the majority of Americans (53 percent) supported gay marriage (Newport, 2011). While attitudes may be changing, public policy changes remain slow to catch up. It was in the very recent past (2003) that the Supreme Court ruled in *Lawrence v. Texas* that the state of Texas's prohibition on homosexual sex was a violation of the constitutional right to privacy, and in many states, homosexuality was still a legally punishable crime.

THE MOVEMENT FOR GAY AND LESBIAN CIVIL RIGHTS

Until recently, most gays and lesbians hid their sexual orientation for fear that "coming out of the closet"—publicly revealing one's sexual orientation—would cost them their jobs, families, and friends and leave them open to verbal and physical abuse. Yet, since the late 1960s, many gays and lesbians have acknowledged their homosexuality openly, and in some cities the lives of lesbian and gay Americans have become quite normalized (Seidman et al., 1999). Celebrities—ranging from pop singer Ricky Martin to news anchor Anderson Cooper—"came out" publicly, with little fanfare. New York City, San Francisco, London, and other large metropolitan areas worldwide have thriving gay and lesbian communities. Coming out may be important not only for the person who does so but also for others in the larger society: Previously closeted lesbians and gays discover they are not alone, while heterosexuals recognize that people whom they admire and respect are homosexual.

The current global wave of gay and lesbian civil rights movements began partly as an outgrowth of the U.S. social movements of the 1960s, which emphasized pride in racial and ethnic identity. One pivotal event was the Stonewall riots in June 1969, when New York City's gay community, angered by continual police harassment, fought the New York Police Department for two days (D'Emilio, 1983; Weeks, 1977). The Stonewall riots became a symbol of gay pride. In 1994, on the twenty-fifth anniversary of the Stonewall riots, 100,000 people attended the International March on the United Nations to Affirm the Human Rights of Lesbian and Gay People. In May 2005, the International Day Against Homophobia (IDAHO) was first celebrated, with events held in more than 40 countries. Clearly, significant strides have been made, although discrimination and homophobia remain serious problems for many lesbian, gay, and bisexual Americans.

There are enormous differences between countries in the degree to which homosexuality is legally punishable. As of September 2012, 11 out of 194 countries for which data are available allow same-sex couples to marry: the Netherlands (2000), Belgium (2003), Canada (2005), Spain (2005), South Africa (2006), Norway (2009), Sweden (2009), Argentina (2010), Iceland (2010), and Portugal (2010). Gay couples are allowed to wed in parts of Brazil and Mexico (Lambda Legal, 2010).Yet many other nations still ban same-sex relations. In Africa, male homosexual acts have been legalized in only a handful of countries, whereas female homosexuality is seldom mentioned in the law at all. In South Africa, the official policy of the former white government was to regard homosexuality as a psychiatric problem that threatened national security. Once the black government took power, however, it legislated full equality. In Asia and the Middle East, male homosexuality is banned in most countries, including all those that are predominantly Islamic. For example, as recently as 2012, four Iranian men were found guilty of sodomy and were sentenced to death. In contrast, Europe has some of the most liberal laws in the world: Homosexuality has been legalized in nearly all countries, and several European nations legally recognize same-sex marriages. (See Chapter 15 for further information on the legalization of gay marriage.)

Today there is a growing movement worldwide for the civil rights of gays and lesbians. The International Lesbian, Gay, Bisexual, Trans and Intersex Association (2007), which was founded in 1978, has more than 600 member organizations in some 90 countries. It holds international conferences, supports lesbian and gay social movement organizations, and lobbies international organizations. For example, it persuaded the Council of Europe to require all its member nations to repeal laws banning homosexuality. In general, active lesbian and gay social movements thrive in countries that emphasize individual rights and liberal state policies (Frank and McEneaney, 1999). Social change is occurring, slowly but steadily.

Reproduction in the Twenty-First Century: Pushing the Limits of Technology

Another area of research among contemporary scholars is the ways that science and technology shape experiences of the body. The development of technologies—ranging from reproductive technologies to the development of medications that help our mental health, physical health, and even sexual performance—has created a context where we have much more control over our bodies today than in the past. Yet this "control" presents us with both exciting possibilities and new anxieties and problems. All this is part of what sociologists call the **socialization of nature**—a process in which phenomena that used to be "natural" or given in nature become social, in that they depend on our personal decisions.

Childbirth is a key example. Giving birth is often described as a "natural" and "beautiful" part of life. For hundreds of years, most women's lives were dominated by childbirth and child rearing. In premodern times, contraception was ineffective or unknown. Even in Europe and the United States as late as the eighteenth century, women commonly experienced as many as 20 pregnancies (often involving miscarriages and infant deaths). Today, owing to improved methods of contraception, women in industrialized countries no longer have so many pregnancies. Advances in contraceptive technology enable most women and men to control whether and when to have children. Contraception is only one **procreative technology**. In recent years, women who delay childbearing until their thirties and older turn to technologies that enhance, rather than limit, their reproductive behavior. This and other areas in which natural processes have become social are described here.

CHILDBIRTH

The medicalization of pregnancy and childbirth developed slowly, as obstetric specialists replaced local physicians and midwives. Today in industrialized societies, most births occur in a hospital, with the help of a specialized medical team.

In the past, new parents had to wait until the birth to learn the sex of their baby and whether it would be healthy. Today, prenatal tests such as the sonogram (an image of the fetus produced by ultrasonic waves) and amniocentesis (which samples amniotic fluid from around the fetus) can reveal structural or chromosomal abnormalities before birth. Such new technology introduces new ethical and legal decisions. For example, when a disorder is detected, the couple must decide whether to have the baby, knowing it may be seriously disabled.

Prospective parents also are turning to technologies that increase their chances of conceiving a child. Fertility drugs, in vitro fertilization (IVF), artificial insemination, and hormone treatments are among the technologies that are assisting reproductively challenged couples in their desire to start a family. The use of such technologies also is altering the nature of family life; the number of twins born in the United States increased by roughly 50 percent, and the number of triplet or higher-number births soared by 404 percent, between 1980 and 1997 (Martin and Park, 1999). This rise in multiple births is partially explained by the growing popularity of fertility drugs such as clomiphene and procedures such as in vitro fertilization, which result in multiple births more frequently than unassisted fertilizations do.

GENETIC ENGINEERING: DESIGNER BABIES

Considerable scientific resources are being devoted to intervening in the genetic makeup of the fetus to influence its subsequent development. The likely social effect of such genetic engineering is provoking debates almost as intense as those over abortion. According to supporters, genetic engineering will bring many benefits—for example, identifying the genetic factors that make some people vulnerable to certain diseases. Genetic reprogramming would ensure that these illnesses no longer passed from generation to generation. It would be possible to "design" our children's bodies before birth in terms of skin color, hair and eye color, weight, and so forth.

socialization of nature • A process in which phenomena that used to be "natural" or given in nature become social, in that they depend on our personal decisions.

procreative technology • Techniques for influencing the human reproductive process.

This issue is a prime example of the opportunities and problems that the increasing socialization of nature creates. What choices will parents make if they can design their babies, and what limits should be placed on those choices? Genetic engineering is unlikely to be cheap. Will this mean that those who can afford to pay will program out from their children any traits they see as socially undesirable? What will happen to the children of more deprived groups, who will continue to be born unaltered?

Some sociologists argue that differential access to genetic engineering might lead to the emergence of a "biological underclass." Those who don't have the physical advantages genetic engineering can bring might be subject to prejudice and discrimination and might have difficulty finding employment and life or health insurance (Duster, 1990).

THE ABORTION DEBATE

The most controversial ethical dilemma created by modern reproductive technologies is abortion. Under what conditions should abortion be available to women? The abortion debate has become highly intense because it centers on basic ethical questions to which there are no easy solutions. Those who are "pro-life" believe that abortion is always wrong except in extreme circumstances, because it is equivalent to murder. For them, ethical issues must be subject to the value placed on human life. Those who are "pro-choice" argue that the woman's control over her own body—her own right to live a rewarding life—must be the primary consideration.

The debate has led to numerous episodes of violence, including the 1998 murder of obstetrician Barnett Slepian in Buffalo, New York. Slepian had been one of just three doctors in the area who performed abortions. Can this debate ever be resolved? One prominent social and legal theorist, Ronald Dworkin (1993), has suggested that it can. The intense divisions between those who are pro-life and those who are pro-choice, he argues, hide deeper areas of agreement between the two sides, and therein is a source of hope. In current times, we place a high value on the sanctity of human life. Each side agrees with this value but interprets it differently— the one emphasizing the interests of the child, the other the interests of the woman. If the two sides can be persuaded that they share a common ethical value, a more constructive dialogue may be possible.

CONCEPT CHECKS ✓

1. How do race, class, and gender affect health?
2. Why are infectious diseases more common in developing nations than in the United States today?
3. Describe patterns of adolescent sexual behavior in contemporary U.S. society.
4. Provide two pieces of evidence that homophobia has declined in recent decades.
5. Describe two ways that the development of new technologies has led to the "socialization of nature."

4 UNANSWERED QUESTIONS ON HEALTH, ILLNESS, AND SEXUALITY

As you have learned throughout this chapter, the sociological study of the body and sexuality is a fascinating and rapidly evolving field. Each day, social scientists struggle with new and vexing questions about the ways that social, biological, technological, economic, and cultural forces transpire to promote (or constrain) physical and sexual well-being. We briefly describe here four unanswered questions that sociologists are now investigating, using the most sophisticated data, methods, and conceptual models.

Does Income Inequality Threaten Health?

As we learned in Chapter 8, the distribution of income in the United States is highly unequal, and this disparity is widening. In 2010 the top 5 percent of households in the United States received 21.3 percent of total income; the highest 20 percent obtained 50.2 percent; and the bottom 20 percent received only 3.3 percent (U.S. Bureau of the Census, 2012o).Some researchers have argued that societies with a vastly unequal distribution of economic resources are unhealthy societies, and that disparities take a toll on all.

British researcher Richard Wilkinson (1996) is one of the most vocal advocates of the argument that the healthiest societies are not necessarily the richest ones, but those in which income is distributed most evenly and levels of social integration are highest. In surveying empirical data from countries worldwide, Wilkinson notes a clear relationship between mortality rates and patterns of income distribution. Inhabitants of countries such as Japan and Sweden, which are among the most egalitarian societies in the world, enjoy better levels of health than do citizens of countries with a more pronounced gap between rich and poor, such as the United States. In Wilkinson's view, the widening gap in income distribution undermines social cohesion and makes it more difficult for people to manage risks and challenges. Wilkinson argues that social factors—the strength of social contacts, ties within communities, a sense of security—are the main determinants of the health of a society.

Wilkinson's thesis—that income inequality harms health—has provoked energetic responses. Some claim that his work should become required reading for policy makers and politicians. They agree that the drive toward prosperity has failed many members of society; it is time to consider more humane and socially responsible policies to support those who are disadvantaged (Kawachi and Kennedy, 1997). Others criticize his study on methodological grounds and argue that he has not demonstrated a clear causal relationship between income inequality and poor health (Judge, 1995). Illness, critics contend, could be caused by any number of other factors. They argue that the empirical evidence for Wilkinson's claims remains suggestive at best.

Yet two very recent studies may help to successfully resolve this debate. Zheng (2012) tracked income inequality in the United States from 1986 through 2004 and then examined whether these trends predicted increases in poor health and mortality several years into the future. This approach allowed him to address the main concern raised by Wilkinson's critics—that he had not effectively established causal ordering. Zheng found that for every .01 increase in the **Gini coefficient**—a standard measure of a country's economic disparity where 0 represents perfect equality and 1 represents maximum inequality—an average person's cumulative risk of death increased by 112 percent over the next 12 years. Zheng (2009) also found that a dramatic increase in income inequality between 1972 and 2004 increased Americans' perceptions that their health was suffering.

Although scholars and policy makers may find Zheng's research to be compelling evidence that income inequality undermines health, we still don't know the reasons for this. Some scholars have hypothesized that in countries with rising

Gini coefficient • A standard measure of a country's economic disparity where 0 represents perfect equality (everyone has the same income) and 1 represents maximum inequality.

income inequality, the interests of the wealthy tend to diverge from those of the rest of society. The wealthiest people may push government for more services for themselves, rather than invest in public goods such as education or affordable medical services—services that can affect health for the majority of people (Zheng, 2009, 2012). Others argue that inequality may create a culture of upward comparison, where many people see the lifestyles of the rich and feel they can't live up to expectations. This can lead to negative views of oneself, frustration, and depression, which have been linked to sickness and mortality (Kawachi and Kennedy, 1997).

Is Alternative Medicine as Effective as "Traditional" Medicine?

Actress and television host Jenny McCarthy made headlines in 2007 when she refused doctors' advice for how to treat her autistic son. Instead, she worked with nutritionists and placed her son, Evan, on a strict gluten- and casein-free diet, in the hope that it would minimize his autism symptoms. Alternative therapies, such as the one McCarthy followed, are being explored by a record high number of people today and are slowly gaining acceptance by the mainstream medical community. Physicians increasingly believe that such unorthodox therapies may be an important complement to (although not a substitute for) traditional medicine, provided they are held to rigorous scientific evaluation. Yet devoted adherents to nontraditional health regimens believe that such practices are effective and that their personal experiences are more meaningful than are the results of controlled trials. Which position, if either, is correct?

Medical sociologists refer to such unorthodox medical practices as **complementary and alternative medicine (CAM)**. CAM encompasses a diverse set of approaches and therapies for treating illness and promoting well-being that generally falls outside standard medical practices. These approaches are usually not taught in medical schools and not practiced by physicians or other professionals trained in medical programs. However, in recent years several medical and nursing schools have started offering courses in alternative medicine (Fenton and Morris, 2003; Wetzel et al., 1998). Examples of common CAM therapies include chiropractic, massage, deep breathing techniques, homeopathy, reflexology, herbal remedies, and acupuncture. Complementary medicine is distinct from alternative medicine in that the former is meant to be used in conjunction with medical procedures to increase their efficacy or reduce side effects, while the latter is meant to be used in place of standard medical procedures (Saks, 1992). Many people use CAM approaches in addition to, rather than in place of, orthodox treatments (although some alternative approaches, such as homeopathy, reject the basis of orthodox medicine entirely).

Industrialized countries have some of the best-developed, best-resourced medical facilities in the world. Why, then, are a growing number of people exploring treatments that have not yet proven effective in controlled clinical trials, such as aromatherapy and hypnotherapy? It has been estimated that as many as 1 in 10 Americans has at some time consulted an alternative practitioner. An even larger proportion of Americans have sought out CAM treatments on their own. A recent survey found that 38 percent of all Americans said that they had used some form of CAM in 2007. The profile of the typical individual who seeks alternative forms of healing is female, middle-aged, and middle class. Whites

complementary and alternative medicine (CAM) • A diverse set of approaches and therapies for treating illness and promoting well-being that generally falls outside standard medical practices.

and Native Americans are most likely to use such treatments. The most common reasons people use such treatments are back, neck, and joint pain (Barnes, Bloom, and Nahin, 2008).

There are many reasons for seeking the services of an alternative medicine practitioner or pursuing CAM regimens on one's own. Some people perceive orthodox medicine to be deficient or ineffective in relieving chronic pain or symptoms of stress and anxiety. Others are dissatisfied with features of modern health care systems such as long waits, referrals through chains of specialists, and financial restrictions. Connected to this are concerns about the harmful side effects of medication and the intrusiveness of surgery, both staples of modern Western medicine. The asymmetrical power relationship between doctors and patients also drives some people to seek alternative medicine. Those people feel that the role of the passive patient does not grant them enough input into their own treatment and healing. Finally, some individuals profess religious or philosophical objections to orthodox medicine, which treats the mind and body separately. They believe that orthodox medicine often overlooks the spiritual and psychological dimensions of health and illness. All these concerns are critiques of the **biomedical model of health** (the foundation of the Western medical establishment), which defines disease in objective terms and believes that scientifically based medical treatment can restore the body to health (Beyerstein, 1999).

The growth of alternative medicine is a fascinating reflection of the transformations occurring within modern societies. We are living in an age where much more information is available to draw on in making choices. The proliferation of health-related websites such as WebMD and MedicineNet provides instant access to information on health symptoms and treatments. Thus individuals are increasingly becoming health consumers, adopting an active stance toward their own health and well-being. Not only are we choosing the type of practitioners to consult, but we are also demanding more involvement in our own care and treatment.

Members of the traditional medical community, once viewed as completely resistant to the notion of alternative medicine, are increasingly taking a more open-minded approach to such therapies. Many now cautiously endorse patients' desires to consult an ever-expanding array of medical information. However, medical leaders believe that CAM should be treated to the same level of scientific scrutiny as traditional medicine: It should be held up to rigorous scientific evaluation. Former editors of *The New England Journal of Medicine* Marcia Angell and Jerome Kassirer (1998) have observed that "many alternative remedies have recently found their way into the medical mainstream. . . . There cannot be two kinds of medicine—conventional and alternative. There is only medicine that has been adequately tested and medicine that has not, medicine that works and medicine that may or may not work. Once a treatment has been tested rigorously, it no longer matters whether it was considered alternative at the outset. If it is found to be reasonably safe and effective, it will be accepted." Most experts conclude that alternative medicine is unlikely to overtake mainstream health care altogether, but that its usage will continue to grow.

Why Are Eating Disorders a "Women's" Problem?

We learned earlier in this chapter that one of the most serious concerns threatening the health of Americans today is the obesity epidemic. Yet

biomedical model of health • The set of principles underpinning Western medical systems and practices. The biomedical model of health defines diseases objectively, in accordance with the presence of recognized symptoms, and believes that the healthy body can be restored through scientifically based medical treatment. The human body is likened to a machine that can be returned to working order with the proper repairs.

as college students, you may notice that some of your classmates are dieting or exercising excessively, striving to look like the models gracing the covers of fashion magazines such as *Vogue*. You may think that another equally important body weight issue faces our nation: excessive slenderness and eating disorders such as anorexia nervosa and bulimia. Anorexia and bulimia are serious social problems, and ones that disproportionately strike women—but why?

It's important first to step back and consider the history of such conditions. Anorexia, an eating disorder characterized by extreme food restriction and an irrational fear of gaining weight, is thought of as a contemporary social problem, but the condition was first identified as a disorder in France in 1874. It remained obscure until the past 30 or 40 years and has since become increasingly common among young women (Brown and Jasper, 1993). So has bulimia—bingeing on large portions of food, followed by self-induced vomiting. Anorexia and bulimia often occur in the same individual. A recent study estimates that 1.3 million women and 450,000 men suffer from anorexia, 2.25 million women and 750,000 men suffer from bulimia, and 5.25 million women and 3.0 million men suffer from binge eating. A total of 11 million Americans, or about 3.7 percent of the population, suffer from one or more forms of eating disorders (Eating Disorders Coalition [EDC], 2009).

Anorexia has the highest mortality rate of any psychological disorder; 20 percent of anorexics will die from it (EDC, 2009). Once a young woman starts to diet and exercise compulsively, she can become locked into a pattern of refusing food or vomiting up what she has eaten. As the body loses muscle mass, it loses heart muscle, so the heart gets smaller and weaker, which ultimately leads to heart failure. About half of all anorexics also have low white blood cell counts, and about a third are anemic. Both conditions can lower the immune system's resistance to disease, leaving an anorexic vulnerable to infections. However, these harmful patterns may be broken through psychotherapy and medical treatment.

These harmful consequences are particularly devastating when one considers that the occurrence of eating disorders in the United States has doubled since 1960 (EDC, 2009). On any given day, 25 percent of men and 45 percent of women are dieting; Americans spend over $40 billion each year on dieting and dieting-related products (National Eating Disorders Association, 2002). About 95 percent of U.S. college women say they want to lose weight, and up to 85 percent suffer serious problems with eating disorders during their college years. Around 25 percent experience bulimic episodes or anorexia. In American society, 60 percent of girls age 13 have already begun to diet; this proportion rises to over 80 percent for women age 18. College men suffer similar experiences, but to a lesser extent. About 50 percent of American male college students want to lose weight, while about 30 percent are on diets (Hesse-Biber, 1997). Over 80 percent of 10-year-old children are afraid of being fat (EDC, 2003).

Obsession with slenderness—and the resulting eating disorders—extends beyond the United States and Europe. Fashion magazines today regularly show images of models who are severely underweight, yet they uphold these women as paragons of beauty. The average fashion model today is 23 percent thinner than the average American woman, yet 25 years ago that number was 8 percent (Derenne and Beresin, 2006). As Western images of feminine beauty have spread to the rest of the world, so have associated illnesses. Eating problems also have surfaced among young, primarily affluent women in Hong Kong and Singapore, and in urban areas in China, India, Pakistan, the Philippines, and Taiwan (Efron, 1997).

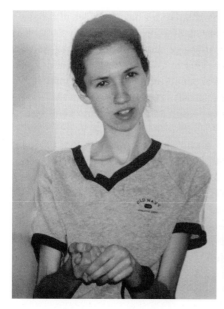
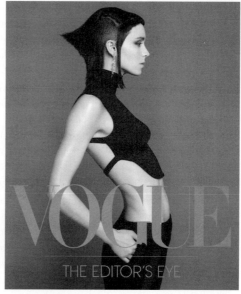

An anorexic woman, left, has starved herself thin; people suffering from anorexia feel compelled to lose weight by a variety of social and personal pressures, often continuing to view themselves as overweight even when they have reached a state of emaciation. Eating disorders are unlikely to disappear as long as severely underweight fashion models, right, are upheld as paragons of beauty.

Given how harmful eating disorders are, why do they persist and why do they affect young women most acutely? Although roughly 10 percent of those with eating disorders are men, they don't suffer from anorexia or bulimia as often as women—partly because social norms stress the importance of physical attractiveness more for women than for men and partly because desirable body images of men differ from those of women. Anorexia and other eating disorders reflect the fact that women now play a larger part in the wider society but are still judged as much by their appearance as by their accomplishments. Eating disorders are rooted in feelings of shame and a desire to have control over one's body. The individual feels inadequate and imperfect, and her anxieties about how others perceive her become focused through feelings about her body. At that point, shedding weight becomes the means of making everything right in her world. Sociologists believe that as long as young women are raised to equate their self-worth with their physical appearance, eating disorders will persist.

Is Sexual Orientation Inborn or Learned?

Most sociologists believe that sexual orientation—whether homosexual, heterosexual, or bisexual—results from a complex interplay between biological factors and social learning. Since heterosexuality is the norm for most people in U.S. culture, considerable research has focused on why some people become homosexual. Some scholars argue that biological influences predispose certain people to become homosexual from birth (Bell, Weinberg, and Hammersmith, 1981; Green, 1987). Biological explanations have included differences in brain characteristics of homosexuals (LeVay, 1996; Maugh and Zamichow, 1991) and the effect on fetal development of the mother's hormone production during pregnancy (Blanchard and Bogaert, 1996; Manning, Koukourakis, and Brodie, 1997; McFadden and Champlin, 2000). Such studies, which are based on small numbers of cases, give highly inconclusive (and highly controversial) results (Healy, 2001). It is virtually impossible to separate biological from early social influences in determining a person's sexual orientation.

Studies of twins may shed light on any genetic basis for homosexuality, since identical twins share identical genes. In two related studies, Bailey and Pillard (1991) examined 167 pairs of brothers and 143 pairs of sisters, with each pair of siblings raised in the same family, in which at least one sibling defined himself or herself as homosexual. Some of these pairs were identical twins (who share all genes), some were fraternal twins (who share some genes), and some were adoptive brothers or sisters (who share no genes). The researchers reasoned that if sexual orientation is determined entirely by biology, then since in each case at least one of the identical twins was homosexual, all the study's identical twins, having the identical genetic makeup, should be homosexual. Among the fraternal twins, some pairs would be homosexual, since some genes are shared. The lowest rates of homosexuality were predicted for the adoptive brothers and sisters.

The results seem to show that homosexuality, like heterosexuality, results from a combination of biological and social factors. Among the men and the women studied, in roughly one out of every two identical twin pairs, the second twin was also homosexual, compared with 1 out of every 5 fraternal twins and 1 out of every 10 adoptive brothers and sisters (Bailey and Pillard, 1991; see also Burr, 1993; Maugh, 1991, 1993). In other words, a woman or man is five times as likely to be gay if her or his identical twin is gay than if her or his sibling is gay but related only through adoption. These results offer some support for the importance of biological factors, since the higher the percentage of shared genes, the greater the percentage of cases in which both siblings were homosexual. However, because approximately half of the identical twin brothers and sisters of homosexuals were not themselves homosexual, social learning must also be involved; otherwise one would expect all identical twin siblings of homosexuals to be homosexual as well.

Clearly, even studies of identical twins cannot fully isolate biological from social factors. It is often the case that even in infancy, identical twins are treated more like one another by parents, peers, and teachers than are fraternal twins, who in turn are treated more like one another than are adoptive siblings. Thus identical twins may have more than genes in common: They may also share a higher proportion of similar socializing experiences. Sociologist Peter Bearman (2002) has shown the intricate ways that genetics and social experience are intertwined. Bearman found that males with a female twin are twice as likely to report same-sex attractions. He theorized that parents of opposite-sex twins are more likely to give them unisex treatment, leading to a less traditionally masculine influence on the males. Having an older brother decreases the rate of homosexuality. Bearman hypothesized that an older brother establishes gender-socializing mechanisms for the younger brother to follow, which allows him to compensate for unisex treatment. Bearman's work is consistent with the statements offered by professional organizations such as the American Academy of Pediatrics, which concludes that "sexual orientation probably is not determined by any one factor but by a combination of genetic, hormonal, and environmental influences" (American Academy of Pediatrics, 2004).

Scholarly debates over the "cause" of sexual orientation underscore the very themes that have provided the foundation for this chapter and for the sociological study of the body and sexuality more generally. It is simplistic to think that there is a "single-bullet" explanation for phenomena as complex as health, sexuality, and illness; rather, a complex array of cultural, biological, technological, social, and economic factors plays a dynamic and essential role.

CONCEPT CHECKS ✓

1. What are two possible reasons income inequality affects health?

2. Compare complementary and alternative medicine.

3. Describe two to three characteristics of persons with the greatest risk of anorexia and bulimia.

4. Contrast biological and social explanations as possible "causes" of homosexuality.

1 **Basic Concepts**

p. 552

2 **Theories and Historical Approaches to Understanding Health, Illness, and Sexuality**

p. 556

LEARNING OBJECTIVES

Understand how social, cultural, and historical contexts shape attitudes toward health, illness, and sexual behavior.

Learn about theoretical perspectives on health and illness in contemporary society, as well as the approaches to studying sexuality throughout history.

TERMS TO KNOW

Obesity • Body mass index (BMI) • Sociology of the body • Sociology of sexuality • Health

Sick role

CONCEPT CHECKS

1. Define the term *health*.
2. Name two ways that modern medicine differs from folk medicine.
3. Contrast the terms *sexual orientation* and *sexual preference*.
4. How would you define the term *homosexuality?*

1. Describe how the primary causes of death have changed between colonial times and the present day.
2. How do functionalist theorists and symbolic interactions differ in their perspectives on health and illness?
3. Describe several changes in sexual practices over the past two centuries.
4. What are the most important contributions of Alfred Kinsey's research on sexuality?

Exercises: Thinking Sociologically

1. Statistical studies of our national health show a gap in life expectancies between the rich and the poor. Review all the major factors that would explain why rich people live about eight years longer than poor people.

2. This text discusses the biological and sociocultural factors associated with sexual orientation. Why are twin studies the most promising type of research on the genetic basis of sexual orientation? Summarize the analysis of these studies, and show whether it presently appears that sexual orientation results from genetic differences, sociocultural practices and experiences, or both.

3

Research on Health, Illness, and Sexuality Today

p. 562

Learn about the social and cultural differences in the distribution of disease. Understand the causes underlying high rates of infectious diseases in developing nations. Learn more about HIV/AIDS as a sociological phenomenon. Explore the cultural differences in sexual behavior and patterns of sexual behavior today.

Epidemiology • Health literacy • Homophobia • Socialization of nature • Procreative technology

1. How do race, class, and gender affect health?
2. Why are infectious diseases more common in developing nations than in the United States today?
3. Describe patterns of adolescent sexual behavior in contemporary U.S. society.
4. Provide two pieces of evidence that homophobia has declined in recent decades.
5. Describe two ways that the development of new technologies has led to the "socialization of nature."

4

Unanswered Questions on Health, Illness, and Sexuality

p. 578

Understand the debates over the relationships between health inequality and income, the relationships between traditional medicine and complementary and alternative medicine (CAM), as well as the debate about the importance of biological versus social and cultural influences on human sexual behavior.

Gini coefficient • Complementary and alternative medicine (CAM) • Biomedical model of health

1. What are two possible reasons income inequality affects health?
2. Compare complementary and alternative medicine.
3. Describe two to three characteristics of persons with the greatest risk of anorexia and bulimia.
4. Contrast biological and social explanations as possible "causes" of homosexuality.

Population, Urbanization, and the Environment

19

It took nearly all of human history to add the first billion people to our planet, a number that was reached only two centuries ago, in roughly 1800. It took another 130 years (until 1930) to add the second billion; 30 years (until 1960) to add the third billion; 15 years (until 1975) to add the fourth billion; 12 years (until 1987) to add the fifth billion, and another 12 years (until 1999) to add the sixth billion. By 2011 the human population had reached 7 billion people. Given past and recent rates of exploding population growth, what do you think is the most widely accepted official prediction for the global population in 2050?

a 9–10 billion

b 14–15 billion

c 19–20 billion

d 24–25 billion

e 29–30 billion

Turn the page for the correct answer.

It is difficult to predict with any precision the rate at which the world population will rise, but United Nations researchers have produced several scenarios. Their most likely estimate assumes "medium" levels of fertility: roughly two children being born, on average, to women throughout the world. (Obviously some women will have more children, and some fewer; this is an average figure, based on current trends.) According to this scenario, world population will reach 9.3 billion people by 2050, before stabilizing at roughly 10.0 billion by the end of the century. The correct answer, then, is 9–10 billion (UN FAO, 2011b). The UN also has a "high" scenario that assumes an average of 2.5 children per woman, which places the world's population at 10.6 billion people by 2050, but this seems unlikely. And it has a "low" (and equally unlikely) scenario that assumes an average of 1.5 children per woman—a result that would actually result in eventual population decline (UN FAO, 2011b).

There are currently an estimated 7 billion people in the world. It was estimated that "baby number 7 billion" was born on approximately October 31, 2011; the 6 billionth baby was born only 12 years earlier, in October 1999. Paul Ehrlich calculated in the 1960s that if the rate of population growth at that time continued, 900 years from now (not a long period in world history as a whole) there would be 60,000,000,000,000,000 (60 quadrillion) people on the face of the earth. There would be 100 people for every square yard of the earth's surface, including both land and water. The physicist J. H. Fremlin (1964) speculated that housing such a population would require a continuous 2,000-story building covering the entire planet. Even such a mammoth structure would have only three or four yards of floor space per person.

Such a picture, of course, is nothing more than nightmarish fiction designed to drive home how cataclysmic the consequences of continued population growth would be. The

LEARNING OBJECTIVES

1 BASIC CONCEPTS

Learn about the most important concepts that demographers use to understand world population growth and the changes in cities.

2 URBAN SOCIOLOGY: SOME INFLUENTIAL THEORIES

Understand how theories of urbanism have placed increasing emphasis on the influence of socioeconomic factors on city life.

3 RECENT RESEARCH ON POPULATION, URBANIZATION, AND THE ENVIRONMENT

See how cities have changed as a result of industrialization and urbanization. Recognize the challenges of urbanization in the global south. Learn about the recent key developments affecting American cities, suburbs, and rural communities in the last several decades. See that the environment is a sociological issue related to urbanization and population growth.

4 UNANSWERED QUESTIONS

Learn more about the sociological debates about the causes of urban poverty and whether global population growth will outstrip our resources.

real issue is what will happen over the next 30 or 40 years, by which time, if current trends are not reversed, the world's population will already have grown to unsustainable levels. Partly because governments and other agencies heeded the warnings of Ehrlich and others 30 years ago by introducing population control programs, there are grounds for supposing that world population growth is beginning to trail off. And population control policies, especially China's one-child policy, have been so effective at reducing birthrates that policy makers now fear that China will not have a large enough pool of young people to care for their aging parents in future decades. Estimates calculated in the 1960s of the likely world population by the year 2000 turned out to be inaccurate and highly overstated, because these estimates presumed that the high growth rates of the 1960s—topping out at 2.2 percent in 1963—would persist into future decades. The United Nations Population Fund (UNFPA, 2011) estimated that the world population reached 7 billion in 2011. Nevertheless, considering that a century ago there were only 1.5 billion people in the world, this still represents growth of staggering proportions. Moreover, the factors underlying population growth are by no means completely predictable, and all estimates have to be interpreted with caution.

In this chapter we will answer this question by examining the complex ways in which population growth, urbanization, and our planet's fragile environment go hand in hand, particularly against the backdrop of rapid industrialization that is transforming many parts of the world. We begin by discussing some of the basic concepts used in explaining population growth, before turning to a review of some of the most influential theories of urban life. Our discussion of current research begins with an examination of global population growth, one result of which is the rise of megacities in the global south (see Chapter 3). We then turn to some recent research on rural, urban, and suburban life in the United States, before discussing the relationship between population growth, industrialization, and environmental challenges. We conclude with two unanswered questions—one focusing on urban poverty in the United States, the other on the likely relationship between global population growth and global food production.

THE ANSWER IS A.

1 BASIC CONCEPTS

The study of population is referred to as **demography**. The term was invented about a century and a half ago, at a time when nations were beginning to keep official statistics on the nature and distribution of their populations. Demography is concerned with measuring the size of populations, explaining their rise or decline, and documenting the distribution of such populations both within and across continents, nations, states, cities, and even neighborhoods. Population patterns are governed by three factors: births, deaths, and migrations. Demography is customarily treated as a branch of sociology, because the factors that influence the level of births and deaths in a given group or society, and migrations of population, are largely social and cultural.

Much demographic work tends to be statistical, relying on large-sample surveys as well as official birth and death records. All the industrialized countries today gather and analyze basic statistics on their populations

demography • The study of populations.

by carrying out *censuses*, systematic surveys designed to find out about the whole population of a given country. Although rigorous modes of data collection are used, and every effort is made to count each and every person in a population, censuses still are not 100 percent accurate, nor is every individual adequately represented. In the United States, for example, a comprehensive population census every 10 years (i.e., the decennial census) and sample studies are regularly conducted. Yet for various reasons, many people are not counted in the official population statistics, including illegal immigrants, homeless people, transients, and others who for one reason or another either did not complete their survey or were not located by census enumerators. In many countries in the global south, particularly those with recent high rates of population growth, demographic statistics are much more unreliable.

Among the basic concepts used by demographers, the most important are crude birthrates, fertility, fecundity, and crude death rates. **Crude birthrates** are expressed as the number of live births per year per 1,000 persons in the population. They are called "crude" rates because of their very general character. Crude birthrates do not tell us what proportions of a population are male or female or what the age distribution of a population is (the relative proportions of young and old people in the population). A population with a high percentage of young women can be expected to have a much higher birthrate than one in which older men predominate. Where statistics are collected that relate birth or death rates to such categories, demographers speak of "specific" rather than "crude" rates. For instance, an age-specific birthrate might specify the number of births per 1,000 women in the 25-to-34-four-year-old age group.

If we wish to understand population patterns in any detail, the information provided by specific birthrates is normally necessary. Crude birthrates may, however, be useful for making overall comparisons between different groups, societies, and regions. The crude birthrate in the United States is 13 per 1,000. Other industrialized countries have lower rates: for example, 8 per 1,000 in Germany and 10 in Hungary and Italy. In many other parts of the world, crude birthrates are much higher. In India, for instance, the crude birthrate is 23 per 1,000; in Ethiopia it is 37 per 1,000 (Population Reference Bureau, 2011a).

Birthrates are an expression of the fertility of women. **Fertility** refers to how many live-born children the average woman has. A fertility rate is usually calculated as the average number of births per 1,000 women of childbearing age. Fertility is distinguished from **fecundity**, which means the number of children women are biologically capable of bearing. It is physically possible for a normal woman to bear a child every year during the period when she is capable of conception. There are variations in fecundity according to the age at which women reach puberty and menopause, both of which differ between countries as well as between individuals. Although there may be families in which a woman bears 20 or more children, fertility rates in practice are always much lower than fecundity rates, because social and cultural factors limit breeding. Even women in cultures who do not use birth control fail to meet their maximum reproductive potential. For instance, breastfeeding one's newborn infant causes a woman to have amenorrhea (i.e., a cessation of menstruation) and, in turn, temporary natural postpartum infertility.

crude birthrates • Statistical measures representing the number of births within a given population per year, normally calculated in terms of the number of births per 1,000 members. Although the crude birthrate is a useful index, it is only a general measure, because it does not specify numbers of births in relation to age distribution.

fertility • The average number of live-born children produced by women of childbearing age in a particular society.

fecundity • A measure of the number of children that it is biologically possible for a woman to produce.

Crude death rates (also called "mortality rates") are calculated in the same way as birthrates—the number of deaths per 1,000 of the population per year. Again, there are major variations among countries, but death rates in many societies in the global south are falling to levels comparable to those of the West. The death rate in the United States and India in 2010 was 8 and 7 per 1,000, respectively. In Malawi it was 15 per 1,000. A few countries have much higher death rates. In Zambia, for example, the death rate is 20 per 1,000 due in part to AIDS and high infant mortality rates (Population Reference Bureau, 2010). Like crude birthrates, crude death rates provide only a very general index of **mortality** (the number of deaths in a population), and can be very misleading. For example, the number of deaths per 1,000 people can be higher for industrial nations than for countries in the global south, despite standards of health being better in industrial countries. This is because industrial countries have a higher percentage of older people, who are more likely to die in a given year; the overall mortality rate can then be higher even if the mortality rate at any given age is lower. Thus specific death rates give more precise information.

A particularly important specific death rate is the **infant mortality rate**—the number of babies per 1,000 births in any year who die before reaching age one. One of the key factors underlying the population explosion has been the reduction in infant mortality rates. Declining rates of infant mortality are the most important influence on increasing **life expectancy**—that is, the number of years the average person can expect to live. In 1900, life expectancy at birth in the United States was about 40 years. Today it has increased to 78 years. This does not mean, however, that most people at the turn of the century died when they were about 40 years of age. When there is a high infant mortality rate, as there is in many countries in the global south, the average life expectancy—which is a statistical average—is brought down by deaths that occurred before the age of one. If we look at the life expectancy of only those people who survive the first year of life, we find that in 1900 the average person could expect to live to age 58. Illness, nutrition, and natural disasters are the other factors influencing life expectancy. Life expectancy has to be distinguished from **life span**, which is the maximum number of years that an individual could live. Although life expectancy has increased in most societies in the world, life span has remained unaltered. Only a small proportion of people lives to be 100 or more.

Rates of population growth or decline are measured by subtracting the yearly number of deaths per 1,000 from the number of births per 1,000. (Actual population growth or decline also requires taking into account the number of people who have migrated into the country as well as the number who have emigrated out of the country.) Some European countries have negative growth rates—in other words, their populations are declining. Virtually all the industrialized countries have growth rates of less than 0.5 percent. Rates of population growth were high in the eighteenth and nineteenth centuries in Europe and the United States but have since leveled off. Many countries in the global south today have rates of between 2 and 3 percent. These

crude death rates • Statistical measures representing the number of deaths that occur annually in a given population per year, normally calculated as the ratio of deaths per 1,000 members. Crude death rates give a general indication of the mortality levels of a community or society, but are limited in their usefulness because they do not take into account the age distribution.

mortality • The number of deaths in a population.

infant mortality rate • The number of infants who die during the first year of life, per 1,000 live births.

life expectancy • The number of years the average person can expect to live.

life span • The maximum length of life that is biologically possible for a member of a given species.

rates of population growth or decline • A measurement of population growth calculated by subtracting the yearly number of deaths per 1,000 from the number of births per 1,000.

may not seem very different from the rates of the industrialized countries, but in fact the difference is enormous.

The reason is that growth in population is **exponential** rather than arithmetic. An ancient Persian myth helps illustrate this concept. A courtier asked a ruler to reward him for his services by giving him twice as many grains of rice for each service as he had the time before, starting with a single grain on the first square of a chess board. Believing he was on to a good thing, the king commanded that grain be brought up from his storehouse. By the twenty-first square, the storehouse was empty; the fortieth square required 10 billion grains of rice (Meadows et al., 1972). In other words, starting with one item and doubling it, doubling the result, and so on, rapidly leads to huge figures: 1:2:4:8:16:32:64:128, and so on. In only seven operations the figure had grown 128 times as large as originally. Exactly the same principle applies to population growth. We can measure this effect by means of the **doubling time**—the period of time it takes for the population to double. The formula used to calculate doubling time is 70 divided by the current growth rate. For example, a population growth of 1 percent will produce a doubling of numbers in 70 years. At 2 percent growth, a population will double in 35 years, while at 3 percent it will double in 23 years.

Demographers often refer to the changes in the ratio of births to deaths in the industrialized countries from the nineteenth century onward as the **demographic transition**. The notion was first worked out by Warren S. Thompson (1929), who described a three-stage process in which one type of population stability would eventually be replaced by another, as a society reached an advanced level of economic development.

Stage one refers to the conditions characteristic of most traditional societies, in which both birthrates and death rates are high and the infant mortality rate is especially high. Population grows little if at all, as the high number of births is more or less balanced by the level of deaths. Although there were sometimes periods of marked population increase, these were followed by increases in death rates. In medieval Europe, for example, when harvests were bad, marriages tended to be postponed and the number of conceptions fell, while deaths increased. These complementary trends reduced the number of mouths to be fed. No preindustrial society was able to escape from this self-regulating rhythm (Wrigley, 1968).

Stage two, which began in Europe and the United States in the early part of the nineteenth century (with wide regional variations), occurs when death rates fall while fertility remains high. This is, therefore, a phase of marked population growth. It is subsequently replaced by *stage three*, in which, with industrial development, birthrates drop to a level such that population is again fairly stable.

Demographers do not fully agree about how this sequence of change should be interpreted or how long-lasting stage three is likely to be. Fertility in the Western countries has not been completely stable over the past century or so; considerable differences in fertility remain among the industrialized nations, and between classes or regions within them. Nevertheless, it is generally accepted that this sequence accurately describes a major transformation in the demographic character of modern societies.

exponential • Involving a geometric, rather than linear, rate of progression; producing a fast rise in the numbers of a population experiencing such growth.

doubling time • The time it takes for a particular level of population to double.

demographic transition • An interpretation of population change that holds that a stable ratio of births to deaths is achieved once a certain level of economic prosperity has been reached. According to this notion, in pre-industrial societies there is a rough balance between births and deaths, because population increase is kept in check by a lack of available food, by disease, or by war. In modern societies, by contrast, population equilibrium is achieved because families are moved by economic incentives to limit the number of children they produce.

In recent decades, demographers have debated whether a **"second demographic transition"** has begun. Under this new model, fertility rates continue to fall because of shifts in family structure. Key influences on the second demographic transition include delayed marriage, delayed childbearing, rising rates of cohabitation, and high, steady rates of divorce. The last two patterns arguably lead to lower birthrates, because most women prefer not to conceive a child when they are cohabiting or are divorced (and thus between relationships). As a result, women may be more "vigilant" about their contraception, and thus birthrates will remain low among increasingly large numbers of unmarried persons (van de Kaa, 2003).

CONCEPT CHECKS ✓

1. What is the difference between fertility and fecundity?
2. What are the stages of a demographic transition, and why do some demographers believe that we've begun a second demographic transition?

② URBAN SOCIOLOGY: SOME INFLUENTIAL THEORIES

Urbanization results when cities grow in population—perhaps partly through natural increase, but mainly through migration from rural areas by people in search of the economic opportunities associated with urban life. Scholars associated with the University of Chicago from the 1920s to the 1940s—especially Robert Park, Ernest Burgess, and Louis Wirth—developed ideas that were for many years the chief basis of theory and research in urban sociology. Some important ideas, however, came from outside universities—for example, in the work of Jane Jacobs.

The Chicago School

Two concepts developed by the "Chicago School" are worthy of special attention. One is the so-called **ecological approach** to urban analysis (Park, 1952); the other is the characterization of urbanism as a *way of life*, developed by Wirth (1938). It is important to understand these ideas as the Chicago School initially conceived them and to see how they have been revised and even replaced by sociologists in more recent decades.

Urban Ecology

Ecology is a term taken from a physical science—the study of the adaptation of plant and animal organisms to their environment. In the natural world, organisms tend to be distributed in systematic ways over the terrain such that a balance or equilibrium between different species is achieved. The Chicago School believed that the locations of major urban settlements and the distribution of different types of neighborhoods within them can be understood in terms of similar principles. Cities do not grow up at random but in response to advantageous features of the environment. For example, large urban areas in modern

second demographic transition • A new demographic model that calls for fertility rates that may continue to fall because of shifts in family structure.

ecological approach • In the field of urban analysis, a perspective emphasizing the "natural" distribution of city neighborhoods into areas having contrasting characteristics.

Robert Park of the Chicago School applied an ecological approach to urban analysis. How did a turn-of-the-century metropolis like Chicago embody the processes of competition, invasion, and succession?

societies tend to develop along the shores of rivers, in fertile plains, or at the intersection of trading routes or railways.

"Once set up," in Park's (1952) words, "a city is, it seems, a great sorting mechanism which . . . infallibly selects out of the population as a whole the individuals best suited to live in a particular region or a particular milieu." Cities become ordered into "natural areas," through processes of competition, invasion, and succession—all of which occur in biological ecology. If we look at the ecology of a lake in the natural environment, we find that competition between various species of fish, insects, and other organisms operates to reach a fairly stable distribution among them. This balance is disturbed if new species invade—try to make the lake their home. Some of the organisms that used to proliferate in the central area of the lake are driven out, to eke out a more precarious existence around its fringes. The invading species are their successors in the central sections.

Patterns of location, movement, and relocation in cities, according to the ecological view, have a similar form. Different neighborhoods develop through the adjustments made by inhabitants as they struggle to gain their livelihoods. According to mid-twentieth-century writings, a city can be pictured as a map of areas with distinct and contrasting social characteristics. Cities can be seen as formed in concentric rings broken up into segments. In the center are the **inner-city** areas, a mixture of big-business prosperity and decaying private homes. Beyond these are older established neighborhoods, housing workers employed in stable manual occupations. Farther out still are the suburbs, in which higher-income groups tend to live. Processes of invasion and succession occur within the segments of the concentric rings. Thus as property decays in a central or near-central area, ethnic minority groups might start to move into it. As they do so, more of the preexisting population starts to leave, precipitating a wholesale flight to neighborhoods elsewhere in the city or out to the suburbs. However, as we will see later in this chapter, these traditional patterns are starting

inner city • The areas composing the central neighborhoods of a city, as distinct from the suburbs. In many modern urban settings in the developed world, inner-city areas are subject to dilapidation and decay, with the more affluent residents having moved to outlying areas.

to change—as wealthy persons and the young flood into urban areas, seeking amenities such as arts and culture, and suburban areas become more desirable (and affordable) to poor and working-class persons.

Another aspect of the **urban ecology** approach emphasized the *interdependence* of different city areas. *Differentiation*—the specialization of groups and occupational roles—is the main way in which human beings adapt to their environment. Groups on which many others depend will have a dominant role, often reflected in their central geographical position. Business groups, for example, such as large banks or insurance companies, provide key services for many in a community and hence are usually to be found in the central areas of settlements (Hawley, 1950, 1968).

Part of what it means to think like an urban sociologist today is to ask whether and how the conditions observed in cities are socially constructed or natural. We have seen that the early Chicago School favored the idea that spatial patterns were natural outcomes. This all began to change when two black graduate students at the University of Chicago published the book *Black Metropolis* (Drake and Cayton, 1945), which posed a challenge to the human-ecology framework.

Drake and Cayton's massive study, based on extensive historical and ethnographic data, showed that the black residential neighborhoods of Chicago were by no means the result of "natural forces" but were instead shaped by unnatural, social forces. These areas were called *ghettos*, a term that has come to mean many things to many people but that can be most usefully defined as a residential area where a racial or ethnic group initially comes to live as a consequence of systematic exclusion from more desirable places. Drake and Cayton showed that the poor living conditions in the ghetto were due to the fact not that the people living there were black, but that the blacks had been given no choice but to live in the worst areas of the city. There was nothing natural about this placement, and it would not have occurred if not for social forces such as exclusion, violence, and restrictive covenants where neighborhood "improvement" associations passed laws making it illegal to sell land in a community to blacks. After the publication of Drake and Cayton's *Black Metropolis*, it was harder for sociologists to think of the distributions of populations in urban areas as natural.

URBANISM AS A WAY OF LIFE

Wirth's thesis of **urbanism** as a *way of life* (1938) is concerned less with whether cities are natural or socially constructed than with what urbanism is as a form of social existence. Urbanism focuses on the ways that life in cities is different from life elsewhere. Wirth also asserted that the effects of life in cities can be felt outside cities as well. For example, have you ever noticed that many young people today dress in garments that were once thought to be distinctive to urban minority youth? It is not uncommon to find some teenagers in suburban high schools all over America dressing in baggy pants, untucked T-shirts, and high-top sneakers. If Wirth were writing today he might cite this as an example of his claim that the cultural life that begins in cities draws in the outlying population so that urbanism is "a way of life" in many places outside cities as well.

Wirth's theory is important because it acknowledges that urbanism not only is part of a society but expresses and influences the nature of the wider social system.

urban ecology • An approach to the study of urban life based on an analogy with the adjustment of plants and organisms to the physical environment. According to ecological theorists, the various neighborhoods and zones within cities are formed as a result of natural processes of adjustment on the part of populations as they compete for resources.

urbanism • A term used by Louis Wirth to denote distinctive characteristics of urban social life, such as its impersonality.

Features of the urban way of life are characteristic of social life in modern societies as a whole, not just the activities of those who happen to live in big cities.

A second facet of Wirth's argument focused on proximity and anonymity, aspects of social life that he viewed as distinctive to cities. In cities, Wirth points out, large numbers of people live in close proximity to one another without knowing most others personally—a fundamental contrast to small, traditional villages. Most contacts between city dwellers are fleeting and partial and are means to other ends rather than being satisfying relationships in themselves. Interactions with sales clerks in stores, baristas at coffee shops, or passengers or ticket collectors on trains are passing encounters, entered into not for their own sake but as means to other aims.

Because those who live in urban areas tend to be highly mobile, there are relatively weak bonds between them. People are involved in many different activities and situations each day—the pace of life is faster than in rural areas. Competition prevails over cooperation. Wirth accepts that the density of social life in cities leads to the formation of neighborhoods having distinct characteristics, some of which may preserve the characteristics of small communities. In immigrant areas, for example, traditional types of connections between families are found, with most people knowing most others on a personal basis. The more such areas are absorbed into wider patterns of city life, however, the less these characteristics survive.

Wirth was among the first to address the "urban interaction problem" (Duneier and Molotch, 1999), the necessity for city dwellers to respect social boundaries when so many people are in close physical proximity all the time. Wirth elaborates that "the reserve, the indifference, and the blasé outlook that urbanites manifest in their relationships may thus be regarded as devices for immunizing themselves against the personal claims and expectations of others." Many people walk down the street in cities, acting unconcerned about the others near them, often talking on cell phones or listening to iPods that block out the sounds of urban life. Through such appearance of apathy, they can avoid unwanted transgression of social boundaries. Wirth's ideas have deservedly enjoyed wide currency. The impersonal nature of many day-to-day contacts in modern cities is undeniable—but to some degree this is true of social life in general in modern societies. Although one might assume that the "immunization" urban dwellers engage in to distance themselves from others is unique to city life, urban interaction may be only a subtype of the universal social condition. While the presence of strangers is more common in cities (Lofland, 1973, 1998), all people must manage social boundaries in their face-to-face interactions with others—as has been found as far afield as western Samoa (Duranti, 1994) or among the African Poro people (Bellman, 1984). It is always necessary to ask whether the problems one associates with cities are aspects of social life more generally. In assessing Wirth's ideas, we must also ask whether his generalizations about urban life hold true for all cities during all times.

Yet neighborhoods marked by close kinship and personal ties often are actively created by city life; they are not just remnants of a preexisting way of life that survive for a period within the city. Claude Fischer (1984) has put forward an explanation for why large-scale urbanism helps to promote diverse subcultures, rather than swamping everyone within an anonymous mass. Those who live in cities, he points out, are able to collaborate with others of like background or interests to develop local connections; and they can join distinctive religious, ethnic, political, and other subcultural groups. A small town or village does not allow the development of such subcultural diversity. Those who form ethnic communities within cities, for instance, might have had little or no knowledge of one another in their land of origin. When they arrive in a new country, they gravitate to areas where others from a similar linguistic and cultural background are living, and new subcommunity structures are formed. An artist might find few others in a village or small town with whom to associate but may find a community of like-minded artistic or intellectual peers in neighborhoods such as Williamsburg in Brooklyn, New York. Likewise, some gay and lesbian young people may find more hospitable communities in cities that have large gay subcultures, such as San Francisco, compared to the small towns where they may have grown up.

A large city is a world of strangers, yet it supports and creates personal relationships. This is not paradoxical. We have to separate urban experience into the public sphere of encounters with strangers and the more private world of family, friends, and work colleagues. It may be difficult to meet people when one first moves to a large city. But anyone moving to a small, established rural community may find the friendliness of the inhabitants largely a matter of public politeness—it may take years to become accepted when one is "new" in town. This is not the case in the city, because cities are continually welcoming new, geographically mobile residents. Although one finds a diversity of strangers, each is a potential friend. And once someone is within a group or network, the possibilities for expanding his or her personal connections increase considerably.

Wirth's ideas retain some validity, but in light of subsequent contributions it is clear that they are overgeneralized. Modern cities frequently involve impersonal, anonymous social relationships, but they are also sources of diversity—and, sometimes, intimacy.

Jane Jacobs: "Eyes and Ears upon the Street"

Like most sociologists in the twentieth century, the Chicago School researchers were professors who saw their mission as contributing to a scholarly literature and advancing the field of social science.

At certain moments in the history of sociology, however, advances have also come from thinkers working outside universities without formal training in sociology. One such person was Jane Jacobs, who published *The Death and Life of Great American Cities* in 1961.

Jacobs was an architecture critic with a high school education, but through her own independent reading and research in the 1950s, she transformed herself into one of the most learned figures in the emerging field of urban studies. She is known as a public intellectual because her main goal was to speak to the educated public rather than to contribute to a scholarly literature. Nevertheless, her work has had an impact on scholarship in sociology as well.

Like sociologists such as Wirth of the Chicago School before her, Jacobs noted that "cities are, by definition, full of strangers," some of whom are dangerous. She tried to explain what makes it possible for cities to meet the challenge of "assimilating strangers" in such a way that strangers can feel comfortable together. She argued that cities are most habitable when they feature a diversity of uses, thereby ensuring that many people will be coming and going on the streets at any time. When enough people are out and about, Jacobs wrote, "respectable" eyes and ears dominate the street and are fixed on strangers, who will thus not get out of hand. Underneath the seeming disorder of a busy street is the very basis for order in "the intricacy of sidewalk use, bringing with it a constant succession of eyes." The more people are out, or looking from their windows at the people who are out, the more their gazes will safeguard the street.

Although Jacobs's ideas seem to cover a broad range of urban situations, there have been notable exceptions: Only three years after her book was published, for example, a young woman named Kitty Genovese was stabbed to death in Queens, New York, while 38 people watched from their windows (Rosenthal, 1999).

It is very common for people to make the mistake of believing that certain principles are natural to social life, only to discover later on that these principles hold up only under particular social conditions. The world has changed a great deal since Jacobs wrote *The Death and Life of Great American Cities*. When Jacobs was writing, most of the people on the sidewalks she discussed were similar in many respects, yet today homeless people, drug users, panhandlers, and others representing economic inequalities, cultural differences, and extremes of behavior can make sidewalk life unpredictable (Duneier, 1999). Under these conditions, strangers do not necessarily feel the kind of solidarity and mutual assurance she described. Sociologists today must ask: What happens to urban life when "the eyes and ears upon the street" represent vast inequalities and cultural differences? Do the assumptions Jacobs made still hold up? In many cases the answer is yes, but in other cases the answer is no. More than five decades after her book was published, Jacobs's ideas remain extremely influential.

Urbanism and the Created Environment

Whereas the earlier Chicago School of sociology emphasized that the distribution of people in cities occurs naturally, scholars such as Drake and Cayton (1945), in their previously mentioned book *Black Metropolis*, countered that this is not true with regard to the black population. They demonstrated that blacks often did not get to live in neighborhoods they desired, even if their incomes allowed them to do so, because of subtle and institutional forms of discrimination. More recent theories of the city have stressed that urbanism is not a natural process but has to be analyzed in relation to major patterns of political and economic change.

According to this view, it is not the stranger on the sidewalk who is most threatening to many urban dwellers, especially the poor; instead, it is the stranger far away, working in a bank or real estate development company, who has the power to make decisions that transform whole blocks or neighborhoods (Logan and Molotch, 1987). This focus on the political economy of cities, and on different kinds of strangers, represented a new and critical direction for urban sociology.

HARVEY: THE RESTRUCTURING OF SPACE

Urbanism is one aspect of the **created environment** brought about by the spread of industrial capitalism, according to David Harvey (1973, 1982, 1985). In traditional societies, city and countryside were clearly differentiated. In the modern world, industry blurs the division between city and countryside. Agriculture becomes mechanized and is run according to considerations of price and profit, just like industrial work, and this process lessens the differences in modes of social life between urban and rural people.

Harvey points out that in modern urbanism, space is continually *restructured*. The process is determined by where large firms choose to place their factories, research and development centers, and so forth; the controls that governments operate over both land and industrial production; and the activities of private investors, buying and selling houses and land. Business firms, for example, are constantly weighing the relative advantages of new locations against existing ones. As production becomes cheaper in one area than another, or as the firm moves from one product to another, offices and factories will be closed down in one place and opened up elsewhere. Thus at one period, when there are considerable profits to be

created environment • An environment made up of constructions established by human beings to serve their needs, derived from the use of man-made technology—including, for example, roads, railways, factories, offices, private homes, and other buildings.

made, there may be a spate of office block buildings in the center of large cities. Once the offices have been built and the central area redeveloped, investors look for the potential for further speculative building elsewhere. Often what is profitable in one period will not be so in another, when the financial climate changes.

The activities of private homebuyers are strongly influenced by how far, and where, business interests buy up land, and by rates of loans and taxes fixed by local and central government. After World War II, for instance, there was vast expansion of suburban development outside major cities in the United States. This was due partly to ethnic discrimination and the tendency of whites to move away from inner-city areas. However, it was made possible, Harvey argues, only because of government decisions to provide tax breaks to homebuyers and construction firms and by the setting up of special credit arrangements by financial organizations. These provided the basis for the building and buying of new homes on the peripheries of cities and at the same time promoted demand for industrial products such as the automobile.

CASTELLS: URBANISM AND SOCIAL MOVEMENTS

Like Harvey, Manuel Castells (1977, 1983) stresses that the spatial form of a society is closely linked to the overall mechanisms of its development. But in contrast to the Chicago sociologists, Castells sees the city not only as a distinct *location* (the urban area) but as an integral part of processes of **collective consumption**, which in turn are an inherent aspect of industrial capitalism. Homes, schools, transport services, and leisure amenities are ways in which people consume the products of modern industry. The taxation system influences who is able to buy or rent where and who builds where. Large corporations, banks, and insurance companies, which provide capital for building projects, have a great deal of power over these processes. But government agencies also directly affect many aspects of city life, by building roads and public housing, planning parks, and so forth. The physical shape of cities is thus a product of both market forces and the power of government.

But the nature of the created environment is not just the result of the activities of wealthy and powerful people. Castells stresses the importance of the struggles of underprivileged groups to alter their living conditions. Urban problems stimulate a range of social movements, concerned with improving housing conditions, protesting against air pollution, defending parks, and combating building development that changes the nature of an area. For example, Castells has studied the gay movement in San Francisco, which succeeded in restructuring neighborhoods around its own cultural values—allowing many gay organizations, clubs, and bars to flourish—and gained a prominent position in local politics.

Cities, Harvey and Castells both emphasize, are almost wholly artificial environments, constructed by people. In some ways, the views set out by Harvey and Castells and those of the Chicago School usefully complement each other and can be combined to give a comprehensive picture of urban processes. The contrasts between city areas described in the urban ecology approach do exist, as does the overall impersonality of city life. But these are more variable than the members of the Chicago School believed and are governed primarily by the social and economic influences analyzed by Harvey and Castells. John Logan and Harvey Molotch (1987) have suggested an approach that directly connects the perspectives of authors such as Harvey and Castells with some features of the ecological standpoint. They agree with Harvey and Castells that broad features of economic development, stretching nationally and internationally, affect urban life in a quite direct way. But these wide-ranging economic factors, they argue, are

collective consumption • A concept used by Manuel Castells to refer to processes of urban consumption—such as the buying and selling of property.

focused through local organizations, including neighborhood businesses, banks, and government agencies, together with the activities of individual home buyers.

Places (land and buildings) are bought and sold, according to Logan and Molotch, just like other goods in modern societies, but the markets that structure city environments are influenced by how different groups of people want to use the property they buy and sell. Many tensions and conflicts arise as a result of this process—and these are the key factors structuring city neighborhoods. For instance, an apartment house is seen as a home by its residents but as a source of income by its landlord. Businesses are most interested in buying and selling property in an area to obtain the best production sites or to make profits in land speculation. Their interests and concerns are quite different from those of residents, for whom the neighborhood is a place to live.

Saskia Sassen: Global Cities

Globalization is transforming cities into vital hubs within the global economy. Urban centers have become critical in coordinating information flows, managing business activities, and innovating new services and technologies. There has been a simultaneous dispersion and concentration of activity and power within a set of cities around the globe (Castells, 1996).

The role of cities in the new global order has been attracting a great deal of attention from sociologists. Globalization is often thought of in terms of a duality between the national level and the global, yet it is the largest *cities* of the world that make up the main circuits through which globalization occurs (Sassen, 1998). The functioning of the new global economy is dependent on a set of central locations with developed informational infrastructures and a hyperconcentration of facilities. It is in such points that the "work" of globalization is performed and directed. As business, production, advertising, and marketing assume a global scale, an enormous amount of organizational activity must be done in order to maintain and develop these global networks.

Saskia Sassen has been one of the leading contributors to theoretical debates on cities and globalization. She uses the term **global city** to refer to urban centers that are home to the headquarters of large, transnational corporations and a superabundance of financial, technological, and consulting services. In *The Global City* (1991), Sassen bases her work on the study of three such cities: New York, London, and Tokyo. The contemporary development of the world economy, she argues, has created a novel strategic role for major cities. Most such cities have long been centers of international trade, but they now have four new traits:

1. They have developed into command posts—centers of direction and policy making—for the global economy.
2. They are the key locations for financial and specialized service firms, which have become more important than manufacturing in influencing economic development.
3. They are the sites of production and innovation in these newly expanded industries.
4. They are markets in which the "products" of financial and service industries are bought, sold, or otherwise disposed of.

global city • A city—such as London, New York, or Tokyo—that has become an organizing center of the new global economy.

New York, London, and Tokyo have very different histories, yet we can trace comparable changes in their nature over the past two or three decades. Within the highly dispersed world economy of today, cities such as these provide for central control of crucial operations. Global cities are much more than simply places of coordination, however; they are also contexts of production. What is important here is the production not of material goods, but of the specialized services required by business organizations for administering offices and factories scattered across the world, and of financial innovations and markets. Services and financial goods are the "things" the global city makes.

The downtown areas of global cities provide concentrated sites within which whole clusters of "producers" can work in close interaction, often including personal contact, with one another. In the global city, local firms mingle with national and multinational organizations, including a multiplicity of foreign companies. Thus 350 foreign banks and 2,500 other foreign financial corporations have offices in New York City; one out of every four bank employees in the city works for a foreign bank. Global cities compete with one another, but they also constitute an interdependent system, partly separate from the nations in which they are located.

Other authors have built on Sassen's work, noting that as globalization progresses, more and more cities are joining New York, London, and Tokyo in the ranks of the global cities. Castells has described the creation of a tiered hierarchy of world cities—with places such as Chicago, Frankfurt, Hong Kong, Los Angeles, Milan, Osaka, Singapore, and Zurich serving as major global centers for business and financial services. Beneath these, new sets of regional centers are developing as key nodes within the global economy. Cities such as Buenos Aires, Jakarta, Madrid, Moscow, São Paulo, and Seoul are becoming important hubs for activity within the so-called emerging markets.

Sassen (1998) argues that global cities have produced a new dynamic of inequality: a prosperous central business district with a nearby impoverished area. These should be seen as interrelated phenomena. The growth sectors of the new economy—financial services, marketing, high technology—are reaping profits far greater than any found within traditional economic sectors. As the salaries and bonuses of the very affluent continue to climb, the wages of those employed to clean and guard their offices are dropping. Sassen (1998) argues that we are witnessing the "valorization" of work located at the forefront of the new global economy and the "devalorization" of work that occurs behind the scenes.

Disparities in profit-making capabilities are expected in market economies, but the magnitude of the disparities in the new global economy is having a negative effect on many aspects of the social world, from housing to the labor market. Those who work in finances and global services receive high salaries, and the areas where they live become gentrified. At the same time, orthodox manufacturing jobs are lost, and the very process of gentrification creates a vast supply of low-wage jobs—in restaurants, hotels, and boutiques. Affordable housing is scarce in gentrified areas, forcing an expansion of low-income neighborhoods. Whereas central business districts are the recipients of massive influxes of investment in real estate, development, and telecommunications, marginalized areas are left with few resources. Within global cities, a geography of "centrality and marginality" is taking shape—as Mitch Duneier's (1999) study in New York's Greenwich Village revealed. Alongside resplendent affluence there is acute poverty. Yet although these two worlds coexist side by side, the actual contact between them can be surprisingly minimal. As Mike Davis (1990) noted in his study of Los Angeles, there has been a "conscious 'hardening' of the city surface against the poor." Walled compounds, neighborhoods guarded by electronic surveillance, and "corporate citadels" have replaced accessible public spaces. In Davis's (1990) words:

> To reduce contact with untouchables, urban redevelopment has converted once vital pedestrian streets into traffic sewers and transformed public parks into

temporary receptacles for the homeless and wretched. The American city . . . is being systematically turned inside out—or, rather, outside in. The valorized spaces of the new megastructures and super-malls are concentrated in the center, street frontage is denuded, public activity is sorted into strictly functional compartments, and circulation is internalized in corridors under the gaze of private police.

According to Davis, life is made as "unlivable" as possible for the poorest and most marginalized residents of Los Angeles. Benches at bus stops are short or barrel-shaped to prevent people from sleeping on them, the number of public toilets is fewer than in any other North American city, and sprinkler systems have been installed in many parks to deter the homeless from living in them. Police and city planners have attempted to contain the homeless population within certain regions of the city, but in periodically sweeping through and confiscating makeshift shelters, they have effectively created a population of "urban Bedouins."

CONCEPT CHECKS

1. How does urban ecology use physical science analogies to explain life in modern cities?

2. What is the urban interaction problem?

3. According to Jane Jacobs, the more people there are on the streets, the more likely the street life will be safe. Do you agree with Jacobs's hypothesis and her explanation for this proposed pattern?

4. What are the four main characteristics of global cities?

---

3 RECENT RESEARCH ON POPULATION, URBANIZATION, AND THE ENVIRONMENT

Cities are the capitals of civilization: They are culturally lively, commercially dynamic, and alluring. They are efficient at providing for a large proportion of the population in a small amount of space. They are also often rife with problems of poverty, racial and ethnic exclusion and antagonism, and crime. And in countries of the global south, such as India and China, cities are exploding in population, serving as magnets for the largest rural-urban migration in human history. At the beginning of the twentieth century, fewer than one out of every seven people on the planet lived in cities. By 2008 the number of people living in cities had surpassed the number living in rural areas, and over the next 30 years as many as two-thirds of the human population may be urban. As population growth continues and globalization results in the spread of manufacturing throughout the world, we can expect the growth of cities, many of them gigantic in size, to continue.

Premodern Cities

In premodern times, cities were self-contained entities that stood apart from the predominantly rural areas in which they were located. Road systems sometimes linked major urban areas, but travel was a specialized affair for merchants, soldiers, and others who needed to cross distances with some regularity. Communication between cities was limited.

The world's first cities appeared about 3500 B.C.E., in the river valleys of the Nile in Egypt, the Tigris and Euphrates in what is now Iraq, and the Indus in what is today Pakistan. Cities in traditional societies were very small by modern standards. Babylon, for example, one of the largest ancient Near Eastern cities, extended over an area of only 3.2 square miles and at its height, around 2000 B.C.E., probably numbered no more than 15,000 to 20,000 people. Rome under Emperor Augustus in the first century B.C.E. was easily the largest premodern city outside China, with some 300,000 inhabitants—the population of Bakersfield, California, or Toledo, Ohio, today.

Most cities of the ancient world shared certain features. Walls that served as a military defense, and emphasized the separation of the urban community from the countryside, usually surrounded them. A religious temple, a royal palace, government and commercial buildings, and a public square almost always occupied the central area of the city. This ceremonial, commercial, and political center was sometimes enclosed within a second, inner wall and was usually too small to hold more than a minority of the citizens. Although it usually contained a market, the center was different from the business districts found at the core of modern cities, because the main buildings were nearly always religious and political rather than commercial (Fox, 1964; Sjoberg, 1960, 1963; Wheatley, 1971).

The dwellings of the ruling class or elite tended to be concentrated in or near the center. Less privileged groups lived toward the perimeter of the city or outside the walls, moving inside if the city came under attack. Different ethnic and religious communities were often segregated in separate neighborhoods, where their members lived and worked. Sometimes walls also surrounded these neighborhoods. Communication among city dwellers was erratic. Lacking any form of printing press, public officials had to shout at the tops of their voices to deliver pronouncements. "Streets" were usually strips of land on which no one had yet built. A few traditional civilizations boasted sophisticated road systems linking particular cities, but these existed mainly for military purposes, and transportation for the most part was slow and limited. Merchants and soldiers were the only people who regularly traveled over long distances.

Although cities became the main centers for science, the arts, and cosmopolitan culture, their influence over the rest of the country was always weak. No more than a tiny proportion of the population lived in the cities, and the division between cities and the countryside was pronounced. By far the majority of people lived in small rural communities and rarely came into contact with more than the occasional state official or merchant from the towns.

Urbanization in the Global South

The picture at the start of the twenty-first century could hardly be more different. Globalization has had a profound effect on cities by making them more interdependent and encouraging the proliferation of links among cities across national borders. Physical and virtual ties between cities now abound, and global networks of cities are emerging.

Between 1920 and 2010 the world's urban population increased from about 270 million to 3.49 billion, and roughly half the world's population now lives in cities (U.N. Habitat, 2010). By 2050 the global urban population is expected to increase as much as it has since 1920, by 3.1 billion—bringing the total urban population to more than 6.0 billion, or roughly 70 percent of the world population in 2050. Levels of urbanization vary by region, yet the majority of residents in all continents is expected to live in urban areas by 2050. Industrial nations now have the highest levels of urbanization today, surpassing 80 percent in Australia, New Zealand, and North America in 2007. Europe is the least urbanized major area in the industrialized world, with just 73 percent of its population living in urban areas. Among the regions in the global south, Latin America and the

Caribbean each has a very high level of urbanization (78 percent)—higher than Europe. By contrast, Africa and Asia remain mostly rural, with 38 percent and 41 percent of their populations, respectively, living in urban areas. However, given the very large population of Asia, half the world's urban population lived in Asia in 2007, while only 16 percent lived in Europe.

In coming decades, levels of urbanization are expected to rise even higher, with Africa and Asia urbanizing more rapidly than other regions. By 2050 an estimated 54 percent of the world's urban population will be concentrated in Asia, with 19 percent in Africa. Most of the 10 cities projected to have more than 10 million residents in 2025 are located in the global south. Most people in industrialized countries already live in cities. In 2011 the population living in urban areas was 3.6 billion (51 percent). This number is projected to gain 2.6 billion, meaning 6.3 billion people living in cities by 2050 (U.N., 2012).

Why is the rate of urban growth in the world's less industrialized regions so much higher than elsewhere? According to UN projections, the urban share is likely to rise from 75 to 81 percent in more industrialized countries and from 44 to 56 percent in less industrialized countries (U.N. Population Division, 2008b). In 1920, less than one-third percent of the population of industrialized countries was urban, and by 1950, more than 50 percent of their population was urbanized. By 2011 the urban populations of New Zealand, Australia, and North America surpassed 80 percent. Europe, with 73 percent of its population living in urban areas, was the least urbanized major area in the industrialized world. The proportion of urban dwellers living in small cities is between 49 percent and 47 percent in Asia and in Latin America and the Caribbean (U.N., 2012).

Two factors in particular must be taken into account. First, rates of population growth are higher in the global south than in industrialized nations. Although fertility rates tend to be lower in urban areas than rural areas worldwide, the higher overall fertility rates in the global south versus industrial nations account for some of the more rapid urban growth in those nations. Thus, urban growth is fueled by high fertility rates among people already living in cities. In the 1980s, natural increase (or the difference between birth rates and death rates) accounted for more than 70 percent of all urban growth in an estimated one-quarter of African nations and one-half of Asian nations (UNDP, 2007). Some claim that the demographic changes that will occur over the next century will be greater than any before in all of human history. However difficult it may be to predict future population growth, as we saw at the beginning of this chapter, the current "best guess" is roughly 9.3 billion people by 2050, stabilizing slightly higher by the end of the century.

Second, there is widespread *internal migration* from rural areas to urban ones—as in the case of the developing Hong Kong–Guangdong megacity. People are drawn to cities in the global south either because their traditional systems of rural production have disintegrated or because the urban areas offer superior job opportunities. Rural poverty prompts many people to try their hand at city life. They may intend to migrate to the city only for a relatively short time, aiming to return to their villages once they have earned enough money. Some actually do return, but most find themselves forced to stay, having for one reason or another lost their position in their previous communities.

Challenges of Urbanization in the Global South

As can be imagined, the rapid urbanization in the global south has brought with it many economic, environmental, and social challenges.

ECONOMIC CHALLENGES

Urbanization carries both positive and negative economic consequences. Urbanization is driven, in part, by the concentration of both employment and investment opportunities in cities. According to some estimates, roughly 80 percent of the world's gross domestic product (GDP) is generated by urban areas. As cities draw more jobs and businesses, they become magnets for migrants seeking better opportunities and provide a fertile setting for entrepreneurs to generate new innovations and use technology in productive ways. For example, in countries of the Organisation for Economic Co-operation and Development (OECD), urban residents file more than 81 percent of patents (OECD, 2006).

Yet as a growing number of unskilled and agricultural workers migrate to urban centers, the formal economy often struggles to absorb the influx into the workforce. In most cities in the global south, it is the *informal economy* that allows those who cannot find formal work to make ends meet. From casual work in manufacturing and construction to small-scale trading activities, the unregulated informal sector offers earning opportunities to poor or unskilled workers.

Informal economic opportunities are important for helping thousands of families (and women especially) to survive in urban conditions, but they have problematic aspects as well. The informal economy is untaxed and unregulated. It is also less productive than the formal economy. Countries where economic activity is concentrated in this sector fail to collect much-needed revenue through taxation. The low level of productivity also hurts the general economy—the proportion of the GDP generated by informal economic activity is much lower than the percentage of the population involved in the sector.

The OECD estimates that a billion new jobs will be needed by 2025 to sustain the estimated population growth in cities in the global south. It is unlikely that all these jobs will be created within the formal economy. Some development analysts argue that attention should be paid to formalizing or regulating the large informal economy, where much of the excess workforce is likely to cluster in the years to come.

ENVIRONMENTAL CHALLENGES

The rapidly expanding urban areas in the global south differ dramatically from cities in the industrialized world. Although cities everywhere are faced with environmental problems, those in the global south are confronted by particularly severe risks. Pollution, housing shortages, inadequate sanitation, and unsafe water supplies are chronic problems for cities in less industrialized countries.

Housing is one of the most acute problems in many urban areas. Cities such as Calcutta, India, and São Paulo, Brazil, are massively congested; the rate of internal migration is much too high for the provision of permanent housing. Migrants crowd into squatters' zones that mushroom around the edges of cities. In urban areas in the West, newcomers are most likely to settle close to the central parts of the city, but the reverse tends to happen in the global south, where migrants populate what has been called the "septic fringe" of the urban areas. Shanty dwellings made of burlap or cardboard are set up around the edges of the city wherever there is a little space.

In São Paulo it is estimated that there was a 5.4 million shortfall in habitable homes in 1996. Some scholars estimate that the shortage is as high as 20 million, if the definition of "habitable housing" is interpreted more strictly. Since the 1980s the chronic deficit of housing in São Paulo has produced a wave of unofficial occupations of empty buildings. Groups of unhoused families initiate mass squats in abandoned hotels, offices, and government buildings. Many families believe that it is better to share limited kitchen and toilet facilities with hundreds of others than to live on the streets or in *favelas*, the makeshift shantytowns on the edges of the city. In 2010, Brazil had 6,329 slums that housed 6 percent of the total population (Brazilian Institute of Geography and Statistics, 2010).

City and regional governments in less industrialized countries are hard pressed to keep up with the spiraling demand for housing. In cities such as São Paulo there are disagreements among housing authorities and local governments about how to address the housing problem. Some argue that the most feasible route is to improve conditions within the *favelas*—to provide electricity and running water, pave the streets, and assign postal addresses. Others fear that makeshift shantytowns are fundamentally uninhabitable and should be demolished to make way for proper housing for poor families.

Congestion and overdevelopment in city centers lead to serious environmental problems in many urban areas. Mexico City is a prime example. About 94 percent of Mexico City consists of built-up areas, with only 6 percent of land being open space. The level of green spaces (parks and open stretches of green land) is far below that found in even the most densely populated U.S. or European cities. Pollution is a major problem, coming mostly from the cars, buses, and trucks that pack the inadequate roads of the city, the rest deriving from industrial pollutants. It has been estimated that living in Mexico City is equivalent to smoking 40 cigarettes a day. In March 1992, pollution reached its highest level ever. Whereas an ozone level of just under 100 points was deemed "satisfactory" for health, in that month the level climbed to 398 points. The government had to order factories to close down for a period, schools were shut, and 40 percent of cars were banned from the streets on any one day. The city did not meet acceptable air quality standards for ozone limits 209 days in 2006. Yet this was a substantial improvement from 304 days in 1994.

SOCIAL CHALLENGES

A vast social and economic divide between the haves and the have-nots increasingly distinguishes urban areas, with poor people bearing the brunt of the negative aspects of urbanization (UNDP, 2007). Overall, urban residents, even in the global south, tend to fare better than rural dwellers along a host of outcomes, including infant and child mortality rates, adult health and mortality, and access to effective birth control and reproductive health services. Better urban public infrastructure, higher levels of maternal education, and better access to health care in cities are responsible for these health advantages. However, for poor urban dwellers, especially in the global south, neighborhoods are overcrowded and social programs under-resourced. Poverty is widespread, and existing social services cannot meet the demands for health care, family planning advice, education, and training.

Because of stark income inequalities in urban areas, especially in the global south, the plight of the urban poor is growing worse, and the size of the urban poor population is growing more rapidly than the overall urban population. Because of high housing costs, poor people in cities often have little choice but to live in overcrowded slums, where sanitation and water facilities are inadequate. The United Nations (2012) estimates that more than a billion persons lived in urban slums in 2010, and one in three city dwellers lived in inadequate housing, with no or few basic services. Furthermore, they estimate that by 2030, 2 billion people will live in slums (U.N. Habitat, 2007). The largest number of urban slum dwellers can be found in Asia (505 million), followed by sub-Saharan Africa (200 million) and Latin America and the Caribbean (111 million) (U.N. Habitat, 2010). The pressures of urban living also are associated with increasing prevalence of chronic diseases (including cardiovascular disease, cancers, and diabetes) and accidents. Traffic accidents, in particular, are growing as a cause of injury or death in cities. Unhealthy behaviors also are thriving in urban areas. Growing consumption of fats and sweeteners in the more urbanized countries of the global south is contributing to high levels of obesity and cardiovascular disease (UNDP, 2007).

The unbalanced age distribution in the global south adds to their social and economic difficulties. Compared to industrialized countries, a much larger proportion of the population in the global south is under the age of 15. A youthful population needs support and education, and during that time its members are not economically productive. But many countries in the global south lack the resources to provide universal education. When their families are poor, many children must work full time, and others have to eke out a living as street children, begging for whatever they can. Poor urban children fare worse than more well-off urban children and rural children in terms of health, are more likely to be underweight, and are less likely to receive important vaccinations. These disadvantages experienced by children in urban slums set off lifelong patterns of disadvantage. When the street children mature, most become unemployed, homeless, or both.

THE FUTURE OF URBANIZATION IN THE GLOBAL SOUTH

In considering the scope of the challenges facing urban areas in the global south, it can be difficult to see prospects for change and development. Conditions of life in many of the world's largest cities seem likely to decline even further in the years to come. But the picture is not entirely negative.

First, although birthrates remain high in many countries, they are likely to drop in the years to come as urbanization proceeds. This in turn will feed into a gradual decrease in the rate of urbanization itself. In Africa, for example, from 1970 to 2011, the percentage rate of urbanization was 1.27; that is expected to drop to .96 by 2030–2050 (United Nations, 2012).

Second, globalization is presenting important opportunities for urban areas in the global south. With economic integration, cities around the world are able to enter international markets, to promote themselves as locations for investment and development, and to create economic links across the borders of nation-states. Globalization presents one of the most dynamic openings for growing urban centers to become major forces in economic development and innovation. Indeed, many cities in the global south are already joining the ranks of the world's global cities.

Third, migrants to urban areas are often "positively selected" in terms of traits such as higher levels of educational attainment. Thus, migration may be beneficial to those persons who find better work opportunities and for their families who benefit from remittances—the money that migrant workers send back home. Urban migration may also provide opportunities for educated women in industrial nations who face obstacles in rural areas, thereby giving them access to jobs outside the home and contributing to their empowerment.

The Rise of the Megalopolis

Britain was the first society to undergo industrialization, beginning in the mid-eighteenth century. The process of industrialization generated increasing **urbanization**—the movement of the population into towns and cities, away from the land. In 1800, fewer than 20 percent of the British population lived in towns or cities with more than 10,000 inhabitants. By 1900, this proportion had risen to 74 percent. London held about 1.1 million people in 1800; by the beginning of the twentieth

urbanization • The development of towns and cities.

conurbation • An agglomeration of towns or cities into an unbroken urban environment.

megalopolis • The "city of all cities" in ancient Greece—used in modern times to refer to very large conurbations.

megacities • A term favored by Manuel Castells to describe large, intensely concentrated urban spaces that serve as connection points for the global economy. It is projected that by 2015 there will be 36 megacities with populations of more than 8 million residents.

century, it had increased in size to a population of more than 7 million, at that date the largest city ever seen in the world. It was a vast manufacturing, commercial, and financial center at the heart of the still-expanding British Empire.

The urbanization of most other European countries and the United States took place somewhat later. In 1800 the United States was more of a rural society than were the leading European countries. Fewer than 10 percent of Americans lived in communities with populations of more than 2,500 people. Today, 84 percent of Americans reside in metropolitan areas (Kaiser Family Foundation, 2008). Between 1800 and 1900, as industrialization grew in the United States, the population of New York City leapt from 60,000 people to 4.8 million.

The contrast in size between the largest modern cities today and those of premodern civilizations is extraordinary. The most populous cities in the industrialized countries number more than 10 million inhabitants. A **conurbation**—a cluster of cities and towns forming a continuous network—may include even larger numbers of people. The peak of urban life today is represented by what is called the **megalopolis**, the "city of cities." The term was originally coined in ancient Greece to refer to a city-state that was planned to be the envy of all civilizations. The current megalopolis, though, bears little relation to that utopia. The term was first used in modern times to refer to the Northeast Corridor of the United States, an area covering some 450 miles from north of Boston to south of Washington, D.C. In this region, about 44 million people live at a density of over 700 persons per square mile. An urban population almost as large and dense is concentrated in the lower Great Lakes region surrounding Chicago.

Manuel Castells (1996) refers to **megacities** as one of the main features of third-millennium urbanization. They are defined not by their size alone—although they are vast agglomerations of people—but also by their role as connection points between enormous human populations and the global economy. Megacities are intensely concentrated pockets of activity through which politics, media, communications, finances, and production flow. According to Castells, megacities function as magnets for the countries or regions in which they are located. People are drawn to large urban areas for various reasons; within megacities are those who succeed in tapping into the global system and those who do not. Besides serving as nodes in the global economy, megacities also become "depositories of all these segments of the population who fight to survive." These "pulls" to urban life

---

Traffic outside the Bank of England in the financial district of London in 1896. In only one century, the population of London grew from over 1 million people to over 7 million.

are supported by countless empirical studies. Average urban incomes are higher than those in rural areas. Urban dwellers also have better access to public services, including education, health, transportation, communication, water supply, sanitation, and waste management. Because of economies of scale, cities are better equipped to provide such services efficiently and cheaply to large, concentrated populations (UNDP, 2007).

Urbanization in the twenty-first century is a global process, into which the global south is being drawn more and more (Kasarda and Crenshaw, 1991). From 1900 to 1950, world urbanization increased by 239 percent, compared with a global population growth of 49 percent. The six decades since 1950 have seen a greater acceleration in the proportion of people living in cities. From 1950 to 1986, urban growth worldwide was 320 percent, while the population grew by 54 percent. Most of this growth has occurred in cities in the global south. In 1975, 39 percent of the world's population lived in urban areas. By 2008 the proportion had increased to over 50 percent, with more than 3.3 billion persons living in urban areas worldwide. This number is expected to reach 5.0 billion by 2030. The trend will be most marked in Africa and Asia, where the urban population will double between 2000 and 2030. By 2030 the towns and cities of the global south will account for 81 percent of the worldwide urban population (Global Map 19.1) (UNFPA, 2008).

Along with this worldwide urbanization come the effects of globalization. For example, the rise of urban-industrial areas in the global south has brought intensified economic

Global Map 19.1
The Ten Cities Expected to Have Over Ten Million Inhabitants in 2025

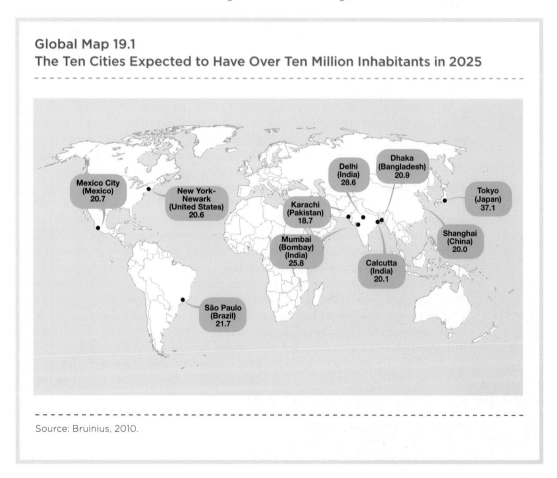

Source: Bruinius, 2010.

competition to industries in U.S. cities. South Korea's shoe industry has led to the impoverishment of urban areas in northeastern Massachusetts that formerly relied on that industry for their prosperity. Similarly, Pittsburgh and Baltimore have had to adjust to losing much of the market for their steel industry to Japan. We will examine later in the chapter how the global economy has influenced forms of city life in recent years.

Rural, Suburban, and Urban Life in the United States

What are the main trends that have affected city, suburban, and rural life in the United States over the past several decades? How can we explain patterns such as suburban sprawl, the disappearance of traditional rural life, and population declines in central cities and older suburbs? These are questions we will take up in the following sections. One of the major changes in population distribution in the period since World War II is the movement of large parts of city populations to newly constructed suburbs; this movement outward has been a particularly pronounced feature of American cities and is related directly to central-city decay. At the same time, rural populations have continued to decline as young people seek richer professional and personal opportunities in our nation's large and small cities. We therefore begin with a discussion of rural America and suburbia before moving on to look at the inner city.

THE DECLINE OF RURAL AMERICA?

Rural life has long been the focus of romanticized images among Americans. Close-knit communities and families, stretches of picturesque cornfields, and isolation from social problems such as poverty and crime round out the stereotype of rural life. Yet these stereotypes stand in stark contrast to life in many parts of rural America today.

Rural areas of the United States are defined by the U.S. Bureau of the Census as those areas located outside urbanized areas or urban clusters. Rural areas have fewer than 2,500 people and typically are areas where people live in open country. Rural America contains over 75 percent of the nation's land area yet holds just 19.3 percent of the total U.S. population (U.S. Bureau of the Census, 2010h). For most of the twentieth century, rural communities experienced significant population losses, despite several modest short-term reversals in the 1970s and the 1990s. Of the 1,346 U.S. counties that shrank in population between 2000 and 2007, 85 percent were located outside metropolitan areas, and 59 percent rely heavily on farming, manufacturing, and mining as their main revenue sources (Mather, 2008).

Population losses in rural areas are attributed to declines in farming and other rural industries, high poverty rates, scarce economic opportunities or lifestyle amenities for young people, lack of government services, and, in some regions, a dearth of natural amenities such as forests, lakes, or temperate winters. Population losses are compounded by the fact that most people leaving rural areas are young people, meaning that fewer babies are born to replace the aging population (Johnson, 2006). Many rural areas have disproportionately high numbers of older adults, because young persons seek opportunities elsewhere and leave the older persons behind. This phenomenon, called **aging in place**, explains the relatively old populations in rural areas in the Rust Belt and upper Midwest (McGranahan and Beale, 2002). Rural areas now face the difficult task of attracting and retaining residents and businesses. This is a

aging in place • A phenomenon in which many rural areas have disproportionately high numbers of older adults because young persons seek opportunities elsewhere and leave the older persons behind.

Global Map 19.2
Population Distribution by Urbanized Areas and Urban Clusters

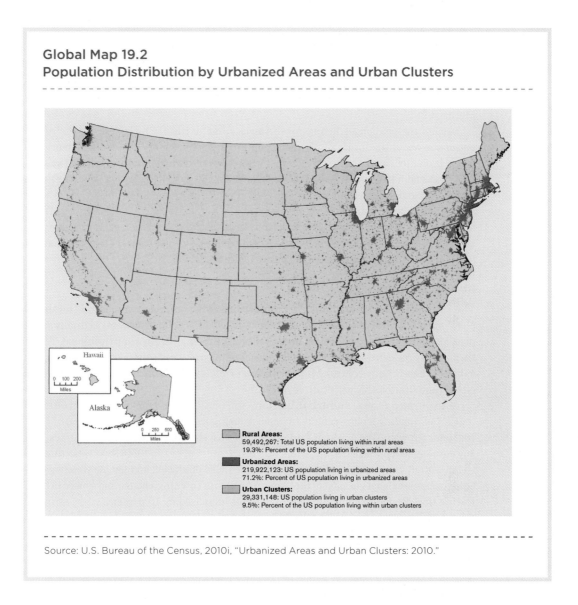

Rural Areas:
59,492,267: Total US population living within rural areas
19.3%: Percent of the US population living within rural areas

Urbanized Areas:
219,922,123: US population living in urbanized areas
71.2%: Percent of US population living in urbanized areas

Urban Clusters:
29,331,148: US population living in urban clusters
9.5%: Percent of the US population living within urban clusters

Source: U.S. Bureau of the Census, 2010i, "Urbanized Areas and Urban Clusters: 2010."

daunting challenge, though, as many rural areas lack the job opportunities or cultural amenities that young people desire.

Yet more troubling than the loss of population in rural areas are concerns about social problems, including high levels of child poverty, high rates of motor vehicle fatalities and other accidental deaths, and low levels of health and educational services (Mather, 2008). Child poverty is usually perceived as an urban problem, yet 2005 data from the U.S. Bureau of the Census reveal that of the 100 counties with the highest child poverty rates, 95 are rural. While the national child poverty rate averaged 18.5 percent in 2005, rates were as high as 70.1 percent in rural Ziebach County, South Dakota, and 61.9 percent in Owsley County, Kentucky. Not all areas are equally likely to be poverty stricken, however. Child poverty rates are highest in the most remote rural counties with the lowest population densities. Race also shapes rural poverty, just as it shapes urban poverty. Rural counties with the highest child poverty rates often are "majority minority" counties, where fewer than 50 percent of the population are non-Hispanic whites. These areas include black-majority counties in the Mississippi Delta and counties in the Midwest and West that have large Native American populations, often dwelling on Indian reservations (O'Hare and Mather, 2008).

Despite the challenges facing rural America, many rural sociologists are guardedly optimistic about the future of nonmetropolitan life. Some surveys show that Americans would prefer to live in remote areas rather than cities. Technological innovations in transportation and telecommunications afford people flexibility to work away from their urban offices. A number of government programs offer young people financial incentives to serve as teachers or health care professionals in remote areas, while not-for-profits such as Teach for America place young teachers in schools in rural areas. However, such programs are likely to be effective at attracting workers and businesses only to rural areas that have at least some natural or recreational amenities (Johnson, 2006).

SUBURBANIZATION

The word *suburb* has its origins in the Latin term *sub urbe*, or "under city control," an appropriate meaning throughout most of the history of urbanism. Suburbs were originally small pockets of dwellings dependent on urban centers for their amenities and livelihood. Today, they are any residential or commercial area adjoining a city, regardless of whether they are subject to central-city control. Many suburbs are effectively autonomous areas over which city administrations have little direct influence.

In the United States, **suburbanization**—the massive development and inhabiting of towns surrounding a city—rapidly increased during the 1950s and 1960s, a time of great economic growth. World War II had previously absorbed most industrial resources, and any development outside the war effort was restricted. But by the 1950s, war rationing had ended, automobiles instead of tanks were being mass produced, and people were encouraged to pursue at least one part of the "American dream": owning a house and a piece of land. During that decade, the population in the cities increased by 10 percent, whereas in the suburban areas it grew by no less than 48 percent.

The History of Suburbs The prevailing economic scene also facilitated moving out of the city. The Federal Housing Administration (FHA) provided assistance in obtaining mortgage loans, making it possible in the early postwar period for families to buy housing in the suburbs for less than they would have paid for rent in the cities. The FHA did not offer financial assistance to improve older homes or to build new homes in the central areas of ethnically mixed cities; its large-scale aid went only to the builders and buyers of suburban housing. The FHA, together with the Veterans Administration, funded almost half of all suburban housing built during the 1950s and 1960s.

Early in the 1950s, lobbies promoting highway construction launched Project Adequate Roads, aimed at inducing the federal government to support the building of highways. President Eisenhower responded with a giant construction program for interstate roadways, and in 1956, the Federal-Aid Highway Act was passed, authorizing $32 billion to be used for building such highways. This coincided with a period of expansion in the automobile industry such that families came to own more than one car; the result was that previously

suburbanization • The development of suburbia, areas of housing outside inner cities.

out-of-the-way suburban areas, with lower property taxes, became accessible to places of work. At the same time, the highway program led to the establishment of industries and services in suburban areas themselves. Consequently, the movement of businesses from the cities to the suburbs took jobs in the manufacturing and service industries with them. Many suburban towns became essentially separate cities, connected by rapid highways to the other suburbs around them. From the 1960s on, the proportion of people commuting between suburbs increased more steadily than the proportion commuting to cities.

Evolving Suburbs in the Twenty-First Century Scholars are currently debating whether the divide between "suburb" and "city" is meaningful, as many older suburbs, often on the fringes of major cities, share many characteristics that were once hallmarks of city life—including racial, ethnic, and social class diversity. These "first suburbs," or "inner-ring" suburbs, are home to an estimated 20 percent of all Americans and include places such as Prince George's County, Maryland; Essex County, New Jersey; and Cuyahoga County, Ohio (Puentes and Warren, 2006). First suburbs have pockets of poverty (despite generally high levels of household income and wealth among residents), an aging housing stock, old infrastructure, growing populations of immigrants, sizeable populations of older adults who bought their homes when housing prices were still reasonable, and little land left for new development that will generate property-tax revenue. These aging suburbs stand in stark contrast to outer suburbs that have new housing stock, expanses of open land, and populations that tend to be more racially and ethnically homogeneous. As a result, researchers increasingly use the term *urban area* or *metropolitan area* to describe regions that encompass central cities and their immediate outskirts.

When social scientists today talk about movement away from cities to suburbs, they are also describing the move from "first suburbs" to newer, outer-ring suburbs and to smaller urban areas. A report by the Census Bureau found that between 2000 and 2004, 18 of the nation's largest 25 metropolitan areas witnessed population declines. Outflow was heaviest from the New York, Los Angeles, Chicago, and San Francisco/Oakland metropolitan areas. Inflow was most substantial in counties that are more than 40 miles away from metropolitan areas, and to smaller cities, dubbed *micropolitan* areas—or areas with populations between 10,000 and 49,999 and that have strong commuting networks with neighboring counties. Movement to bedroom communities such as Stroudsburg, Pennsylvania, or retirement communities such as Traverse City, Michigan, reflect several major social forces, including rising housing prices and the aging of the baby boom population. Young families in particular are seeking out places where they can get a good home value yet still commute to their city jobs (U.S. Bureau of the Census, 2006).

Another important change in suburbs today, even outer suburbs, is that more and more members of racial and ethnic minorities are moving there. From 1980 to 1990, the suburban population of blacks grew by 34.4 percent, of Latinos by 69.3 percent, and of Asians by 125.9 percent. In contrast, the suburban white population grew by only 9.2 percent. In the decade from 2000 to 2009, the movement of racial and ethnic minority groups to the suburbs slowed, but it remained diverse. The suburban population of blacks grew by 27.0 percent, Latinos by 47.0 percent, Asians by 45.9 percent, and whites by 3.1 percent (Brookings Institution, 2010). This steady increase in minority suburban populations was concentrated in so-called melting pot metros, or the metropolitan regions of New York, Los Angeles, Chicago, San Francisco, Miami, and other immigrant gateway cities (Frey, 2001).

Members of minority groups move to the suburbs for reasons similar to those who preceded them: better housing, schools, and amenities. Like the people who began the exodus to suburbia in the 1950s, they are mostly middle-class professionals. According to the chairman of the Chicago Housing Authority, "Suburbanization isn't about race now; it's about class. Nobody wants to be around poor people because of all the problems that go along with poor people: poor schools, unsafe streets, gangs" (DeWitt, 1994).

Nevertheless, the suburbs remain mostly white. Minority groups constituted only 34 percent of the total suburban population and 36 percent of suburban populations in the nation's largest metropolitan areas in 2009, although they accounted for 35 percent of the total U.S. population the prior year. By contrast, whites accounted for 66 percent of the suburban population in 2009 but just under half of the population in central cities (Brookings Institution, 2010). Twenty-one percent of African Americans continue to live in the central cities, compared with 42 percent of whites. Most black suburban residents live in black-majority neighborhoods in towns bordering the city.

While the last several decades saw a movement from the cities to the suburbs, they also witnessed a shift in the regional distribution of the U.S. population from north to south and east to west. Between 2000 and 2010, regional growth was much more rapid in the South (14.3 percent) and West (13.8 percent) than in the Northeast (3.2 percent) and Midwest (3.9 percent). Overall, the South and West accounted for 84.4 percent of the total U.S. population growth between 2000 and 2010 (U.S. Bureau of the Census, 2010f).

URBAN PROBLEMS

Innercity decay is partially a consequence of the social and economic forces involved in the movement of businesses, jobs, and middle-class residents from major cities to the outlying suburbs since the 1950s. The manufacturing industries that provided employment for the urban blue-collar class largely vanished and were replaced by white-collar service industries. Millions of blue-collar jobs disappeared, and this affected in particular the poorly educated, drawn mostly from minority groups. Although the overall educational levels of minority groups improved over this period, the improvement was not sufficient to keep up with the demands of an information-based economy (Kasarda, 1993). William Julius Wilson (1991, 1996) has argued that the problems of the urban underclass grew out of this economic transformation (see Chapter 8).

These economic changes also contributed to increased residential segregation of different racial and ethnic groups and social classes, as we saw in Chapter 11. Discriminatory practices by home sellers, real estate agents, and mortgage lending institutions further added to this pattern of segregation (Massey and Denton, 1993). From 1980 to 2000 the share of African Americans in the United States living in predominantly black neighborhoods decreased from 57 to 47 percent. Over the same period, the share of African Americans living in black/Hispanic neighborhoods rose from 18 to 28 percent (Orfield, 2005). The decade from 1990 to 2000 has shown a modest decline in black-white segregation, yet segregation continues to be high among lower-income quartiles, the poor, those with less education, and those in service occupations (Iceland et al., 2003). Yet, in the decade from 2000 to 2010, black-white segregation barely declined (Logan and Stults, 2011). The social isolation of minority groups, particularly those in the underclass, or "ghetto poor," can escalate urban problems such as crime, lack of economic opportunities, poor health, and family breakdown (Massey, 1996).

Adding to these difficulties is the fact that city governments today operate against a background of almost continual financial crisis. As businesses and middle-class residents moved to the suburbs, the cities lost major sources of tax revenue. High rates of crime and unemployment in the city require it to spend more on welfare services, schools, police, and overall upkeep. Yet because of budget constraints, cities are forced to cut back many of these services. A cycle of deterioration develops in which the more suburbia expands, the greater the problems faced by city dwellers become.

THE GHETTO AS A SOCIAL AND HISTORICAL PROBLEM

Thus far, we have used the word *ghetto* without defining it. What are ghettos, and how did ghettoized poverty influence the results of the disaster in New Orleans? Many people mistakenly believe that *ghetto* means a place where African Americans or Latinos live, but the word originated in sixteenth-century Italy and applied to areas of Rome and Venice where Jews were forced to live, as a way of isolating them from mainstream Christian society, by official decree.

Sociologists originally drew a distinction between ghettos on the one hand and slums on the other. Ghettos were residential zones where particular groups were forced to live. The people who lived in these zones were not necessarily impoverished but simply of a particular ethnic or racial group who were viewed as inferior and in need of being forcibly cordoned off by the wider society. Slums were zones inhabited by poor people, including members of a dominant, nonstigmatized race, such as poor whites in the United States. In recent years, many sociologists have started using the terms *ghetto* and *slum* interchangeably, but it is better to retain the analytical clarity inherent in the former distinction.

A crucial criterion for the definition of the ghetto is that the people who live there must have been forced to do so. Indeed, this was the situation of blacks in the United States and Jews in Rome. In the United States, blacks were forced to live in certain parts of the northern cities because of restrictive covenants that made it illegal to sell them land in certain neighborhoods. Jews were forced to live in ghettos because of decrees by the popes. During the fourteenth century, most Jews were also forced to wear insignias when they traveled outside the zone where they lived, to indicate that they were Jews.

Force or compulsion is a historical rather than a contemporary factor in defining the idea of a ghetto. In other words, whereas the inhabitants of the original ghettos were given little choice of where they could live, inhabitants of today's ghettos may feel that they live in their highly segregated and impoverished neighborhoods by choice. Sociological studies have demonstrated over and again that when poor people have an opportunity to move, they will often resist every chance to do so. This is not because they do not want to improve their life chances, but because they do not believe their lives would be better independent of the social networks and neighborhood institutions that sustain them.

Are ghettos necessarily zones for the economically marginalized and exploited populations of stigmatized people? Whereas the U.S. ghetto was used to warehouse a significant labor supply for growing factories during the two world wars, the Jewish ghetto of Venice did not originally seem to have such a mission. Jews were very successful, and they continued to have significant economic ties to the wider society long after they were ghettoized (Stow, 2000). Ultimately, laws were enacted that made it difficult for Jews to carry on their occupations, but these were not intrinsic to ghettoization.

There have been many ghettos in the history of the world, but there are no sociological studies that compare ghettos in more than a few societies. For this reason, there is still much to know about the characteristics that would define the ghetto concept. From what we know, a ghetto is a residential zone in which stigmatized racial or religious groups are compelled to live by the wider society.

This takes us to an example in the contemporary United States. When Hurricane Katrina struck New Orleans, Louisiana, in August 2005, the victims of the floods that ravaged the city in the storm's aftermath were mainly poor blacks who lived in the most impoverished ghettos of the city. Why were these poor people disproportionately affected by the extreme weather conditions? The answer has mainly to do with the social and political history of these particular residential zones, which were always given fewer resources for drainage and pumping systems after past storms. It also has to do with the limited resources that poor people have to evacuate and the limited networks they have outside the zones where they live. By contrast with the poor blacks who were trapped inside the ghettos as they flooded, many middle-class whites had the resources and social connections to leave the city when warnings first appeared on the national news. The effect of Hurricane Katrina followed the fault lines of the larger urban problems associated with racial segregation and ghettoization in the inner cities today, a subject we return to later in this chapter.

Urban Renewal and Gentrification

Urban decay is not wholly a one-way process; it can stimulate countertrends, such as **urban renewal** or **gentrification**. Dilapidated areas or buildings may become renovated as more affluent groups move back into cities. Such a renewal process is called *gentrification* because those areas or buildings become upgraded and return to the control of the urban "gentry"—high-income dwellers—rather than remaining in the hands of the poor.

In *Streetwise: Race, Class, and Change in an Urban Community* (1990), sociologist Elijah Anderson analyzed the effect of gentrification on cities. Although the renovation of a neighborhood generally increases its value, it rarely improves the living standards of its current low-income residents, who are usually forced to move out. In the Philadelphia neighborhood that Anderson studied, close to the ghetto, many black residences were condemned, forcing more than 1,000 people to leave. Although they were told that their property would be used to build low-cost housing, which they would be given the first opportunity to buy, large businesses and a high school now stand there.

The poor residents who continued to live in the neighborhood received some benefits, in the form of improved schools and police protection, but the resulting increase in taxes and rents also forced them to leave for more affordable neighborhoods, most often deeper into the ghetto. African American residents whom Anderson interviewed expressed resentment at the influx of "yuppies," whom they held responsible for the changes that drove the poorer people away.

The white newcomers had come to the city in search of cheap "antique" housing, closer access to their city-based jobs, and a trendy urban lifestyle. They professed to be "open-minded" about racial and ethnic differences; in reality, however, little fraternizing took place between the new and old residents unless they were of the same social class. Because the African American residents were mostly poor and the white residents were middle class, class differences were compounded by racial ones. Though some middle-class blacks lived in the area, most chose to live far from the ghetto, fearing they would receive the same treatment that whites reserved for the black underclass. Over time, the neighborhood was gradually transformed into a white middle-class enclave.

urban renewal • The process of renovating deteriorating neighborhoods by encouraging the renewal of old buildings and the construction of new ones.

gentrification • A process of urban renewal in which older, deteriorated housing is refurbished by affluent people moving into the area.

It is important to note that the process of gentrification parallels another trend discussed earlier: the transformation of the urban economy from a manufacturing to a service industries base. Addressing the concerns of the victims of these economic changes is critical for the survival of the cities.

Population Growth, Urbanization, and Environmental Challenges

Since the beginning of the practice of agriculture thousands of years ago, human beings have left an imprint on nature. Hunting and gathering societies lived mainly from nature; they existed on what the natural environment provided and made little attempt to change the world around them. With the coming of agriculture, this situation was altered. For crops to grow, land must be cleared, trees cut down, and encroaching weeds and wild foliage kept at bay. Even primitive farming methods can lead to soil erosion. Once natural forests are cut down and clearings made, the wind may blow away the topsoil. The farming community then clears some fresh plots of land, and so the process goes on. Some landscapes that we today think of as natural, such as the rocky areas and scrubland in southwestern Greece, are actually the result of soil erosion created by farmers 5,000 years ago.

Yet before the development of modern industry and its associated urbanization, nature dominated human life far more than the other way around. Today the human onslaught on the environment is so intense that few natural processes are uninfluenced by human activity. Nearly all cultivable land is under agricultural production. What used to be almost inaccessible wildernesses are now often nature reserves, visited routinely by thousands of tourists. Modern industry, still expanding worldwide, has led to steeply climbing demands for sources of energy and raw materials. Yet the world's supply of such energy sources and raw materials is limited, and some key resources are bound to run out if global consumption is not restricted. Even the world's climate, as we shall see, has probably been affected by the global development of industry.

The Environment: A Sociological Issue?

Why should the environment be a concern for sociologists? Aren't we talking of issues that are the province purely of scientists or technologists? Isn't the effect of human beings on nature a physical one, created by modern technologies of industrial production? Yes, but modern industry and technology have come into being in relation to distinctive social institutions. The origins of our effect on the environment are social, and so are many of its consequences.

Much of the debate surrounding the environment and economic development hinges on the issue of consumption patterns. *Consumption* refers to the goods, services, energy, and resources that are used up by people, institutions, and societies. It is a phenomenon with both positive and negative dimensions. On the one hand, rising levels of consumption around the world mean that people are living under better conditions than in times past. Consumption is linked to economic development—as living standards rise, people are able to afford more food, clothing, personal items, leisure time, vacations, cars, and so forth. On the other hand, consumption can have negative impacts as well. Consumption patterns can damage the environmental resource base and exacerbate patterns of inequality. As we saw in Chapter 9 (Global Inequality), the gap between rich and poor in the world has grown during recent decades. To take one measure, the average per-person consumption of goods and services in the world's poorest economies grew only half as fast as in advanced industrial economies between 1975 and 2005 (slightly less than 1 percent per year, in comparison with 2 percent per year). The poorest region of the world, sub-Saharan Africa, actually experienced economic decline: Per-person consumption shrank by a half a percent per year during the period. Even in East Asia, the world's fastest-growing region (where growth averaged more than 6 percent per year), significant inequalities emerged within countries such as China (UNDP, 2007).

Finally, although the rich are the world's main consumers, the environmental damage that is caused by growing consumption has the heaviest effect on the poor. The wealthy are in a better position to enjoy the many benefits of consumption without having to deal with its negative effects. On a local level, affluent groups can usually afford to move away from problem areas, leaving the poor to bear most of the costs. Chemical plants, power stations, major roads, railways, and airports are often sited close to low-income areas. On a global level, we can see a similar process at work: Soil degradation, deforestation, water shortages, lead emissions, and air pollution are all concentrated within the global south. Poverty also intensifies these environmental threats. People with few resources have little choice but to maximize the resources that are available to them. As a result, more and more pressures are put on a shrinking resource base as the human population increases.

Rescuing the global environment will thus mean social as well as technological change. Given the vast global inequalities that exist, there is little chance that the poor countries in the global south will sacrifice their own economic growth because of environmental problems created largely by the rich ones. Yet the earth does not seem to possess sufficient resources for everyone on the planet to live at the standard of living most people in the industrialized societies take for granted. Hence if the impoverished sectors of the world are to catch up with the richer ones, the richer ones likely will have to revise their expectations about constant economic growth. Some "green" or environmental advocates argue that if global ecological disaster is to be avoided, people in the rich countries must react against consumerism and return to simpler ways of life.

GLOBAL ENVIRONMENTAL THREATS

One problem we all face concerns **environmental ecology**. The spread of industrial production may already have done irreparable damage to the environment. Ecological questions concern not only how we can best cope with and contain environmental damage but also the very ways of life within industrialized societies. According to one popular website, Global Footprint Network, if all people on earth were somehow to achieve the standard of living of the average American, it would require seven planets to feed, clothe, shelter, and provide the countless consumer items that make up what most of us consider a decent life. While such calculations are perhaps somewhat fanciful, the overall message is not: Our current path, whether as a nation or as all humanity, is no longer sustainable. Technological progress is, of course, unpredictable, and it may be that the earth will in fact yield sufficient resources to permit global industrialization without it resulting in irreversible ecological changes to the planet. At the moment, however, this does not seem feasible, and if the countries in the global south are to achieve living standards comparable to those currently enjoyed in the West, global readjustments will be necessary.

environmental ecology • The scientific study of the distribution and abundance of life and the interactions between organisms and their natural environment.

BIODIVERSITY

According to the International Union for the Conservation of Nature (IUCN), the most widely accepted authoritative source, more than 16,306 species are currently threatened with extinction. Hundreds of animal species have already become extinct even since the 1950s. On a list of 41,415 species that are being actively monitored by the IUCN, one out of every four mammals, one in eight birds, and nearly three-quarters of all plants are endangered. Human population growth, urbanization, and industrialization are resulting in rapid deforestation, threatening biodiversity, from gorillas to coral, everywhere on the planet. The loss of biodiversity, in turn, means more to humans than the loss of natural habitat—although many would agree with the nineteenth-century American writer Henry David Thoreau's spiritual musing, "In wilderness lies the preservation of the world." Biodiversity also provides humans with new medicines and sources and varieties of food and plays a role in regulating

Kids play on a merry-go-round near an oil refinery at the Carver Terrace housing project playground in West Port Arthur, Texas. West Port Arthur sits squarely on a two-state corridor routinely ranked as one of the country's most polluted regions.

atmospheric and oceanic chemistry. The International Union for the Conservation of Nature, which draws on the support of the governments of 140 different countries, more than 800 nongovernmental organizations, and some 10,000 scientists and experts from around the world, concludes its 2007 report with these chilling words: "Life on Earth is disappearing fast and will continue to do so unless urgent action is taken" (IUCN, 2007).

Global environmental threats are of several basic sorts: pollution, the creation of waste that cannot be disposed of in the short term or recycled, and the depletion of resources that cannot be replenished. The amount of domestic waste—what goes into our garbage cans—produced each day in industrialized societies is staggering; these countries have sometimes been called "throwaway societies" because the volume of items discarded as a matter of course is so large. For instance, food is mostly bought in packages that are thrown away at the end of the day. Some of these can be reprocessed and reused, but most cannot. Some kinds of widely employed plastics simply become unusable waste; there is no way of recycling them, and they have to be buried in garbage dumps. Or, to take another example, the disposal of electronic waste—computers, mobile phones, MP3 players, and the host of toys and gadgets that contain electronic circuits—is a growing problem. Discarded electronics, which contain toxins that cause cancer and other illnesses, are routinely "recycled" to landfills in China, India, and other poor countries, where there are few if any safeguards against contaminating local watersheds, farmlands, and communities.

Global green movements and parties (such as Friends of the Earth, Greenpeace, and Conservation International) have developed in response to the new environmental hazards. Although green philosophies are varied, a common thread concerns taking action to protect the world's environment, conserve rather than exhaust its resources, and protect the remaining animal species.

GLOBAL WARMING AND CLIMATE CHANGE

When environmental analysts speak of waste materials, however, they mean not only goods that are thrown away but also gaseous wastes pumped into the atmosphere. Examples are the carbon dioxide released into the atmosphere by the burning of fuels such as oil and coal in cars and power stations, and gases released into the air by the use of such things as aerosol cans, material for insulation, and air-conditioning units. Carbon dioxide is the main influence on the process of global warming that many scientists believe is occurring, while the other gases attack the ozone layer around the earth.

Global warming is thought to happen in the following way. The buildup of carbon dioxide in the earth's atmosphere functions like the glass of a greenhouse. It allows the sun's rays to pass through but acts as a barrier to prevent them from passing back out. The effect is to heat up the earth; global warming is sometimes termed the "greenhouse effect" for this reason. There is no longer any question that human activities play a key role in global warming. In 2007 the Intergovernmental Panel on Climate Change (IPCC) issued its fourth assessment since 1990 on the state of the planet's climate. The IPCC—a blue-ribbon group of scientists created by the UNDP and the United Nations' World Meteorological Organization in 1988— took the planet's temperature and found it to be rapidly rising.

The IPCC report concluded that "warming of the planet is unequivocal, as is now evident from observations of increases in global average air and ocean temperatures, widespread melting of snow and ice, and rising global average sea level" (IPCC, 2007). The report noted that 11 of the past 12 years had been the warmest on record, and that Northern Hemisphere temperatures during the second half of the twentieth century were likely the highest in the past 13 centuries—or longer. Rising temperatures were resulting in the rapid shrinking of polar ice caps, along with mountain glaciers; long-term droughts in some regions, with greater rainfall in others; an increase in hurricane activity in the North Atlantic; and in general more turbulence in global weather. Most significantly, the IPCC report stated unequivocally that human activity is the principal source of global warming, very likely causing most of the temperature increase over the last century. It found, for example, that human-caused global greenhouse gas emissions have grown since the Industrial Revolution, increasing 70 percent in the past several decades alone (IPCC, 2007).

The U.S. government, which had generally refused to accept as conclusive the link between human activity and global warming, finally joined more than 100 other countries in accepting the report's conclusions (Rosenthal and Revkin, 2007). In recognition of its work, the IPCC—along with former U.S. vice president Al Gore, whose Academy Award–winning film *An Inconvenient Truth* popularized the issue of global warming—received the 2007 Nobel Peace Prize.

Why should global warming matter? Apart from requiring American snowboarders to travel much farther north for good conditions, won't rising temperatures result in more moderate climates in most places? The IPCC report documents the many dangers that global warming will bring. Apart from severe droughts—which will turn once-fertile lands into deserts—global warming will threaten the water supplies of hundreds of millions of people, increase the danger of flooding for others, adversely affect agriculture in parts of the world, and further reduce planetary biodiversity. It will likely have devastating consequences for low-lying areas, as melting polar ice caps, particularly in Greenland and the Antarctic, lead to rising sea levels. Cities that lie near the coasts or in low-lying areas will be flooded and become uninhabitable. Under some scenarios, for example, most of Florida will disappear beneath the rising seas; a number of South Sea islands have already been affected. The IPCC specifically identified the following impacts as likely:

- warming greatest over land and at most high northern latitudes and least over the Southern Ocean and parts of the North Atlantic Ocean, continuing recent observed trends;
- contraction of snow cover area, increases in thaw depth over most permafrost regions, and decrease in sea ice extent; in some projections . . . Arctic late-summer sea ice disappears almost entirely by the latter part of the 21st century;
- *very likely* increase in frequency of hot extremes, heat waves, and heavy precipitation;
- *likely* increase in tropical cyclone intensity; less confidence in global decrease of tropical cyclone numbers;
- poleward shift of extra-tropical storm tracks with consequent changes in wind, precipitation, and temperature patterns and;
- *very likely* precipitation increases in high latitudes and *likely* decreases in most subtropical land regions, continuing observed recent trends. (IPCC, 2007)

The IPCC (2007) also offers some hope that the worst consequences of global warming can be mitigated, since it concludes that there is still time for changes to be made. But these changes will require concerted action by governments and people around the world. They include national policies that encourage water, land, and energy conservation, the development of alternative energy sources, and in general incorporating scientific thinking about global climate change into our ways of thinking about everything from tourism to transportation. While the IPCC report addresses governments, it also stands to reason that individual behavior can make a difference, even if that difference is small. Because individuals in the United States and other advanced industrial nations consume far more than the average person in the global south, their ecological footprint is much greater. Recycling, walking or riding a bicycle rather than driving whenever possible, buying fuel-efficient cars, turning the heat down and the air-conditioning off—all these are small steps that can add up, if practiced by a large enough number of people. As the IPCC report makes clear, the time for concerted action may be running out.

ENERGY

Modern industry, still expanding worldwide, has led to steeply climbing demands for sources of energy and raw materials. Yet the world's supply of such energy sources and raw materials is limited. Even at current rates of use, for example, the known oil resources of the world will be completely consumed by the year 2050. New reserves of oil may be discovered, or alternative sources of cheap energy invented, but there is plainly a point at which some key resources will run out if global consumption is not limited.

The United States is the largest consumer of energy in the world, and the world's largest producer of greenhouse gases, accounting for perhaps a quarter of the world's total (although, as mentioned previously, China is rapidly catching up and may have surpassed

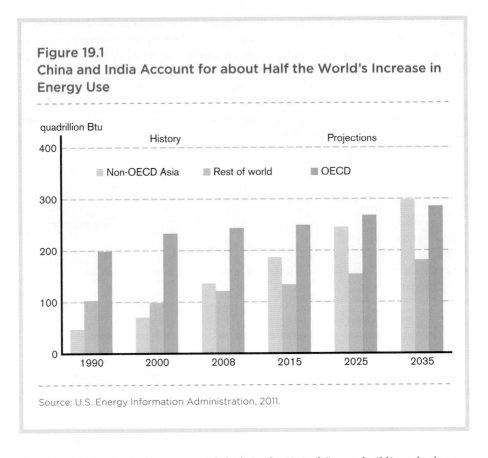

Figure 19.1
China and India Account for about Half the World's Increase in Energy Use

quadrillion Btu

History   Projections

Non-OECD Asia   Rest of world   OECD

Source: U.S. Energy Information Administration, 2011.

the United States by the time you read this). In the United States, buildings, both commercial and residential, represent 41 percent of energy use, while industrial uses account for 30 percent of energy use, and transportation, 28 percent (U.S. Department of Energy, 2011). Most of America's energy comes from nonrenewable fossil fuels—mainly petroleum, and to a lesser degree coal and natural gas. According to U.S. government figures, the United States in 2008 consumed 22 percent of the world's petroleum, 21 percent of its natural gas, 16 percent of its coal, and 23 percent of its electricity—and produced 20 percent of all carbon emissions that result from fossil fuel consumption (U.S. Energy Information Administration [EIA], 2010). Since the United States has only 8 percent of the world's population, it is clearly consuming a greatly disproportionate share of global energy reserves.

Although the United States accounts for much of the current worldwide energy consumption, the fastest and biggest increases in energy use are in China and India. The U.S. Energy Information Administration (EIA, 2011) projects that worldwide energy use will increase by 53 percent between 2011 and 2035, and half of that increase will occur in China and India. In 2008 those two countries accounted for 21 percent of the total growth in energy use. If current trends continue, the EIA predicts that by 2035, China will be using 68 percent more energy than the United States. However, natural gas has the fastest growth rate among the fossil fuels, and the United States has a larger supply and more developed industry than any other country. Nonetheless, the increase in energy use will put tremendous strain on world resources. Despite breakthroughs in renewable energy, it is predicted that fossil fuels will still comprise 78 percent of global energy consumption. It is also clear that as the poor nations of the world pursue economic development, if their per-person levels of energy consumption approach that of the United States—or even that of more energy-efficient industrial countries such as Germany or Japan—the world's energy sources will be severely challenged. Whether or not the world's oil reserves, for example, will be greatly reduced or even depleted over the next 25 to 50 years is much debated, but there is little disagreement over the fact that if continued economic growth in China and India depends heavily on the use of petroleum—and if the United States and other advanced industrial countries fail to develop alternative sources of energy—the cost of oil and gasoline will greatly increase. As petroleum becomes increasingly scarce, the cost of extracting and refining it rises. Coal—one alternative energy source that remains in relative abundance—is, as we have already noted, a highly polluting source of greenhouse gases. While "clean coal" technology exists, it remains costly. Nuclear energy is another alternative to petroleum. Although widely used in Europe—more than a third of France's energy comes from nuclear plants—nuclear energy has a number of potential drawbacks: An accident in a nuclear plant could release the spread of deadly radiation, as happened in Chernobyl, Ukraine, in 1986, exposing more than 6 million people and requiring the resettlement of some 300,000; there are problems of disposing of radioactive waste from spent nuclear fuel, which remains highly toxic for thousands of years; there is the danger that nuclear fuel could be stolen and used to make nuclear weapons. The future of nuclear energy is unclear. In 2011 an earthquake and tsunami caused three nuclear reactors to experience meltdown at the Fukushima Daiichi nuclear power plant in Japan. Many countries halted planned nuclear energy expansions. Germany took the dramatic step of phasing out nuclear power; a goal that it hopes to achieve by 2020 (*New York Times*, 2012b).

There is an emerging consensus among scientists and policy makers around the world that if economic development is to occur, it has to be concerned increasingly with conservation of scarce resources and with reducing the production of greenhouse gases and other pollutants.

SUSTAINABLE DEVELOPMENT

Rather than calling for a reining in of economic growth, more recent developments turn on the notion of **sustainable development**. Sustainable development means that growth should, at least minimally, be carried on in such a way as to recycle physical resources rather than deplete them and to keep levels of pollution to a minimum; ideally, development would be based largely on renewable resources such as wind, sun, and water, rather than fossil fuels that will eventually become depleted. The term *sustainable development* was first introduced in a 1987 report commissioned by the United Nations, *Our Common Future* (also known as the Brundtland Report, because the organizing committee that produced the report was chaired by Gro Harlem Brundtland, at that time the prime minister of Norway). Sustainable development was defined as the use of renewable resources to promote economic growth, the protection of animal species and biodiversity, and the commitment to maintaining clean air, water, and land. The Brundtland Commission regarded

sustainable development • The limiting of economic growth to proceed only insofar as natural resources are recycled rather than depleted; biodiversity is maintained; and clean air, water, and land are protected.

sustainable development as "meeting the needs of the present, without compromising the ability of future generations to meet their own needs."

After the publication of *Our Common Future*, the term *sustainable development* came to be widely used by environmentalists and governments. It was employed at the UN Earth Summit in Rio de Janeiro in 1992 and has subsequently appeared in other ecological summit meetings organized by the United Nations.

The Brundtland Report attracted much criticism. Critics see the notion of sustainable development as too vague and as neglecting the specific needs of poorer countries. According to the critics, the idea of sustainable development tends to focus attention only on the needs of richer countries; it does not consider the ways in which the high levels of consumption in the more affluent countries are satisfied at the expense of other people. For instance, demands on Indonesia to conserve its rain forests could be seen as unfair, because Indonesia has a greater need than the industrialized countries for the revenue it would have to forgo by accepting conservation measures.

Still, the hope for globally sustainable development is far from abandoned. Despite the early criticisms of the Brundtland Report, progress has been made in better understanding how renewable resources and conservation can—indeed, must—play a key role in any country's development strategy, for the many reasons outlined in this chapter: If the cost of development is toxic air and water, cities choked with traffic congestion, and the global depletion of key sources of energy, another path must be sought. In 2007 the United Nations Division for Sustainable Development, which provides technical assistance to countries in the global south, issued a report addressing such issues as energy, industrial development, air quality, and climate change (UN CSD, 2007). The UN Human Development Report of 2011 focused on the intersection of sustainability and equity, further exploring the links between global social well-being and the state of the environment (UNDP, 2011).

China, whose rapid economic growth has brought severe energy and environmental challenges, also has an emerging grassroots environmental movement (Birnbaum and Yu, 2007; Wu, 2009). The country's current (eleventh) Five-Year Plan, for the period 2007–2012, calls for a 20 percent reduction in energy consumption in relation to the size of its economy over the plan period; the country has enacted legislation requiring far stricter fuel economy standards for cars than exist in the United States (Niederberger et al., 2007). In 2005, China's president, Hu Jintao, called on China's leadership to build a "harmonious society"—both among people (by addressing the growing economic inequality) and with nature. In Hu's words, "The present ecological and environmental situations in China are rather tough and grave in some places. Without a sound natural environment, people will have no clean water to drink, fresh air to breathe, healthy food to eat, which will result in serious social problems" (*Xinhua*, 2005). Whether China is able to achieve the lofty goal of continuing rapid economic growth—including elevating hundreds of millions of people out of poverty—while at the same time achieving some sort of balance with nature remains to be seen.

CONCEPT CHECKS ✓

1. What is urbanization? How is it related to globalization?

2. Urban growth in the global south is much higher than elsewhere. Discuss several economic, social, and environmental consequences of such rapid expansion of cities in the global south.

3. What are the two unintended consequences of urbanization? How do they deepen socioeconomic and racial inequalities?

4. Define sustainable development and provide at least one criticism of the concept.

UNANSWERED QUESTIONS

Population growth, industrialization, urbanization, and the resulting environmental disruptions provide many challenges for sociological research. In this final section we consider two questions whose answers remain contested—one concerning urban poverty in the United States, the other whether global population growth will outstrip global food production, resulting in widespread famine.

Explaining Urban Poverty: The Sociological Debate

The plight of the American inner city has grown bleak in recent times. According to U.S. Census data, the proportion of our nation's poor who live in central cities increased from 34 percent in 1970 to 43 percent in 1990 (U.S. Bureau of the Census, 2003a). Not only are the poor increasingly concentrated in urban areas, but the poor living in the inner city are clustered in neighborhoods overwhelmingly inhabited by other poor families. The consequences are that the urban poor, particularly the black urban poor, live in very poor, socially isolated, racially homogeneous neighborhoods, which are increasingly plagued with troubles such as joblessness, crime, and poor quality of life. From 2000 to 2010, the overall population living in central cities increased by 3 percentage points. In 2010, roughly one-third of the total U.S. population lived in central cities, the highest proportion since 1950 (Population Reference Bureau, 2011b). From 2000 to 2010, the population in extreme poverty rose twice as fast in the suburbs as in central cities. Still, poor people are four times more likely to be in concentrated poverty in an urban area than are the poor in the suburbs (Brookings Institution, 2011).

William Julius Wilson's (1987, 1996) position can be described as the "economic restructuring" hypothesis. He argues that persistent urban poverty stems primarily from the structural transformation of the inner-city economy. The decline of manufacturing industries, the "suburbanization" of employment, and the rise of a low-wage service sector have dramatically reduced the number of entry-level jobs that pay wages sufficient to support a family. The high rate of joblessness resulting from economic shifts has led to a shrinking pool of marriageable men (those financially able to support a family). Thus marriage has become less attractive to poor women, unwed childbearing has increased, and female-headed households have proliferated. New generations of children are born into poverty, and the vicious circle is perpetuated. Wilson argues that blacks suffer disproportionately due to past discrimination and because they are concentrated in locations and occupations particularly affected by economic restructuring.

Wilson elaborated that these economic changes were accompanied by an increase in the spatial concentration of poverty within black neighborhoods. This new geography of poverty, he felt, was due in part to the civil rights movement of the 1960s, which provided middle-class blacks with new opportunities outside the ghetto. The out-migration of middle-class families from ghetto areas left behind a destitute community lacking the institutions, resources, and values necessary for success in postindustrial society. He also acknowledges that such neighborhoods lack locally available training and education and have suffered from the dissolution of government and private support of the local organizations that once supplied job information as well as employment opportunities. Thus the urban underclass arose from a complex interplay of civil rights policy, economic restructuring, and a historical legacy of discrimination.

While Wilson emphasizes macro-level economic shifts as the cause underlying the concentration of urban poverty, Douglas Massey and Nancy Denton support the "racial residential segregation" hypothesis. This view holds that high levels of racial residential segregation may increase minority poverty by limiting access to employment opportunities. Segregation in ghettos exacerbates employment problems because it leads to weak informal employment networks and contributes to the social isolation of individuals and families, thereby reducing their chances of acquiring the skills, including adequate educational training, that facilitate mobility in a society. Because no other group in society experiences the degree of segregation, isolation, and poverty concentration that African Americans do, African Americans are far more likely to be disadvantaged when they have to compete with other groups in society for resources and privileges.

Massey and Denton argue further that in the absence of residential segregation, the structural and economic changes observed by Wilson would not have produced the disastrous social and economic consequences observed in inner cities during the past 30 years. Although the economic dislocations Wilson identifies drove up rates of black poverty, it was segregation that confined the higher levels of deprivation to a small number of densely settled, tightly packed, and geographically isolated areas.

Massey and Denton (1993) also dispute Wilson's claim that concentrated poverty arose because the civil rights revolution allowed middle-class blacks to move out of the ghetto. Their principal objection to Wilson's focus on middle-class out-migration is that it deflects attention from the "real issue, which is the limitation of black residential options through segregation."

This debate highlights an important aspect of sociology—namely, that many of its leading practitioners are trying to think like scientists. Douglas Massey and William Julius Wilson are two of the leading sociologists of the past 50 years. From the standpoint of many Americans who would see both of their arguments as supporting the same progressive political agenda, it would not matter whether poverty were caused by segregation or joblessness. Either cause requires a major shift in political priorities and a significant role for the U.S. government in solving the problem. In their political sympathies, Wilson and Massey have a tremendous amount in common, so why has their debate been so fierce?

The answer is that one of their highest shared priorities is the scientific goal of explanation. Each of them is trying to explain the root causes of the contemporary ghetto. But ultimately, they have a great deal in common. Both of them agree that if you are poor, the neighborhood you live in has a major effect on your life chances, above and beyond other aspects of your life. These "neighborhood effects" must be addressed, regardless of how they came into being.

Will Global Population Growth Outstrip Resources?

During the rise of industrialism, many looked forward to a new age in which food scarcity would be a phenomenon of the past. The development of modern industry, it was widely supposed, would create a new era of abundance. In his celebrated work *Essay on the Principle of Population* (2003; orig. 1798), Thomas Malthus criticized these ideas and initiated a debate about the connection between population and food resources that continues to this day. At the time Malthus wrote, the population in Europe was growing rapidly. Malthus pointed out that whereas population increase is exponential, food supply depends on fixed resources that can be expanded only by developing new land for cultivation. Population growth therefore tends to outstrip the means of support available. The inevitable outcome is famine, which, combined with the influence of war and plagues, acts as a natural limit to population increase. Malthus predicted that human beings would always live in circumstances of misery and starvation, unless they practiced what he called "moral restraint." His cure for excessive population growth was for people to delay marriage and to strictly limit their frequency of sexual intercourse. (The use of contraception he proclaimed to be a "vice.")

For a while, **Malthusianism** was ignored, because the population development of the Western countries followed a quite different pattern from that which he had anticipated. Rates of population growth trailed off in the nineteenth and twentieth centuries. Indeed, in the 1930s there were major worries about population decline in many industrialized countries, including the United States. Malthus also failed to consider that technology that fostered increases in food production would be developed in the modern era. However, the upsurge in world population growth in the twentieth century has again lent some credence to Malthus's views. Population expansion in the global south seemed to be outstripping the resources that those countries could generate to feed their citizenry—especially in nations that suffered from such natural disasters as droughts and floods that hurt local food supplies.

Malthusian arguments got a boost when the biologist Paul Ehrlich published a best-selling book, *The Population Bomb,* in 1968. Ehrlich (1968) predicted a catastrophic global collapse, as an exploding world population vastly outstripped global food production. Famine would overtake India and other populous countries, and hundreds of millions of people would perish in the coming decades. His arguments received support from another study published a few years later. *The Limits to Growth* (Meadows et al., 1972) used advanced (for the time) computer simulation modeling to project the complex interaction of five factors the authors believed to be key to understand the earth–human system interrelationship: population, industrialization, pollution, food production, and resource depletion. Their predictions were dire: a high likelihood of global agricultural and economic collapse by the mid- to late-twenty-first century. Ehrlich updated (and reaffirmed) his arguments some 20 years later in *The Population Explosion* (Ehrlich and Ehrlich, 1990), and gave even more dire predictions in a keynote address to the annual meeting of the American Sociological Association in 2012.

Famine and food shortages are indeed a serious concern. There are already 925 million people in the world who suffer from hunger or undernourishment (UN FAO, 2011a). In some parts of the world, more than a third of the population is under-nourished (Figure 19.2). As the population rises, levels of food output will need to rise accordingly to avoid widespread scarcity. Yet many of the world's poorest areas are particularly affected by water shortages, shrinking farmland, and soil degradation—processes that reduce, rather than enhance, agricultural productivity. It is almost certain in such areas that food production will not occur at a level to ensure self-sufficiency. Large amounts of food and grain will need to be imported from areas where there are surpluses.

On the other hand, as noted at the beginning of this chapter, the most widely accepted prediction of global population growth sees a leveling-off at 9–10 billion people by the end of the century, the result of a "second demographic transition," which, contrary to Malthusian predictions, would result in lower (rather than higher) fertility. Having a large number of children may make sense in pre-industrial countries, where child mortality is high and children provide an important source of labor on family farms, but in modern industrial

Malthusianism • A doctrine about population dynamics developed by Thomas Malthus, according to which population increase comes up against "natural limits," represented by famine and war.

Figure 19.2
Shares of World Consumption of the Richest 20 Percent and the Poorest 20 Percent, 1995

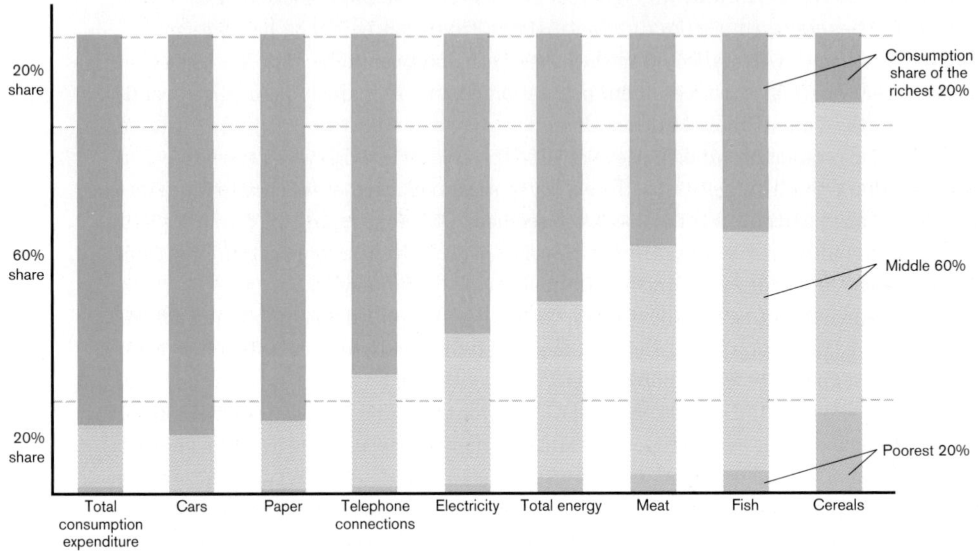

Source: UNDP, 1998, "Human Development Report 1999."

societies, large families can be an economic cost rather than an asset: children tend to be economic consumers rather than producers. As more and more countries in the global south are brought into the global economy, the reasoning goes, they will undergo their own demographic transition to a low mortality/low fertility equilibrium, thereby radically slowing population growth. Population may in fact initially surge: As modern farming technology and public health measures developed in industrial nations are adopted by countries in the global south, mortality will decline. But eventually fertility will follow suit, and a low-growth equilibrium will result. Among industrial economies, such as Germany, Italy, Japan, and Russia, fertility has dropped below replacement levels, resulting in a declining population, at least among the native-born population. (Growth in such cases can occur only through immigration.)

Moreover, doomsday predictions have long underestimated global increases in food production, which, thanks in part to advances in farming technology, have so far managed to keep pace with population growth. According to the UN Food and Agricultural Organization, even the projected population growth to 2050 can be accommodated by increased food supply—if certain conditions are met: drawing on additional (but available) land and water resources, higher crop yields, and preserving biodiversity. The study concludes that

According to FAO's baseline projections, it should be possible to meet the future food and feed demand of the projected world population in 2050 within realistic rates for land and water use expansion and yield development. However, achieving this will not at all be automatic and several significant challenges will have to be met . . . The conditions under which this can be achieved are strong economic growth, global expansion of food supplies by about 70 percent, relatively high production growth in many developing countries achievable through growing capital stock, higher productivity and global trade helping the low income food deficit countries to close their import gaps for cereals and other food products at affordable prices (UN FAO, 2011a).

The key problem, according to this view, is not that population growth is outstripping food production, as Malthus predicted more than 200 years ago; it is that the results of increased agricultural productivity are not equitably distributed. The counterargument to Malthusian pessimism, simply stated, lies neither with the biological food-producing capacity of the planet nor with the failure of agricultural technology to keep pace. It lies with the fact that a small proportion of the world's population consumes a vastly unequal proportion of the world's natural resources. The solutions, in other words, are to be found in societal terms, not a biological imperative.

What will be the consequences of these changes? Some observers see the makings of widespread social upheaval—particularly in countries in the global south undergoing demographic transition. Changes in the economy and labor markets may prompt widespread internal migration as people in rural areas search for work. The rapid growth of cities will be likely to lead to environmental damage, new public health risks, overloaded infrastructures, rising crime, and impoverished squatter settlements. Technological advances in agriculture and industry are unpredictable, so no one can be sure how large a population the world might eventually be able to support. Even if technological solutions are found, will they be used to benefit those in the poorest regions of the world, who face the most dire Malthusian prospects—or to increase the consumption of those in relatively wealthy countries, who are most likely to be insulated from catastrophic collapse?

CONCEPT CHECKS

1. Explain Malthus's position on the relationship between population growth and the food supply.

2. Compare and contrast Massey and Denton's explanations for urban poverty with William Julius Wilson's.

1

Basic Concepts

p. 591

2

Urban Sociology: Some Influential Theories

p. 595

LEARNING OBJECTIVES

Learn about the most important concepts that demographers use to understand world population growth and the changes in cities.

Understand how theories of urbanism have placed increasing emphasis on the influence of socioeconomic factors on city life.

TERMS TO KNOW

Demography • Crude birthrates • Fertility • Fecundity • Crude death rates • Mortality • Infant mortality rate • Life expectancy • Life span • Rates of population growth or decline • Exponential • Doubling time • Demographic transition • Second demographic transition

Ecological approach • Inner city • Urban ecology • Urbanism • Created environment • Collective consumption • Global city

CONCEPT CHECKS

1. What is the difference between fertility and fecundity?
2. What are the stages of a demographic transition, and why do some demographers believe that we've begun a second demographic transition?

1. How does urban ecology use physical science analogies to explain life in modern cities?
2. What is the urban interaction problem?
3. According to Jane Jacobs, the more people there are on the streets, the more likely the street life will be safe. Do you agree with Jacobs's hypothesis and her explanation for this proposed pattern?
4. What are the four main characteristics of global cities?

1. Explain what makes the urbanization now occurring in developing countries, such as Brazil and India, different from and more problematic than the urbanization that took place a century ago in New York, London, Tokyo, and Berlin.

2. Following analysis presented in this chapter, concisely explain how the expanded quest for cheap energy and raw materials and present-day dangers of environmental pollution and resource depletion threaten not only the survival of people in developed countries but also that of people in less developed countries.

3

Recent Research on Population, Urbanization, and the Environment

p. 604

4

Unanswered Questions

p. 627

See how cities have changed as a result of industrialization and urbanization. Recognize the challenges of urbanization in the global south. Learn about the recent key developments affecting American cities, suburbs, and rural communities in the last several decades. See that the environment is a sociological issue related to urbanization and population growth.

Learn more about the sociological debates about the causes of urban poverty and whether global population growth will outstrip our resources.

Urbanization • Conurbation • Megalopolis • Megacities • Aging in place • Suburbanization • Urban renewal • Gentrification • Environmental ecology • Sustainable development

Malthusianism

1. What is urbanization? How is it related to globalization?

2. Urban growth in the global south is much higher than elsewhere. Discuss several economic, social, and environmental consequences of such rapid expansion of cities in the global south.

3. What are the two unintended consequences of urbanization? How do they deepen socioeconomic and racial inequalities?

4. Define sustainable development and provide at least one criticism of the concept.

1. Explain Malthus's position on the relationship between population growth and the food supply.

2. Compare and contrast Massey and Denton's explanations for urban poverty with William Julius Wilson's.

Globalization in a Changing World

20

Which of these countries has the largest movie industry, as measured by the number of major films produced each year? (For extra credit, rank them in descending order of the size of the film industry)

a United States

b China

c Japan

d India

e Nigeria

Turn the page for the correct answer.

If you guessed the United States and Hollywood, you are not even close! India tops the list by far. According to a 2009 UN study of the global film industry (the most recent year for which comparative statistics are available), India produced 1,288 feature films that year, resulting in nearly 3 billion admissions, accounting for two out of every five movie tickets that were sold in the world (UNESCO, 2012b, tables 3 and 11). India's film industry produces films in more than a dozen different languages, reflecting the extraordinary cultural and linguistic diversity of a country that is well known locally and globally for its Hindi-language "Bollywood" films, based in the city of Mumbai (Bombay). Bollywood films are truly global in origin: They draw from such wide-ranging sources as twentieth-century Hollywood musicals, ancient Sanskrit dramas that combined lavish music and dance, Indian folk theater, and even MTV. The results are rich, elaborate films with romantic characters, numerous plots and subplots, lavish costuming, highly theatrical performances, and lots of dancing. Indian films have had widespread impact outside India: Satyajit Ray's *Apu Trilogy* was released in the 1950s to critical acclaim and was ranked among the top 100 movies ever made by *Time* magazine in 2005. More recently, British filmmaker Danny Boyle's film *Slumdog Millionaire*, based on an Indian novel, was filmed in Mumbai; Boyle— who also orchestrated the opening ceremony for the 2012 Olympics in London—credits Indian film as a major influence.

Nigeria comes in second on the list, producing 987 feature films in 2009. Unlike in India, many films in Nigeria are low budget: they are usually shot using digital hand-held cameras, burned onto CDs, and sold inexpensively throughout Africa. The country's burgeoning film industry, sometimes dubbed Nollywood, provides significant

LEARNING OBJECTIVES

1 BASIC CONCEPTS

Recognize that numerous factors influence social change, including physical environment, political organization, culture, and economic factors.

2 CURRENT THEORIES: IS GLOBALIZATION TODAY SOMETHING NEW— OR HAVE WE SEEN IT ALL BEFORE?

Understand the debates between skeptics, hyperglobalizers, and transformationalists over whether globalization differs radically from anything in human history.

3 RECENT RESEARCH ON GLOBALIZATION AND SOCIAL CHANGE

Recognize the importance of information flows, political changes, and transnational corporations. Appreciate how globalization has influenced the rise of individualism, changing work patterns, popular culture, risk, and inequality in modern society.

4 UNANSWERED QUESTIONS

Evaluate the notion that social change is leading into a postindustrial or postmodern stage of social organization. Understand why new forms of global governance are needed to address the risks, challenges, and inequalities produced by globalization.

employment in the job-starved country. It has its own Academy Awards, enlivened with visits from Hollywood movie stars such as Danny Glover and Forest Whitaker. While the films deal with a range of topics, they often draw on local themes and are shot on location, rather than in studios. By some estimates, Nigeria's film industry is a half-billion-dollar business (Rice, 2012).

In the global sweepstakes of feature films, the United States ranked only third in 2009, producing 734 feature films—although its blockbuster, high-budget (and high-special-effects) films are popular throughout the world, accounting for the highest revenues. China, despite its large population, came in only fourth (with 475 films), and Japan, fifth (with 448 films).

Films around the world draw on one another for themes, cinematographic techniques, and technology. While Hollywood remains an important influence, each country (indeed, in many countries, each region) has developed its own style and approach. The global film industry is an example of **hybridity**—a notion borrowed from biology to capture the fact that cultures are neither isolated nor wholly distinct, but in fact involve numerous borrowings from one another. This has been true historically and arguably has accelerated in recent years. Globalization today brings people, and their cultures, into intimate contact with one another, whether through travel or migration, economic interdependence, mass media, or popular culture. Social media play a key role in connecting people, films, and popular music across a global space:

> Fairly recent on the horizon, after Latino rock, is Mandarin pop, a Cantonese and Pacific American combination of styles. One of its original inspirations is Hong Kong crooners doing Mandarin cover versions of Japanese popular ballads. The Japanese ballads were already a mixture of Japanese and American styles that featured, for instance, saxophone backgrounds. Mandarin pop (or Mandopop) is part of the soundscape of the Pacific Chinese diaspora. Its audience ranges from youngsters in China, Hong Kong and Taiwan to prosperous second-generation Chinese immigrants in the United States. (Nederveen Pieterse, 2001)

In this chapter we examine the ways in which globalization affects our lives on many levels, contributing to the social changes that are sweeping the world today.

THE ANSWER IS D.

① BASIC CONCEPTS

Imagine standing before a clock that measures time on a cosmic scale, in which each second represents 60,000 years. On such a clock it would take 24 hours for the 5-billion-year history of our planet to unfold. Humanlike apes would not even appear until the last two minutes, and human beings only in the last four seconds. Compared to us, even the dinosaurs would look like long-term residents of the planet—they roamed the earth for nearly three-quarters of an hour on our 24-hour clock, before disappearing forever. Will human beings—whose great civilizations appeared only in the last quarter second—do nearly as well?

Human beings are very recent residents of planet Earth, yet we have unquestionably made our presence known. Our numbers have exploded to some 7 billion people and will probably increase by half again over the next 50 years. We have spread to every nook and cranny on the planet. Thanks to modern science and industry, each of us uses up a vastly greater amount of the planet's limited resources than did our apelike ancestors. Indeed, the combination of population explosion and modern industrial expansion threatens both our planet and our human civilization.

Humans have shown a unique ability to create massive problems—and then find ways to solve them. Today our problems are global, requiring global solutions. Globalization has contributed to such challenges as global warming and climate change, the worldwide spread of HIV/AIDS, conflict among nations, terrorism, and global poverty. Yet globalization can also contribute to their solution. All human beings share a common home and, therefore, a common interest in its preservation.

Social Change

Social change can be defined as the transformation over time of the institutions and culture of a society. Globalization has accelerated these processes of social change, affecting virtually all of humanity. As a result, far more than any generation before us, we face an uncertain future. To be sure, previous generations were at the mercy of natural disasters, plagues, and famines. Yet, although these problems still trouble much of the world, today we must also deal with the social forces that we ourselves have unleashed. During a period of only two or three centuries—a sliver of time in the context of human history—human social life has been wrenched away from the types of social order in which people lived for thousands of years.

Social theorists have tried for the past two centuries to develop a single grand theory that explains social change. Marx, for example, emphasized the importance of economic factors in shaping social life, including politics and culture. But no single-factor theory can account for the diversity of human social development from hunting and gathering and pastoral societies, to traditional civilizations, to the highly complex social systems of today. In analyzing social change, we can accomplish two tasks: We can identify major factors that have consistently influenced social change, such as the physical environment, economics, political organization, and culture; and we can develop theories that explain particular periods of change, such as modern times.

THE PHYSICAL ENVIRONMENT

The physical environment often affects the development of human social organization. This is clearest in extreme environmental conditions. For example, people in polar regions develop different practices from those living in subtropical areas. Residents of Alaska, where the winters are long and cold and winter days very short, follow different patterns of social life from residents of the much warmer U.S. South. Most Alaskans spend more of their lives indoors and, except in summer months, plan outdoor activities carefully, given the inhospitable environment.

Less extreme physical conditions can also affect society. The indigenous population of

social change • Alteration in basic structures of a social group or society. Social change is an ever-present phenomenon in social life but has become especially intense in the modern era. The origins of modern sociology can be traced to attempts to understand the dramatic changes shattering the traditional world and promoting new forms of social order.

Australia has remained hunters and gatherers because the continent has hardly any indigenous plants suitable for cultivation or animals suitable for pastoral production. Most of the world's early civilizations originated in areas with rich agricultural land—for instance, in river deltas. The ease of communications across land and the availability of sea routes are also important: Societies cut off from others by mountain ranges, impassable jungles, or deserts often remain relatively unchanged over long periods.

Jared Diamond (2005) makes a strong case for the importance of environment in his book *Collapse: How Societies Choose to Fail or Succeed*. Diamond, a physiologist, biologist, and geographer, examines more than a dozen past and present societies, some of which collapsed (past examples include Easter Island and the Anasazi of the southwestern United States; more recent examples include Rwanda and Haiti) and some of which overcame serious challenges to succeed. Diamond identifies five factors contributing to a society's collapse: the presence of hostile neighbors, the absence (or collapse) of trading partners for essential goods, climate change, environmental problems, and an adequate response to environmental problems. Three of these factors involve environmental conditions. The first four factors are often outside a society's control and need not always result in collapse. The final factor, however, is always crucial, as success or failure depends on the choices made by a society and its leaders.

The collapse of Rwanda, for example, is typically attributed to ethnic rivalries fueled by Rwanda's colonial past. According to some explanations of the genocide that left more than 800,000 Tutsis dead after a few horrific months in 1994, much of the cause lay in the legacy of colonialism. During the first part of the twentieth century, Belgium ran Rwanda through Tutsi administrators because, according to prevailing European racial theories, the Belgians considered the Tutsis—somewhat taller and lighter-skinned than the Hutus and, therefore, closer in resemblance to Europeans—to be more "civilized." This led to resentment and hatred, which boiled over in 1994, fueled by Hutu demagogues urging the killing of all Tutsis.

Diamond holds that this explanation is only part of the story. Through careful analysis of patterns of landholding, population, and killing, he argues that the root causes are found in overpopulation and the resulting environmental destruction. The population of Rwanda, he shows, was one of the fastest growing on earth, with disastrous consequences for the country's land and people, who had become one of the planet's most impoverished populations. Faced with starvation—and the absence of land to share among the growing number of (male) children—Rwanda was ripe for violence and collapse. Although ethnic rivalries may have fueled the fires of rage, Diamond also shows that in some hard-hit provinces, Hutus killed other Hutus, as young men sought to acquire scarce farmland by any means.

Some have criticized Diamond for overemphasizing the environment at the expense of other factors. By itself—except perhaps for extreme circumstances, such as the extended drought that doomed the Anasazi early in the fourteenth century—the environment does not necessarily determine how a society develops. Today especially, when humans can control much of their immediate living conditions, environment seems less important: Modern cities have sprung up in the arctic cold and the harshest deserts.

POLITICAL ORGANIZATION

Another factor influencing social change is the type of political organization a society has. In hunting and gathering societies, this influence is minimal because no political authorities can mobilize the community. In other types of society, however, distinct political agents—chiefs, lords, monarchs, and governments—strongly affect the course of social development. How a people respond to a crisis can determine whether they thrive or fail, and leadership is crucial to success or failure. A leader capable of pursuing dynamic policies and generating a mass following or radically altering preexisting modes of thought can overturn a previously established order. However, individuals can reach positions of leadership and become effective only under favorable social conditions. Mohandas Gandhi, the famous pacifist leader in India, succeeded in securing his country's independence from Britain because World War II and other events had unsettled the existing colonial institutions in India.

Japan illustrates how effective leadership averted possible ecological and economic collapse (Diamond, 2005). Political and military stability under the Tokugawa *shoguns* (military rulers from 1603 to 1867) ushered in a period of prosperity. This economic growth, however, contributed to massive deforestation of the island country. Its leaders (the celebrated *samurai* warriors) instituted programs of conservation and reforestation, and today—despite having one of the highest population densities of any industrial country—nearly three-quarters of Japan is covered with forests (Diamond, 2005).

Military strength played a fundamental part in the establishment of most traditional states, but the connections between level of production and military strength are indirect. A ruler may channel resources into building up the military, for example, even when this impoverishes the rest of the population—as happened in Iraq in the 1980s under the rule of Saddam Hussein and in North Korea during the 1990s under Kim Jong Il.

The most important political factor that has promoted change in the modern era is the emergence of the modern state, a vastly more efficient mechanism of government than those of premodern societies. Government plays a much bigger role in our lives, for better or worse, than it did before modern industrial societies arose.

Globalization today may be challenging national governments' ability to effectively exert leadership. A number of theorists argue that political power is becoming increasingly uncoupled from geography (Sassen, 1996; Shaw, 2000). Sociologist William Robinson (2004), for example, claims that as economic power has become deterritorialized, so, too, has political power: Just as transnational corporations operate across borders, with few or no national allegiances, transnational political organizations are becoming stronger as national governments are becoming weaker. The World Trade Organization (WTO) has the power to punish countries that violate its principles of free trade (Conti, 2008). European countries have opened their borders to one another, established a common currency, and given up substantial political power to the European Union (EU), a regional form of governance.

Will the twenty-first century see new forms of political organization better suited to a world in which people, products, knowledge, religious beliefs, pop culture, and pollution all cross borders easily? Although it is too soon to tell, most likely the most important forms of political organization of this century will bear little resemblance to those of the twentieth.

CULTURAL FACTORS

Another major influence on social change consists of cultural factors, such as modern communications systems or religious and other belief systems.

A particularly important cultural influence is the nature of communications systems. The invention of writing, for instance, promoted record keeping, facilitating the control of material resources and the development of large-scale organizations. In addition, writing altered people's perception of the relationship between past, present, and future. Societies that write keep a record of past events, through which they gain a sense of their evolution. The existence of a written constitution and laws enables a country to have a legal system based on the interpretation of legal precedents—just as written scriptures enable religious leaders to justify their beliefs by citing chapters and verses from religious texts, such as the Bible or Koran.

We saw in Chapters 6, 13, and 16 how the Internet has changed our personal relationships, our forms of recreation, the ways in which we learn and work, the nature of politics and social movements—in fact, almost every aspect of modern life. These changes, among the most rapid in human history, have caused what geographer David Harvey (1989) calls the compression of time and space. And they have all occurred within a single generation.

Religion may be either a conservative or an innovative force in social life. Some forms of religious belief and practice have acted as a brake on change, emphasizing traditional values and rituals. Yet, as Max Weber held, religious convictions frequently mobilize pressures for social change. For instance, many American church leaders promote attempts to reduce poverty or diminish inequalities in society. Religious leaders such as Dr. Martin Luther King Jr. were in the forefront of the American civil rights movement, and adherents of liberation theology fought for better schools, water supplies, health services, and democracy in Latin America—often at the cost of their lives.

Yet at the same time, many religious communities today have resisted many of the cultural aspects of globalization. Islamists, fundamentalist Christians, and ultraorthodox Jewish *Haredim* all reject what they regard as the corrupting influences of modern secular culture, now spreading globally through mass media and the Internet (Juergensmeyer, 1993, 2008). Islamists call this "Westoxification"—literally, getting drunk on the temptations of modern Western culture. While such religious communities usually embrace modern technology, which they sometimes use to disseminate their ideas, they reject the corruptions that go along with it.

Political scientist Samuel Huntington (1993, 1998) advanced the controversial thesis that such differences are part of seismic fault lines between entire civilizations. According to his "clash of civilizations" thesis,

An Egyptian girl walks next to the Muslim Fulla dolls at a kids' shop in Cairo. Two years after she first came on the market, Fulla is now thought to be the best-selling girls' toy in the Arab world, displacing her Western rival, Barbie.

The great divisions among humankind and the dominating source of conflict will be cultural. Nation states will remain the most powerful actors in world affairs, but the principal conflicts of global politics will occur between nations and groups of different civilizations. The clash of civilizations will dominate global politics. The fault lines between civilizations will be the battle lines of the future. (1993)

Huntington identified several major civilizations as having great potential for future conflict: Christianity, subdivided into Western Christianity and Eastern Orthodox; Islam; Hindu; Chinese; African; Buddhist; and Japanese. Although his thesis seems especially plausible after the events of September 11, 2001, it has been criticized as overly simplistic. Each of his so-called civilizations encompasses enormous differences in beliefs and practices, while old-fashioned geopolitical interests (for example, involving scarce resources such as oil and water) will likely shape international conflicts well into the twenty-first century. Moreover, to the extent that national policies are influenced by a belief in the clash of civilizations, Huntington's thesis may become a self-fulfilling prophecy, as different sides square off for a cosmic war against what each believes to be the forces of unmitigated evil (Juergensmeyer, 1993).

In fact, the principal cultural clashes of the twenty-first century may not be between so-called civilizations but between those who believe that truthful understanding derives from religious faith and those who find such understanding in science, critical thinking, and secular thought (Juergensmeyer, 1993). Secular ideals, such as self-betterment, freedom, equality, and democratic participation, are largely creations of the past two or three centuries.

ECONOMIC FACTORS

Of economic influences, the farthest reaching is the effect of industrial capitalism. Capitalism differs fundamentally from previous production systems because it involves the constant expansion of production and the ever-increasing accumulation of wealth. In traditional production systems, levels of production were fairly unchanging because they were geared to customary needs. Capitalism requires the constant revision of the technology of production, a process that increasingly involves science. The rate of technological innovation fostered in modern industry is vastly greater than that in any previous type of economic order. And such technological innovation has helped create a global economy whose production lines draw on a worldwide workforce.

Economic changes affect other changes as well. Science and technology, for example, are driven in part by economic factors. Corporations, to remain competitive, must spend large sums on research and development to commercialize scientific insights. Governments often spend far more money than individual businesses can afford in an effort to ensure that their countries don't fall behind militarily or economically. For instance, when the Soviet Union launched the world's first satellite, *Sputnik*, in 1957, the United States responded with a massive and costly space program, inspired by fear that the Russians were winning the "space race." During the 1960 presidential campaign, John F. Kennedy heightened that fear by repeatedly accusing the Republicans of being lax on Russian missile technology, suggesting that a "missile gap" made us vulnerable to nuclear attack. The arms race, fueled by government contracts with corporations, has provided major economic support for scientific research and more general support for the U.S. economy.

Most recently, governments worldwide are spending vast sums to win the next technological race, whether it be information technology, biotechnology, or—the latest area that promises solutions to a wide range of problems all societies confront today— nanotechnology. *Nanotechnology* involves working with matter at the atomic, or "nano," scale (a billionth of a meter), creating new materials that have novel properties: tiny particles that can enter the bloodstream and "search and destroy" particular cancer cells, replacing much more toxic chemotherapy; ultra-strong, lightweight carbon fibers, which have already found their way into golf clubs, tennis rackets, and bicycle frames, and which promise to revolutionize aircraft; data storage devices that can store a hundred times as much data as the most powerful electronics currently available; and highly efficient nanoscale filtration devices that can remove major industrial contaminants from groundwater. Countries are investing significant public funds in support of research, development, and commercialization of advanced technologies, hoping to profit while solving some of the world's most vexing problems.

CONCEPT CHECKS

1. Name two examples of cultural factors that may influence social change.
2. How does industrial capitalism affect social change?
3. What are the most important political factors that influence social change?

② CURRENT THEORIES: IS GLOBALIZATION TODAY SOMETHING NEW—OR HAVE WE SEEN IT ALL BEFORE?

Most people accept that important transformations are occurring, but the extent to which one can explain them as "globalization" is contested. This is not surprising, given the unpredictable and turbulent process that globalization involves. David Held and his colleagues (1999) have identified three schools of thought: skeptics, hyperglobalizers, and transformationalists. These approaches to the globalization debate are summarized in Table 20.1.

The Skeptics

Skeptics in the globalization controversy believe that present levels of economic interdependence are not unprecedented. Pointing to nineteenth-century statistics on world trade and investment, they contend that modern globalization differs from the past only in the intensity of interaction among nations. They agree that there may be more contact among countries today than in previous eras, but in their eyes the current world economy is not sufficiently integrated to constitute a truly globalized economy. This is because the bulk of trade occurs within three regional groups—Europe, Asia-Pacific, and North America. The countries of the EU, for example, trade predominantly among themselves. The same is true of the other regional groups, thereby invalidating the notion of a single global economy (Hirst, 1997).

Many skeptics focus on *regionalization* within the world economy—such as the emergence of major financial and trading blocs—as evidence that the world economy has become less integrated rather than more (Boyer and Drache, 1996; Hirst and Thompson, 1999). Compared with the patterns of trade that prevailed a century ago, they argue, the world economy is less global in its geographical scope and more concentrated on intense pockets of activity. They strongly reject the view held by some, such as the hyperglobalizers, that globalization is producing a world order in which national governments are less central. According to the skeptics, national governments continue to be key players because of their involvement in regulating and coordinating economic activity. Governments, for example, are the driving force behind many trade agreements and policies of economic liberalization.

Table 20.1
Conceptualizing Globalization: Three Tendencies

CHARACTERISTIC	SKEPTICS	TRANSFORMATIONALISTS	HYPERGLOBALIZERS
What's new?	Trading blocs, weaker geogovernance than in earlier periods	Historically unprecedented levels of global interconnectedness	A global age
Dominant features global	World less interdependent than in 1890s	"Thick" (intensive and extensive) globalization	Global capitalism, governance, global civil society
Power of national government	Reinforced or enhanced	Reconstituted, restructured	Declining or eroding
Driving forces of globalization	Governments and markets	Combined forces of modernity	Capitalism and technology
Pattern of hierarchies stratification	Increased marginalization of global south	New architecture of world order	Erosion of old
Dominant motif	National interest	Transformation of political community	McDonald's, Apple, etc.
Conceptualization of globalization	As internationalization and regionalization	As the reordering of interregional relations and action at a distance	As a reordering of the framework of human action
Historical trajectory	Regional blocs/clash of civilizations	Indeterminate: global integration and fragmentation	Global civilization
Summary argument	Internationalization depends on government acquiescence and support	Globalization transforming government power and world politics	The end of the nation-state

Source: Adapted from Held et al., 1999.

The Hyperglobalizers

The hyperglobalizers argue that globalization is a very real phenomenon with consequences almost everywhere. They see globalization as a process that is indifferent to national borders. In their view, globalization is producing a new global order, swept along by powerful flows of cross-border trade and production. They argue that individual countries no longer control their economies because of the vast growth in world trade. National governments and the politicians within them have decreasing control over the issues that cross their borders, such as volatile financial markets and environmental threats. Citizens recognize that politicians' ability to address these problems is limited and, as a result, lose faith in existing systems of governance. Some hyperglobalizers believe that the power of national governments is also being challenged from above—by new regional and international institutions, such as the EU and the WTO. These shifts signal the dawning of a global age (Albrow, 1997) in which national governments decline in importance and influence.

Sociologists such as William Robinson (2001, 2004), Leslie Sklair (2002a, 2002b, 2003), and Saskia Sassen (1996, 2005) tend to reject the label of *hyperglobalist*, a term they associate with such popular writers or journalists as Thomas Friedman (2000, 2005). Nonetheless, they do argue that transnational economic actors and political institutions are challenging the dominance of national ones. Robinson has studied these changes throughout the world, with a special focus on Latin America. He argues that the most powerful economic actors today are not bound by national boundaries; they are transnational. For example, the "transnational capitalist class" is emerging out of (and is transforming) the capitalist classes of individual countries, because the transnational corporations they manage are global rather than national. By the same token, he argues that nation-states are becoming "component elements" of a transnational state—exemplified, for example, by the WTO, which serves the interests of global businesses as a whole by ensuring that individual countries adhere to the principles of free trade. Robinson (2001) concludes that "the nation-state is a historically-specific form of world social organization in the process of becoming transcended by globalization."

The Transformationalists

The transformationalists take more of a middle position. Writers such as David Held and Anthony G. McGrew (Held et al., 1999), and Anthony Giddens, one of the authors of this textbook (1990), see globalization as the central force behind a broad spectrum of change. According to them, the global order is being transformed, but many of the old patterns remain. Governments, for instance, still retain a good deal of power in spite of global interdependence. These transformations are not restricted to economics but are equally prominent within politics, culture, and personal life. Transformationalists contend that the current level of globalization is breaking down established boundaries between internal and external, international and domestic. In adjusting to this new order, societies, institutions, and individuals must navigate contexts where previous structures have been shaken up.

Unlike hyperglobalizers, transformationalists see globalization as a dynamic and open process that is subject to influence and change. It is developing in a contradictory fashion, encompassing tendencies that frequently operate in opposition to one another. Globalization is a two-way flow of images, information, and influences. Global migration, media, and telecommunications are contributing to the diffusion of cultural influences. According to transformationalists, globalization is a decentered process characterized by links and cultural flows that work in a multidirectional way. Because globalization is the product of numerous intertwined global networks, it is not driven from one particular part of the world. Rather than losing sovereignty, countries are restructuring in response to new, nonterritorial forms of economic and social organization (e.g., corporations, social movements, and international bodies). Transformationalists argue that we are no longer living in a state-centric world; instead, governments must adopt a more active, outward-looking stance under the complex conditions of globalization (Cerny, 2005; Rosenau, 1997). In other words, nation-states remain relevant actors, but their function is changing. Globalization can perhaps be best understood as a tension between *inter*national (between nation-states) and *trans*national (borderless) social forces.

Whose View Is Most Nearly Correct?

There are elements of truth in all three views, although those of the transformationalists are perhaps the most balanced. The skeptics underestimate how far the world is changing; world finance markets, for example, are organized on a global level much more than ever before. Yet at the same time, the world has undergone periods of globalization before—only to withdraw into periods when countries protected their markets and closed their borders to trade. Although the march of globalization seems inevitable, it may not continue unabated: Countries that find themselves losing out may attempt to stem the tide. Many countries in Latin America, for example, have recently elected left-wing governments that reject free trade, arguing instead for protections for their citizens.

The hyperglobalizers are correct in pointing to the current strength of globalization as dissolving many national barriers, changing the nature of state power, and creating powerful transnational social classes. However, they often see globalization too much in economic terms and as too much of a one-way process. In reality, globalization is much more complex. World-systems theorists such as Immanuel Wallerstein (2004) and Giovanni Arrighi (1994) argue that while countries remain important actors on the global field, so, too, are transnational corporations. National governments will neither dissolve under the weight of a globalized economy (as some hyperglobalizers argue) nor reassert themselves as the dominant political force (as some skeptics argue), but rather will seek to steer global capitalism to their own advantage. According to this argument, U.S. dominance of the world economy is seriously challenged by the rise of East Asia, and particularly China, whose economy has been expanding at more than 9 percent per year for nearly two decades. The world economy of the future may be much more globalized than today's, with multinational corporations and global institutions playing increasingly important roles. But some countries in the world economy may still be more powerful than even the most powerful transnational actors.

The world is in the midst of a highly dynamic and turbulent transformation. It is not surprising, perhaps, that scholars cannot agree on the social forces that are reshaping it.

CONCEPT CHECKS

1. Compare and contrast how the skeptics, the hyperglobalizers, and the transformationalists explain the phenomenon of globalization.
2. How might skeptics, hyperglobalizers, and transformationalists interpret differently the growing global prominence of China?

③ RECENT RESEARCH ON GLOBALIZATION AND SOCIAL CHANGE

As we have emphasized throughout this textbook, *globalization* refers to the fact that we increasingly live in one world, so that individuals, groups, and nations become more *interdependent*—that is, what happens 12,000 miles away is likely to have enormous consequence for our daily lives. In this chapter we examine these global processes and see what leading sociologists and other social scientists have had to say about them. We go beyond our discussions from elsewhere in the book, considering why the modern period is associated with especially profound and rapid social change. We explore how globalization has contributed to this change and consider what the future is likely to bring.

Factors Contributing to Globalization

Although globalization is often portrayed solely as an economic phenomenon, it is in fact created by the coming together of technological, political, and economic factors. It has been driven above all by the development of information and communications technologies that have intensified the speed and scope of interaction among people worldwide.

INFORMATION FLOWS

Important advances in technology and the world's telecommunications infrastructure have facilitated the explosion in global communications. The post–World War II era has seen a transformation in the scope and intensity of telecommunications flows. Traditional telephone communication, which depended on analog signals sent through wires and cables, has been replaced by integrated systems in which vast amounts of information are compressed and transferred digitally. Cable technology has become more efficient and less expensive. The development of fiber-optic cables, for example, has dramatically expanded the number of channels that can be carried, and even this recent technology has achieved significant advances: While the first transoceanic fiber-optic cables could carry the equivalent of 35,000 telephone circuits, the most recent have 10,000 times that capacity (Hecht, 2003). The spread of communications satellites has also helped expand international communications. Today a network of more than 200 satellites facilitates the transfer of information around the globe.

The effect of these communications systems has been staggering. In countries with highly developed telecommunications infrastructures, homes and offices have multiple links to the outside world, including telephones (both land lines and mobile phones), fax machines, digital and cable television, electronic mail, and the Internet. The Internet is the fastest-growing communication tool ever developed—more than 1.8 billion people worldwide (over one-quarter of the world's population) were estimated to be using the Internet at the end of 2009, four times the number online in 2000 (Internet World Stats, 2010).

These forms of technology facilitate the compression of time and space: Two individuals located on opposite sides of the planet can not only hold a conversation in real time but also send documents and images to each other with the help of satellite technology. Widespread use of the Internet and mobile phones is accelerating processes of globalization; more people are becoming interconnected through these technologies in places that have previously been isolated or poorly served by traditional communications. Although the telecommunications infrastructure is not evenly developed around the world, a growing number of countries now have access to international communications networks.

Globalization is also being driven forward by the electronic integration of the world economy. The global economy increasingly involves activity that is *weightless* and *intangible* (Quah, 1999), because so many products have their base in information, as with computer software, media and entertainment products, and Internet-based services. A variety of new terms describe this new social order, such as *information society*, *service society*, and *knowledge society*. The emergence of this "knowledge society" reflects a broad base of consumers who are technologically literate and who integrate new advances in computing, entertainment, and telecommunications into their everyday lives.

The very operation of the global economy reflects the changes characteristic of the information age. Many aspects of the economy now require networks that cross national boundaries (Castells, 1996). To be competitive in globalizing conditions, businesses and corporations have become more flexible and less hierarchical. Production practices and organizational patterns have become more flexible, partnering arrangements with other firms have become commonplace, and participation in worldwide distribution networks has become essential.

Whether in a factory or a call center, today the job can be done more cheaply in China, India, or some other country in the global south. The same is true for software engineering, graphic design, and financial advice. Of course, to the extent that global competition for labor reduces the cost of goods and services, it also provides for a wealth of cheaper products (Roach, 2005). As consumers, we all benefit from low-cost flat-panel TVs made in China or inexpensive computer games programmed in India. It is an open question, however, whether the declining cost of consumption will balance out wage and job losses due to globalization.

POLITICAL CHANGES

Political changes are driving forces behind contemporary globalization. One of the most significant is the collapse of Soviet-style communism, which occurred in Eastern Europe in 1989 and in the Soviet Union itself in 1991. Since then, countries in the former Soviet bloc—including Russia, Ukraine, Poland, Hungary, the Czech Republic, the Baltic states, and the states of the Caucasus and Central Asia—have been moving toward Western-style political and economic systems and are increasingly integrated into the global community. In fact, the collapse of communism not only hastened processes of globalization but also was a result of it. The centrally planned Communist economies and the ideological and cultural control of Communist political authority ultimately could not survive in an era of global media and an electronically integrated world economy.

A second political factor leading to intensifying globalization is the growth of international and regional mechanisms of government. The United Nations (UN) and the EU are two prominent examples of international organizations that bring together nation-states into a common political forum. Whereas the UN does this as an association of individual nation-states, the EU is a form of transnational governance in which some national sovereignty is relinquished by its member states. The governments of EU states are bound by directives, regulations, and court judgments from common EU bodies, but they also reap economic, social, and political benefits from their participation in the regional union.

A third political factor is the growing importance of **international governmental organizations (IGOs)** and **international nongovernmental organizations** (**INGOs**; see also Chapter 6). An *international governmental organization* is a body that is established by participating governments and given responsibility for regulating or overseeing a domain of activity that is transnational in scope. Such bodies regulate issues ranging from civil aviation to broadcasting to the disposal of hazardous waste. In 1909 there were 37 IGOs in existence to regulate transnational affairs; by 2005 there were more than 7,000 (Union of International Associations, 2005). INGOs differ from IGOs in that they are not affiliated with government institutions. Rather, they are independent organizations that work alongside governmental bodies in making policy decisions and addressing international issues. Some of the best-known INGOs—such as Greenpeace, Médecins Sans Frontières (Doctors without Borders), the International Committee of the Red Cross, and Amnesty International—are involved in environmental protection and humanitarian relief efforts. But the activities of the nearly 59,000 lesser-known groups also link countries and communities (Figure 20.1).

Finally, the spread of information technology has expanded the possibilities for contact among people worldwide, while also facilitating the flow of information about people and events in distant places. Some of the most gripping events of recent decades—such as the fall of the Berlin Wall, the violent crackdown on democratic protesters in China's Tiananmen Square, and the terrorist attacks of September 11, 2001—unfolded through

international governmental organizations (IGOs) • International organizations established by treaties between governments for purposes of conducting business between the nations making up their membership.

international nongovernmental organizations (INGOs) • International organizations established by agreements between the individuals or private organizations making up their membership.

the media before a truly global audience. Such events, along with less dramatic ones, have caused a reorientation in people's thinking from the level of the nation-state to the global stage.

This shift has two significant consequences. First, as members of a global community, people increasingly perceive that social responsibility extends beyond national borders. There is a growing assumption that the international community has an obligation to act in crisis situations to protect the physical well-being or human rights of people whose lives are under threat. In the case of natural disasters, such interventions take the form of humanitarian relief and technical assistance. In recent years, earthquakes in Haiti, floods in Mozambique, famine in Africa, hurricanes in Central America, and the tsunami that hit Asia and Africa have been rallying points for global assistance.

There have also been stronger calls for interventions in the case of war, ethnic conflict, and the violation of human rights, although such mobilizations are more problematic than with natural disasters. In the case of the Gulf War in 1991 and the violent conflicts in Bosnia and Kosovo (in the former Yugoslavia), many people saw military intervention as justified in the interest of defending human rights and national sovereignty.

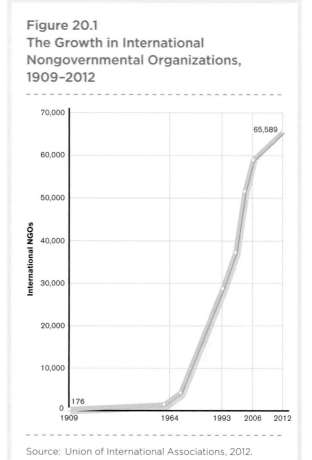

Figure 20.1

The Growth in International Nongovernmental Organizations, 1909–2012

Source: Union of International Associations, 2012.

Second, a global outlook means that people increasingly look to sources other than the nation-state in formulating their own sense of identity. This phenomenon both is produced by and further accelerates processes of globalization. Local cultural identities in various parts of the world are experiencing powerful revivals at a time when the traditional hold of the nation-state is undergoing profound transformation. In Europe, for example, inhabitants of Scotland and the Basque region of Spain might be more likely to identify themselves as Scottish or Basque (or simply as Europeans) rather than as British or Spanish.

ECONOMIC CHANGES: THE GROWING IMPORTANCE OF TRANSNATIONAL CORPORATIONS

Transnational corporations are companies that produce goods or market services in more than one country. These may be small firms with one or two factories outside the country

transnational corporations • Business corporations located in two or more countries.

where they are based or gigantic international ventures whose operations crisscross the globe. Some of the biggest transnational corporations are BMW, Coca-Cola, Disney, Exxon-Mobil, Ford, Google, McDonald's, Nike, Starbucks, Toyota, and Walmart. Even when transnational corporations have a clear national base, they are oriented toward global markets and global profits.

Transnational corporations account for two-thirds of all world trade, are instrumental in diffusing new technology around the globe, and are major actors in international financial markets. As one group of writers has noted, they are "the linchpins of the contemporary world economy" (Held et al., 1999). Well over 700 transnational corporations had annual sales of more than $10 billion in 2009, whereas only 118 countries could boast a gross domestic product (GDP) of at least that amount. In other words, the world's leading transnational corporations are larger economically than most of the world's countries. Royal Dutch Shell and Walmart, two of the world's largest corporations in terms of sales, had revenues that surpassed the GDPs of all but a couple dozen. Among the world's 75 largest economies, 22 are transnational corporations (*Forbes*, 2009; International Monetary Fund, 2009). Over the last few years, total assets of transnational corporations rose from $7 trillion to $82 trillion. Due mainly to economic uncertainty, transnational companies, it is believed, hoard some $5 trillion in cash and are not using it for investment (UNCTAD, 2010).

Transnational corporations became a global phenomenon after World War II. Expansion initially came from firms based in the United States, but by the 1970s European and Japanese firms also began to invest abroad. In the late 1980s and '90s, transnational corporations expanded dramatically with the establishment of three powerful regional markets: Europe (the Single European Market), Asia-Pacific (the Osaka Declaration guaranteed free and open trade by 2010), and North America (the North American Free Trade Agreement, or NAFTA). Since the early 1990s, countries in other areas have also eased restrictions on foreign investment. By the turn of the twenty-first century, few economies were beyond the reach of transnational corporations. Over the past decade, transnational corporations based in industrialized economies have been expanding their operations in countries in the global south as well as in countries that were part of the former Soviet Union and Eastern Europe.

The "electronic economy" also underpins economic globalization. Banks, corporations, fund managers, and individual investors can now shift funds internationally with the click of a mouse. This new ability carries great risks, however. Transfers of vast amounts of capital can destabilize economies and trigger international financial crises. As the global economy becomes increasingly integrated, a financial collapse in one part of the world can have an enormous effect on distant economies.

The Effect of Globalization on Our Lives

Although globalization is often associated with changes within big systems—such as world financial markets, production and trade, and telecommunications—its effects are felt equally strongly in the private realm. Inevitably, our personal lives have been altered as globalizing forces enter into our local contexts, our homes, and our communities through impersonal sources—such as the media, the Internet, and popular culture—as well as through personal contact with individuals from other countries and cultures.

As the societies in which we live undergo profound transformations, the institutions that underpin them have become outdated. This is forcing a redefinition of the family, gender roles, sexuality, personal identity, our interactions with others, and our relationships to work. The political, economic, social, and technological factors just described are producing a phenomenon without parallel in terms of intensity and scope. Before considering the consequences of globalization, let's examine the main views about globalization that have been expressed in recent years.

THE RISE OF INDIVIDUALISM

In the current age, individuals have much more opportunity to shape their own lives than previously. At one time, tradition and custom strongly influenced them. Factors such as social class, gender, ethnicity, and religious affiliation could close off certain avenues for individuals or open up others. The values, lifestyles, and ethics prevailing in one's community provided fixed guidelines for living.

Conditions of globalization, however, bring a new *individualism* in which people actively construct their own identities. The weight of tradition and established values is lessening as local communities interact with a new global order. The social codes that formerly guided people's choices and activities have significantly loosened.

Traditional frameworks of identity are dissolving; new patterns of identity are emerging. Globalization is forcing people constantly to respond and adjust to the changing environment; as individuals, we now evolve within the larger context. Even small choices in daily life—what to wear, how to spend leisure time, and how to care for our health and our bodies—are part of an ongoing process of creating and re-creating our self-identities.

WORK PATTERNS

Although we may regard work as a chore or a necessary evil, it is undeniably a crucial element in our lives. Not only our jobs but also many other aspects of our existence—from our friends to our leisure pursuits—are shaped by our work patterns.

Globalization has unleashed profound transformations within the world of work. New patterns of international trade and the move to a knowledge economy have significantly impacted long-standing employment patterns. Many traditional industries have become obsolete or are losing their share of the market to competitors abroad. Global trade and new forms of technology have affected traditional manufacturing communities, where industrial workers have been left unemployed and without the skills required by the knowledge-based economy. These communities are facing new social problems, including long-term unemployment and rising crime rates, as a result of economic globalization.

If at one time people's working lives were dominated by employment with one employer over several decades—the so-called job-for-life framework—today more individuals are creating their own career paths. Often this involves changing jobs several times over the course of a career, building up new skills and abilities, and transferring them to diverse work contexts. Standard patterns of full-time work are dissolving into more flexible arrangements: working from home via information technology, job sharing, short-term consulting projects, flextime, and so forth (Kalleberg, 2003). While this affords new opportunities for some, for most it means greater uncertainty. Job security and attendant health care and retirement benefits have largely become things of the past.

Women's entering the workforce in large numbers has strongly affected the personal lives of people of both sexes. Expanded professional and educational opportunities have led many women to put off marriage and children until after they have begun a career. Also, many women return to work shortly after having children, instead of remaining at home. These shifts have required important adjustments within families, in terms of the domestic division of labor, the role of men in child rearing, and the emergence of more family-friendly working policies to accommodate the needs of dual-earner households.

POPULAR CULTURE

The cultural effects of globalization have received much attention. Images, ideas, goods, and styles are now disseminated worldwide more rapidly than ever. Trade, new information technologies, the international media, and global migration have all promoted the free movement of culture across national borders. Many people believe that we now live in a single information order—a massive global network where information is shared quickly and in great volumes. A simple example illustrates this point.

The film *Avatar* is a 2009 3-D science fiction epic in which a greedy Earth-based corporation threatens to destroy a lush forest on the habitable moon Pandora, along with the humanlike Na'vi who live there in peaceful harmony with nature, in order to obtain the precious mineral called (appropriately) "unobtainium." *Avatar* quickly became the highest-grossing film in history, garnering $2.8 billion as of 2012, three-quarters from outside the United States. The film is one of many cultural products that has succeeded in cutting across national boundaries and creating a truly international phenomenon.

What accounts for the enormous popularity of a film such as *Avatar*? And what does its success tell us about globalization? At one level, *Avatar* was popular for straightforward reasons: It combined romance (one of the humans who assumed the bodily shape (avatar) of a Na'vi in order to infiltrate their community predictably falls in love with a beautiful Na'vi woman) and drama (will the avatar go native and side with the Na'vis? Will the primitive weaponry of the Na'vi triumph over the high-tech weaponry of the humans?). The film was also lavishly produced and included dazzling state-of-the-art special effects. But another reason for *Avatar's* popularity is that it reflected ideas and values that resonated with audiences worldwide. One of the film's central themes is the possibility of romantic love prevailing over vast cultural (indeed, racial) differences and community traditions. Can a human male, even occupying the body of an avatar, truly find love with a ten-foot-tall blue-skinned Na'vi woman? The film, happily in the eyes of its many viewers, shows that true love can indeed conquer all, including a galactic version of racial prejudice and the power of transgalactic corporations that will stop at nothing to satisfy their greed.

These themes undoubtedly resonated both with widely shared romantic yearnings and with growing environmentalist concerns shared by many people around the globe. The success of a film such as *Avatar* reflects changing values and may also *contribute* to this shift in values. Western-made films and television programs, which dominate the global media, advance political, social, and economic agendas that reflect a specifically Western worldview. Some people worry that globalization is fostering a global culture in which the values of the most powerful and affluent—in this instance, Hollywood filmmakers—overwhelm local customs and tradition. According to this view, globalization is a form of cultural imperialism in which Western values, styles, and outlooks smother individual national cultures.

Others, by contrast, have linked globalization to a growing *differentiation* in cultural traditions and forms, as is seen in the Indian Bollywood and Nigerian Nollywood film industries discussed at the beginning of this chapter. Global society is characterized by an enormous diversity of cultures existing side by side. Local traditions are joined by a host of additional cultural forms from abroad, presenting a bewildering array of lifestyle options. Rather than a unified global culture, what we are witnessing is the fragmentation of cultural forms (Friedman, 1994). Established identities and ways of life grounded in local communities and cultures are giving way to hybrid identities composed of elements from contrasting cultural sources (Hall, 1992). Thus a black urban South African today might be strongly influenced by the traditions and cultural outlooks of his tribal roots at the same time that he adopts cosmopolitan styles and tastes—in dress, leisure pursuits, hobbies, and so forth—that have been shaped by globalizing forces.

Globalization and Risk

Because globalization is an open-ended and internally contradictory process, it produces outcomes that are difficult to predict and control. Another way of thinking of this dynamic is in terms of *risk*. Many of the changes wrought by globalization present new forms of risk. Unlike risks from the past, which had established causes and known effects, today's risks are incalculable in origin and indeterminate in their consequences.

THE SPREAD OF "MANUFACTURED RISK"

Humans have always had to face risks, but today's risks are qualitatively different from those of earlier times. Until recently, human societies were threatened by **external risk** from the natural world—dangers such as drought, earthquakes, famines, and storms. Today, however, we increasingly face various types of **manufactured risk**—risks created by the effect of our own knowledge and technology on the natural world. Many current environmental and health risks are the outcomes of our own interventions into nature.

Environmental Risks One of the clearest illustrations of manufactured risk involves threats posed by the natural environment (see Chapter 19). One of the consequences of accelerating industrial and technological development has been the steady spread of human intervention in nature—for example, through urbanization, industrial production and pollution, large-scale agricultural projects, the construction of dams and hydroelectric plants, and nuclear power. The collective outcome of such processes has been widespread environmental destruction whose precise cause is indeterminate and whose consequences are difficult to calculate.

In the globalizing world, ecological risk takes many forms. One example of ecological risk is global warming. Concern over global warming has been mounting in the scientific community; it is now generally accepted that the earth's temperature has increased from the buildup of greenhouse gases within the atmosphere. If polar ice caps continue to melt as they currently are, sea levels will rise and may threaten low-lying land masses and their human populations. Changes in climate patterns may have caused the severe floods that afflicted parts of China in 1998 and Mozambique in 2000, the record number of hurricanes that swept through the Atlantic and Gulf of Mexico in the fall of 1995, or Superstorm Sandy that devastated the Northeast portion of the United States in 2012.

Because environmental risks are diffuse in origin, it is unclear how to address them or who bears responsibility for remedying them. For example, although scientists have found that chemical pollution levels have harmed Antarctic penguin colonies, it is impossible to identify either the exact origins of the pollution or its

external risk • Dangers that spring from the natural world and are unrelated to the actions of humans. Examples of external risk include droughts, earthquakes, famines, and storms.

manufactured risk • Dangers that are created by the impact of human knowledge and technology on the natural world. Examples of manufactured risk include global warming and genetically modified foods.

possible consequences for the penguins in the future. In such an instance—and in hundreds of similar cases—action to address the risk is unlikely because the extent of both the cause and the outcome is unknown (Beck, 1995).

Health Risks Lately, the dangers posed to human health by manufactured risks have attracted great attention. The media and public health campaigns, for example, urge people to limit their exposure to harmful ultraviolet rays and to apply sunscreen to prevent burning. Sun exposure has been linked to a heightened risk of skin cancer, possibly due to the depletion of the ozone layer—the layer of the earth's atmosphere that filters out ultraviolet light. Because of the high volume of chemical emissions produced by human activities and industry, the concentration of ozone in the atmosphere has been diminishing, and in some cases ozone holes have opened up.

Many examples of manufactured risk are linked to food, because advances in science and technology have heavily influenced modern farming and food production techniques. For example, chemical pesticides and herbicides are widely used in commercial agriculture, and chickens, pigs, and many other animals raised for food are pumped full of hormones and antibiotics. Some people have suggested that such farming techniques compromise food safety and could adversely affect humans. Two particular controversies have raised widespread public concern: the debate over genetically modified foods and mad cow disease.

The saga of genetically modified foods began over 10 years ago, when some of the world's leading chemical and agricultural firms decided that new knowledge about genes could transform the world's food supply. These companies had been making pesticides and herbicides but wanted to develop a major market for the future. The American firm Monsanto was the leader in developing much of the new technology. Monsanto bought up seed companies, sold off its chemical division, worked to bring the new crops to market, and launched a gigantic advertising campaign promoting the benefits of its genetically modified crops to farmers and consumers. The early responses were just as the company had confidently anticipated. By early 1999, 55 percent of the soybeans and 35 percent of the corn produced in the United States contained genetic alterations. From 1996 to 2010, genetically modified foods experienced an unprecedented 87-fold increase in worldwide production (International Service for the Acquisition of Agri-biotech Applications, 2011).

It is currently estimated that between 70 and 75 percent of all processed foods sold in grocery stores contain some genetically modified components (Center for Food Safety, 2010). In addition to North America, genetically modified crops are being widely grown in China. Since genetically modified crops are new, no one can be certain about their effects once they are introduced into the environment. Many ecological and consumer groups are concerned about the potential risks involved with the adoption of this largely untested technology.

Bovine spongiform encephalopathy (BSE), known popularly as mad cow disease, was first detected in British cattle in 1986. Scientists have linked BSE infection to the practice of raising cattle, normally herbivores, on feed containing traces of the parts of other animals. After the outbreak, the British government took steps to control the disease among cattle, but it claimed that eating beef was safe for humans. Only in the mid-1990s was it admitted that several human deaths from Creutzfeldt-Jakob disease, a degenerative brain condition, had been linked to the consumption of beef from infected cattle. Thousands of British cattle were killed, and strict new legislation was passed to regulate cattle farming and the sale of beef products. Most recently, cattle infected with BSE have been discovered in Canada and the United States, sparking widespread fears about the safety of the food supply.

Although extensive scientific research has explored the risks to humans from BSE, the findings remain inconclusive. There is a risk that individuals who consumed British beef in the years preceding the discovery of BSE may have been exposed to infection. Calculating the risks to humans from BSE is an example of the complexity of risk assessment in the contemporary world. It is necessary to know if and when infected cattle were part of a certain food chain, the level and distribution of the infection present in the cattle, how the beef was processed, and many other details. The sheer quantity of unknown factors has complicated the task.

THE GLOBAL "RISK SOCIETY"

Global warming, the BSE crisis, the debate over genetically modified foods, and other manufactured risks present new choices and challenges. Individuals, countries, and transnational organizations must negotiate risks as they make choices about how to live and conduct business. Because there are no definitive answers about the causes and outcomes of such risks, this can be a bewildering endeavor. Should we use food and raw materials if their production or consumption might harm our health and the natural environment?

German sociologist Ulrich Beck (1992) sees these risks contributing to a global "risk society." As technological change progresses and produces new forms of risk, we must constantly respond and adjust to these changes. The risk society, he argues, is not limited to environmental and health risks; it includes a series of interrelated changes within contemporary social life: shifting employment patterns, heightened job insecurity, the declining influence of tradition and custom on self-identity, the erosion of traditional family patterns, and the democratization of personal relationships. Because personal futures are much less fixed than they were in traditional societies, decisions of all kinds present risks. Getting married, for example, is a riskier endeavor today than when marriage was a lifelong institution. Decisions about educational qualifications and career paths can also feel risky: It is difficult to predict what skills will be valuable in an economy that is changing so rapidly.

According to Beck (1995), an important aspect of the risk society is that its hazards are not restricted spatially, temporally, or socially. Today's risks have global, not merely personal, consequences. Many forms of manufactured risk, such as those concerning human health and the environment, cross national boundaries. Consider the disaster at the Fukushima Daiichi nuclear power plant in Japan in 2011. Everyone living in the immediate vicinity—regardless of age, class, gender, or status—was exposed to dangerous levels of radiation.

Globalization and Inequality

Beck and other scholars have identified risk as one of the main outcomes of globalization and technological advance. Yet globalization is generating other important challenges, because its effect is differential—and some of its consequences are not benign. Next to mounting ecological problems, the expansion of inequalities within and between societies is one of the most serious challenges today.

The majority of the world's wealth is concentrated in the industrialized countries of the global north, whereas countries in the global south suffer from widespread poverty, overpopulation, inadequate educational and health care systems, and crippling foreign debt. The disparity between the industrial north and the global south widened steadily over the course of the twentieth century and is now the largest it has ever been.

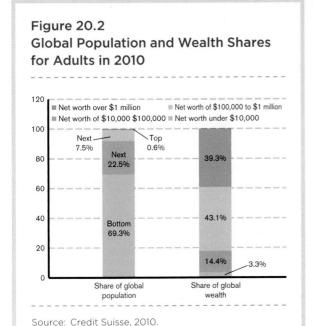

Figure 20.2
Global Population and Wealth Shares for Adults in 2010

- Net worth over $1 million
- Net worth of $100,000 to $1 million
- Net worth of $10,000 $100,000
- Net worth under $10,000

Top 0.6%
Next 7.5%
Next 22.5%
Bottom 69.3%

39.3%
43.1%
14.4%
3.3%

Share of global population

Share of global wealth

Source: Credit Suisse, 2010.

A recent report on global wealth shows that global inequality is at extreme levels. The top 0.6 percent of the richest people in the world own 39.3 percent of total shares of global wealth, while the bottom 69.3 percent of the world's population owns only 3.3 percent of total global wealth (Figure 20.2). The top 8.1 percent own roughly 82.4 percent of the world's wealth (Credit Suisse, 2010). Additionally, the World Development Indicators (WDI) 2010 says that nearly 75 percent of the population in South Asia and sub-Saharan Africa lives on less than two dollars a day, a level of poverty that is nonexistent for industrial nations in Europe and North America (World Bank, 2010b).

In much of the global south, levels of economic growth and output over the past century have not kept up with the rate of population growth, whereas the level of economic development in industrialized countries has far outpaced it. These opposing tendencies have caused a marked divergence between the richest and poorest countries. The gap between the world's richest and poorest countries was approximately 3 to 1 in 1820, 11 to 1 in 1913, 35 to 1 in 1950, 72 to 1 in 1992, 173 to 1 in 2001, and 209 to 1 in 2011 (Figure 20.3). The figure for 2006 using gross national income (GNI) per capita is 760.4 to 1 (World Bank, 2008). The WDI 2010 shows that the mortality rate for children under age five is 15 times higher in low-income countries than in high-income countries (World Bank, 2010b). Over the past century, among the richest quarter of the world's population, income per capita has increased almost sixfold, while among the poorest quarter, the increase has been less than threefold.

Globalization seems to be exacerbating these trends by further concentrating income, wealth, and resources within a small core of countries (Figure 20.3). The expansion of global trade has been central to this process—between 2000 and 2007, the volume of global trade grew about 5 percent a year; the volume of exports and imports in 2005 exceeded $26 trillion, or 58 percent of total global output, up from 44 percent in 1980. In 2011, the growth was 5 percent again, after an unprecedented increase in 2010 of 14 percent, caused by a rebound from the economic downturn of 2008–2009 (WTO, 2008; World Bank 2008; WTO, 2012). Only a handful of countries in the global south have managed to benefit from the overall rapid growth—the global south accounts for only a third of global trade—and the process of integration into the global economy has been uneven. Some countries—such as the East Asian economies, Chile, India, and Poland—have fared well, with significant growth in exports. Other countries—such as Algeria, Russia, Venezuela, and most of sub-Saharan Africa—have seen few benefits from expanding trade and globalization (UNDP, 2006). There is a danger that many of the countries most in need of economic growth will be left further behind as globalization progresses.

Many scholars see free trade as the key to economic development and poverty relief. Organizations such as the WTO work to liberalize trade regulations and to reduce trade barriers. Free trade across borders is viewed as a win-win proposition for countries in the global north

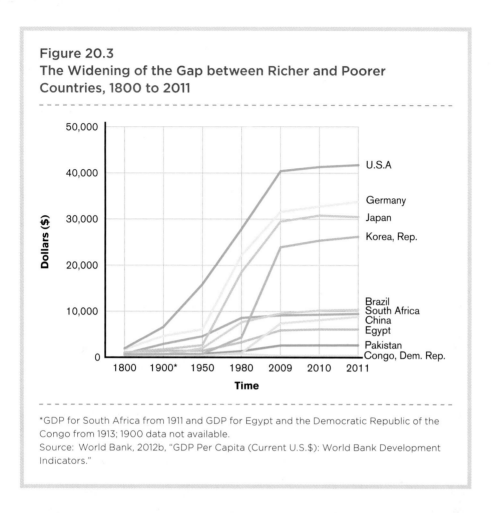

Figure 20.3
The Widening of the Gap between Richer and Poorer Countries, 1800 to 2011

*GDP for South Africa from 1911 and GDP for Egypt and the Democratic Republic of the Congo from 1913; 1900 data not available.
Source: World Bank, 2012b, "GDP Per Capita (Current U.S.$): World Bank Development Indicators."

and south. While the industrialized economies are able to export their products to markets worldwide, it is claimed that countries in the global south will benefit by gaining access to world markets. This, in turn, would improve their prospects for integration into the global economy.

THE CAMPAIGN FOR GLOBAL JUSTICE

Many critics argue that free trade is a one-sided affair that benefits those who are already well off and exacerbates poverty and dependency within the global south. Recently, much of this criticism has focused around the WTO, which is at the forefront of efforts to increase global trade.

In 1999, more than 50,000 people from around the world took to the streets of Seattle to protest during the WTO's Millennium Round of trade talks. Trade unionists, environmentalists, human rights campaigners, antinuclear activists, farmers, and representatives from hundreds of local and international nongovernmental organizations joined forces to voice their frustration with the WTO—an organization seen by many as favoring economic imperatives over all other concerns, including human rights, labor rights, the environment, and sustainable development.

Negotiators from the WTO's 134 member states—the number of members has since risen to 153—had come together to discuss measures to liberalize conditions for global trade and investment in agriculture and forest products, among other issues. Yet the talks broke off early with no agreements reached. The organizers of the protests were triumphant—not only had the demonstrations succeeded in disrupting the talks, but internal disputes among delegates had also surfaced. The Seattle protests were heralded as the biggest victory to date for campaigners for global justice. Since that time, every ministerial meeting of the WTO has faced massive demonstrations by those excluded from the processes of setting the rules for global trade.

Does this campaign represent the emergence of a powerful anti-globalization movement, as some commentators have suggested? Protesters in other cities, such as London and Washington, D.C., argue that free trade and economic globalization further concentrate wealth in the hands of a few, while increasing poverty for the majority of the world's population. Most of these activists agree that global trade is necessary and potentially beneficial for national economies, but they claim that it needs to be regulated by *different* rules: trade rules oriented toward protecting human rights, the environment, labor rights, and local economies—not toward ensuring larger profits for already rich corporations.

The protesters claim that the WTO is an undemocratic organization dominated by the interests of the world's richest nations, particularly the United States. Although the members of the WTO include many countries in the global south, many have no influence over the

----

Indian farmers and labor unionists march at an anti-WTO protest in New Delhi, India, in September 2009. What are some of the criticisms that activists level at the WTO?

organization's policies because the agenda is set by the richest nations. Poorer nations have fewer resources, in terms of money and trained personnel, to confront the highly complex issues related to international trade. The president of the World Bank has pointed out that 19 of the 42 African states that are members of the WTO have little or no representation at its headquarters in Geneva (World Bank, 2000). Such imbalances have very real consequences. For example, although the WTO has insisted that countries in the global south open their markets to imports from industrialized countries, it has allowed industrialized countries to maintain high barriers to agricultural imports and to provide vast subsidies for their domestic agriculture production to protect their own agricultural sectors (Stiglitz, 2007).

Since 1994 the U.S. government has spent $194 billion to boost the income of crop and livestock farmers (Environmental Working Group, 2012). The EU spends $68 billion each year on their farmers, and the farm budget takes up to 40 percent of the EU's yearly expenditures (Dunmore, 2012).In fact, the average European cow gets a subsidy of approximately two dollars a day; more than half of the people in the global south live on less than that (Stiglitz, 2007). This means that the world's poorest (and predominantly agricultural) countries do not have access to the large markets for agricultural goods in industrialized countries. This issue has confounded the expansion of WTO rules covering trade in services, foreign investment, government procurement, and other areas. Beginning with the 2003 WTO ministerial meeting in Mexico, the "Group of 21" countries in the global south, led by Brazil and India, have refused to consider the expansion of WTO rules until the United States and the EU eliminate subsidies for agriculture production and allow greater access to other agriculture markets, such as cotton. The issue of agriculture subsidies still has not been resolved. A group of countries in the global south, again led by Brazil, won two major disputes at the WTO over subsidies for European sugar and American cotton. Despite these rulings, the issue of illegal subsidies used by Europe and the United States to support their farmers continues to hamper WTO ministerial meetings.

A similar divide exists over the protection of intellectual property rights—an issue monitored by a WTO multilateral agreement called TRIPS (Trade-Related Aspects of Intellectual Property Rights). In 2010, high-income countries accounted for 70 percent of patent applications. Only five patent offices (United States, China, Japan, South Korea, and the European patent office) accounted for 79 percent of patent applications (World Intellectual Property Organization, 2012), but the concept of intellectual property rights is alien to the global south. Recently there has been a significant increase in the number of patent claims as biotechnology companies and research institutes push to control and "own" more forms of knowledge, technology, and biodiversity. Many samples of plant material, for example, have been taken from biodiverse areas such as rain forests and developed by pharmaceutical companies into profitable, and patented, medicines. Local knowledge about the medicinal uses of the plants is often used in developing and marketing the medicines, yet the indigenous people receive no compensation for their contribution. As industrialized countries within the WTO push to strengthen intellectual property laws, many people in the global south argue that such a move works against the needs of their countries. Research agendas are dictated by profit interests, not human interests, and valuable forms of technology may end up inaccessible to poorer countries that could benefit from their use.

Another criticism of the WTO is that it operates in secret and is not accountable to citizens who are affected by its decisions. In many ways, this criticism is valid. Trade disputes between members of the WTO are decided behind closed doors by a committee of "experts" who are appointed rather than elected. When a decision is handed down, it is legally binding on all member states and enforceable through a mechanism that authorizes WTO member nations to enact punitive trade policies unless the losing nation complies with the decision. The WTO can also challenge or override laws that are seen as barriers to trade. This includes national laws or bilateral agreements designed to protect the environment, conserve scarce resources, safeguard public health, or guarantee labor standards and human rights. For example, the WTO has ruled against the EU's ban on U.S. hormone-treated beef (because of its possible links to cancer) and has challenged a law passed in Massachusetts that prohibits companies from investing in Myanmar (Burma) because of its government's human rights violations. In another instance, the United States and the EU attempted to use the TRIPS provision to block the importation of inexpensive generic HIV/AIDS medication into countries in sub-Saharan Africa, whose populations are being devastated by this epidemic. This move produced worldwide public outrage, which forced the WTO to reconsider its rules that regulate patent rights when public health is at stake.

A final concern is the undue influence wielded by the United States over the activities of the WTO and other international bodies such as the World Bank and the International Monetary Fund. With its overwhelming economic, political, and military might, the United States is able to influence debates and decision making in many international institutions. The unevenness of globalization in part reflects the fact that political and economic power is concentrated in the hands of a few core states. Even as the United States influences the WTO, the United States is also subject to the WTO's rules and decisions. In fact, the United States almost always loses when it is forced to defend its trading practices before a WTO appellate panel (Conti, 2008). For example, in 2003 the WTO determined that high tariffs placed on imports of steel into the United States violated the rights of WTO member nations. Under heavy pressure from its trading partners, the United States eventually rescinded the tariffs and complied with WTO law. This example highlights a tension between the nature of power and the processes of globalization: Can we expect the world's sole superpower to play by the rules when the rules go against the interests of that superpower? What effect will this tension have on the creation of a just and equitable global legal and political system?

CONCEPT CHECKS ✓

1. How has technology facilitated the compression of time and space?
2. What are the three causes of increasing globalization?
3. Briefly describe the history of transnational corporations since the 1970s.
4. What effect does globalization have on our everyday lives?
5. Why is globalization associated with new forms of risk? What are the new forms of risk?
6. Briefly describe the debate over the role that free trade plays in global inequality.

4 UNANSWERED QUESTIONS

We are in the midst of a global transformation, so it is difficult to see where we are headed and how these changes can be managed. There are important sociological debates over what comes next, and what steps should be taken to best address the social, economic, and environmental challenges that have resulted from globalization. In this section we consider differing views on what comes after modern industrialism and how globalization's rough edges might be best softened.

What Comes after Modern Industrial Society?

If social theorists do not agree on the nature of globalization, they also differ on where these changes are leading us. According to one argument, we have become a postindustrial society; according to another, we are not so much postindustrial as **postmodern**. **Postindustrial society** is said to be the next phase of development beyond industrial society, a term first employed by Daniel Bell (1976) in the United States and Alain Touraine (1974) in France. (*Post* means "after," suggesting that we are moving beyond old forms of industrial development.) A variety of new terms describes this new social order, such as **information society**, **service society**, and **knowledge society**. The diversity of terms reflects the countless ideas put forward to interpret current social changes. But one consistent theme is the significance of *information* or *knowledge* in the society of the future. Our ways of life throughout the nineteenth and twentieth centuries, based largely on machine power (the manufacture of material goods in factories), is being displaced by one in which information underlies the production system.

In his now-classic *The Coming of Post-Industrial Society*, Bell (1976) argues that the postindustrial order is distinguished by a growth of service occupations at the expense of jobs that produce material goods. The blue-collar worker is no longer the most essential type of employee. White-collar (clerical and professional) workers outnumber blue-collar (factory) workers, with professional and technical occupations growing fastest of all. People working in higher-level white-collar occupations specialize in the production of information and knowledge. The production and control of what Bell calls "codified knowledge"—systematic, coordinated information—is society's main productive resource. Those who create and distribute this knowledge—scientists, computer specialists, economists, engineers, and professionals of all kinds—increasingly become the leading social groups, replacing industrialists and entrepreneurs. On the level of culture, there is a shift away from the work ethic characteristic of industrialism; people are freer to innovate and enjoy themselves in both their work and their domestic lives.

Postmodern society, on the other hand, is said to involve changes even more profound than the end of industrialism. Postmodern scholars claim that we are witnessing a movement beyond *modernity*—the attitudes and ways of life associated with modern societies, such as our belief in progress, the benefits of science, and our capability to control the modern world. Advocates of this view claim that modern societies drew inspiration from the idea that history has a shape—it "goes somewhere" and leads to progress—and that now this notion has collapsed. There are no longer any overall conceptions of history that make sense (Lyotard, 1985). Not only is there no general notion of progress that can be defended, but there is no such thing as history. The postmodern world is thus highly pluralistic and diverse. In countless films, videos, and

postmodern • Quality of a technologically sophisticated society that is preoccupied with consumer goods and media images.

postindustrial society • A notion advocated by those who believe that processes of social change are taking us beyond the industrialized order. A postindustrial society is based on the production of information rather than material goods. According to postindustrialists, we are currently experiencing a series of social changes as profound as those that initiated the industrial era some 200 years ago.

information society • A society no longer based primarily on the production of material goods but on the production of knowledge. The notion of the information society is closely bound up with the rise of information technology.

service society • A concept related to postindustrial society, it refers to a social order distinguished by the growth of service occupations at the expense of industrial jobs that produce material goods.

knowledge society • A common term for information society—referring to a society based on the production and consumption of knowledge and information.

TV programs, images circulate worldwide. We encounter many ideas and values, but these have little connection with the history of the areas we live in, or indeed with our own personal histories. Everything seems constantly in flux. According to one group of authors,

> Our world is being remade. Mass production, the mass consumer, the big city, big-brother state, the sprawling housing estate, and the nation-state are in decline: flexibility, diversity, differentiation, and mobility, communication, decentralization and internationalization are in the ascendant. In the process our own identities, our sense of self, our own subjectivities are being transformed. We are in transition to a new era. (Hall et al., 1988)

While both the postindustrial and postmodern theorists provide important insights, each has shortcomings as well. Critics of the postindustrial argument claim that the trend toward service occupations began with the Industrial Revolution and that service workers have replaced not industrial workers so much as agricultural workers. Moreover, the notion that creative and challenging white-collar work is replacing highly routinized factory work is incorrect; much service-sector employment today is just as routinized and unsatisfying as factory work was in the past (and pays less). The postindustrial society thesis is also criticized for exaggerating the importance of economic factors in producing social change. Finally, the very concept of *postindustrial* implies that we are somehow at the end of history—after all, what can come after "post"? Any attempt to divide history into before and after stages is bound to be proven wrong over time as new (and unanticipated) technological breakthroughs, and their associated social changes, occur.

Postmodern theorists agree with this final criticism, seeing societies as moving into a stage that is so radically different that any attempt to understand general processes in the social world is doomed, as is the notion that we can change the world for the better. Writers such as Ulrich Beck and Anthony Giddens have strongly criticized this position, arguing instead that as much as ever, general theories of the social world allow us to intervene to shape it in a positive way. Such theories have considered how contemporary societies are becoming globalized, while everyday life is breaking free from tradition and custom. But these changes should not spell the end of social and political reform. Values, such as a belief in the importance of social community, equality, and caring for the weak and vulnerable, are still very much alive worldwide.

Is There a Need for Global Governance?

Globalization has brought with it violence, internal conflict, and chaotic transformations in many areas of the world. The existing political structures and models appear unequipped to manage the risks, inequalities, and challenges that transcend national borders. Individual governments cannot control the spread of HIV/AIDS, counter the effects of global warming, or regulate volatile financial markets. Critics of globalization see global organizations such as transnational corporations or the World Trade Organization as responsible. Others see opportunities to harness globalizing forces in the pursuit of greater equality, democracy, and prosperity.

Protesters against the WTO and other international financial institutions argue that exuberance over global economic integration and free trade is forcing people to live in an economy rather than a society. Many are convinced that such moves will further weaken the economic position of poor societies by allowing transnational corporations to operate with few or no safety and environmental regulations. Commercial interests, they claim, are increasingly taking precedence over concern for human well-being. Not only within countries in the global south, but in industrialized ones as well, the call is for greater investment in "human capital" (public health, education, and training) if global divisions are not to deepen. In their view, a key challenge for the twenty-first century is to ensure that globalization works for people everywhere, not only for those who are already well placed to benefit from it.

Walden Bello is a sociologist, member of the Philippine Parliament, and anti-globalization activist. Bello (2005) has called for **deglobalization**—reducing global interdependence by rendering economies less dependent on trade and global supply chains, instead making them as local as possible. Bello envisions democratically controlled local economies, where greater equality, rather than profit maximization, would be the goal. This would be achieved by subjecting key economic decisions to democratic choice rather than the marketplace. In Bello's deglobalized world there would be income redistribution, community cooperatives, small and medium-size businesses, and state enterprises—but no transnational corporations. Bello regards deglobalization as necessary on ecological as well as moral grounds. He argues that today's global economy, where products move thousands of miles, is in large part responsible for fossil fuel depletion, pollution, greenhouse gases, and global climate change. As he sees it,

> We must no longer think simply in terms of neutralizing the multilateral agencies that form the outer trenches of the system but of disabling the transnational corporations that are fortresses and the earthworks that constitute the core of the global economic system. I am talking about disabling not just the WTO, the IMF, and the World Bank but the transnational corporation itself. And I am not talking about a process of "reregulating" the TNCs but of eventually disabling or dismantling them as fundamental hazards to people, society, the environment, to everything we hold dear. (Bello, 2005)

Bello's views on deglobalization would be regarded as completely wrongheaded by those who argue that global capitalism is not only here to stay, but has resulted in higher living standards for hundreds of millions of people. Even those who share many of his criticisms of globalization would most likely regard his call for deglobalization as utopian. They would argue that the challenge is to make globalization work better for everyone—to establish institutions that would more effectively regulate the global economy, instead of leaving it to the marketplace. The Nobel Prize–winning economist Joseph Stiglitz (2003, 2007, 2010) and the philanthropist George Soros (2000, 2005, 2009) have both called for reforms of the current system, rather than overturning it completely.

New forms of global governance could help promote a cosmopolitan world order in which transparent rules and standards for international behavior, such as the defense of human rights, are established and observed. Yet the existing institutions of global governance hardly seem up to the task of reform: The United Nations and its affiliated organizations, such as the International Labor Organization, have little or no enforcement power, while the WTO, as presently constituted, seeks to promote free trade and economic deregulation (although Stiglitz and others have proposed reforms that could make it more responsive to social concerns).

deglobalization • The reduction of global interdependence by making economies as local as possible.

Uganda-based Good African Coffee is a model of deglobalization. CEO Andrew Rugasira has helped organize local farmers and worked with them to improve yields through better agricultural practices—ensuring that their coffee reaches global markets through a sustainable business model.

Erik Olin Wright's 2012 presidential address to the American Sociologist Association called for "envisioning real utopias"—nonreformist reforms that would move us incrementally toward a more egalitarian world. In his book by that name (2010), Wright critically evaluates the pros and cons of numerous proposals for reform, as well as specific organizations (such as worker-owned cooperatives or a guaranteed minimal income) that provide concrete examples of what might be possible. This is important, he argues, because

> most people in the world today, especially in the economically developed regions of the world, no longer believe in this possibility. Capitalism seems to most people part of the natural order of things . . . This book hopes to contribute to rebuilding a sense of possibility for emancipatory social change by investigating the feasibility of radically different kinds of institutions and social relations that could potentially advance the democratic egalitarian goals historically associated with the idea of socialism. In part this investigation will be empirical, examining cases of institutional innovations that embody in one way or another emancipatory alternatives to the dominant forms of social organization. In part it will be more speculative, exploring theoretical proposals that have not yet been implemented but nevertheless are attentive to realistic problems of institutional design and

social feasibility. The idea is to provide empirical and theoretical grounding for radical democratic egalitarian visions of an alternative social world. (Wright, 2010)

The move toward global governance and more effective regulatory institutions, and the search for alternatives to the present system, are clearly warranted at a time when global interdependence and the rapid pace of change link all people together more than ever before. Whether such changes should take the form of a move toward less global interdependence, as envisioned by Bello and the global justice movement, or reforming the current system, as called for by Soros, Stiglitz, and Wright, is open for discussion and debate.

It is not beyond our abilities to reassert our will on the social world. Indeed, such a task appears to be both the greatest necessity and the greatest challenge facing human societies in the twenty-first century.

CONCEPT CHECKS

1. What is the "postindustrial society"?
2. What is the "postmodern era"? What is the main criticism of this concept?
3. What are some examples of a move toward a global democratic structure?
4. Summarize optimistic versus pessimistic views toward global governance.

1 **Basic Concepts**

p. 637

2 **Current Theories: Is Globalization Today Something New—or Have We Seen It All Before?**

p. 643

LEARNING OBJECTIVES

Recognize that numerous factors influence social change, including physical environment, political organization, culture, and economic factors.

Understand the debates between skeptics, hyperglobalizers, and transformationalists over whether globalization differs radically from anything in human history.

TERMS TO KNOW

Hybridity • Social change

CONCEPT CHECKS

1. Name two examples of cultural factors that may influence social change.
2. How does industrial capitalism affect social change?
3. What are the most important political factors that influence social change?

1. Compare and contrast how the skeptics, the hyperglobalizers, and the transformationalists explain the phenomenon of globalization.
2. How might skeptics, hyper-globalizers and transformationalists interpret differently the growing global prominence of China?

Exercises: Thinking Sociologically

1. Discuss the many influences on social change: environmental, political, and cultural factors. Summarize how each element can contribute to social change.

2. According to this chapter, we now live in a society where we increasingly face various types of manufactured risks. Briefly explain what these risks consist of. Do you think the last decade has brought us any closer to or further away from confronting the challenges of manufactured risks? Explain.

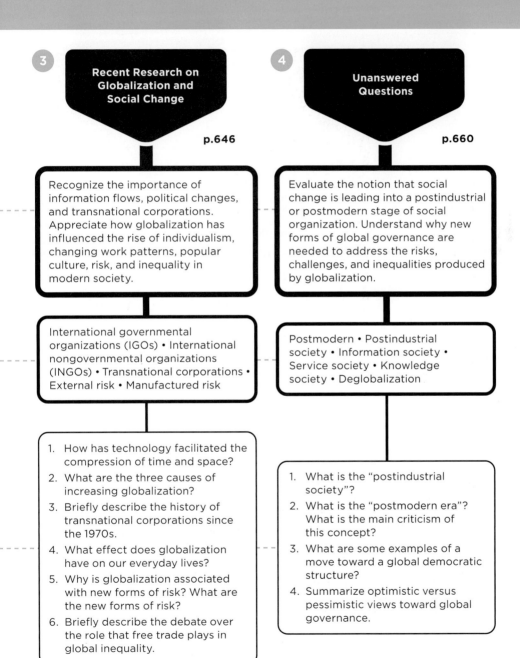

3

Recent Research on Globalization and Social Change

p.646

Recognize the importance of information flows, political changes, and transnational corporations. Appreciate how globalization has influenced the rise of individualism, changing work patterns, popular culture, risk, and inequality in modern society.

International governmental organizations (IGOs) • International nongovernmental organizations (INGOs) • Transnational corporations • External risk • Manufactured risk

1. How has technology facilitated the compression of time and space?
2. What are the three causes of increasing globalization?
3. Briefly describe the history of transnational corporations since the 1970s.
4. What effect does globalization have on our everyday lives?
5. Why is globalization associated with new forms of risk? What are the new forms of risk?
6. Briefly describe the debate over the role that free trade plays in global inequality.

4

Unanswered Questions

p.660

Evaluate the notion that social change is leading into a postindustrial or postmodern stage of social organization. Understand why new forms of global governance are needed to address the risks, challenges, and inequalities produced by globalization.

Postmodern • Postindustrial society • Information society • Service society • Knowledge society • Deglobalization

1. What is the "postindustrial society"?
2. What is the "postmodern era"? What is the main criticism of this concept?
3. What are some examples of a move toward a global democratic structure?
4. Summarize optimistic versus pessimistic views toward global governance.

Glossary

Words in **bold** type within entries refer to terms found elsewhere in the glossary.

AARP: U.S. advocacy group for people age 50 and over; formerly the American Association of Retired Persons.

absolute poverty: The minimal requirements necessary to sustain a healthy existence.

abstract and concrete attitudes: Abstract attitudes are ideas that are consistent with mainstream societal views, while concrete attitudes are ideas that are based on actual experience.

achievement gap: Disparity on a number of educational measures between the performance of groups of students, especially groups defined by **gender**, **race**, **ethnicity**, ability, and socioeconomic status.

"acting white" thesis: The thesis that black students do not aspire to or strive to get good grades because it is perceived as "acting white."

activity theory: A functionalist theory of **aging** which holds that busy, engaged people are more likely to lead fulfilling and productive lives.

affective individualism: The belief in romantic attachment as a basis for contracting **marriage** ties.

age-grade: The system found in small traditional **cultures** by which people belonging to a similar age group are categorized together and hold similar rights and obligations.

ageism: Discrimination or **prejudice** against a person on the grounds of age.

agents of socialization: Groups or social contexts within which processes of **socialization** take place.

aging: The combination of biological, psychological, and social processes that affect people as they grow older.

aging in place: A phenomenon in which many rural areas have disproportionately high numbers of older adults because young persons seek opportunities elsewhere and leave the older persons behind.

agrarian societies: Societies whose means of subsistence are based on agricultural production (crop growing).

alienation: The sense that our own abilities as human beings are taken over by other entities. The term was originally used by Karl Marx to refer to the projection of human powers onto gods. Subsequently he used the term to refer to the loss of workers' control over the nature and products of their labor.

Alzheimer's disease: A degenerative disease of the brain resulting in progressive loss of mental capacity.

anomie: A concept first brought into wide usage in sociology by Durkheim that refers to a situation in which social **norms** lose their hold over individual behavior.

antiracism: Forms of thought and/or practice that seek to confront, eradicate, and/or ameliorate **racism.**

apartheid: The system of racial **segregation** established in South Africa.

assimilation: The acceptance of a **minority group** by a majority **population** in which the new group takes on the **values** and **norms** of the dominant **culture**.

authority: A government's legitimate use of **power**.

automation: Production processes monitored and controlled by machines with only minimal supervision from people.

back region: Areas apart from **front region** performance, as specified by Erving Goffman, in which individuals are able to relax and behave informally.

biomedical model of health: A model of health that defines diseases objectively, in accordance with the presence of recognized symptoms, and believes that the healthy body can be restored through scientifically based medical treatment.

black feminism: A strand of **feminist theory** that highlights the multiple disadvantages of **gender**, **class**, and **race** that shape the experiences of nonwhite women. Black feminists reject the idea of a single, unified gender oppression that is experienced evenly by all women, and they argue that early feminist analysis reflected the specific concerns of white, **middle-class** women.

body mass index (BMI): A measure of body fat based on height and weight.

bureaucracy: A type of **organization** marked by a clear hierarchy of **authority** and the existence of written rules of procedure and staffed by full-time, salaried officials.

capitalism: An economic system based on the private ownership of **wealth**, which is invested and reinvested in order to produce profit.

capitalists: People who own companies, land, or stocks (shares) and use these to generate economic returns.

caste: A social system in which one's social **status** is held for life.

charismatic: The inspirational quality of leaders that makes them capable of capturing the imagination and devotion of a mass of followers.

churches: Large bodies of people belonging to an established religious **organization**. The term is also used to refer to the place in which religious ceremonies are carried out.

citizens: Members of a political community, having both rights and duties associated with that membership.

civil inattention: The process whereby individuals in the same physical setting glance at each other and quickly look away to indicate awareness of each other but not intrusiveness.

civil religion: A set of religious beliefs through which a **society** interprets its own history in light of some conception of ultimate reality.

civil rights: Legal rights held by all **citizens** in a given national community.

civil society: The realm of activity that lies between the **state** and the market, including the **family**, schools, community associations, and noneconomic institutions. Civil society, or civic culture, is essential to vibrant democratic societies.

class: Although it is one of the most frequently used concepts in sociology, there is no clear agreement about how the notion should be defined. Most sociologists use the term to refer to socioeconomic variations between groups of individuals that create variations in their material prosperity and **power**.

class systems: Large-scale, interpersonal, and fluid systems of social hierarchy based on wealth, occupation, income, and education.

clock time: Time as measured by the clock, in terms of hours, minutes, and seconds, as opposed to the rising and setting of the sun.

cognition: Human thought processes involving perception, reasoning, and remembering.

cohabitation: Two people living together in a sexual relationship of some permanence without being married to one another.

collective action: Action undertaken in a relatively spontaneous way by a large number of people assembled together.

collective consumption: A concept used by Manuel Castells to refer to processes of urban consumption—such as the buying and selling of property.

colonialism: The process whereby Western nations established their rule in parts of the world away from their home territories.

community policing: A renewed emphasis on crime prevention rather than law enforcement to reintegrate policing within the community.

comparable-worth policies: Policies that attempt to remedy the **gender** pay gap by adjusting pay so that those in female-dominated jobs are not paid less for equivalent work.

comparative research: Research that compares one set of findings on one **society** with the same type of findings on other societies.

complementary and alternative medicine (CAM): A diverse set of approaches and therapies for treating illness and promoting well-being that generally falls outside standard medical practices.

compulsion of proximity: People's need to interact with others in their presence.

concrete operational stage: A stage of cognitive development, as formulated by Piaget, in which a child's thinking is based primarily on physical perception of the world. In this phase, the child is not yet capable of dealing with abstract concepts or hypothetical situations.

conflict theories of aging: Arguments that emphasize the ways in which the larger **social structure** helps to shape the opportunities available to the elderly. Unequal opportunities are seen as creating the potential for conflict.

conflict theory: The argument that **deviance** is deliberately chosen and often political in nature.

constitutional monarchs: Kings or queens who are largely figureheads. Real **power** rests in the hands of other political leaders.

continuity theory: The theory that older adults' well-being is enhanced when their activities are consistent with their personality, preferences, and activities earlier in life.

contradictory class locations: Positions in the class structure, particularly routine white-collar and lower managerial jobs, that share characteristics of the class positions both above and below them.

control theory: The theory that views **crime** as the outcome of an imbalance between impulses toward criminal activity and controls that deter it. Control theorists hold that criminals are rational beings who will act to maximize their own reward unless they are rendered unable to do so through either social or physical controls.

conurbation: An agglomeration of towns or cities into an unbroken urban environment.

conversation analysis: The empirical study of conversations, employing techniques drawn from **ethnomethodology**. Conversation analysis examines details of naturally occurring conversations to reveal the organizational principles of talk and its role in the production and reproduction of social order.

core: According to **world-systems theory**, the most advanced industrial countries, which take the lion's share of profits in the world economic system.

corporate crime: Offenses committed by large **corporations** in society. Examples of corporate crime include pollution, false advertising, and violations of **health** and safety regulations.

corporations: Business firms or companies.

correlation coefficients: The measure of the degree of correlation between variables.

created environment: Constructions established by human beings to serve their needs, derived from the use of man-made **technology**—including, for example, roads, railways, factories, offices, private homes, and other buildings.

crime: Any action that contravenes the **laws** established by a political **authority**. Although we may think of criminals as a distinct subsection of the **population**, there are few people who have not broken the law in one way or another during their lives. While laws are formulated by state authorities, it is not unknown for those authorities to engage in criminal behavior in certain situations.

crude birthrates: Statistical measures representing the number of births within a given **population** per year, normally calculated in terms of the number of births per 1,000 members. Although the crude birthrate is a useful index, it is only a general measure because it does not specify numbers of births in relation to age distribution.

crude death rates: Statistical measures representing the number of deaths that occur annually in a given **population** per year, normally calculated as the ratio of deaths per 1,000 members. Crude death rates give a general indication of the **mortality** levels of a community or **society**, but are limited in their usefulness because they do not take into account the age distribution.

cults: Fragmentary religious groupings to which individuals are loosely affiliated but that lack any permanent structure.

cultural capital: The advantages that well-to-do parents usually provide their children.

cultural navigators: People who draw from both their home **culture** and mainstream culture to create an attitude that allows them to succeed.

cultural relativism: The practice of judging a **society** by its own standards.

cultural turn: Sociology's recent emphasis on the importance of understanding the role of **culture** in daily life.

cultural universals: Values or **modes** of behavior shared by all human **cultures**.

culture: The **values**, **norms**, and material goods characteristic of a given group. Like the concept of **society**, the notion of culture is widely used in sociology and the other social sciences (particularly anthropology). Culture is one of the most distinctive properties of human social association.

culture of poverty: The thesis, popularized by Oscar Lewis, that poverty is not a result of individual inadequacies but is instead the outcome of a larger social and cultural atmosphere into which successive generations of children are socialized. The culture of poverty refers to the **values**, beliefs, lifestyles, habits, and traditions that are common among people living under conditions of material deprivation.

cybercrime: Criminal activities by means of electronic **networks** or involving the use of new information **technologies**. Electronic money laundering, personal **identity** theft, electronic vandalism, and monitoring electronic correspondence are all emergent forms of cybercrime.

cyberspace: Electronic networks of interaction between individuals at different computer terminals.

deglobalization: The reduction of global interdependence by making economies as local as possible.

degree of dispersal: The range or distribution of a set of figures.

democratic elitism: A theory of the limits of democracy that holds that in large-scale societies democratic participation is necessarily limited to the regular election of political leaders.

demographic transition: An interpretation of **population** change that holds that a stable ratio of births to deaths is achieved once a certain level of economic prosperity has been reached. According to this notion, in preindustrial

societies there is a rough balance between births and deaths because population increase is kept in check by a lack of available food, by disease, or by war. In modern societies, by contrast, population equilibrium is achieved because **families** are moved by economic incentives to limit the number of children.

demography: The study of **populations**.

denomination: A religious **sect** that has lost its revivalist dynamism and become an institutionalized body, commanding the adherence of significant numbers of people.

dependency culture: A term popularized by Charles Murray to describe individuals who rely on state welfare provision rather than entering the labor market. The dependency culture is seen as the outcome of the "paternalistic" **welfare state** that undermines individual ambition and people's capacity for self-help.

dependency theories: Marxist theories of economic development arguing that the poverty of low-income countries stems directly from their exploitation by wealthy countries and the **transnational** (or multinational) corporations that are based in wealthy countries.

dependent development: The theory that poor countries can still develop economically, but only in ways shaped by their reliance on wealthier countries.

deviance: Modes of action that do not conform to the **norms** or **values** held by most members of a group or **society**. What is regarded as deviant is as variable as the norms and values that distinguish different **cultures** and **subcultures** from one another. Forms of behavior that are highly esteemed by one group may be regarded negatively by others.

deviant subcultures: Subcultures whose members hold **values** that differ substantially from those of the majority.

diaspora: The dispersal of an ethnic **population** from an original homeland into foreign areas, often in a forced manner or under traumatic circumstances.

differential association: An interpretation of the development

of criminal behavior proposed by Edwin H. Sutherland, according to whom criminal behavior is learned through association with others who regularly engage in **crime**.

direct democracy: A form of **participatory democracy** that allows **citizens** to vote directly on **laws** and policies.

discrimination: Behavior that denies to the members of a particular group resources or rewards that can be obtained by others. Discrimination must be distinguished from **prejudice**. Individuals who are prejudiced against others may not engage in discriminatory practices against them; conversely, people may act in a discriminatory fashion toward a group even though they are not prejudiced against that group.

disengagement theory: A functionalist theory of **aging** that holds that it is functional for **society** to remove people from their traditional **roles** when they become elderly, thereby freeing up those roles for others.

disestablishment: A period during which the political influence of established **religions** is successfully challenged.

displacement: The transferring of ideas or emotions from their true source to another object.

division of labor: The specialization of **work** tasks by means of which different **occupations** are combined within a production system. All **societies** have at least some rudimentary form of division of labor, especially between the tasks allocated to men and those performed by women. With the development of industrialism, the division of labor became vastly more complex than in any prior type of production system. In the modern world, the division of labor is international in scope.

doubling time: The time it takes for a particular level of **population** to double.

dyad: A group consisting of two persons.

ecological approach: In the field of urban analysis, a perspective emphasizing the "natural" distribution of city neighborhoods into areas having contrasting characteristics.

economic interdependence: The fact that in the **division of labor**, individuals depend on others to produce many or most of the goods they need to sustain their lives.

economy: The system of production and exchange that provides for the material needs of individuals living in a given **society**. Economic institutions are of key importance in all social orders. What goes on in the economy usually influences other areas of social life. Modern economies differ substantially from traditional ones because the majority of the **population** is no longer engaged in agricultural production.

egocentric: According to Piaget, the characteristic quality of a child during the early years of her life. Egocentric thinking involves understanding objects and events in the environment solely in terms of the child's own position.

elderly: Adults 65 and older.

emerging economies: Formerly impoverished countries that over the past two or three decades have begun to develop a strong industrial base, such as India or Singapore.

emigration: The movement of people out of one country in order to settle in another.

emotional intelligence: The ability to identify, assess, and control one's own emotions or the emotions of others.

emotional loneliness: The absence of an intimate confidant.

empirical investigation: A factual inquiry carried out in any area of sociological study.

encounter: A meeting between two or more people in a situation of face-to-face interaction. Our daily lives can be seen as a series of different encounters strung out across the course of the day. In modern societies, many of these encounters are with strangers rather than people we know.

entrepreneur: The owner/founder of a business firm.

environmental ecology: The scientific study of the distribution and abundance of life and the interactions between organisms and their natural environment.

epidemiology: The study of the distribution and incidence of disease and illness within a **population**.

ethnic cleansing: The creation of ethnically homogeneous territories through the mass expulsion of other ethnic **populations**.

ethnicity: Cultural **values** and **norms** that distinguish the members of a given group from others. An ethnic group is one whose members share a distinct awareness of a common cultural **identity**, separating them from other groups. In virtually all **societies**, ethnic differences are associated with variations in **power** and material **wealth**. Where ethnic differences are also racial, such divisions are sometimes especially pronounced.

ethnocentrism: The tendency to look at other **cultures** through the eyes of one's own culture, and thereby misrepresent them.

ethnography: The firsthand study of people using **participant observation** or interviewing.

ethnomethodology: The study of how people make sense of what others say and do in the course of day-to-day **social interaction**. Ethnomethodology is concerned with the "ethnomethods" by which people sustain meaningful interchanges with one another.

evangelicalism: A form of Protestantism characterized by a belief in spiritual rebirth (being "born again").

exchange mobility: The exchange of positions on the socioeconomic scale such that talented people move up the economic hierarchy while the less talented move down.

experiment: A **research method** in which variables can be analyzed in a controlled and systematic way, either in an artificial situation constructed by the researcher or in naturally occurring settings.

exponential: A geometric, rather than linear, rate of progression, producing a fast rise in the numbers of a **population** experiencing such growth.

extended family: A **family** group consisting of more than two generations of relatives living either within the same household or very close to one another.

external risk: Dangers that spring from the natural world and are unrelated to the actions of humans. Examples of external risk include droughts, earthquakes, famines, and storms.

failed states: States in which the central government has lost authority and resorts to deadly force to retain power.

families of orientation: The families into which individuals are born.

families of procreation: The families individuals initiate through **marriage** or by having children.

family: A group of individuals related to one another by blood ties, **marriage**, or adoption, who form an economic unit, the adult members of which are responsible for the upbringing of children. All known **societies** involve some form of family system, although the nature of family relationships varies widely. While in modern societies the main family form is the **nuclear family**, **extended family** relationships are also found.

family capitalism: Capitalistic enterprise owned and administered by entrepreneurial **families**.

fecundity: A measure of the number of children that it is biologically possible for a woman to produce.

feminist theories: Sociological perspectives that emphasize the centrality of **gender** in analyzing the social world and particularly the uniqueness of the experience of women. There are many strands of feminist theory, but they all share the desire to explain **gender inequality** in **society** and to work to overcome it.

feminization of poverty: An increase in the proportion of the poor who are female.

fertility: The average number of live-born children produced by women of childbearing age in a particular **society**.

field of action: The arena within which **social movements** interact with established **organizations**, often producing a modification of the ideas and outlook of the members of both.

flexible production: Process in which computers design customized products for a mass market.

focused interaction: Interaction between individuals engaged in a common activity or in direct conversation with one another.

Fordism: The system of production pioneered by Henry Ford, in which the assembly line was introduced.

formal operational stage: According to Piaget's theory, a stage of cognitive development at which a growing child becomes capable of handling abstract concepts and hypothetical situations.

formal organization: A group that is rationally designed to achieve its objectives, often by means of explicit rules, regulations, and procedures.

formal relations: Relations that exist in groups and **organizations** laid down by the **norms**, or as rules, of the official system of **authority**.

front region: Settings of social activity in which people seek to put on a definite "performance" for others.

functionalism: A theoretical perspective based on the notion that social events can best be explained in terms of the functions they perform—that is, the contributions they make to the continuity of a **society**.

fundamentalists: Evangelists who are highly antimodern in many of their beliefs and adhere to strict codes of morality and conduct.

gender: Social expectations about behavior regarded as appropriate for the members of each **sex**. Gender refers not to the physical attributes distinguishing men and women but to socially formed traits of masculinity and femininity. The study of gender relations has become one of the most important areas of sociology in recent years.

gender gap: The differences between women and men, especially as reflected in social, political, intellectual, cultural, or economic attainments or attitudes.

gender inequality: The inequality between men and women in terms of **wealth**, **income**, and **status**.

gender roles: Social roles assigned to each **sex** and labeled as masculine or feminine.

gender role socialization: The learning of **gender roles** through social factors such as schooling, the media, and **family**.

gender typing: Women holding **occupations** of lower **status** and pay, such as secretarial and retail positions, and men holding jobs of higher status and pay, such as managerial and professional positions.

generalized other: A concept described by George Herbert Mead according to which the individual comes to understand the general **values** and moral rules of a given group or **society** during the **socialization** process.

generational equity: The striking of a balance between the needs and interests of members of different generations.

genocide: The systematic, planned destruction of a racial, political, or cultural group.

gentrification: A process of **urban renewal** in which older, deteriorated housing is refurbished by affluent people moving into the area.

Gini coefficient: A standard measure of a country's economic disparity where 0 represents perfect equality and 1 represents maximum inequality.

glass ceiling: A promotion barrier that prevents a woman's upward mobility within an **organization**.

global city: A city—such as London, New York, or Tokyo—that has become an organizing center of the new global **economy**.

global commodity chains: Worldwide **networks** of labor and production processes yielding a finished product.

global inequality: The systematic differences in **wealth** and **power** between countries.

globalization: The development of social and economic relationships stretching worldwide. In current times, we are all influenced by **organizations** and social **networks** located thousands of miles away. A key part of the study of globalization is the emergence of a world system—for some purposes, we need to regard the world as forming a single social order.

graying: A term used to indicate that an increasing proportion of a **society**'s **population** is elderly.

health: Complete physical, mental, and social well-being rather than merely the absence of disease or infirmity.

health literacy: One's capacity to obtain, process, and understand basic health information and services needed to make appropriate health decisions.

hidden curriculum: Traits of behavior or attitudes that are learned at school but not included within the formal curriculum—for example, **gender** differences.

high-trust systems: Organizations or **work** settings in which individuals are permitted a great deal of autonomy and control over the work task.

historicity: The use of an understanding of history as a basis for trying to change history—that is, producing informed processes of **social change**.

homeless: People who have no place to sleep and either stay in free shelters or sleep in public places not meant for habitation.

homophobia: An irrational fear of or disdain for homosexuals.

human capital theory: The argument that individuals make investments in their own "human capital" in order to increase their productivity and earnings.

hunting and gathering societies: Societies whose mode of subsistence is gained from hunting animals, fishing, and gathering edible plants.

hybridity: The fact that cultures are neither wholly isolated nor entirely distinct, but instead constantly borrow from one another.

hypotheses: Ideas or guesses about a given state of affairs, put forward as bases for empirical testing.

ideal type: A "pure type," constructed by emphasizing certain traits of a social item that do not necessarily exist in reality. An example is Max Weber's ideal type of bureaucratic **organization**.

identity: The distinctive characteristics of a person's or group's character that relate to who they are and what is meaningful to them. Some of the main sources of identity include **gender**, sexual orientation, nationality or **ethnicity**, and social **class**.

ideologies: Shared ideas or beliefs that serve to justify the interests of dominant groups. Ideologies are found in all **societies** in which there are systematic and ingrained inequalities between groups. The concept of ideology connects closely with that of **power**, since ideological systems serve to legitimize the power that groups hold.

immigration: The movement of people into one country from another for the purpose of settlement.

impression management: Preparing for the presentation of one's **social role**.

income: Payment, usually derived from wages, salaries, or investments.

industrialization: The process of the machine production of goods. See also **industrialized societies**.

industrialized societies: Strongly developed **nation-states** in which the majority of the **population** works in factories or offices rather than in agriculture, and most people live in urban areas.

infant mortality rate: The number of infants who die during the first year of life, per 1,000 live births.

informal economy: Economic transactions carried on outside the sphere of orthodox paid employment.

informal relations: Relations that exist in groups and **organizations** developed on the basis of personal connections; ways of doing things that depart from formally recognized modes of procedure.

information and communication technology: Forms of **technology** based on information processing and requiring microelectronic circuitry.

information poverty: The "information poor" are those people who have little or no access to information **technology**, such as computers.

information society: A **society** no longer based primarily on the production of material goods but rather on the production of knowledge. The notion of the information society is closely bound up with the rise of information **technology**.

in-groups: Groups toward which one feels particular loyalty and respect—the groups to which "we" belong.

inner city: The areas composing the central neighborhoods of a city, as distinct from the suburbs. In many modern urban settings in the developed world, inner-city areas are subject to dilapidation and decay, with the more affluent residents having moved to outlying areas.

instincts: Fixed patterns of behavior that have genetic origins and that appear in all normal animals within a given species.

institutional capitalism: Capitalistic enterprise organized on the basis of institutional shareholding.

institutional racism: Patterns of **discrimination** based on

ethnicity that have become structured into existing social institutions.

intelligence: Level of intellectual ability, particularly as measured by **IQ (intelligence quotient)** tests.

interactional vandalism: The deliberate subversion of the tacit rules of conversation.

interest group: A group organized to pursue specific interests in the political arena, operating primarily by lobbying the members of legislative bodies.

intergenerational mobility: Movement up or down a **social stratification** hierarchy from one generation to another.

international division of labor: The specialization in producing goods for the world market that divides regions into zones of industrial or agricultural production or high- or low-skilled labor.

international governmental organizations (IGOs): International organizations established by treaties between governments for purposes of conducting business between the nations making up their membership.

international nongovernmental organizations (INGOs): International organizations established by agreements between the individuals or private **organizations** making up their membership.

intragenerational mobility: Movement up or down a **social stratification** hierarchy within the course of a personal career.

IQ (intelligence quotient): A score attained on tests of symbolic or reasoning abilities.

iron law of oligarchy: A term coined by Weber's student Robert Michels meaning that large **organizations** tend toward centralization of **power**, making **democracy** difficult.

kinship: A relation that links individuals through blood ties, **marriage**, or adoption. Kinship relations are by definition part of marriage and the **family**, but extend much more broadly. While in most modern societies few social obligations are involved in kinship relations extending beyond the immediate family, in other **cultures** kinship is of vital importance to social life.

knowledge economy: A **society** no longer based primarily on the

production of material goods but instead on the production of knowledge. Its emergence has been linked to the development of a broad base of consumers who are technologically literate and have made new advances in computing, entertainment, and telecommunications part of their lives.

knowledge society: A common term for **information society** referring to a **society** based on the production and consumption of knowledge and information.

Kuznets curve: A formula showing that inequality increases during the early stages of capitalist development, then declines, and eventually stabilizes at a relatively low level; advanced by the economist Simon Kuznets.

labeling theory: An approach to the study of **deviance** that suggests that people become "deviant" because certain labels are attached to their behavior by political authorities and others.

language: The primary vehicle of meaning and communication in a **society**; a system of **symbols** that represent objects and abstract thoughts.

latent functions: Functional consequences that are not intended or recognized by the members of a social system in which they occur.

laws: Rules of behavior established by a political **authority** and backed by state **power**.

legitimation crisis: The failure of a political order to generate a sufficient level of commitment and involvement on the part of its **citizens** to be able to govern properly.

liberal democracies: Systems of democracy based on parliamentary institutions, coupled to the free-market system in the area of economic production.

liberal feminism: The form of **feminist theory** that believes that **gender inequality** is produced by unequal access to **civil rights** and certain social resources, such as education and employment, based on **sex**. Liberal feminists tend to seek solutions through changes in legislation that ensure that the rights of individuals are protected.

liberation theology: An activist Catholic **religious movement** that combines Catholic beliefs with a passion for social justice for the poor.

life course: The various transitions people experience during their lives.

life expectancy: The number of years the average person can expect to live.

life span: The maximum length of life that is biologically possible for a member of a given species.

linguistic relativity hypothesis: A **hypothesis**, based on the **theories** of Sapir and Whorf, that perceptions are relative to **language**.

local nationalism: The belief that communities that share a cultural **identity** should have political autonomy, even within smaller units of **nation-states**.

lower class: A social class comprised of those who work part time or not at all and whose household income is typically lower than $30,000 a year.

low-trust systems: Organizational or **work** settings in which people are allowed little responsibility for, or control over, the work task.

macrosociology: The study of large-scale groups, **organizations**, or social systems.

Malthusianism: A doctrine about **population** dynamics developed by Thomas Malthus, according to which population increase comes up against "natural limits," represented by famine and war.

managerial capitalism: Capitalistic enterprises administered by managerial executives rather than by owners.

manifest functions: The functions of a type of social activity that are known to and intended by the individuals involved in the activity.

manufactured risk: Dangers that are created by the impact of human knowledge and **technology** on the natural world. Examples of manufactured risk include global warming and genetically modified foods.

market-oriented theories: Theories about economic development that assume that the best possible economic consequences will result if individuals are free to make their own economic decisions, uninhibited by governmental constraint.

marriage: A socially approved sexual relationship between two individuals. Marriage almost always involves two persons of opposite sexes, but in some **cultures**, types of homosexual marriage are tolerated. Marriage normally forms the basis of a **family of procreation**—that is, it is expected that the married couple will produce and bring up children. Some societies permit **polygamy**, in which an individual may have several spouses at the same time.

Marxism: A body of thought deriving its main elements from the ideas of Karl Marx.

mass media: Forms of communication, such as newspapers, magazines, radio, and television, designed to reach mass audiences.

material culture: The physical objects that a **society** creates that influence the ways in which people live.

materialist conception of history: The view developed by Marx, according to which material, or economic, factors have a prime role in determining historical change.

matrilocal: A **family** system in which the husband is expected to live near the wife's parents.

mean: A statistical measure of central tendency, or average, based on dividing a total by the number of individual cases.

means of production: The means whereby the production of material goods is carried on in a **society**, including not just **technology** but also the social relations between producers.

measures of central tendency: The ways of calculating averages.

median: The number that falls halfway in a range of numbers—a way of calculating central tendency that is sometimes more useful than calculating a **mean**.

Medicare: A program under the U.S. **Social Security** Administration that reimburses hospitals and physicians for medical care provided to qualifying people over 65 years old.

megacities: A term favored by Manuel Castells to describe large, intensely concentrated urban spaces that serve as connection points for the global **economy**. It is projected that by 2015 there will be 36 megacities with **populations** of more than 8 million residents.

megalopolis: The "city of all cities" in ancient Greece—used in modern times to refer to very large **conurbations**.

melting pot: The idea that ethnic differences can be combined to create new patterns of behavior drawing on diverse cultural sources.

microsociology: The study of human behavior in contexts of face-to-face interaction.

middle class: A social **class** composed broadly of those working in white-collar and lower managerial **occupations**.

minority group: A group of people in a given **society** who, because of their distinct physical or cultural characteristics, find themselves in situations of inequality compared with the dominant group within that society.

mode: The number that appears most often in a given set of data. This can sometimes be a helpful way of portraying central tendency.

modernization theory: A version of market-oriented development theory that argues that low-income societies develop economically only if they give up their traditional ways and adopt modern economic institutions, **technologies**, and cultural **values** that emphasize savings and productive investment.

monarchies: Systems of government in which unelected kings or queens rule.

monogamy: A form of **marriage** in which each married partner is allowed only one spouse at any given time.

monopoly: A situation in which a single firm dominates in a given industry.

monotheism: Belief in a single god.

mortality: The number of deaths in a **population**.

multiculturalism: A condition in which ethnic groups exist separately and share equally in economic and political life.

multiple sovereignty: A situation in which there is no single sovereign **power** in a **society**.

nation: People with a common identity that ideally includes a shared culture, language, and feelings of belonging.

nationalism: A set of beliefs and **symbols** expressing identification with a national community.

nation-states: Particular types of **states**, characteristic of the modern world, in which governments have sovereign **power** within defined territorial areas and **populations** comprise **citizens**

who know themselves to be part of single nations. Nation-states are closely associated with the rise of **nationalism**, although nationalist loyalties do not always conform to the boundaries of specific states. Nation-states developed as part of an emerging nation-state system, originating in Europe; in current times, they span the whole globe.

nations without states: Instances in which the members of a nation lack political **sovereignty** over the area they claim as their own.

neoliberalism: The economic belief that free-market forces, achieved by minimizing government restrictions on business, provide the only route to economic growth.

networks: Sets of informal and formal social ties that link people to each other.

New Age movement: A general term to describe the diverse spectrum of beliefs and practices oriented on inner spirituality. Paganism, Eastern mysticism, shamanism, alternative forms of healing, and astrology are all examples of New Age activities.

newly industrializing economies (NIEs): Developing countries that over the past two or three decades have begun to develop a strong industrial base, such as Singapore and Hong Kong.

new religious movements: The broad range of religious and spiritual groups, **cults**, and **sects** that have emerged alongside mainstream **religions**. New religious movements range from spiritual and self-help groups within the **New Age movement** to exclusive sects such as the Hare Krishnas.

new social movements: A set of **social movements** that have arisen in Western **societies** since the 1960s in response to the changing risks facing human societies. New social movements such as **feminism**, environmentalism, the antinuclear movement, opposition to genetically modified food, and the antiglobalization movement differ from earlier social movements in that they are single-issue campaigns oriented to nonmaterial ends and draw support from across class lines.

nonverbal communication: Communication between individuals based on facial expression or bodily gesture rather than on **language**.

norms: Rules of conduct that specify appropriate behavior in a given range of social situations. A norm either prescribes a given type of behavior or forbids it. All human groups follow definite norms, which are always backed by **sanctions** of one kind or another, varying from informal disapproval to physical punishment.

nuclear family: A **family** group consisting of a wife, a husband (or one of these), and dependent children.

obesity: Excessive body weight, indicated by a **body mass index (BMI)** over 30.

occupation: Any form of paid employment in which an individual regularly works.

oldest old: Sociological term for persons aged 85 and older.

old old: Sociological term for persons aged 75 to 84.

oligarchy: Rule by a small minority within an **organization** or **society**.

oligopoly: The domination of a small number of firms in a given industry.

organic solidarity: According to Émile Durkheim, the social cohesion that results from the various parts of a **society** functioning as an integrated whole.

organization: A large group of individuals with a definite set of **authority** relations. Many types of organizations exist in **industrialized societies**, influencing most aspects of our lives. While not all organizations are bureaucratic, there are close links between the development of organizations and bureaucratic tendencies.

out-groups: Groups toward which one feels antagonism and contempt— "those people."

outsourcing: A business practice that sends production of materials to factories around the world. The components of one final product often originate from many different countries and then are sent elsewhere to be put together and sold. Factories from different countries must compete with one another to obtain business.

pariah groups: Groups who suffer from negative **status discrimination**—they are looked down on by most other members of **society**. The Jews, for example, have been a pariah group throughout much of European history.

participant observation: A method of research widely used in sociology and anthropology, in which the researcher takes part in the activities of the group or community being studied.

participatory democracy: A system of democracy in which all members of a group or community participate collectively in making major decisions.

pastoral societies: Societies whose subsistence derives from the rearing of domesticated animals.

patriarchy: The dominance of men over women. All known **societies** are patriarchal, although there are variations in the degree and nature of the **power** men exercise as compared with women. One of the prime objectives of women's movements in modern societies is to combat existing patriarchal institutions.

patrilocal: A **family** system in which the wife is expected to live near the husband's parents.

peer group: A friendship group composed of individuals of similar age and social **status**.

periphery: Describes countries that have a marginal role in the world **economy** and are thus dependent on the **core** producing societies for their trading relationships.

personality stabilization: According to the theory of **functionalism**, the **family** plays a crucial role in assisting its adult members emotionally. **Marriage** between adult men and women is the arrangement through which adult personalities are supported and kept healthy.

personal space: The physical space individuals maintain between themselves and others.

pilot study: A trial run in **survey** research.

pluralism: A model for ethnic relations in which all ethnic groups in the United States retain their independent and separate identities yet share equally in the rights and **powers** of citizenship.

political rights: Rights of political participation, such as the right to vote in local and national elections, held by **citizens** of a national community.

polyandry: A form of **marriage** in which a woman may simultaneously have two or more husbands.

polygamy: A form of **marriage** in which a person may have two or more spouses simultaneously.

polygyny: A form of marriage in which a man may simultaneously have two or more wives.

polytheism: Belief in two or more gods.

population: The people who are the focus of social research.

portfolio workers: Workers who possess a diversity of skills or qualifications and are therefore able to move easily from job to job.

post-Fordism: A general term used to describe the transition from mass industrial production, characterized by Fordist methods, to more flexible forms of production favoring innovation and aimed at meeting market demands for customized products.

postindustrial society: A notion advocated by those who believe that processes of **social change** are taking us beyond the industrialized order. A postindustrial society is based on the production of information rather than material goods. According to postindustrialists, we are currently experiencing a series of social changes as profound as those that initiated the industrial era some 200 years ago.

postmodern: Quality of a technologically sophisticated **society** that is preoccupied with consumer goods and media images.

postmodern feminism: The feminist perspective that challenges the idea of a unitary basis of **identity** and experience shared by all women. Postmodern feminists reject the claim that there is a grand theory that can explain the position of women in **society**, or that there is any single, universal essence or category of "woman." Instead, they encourage the acceptance of many different standpoints as equally valid.

postmodernism: The belief that **society** is no longer governed by history or progress. **Postmodern** society is highly pluralistic and diverse, with no "grand narrative" guiding its development.

poverty line: An official government measure to define those living in poverty in the United States.

power: The ability of individuals or the members of a group to achieve aims or further the interests they hold. Power is a pervasive element in all human relationships. Many conflicts in **society** are struggles over power, because how much power an individual or group is able to achieve governs how far they are able to put their wishes into practice.

power elite: Small **networks** of individuals who, according to C. Wright Mills, hold concentrated **power** in modern **societies**.

prejudice: The holding of preconceived ideas about an individual or group, ideas that are resistant to change even in the face of new information. Prejudice may be either positive or negative.

preoperational stage: A stage of cognitive development, in Piaget's theory, in which a child has advanced sufficiently to master basic modes of logical thought.

primary deviation: According to Edwin Lemert, the actions that cause others to label one as a deviant.

primary groups: Groups that are characterized by intense emotional ties, face-to-face interaction, intimacy, and a strong, enduring sense of commitment.

primary socialization: The process by which children learn the cultural **norms** of the **society** into which they are born. Primary socialization occurs largely in the **family**.

procreative technology: Techniques for influencing the human reproductive process.

profane: That which belongs to the mundane, everyday world.

race: Differences in human physical characteristics used to categorize large numbers of individuals.

racialization: The process by which understandings of **race** are used to classify individuals or groups of people. Racial distinctions are more than ways of describing human differences; they are also important factors in the reproduction of patterns of **power** and inequality.

racial literacy: The skills taught to children of multiracial families to help them cope with racial hierarchies and to integrate multiple ethnic identities.

racism: The attribution of characteristics of superiority or inferiority to a **population** sharing certain physically inherited characteristics. Racism is one specific form of **prejudice**, focusing on physical variations between people. Racist attitudes became entrenched during the period of Western colonial expansion but seem also to rest on mechanisms of prejudice and **discrimination** found in human **societies** today.

radical feminism: The form of **feminist theory** that believes that **gender inequality** is the result of male domination in all aspects of social and economic life.

random sampling: Sampling method in which a sample is chosen so that every member of the **population** has the same probability of being included.

rape: The forcing of nonconsensual vaginal, oral, or anal intercourse.

rates of population growth or decline: A measurement of population growth calculated by subtracting the yearly number of deaths per 1,000 from the number of births per 1,000.

rational choice approach: More broadly, the theory that an individual's behavior is purposive. Within the field of criminology, rational choice analysis argues that deviant behavior is a rational response to a specific social situation.

rationalization: A concept used by Max Weber to refer to the process by which modes of precise calculation and organization, involving abstract rules and procedures, increasingly come to dominate the social world.

reference group: A group that provides a standard for judging one's attitudes or behaviors.

regionalization: The division of social life into different regional settings or zones.

relative deprivation: Deprivation a person feels by comparing himself with a group.

relative poverty: Poverty defined according to the living standards of the majority in any given society.

religion: A set of beliefs adhered to by the members of a community, incorporating **symbols** regarded with a sense of awe or wonder together with ritual practices. Religions do not universally involve a belief in supernatural entities.

religious economy: A theoretical framework within the sociology of

religion that argues that religions can be fruitfully understood as **organizations** in competition with one another for followers.

religious movements: Associations of people who join together to seek to spread a new **religion** or to promote a new interpretation of an existing religion.

religious nationalism: The linking of strongly held religious convictions with beliefs about a people's social and political destiny.

research methods: The diverse methods of investigation used to gather empirical (factual) material. Different research methods exist in sociology, but the most commonly used are fieldwork (or **participant observation**) and **survey** methods. For many purposes, it is useful to combine two or more methods within a single research project.

response cries: Seemingly involuntary exclamations individuals make when, for example, they are taken by surprise, drop something inadvertently, or want to express pleasure.

revolutions: Processes of political change involving the mobilizing of a mass **social movement**, which, by the use of violence, successfully overthrows an existing regime and forms a new government.

roles: The expected behaviors of people occupying particular **social positions**. The idea of **social role** originally comes from the theater, referring to the parts that actors play in a stage production. In every **society**, individuals play a number of **social roles**.

sacred: That which inspires attitudes of awe or reverence among believers in a given set of religious ideas.

sample: A small proportion of a larger **population**.

sampling: Studying a proportion of individuals or cases from a larger **population** as representative of that population as a whole.

sanction: A mode of reward or punishment that reinforces socially expected forms of behavior.

scapegoats: Individuals or groups blamed for wrongs that were not of their doing.

science: In the sense of physical science, the systematic study of the physical world. Science involves the disciplined marshaling of empirical data, combined with theoretical approaches and theories

that illuminate or explain those data. Scientific activity combines the creation of bold new modes of thought with the careful testing of **hypotheses** and ideas. One major feature that helps distinguish science from other idea systems is the assumption that all scientific ideas are open to criticism and revision.

secondary deviation: According to Edwin Lemert, following the act of **primary deviation**, secondary deviation occurs when an individual accepts the label of deviant and acts accordingly.

secondary groups: Groups characterized by large size and by impersonal, fleeting relationships.

second demographic transition: A new demographic model that calls for **fertility** rates that may continue to fall because of shifts in **family** structure.

sects: Religious movements that break away from orthodoxy.

secularization: A process of decline in the influence of **religion**. Although modern **societies** have become increasingly secularized, tracing the extent of secularization is a complex matter. Secularization can refer to levels of involvement with religious **organizations** (such as rates of **church** attendance), the social and material influence wielded by religious organizations, and the degree to which people hold religious beliefs.

secular thinking: Worldly thinking particularly as seen in the rise of **science**, **technology**, and rational thought in general.

segregation: The practice of keeping racial and ethnic groups physically separate, thereby maintaining the superior position of the dominant group.

self-consciousness: Awareness of one's distinct **social identity** as a person separate from others. Human beings are not born with self-consciousness but acquire an awareness of self as a result of early **socialization**. The learning of **language** is of vital importance to the processes by which a child learns to become a self-conscious being.

self-identity: The ongoing process of self-development and definition of our personal **identity** through which we formulate a unique sense of ourselves and our relationship to the world around us.

semiotics: The study of the ways in which nonlinguistic phenomena can generate meaning—as in the example of a traffic light.

semiperiphery: Describes countries that supply sources of labor and raw materials to the **core** industrial countries and the world **economy** but are not themselves fully **industrialized societies**.

sensorimotor stage: According to Piaget, a stage of human cognitive development in which a child's awareness of his environment is dominated by perception and touch.

service society: A concept related to the one of **postindustrial society**, it refers to a social order distinguished by the growth of service **occupations** at the expense of industrial jobs that produce material goods.

sex: The biological and anatomical differences distinguishing females from males.

sex segregation: The concentration of men and women in different **occupations**.

sexual harassment: Unwanted sexual advances made by one individual toward another, in which the first person persists even though it is clear that the other party is resistant.

shaming: A way of punishing criminal and deviant behavior based on rituals of public disapproval rather than incarceration. The goal of shaming is to maintain the ties of the offender to the community.

sick role: A term associated with the functionalist Talcott Parsons to describe the patterns of behavior that a sick person adopts in order to minimize the disruptive impact of his illness on others.

signifier: Any vehicle of meaning and communication.

slavery: A form of **social stratification** in which some people are literally owned by others as their property.

social aggregate: A simple collection of people who happen to be together in a particular place but do not significantly interact or identify with one another.

social aging: The **norms**, **values**, and **roles** that are culturally associated with a particular chronological age.

social category: People who share a common characteristic (such as **gender** or **occupation**) but do not necessarily interact or identify with one another.

social change: Alteration in basic structures of a **social group** or **society**. Social change is an ever-present phenomenon in social life, but it has become especially intense in the modern era. The origins of modern sociology can be traced to attempts to understand the dramatic changes shattering the traditional world and promoting new forms of social order.

social constraint: The conditioning influence on our behavior of the groups and **societies** of which we are members. Social constraint was regarded by Émile Durkheim as one of the distinctive properties of **social facts**.

social construction: An idea or practice that a group of people agree exists and that is maintained over time because people take its existence for granted.

social construction of gender: The learning of **gender roles** through **socialization** and interaction with others.

social facts: According to Émile Durkheim, the aspects of social life that shape our actions as individuals. Durkheim believed that social facts could be studied scientifically.

social gerontology: The study of **aging** and the elderly.

social group: A collection of people who regularly interact with one another on the basis of shared expectations concerning behavior and who share a sense of common **identity**.

social identity: The characteristics that are attributed to an individual by others.

social interaction: The process by which we act and react to those around us.

socialization: The social processes through which children develop an awareness of social **norms** and **values** and achieve a distinct sense of self. Although socialization processes are particularly significant in infancy and childhood, they continue to some degree throughout life. No individuals are immune from the reactions of others around them, which influence and modify their behavior at all phases of the **life course**.

socialization of nature: The process by which we control phenomena

regarded as "natural," such as reproduction.

social loneliness: The absence of a broader social network.

social mobility: Movement of individuals or groups between different **social positions**.

social movements: Large groups of people who seek to accomplish, or to block, a process of **social change**. Social movements normally exist in conflict with **organizations** whose objectives and outlook they oppose. However, movements that successfully challenge **power**, once they become institutionalized, can develop into organizations.

social position: The **social identity** an individual has in a given group or **society**. Social positions may be general in nature (those associated with **gender roles**) or more specific (occupational positions).

social reproduction: The process of perpetuating **values**, **norms**, and social practices through **socialization**, which leads to structural continuity over time.

social rights: Rights of social and welfare provision held by all **citizens** in a national community, including, for example, the right to claim unemployment benefits and sickness payments provided by the **state**.

social roles: Socially defined expectations of an individual in a given **status**, or **social position**.

Social Security: A government program that provides economic assistance to persons faced with unemployment, disability, or agedness.

social self: The basis of **self-consciousness** in human individuals, according to the theory of George H. Mead. The social self is the **identity** conferred upon an individual by the reactions of others. A person achieves self-consciousness by becoming aware of this **social identity**.

social stratification: The existence of **structured inequalities** between groups in **society** in terms of their access to material or symbolic rewards. While all societies involve some forms of stratification, only with the development of state-based systems did wide differences in **wealth** and **power** arise. The most distinctive

form of stratification in modern societies is **class** divisions.

social structure: The underlying regularities or patterns in how people behave in their relationships with one another.

society: A group of people who live in a particular territory, are subject to a common system of political **authority**, and are aware of having a distinct **identity** from other groups. Some societies, such as **hunting and gathering societies**, are small, numbering no more than a few dozen people. Others are large, numbering millions—modern Chinese society, for instance, has a **population** of more than a billion people.

sociobiology: An approach that attempts to explain the behavior of both animals and human beings in terms of biological principles.

socioemotional selectivity theory: The theory that adults maintain fewer relationships as they age, but that those relationships are of higher quality.

sociological imagination: The application of imaginative thought to the asking and answering of sociological questions. Someone using the sociological imagination "thinks himself away" from the familiar routines of daily life.

sociology of sexuality: A field that explores and debates the importance of biological versus social and cultural influences on human sexual behavior.

sociology of the body: A field that focuses on how our **health** and illness are affected by social and cultural influences.

sovereignty: The undisputed political rule of a **state** over a given territorial area.

standard deviation: A way of calculating the spread of a group of numbers.

standardized testing: A situation in which all students take the same test under the same conditions.

state: A political apparatus (government institutions plus civil service officials) ruling over a given territorial order, whose **authority** is backed by **law** and the ability to use force. Not all societies are characterized by the existence of a state. **Hunting and gathering societies** and smaller **agrarian societies** lack state institutions. The emergence of the state marked a distinctive transition in human history, because the centralization of political **power** involved in state formation introduced new dynamics into processes of **social change**.

state overload: A **theory** that holds that modern **states** face major difficulties as a result of being overburdened with complex administrative decisions.

status: The social honor or prestige that a particular group is accorded by other members of a **society**. Status groups normally display distinct styles of life—patterns of behavior that the members of a group follow. Status privilege may be positive or negative. **Pariah groups** are regarded with disdain or treated as outcasts by the majority of the **population**.

stepfamily: A **family** in which at least one partner has children from a previous **marriage**, living either in the home or nearby.

stereotype threat: The idea that when African American students believe they are being judged not as individuals but as members of a negatively stereotyped **social group**, they will do worse on tests.

stereotyping: Thinking in terms of fixed and inflexible categories.

strike: A temporary stoppage of **work** by a group of employees in order to express a grievance or enforce a demand.

structural mobility: Mobility resulting from changes in the number and kinds of jobs available in a **society**.

structural strain: Tensions that produce conflicting interests within **societies**.

structured inequalities: Social inequalities that result from patterns in the **social structure**.

subcultures: **Values** and **norms** distinct from those of the majority, held by a group within a wider **society**.

suburbanization: The development of suburbia, areas of housing outside **inner cities**.

surplus value: The value of a worker's labor **power**, in **Marxist** theory, left over when an employer has repaid the cost of hiring the worker.

surveillance: The supervising of the activities of some individuals or groups by others in order to ensure compliant behavior.

survey: A method of sociological research in which questionnaires are administered to the **population** being studied.

sustainable development: The limiting of economic growth to proceed only insofar as natural resources are recycled rather than depleted; biodiversity is maintained; and clean air, water, and land are protected.

symbol: One item used to stand for or represent another—as in the case of a flag, which symbolizes a nation.

symbolic interactionism: A theoretical approach in sociology developed by George Herbert Mead that emphasizes the role of **symbols** and **language** as core elements of all human interaction.

Taylorism: A set of ideas, also referred to as "scientific management," developed by Frederick Winslow Taylor, involving simple, coordinated operations in industry.

technology: The application of knowledge of the material world to production; the creation of material instruments (such as machines) used in human interaction with nature.

theism: A belief in one or more supernatural deities.

time-space: When and where events occur.

timetables: The means by which **organizations** regularize activities across time and space.

total institutions: Groups who exercise control over their members by making them subsume their individual **identities** in that of the group, compelling them to adhere to strict ethical codes or rules, and sometimes forcing them to withdraw from activity in the outside world.

tracking: Dividing students into groups that receive different instruction on the basis of assumed similarities in ability or attainment.

transnational (or multinational) corporations: Business **corporations** located in two or more countries.

triad: A group consisting of three persons.

underclass: A **class** of individuals situated at the bottom of the class system, normally composed of people from **ethnic minority** backgrounds.

unfocused interaction: Interaction occurring among people present in a particular setting but not engaged in direct face-to-face communication.

union density: A statistic that represents the number of union members as a percentage of the number of people who could potentially be union members.

upper class: A social **class** broadly composed of the more affluent members of **society**, especially those who have inherited **wealth**, own businesses, or hold large numbers of stocks (shares).

urban ecology: An approach to the study of urban life based on an analogy with the adjustment of plants and organisms to the physical environment. According to ecological theorists, the various neighborhoods and zones within cities are formed as a result of natural processes of adjustment on the part of **populations** as they compete for resources.

urbanism: A term used by Louis Wirth to denote distinctive characteristics of urban social life, such as its impersonality.

urbanization: The development of towns and cities.

urban renewal: The process of renovating deteriorating neighborhoods by encouraging the renewal of old buildings and the construction of new ones.

values: Ideas held by individuals or groups about what is desirable, proper, good, and bad. What individuals value is strongly influenced by the specific **culture** in which they happen to live.

wealth: Money and material possessions held by an individual or group.

welfare capitalism: The practice by which large **corporations** protect their employees from the vicissitudes of the market.

welfare state: A political system that provides a wide range of welfare benefits for its **citizens**.

white-collar crime: Criminal activities carried out by those in white-collar, or professional, jobs.

work: The activity by which people produce from the natural world and so ensure their survival. Work should not be thought of exclusively as paid employment. In traditional **cultures**, there was only a rudimentary monetary system, and few people worked for money. In modern **societies**, there remain types of work that do not involve direct payment (e.g., housework).

working class: A social **class** broadly composed of people working in blue-collar, or manual, **occupations**.

working poor: People who work but whose earnings are not enough to lift them above the **poverty line**.

world-accommodating movements: Religious movements that emphasize the importance of inner religious life and spiritual purity over worldly concerns.

world-affirming movements: Religious movements that seek to enhance followers' ability to succeed in the outside world by helping them to unlock their human potential.

world-rejecting movements: Religious movements that are exclusive in nature, highly critical of the outside world, and demanding of their members.

world-systems theory: Pioneered by Immanuel Wallerstein, this **theory** emphasizes the interconnections among countries based on the expansion of a capitalist world **economy.** This economy is made up of **core**, **semiperiphery**, and **periphery countries**.

young old: Sociological term for persons aged 65 to 74.

Bibliography

ABC News/Washington Post Poll. (2006). "Which Punishment Do You Prefer for People Convicted of Murder: The Death Penalty or Life in Prison with No Chance of Parole?" Accessed fall 2007. www.pollingreport.com/crime.htm.

Abdul-Rauf, M. (1975). *Islam: Creed and Worship.* Washington, DC: Islamic Center.

Abeles, R. P., and M. W. Riley. (1987). "Longevity, Social Structure, and Cognitive Aging." In C. Schooler and K. Warner Schaie, eds., *Cognitive Functioning and Social Structure over the Life Course.* Norwood, NJ: Ablex.

Achen, Alexandra C., and Frank P. Stafford. (2005). "Data Quality of Housework Hours in the Panel Study of Income Dynamics: Who Really Does the Dishes." *Panel Study of Income Dynamics Report.* Ann Arbor, MI: Institute for Social Research. Accessed December 10, 2010. http://psidonline.isr.umich.edu/publications/papers/achenproxyreports04.pdf.

Acs, Gregory. (2011). "Downward Mobility from the Middle Class: Waking Up from the American Dream." Washington, DC: The Pew Charitable Trusts, Economic Mobility Project (September 2011). Accessed June 18, 2012. www.pewstates.org/uploadedFiles/PCS_Assets/2011/MiddleClassReport.pdf.

Agree, E. M., and V. A. Freedman. (2000). "Incorporating Assistive Devices into Community-Based Long-Term Care: An Analysis of the Potential for Substitution and Supplementation." *Journal of Health and Aging* 12: 426–50.

AIDS Orphans Educational Trust. (2003). "AIDS Orphans Educational Trust–Uganda." Accessed December 28, 2004. www.orphanseducation.org (site discontinued).

Al Ahmad, J. (1997; orig. 1962). *Gharbzadegi: Weststruckedness.* Costa Mesa, CA: Mazda Publications.

Albrow, M. (1997). *The Global Age: State and Society Beyond Modernity.* Stanford, CA: Stanford University Press.

Aldrich, H. E., and P. V. Marsden. (1988). "Environments and Organizations." In N. J. Smelser, ed., *Handbook of Sociology.* Newbury Park, CA: Sage.

Alexander, M. (2011). "The New Jim Crow: How Mass Incarceration Turns People of Color into Permanent Second-Class Citizens." *The American Prospect* 22(1).

Ali, T. (2003). "Re-Colonizing Iraq." *New Left Review* 21 (May–June): 5–19.

Allen, B. (1996). *Rape Warfare: The Hidden Genocide in Bosnia-Herzegovina and Croatia.* Minneapolis: University of Minnesota Press.

Allen, M. P. (1981). "Managerial Power and Tenure in the Large Corporation." *Social Forces* 60: 482–94.

Alliance for Excellent Education. (2010). *High School Dropouts in America.* Washington, DC: Alliance for Excellent Education. Accessed October 8, 2012. www.all4ed/files/HighSchoolDropouts.pdf.

Alliance for Excellent Education. (2011). *The High Cost of High School Dropouts: What the Nation Pays for Inadequate High Schools.* Washington, DC: Alliance for Excellent Education. Accessed October 9, 2012. www.all4ed.org/files/HighCost.pdf.

Alvarez, R., L. Robin, M. Tuan, M., and S.-I. Huang. (1996). "Women in the Professions: Assessing Progress." In P. J. Dubeck and K. Borman, eds., *Women and Work: A Handbook.* New York: Garland.

Alwin, Duane F. (2008). "History, Cohort, and Patterns of Cognitive Aging." In Hofer S. M. and D. F. Alwin, eds., *Handbook of Cognitive Aging: Interdisciplinary Perspectives* (pp. 9–38). Thousand Oaks, CA: Sage.

Alzheimer's Association. (2012). "2012 Alzheimer's Disease Facts and Figures." Washington, DC. Accessed August 7, 2012. www.alz.org/downloads/facts_figures_2012.pdf.

Amato, P. (2000). "The Consequences of Divorce for Adults and Children." *Journal of Marriage and the Family* 62: 1269–87.

Amato, P., L. S. Loomis, and A. Booth. (1995). "Parental Divorce, Marital Conflict, and Offspring Well-Being during Early Adulthood." *Social Forces* 73: 895–915.

Amenta, E. (1998). *Bold Relief: Institutional Politics and the Origins of Modern American Social Policy.* Princeton, NJ: Princeton University Press.

American Academy of Pediatrics. (2004). "Sexual Orientation and Adolescents." *Pediatrics* 113 (6): 1827–32.

American Association of University Women (AAUW). (1992). *How Schools Shortchange Girls.* Washington, DC: American Association of University Women Educational Foundation.

American Community Survey. (2012). "The Foreign-Born Population in the United States: 2010." Accessed summer 2012. www.census.gov/prod/2012pubs/acs-19.pdf.

American Council on Education (ACE). (2001). "The American Freshman: National Norms for Fall 2000." Los Angeles, CA: UCLA Higher Education Research Institute and ACE. Results also published in "This Year's Freshmen at 4-Year Colleges: Their Opinions, Activities, and Goals." *Chronicle of Higher Education* (January 26): A49.

American Council on Education (ACE). (2008). "Mapping New Directions: Higher Education for Older Adults." Washington, DC: American Council on Education. Accessed August 8, 2012. www.acenet.edu/Content/NavigationMenu/ProgramsServices/CLLL/Reinvesting/MapDirections.pdf.

American Express OPEN. (2013). *The 2013 State of Women-Owned Businesses Report.* Commissioned Report. Accessed spring 2013. https://c401345.ssl.cf1.rackcdn.com/wp-content/uploads/2013/03/13ADV-WBI-E-StateOfWomenReport_FINAL.pdf.

American Federation of Labor and Congress of Industrial Organizations (AFL-CIO). (2011). "About Us." Accessed spring 2011. http://www.aflcio.org/About.

American Psychiatric Association. (2000). *Diagnostic and Statistical Manual of Mental Disorders*, 4th ed., text rev. Washington, DC: American Psychiatric Association.

American Psychological Association. (2005). *Lesbian and Gay Parenting*. Accessed spring 2013. www.apa.org/pi/lgbt/resources /parenting-full.pdf.

Amin, S. (1974). *Accumulation on a World Scale*. New York: Monthly Review Press.

Ammons, S. K., and W. T. Markham. (2004). "Working at Home: Experiences of Skilled White-Collar Workers." *Sociological Spectrum* 24 (2): 191–238.

Amsden, A. H. (1989). *Asia's Next Giant: South Korea and Late Industrialization*. New York: Oxford University Press.

Amsden, A. H., J. Kochanowicz, and L. Taylor. (1994). *The Market Meets Its Match: Restructuring the Economies of Eastern Europe*. Cambridge, MA: Harvard University Press.

Anderson, B. (1991). *Imagined Communities: Reflections on the Origin and Spread of Nationalism*, rev. ed. New York: Routledge.

Anderson, E. (1990). *Streetwise: Race, Class, and Change in an Urban Community*. Chicago: University of Chicago Press.

Anderson, P. B., and C. Struckman-Johnson, eds. (1998). *Sexually Aggressive Women: Current Perspectives and Controversies*. New York: Guilford Press.

Angell, M., and J. P. Kassirer. (1998). "Alternative Medicine: The Risks of Untested and Unregulated Remedies." *New England Journal of Medicine* 339: 839.

Annie E. Casey Foundation. (2011). *Kids Count Data Center*. Accessed August 31, 2011. http://datacenter .kidscount.org/.

Anyon, J. (2006). "Social Class, School Knowledge, and the Hidden Curriculum Revisited." In L. Weiss and G. Dimitriadis, eds., *The New Sociology of Knowledge*. New York: Routledge.

Anzaldua, G. (1990). *Making Face, Making Soul: Haciendo Caras: Creative and Critical Perspectives by Feminists of Color*. San Francisco: Aunt Lute Foundation.

Appadurai, A. (1986). "Introduction: Commodities and the Politics of Value." In A. Appadurai ed., *The Social Life of Things*. Cambridge, UK: Cambridge University Press.

Appelbaum, E., R. Murnane, and A. Bernhardt, eds. (2003). *Low-Wage America: How Employers Are Reshaping Opportunity in the Workplace*. New York: Russell Sage Foundation.

Appelbaum, R. (1988). *Karl Marx*. Thousand Oaks, CA: Sage.

Appelbaum, R. (1990). "Counting the Homeless." In J. A. Momeni (Ed.), *Homeless in the United States* (Vol. 2). New York: Praeger.

Appelbaum, R. P., and B. Christerson. (1997). "Cheap Labor Strategies and Export-Oriented Industrialization: Some Lessons from the East Asia/Los Angeles Apparel Connection." *International Journal of Urban and Regional Research* 21(2): 202–17.

Appelbaum, R. P., and J. Henderson, eds. (1992). *States and Development in the Asian Pacific Rim*. Newbury Park, CA: Sage.

Appelbaum, R., and N. Lichtenstein. (2006). "A New World of Retail Supremacy: Supply Chains and Workers' Chains in the Age of Wal-Mart." *International Labor and Working-Class History* 70: 106–25.

Arias, E. (2007). "United States Life Tables, 2003." *National Vital Statistics Reports* 54. Accessed January 2008. www.cdc.gov /nchs/data/nvsr/nvsr54 /nvsr54_14.pdf.

Arias, E. (2010). "United States Life Tables by Hispanic Origin." *National Vital Statistics* 2 (152).

Arias, E. (2012). "United States Life Tables, 2008. *National Vital Statistics* 61 (3). Accessed summer 2013. www.cdc.gov/nchs/data /nvsr/nvsr61/nvsr61_03.pdf.

Ariès, P. (1965). *Centuries of Childhood*. New York: Random House.

Arjomand, S. A. (1988). *The Turban for the Crown: The Islamic Revolution in Iran*. New York: Oxford University Press.

Aronowitz, S., and H. A. Giroux. (1985). *Education under Siege: The Conservative, Liberal and Radical Debate over Schooling*. London: Routledge.

Arrighi, G. (1994). *The Long Twentieth Century: Money, Power, and the Origin of Our Times*. New York: Verso.

Asch, S. (1952). *Social Psychology*. Englewood Cliffs, NJ: Prentice-Hall.

Aslan, R. (2006). *No God but God: The Origins, Evolution, and Future of Islam*. New York: Random House.

Aslan, R. (2009). *How to Win a Cosmic War: God, Globalization, and the End of the War on Terror*. New York: Random House.

Atchley, R. (1989). "A Continuity Theory of Normal Aging." *Gerontologist* 29: 183–90.

Atchley, R. C. (2000). *Social Forces and Aging: An Introduction to Social Gerontology*, 9th ed. Belmont, CA: Wadsworth.

Attaran, M. (2004). "Exploring the Relationship between Information Technology and Business Process Reengineering." *Information and Management* 41(5): 585–96.

August, K. J., and D. H. Sorkin. (2010). "Racial and Ethnic Disparities in Indicators of Physical Health Status: Do They Still Exist Throughout Late Life?" *Journal of the American Geriatrics Society* 58: 2009–2015.

Avert.org. (2010). *Global HIV and AIDS Estimates*. End of 2009. Accessed August 23, 2011. www.avert.org /worldstats.htm.

Avery, R. B., G. B. Canner, and R. E. Cook. (2005). "New Information Reported under HMDA and Its Application in Fair Lending Enforcement." *Federal Reserve Bulletin* 91 (2): 344-394. Accessed spring 2006. www.federalreserve .gov/pubs/bulletin/2005/3–05hmda .pdf (site discontinued).

Baden, Ben. (2011). "Temporary Workers Could Become the New Norm." *U.S. News and World Report*, November 17. Accessed summer 2012. money.usnews .com/money/careers/articles /2011/11/17/larger-temporary -workforce-could-be-new-normal.

Bailey, J. M., and R. C. Pillard. (1991). "A Genetic Study of Male Sexual Orientation." *Archives of General Psychiatry* 48: 1089–96.

Bair, Jennifer, ed. (2009). *Frontiers of Commodity Chain Research.* Stanford, CA: Stanford University Press.

Bales, R. F. (1953). "The Egalitarian Problem in Small Groups." In T. Parsons, ed., *Working Papers in the Theory of Action.* Glencoe, IL: Free Press.

Bales, Robert Freed. (1970). *Personality and Interpersonal Behavior.* New York: Holt, Rinehart, and Winston.

Balfanz, Robert, John M. Bridgeland, Mary Bruce, and Joanna Horning Fox. (2012). *Building a Grad Nation: Progress and Challenge in Ending the High School Dropout Epidemic: Annual Update 2012.* Baltimore, MD: Civic Enterprises. Accessed October 9, 2012. www.americaspromise.org /our-work/gradnation/-/media /Files/Our%20Work/Grad %20Nation/Building%20a %20Grad%20Nation/ BuildingAGradNation2012.ashx.

Balmer, R. (1989). *Mine Eyes Have Seen the Glory: A Journey into the Evangelical Subculture in America.* New York: Oxford University Press.

Balswick, J. O. (1983). "Male Inexpressiveness." In K. Soloman and N. B. Levy, eds., *Men in Transition: Theory and Therapy.* New York: Plenum Press.

Baltic 21 Secretariat. (2000). "Passenger Car Density." Accessed spring 2006. www.baltic21.org/reports /indicators/tr08.htm (site discontinued).

Barker, M. (1981). *The New Racism: Conservatives and the Ideology of the Tribe.* Frederick, MD: University Press of America.

Barnes, H., and J. Parry. (2004). "Renegotiating Identity and Relationships: Men's and Women's Adjustment to Retirement." *Ageing and Society* 24: 213–33.

Barnes, P. M., B. Bloom, and R. Nahin. (2008). "The Use of Complementary and Alternative Medicine in the United States." Figure 1. CAM Use by U.S. Adults and Children, 2007. *CDC National Health Statistics Report No. 12,* December. Accessed September 24, 2012. http://nccam.nih.gov/sites/nccam .nih.gov/files/camuse.pdf.

Barnes, Taylor. (2009). "America's 'Shadow Economy' Is Bigger Than You Think—and Growing." *Christian Science Monitor,* November 12. Accessed spring 2013. www.csmonitor.com/Business /2009/1112/americas-shadow -economy-is-bigger-than-you -think-and-growing.

Barnet, R. J., and J. Cavanagh. (1994). *Global Dreams: Imperial Corporations and the New World Order.* New York: Simon and Schuster.

Bartels, L. M. (2006). "What's the Matter with *What's the Matter with Kansas?*" *Quarterly Journal of Political Science* 1 (March): 201–26.

Bartels, L. M. (2008). *Unequal Democracy: The Political Economy of the New Gilded Age.* Princeton, NJ: Princeton University Press.

Barzilai-Nahon, Karine, and Gad Barzilai. (2005) . "Cultured Technology: Internet and Religious Fundamentalism." *The Information Society* 21(1): 25-40.

Basham, A. L. (1989). *The Origins and Development of Classical Hinduism.* Boston: Beacon Press.

Bates, T. (2010). "Vatican Angers Many with 'Grave Crimes' List." *AOLNews,* July 16. Accessed spring 2013. www.aolnews.com/2010/07 /16/vatican-puts-ordaining -women-priests-on-par-with-child -sex-abuse/.

Baxter, J. (1997). "Gender Inequality and Participation in Housework: A Cross-National Perspective." *Journal of Comparative Family Issues* 28: 220–28.

BBC News. (2001). *Bin Laden's Warning: Full Text.* Accessed January 10, 2005. http://news.bbc.co .uk/1/hi/world/south_asia /1585636.stm.

Bean, F. D., R. Chanove, R. Cushing, R. de la Garza, C. Haynes, G. Freeman, and D. Spener. (1994). *Illegal Mexican Migration and the United States/Mexico Border: Operation Hold-the-Line and El Paso/ Juarez.* Washington, DC: U.S. Commission on Immigration Reform.

Bearman, P. (2002). "Opposite-Sex Twins and Adolescent Same-Sex Attraction." *American Journal of Sociology* 107: 1179–1205.

Beasley, C. (1999). *What Is Feminism?* Thousand Oaks, CA: Sage.

Beck, U. (1992). *Risk Society.* London: Sage.

Beck, U. (1995). *Ecological Politics in an Age of Risk.* Cambridge, UK: Polity Press.

Becker, G. (1964). *Human Capital.* New York: National Bureau of Economic Research.

Becker, G. (1991). *A Treatise on the Family.* Cambridge, MA: Harvard University Press.

Becker, H. S. (1963). *Outsiders: Studies in the Sociology of Deviance.* New York: Macmillan.

Becker, Kristina Floodman. (2004). *The Informal Economy.* Swedish International Development Cooperation Agency (SIDA). March. Accessed spring 2013. http://rru.worldbank.org /Documents/PapersLinks/Sida.pdf.

Becker, M. H., ed. (1974). "The Health Belief Model and Personal Health Behavior." *Health Education Monographs* 2: 324–473.

Bell, A., M. Weinberg, and S. Hammersmith. (1981). *Sexual Preference: Its Development in Men and Women.* Bloomington, IN: Indiana University Press.

Bell, D. (1976). *The Coming of Post-Industrial Society: A Venture in Social Forecasting.* New York: Basic Books.

Bell, N. (2010). *Graduate Enrollment and Degrees: 1999 to 2009.* Washington, DC: Council of Graduate Schools. Accessed September 20, 2010. www.cgsnet.org/portals/0 /pdf/R_ED2009.pdf (site discontinued).

Bellah, R. N. (1968). "Civil Religion in America." In W. G. McLoughlin and R. N. Bellah, eds., *Religion in America.* Boston: Houghton Mifflin.

Bellah, R. N. (1975). *The Broken Covenant.* New York: Seabury Press.

Bellah, R. N., et al. (1985). *Habits of the Heart: Individualism and Commitment in American Life.* New York: Harper and Row.

Bellman, B. (1984). *The Language of Secrecy: Symbols and Metaphors in Poro Ritual.* New Brunswick, NJ: Rutgers University Press.

Bello, Walden. (2000). "From Melbourne to Prague: The Struggle for a Deglobalized World." International Network on Disarmament and Globalization. Vancouver, Canada. Accessed spring 2013. http://ratical.org/co-globalize /WB0900.html.

Bello, Walden. (2005). *Deglobalization: Ideas for a New World Economy.* London: Zed Book.

Belsky, Jay, Deborah Lowe Vandell, Margaret Burchinal, K. Alison Clarke-Stewart, Kathleen McCartney, Margaret Tresch Owen and the NICHD Early Child Care Research Network. (2007). "Are There Long-Term Effects of Early Child Care?" *Child Development* 78 (2): 681-701.

Bengston, V. L., N. M. Putney, and M. Johnson. (2005). "The Problem of Theory in Gerontology Today." In M. Johnson, V. Bengtson, P. G. Coleman, and T. B. L. Kirkwood, eds., *The Cambridge Handbook of Age and Ageing*. Cambridge, UK: Cambridge University Press.

Benjamin, M. (2012). *Drone Warfare: Killing by Remote Control*. New York: OR Books.

Bennett, J. W. (1976). *The Ecological Transition: Cultural Anthropology and Human Adaptation*. New York: Pergamon Press.

Berger, P. L. (1967). *The Sacred Canopy: Elements of a Sociological Theory of Religion*. Garden City, NY: Anchor Books.

Berger, P. L. (1986). *The Capitalist Revolution: Fifty Propositions about Prosperity, Equality, and Liberty*. New York: Basic Books.

Berger, P. L. (1988). "An East Asian Development Model?" In P. L. Berger and H. M. Hsiao, eds., *In Search of an East Asian Development Model*. New Brunswick, NJ: Transaction Books.

Berlan E. D., H. L. Corliss, A. E. Field, E. Goodman, and S. Bryn Austin. (2010). "Sexual Orientation and Bullying among Adolescents in the Growing Up Today Study." *Journal of Adolescent Health* 46 (4): 366–71.

Berle, A., and G. C. Means. (1982; orig. 1932). *The Modern Corporation and Private Property*. Buffalo, NY: Heim.

Berryman, P. (1987). *Liberation Theology: Essential Facts about the Revolutionary Movement in Central America and Beyond*. Philadelphia: Temple University Press.

Bertakis, K., et al. (2000). "Gender Differences in the Utilization of Health Care Services." *Journal of Family Practice* 29 (2): 147–52.

Beyer, P. (1994). *Religion and Globalization*. Thousand Oaks, CA: Sage.

Beyerstein, B. L. (1999). "Psychology and 'Alternative Medicine': Social and Judgmental Biases That Make Inert Treatments Seem To Work." *Scientific Review of Alternative Medicine* 3 (2).

Biddle, B. J. (1986). "Recent Developments in Role Theory." *Annual Review of Sociology* 12:67–92.

Birditt, K. S., L. M. H. Jackey, and T. C. Antonucci. (2009). "Longitudinal Patterns of Negative Relationship Quality Across Adulthood." *Journals of Gerontology* 64B: 55–64.

Birnbaum, E., and Yu Xiubo. (2007). "Special Report: NGO Strategies to Promote River Protection and Restoration." Princeton, NJ: Woodrow Wilson International Center for Scholars. Accessed May 18, 2011. www.wilsoncenter.org/topics /pubs/CEF_SpecialReport.2.pdf.

Birnbaum, J. H. (2005). "AARP Leads with Wallet in Fight over Social Security." *Washington Post*, March 30. Accessed December 6, 2005. www.washingtonpost .com/wp-dyn/articles/A11076 -2005Mar29.html.

Birren, J. E., and V. L. Bengston, eds. (1988). *Emerging Theories of Aging*. New York: Springer.

Bjorkqvist, K. (1994). "Sex Differences in Physical, Verbal, and Indirect Aggression: A Review of Recent Research." *Sex Roles* 30 (3/4): 177–88.

Bjorkqvist, K., K. M. Lagerspetz, and K. Osterman. (2006). "Sex Differences in Covert Aggression." *Aggressive Behavior* 202 (December 6): 27–33.

Blanchard, R., and A. F. Bogaert. (1996). "Homosexuality in Men and Number of Older Brothers." *American Journal of Psychiatry* 153: 27–31.

Blau, P. (1963). *Bureaucracy in Modern Society*. New York: Random House.

Blau, P. (1977). *Inequality and Heterogeneity: A Primitive Theory of Social Structure*. New York: Free Press.

Blau, P., and O. D. Duncan. (1967). *The American Occupational Structure*. New York: Wiley.

Blau, Francine D., and Lawrence M. Kahn. (2005). "Changes in the Labor Supply Behavior of Married Women: 1980-2000." *NBER Working Paper 11230*. National Bureau of Economic Research. Accessed spring 2013. www.nber .org/papers/w11230.pdf.

Blauner, R. (1964). *Alienation and Freedom*. Chicago: University of Chicago Press.

Blickman, Tom. (2003). "The Economic Impact of the Illicit Drug Industry." The Transnational Institute. Accessed spring 2013. www.tni.org/archives/acts /impact.pdf.

Block, F. (1990). *Postindustrial Possibilities: A Critique of Economic Discourse*. Berkeley, CA: University of California Press.

Blum, L. M. (1991). *Between Feminism and Labor: The Significance of the Comparable Worth Movement*. Berkeley, CA: University of California Press.

Bochenek, M. A., and W. Brown. (2001). *Hatred in the Hallways: Violence and Discrimination against Lesbian, Gay, Bisexual, and Transgender Students in U.S. Schools*. New York: Human Rights Watch, May 30. Accessed December 28, 2004. www.hrw.org/reports/2001 /uslgbt/toc.htm.

Boden, D., and H. Molotch. (1994). "The Compulsion of Proximity." In D. Boden and R. Friedland, eds., *Nowhere: Space, Time, and Modernity*. Berkeley: University of California Press.

Bohan, S. (1999). "Bohemian Grove and Global Elite." *Sacramento Bee*, August 2. Accessed December 28, 2004. www.mt.net/~watcher /bohemiangrove.html.

Bonacich, E., and R. P. Appelbaum. (2000). *Behind the Label: Inequality in the Los Angeles Garment Industry*. Berkeley, CA: University of California Press.

Bonnell, V. E., and L. Hunt, eds. (1999). *Beyond the Cultural Turn*. Berkeley, CA: University of California Press.

Bonnett, A. (2000). *Anti-Racism*. New York: Routledge.

Bonnie, R., and R. Wallace, eds. (2003). "Elder Mistreatment: Abuse, Neglect, and Exploitation in an Aging America." *Panel to Review Risk and Prevalence of Elder Abuse and Neglect*. Washington, DC: National Academies Press.

Booth, A. (1977). "Food Riots in the North-West of England, 1770–1801." *Past and Present* 77: 90.

Bositis, D. (2001). "Black Elected Officials: A Statistical Summary: 2001." *Joint Center for Political and Economic Studies*. Accessed January 2008. www.jointcenter .org/publications1/publication -PDFs/BEO-pdfs/2001-BEO.pdf (site discontinued).

Boswell, J. (1995). *The Marriage of Likeness: Same-Sex Unions in Pre-Modern Europe*. London: Fontana.

Bourdieu, P. (1984). *Distinction: A Social Critique of Judgment of Taste*. Cambridge, MA: Harvard University Press.

Bourdieu, P. (1988). *Language and Symbolic Power*. Cambridge, UK: Polity Press.

Bourdieu, P. (1990). *The Logic of Practice*. Palo Alto, CA: Stanford University Press.

Boushey, Heather, and Adam S. Hersh. (2012). *The American Middle Class, Income Inequality, and the Strength of Our Economy: New Evidence in Economics*. Washington, DC: Center for American Progress. Accessed June 18, 2012. www.americanprogress.org /issues/2012/05/pdf/middleclass _growth.pdf.

Bowen, William G., and James Shulman. (2001a). *The Game of Life: College Sports and Educational Values*. Princeton, NJ: Princeton University.

Bowen, William G., and James Shulman. (2001b). "Playing Their Way In." *New York Times*, February 22.

Bowen, K. (1996). *Evangelism and Apostasy: The Evolution and Impact of Evangelicals in Modern Mexico*. Montreal, Canada: McGill-Queens University Press.

Bowlby, J. (1953). *Child Care and the Growth of Love*. Baltimore, MD: Penguin.

Bowles, S., and H. Gintis. (1976). *Schooling in Capitalist America*. New York: Basic Books.

Boyer, R., and D. Drache, eds. (1996). *States against Markets: The Limits of Globalization*. New York: Routledge.

Bradsher, K. (2000). "Efficiency on Wheels: U.S. Auto Industry Is Catching Up with the Japanese." *New York Times*, June 16.

Braithwaite, J. (1996). "Crime, Shame, and Reintegration." In P. Cordella and L. Siegel, eds., *Readings in Contemporary Criminological Theory*. Boston: Northeastern University Press.

Bramlett, M. D., and W. D. Mosher. (2002). "Cohabitation, Marriage, Divorce, and Remarriage in the United States." National Center for Health Statistics (NCHS). *Vital Health Statistics* 23: 22.

Branch, T. (1989). *Parting the Waters: America in the King Years 1954–1963*. New York: Simon and Schuster.

Branch, T. (1999). *Pillar of Fire: America in the King Years 1963–1965*. New York: Simon and Schuster.

Branch, T. (2007). *At Canaan's Edge: America in the King Years 1965–1968*. New York: Simon and Schuster.

Brass, D. J. (1985). "Men's and Women's Networks: A Study of Interaction Patterns and Influence in an Organization." *Academy of Management Journal* 28: 327–43.

Braverman, H. (1974). *Labor and Monopoly Capital: The Degradation of Work in the Twentieth Century*. New York: Monthly Review Press.

Brazilian Institute of Geography and Statistics. (2010). *Subnormal Agglomerates*. Accessed summer 2012. www.ibge.gov.br/english /presidencia/noticias/noticia _impressao.php?id_noticia=2057=1.

Brekhus, W. H. (2003). *Peacocks, Chameleons, Centaurs: Gay Suburbia and the Grammar of Social Identity*. Chicago: University of Chicago Press.

Bremner, Jason, Ashley Frost, Carl Haub, Mark Mather, Karen Ringheim, and Eric Zuehlke. (2010). "World Population Highlights: Key Findings from PRB's World Population Data Sheet." *Population Bulletin* 65 (2). Accessed August 10, 2012. www.prb.org/pdf10/65 .2highlights.pdf.

Brennan, T. (1988). "Controversial Discussions and Feminist Debate." In N. Segal and E. Timms, eds., *The Origins and Evolution of Psychoanalysis*. New Haven, CT: Yale University Press.

Bresnahan, T., E. Brynjolfsson, and L. Hitt. (2002). "Information Technology, Workplace Organization, and the Demand for Skilled Labor: Firm-Level Evidence." *Quarterly Journal of Economics* 117 (1): 339–76.

Brewer, R. M. (1993). "Theorizing Race, Class and Gender: The New Scholarship of Black Feminist Intellectuals and Black Women's Labor." In S. M. James and A. P. A. Busia, eds., *Theorizing Black Feminisms: The Visionary Pragmatism of Black Women*. New York: Routledge.

Bricker, Jesse, Arthur B. Kennickell, Kevin B. Moore, and John Sabelhaus. (2012). "Changes in Family Finances from 2007 to 2010: Evidence from the Survey of Consumer Finances." *Federal Reserve Bulletin* 98 (2): 1–80. Accessed August 17, 2010. www.federal reserve.gov/pubs/bulletin/2012 /pdf/scf12.pdf.

Bricourt, J. C. (2004). "Using Telework to Enhance Return to Work Outcomes for Individuals with Spinal Cord Injuries." *Neurorehabilitation* 19 (2): 147–59.

Bridgeman, Benjamin, Andrew Dugan, Mikhael Lal, Matthew Osborne, and Shaunda Villones. (2012). "Accounting for Household Production in the National Accounts, 1965–2010." *Survey of Current Business* (May): 23–36. Accessed spring 2013. www.bea.gov/scb /pdf/2012/05%20May/0512 _household.pdf.

Brimelow, P. (1995). *Alien Nation: Common Sense about America's Immigration Disaster*. New York: Random House.

Britain, S. (1975). "The Economic Contradictions of Democracy." *British Journal of Political Science* 15: 129–59.

Brizendine, L. (2007). *The Female Brain*. New York: Broadway.

Brizendine, L. (2010). *The Male Brain*. New York: Broadway.

Bronson, Po, and Ashley Merryman. (2009). *NurtureShock: New Thinking about Children*. New York: Twelve.

Brookings Institution. (2010). "Change in Non-Hispanic White Population since 2000." *State of Metropolitan America*. Accessed spring 2011. www.brookings.edu/metro /StateOfMetroAmerica/Map .aspx#/?subject=9&ind=91&dist =0&data=Percent&year=2009&geo =suburb&zoom=0&x=0&y=0

Brookings Institution. (2011). "The Re-Emergence of Concentrated Poverty: Metropolitan Trends in the 2000s." *Metropolitan Opportunity Series*. Accessed summer 2012. www.brookings.edu/~/media /research/files/papers/2011/11 /03%20poverty%20kneebone%20 nadeau%20berube/1103_poverty _kneebone_nadeau_berube.

Brooks, Jennifer, and Kerry Weidrich. (2012). "Assets and Opportunity Scorecard: A Portrait of Financial Insecurity and Policies to Rebuild

Prosperity in America. Four-Year Degree by Income." *Corporation for Enterprise Development: 2010 American Community Survey.* Washington, DC: U.S. Department of Commerce, Census Bureau, 2010. Data calculated by the Bay Area Council Economic Institute. Accessed September 21, 2012. http://scorecard.assetsand opportunity.org/2012/measure /four-year-degree-by-income.

Brooks-Gunn, J., W. Han, and J. Waldfogel. (2010). "First-Year Maternal Employment and Child Development in the First Seven Years." *Monographs of the Society for Research in Child Development* 75 (2).

Brown, C., and K. Jasper, eds. (1993). *Consuming Passions: Feminist Approaches to Eating Disorders and Weight Preoccupations.* Toronto, Canada: Second Story Press.

Brown, D. E. (1991). *Human Universals.* New York: McGraw-Hill.

Brown, S. L. (2004). "Family Structure and Child Well-Being: The Significance of Parental Cohabitation." *Journal of Marriage and Family* 66: 351–67.

Brownell, K., and K. Horgen. (2004). *Food Fight: The Inside Story of the Food Industry, America's Obesity Crisis, and What We Can Do about It.* New York: McGraw-Hill.

Brownmiller, S. (1975). *Against Our Will: Men, Women, and Rape.* New York: Simon and Schuster.

Brubaker, R. (1992). *The Politics of Citizenship.* Cambridge, MA: Harvard University Press.

Bruinius, H. (2010). "Megacities of the World: A Glimpse of How We'll Live Tomorrow. *Christian Science Monitor,* May 5. Accessed spring 2011. www.csmonitor.com/World /Global-Issues/2010/0505 /Megacities-of-the-world-a -glimpse-of-how-we-ll-live -tomorrow.

Bryan, B., S. Dadzie, and S. Scafe. (1987). "Learning to Resist: Black Women and Education." In G. Weiner and M. Arnot, eds., *Gender under Scrutiny: New Inquiries in Education.* London: Hutchinson.

Bryson, V. (1999). *Feminist Debates: Issues of Theory and Political Practice.* Basingstoke: Macmillan.

Bull, P. (1983). *Body Movement and Interpersonal Communication.* New York: Wiley.

Bullock, C., III. (1984). "Equal Education Opportunity." In C. S. Bullock III and C. M. Lamb, eds., *Implementation of Civil Rights Policy.* Monterey, CA: Brooks and Cole.

Bumpass, L., J. A. Sweet, and A. Cherlin. (1991). "The Role of Cohabitation in Declining Rates of Marriage." *Journal of Marriage and the Family* 53: 913–27.

Burke, Jason. (2010). "More of World's Poor Live in India Than in All Sub-Saharan Africa, Says Study." *The Guardian,* July 13. Accessed summer 2012. www.guardian.co.uk /world/2010/jul/14/poverty-india -africa-oxford.

Burman, D. D. et al. (2007). "Sex Differences in Neural Processing of Language among Children." *Neuropsychologia* 46 (5): 1349–62.

Burns, John. (2012). "For Prince Harry, Vegas Exploits Didn't Stay There." *New York Times,* April 22. Accessed October 8, 2012. www .nytimes.com/2012/08/23/world /europe/for-prince-harry-what -happened-in-vegas-didnt-stay -there.html?_r=0.

Burr, C. (1993). "Homosexuality and Biology." *Atlantic Monthly* 271: 47–65.

Burris, B. H. (1993). *Technocracy at Work.* Albany, NY: State University of New York Press.

Burris, B. H. (1998). "Computerization of the Workplace." *Annual Review of Sociology* 24: 141–57.

Burtless, Gary, and Tracy Gordon. (2011). "The Federal Stimulus Programs and Their Effects." In David B. Grusky, Bruce Western, and Christopher Wimer, eds. *The Great Recession* (pp. 249–93). New York: Russell Sage Foundation.

Buss, D. M. (2003). *Evolution of Desire: Strategies of Human Mating.* New York: Basic Books.

Butler, J. (1989). *Gender Trouble: Feminism and the Subversion of Identity.* New York: Routledge.

Butler, R. (2010). *The Longevity Prescription: The 8 Proven Keys to a Long, Healthy Life.* New York: Avery.

Butterfield, F. (1998). "Decline of Violent Crimes Is Linked To Crack Market." *New York Times,* December 28, p. A18.

Byrne, Anne, and Deborah Carr. (2005). "Caught in the Cultural Lag: The Stigma of Singlehood." *Psychological Inquiry* 16: 84–90.

Cacioppo, J. T., L. C. Hawkley, L. E. Crawford, J. M. Ernst, M. H. Burleson, R. B. Kowalewski, W. B. Malarkey, E. Van Cauter, and G. G. Berntson. (2002). "Loneliness and Health: Potential Mechanisms." *Psychosomatic Medicine* 64: 407–17.

C-SPAN. (2012). "NCPSSM Releases Report on Women and Social Security." May 11. Accessed spring 2013. www.c-span.org/Events /NCPSSM-Releases-Report-on -Women-and-Social-Security /10737430628/.

Cahn, Naomi, and June Carbone. (2010). *Red Families v. Blue Families: Legal Polarization and the Creation of Culture.* New York: Oxford University Press.

Campos, P., A. Saguy, P. Ernsberger, E. Oliver, and G. Gaesser. (2006). "The Epidemiology of Overweight and Obesity: Public Health Crisis or Moral Panic?" *International Journal of Epidemiology* 35: 55–60.

Caplow, T. (1956). "A Theory of Coalitions in the Triad." *American Sociological Review* 21: 489–93.

Caplow, T. (1959). "Further Development of a Theory of Coalitions in Triads." *American Journal of Sociology* 64: 488–93.

Caplow, T. (1969). *Two Against One: Coalitions in Triads.* Englewood Cliffs, NJ: Prentice Hall.

Cardoso, F. H., and E. Faletto. (1979). *Dependency and Development in Latin America.* Berkeley: University of California Press.

Carr, D. (2004). "The Desire to Date and Remarry among Older Widows and Widowers." *Journal of Marriage and Family* 66: 1051–68.

Carr, Deborah. (2008). "Gender Politics." *Contexts* 7 (3): 58–59.

Carr, Deborah. (2010). "Golden Years? Poverty among Older Americans." *Contexts* 9 (1): 62–63.

Carr, D., and M. Friedman. (2005). "Is Obesity Stigmatizing? Body Weight, Perceived Discrimination and Psychological Well-Being in the United States." *Journal of Health and Social Behavior* 46: 244–59.

Carr, Deborah, and Sara M. Moorman. (2011). "Social Relations and Aging." In Richard A. Settersten Jr., and Jacqueline L. Angel, eds., *Handbook of Sociology of Aging* (pp. 145–60). New York: Springer.

Carr, Deborah, and Kristen Springer. (2010). "Advances in Families and Health Research in the 21st Century." *Journal of Marriage and Family* (Decade in Review Special Issue) 72: 744–62.

Carstensen, L. L., D. Isaacowitz, and S. T. Charles. (1999). "Taking Time Seriously: A Theory of Socio-emotional Selectivity." *American Psychologist* 54: 165–81.

Carter, P. (2005). *Keepin' It Real: School Success Beyond Black and White*. New York: Oxford University Press.

Castells, M. (1977). *The Urban Question: A Marxist Approach*. Cambridge, MA: MIT Press.

Castells, M. (1983). *The City and the Grass Roots: A Cross-Cultural Theory of Urban Social Movements*. Berkeley, CA: University of California Press.

Castells, M. (1996). *The Rise of the Network Society*. Malden, MA: Blackwell.

Castells, M. (1997). *The Power of Identity*. Malden, MA: Blackwell.

Castells, M. (2000). *The Rise of the Network Society* (Vol. 1). New York: Wiley-Blackwell.

Castells, M. (2001). *The Internet Galaxy*. Oxford, UK: Oxford University Press.

Castles, S., and M. J. Miller. (1993). *The Age of Migration: International Population Movements in the Modern World*. London: Macmillan.

Catalano, S. M. (2005). "Criminal Victimization, 2004." Accessed October 5, 2005. www.ojp.usdoj .gov/bjs/pub/pdf/cv04.pdf (site discontinued).

Catalyst. (2012). "Women CEOs of the *Fortune* 1000." Catalyst. org. Accessed November 2, 2012. www.catalyst.org/publication /271/women-ceos-of-the-fortune -1000.

Catholic Women's Ordination (CWO). (2010). CWO e-news. June 2010 (issue 28). Accessed spring 2010. www.catholic-womens-ordination .org.uk/cutenews/data/upimages /Enews%201007.pdf.

Census of India. (2011). "Religious Composition." Accessed summer 2012. http://censusindia.gov.in/Ad _Campaign/drop_in_articles/04 -Distribution_by_Religion.pdf.

Center for American Women and Politics (CAWP). (2013a). "Fact Sheet: Statewide Elective Executive Women 2013." Accessed spring 2013. www.cawp.rutgers.edu /fast_facts/levels_of_office /documents/stwide.pdf.

Center for American Women and Politics. (CAWP). (2013b). "Gaining Momentum? Taking Stock on International Women's Day." Accessed spring 2013. http:// cawp.rutgers.edu/footnotes /international-womens-day.

Center for Food Safety. (2010). "Genetically Engineered Food." Accessed April 2010. www.centerforfood safety.org/geneticall7.cfm (site discontinued).

Center for Immigration Studies. (2012). "Immigrants in the United States: A Profile of America's Foreign-Born Population." Accessed summer 2012. www.cis .org/articles/2012/immigrants-in -the-united-states-2012.pdf.

Center for Information and Research on Civic Learning and Engagement (Circle). (2012). "Youth Turnout: At Least 49%, 22-23 Million Under-30 Voted." Accessed spring 2013. www.civicyouth.org/youth -turnout-at-least-49-22-23 -million-under-30-voted/.

Center for Public Integrity. (2010). "Lobbying Database." Accessed June 20, 2010. www.opensecrets .org/lobby/index.php.

Center for Responsive Politics (CRP). (2003). "2000 Presidential Race: Total Raised and Spent. Center for Responsive Politics." Accessed December 29, 2004. www .opensecrets.org/2000elect/index /AllCands.htm.

Center for Responsive Politics (CRP). (2008). "Banking on Becoming President." Accessed November 2008. www.opensecrets .org/pres08/index.php.

Center for Responsive Politics (CRP). (2010). "Reelection Rates over the Years: Incumbent Advantage." Accessed spring 2011. www .opensecrets.org/bigpicture /incumbs.php?cycle=2008&Type =G&Party=S.

Center for Responsive Politics (CRP). (2011). "Incumbent Advantage." Accessed spring 2013. www.opensecrets.org /bigpicture/incumbs. php?cycle=2010.

Center for Responsive Politics (CRP). (2012a). "Barack Obama (D)." Accessed spring 2013. www .opensecrets.org/pres12 /candidate.php?cycle=2012&id= N00009638.

Center for Responsive Politics (CRP). (2012b). "527s: Advocacy Group Spending." Accessed spring 2013. www.opensecrets.org/527s/.

Center for Responsive Politics (CRP). (2012c). "Mitt Romney (R)." Accessed spring 2013. www .opensecrets.org/pres12/candidate .php?cycle=2012&id=N00000286.

Center for Responsive Politics (CRP). (2012d). "Reelection Rates over the Years." Accessed spring 2013. www.opensecrets.org/bigpicture /reelect.php?cycle=2010.

Center for Responsive Politics (CRP). (2013a). "American Federation of State, County and Municipal Employees." Accessed spring 2013. http://www.opensecrets.org/orgs /summary.php?id=D000000061.

Center for Responsive Politics (CRP). (2013b). "Top PACs." Accessed spring 2013. www.opensecrets .org/pacs/toppacs.php.

Center for Responsive Politics (CRP). (2013c). "2012 Overview: Stats at a Glance." Accessed spring 2013. www.opensecrets.org/overview /blio.php.

Center for Technology and Aging. (2010). "Fact Sheet: Highlights from the Assistive Technologies for Functional Improvement Technology Review." Public Health Institute. Accessed August 7, 2012. www.techandaging.org /ATfactsheet.pdf.

Centers for Disease Control and Prevention (CDC). (2007). "Adult Cigarette Smoking in the United States: Current Estimates." Accessed September 19, 2008. www.cdc.gov /tobacco/data_statistics/fact _sheets/adult_data/adult_cig _smoking.htm (site discontinued).

Centers for Disease Control and Prevention (CDC). (2010a). "Births: Preliminary Data for 2008." Accessed June 20, 2010. www.cdc .gov/nchs/nvss/birth_products .htm (site discontinued).

Centers for Disease Control and Prevention (CDC). (2010b). "Cigarette Smoking: United States, 1965– 2008." Accessed October 1, 2012. www.cdc.gov/mmwr/preview /mmwrhtml/su6001a24.htm# tab2.

Centers for Disease Control and Prevention (CDC). (2010c). "U.S. Obesity Trends 1986–2009." Accessed June 20, 2010. www.cdc.gov /obesity/data/trends.html#State.

Centers for Disease Control and Prevention (CDC). (2011a). "Estimates of New HIV Infections in the United States, 2006-2009." Accessed summer 2013. www.cdc .gov/nchhstp/newsroom/docs /Hiv-infections-2006-2009.pdf.

Centers for Disease Control and Prevention (CDC). (2011b). "Prevalence of Hypertension and Controlled Hypertension: United States, 2005–2008." Accessed October 1, 2012. www.cdc.gov /mmwr/preview/mmwrhtml /su6001a21.htm.

Centers for Disease Control and Prevention (CDC). (2012a). "Breast Cancer Screening Rates." Accessed summer 2013. www.cdc.gov/cancer/breast /statistics/screening.htm.

Centers for Disease Control and Prevention (CDC). (2012b). "Monitoring Selected National HIV Prevention and Care Objectives by Using HIV Surveillance Data—United States and 6 U.S. Dependent Areas—2010." *HIV Surveillance Supplemental Report 2012*: 17 (No. 3, part A). Accessed August 20, 2013. http:// www.cdc.gov/hiv/topics /surveillance/resources/reports/.

Centers for Disease Control and Prevention (CDC). (2012c). "Pertussis Outbreaks, July 2012." Accessed summer 2012. www .cdc.gov/pertussis/outbreaks .html#activity.

Centers for Disease Control and Prevention (CDC). (2012d). "Prevalence of Obesity in the United States, 2009–2010." *NCHS Data Brief* (No. 82, January). Accessed summer 2012. www.cdc.gov/nchs /data/databriefs/db82.pdf.

Centers for Disease Control and Prevention (CDC). (2012e). "Prevalence of Self-Reported Obesity among U.S. Adults." Accessed April 14, 2013. www.cdc.gov /obesity/data/adult.html.

Centers for Disease Control and Prevention (CDC). (2012f). "Provisional Number of Marriages and Marriage Rate: United States, 2000–2010." National Center for Health Statistics. Last updated January 10, 2012. Accessed September 31, 2012. www.cdc.gov/nchs/nvss /marriage_divorce_tables.htm.

Centers for Disease Control and Prevention (CDC). (2013). "Smoking and Tobacco Use: Fast Facts." Accessed spring 2013. www.cdc .gov/tobacco/data_statistics /fact_sheets/fast_facts/.

Central Intelligence Agency (CIA). (2000). "CIA World Factbook." Accessed December 29, 2004. www.cia.gov/cia/publications /factbook/geos/rs.html#Econ (site discontinued).

Central Intelligence Agency (CIA). (2012). "CIA World Factbook." Accessed summer 2013. www .cia.gov/library/publications/the -world-factbook/index.html.

Central Intelligence Agency. (2013). "Field Listing: Sex Ratio." CIA World Factbook. Accessed spring 2013. www.cia.gov/library /publications/the-world-factbook /fields/2018.html.

Cerny, P. (2005). "Political Globalization and the Competition State." In R. Stubbs and G. Underhill, eds., *The Political Economy of the Changing Global Order*. Oxford: Oxford University Press.

Chafetz, J. S. (1990). *Gender Equity: An Integrated Theory of Stability and Change*. Newbury Park, CA: Sage.

Chaliand, G., and J. Rageau. (1992). *Strategic Atlas: A Comparative Geopolitics of the World's Powers*. New York: Harper and Row.

Chambliss, W. J. (1988). *On the Take: From Petty Crooks to Presidents*. Bloomington, IN: Indiana University Press.

Chaney, D. (1994). *The Cultural Turn: Scene-Setting Essays in Contemporary Cultural History*. New York: Routledge.

Chang, I., and W. C. Kirby. (1997). *The Rape of Nanking: The Forgotten Holocaust of World War II*. New York: Basic Books.

Chapman, C., J. Laird, N. Ifill, and A. Kewal Ramani. (2011). "Trends in High School Dropout and Completion Rates in the United States: 1972–2009." *NCES 2012-006*. U.S. Department of Education. Washington, DC: National Center for Education Statistics. Accessed August 27, 2012. http://nces.ed.gov/pubs2012 /2012006.pdf.

Chapman, James C., and Li Linlin. (2011). "Mergers and Acquisitions in China: Current Trends and Challenges in the Middle Kingdom." Association for Corporate Growth. Accessed spring 2013. www.acg .org/UserFiles/file/global /Advisor%20Link/January %202011/Mergers%20and %20Acquisitions%20in% 20China-1-10-11_2.pdf.

Chase-Dunn, C. (1989). *Global Formation: Structures of the World Economy*. Cambridge, MA: Basil Blackwell.

Chaves, M. (1993). "Intraorganizational Power and Internal Secularization in Protestant Denominations." *American Journal of Sociology* 99: 1–48.

Chaves, M. (1994). "Secularization as Declining Religious Authority." *Social Forces* 72: 749–74.

Cherlin, A. (1990). "Recent Changes in American Fertility, Marriage, and Divorce." *Annals of the American Academy of Political and Social Science* 510: 145–54.

Cherlin, A. (1992). *Marriage, Divorce, Re-Marriage*, rev. ed. Cambridge, MA: Harvard University Press.

Cherlin, A. (1999). *Public and Private Families: An Introduction*, 2nd ed. New York: McGraw-Hill.

Cherlin, A., P. Chase-Lansdale, and C. McRae. (1998). "Effects of Parental Divorce on Mental Health Throughout the Life Course." *American Sociological Review* 63: 239–49.

Child Trends. (2012). "Percentage of Births to Unmarried Women." Accessed September 10, 2012. www.childtrendsdatabank .org/?q=node/196.

Child Welfare Information Gateway. (2012). "Child Maltreatment 2010: Summary of Key Findings." Accessed September 29, 2012. www.childwelfare.gov/pubs /factsheets/canstats.pdf.

Chodorow, N. (1978). *The Reproduction of Mothering*. Berkeley, CA: University of California Press.

Chodorow, N. (1988). *Psychoanalytic Theory and Feminism*. Cambridge, UK: Polity Press.

Choo, H. Y., and M. M. Ferree. (2010). "Practicing Intersectionality in Sociological Research: A Critical Analysis of Inclusions, Interactions, and Institutions in the Study of Inequalities." *Sociological Theory* 28: 129–49.

Christakis, Nicholas A., and James H. Fowler. (2007). "The Spread of Obesity in a Large Social Network over 32 Years." *New England Journal of Medicine* 357: 370–79.

Chronicle of Higher Education. (2010). "China Begins to Reform Its Controversial College-Entrance Exam." July 7. Accessed July 23, 2012. http://chronicle.com/article

/China-Begins-to-BMREForm
-Its/65804/.

Chua, A. (2003). *World on Fire: How Exporting Free Market Democracy Breeds Ethnic Hatred and Global Instability*. New York: Doubleday.

Cisco. (2009). "Cisco Study Finds Telecommuting Significantly Increases Employee Productivity, Work-Life Flexibility and Job Satisfaction." Press release, June 25. Accessed fall 2010. http://newsroom.cisco.com/dlls/2009/prod_062609.html.

Clawson, D., and M. A. Clawson. (1999). "What Has Happened to the U.S. Labor Movement? Union Decline and Renewal." *Annual Review of Sociology* 25: 95–119.

Cleary, P. D. (1987). "Gender Differences in Stress-Related Disorders." In R. C. Barnett, ed., *Gender and Stress*. New York: Free Press.

Cleveland, J. N. (1996). "Women in High-Status Nontraditional Occupations." In P. J. Dubeck and K. Borman, eds., *Women and Work: A Handbook*. New York: Garland.

Cloward, R. A., and L. E. Ohlin. (1960). *Delinquency and Opportunity*. New York: Free Press.

CNN. (2004). "Bush Calls for Ban on Same-Sex Marriages," February 25. Accessed December 29, 2004. http://edition.cnn.com/2004/ALLPOLITICS/02/24/elec04.prez.bush.marriage/index.html.

CNN. (2012a). "Global 500, 2012." *Fortune,* July 23. Accessed summer 2012. http://money.cnn.com/magazines/fortune/global500/2012/full_list/.

CNN. (2012b). "Top Companies: Most Profitable." *Fortune,* July 23. Accessed summer 2012. http://money.cnn.com/magazines/fortune/global500/2012/performers/companies/profits/.

Coate, J. (1994). "Cyberspace Innkeeping: Building Online Community." Accessed December 29, 2004. www.well.com:70/0/Community/innkeeping.

Cohen, A. (1955). *Delinquent Boys: The Culture of the Gang*. Glencoe, IL: Free Press.

Cohen, G. D. (2005). *The Mature Mind: The Positive Power of the Aging Brain*. New York: Basic Books.

Cohen, J., and G. Langer. (2005). "Poll: Will You Live Longer and Better?" ABC News, October 24. Accessed December 6, 2005. http://abcnews.go.com/Health/PollVault/story?id=1232993&CMP=OTC-RSSFeeds0312.

Cohen, L. E., Broschak, J. P., & Haveman, H. A. (1998). "And Then There Were More? The Effect of Organizational Sex Composition on the Hiring and Promotion of Managers." *American Sociological Review* 63: 5.

Cohen, R. (1997). *Global Diasporas: An Introduction*. London: UCL Press.

Coleman, J. S. (1987). "Families and Schools." *Educational Researcher* 16: 6.

Coleman, J. S., et al. (1966). *Equality of Educational Opportunity*. Washington, DC: U.S. Government Printing Office.

College Board. (2012). *2012 College-Bound Seniors: Total Group Profile Report*. New York: College Board. Accessed October 8, 2012. http://media.collegeboard.com/digitalServices/pdf/research/TotalGroup-2012.pdf.

Collins, D. (2004). "Strong Plea from a Strong Lady: Nancy Reagan Urges Expanded Stem Cell Research." CBS News, May 10. Accessed July 30, 2010. www.cbsnews.com/stories/2004/05/10/health/main616473.shtml.

Collins, P. H. (2008). *Black Feminist Thought: Knowledge, Consciousness, and the Politics of Empowerment*. New York: Routledge Classics.

Collins, R. (1979). *The Credential Society: An Historical Sociology of Education*. New York: Academic Press.

Combat 18. (1998). "Blood and Honour." Accessed January 10, 2005. www.combat18.org.

Common Cause. (2002). "Campaign Finance Reform: Election 2002—Incumbent Advantage." Accessed November 6, 2005. www.commoncause.org/news/default.cfm?ArtID538 (site discontinued).

Computer Security Institute. (2007). "CSI Survey 2007: The 12th Annual Computer Crime and Security Survey." Accessed May 2007. http://i.cmpnet.com/v2.gocsi.com/pdf/CSISurvey2007.pdf.

Computer World. (2002). "The Best Places to Work in IT: United States." Accessed January 20, 2005. www.computerworld.com/departments/surveys/bestplaces/bestplaces_us_region_sort/0,10984,,00.html (site discontinued).

Conley, D. (1999). *Being Black, Living in the Red: Race, Wealth, and Social Policy in America*. Berkeley and Los Angeles: University of California Press.

Connell, R. W. (1987). *Gender and Power: Society, the Person, and Sexual Politics*. Boston: Allen and Unwin.

Conti, J. (2008). "The Good Case: Decisions to Litigate at the World Trade Organization." *Law and Society Review* 42 (1): 145–82.

Cooley, C. H. (1964; orig. 1902). *Human Nature and the Social Order*. New York: Schocken Books.

Coontz, S. (1992). *The Way We Never Were: American Families and the Nostalgia Trap*. New York: Basic Books.

Coontz, S. (2005). *Marriage: A History*. New York: Viking.

Copen, C. E., K. Daniels, J. Vespa, and W. D. Mosher. (2012). "First Marriages in the United States: Data from the 2006–2010 National Survey of Family Growth." *National Health Statistics Report, No. 49*. National Center for Health Statistics, Hyattsville, MD.

Corbin, J., and A. Strauss. (1985). "Managing Chronic Illness at Home: Three Lines of Work." *Qualitative Sociology* 8: 224–47.

Cornman, J. C., V. A. Freedman, and E. M. Agree. (2005). "Measurement of Assistive Device Use: Implications for Estimates of Device Use and Disability in Late Life." *Gerontologist* 45: 347–58.

Correll, S. J., S. Benard, and I. Paik. (2007). "Getting a Job: Is There a Motherhood Penalty?" *American Journal of Sociology* 112: 1297–338.

Corsaro, W. (1997). *The Sociology of Childhood*. Thousand Oaks, CA: Pine Forge Press.

Cosmides, L., and J. Tooby. (1997). "Evolutionary Psychology: A Primer." University of California at Santa Barbara: Institute for Social, Behavioral, and Economic Research Center for Evolutionary Psychology. Accessed January 11, 2005. www.psych.ucsb.edu/research/cep/primer.html.

Coward, R. (1984). *Female Desire: Women's Sexuality Today*. London: Paladin.

Cowgill, D. O. (1968). "The Social Life of the Aged in Thailand." *Gerontologist* 8: 159–63.

Cowgill, D. O. (1986). *Aging around the World*. Belmont, CA: Wadsworth.

Credit Suisse. (2010). "Global Wealth Report, 2010." Accessed summer 2012. www.credit-suisse.com /news/en/media_release.jsp?ns =41610 (site discontinued).

Crompton, R. (1998). *Class and Stratification: An Introduction to Current Debates,* 2nd ed. Cambridge, UK: Polity Press.

Cumings, B. (1997). *Korea's Place in the Sun: A Modern History.* New York: W.W. Norton.

Cumming, E. (1963). "Further Thoughts on the Theory of Disengagement." *International Social Science Journal* 15: 377–93.

Cumming, E. (1975). "Engagement with an Old Theory." *International Journal of Aging and Human Development* 6: 187–91.

Cumming, E., and W. E. Henry. (1961). *Growing Old: The Process of Disengagement.* New York: Basic Books.

D'Andrade, R. (1995). *The Development of Cognitive Anthropology.* New York: Cambridge University Press.

Danziger, S. H., and P. Gottschalk. (1995). *America Unequal.* Cambridge, MA: Harvard University Press.

Davies, B. (1991). *Frogs and Snails and Feminist Tales.* Sydney, Australia: Allen and Unwin.

Davies, J. C. (1962). "Towards a Theory of Revolution." *American Sociological Review* 27: 5–19.

Davies, M. W. (1983). *Women's Place Is at the Typewriter: Office Work and Office Workers, 1870–1930.* Philadelphia: Temple University Press.

Davis, D., and K. Polonko. (2001). "Telework America 2001 Summary." International Telework Association and Council. Accessed January 20, 2005. www .telecommute.org/telework /twa2001.html.

Davis, K., and W. E. Moore. (1945). "Some Principles of Stratification." *American Sociological Review* 10: 242–49.

Davis, M. (1990). *City of Quartz: Excavating the Future in Los Angeles.* New York: Verso.

Davis, S. (1988). *2001 Management: Managing the Future Now.* New York: Simon and Schuster.

Deacon, T. W. (1998). *The Symbolic Species: The Co-Evolution of Language and the Brain.* New York: W. W. Norton.

Death Penalty Information Center. (2012). "Facts about the Death Penalty." Updated September 26. Accessed summer 2012. www .deathpenaltyinfo.org/documents /FactSheet.pdf.

Defense of Marriage Act. (1996). H.R. 3396—Defense of Marriage Act (Enrolled Bill [Final as Passed Both House and Senate]—ENR). Library of Congress. Accessed July 1, 2013. http://thomas.loc.gov/cgi-bin /query/z?c104:H.R.3396.ENR.

Dejong, W. (1993). "Obesity as a Characterological Stigma: The Issue of Responsibility and Judgments of Task Performance." *Psychological Reports* 73: 963–70.

de Jong Gierveld, J., M. Broese van Groenou, A. W. Hoogendoorn, and J. H. Smit. (2009). "Quality of Marriages in Later Life and Emotional and Social Loneliness." *Journals of Gerontology* 64B: 497–506.

de Jong Gierveld, J., and B. Havens. (2004). "Cross-National Comparisons of Social Isolation and Loneliness: Introduction and Overview." *Canadian Journal on Aging* 23: 109–13.

D'Emilio, J. (1983). *Sexual Politics, Sexual Communities: The Making of a Homosexual Minority in the United States, 1940–1970.* Chicago: University of Chicago Press.

DeNavas-Walt, C., B. D. Proctor, and C. H. Lee. (2005). "Income, Poverty, and Health Insurance Coverage in the United States: 2004." *Current Population Reports,* P60–229. Washington, DC: U.S. Government Printing Office. Accessed spring 2006. www.census.gov/prod/2005pubs /p60–229.pdf.

DeNavas-Walt, C., B. D. Proctor, and J. C. Smith. (2011). "Income, Poverty, and Health Insurance Coverage in the United States: 2010." *Current Population Reports, P60-239.* Washington, DC: U.S. Government Printing Office. Accessed August 17, 2012. www.census.gov/prod/2011pubs /p60-239.pdf.

DeNavas-Walt, C., B. D. Proctor, and J. C. Smith. (2012). "Income, Poverty, and Health Insurance Coverage in the United States: 2011." *Current Population Reports, P60-243.* Washington, DC: U.S. Government Printing Office. Accessed spring 2013. www.census.gov /prod/2012pubs/p60-243.pdf.

Derenne, J. L., and E. Beresin. (2006). "Body Image, Media, and Eating Disorders." *Academic Psychiatry* 30: 257–61.

de Tocqueville, A. (1969; orig. 1835). *Democracy in America.* New York: Doubleday.

Deyo, F. C. (1989). *Beneath the Miracle: Labor Subordination in the New Asian Industrialism.* Berkeley, CA: University of California Press.

DeWitt, K. (1994). "Wave of Suburban Growth Is Being Fed by Minorities." *New York Times,* August 15, pp. A1, B6.

Diamond, J. (1999). *Guns, Germs, and Steel: The Fates of Human Societies.* New York: W. W. Norton.

Diamond, J. (2005). *Collapse: How Societies Choose to Fail or Succeed.* New York: Penguin.

Dickens, W. T., and J. S. Leonard. (1985) "Accounting for the Decline in Union Membership." NBER Working Paper Series, 1275. *Industrial and Labor Relations Review* 38 (April): 323–34.

Dillon, Sam. (2010). "Formula to Grade Teachers' Skill Gains Acceptance, and Critics." *New York Times,* August 31. Accessed October 19, 2012. www.nytimes.com/2010/09 /01/education/01teacher.html.

DiMaggio, P. (1997). "Culture and Cognition." *Annual Review of Sociology* 23: 263–87.

Dimitrova, D. (2003). "Controlling Teleworkers: Supervision and Flexibility Revisited." *New Technology Work and Employment* 18 (3): 181–95.

Dobash, R. E., and R. P. Dobash. (1992). *Women, Violence, and Social Change.* New York: Routledge.

Dogloff, Joanna. (2010). "Should Schools Send Home 'Weight Report Cards'?" *Huffington Post,* February 19. Accessed September 24, 2012. www.huffingtonpost .com/joanna-dolgoff-md/should -schools-send-home_b_468848 .html.

Dolan, Kerry A. (2012). "Facebook's IPO Pricing Drops Zuckerberg's Net Worth to $15.5 Billion." *Forbes,* March 3. Accessed June 18, 2012. www.forbes.com/sites /kerryadolan/2012/05/03 /facebook-ipo-pricing-puts -zuckerbergs-net-worth-at-15-5 -billion/.

Dolbeare, C. (1995). *Out of Reach: Why Everyday People Can't*

Find Affordable Housing. Washington, DC: Low Income Housing Information.

Domhoff, G. W. (1971). *The Higher Circles: The Governing Class in America.* New York: Vintage Books.

Domhoff, G. W. (1974). *The Bohemian Grove and Other Retreats.* New York: Harper and Row.

Domhoff, G. W. (1979). *The Powers That Be: Processes of Ruling Class Domination in America.* New York: Vintage Books.

Domhoff, G. W. (1983). *Who Rules America Now? A View for the '80s.* New York: Prentice Hall.

Domhoff, G. W. (1998). *Who Rules America? Power and Politics in the Year 2000.* Belmont, CA: Mayfield.

Domhoff, G. W. (2005). "Power in America: Wealth, Income, and Power." Accessed spring 2006. http://sociology.ucsc.edu /whorulesamerica/power/wealth .html.

Dow, J. W. (2005). "The Expansion of Protestantism in Mexico: An Anthropological View." *Anthropological Quarterly* 78 (4): 827–51.

Dowling H. (1977). *Fighting Infection: Conquests of the Twentieth Century.* Cambridge, MA: Harvard University Press.

Drake, S., and H. Cayton. (1945). *Black Metropolis: A Study of Negro Life in a Northern City.* New York: Harcourt, Brace.

Draper, P. (1975). "!Kung Women: Contrasts in Sexual Egalitarianism in Foraging and Sedentary Contexts. In R. R. Reiter (Ed.), *Toward an Anthropology of Women.* New York: Monthly Review Press.

Dreier, P., and R. P. Appelbaum. (1992). "The Housing Crisis Enters the 1990s." *New England Journal of Public Policy* 8: 155–67.

Drentea, P. (1998). "Consequences of Women's Formal and Informal Job Search Methods for Employment in Female-Dominated Jobs." *Gender and Society* 12: 321–38.

Du Bois, W. E. B. (1903). *The Souls of Black Folk.* New York: Dover.

Dubos, R. (1959). *Mirage of Health.* New York: Doubleday/Anchor.

Duncan, G. J., J. Brooks-Gunn, W. J. Yeung, and J. R. Smith. (1998). "How Much Does Childhood Poverty Affect the Life Chances of Children?" *American Sociological Review* 63 (3): 406–23.

Duncan, G. J., K. M. Ziol-Guest, and A. Kalil. (2010). "Early-Childhood Poverty and Adult Attainment, Behavior, and Health." *Child Development* 81: 306-25.

Duneier, M. (1999). *Sidewalk.* New York: Farrar, Straus and Giroux.

Duneier, M., and H. Molotch. (1999). "Talking City Trouble: Interactional Vandalism, Social Inequality, and the Urban Interaction Problem." *American Journal of Sociology* 104: 1263–95.

Dunmore, Charlie. (2012). "EU Quest for Growth Could Hit Farm Subsidies." *Reuters,* July 2. Accessed summer 2012. www.reuters .com/article/2012/07/02/eu -budget-agriculture -idUSL6E8HSJU720120702.

Duranti, A. (1994). *From Grammar to Politics: Linguistic Anthropology in a Western Samoan Village.* Berkeley: University of California Press.

Durkheim, É. (1964; orig. 1893). *The Division of Labor in Society.* New York: Free Press.

Durkheim, É. (1965; orig. 1912). *The Elementary Forms of Religious Life.* New York: Free Press.

Durkheim, É. (1966; orig. 1897). *Suicide.* New York: Free Press.

Dush, C. M. K., C. L. Cohan, and P. R. Amato. (2003). "The Relationship between Cohabitation and Marital Quality and Stability: Change Across Cohorts?" *Journal of Marriage and Family* 65: 539–49.

Duster, T. (1990). *Backdoor to Eugenics.* New York: Routledge.

Duverger, M. (1954). *Political Parties.* London: Methuen.

Dworkin, A. (1987). *Intercourse.* New York: Free Press.

Dworkin, R. M. (1993). *Life's Dominion: An Argument about Abortion, Euthanasia, and Individual Freedom.* New York: Knopf.

Dye, T. R. (1986). *Who's Running America?* 4th ed. Englewood Cliffs, NJ: Prentice Hall.

Early, Steve. (2011). *The Civil Wars in U.S. Labor.* Chicago: Haymarket Books.

Easterlin, Richard A. (2001). "Income and Happiness. Towards a Unified Theory." *Economic Journal* 111: 465–84.

Easterlin, Richard A. (2003). "Explaining Happiness." *Proceedings of the National Academy of Sciences* 100: 11176–83.

Easterlin, Richard A. (2010). *Happiness, Growth, and the Life Cycle.* New York: Oxford University Press.

Easterlin, Richard A., Laura Angelescu McVey, Malgorzata Switek, Onnicha Sawangfa, and Smith Zweig. (2010). "The Happiness–Income Paradox Revisited." *Proceedings of the National Academy of Sciences* 107: 22463–68.

Easterlin, Richard A., Robson Morgan, Malgorzata Switek, and Fei Wang. (2012). "China's Life Satisfaction, 1990–2010." *Proceedings of the National Academy of Sciences* 109 (25): 9775–80.

Easterlin, Richard A., and Onnicha Sawangfa. (2010). "Happiness and Economic Growth: Does the Cross Section Predict Time Trends? Evidence from Developing Countries." In Ed Diener, Daniel Kahneman, and John Helliwell, eds., *International Differences in Well-Being* (pp. 166–216). New York: Oxford University Press.

Eating Disorders Coalition (EDC). (2003). "Statistics." Accessed December 29, 2004. www .eatingdisorderscoalition.org /reports/statistics.html (site discontinued).

Eating Disorders Coalition (EDC). (2009). "Statistics." Accessed May 15, 2010. www.eating disorderscoalition.org/reports /statistics (site discontinued).

Eaton, J., and M. B. Pell. (2010). "Lobbyists Swarm Capitol to Influence Health Care Reform." Center for Public Integrity, February 24. Accessed spring 2011. www .publicintegrity.org/articles /entry/1953/.

Ebomoyi, E. (1987). "The Prevalence of Female Circumcision in Two Nigerian Communities." *Sex Roles* 17: 3–4.

Edin, K., and M. Kefalas. (2005). *Promises I Can Keep: Why Poor Women Put Motherhood before Marriage.* Berkeley: University of California Press.

Edin, K., & Lein, L. (1997). "Work, Welfare, and Single Mothers' Economic Survival Strategies." *American Sociological Review* 62: 2.

Education Week. (2004). "Tracking." Accessed October 11, 2012. www .edweek.org/ew/issues/tracking/.

The Economist. (1996). *Pocket World in Figures: 1997.* London: Profile Books.

The Economist. (2007). *Pocket World in Figures: 2008.* London: Profile Books.

The Economist. (2012a). "Points of Light." *The Economist,* July 14, p. 22.

The Economist. (2012b). "A Fall to Cheer: for the First Time Ever, the Number of Poor People Is Declining Everywhere," *The Economist,* May 3. Accessed March 4, 2013. www.economist.com/node /21548963.

Efron, S. (1997). "Eating Disorders Go Global." *Los Angeles Times,* October 18, p. A-1.

Eggen, D. (2009). "Lobbyists Spend Millions to Influence Health Care Reform." *Washington Post,* July 21. Accessed fall 2010. http://voices .washingtonpost.com/health -care-reform/2009/07/health _care_continues_its_inte.html.

Ehrlich, Paul. (1968). *The Population Bomb.* New York: Ballantine Books.

Ehrlich, Paul, and Anne H. Ehrlich. (1990). *The Population Explosion.* New York: Touchstone.

Eibl-Eibesfeldt, I. (1972). "Similarities and Differences between Cultures in Expressive Movements." In R. A. Hinde, ed., *Nonverbal Communication.* New York: Cambridge University Press.

Eisenhower, D. D. (1961). "Military-Industrial Complex Speech, Dwight D. Eisenhower, 1961." *Public Papers of the Presidents.* Accessed fall 2010. www.h-net .org/~hst306/documents/indust .html.

Ekman, P., and W. V. Friesen. (1978). *Facial Action Coding System.* New York: Consulting Psychologists Press.

el Dareer, A. (1982). *Woman, Why Do You Weep? Circumcision and Its Consequences.* Westport, CT: Zed.

Elias, N. (1987). *Involvement and Detachment.* London: Oxford University Press.

Elias, N., and E. Dunning. (1987). *Quest for Excitement: Sport and Leisure in the Civilizing Process.* Oxford, UK: Blackwell.

Elliott, A. (2008). *Making the Cut: How Cosmetic Surgery Is Transforming Our Lives.* London: Reaktion Books.

Elver, H. (2012). *The Headscarf Controversy: Secularism and Freedom of Religion.* New York: Oxford University Press.

Elwert, F. (2005). *How Cohabitation Does—And Does Not—Reduce the Risk of Divorce.* Unpublished manuscript.

Emmanuel, A. (1972). *Unequal Exchange: A Study of the Imperialism of Trade.* New York: Monthly Review Press.

England, P. (1992). *Comparable Worth: Theories and Evidence.* New York: Aldine de Gruyter.

Ennis, Sharon R., Merarys Ríos-Vargas, and Nora G. Albert. (2011). *The Hispanic Population: 2010.* C2010BR-04. Washington, DC: U.S. Bureau of the Census. Accessed September 29, 2012. www.census.gov/prod/cen2010 /briefs/c2010br-04.pdf.

Entertainment Software Association. (2011). "Essential Facts about the Computer and Video Game Industry." Accessed summer 2012. www.theesa.com/facts/pdfs/ESA _EF_2011.pdf.

Environmental Working Group. (2012). "Farm Subsidy Database." Accessed summer 2012. http:// farm.ewg.org/.

Ericson, R., and K. Haggerty. (1997). *Policing the Risk Society.* Toronto: University of Toronto Press.

Erikson, K. (1966). *Wayward Puritans: A Study in the Sociology of Deviance.* New York: Wiley.

Esposito, J. L. (1984). *Islam and Politics.* Syracuse, NY: Syracuse University Press.

Estes, Carol. (2011). "Crises and Old Age Policy." In Richard A. Settersten Jr., and Jacqueline L. Angel, *Handbook of Sociology of Aging* (pp. 297–320). New York: Springer.

Estes, C. L., E. A. Binney, and R. A. Culbertson. (1992). "The Gerontological Imagination: Social Influences on the Development of Gerontology, 1945–Present." *Journal of Aging and Human Development* 35: 49–67.

Estlund, C. L. (2006). "The Death of Labor Law?" *Annual Review of Law and Social Science* 2: 105–23.

Estrich, S. (1987). *Real Rape.* Cambridge, MA: Harvard University Press.

Etzioni-Halévy, E. (1985). *Bureaucracy and Democracy: A Political Dilemma.* New York: Routledge, Chapman and Hall.

Evans, P. (1979). *Dependent Development.* Princeton, NJ: Princeton University Press.

Evans, P. (1995). *Embedded Autonomy: States and Industrial Transformation.* Princeton, NJ: Princeton University Press.

Evans-Pritchard, E. E. (1970). "Sexual Inversion among the Azande." *American Anthropologist* 72: 1428–34.

Fadiman, A. (1997). *The Spirit Catches You and You Fall Down.* New York: Farrar, Straus and Giroux.

Falk, G., U. Falk, and V. Tomashevich. (1981). *Aging in America and Other Cultures.* Saratoga, CA: Century Twenty-One.

Federal Bureau of Investigation (FBI). (2011). "Hate Crime Statistics." Accessed February 16, 2013. www .fbi.gov/about-us/cjis/ucr/hate -crime/2011/narratives/victims.

Federal Bureau of Investigation (FBI). (2012a). "Crime in the United States by Volume and Rate per 100,000 Inhabitants, 1992–2011." Table 1. www.fbi.gov/about-us/cjis /ucr/crime-in-the-u.s/2011/crime -in-the-u.s.-2011/tables/table-1.

Federal Bureau of Investigation (FBI). (2012b). "Murder Victims by Race and Sex." "Expanded Homicide Data Table 1. Accessed spring 2013. www.fbi.gov/about-us/cjis/ucr /crime-in-the-u.s/2011/crime-in -the-u.s.-2011/tables/expanded -homicide-data-table-1.

Federal Bureau of Investigation (FBI). (2012c). "Persons Arrested." Accessed spring 2013. www.fbi.gov /about-us/cjis/ucr/crime-in-the -u.s/2011/crime-in-the-u.s.-2011 /persons-arrested/persons -arrested.

Federal Interagency Forum on Aging-Related Statistics (FIFARS). (2010). *Older Americans 2010: Key Indicators of Well-Being.* Washington, DC: U.S. Government Printing Office. Accessed July 30, 2010. www.agingstats.gov/agingstatsdot net/main_site/default.aspx.

Federal Interagency Forum on Aging-Related Statistics (FIFARS). (2012). *Older Americans 2012: Key Indicators of Well-Being.* Washington, DC: U.S. Government Printing Office. Accessed spring 2013. www .agingstats.gov/Main_Site/Data /2012_Documents/docs/Entire Chartbook.pdf.

Federal Register. (2011). "The 2011 Poverty Guidelines for the 48 Contiguous States and the District of Columbia." Accessed August 23, 2011. http://aspe.hhs .gov/poverty/11fedreg.shtml.

Federal Reserve Board. (2012). "Changes in U.S. Family Finances from 2007 to 2010: Evidence from the Survey of Consumer Finances."

www.federalreserve.gov/pubs/bulletin/2012/PDF/scf12.pdf.

Fenton M. V., and D. L. Morris. (2003). "The Integration of Holistic Nursing Practices and Complementary and Alternative Modalities into Curricula of Schools of Nursing." *Alternative Therapies in Health and Medicine* 9 (4): 62–67.

Ferguson, A. (2000). *Bad Boys: Public Schools in the Making of Black Masculinity*. Ann Arbor: University of Michigan Press.

Ferguson, Christopher. (2011). "The Influence of Television and Video Game Use on Attention and School Problems: A Multivariate Analysis with Other Risk Factors Controlled." *Journal of Psychiatric Research* 45 (6): 808–13.

Fifth World Conference on Women. (2010). "Establishment of UN Entity for Gender Equality and Empowerment." Accessed September 20, 2010. www.5wcw.org/docs/UN_Women.html.

Filkins, D. (1998). "Afghans Pay Dearly for Peace." *Los Angeles Times*, October 22, p. A-1.

Findsen, B., and M. Formosa. (2011). *Lifelong Learning in Later Life: A Handbook on Older Adult Learning*. Boston: Sense Publishers.

Finke, R., and R. Stark. (1988). "Religious Economies and Sacred Canopies: Religious Mobilization in American Cities, 1906." *American Sociological Review* 53: 41–49.

Finke, R., and R. Stark. (2005). *The Churching of America, 1776–1990: Winners and Losers in Our Religious Economy*. New Brunswick, NJ: Rutgers University Press.

Firestone, S. (1970). *The Dialectic of Sex: The Case for Feminist Revolution*. New York: William Morrow & Company.

Fischer, C. S. (1984). *The Urban Experience*, 2nd ed. New York: Harcourt Brace Jovanovich.

Fischer, C. S., M. Hout, M. Sánchez Jankowski, S. R. Lucas, A. Swidler, and K. Vos. (1996). *Inequality by Design: Cracking the Bell Curve Myth*. Princeton, NJ: Princeton University Press.

Fisher, B. S., F. T. Cullen, and M. G. Turner. (2000). *The Sexual Victimization of College Women*. Bureau of Justice Statistics, NCJ 182369, December. Washington, DC: U.S. Department of Justice, National Institute of Justice. Accessed December 29, 2004. www.ncjrs.org/pdffiles1/nij/182369.pdf.

Flegal, Katherine M., Margaret D. Carroll, Brian K. Kit, and Cynthia L. Ogden. (2012). "Prevalence of Obesity and Trends in the Distribution of Body Mass Index among U.S. Adults: 1999–2010." *Journal of American Medical Association* 307: 491–497.

Foley, D. (1994). *Learning Capitalist Culture: Deep in the Heart of Tejas*. Philadelphia: University of Pennsylvania Press.

Foner, N. (1984). *Ages in Conflict: A Cross-Cultural Perspective on Inequality between Old and Young*. New York: Columbia University Press.

Foran, J., ed. (1997). *Theorizing Revolutions*. New York: Routledge.

Foran. J. (2005). *Taking Power: On the Origins of Third World Revolutions*. Cambridge, UK: Cambridge University Press.

Forbes. (2007). "Special Report: CEO Compensation." Accessed fall 2007. www.forbes.com/2007/05/03/highest-paid-ceos-lead-07ceo-cz_sd_0503ceo_land.html.

Forbes. (2009). "The World's Biggest Companies." Accessed May 2010. www.forbes.com/2009/04/08/worlds-largest-companies-business-global-09-global_land.html.

Forbes. (2011). "The Forbes 400." Accessed August 16, 2011. www.forbes.com/wealth/forbes-400/list.

Forbes. (2012). "The World's Billionaires," *Forbes*, July 23. Accessed March 4, 2013. www.forbes.com/sites/luisakroll/2011/03/09/the-worlds-billionaires-2011-inside-the-list/.

Ford, C. S., and Beach, F. A. (1951). *Patterns of Sexual Behavior*. New York: Harper and Row.

Foreign Policy. (2007). "The List: The World's Fastest-Growing Religions." *Foreign Policy*, May 14. Accessed spring 2013. www.foreignpolicy.com/articles/2007/05/13/the_list_the_worlds_fastest_growing_religions.

Foreign Policy. (2012). "Failed States." *Foreign Policy*, October 7. Accessed spring 2013. www.foreignpolicy.com/failed_states_index_2012_interactive.

Foucault, M. (1971). *The Order of Things: An Archaeology of the Human Sciences*. New York: Pantheon.

Foucault, M. (1975). *Discipline and Punish: The Birth of the Prison*. Paris: Gallimard.

Foucault, M. (1988). "Technologies of the Self." In L. H. Martin, H. Gutman, and P. H. Hutton, eds., *Technologies of the Self: A Seminar with Michel Foucault*. Amherst: University of Massachusetts Press.

Fox, O. C. (1964). "The Pre-Industrial City Reconsidered." *Sociological Quarterly* 5.

Francia, P., and N. Bigelow. (2010). "What's the Matter with the White Working Class? The Effects of Union Membership in the 2004 Presidential Election." *Presidential Studies Quarterly* 41: 140–58.

Frank, A. G. (1966). "The Development of Underdevelopment." *Monthly Review* 18.

Frank, A. G. (1969a). *Capitalism and Underdevelopment in Latin America: Historical Studies of Chile and Brazil*. New York: Monthly Review Press.

Frank, A. G. (1969b). *Latin America: Underdevelopment or Revolution*. New York: Monthly Review Press.

Frank, A. G. (1979). *Dependent Accumulation and Underdevelopment*. London: Macmillan.

Frank, D. J., and E. H. McEneaney. (1999). "The Individualization of Society and the Liberalization of State Policies on Same-Sex Sexual Relations, 1984–1995." *Social Forces* 7 (3): 911–44.

Frank, T. (2004). *What's the Matter with Kansas? How Conservatives Won the Heart of America*. New York: Metropolitan Books.

Frank, T. (2005). "Class Is Dismissed." Accessed fall 2010. www.google.com/url?sa=t&source=web&cd=1&ved=0CBoQFjAA&url=http%3A%2F%2Fuserwww.service.emory.edu%2F-dlinzer%2FFrank-ClassDismissd.pdf&ei=52xhTOPfJ4uCsQOB4Y24CA&usg=AFQjCNF7H96XIOzUBnwojH9iI-sXrD4MCg&sig2=8XnbyZGOcf_eVGeKTFq3XA.

Franzini, L., J. C. Ribble, and A. M. Keddie. (2001). "Understanding the Hispanic Paradox." *Ethnicity and Disease* 11 (3): 496–518.

Freedom House. (2012). "Freedom in the World 2012: The Arab Uprisings

and Their Global Repercussions."
Accessed summer 2012. www.
freedomhouse.org/report/freedom-
world/freedom-world-2012.

Freeman, R. B., and J. Rogers. (1999).
What Workers Want. Ithaca,
NY: ILR Press and Russell Sage
Foundation.

Freidson, E. (1970). *Profession of
Medicine: A Study of the Sociology
of Applied Knowledge.* New York:
Dodd, Mead.

Fremlin, J. H. (1964). "How Many
People Can the World Support?"
New Scientist 24 : 285–87.

French, H. W. (2001). "Diploma at
Hand, Japanese Women Find Glass
Ceiling Reinforced with Iron." *New
York Times,* January 1, p. A1.

French, H. W. (2006). "As Chinese
Cities Boom, Old Are Left Behind."
New York Times, November 3.
http://www.nytimes.com/2006/11
/03/world/asia/03iht-age.3383555
.html?_r=0.

Frey, W. (2001). "Melting Pot Suburbs:
A Census 2000 Study of Subur-
ban Diversity." *Census 2000 Series.*
Washington, DC: The Brookings
Institution.

Frey, W. (2011). "The Great American
Migration Slowdown: Regional and
Metropolitan Dimensions." Brookings Institution. Accessed summer
2012. www.brookings.edu/~/media
/research/files/opinions/2011/1/12
%20migration%20frey/1209
_migration_frey.pdf.

Fried, Amy, and Douglas B. Harris.
(2001). "On Red Capes and
Charging Bulls: How and Why
Conservative Politicians and
Interest Groups Promoted Public
Anger." In John R. Hibbing and
Elizabeth Theiss-Morse, *What Is It
about Government That Americans
Dislike?* (pp. 157–74). New York:
Cambridge University Press.

Friedman, J. (1994). *Cultural Identity
and Global Process.* London: Sage.

Friedman, R. A., and S. C. Currall.
(2003). "Conflict Escalation:
Dispute Exacerbating Elements of
E-mail Communication." *Human
Relations* 56 (11): 1325–47.

Friedman, T. (2000). *The Lexus and the
Olive Tree: Understanding Globalization.* New York: Anchor.

Friedman, T. (2005). *The World Is Flat:
A Brief History of the Twenty-First
Century.* New York: Farrar, Straus
and Giroux.

Fries, J. F. (1980). "Aging, Natural
Death, and the Compression of
Morbidity." *New England Journal
of Medicine* 303: 130–35.

Fröbel, F., J. Heinrichs, and O. Kreye.
(1979). *The New International Division of Labor.* New York: Cambridge
University Press.

Fry, C. L. (1980). *Aging in Culture and
Society.* New York: Bergin.

Fryer, D., and S. McKenna. (1987).
"The Laying Off of Hands—
Unemployment and the
Experience of Time." In S. Fine-
man, ed., *Unemployment: Personal
and Social Consequences.* London:
Tavistock.

Furstenberg, F. F., Jr., and A. J.
Cherlin. (1991). *Divided Families.*
Cambridge, MA: Harvard
University Press.

Gallup. (1998). "Have and Have-
Nots: Perceptions of Fairness
and Opportunity—1998." July 6.
Accessed spring 2013. www
.gallup.com/poll/9877/havenots
-perceptions-fairness-opportunity
-1998.aspx?version=print.

Gallup. (2012). "Party Affiliation,"
July 9–22. Accessed summer 2012.
www.gallup.com/poll/15370
/party-affiliation.aspx.

Gamoran, A., and M. Nystrand. (1995).
"An Organizational Analysis of
the Effects of Ability Grouping."
*American Educational Research
Journal* 32(4): 687–715.

Gans, D., and M. Silverstein. (2006).
"Norms of Filial Responsibility
for Aging Parents across Time and
Generations." *Journal of Marriage
and Family* 68 (4): 961–76.

Gardner, C. B. (1995). *Passing By:
Gender and Public Harassment.*
Berkeley, CA: University of Califor-
nia Press.

Gardner, H., and T. Hatch. (1989).
"Multiple Intelligences Go to
School: Educational Implications
of the Theory of Multiple Intelligences." *Educational Researcher*
18 (8): 4–9.

Garfinkel, H. (1963). "A Conception
of, and Experiments with, 'Trust'
as a Condition of Stable Concerted Actions." In O. J. Harvey,
ed., *Motivation and Social
Interaction.* New York: Ronald
Press.

Gates, Gary J. (2012). "LGBT Identity:
A Demographer's Perspective."
Loyola of Los Angeles Law Review
45 (693). Accessed September 25,
2012. http://digitalcommons.lmu
.edu/llr/vol45/iss3/2.

Gavron, H. (1966). *The Captive
Wife: Conflicts of Housebound
Mothers.* London: Routledge and
Kegan Paul.

Geary, D. (1981). *European Labor
Protest, 1848–1939.* New York:
St. Martin's Press.

Geertz, C. (1973). *The Interpretation
of Cultures.* New York: Basic
Books.

Gelb, I. J. (1952). *A Study of Writing.* Chicago: University of Chicago Press.

Genworth Financial. (2012). "Gen-
worth 2012 Cost of Care Survey:
Home Care Providers, Adult Day
Health Care Facilities, Assisted
Living Facilities, and Nursing
Homes." New York: Genworth.

Gerbner, G., L. Gross, M. Morgan,
and N. Signorielli. (1986).
"Television's Mean World:
Violence Profile No. 14–15."
Philadelphia: Annenberg School
of Communication, University of
Pennsylvania.

Gereffi, G. (1995). "Contending Para-
digms for Cross-Regional Comparison: Development Strategies and
Commodity Chains in East Asia
and Latin America." In P. H. Smith,
ed., *Latin America in Comparative
Perspective: New Approaches to
Methods and Analysis.* Boulder,
CO: Westview Press.

Gereffi, G. (1996). "Commodity Chains
and Regional Divisions of Labor in
East Asia." *Journal of Asian Business* 12 (1): 75–112.

Gershuny, J., M. Godwin,
and S. Jones. (1994). "The Domestic Labour Revolution: A Process of
Lagged Adaptation?" In M. Anderson, F. Bechofer, and J. Gershuny,
eds., *The Social and Political
Economy of the Household.* Oxford,
UK: Oxford University Press.

Gertz, Geoffrey, and Laurence
Chandy. (2011). "Two Trends in
Global Poverty." Brookings Institution, May 2011. Accessed summer
2012. www.brookings.edu/~/media
/research/files/opinions/2011
/5/17%20global%20poverty
%20trends%20chandy/0517
_trends_global_poverty.

Gibson, P. (1989). "Gay Male and
Lesbian Youth Suicide." *Report
of the Secretary's Task Force
on Youth Suicide.* Washington,
DC: U.S. Department of Health and
Human Services.

Giddens, A. (1984). *The Constitution
of Society.* Cambridge, UK: Polity
Press.

Giddens, A. (1990). *The Consequences of Modernity*. Cambridge, UK: Polity Press.

Gilligan, C. (1982). *In a Different Voice: Psychological Theory and Women's Development*. Cambridge, MA: Harvard University Press.

Giuffre, P. A., and C. L. Williams. (1994). "Boundary Lines: Labeling Sexual Harassment in Restaurants." *Gender and Society* 8: 378–401.

Gladwell, M. (2005). "Getting in: The Social Logic of Ivy League Admissions." *The New Yorker*, October 15.

Glassner, B. (1999). *The Culture of Fear: Why Americans Are Afraid of the Wrong Things*. New York: Basic Books.

Global Health Facts. (2009). "Estimated Global Malaria Deaths." Accessed May 20, 2010. www.globalhealthfacts.org/topic.jsp?i=31 (site discontinued).

Global Times. (2010). "Cops Revoke Warrant for Fugitive Reporter." *Global Times,* July 30. Accessed spring 2011. http://english.sina.com/china/2010/0729/331563.html.

Glock, C. Y. (1976). "On the Origin and Evolution of Religious Groups." In C. Y. Glock and R. N. Bellah, eds., *The New Religious Consciousness*. Berkeley, CA: University of California Press.

Goffard, Christopher, and Molly Hennessy-Fiske. (2012). "The Nonthreatening Path of a Future Mass Murder." *Los Angeles Times*, August 9. Accessed spring 2013. www.latimes.com/news/nationworld/nation/la-na-wisconsin-gunman-20120809,0,6250188,full.story (site discontinued).

Goffman, A. (2009). "On the Run." *American Sociological Review* 74 (3): 339–57.

Goffman, E. (1963). *Stigma: Notes on the Management of Spoiled Identity*. Englewood Cliffs, NJ: Prentice-Hall.

Goffman, E. (1967). *Interaction Ritual*. New York: Doubleday/Anchor.

Goffman, E. (1971). *Relations in Public: Microstudies of the Public Order*. New York: Basic Books.

Goffman, E. (1973). *The Presentation of Self in Everyday Life*. New York: Overlook Books.

Goffman, E. (1981). *Forms of Talk*. Philadelphia: University of Pennsylvania Press.

Goldberg, C. (1997). "Hispanic Households Struggle amid Broad Decline in Income." *New York Times*, January 30, pp. A1, A16.

Goldberg, S. (1999). "The Logic of Patriarchy." *Gender Issues*, 17, 53–69.

Goldscheider, F. K., and L. J. Waite. (1991). *New Families, No Families? The Transformation of the American Home*. Berkeley, CA: University of California Press.

Goldstein, J., and A. Morning. (2000). "The Multiple-Race Population of the United States: Issues and Estimates." *Proceedings of the National Academy of Sciences* 97 (11): 6230–35.

Goldstein, S., and A. Goldstein. (1996). *Jews on the Move: Implications for Jewish identity*. Albany, NY: State University of New York Press.

Goleman, Daniel. (1996). *Emotional Intelligence: Why It Can Matter More Than IQ*. New York: Bantam Books.

Goode, W. J. (1963). *World Revolution in Family Patterns*. New York: Free Press.

Gornick, J.C., and M. K. Meyers. (2003). "Welfare Regimes in Relation to Paid Work and Care." In J. Z. Giele and E. Holst, eds., *Changing Life Patterns in Western Societies*. Netherlands: Elsevier.

Gottfredson, M. R., and T. Hirschi. (1990). *A General Theory of Crime*. Stanford, CA: Stanford University Press.

Granovetter, M. (1973). "The Strength of Weak Ties." *American Journal of Sociology* 78: 1360–80.

Grant Thornton Business Report. (2011). "Proportion of Women in Senior Management Falls to 2004 Levels." Accessed summer 2013. www.internationalbusinessreport.com/Press-room/2011/women_in-senior_management.asp.

Green, F. (1987). *The "Sissy Boy" Syndrome and the Development of Homosexuality*. New Haven, CT: Yale University Press.

Greenfield, P. M. (1993). "Representational Competence in Shared Symbol Systems." In R. R. Cocking and K. A. Renninger, eds., *The Development and Meaning of Psychological Distance*. Hillsdale, NJ: Erlbaum.

Greenhouse, S. (2010). "Report Warned Wal-Mart of Risks before Bias Suit." *New York Times*, June 3. Accessed spring 2011. www.nytimes.com/2010/06/04/business/04lawsuit.html.

Greenhouse, S., and M. Barbaro. (2007). "Costco Bias Suit Is Given Class-Action Status." *New York Times*, January 12.

Griffin, S. (1979). *Rape, the Power of Consciousness*. New York: Harper and Row.

Gross, J. (1992). "Suffering in Silence No More: Fighting Sexual Harassment." *New York Times*, July 13, p. A1.

Grossman, Jonathan. (1978). "Fair Labor Standards Act of 1938: Maximum Struggle for a Minimum Wage." United States Department of Labor: History. Accessed summer 2013. www.dol.gov/oasam/programs/history/flsa1938.htm.

Grosz, E. (1994). *Volatile Bodies: Toward a Corporeal Feminism*. Bloomington: Indiana University Press.

Grusky, David B., Bruce Western, and Christopher Wimer. (2011). "The Consequences of the Great Recession." In David B. Grusky, Bruce Western, and Christopher Wimer, eds. *The Great Recession* (pp. 3–20). New York: Russell Sage Foundation.

The Guardian. (2002). "Top 1% Earn as Much as the Poorest 57%." Accessed January 10, 2005. www.guardian.co.uk/business/story/0,,635292,00.html.

Guerino, Paul, Paige M. Harrison, and William J. Sabol. (2012). "Prisoners in 2010." Washington, DC: Bureau of Justice Statistics. Accessed summer 2012. http://www.bjs.gov/index.cfm?ty=pbdetail&iid=2230.

Guibernau, M. (1999). *Nations without States: Political Communities in a Global Age*. Cambridge, MA: Blackwell.

Ha, J.-H. (2008). "Changes in Support from Confidantes, Children, and Friends Following Widowhood." *Journal of Marriage and Family* 70: 306–18.

Habermas, J. (1975). *Legitimation Crisis* (T. McCarthy, trans.). Boston: Beacon Press.

Haberstick, Brett C., Jeffery M. Lessem, Matthew McQueen, Jason D. Boardman, Christian J. Hopfer, Andrew Smolen, and John K. Hewitt. (2010). "Stable Genes and Changing Environments: Body Mass Index Across Adolescence and Young

Adulthood." *Behavior Genetics* 40: 495–504.

Hacker, J. David. (2010). "Decennial Life Tables for the White Population of the United States, 1790–1900." *Historical Methods* 43(2): 45-79. Accessed summer 2013. www.ncbi.nlm.nih.gov/pmc /articles/PMC2885717/.

Hadden, J. (1997a). "The Concepts 'Cult' and 'Sect' in Scholarly Research and Public Discourse." New Religious Movements. Accessed January 10, 2005. http:// religiousmovements.lib.virginia .edu/cultsect/concult.htm (site discontinued).

Hadden, J. (1997b). "New Religious Movements Mission Statement." New Religious Movements. Accessed January 10, 2005. http:// religousmovements.lib.virginia .edu/welcome/mission.htm (site discontinued).

Hadden, J. (2004). "Televangelism." Religious Broadcasting Website. Accessed January 3, 2005. http://religious broadcasting.lib .virginia.edu/televangelism.html (site discontinued).

Hagan, J., and B. McCarthy. (1992). "Mean Streets: The Theoretical Significance of Situational Delinquency among Homeless Youth." *American Sociological Review* 98: 597–627.

Haggerty, Roseann. (2012). "To Cut Homelessness, Cut the Red Tape." *New York Times,* May 24. Accessed March 1, 2013. www.nytimes.com/ roomfordebate/2012/05/24/how-should-the-us-support-returning-veterans/to-cut-veteran-homelessness-cut-the-red-tape.

Hall, E. T. (1969). *The Hidden Dimension.* New York: Doubleday.

Hall, E. T. (1973). *The Silent Language.* New York: Doubleday.

Hall, S. (1992). "The Question of Cultural Identity." In S. Hall, D. Held, and T. McGrew, eds., *Modernity and its Futures.* Cambridge, UK: Polity Press.

Hall, S., D. Held, and T. McGrew. (1988). "New Times." *Marxism Today,* October.

Halpern, C. T., et al. (2000). "Smart Teens Don't Have Sex (Or Kiss Much Either)." *Journal of Adolescent Health* 26 (3): 213–25.

Hamel, G. (1991). "Competition for Competence and Inter-Partner Learning within International Strategic Alliances." *Strategic Management Journal* 12 (Summer Special Issue): 83–103.

Hamilton, M. (2001). *The Sociology of Religion: Theoretical and Comparative Perspectives,* 2nd ed. Florence, KY: Routledge.

Hammond, P. E. (1992). *Religion and Personal Autonomy: The Third Disestablishment in America.* Columbia: University of South Carolina Press.

Handy, C. (1994). *The Empty Raincoat: Making Sense of the Future.* London: Hutchinson.

Harknett, K., and S. McLanahan. (2004). "Racial and Ethnic Differences in Marriage after the Birth of a Child." *American Sociological Review* 69: 790–811.

Harper, S., D. Rusahni, and J. S. Kaufman. (2012). "Trends in the Black-White Life Expectancy Gap, 2003–2008." (sam.harper@ mcgill.ca). *Journal of the American Medical Association* 307(21): 2257–59.

Harris, D. (2003). "Racial Classification and the 2000 Census." Commissioned paper. Panel to Review the 2000 Census, Committee on National Statistics. University of Michigan, Ann Arbor.

Harris, D. R., and J. J. Sim. (2000). "An Empirical Look at the Social Construction of Race: The Case of Mixed-Race Adolescents." *Population Studies Center Research Report 00–452.* University of Michigan, Ann Arbor.

Harris, J. R. (1998). *The Nurture Assumption: Why Children Turn Out the Way They Do.* New York: Free Press.

Harris, M. (1975). *Cows, Pigs, Wars, and Riches: The Riddles of Culture.* New York: Random House.

Harris, M. (1978). *Cannibals and Kings: The Origins of Cultures.* New York: Random House.

Harris, M. (1980). *Cultural Materialism: The Struggle for a Science of Culture.* New York: Vintage Books.

Hartig, T., G. Johansson, and C. Kylin. (2003). "Residence in the Social Ecology of Stress and Restoration." *Journal of Social Issues* 59 (3): 611–36.

Hartman, M., and H. Hartman. (1996). *Gender Equality and American Jews.* Albany, NY: State University of New York Press.

Hartmann, H. I. et al. (1985). "An Agenda for Basic Research on Comparable Worth." In H. I. Hartmann et al., eds., *Comparable Worth: New Directions for Research.* Washington, DC: National Academy Press.

Harvey, D. (1973). *Social Justice and the City.* Oxford, UK: Blackwell.

Harvey, D. (1982). *The Limits to Capital.* Oxford, UK: Blackwell.

Harvey, D. (1985). *Consciousness and the Urban Experience: Studies in the History and Theory of Capitalist Urbanization.* Oxford, UK: Blackwell.

Harvey, D. (1989). *The Condition of Postmodernity.* Cambridge, MA: Blackwell.

Haslam, D. W., and W. P. James. (2005). "Obesity." *Lancet* 366 (9492): 1197–1209.

Hatch, N. O. (1989). *The Democratization of American Christianity.* New Haven, CT: Yale University Press.

Hathaway, A. D. (1997). "Marijuana and Tolerance: Revisiting Becker's Sources of Control." *Deviant Behavior* 18 (2): 103–24.

Haub, Carl. (2011). "World Population Aging: Clocks Illustrate Growth in Population under Age 5 and over Age 65." Washington, DC: Population Reference Bureau. Accessed August 10, 2012. www.prb.org /Articles/2011/agingpopulation clocks.aspx.

Hawkes, T. (1977). *Structuralism and Semiotics.* Berkeley, CA: University of California Press.

Hawley, A. H. (1950). *Human Ecology: A Theory of Community Structure.* New York: Ronald Press Company.

Hawley, A. H. (1968). "Human Ecology." *International Encyclopedia of Social Science* (Vol. 4). New York: Free Press.

Hayden, R. M. (2000). "Rape and Rape Avoidance in Ethno-National Conflicts: Sexual Violence in Liminalized States." *American Anthropologist* 102 (1): 27–41.

Hayflick, L. (1994). *How and Why We Age.* New York: Ballantine Books.

Hays, S. (2000). "Constructing the Centrality of Culture—and Deconstructing Sociology?" *Contemporary Sociology* 29 (4): 594–602.

Headhoncha. (2012). "How Many Countries Have Women Heads of State?" Accessed spring 2013.

www.headhoncha.com/2012/09
/how-many-countries-have
-women-heads-of.html.

Healthful Life Project. (2003).
"The World's Ageing Population
and Scientific Attempts to Make
It an Even Greater Problem."
Accessed December 7, 2005. http://
healthfullife.umdnj.edu
/archives/aging_pop%20
_archive.htm (site discontinued).

Healy, M. (2001). "Pieces of the
Puzzle." *Los Angeles Times*,
May 21. Accessed January 10,
2005. http://articles.latimes
.com/2001/may/21/health/he-533.

Hebl, M. R., and T. F. Heatherton.
(1998). "The Stigma of Obesity in
Women: The Difference Is Black
and White." *Personality and Social
Psychology Bulletin* 24: 417–26.

Hecht, J. (2003). "New Life for
Undersea Fiber." *Technology
Review*, May 16. Massachusetts
Institute of Technology. Accessed
spring 2006. www.techreview
.com/NanoTech/wtr_13185
,318,p1.html.

Heidensohn, F. (1985). *Women and
Crime*. London: Macmillan.

Held, D. (2006). *Models of Democracy*,
3rd ed. Stanford, CA: Stanford
University Press.

Held, D., A. McGrew, D. Goldblatt,
and J. Perraton. (1999). *Global
Transformations: Politics,
Economics, and Culture*.
Cambridge, UK: Polity Press.

Hendricks, J. (1992). "Generation and
the Generation of Theory in Social
Gerontology." *Aging and Human
Development* 35: 31–47.

Hendricks, J., and C. D. Hendricks.
(1986). *Aging in Mass Society:
Myths and Realities*. Boston: Little,
Brown.

Henry J. Kaiser Family Foundation. (2011). "Pulling It Together:
Medicare, Medicaid, and the Mul-
tiplier Effect." June 9. Accessed
spring 2013. http://kff.org
/health-BMREForm/perspective
/pulling-it-together-medicare
-medicaid-and-the/.

Henry J. Kaiser Family Foundation. (2012). "Medicare Spending and Financing Fact Sheet."
November 14. Accessed spring
2013. http://kff.org/medicare/fact
-sheet/medicare-spending-and
-financing-fact-sheet/.

Henry, W. E. (1965). *Growing Older:
The Process of Disengage-
ment*. New York: Basic Books.

Henslin, J. M., and M. A. Biggs. (1971).
"Dramaturgical Desexualiza-
tion: The Sociology of the Vaginal
Examination." In J. M. Henslin,
ed., *Studies in the Sociology of
Sex*. New York: Appleton-Century-
Crofts.

Henslin, J. M., and M. A. Biggs.
(1997). "Behavior in Public Places:
The Sociology of the Vaginal
Examination." In J. M. Henslin, ed.,
*Down to Earth Sociology: Introduc-
tory Readings*, 9th ed. New York:
Free Press.

Hentoff, N. (2002). "The FBI's
Magic Lantern: Ashcroft Can Be
in Your Computer." *Village Voice*,
May 24.

Herdt, G. (1981). *Guardians of the
Flutes: Idioms of Masculinity*. New
York: McGraw-Hill.

Herdt, G. (1984). *Ritualized Homosexuality in Melanesia*. Berkeley, CA:
University of California Press.

Herdt, G. (1986). *The Sambia: Ritual
and Gender in New Guinea*. New
York: Holt, Rinehart and Winston.

Herdt, G., and J. Davidson. (1988).
"The Sambia 'Urnim-Man':
Sociocultural and Clinical Aspects
of Gender Formation in Papua,
New Guinea." *Archives of Sexual
Behavior* 17.

Heritage, J. (1985). *Garfinkel and
Ethnomethodology*. New York:
Basil Blackwell.

Hernandez, D. J. (1993). *America's
Children: Resources from Family,
Government, and Economy*. New
York: Russell Sage Foundation.

Herrnstein, R. J., and C. Murray. (1994).
*The Bell Curve: Intelligence and
Class Structure in American
Life*. New York: Free Press.

Hesse-Biber, S. (1997). *Am I Thin
Enough Yet? The Cult of Thinness
and the Commercialization of Identity*. New York: Oxford University
Press.

Hexham, I., and K. Poewe. (1997). *New
Religions as Global Cultures*. Boulder, CO: Westview Press.

Hewitt, Karen. (2001). "Blocks as a
Tool for Learning." National Asso-
ciation for the Education of Young
Children. Accessed summer 2013.
www.naeyc.org/files/yc/file
/Hewitt0101.pdf.

Hibbing, John R., and Elizabeth
Theiss-Morse. (2001.) *What Is
It about Government That Ameri-
cans Dislike?* New York and Cam-
bridge, UK: Cambridge University
Press.

Hill, K., and D. M. Upchurch. (1995).
"Gender Differences in Child
Health: Evidence from the Demo-
graphic and Health Surveys."
*Population and Development
Review* 21: 127–51.

Himes, C. L. (1999). "Racial Differ-
ences in Education, Obesity,
and Health in Later Life."
In N. E. Adler, M. Marmot,
B. S. McEwen, and J. Stewart , eds.,
*Socioeconomic Status and Health
in Industrial Nations: Social,
Psychological, and Biological
Pathways. Annals of the New York
Academy of Sciences* 896: 370–72.

Hines, M. (2003). *Brain Gender*. New
York: Oxford University Press.

Hirschi, T. (1969). *Causes of Delinquency*. Berkeley, CA: University of
California Press.

Hirst, P. (1997). "The Global Economy:
Myths and Realities." *International Affairs* 73: 409–25.

Hirst, P., and G. Thompson. (1992).
"The Problem of 'Globalization':
International Economic Relations,
National Economic Management,
and the Formation of Trading
Blocs." *Economy and Society* 24:
357–96.

Hirst, P., and G. Thompson. (1999). *Globalization in Question: The International Economy and the Possibilities
of Governance*, rev. ed. Cambridge,
UK: Polity Press.

Hochschild, A. R. (1975). "Disengage-
ment Theory: A Critique and
Proposal." *American Sociological
Review* 40: 553–69.

Hochschild, A. R., with A. Machung.
(1989). *The Second Shift: Working
Parents and the Revolution at
Home*. New York: Viking.

Hodge, R., and D. Tripp. (1986). *Chil-
dren and Television: A Semiotic
Approach*. Cambridge, UK: Polity
Press.

Hofstede, G. (1997). *Cultures and
Organizations: Software of the
Mind*. New York: McGraw-Hill.

Holmes, L.D. (1983). *Other Cultures,
Elder Years: An Introduction to
Cultural Gerontology*. Minneapo-
lis, MN: Burgess.

Holmes, S. A. (1997). "New Reports
Say Minorities Benefit in Fiscal
Recovery." *New York Times*, Sep-
tember 30, p. A1.

Holton, R. J. (1978). "The Crowd in History: Some Problems of Theory and
Method." *Social History* 3: 219–33.

Homans, G. (1950). *The Human Group*.
New York: Harcourt, Brace.

Homans, H. (1987). "Man-Made Myth: The Reality of Being a Woman Scientist in the NHS." In A. Spencer and D. Podmore, eds., *In a Man's World: Essays on Women in Male-Dominated Professions*. London: Tavistock.

Hood, J. R. (2002). "More Abuse Seen as Elder Population Grows." *Caregiver USA News*, December 16. Accessed December 7, 2005. www.andthoushalthonor.org /news/abuse.html (site discontinued).

Hooks, B. (1981). *Ain't I a Woman: Black Women and Feminism*. Boston: South End Press.

Hopkins, T. K., and I. Wallerstein. (1996). *The Age of Transition: Trajectory of the World-System, 1945–2025*. London: Zed Books.

Hout, M. (1988). "More Universalism, Less Structural Mobility: The American Occupational Structure in the 1980s." *American Journal of Sociology* 93, 1358–1400.

Hout, M., and S. R. Lucas. (1996). "Education's Role in Reducing Income Disparities." *Education Digest* 62(3): 29–32.

Hughes, Mary E., Linda J. Waite, Tracey A. LaPierre, and Ye Luo. (2007). "All in the Family: The Impact of Caring for Grandchildren on Grandparents' Health." *Journals of Gerontology* 62B: S108–19.

Hunter, J. D. (1987). *Evangelism: The Coming Generation*. Chicago: University of Chicago Press.

Huntington, S. P. (1993). "The Clash of Civilizations?" *Foreign Affairs* 72 (3): 22–49.

Huntington, S. P. (1998). *The Clash of Civilizations and the Remaking of World Order*. New York: Simon and Schuster.

Hursh, David. (2007). "Assessing No Child Left Behind and the Rise of Neoliberal Education Policies." *American Educational Research Journal* 44: 493–518.

Hurtado, A. (1995). "Variation, Combinations, and Evolutions: Latino Families in the United States." In R. Zambrana, ed., *Understanding Latino Families*. Thousand Oaks, CA: Sage.

Hyman, H. H., and E. Singer. (1968). *Readings in Reference Group Theory and Research*. New York: Free Press.

Hyman, R. (1984). *Strikes*, 2nd ed. London: Fontana.

Iceland, J., C. Sharpe, and E. Steinmetz. (2003). "Class Differences in African American Residential Patterns in U.S. Metropolitan Areas: 1990–2000." U.S. Census Bureau. Paper presented at the Annual Meetings of the Population Association of America. Minneapolis, MN.

Idler, E. L. (1993). "Age Differences in Self-Assessments of Health: Age Changes, Cohort Differences, or Survivorship?" *Journals of Gerontology: Series B: Psychological Sciences and Social Sciences* 48: P289–P300.

Illich, I. D. (1983). *Deschooling Society*. New York: Harper and Row.

Independent Sector. (2012). "Independent Sector's Value of Volunteer Time." Washington, DC: Independent Sector. Accessed April 16, 2013. www.independentsector.org /volunteer_time.

Inglehart, R. (1997). *Modernization and Postmodernization: Cultural, Economic and Political Change in 43 Societies*. Princeton, NJ: Princeton University Press.

Inglis, D. (2005). *Culture and Everyday Life*. New York: Routledge.

Institute for Women's Policy Research (IWPR). (2010). "The Gender Wage Gap by Occupation." IWPR Fact Sheet #C350a. Washington, DC: Institute for Women's Policy Research. Accessed August 13, 2010. www.iwpr.org/pdf/C350a .pdf (site discontinued).

Institute of International Education (IIE). (2011). "Open Doors 2011: Report on International Educational Exchange." Accessed October 19, 2012. www.iie.org /Research-and-Publications /Open-Doors (site discontinued).

Institute of International Education (IIE). (2012). "Open Doors 2012: Fast Facts." Accessed spring 2013. http://www.iie.org/~/media/Files /Corporate/Open-Doors/Fast -Facts/Fast%20Facts%202012 -final.ashx.

International Centre for Prison Studies (ICPS). (2007). "Highest to Lowest Rates." Prison Brief. Accessed fall 2007. www .kcl.ac.uk/depsta/law/research /icps/worldbrief/wpb_stats.php ?area=all&category=wb_poprate (site discontinued).

International Centre for Prison Studies (ICPS). (2012). "Prison Population Rates per 100,000 of the National Population." World Prison Brief. Accessed summer 2012. www.prisonstudies.org /info/worldbrief/wpb_stats.php ?area=all&category=wb_poprate.

International Institute for Democracy and Electoral Assistance (IIDEA). (2004). *Voter Turnout in Western Europe since 1945*. Stockholm: International Institute for Democracy and Electoral Assistance.

International Labour Organization (ILO). (2004a). "Breaking through the Glass Ceiling: Women in Management." Accessed December 4, 2005. www.ilo.org/dyn/gender /docs/RES/292/F267981337 /Breaking%20Glass%20PDF %20English.pdf.

International Labour Organization (ILO). (2004b). "More Women Are Entering the Global Labour Force Than Ever Before, But Job Equality, Poverty Reduction Remain Elusive." Accessed October 9, 2008. www.ilo.org/global/About _the_ILO/Media_and_public _information/Press_releases /lang—en/WCMS_005243/index .htm (site discontinued).

International Labour Organization (ILO). (2007). "Global Employment Trends for Women." Brief. Accessed fall 2007. www.ilo .org/wcmsp5/groups/public/—ed _emp/—emp_elm/—trends /documents/publication/wcms _114287.pdf.

International Labour Organization (ILO). (2008). "Global Employment Trends for Women." Accessed August 8, 2011. www.ilo.org /wcmsp5/groups/public /@dgreports/@dcomm /documents/publication/wcms _091225.pdf.

International Lesbian and Gay Association (ILGA). (2007). "About ILGA." Accessed January 2008. www.ilga.org/aboutilga.asp.

International Monetary Fund (IMF). (2005). "World Economic Lookout." Accessed spring 2006. www .imf.org/external/pubs/ft/weo /2005/01/pdf/chapter4.pdf.

International Monetary Fund (IMF). (2009). "World Economic and Financial Surveys." Accessed May 2010. www.imf.org/external /pubs/ft/weo/2009/01/weodata /index.aspx.

International Monetary Fund (IMF). (2010). "World Economic Outlook

Database, April 2010: Nominal GDP List of Countries." Accessed August 15, 2010. www.imf.org /external/pubs/ft/weo/2010/01 /weodata/weorept (site discontinued).

International Panel on Climate Change (IPCC). (2007). "Climate Change 2007: Synthesis Report, Summary for Policymakers." Intergovernmental Panel on Climate Change Fourth Assessment Report. Accessed fall 2010. www .ipcc.ch/pdf/assessment-report /ar4/syr/ar4_syr_spm.pdf.

International Road Federation (IRF). (1987). "United Nations Annual Bulletin of Transport Statistics." *Social Trends* 17. London: Her Majesty's Stationery Office (HMSO).

International Service for the Acquisition of Agri-Biotech Applications (ISAAA). (2011)."Crop Biotech Update." Accessed summer 2012. www.isaaa.org/kc/cropbiotech update/specialedition/2011 /default.asp.

International Telework Association and Council (ITAC). (2004). "Telework Facts and Figures." Accessed January 20, 2005. www .telecommute.org/ resources /abouttelework.htm.

International Union for Conservation of Nature (IUCN). (2007). "Extinction Crisis Escalates: Red List Shows Apes, Corals, Vultures, Dolphins All in Danger." Accessed spring 2008. http://cms.iucn.org /what/species/wildlife/index .cfm?uNewsID=81 (site discontinued).

Internet World Stats. (2010). "Internet Usage Statistics: World Internet Users and Population Stats." Accessed May 2010. www .internetworldstats.com/stats .htm.

Internet World Stats. (2012). "Internet Users in the World, Distribution by World Regions, 2011." Accessed summer 2012. www.internetworldstats.com /stats.htm.

Inter-Parliamentary Union (IPU). (2010). "Women in National Parliaments." Geneva: Inter-Parliamentary Union. Accessed fall 2010. www.ipu.org/wmn-e /classif.htm#2.

Inter-Parliamentary Union (IPU). (2012). "Women in National Parliaments." Accessed summer 2012.

www.ipu.org/wmn-e/classif .htm#2.

Ipsos/Reuters. (2012). "The World of Work: Global Study of Online Employees Shows One in Five (17%) Work from Elsewhere." Accessed spring 2013. www .ipsos-na.com/news-polls /pressrelease.aspx?id=5486.

Issa, P., and S. R. Zedlewski. (2011). "Poverty among Older Americans, 2009." *Retirement Security Data Brief* (February 2011). Washington, DC: Urban Institute Program on Retirement Policy.

Jacobs, J. (1961). *The Death and Life of Great American Cities.* New York: Random House.

Jacoby, S. (1998). *Modern Manors: Welfare Capitalism since the New Deal.* Princeton, NJ: Princeton University Press.

Jaher, F. C., ed. (1973). *The Rich, the Well Born, and the Powerful.* Urbana, IL: University of Illinois Press.

Jameson, K. H., and J. N. Cappella. (2009). *Echo Chamber: Rush Limbaugh and the Conservative Media Establishment.* New York: Oxford University Press.

Jarvis, P. (2007). *Globalization, Lifelong Learning and the Learning Society: Sociological Perspectives.* New York: Routledge.

Jencks, C., M. Smith, H. Acland, M. J. Bane, D. Cohen, H. Gintis et al. (1972). *Inequality: A Reassessment of the Effects of Family and School in America.* New York: Basic Books.

Jensen, A. (1979). *Bias in Mental Testing.* New York: Free Press.

Jobling, R. (1988). "The Experience of Psoriasis under Treatment." In M. Bury and R. Anderson, eds., *Living with Chronic Illness: The Experience of Patients and Their Families.* London: Unwin Hyman.

Johnson, D. (2010). "Will Supreme Court Rule for One Dollar, One Vote?" *Campaign for America's Future,* January 9. Accessed spring 2011. www.ourfuture. org/blog-entry/2010010109/will-supreme-court-rule-one-dollar-one-vote.

Johnson, K. (2006). "Demographic Trends in Rural and Small Town America." *Institute Reports on Rural America* 1.

Johnson, M. P. (1995). "Patriarchal Terrorism and Common Couple

Violence: Two Forms of Violence against Women in U.S. Families." *Journal of Marriage and Family* 57: 283–94.

Johnson, M., and J. Morton. (1991). *Biology and Cognitive Development: The Case of Face Recognition.* Oxford, UK: Blackwell.

Johnson-Odim, C. (1991). "Common Themes, Different Contexts: Third World Women and Feminism." In C. Mohanty et al., eds., *Third World Women and the Politics of Feminism.* Bloomington, IN: Indiana University Press.

Joint Center for Housing Studies of Harvard University (JCHS). (2005). "The State of the Nation's Housing, 2005." Accessed spring 2006. www.jchs.harvard.edu /publications/markets/son2005 /son2005.pdf.

Joint Center for Housing Studies of Harvard University (JCHS). (2011). "Rental Market Stresses: Impacts of the Great Recession on Affordability and Multifamily Lending." Accessed August 23, 2011. www .urban.org/UploadedPDF/1001550 -Rental-Market-Stresses.pdf.

Jones, J. (1986). *Labor of Love, Labor of Sorrow: Black Women, Work, and the Family from Slavery to the Present.* New York: Random House.

Jones, S. G. (1995). "Understanding Community in the Information Age." In S. G. Jones, ed., *Cyber-Society: Computer-Mediated Communication and Community.* Thousand Oaks, CA: Sage.

Judge, K. (1995). "Income Distribution and Life Expectancy: A Critical Appraisal." *British Medical Journal* 311: 1282–87.

Juergensmeyer, M. (1993). *The New Cold War? Religious Nationalism Confronts the Secular State.* Berkeley, CA: University of California Press.

Juergensmeyer, M. (1995). "The New Religious State." *Comparative Politics* 27: 379–91.

Juergensmeyer, M. (2001). *Terror in the Mind of God: The Global Rise of Religious Violence.* Berkeley, CA: University of California Press.

Juergensmeyer, M. (2008). *Global Rebellion: Religious Challenges to the Secular State, from Christian Militias to al Qaeda.* Berkeley, CA: University of California Press.

Kaiser Family Foundation. (2008). "State Health Facts: Population Distribution by Metropolitan Status, States (2006–2007), U.S. (2007)." Accessed spring 2008. www.statehealthfacts.org/comparebar.jsp?cat=1&ind=18.

Kalleberg, Arne. (2003). 'Flexible Firms and Labor Market Segmentation." *Work and Occupations* 30 (2): 154–75.

Kanellos, M. (2007). "Intel to Produce Chips in China." *CNET News*, March 25. Accessed fall 2007. www.news.com/Intel-to-produce-chips-in-China/2100–1006_3-6170016.html?tag=ne.gall.related (site discontinued).

Kanter, R. M. (1991). "The Future of Bureaucracy and Hierarchy in Organizational Theory." In P. Bourdieu and J. Coleman, eds., *Social Theory for a Changing Society*. Boulder, CO: Westview Press.

Kaplan, G., and S. Schulhofer-Wohl. (2012). "Understanding the Long Run Decline in Interstate Migration." Working Paper 697. Federal Reserve Bank of Minneapolis.

Kaplan, Thomas, and John Eligon. (2012). "In Albany, Lawmakers Vote to Limit Public Pensions." *New York Times*, March 14. Accessed June 18, 2012. www.nytimes.com/2012/03/15/nyregion/plan-to-reduce-pensions-for-new-public-workers-takes-shape-in-albany.html?_r=1&pagewanted=all.

Kasarda, J. (1993). "Urban Industrial Transition and the Underclass." In W. J. Wilson, ed., *The Ghetto Underclass*. Newbury Park, CA: Sage.

Karabel, J. (2005). *The Chosen: The Hidden History of Admission and Exclusion at Harvard, Yale, and Princeton*. Boston: Houghton Mifflin Company.

Kasarda, J., and E. M. Crenshaw. (1991). "Third World Urbanization: Dimensions, Theories, and Determinants. *Annual Review of Sociology 1991* 17. Palo Alto, CA: Annual Reviews.

Katz, J. (1999). *How Emotions Work*. Chicago: University of Chicago Press.

Kautsky, J. (1982). *The Politics of Aristocratic Empires*. Chapel Hill, NC: University of North Carolina Press.

Kawachi, I., and B. P. Kennedy. (1997). "Socioeconomic Determinants of Health: Health and Social

Cohesion: Why Care about Income Inequality?" *British Medical Journal* 314: 1037.

Kedouri, E. (1992). *Politics in the Middle East*. New York: Oxford University Press.

Keeter, S. (2008). "Young Voters in the 2008 Election." November 12. Accessed fall 2010. http://pewresearch.org/pubs/1031/young-voters-in-the-2008-election.

Kelley, J., and M. D. R. Evans. (1995). "Class and Class Conflict in Six Western Nations." *American Review of Sociology* 60 (2): 157–78.

Kelling, G. L., and C. M. Coles. (1997). *Fixing Broken Windows: Restoring Order and Reducing Crime in Our Communities*. New York: Free Press.

Kelly, M. P. (1992). *Colitis: The Experience of Illness*. London: Routledge.

Kenkel, D., D. Lillard, and A. Mathios. (2006). "The Roles of High School Completion and GED Receipt in Smoking and Obesity." *Journal of Labor Economics* 24 (3): 635–60.

Kenway, J., et al. (1995). "Pulp Fictions? Education, Markets, and the Information Superhighway." *Australian Educational Researcher* 22.

Kenworthy, L., and M. Malami. (1999). "Gender Inequality in Political Representation: A Worldwide Comparative Analysis." *Social Forces* 78 (1): 235–69.

Kernaghan, Charles. (2012). "Chinese Sweatshop Labor in Bangladesh." Institute for Global Labour and Human Rights, March. Accessed March 4, 2013. www.globallabourrights.org/admin/reports/files/1203-Chinese-Sweatshop-in-Bangladesh.pdf.

Khan, Shamus. (2012). "The Sociology of Elites." *Annual Review of Sociology* 38: 361–77.

Kiecolt, K. J., and N. M. Nelson. (1991). "Evangelicals and Party Realignment, 1976–1988." *Social Science Quarterly* 72: 552–69.

Kiger, Patrick. (2012). "Boomers' 'Anxiety Index' High, Voter Survey Reveal Retirement Prospects Top Economic Issues, Concerns." American Association of Retired Persons (August 8, 2012). Accessed August 9, 2012. www.aarp.org/politics-society/government-elections/info-08-2012/aarp-2012-voter-survey.html?cmp=RDRCT-VTR50PL_JUL30_012.

Kilbourne, J. (2010). *Killing Us Softly 4: Advertising's Image of Women*. Media Education Foundation.

Kimmel, M. S. (2003). *The Gender of Desire: Essays on Male Sexuality*. Albany, NY: State University of New York Press.

Kinder, M. (1993). *Playing with Power in Movies, Television, and Video Games*. Berkeley, CA: University of California Press.

King, Gary, Robert O. Keohane, and Sidney Verba. (1994). *Designing Social Inquiry: Scientific Inference in Qualitative Research*. Princeton, NJ: Princeton University Press.

King, N. R. (1984). "Exploitation and Abuse of Older Family Members: An Overview of the Problem." In J. J. Cosa, ed., *Abuse of the Elderly*. Lexington, MA: Lexington Books.

Kinsey, A. C. (1953). *Sexual Behavior in the Human Female*. Philadelphia: Saunders.

Kinsey, A. C., W. R. Pomeroy, and C. E. Martin. (1948). *Sexual Behavior in the Human Male*. Philadelphia: Saunders.

Kinsley, D. (1982). *Hinduism: A Cultural Perspective*. Englewood Cliffs, NJ: Prentice Hall.

Kjekshus, H. (1977). *Ecology, Control, and Economic Development in East African History*. Berkeley, CA: University of California Press.

Klasen, Stephan, and Claudia Wink. (2003). "'Missing Women': Revisiting the Debate." *Feminist Economics* 9(2-3): 263–299. Accessed spring 2013. http://csde.washington.edu/~scurran/files/readings/April28/recommended/MissingWomen.pdf.

Klinenberg, Eric. (2012a). *Going Solo: The Extraordinary Rise and Surprising Appeal of Living Alone*. New York: Penguin.

Klinenberg, Eric. (2012b). "One's a Crowd." *New York Times*, February 4. Accessed September 21, 2012. www.nytimes.com/2012/02/05/opinion/sunday/living-alone-means-being-social.html?pagewanted=print.

Kling, R. (1996). "Computerization at Work." In R. Kling, ed., *Computers and Controversy*, 2nd ed. New York: Academic Press.

Kluckhohn, C. (1949). *Mirror for Man*. Tucson, AZ: University of Arizona Press.

Knodel, J. (2006). "Parents of Persons with AIDS:

Unrecognized Contributions and Unmet Needs." *Journal of Global Ageing* 4: 46–55.

Knoke, D. (1990). *Political Networks: The Structural Perspective.* New York: Cambridge University Press.

Knop, Karen, Ralf Michaels, and Annelise Riles. (2012). "From Multiculturalism to Technique: Feminism, Culture, and the Conflict of Laws Style." *Stanford Law Review* 64: 589–656.

Knorr-Cetina, K., and A. V. Cicourel, eds. (1981). *Advances in Social Theory and Methodology: Towards an Integration of Micro- and Macro-Sociologies.* Boston: Routledge and Kegan Paul.

Kobrin, S. J. (1997). "Electronic Cash and the End of National Markets." *Foreign Policy* 107: 65–77.

Kohn, M. (1977). *Class and Conformity,* 2nd ed. Homewood, IL: Dorsey Press.

Kohut, A. (2008). "Post-Election Perspectives." November 13. Pew Research Center for the People and the Press. Accessed fall 2010. http://pewresearch.org/pubs/1039/post-election-perspectives.

Kollmeyer, C. (2003). "Globalization, Class Compromise, and American Exceptionalism: Political Change in 16 Advanced Capitalist Countries." *Critical Sociology* 29 (3): 369–91.

Kollock, P., and M. A. Smith. (1996). "Managing the Virtual Commons: Cooperation and Conflict in Computer Communities." In S. Herring, ed., *Computer-Mediated Communication.* Amsterdam: John Benjamins.

Kosmin, B. A., E. Mayer, and A. Keysar. (2001). "American Religious Identification Survey (ARIS)." December 19, 2001. New York: CUNY Graduate Center. Accessed January 3, 2005. www.gc.cuny.edu/studies/aris.pdf (site discontinued).

Kosmin, Barry A., and Ariela Keysar. (2009). "American Religious Identification Survey (ARIS 2008)." Accessed spring 2013. http://commons.trincoll.edu/aris/files/2011/08/ARIS_Report_2008.pdf.

Kotlikoff, Laurence J., and Scott Burns. (2012). *The Clash of Generations: Saving Ourselves, Our Kids, and Our Economy.* Cambridge, MA: MIT Press.

Kozol, J. (1991). *Savage Inequalities: Children in America's Schools.* New York: Crown.

Kozol, J. (1995). *Amazing Grace: The Lives of Children and the Conscience of a Nation.* New York: Crown.

Kozol, J. (2012). *Fire in the Ashes: Twenty-Five Years among the Poorest Children in America.* New York: Crown.

Kreider, Rose. (2010). "Increase in Opposite-Sex Couples from 2009 to 2010 in the Annual Social and Economic Supplement (ASEC) to the Current Population Survey (CPS)." Accessed September 17, 2012. www.census.gov/population/www/socdemo/Inc-Opp-sex-2009-to-2010.pdf.

Kristof, N. D. (2010). "The World Capital of Killing." *New York Times,* February 6.

Kristof, Nicholas D., and Sheryl WuDunn. (2009). *Half the Sky: Turning Oppression into Opportunity for Women Worldwide.* New York: Knopf.

Krueger, Alan, and Stacy Dale. (1999). "Estimating the Payoff to Attending a More Selective College: An Application of Selection on Observables and Unobservables." *National Bureau of Economic Research,* Working Paper No. 7322, August.

Krueger, Alan, and Stacy Dale. (2002). "Estimating the Payoff to Attending a More Selective College: An Application of Selection on Observables and Unobservables." *Quarterly Journal of Economics* 117(4): 1491–1527.

Krueger, C. (1995). "Retirees with Company Health Plans on Decline." *Los Angeles Times,* September 22.

Kuefler, Mathew. (2007). *The History of Sexuality Sourcebook.* Toronto: University of Toronto Press.

Kuhn, D. P. (2008). "That Huge Voter Turnout: Didn't Happen." Politico.com, November 8. Accessed fall 2010. www.politico.com/news/stories/1108/15422.html.

Kumagai, Fumie. (2010). "Forty Years of Family Change in Japan: A Society Experiencing Population Aging and Declining Fertility." *Journal of Comparative Family Studies* 41 (4): 581–610.

Lacy, K. R. (2007). *Blue-Chip Black: Race, Class, and Status in the New Black Middle Class.* Berkeley, CA: University of California Press.

LaFraniere. (2012). "All iPhone Sales Suspended at Apple Stores in China." *New York Times,* January 13. Accessed spring 2013. www.nytimes.com/2012/01/14/technology/apple-suspends-iphone-4s-sales-in-mainland-china-stores.html?_r=0.

Laing, R. D. (1971). *Self and Others.* London: Tavistock.

Lake, R. (1981). *The New Suburbanites: Race and Housing in the Suburbs.* New Brunswick, NJ: Center for Urban Policy Research, Rutgers University Press.

Lalich, J. (2004). *Bounded Choice: True Believers and Charismatic Cults.* Berkeley, CA: University of California Press.

Lambda Legal. (2010). *Recognition of Same-Sex Couples Worldwide. Recognition of Same-Sex Couples in the United States.* Accessed October 2, 2012. http://gaymarriage.procon.org/sourcefiles/lambda-gay-marriage-report.pdf.

Lammers, C., M. Ireland, M. Resnick, and V. Blum. (2000). "Influences on Adolescents' Decision to Postpone Onset of Sexual Intercourse: A Survival Analysis of Virginity among Youths Aged 13 to 18 Years." *Journal of Adolescent Health* 26 (1): 42–48.

Land, K. C., G. Deane, and J. R. Blau. (1991). "Religious Pluralism and Church Membership." *American Sociological Review* 56: 237–49.

Landale, N., and K. Fennelly. (1992). "Informal Unions among Mainland Puerto Ricans: Cohabitation or an Alternative to Legal Marriage?" *Journal of Marriage and Family* 54: 269–80.

Landry, Bart, and Kris Marsh. (2011). "The Evolution of the New Black Middle Class." *Annual Review of Sociology* 37: 373–94.

Lappe, F. M., J. Collins, and P. Rosset. (1998). *World Hunger: 12 Myths,* 2nd ed. New York: Grove Press.

Lareau, Annette. (2011). *Unequal Childhoods: Class, Race and Family Life,* 2nd ed. Berkeley, CA: University of California Press.

Latner, J. D., and A. J. Stunkard. (2003). "Getting Worse: The Stigmatization of Obese Children." *Obesity Research* 11: 452–56.

Lattman, P. (2010). "3 Women Claim Bias at Goldman." *New York Times,* September 15. Accessed spring 2011. www.nytimes.com/2010/09/16/business/16bias.html.

Laumann, E. O., J. H. Gagnon, R. T. Michael, and S. Michaels. (1994). *The Social Organization of Sexuality: Sexual Practices in the United States*. Chicago: University of Chicago Press.

Laumann, E. O., S. A. Leitsch, and L. J. Waite. (2008). "Elder Mistreatment in the United States: Prevalence Estimates from a Nationally Representative Study." *Journal of Gerontology: Social Sciences* 63: 248–54.

Lawrence, B. B. (1989). *Defenders of God: The Fundamentalist Revolt Against the Modern Age*. San Francisco: Harper and Row.

Leach, E. (1976). *Culture and Communication: The Logic By Which Symbols Are Connected*. New York: Cambridge University Press.

Lee, G. (1982). *Family Structure and Interaction: A Comparative Analysis*, 2nd ed. Minneapolis: University of Minnesota Press.

Lemert, E. (1972). *Human Deviance, Social Problems, and Social Control*. Englewood Cliffs, NJ: Prentice-Hall.

Leonhardt, D. (2001). "Belt Tightening Seen as Threat to the Economy." *New York Times*, July 15, p. 1.

Lessig, Lawrence. (2011). *Republic, Lost: How Money Corrupts Congress—and a Plan to Stop It*. Mission Viejo, CA: Twelve.

Leupp, G. P. (1995). *Male Colors: The Construction of Homosexuality in Tokugawa Japan*. Berkeley, CA: University of California Press.

Levay, S. (1996). *Queer Science: The Uses and Abuses of Research into Homosexuality*. Cambridge, MA: MIT Press.

LeVine, R., and D. T. Campbell. (1972). *Ethnocentrism: Theories of Conflict, Attitudes and Group Behavior*. New York: Wiley.

Levy, Becca, Martin D. Slade, Suzanne R. Kunkel, and Stanislav V. Kasl. (2002). "Longevity Increased by Positive Self-Perceptions of Aging." *Journal of Personality and Social Psychology* 83 (2): 261–70.

Lewis, O. (1968). "The Culture of Poverty." In D. P. Moynihan, ed., *On Understanding Poverty: Perspectives from the Social Sciences*. New York: Basic Books.

Lichtenstein, N. (2006). "Wal-Mart: A Template for Twenty-First-Century Capitalism." In N. Lichtenstein, ed., *Wal-Mart: The Face of Twenty-First-Century Capitalism*. New York: New Press.

Lightfoot-Klein, H. (1989). *Prisoners of Ritual: An Odyssey into Female Genital Circumcision in Africa*. New York: Haworth.

Lin, Ann Chih, and David R. Harris, eds. (2010). *The Colors of Poverty: Why Racial and Ethnic Disparities Persist*. New York: Russell Sage Foundation.

Lindau, S. T., P. Schumm, E. O. Laumann, W. Levinson, C. A. O'Muircheartaigh, and L. J. Waite. (2007). "A Study of Sexuality and Health among Older Adults in the United States." *New England Journal of Medicine* 357: 762–74.

Linden, G., K. L. Kraemer, and J. Dedrick. (2007). "Who Captures Value in a Global Innovation System? The Case of Apple's iPod." Alfred P. Sloan Foundation: Personal Computing Industry Center. Accessed fall 2007. http://pcic.merage.uci.edu/papers/2007/AppleiPod.pdf (site discontinued).

Lipset, S. M., ed. (1981). *Party Coalitions in the 1980s*. San Francisco: Institute for Contemporary Affairs.

Lipsky, D. (2003). *Absolutely American: Four Years at West Point*. Boston: Houghton Mifflin.

Liptak, A. (2010). "Justices, 5–4, Reject Corporate Spending Limit." *New York Times*, January 21. Accessed spring 2011. www.nytimes.com/2010/01/22/us/politics/22scotus.html.

Locke, J., and E. Pascoe. (2000). "Can a Sense of Community Flourish in Cyberspace?" *The Guardian*, March 11.

Loe, M. (2004). *The Rise of Viagra: How the Little Blue Pill Changed Sex in America*. New York: New York University Press.

Lofland, L. H. (1973). *A World of Strangers*. New York: Basic Books.

Lofland, L. H. (1998). *The Public Realm: Exploring the City's Quintessential Social Territory*. New York: Aldine de Gruyter.

Lofquist, Daphne. (2011). "Same-Sex Couple Households." *American Community Survey Briefs*. Washington, DC: U.S. Department of the Census. Accessed September 20, 2012. www.census.gov/prod/2011pubs/acsbr10-03.pdf.

Logan, J. R., and H. L. Molotch. (1987). *Urban Fortunes: The Political Economy of Place*. Berkeley, CA: University of California Press.

Logan, J., and B. Stults. (2011). "The Persistence of Segregation in the Metropolis: New Findings from the 2010 Census." *U.S. 2010: Discover America in a New Century*. Accessed summer 2012. www.s4.brown.edu/us2010/Data/Report/report2.pdf.

Long, E., ed. (1997). *From Sociology to Cultural Studies: New Perspectives*. Malden, MA: Blackwell.

Loprest, P. (1999). "Families Who Left Welfare: Who Are They and How Are They Doing?" Washington, DC: Urban Institute. Accessed January 3, 2005. www.urban.org/Template.cfm?NavMenuID=24&template=/TaggedContent/ViewPublication.cfm&PublicationID=7297.

Lorber, J. (1994). *Paradoxes of Gender*. New Haven, CT: Yale University Press.

Lowe, G. S. (1987). *Women in the Administrative Revolution: The Feminization of Clerical Work*. Toronto: University of Toronto Press.

Louise, Kimberly. (2010). "Toys R Us Releases List of Hot Toys for Christmas 2010." Accessed summer 2013. http://voices.yahoo.com/toys-r-us-releases-list-hot-toys-christmas-6826942.html?cat=25.

Lucy. (1997). "Linguistic Relativity." *Annual Review of Anthropology*, 26: 291-312.

Luhby, T. (2011). "Social Security Payments to See First Increase since 2009." CNN, October 18. Accessed August 9, 2012. http://money.cnn.com/2011/10/18/news/economy/Social_security_cola_increase/index.htm.

Luo, Y., J. Xu, E. Granberg, and W. M. Wentworth. (2011). "A Longitudinal Study of Social Status, Perceived Discrimination, and Physical and Emotional Health among Older Adults." *Research on Aging*. Advance online publication doi: 10.1177/0164027511426151.

Lyons, R. (2011). "The Spread of Evidence-Poor Medicine via Flawed Social-Network Analysis." *Statistics, Politics, and Policy* 2(1), Article 2.

Lyotard, J. (1985). *The Post-Modern Condition: A Report on Knowledge*. Minneapolis: University of Minnesota Press.

MacEnoin, D., and A. al-Shahi, eds. (1983). *Islam in the Modern World*. New York: St. Martin's Press.

Maddox, G. L. (1965). "Fact and Artifact: Evidence Bearing on Disengagement from the Duke Geriatrics Project." *Human Development* 8: 117–30.

Maddox, G. L. (1970). "Themes and Issues in Sociological Theories of Human Aging." *Human Development* 13: 17–27.

Madigan, F. C. (1957). "Are Sex Mortality Differentials Biologically Caused?" *Millbank Memorial Fund Quarterly* 25: 202–23.

Mahalik, J. R., S. M. Burns, and M. Syzdek. (2007). "Masculinity and Perceived Normative Health Behaviors as Predictors of Men's Health Behaviors." *Social Science and Medicine* 64 (11): 2201–2209.

Malthus, T. (2003; orig. 1798). *Essay on the Principle of Population: A Norton Critical Edition*, rev. ed. (P. Appleman, ed.). New York: W. W. Norton.

Manchin, R. (2004). "Religion in Europe: Trust Not Filling the Pews." Gallup Poll, September 21. Accessed fall 2010. www.gallup.com/poll/13117/religion-europe-trust-filling-pews.aspx.

Manjoo, Farhad. (2008). *True Enough: Learning to Live in a Post-Fact Society*. New York: Wiley.

Manning, J. T., K. Koukourakis, and D. A. Brodie. (1997). "Fluctuating Asymmetry, Metabolic Rate and Sexual Selection in Human Males." *Evolution and Human Behavior* 18 (1): 15–21.

Manning, Wendy D., and Susan L. Brown. (2011). "The Demography of Unions among Older Americans, 1980–Present: A Family Change Approach." In Richard A. Settersten, Jr., and Jacqueline L. Angel, eds. *Handbook of Sociology of Aging* (pp. 193–212). New York: Springer.

Manpower, Inc. (2008). Company Overview. Accessed spring 2008. www.manpower.com/about/companyoverview.cfm (site discontinued).

Manton K. G., X. Gu, and G. R. Lowrimore. (2008). "Cohort Changes in Active Life Expectancy in the U.S. Elderly Population: Experience from the 1982–2004 National Long-Term Care Survey." *Journals of Gerontology: Series B: Psychological Sciences and Social Sciences* 63: P269–81.

Markoff, John. (2012). "Skilled Work, without the Worker." *New York Times*, April 18. Accessed spring 2013. www.nytimes.com/2012/08/19/business/new-wave-of-adept-robots-is-changing-global-industry.html?pagewanted=all.

Marsden, P. (1987). "Core Discussion Networks of Americans." *American Sociological Review* 52: 122–31.

Marsden, P., and N. Lin. (1982). *Social Structure and Network Analysis*. Beverly Hills, CA: Sage.

Marsh, Bill. (2012). "Jobs Where Gender Segregation Persists." *New York Times*, September 30. Accessed November 14, 2012. www.nytimes.com/imagepages/2012/09/30/opinion/30coontz-gr1.html?BMREF=sunday.

Marsh, Kris, William A. Darity Jr., Philip N. Cohen, Lynne M. Casper, and Danielle Salters. (2007). "The Emerging Black Middle Class: Single and Living Alone." *Social Forces* 86: 735–62.

Marshall, T. H. (1973). *Class, Citizenship, and Social Development: Essays by T. H. Marshall*. Westport, CT: Greenwood Press.

Martin, J. A., and M. M. Park. (1999). "Trends in Twin and Triplet Births: 1980–1997." *National Vital Statistics Reports* 47 (24).

Martin, Joyce A., Brady E. Hamilton, Stephanie J. Ventura, Michelle J. K. Osterman, Elizabeth C. Wilson, T. J. Mathews, and Division of Vital Statistics. (2012). "Births: Final Data for 2010." *National Vital Statistics Reports* 6 (1): 51. Accessed September 29, 2012. www.cdc.gov/nchs/data/nvsr/nvsr61/nvsr61_01.pdf.

Martin, R. C. (1982). *Islam: A Cultural Perspective*. Englewood Cliffs, NJ: Prentice Hall.

Martineau, H. (1962; orig. 1837). *Society in America*. Garden City, NY: Doubleday.

Martinez, G. M., K. Daniels, and A. Chandra. (2012). "Fertility of Men and Women Aged 15–44 Years in the United States: National Survey of Family Growth, 2006–2010." *National Health Statistics Reports No. 51*. Hyattsville, MD: National Center for Health Statistics. Accessed September 30, 2012. www.cdc.gov/nchs/data/nhsr/nhsr051.pdf.

Marx, K. (1977; orig. 1867). *Capital: A Critique of Political Economy* (Vol. 1). New York: Random House.

Marx, K. (1983). *The Portable Karl Marx*. New York: Penguin.

Marx, K. (1994; orig. 1843–1844). "A Contribution to the Critique of Hegel's *Philosophy of Right*: Introduction." In J. J. O'Malley, ed., *Marx: Early Writings*. New York: Cambridge University Press.

Marx, K. (2000; orig. 1844). "The Economic and Philosophical Manuscripts." In D. McLellan, ed., *Karl Marx: Selected Writings*. New York: Oxford University Press.

Marx, K. (2008; orig. 1867). *Capital: A New Abridgement* (D. McClellan, ed.). New York: Oxford University Press.

Marx, K., and F. Engels. (2008; orig. 1848). *The Communist Manifesto*. New York: Oxford University Press.

Mascia, J. (2009). "A Landlord's Foreclosure Puts a Tenant in Trouble." *New York Times*, November 26. Accessed August 1, 2010. ww.nytimes.com/2009/11/26/nyregion/26neediest2.html.

Mason, A., and A. Palmer. (1996). *Queer Bashing: A National Survey of Hate Crimes against Lesbians and Gay Men*. London: Stonewall.

Massey, D. S. (1996). "The Age of Extremes: Concentrated Affluence and Poverty in the Twenty-First Century." *Demography* 33 (4): 395–412.

Massey, D. S., and N. A. Denton. (1993). *American Apartheid: Segregation and the Making of the Underclass*. Cambridge, MA: Harvard University Press.

Mather, M. (2008). *Population Losses Mount in U.S. Rural Areas*. Washington, DC: Population Reference Bureau.

Mathews, T. M., and M. F. MacDorman. (2012). "Infant Mortality Statistics from the 2008 Period Linked Birth/Infant Death Data Set." *National Vital Statistics Reports* 60 (5). Hyattsville, MD: National Center for Health Statistics. Accessed October 1, 2012. www.cdc.gov/nchs/data/nvsr/nvsr60/nvsr60_05.pdf.

Matsueda, R. L. (1992). "Reflected Appraisals, Parental Labeling, and Delinquency: Specifying a Symbolic Interaction Theory." *American Journal of Sociology* 97: 1577–1611.

Maugh, T. H., II. (1991). "Survey of Identical Twins Links Biological Factors with Being Gay." *Los Angeles Times,* December 15.

Maugh, T. H., II. (1993). "Genetic Compound Found in Lesbianism, Study Says." *Los Angeles Times,* March 12.

Maugh, T. H., II, and N. Zamichow. (1991). "Medicine: San Diego's Researcher's Findings Offer First Evidence of a Biological Cause for Homosexuality." *Los Angeles Times,* August 30.

McCullough, J.J. (2013). "Female World Leaders Currently in Power." Accessed spring 2013. www.filibustercartoons.com /charts_rest_female-leaders.php.

McDonald, M. P., and S. L. Popkin. (2001). "The Myth of the Vanishing Voter." *American Political Science Review* 95 (4): 963–74.

McDonough, S. (2005). "U.S. Prison Population Soars in 2003, 2004." ABC News, April 25. Accessed spring 2006. http://abcnews.go .com/US/LegalCenter/wireStory ?id=699808&CMP=OTC-RSS Feeds0312 (site discontinued).

McFadden, D., and C. A. Champlin. (2000). "Comparison of Auditory Evoked Potentials in Heterosexual, Homosexual, and Bisexual Males and Females." *Journal of the Association for Research in Otolaryngology* 1: 89–99.

McGranahan, D.A., and C. L. Beale. (2002). "Understanding Rural Population Loss." *Rural America* 17.

McLanahan, S., and G. Sandefur. (1994). *Growing Up with a Single Parent: What Hurts, What Helps.* Cambridge, MA: Harvard University Press.

McLaren, P. (1985). "The Ritual Dimensions of Resistance: Clowning and Symbolic Inversion." *Journal of Education* 167 (2): 84–97.

McLeod, J. (1995). *Ain't No Makin' It.* Boulder, CO: Westview Press.

McMichael, P. (1996). *Development and Social Change: A Global Perspective.* Thousand Oaks, CA: Pine Forge.

McMurrer, J. (2007). *Choices, Changes, and Challenges: Curriculum and Instruction in the NCLB Era.* Washington, DC: Center on Education Policy). Accessed spring 2008. http://www.cep-dc.org

/displayDocument.cfm ?DocumentID=312.

McPherson, J. Miller, Lynn Smith-Lovin, and Matthew E. Brashears. (2006). "Social Isolation in America: Changes in Core Discussion Networks over Two Decades." *American Sociological Review* 71 (3): 185–203.

Mead, M. (1966). "Marriage in Two Steps." *Redbook Magazine* (July): 48–49, 84, 86.

Mead, M. (1972). *Blackberry Winter: My Earlier Years.* New York: William Morrow.

Meadows, D. H., D. L. Meadows, J. Randers, and W. W. Behrens III. (1972). *The Limits to Growth.* New York: Universe Books.

Melton, J. G. (1989). *The Encyclopedia of American Religions,* 3rd ed. Detroit, MI: Gale Research Co.

Melton, J. G. (1996). *The Encyclopedia of American Religions,* 5th ed. Detroit, MI: Gale Research Co.

Merkyl, P. H., and N. Smart, eds. (1983). *Religion and Politics in the Modern World.* New York: New York University Press.

Merton, R. K. (1957). *Social Theory and Social Structure,* rev. ed. New York: Free Press.

Merton, R. K. (1968; orig. 1938). "Social Structure and Anomie." *American Sociological Review* 3.

Meyer, J. W., and B. Rowan. (1977). "Institutionalized Organizations: Formal Structure as Myth and Ceremony." *American Journal of Sociology* 83: 340–63.

Michels, R. (1967; orig. 1911). *Political Parties.* New York: Free Press.

Michigan Department of Community Health. (2010). "Watch Out for Date Rape Drugs." Accessed September 20, 2010. www.michigan .gov/documents/publications _date_rape_drugs_8886_7.pdf (site discontinued).

Mickelson, R. A (1990). "The Attitude-Achievement Paradox among Black Adolescents." *Sociology of Education* 63: 44–61.

Migration Policy Institute (MPI). (2007). "Annual Immigration to the United States: The Real Numbers." Accessed January 2008. www.migrationpolicy.org/pubs /FS16_USImmigration_051807 .pdf.

Milgram, S. (1963). "Behavioral Study of Obedience." *Journal of Abnormal and Social Psychology* 67: 371–78.

Mills, C. W. (1956). *The Power Elite.* New York: Oxford University Press.

Mills, C. W. (2000; orig. 1959). *The Sociological Imagination.* New York: Oxford University Press.

Mills, T. J. (1967). *The Sociology of Small Groups.* Englewood, NJ: Prentice-Hall.

Minkov, Michael, and Geert Hofstede. (2012). "Is National Culture a Meaningful Concept? Cultural Values Delineate Homogeneous National Clusters of In-Country Regions." *Cross-Cultural Research* 46 (2): 133–59.

Mintz, Steven. (2010). "American Childhood as a Social and Cultural Construct." In Barbara J. Risman, ed., *Families As They Really Are.* New York: W. W. Norton.

Mirowsky, J., and Ross, C. E. (2005). Education, Cumulative Advantage, and Health. *Ageing International* 30 (1): 27–62.

Mitchell, J. (1975). *Psychoanalysis and Feminism.* New York: Random House.

Miyazaki, Ichisada. (1981). *China's Examination Hell: The Civil Service Examinations of Imperial China.* (Conrad Schirokauer, trans). New Haven, CT: Yale University Press.

Moen, P. (1995). "A Life Course Approach to Postretirement Roles and Well-Being." In L. A. Bond, S. J. Cutler, and A. Grams, eds., *Promoting Successful and Productive Aging.* Newbury Park, CA: Sage.

Moore, G. (1990). "Structural Determinants of Men's and Women's Personal Networks." *American Sociological Review* 55: 726–35.

Moore, L. R. (1994). *Selling God: American Religion in the Marketplace of Culture.* New York: Oxford University Press.

Morin, Rich. (2012). *Rising Share of Americans See Conflict between Rich and Poor.* Washington, DC: Pew Research Center. Accessed June 18, 2012. www.pewsocial trends.org/2012/01/11/rising -share-of-americans-see-conflict -between-rich-and-poor/.

Morland, K., S. Wing, A. Diez-Roux, and C. Poole. (2002). "Neighborhood Characteristics Associated with the Location of Food Stores and Food Service Places." *American Journal of Preventive Medicine* 22 (1): 23–29.

Moynihan, D. P. (1965). *The Negro Family: A Case for National Action.* Washington, DC: U.S. Government Printing Office.

Moynihan, D. P. (1993). "Defining Deviancy Down: How We've Become Accustomed to Alarming Levels of Crime and Destructive Behavior." *American Scholar* Winter: 19–30.

Mumford, L. (1973). *Interpretations and Forecasts.* New York: Harcourt Brace Jovanovich.

Muncie, J. (1999). *Youth and Crime: A Critical Introduction.* London: Sage.

Murdock, G. P. (1949). *Social Structure.* New York: Macmillan.

Murphy, Joseph. (2012). *Homeschooling in America: Capturing and Assessing the Movement.* Thousand Oaks, CA: Sage.

Murray, C. A. (1984). *Losing Ground: American Social Policy, 1950–1980.* New York: Basic Books.

Murray, Liz. (2010). *Breaking Night: A Memoir of Forgiveness, Survival, and My Journey from Homeless to Harvard.* New York: Hyperion.

Najman, J. M. (1993). "Health and Poverty: Past, Present, and Prospects for the Future." *Social Science and Medicine* 36 (2): 157–66.

Narayan, D. (1999). *Can Anyone Hear Us? Voices from 47 Countries.* Washington, DC: World Bank Poverty Group, PREM, December.

National Alliance to End Homelessness. (2009). "Changes in Homelessness 05-07 Map." Accessed August 23, 2011. www.endhomelessness.org/content/article/detail/2797.

National Alliance to End Homelessness. (2012). "State of Homelessness in America, 2012." Washington, DC.

National Center for Education Statistics (NCES). (2005). "Digest of Education Statistics, 2004." Accessed January 20, 2006. http://nces.ed.gov/programs/digest/d04/tables/dt04_298.asp (site discontinued).

National Center for Education Statistics (NCES). (2009). "NAEP 2009 High School Transcript Study, 2009." Accessed October 19, 2012. http://nationsreportcard.gov/hsts_2009/.

National Center for Education Statistics (NCES). (2011). "Condition of Education 2011." Accessed October 19, 2012. http://nces.ed.gov/programs/coe/analysis/2010-section3b.asp (site discontinued).

National Center for Health Statistics. (2005). "Health, United States, 2005." Accessed spring 2006. www.cdc.gov/nchs/data/hus/hus05.pdf.

National Center for Health Statistics. (2008a). "National Marriage and Divorce Rate Trends." Accessed spring 2011. www.cdc.gov/nchs/nvss/mardiv_tables.htm.

National Center for Health Statistics. (2008b). "Women's Health." Accessed May 15, 2010. www.cdc.gov/nchs/fastats/womens_health.htm.

National Center for Health Statistics. (2009). "Health, United States 2009." Accessed spring 2010. www.cdc.gov/nchs/hus.htm.

National Center for Health Statistics. (2010). "Deaths: Preliminary Data from 2008." *National Vital Statistics Report* (*NVSR*) 59 (2).

National Center for Health Statistics. (2012). "Health, United States, 2012." Accessed summer 2013. www.cdc.gov/nchs/data/hus/hus12.pdf#018.

National Center on Elder Abuse (NCEA). (2005). "Fact Sheet: Elder Abuse Prevalence and Incidence." Accessed December 7, 2005. www.elderabusecenter.org/pdf/publication/FinalStatistics050331.pdf (site discontinued).

National Coalition for Homeless Veterans (NCHV). (2011). "FAQ about Homeless Veterans." Accessed August 23, 2011. www.nchv.org/background.cfm (site discontinued).

National Conference of State Legislatures (NCSL). (2011). "Legislator Demographics." Accessed spring 2013. www.ncsl.org/legislatures-elections/legisdata/legislator-demographics.aspx.

National Conference of State Legislatures (NCSL). (2013). "Defining Marriage: Defense of Marriage Acts and Same-Sex Marriage Laws." March 21. Accessed spring 2013. www.ncsl.org/issues-research/human-services/same-sex-marriage-overview.aspx.

National Coordinator for Counterterrorism (NCTb). (2007). *Jihadists and the Internet.* The Hague, The Netherlands: Ministry of Security and Justice, National Coordinator for Counterterrorism and Security. www.investigativeproject.org/documents/testimony/226.pdf

National Crime Records Bureau (NCRB). (2008). "All India Figures at a Glance–2008." Accessed spring 2011. http://ncrb.nic.in/cii2008/cii-2008/figure%20at%20a%20glance.pdf.

National Eating Disorders Association. (2002). "Statistics: Eating Disorders and Their Precursors." Accessed January, 29, 2006. www.nationaleatingdisorders.org/p.asp?WebPage_ID=286&Profile_IS=41138.

National Election Studies (NES). (2003). "The NES Guide to Public Opinion and Electoral Behavior—Voter Turnout 1948–2002." Accessed January 3, 2005. www.umich.edu/,nes/nesguide/toptable/tab6a_2.htm (site discontinued).

National Heart, Lung, and Blood Institute. (2008). "Aim for a Healthy Weight: Information for Patients and the Public." Accessed spring 2008. www.nhlbi.nih.gov/health/public/heart/obesity/lose_wt/risk.htm.

National High-Tech Crime Unit (NHTCU). (2005). "High-Tech Crime: The Impact on UK Business 2005." Accessed October 5, 2005. www.nhtcu.org/media/documents/publications/8817_Survey.pdf (site discontinued).

National Law Center on Homelessness and Poverty (NLCHP). (2004). "Key Data Concerning Homeless Persons in America," July. Accessed spring 2006. www.nlchp.org/FA_HAPIA/HomelessPersoninAmerica.pdf (site discontinued).

National Law Center on Homelessness and Poverty (NLCHP). (2009). "Indicators of Increasing Homelessness Due to the Foreclosure and Economic Crises." Accessed December 9, 2009. www.nlchp.org/content/pubs/foreclosure_effects_homelessness.pdf.

National Low Income Housing Coalition (NLIHC). (2000). "Out of Reach: The Growing Gap between Housing Costs and Income of Poor People in the United States." Washington, DC: The National Low Income Housing Coalition/Low Income Housing Information Service. Accessed January 3, 2005. www.nlihc.org/oor2000/index.htm.

National Opinion Research Center (NORC). (2001). "General Social Surveys 1972-2000: Cumulative Codebook." Storrs, CT: Roper Center for Public Opinion Research.

National Organization for Women (NOW). (2010). "The Paycheck Fairness Act: The Next Step in the Fight for Fair Pay." Accessed September 20, 2010. www.now.org /issues/economic/022709pfa.html.

National Public Radio (NPR). (2001). "Poverty in America. NPR/Kaiser/ Kennedy School Poll." Accessed spring 2013. www.npr.org /programs/specials/poll/poverty/.

National Public Radio (NPR). (2009). Is Vaccine Refusal Worth the Risk? *NPR Morning Edition.* Accessed summer 2010. www.npr.org /templates/story/story.php ?storyId=104523437.

Nederveen Pieterse, Jan. (2011). "Global Rebalancing and the East-South Turn." *Development and Change* 42 (1): 22-48.

Nesiah, D. (1997). *Discrimination with Reason? The Policy of Reservations in the United States, India and Malaysia.* New York: Oxford University Press.

Ness, R. B., and L. H. Kuller. (1999). *Health and Disease among Women: Biological and Environmental Influences.* New York: Oxford University Press.

New York City Gay and Lesbian Anti-Violence Project. (1996). "Project Annual." Accessed January 3, 2005. www.avp.org.

New York Times. (2012a). "How Obama Won Re-election: Romney's Shift Wasn't Enough." *New York Times,* November 7. Accessed March 3, 2013. www.nytimes.com /interactive/2012/11/07/us /politics/obamas-diverse-base-of -support.html?_r=0.

New York Times. (2012b). "Nuclear Power." *New York Times,* July 5. Accessed August 10, 2012. http:// topics.nytimes.com/top /news/business/energy -environment/atomic-energy /index.html.

Newman. K. S. (1999). *Falling from Grace: Downward Mobility in the Age of Affluence.* Berkeley, CA: University of California Press.

Newman, K. S. (2000). *No Shame in My Game: The Working Poor in the Inner City.* New York: Vintage.

Newman, Katherine S., and David Pedulla. (2010). "An Unequal Opportunity Recession." *The Nation,* July 19. Accessed March 1, 2013. www.thenation.com/article /36883/unequal-opportunity -recession.

Newport, Frank. (2010). "Americans' Church Attendance Inched Up in 2010." Gallup Poll, June 25. Accessed summer 2012. www .gallup.com/poll/141044 /americans-church-attendance -inches-2010.aspx.

Newport, Frank. (2011). "For First Time, Majority of Americans Favor Legal Gay Marriage." Gallup Poll, May 20. Accessed summer 2013. www.gallup.com/poll/147662 /First-Time-Majority-Americans -Favor-Legal-Gay-Marriage.aspx.

Niahh, Sonjah Stanley. (2010). *Dancehall: From Slave Ship to Ghetto.* Ottawa: University of Ottawa Press.

Nibley, Lidia. (2011). "Two Spirits." Accessed August 25, 2011. www .pbs.org/independentlens/two -spirits/resources/two-spirits -discussion.pdf.

Nie, N., and L. Ebring. (2000). "Internet and Society—A Preliminary Report." Stanford Institute for the Quantitative Study of Society (SIQSS). Accessed September 23, 2005. www.stanford.edu/group /siqss/Press_Release/Preliminary _Report.pdf (site discontinued).

Nie, N., A. Simpser, I. Stepanikova, and L. Zheng. (2004). "Ten Years after the Birth of the Internet, How Do Americans Use the Internet in Their Daily Lives?" Draft Report. Stanford University. Accessed September 23, 2005. www.stanford.edu/group/siqss /SIQSS_Time_Study_04.pdf (site discontinued).

Niebuhr, H. R. (1929). *The Social Sources of Denominationalism.* New York: Holt.

Niederberger, A., C. U. Brunner, K. Jiang, and Y. Chen. (2007). "Energy Efficiency in China—The Business Case for Mining an Untapped Resource." *Greener Management International* 50: 25–40.

Nielsen, F. (1994). "Income Inequality and Industrial Development: Dualism Revisited." *American Sociological Review 59,* 654–677.

Nielsen Company. (2001). "Internet Access for Blue-Collar Workers Spikes 52 Percent, According to Nielsen//Net Ratings." Accessed May 3, 2001. http://209.249.142.22/press _releases/PDF/pr_010412.pdf (site discontinued).

Nielsen Company. (2011). "State of the Media: The Social Media Report Q3." Accessed spring 2013. www .nielsen.com/us/en/reports/2011 /social-media-report-q3.html.

Nielsen Company. (2012). "State of the Media: The Social Media Report." Accessed spring 2013. www .nielsen.com/content/dam /corporate/us/en/reports -downloads/2012-Reports/The -Social-Media-Report-2012.pdf.

Nien Hsing. (2007). "Global Distribution: Nien Hsing Textile Co. Ltd." Accessed December 2007. www .nht.com.tw/en/about-2.htm (site discontinued).

Nien Hsing. (2012). "Our Customers." Accessed March 18, 2013. www .nhjeans.com/en/client.php.

Nolan, K, and J. Anyon. (2004). "Learning to Do Time: Willis' Cultural Reproduction Model in an Era of Deindustrialization, Globalization, and the Mass Incarceration of People of Color." In N. Dolby, G. Dimitriadis, and P. Willis, eds., *Learning to Labor in New Times.* New York: Routledge.

Nordberg, J. (2010). "Afghan Boys Are Prized, So Girls Live the Part." *New York Times,* September 21. Accessed September 22, 2010. www.nytimes.com/2010/09/21 /world/asia/21gender.html.

Nordhaus, W. D. (1975). "The Political Business Cycle." *Review of Economic Studies* 42: 169–90.

Norris, P., and R. Inglehart. (2004). *Sacred and Secular: Religion and Politics Worldwide.* New York: Cambridge University Press.

NPR/Kaiser/Kennedy School Poll, 2001. "Poverty in America." Accessed August 23, 2011. www .npr.org/programs/specials/poll /poverty/staticresults1.html.

Nugent, Colleen. (2012). "Parents' Preferences for Mixed-Sex Children: Motivations, Fertility Behavior, and Psychological Well-Being." Unpublished doctoral dissertation. New Brunswick, NJ: Rutgers University.

Oakes, J. (1985). *Keeping Track: How Schools Structure Inequality.* New Haven, CT: Yale University Press.

Oakes, J. (1990). *Multiplying Inequalities: The Effects of Race, Social*

Class, and Tracking on Opportunities to Learn Mathematics and Science. Santa Monica, CA: Rand.

Oakley, A. (1974). The Sociology of Housework. New York: Pantheon.

O'Connor, Anahad. (2011). "Surgeon General Calls for Health over Hair." New York Times, August 25. Accessed October 1, 2012. http://well.blogs.nytimes.com/2011/08/25/surgeon-general-calls-for-health-over-hair/.

O'Connor, Michael. (2012). "Boy or Girl? Only the Cake Knows." Omaha World-Herald, January 17. Accessed March 5, 2013. www.omaha.com/article/20120117/LIVING/701179974.

Offe, C. (1984). Contradictions of the Welfare State. Cambridge, MA: MIT Press.

Offe, C. (1985). Disorganized Capitalism. Cambridge, MA: MIT Press.

Ogbu, J. U., and S. Fordham. (1986). "Black Students' School Success: Coping with the 'Burden of Acting White.'" Urban Review 18: 176–206.

Ogburn, W. F. (1930). "The Folkways of a Scientific Sociology." Publications of the American Sociological Society 24: 1–11.

Ogden, C. L., M. D. Carroll, L. R. Curtin, M. A. McDowell, C. J. Tabak, and K. M. Flegal. (2006). "Prevalence of Overweight and Obesity in the United States, 1999–2004." Journal of the American Medical Association 495: 1549–55.

Ogden, C. L., M. D. Carroll, B. K. Kit, and K. M. Flegal. (2012). "Prevalence of Obesity and Trends in Body Mass Index among U.S. Children and Adolescents, 1999–2010." Journal of the American Medical Association 307: 483–90.

O'Hare, W., and M. Mather. (2008). "Child Poverty Is Highest in Rural Counties in U.S." Population Reference Bureau. Accessed spring 2011. www.prb.org/Articles/2008/childpoverty.aspx.

Ohmae, K. (1995). The End of the Nation-State: How Regional Economies Will Soon Reshape the World. New York: Simon and Schuster.

Oliver, M. L., and T. M. Shapiro. (1995). Black Wealth/White Wealth: A New Perspective on Racial Inequality. New York: Routledge.

Oliver, M. L., and T. M. Shapiro. (2006). Black Wealth/White Wealth, 2nd ed. New York: Routledge.

Olshansky, S. J., T. Antonucci, L. Berkman et al. (2012). "Differences in Life Expectancy Due to Race and Educational Differences Are Widening, and Many May Not Catch Up." Health Affairs 31 (8): 1803–13.

Olshansky, S. J., B. A. Carnes, and D. Grahn. (2003). "Biological Evidence for Limits to the Duration of Life." Biogerontology 4 (1): 31–45.

Olson, M. H. (1989). "Work at Home for Computer Professionals: Current Attitudes and Future Prospects." ACM Transactions on Information Systems 7 (4): 317–38.

Olson, M. H., and S. B. Primps. (1984). "Working at Home with Computers." Journal of Social Issues 40 (3): 97–112.

O'Neill, Greg. (2009). "The Baby Boom Age Wave: Population Success or Tsunami?" In Robert B. Hudson, ed., Boomer Bust? Economic and Political Issues of the Graying Society (pp. 3–22). Westport, CT: Praeger Press.

Online Schools. (2011). "Obsessed with Facebook." Accessed summer 2012. www.onlineschools.org/visual-academy/facebook-obsession/ (site discontinued).

Oplinger, Douglas, and Dennis J. Willard. (2004). "Claims of Academic Success Rely on Anecdote, Flawed Data Analysis." Akron Beacon Journal, November 15.

Oppenheimer, V. K. (1970). The Female Labor Force in the United States. Westport, CT: Greenwood Press.

Orfield, G. (2005). Segregation and Its Consequences: Race and Regionalism. Minneapolis, MN: Institute on Race and Poverty.

Organisation for Economic Co-operation and Development (OECD). (2005). "Factbook: Economic, Environmental, and Social Statistics." Accessed spring 2006. http://oberon.sourceoecd.org/vl=820148/cl=43/nw=1/rpsv/fact2005/ (site discontinued).

Organisation for Economic Co-operation and Development (OECD). (2006). "OECD Territorial Reviews: Competitive Cities in the Global Economy." Accessed spring 2008. www.oecd.org/document/2/0,3343,en_2649_34413_37801602_1_1_1_37429,00.html.

Organisation for Economic Co-operation and Development (OECD). (2009). OECD Programme for International Student Assessment (PISA). "PISA 2009 Results: What Students Know and Can Do." Paris: OECD Publishing. www.oecd.org/pisa/.

Organisation for Economic Co-operation and Development (OECD). (2010). "Income Inequality." OECD Factbook 2010: Economic, Environmental and Social Statistics. Paris: OECD Publishing. Accessed spring 2013. www.oecd-ilibrary.org/economics/oecd-factbook-2010/income-inequality-table_fact book-2010-table254-en.

Organisation for Economic Co-operation and Development (OECD). (2011). Education at a Glance 2011: OECD Indicators. Paris: OECD Publishing. Accessed October 9, 2012. www.oecd-ilibrary.org/education/education-at-a-glance-2011_eag-2011-en.

Orloff, A. S. (1993). The Politics of Pensions: A Comparative Analysis of Britain, Canada, and the United States, 1880–1940. Madison: University of Wisconsin Press.

Padavic, I., and B. Reskin. (2002). Women and Men at Work, 2nd ed. Thousand Oaks, CA: Pine Forge Press.

Pahl, J. (1989). Money and Marriage. London: Macmillan.

Palazzolo, J. (2013). "Cost of Housing Federal Prisoners Continues to Rise." Wall Street Journal. Accessed spring 2013. http://blogs.wsj.com/law/2013/03/15/cost-to-house-federal-prisoners-continues-to-rise/.

Paludi, M. A., and R. B. Barickman. (1991). Academic and Workplace Sexual Harassment: A Resource Manual. Albany, NY: State University of New York Press.

Parekh, B. (2010). "What Is Multiculturalism?" In Montserrat Guibernau and John Rex, eds., The Ethnicity Reader: Nationalism, Multiculturalism, and Migration, 2nd ed. (pp. 238-41). Malden, MA: Polity Press.

Park, R. E. (1952). Human Communities: The City and Human Ecology. New York: Free Press.

Parker, R., and R. P. Appelbaum. (2012). "The Chinese Century? Some Policy Implications of China's Move Toward 'Indigenous Innovation.'" In Barbara Herr Harthorn and John Mohr, eds., The Social Life of

Nanotechnology (pp. 134–65).
New York: Routledge.

Parker, Kim. (2012). *The Boomerang Generation Feeling OK about Living with Mom and Dad.* Washington, DC: Pew Social and Demographic Trends. Accessed August 7, 2012. www.pewsocialtrends.org/2012/03/15/the-boomerang-generation/.

Parsons, T. (1964; orig. 1951). *The Social System.* Glencoe, IL: Free Press.

Parsons, T. (1960). "Towards a Healthy Maturity." *Journal of Health and Social Behavior* 1: 163–73.

Parsons, T., and R. F. Bales. (1955). *Family, Socialization, and Interaction Process.* Glencoe, IL: Free Press.

Passel, J. S., and D. Cohn. (2008). "U.S. Population Projections: 2005–2050," February 11. Washington, DC: Pew Research Center: Social and Demographic Trends. Accessed spring 2011. http://pewhispanic.org/files/reports/85.pdf.

Pattillo-McCoy, M. (1999). *Black Picket Fences: Privilege and Peril among the Black Middle Class.* Chicago: University of Chicago Press.

Paul, D. Y. (1985). *Women in Buddhism: Images of the Feminine in the Mahayana Tradition.* Berkeley, CA: University of California Press.

PBS *NewsHour.* (2000). "Background: AOL–Time Warner Merger." January 10. http://www.pbs.org/newshour/bb/business/jan-june00/aol_01-10.html

PBS *NewsHour.* (2003). "AOL Time Warner Posts Record $99 Billion Annual Loss." Online NewsHour update, January 30. Accessed fall 2010. www.pbs.org/newshour/updates/aoltw_01-30-03.html.

PBS *NewsHour.* (2009). "Cyber Crime and Spying Threaten National Security." Accessed spring 2011. www.pbs.org/newshour/extra/features/us/jan-june09/cybercrime_04-10.html.

Pear, Robert. (2011). "Reshaping Medicare Brings Hard Choices." *New York Times,* April 12. Accessed August 10, 2012. www.nytimes.com/2011/04/13/us/politics/13medicare.html?_r=1&pagewanted=print.

Pearce, F. (1976). *Crimes of the Powerful: Marxism, Crime, and Deviance.* London: Pluto Press.

Peralta, Eyder. (2013). "Court Overturns DOMA, Sidesteps Broad Gay Marriage Ruling." NPR. Accessed July 1, 2013. www.npr.org/blogs/thetwo-way/2013/06/26/195857796/supreme-court-strikes-down-defense-of-marriage-act.

Peterson, R. (1996). "A Re-Evaluation of the Economic Consequences of Divorce." *American Sociological Review* 61: 528–36.

Petrovic, M., and G. G. Hamilton. (2006). "Making Global Markets: Wal-Mart and Its Suppliers." In N. Lichtenstein, ed., *Wal-Mart: The Face of Twenty-First-Century Capitalism.* New York: New Press.

Pew Research Center. (2005). "Internet: The Mainstreaming of Online Life." Pew Internet and American Life Project. Accessed spring 2006. www.pewinternet.org/pdfs/Internet_Status_2005.pdf (site discontinued).

Pew Research Center. (2008). "U.S. Religious Landscape Survey." Pew Forum on Religion and Public Life, February. Accessed spring 2011. http://religions.pewforum.org/reports.

Pew Research Center. (2009a). "Faith in Flux: Changes in Religious Affiliation in the U.S." Pew Forum on Religion and Public Life, April. Accessed spring 2011. http://pewforum.org/uploadedfiles/Topics/Religious_Affiliation/fullreport.pdf.

Pew Research Center. (2009b). "Mapping the Global Muslim Population." Pew Forum on Religion and Public Life, October. Accessed spring 2011. http://pewforum.org/uploadedfiles/Topics/Demographics/Muslimpopulation.pdf.

Pew Research Center. (2009c). "Online Politics Reserved for the Rich." Pew Internet and American Life Survey, September 2. Accessed spring 2011. www.pewinternet.org/Media-Mentions/2009/Online-politics-reserved-for-rich.a.

Pew Research Center. (2009d). "Pew Internet Project Data Memo." Pew Internet and American Life Survey, January 28. Accessed spring 2011 http://pewinternet.org/~/media//Files/Reports/2009/PIP_Generations_2009.pdf.

Pew Research Center. (2010a). "Minorities More Likely to Use the Mobile Web." Pew Internet and American Life Survey, July 7. Accessed spring 2011. www.pewinternet.org/Media-Mentions/2010/The-Hill-Minorities-more-likely-to-use-mobile-web.aspx.

Pew Research Center. (2010b). "Prison Count 2010: State Population Declines for the First Time in 38 Years." Pew Center on the States. Accessed spring 2013. www.pewstates.org/research/reports/prison-count-2010-85899372907.

Pew Research Center. (2010c). "Religion among the Millennials: Less Religiously Active Than Older Americans, but Fairly Traditional in Other Ways." Forum on Religion and Public Life, February 17. Accessed summer 2012. www.pewforum.org/uploadedFiles/Topics/Demographics/Age/millennials-report.pdf.

Pew Research Center. (2011a). "American Muslims: No Signs in Growth in Alienation or Extremism." Pew Forum on Religion and Public Life, August 30. Accessed spring 2013. www.people-press.org/files/legacy-pdf/Muslim-American-Report.pdf.

Pew Research Center. (2011b). "Common Concerns about Muslim Extremism: Muslim-Western Tensions Persist." Pew Global Attitudes Project, July 21. Accessed spring 2013. www.pewglobal.org/files/2011/07/Pew-Global-Attitudes-Muslim-Western-Relations-FINAL-FOR-PRINT-July-21-2011.pdf.

Pew Research Center. (2011c). "The Future of the Global Muslim Population: Projections for 2010–2030." Pew Forum on Religion and Public Life, January 27. Accessed summer 2012. www.pewforum.org/uploadedFiles/Topics/Religious_Affiliation/Muslim/FutureGlobalMuslimPopulation-WebPDF-Feb10.pdf.

Pew Research Center. (2011d). "Global Survey of Evangelical Protestant Leaders." Pew Forum on Religion and Public Life, June 22. Accessed spring 2013. www.pewforum.org/uploadedFiles/Topics/Religious_Affiliation/Christian/Evangelical_Protestant_Churches/Global%20Survey%20of%20Evan.%20Prot.%20Leaders.pdf.

Pew Research Center. (2012a). "A Closer Look at Gadget Ownership: Demographics." Pew Internet and American Life Project, June 28.

Accessed summer 2012. http://
pewinternet.org/Infographics
/2012/A-Closer-Look-at-Gadget
-Ownership.aspx.

Pew Research Center. (2012b).
"Global Opinion of Obama Slips,
International Policies Faulted:
Drone Strikes Widely Opposed."
Global Attitudes Project (June 13).
Accessed summer 2012. www
.pewglobal.org/files/2012/06
/Pew-Global-Attitudes-U.S.-Image
-Report-FINAL-June-13-2012.pdf.

Pew Research Center. (2012c). "The
Global Religious Landscape." Pew
Forum on Religion and Public
Life. Accessed summer 2013. www
.pewforum.org/uploadedFiles
/Topics/Religious_Affiliation
/globalReligion-full.pdf.

Pew Research Center. (2012d). "Inter-
net Use and Home Broadband
Connections: Demographics."
Pew Internet and American Life
Project, July 24. Accessed summer
2012. http://pewinternet.org
/Infographics/2012/Internet
-Use-and-Home-Broadband
-Connections.aspx.

Pew Research Center. (2012e). "Most
Muslims Want Democracy, Personal Freedoms, and Islam in Public Life." Pew Forum on Religion
and Public Life, July 10. Accessed
spring 2013. www.pewglobal.org
/files/2012/07/Pew-Global
-Attitudes-Project-Arab-Spring
-Report-FINAL-Tuesday-July-10
-2012.pdf.

Pew Research Center (2012f).
"Smartphone Ownership Update:
2012." Pew Internet and American
Life Project. Accessed summer
2012. http://pewinternet.org
/Reports/2012/Smartphone-Update
-Sept-2012/Findings.aspx.

Pew Research Center. (2012g). "The
World's Muslims: Unity and
Diversity." Pew Forum on Religion
and Public Life, August 9. Accessed
summer 2012. www.pewforum
.org/Muslim/the-worlds-muslims
-unity-and-diversity-executive
-summary.aspx.

Pew Research Center. (2013). "Gay
Marriage Around the World." Pew
Forum on Religion and Public Life,
June. Accessed July 1, 2013. www
.pewforum.org/Gay-Marriage
-and-Homosexuality/Gay
-Marriage-Around-the-World
-2013.aspx#mexico.

Pew Research Center for the People
and the Press. (2003). "The 2004

Political Landscape: Evenly
Divided and Increasingly Polarized." November 5. Accessed
January 3, 2005. http://people-
press.org/reports/display.
php3?ReportID5196 (site
discontinued).

Pew Research Center for the People
and the Press. (2005). "GOP Makes
Gains among the Working Class,
While Democrats Hold On to the
Union Vote," August 2. Accessed
spring 2011. http://people-press
.org/commentary/?analysisid=114
(site discontinued).

Pew Research Center for the People and
the Press. (2009). "Mixed Views
of Economic Policies and Health
Care Reform Persist," October 8.
Accessed spring 2011. http://people
-press.org/report/551/.

Pew Research Center for the People
and the Press. (2010a). "Growing
Number of Americans Say Obama
Is a Muslim," August 19. Accessed
spring 2011. http://people-press
.org/report/645/.

Pew Research Center for the People
and the Press. (2010b). "The People
and Their Government: Distrust,
Discontent, Anger, and Partisan
Rancor," April 18. Accessed spring
2011. http://people-press.org
/reports/pdf/606.pdf.

Pew Research Center for the
People and the Press. (2011a).
"Fewer Are Angry at Government,
but Discontent Remains High,"
March 3. Accessed summer 2012.
www.people-press.org/2011/03
/03/fewer-are-angry-at
-government-but-discontent
-remains-high/.

Pew Research Center for the People
and the Press. (2011b). "Frustration with Congress Could Hurt
Republican Incumbents." Accessed
spring 2013. www.people-press
.org/2011/12/15/frustration-with
-congress-could-hurt-republican
-incumbents/.

Pew Research Center for the People
and the Press. (2011c). "Occupy
Wall Street and Inequality,"
December 15. Accessed summer
2012. www.people-press.org/2011
/12/15/section-2-occupy-wall
-street-and-inequality/.

Pew Research Center for the People
and the Press. (2011d). "Public
Wants Changes in Entitlements,
Not Changes in Benefits: GOP
Divided over Benefit Reductions."
Accessed August 9, 2012. http://

pewresearch.org/pubs/2051
/medicare-medicaid-social
-security-republicans
-entitlements-budget-deficit.

Pew Research Center for the People
and the Press. (2012a). "Continued
Majority Support for Death Penalty." Accessed summer 2012.
www.people-press.org/2012/01
/06/continued-majority-support
-for-death-penalty/.

Pew Research Center for the People
and the Press. (2012b). "The Rise of
Asian Americans." Pew Social
and Demographic Trends.
Accessed September 17, 2012. www
.pewsocialtrends.org/files/2012
/06/SDT-The-Rise-of-Asian
-Americans-Full-Report.pdf.

Pew Research Hispanic Center. (2010a). "Hispanics, High
School Dropouts and the GED,"
May 13. Accessed summer
2010. www.pewhispanic.org
/2010/05/13/hispanics-high-school
-dropouts-and-the-ged/.

Pew Research Hispanic Center.
(2010b). "Latinos by Country of
Origin." Accessed summer 2010.
http://pewhispanic.org/.

Pew Research Hispanic Center.
(2011a). "Hispanic Poverty Rate
Highest in New Supplemental
Census Measure." Accessed summer 2012. www.pewhispanic.org
/2011/11/08/hispanic-poverty
-rate-highest-in-new-supplemental
-census-measure/.

Pew Research Hispanic Center.
(2011b). "Hispanics Account for
More Than Half of Nation's Growth
in Past Decade." Accessed spring
2013. www.pewhispanic.org
/2011/03/24/hispanics-account
-for-more-than-half-of-nations
-growth-in-past-decade/.

Pew Research Hispanic Center.
(2012a). "Net Migration from
Mexico Falls to Zero, and Perhaps
Less." Accessed summer 2012.
www.pewhispanic.org/files
/2012/04/Mexican-migrants
-report_final.pdf.

Pew Research Hispanic Center. (2012b). "The 10 Largest
Hispanic Origin Groups: Characteristics, Rankings, Top Counties."
Accessed summer 2012. www
.pewhispanic.org/2012/06/27
/the-10-largest-hispanic-origin
-groups-characteristics-rankings
-top-counties/.

Pine, J. (1999). *Mass Customization:
The New Frontier in Business Com-*

petition. Cambridge, MA: Harvard Business School Press.

Pinquart, M., and S. Sorensen. (2006). "Gender Differences in Caregiver Stressors, Social Resources, and Health: An Updated Meta-Analysis." *Journals of Gerontology, Series B (Psychological Sciences and Social Sciences)* 61 (1): 33–45.

Pintor, R. L., and M. Gratschew. (2002). "Voter Turnout since 1945: A Global Report." Stockholm, Sweden: International Institute for Democracy and Electoral Assistance (International IDEA). Accessed January 3, 2005. www .idea.int/publications/vt/upload /VT_screenopt_2002.pdf.

Piore, M. J., and C. F. Sabel. (1984). *The Second Industrial Divide: Possibilities for Prosperity*. New York: Basic Books.

Pitts, Steven. (2011). "Research Brief: Black Workers and the Public Sector." Berkeley, CA: University of California–Berkeley Center for Labor Research and Education. Accessed June 18, 2012. http:// laborcenter.berkeley.edu/black workers/blacks_public_sector11.pdf.

Pollak, O. (1950). *The Criminality of Women*. Philadelphia: University of Pennsylvania Press.

Pollard, Kelvin. (2011). *The Gender Gap in College Enrollment and Graduation*. Washington, DC: Population Reference Bureau. Accessed October 19, 2012. www.prb.org/Articles/2011 /gender-gap-in-education.aspx.

Polletta, F., and J. M. Jasper. (2001). "Collective Identity and Social Movements." *Annual Review of Sociology* 27: 283–305.

Popenoe, D. (1993). "American Family Decline, 1960–1990: A Review and Appraisal." *Journal of Marriage and Family* 55: 527–55.

Popenoe, D. (1996). *Life without Father: Compelling New Evidence That Fatherhood and Marriage Are Indispensable for the Good of Children and Society*. New York: Martin Kessler Books.

Population Reference Bureau. (2010). "2010 World Population Data Sheet." August 2, 2010. www.prb .org/Publications/Datasheets /2010/2010wpds.aspx.

Population Reference Bureau. (2011a). "2011 World Population Data Sheet." Accessed summer 2012. www .prb.org/pdf11/2011population -data-sheet_eng.pdf.

Population Reference Bureau. (2011b). "PRB Reports on America: First Results from the 2010 Census." Accessed summer 2012. www.prb .org/pdf11/reports-on-america -2010-census.pdf.

Potter, K. H. (1992). "Hinduism." *The American Academic Encyclopedia* (online ed.). Danbury, CT: Grolier Electronic.

Powell, M. (2009). "Bank Accused of Pushing Mortgage Deals on Blacks." *New York Times*, June 6. Accessed spring 2011. www .nytimes.com/2009/06/07/us /07baltimore.html?pagewanted =1&_r=1.

Powell, W. W., and P. Brantley. (1992). "Competitive Cooperation in Biotechnology: Learning through Networks?" In N. Nohria and R. Eccles, eds., *Networks and Organizations: Structure, Form and Action*. Boston: Harvard Business School Press.

Powell, W. W., K. W. Koput, and L. Smith-Doerr. (1996). "Interorganizational Collaboration and the Locus of Innovation: Networks of Learning in Biotechnology." *Administration Science Quarterly* 41.

Prebisch, R. (1967). *Hacia Una Dinamica del Desarollo Latino-americano*. Montevideo, Uruguay: Ediciones de la Banda Oriental.

Prebisch, R. (1971). "Change and Development—Latin America's Great Task." Report Submitted to the Inter-American Bank. New York: Praeger.

President's Commission on Organized Crime. (1986). "Records of Hearings, June 24–26, 1985." Washington, DC: U.S. Government Printing Office.

Provenzo, E. F., Jr. (1991). *Video Kids: Making Sense of Nintendo*. Cambridge, MA: Harvard University Press.

Puentes, R., and D. Warren (2006). "One-Fifth of America: A Comprehensive Guide to America's First Suburbs." Washington, DC: Metropolitan Policy Program, The Brookings Institution.

Quadagno, J. (1989). "Generational Equity and the Politics of the Welfare State." *Politics and Society* 17: 353–76.

Quah, D. (1999). *The Weightless Economy in Economic Development*. London: Centre for Economic Performance.

Ramirez, F. O., and J. Boli. (1987). "The Political Construction of Mass Schooling: European Origins and Worldwide Institutionalism." *Sociology of Education* 60.

Rampell, Catherine. (2009). "As Lay-offs Surge, Women May Pass Men in Job Force." *New York Times*, February 5. Accessed September 16, 2012. www.nytimes .com/2009/02/06/business /06women.html.

Ranis, G. (1996). *Will Latin America Now Put a Stop to "Stop-and-Go"?* New Haven, CT: Yale University, Economic Growth Center.

Ranis, G., and S. A. Mahmood. (1992). *The Political Economy of Development Policy Change*. Cambridge, MA: Blackwell.

Reich, R. (1991). *The Work of Nations: Preparing Ourselves for 21st Century Capitalism*. New York: Knopf.

Renzetti, C., and D. Curran. (1995). *Women, Men, and Society*, 3rd ed. Needham, MA: Allyn and Bacon.

Reporters without Borders. (2010). "2010: 116 Netizens Imprisoned." Accessed spring 2011. http://en.rsf .org/press-freedom-barometer -netizens-imprisoned.html?annee =2010.

Reskin, B., and P. A. Roos. (1990). *Job Queues, Gender Queues: Explaining Women's Inroads into Male Occupations*. Philadelphia: Temple University Press.

Reuter, Peter, and Victoria Greenfield. (2001). "Measuring Global Drug Markets: How Good Are the Numbers and Why Should We Care about Them?" *World Economics* 2 (4).

Reuters. (2011). "Casey Anthony Is Most Hated Person in America: Poll." Reuters, August 10, 2011. Accessed October 8, 2012. www.reuters.com/article/2011 /08/10/us-caseyanthony -idUSTRE77934O20110810.

Rhoades, Galena K., Scott M. Stanley, and Howard J. Markman. (2009). "Couples' Reasons for Cohabitation: Associations with Individual Well-Being and Relationship Quality." *Journal of Family Issues* 30: 233–58.

Rice, Andrew. (2012). "A Scorsese in Lagos: The Making of Nigeria's Film Industry." *New York Times*, February 23.

Richardson, D., and H. May. (1999). "Deserving Victims? Sexual Status and the Social Construction of Violence." *Sociological Review* 47: 308–31.

Richardson, S. A., N. Goodman, A. H. Hastorf, and S. M. Dornbusch. (1961). "Cultural Uniformity in Reaction to Physical Disabilities." *American Sociological Review* 26: 241–47.

Riley, M. W., A. Foner, and J. Waring. (1988). "Sociology of Age." In N. J. Smelser, ed., *Handbook of Sociology*. Newbury Park, CA: Sage.

Risen, J., and E. Lichtblau. (2005). "Bush Lets U.S. Spy on Callers without Courts." *New York Times*, December 16.

Ritzer, G. (1993). *The McDonaldization of Society*. Newbury Park, CA: Pine Forge Press.

Roach, S. S. (2005). "The New Macro of Globalization." *Global: Daily Economic Comment*, June 6.

Roberts, S. (1995). "Women's Work: What's New, What Isn't." *New York Times*, April 27, p. B6.

Robinson, W. I. (2001). "Social Theory and Globalization: The Rise of a Transnational State." *Theory and Society* 30 (2): 157–200.

Robinson, W. I. (2004). *A Theory of Global Capitalism: Production, Class and State in a Transnational World*. Baltimore, MD: Johns Hopkins University Press.

Rocheleau, M. (2010). "Senior Citizens Carve Their Own Niche with Laptops and Facebook." *Christian Science Monitor*, July 24. Accessed August 1, 2010. www.csmonitor .com/Innovation/Tech/2010/0724 /Senior-citizens-carve-their-own -niche-with-laptops-and -Facebook.

Rodriguez, C. D. (2004). "The Immigrant Contribution." *La Prensa San Diego*, June 11. Accessed spring 2006. www.laprensa-sandiego.org /archieve/june11–04/imigrant .htm (site discontinued).

Roof, W. C. (1993). *A Generation of Seekers: The Spiritual Journeys of the Baby Boom Generation*. San Francisco: Harper San Francisco.

Roof, W. C. (1999). *Spiritual Marketplace: Baby Boomers and the Remaking of American Religion*. Princeton, NJ: Princeton University Press.

Roof, W. C., J. W. Carroll, and D. A. Roozen, eds. (1995). *The Post-War Generation and Establishment Religion: Cross-Cultural Perspectives*. Boulder, CO: Westview Press.

Roof, W. C., and W. McKinney. (1990). *American Mainline Religion: Its Changing Shape and Future Prospects*. New Brunswick, NJ: Rutgers University Press.

Roos, P., and B. Reskin. (1992). "Occupational Desegregation in the 1970s—Integration and Economic Equity." *Sociological Perspectives* 35: 69–91.

Rosen, David. (2008). "Rape as an Instrument of Total War." *Counterpunch*. Accessed spring 2013. www.counterpunch .org/2008/04/04/rape-as-an -instrument-of-total-war/.

Rosenau, J. N. (1997). *Along the Domestic-Foreign Frontier: Exploring Governance in a Turbulent World*. Cambridge, UK: Cambridge University Press.

Rosenfeld, Michael J. (2010). "Nontraditional Families and Childhood Progress through School." *Demography* 47: 755–75.

Rosenstock, I. (1974). "Historical Origins of the Health Belief Model." *Health Education Monographs* 2 (4).

Rosenthal, A. M. (1999). *Thirty-Eight Witnesses: The Kitty Genovese Case*. Berkeley, CA: University of California Press.

Rosenthal, E., and A. C. Revkin. (2007). "Science Panel Calls Global Warming "Unequivocal." *New York Times*, February 3.

Rosin, Hannah. (2012). "Who Wears the Pants in This Economy?" *New York Times*, August 30. Accessed September 10, 2012. www.nytimes .com/2012/09/02/magazine/who -wears-the-pants-in-this -economy.html?pagewanted=all.

Rossi, A. (1973). "The First Woman Sociologist: Harriett Martineau." In the *Feminist Papers: from Adams to de Beauvoir*. New York: Columbia University Press.

Rostow, W. W. (1961). *The Stages of Economic Growth*. Cambridge, UK: Cambridge University Press.

Rothenberg, P. (2007). *Race, Class and Gender in the United States*, 7th ed. New York: Worth.

Rothschild, J. (2000). "Creating a Just and Democratic Workplace: More Engagement, Less Hierarchy." *Contemporary Sociology: Utopian Visions: Engaged Sociologies for the 21st Century* 29 (1): 195–213.

Rousselle, R. (1999). "Defining Ancient Greek Sexuality. *Digital Archives of Psychohistory* 26 (4). Accessed January 11, 2005. www.geocities

.com/kidhistory/ja/defining.htm (site discontinued).

Rowe, R. H., and R. L. Kahn. (1987). "Human Aging: Usual and Successful." *Science* 237: 10143–49.

Rubin, L. B. (1990). *Erotic Wars: What Happened to the Sexual Revolution?* New York: Farrar, Straus and Giroux.

Rubinstein, W. D. (1986). *Wealth and Inequality in Britain*. Winchester, MA: Faber and Faber.

Rudé, G. (1964). *The Crowd in History: A Study of Popular Disturbances in France and England, 1730–1848*. New York: Wiley.

Rudner, Lawrence. (1999). "Scholastic Achievement and Demographic Characteristics of Home Schooled Students in 1998." *Educational Policy Analysis Archive* 7 (8).

Russell, John. (2012). "Internet Usage Surges 11% in China." *USA Today*, Tech Section, July 19. Accessed summer 2012. www .usatoday.com/tech/news /story/2012-07-19/china-internet -usage/56329450/1.

Rutter, M., and H. Giller (1984). *Juvenile Delinquency: Trends and Perspectives*. New York: Guilford Press.

Ryan, T. (1985). "The Roots of Masculinity." In A. Metcalf and M. Humphries, eds., *Sexuality of Men*. London: Pluto.

Saad, L. (2007). "Tolerance for Gay Rights at High-Water Mark." Gallup News Service, May 29. Accessed February 17, 2008. www.gallup.com/poll/27694 /Tolerance-Gay-Rights -HighWater-Mark.aspx.

Saad, L. (2009). "Churchgoing among U.S. Catholics Slides to Tie Protestants." Gallup, April 9. Accessed August 24, 2009. www .gallup.com/poll/117382/church -going-among-catholics-slides-tie -protestants.aspx.

Sachs, J. (2000). "A New Map of the World." *The Economist*, June 22, 81–83.

Sackmann, R., and M. Wingens. (2003). "From Transitions to Trajectories: Sequence Types." In W. R. Heinz, ed., *Social Dynamics of the Life Course: Transitions, Institutions, and Interrelations*. New York: Aldine de Gruyter.

Sadker, M., and D. Sadker. (1994). *Failing at Fairness*. New York: Scribner.

Saguy, Abigail. (2012). *What's Wrong with Fat?* New York: Oxford University Press.

Sahliyeh, E., ed. (1990). *Religious Resurgence and Politics in the Contemporary World.* Albany, NY: State University of New York Press.

Saks, M., ed. (1992). *Alternative Medicine in Britain.* Oxford, UK: Clarendon.

Salganik, Matthew J., Peter S. Dodds, and Duncan J. Watts. (2006). "Experimental Study of Inequality and Unpredictability in an Artificial Cultural Market." *Science* 311 (5762): 854–56.

Sallie Mae. (2012). *How America Pays for College 2012: Sallie Mae's National Study of College Students and Parents.* Newark, DE: Sallie Mae, Inc.

Sampson, R. J., and J. Cohen. (1988). "Deterrent Effects of the Police on Crime: A Replication and Theoretical Extension." *Law and Society Review* 22 (1).

Sandefur, G., and C. Liebler. (1997). "The Demography of American Indian Families." *Population Research and Policy Review* 16: 95–114.

Sarkisian, N., and N. Gerstel. (2004). "Kin Support among Blacks and Whites: Race and Family Organization." *American Sociological Review* 69: 812–37.

Sartre, J. (1965; orig. 1948). *Anti-Semite and Jew.* New York: Schocken Books.

Sassen, S. (1991). *The Global City: New York, London, Tokyo.* Princeton, NJ: Princeton University Press.

Sassen, S. (1996). *Losing Control: Sovereignty in the Age of Globalization.* New York: Columbia University Press.

Sassen, S. (1998). *Globalization and Its Discontents.* New York: New Press.

Sassen, S. (2005). *Denationalization: Territory, Authority and Rights.* Princeton, NJ: Princeton University Press.

Sassler, S. (2004). "The Process of Entering in Cohabitating Unions." *Journal of Marriage and Family* 66: 491–505.

Savage, D. G. (1998). "Same-Sex Harassment Illegal, Says High Court." *Los Angeles Times*, March 5.

Savitz, E. (2012). "China's Mobile Market Tops 1 Billion Subs; Bullish for Apple." Forbes.com, April 27,

2012. Accessed summer 2013. www .forbes.com/sites/ericsavitz/2012 /04/27/chinas-mobile-market -tops-1-billion-subs-bullish-for -apple/.

Sayers, J. (1986). *Sexual Contradiction: Psychology, Psychoanalysis, and Feminism.* New York: Methuen.

Schaie, K. W. (1983). *Longitudinal Studies of Adult Psychological Development.* New York: Guilford Press.

Schaie, K. W., and S. L. Willis. (2010). *Handbook of the Psychology of Aging*, 7th ed. New York: Academic Press.

Scheff, T. (1966). *Being Mentally Ill.* Chicago: Aldine.

Schmidt, R. (1980). *Exploring Religion.* Belmont, CA: Wadsworth.

Schmidt, Roger, Gerald Carney, Gene Sager, and Albert Muller. (2005). *Patterns of Religion*, 2nd ed. New York: Wadsworth Publishing.

Schneider, Friedrich, and Dominik Enste. (2002). "Hiding in the Shadows: The Growth of the Underground Economy." *International Monetary Fund*, March. Accessed spring 2013. www.imf.org /external/pubs/ft/issues /issues30/index.htm#3.

Schumpeter, J. (1983; orig. 1942). *Capitalism, Socialism, and Democracy.* Magnolia, MA: Peter Smith.

Schwartz, G. (1970). *Sect Ideologies and Social Status.* Chicago: University of Chicago Press.

Schwarz, J. E., and T. J. Volgy. (1992). *The Forgotten Americans.* New York: W. W. Norton.

Scott, S., and D. Morgan. (1993). "Bodies in a Social Landscape." In S. Scott and D. Morgan, eds., *Body Matters: Essays on the Sociology of the Body.* Washington, DC: Falmer Press.

Scully, D. (1990). *Understanding Sexual Violence: A Study of Convicted Rapists.* Boston: Unwin Hyman.

Sedlak, A., and D. Broadhurst. (1996). *Third National Incidence Study of Child Abuse and Neglect.* Washington, DC: U.S. Department of Health and Human Services.

Seeman, T. E., S. S. Merkin, E. M. Crimmins, and A. S. Karlamangla. (2009). "Disability Trends among Older Americans: National Health and Nutrition Examination Surveys, 1988–1994 and 1999–2004." *American Journal of Public Health* 100: 100–107.

Segura, D. A., and J. L. Pierce. (1993). "Chicana/o Family Structure and Gender Personality: Chodorow, Familism, and Psychoanalytic Sociology Revisited." *Signs* 19: 62–91.

Seidman, S. (1997). "Relativizing Sociology: The Challenge of Cultural Studies." In E. Long, ed., *From Sociology to Cultural Studies: New Perspectives.* Malden, MA: Blackwell.

Seidman, S., C. Meeks, and F. Traschen. (1999). "Beyond the Closet? The Changing Social Meaning of Homosexuality in the United States." *Sexualities* 2 (1): 9–34.

Sennett, R. (1998). *The Corrosion of Character: The Personal Consequences of Work in the New Capitalism.* New York: W. W. Norton.

Service Employees International Union (SEIU). (2012). "A Look inside America's Fastest Growing Union." Accessed summer 2012. www.seiu.org/a/ourunion /a-closer-look-inside-labors -fastest-growing-union.php.

Seville Statement on Violence. (1990). *American Psychologist* 45 (10): 1167–68. Accessed January 3, 2005. www.lrainc.com/swtaboo /taboos/seville1.html (site discontinued).

Sewell, W. H., Jr. (1992). "A Theory of Structure: Duality, Agency, and Transformation." *American Journal of Sociology* 98: 1–29.

Sewell, W. H., Jr. (1999). "The Concept of Culture." In V. E. Bonnell and L. Hunt, eds., *Beyond the Cultural Turn.* Berkeley, CA: University of California Press.

Sewell, W. H., and R. M. Hauser. (1980). "The Wisconsin Longitudinal Study of Social and Psychological Factors in Aspirations and Achievements." In A. C. Kerckhoff, ed., *Research in Sociology of Education and Socialization* (Vol. 1). Greenwich, CT: JAI Press.

Sezgin, S. (2012). "Assimilation versus Absorption." In Patrick Hayes (ed.), *The Making of Modern Immigration* (pp. 29–61). Santa Barbara, CA: ABC-CLIO.

Shah, A. (2011). "World Military Spending." *Global Issues.* Accessed spring 2011. www.globalissues .org/article/75/world-military -spending.

Shao, M. (2011). "Who Is More Digital? Teenagers in China or

Silicon Valley?" Stanford Graduate School of Business, News (October 1). Accessed summer 2013. www.gsb.stanford.edu/news /headlines/digital_teenagers _2011.html.

Shariati, A. (1971). *Fatima Is Fatima.* Tehran, Iran: The Shariati Foundation. Accessed spring 2011.www.al -islam.org/fatimais fatima/.

Shaw, Martin. (2000). *Theory of the Global State: Globality as an Unfinished Revolution.* Cambridge, UK: Cambridge University Press.

Shea, S., A. D. Stein, C. E. Basch, R. Lantigua, C. Maylahn, D. Strogatz et al. (1991). "Independent Associations of Educational Attainment and Ethnicity with Behavioral Risk Factors for Cardiovascular Disease." *American Journal of Epidemiology* 134 (6): 567–82.

Shelton, B. A. (1992). *Women, Men, and Time: Gender Differences in Paid Work, Housework, and Leisure.* Westport, CT: Greenwood.

Shils, E. (1972). *The Intellectuals and the Powers and Other Essays.* Chicago: University of Chicago Press.

Shin, Hyon B., and Robert A. Kominski. (2010). *Language Use in the United States: 2007. American Community Survey Reports,* ACS-12. Washington, DC: U.S. Bureau of the Census. Accessed May 19, 2010. www.census.gov/prod/2010pubs /acs-12.pdf.

Shkolnikov, V. D. (2010). *Nations in Transit 2009: Democracy's Dark Year.* Washington, DC: Freedom House.

Sigmund, P. E. (1990). *Liberation Theology at the Crossroads: Democracy or Revolution?* New York: Oxford University Press.

Simmel, G. (1955). *Conflict and the Web of Group Affiliations* (K. Wolff, Trans.). Glencoe, IL: Free Press.

Simon, J. (1981). *The Ultimate Resource.* Princeton, NJ: Princeton University Press.

Simon, J. (1989). *The Economic Consequences of Immigration.* Cambridge, MA: Basil Blackwell.

Simpson, G. E., and J. M. Yinger. (1986). *Racial and Cultural Minorities: An Analysis of Prejudice and Discrimination.* New York: Plenum Press.

Simpson, J. H. (1985). "Socio-Moral Issues and Recent Presidential Elections." *Review of Religious Research* 27: 115–23.

Singer, P.W. (2009). *Wired for War: The Robotics Revolution and Conflict*

in the 21st Century. New York: Penguin.

SIPRI. (2011). "The 15 Countries with the Highest Military Expenditure in 2011." Accessed summer 2012. www.sipri.org/databases/milex/.

Siwek, Stephen E. (2010). "Video Games in the 21st Century: The 2010 Report." Entertainment Software Association. Accessed spring 2013. www.theesa.com/facts/pdfs /videogames21stcentury_2010 .pdf.

Sjoberg, G. (1960). *The Pre-Industrial City: Past and Present.* New York: Free Press.

Sjoberg, G. (1963). "The Rise and Fall of Cities: A Theoretical Perspective." *International Journal of Comparative Sociology* 4: 107–20.

Sklair, L. (2000). *The Transnational Capitalist Class.* New York: Wiley-Blackwell.

Sklair, L. (2002a). Democracy and the Transnational Capitalist Class. *Annals of the American Academy of Political and Social Science* 581: 144–57.

Sklair, L. (2002b). *Globalization: Capitalism and Its Alternatives,* 3rd ed. New York: Oxford University Press.

Sklair, L. (2003). "Transnational Practices and the Analysis of the Global System." In A. Hulsemeyer, *Globalization in the Twenty-First Century.* New York: Palgrave Macmillan.

Skocpol, Theda. (1979). *States and Social Revolutions: A Comparative Analysis of France, Russia, and China.* New York: Cambridge University Press.

Skocpol, Theda. (1992). *Protecting Soldiers and Mothers: The Political Origins of Social Policy in the United States.* Cambridge, MA: Harvard University Press.

Slapper, G., and S. Tombs. (1999). *Corporate Crime.* Essex, UK: Longman.

Slavich G. M., S. M. Monroe, and I. H. Gotlib. (2011). "Early Parental Loss and Depression History: Associations with Recent Life Stress in Major Depressive Disorder." *Journal of Psychiatric Research,* 45(9):1146–52.

Slevin, P. (2005). "Prison Experts See Opportunity for Improvement." *Washington Post,* July 26. Accessed spring 2006. www.washingtonpost .com/wpdyn/content/article/2005 /07/25/AR2005072501484.html (site discontinued).

Slopen, N., T. T. Lewis, T. L. Gruenewald, M. S. Mujahid, C. D. Ryff, M. A. Albert, and D. R. Williams. (2010). "Early Life Adversity and Inflammation in African Americans and Whites in the Midlife in the United States Survey." *Psychosomatic Medicine* 72: 694–701.

Smart, N. (1989). *The World Religions.* Englewood Cliffs, NJ: Prentice Hall.

Smeeding, Timothy M., Jeffrey P. Thompson, Asaf Levanon, and Esra Burak. (2011). "Poverty and Income Inequality in the Early Stages of the Great Recession." In David B. Grusky, Bruce Western, and Christopher Wimer, eds., *The Great Recession* (pp. 82–126). New York: Russell Sage Foundation,

Smelser, N. J. (1963). *Theory of Collective Behavior.* New York: Free Press.

Smith, A. (1776). *An Inquiry into the Nature and Causes of the Wealth of Nations.* London: Methuen and Co., Ltd.

Smith, A. (1988). *The Ethnic Origins of Nations.* Boston: Blackwell.

Smith, P., and B. West. (2000). "Cultural Studies." In *Encyclopedia of Naturalism* (Vol. 1). San Diego, CA: Academic Press.

Smith, T. W. (1998). "American Sexual Behavior: Trends, Socio-Demographic Differences, and Risk Behavior." In J. Garrison, M. D. Smith, and D. Bersharov, eds., *The Demography of Social Behavior.* Menlo Park, CA: Kaiser Family Foundation.

Smith-Bindman, R., et al. (2006). "Does Utilization of Screening Mammography Explain Racial and Ethnic Differences in Breast Cancer?" *Annals of Internal Medicine* 144 (8): 541–53.

Smolowe, J. (1994). " . . . and Throw Away the Key." *Time,* February 7.

So, A. (1990). *Social Change and Development: Modernization, Dependency, and World-Systems Theories.* Newbury Park, CA: Sage.

Social Security Administration (SSA). (2005). "Frequently Asked Questions about Social Security's Future." Accessed December 7, 2005. www.ssa.gov/qa.htm (site discontinued).

Social Security Administration (SSA). (2012a). "Fact Sheet: Social Security." Washington, DC: Social Security Administration. Accessed April 16,

2013. www.ssa.gov/pressoffice /factsheets/colafacts2012 .pdf.

Social Security Administration (SSA). (2012b). "Income of the Aged Chartbook, 2010." *SSA Publication No. 13-11727*. Washington, DC. Accessed September 15, 2012. www.ssa.gov/policy/docs /chartbooks/income_aged/2010 /iac10.pdf.

Social Security Administration (SSA). (2013a). "Social Security Basic Facts." Accessed spring 2013. www.ssa.gov/pressoffice/basic fact.htm.

Social Security Administration (SSA). (2013b). "Social Security Board of Trustees: No Change in Projected Year of Trust Fund Reserve Depletion." Accessed spring 2013. www .ssa.gov/pressoffice/pr/trustee13 -pr.html.

Solomon, R. P. (1992). *Black Resistance in High School: Forging a Separatist Culture*. Albany, NY: State University of New York Press.

Soros, George. (2000). *Open Society: Reforming Global Capitalism*. Jackson, TN: Public Affairs Books.

Soros, George. (2005). *George Soros on Globalization*. Jackson, TN: Public Affairs Books.

Soros, George. (2009). *The Crash of 2008 and What It Means: The New Paradigm for Financial Markets*. Jackson, TN: Public Affairs Books.

Southern Poverty Law Center. (2001). "Intelligence Report." *Reevaluating the Net* 102 (Summer).

Southwick, S. (1996). "Liszt: Searchable Directory of E-Mail Discussion Groups." Accessed January 3, 2005. www.liszt.com (site discontinued).

Spenner, K. (1983). "Deciphering Prometheus: Temporal Change in the Skill Level of Work." *American Sociological Review* 48: 824–37.

Springer, Kristen W., and Dawne Mouzon. (2011). "'Macho Men' and Preventive Healthcare: Implications for Older Men in Different Social Classes." *Journal of Health and Social Behavior* 50 (2): 212–27.

Stacey, Judith. (1998). *Brave New Families: Stories of Domestic Upheaval in Late Twentieth-Century America*, 2nd ed. Berkeley: University of California Press.

Stacey, Judith. (2011). *Unhitched: Love, Marriage and Family Values from West Hollywood to Western China*. New York: New York University Press.

Stacey, Judith, and Timothy Biblarz. (2001). "(How) Does the Sexual Orientation of Parents Matter?" *American Sociological Review* 66 (2): 159–83.

Stack, C. B. (1997). *All Our Kin: Strategies for Survival in a Black Community*. New York: Harper Colophon.

Stampp, K. (1956). *The Peculiar Institution*. New York: Knopf.

Stark, R., and W. S. Bainbridge. (1980). "Towards a Theory of Religious Commitment." *Journal for the Scientific Study of Religion* 19: 114–28.

Stark, R., and W. S. Bainbridge. (1985). *The Future of Religion, Secularization, Revival, and Cult Formation*. Berkeley, CA: University of California Press.

Stark, R., and W. S. Bainbridge. (1987). *A Theory of Religion*. New Brunswick, NJ: Rutgers University Press.

Statham, J. (1986). *Daughters and Sons: Experiences of Non-Sexist Childraising*. New York: Basil Blackwell.

Statistical Office of the European Communities. (1991). *Basic Statistics of the Community*. Luxembourg: European Union.

Statistics Bureau Japan. (2012). *Statistical Handbook of Japan, 2011*, Chapter 2: "Population." Accessed August 10, 2012. www.stat.go.jp /english/data/handbook/pdf /c02cont.pdf.

Steele, C. M., and J. Aronson. (1995). "Stereotype Threat and the Intellectual Test Performance of African-Americans." *Journal of Personality and Social Psychology* 69: 797–811.

Steele, C. M., and J. A. Aronson. (2004). "Stereotype Threat Does Not Live by Steele and Aronson (1995) Alone." *American Psychologist* 59: 47–48.

Steinberg, R. J. (1990). "Social Construction of Skill: Gender, Power, and Comparable Worth." *Work and Occupations* 17: 449–82.

Steinmetz, S. K. (1983). "Family Violence toward Elders." In S. Saunders, A. Anderson, and C. Hart, eds., *Violent Individuals and Families: A Practitioner's Handbook*. Springfield, IL: Charles C. Thomas.

Sternheimer, Karen. (2003). *It's Not the Media: The Truth about Pop Culture's Influence on Children*. Boulder, CO: Westview Press.

Stetz, M., and B. Oh, eds. (2001). *Legacies of the Comfort Women of World War II*. Armonk, NY: M.E. Sharpe.

Stevens, Mitchell L. (2009). *Creating a Class: College Admissions and the Education of Elites*. Cambridge, MA: Harvard University Press.

Stiglitz, Joseph. (2003). *Globalization and Its Discontents*. New York: W. W. Norton.

Stiglitz, Joseph. (2007). *Making Globalization Work*. New York: W. W. Norton.

Stiglitz, Joseph. (2010). *Freefall: America, Free Markets, and the Sinking of the World Economy*. New York: W. W. Norton.

Stiles, Joan. (2011). "Brain Development and the Nature versus Nurture Debate." *Progress in Brain Research* 189: 3–22.

Stillwagon, E. (2001). "AIDS and Poverty in Africa." *The Nation*, May 21.

Stinner, W. F. (1979). "Modernization and the Family Extension in the Philippines: A Social-Demographic Analysis." *Journal of Marriage and Family* 41: 161–68.

Stone, L. (1980). *The Family, Sex, and Marriage in England, 1500–1800*. New York: Harper and Row.

Stonecash, J. M. (2000). *Class and Party in American Politics*. Boulder, CO: Westview Press.

Stop Violence Against Women (STOPVAW). (2006). "Prevalence of Domestic Violence." Accessed fall 2007. www.stopvaw.org /Prevalence_of_Domestic _Violence.html.

Stow, K. (2000). *Theater of Acculturation: The Roman Ghetto in the Sixteenth Century*. Seattle, WA: University of Washington Press.

Street, D., and J. S. Cossman. (2006). "Greatest Generation or Greedy Geezers? A Life Course Approach to Social Spending Preferences." *Social Problems* 53 (1): 75–96.

Stryker, R. (1996). "Comparable Worth and the Labor Market." In P. J. Dubeck and K. Borman, eds., *Women and Work: A Handbook*. New York: Garland.

Sudworth, John. (2012). "China's Students Take on Tough Gaokao University Entrance Exam." BBC World News Website (June 8). Accessed July 8, 2012. www.bbc .co.uk/news/world-asia-china -18349873.

Suitor, J. Jill, Jori Sechrist, Megan Gilligan, and Karl Pillemer. (2011). "Intergenerational Relations in Later Life Families." In Richard A. Settersten Jr. and Jacqueline L. Angel, eds., *Handbook of Sociology of Aging* (pp. 161–78). New York: Springer.

Sullivan, O. (1997). "Time Waits for No (Wo)man: An Investigation of the Gendered Experience of Domestic Time. *Sociology* 31: 221–39.

Sullivan, Paul. (2012). "The Tightwire Act of Living Only on Social Security." *New York Times*, September 11. Accessed spring 2013. www.nytimes.com/2012 /09/12/business/retirement special/living-only-on-social -security-is-a-tightwire-act .html?pagewanted=all.

Sung, Kyu-taik. (2000). "Respect for Elders: Myths and Realities in East Asia." *Journal of Aging and Identity* 5: 197–205.

Sunstein, Cass. (2012). *Republic.com 2.0.* Princeton, NJ: Princeton University Press.

"Super PAC Spending." *Los Angeles Times*, August 10. Accessed summer 2012. graphics.latimes .com/2012-election-superpac -spending/.

Sutherland, E. H. (1949). *Principles of Criminology.* Chicago: Lippincott.

Swanbrow, D. (2003). "U.S. One of the Most Religious Countries." *The University Record Online* (University of Michigan). Accessed spring 2011. www.umich.edu/~urecord /0304/Nov24_03/15.shtml.

Swartley, A. (2009). "Red, White and Bruce." *AARP Magazine*, September. Accessed August 1, 2010. www .aarp.org/politics-society/news makers/info-09-2009/bruce _springsteen.html.

Sweeney, Megan. (2010). "Remarriage and Stepfamilies: Strategic Sites for Family Scholarship in the 21st Century." *Journal of Marriage and Family* 72: 667–684.

Swidler, A. (1986). "Culture in Action: Symbols and Strategies." *American Sociological Review* 51: 273–86.

Swidler, A. (2001). *Talk of Love: How Culture Matters.* Chicago: University of Chicago Press.

Tabor, J. D., and E. V. Gallagher. (1995). *Why Waco? Cults and the Battle for Religious Freedom in America.* Berkeley, CA: University of California Press.

Tang, S., and J. Zuo. (2000). Dating Attitudes and Behaviors of American and Chinese College Students. *Social Science Journal* 37 (1): 67–78.

Tavernise, Sabrina. (2011). "Adoptions by Gay Couples Rise, Despite Barriers." *New York Times*, June 13. Accessed September 20, 2012. www.nytimes.com/2011/06/14/us /14adoption.html?pagewanted =all.

Tavernise, Sabrina. (2012). "Life Spans Shrink for Least-Educated Whites in the U.S." *New York Times*, September 20. Accessed September 22, 2012. www.nytimes .com/2012/09/21/us/life -expectancy-for-less-educated -whites-in-us-is-shrinking.html ?pagewanted=all&_moc.semityn .www&pagewanted=print.

Taylor, Paul, Rakesh Kochhar, Richard Fry, Gabriel Velasco, and Seth Motel. (2011). "Twenty-to-One: Wealth Gaps Rise to Record Highs between Whites, Blacks, and Hispanics." Washington, D.C.: Pew Research Center. Accessed October 3, 2012. www.pewsocial trends.org/files/2011/07/SDT -Wealth-Report_7-26-11_FINAL .pdf.

Teachman, J. (2003). "Premarital Sex, Premarital Cohabitation, and the Risk of Subsequent Marital Dissolution among Women." *Journal of Marriage and Family* 65: 444–55.

Telework Coalition. (2004). "Telework Facts." Accessed September 23, 2005. www.telcoa.org/id33.htm.

Telework Research Network. (2011). "The State of Telework in the U.S." Accessed spring 2013. www.work shifting.com/downloads/down loads/Telework-Trends-US.pdf.

Telework Research Network. (2012). "The Latest Telecommuting Statistics." Accessed summer 2012. www.teleworkresearchnetwork .com/telecommuting-statistics.

Tempest, R. (1996). "Barbie and the World Economy." *Los Angeles Times*, September 22.

Thompson, B. (2001). *A Promise and a Way of Life.* Minneapolis, MN: University of Minnesota Press.

Thompson, E. P. (1971). "The Moral Economy of the English Crowd in the Eighteenth Century." *Past and Present* 50: 76–136.

Thompson, W. S. (1929). "Population." *American Journal of Sociology* 34: 959–75.

Thorne, B. (1993). *Gender Play: Girls and Boys in School.* New Brunswick, NJ: Rutgers University Press.

Thoumi, Francisco. (2003). "The Numbers Game: Let's All Guess the Size of the Illegal Drugs Industry!" Paper prepared for TNI seminar on the Economic Impact of the Illicit Drug Industry, December. Accessed spring 2013. http:// jod.sagepub.com/content/35/1 /185.abstract

Tilly, C. (1978). *From Mobilization to Revolution.* Reading, MA: Addison-Wesley.

Tilly, C. (1992). "How to Detect, Describe, and Explain Repertoires of Contention." Working Paper No. 150. Center for the Study of Social Change. New York: New School for Social Research.

Time. (2011). "Special Report: The World at 7 Billion." Accessed summer 2012. www.time.com/time /specials/packages/0,28757, 2097720,00.html.

Tjaden, P., and N. Thoennes. (2010). "Full Report of the Prevalence, Incidence, and Consequences of Violence Against Women," November. Washington, DC: U.S. Department of Justice. Accessed spring 2011. www.ncjrs.gov/pdffiles1 /nij/183781.pdf.

Tong, R. (2009). *Feminist Thought: A More Comprehensive Introduction.* Philadelphia: Westview Press.

Toobin. (2011). "Betty Dukes v. Walmart." *The New Yorker,* June 20. Accessed spring 2013. www.newyorker.com/online /blogs/newsdesk/2011/06 /betty-dukes-v-walmart.html.

Torregrossa, Luisita Lopez. (2012). "On Wall Street, Gender Bias Runs Deep." *New York Times*, July 24. Accessed November 7, 2012. www.nytimes .com/2012/07/25/us/25iht -letter25.html?_r=2&adxnnl=1 &adxnnlx=1343214042-69ZdKa KnUsQxP0DFDC/2Ug&page wanted=print&.

Toufexis, A. (1993). "Sex Has Many Accents." *Time,* May 24.

Touraine, A. (1974). *The Post-Industrial Society.* London: Wildwood.

Touraine, A. (1977). *The Self-Production of Society.* Chicago: University of Chicago Press.

Touraine, A. (1981). *The Voice and the Eye: An Analysis of Social*

Movements. New York: Cambridge University Press.

Townsend, E. (2002). "E-activism Connects Protest Groups." *Hartford Courant*, December 4. Accessed September 23, 2005. www.global policy.org/ngos/advocacy/protest /iraq/2002/1204activism.htm.

Townsend, P., and N. Davidson, eds. (1982). *Inequalities in Health: The Black Report.* Harmondsworth, UK: Penguin.

Toyota Corporation. (2001). "2001 Number and Diffusion Rate for Motor Vehicles in Major Countries." Accessed spring 2006. www .toyota.co.jp/IRweb/corp_info /and_the_word/pdf/2003_c07.pdf (site discontinued).

Toyota Corporation. (2012). "2012 U.S. Operations." Accessed summer 2012. www.toyota.com /about/our_business/our_numbers /images/TMOB0154_2012 _BROCHURE_lores_panelsw _mapspread.pdf.

Treiman, D. (1977). *Occupational Prestige in Comparative Perspective.* New York: Academic Press.

Troeltsch, E. (1931). *The Social Teaching of the Christian Churches* (2 vols.). New York: Macmillan.

Truman, D. B. (1981). *The Governmental Process.* Westport, CT: Greenwood Press.

Tu, W. (1989). "The Rise of Industrial East Asia: The Role of Confucian Values." *Copenhagen Journal of Asian Studies* 4: 81–97. Accessed spring 2011. http://rauli.cbs.dk /index.php/cjas/article/view /1767/1787.

Tuller, D. (2009). "My Mother, the Octogenarian Activist." *New York Times*, December 11. Accessed August 1, 2010. http://well.blogs .nytimes.com/2009/12/11/my -mother-the-octogenarian -activist/.

Tumin, M. M. (1953). "Some Principles of Stratification: A Critical Analysis." *American Sociological Review* 18: 387–94.

Turnbull, C. (1983). *The Human Cycle.* New York: Simon and Schuster.

Turowski, J. (1977). "Inadequacy of the Theory of the Nuclear Family: The Polish Experience." In L. L. Otero, ed., *Beyond the Nuclear Family Model: Cross-Cultural Perspectives.* Beverly Hills, CA: Sage.

Twine, F. W. (1991). *Just Black? Multiracial Identity.* Motion picture; color, 57 minutes. (Available from Filmmakers Library, New York.)

Twine, F. W. (1997). *Racism in a Racial Democracy: The Maintenance of White Supremacy in Brazil.* New Brunswick, NJ: Rutgers University Press.

Twine, F. W. (2003). "Racial Literacy in Britain: Antiracist Projects, Black Children, White Parents." *Contours: A Journal of the African Diaspora* 1 (2): 129–53.

Twine, F. W. (2004). "A White Side of Black Britain: The Concept of Racial Literacy." *Ethnic and Racial Studies (A Special Issue on Racial Hierarchy)* 27 (6): 1–30.

U. K. Statistics Authority. (2001). "Ethnicity and Identity: Inter-Ethnic Marriage." Accessed spring 2008. www.statistics.gov.uk/CCI /nugget.asp?ID=1090&Pos=1& ColRank=2&Rank=416 (site discontinued).

Umberson, D., C. B. Wortman, and R. C. Kessler. (1992). "Widowhood and Depression: Explaining Long-Term Gender Differences in Vulnerability." *Journal of Health and Social Behavior* 33: 10–24.

U.N. (2004). "World Population to 2300." Department of Economic and Social Affairs/Population Division, New York. Accessed spring 2013. www.un.org/esa /population/publications /longrange2/WorldPop2300final .pdf

U. N. (2005). "Population Challenges and Development Goals." Accessed January 2008. www.un.org/esa /population/publications /pop_challenges/Population _Challenges.pdf.

U. N. (2009). "The Millennium Development Goals Report." Accessed spring 2011. http://unstats.un.org /unsd/mdg/Resources/Static /Products/Progress2009/MDG _Report_2009_En.pdf.

U. N. (2012). "World Urbanization Prospects, the 2011 Revision: Highlights. Development Indicators." Department of Economic and Social Affairs, Population Division, New York. Accessed summer 2013. http://esa.un.org /unup/pdf/WUP2011_Highlights .pdf.

U. N. Commission on Sustainable Development (UN CSD). (2007). "CSD-15 Session." U. N. Department of Economic and Social Affairs, Division for Sustainable Development. December 26, 2007. http://sustainabledevelopment .un.org/index.php?menu=1124.

U. N. Conference on Trade and Development (UNCTAD). (2005). "World Investment Report 2005: Transnational Corporations, Extractive Industries and Development." New York. Accessed spring 2013. http:// unctad.org/en/docs/diaeia20104 _en.pdf.

U. N. Conference on Trade and Development (UNCTAD). (2010). "World Investment Prospects Survey, 2010–2012." New York. Accessed summer 2012. http://unctad.org /en/docs/diaeia20104_en.pdf.

U. N. Development Programme (UNDP). (1998). "Human Development Report 1998." New York: Oxford University Press.

U. N. Development Programme (UNDP). (1999). "Human Development Report 1999." New York/Oxford: Oxford University Press.

U. N. Development Programme (UNDP). (2006). "Human Development Report, 2006." Accessed May 2010. http://hdr.undp.org/en/reports /global/hdr2006/.

U. N. Development Programme (UNDP). (2007). "Human Development Report: 2007." Accessed fall 2007. http://hdr.undp.org/en/reports /global/hdr2007-8/.

U. N. Development Programme (UNDP). (2011). "Sustainability and Equity: A Better Future for All." Human Development Report 2011. Accessed summer 2012. http://hdr.undp.org/en/reports /global/hdr2011/download/.

U. N. Development Programme (UNDP). (2013). "Human Development Report 2013: The Rise of the South: Human Progress in a Diverse World." Table 15. Accessed spring 2013. http://hdr.undp.org /en/media/HDR_2013_EN _complete.pdf

U. N. Development Report. (2011). "The Real Wealth of Nations: Pathways to Human Development." Accessed summer 2012. http://hdr.undp .org/en/reports/global/hdr2010 /chapters/.

U. N. Economic Commission for Europe (UNECE). (2003). "Ireland." Accessed spring 2006. www .unece.org/stats/trend/irl.pdf (site discontinued).

U. N. Economic and Social Commission for Asia and the Pacific

[UNESCAP]. (2010). "Global Financial Crisis Derails MDG Progress in Asia-Pacific Region." Press Release. Accessed spring 2011. http://mediaglobal.org/article/2010-02-23/global-financial-crisis-derails-mdg-progress-in-asia-pacific-region (site discontinued).

UNESCO. (2012a). "Adult and Youth Literacy: UIS Fact Sheet." September 20. Accessed October 19, 2012. www.uis.unesco.org/literacy/Documents/fs20-literacy-day-2012-en-V3.pdf.

UNESCO. (2012b). "From International Blockbusters to National Hits: An Analysis of the 2010 UIS Survey on Feature Film Statistics." *UIS Information Bulletin,* No. 8, Paris, France. Accessed spring 2013. www.google.com/url?sa=t&rct=j&q=&esrc=s&source=web&cd=1&cad=rja&ved=0CCIQFjAA&url=http%3A%2F%2Fwww.uis.unesco.org%2Fculture%2FDocuments%2Fib8-analysis-cinema-production-2012-en2.pdf&ei=5tJIUOSdMKvFiwLmz4DwBA&usg=AFQjCNHzvq1TPFCnDpQSotLz9b1ExJ-pTg&sig2=E_NntukUUZLYZiAN3KjoHA.

U. N. Food and Agriculture Organization (UN FAO). (2001). "The Impact of HIV/AIDS on Food Security." Conference on World Food Security, May 28–June 1, Rome.

U. N. Food and Agriculture Organization (UN FAO). (2005). "Armed Conflicts Leading Cause of World Hunger Emergencies." Accessed December 1, 2005. www.fao.org/newsroom/en/news/2005/102562/index.html.

U. N. Food and Agriculture Organization (UN FAO). (2007). "Hunger Facts." Accessed fall 2007. www.wfp.org/aboutwfp/facts/hunger_facts.asp (site discontinued).

U. N. Food and Agriculture Organization (UN FAO). (2010). "The State of Food Insecurity in the World 2010." Accessed summer 2012. www.fao.org/docrep/013/i1683e/i1683e.pdf.

U. N. Food and Agriculture Organization (UN FAO). (2011a). "How to Feed the World in 2050." UN Issue Brief, October 12–13. Accessed spring 2013. www.fao.org/fileadmin/templates/wsfs/docs/expert_paper/How_to_Feed_the_World_in_2050.pdf.

U. N. Food and Agriculture Organization (UN FAO). (2011b). "World Population to Reach 10 Billion by 2100 if Fertility in All Countries Converges to Replacement Level." FAO Press Release. May 3.

U. N. Food and Agriculture Organization (UN FAO). (2012). "The State of Food Insecurity in the World 2012. Economic Growth Is Necessary But Not Sufficient to Accelerate Reduction of Hunger and Malnutrition." Joint Document with World Food Programme (WFP) and Institute for Agricultural Development (IFAD), Rome. Accessed March 8, 2013. www.fao.org/docrep/016/i3027e/i3027e.pdf.

U. N. Food and Agriculture Organization (UN FAO). (2013). Hunger Map 2013. Accessed fall 2013. http://home.wfp.org/stellent/groups/public/documents/communications/wfp229327.pdf.

U. N.-Habitat. (2007). "Slum Dwellers to Double by 2030: Millennium Development Goal Could Fall Short." Accessed spring 2013. www.unhabitat.org/downloads/docs/4631_46759_GC%2021%20Slum%20dwellers%20to%20double.pdf.

U. N.-Habitat. (2010). "Urban World: Ten Years into the Millennium." August 2, 2010. www.unhabitat.org/pmss/listItemDetails.aspx?publicationID=2980.

UNICEF. (2005). "Female Genital Mutilation/Cutting: A Statistical Exploration." Accessed fall 2007. www.unicef.org/publications/files/FGM-C_final_10_October.pdf.

UNICEF. (2006). "Equality in Employment." Accessed August 16, 2011. www.unicef.org/sowc07/docs/sowc07_chap3.pdf.

UNICEF. (2012). "Measuring Child Poverty: New League Tables of Child Poverty in the World's Rich Countries." May 2012. Accessed June 19, 2012. www.unicef-irc.org/publications/pdf/rc10_eng.pdf.

Union of International Associations (UIA). (2005). "Statistics on International Organizations and NGOs." Accessed spring 2008. www.uia.org/statistics/organizations/types-2004.pdf.

Union of International Associations (UIA). (2012). "Yearbook of International Organizations, 2012–2013." Accessed summer 2012. www.uia.be/yearbook.

United Steelworkers (USW). (2008). "Who We Are." Accessed spring 2008. www.usw.org/our_union/who_we_are.

University of Michigan Institute for Social Research. (2008). "Chore Wars: Men, Women, and Housework." National Science Foundation. Accessed August 16, 2011. www.nsf.gov/discoveries/disc_summ.jsp?cntn_id=111458.

U. N. Joint Programme on HIV/AIDS (UNAIDS). (2003). "AIDS Epidemic Update." December 2003. Accessed January 10, 2005. http://data.unaids.org/Publications/IRC-pub06/JC943-EpiUpdate2003_en.pdf.

U. N. Joint Programme on HIV/AIDS (UNAIDS). (2005). "AIDS Epidemic Update." December 2005. Accessed spring 2006. www.unaids.org/epi/2005/doc/EPIupdate2005_pdf_en/Epi05_10_en.pdf (site discontinued).

U. N. Joint Programme on HIV/AIDS (UNAIDS). (2010a). "Report on the Global AIDS Epidemic." Accessed summer 2012. www.unaids.org/globalreport/global_reports.htm.

U. N. Joint Programme on HIV/AIDS (UNAIDS). (2010b). "WHO Library Cataloguing-in-Publication Data Global Report: UNAIDS Report on the Global AIDS Epidemic." Accessed March 13, 2013. www.unaids.org/documents/20101123_globalreport_em.pdf.

U. N. Joint Programme on HIV/AIDS (UNAIDS). (2011). Homepage. Accessed August 25, 2011. www.unaids.org/en/.

U. N. Office on Drugs and Crime (UNODC). (2005). "World Drug Report, 2005." Accessed spring 2006. www.unodc.org/unodc/en/world_drug_report.html (site discontinued).

U. N. Office on Drugs and Crime (UNODC). (2011). "Estimating Illicit Financial Flows Resulting from Drug Trafficking and Other Transnational Organized Crimes." October. Accessed spring 2013. www.unodc.org/documents/data-and-analysis/Studies/Illicit_financial_flows_2011_web.pdf.

U. N. Population Division. (2008a). "International Migrant Stock: The 2008 Revision." Accessed summer 2010. http://esa.un.org/migration/.

U. N. Population Division. (2008b). "An Overview of Urbanization, Internal Migration, Population Distribution, and Development in the World." Accessed spring 2011. www.un.org/esa/population /meetings/EGM_PopDist /P01_UNPopDiv.pdf.

U. N. Population Fund (UNFPA). (2005). "Gender-Based Violence: A Price Too High." *State of the World Population, 2005.* Accessed December 4, 2005. www.unfpa .org/swp/2005/english/ch7/index .htm.

U. N. Population Fund (UNFPA). (2008). "Unleashing the Potential of Urban Growth." *State of the World Population 2007.* Accessed spring 2008. www.unfpa.org /swp/2007/english/introduction .html.

U. N. Population Fund (UNFPA). (2011). *State of the World, Population 2011.* Accessed summer 2012. http://foweb.unfpa.org/SWP2011 /reports/EN-SWOP2011-FINAL .pdf.

U. N. World Food Programme (UNWFP). (2004). "Paying the Price of Hunger: The Impact of Malnutrition on Women and Children." Accessed December 1, 2005. http://documents.wfp.org /stellent/groups/public /documents/newsroom/wfp 076313.pdf.

Urahn, Susan K., Erin Currier, Dana Elliott, Lauren Wechsler, Denise Wilson, Daniel Colbert, and Pew Charitable Trusts. (2012). "Pursuing the American Dream: Economic Mobility across Generations. Project Report." Accessed September 21, 2012. www .pewstates.org/uploadedFiles /PCS_Assets/2012/Pursuing _American_Dream.pdf.

Urban Institute. (2005). "Low-Income Working Families: Facts and Figures," August 25. Accessed spring 2006. www.urban.org/Uploaded PDF/900832.pdf.

Urban Institute. (2010). "The Future of Social Security: Solvency, Work, Adequacy, and Equity." Washington, DC: Program on Retirement Policy. Accessed August 9, 2012. www.urban.org/uploadedpdf /412253-Social-Security -Solvency.pdf.

U.S. Administration on Aging (AOA). (2010). "Older Population as a Percentage of the Total Population: 1900 to 2050." Accessed spring 2011. www.aoa.gov/aoaroot/aging _statistics/future_growth/docs /By_Age_Total_Population.xls.

U.S. Administration on Aging (AOA). (2011). *A Profile of Older Americans: 2011.* Washington, DC: U.S. Department of Health and Human Services. Accessed spring 2013. www.aoa.gov/Aging _Statistics/Profile/2011/docs /2011profile.pdf.

USA Today. (2009). "Credit Card Debt Rises Faster for Those 65 and Older." Accessed spring 2011. www.usatoday.com/money/perfi /credit/2009-07-27-credit-card -debt-seniors_N.htm.

U.S. Bureau of Justice Statistics (BJS). (2005a). "Justice Expenditure and Employment Extracts: Direct Expenditure by Level of Government, 1982–2005." Accessed fall 2007. www.ojp.usdoj.gov/bjs /glance/tables/expgovtab.htm (site discontinued).

U.S. Bureau of Justice Statistics (BJS). (2005b). "Violent Crime Rate Unchanged during 2005, Theft Rate Declined." Accessed fall 2007. www.ojp.usdoj.gov/bjs/pub/press /cv05pr.htm (site discontinued).

U.S. Bureau of Justice Statistics (BJS). (2007). "Justice Expenditure and Employment Extracts, 2007." Accessed spring 2011. http://bjs.ojp.usdoj.gov/index .cfm?ty=pbdetail&iid=2315.

U.S. Bureau of Justice Statistics (BJS). (2008). "Violent Crime Rates Overall Fell by 41% from 1999 to 2008." *Criminal Victimization, 2008,* Figure 1. Accessed spring 2011. http://bjs.ojp.usdoj.gov/content /pub/pdf/cv08.pdf.

U.S. Bureau of Labor Statistics (BLS). (2005). "Contingent and Alternative Employment Arrangements." Accessed March 13, 2006. www.bls .gov/news.release/conemp.toc.htm.

U.S. Bureau of Labor Statistics (BLS). (2007). "Median Weekly Earnings of Full-Time Wage and Salary Workers by Selected Characteristics." *Data Annual Averages,* Table 37. Accessed fall 2007. www.bls .gov/cps/cpsaat37.pdf.

U.S. Bureau of Labor Statistics (BLS). (2009). "Women in the Labor Force: A Databook." Report 1018. Accessed spring 2011. www.bls .gov/cps/wlf-databook-2009.pdf.

U.S. Bureau of Labor Statistics (BLS). (2010a). "Employed Persons by Detailed Occupation, Sex, Race, and Hispanic or Latino Ethnicity." Accessed spring 2011. www.bls .gov/cps/cpsaat11.pdf.

U.S. Bureau of Labor Statistics (BLS). (2010b). "Employment Status of the Civilian Noninstitutional Population 16 Years and Over by Sex, 1973 to Date." Table 607. Accessed spring 2011. www.bls .gov/cps/cpsaat2.pdf.

U.S. Bureau of Labor Statistics (BLS). (2010c). "Median Weekly Earnings of Full-Time Wage and Salary Workers by Selected Characteristics." Accessed spring 2011. www .bls.gov/cps/cpsaat37.pdf.

U.S. Bureau of Labor Statistics (BLS). (2010d). "Union Members Summary 2010." Accessed August 15, 2010. www.bls.gov/news.release /union2.nr0.htm.

U.S. Bureau of Labor Statistics (BLS). (2011a). "American Time Use Survey—2011 Results." Accessed August 27, 2012. www.bls.gov /news.release/pdf/atus.pdf.

U.S. Bureau of Labor Statistics (BLS). (2011b)." Highlights of Women's Earnings in 2010." July. Accessed spring 2013. www.bls.gov/cps /cpswom2010.pdf.

U.S. Bureau of Labor Statistics (BLS). (2011c). "Major Work Stoppages 2011 (Annual)." Accessed summer 2012. www.bls.gov/news.release /wkstp.htm.

U.S. Bureau of Labor Statistics (BLS). (2011d). "Union Members Summary 2011." Accessed summer 2012. www.bls.gov/news.release /union2.nr0.htm.

U.S. Bureau of Labor Statistics (BLS). (2011e). "Women in the Labor Force: A Databook." Report 1034, December. Accessed November 19, 2012. www.bls.gov/cps/wlf -databook-2011.pdf.

U.S. Bureau of Labor Statistics (BLS). (2012a). "American Time Use Survey—2011 Results." Accessed August 27, 2012. www.bls.gov /news.release/pdf/atus.pdf.

U.S. Bureau of Labor Statistics (BLS). (2012b). "Employed Persons by Detailed Occupation, Sex, Race, and Hispanic or Latino Ethnicity." Accessed spring 2013. www.bls. gov/cps/cpsaat11.htm.

U.S. Bureau of Labor Statistics (BLS). (2012c). "Employment by Major Industry Sector." Table 620. Accessed summer 2012. www.bls .gov/emp/ep_table_201.htm.

U.S. Bureau of Labor Statistics (BLS). (2012d). "The Employment Situation, July 2012." Accessed summer 2012. www.bls.gov/news.release /pdf/empsit.pdf.

U.S. Bureau of Labor Statistics (BLS). (2012e). "Employment Status of the Civilian Non-Institutional Populations by Hispanic or Latino Ethnicity, Sex, and Race, 2011." *Labor Force Characteristics by Race and Ethnicity, 2011,* Table 2. Accessed September 29, 2012. www.bls.gov/cps/cpsrace2011.pdf.

U.S. Bureau of Labor Statistics (BLS). (2012f). "Median Weekly Earnings of Full-Time Wage and Salary Workers by Selected Characteristics." Accessed spring 2013. www .bls.gov/cps/cpsaat37.htm.

U.S. Bureau of Labor Statistics (BLS). (2012g). "National Census of Fatal Occupational Injuries in 2011." Accessed October 1, 2012. www .bls.gov/news.release/pdf/cfoi.pdf.

U.S. Bureau of Labor Statistics (BLS). (2012h). "A Profile of the Working Poor 2010." Accessed September 3, 2011. www.bls.gov/cps/cpswp2010 .pdf.

U.S. Bureau of Labor Statistics (BLS). (2013a). "Employment Characteristics of Families Summary." Accessed spring 2013. www.bls .gov/news.release/famee.nr0 .htm.

U.S. Bureau of Labor Statistics (BLS). (2013b). "Usual Weekly Earnings of Wage and Salary Workers First Quarter 2013." Accessed spring 2013. www.bls.gov/news.release /pdf/wkyeng.pdf.

U.S. Bureau of Labor Statistics (BLS). (2013c). "Women in the Labor Force: A Databook." Accessed spring 2013. www.bls.gov/cps/wlf -databook-2012.pdf.

U.S. Bureau of the Census. (1979). "Nonagricultural Establishments—Employees and Average Weekly Hours: 1960 to 1979." *Statistical Abstract of the United States: 1980.* Accessed March 18, 2013. www.census.gov/prod /www/statistical_abstract .html.

U.S. Bureau of the Census. (1996). "65+ in the United States." *Current Population Reports: Special Studies: P23–190.* Washington, DC: U.S. Government Printing Office.

U.S. Bureau of the Census. (1998). "Voting and Registration in the Elec-tion of November 1996." Accessed spring 2013. www.census.gov /prod/3/98pubs/p20-504.pdf.

U.S. Bureau of the Census. (2003a). "Number in Poverty and Poverty Rate by Race and Hispanic Origin: 2001 and 2002." Accessed January 4, 2005. www.census.gov /hhes/poverty/poverty02/table1 .pdf (site discontinued).

U.S. Bureau of the Census. (2003b). "Poverty Status: Status of Families, by Type of Family, Presence of Related Children, Race, and Hispanic Origin: 1959 to 2002." Accessed January 4, 2005. www .census.gov/hhes/poverty/histpov /hstpov4.html (site discontinued).

U.S. Bureau of the Census. (2004). "Interim Projections of the U.S. Population by Age, Race, Sex, and Hispanic Origin." *2004 Interim National Population Projections.* Accessed January 2008. http:// www.census.gov/population /projections/files/methodology /idbsummeth.pdf.

U.S. Bureau of the Census. (2006). *Statistical Abstract of the United States: 2005.* Accessed spring 2013. www.census.gov/compendia /statab/.

U.S. Bureau of the Census. (2008a). *American Community Survey: 2007.* Accessed January 2008. http://factfinder.census.gov /servlet/DatasetMainPageServlet ?_program=ACS&_submenuId =&_lang=en&_ts= (site discontinued).

U.S. Bureau of the Census. (2008b). "Employed Civilians by Sex, Race, and Hispanic Origins." *Statistical Abstract of the United States: 2008,* Table 598. Accessed January 2008. www.census.gov/compendia /statab/tables/08s0598.pdf (site discontinued).

U.S. Bureau of the Census. (2008c). "Employment by Industry: 2000 to 2006." *Statistical Abstract of the United States: 2008,* Table 602. Accessed spring 2008. www .census.gov/compendia/statab /tables/08s0602.pdf (site discontinued).

U.S. Bureau of the Census. (2008d). "Employment Projections by Occupation: 2004 and 2014." *Statistical Abstract of the United States: 2008,* Table 600. Accessed spring 2008. www.census.gov/compendia /statab/tables/08s0600.pdf (site discontinued).

U.S. Bureau of the Census. (2008e). "Median Income of People with Income in Constant (2005) Dollars, Sex, Race and Hispanic Origin: 1990 to 2005." *Statistical Abstract of the United States: 2008,* Table 679. Accessed January 2008. www.census.gov/compendia /statab/tables/08s0679.pdf (site discontinued).

U.S. Bureau of the Census. (2008f). *An Older and More Diverse Nation by Midcentury.* August 14. Accessed summer 2013. www.census.gov /newsroom/releases/archives /population/cb08-123.html.

U.S. Bureau of the Census. (2008g). "Unemployed and Unemployment Rates by Educational Attainment, Sex, Race and Hispanic Origin: 1992 to 2006." *Statistical Abstract of the United States: 2008,* Table 609. Accessed January 2008. www.census.gov/compendia /statab/tables/08s0609.pdf (site discontinued).

U.S. Bureau of the Census. (2009). "Race and Hispanic Origin of People by Median Income and Sex: 1947 to 2008." Historical Income Tables: People, Table P-2. Accessed June 1, 2010. www.census.gov /hhes/www/income/data /historical/people/index.html.

U.S. Bureau of the Census. (2010a). "Births, Deaths, Marriages, and Divorces: Marriages and Divorces." *Statistical Abstract of the United States: 2010,* Table 126. Accessed spring 2011. www.census.gov /compendia/statab/cats/births _deaths_marriages_divorces /marriages_and_divorces.html

U.S. Bureau of the Census. (2010b). "Expectation of Life at Birth, 1970 to 2006, and Projection, 2010 to 2020." *Statistical Abstract of the United States: 2010,* Table 102. Accessed August 10, 2010. www.census.gov/compendia /statab/cats/births_deaths _marriages_divorces/life _expectancy.html.

U.S. Bureau of the Census. (2010c). "Labor Force, Employment, and Earnings: Employment by Industry." *Statistical Abstract of the United States: 2010,* Table 607. Accessed spring 2011. www .census.gov/compendia/statab /2010/tables/10s0607.pdf.

U.S. Bureau of the Census. (2010d). "The Next Four Decades: The Older Population in the United States:

2010 to 2050." Accessed April 12, 2013. www.census.gov/prod /2010pubs/p25-1138.pdf.

U.S. Bureau of the Census. (2010e). "Participation in Elections for President and U.S. Representatives." *Statistical Abstract of the United States: 2010*, Table 408. http://www .census.gov/compendia/statab /2010/tables/10s0408.pdf

U.S. Bureau of the Census. (2010f). "Population and Distribution Change, 2000–2010." Accessed summer 2012. www.census.gov /prod/cen2010/briefs/c2010br-01 .pdf.

U.S. Bureau of the Census. (2010g). "Selected Social Characteristics in the United States." *American Community Survey: 2010.* Accessed spring 2011. http://www .culvercity.org/-/media/Files /Planning/Census2010/US %20Census%20DP-02%20Selected %20Social%20Char.%202010.ashx.

U.S. Bureau of the Census. (2010h). "Urban and Rural Classification and Urban Area Criteria." Accessed summer 2012. www .census.gov/geo/www/ua /2010urbanruralclass.html (site discontinued).

U.S. Bureau of the Census. (2010i). "Urbanized Areas and Urban Clusters: 2010." Accessed summer 2012. www.census.gov/geo/www /ua/2010urbanruralclass .html (site discontinued).

U.S. Bureau of the Census. (2010j). "U.S. Census Bureau Reports Men and Women Wait Longer to Marry." Accessed August 29, 2012. www.census.gov/newsroom /releases/archives/families _households/cb10-174.html.

U.S. Bureau of the Census. (2011a). "Age and Sex of All People, Family Members and Unrelated Individuals Iterated by Income-to-Poverty Ratio and Race: 2010." *Annual Social and Economic (ASEC) Supplement.* Accessed September 3, 2012. www.census.gov/hhes/www /cpstables/032011/pov/new01 _100.htm.

U.S. Bureau of the Census. (2011b). *America's Families and Living Arrangements: 2010.* Accessed September 10, 2012. www .census.gov/compendia/ statab/2012/tables/12s0057.pdf.

U.S. Bureau of the Census. (2011c). "Educational Attainment in the United States: 2011." Accessed

April 12, 2013. www.census.gov /hhes/socdemo/education/data /cps/2011/tables.html.

U.S. Bureau of the Census. (2011d). "Homicide Victims by Race and Sex: 1980 to 2006." *Statistical Abstract of the United States: 2011,* Table 309. Accessed October 1, 2012. www.census.gov/compendia /statab/2011/tables/11s0309.pdf.

U.S. Bureau of the Census. (2011e). "Income, Poverty, and Health Insurance Coverage in the United States: 2010." Accessed spring 2013. www.census.gov/prod /2011pubs/p60-239.pdf.

U.S. Bureau of the Census. (2011f). "Living Alone." Accessed spring 2013. www.census.gov/hhes/www /housing/census/historic/livalone .html.

U.S. Bureau of the Census. (2011g). "Marital Status of People Age 15 and Older by Age, Sex, Personal Earnings, Race, and Hispanic Origin: 2010." *America's Families and Living Arrangements: 2010,* Table 1a. Accessed September 30, 2012. www.census.gov/compendia /statab/2012/tables/12s0057.pdf.

U.S. Bureau of the Census. (2011h). "Number, Timing, and Duration of Marriages and Divorces: 2009." *Household Economic Studies, Current Reports.* Accessed summer 2012. www.census.gov/prod /2011pubs/p70-125.pdf.

U.S. Bureau of the Census. (2011i). "Overview of Race and Hispanic Origin: 2010." Accessed summer 2013. www.census.gov/prod /cen2010/briefs/c2010br-02.pdf.

U.S. Bureau of the Census. (2011j). "People in Families by Family Structure, Age, and Sex, Iterated by Income-to-Poverty Ratio and Race: 2010." *Annual Social and Economic (ASEC) Supplement.* Accessed September 3, 2012. www.census .gov/hhes/www/cpstables/032011 /pov/new02_100.htm.

U.S. Bureau of the Census. (2011k). "Population: Religion." *Statistical Abstract of the United States: 2011.* Accessed spring 2011. www .census.gov/compendia/statab /cats/population/religion.html.

U.S. Bureau of the Census. (2011l). "Poverty Status of Families by Type of Family, Presence of Related Children, Race, and Hispanic Origin: 1959 to 2010." Historical Poverty Tables: Families, Table 4. Accessed Septem-

ber 4, 2012. www.census.gov/hhes /www/poverty/data/historical /families.html.

U.S. Bureau of the Census. (2011m). "Poverty Status of People by Age, Race, and Hispanic Origin: 1959 to 2010." Historical Poverty Tables: People, Table 3. Accessed September 4, 2012. www.census.gov /hhes/www/poverty/data /historical/people.html.

U.S. Bureau of the Census. (2011n). Poverty Status of People by Family Relationship, Race, and Hispanic Origin: 1959 to 2010. Historical Poverty Tables: People, Table 2. Accessed September 4, 2012. www .census.gov/hhes/www/poverty /data/historical/people.html.

U.S. Bureau of the Census. (2011o). *Quick Facts from U.S. Census Bureau.* Accessed summer 2012. http://quickfacts.census.gov/qfd /states/00000.html.

U.S. Bureau of the Census. (2012a). "All Parent/Child Situations, by Type, Race, and Hispanic Origin of Householder or Reference Person: 1970 to Present." *America's Families and Living Arrangements: 2011,* Table FM-2. Accessed summer 2013. www .census.gov/hhes/families/data /families.html.

U.S. Bureau of the Census. (2012b). *America's Families and Living Arrangements: 2011.* Accessed September 29, 2012. www.census.gov /population/www/socdemo/hh -fam/cps2011.html.

U.S. Bureau of the Census. (2012c). "Detailed Years of School Completed by People 25 Years and Over by Sex, Age Groups, Race and Hispanic Origin: 2011." Table 3. *Educational Attainment in the United States: 2011.* Accessed summer 2012. www.census.gov/hhes /socdemo/education/data/cps /2011/Table3.xls.

U.S. Bureau of the Census. (2012d). "Employed Civilians and Weekly Hours: 1980 to 2010." *Statistical Abstract of the United States: 2012,* Table 602. Accessed summer 2013. http://www.census.gov /compendia/statab/2012 /tables/12s0602.pdf

U.S. Bureau of the Census. (2012e). "Expectation of Life at Birth, 1970 to 2008, and Projections, 2010 to 2020." *Statistical Abstract of the United States: 2012,* Table 104. Accessed October 1, 2012.

www.census.gov/compendia/statab/2012/tables/12s0105.pdf.

U.S. Bureau of the Census. (2012f). "Family Households by Type, Age of Own Children, Age of Family Members, and Age, Race and Hispanic Origin of Householder: 2011." *America's Families and Living Arrangements: 2011,* Table F1. Accessed summer 2013. www.census.gov/hhes/families/files/cps2011/tabF1-all.xls.

U.S. Bureau of the Census. (2012g). "Households by Total Money Income, Race, and Hispanic Origin of Householder: 1967 to 2011." Historical Income Tables: Households, Table H-17. Accessed September 23, 2012. www.census.gov/hhes/www/income/data/historical/household/.

U.S. Bureau of the Census. (2012h). "Income Limits for Each Fifth and Top 5 Percent of All Households: 1967 to 2010." Historical Income Tables: Households, Table H-1. Accessed September 3, 2012. www.census.gov/hhes/www/income/data/historical/household/index.html.

U.S. Bureau of the Census. (2012i). "Living Arrangements of Children under 18 Years and Marital Status of Parents, by Age, Sex, Race, and Hispanic Origin and Selected Characteristics of the Child for All Children: 2011." *America's Families and Living Arrangements: 2011,* Table C3. Accessed summer 2013. www.census.gov/hhes/families/files/cps2011/tabC3-all.xls.

U.S. Bureau of the Census. (2012j). "Mean Household Income Received by Each Fifth and Top 5 Percent, All Races: 1967 to 2010." Historical Income Tables: Households, Table H-3. Accessed August 27, 2012. www.census.gov/hhes/www/income/data/historical/household/index.html.

U.S. Bureau of the Census. (2012k). "One-Parent Unmarried Family Groups with Own Children under 18, by Marital Status of the Reference Person: 2011." *America's Families and Living Arrangements: 2011,* Table FG6. Accessed summer 2013. www.census.gov/hhes/families/files/cps2011/tabFG6-all_one.xls.

U.S. Bureau of the Census. (2012l). "Persons Living Alone by Sex and Age: 1990 to 2010." *Statistical Abstract of the United States: 2012,* Table 72. Accessed June 20, 2013. www.census.gov/compendia/statab/2012/tables/12s0072.pdf.

U.S. Bureau of the Census. (2012m). "Resident Population Projections by Sex and Age: 2010 to 2050." *Statistical Abstract of the United States: 2012,* Table 9. Accessed spring 2013. www.census.gov/compendia/statab/2012/tables/12s0009.pdf.

U.S. Bureau of the Census. (2012n). "Self-Described Religious Affiliation of Adult Population: 1990, 2001, and 2008." *Statistical Abstract of the United States: 2012,* Table 75. Washington, DC: U.S. Bureau of the Census. Accessed spring 2013. www.census.gov/compendia/statab/2012/tables/12s0075.pdf.

U.S. Bureau of the Census. (2012o). "Share of Aggregate Income Received by Each Fifth and Top 5 Percent of Households, All Races: 1967 to 2010." Historical Income Tables: Households, Table H-2. August 27, 2012. www.census.gov/hhes/www/income/data/historical/household/index.html.

U.S. Bureau of the Census. (2012p). "Unemployed and Unemployment Rates by Educational Attainment, Sex, Race, and Hispanic Origin: 2000 to 2010." *Statistical Abstract of the United States: 2012,* Table 627. Accessed spring 2013. www.census.gov/compendia/statab/2012/tables/12s0627.pdf.

U.S. Bureau of the Census. (2012q). "Voting and Registration in the Election of November 2012 – Detailed Tables." Accessed spring 2013. www.census.gov/hhes/www/socdemo/voting/publications/p20/2012/tables.html.

U.S. Bureau of the Census. (2013). "Blacks Voted at a Higher Rate Than Whites in 2012 Election – A First, Census Bureau Reports." Accessed spring 2013. www.census.gov/newsroom/releases/archives/voting/cb13-84.html.

U.S. Congress. (2010). Senate Special Committee on Aging. "Social Security Modernization: Options to Address Solvency and Benefit Adequacy." Report 111-187. 111th Cong., 2d sess., May 18.

U.S. Department of Commerce. (2010). "Middle Class in America." Washington, DC: U.S. Department of Commerce Economics and Statistics Administration for the Office of the Vice President of the United States Middle Class Task Force.

U.S. Department of Defense. (2012a). Fiscal Year 2013 Budget Request. Accessed March 3, 2013. http://comptroller.defense.gov/defbudget/fy2013/FY2013_Budget_Request_Overview_Book.pdf.

U.S. Department of Defense. (2012b). "National Defense Budget Estimates for FY 2013." Accessed spring 2013. http://comptroller.defense.gov/defbudget/fy2013/FY13_Green_Book.pdf.

U.S. Department of Education. (2008). "1.5 Million Homeschooled Students in the United States in 2007." Washington, DC: Institute of Education Sciences, December. Accessed August 28, 2011. http://nces.ed.gov/pubs2009/2009030.pdf.

U.S. Department of Education. (2012). "Fast Facts: Degrees Conferred by Race and Sex." National Center for Education Statistics. Accessed summer 2012. http://nces.ed.gov/fastfacts/display.asp?id=72.

U.S. Department of Energy. (2011). "Renewable Energy Data Book 2010." National Renewable Energy Laboratory. Accessed summer 2012. www.nrel.gov/analysis/pdfs/51680.pdf.

U.S. Department of Health and Human Services (DHHS). (2004). "Indicators of Welfare Dependence: Annual Report to Congress, 2004." Table 2. Accessed spring 2006. http://aspe.hhs.gov/hsp/indicators04.

U.S. Department of Health and Human Services (DHHS). (2008). "Summary: Child Maltreatment 2008." Accessed June 20, 2010. www.acf.hhs.gov/programs/cb/pubs/cm08/ (site discontinued).

U.S. Department of Justice. (2003). "Budget Trend Data 1975 through the President's 2003 Request to the Congress." Accessed fall 2007. www.justice.gov/archive/jmd/1975_2002/btd02tocpg.htm.

U.S. Department of Justice. (2011). "Correctional Population in the United States, 2010." Accessed summer 2012. http://bjs.ojp.usdoj.gov/content/pub/pdf/cpus10.pdf.

U.S. Department of Labor. (2010a). "Wage and Hour Division (WHD):

Minimum Wage Laws in the States." Accessed spring 2011. www.dol.gov/whd/minwage /america.htm.

U.S. Department of Labor (2010b). "Women in the Labor Force: A Data Handbook." Accessed summer 2012. www.bls.gov/cps/wlf -databook-2010.pdf.

U.S. Department of Labor. (2011). "Minimum Wage Laws in the States: January 1, 2011." Accessed March 1, 2013. www.dol.gov/whd /minwage/america.htm.

U.S. Department of Labor. (2012). "Women in the Labor Force: A Data Handbook." Accessed summer 2012 . www.bls.gov/cps/wlf -databook-2010.pdf.

U.S. Election Project. (2010). "2008 Current Population Survey Voting and Registration Supplement." Accessed August 3, 2010. http://elections.gmu.edu /CPS_2008.html.

U.S. Energy Information Administration (US EIA). (2010). "United States Energy Profile." Accessed August 5, 2010. http://tonto.eia .doe.gov/country/country_energy _data.cfm?fips=US (site discontinued).

U.S. Energy Information Administration (US EIA). (2011). "International Energy Outlook, 2011." Accessed summer 2012. www.eia .gov/forecasts/ieo/.

U.S. Equal Employment Opportunity Commission (EEOC). (2011). "Sexual Harassment Charges EEOC & FEPAs Combined: FY 1997–FY 2011." Accessed November 19, 2012. www.eeoc.gov/eeoc /statistics/enforcement/sexual _harassment.cfm.

U.S. Equal Employment Opportunity Commission (EEOC). (2012). "Sexual Harassment Charges, FY 2010–FY 2012." Accessed spring 2013. http://www .eeoc.gov/eeoc/statistics /enforcement/sexual _harassment_new.cfm

U.S. Government Accountability Office (GAO). (2011). "Income Security: Older Adults and the 2007–2009 Recession." Accessed spring 2013. www.gao.gov/products /GAO-12-76.

U.S. Supreme Court. (2011). Wal-Mart Stores, Inc. v. Dukes et al. No. 10-277. Accessed spring 2013. www .supremecourt.gov/opinions /10pdf/10-277.pdf.

Valenzuela, A. (1999). Subtractively Schooling: U.S. Mexican Youth and the Politics of Caring. Albany, NY: State University of New York Press.

Vallas, S., and J. Beck. (1996). "The Transformation of Work Revisited: The Limits of Flexibility in American Manufacturing." Social Problems 43 (3): 339–61.

Vanacore, Andrew. (2012). "Recovery School District Will Lay off Almost 200 Teachers." Times-Picayune, June 18. Accessed June 18, 2012. www.nola.com/education/index .ssf/2012/06/recovery_school _district_will_2.html.

van de Kaa, D. J. (2003). "Second Demographic Transition." In P. Demeny and G. McNicoll, eds., Encyclopedia of Population (Vol. 2, pp. 872–75). New York: Macmillan.

van den Hoonard, D. K. (2002). "Attitudes of Older Widows and Widowers in New Brunswick, Canada toward New Partnerships." Ageing International 27: 79–92.

van der Veer, P. (1994). Religious Nationalism: Hindus and Muslims in India. Berkeley, CA: University of California Press.

van Gennep, A. (1977; orig. 1908). The Rites of Passage. London: Routledge and Kegan Paul.

Van Horn, Carl, Cliff Zukin, Mark Szeltner, and Charley Stone. (2012). Left Out, Forgotten? Recent High School Graduates and the Great Recession (June 2012). New Brunswick, NJ: John J. Heldrich Center for Workforce Development. Accessed June 18, 2012. www .heldrich.rutgers.edu/sites/default /files/content/Left_Out_Forgotten _Work_Trends_June_2012 .pdf.

Vartanian, T. P., and L. Houser. (2010). "The Effects of Childhood Neighborhood Conditions on Self-Reports of Adult Health." Journal of Health and Social Behavior 51: 291–306.

Vaughan, D. (1986). Uncoupling: Turning Points in Intimate Relationships. New York: Oxford University Press.

Vaupel, J. W., et al. (1998). "Biodemographic Trajectories of Longevity." Science 280 (5365): 855–60.

Venkatesh, Sudhir Alladi. (2008). Gang Leader for a Day: A Rogue Sociologist Takes to the Streets. New York: Penguin Press.

Veracini, Lorenzo. (2010). Settler Colonialism: A Theoretical

Overview. New York: Palgrave Macmillan.

Vincent, N. (2006). Self-Made Man: One Woman's Year Disguised as a Man. New York: Penguin.

Viorst, J. (1986). "And the Prince Knelt Down and Tried to Put the Glass Slipper on Cinderella's Foot." In J. Zipes, ed., Don't Bet on the Prince: Contemporary Feminist Fairy Tales in North America and England. New York: Methuen.

Vitali, Stefania, James Glattfelder, and Stefano Battiston. (2011). "The Network of Global Corporate Control." Accessed summer 2012. http://arxiv.org/pdf/1107.5728v2 .pdf.

Wacquant, L. J. D. (1993). "Redrawing the Urban Color Line: The State of the Ghetto in the 1980s." In C. Calhoun and G. Ritzer, eds., Social Problems. New York: McGraw-Hill.

Wacquant, L. J. D. (1996). "The Rise of Advanced Marginality: Notes on Its Nature and Implications." Acta Sociologica 39 (2): 121–39.

Wacquant, L. J. D. (2002). "Scrutinizing the Street: Poverty, Morality, and the Pitfalls of Urban Ethnography." American Journal of Sociology 107: 1468–532.

Wacquant, L. J. D., and Wilson, W. J. (1993). "The Cost of Racial and Class Exclusion in the Inner City." In W. J. Wilson, ed., The Ghetto Underclass: Social Science Perspectives. Newbury Park, CA: Sage.

Wade, Lisa. (2011). "Separating the Heat from the Light: Lessons from 30 Years of Academic Discourse about Female Genital Cutting" Ethnicities 12(1): 26-49.

Wadud, A. (1999). Qur'an and Women: Rereading the Sacred Text from a Woman's Perspective. New York: Oxford University Press.

Wagar, W. (1992). A Short History of the Future. Chicago: University of Chicago Press.

Wagner, Carolyn. (2008). The New Invisible College: Science for Development. Washington, DC: Brookings Institution.

Waldron, I. (1986). "Why Do Women Live Longer Than Men?" In P. Conrad and R. Kern, eds., The Sociology of Health and Illness. New York: St. Martin's.

Wallerstein, I. (1974a). Capitalist Agriculture and the Origins of the European World-Economy in the Sixteenth Century. New York: Academic Press.

Wallerstein, I. (1974b). *The Modern World-System.* New York: Academic Press.

Wallerstein, I. (1979). *The Capitalist World Economy.* Cambridge, UK: Cambridge University Press.

Wallerstein, I. (1990). *The Modern World-System II.* New York: Academic Press.

Wallerstein, I. (1996). *Historical Capitalism with Capitalist Civilization.* New York: W. W. Norton.

Wallerstein, I. (2004). *World-System Analysis: An Introduction.* Durham, NC: Duke University Press.

Wallerstein, Judith. (2000). *The Unexpected Legacy of Divorce: A 25-Year Landmark Study.* New York: Hyperion.

Wallerstein, Judith, and Sandra Blakeslee. (1989). *Second Chances: Men, Women and Children a Decade after Divorce.* New York: Houghton-Mifflin.

Wallerstein, J. S., & Kelly, J. B. (1980). *Surviving the Breakup: How Parents and Children Cope with Divorce.* New York: Basic Books.

Wallis, R. (1984). *The Elementary Forms of New Religious Life.* London: Routledge and Kegan Paul.

Wallsten, K. (2005). "Political Blogs: Is the Political Blogosphere an Echo Chamber?" Paper presented at the annual meetings of the American Political Science Association, Washington, DC.

Walum, L. R. (1977). *The Dynamics of Sex and Gender: A Sociological Perspective.* Chicago: Rand McNally.

Wang, H., R. Appelbaum, F. de Giuli, and N. Lichtenstein. (2009). "China's New Contract Labor Law: Is China Moving towards Increased Power for Workers?" *Third World Quarterly* 30 (3): 485–501.

Wang, Gao-hua. (2010). "China's Higher Education Reform," China Currents Special Edition. Accessed July 23, 2012. www.chinacurrents.com/spring_2010/cc_wang.htm.

Warner, Judith. (2010). "What the Great Recession Has Done to Family Life." *New York Times,* August 6. Accessed June 18, 2012. www.nytimes.com/2010/08/08/magazine/08FOB-wwln-t.html.

Warner, S. (1993). "Work in Progress toward a New Paradigm for the Sociological Study of Religion in

the United States." *American Journal of Sociology* 98: 1044–93.

Warren, B. (1980). *Imperialism: Pioneer of Capitalism.* London: Verso.

Washington Post. (2012). "Exit Polls 2012: How the Vote Has Shifted." Campaign 2012. Accessed spring 2013. www.washingtonpost.com/wp-srv/special/politics/2012-exit-polls/table.html.

Watts, Duncan J. (2007). "Is Justin Timberlake a Product of Cumulative Advantage?" *New York Times,* April 15. Accessed March 14, 2013. www.nytimes.com/2007/04/15/magazine/15wwlnidealab.t.html?_r=2&pagewanted=all.

Waxman, L., and S. Hinderliter. (1996). *A Status Report on Hunger and Homelessness in America's Cities.* Washington, DC: U.S. Conference of Mayors.

Weber, M. (1947; orig. 1922). *The Theory of Social and Economic Organization.* New York: Free Press.

Weber, M. (1963; orig. 1922). *The Sociology of Religion.* Boston: Beacon Press.

Weber, M. (1977; orig. 1904). *The Protestant Ethic and the Spirit of Capitalism.* New York: Macmillan.

Weber, M. (1979; orig. 1921). *Economy and Society: An Outline of Interpretive Sociology* (2 vols.). Berkeley, CA: University of California Press.

Weeks, J. (1977). *Coming Out: Homosexual Politics in Britain, from the Nineteenth Century to the Present.* New York: Quartet.

Weitzman, L. (1985). *Divorce Revolution: The Unexpected Social and Economic Consequences for Women and Children in America.* New York: Free Press.

Weitzman, L., et al. (1972). "Sex-Role Socialization in Picture Books for Preschool Children." *American Journal of Sociology* 77: 1125–50.

Wellman, B. (1994). "I Was a Teenage Network Analyst: The Route from the Bronx to the Information Highway." *Connections* 17 (2): 28–45.

Wellman, B., P. J. Carrington, and A. Hall. (1988). "Networks as Personal Communities." In B. Wellman and S. D. Berkowitz, eds., *Social Structures: A Network Approach.* New York: Cambridge University Press.

Wellman, B., J. Salaff, D. Dimitrova, L. Garton, M. Gulia, and C. Haythornthwaite. (1996). "Computer Networks as Social Networks: Collaborative Work,

Telework, and Virtual Community." *Annual Review of Sociology* 22: 213–38.

West, C., and D. H. Zimmerman. (1987). "Doing Gender." *Gender and Society* 1 (2): 125–51.

Western, B. (1997). *Between Class and Market: Postwar Unionization in the Capitalist Democracies.* Princeton, NJ: Princeton University Press.

Wetzel, M. S., D. M. Eisenberg, and T. J. Kaptchuk. (1998). "Courses Involving Complementary and Alternative Medicine at U.S. Medical Schools." *Journal of the American Medical Society* 280 (9): 784–87.

Wheary, Jennifer, Thomas M. Shapiro, and Tamara Draut. (2010). "By a Thread: The New Experience of America's Middle Class." New York: Demos and Institute on Assets and Social Policy at Brandeis University. Accessed August 31, 2011. http://iasp.brandeis.edu/pdfs/byathread_web.pdf (site discontinued).

Wheatley, P. (1971). *The Pivot of the Four Quarters.* Edinburgh: Edinburgh University Press.

White, L. K. (1990). "Determinants of Divorce: A Review of Research in the Eighties. *Journal of Marriage and Family* 52: 904–912.

White House. (2010). "First Lady Michelle Obama Launches Let's Move: America's Move to Raise a Healthier Generation of Kids." February 9. Office of the First Lady, Washington, D.C. Accessed August 31, 2011. www.whitehouse.gov/the-press-office/first-lady-michelle-obama-launches-lets-move-americas-move-raise-a-healthier-genera.

Wilken, Carolyn S. (2008). *Myths and Realities of Aging.* Gainesville, FL: University of Florida IFAS Extension. Accessed August 9, 2012. http://edis.ifas.ufl.edu/pdffiles/FY/FY52400.pdf.

Wilkinson, R. (1996). *Unhealthy Societies: The Afflictions of Inequality.* New York: Routledge.

Will, J., P. Self, and N. Datan. (1976). "Maternal Behavior and Perceived Sex of Infant." *American Journal of Orthopsychiatry* 46: 135–39.

Williams, Alex. (2012). "Just Wait Until Your Mother Gets Home." *New York Times,* August 10. Accessed September 16, 2012. www.nytimes.com/2012/08/12/fashion/dads-are-taking-over

-as-full-time-parents.html
?pagewanted=all.

Williams, C. L. (1992). "The Glass
Escalator: Hidden Advantages for
Men in the 'Female' Professions."
Social Problems 39: 253–67.

Williams, S. J. (1993). *Chronic Respiratory Illness.* London: Routledge.

Williams, Timothy. (2012). "For
Native American Women, Scourge
of Rape, Rare Justice." *New
York Times*, May 22. Accessed
September 10, 2012. www.nytimes
.com/2012/05/23/us/native
-americans-struggle-with-high
-rate-of-rape. html?pagewanted
=all.

Willis, P. (1977). *Learning to Labor.* Lexington, MA: Lexington Books.

Wilsdon, James, and James
Keeley. (2007). *China: The Next
Science Superpower?* London:
Demos. Accessed summer 2013.
www.google.com/url?sa=t&rct
=j&q=&esrc=s&source=web&cd
=2&ved=0CGQQFjAB&url=http
%3A%2F%2Fwww.naider.com
%2Fupload%2F82_china_final
.pdf&ei=dz8cUM-vG-n
_igKi04D4Dg&usg=AFQjCNG
_GZ6E6_9NIWk0ftR-ifla276GCA
&sig2=8_7eKS0i7OaZvHOC6
KDM0A.

Wilson, B. (1982). *Religion in Sociological Perspective.* New York: Oxford
University Press.

Wilson, J. Q., and G. Kelling. (1982).
"Broken Windows." *Atlantic
Monthly*, March.

Wilson, W. J. (1978). *The Declining
Significance of Race: Blacks and
Changing American Institutions.* Chicago: University of
Chicago Press.

Wilson, W. J. (1987). *The Truly Disadvantaged: The Inner City, the
Underclass, and Public Policy.* Chicago: University of Chicago Press.

Wilson, W. J. (1991). "Studying Inner-
City Social Dislocations: The Challenge of Public Agenda Research."
American Sociological Review 56:
1–14.

Wilson, W. J. (1996). *When Work
Disappears: The World of the New
Urban Poor.* New York: Knopf.

Wilson, W. J. (2011). "Being Poor,
Black, and American: The Impact
of Political, Economic, and Cultural Forces." *American Educator*
(Spring): 10–23, 46.

Wimmer, Andreas. (2012). *Waves of
War: Nationalism, State Formation, and Ethnic Exclusion in the
Modern World.* New York: Cambridge University Press.

Winkleby, M. A., D. E. Jatulis, E. Frank,
and S. P. Fortmann. (1992). "Socioeconomic Status and Health: How
Education, Income, and Occupation Contribute to Risk Factors for
Cardiovascular Disease." *American
Journal of Public Health* 82: 816–20.

Wirth, L. (1938). "Urbanism as a Way
of Life." *American Sociological
Review* 44: 1–24.

Wolf, N. (1992). *The Beauty Myth: How
Images of Beauty Have Been Used
against Women.* New York: Anchor
Books.

Wolfers, Justin. (2008). "Economic
Growth and Subjective Well-
Being: Reassessing the Easterlin
Paradox." *Brookings Papers on
Economic Activity*: 1–87.

Wolff, Edward N. (2010). "Recent
Trends in Household Wealth in the
United States: Rising Debt and
the Middle-Class Squeeze: An
Update to 2007." Working Paper
Number 589. Levy Economics
Institute of Bard College,
Annandale-on-Hudson, NY.
Accessed September 26, 2012.
www.levyinstitute.org/pubs
/wp_589.pdf.

Wolff, Edward N., Lindsay A. Owens,
and Esra Burak. (2011). "How
Much Wealth Was Destroyed
in the Great Recession?" In
David B. Grusky, Bruce Western,
and Christopher Wimer, eds. *The
Great Recession* (pp. 127–58). New
York: Russell Sage Foundation.

Wolff, Phillip M., and Kevin J.
Holmes. (2011). "Linguistic Relativity." *Wiley Interdisciplinary
Reviews: Cognitive Science* 2 (May/
June).

Women in National Parliaments
(WNP). (2011). Accessed August 8,
2011. www.ipu.org/wmn-e/world
.htm; http://www.ipu.org/wmn-e
/classif.htm.

Woodrum, E. (1988). "Moral Conservatism and the 1984 Presidential
Election." *Journal for the Scientific
Study of Religion* 27: 192–210.

Woolsey, Ben, and Matt Schulz. (2012).
"Credit Card Statistics, Industry
Facts, Debt Statistics." Accessed
August 26, 2012. www.creditcards
.com/credit-card-news/credit
-card-industry-facts-personal
-debt-statistics-1276.php.

WorldatWork. (2009). "Telework
Trendlines 2009: A Survey Brief
by WorldatWork." Data collected
by the Dieringer Research Group,
Inc. February. Accessed spring
2011. www.worldatwork.org/waw
/adimLink?id=31115.

World Bank. (1997). *World Development Report: 1997: The State in a
Changing World.* New York: Oxford
University Press.

World Bank. (1999). "World Development Indicators 1999." Washington, DC.: International Bank
for Reconstruction and
Development.

World Bank. (2000). *World Development Report: 2000.* New York:
Oxford University Press.

World Bank. (2000–2001). "World
Development Indicators: 2000-
2001." *World Development Report
2000–2001: Attacking Poverty.*
Accessed January 4, 2005.
http://poverty.worldbank.org
/library/topic/3389/ (site discontinued).

World Bank. (2005). "World Development Indicators: 2005." Accessed
spring 2006. http://devdata
.worldbank.org/wdi2005/cover.ht
(site discontinued).

World Bank. (2008). "World Development Indicators: 2007." Accessed
fall 2008. http://data.worldbank
.org/sites/default/files/wdi07
fulltext.pdf.

World Bank. (2010a). "Millennium
Development Goals." Accessed
spring 2011. http://web.worldbank
.org/WBSITE/EXTERNAL
/EXTABOUTUS/0,,contentMD
K:20104132-menuPK:250991
-pagePK:43912-piPK:44037
-theSitePK:29708,00.html.

World Bank. (2010b). "World Development Indicators: Poverty."
Accessed April 2010. http://data
.worldbank.org/topic/poverty.

World Bank.(2011a). "Data by Income
Level." Accessed summer 2012.
http://wdronline.worldbank.org
/worldbank/a/incomelevel.

World Bank. (2011b). "GNI Per Capita,
Atlas Method (Current US$)."
Accessed March 8, 2013. http://
data.worldbank.org/indicator
/NY.GNP.PCAP.CD.

World Bank. (2011c). "Life Expectancy
at Birth, Total (Years)." Accessed
spring 2013. http://data.worldbank
.org/indicator/SP.DYN.LE00
.IN

World Bank. (2011d). "Passenger Cars
Per 1,000 People." Accessed fall
2012. http://data.worldbank.org
/indicator/IS.VEH.PCAR.P3.

World Bank. (2012a). "Country Classification." Accessed summer 2012.
http://data.worldbank.org/about
/country-classifications.

World Bank. (2012b). "GDP (Current
US$)." World Bank Development
Indicators. Accessed summer
2012. http://data.worldbank.org
/indicator/NY.GDP.MKTP.CD.

World Bank. (2012c). "GDP 2011."
World Bank Development Indicators. Accessed summer 2012.
http://data.worldbank.org
/indicator/NY.GDP.MKTP.CD.

World Bank. (2012d). "GDP Per Capita
(Current US$): World Bank
Development Indicators."
Accessed summer 2012. http://
data.worldbank.org/indicator
/NY.GDP.PCAP.CD.

World Bank. (2012e). "GNI Per Capita,
Atlas Method (Current US$)."
Accessed summer 2012. http://
data.worldbank.org/indicator
/NY.GNP.PCAP.CD.

World Bank Institute. (2012f). "Knowledge Economy Index." Accessed
summer 2012. http://info
.worldbank.org/etools/kam2/
KAM_page5.asp.

World Bank. (2012g). "List of Economies (July)." Accessed summer
2012. http://data.worldbank
.org/about/country
-classifications/country-and
-lending-groups.

World Bank. (2012h). "Literacy Rate,
Adult Total (% of People Ages
15 and Above)." World Bank Development Indicators. Accessed summer 2012. http://data.worldbank
.org/indicator/SE.ADT.LITR.ZS.

World Bank. (2012i). "Regional
Aggregation Using 2005 PPP and
$1.25/day Poverty Line." Calcula-
tions done at http://iresearch.
worldbank.org/PovcalNet/index
.htm?1.

World Bank. (2012j). "World Bank Sees
Progress Against Extreme Poverty,
but Flags Vulnerabilities." Press
release, February 29. Accessed
March 4, 2013. http://web.world
bank.org/WBSITE/EXTERNAL
/NEWS/0,,contentMDK:23130032
~pagePK:64257043~piPK:437376
~theSitePK:4607,00.html.

World Bank. (2013a). "GNI Per Capita,
Atlas Method (Current US$)."
Accessed March 8, 2013. http://
databank.worldbank.org/data
/views/reports/tableview.aspx
?isshared=true&ispopular
=series&pid=4.

World Bank. (2013b). "World Data-
Bank: 2011." Accessed summer
2013. http://databank.worldbank
.org/data/home.aspx.

World Health Organization. (1948).
"Preamble to the Constitution of
the World Health Organization
as Adopted by the International
Health Conference, New York,
19-22." June, 1946; signed on
22 July 1946 by the representa
tives of 61 States (Official Records
of the World Health Organization,
no. 2, p. 100) and entered into force
on 7 April 1948. Accessed spring
2013. www.who.int/about
/definition/en/print.html.

World Health Organization and
UNICEF. (2012)." Progress on
Drinking Water and Sanitation:
2012 Update." Accessed spring
2013. www.unicef.org/media
/files/JMPreport2012.pdf. www
.wipo.int/freepublications/en
/statistics/943/wipo_pub_943
_2012.pdf.

World Health Organization, UNICEF,
and the United Nations Joint
Programme on HIV/AIDS
(UNAIDS). (2011). "Progress
Report 2011: Global HIV/AIDS
Response." Accessed summer
2013. www.who.int/hiv/pub
/progress_report2011/en/index
.html.

World Intellectual Property Organiza-
tion. (2012). "2012 Intellectual
Property Facts and Figures."
Accessed summer 2012.

Worldsteel.org. (2008). "Major Steel
Producing Countries, 2005 and
2006." Accessed spring 2008.
www.worldsteel.org/?action
=storypages&id=195.

World Trade Organization (WTO).
(2008). International Trade Statistics. Accessed spring 2013. www
.wto.org/english/res_e/statis_e
/its2008_e/its2008_e.pdf.

World Trade Organization (WTO).
(2011a). "International Statistics,
2010: Share of Manufactures
in Total Merchandise Trade by
Region. Table A1." Accessed summer 2012. www.wto.org/english
/res_e/statis_e/its2011_e/its11
_merch_trade_product_e.htm.

World Trade Organization (WTO).
(2011b). "International Trade
Statistics."Accessed spring 2013.
www.wto.org/english/res_e
/statis_e/its2011_e/its2011_e.pdf.

World Trade Organization (WTO).
(2012). "International Trade

Statistics 2012." Accessed spring
2013. www.wto.org/english
/res_e/statis_e/its2012_e
/its2012_e.pdf.

Worrall, A. (1990). *Offending Women:
Female Lawbreakers and the
Criminal Justice System*. London:
Routledge.

Wray, L. A., A. R. Herzog, R. J. Willis,
and R. B. Wallace. (1998). "The
Impact of Education and Heart
Attack on Smoking Cessation
among Middle-Aged Adults." *Journal of Health and Social Behavior*
39 (4): 271–94.

Wright, E. O. (1978). *Class, Crisis, and
the State*. London: New Left Books.

Wright, E. O. (1985). *Classes*. New York:
Schocken.

Wright, E. O. (1997). *Class Counts:
Comparative Studies in Class
Analysis*. New York: Cambridge
University Press.

Wright, E. O. (2010). *Envisioning
Real Utopias*. New York: Verso.
Accessed spring 2013. www.scribd
.com/doc/55940923/Erik-Olin
-Wright-Envisioning-Real-Utopias
-Verso.

Wrigley, E. A. (1968). *Population and
History*. New York: McGraw-Hill.

Wu, Fengshi. (2009). "Environmental
Activism in China: Fifteen Years in
Review, 1994–2008." Cambridge,
MA: Harvard. Accessed spring
2011. www.harvard-yenching.org
/sites/harvard-yenching.org/files
/WU%20Fengshi_Environmental
%20Civil%20Society%20in%20
China2.pdf.

Wuthnow, R. (1976). *The Consciousness Reformation*. Berkeley, CA:
University of California Press.

Wuthnow, R. (1978). *Experimentation
in American Religion*. Berkeley,
CA: University of California
Press.

Wuthnow, R. (1988). "Sociology of
Religion." In N. J. Smelser, ed.,
Handbook of Sociology. Newbury
Park, CA: Sage.

Wuthnow, R. (1990). *The Restructuring
of American Religion*. Princeton,
NJ: Princeton University Press.

Wuthnow, R. (1998). *After Heaven:
Spirituality in America since the
1950s*. Berkeley, CA: University of
California Press.

Wuthnow, R. (2007). *America and the
Challenges of Religious Diver-
sity*. Princeton, NJ: Princeton
University Press.

Wuthnow, R. (2010). *Boundless Faith:
The Global Outreach of American*

Churches. Berkeley: University of California Press.

Xinhua. (2005). "Building Harmonious Society Crucial for Progress," June 26. Accessed spring 2011. http://news.xinhuanet.com /english/2005-06/26/content _3139097.htm.

Xinhua. (2010). "IMF Raises China's 2010 GDP Growth Projection to 10.5%." Accessed summer 2010. http://news.xinhuanet.com /english2010/china/2010 -07/08/c_13389941.htm.

Yankelovich, C. S. (1991). "What's OK on a Date: Survey for Time and CNN," May 8.

Young, M., and P. Willmott. (1973). *The Symmetrical Family: A Study of Work and Leisure in the London Region*. London: Routledge and Kegan Paul.

Yue Yuen. (2007). "Yue Yuen Industrial (Holdings) Ltd: About Us: Corporate Profile." Accessed December 2007. www.yueyuen .com/about_corporateProfile .htm.

Zablocki, B., and T. Robbins. (2001). *Misunderstanding Cults: Searching for Objectivity in a Controversial Field*. Toronto: University of Toronto Press.

Zakaria, Fareed. (2009). *The Post-American World and the Rise of the Rest*. New York: Penguin.

Zammuner, V. (1986). "Children's Sex-Role Stereotypes: A Cross-Cultural Analysis." In P. Shaver and C. Hendrick, eds., *Sex and Gender*. Beverly Hills, CA: Sage.

Zarcadoolas, C., A. Pleasant, and D. Greer. (2006). *Advancing Health Literacy: A Framework for Understanding and Action*. San Francisco: Jossey-Bass.

Zerubavel, E. (1979). *Patterns of Time in Hospital Life*. Chicago: University of Chicago Press.

Zerubavel, E. (1982). "The Standardization of Time: A Sociohistorical Perspective." *American Journal of Sociology* 88: 1–23.

Zheng, Hui. (2009). "Rising U.S. Income Inequality, Gender, and Individual Self-Rated Health, 1972–2004." *Social Science and Medicine* 69: 1333–42.

Zheng, Hui. (2012). "Do People Die from Income Inequality of a Decade Ago?" *Social Science and Medicine* 75: 36–45.

Zickhur, Kathryn, and Aaron Smith. (2012). *Digital Differences*. Washington, DC: Pew Internet and American Life Project. Accessed October 19, 2012. www.pewinternet.org/~/media// Files/Reports/2012/PIP _Digital_differences_041312.pdf.

Zimbardo, P. G. (1969). "The Human Choice: Individuation, Reason, and Order Versus Deindividuation, Impulse, and Chaos." In W. J. Arnold and D. Levine, eds., *Nebraska Symposium on Motivation* 17. Lincoln, NE: University of Nebraska Press.

Zimbardo, P. G. (1992). *Quiet Rage: The Stanford Prison Experiment* (documentary). Available from www.prisonexp.org/.

Zimbardo, P. G, E. B. Ebbesen, and C. Maslach. (1977). *Influencing Attitudes and Changing Behavior*. Reading, MA: Addison-Wesley.

Zimmerman, J. (2010). "College Admissions: What Matters Most—SAT Scores, Grades, or Just Luck?" *Christian Science Monitor*, April 13. Accessed spring 2011. www.csmonitor.com /Commentary/Opinion/2010/0413 /College-admissions-What -matters-most-SAT-scores -grades-or-just-luck.

Zuboff, S. (1988). *In the Age of the Smart Machine: The Future of Work and Power*. New York: Basic Books.

Photo Credits

Chapter 1: Page 2: Joseph Sohm/Agefotostock; p. 7: Michael S. Quinton/National Geographic Stock; p. 10: Granger Collection; p. 11: Corbis; p. 12: Corbis; p. 14: Granger Collection; p. 15 (top): Corbis; (bottom): Library of Congress; p. 19: Pictorial Parade/Getty Images; p. 23 (left): Kevin Dodge/Corbis; (right): Gavriel Jecan/Corbis.

Chapter 2: Page 28: Reena Rose Sibayan/The Jersey Journal/Landov; p. 34 (both): The University of Chicago Library Special Collections Research Center; p. 41: Philip G. Zimbardo/Stanford Prison Experiment.

Chapter 3: Page 50: Tom Salyer/Alamy; p. 57: AP Photo; p. 67: Tim Graham / Alamy; p. 72 (left): © Atsuko Tanaka; (right): Christopher Polk/Getty Images; p. 78: STR/AFP/Getty Images.

Chapter 4: Page 82: Andrew Olney/Getty Images; p. 91: Alinari Archives/Corbis; p. 94: courtesy of Dan Bartell; p. 99: Harold M. Lambert/Lambert/Getty Images.

Chapter 5: Page 106: Jon Hicks/Corbis; p. 110: Charles Gullung/zefa/Corbis; p. 114 (all): Paul Ekman; p. 119: Pankaj & Insy Shah/Getty Images; p. 123: Ovie Carter from SIDEWALK; p. 129: Khaled El Fiqi/EPA/Landov.

Chapter 6: Page 132: Mike Strasser/West Point Public Affairs; http://creativecommons.org/licenses/by/2.0/deed.en; p. 139 (all): Courtesy of Alexandra Milgram; p. 146: Ed Kashi/Corbis.

Chapter 7: Page 160: Benoit Decout/REA/Redux; p. 167: Randy Tepper/© Showtime / Courtesy: Everett Collection; p. 175: Sanjit Das/Barcroft Media/Landov; p. 178: Hiroko Masuike/Getty Images.

Chapter 8: Page 192: AP Photo.

Chapter 9: Page 228: Miguel Caibarien/Agefotostock; p. 237: Popperfoto/Getty Images; p. 242 (left): AP Photo; (right): Jeff Greenberg "0 people images" / Alamy.

Chapter 10: Page 254: AP Photo; p. 257: AP Photo; p. 264: Adam Ferguson/The New York Times/Redux; p. 268: Librado Romero/The New York Times/Redux; p. 280: Fang Zhe/Xinhua/Landov; p. 283: Fancy/Alamy.

Chapter 11: Page 290: AP Photo; p. 294: Alain Nogues/Corbis Sygma; p. 301: Hulton-Deutsch/Corbis; p. 304: National Archives.

Chapter 12: Page 320: Scott Jones Event Photography; p. 340: Courtesy AARP. Photo: Getty Images; p. 344: AP Photo.

Chapter 13: Page 352: ITAR-TASS / Landov; p. 358: AP Photo; p. 362: Granger Collection; p. 377: Polaris Images; p. 384: Joe Raedle/Getty Images.

Chapter 14: Page 394: AP Photo; p. 403: Bettmann/Corbis; p. 409: Greg Ruffing/Redux.

Chapter 15: Page 434: AP Photo; p. 443: Everett Collection; p. 460: AP Photo.

Chapter 16: Page 470: The Washington Post/Getty Images; p. 486: Ted Streshinsky/Corbis; p. 491: Granger Collection.

Chapter 17: Page 500: Lorenzo Moscia/archivolatino/Redux; p. 510: Bennett Dean/Eye Ubiquitous/Corbis; p. 528: Edu Nividhia-PHOTOlink.org/Newscom.

Chapter 18: Page 546: AP Photo; p. 572: Gideon Mendel/Corbis; p. 575: New York Daily News; p. 583 (left): Ed Quinn/Corbis; (right): AP Photo.

Chapter 19: Page 588: AP Photo; p. 596: akg-images / The Image Works; p. 610: London Stereoscopic Company/Getty Images; p. 621: AP Photo.

Chapter 20: Page 634: Jonathan Torgovnik/Getty Images; p. 641: Khaled Desouki/AFP/Getty Images; p. 658: Subir Halder/India Today Group/Getty Images; p. 664: Jonathan Torgovnik/Getty Images.

Index

hip-hop, 70–71
Hirschi, Travis, 169
Hispanics, *see* Latinos/Hispanics
historicity, 378
HIV/AIDS, 244, 347, 569–70
    in Africa, 244, 245–46
    stigma of, 559, 560, 561, 570, 572
Hodge, Robert, 88
Hofstadter, Judy, 322–24
Holocaust, 137, 150, 315, 519
homelessness, 166, 218–19
home ownership, 197, 198
homeschooling, 495–96
homophobia, 574–75
homosexuality, 554, 555, 576, 584
    see also gays and lesbians
Honda, 416
Hong Kong, 66
    as a high-income country, 232
    as newly industrializing, 240, 248
Hong Kong-Guangdong megacity, 606
hooks, bell, 268, 269
Hopi tribe, 19
horticulture, 63
hospitals, 146–47
housework, 278–80, 399
housing, 219
    see also homelessness
HP, 426
Hubbard, L. Ron, 528
human capital theory, 283–84
human subjects, 43
hunger, malnutrition, and famine,
    global, 244–46
hunting and gathering societies,
    61–63
Huntington, Samuel, 641–42
Hurricane Katrina, 618
Hussein, Saddam, 640
Hutus, 316, 639
hybridity, 637
hyperglobalizers, 644–45
hypertension, 566
hypotheses, 32

I
IBM, 157, 214, 414, 415
Iceland, 576
ideal type, 144–45
identical twin studies, 261, 584
identity, 89–90
ideologies, 20
IGOs, *see* international governmental
    organizations (IGOs)
illegal models of immigration, 307
illegitimate sick role, 559
illness, *see* health and illness
ILO, *see* United Nations International
    Labor Organization (ILO)
immigration
    anti-immigrant sentiment against,
    310–11
    definition of, 307
    to the United States, 303

economy and, 310–11
    immigration law, 303, 306
Immigration and Nationality Act
    Amendments, 310
impression management ("striking a
    pose"), 110, 126–27
incarceration, *see* prisons
income, 196
    definition of, 194
    inequality
        gender and, 271–78
        health and, 579–80
        race and, 313, 314
        in the United States, 196, 197,
        207–8, 220–22
    of lower class, 209
    of middle class, 207, 208
    real, 196
    of upper class, 206
    of working class, 208, 209
Inconvenient Truth, An (Gore), 623
India
    antiracism in, 297–98
    caste in, 195, 520
    energy consumption of, 624–25
    film industry in, 636
    independence of, 67
    religious conflict within, 506
    transnational corporations and, 413
individualism, 443, 651
Indonesia, 245, 536
    Chinese ethnic minority in, 317
    as newly industrializing
    economy, 248
industrialization, 10, 64, 619–26
industrialized societies, 64–65, 66,
    68–71
Industrial Revolution, 12, 64
inequality
    in education, 479–86
    gap between rich and poor
    global, 248–49
    in the United States, 220–22
    gender, *see* gender inequality
    global, *see* global inequality
    globalization and, 655–60
    in health and illness, 563–68
        gender-based, 566–68
        income-based, 579–80
        race-based, 313–14, 565–66
        social class-based, 563–65
    income, *see* income: inequality
    racial and ethnic, 311–15
Inequality by Design (Fischer
    et al.), 494
infant mortality rate, 233, 244, 562,
    565, 593
infectious diseases, 556–57
informal economy, 408–10, 607
informal relations within
    bureaucracies, 145–47
Information Awareness Office, 387
information poverty, 491–92
information society, 647, 661

information technology
    modern organizations and, 154–56
    workplace and, 406
Inglehart, Ronald, 514, 515
INGOs, *see* international
    nongovernmental
    organizations (INGOs)
in-groups, 141
inner-city areas, 596
innovators, 165
instincts, 74
institutional capitalism, 402
institutional racism, 295–96
Intel, 415, 416
intelligence, 475–76, 493–95
interactional vandalism, 122–25
interactionist theories on crime and
    deviance, 167–68
interest groups, 367–69
intergenerational mobility, 210,
    212
Intergovernmental Panel on Climate
    Change (IPCC), 622, 623
international division of labor, 413
international education, 496–97
international governmental
    organizations (IGOs), 648
International Institute for
    Democracy and Electoral
    Assistance, 385
International Lesbian, Gay, Bisexual,
    Trans and Intersex
    Association, 576
international nongovernmental
    organizations (INGOs), 648
International Union for the
    Conservation of Nature
    (IUCN), 621
Internet
    access, 647
    American culture and, 53–54
    in China, 53
    cybercrime and, 179
    democracy and, 386–87
    democratization and, 371–72
    global culture and, 75–76
    political participation and, 371–72
    social interaction and (*see* social
        interaction)
    as social network, 140, 152–53
internment camps, 304, 305
Inter-Parliamentary Union, 370
interpersonal aggression, 260
intragenerational mobility, 210, 212
in vitro fertilization (IVF), 577
iPads, 53, 416
IPCC, *see* Intergovernmental Panel on
    Climate Change (IPCC)
iPhones, 53
IQ (intelligence quotient), 475–76,
    494–95
Iran
    Green Movement and, 386
    religion in, 535